MODERN EQUITY

of England and Wales

LIBRARY SERVICES

The College of Law, 133 Great Hampton Street, Birmingham, B18 6AQ
Telephone: 01483 216041   E-mail: library.brm@lawcol.co.uk

**This book MUST be returned on or before the last date stamped below.
Failure to do so will result in a fine.**

18/02/17

Birmingham • Bristol • Chester • Guildford • London • Manchester • York

HANBURY & MARTIN

MODERN EQUITY

NINETEENTH EDITION

BY

JILL E MARTIN, LL.D. (Lond.)

Barrister, Lincoln's Inn

SWEET & MAXWELL

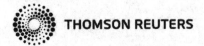

THOMSON REUTERS

First Edition	1935	Tenth Edition	1976
Second Edition	1937	Second Impression	1979
Third Edition	1943	Eleventh Edition	1981
Fourth Edition	1946	Twelfth Edition	1985
Fifth Edition	1949	Thirteenth Edition	1989
Sixth Edition	1952	Second Impression	1990
Seventh Edition	1957	Fourteenth Edition	1993
Eighth Edition	1962	Fifteenth Edition	1997
Ninth Edition	1969	Sixteenth Edition	2001
Second Impression	1971	Seventeenth Edition	2005
Third Impression	1973	Eighteenth Edition	2009
Fourth Impression	1974	Nineteenth Edition	2012
Fifth Impression	1975		

Published in 2012 by Sweet & Maxwell, 100 Avenue Road, London NW3 3PF
Part of Thomson Reuters (Professional) UK Limited
(Registered in England & Wales, Company No 1679046.
Registered Office and address for service:
Aldgate House, 33 Aldgate High Street, London EC3N 1DL)
For further information on our products and services, visit
www.sweetandmaxwell.co.uk

Typeset by Interactive Sciences Ltd, Gloucester
Printed and bound by CPI Group (UK) Ltd
Croydon, CR0 4YY

A CIP catalogue record for this book is available from the British Library

ISBN: 978 184 7039538

PREFACE

This edition is the first for many years to appear after an interval of only three years. Some of the first few editions by Harold Hanbury were published at intervals of three or even two years, but since then the pattern has been at least four years. It is also the last I will edit. I have been a contributor since the tenth edition in 1976 and the sole editor since 1981 and feel that the time has come to hand it over to a new editor.

For me the most interesting and significant decisions during the three years since the last edition were *Jones v Kernott, Pitt v Holt* (heard with *Futter v Futter*) and *Sinclair Investments (UK) Ltd v Versailles Trade Finance Ltd (in Administration)*, all decided in 2011. In *Jones* the question for the Supreme Court was whether the joint beneficial ownership of a family home owned by an unmarried couple had changed subsequently after their separation. There was a six month wait for the ruling, which met a mixed reception. The court boldly embraced the notion of imputing intentions to the parties to achieve a "fair" result, but the decision is unlikely to stem the flow of litigation in this area. Legislation is unlikely for the foreseeable future, as the Government has recently declined to implement the Law Commission's 2007 report on *Cohabitation: The Financial Consequences of Relationship Breakdown.*

In *Pitt v Holt* the Court of Appeal thoroughly analysed the so-called "rule in *Re Hastings-Bass*", and decided that the case had been misinterpreted. The "rule" dealt with the setting aside of dispositions made by trustees under some mistake, typically as to the tax consequences. The result of the decision, which also clarified the law on the setting aside of dispositions made by settlors under some misapprehension, is that fewer dispositions will be set aside, and the remedy (if any) is more likely to be against negligent professional advisers. Leave to appeal to the Supreme Court has been given.

Sinclair settled (at Court of Appeal level) the conflict between *Lister & Co v Stubbs* and the later decision of the Privy Council in

Attorney General for Hong Kong v Reid. In *Lister* it was held that, where an agent or other fiduciary took a bribe or secret commission, the principal's remedy was personal only. In *Reid* the remedy was held to be proprietary. Both decisions have attracted criticism, but the Court of Appeal in *Sinclair* was surely right to follow *Lister*, for reasons of precedent and principle. It also confirmed that the remedial constructive trust is not recognised in this jurisdiction.

Other noteworthy decisions since the last edition include *Fisher v Brooker*, where the House of Lords clarified the principles of laches and acquiescence, and *Thorner v Major*, which could only be included at Court of Appeal level in the last edition. The House of Lords reversed the Court of Appeal, and confirmed that the principles governing proprietary estoppel remained flexible in the family context, thus confining the approach of the House of Lords in *Yeoman's Rowe Management Ltd v Cobbe* to the commercial context and relieving fears that the doctrine had been emasculated. The Privy Council provided valuable guidance on interlocutory injunctions in *National Commercial Bank Jamaica Ltd v Olint Corporation Ltd*. Also of interest were the decisions of the Court of Appeal in *Zeital v Kaye* on imperfect gifts (where the waters have been muddied by that court's decision in *Pennington v Waine*), and in *Araci v Fallon* on interim injunctions to restrain a breach of contract.

Turning to legislation, the Equality Act 2010 abolished the presumption of advancement in relation to future transfers, though the relevant section has not come into force at the time of writing. The Perpetuities and Accumulations Act 2009, implementing Law Commission recommendations, abolished the rule against excessive accumulations and replaced the common law perpetuity period with a fixed period of 125 years. The Charities Act 2011 consolidated much of the legislation previously found in the Charities Acts of 1993 and 2006 and the Recreational Charities Act 1958. The Act received Royal Assent on December 14, 2011, thus requiring considerable last minute amendments to the proofs.

Another headache, from an editor's point of view, was the recent withdrawal by the Charity Commission of some of its guidance on public benefit. A judicial review application (along with a reference by the Attorney General) was heard earlier in 2011 but the ruling in *Independent Schools Council v Charity Commission* was not available until November 2011, after delivery of the manuscript. The Tribunal required the Commission to amend some of its guidance, but the Commission did not move sufficiently quickly. The Tribunal then gave further directions to the effect that, if the offending passages were not withdrawn by December 21, 2011, the guidance would be quashed. The Commission duly excised the relevant passages on that date, but revised guidance will not be available until later this year.

The Law Commission's report on *Capital and Income in Trusts: Classification and Apportionment* (No 315) was published in 2009. The Commission's long awaited final report on *The Illegality Defence* (No 320), which was available only in draft at the date of the last edition, appeared in 2010. The recent report on *Intestacy and Family Provision Claims on Death* (No 331) recommends amendments to sections 31 and 32 of the Trustee Act 1925 on trustees' powers of maintenance and advancement. These proposals, which resulted from a supplementary consultation paper, are not confined to trusts arising on intestacy but will apply generally. Another interesting report, though not from the Law Commission, came from Lord Neuberger's Committee on Super-Injunctions, *Super-Injunctions, Anonymised Injunctions and Open Justice* (2011).

As always, thanks are due to the editorial staff of Sweet & Maxwell for their hard work on this edition and throughout the many years of my editorship. I hope that the new editor will enjoy working on the book as much as I have.

This edition aims to state the law as at January 1, 2012.

Jill Martin
Lincoln's Inn
January 1, 2012

CONTENTS

PART I

INTRODUCTION

PART II

TRUSTS AND POWERS

PART III

TRUSTEES

PART IV

MISCELLANEOUS EQUITABLE REMEDIES AND DOCTRINES

TABLE OF ABBREVIATIONS

Books

Annual Report	*Annual Report of the Charity Commission.*
A.S.C.L.	*Annual Survey of Commonwealth Law.*
Chambers	Chambers, *Resulting Trusts*, 1997.
Cheshire	Cheshire and Burn, *The Modern Law of Real Property*, 18th edn, 2011.
Goff and Jones	Goff and Jones, *The Law of Restitution*, 7th edn, 2007.
Halsbury	Halsbury, *Halsbury's Laws of England*, 4th edn, 1973–1985, 4th edn reissue, 1988–2008 and 5th edn, 2008 onwards.
Harris	Harris, *Variation of Trusts*, 1975.
Hayton and Marshall	Hayton and Marshall, *Commentary and Cases on the Law of Trusts and Equitable Remedies*, 12th edn, 2005.
Heydon, Gummow & Austin	Heydon, Gummow & Austin, *Cases and Materials on Equity & Trusts*, 4th edn, 1993.
Holdsworth *H.E.L.*	Holdsworth, *History of English Law.*
Maitland	*Maitland's Equity*, 2nd edn, 1936.
Maudsley	Maudsley, *The Modern Law of Perpetuities*, 1979.
M. & W.	Megarry and Wade, *The Law of Real Property*, 7th edn, 2008.
Meagher, Gummow & Lehane	Meagher, Gummow & Lehane, *Equity: Doctrines & Remedies*, 4th edn, 2002.
Milsom	Milsom, *Historial Foundations of the Common Law*, 2nd edn, 1981.
Morris and Leach	Morris and Leach, *The Rule Against Perpetuities*, 2nd edn, 1962.
Oakley	Oakley, *Constructive Trusts*, 3rd edn, 1997.

Parker and Mellows	Parker and Mellows, *The Modern Law of Trusts*, 9th edn, 2008.
Pettit	Pettit, *Equity and the Law of Trusts*, 10th edn, 2005.
Picarda	Picarda, *The Law and Practice Relating to Charities*, 4th edn, 2011.
Preston and Newsom	Preston and Newsom, *Limitation of Actions*, 3rd edn, 1953.
Smith	Smith, *The Law of Tracing*, 1997.
Snell	Snell, *Principles of Equity*, 32nd edn, 2010.
Spry	Spry, *Equitable Remedies*, 8th edn, 2010.
Thomas	Thomas, *Powers*, 1998.
Tudor	*Tudor on Charities*, 9th edn, 2003.
Underhill and Hayton	Underhill and Hayton, *Law Relating to Trusts and Trustees*, 18th edn, 2010.

Journals and Reports

All E.R. Rev.	All England Law Reports Annual Review.
B.T.R.	British Tax Review.
Bus.L.R.	Business Law Reports.
C.F.L.Q.	Child and Family Law Quarterly.
C.L.J.	Cambridge Law Journal.
C.B.R.	Canadian Bar Review.
Col. L.R.	Columbia Law Review.
Conv.	Conveyancer and Property Lawyer.
C.L.P.	Current Legal Problems.
E.G.	Estates Gazette.
Fam. Law.	Family Law.
F.L.R.	Family Law Reports.
H.L.R.	Harvard Law Review.
I.C.L.Q.	International and Comparative Law Quarterly.
I.C.R.	Industrial Cases Reports.
J.B.L.	Journal of Business Law.
J.L.H.	Journal of Legal History.
K.C.L.J.	King's College Law Journal.
L.M.C.L.Q.	Lloyd's Maritime and Commercial Law Quarterly.
L.Q.R.	Law Quarterly Review.
L.S.	Legal Studies.
L.S.Gaz.	Law Society's Gazette.

M.L.R.	Modern Law Review.
N.L.J.	New Law Journal.
R.L.R.	Restitution Law Review.
S.J.	Solicitors' Journal.
T.L.I.	Trust Law International.
U.W.A.L.R.	University of Western Australia Law Review.
W.T.L.R.	Wills and Trusts Law Reports.

Acts of Parliament

AEA	Administration of Estates Act.
AJA	Administration of Justice Act.
FA	Finance Act.
FLRA	Family Law Reform Act.
ICTA	Income and Corporation Taxes Act.
IHTA	Inheritance Tax Act.
ITA	Income Tax Act.
LCA	Land Charges Act.
LGFA	Local Government Finance Act.
LPA	Law of Property Act.
LP(A)A	Law of Property (Amendment) Act.
LRA	Land Registration Act.
MCA	Mental Capacity Act.
PAA	Perpetuities and Accumulations Act.
SLA	Settled Land Act.
TA	Trustee Act.
TCGA	Taxation of Chargeable Gains Act.
TLATA	Trusts of Land and Appointment of Trustees Act.
VTA	Variation of Trusts Act.

General

BS	Building Society.
Comm	Commissioners.
CPR	Civil Procedure Rules
IRC	Inland Revenue Commissioners.
S	Section.
SE	Settled Estates.
ST	Settlement Trusts.
WT	Will Trusts.

TABLE OF CASES

TABLE OF STATUTES

TABLE OF STATUTORY INSTRUMENTS

TABLE OF TREATIES AND CONVENTIONS

TABLE OF FOREIGN LEGISLATION

PART I

INTRODUCTION

HISTORY AND PRINCIPLES

1. GENERAL

EQUITY is a word with many meanings. In a wide sense, it means **1–001** that which is fair and just, moral and ethical; but its legal meaning is much narrower. Equity is the branch of the law which, before the Judicature Act of 1873 came into force, was applied and administered by the Court of Chancery.[1] It is not synonymous with justice in a broad sense. A litigant asserting some equitable right or remedy must show that his claim has:

"[A]n ancestry founded in history and in the practice and precedents of the court administering equity jurisdiction. It is not sufficient that because we may think that the 'justice' of the present

---

[1] This is "but a poor thing to call a definition"; Maitland, p.1.

3

case requires it, we should invent such a jurisdiction for the first time."[2]

Developed systems of law have often been assisted by the introduction of a discretionary power to do justice in particular cases where the strict rules of law cause hardship.[3] Rules formulated to deal with particular situations may subsequently work unfairly as society develops. Equity is the body of rules which evolved to mitigate the severity of the rules of the common law. Its origin was the exercise by the Chancellor of the residual discretionary power of the King to do justice among his subjects in circumstances in which, for one reason or another, justice could not be obtained in a common law court.

1–002 Principles of justice and conscience are the basis of equity jurisdiction, but it must not be thought that the contrast between law and equity is one between a system of strict rules and one of broad discretion.[4] Equity has no monopoly of the pursuit of justice. As Harman L.J. has said, equitable principles are:

> "[R]ather too often bandied about in common law courts as though the Chancellor still had only the length of his own foot to measure when coming to a conclusion. Since the time of Lord Eldon, the system of equity for good or evil has been a very precise one, and equitable jurisdiction is exercised only on well-known principles."[5]

In similar vein Lord Radcliffe, speaking of common lawyers, said that equity lawyers were "both surprised and discomfited by the plenitude of jurisdiction and the imprecision of rules that are attributed to 'equity' by their more enthusiastic colleagues."[6] More recently, Neuberger L.J. said:

> "The fact that a particular type of right or relief is equitable does not, *pace* some judicial observations to the contrary, operate as a green light to invent new general or specific rules in order to achieve what one judge might regard as a fair result in a particular case or, to put it another way, to achieve 'a form of palm-tree justice' ".[7]

---

[2] *Re Diplock* [1948] Ch. 465 at 481, 482. See also Jessel M.R. in *Re National Funds Assurance Co* (1878) 10 Ch.D. 118 at 128: "This court is not, as I have often said, a Court of Conscience, but a Court of Law."

[3] The Praetor performed such a function in Roman Law: Buckland and McNair, *Roman Law and Common Law*, 2nd edn, 1965, pp.1–6.

[4] See generally A. Duggan (1997) 113 L.Q.R. 601.

[5] *Campbell Discount Co Ltd v Bridge* [1961] 1 Q.B. 445 at 459.

[6] *Bridge v Campbell Discount Co Ltd* [1962] A.C. 600 at 626.

[7] *Edlington Properties Ltd v J H Fenner & Co Ltd* [2006] 1 W.L.R. 1583 at pp.1595/1596, quoting from *Muscat v Smith* [2003] 1 W.L.R. 2853 at 2865.

Returning to the theme, his Lordship added:

> "But equity is not a sort of moral US fifth cavalry riding to the rescue every time a claimant is left worse off than he anticipated as a result of the defendants behaving badly, and the common law affords him no remedy."[8]

Just as the common law has escaped from its early formalism, so over the years equity has established strict rules for the application of its principles. Indeed, at one stage the rules became so fixed that a *"rigor aequitatis"*[9] developed; equity itself displayed the very defect which it was designed to remedy. We will see that today some aspects of equity are strict and technical, while others leave considerable discretion to the court.

The field of equity is delineated by a series of historical events, and not by a pre-conceived theory; an outline of these events will be given in the next section. We will then see that, until the Judicature Act 1873, the Court of Chancery had almost exclusive equity jurisdiction[10]; rules of equity were not enforced in the common law courts. If a defendant to a common law action had an equitable defence to it, he had to go to Chancery to obtain an injunction to stay the proceedings in the common law court and then start a new action in Chancery to establish his equitable rights. This complicated system led to a number of difficulties, as we shall see. The Judicature Acts of 1873 and 1875 created the Supreme Court of Judicature, all of whose branches exercise common law and equity jurisdiction. The division between law and equity is less marked, therefore, than it was prior to those Acts, but it is still necessary for various reasons to know whether a rule has its origins in law or in equity.[11]

2. HISTORICAL OUTLINE

The long history of the Court of Chancery is a fascinating story, the details of which must be sought elsewhere[12]; it is not possible here

1–003

---

[8] (2009) 68 C.L.J. 537 at 540.

[9] Allen's *Law in the Making*, 7th edn, p.417.

[10] For the equity jurisdiction of the Court of Exchequer, see *Halsbury*, Vol.10, para.606, fn.4. The Common Law Procedure Act 1854 had given common law courts a limited power to issue injunctions.

[11] Below, paras 1–020–1–023.

[12] Maitland Lectures, *The Constitutional History of England*, 1908 I–IV; Holdsworth; *H.E.L.* i, Ch.5; iv, pp.407–480; v, pp.215–338; vi, pp.518–551, 640–671; ix, pp.335–408; xii, pp.178–330; xiii, pp.574–668; xvi, pp.5–135; Plucknett, *Concise History of the Common Law*, 5th edn, Pt 5; Milsom, *Historical Foundations of the Common Law*, 2nd edn, 1981, Chs 4, 9; Jones, *The Elizabethan Court of Chancery*, 1967; (1965) 81 L.Q.R. 562; J. Barton (1966) 82 L.Q.R. 215; Keeton and Sheridan's *Equity*, 3rd edn, 1985, Ch.2; Klinck, *Conscience, Equity and the Court of Chancery in Early Modern England*, 2010.

to do more than mention, in broad outline, those aspects which are
essential to the understanding of modern equity.

A. The Medieval Chancellor

1–004   In the medieval period the Chancellor was the most important
person in the country next to the King himself: Maitland described
him as "the king's prime minister",[13] "the king's secretary of state
for all departments".[14] One very important function of the Chancery
was to issue the royal writs which began an action at law.[15] By
varying existing writs or inventing new ones, the Chancellor could
have some influence on the development of the law; a limited influence, however, for the decision to issue a writ (now called a claim
form in the Civil Procedure Rules 1998) did not create a new form
of action. The litigant could not proceed without it; but the common
law court could still decide that the writ disclosed no claim recognised by the law.

B. Petitions to the Chancellor[16]

1–005   A claimant could only sue at common law if his complaint came
within the scope of an existing writ. In the 13th century the available
writs covered very narrow ground. Even if the claim came within
the scope of an existing writ, it may have been that for some reason,
such as the power and influence of the defendant, his opponent
could not get justice before a common law court. The King in his
Council still retained wide discretionary power to do justice among
his subjects, and the claimant could petition to the King and Council
praying for a remedy.

Petitions were addressed to the Chancellor in situations in which
a petitioner complained that his case was beyond the ordinary mechanism, and he sought another way. Milsom points out that, in its
origins, this would not be regarded as an application of a separate
and superior body of rules to those applied by the common law
courts.

> "Not only was there no equity as a nascent body of rules different
> from those of the common law. There was no common law, no
> body of substantive rules from which equity could be dif-
> ferent."[17]

---

[13] Maitland, p.3.
[14] Maitland, p.2.
[15] See Maitland, *Forms of Action at Common Law*, 1909.
[16] Holdsworth, *H.E.L.* i, pp.402 et seq.; Milsom, p.82.
[17] Milsom, p.84.

If the mechanism appeared to work unfairly, as where juries were misled, corrupted or intimidated, the petitioner would seek another way. The Chancery:

> "[W]as the head office of the organisation, and it was here that application was made when the ordinary mechanisms appeared to be incapable of working. The approach to the chancellor has no more mysterious origin than that."[18]

Later the petition was used to obtain relief in cases where the common law was inflexible and incapable of providing a remedy. The common law developed into a comprehensive system, but a litigant could only sue at common law if his complaint came within the scope of an existing writ. By the 16th century local jurisdictions, where many matters not covered by common law writs had been dealt with, played a much smaller part. The common law was taking on the aspect of a substantive as well as a comprehensive system, and the application to Chancery was ceasing to look like a request for the same justice, withheld below by some mechanical fault. There seemed to be two parallel systems, and the relationship between them had to be explained in theory and worked out in practice.

C. The Chancellor's Discretion

Maitland points out that in the 13th and 14th centuries the Chancellor probably did not regard himself as administering a new body of law.[19] He was trying to give relief in hard cases, and the medieval Chancellor was peculiarly well fitted for this work. He was usually an ecclesiastic, generally a bishop, and learned in the civil and canon law.[20] The Chancellor would give or withhold relief, not according to any precedent, but according to the effect produced upon his own individual sense of right and wrong by the merits of the particular case before him. No wonder that Selden could say that:

1–006

> "Equity is a roguish thing. For law we have a measure . . . equity is according to the conscience of him that is Chancellor, and as that is longer or narrower, so is equity. 'Tis all one as if they should make the standard for the measure a Chancellor's foot."[21]

---

[18] Milsom, p.84.

[19] Maitland, p.5.

[20] There were some lay Chancellors at this period; see Trevelyan, *England in the Age of Wycliffe* (1899).

[21] Pollock (ed.) *Table Talk of John Selden*, (1927), p.43; quoted Holdsworth, *H.E.L.* i, pp.467–468.

D. Attendance of the Defendant

1–007   In exercising this jurisdiction, the Chancellor was faced with the problem of ensuring the attendance of the defendant without the issue of a royal writ.

> "The Chancellor, having considered the petition or bill as it is called, orders the (defendant) to come before him and answer the complaint. The writ whereby he does this is called a *subpoena* —because it orders the man to appear upon pain of forfeiting a sum of money—*e.g. subpoena centum librarum.*"[22]

The examination was made under oath; it did not need to be restricted to specific questions raised in the complaint; and issues of fact as well as issues of law were decided by the Chancellor.

E. Enforcement

1–008   A further question was that of enforcement. If the petition was successful, the Chancellor's conclusion would usually be different from that which the common law court would have reached; otherwise the matter would have been litigated at common law. If the Chancellor found that Blackacre was owned by A, but that, in conscience, it should be beneficially owned by B, he could order A to convey the land to B, or to hold the legal estate for the exclusive benefit of B. The Chancellor did not and could not in these circumstances hold that B was the owner. A's right at law was undoubted, and the Chancellor could not change the law. What the Chancellor did was to issue an order to A either to convey the land to B, or to refrain from action interfering with B's right. The Chancellor's jurisdiction was against the person—*in personam*[23]—and directed to the conscience of the individual in question. The Chancellor had the power to back up his orders with the threat of imprisonment for those in contempt. Although there was, theoretically, no interference with common law property rights, there was in substance an interference with common law jurisdiction. This was the subject of dispute later on.[24]

F. The Use[25]

1–009   "If we were asked what is the greatest and most distinctive

---

[22] Maitland, p.5.
[23] Below, para.1–018.
[24] Below, para.1–013.
[25] Holdsworth, *H.E.L.* iv, pp.407–480; Ames, *Lectures on Legal History*, 1913, pp.233–247; Plucknett, *Concise History of the Common Law*, 5th edn, 1956, p.575; Milsom, Ch.9; (1965) 81 L.Q.R. 562; J. Barton (1966) 82 L.Q.R. 215; N. Jones (1997) 56 C.L.J. 175.

achievement performed by Englishmen in the field of jurisprudence I cannot think that we should have any better answer to give than this, namely the development from century to century of the trust idea."[26]

Such was the view of Maitland. A more recent statement is that "Trust law is the finest legal concept we have given to a civilised world."[27] Let us now examine the origins of that concept.

In medieval times, the Chancellor's jurisdiction was vague and undefined; as wide as the subject-matter of the petitions which invoked it. The basis of intervention was that it was necessary on grounds of conscience. His authority was unquestioned in cases of fraud and breach of confidence. As stated above, the most significant and far-reaching sphere of his jurisdiction was the enforcement of the use of land.

If land was given to A on A's undertaking to hold the land to the use and benefit of B, it was unconscionable for A to keep it for his own benefit. B however had no legal claim or title to the land. The conveyance to A gave him whatever legal estate was conveyed, and, at common law, A could exercise all the rights which that estate gave him.

Land might be given to A to the use of B for various reasons. If B were going on a crusade, then there had to be someone to perform and receive the feudal services. If B were a community of Franciscan friars which, because of the rule of poverty, was incapable of holding property, it was necessary for someone to hold the land for its benefit.[28] Perhaps, however, B was trying to escape from his creditors; or feared that a conviction for felony would result in the loss of his lands.[29] For various reasons it may have been advisable or necessary to put the legal title to B's land in A. If B conveyed to A subject to an undertaking to hold to the use of B, B would have no protection at common law beyond that given in the 14th century to covenants under seal; and if a third party conveyed the land to A to hold to the use of B, no relationship recognised by the common law existed between A and B.

The Chancellor interfered to compel A to hold the land for the exclusive use and benefit of B. The Chancellor could not say that B was the owner; A was. But all the beneficial interest in the land could be given to B by compelling A to keep the legal title only, and to give all the benefit of the land to B. This is what happened when the use was enforced. And, although the jurisdiction against A was a jurisdiction *in personam*, the Chancellor would enforce B's rights,

---

[26] *Selected Essays*, p.129.
[27] J. Quarrell (1995) 9 T.L.I. 33.
[28] Maitland, p.25; Holdsworth, *H.E.L.* iv, p.415; Milsom, p.203.
[29] *Davies v Otty (No.2)* (1865) 35 Beav. 208.

not only against A, but against other persons who took the land from A.[30] It was not long before it was said that A was the owner at law, B the owner in equity. In the terminology of the time, A was the feoffee to uses, B the *cestui que use*. The use was the forerunner, as we will see, of the trust.

Gradually the Chancellors established the circumstances in which uses would be enforced. They had to decide also what equitable estates they would recognise; for example, if land were conveyed to A to the use of B for life and then to the use of C, should this be enforced? Broadly, the answer was that, in accordance with the maxim that equity follows the law, the estates and interests which could be created in equity corresponded with those which existed at law.

G. The Advantages of the Use

1–010   The employment of the use made it possible to avoid some of the feudal incidents. Under feudal law, the lord was entitled to a payment when an heir succeeded to feudal land, and to other valuable rights arising when the land was held by an under-age heir, and the right of escheat where there was no heir. These burdens could be avoided if the land was vested in a number of feoffees to uses. They were unlikely to die together or without heirs. Those who died could be replaced, and the feoffees would never be children. Thus, the use, to feudal land owners, had something of the appeal of tax planning techniques at the present day. It was possible also, in spite of the rule that freehold land could not be devised, to create effective dispositions of equitable interests on death by vesting the land in feoffees and declaring the uses on which the land was to be held after the settlor's death. Further, uses made possible the creation of new types of interests in land which were not possible at common law.[31] For a time also, until prevented by statute, land held to uses could be enjoyed by religious houses in defiance of the Statutes of Mortmain,[32] or be placed beyond the reach of creditors.

H. The Statute of Uses 1535

1–011   Henry VIII found that his purse was being emptied by the avoidance of feudal incidents which the system of uses made possible. To small tenants who had no tenants of their own, the system of uses was entirely beneficial. To large landowners, it was beneficial in so

---

[30] Except a bona fide purchaser of a legal estate for value without notice, below, para.1–039; Maitland, pp.113–115.

[31] e.g. springing and shifting interests; Cheshire and Burn, p.69.

[32] Which forbade the conveyance of land to religious houses without permission of the Crown. Milsom, p.204.

far as they were tenants, and harmful in so far as they were lords. To the King, it was entirely harmful, because he was lord of all and tenant of none. The first part of Henry VIII's reign had been expensive, and he was determined to restore the revenues of the Crown by attacking uses. The Statute of Uses of 1535 was intended to reduce greatly the scope of the use. After a grandiloquent preamble it provided, according to Maitland's summary of the first clause[33]:

> "[W]here any person or persons shall be seised of any lands or other hereditaments to the use, confidence, or trust of any other person or persons, in every such case such person and persons that shall have any such use, confidence or trust in fee simple, fee tail, for term of life or for years or otherwise shall stand and be seised deemed and adjudged in lawful seisin estate and possession of and in the same lands and hereditaments in such like estates as they had or shall have in the use."

In other words, the feoffees to uses were to disappear. The *cestui que use* was to have the legal estate.

The Statute did not however suppress all uses.[34] It only applied where the feoffee was *seised* to the use of another. If the feoffee held only a lease, he would not be seised, and the Statute would not apply. Again it did not apply to situations where the feoffees had active duties to perform. The feoffees were then necessary participants, and the Chancellor held that a duty to sell the land, or to collect the rents and profits of the land and pay them to X, was a sufficiently active duty to exclude the Statute.[35]

I. A Use upon a Use. The Trust

It was possible, after the Statute, to create equitable interests in land by imposing a use upon a leasehold, or by requiring the legal owners of freehold land to collect the rents and profits and to pay them over to the beneficiaries. Such uses were not executed; nor were they invalid.[36] Passive uses of freehold land were, however, executed by the Statute, so that the beneficiary held the legal estate. What would happen if a second use were imposed? If land were limited to A to the use of B to the use of C, is it possible to argue that the first use will be executed, and that B will hold the legal estate to the use of C? Such a solution was reached by about 1700[37]; the second use is called a trust. A shorter form, which became settled

1–012

---

[33] Maitland, p.35.
[34] Holdsworth, *H.E.L.* iv, pp.467–473.
[35] Maitland, pp.38–41; M & W., p.1167.
[36] Simpson, *A History of The Land Law*, 2nd edn, 1986, p.195.
[37] Simpson, *A History of The Land Law*, 2nd edn, 1986, p.203.

practice, was to omit A, and to make the disposition "unto and to the use of B in trust for C".

The story of this development is confused and uncertain.[38] Most accounts start with the proposition that through the 16th century, the second use was repugnant to the first, and void.[39] When the turning-point came is unsettled, but it is clear that after the Restoration in 1660, a number of factors combined to facilitate the recognition of passive trusts of freeholds. The abolition of military tenures[40] and the consequent freedom to devise all freehold land,[41] the reduction in the value of money which followed the development of the New World, and the changes in the constitutional and financial structure of the country in the 17th century, all helped to make the collection of feudal dues a minor factor in the royal revenues. The Civil War determined once and for all that the Government was to be financed by Parliamentary vote. There was now no reason of policy why passive trusts of freeholds should not be enforced as were active trusts and trusts of leaseholds. The enforcement of the second use as a trust was so similar to that of the enforcement of the use against a feoffee to uses centuries before that Lord Hardwicke was able to say, in 1738, in a remark of greater dramatic power than legal or mathematical accuracy:

> " . . . [B]y this means a statute made upon great consideration, introduced in a solemn and pompous manner, by this strict construction, has had no other effect than to add at most, three words to a conveyance."[42]

J. The Struggle over Injunctions

1–013   The story of the use and of the trust has taken us away from the chronological sequence. For it was at the close of the 16th century that the quarrel over the power of the Chancery to issue injunctions came to a head. The use of the injunction had the effect of rendering the common law inoperative. That the clash did not come earlier was due partly to the statesmanlike qualities of men like More; and no doubt also to the reluctance to challenge the powers of royal officers in Tudor times. Chief Justice Coke was not willing to see the common law treated in this way, and in a number of cases decided

---

[38] Milsom, p.208 suggests that the origin is in a situation in which a settlor wishes to settle upon himself with remainders over; J. Baker (1977) 93 L.Q.R. 33.
[39] Maitland, p.42; Ames, *Lectures on Legal History*, 1913, pp.243–247; Holdsworth, *H.E.L.* iv, pp.471–473; *Jane Tyrell's Case* (1557) Dyer 155a.
[40] Tenures Abolition Act 1660.
[41] Previously only two-thirds of land held by knight service could be devised.
[42] *Hopkins v Hopkins* (1739) 1 Atk. 581 at 591; see Holdsworth, *H.E.L.* iv, p.449.

that imprisonment for disobedience to injunctions issued by Chancery was unlawful.[43] In one case it was said that "if any court of equity doth inter-meddle with any matters properly triable at the common law, or which concern freehold, they are to be prohibited."[44] Lord Chancellor Ellesmere, equally determined, claimed that he was in no sense interfering with the common law; he was merely acting *in personam*, directing the individual that, on equitable grounds, he must not proceed to sue at law or enforce a judgment already obtained at law.

James I stepped in and referred the matter to Bacon, then Attorney General, and others learned in the law. Acting on their recommendations, and no doubt in accordance with his own political views and interests, he decided in favour of the Chancery.[45] The victory did not remain long unchallenged. The success of the Parliament and of the common lawyers in the political struggles of the 17th century provided further impetus for the attack on the Chancery. As late as 1690, following the Revolution, a Bill was introduced in the House of Commons to restrain the interference by Chancery in any suit for which the proper remedy was at common law.[46] The Bill was not passed, and from that time the Chancellor's jurisdiction was not seriously challenged. Thereafter, law and equity worked together, as parts of a consistent whole; and this enabled Maitland to say that equity had come, not to destroy the law, but to fulfil it.[47]

K. The Transformation of Equity into the Modern System[48]

From the beginning of the Chancellorship of Lord Nottingham in 1673 and to the end of that of Lord Eldon in 1827, equity was transformed from a jurisdiction based upon the personal interference of the Chancellor into a system of established rules and principles. We have seen that the early Chancellors were ecclesiastics. Lawyers and others were sometimes appointed during the Tudor and Stuart periods. The retirement of Lord Shaftesbury[49] in 1672 was the last occasion on which a non-lawyer held the Great Seal.[50] This factor influenced the development of the system into one based on rules

1–014

---

[43] *Heath v Rydley* (1614) Cro.Jac. 335; *Bromage v Genning* (1617) 1 Rolle 368; *Throckmorton v Finch* (1598) Third Institute 124 at 25.

[44] i.e. liable to be subject to the writ of Prohibition; *Heath v Rydley* (1614) Cro.Jac. 335.

[45] *Reports of Cases in Chancery*, App.1, p.49; 21 E.R. 588.

[46] Holdsworth, *H.E.L.* i, pp.463–465.

[47] Maitland, p.19.

[48] Pollock, *Essays in Legal History*, 1907, p.286.

[49] A member of the Cabal of Charles II; he had been educated as a lawyer, but never practised; Holdsworth, *H.E.L.* i, p.411; vi, pp.525–526.

[50] Since the Constitutional Reform Act 2005 the Lord Chancellor need not be a lawyer. He must be "qualified by experience"; s.2. See generally Lord Bingham (2006) 122 L.Q.R. 211.

and precedents rather than on individual conscience. The first reported Chancery cases are dated 1557[51] and these cases are treated as authorities and followed.[52]

Lord Nottingham did much to weld together and consolidate the whole system. To him we owe the doctrine that there can be no "clog on the equity of redemption",[53] a classification of trusts,[54] and the modern rule against perpetuities.[55] Throughout the 18th century, equity, in a period of legislative stagnation, became the great force that moulded the progress of the law right up to the beginning of the 19th century. In this period the modern law of trusts developed and was shaped to meet entirely new conditions of social life; equity took in hand the administration of the estates of deceased persons, on which depended the doctrines of election,[56] satisfaction,[57] ademption,[58] marshalling of assets,[59] and performance,[60] and in many cases it is possible to point to the Chancellor who first applied them.[61] In this period there were many great Chancellors, culminating in Lord Eldon (1801–1806, 1807–1827), one of the greatest equity lawyers. His decisions were thorough, painstaking, learned and clear. As Holdsworth said:

> "He had a thorough grasp of existing rules and principles; but he looked as anxiously into all the facts and circumstances of each case . . . as if there were no such rules and as if, therefore, he was under the necessity of determining each case as one of first impression."[62]

The judgments were masterly. But it is hardly surprising that the business of the court was scandalously in arrears. The pattern and principles of equity were now established. "Nothing would inflict on me greater pain in quitting this place," he said, "than the recollection that I had done anything to justify the reproach that the equity of this court varies like the Chancellor's foot."[63]

---

[51] "Choyce Cases in Chancery"; Holdsworth, *H.E.L.* v pp.274–278; Jones, *The Elizabethan Court of Chancery*, 1967, p.3.

[52] In the preface to Nelson's reports, at pp.2–3, the author said that "Equity became artificial Reason, and hath ever since such a mixture of law in it, that it woud be much easier now for a Lawyer to preach, than for a Prelate to be a Judge of that Court"; Holdsworth, *H.E.L.* vi, p.669.

[53] *Howard v Harris* (1681) 1 Vern. 33.

[54] *Cook v Fountain* (1676) 3 Swan. 585.

[55] *Duke of Norfolk's Case* (1683) 2 Swan. 454.

[56] Snell, para.6–012.

[57] Snell, para.6–056.

[58] Snell, para.35–005.

[59] Snell, para.32–045.

[60] Snell, para.6–040.

[61] *Re Hallet's Estate* (1880) 13 Ch.D. 696 at 710.

[62] Holdsworth, *H.E.L.* i, p.468.

[63] Holdsworth, *H.E.L.* i, pp.468–469; *Gee v Pritchard* (1818) 2 Swan. 402 at 414.

L. The 19th Century and the Judicature Acts 1873 and 1875

The 19th century was a period of great development of the equita- **1–015**
ble jurisdiction, based upon the principles established by the end of
Lord Eldon's tenure. The enormous industrial, international and
imperial expansion of Britain in this period necessitated developments in equity to deal with a host of new problems. The accumulation of business fortunes required rules for the administration of
companies and partnerships; and the change in emphasis from
landed wealth to stocks and shares necessitated the development of
new concepts of property settlements.

Clearly the old organisation of the Chancery Court, overloaded in
Lord Eldon's time, could not hope to deal with the mass of business.
"Remember this," said Maitland to his students at the turn of the
20th century:

> "[T]hat until 1813 there were only two judges in the Court of
> Chancery. There was the Lord Chancellor, and there was the
> Master of the Rolls, and it was but by degrees that the latter had
> become an independent judge; for a long time he appears merely
> as the Chancellor's assistant. In 1813 a Vice-Chancellor was ap-
> pointed. In 1841 two more Vice-Chancellors. In 1851 two Lords
> Justices of Appeal in Chancery. When the Court was abolished in
> 1875, it had seven judges. Cases in the first instance were taken
> before the Master of the Rolls, or one of the three Vice-Chancel-
> lors, and there was an Appeal Court constituted by the Chancellor
> and the two Lords Justices; but the Chancellor could sit as a judge
> of first instance if he pleased and sometimes did so."[64]

At least, however, the judges could deal with their work without the
fear of opposition from the common law. The two courts had now
become "not rivals but partners in the work of administering justice."[65] The time had come for the fusion of these jurisdictions into a
single Supreme Court.

Some limited steps were taken towards this fusion in the middle
of the 19th century. The Common Law Procedure Act 1854 gave to
the common law courts a certain power to give equitable remedies,
and the Chancery Amendment Act 1858, commonly known as Lord
Cairns' Act, gave to the Court of Chancery power to award damages
in addition to, or in substitution for, an injunction or an order for
specific performance.[66] The major change however came with the

---

[64] Maitland, p.14. There are now 18 judges, headed by the Chancellor of the High Court,
allocated to the Chancery Division.
[65] Holdsworth, *H.E.L.* v p.668.
[66] Below, paras 24–044, 25–048.

Judicature Acts 1873 and 1875. These Acts abolished the old separate Courts of Queen's Bench, Exchequer, Common Pleas, Chancery, Probate, the Divorce Court, and the Court of Admiralty; it created the Supreme Court of Judicature with a High Court divided into Divisions known as the Queen's Bench Division, Chancery Division, and the Probate, Divorce and Admiralty Division. The latter was re-named the Family Division in 1970.[67] Its Admiralty jurisdiction was assigned to the Queen's Bench Division, and Probate business, other than non-contentious and common form probate business, to the Chancery Division. Each division exercises both legal and equitable jurisdiction.[68] Thus any issue can be adjudicated in any division; and any point of law or equity can be raised and determined in any division; but, for the sake of administrative convenience, cases are allocated to the divisions according to their general subject-matter.[69] Thus the court "is now not a Court of Law or a Court of Equity, it is a Court of complete jurisdiction."[70]

1–016   It was foreseen that a court which applied the rules both of common law and of equity would face a conflict where the common law rules would produce one result, and equity another. Section 25 of the Supreme Court of Judicature Act 1873 therefore provided for the solution of many problems in which those rules would conflict.[71] Subsection 11 contained a general residual clause:

> "Generally, in all matters not hereinbefore particularly mentioned in which there is any conflict or variance between the rules of equity and the rules of common law with reference to the same matter, the rules of equity shall prevail."

The effect of the Judicature Act is best shown by the leading case of *Walsh v Lonsdale*.[72]

> The landlord agreed in writing to grant to the tenant a lease of a mill for seven years. The agreement provided that the rent was

---

[67] Administration of Justice Act 1970 s.1.

[68] Judicature Act 1873 s.24; Judicature Act 1925 ss.36–44; Senior Courts Act 1981 s.49.

[69] See Senior Courts Act 1981 Sch.1, below, para.1–049. The Court of Protection was established as a court of record by the Mental Capacity Act 2005.

[70] *Pugh v Heath* (1882) 7 App.Cas. 235 at 237, per Lord Cairns. Thus the three-fold division of the content of equity into the exclusive, concurrent and auxiliary jurisdictions lost importance after the Judicature Acts.

[71] Now Senior Courts Act 1981 s.49. Examples are found in s.25(1) of the Act of 1873, dealing with the order of priority of payment of debts of a person dying insolvent; and the refusal of common law but not of equity to recognise the assignment of debts and choses in action (s.25(6)). These matters are now dealt with by the AEA 1925 s.34(1) and LPA 1925 s.136 respectively. See *Job v Job* (1877) 6 Ch.D. 562; *Lowe v Dixon* (1885) 16 Q.B.D. 455; *Berry v Berry* [1929] 2 K.B. 316. See also LPA 1925 s.41.

[72] (1882) 21 Ch.D. 9; *Warmington v Miller* [1973] Q.B. 877; *Tottenham Hotspur Football and Athletic Co Ltd v Princegrove Publishers Ltd* [1974] 1 W.L.R. 113; M. Albery (1974) 90 L.Q.R. 149; S. Gardner (1987) 7 O.J.L.S. 60.

payable in advance if demanded. No grant by deed of the lease—as required for a lease exceeding three years *at law*—was ever made.

The tenant entered and paid rent quarterly, not in advance. He became in arrears and the landlord demanded a year's rent in advance. It was not paid, and the landlord distrained. The tenant brought this action for illegal distress.[73]

The action failed. The distress would have been illegal at law, because no seven-year lease had been granted, and the yearly legal tenancy which arose because of the entering into possession and payment of rent did not include the provision for payment of rent in advance.[74] In equity, however, the agreement for the lease was as good as a lease. The tenant was liable to pay a year's rent in advance and the distress was lawful.

It will be seen that the effect of the Act is procedural only.[75] The rights of the parties, whether dependent on the rules of law or of equity, were under the Act determined at a single trial. But the same result would ultimately have been reached if the case had arisen before 1875; the procedure only would have differed. The claim, being one for damages for illegal distress, would have been brought at common law. To the tenant's argument that he held only on a lease from year to year, of which the covenant to pay rent a year in advance was not a term, the landlord would have had no reply in a court of law. The claim to specific performance of the agreement to take a lease was one that could only have been made in equity. The landlord would have had to obtain an injunction to stop the tenant's action at law, and then to obtain specific performance of the agreement; and then to have returned to the common law court with the lease duly created by deed in conformity with the decree of Chancery. The landlord would then have had a good defence in the common law court. The effect of the Judicature Acts was to enable the court to treat as done that which ought to be done, and to allow the landlord to use his equitable defence (based on his right to specific performance) to the common law claim. The principle that equity treats as done that which ought to be done was not new. The significance of the case is the recognition of that principle in a case involving a legal claim. The principle is not limited to agreements for leases, but is applicable to all cases where there is a specifically

---

[73] A landlord could distrain (i.e. issue a distress) upon a tenant who was in arrear, and in doing so could take and sell sufficient goods of the tenant (with exceptions) as were necessary to pay the arrears; M. & W., p.878. (This common law remedy was abolished by Tribunals, Courts and Enforcement Act 2007 s.71.)

[74] A yearly tenancy which arises in these circumstances includes only such terms of any agreement as are consistent with a yearly tenancy. An agreement to pay a year's rent in advance is not consistent with a yearly tenancy; M. & W., p.774.

[75] See J. Coté (1966) 4 Alberta L.R. 134.

enforceable contract by a legal owner to convey or create a legal estate, such as a contract to sell, to grant a lease or a mortgage. The principle has been applied "once removed"; as where A agreed to sell Blackacre to B who had agreed to grant a lease to C. C was treated as the lessee in equity of the land.[76] C would not become a lessee at law until the legal lease had been properly granted.

Whether developments since the Judicature Acts have had the effect of fusing not only the jurisdictions but law and equity themselves is a disputed question which can best be considered after looking into the nature of equitable rights.

M. Current Role of the Lord Chancellor

1–017   In 2003 the Prime Minister unexpectedly and controversially announced that the historic office of Lord Chancellor was to be abolished. This led to much debate concerning the propriety of the same office-holder appointing the judiciary, sitting (occasionally) as a judge in the Judicial Committee of the House of Lords, sitting in the House of Lords and being a government Minister. The Constitutional Reform Bill was introduced, providing for the abolition of the office of Lord Chancellor and the transfer of his functions to the Secretary of State for Constitutional Affairs,[77] the Lord Chief Justice and others.

The proposal to abolish the office of Lord Chancellor met with resistance, and the Constitutional Reform Act 2005 retained the office, although the Lord Chancellor's judicial functions passed to the Lord Chief Justice.[78]

The other main provisions of the Act were the creation of the Judicial Appointments Commission and the replacement of the Judicial Committee of the House of Lords by a Supreme Court.

3. THE NATURE OF EQUITABLE RIGHTS

1–018   There has for many years been a learned and unsettled controversy on the question of the nature of equitable rights; and particularly of the nature of the interest of a beneficiary under a trust. In its simplest form, one view emphasises the fact that a beneficiary's remedy, historically and practically, is in the form of an action against the trustee; a right *in personam*. On the other hand, equitable interests under trusts are equitable proprietary interests, corresponding to

---

[76] *Industrial Properties (Barton Hill) Ltd v Associated Electrical Industries Ltd* [1977] Q.B. 580; P. Jackson (1977) 40 M.L.R. 718.

[77] The Department for Constitutional Affairs became the Ministry of Justice in 2007.

[78] Constitutional Reform Act 2005 s.7. The Lord Chancellor need not be a lawyer or a peer; s.2. See generally Lord Bingham (2006) 122 L.Q.R. 211.

legal estates, and the beneficiary can properly be regarded as the owner of the beneficial interest; and ownership is a right *in rem*. The controversy attracted many great scholars; with Langdell, Ames, Maitland and Holland on one side, and Austin, Salmond, Pomeroy and Scott on the other.[79]

Much of this controversy centred upon whether the beneficiary's right was a right *in personam* or a right *in rem*. This was because Austin, following the classifications of Roman law, laid down that rights must be of one type or the other. But, for the discussion to become meaningful, it is necessary to know what these terms mean. They mean different things in different contexts. It seems that the proper meaning of a right *in rem* in the present context is "a right enforceable against the world with respect to a particular thing".[80] It is assumed throughout that a legal owner does have rights *in rem*. Rights, that is, against all the world with respect to property. How, then, does a beneficiary under a trust measure up to this test?

The basis of equitable jurisdiction, historically and presently, is that, in accordance with the maxim, equity acts *in personam*, equitable rights grew up where the Chancellor was willing to intervene. The use has its origin in the insistence of the Chancellor that the feoffees to uses should administer the property for the benefit of the *cestui que use*. Similarly with the trust.

> "Equity did not say that the *cestui que trust* was the owner of the land, it said that the trustee was the owner of the land, but added that he was bound to hold the land for the benefit of the *cestui que trust*."[81]

This raised the question of the effect of the sale of the land by the trustee. The answer was that the beneficiary's interest was effective against everyone except a bona fide purchaser for valuable consideration without notice, actual or constructive, of the equitable interest.

Indeed equity could not have done differently. Its remedies of specific performance and injunction were orders *in personam*. They ordered the defendant to do something or to refrain from doing something; and behind them was the threat that a recalcitrant defendant would be put in prison for contempt.

There is no space here to run through every aspect of equity jurisdiction to establish the point that equity acts *in personam*. One practical application of this proposition is the fact that a court of equity will exercise jurisdiction to order specific performance of a

---

[79] D. Waters (1967) 45 C.B.R. at 221; A. Scott (1917) 17 Col.L.R. 269; H. Stone (1917) 17 Col.L.R. 467; E. Mockler (1962) 40 C.B.R. at 270.

[80] (1962) 40 C.B.R. at 279.

[81] Maitland, p.17.

contract for the sale of land abroad,[82] or to administer assets abroad
if the executors are in England.[83] Where a father bought a flat in
France in his son's name and sought a declaration that the son was a
trustee and an order to vest the property in the father, his action was
classified as *in personam* for the purposes of the 1968 Brussels
Convention,[84] so that the son's claim that only the French courts had
jurisdiction failed.[85] Where a wife sought a declaration in the English courts as to her beneficial interest in land in England, her claim
was classified as *in personam*. Thus the English courts did not have
exclusive jurisdiction and the action was stayed because her husband had already commenced divorce and ancillary relief proceedings in France.[86] In *Re Hayward*,[87] on the other hand, the claim by
the trustee in bankruptcy of a deceased legal and beneficial co-
owner of a villa in Spain to his share of the property was held to be
in rem, so that the Spanish court had exclusive jurisdiction under the
Convention. It has been noted that the fact that English law has been
incapable of determining conclusively whether trust interests are *in
rem* or *in personam* "is a deficiency only exacerbated when the
concepts are carried into private international law".[88]

1–019   This debate does not prevent us from treating a beneficiary under
a trust as having equitable ownership. A beneficiary's interest behind a trust has long been treated as having the basic characteristics
of a proprietary interest in that it can be bought, sold, mortgaged,
and devised or bequeathed. Even though, historically, the protection
of the beneficiary was based on the Chancellor's willingness to
proceed *in personam* against the trustee, that protection has ended
up by creating rights in the nature of ownership.[89] To argue that a
beneficiary's rights are proprietary is not to say that legal rights are
the same as equitable, or that equitable ownership is the same as
legal. Rather, it is to accept the basic peculiarity of ownership under
the English law of trusts. The trustee is the owner at law; and the
beneficiary is the owner in equity. A recent analysis is that the
interest of the beneficiary is negative, or "exclusionary": it is a
negative right to exclude non-beneficiaries from the assets as opposed to a positive right to impose trustee duties on them.[90] Another

---

[82] *Penn v Lord Baltimore* (1750) 1 Ves.Sen. 444; *Richard West and Partners (Inverness) Ltd
v Dick* [1969] Ch. 424; below para.24–003.
[83] *Ewing v Orr-Ewing (No.1)* (1883) 9 App.Cas. 34.
[84] See now art.22 of the Council Regulation (EC) No.44/2001.
[85] *Webb v Webb* [1994] Q.B. 696; A. Briggs (1994) 110 L.Q.R. 526; P. Rogerson (1994) 53
C.L.J. 462; P. Birks (1994) 8 T.L.I. 99; J. Collier All E.R. Rev. 1994 p.81; C. MacMillan
[1996] Conv. 125. See also *Ashurst v Pollard* [2001] Ch. 595; J. Harris [2001]
L.M.C.L.Q. 205.
[86] *Prazic v Prazic* [2006] 2 F.L.R. 1128.
[87] [1997] Ch. 45.
[88] J. Stevens [1998] Conv. 145 at 150.
[89] *Sinclair v Brougham* [1914] A.C. 398 at 444; Lord Evershed M.R. (1954) 70 L.Q.R. 326
at 331; *Tinsley v Milligan* [1994] 1 A.C. 340 at 371.
[90] R. Nolan (2006) 122 L.Q.R. 232.

view is that the beneficiary's interest is "a bundle of *in personam* equitable rights against the trustee".[91]

In relation to some claims affecting the trust property, the trustee is able to sue and not the beneficiary. Thus, the trustee sues for rent,[92] or for possession; and, with personalty, the trustee, not the beneficiary, sues for conversion of the trust property.[93] The beneficiary's right is to compel the trustee to take action; though he may, in some cases, take action himself on behalf of the trust, joining the trustee as defendant.[94] This right may sometimes be inadequate; as where the trustee has sold the property to a bona fide purchaser of the legal estate for value without notice, who will defeat the equitable ownership of the beneficiary.[95] Does this require us to say that his rights are personal against the trustee, and are not properly regarded as proprietary? This was the deciding test for the supporters of the theory that equitable rights must be regarded as being *in personam*. But it shows the inadequacy of the test which is being applied as a means of distinguishing equitable ownership from legal ownership; which is accepted as being a right *in rem*. For legal rights of ownership are not good against all the world. There are many ways in which the legal owner of a chattel or chose in action may be involuntarily deprived of legal ownership.[96] The situation of the bona fide purchaser is not determinative of the question whether the beneficiary's interest is proprietary; or whether his rights are *in rem* or *in personam*. It demonstrates simply that legal and equitable ownership may have different effects. It has recently been held that a duty of care may be owed to a beneficial owner of property just as much as to a legal owner, but this has been criticised as blurring legal and equitable ownership in a manner contrary to principle and authority.[97]

From a practical point of view, it can be said that where the problem involves the working of the trust machinery, so that the

---

[91] S. Aaron (2010) 24 T.L.I. 155 at 173.

[92] *Schalit v Nadler Ltd* [1933] 2 K.B. 79.

[93] *MCC Proceeds Inc v Lehman Brothers International (Europe)* [1998] 4 All E.R. 675. The beneficiary can sue if he has a right to immediate possession; *Healey v Healey* [1915] 1 K.B. 938. See A. Tettenborn (1996) 55 C.L.J. 36.

[94] See *Les Affréteurs Réunis Société Anonyme v Leopold Walford (London) Ltd* [1919] A.C. 801; *Parker-Tweedale v Dunbar Bank Plc* [1991] Ch. 12; *Bradstock Trustee Services Ltd v Nabarro Nathanson (A Firm)* [1995] 1 W.L.R. 1405; *Barbados Trust Co v Bank of Zambia* [2007] 1 Lloyd's Rep. 495; G. Tolhurst [2007] L.M.C.L.Q. 278; M. Smith (2008) 22 T.L.I. 140; R. Goode (2009) L.M.C.L.Q. 300 at 313–315; *Roberts v Gill & Co* [2011] 1 A.C. 240.

[95] The beneficiary will have a personal right against the trustee for compensation and may be able to trace the proceeds; below, Ch.23.

[96] Sale of Goods Act 1979 ss.21, 24; Factors Act 1889 ss.2, 8, 9; Consumer Credit Act 1974 Sch.4, para.22.

[97] *Shell UK Ltd v Total UK Ltd* [2011] Q.B. 86; N. Macklam [2010] Conv. 265; K. Low (2010) 126 L.Q.R. 507; A. Rushworth and A. Scott [2010] L.M.C.L.Q. 536; P. Turner (2010) 69 C.L.J. 445.

beneficiary asserts his rights by an action against the trustees to enforce their duties, the old theory that equity acts *in personam* is wholly acceptable.[98] But, in other cases, usually tax cases,[99] the theoretical view is overtaken by a pragmatic approach; and the result determined by the language of the statute and a number of policy questions relating to the purposes of the particular statute. This is an area where Austin's theoretical analysis is the least helpful. Perhaps the better view is that the beneficiary's interest is sui generis.[100]

4. The Relationship Between Law and Equity: Fusion[101]

1–020　　The Judicature Act clearly "fused" the administration of law and equity by the creation of the High Court of Judicature exercising both law and equity and gave supremacy to equity in cases of conflict. A disputed question is whether that Act, or the subsequent development of law and equity, should be regarded as having effected the fusion of law and equity themselves.

The orthodox view is that only the jurisdictions have been fused. The changes made by the Judicature Act gave rise to no new cause of action, remedy, or defence, which was not available before. In a famous metaphor, Ashburner said that "the two streams of jurisdiction, though they run in the same channel; run side by side, and do not mingle their waters."[102] Thus, legal rights remain legal rights, and equitable rights remain equitable rights, though administered in the same court. Other bills which were introduced prior to the Judicature Act would indeed have fused law and equity; but they failed, and the Judicature Act was a more cautious measure.[103]

There are, however, statements by great judges to the effect that law and equity are fused. Sir George Jessel said, as early as 1881:

> "[T]here are not two estates as there were formerly, one estate in common law by reason of the payment of rent from year to year, and an estate in equity under the agreement. There is only one court, and equity rules prevail in it."[104]

---

[98] D. Waters (1967) 45 C.B.R. at 280.

[99] See *Baker v Archer-Shee* [1927] A.C. 844.

[100] Pettit, p.83.

[101] See generally Degeling and Edelman (eds) *Equity in Commercial Law*, 2005, Pt I.

[102] Ashburner, *Principles of Equity*, 2nd edn, p.18. See also Lord Evershed M.R. (1954) 70 L.Q.R. 326; V. Delaney (1961) 24 M.L.R. 116; T. Watkin (1977) 6 A.A.L.R. 119. For a historical study, see P. Polden (2002) 61 C.L.J. 575.

[103] P. Baker (1977) 93 L.Q.R. 529 at 530; (1870) 14 S.J. 548.

[104] *Walsh v Lonsdale* (1882) 21 Ch.D. 14. He had previously expressed the orthodox view of the effect of the Act, in *Salt v Cooper* (1880) 16 Ch.D. 544 at 549.

Subsequently Lord Diplock[105] discussed Ashburner's metaphor, and declared:

"By 1977, this metaphor has in my view become most mischievous and deceptive. The innate conservatism of English lawyers may have made them slow to recognise that by the Supreme Court of Judicature Act 1873, the two systems of substantive and adjectival law formerly administered by courts of law and Courts of Chancery (as well as those administered by Courts of Admiralty, Probate and Matrimonial Causes), were fused."

In some jurisdictions in recent years, contrary to Lord Diplock's view, the distinction between law and equity "has achieved renewed prominence", as the courts have reasserted the old conscience-based jurisdiction of equity, with its different techniques, policies and doctrines.[106]

Others have expressed views to the effect that we ought to be addressing our minds to the *combined effect* of the systems of law and equity, and that to keep the systems always distinct is pedantic, and an impediment to the natural development of the law.[107]

It is important, in this discussion, to be clear as to what is meant by the claim that law and equity are fused. If it means that there is now no distinction or difference between legal rights and remedies and equitable rights and remedies, it cannot be supported.[108] It is still clear that legal ownership is different from equitable ownership; all the provisions of the legislation of 1925, dealing with unregistered land, are based on that assumption.[109] Again, the law of trusts assumes a distinction between legal and equitable rights. The equitable nature of the duties of a mortgagee has been emphasised,[110] although Sir Richard Scott V.C. has said:

---

[105] *United Scientific Holdings Ltd v Burnley BC* [1978] A.C. 904 at 925. All the members of the House indicated their general acceptance of the principle of fusion. Lord Diplock is described as "the most forceful exponent of the fusion fallacy", in Heydon, Gummow and Austin, *Cases and Materials on Equity and Trusts*, 4th edn, p.27. See also *Chief Constable of Kent v V* [1983] Q.B. 34 at 41.

[106] A. Duggan (1997) 113 L.Q.R. 601 at 601–602. The author goes on, however, to "debunk the myth" of the "new equity rhetoric".

[107] See Lord Evershed (1948) J.S.P.T.L. 180; Lord Denning (1952) C.L.P. 1; *The Court of Appeal in England*, p.13 (Lord Evershed); V. Delaney (1961) 24 M.L.R. 116; Lord Denning, *Landmarks in the Law*, p.86 ("the fusion is complete"). See also A. Burrows (2002) 22 O.J.L.S. 1, S. Worthington (2002) 55 C.L.P. 223.

[108] P. Baker (1977) 93 L.Q.R. 529 at 532.

[109] The distinction between legal and equitable ownership is of little significance in registered land. But that is due to the classification of interests for the purposes of the system, and is unconnected with any question of fusion.

[110] *China and South Sea Bank Ltd v Tan Soon Gin* [1990] 1 A.C. 536; *Parker-Tweedale v Dunbar Bank Plc* [1991] Ch. 12, criticising *Cuckmere Brick Co Ltd v Mutual Finance Ltd* [1971] Ch. 949 (common law damages and duty of care in tort imported); *Downsview Nominees Ltd v First City Corp Ltd* [1993] A.C. 295; *AIB Finance Ltd v Debtors* [1998] 2 All E.R. 929; *Yorkshire Bank Plc v Hall* [1999] 1 W.L.R. 1713.

"I do not, for my part, think that it matters one jot whether the duty is expressed as a common law duty or as a duty in equity. The result is the same."[111]

The result may not always be the same, however.[112] Further, as discussed below,[113] it is still basically true to say that an equitable claim will provide only an equitable remedy. An equitable claim is required for the revived writ[114] *ne exeat regno*.[115] The common law and equitable rules for tracing property are different, as explained in Ch.23; likewise the rules concerning the transmission of the burden of a restrictive covenant.[116] Although common law damages and compensation in equity share the requirement of causation, they differ on remoteness and foreseeability.[117] The illustrations could be multiplied.

1–021   Nor is it true, at the other extreme, to say that rights exercisable in the High Court today are the same as those existing in 1875; nor that the application of equitable doctrines in the court has not had the effect of refining and developing the common law rules.[118] Both legal and equitable rules have developed since 1873; and the development of legal rules has sometimes been influenced by established equitable doctrine, with the effect that a situation which would at one time have been treated differently at law and in equity is now treated in the same manner. If that is what is meant by fusion, there is evidence of it, as shown below. It is a healthy and welcome development; and there are other situations which might be candidates for future inclusion.

In *Boyer v Warbey*,[119] the question arose whether covenants in a lease bound assignees, not only where the lease was by deed, but also where the lease was a valid written lease (not exceeding three years). The Court of Appeal held that, whatever the position before 1875, this was not an area where distinctions based on formalities were now acceptable, and that the covenant should bind. It was further suggested that the same result would follow if there was

[111] *Medforth v Blake* [2000] Ch. 86 at 102; A. Kenny [1999] Conv. 434; L. Sealy (2000) 59 C.L.J. 31; S. Frisby (2000) 63 M.L.R. 413.
[112] *Raja v Lloyds TSB Bank Plc* (2001) 82 P. & C.R. 191 (limitation period).
[113] Below, para.1–022.
[114] Now called a claim form in the Civil Procedure Rules 1998.
[115] See *Felton v Callis* [1969] 1 Q.B. 200; *Allied Arab Bank Ltd v Hajjar* [1988] Q.B. 787; *Ali v Naseem, The Times*, October 3, 2003.
[116] See *Rhone v Stephens* [1994] 2 A.C. 310, especially at 321.
[117] *Target Holdings Ltd v Redferns (A Firm)* [1996] 1 A.C. 421 at 438, below, para.23–007, approving the views of McLachlin J. in *Canson Enterprises Ltd v Boughton* (1991) 85 D.L.R. (4th) 129.
[118] P. Baker (1977) 93 L.Q.R. 536; Sir Anthony Mason (1994) 110 L.Q.R. 238 and (1997–98) 8 K.C.L.J. 1; J. Martin [1994] Conv. 13; Sir Peter Millett (1995) 9 T.L.I. 35 at 37.
[119] [1953] 1 Q.B. 234, especially at 245–247, per Denning and Romer L.JJ. See also *Australian Blue Metal Ltd v Hughes* [1963] A.C. 74 at 101–102.

merely a contract for a lease which was enforceable in equity. Whether it was law or equity that regarded the lease as effective, the rule as to the running of covenants should be the same. In a limited sense this is "fusion" in that the reasons why a particular lease is effective are ignored in favour of a uniform consequential rule.

In *Tinsley v Milligan*[120] the question was whether an equitable interest could be asserted in spite of an element of illegality in its acquisition. Lord Browne-Wilkinson explained that legal and equitable interests had different incidents for historical reasons, but that "fusion" resulted in the adoption of a single rule as to the circumstances in which the court would enforce interests acquired under an illegal transaction. Thus the rule is the same whether the claim is to a legal or equitable title, and can be fully stated without reference to its origins.[121] In *Napier and Ettrick (Lord) v Hunter*[122] the nature of an insurer's subrogation right was in issue. Lord Goff examined the origins of subrogation at law and in equity and concluded that "No doubt our task nowadays is to see the two strands of authority, at law and in equity, moulded into a coherent whole."[123] Similarly, it has been held that set-off, whether legal or equitable, can be raised as a defence whether the relief sought by the claimant is legal or equitable.[124] The House of Lords has recently held that compound interest may be recovered at common law as well as in equity.[125] In the context of limitation periods, it has been held that there is no distinction between an action for fraud at common law and an action in equity for deliberate and dishonest breach of fiduciary duty based on the same facts, which is the equitable counterpart of the common law claim[126]:

"It would have been a blot on our jurisprudence if those self-same facts gave rise to a time bar in the common law courts but none in the court of equity".[127]

Much of the modern development of the law of estoppel, especially promissory estoppel and proprietary estoppel, has been achieved without enquiring whether the doctrines are doctrines of equity, or of law or of both. The doctrine of promissory estoppel

---

[120] [1994] 1 A.C. 340 at 371, 375, 376.

[121] But the Law Commission now recommends a different rule for equitable interests; Law Com. No.320 (2010), *The Illegality Defence*, para.2.54.

[122] [1993] A.C. 713.

[123] [1993] A.C. 713 at 743.

[124] *BICC Plc v Burndy Corp* [1985] Ch. 232; (1985) 101 L.Q.R. 145; *Eller v Grovecrest Investments Ltd* [1995] Q.B. 272. The rules for legal and equitable set-off remain distinct; *Muscat v Smith* [2003] 1 W.L.R. 2853; R. Derham (2006) 122 L.Q.R. 469.

[125] *Sempra Metals Ltd (formerly Metallgesellschaft Ltd) v IRC* [2008] 1 A.C. 561.

[126] *Coulthard v Disco Mix Club Ltd* [2000] 1 W.L.R. 707.

[127] *Coulthard v Disco Mix Club Ltd* [2000] 1 W.L.R. 707 at 730. See also *Cia de Seguros Imperio v Heath (REBX) Ltd* [2000] 1 W.L.R. 112 at 124.

works negatively; to give protection to the party who relied on the promise, but not to give a new cause of action.[128] But proprietary estoppel operates positively[129] and is capable of creating new rights. Such rights are recognised in equity only, and, in unregistered land, cannot bind a bona fide purchaser of a legal estate for value without notice. Proprietary estoppel must be regarded as a development in equity. Other estoppels can be regarded as being based on common law or equity.[130]

1–022　　　One indication of fusion is a situation where the legal remedy of damages may be given for breach of an equitable right. The converse, an equitable remedy for breach of a legal right, such as an injunction to restrain a tort, or specific performance of a contract, is explicable as the exercise of equity's concurrent jurisdiction and is not an example of fusion. However, the House of Lords went further in *Att Gen v Blake*,[131] holding that the equitable remedy of account of profits (which is traditionally associated with a fiduciary relationship) could be awarded in exceptional cases for breach of contract. This remedy, like injunctions and specific performance, could be awarded at the court's discretion where the remedy of damages, based on loss, would be inadequate. Although no direct authority could be found, it was considered a modest step which did not contradict any recognised principle on the grant or withholding of the remedy of account. As Lord Nicholls observed, remedies are the law's response to a wrong. The different remedial responses of the common law and equity arose as "an accident of history".[132]

Prior to the Judicature Act, Lord Cairns' Act authorised, in certain circumstances, courts of common law to grant specific performance or an injunction instead of damages, and courts of equity to award damages. As will be seen, this Act, although overtaken by the Judicature Act, still has scope for operation.[133] Generally, however, the breach of an equitable right will provide an equitable remedy only. Thus, a breach of a restrictive covenant by a non-contracting party is remedied by an injunction, not damages; innocent misrepresentation, apart from the Misrepresentation Act 1967, by rescission and not damages; and breach of trust[134] or other fiduciary duty by various equitable remedies. The stage has not yet been reached at which

---

[128] *Combe v Combe* [1951] 2 K.B. 215, below, para.27–021.

[129] Below, para.27–022.

[130] These distinctions are no longer drawn in Australia; below, para.27–019. See, however, *First National Bank Plc v Thompson* [1996] Ch. 231, emphasising the common law origin of certain types of estoppel.

[131] *Att Gen v Blake* [2001] 1 A.C. 268; P. Birks and W. Swadling All E.R. Rev. 2000, p.315; D. Campbell and J. Devenney (2006) 65 C.L.J. 208. See also *WWF - World Wide Fund for Nature v World Wrestling Federation Entertainment Inc* [2008] 1 W.L.R. 445; below, para.25–052.

[132] *Att Gen v Blake* [2001] 1 A.C. 268 at 280.

[133] Below, para.24–044.

[134] See *Metall und Rohstoff AG v Donaldson Lufkin & Jenrette Inc* [1990] 1 Q.B. 391 at 473 (common law damages not available).

it is immaterial whether a breach is of a legal or equitable duty. This situation was approached in *Seager v Copydex Ltd*,[135] where the defendants had used a technical idea communicated to them in confidence by the claimant in marketing a carpet grip. Equity's remedies in such cases are an injunction and an account of profits. But the circumstances of this case suggested that the most just solution was an assessment of damages. Can an action for common law damages lie, however, for a breach of confidence, which is protected only in equity?[136] The Court of Appeal held that the appropriate remedy must be granted; fictions of implied contracts or notional injunctions were not now necessary[137]; damages were thus ordered to be assessed.

Lord Goff subsequently said that damages are available for breach of confidence, despite the equitable nature of the wrong "through a beneficent interpretation of the Chancery Amendment Act 1858 (Lord Cairns' Act)".[138] Commonwealth courts have gone further, regarding it as now settled that damages may be awarded for breach of confidence[139] or other fiduciary duty[140]:

> "[E]quity and common law are now mingled or merged . . . a full range of remedies should be available as appropriate, no matter whether they originated in common law, equity or statute".[141]

But the compensation in such cases has been classified not as common law damages, but as "equitable compensation".[142]

In *Swindle v Harrison*[143] Hobhouse L.J. confirmed that common   **1–023** law damages were not available for breach of fiduciary duty. Evans

[135] [1967] 1 W.L.R. 923, and *(No.2)* [1969] 1 W.L.R. 809. Heydon, Gummow and Austin, *Cases and Materials on Equity and Trusts*, 4th edn, p.13, treat this case as an example of "fusion fallacies", i.e. cases where the results are explicable by the application of neither law nor equity, and could only result from a legislative change in substantive principles which is not found in the Judicature Act.

[136] There is no tort of invasion of privacy; *Campbell v MGN Ltd* [2004] 2 A.C. 457; below, para.25–069.

[137] i.e. to enable damages to be granted in lieu under Lord Cairns' Act, below, para.24–044. See *Seager v Copydex Ltd*, above, fn.135, at 931–932. See also *Fraser v Thames Television Ltd* [1984] Q.B. 44, where damages were awarded for breach of confidence without any argument on this point; *Stephens v Avery* [1988] Ch. 449; *Dowson & Mason Ltd v Potter* [1986] 1 W.L.R. 1419. In employment cases, of course, use of confidential information may be a breach of contract sounding in damages.

[138] *Att Gen v Guardian Newspapers Ltd (No.2)* [1990] 1 A.C. 109 at 286. See D. Capper (1994) 14 L.S. 313.

[139] *Catt v Marac Australia Ltd* (1986) 9 N.S.W.L.R. 639; *Lac Minerals Ltd v International Corona Resources Ltd* (1989) 61 D.L.R. (4th) 14; G Hammond (1990) 106 L.Q.R. 207.

[140] *Day v Mead* [1987] 2 N.Z.L.R. 443; M McGregor Vennell (1989) 105 L.Q.R. 32; *New Zealand Land Development Co Ltd v Porter* [1992] 2 N.Z.L.R. 462.

[141] *Aquaculture Corp v New Zealand Green Mussel Co Ltd* [1990] 3 N.Z.L.R. 299 at 301; J. Beatson (1991) 107 L.Q.R. 209.

[142] *Day v Mead*, above, fn.140. See further Sir Peter Millett (1998) 114 L.Q.R. 214 at 225.

[143] [1997] 4 All E.R. 705 at 726.

L.J. explained that it was still necessary to take account of the distinction between common law and equity even after the Judicature Act reforms:

"The reason is, of course, that the origins of both common law and equitable rules are always relevant to their scope, although we should endeavour now to identify the underlying common principles".[144]

The issue in *MCC Proceeds Inc v Lehman Brothers International (Europe)*[145] was whether an equitable owner could sue for conversion. It was held that such an owner, who has no title at common law, could not bring such an action. That rule had not been altered by the Judicature Act, which was intended to achieve procedural improvements in the administration of law and equity and not to transform equitable interests into legal titles. Conversion was a common law action, and the common law recognised only the title of the trustee:

"It is of the character of legal remedies that they derive from legal rights. That is one reason why they are not discretionary and may impose strict liabilities upon innocent parties. Equitable rights are of a different character and are recognised by the grant of equitable remedies which too have a different character".[146]

Thus it was impermissible to combine a strict legal remedy with a mere equitable right.

On the New Zealand approach, exemplary damages[147] or damages for mental distress[148] could be awarded for breach of equitable duties, and equitable compensation reduced for contributory negligence.[149] English courts have rejected the defence in cases of deceit and dishonest assistance in a breach of trust, unless the claimant has

---

[144] [1997] 4 All E.R. 705 at 714.

[145] [1998] 4 All E.R. 675; K. Barker [1998] 6 R.L.R. 150.

[146] [1998] 4 All E.R. 675 at 701.

[147] Differing views were expressed in the *Aquaculture* case, above. See P. McDermott (1995) 69 A.L.J. 773; *X v Att Gen* [1997] 2 N.Z.L.R. 623. Lindsay J. in *Douglas v Hello! Ltd (No.3)* [2003] 3 All E.R. 996 at 1073 assumed without deciding that exemplary damages were available for breach of confidence (not discussed on appeal). See further J. Edelman (2003) 119 L.Q.R. 375; S. Elliott and C. Mitchell (2004) 67 M.L.R. 16; J. Edelman and S. Elliott (2004) 18 T.L.I. 116; J. Getzler and A. Burrows in Degeling and Edelman (eds) *Equity in Commercial Law*, 2005, Ch.10 and Ch.15 respectively.

[148] Accepted by Cooke P. in *Mouat v Clark Boyce* [1992] 2 N.Z.L.R. 559 (not discussed on appeal at [1994] 1 A.C. 428). An award of damages for mental distress was upheld by the Court of Appeal in *Douglas v Hello! Ltd (No.3)* [2006] Q.B. 125. The House of Lords did not consider this issue on appeal at [2008] A.C. 1.

[149] Also accepted by Cooke P. in *Mouat*, above, fn.148, in *Day v Mead*, above, fn.137, and in Sir Peter Millett (1995) 9 T.L.I. 35 at 38. Differing views were expressed in *Canson Enterprises Ltd v Boughton* (1991) 85 D.L.R. (4th) 129.

been "the author of his own misfortune".[150] As contributory negligence is not a defence at common law to intentional torts, it has been said that equity should be no less rigorous. Thus if the breach involves conscious disloyalty (as opposed to a breach of the non-fiduciary duty of care), the defendant is disabled from asserting that the claimant contributed to the loss by his own want of care, although there may come a point where the loss is too remote.[151] As one commentator has recently put it: "It would be anathema to the nature and function of fiduciary liability for such pleas to be accepted."[152] Whether a wider view on the applicability of contributory negligence or the availability of heads of damage such as mental distress is acceptable depends on whether the policy of the common law on which such concepts are based is the same policy as that on which equitable compensation is founded. This, it is submitted, is not necessarily so.[153] We should heed the warning of Stevenson J.: "I greatly fear that talk of fusing law and equity only results in confusing and confounding the law."[154]

Sufficient examples have been given to show that law and equity are not fused. What can be said is that more than a century of fused jurisdiction has seen the two systems, whose relationship is "still-evolving",[155] working more closely together; each changing and developing and improving from contact with the other; and each willing to accept new ideas and developments, regardless of their origin. They are coming closer together. But they are not yet fused.

5. THE MAXIMS OF EQUITY

The maxims of equity embody the general principles which evolved   **1–024**
in the Court of Chancery. They are not rules which must be rigorously applied in every case, but are more in the nature of general guidelines illustrating the way in which equitable jurisdiction is exercised. A few examples of their operation must suffice,[156] but

[150] *Corporacion Nacional del Cobre de Chile v Sogemin Metals Ltd* [1997] 1 W.L.R. 1396; *Standard Chartered Bank v Pakistan National Shipping Corp (Nos 2 and 4)* [2003] 1 A.C. 959.

[151] *Nationwide Building Society v Balmer Radmore* [1999] Lloyd's Rep. P.N. 241. It was noted that the topic was highly contentious and academic opinion sharply divided.

[152] M. Conaglen (2010) 126 L.Q.R. 72 at 101.

[153] J. Martin [1994] Conv. 13 at 21–22; cf. per Cooke P. in *Mouat v Clark Boyce*, above, fn.148, at 569. Differing views were expressed in *Canson Enterprises Ltd v Boughton*, above, fn.149.

[154] *Canson Enterprises Ltd v Boughton*, above, fn.149, at 165. See also L. Smith in Degeling and Edelman (eds) *Equity in Commercial Law*, Ch.2.

[155] *Sempra Metals Ltd (formerly Metallgesellschaft Ltd) v IRC* [2008] 1 A.C. 561 at 629.

[156] For a more detailed survey, see Snell, Ch.5.

they should be borne in mind when considering the various rules and doctrines of equity.

1–025   **i. Equity will not suffer a wrong to be without a remedy.** The principle behind this maxim is that equity will intervene to protect a right which, perhaps because of some technical defect, is not enforceable at law. It is not sufficient that the defendant may be guilty of some moral wrong: the claimant's right must be suitable for enforcement by the court. The classic example is the enforcement of trusts. The beneficiary had no remedy at common law if the trustee claimed the property for himself, as the trustee was the legal owner, but he could enforce his rights in equity. The maxim is also reflected in the area of equitable remedies, which may be granted where the defendant's wrong is one not recognised by the common law. In the field of injunctions, for example, the claimant may obtain a *quia timet* injunction to restrain a threatened wrong although he has no cause of action at law until the wrong is committed.[157]

1–026   **ii. Equity follows the law.** Clearly equity may not depart from statute law, nor does it refuse to follow common law rules save in exceptional circumstances.[158] Thus equitable interests in land correspond with the legal estates and interests.[159] As Mummery L.J. recently stated:

> "[I]f an interest in land does not satisfy the basic legal requirements for its existence, then it will not, as a general rule, exist as an interest in land either at law or in equity."[160]

Nor will equity depart from the common law rule that a third party cannot be made to perform a contract.[161] Where the legal title to land is held jointly, the equitable interests follow the legal unless a contrary intention is proved.[162]

1–027   **iii. He who seeks equity must do equity.** A claimant who seeks equitable relief must be prepared to act fairly towards the defendant. A person seeking an injunction will not succeed if he is unable or

---

[157] Below, para.25–042.
[158] For the conflicts between the rules of law and equity, see above, para.1–016.
[159] Equity, however, recognised certain future interests which were not recognised at law. See Cheshire and Burn, pp.515–516.
[160] *Mexfield Housing Co-operative Ltd v Berrisford* [2011] Ch. 244 at 268; K. Low (2011) 127 L.Q.R. 31.
[161] *Rhone v Stephens* [1994] 2 A.C. 310 (positive covenant relating to land).
[162] *Stack v Dowden* [2007] 2 A.C. 432; below, para.11–004.

unwilling to carry out his own future obligations.[163] This maxim is also the foundation of the doctrine of election.[164]

iv. He who comes to equity must come with clean hands.[165] This principle is closely related to the last one, save that the latter looks to the claimant's future conduct, while the "clean hands" principle looks to his previous conduct. Thus equity will not grant relief against forfeiture for breach of covenant where the breach in question was flagrant.[166] Examples abound in the field of equitable remedies: a tenant cannot get specific performance of a contract for a lease if he is already in breach of his obligations[167]; nor could a purchaser if he had taken advantage of the illiteracy of the vendor who was not separately advised[168]; so also in the case of injunctions,[169] but equitable relief will only be debarred on this ground if the claimant's blameworthy conduct has some connection with the relief sought. The court is not concerned with the claimant's general conduct. Thus in *Argyll (Duchess) v Argyll (Duke)*,[170] the fact that the wife's adultery had led to the divorce proceedings was no ground for refusing her an injunction to restrain her husband from publishing confidential material. Nor will unclean hands debar a claim which does not involve reliance on one's own misconduct.[171] If both parties have "unclean hands", the court should consider only those of the applicant, and need not balance the misconduct of one against that of the other.[172]

1–028

v. Where the equities are equal the law prevails.

1–029

vi. Where the equities are equal the first in time prevails. These two related maxims, dealing with the priorities of competing interests, may be dealt with together. They provide the foundation for the doctrine of notice.[173] Thus a prior equitable interest in land can only be defeated by a bona fide purchaser of a legal estate without notice. If the purchaser is bona fide and without notice, then the equities are equal and his legal estate prevails. If he took with

1–030

[163] See *Chappell v Times Newspapers Ltd* [1975] 1 W.L.R. 482, where employees failed to get an injunction to restrain their dismissal where they refused to undertake not to become involved in strikes.

[164] *Snell*, para.6–012.

[165] P. Pettit [1990] Conv. 416; M. Halliwell [2004] Conv. 439.

[166] See *Shiloh Spinners Ltd v Harding* [1973] A.C. 691.

[167] *Coatsworth v Johnson* (1886) 54 L.T. 520.

[168] *Mountford v Scott* [1975] Ch. 258.

[169] See *Hubbard v Vosper* [1972] 2 Q.B. 84.

[170] [1967] Ch. 302.

[171] *Tinsley v Milligan* [1994] 1 A.C. 340; below, para.10–028.

[172] *Sang Lee Investment Co Ltd v Wing Kwai Investment Co Ltd, The Times,* April 14, 1983.

[173] Below, para.1–039. See *Halifax plc v Omar* (2002) 2 P. & C.R. 26.

notice the position is otherwise, as the equities are not equal. If he does not acquire a legal estate then the first in time, i.e. the prior equitable interest, prevails, as equitable interests rank in order of creation. The two maxims have lost some of their importance since the introduction in 1925 of the system of registration of certain interests in land and by the introduction of registered title.[174]

1–031   **vii. Equity imputes an intention to fulfil an obligation.** Where a person is obliged to do some act, and does some other act which could be regarded as a performance of it, then it will be so regarded in equity. This is the basis of the doctrines of performance and satisfaction.[175] For example, if a debtor leaves a legacy to his creditor (of an amount at least as great as the debt), this is presumed to be a repayment of the debt so that, unless the presumption is rebutted, the creditor cannot take the legacy and sue to recover the debt.

1–032   **viii. Equity regards as done that which ought to be done.** Where there is a specifically enforceable obligation equity regards the parties as already in the position which they would be in after performance of the obligation. Therefore in equity a specifically enforceable contract for a lease creates an equitable lease. This is the doctrine of *Walsh v Lonsdale*.[176] Similarly, a specifically enforceable contract for the sale of land transfers the equitable interest to the purchaser, the vendor holding the legal title on constructive trust until completion.[177] The maxim is also the basis of the doctrine of conversion,[178] and the rule in *Howe v Dartmouth*,[179] concerning the duty to sell unauthorised investments. The maxim has been invoked in modern times by the Privy Council and House of Lords. In *Att Gen for Hong Kong v Reid*[180] the issue was whether a fiduciary who took a bribe became constructive trustee of it or was merely personally accountable. Because he was under a duty to hand over the bribe to his principal, it was held that the property belonged to the principal in equity. The difficulty in this is that an obligation to pay money is not normally specifically enforceable.[181] Similarly, in

---

[174] Below, para.1–046.

[175] Snell, para.5–031.

[176] (1882) 21 Ch.D. 9, above para.1–016. A contract relating to land must be in writing; Law of Property (Miscellaneous Provisions) Act 1989.

[177] Below, para.12–035. See also *Davis v Richards & Wallington Industries Ltd* [1990] 1 W.L.R. 1511 (obligation to execute pension trust deed).

[178] Snell, para.5–030.

[179] (1802) 7 Ves. 137, below, Ch.19.

[180] [1994] 1 A.C. 324 (PC); below, para.21–026.

[181] D. Crilley [1994] 2 R.L.R. 57; A. Oakley (1994) 53 C.L.J. 31; P. Watts (1994) 110 L.Q.R. 178; P. Clarke and W. Swadling All E.R. Rev. 1994 respectively pp.252 and 365; S. Gardner (1995) 54 C.L.J. 60; T. Allen (1995) 58 M.L.R. 87. The Court of Appeal considered the decision unsound in *Sinclair Investments (UK) Ltd v Versailles Trade Finance Ltd (in administrative receivership)* [2011] 3 W.L.R. 1153; below, para.21–028.

Napier and Ettrick (Lord) v Hunter[182] it was considered that the duty of an insured person to hand over any damages from the wrongdoer to the insurer was specifically enforceable, so that the insurer had immediate proprietary rights in the form of a lien over the money.

ix. Equity is equality. Where two or more persons are entitled to 1–033 an interest in the same property, then the principle of equity is equal division, if there is no good reason for any other basis for division.[183] Equity, therefore, dislikes the joint tenancy where, by the doctrine of survivorship, the last survivor takes all. This may be contrasted with the tenancy in common, where the interest of each party devolves upon his personal representative on his death. In the absence of an express declaration to the effect that the equitable interest is held jointly, equity presumes a tenancy in common in certain cases where at law the parties are joint tenants: for example, in the case of partnership property.[184] Even where the equitable interest is held jointly, equity leans in favour of severance, meaning that equity is ready to regard an act or dealing as an act of severance, whereby the equitable interest is converted to a tenancy in common, thus excluding the possibility of survivorship.[185]

x. Equity looks to the intent rather than the form. This prin- 1–034 ciple does not mean that formalities may be ignored in equity, but rather that equity looks at the substance rather than the form. Thus equity will regard a transaction as a mortgage even though it is not so described, if in substance it appears that the property was transferred by way of security. Similarly a trust may be created although the word "trust" has not been used.[186] A covenant will be regarded as a restrictive covenant if negative in substance even if it is worded in a positive form.[187] Although a party to a covenant can enforce the contract at law even though no consideration has been given, equity regards such a party as a volunteer and will not order specific performance in his favour.[188]

xi. Delay defeats equities. Equity aids the vigilant and not the 1–035 indolent. This is the foundation of the doctrine of laches, whereby a party who has delayed cannot obtain equitable relief. This doctrine

---

[182] [1993] A.C. 713.
[183] For a modern example, see *Rowe v Prance* [1999] 2 F.L.R. 787 (yacht).
[184] *Lake v Craddock* (1732) 3 P Wms 158.
[185] See *Burgess v Rawnsley* [1975] Ch. 429.
[186] Below, para.3–019.
[187] *Tulk v Moxhay* (1848) 18 L.J.Ch. 83 (covenant "to keep uncovered by buildings" held negative).
[188] *Cannon v Hartley* [1949] Ch. 213.

is superseded where the Limitation Act 1980 deals with the matter.[189] For example, actions against trustees for breach of trust must, by s.21, be brought within six years, and delay short of this will not bar relief. Where, however, the claimant has a legal right, for example, upon a contract, delay may prevent the grant of an equitable remedy such as specific performance even though the legal right is not statute-barred.[190] Interlocutory injunctions must always be sought promptly, but it seems that delay may not prevent the grant of a final injunction where the cause of action is not statute-barred.[191]

The doctrine of laches continues to apply to those equitable claims which are outside the Limitation Act 1980, for example a claim to set aside a purchase of trust property by a trustee.[192] Similarly, claims to rescission and rectification may be barred by delay.[193]

1–036 **xii. Equity acts *in personam*.** Equity has jurisdiction over the defendant personally. The personal nature of the jurisdiction is illustrated by the fact that failure to comply with an order, such as specific performance or an injunction, is a contempt of court punishable by imprisonment. Provided that the defendant is within the jurisdiction (or can be served outside it), it is no objection that the property which is the subject-matter of the dispute is outside it. Thus in the leading case of *Penn v Lord Baltimore*,[194] specific performance was ordered of an agreement relating to land boundaries in Pennsylvania and Maryland, the defendant being in this country.

6. Equitable Remedies

1–037 At common law, the normal form of relief is an award of damages, to which a claimant who has proved his case is entitled as of right. One of the greatest contributions of equity has been to supplement the limited range of legal remedies by introducing wide range of equitable remedies,[195] which can be awarded both to enforce rights

---

[189] Either expressly or by analogy; below, para.23–041.

[190] Below, para.24–036. See Limitation Act 1980 s.36(1).

[191] *Fullwood v Fullwood* (1878) 9 Ch.D. 176; *H P Bulmer Ltd & Showerings Ltd v J Bollinger SA* [1977] 2 C.M.L.R. 625, below, para.25–044.

[192] Below, para.23–041.

[193] Below, paras 26–016, 26–024. See *Humphreys v Humphreys* [2004] W.T.L.R. 1425 (undue influence).

[194] (1750) 1 Ves.Sen. 444, below para.24–004; *Hamlin v Hamlin* [1986] Fam. 11; *Webb v Webb* [1994] Q.B. 696; above, para.1–018. See also Civil Jurisdiction and Judgments Act 1982 s.30(1).

[195] See generally Meagher, Gummow and Lehane, *Equity—Doctrines and Remedies*; Heydon, Gummow and Austin, *Cases and Materials on Equity and Trusts*; Spry, *Equitable Remedies*, Ch.1.

which are exclusively equitable and those which are legal. Their common features are that they are discretionary, their availability depends upon the inadequacy of common law remedies (which, in the case of exclusively equitable rights, will not be available at all) and they are governed by the doctrine that equity acts *in personam*.

The most significant of these remedies are specific performance, whereby the court orders a party to a contract to perform his contractual obligations, and an injunction, whereby the court orders a person to do, or, more commonly, to refrain from doing, some particular act. These, plus the remedies of rescission and rectification of contracts, will be examined in Pt IV. Other equitable remedies include delivery up and cancellation of documents,[196] account[197] and receivers.[198]

The ancient prerogative writ *ne exeat regno*,[199] later adapted by equity, has enjoyed something of a revival in modern times. It prevents the defendant from leaving the jurisdiction before final judgment, its purpose being to coerce him to give security for an equitable debt, on pain of arrest. The stringent conditions for its grant were laid down in *Felton v Callis*,[200] but more recent cases have tended to relax them,[201] perhaps unjustifiably.[202] The conditions may also be sidestepped by the grant of an interlocutory injunction against leaving the jurisdiction.[203]

The remedy of the declaration had some connection with equity in origin,[204] but the jurisdiction to grant it is now governed wholly by statute.[205] Finally, although not remedies in the traditional sense, the constructive trust and the doctrine of tracing are sometimes so described. These will be examined elsewhere.[206]

The differing character of equitable remedies must be appreciated. First, it is obvious that factors such as fraud, misrepresentation and mistake are relevant to the exercise of a discretionary jurisdiction to issue injunctions and orders of specific performance. Here, **1–038**

[196] Snell, para.14–007.
[197] Snell, para.20–003. See *Att Gen v Blake* [2001] 1 A.C. 268; J. Edelman [2001] L.M.C.L.Q. 9.
[198] Snell, para.19–001.
[199] For its history, see *Allied Arab Bank Ltd v Hajjar* [1988] Q.B. 787.
[200] [1969] 1 Q.B. 200.
[201] *Lipkin Gorman v Cass, The Times,* May 29, 1985; *Al Nahkel for Contracting and Trading Ltd v Lowe* [1986] Q.B. 235; cf. *Allied Arab Bank Ltd v Hajjar*, above, fn.199. See also *Thaha v Thaha* (1987) 17 Fam.Law 234; *Re Jeffrey S Levitt Ltd* [1992] Ch. 457.
[202] See C. Harpum (1986) 45 C.L.J. 189; L. Anderson (1987) 103 L.Q.R. 246; N. Andrews (1988) 47 C.L.J. 364; J. Martin (1990) 20 U.W.A.L.R. 143 at 160; *B v B (Injunction: jurisdiction)* [1998] 1 W.L.R. 329.
[203] Below, para.25–015.
[204] See de Smith, *Judicial Review*, 6th edn, 2007, p.806.
[205] *Tito v Waddell (No.2)* [1977] Ch. 106 at 259 (Megarry V.C.). See also *Chapman v Michaelson* [1909] 1 Ch. 238.
[206] Below, paras 12–006, 23–042.

the question is ordinarily one of the manner in which an already existing legal or equitable right is enforced.[207] The right itself is not affected. Thus if equity refuses to order specific performance of a contract due to a defendant's mistake, the claimant's right to sue for damages still subsists[208]: it is merely that a supplementary method of enforcement is denied. But secondly, other equitable remedies are larger in their effect; if equity rescinds a deed or a contract, a right to sue on that contract or deed ceases to be available at law. Equity will exercise this jurisdiction on grounds on which law takes no similar action, for instance, in cases of constructive fraud or wholly innocent misrepresentations, so that the equitable remedy affects the substance of a claimant's rights, and not merely the manner of their enforcement. This is also true when the equitable remedy of rectification is called into operation, a remedy by which a term of a document is varied so as to make it accord with the parties' real intentions. Thirdly, it should be noted that an equitable remedy may fulfil a task intermediate between the situations so far considered, the task of enabling a claimant to take full advantage of a right at common law. A claimant may, for instance, have a right at common law to rescind a contract for fraud, but may be at common law unable to exercise that right[209] because a precise *restitutio in integrum* is not possible. Equity has a wider discretion to rescind in such a case by devising a fair, if not a precise, return of the parties to something approaching their original positions.[210]

As we shall see, it is in the field of remedies that equity displays perhaps the greatest inventiveness and capacity for development, providing relief in new situations as they arise.[211]

7. The Bona Fide Purchaser of the Legal Estate for Value Without Notice

1–039   As we have seen, the use was enforceable against the feoffee to uses because the feoffee's conscience was bound by the undertaking which he had given to hold the property to the use and benefit of the *cestui que use*. Similarly with a trustee and beneficiary. So long as the same person remained trustee, this theory works quite simply. But if the legal estate passes from him to another person, how is the conscience of the transferee affected? The question is then one of determining, as a matter of policy, whether this new holder of the

---

[207] Below, paras 24–033, 25–043.

[208] *Wood v Scarth* (1855) 2 K. & J. 33 (in equity); (1858) 1 F. & F. 293 (at law); *Webster v Cecil* (1861) 30 Beav. 62; *Johnson v Agnew* [1980] A.C. 367, below, para.24–046.

[209] And would be confined to an action for damages.

[210] *Spence v Crawford* [1939] 3 All E.R. 271; a decision showing that equity may be more willing to do so in cases of actual fraud than in others.

[211] See particularly search orders and freezing injunctions, below, paras 25–077, 25–080.

legal estates is to be bound by the trust.[212] Any way in which the equitable ownership of a beneficiary is destroyed is of course a serious weakening of the position of the beneficiary; and equity strives always to protect him.[213]

Thus, a trust is binding on a person to whom the trustee gave the property[214]; or a mere occupier,[215] and also on a purchaser who bought it if he knew or could by reasonable inquiries have found out about the existence of the trust.[216] In short, the trust is binding on everyone coming to the land except the bona fide purchaser of a legal estate for value without notice actual, constructive or imputed.[217]

The doctrine applies to land and personalty. As far as land is concerned, its importance has diminished now that the system of registration of title applies throughout England and Wales. Under this system the doctrine of notice has little scope for application.[218] But some unregistered land remains, because there is no duty to register the title until a transaction of a specified kind after the area has become one of compulsory registration of title.[219] Even with unregistered land, the doctrine of notice was largely replaced, as will be seen, by the Land Charges Act 1925 (now the Act of 1972). In the account which follows, it should thus be borne in mind that in the case of registered land, the traditional doctrine applies only to transactions occurring before the title was registered, although some aspects of the doctrine have wider application.[220]

A. Purchaser for Value

The purchaser must have given consideration in money, or money's worth,[221] or the consideration of marriage.[222] Otherwise he is a donee, and bound by the trust regardless of notice. A purchaser includes a mortgagee[223] or lessee.

1–040

---

[212] Maitland, p.111. See also J. Howell [1997] Conv. 431.

[213] Maitland at 220.

[214] *Re Diplock* [1948] Ch. 465, at 544–545.

[215] *Mander v Falcke* [1891] 2 Ch. 554.

[216] *Pilcher v Rawlins* (1872) L.R. 7 Ch.App. 250.

[217] Such a purchaser can pass his good title to a purchaser with notice under the rule in *Wilkes v Spooner* [1911] 2 K.B. 473.

[218] Interests protected on the register and overriding interests (LRA 2002 s.29 and Sch.3) are binding on a purchaser of registered land, regardless of notice, and whether legal or equitable. LRA 2002 replaced LRA 1925 with effect from October 2003.

[219] LRA 2002 s.4. The occasions for registration include sales, gifts, assents on death and certain mortgages and leases.

[220] Below, para.1–046.

[221] *Thorndike v Hunt* (1859) 3 De G. & J. 563. Nominal consideration does not suffice; *Nurdin & Peacock Plc v D B Ramsden & Co Ltd* [1999] 1 E.G.L.R. 119.

[222] i.e. a future marriage. An ante-nuptial settlement is deemed to be made for value in respect of the spouses and the issue of the marriage, below, para.4–017.

[223] *Kingsnorth Finance Co v Tizard* [1986] 1 W.L.R. 783; see LPA 1925 s.205(xxi).

B. Legal Estate

1–041   This doctrine is based on the maxim that when the equities are equal the law prevails. In the case of a purchase of a legal estate for value without notice, the equities are equal between the purchaser and the beneficiaries; the purchaser's legal estate is allowed to prevail.

The position is different where the purchaser is a purchaser of an *equitable* interest only. The competition then is between two equitable interests; and the rule here is that the first in time prevails.[224] By way of exception, a purchaser of an equitable interest can defeat prior "mere equities", such as rights to rectification or to set aside a voidable contract.[225] It seems that a bona fide purchaser of an equitable interest in the land for value without notice will take free of mere equities,[226] and, a fortiori, a purchaser of a legal estate.[227]

C. Notice

1–042   **i. Meaning of Notice.** Apart from legislation[228] a purchaser is taken to have notice of an equitable interest unless he can show that "he took all reasonable care and made inquiries, and that, having taken that care and made inquiry, he received no notice of the trust which affected the property".[229] He must show that he had no notice actual, constructive or imputed.

Actual notice is the simple case where the purchaser subjectively knew of the equitable interest. Constructive notice exists where knowledge of the equitable interest would have come to him if he had made all such inquiries as a prudent purchaser would have made. Imputed notice covers actual or constructive notice to his agent who was acting as such in the transaction in question.[230]

1–043   **ii. Duty to Make Inquiries.** The inquiries which should be made will depend on the type of property in question. A purchaser, however, should always inspect the premises, and has notice of the interest of a person in occupation of the property.[231]

---

[224] *Re Morgan* (1881) 18 Ch.D. 93; *McCarthy and Stone Ltd v Hodge & Co* [1971] 1 W.L.R. 1547.

[225] *Shiloh Spinners Ltd v Harding* [1973] A.C. at 721. See, however, *Collings v Lee* [2001] 2 All E.R. 332 (where non-consensual transfer procured by fraudulent misrepresentation transferor retains full equitable interest and not a "mere equity" to set aside).

[226] *National Provincial Bank Ltd v Ainsworth* [1965] A.C. 1175 at 1238; D O'Sullivan (2002) 118 L.Q.R. 296.

[227] *Smith v Jones* [1954] 1 W.L.R. 1089. For the position of mere equities in registered land, see LRA 2002 s.116.

[228] Especially LCA 1972, below, para.1–046.

[229] per Fry J. in *Re Morgan* (1881) 18 Ch.D. 93 at 102.

[230] LPA 1925 s.199.

[231] *Barnhart v Greenshields* (1853) 9 Moo.P.C. 18; *Hunt v Luck* [1902] 1 Ch. 428; *Kingsnorth Finance Co Ltd v Tizard* [1986] 1 W.L.R. 783; cf. *Bristol and West Building Society v Henning* [1985] 1 W.L.R. 778.

(a) *Land.* With the unregistered title system, a vendor satisfied a **1–044** purchaser of his ownership of the land by producing title deeds which traced the history of the ownership of the land. The title had to start with a good root of title[232] at least 15 years old.[233] A prudent purchaser would examine that document and every one subsequent to it; he would normally be held to have constructive notice of every equitable interest which appeared on the title,[234] but not of those disclosed by earlier deeds with which he was not concerned. If he agreed to accept a title which began later than the statutory period of 15 years, he did so at his own risk, and would be bound by equitable interests disclosed by documents which were within the statutory period but prior to the agreed date.[235] There was an exception where there were in fact deeds which disclosed an equitable interest, but the vendor was able to produce an apparently perfect title after suppressing some of them.[236]

(b) *Personalty.* The doctrine of notice in the strict conveyancing **1–045** sense does not apply to personalty, because there is no duty on the purchaser to examine the seller's title; and usually there are no documents of title.[237] A purchaser of shares is not required to inquire about beneficial ownership, nor may notice of any trust affecting the shares be entered on the company's register of shareholders. However, where some equitable interest or charge is disclosed to a purchaser of personalty or presents itself to his notice, he will be bound by it if it is not satisfied out of the purchase money.[238] The doctrine of constructive notice applies even to commercial dealings with personalty, where the facts known to the purchaser make it imperative to seek an explanation, without which it is obvious that the transaction is probably improper.[239] It has recently been emphasised that the courts should not interpret or develop the law of notice in such a way as to interfere unacceptably with ordinary and honest commerce.[240]

---

[232] i.e. "a document which describes the land sufficiently to identify it, which shows a disposition of the whole legal and equitable interest contracted to be sold, and which contains nothing to throw any doubt on the title"; M. & W., p.661.

[233] LPA 1969 s.23.

[234] *Carter v Carter* (1857) 3 K. & J. 617.

[235] *Re Nisbet and Potts' Contract* [1906] 1 Ch. 386; affirming [1905] 1 Ch. 391.

[236] *Pilcher v Rawlins* (1872) L.R. 7 Ch.App. 259.

[237] See Factors Act 1889 s.1(4). The registration book of a car is not a document of title: *Joblin v Watkins and Roseveare (Motors) Ltd* [1949] 1 All E.R. 47.

[238] *Nelson v Larholt* [1948] 1 K.B. 339.

[239] *Macmillan Inc v Bishopsgate Investment Trust Plc (No.3)* [1995] 1 W.L.R. 978 at 1014 (shares); affirmed [1996] 1 W.L.R. 387. See also the sequel, *MCC Proceeds Inc v Lehman Brothers International (Europe)* [1998] 4 All E.R. 675; above, para.1–023.

[240] *Sinclair Investments (UK) Ltd v Versailles Trade Finance Ltd (in administrative receivership)* [2011] 3 W.L.R. 1153.

1–046   **iii. Registration.** The Land Charges Act 1925 introduced a system of registration of various interests in unregistered land.[241] Local
land charges are dealt with in the Local Land Charges Act 1975.
Most of the registrable interests are equitable, but a legal mortgage
where the mortgagee did not take possession of the title deeds is
included,[242] and one is a statutory creation.[243] Registration is
deemed to be actual notice to all persons so long as the registration
remains in force[244] whereas failure to register makes the charge void
against a purchaser.[245]

It will be seen that this enactment vitally affected the old doctrine
of notice. A purchaser is deemed to have notice of a charge if it is
registered. If the charge is not registered, it has been held that he
takes free even if he actually knows about it,[246] or if the interest in
question is that of a person who is in actual occupation of the
land,[247] and the House of Lords has held that the court cannot
enquire into the good faith of the purchaser, nor into the adequacy of
the consideration paid by him.[248]

D. Overreaching[249]

1–047   More important for our present purposes than the registration
provisions are the equitable interests enjoyed by beneficial owners
under trusts of land. Under the Law of Property Act 1925 s.1(1), the
only legal estates which can exist in land after 1925 are the fee
simple absolute in possession and the term of years absolute. Thus,
in every case in which the beneficial ownership of land is split into
successive interests (other than leases), the interests are equitable.

The 1925 legislation provided that all successive beneficial interests in land must be held either behind a trust for sale or under a
strict settlement under the Settled Land Act 1925. Under Pt I of the
Trusts of Land and Appointment of Trustees Act 1996, this dual
system was replaced by the single system of the "trust of land".
Although existing strict settlements were unaffected,[250] no new ones

---

[241] LCA 1972 does not apply to registered land; but all the interests contained in it can be
protected by the entry of a notice under LRA 2002 (replacing earlier legislation).

[242] LCA 1972 s.2(4) Class C(i).

[243] Class F. See Family Law Act 1996, re-enacting Matrimonial Homes Act 1983.

[244] LPA 1925 s.198(1).

[245] LCA 1972 s.4; LPA 1925 s.199(1)(i).

[246] *Hollington Brothers v Rhodes* [1951] 2 All E.R. 578.

[247] *Smith v Jones* [1954] 1 W.L.R. 1089; *Lloyd's Bank Plc v Carrick* [1996] 4 All
E.R. 630.

[248] *Midland Bank Trust Co Ltd v Green* [1981] A.C. 513; B. Green (1981) 97 L.Q.R. 518;
C. Harpum (1981) 40 C.L.J. 213; H. Johnson [1981] Conv. 361 (son, holding unregistered
option to purchase valuable land granted by father, not protected when father sold to mother
for £500).

[249] See generally D. Fox in Birks and Pretto (eds) *Breach of Trust*, 2002, Ch.4.

[250] Save that no land held on charitable trusts may be settled land; s.2(5).

may be created. The 1996 Act applies to other trusts of land, when-ever created. The "trust of land" now embraces situations (primarily co-ownership and intestacy) where statutory trusts for sale were imposed before the 1996 Act, expressly created trusts for sale, and bare trusts of land (where the land is held for an adult beneficiary absolutely entitled).[251] The legal estate is vested in trustees, who have a power of sale. When the land is sold by the trustees (or by the tenant for life of an existing strict settlement, in whom the legal estate is vested), the purchaser takes free from the beneficial inter-ests, which are transferred to the proceeds of sale.[252] Thus the bene-ficiaries have interests in the proceeds which are equivalent to those which they had in the land. This is so whether the title is registered or unregistered.

This process of transfer of beneficial interests from the land to the purchase money is called "overreaching". Provided that any capital money which is payable is paid to at least two trustees, the purchaser takes free of the beneficial interests even if he knew of them. There is no room for the application of the doctrine that occupation by the beneficiaries gives constructive notice to the purchaser.[253] Nor, in unregistered land, is there any machinery for the registration of such interests. It has been held that overreaching applies also to interests arising under the doctrine of proprietary estoppel.[254]

Where, however, the purchase money is paid to a sole trustee (for example, a husband who is sole legal owner of a house in which his wife has a share in equity), the doctrine of overreaching cannot apply. In such a case the doctrine of notice remains applicable in unregistered land, so that occupation by the wife is likely to give constructive notice to a purchaser or mortgagee.[255] In the case of an acquisition mortgage, however, where the legal owner could not have bought the property without the mortgage loan, it has been held that a person claiming an equitable interest has no rights against the mortgagee but only against the legal owner, even if in occu-pation.[256]

---

[251] s.1(1), (2).

[252] LPA 1925 s.2(1), as amended by the 1996 Act. See G. Ferris and G. Battersby (2003) 119 L.Q.R. 94, comparing the operation of the doctrine in registered and unregistered land; cf. S. Pascoe [2005] Conv. 140 at p.151.

[253] *City of London Building Society v Flegg* [1988] A.C. 54. Overreaching can occur even if no capital money is payable at the time of the conveyance; *State Bank of India v Sood* [1997] Ch. 276 (mortgage to secure existing and future debts); M. Thompson [1997] Conv. 134; M. Oldham (1997) 56 C.L.J. 494; G. Ferris and G. Battersby [1998] Conv. 168 at 182. See also *HSBC Bank Plc v Dyche* [2010] 2 P. & C.R. 4; N. Gravells [2010] Conv. 169.

[254] *Birmingham Midshires Mortgage Services Ltd v Sabherwal* (2000) 80 P. & C.R. 256.

[255] *Kingsnorth Finance Co Ltd v Tizard* [1986] 1 W.L.R. 783; cf. *Bristol and West Building Society v Henning* [1985] 1 W.L.R. 778; *Abbey National Building Society v Cann* [1991] 1 A.C. 56; *Equity & Law Home Loans Ltd v Prestidge* [1992] 1 W.L.R. 137. (Equitable owner who acquiesced in or impliedly authorised mortgage by legal owner deemed to intend to cede priority to mortgagee).

[256] *Abbey National Building Society v Cann*, above, fn.255.

The doctrine of notice in its conveyancing sense therefore applies only in the cases of equitable interests in unregistered land which are neither registrable nor overreachable, such as a restrictive covenant entered into before 1926 and a few other examples.[257] The cases seem "to show that there may well be rights, of an equitable character outside the provisions as to registration and which are incapable of being overreached."[258]

It is important to appreciate, however, that the doctrine of notice still operates in the context of beneficial interests under a trust of unregistered land where the doctrine of overreaching cannot apply because there is only one trustee.[259] Although such interests cannot be registered, a wife's statutory right to occupy the matrimonial home is registrable.[260] This, however, has no effect on the enforceability of any equitable interest she may have. However, priority disputes governed by unregistered land principles have become increasingly rare.

E. Other Applications of the Doctrine of Notice

1–048   We have seen that the traditional doctrine is now restricted in its application. The doctrine in its wider form, however, remains significant. As discussed above, it can apply even to commercial dealings with personalty.[261] The defence of purchaser without notice operates in the context of personal claims arising from the receipt of trust property transferred in breach of trust and of proprietary tracing claims, as will be explained in Chs 12 and 23 respectively.

The House of Lords applied the doctrine in its wider sense in *Barclays Bank Plc v O'Brien*,[262] where the question was whether a wife could set aside a mortgage or guarantee entered into with the bank as a result of her husband's misrepresentation or undue influence. This was not the traditional doctrine because there was only one transaction. The issue was not whether the bank could take free of a prior interest but whether enforcement of the transaction by the bank would be taking advantage of the husband's equitable fraud.[263] The solution lay in the doctrine of constructive notice, whether the land had a registered or unregistered title. This was: "not the same 'doctrine of notice' so beloved of property lawyers and now largely

---

[257] *Poster v Slough Estates Ltd* [1968] 1 W.L.R. 1518 (right to enter to remove fixtures); *Shiloh Spinners Ltd v Harding* [1973] A.C. 691 (equitable right of entry).
[258] per Lord Wilberforce in *Shiloh Spinners v Harding* [1973] A.C. 691 at 721.
[259] Above, para.1–047.
[260] Land Charges Act 1972 s.2(7) (Class F).
[261] Above, para.1–045.
[262] [1994] 1 A.C. 180; below, para.26–010.
[263] G. Battersby (1995) 15 L.S. 35.

replaced by registration of title."[264] Thus the doctrine has a role to play beyond the confines of unregistered land. Indeed, it "lies at the heart of equity".[265]

8. THE SUBJECT-MATTER OF EQUITY

In this Introduction, it has only been possible to mention certain **1–049** heads of equitable jurisdiction as they became relevant, and it may be helpful to the understanding of equity to list the subjects which should properly be included within it. No list can be exhaustive. Certain matters however are assigned to the Chancery Division by the Senior Courts Act 1981.[266] They are:

- the sale, exchange or partition of land, or the raising of charges on land;
- the redemption or foreclosure of mortgages;
- the execution of trusts;
- the administration of the estates of deceased persons;
- bankruptcy;
- the dissolution of partnerships or the taking of partnership or other accounts;
- the rectification, setting aside or cancellation of deeds or other instruments in writing;
- probate business, other than non-contentious or common form business;
- patents, trade marks, registered designs or copyright;
- all causes and matters involving the exercise of the High Court's jurisdiction under the enactments relating to companies.

All divisions of the High Court, however, exercise co-ordinate jurisdiction. Where a matter arises which has not been assigned to one division, it should go to whichever division is the more appropriate and convenient; in many cases the claimant's counsel will be able to choose. If the action is brought in the wrong division, it may be retained or transferred at the discretion of the judge.[267]

---

[264] M. Dixon and C. Harpum [1994] Conv. 421 at 423. See also W. Swadling All E.R. Rev. 1993 p.367; M. Thompson [1994] Conv. 140; P. O'Hagan (1994) 144 N.L.J. 765; P. Sparkes [1995] Conv. 250; A. Lawson and J. Mee (1995) 54 C.L.J. 280 and 536; J. Howell [1996] Conv. 34.

[265] *Barclays Bank Plc v O'Brien*, above, at 195 (Lord Browne-Wilkinson).

[266] s.61 and Sch.1 (formerly the Supreme Court Act 1981 but renamed by the Constitutional Reform Act 2005).

[267] Senior Courts Act 1981 ss.61(6), 65.

9. THE TRUST IN MODERN LAW[268]

1–050   The Law Commission has recently stated:

"Trusts are the invention of the English courts and have spread throughout the common law world on account of their potential for flexible management of a wide range of financial relationships. Their history goes back centuries, and the modern world of finance and real property is pervaded by them to the extent that many individuals are trustees, or are the beneficiaries of trusts, without having the slightest ideas that this is the case."[269]

Trusts are primarily about money and the preservation of wealth. The idea of the trust developed as a means for providing for the family. Although the trust still plays a significant role in establishing ownership of property on family breakdown,[270] it "can no longer be doubted that equity has moved out of the family home and the settled estate and into the market-place".[271] A major area of activity is in the holding of the property of charities and other non-profit making bodies. A modern and significant role has emerged for the trust in the constitution of pension funds,[272] although such trusts differ from traditional trusts in so far as there is a contractual relationship of employment and the beneficiaries have given consideration.[273] Unit trusts and investment trusts[274] are designed to spread investment risks. Another role is the safeguarding of property belonging to minors and those who lack mental capacity.[275] Thus the trust continues to be a form of property-holding of ever-increasing importance because of its adaptability and convenience in effecting complicated forms of settlement. Indeed, "as the principles of equity permeate the complications of modern life, the nature and variety of trusts ever grow."[276]

If a settlor wishes to give property to his wife for life and after her death to various other members of the family, it would be possible to arrange a system of law by which it could be done without using a

---

[268] See D. Hayton (1990) 106 L.Q.R. 87; Sir Anthony Mason (1994) 110 L.Q.R. 238; W Goodhart (1996) 10 T.L.I. 38.

[269] Law Com. No. 315 (2009), *Capital and Income in Trusts: Classification and Apportionment*, para.1.1.

[270] Below, Ch.11.

[271] Sir Peter Millett (1995) 9 T.L.I. 35 at 36; Sir Anthony Mason (1997–98) 8 K.C.L.J. 1 at 4.

[272] Below. Ch.16.

[273] Below, para.16–005.

[274] Below, para.18–009. For other commercial uses of trusts, see D. Hayton (ed.) *Modern International Developments in Trust Law*, 1999, Ch.8.

[275] Law Com. No.315 (2009), *Capital and Income in Trusts: Classification and Apportionment*, para.1.2.

[276] *Re a Solicitor* [1952] Ch. 328 at 332, per Roxburgh J.

trust. Indeed, the early common law did so, in an elementary form. Roman law did so[277]; as do those countries which have followed modernised systems of Roman law.[278]

In England, full use has been made of the convenience of the system whereby the legal estate is in the trustees and the equitable or beneficial ownership is kept separate. We have seen that this is insisted upon for the creation of successive or concurrent interests in land under the 1925 legislation.[279] The legal title can be kept clear of beneficial interests; the land can be sold free of them to a purchaser, who can overreach them. Thus a most elaborate system of beneficial interests can be created without complicating the title to the land.

The same advantages exist with personalty. Most modern settlements deal wholly or partly with personalty in the form of investments. No system of legal future interests in personalty ever developed; for settlements of personalty did not arise until the system of trusts was well advanced. In this sphere also, it is most convenient to separate legal and equitable ownership; by doing so, the trustees can buy and sell shares without the purchaser being concerned with the beneficial interests.[280] The beneficial interests attach to whatever is held by the trustees for the time being.

Those are the simple cases. Settlors may wish to create other forms of settlement.[281] With a gift for charitable purposes, for example, there is no beneficial owner; such a gift is effected by a special form of trust.[282] A settlor may wish to protect a beneficiary from his own extravagance by making it impossible for creditors to proceed against his limited interest; this is done by protective trust.[283] The settlor may wish to allow his trustees to determine from time to time how the capital and income shall be distributed among the beneficiaries; this is done by a discretionary trust.[284] He may wish to provide for someone, such as his lover, by will without identifying her in that document; this is done by a secret trust.[285] Each sort of trust will be considered in its proper place. It will in each case be seen that the

---

[277] Buckland and McNair: *Roman Law and Common Law*, 2nd edn, 1965, p.173.

[278] See (1980) B. Beinart *Journal of Legal History*, p.6; J. Merryman (1974) 48 Tulane L.Rev. 917.

[279] Above, para.1–047.

[280] No notice of any trust can be entered on the register of shareholders (Companies Act 2006 s.126, re-enacting earlier legislation).

[281] It should not be forgotten that the trust may also be created unintentionally. See Resulting and Constructive Trusts, below, Chs 10, 12.

[282] Below, Ch.15. Also a gift for a non-human object, such as the maintenance of an animal or a tombstone; below, paras 14–010, 14–011.

[283] Below, Ch.7.

[284] Below, Ch.8.

[285] Below, Ch.5. A modern variation is the "blind trust". A politician may receive funding of which the source is not revealed, or may place his assets with trustees to be administered on the basis that he is not informed of investments made. By these means his political decisions are seen to be uninfluenced by personal interests. See further P. Matthews (1998) 3 *Amicus Curiae* 22.

desired result could have been effected without the existence of a
trust; but that the trust is a very satisfactory and convenient way of
effecting it; and that in most cases this has become the only way in
which it can now be effected in English law. In some cases, however, the trust has not afforded a solution, for example, in the case of
gifts for abstract non-charitable purposes.[286] Theoretical difficulties
have also been encountered with the property of unincorporated
associations.[287] Finally, it should never be forgotten that there is one
factor which dominates all others in the context of the creation of
trusts in modern law: taxation. Although the law of equity and trusts
can be understood without it, it will be appreciated that the popular
forms of trust in recent years have been those which reduce to a
minimum the liability to tax.[288] The Chancery lawyer's job is to be
able to advise on these matters and to create the most appropriate
trusts to meet the wishes of the settlor.

10. THE CREATIVITY OF EQUITY

1–051   One question which has arisen is whether the category of equitable
interests is closed, or whether new ones might be created.[289] One
clear example is the restrictive covenant, which, since Lord Eldon's
day, has evolved from a contractual right to an equitable interest
enforceable against the covenantor's successors in title. Another
possibility is the contractual licence, although the matter awaits
clarification in the House of Lords.[290] One view is that the modern
machinery for law reform should be relied upon in preference to
judicial creativity.[291]

Bagnall J., in a case concerning matrimonial property, warned
against unwarranted extensions of equitable jurisdiction in the following words:

> "In any individual case the application of these propositions
> may produce a result which appears unfair. So be it; in my view
> that is not an injustice. I am convinced that in determining rights,

---

[286] Below, Ch.14.

[287] Below, para.14–014.

[288] The Finance Act 2006, however, removed many inheritance tax advantages of trusts;
below, para.9–015.

[289] Eveleigh L.J. in *Pennine Raceway Ltd v Kirklees Metropolitan Council* [1983] Q.B. 382
at 392, said, "there has been a considerable development in the law in relation to equitable
interests and I do not think that it is right to regard the category as closed." But at 397,
Stephenson L.J. preferred to express no view.

[290] Below, para.27–014. See *Ashburn Anstalt v Arnold* [1989] Ch. 1.

[291] As in the case of the matrimonial homes legislation (now Family Law Act 1996),
replacing Lord Denning's "deserted wife's equity".

particularly property rights, the only justice that can be obtained by mortals, who are fallible and are not omniscient, is justice according to law; the justice which flows from the application of sure and settled principles to proved or admitted facts. So in the field of equity, the length of the Chancellor's foot has been measured or is capable of measurement. This does not mean that equity is past childbearing; simply that its progeny must be legitimate—by precedent out of principle. It is well that this should be so; otherwise no lawyer could safely advise on his client's title and every quarrel would lead to a law suit."[292]

Throughout this book it will be seen that the principles of equity have constantly developed and found new fields of application.[293] The reader, when examining these developments, might consider whether the words of Bagnall J. have been heeded. A few examples must suffice here.

Many new developments have been seen in the field of injunctions, notably the evolution of search orders and freezing injunctions, designed respectively to prevent removal or destruction of evidence and to prevent the assets of the defendant from being dissipated.[294] Equity's excursions into the criminal law, however, have been restricted.[295] Similarly, equity's "intrusion" into the common law rules on mistake in contract has been rejected.[296]

The constructive trust has also proved to be a fertile field, assisting in the enforcement of contractual licences against third parties[297]; and allowing unprotected interests to be enforced against purchasers of registered land.[298] Constructive and resulting trusts have operated to give security to unsecured creditors[299]; and to determine the ownership of matrimonial and "quasi-matrimonial" property.[300] Here we saw the "new model constructive trust", a term first used by Lord Denning M.R. in the case concerning the claim of a cohabitant to a share in the home, where he said:

---

[292] *Cowcher v Cowcher* [1972] 1 W.L.R. 425 at 430.

[293] In some fields, however, the role of equity has declined. The entitlement to the funds on dissolution of an unincorporated association, for example, is today treated as more a matter of contract than of trusts. See below, para.10–013.

[294] Below, paras 25–077, 25–080.

[295] *RCA Corp v Pollard* [1983] Ch. 135; below, para.25–013.

[296] *Great Peace Shipping Ltd v Tsavliris Salvage (International) Ltd* [2003] Q.B. 679; below, para.26–003.

[297] *Ashburn Anstalt v Arnold*, above, fn.229; below, para.27–017.

[298] *Peffer v Rigg* [1977] 1 W.L.R. 285; *Lyus v Prowsa Ltd* [1982] 1 W.L.R. 1044. See E. Cooke and P. O'Connor (2004) 120 L.Q.R. 640.

[299] *Barclays Bank Ltd v Quistclose Investments Ltd* [1970] A.C. 567, below, para.2–009. See also *Re Kayford* [1975] 1 W.L.R. 279.

[300] Below, Ch.11.

"Equity is not past the age of childbearing. One of her latest progeny is a constructive trust of a new model. Lord Diplock brought it into the world[301] and we have nourished it".[302]

Other areas where equity's creativity has shown itself in modern times include proprietary estoppel[303] and the restriction of the rights of a mortgagee.[304] This brief survey indicates the dynamism of equity. The developments discussed above, and others, will be examined in the relevant parts of the book.

11. THE RECOGNITION OF TRUSTS ACT 1987[305]

1–052 The trust is an English concept which has spread to common law, but not civil law, jurisdictions.[306] The 1984 Hague Convention on the Law applicable to Trusts and their Recognition establishes common principles between states on the law governing trusts and provides guidelines for their recognition. The United Kingdom, by means of the Recognition of Trusts Act 1987, has ratified the Convention.

The ratification does not have the effect of changing the substantive law of trusts of the United Kingdom, nor of importing trusts into civil law jurisdictions. The Convention seeks to establish uniform conflict of laws principles and to assist civil law states to deal with trust issues arising within their jurisdiction. Recognition implies, for example, that the trustee may sue and be sued in his capacity as trustee, and that the trust property is a separate fund and is not part of the trustee's estate.[307] A trust is to be governed by the law chosen by the settlor, expressly or by implication. In the absence of any such choice, the trust is to be governed by the law with which it is most closely connected.[308] The applicable law governs the validity and construction of the trust, and its effects and administration.[309]

---

[301] In *Gissing v Gissing* [1971] A.C. 886.

[302] *Eves v Eves* [1975] 1 W.L.R. 1338 at 1341; cf. *Allen v Snyder* [1977] 2 N.S.W.L.R. 685 at 701: "the legitimacy of the new model is at least suspect; at best it is a mutant from which further breeding should be discouraged." The "new model" is no longer in use; below, para.12–043.

[303] Below, para.27–022.

[304] *Quennell v Maltby* [1979] 1 W.L.R. 318 (right to possession must be exercised bona fide and to protect security).

[305] D. Hayton (1987) 36 I.C.L.Q. 260; Underhill, Ch.25; M Lupoi (1998) 4 *Trusts & Trustees* 15; D. Hayton (ed.) *Modern International Developments in Trust Law*, 1999, Chs 2, 3.

[306] On February 7, 2007 the French Parliament adopted a new law instituting "La Fiducie", a device similar to the trust but formed contractually. See P. Matthews (2007) 21 T.L.I. 17.

[307] Article 11, as set out in the Schedule to the 1987 Act.

[308] Articles 6 and 7. See *Gomez v Gomez-Monche Vives* [2009] Ch. 245; D. Hayton (2009) 23 T.L.I. 3; *Martin v Secretary of State for Work and Pensions* [2010] W.T.L.R. 671.

[309] Article 8.

CHAPTER 2

NATURE AND CLASSIFICATION OF TRUSTS

1. DISTINCTIONS

MANY attempts have been made to define a trust, but none of them   **2–001** has been wholly successful.[1] It is more useful to describe than to define a trust, and then to distinguish it from related but distinguishable concepts.

A trust is a relationship recognised by equity which arises where property is vested in (a person or) persons called the trustees, which those trustees are obliged to hold for the benefit of other persons called cestuis que trust[2] or beneficiaries. The interests of the beneficiaries will usually be laid down in the instrument creating the trust,

---

[1] Co.Litt. 272b; Underhill and Hayton, 18th edn, p.2; Snell, para.21–001; *Halsbury's Laws of England*, 4th edn, Vol.48, p.343; A. Scott (1955) 71 L.Q.R. 39; P. Parkinson (2002) 61 C.L.J. 657.

[2] This is the correct plural; C. Sweet (1910) 26 L.Q.R. 196.

but may be implied or imposed by law.[3] The beneficiary's interest is proprietary[4] in the sense that it can be sold, given away or disposed of by will; but it will cease to exist if the legal estate in the property comes into the hands of a bona fide purchaser for value without notice of the beneficial interest.[5] The subject-matter of the trust must be some form of property. Commonly, it is legal ownership of land or of invested funds; but it may be of any sort of property—land, money, chattels, equitable interests,[6] choses in action,[7] etc. There may also be trusts for charitable purposes; such trusts are enforced at the suit of the Attorney General.[8] There is much doubt and uncertainty as to the status and validity of trusts for non-charitable purposes—as a trust for the building of a monument[9] or for the maintenance of the testator's horses, dogs, and cats.[10]

A trust must be distinguished from certain other legal phenomena which resemble the trust, but which must be kept separate from it. The point of such distinguishing is threefold: first, to compare the different legal consequences of a trust and the related concept; secondly, to identify the circumstances in which the one concept must exist to the exclusion of the other; and thirdly, to identify the circumstances in which a trust may co-exist with the related concept, as may be the case, for example, with certain contracts and debts.

A. Bailment

2–002　　　Bailment is a relationship recognised by the common law, and arises where a chattel owned by A is, with A's permission, in the possession of B.[11] The rights of the parties may or may not be governed by a contract. A is entitled to a certain standard of care by B in his stewardship of A's chattel. But this is very different from a trust. For there is no transfer of ownership from A to B; B's duties are dependent on the rules of common law and not upon equity; and these duties are entirely different from, and minimal in character as compared with, those which would exist if B held the property as trustee for A. A trustee of shares is the legal owner of the shares and

---

[3] Below, paras 2–032, 2–033.

[4] Above, para.1–018. Discretionary trusts and trusts for persons for particular purposes need separate consideration: below, Chs 8 and 14.

[5] Above, para.1–039.

[6] For example, where a beneficiary under a settlement makes a settlement of his beneficial interest.

[7] For example, a trust of the benefit of a covenant, or of a debt, or of a bank balance.

[8] Below, Ch.15.

[9] *Mussett v Bingle* [1876] W.N. 170; *Re Endacott* [1960] Ch. 232; below, para.14–010.

[10] *Pettingall v Pettingall* (1842) 11 L.J.Ch. 176; *Re Dean* (1889) 41 Ch.D. 552; below, para.14–011.

[11] *Halsbury's Laws of England*, 4th edn, Vol.3(1), p.3; *Aluminium Industrie Vaassen BV v Romalpa Aluminium Ltd* [1976] 1 W.L.R. 676, below, para.23–073; *Re Goldcorp Exchange Ltd* [1995] 1 A.C. 74 at 97.

the certificates, and not a mere bailee of the latter.[12] A bailor, A, could lose his legal ownership only through one of the ways in which legal owners may be deprived.[13] But if the property was held by B on trust for A, A's equitable title could be defeated by the transfer of the legal title in the property to a bona fide purchaser for value without notice of the trust.[14]

B. Agency

The relationship of principal and agent, which is normally con-   **2–003**
tractual, is governed by rules of common law and equity, while the relationship of trustee and beneficiary, which is rarely contractual, is exclusively equitable. The function of an agent is to represent the principal in dealings with third parties, while a trustee does not bring the beneficiaries into any relationship with third parties. There are, however, many similarities.[15] The relationship of trustee and beneficiary is fiduciary; that of principal and agent is normally fiduciary, but not inevitably so.[16] Both trustees and agents must act personally and not delegate their duties[17]; neither may make unauthorised profits from their office.[18]

A significant distinction arises from the fact that the relationship of principal and agent is primarily debtor/creditor, while a trust is proprietary: the trust property vests in the trustee and the beneficiaries are the equitable owners. The crucial point here is that a proprietary right (so long as the property or its proceeds can be identified) is not affected by the defendant's insolvency, whereas a personal claim will abate with the claims of other creditors if the defendant cannot pay in full.

An agent does not necessarily hold any property for the principal. Even if he does, he may merely have possession rather than title. The principal will have proprietary rights against the agent only if the agent has acquired title to property for the benefit of the principal.

"That proposition is clear enough in the abstract, but it is often extremely difficult to gauge, especially where the subject matter is money ... (i) whether the agent has acquired title or mere

---

[12] *MCC Proceeds Inc v Lehman Bros International (Europe)* [1998] 4 All E.R. 675 (beneficiary could not sue third party for conversion of certificates).

[13] e.g. through estoppel, or the operation of the Factors Act 1889 ss.2, 8, 9; Sale of Goods Act 1979 ss.21, 24, or the Consumer Credit Act 1974 Sch.4, para.22.

[14] Above, para.1–039–1–046. See *MCC Proceeds Inc v Lehman Bros International (Europe)* [1998] 4 All E.R. 675, above.

[15] See Fridman's *Law of Agency*, 7th edn, 1996, pp.23–27.

[16] Below, para.21–017.

[17] Below, para.20–012.

[18] Below, Ch.21.

possession, and (ii) if he has acquired title, whether there is an intention to create a trust or to allow the agent to take an absolute title subject to a merely personal monetary obligation."[19]

The above discussion relates to assets lawfully received by the agent on behalf of the principal. Where property is received in breach of fiduciary duty, as in the case of a bribe, it has been held by the Privy Council that the agent holds the property on trust for the principal.[20] The consequence would be that the principal's remedy would not depend on the agent's solvency, and the principal would be entitled to any increase in value of the property, but the Court of Appeal recently declined to follow this decision.[21]

C. Contract

2–004   Trust and contract are quite different concepts. A contract is a common law personal obligation resulting from agreement between the parties. A trust is an equitable proprietary relationship which can arise independently of agreement. However, there are various situations in which the distinction may be difficult to draw, or where the facts may give rise to both[22]; contracts and trusts are not mutually exclusive.[23]

2–005   **i. Settlements and Covenants to Settle.** Property which is vested in the trustees of a settlement is held upon the trusts of the settlement, and the beneficiaries are the owners in equity of their interests under the settlement. But if the property has not yet been conveyed to the trustees, and is merely subject to a covenant to settle, then until recently the beneficiaries could only enforce the covenant if they had given consideration or were parties to the deed.[24] This area is now subject to the development mentioned below.

2–006   **ii. Third Party Rights under a Contract.** There has been much discussion of the question whether the inability of a third party to

---

[19] Heydon, Gummow and Austin, *Cases and Materials on Equity and Trusts*, 4th edn, p.467.

[20] *Att Gen for Hong Kong v Reid* [1994] 1 A.C. 324.

[21] *Sinclair Investments (UK) Ltd v Versailles Trade Finance Ltd (in administrative receivership)* [2011] 3 W.L.R. 1153; below, para.21–028.

[22] As, for example, in the case of a constructive trust arising out of a specifically enforceable contract for sale, below, para.12–035; or possibly in the case of a contractual licence, discussed below. Consideration does not negative a trust; *Carreras Rothmans Ltd v Freeman Mathews Treasure Ltd* [1985] Ch. 207.

[23] *Baird v Baird* [1990] 2 A.C. 548 at 560; *Imperial Group Pension Trust Ltd v Imperial Tobacco Ltd* [1991] 1 W.L.R. 589 at 597. These employee pension fund cases are an important illustration of the co-existence of contractual and trust relationships.

[24] Below, Ch.4.

sue upon a contract can be overcome by finding that one of the parties to the contract contracted as trustee for him. This is not really a question of distinguishing a trust from a contract. The question is whether there is a trust of the benefit of the contract. The answer to that question depends on whether there is an intention to create a trust of the benefit of the contract; this question is discussed elsewhere.[25] The question is of less significance now that third parties may enforce contracts for their benefit in certain circumstances under the Contracts (Rights of Third Parties) Act 1999.

iii. Unincorporated Associations. An unincorporated association is not a legal entity. Where there is a gift to an unincorporated association, there have been doubts as to whether the property is held on trust for the purposes of the association, or whether it belongs absolutely to the members, to be dealt with according to their contract.[26] On the dissolution of such an association the ownership of its funds has sometimes been determined by applying trust principles, but today the matter is more commonly treated as one of contract.[27]

2–007

iv. Contractual Licences. A contractual licence, normally involving the occupation of land, is created by agreement of the parties, applying the normal principles of the law of contract. There is authority,[28] however, especially in the context of enforceability against third parties, that a contractual licence may give rise to a constructive trust, thus giving the licensee an equitable interest in the land in addition to his contractual rights. The development of this theory is discussed elsewhere.[29]

2–008

D. Debt

A debt may or may not be contractual. Whether the obligation is contractual or not, the duty of the debtor is to pay money to the creditor; that of a trustee is to hold the trust property on trust for the beneficiary. The debtor's obligation is personal. The trust is proprietary. We have seen that the distinction becomes crucial on insolvency. Further, a trustee must invest the trust funds, and the beneficiaries are entitled to the income. With a debtor, or a stakeholder, this is a matter of agreement, express or implied.[30]

2–009

---

[25] Below, para.4–020.
[26] Below, para.4–016.
[27] Below, para.10–013.
[28] See *Ashburn Anstalt v Arnold* [1989] Ch. 1.
[29] Below, para.27–016.
[30] *Duggan v Governor of Full Sutton Prison* [2004] 1 W.L.R. 1010.

On the other hand, it may be to a person's own advantage to be a trustee rather than a person subject to a personal obligation. If money is borrowed and then stolen from the borrower, it must still be repaid; but a trustee may not be liable for a loss which is not due to his own lack of care.[31]

A debt may, of course, be the subject-matter of a trust,[32] but the question here considered is whether the making of a loan can create a trust in favour of the lender. Sometimes a form of words is construed as creating both forms of obligation.[33] There is no reason why, in certain circumstances, a debt and a trust cannot co-exist; a loan to be held by the borrower on trust is repayable in debt if the purpose for which the money was lent is carried out, and may be held in trust for the lender if performance is impossible or is for some other reason not carried out. In *Barclays Bank Ltd v Quistclose Investments Ltd*[34]:

> Rolls Razor Ltd, very much indebted to Barclays Bank, was in need of £209,719 to pay dividends which had been declared on its shares. This sum was borrowed from Quistclose under an arrangement whereby the loan was to be used only for that purpose. The money was paid into a separate account at Barclays Bank, the Bank having notice of the nature of the arrangement.
>
> Before the dividend was paid, Rolls Razor went into liquidation. The question was whether the money in the account was owned beneficially by Rolls Razor in which case Barclays Bank claimed to set it off against the overdraft,[35] or whether Rolls Razor had received the money as trustee and still held it on trust for Quistclose.
>
> The House of Lords unanimously decided that the money had been received upon trust to apply it for the payment of dividends; that purpose having failed, the money was held on trust for Quistclose. The fact that the transaction was a loan, recoverable by an action at law, did not exclude the implication of a trust. The legal and equitable rights and remedies could co-exist. The Bank, having notice of the trust, could not retain the money against Quistclose.

---

[31] *Morley v Morley* (1678) 2 Ch.Cas. 2.

[32] For an unusual example, see *Barclays Bank Plc v Willowbrook International Ltd* [1987] 1 F.T.L.R. 386, CA, holding that where A charges to B a debt owed to A by C, any money paid by C to A is held by A on constructive trust for B.

[33] *Welby v Rockcliffe* (1830) 1 Russ. & M. 571; *Wright v Wilkin* (1862) 2 B. & S. 232 at 260.

[34] [1970] A.C. 567; W. Goodhart and G. Jones (1980) 43 M.L.R. 489. For other circumstances where an unsecured creditor can acquire a proprietary interest, see *Swiss Bank Corp v Lloyds Bank Ltd* [1982] A.C. 584. See generally Swadling (ed), *The Quistclose Trust*, 2004.

[35] See Insolvency Act 1986 s.323.

The principle is that:

"[E]quity fastens on the conscience of the person who receives from another property transferred for a specific purpose only and not therefore for the recipient's own purposes, so that such person will not be permitted to treat the property as his own or to use it for other than the stated purpose."[36]

The principle applies also where only part of the money lent is used for the specific purpose: the part not so applied is held on trust for the lender.[37]

Lord Millett in *Twinsectra v Yardley*[38] analysed the position as follows: a resulting trust for the lender arises as soon as the money is transferred to the borrower, but is subject to the borrower's power (or duty) to apply it to the specified purpose. It is not enough that the money has been lent for a specified purpose. The question is whether the parties intended the money to be at the free disposal of the lender. If they did not, the *Quistclose* principle applies.[39]

The court in *Re Kayford Ltd (In Liquidation)*[40] went one step **2–010** further, holding that circumstances apparently giving rise to a debt in fact created a trust which did not co-exist with the debt but excluded it. In that case, customers of a mail-order company paid in advance when ordering goods. The company, being in financial difficulties, decided to protect its customers in the event of its insolvency by opening a separate bank account, called "Customers' Trust Deposit Account", into which the purchase money was paid. In liquidation proceedings it was held that the money was held on trust for the customers and did not form part of the assets of the company. The customer could create a trust by using appropriate words or, as here, the company could do it by taking suitable steps on or before receiving the money, thus transforming the obligations from debt to trust. The customers never became creditors, so no question of a

---

[36] *Carreras Rothmans Ltd v Freeman Mathews Treasure Ltd* [1985] Ch. 207 at p.222.

[37] *Re EVTR Ltd* [1987] B.C.L.C. 647 (loan for buying equipment, part of which was never delivered and money refunded to debtor by vendor). See also *Latimer v Commissioner of Inland Revenue* [2004] 1 W.L.R. 1466; D. Morris (2004) 18 T.L.I. 155; *Re Margaretta Ltd (In Liquidation)* [2006] W.T.L.R. 1271 (money held by solicitors solely for payment of VAT if liability to pay should be established); *Templeton Insurance Ltd v Penningtons Solicitors LLP* [2007] W.T.L.R. 1103.

[38] [2002] 2 A.C. 164; C. Rickett [2002] 10 R.L.R. 112; M. Thompson [2002] Conv. 387; J. Penner and J. Glister respectively (2002) 16 T.L.I. 165 and 223; P. Clarke All E.R. Rev. 2002, p.231; T. Yeo and H. Tjio (2003) 119 L.Q.R. 8.

[39] His Lordship expanded on the views he expressed in (1985) 101 L.Q.R. 269 and rejected the analysis in Chambers, *Resulting Trusts*, 1997, Ch.3 (beneficial interest in borrower, subject to lender's contractual right to restrain misapplication). See also C. Rickett (1991) 107 L.Q.R. 608; J. Glister (2004) 63 C.L.J. 632.

[40] [1975] 1 W.L.R. 279; distinguished in *Re Multi Guarantee Co Ltd* [1987] B.C.L.C. 257, where a separate account was designated but no trust of the money was established because the company contemplated having further resort to the money.

fraudulent preference[41] of creditors could arise.[42] No trust arose, however, where members of a financially troubled club deposited "rescue funds" in a separate account, for use when the club's future was known.[43] *Re Kayford Ltd* was distinguished on the ground that in the present case the circumstances in which the money could be used were not defined. Thus the terms of the intended trust were uncertain and the money was part of the club's assets and therefore available to its creditors.

The payer will not normally have proprietary rights if the money has not yet been paid into the designated account, even though the failure to pay in was a breach of trust.[44] It is otherwise if a trust has been declared of the money awaiting transfer to the account,[45] or if a trust arises on receipt of client funds by an investment firm under a statutory regulatory regime.[46]

2–011 *Re Kayford Ltd* was not referred to in *Customs and Excise Commissioners v Richmond Theatre Management Ltd*,[47] where a different, and somewhat surprising, result was reached in the context not of insolvency but of liability to value added tax. The theatre sold tickets in advance on terms which expressly imposed a trust on the money for the purchasers until the performance took place. Dyson J. held that no trust was created because the terms also provided that the theatre was "not accountable for interest or otherwise in respect of the use of the ticket money after its receipt". It was considered that the effect of this clause was that the purchasers accepted the risk of insolvency and that it would be inequitable to put them in a better position than unsecured creditors in that event. There was no reference to *R. v Clowes (No.2)*[48] where, in the context of theft, the Court of Appeal said that the requirement to keep money separately normally indicates a trust, and the absence of such a requirement normally negatives it *if there were no other indicators of a trust*; the fact

---

[41] The preference rules are now found in Insolvency Act 1986 s.239.

[42] cf. W. Goodhart and G. Jones (1980) 43 M.L.R. 489 at 494. The point that the customers never became creditors seems unconvincing. For this to be so, the trust must already have existed when the company received the money. This has now been recognised in *Re Farepak Food and Gifts Ltd* [2007] W.T.L.R. 1407. See also Heydon, Gummow and Austin, *Cases and Materials on Equity and Trusts*, 4th edn, p.475, suggesting that *Re Kayford Ltd* and the *Quistclose* case "provide startling opportunities for well-advised lenders to obtain protection against the prospect of the borrower's insolvency." There is no proposal that such arrangements should be registrable; Law Com. No.296 (2005), paras 1.60–1.66.

[43] *Re Challoner Club Ltd (In Liquidation)*, *The Times*, November 4, 1997. See also *Re Branston & Gothard Ltd* [2007] W.T.L.R. 85; *OT Computers Ltd v First National Tricity Finance Ltd* [2007] W.T.L.R. 165.

[44] *Re B A Peters Plc (in administration)* [2010] 1 B.C.L.C. 142 (money paid for purchase of yacht which had not been delivered).

[45] *Re Kaupthing Singer & Friedlander Ltd (in administration)* [2010] W.T.L.R. 79.

[46] *Lehman Brothers International (Europe) (in administration) v CRC Credit Fund Ltd* [2011] Bus. L.R. 277; H. McVea [2011] L.M.C.L.Q. 411.

[47] [1995] S.T.C. 257; criticised P. Matthews [1995] B.T.R. 332.

[48] [1994] 2 All E.R. 316. See also *Re Lewis's of Leicester Ltd* [1995] 1 B.C.L.C. 428; *Mills v Sportsdirect.com Retail Ltd* [2010] 2 B.C.L.C. 143.

that the transaction contemplates the mingling of money is not necessarily fatal to a trust. There the terms of an investment brochure were held to establish that investors' money was received on trust for them, to the exclusion of a debtor/creditor relationship.

In the context of informal family transactions, it may be difficult to determine whether a payment was intended to create a debt or not. Thus in *Hussey v Palmer*,[49] where the claimant paid £607 for an extension to her son-in-law's house, Cairns L.J. held that it was a loan, Lord Denning M.R. held that it was not, and Phillimore L.J. thought that it "might be" a loan. The decision of the majority was that the payment gave rise to a resulting (or constructive) trust on the basis that it would be inequitable for the son-in-law to deny that she had an interest in the house.[50] If the payment was neither a gift nor a loan, this conclusion is not surprising, but Phillimore L.J. held that a resulting trust could arise even if it was a loan.[51] There is much force in the dissenting judgment of Cairns L.J., holding that a resulting trust of money paid by way of a loan could not arise. The question arose again in *Re Sharpe*,[52] where an aunt lent money to her nephew towards the purchase of a house on the understanding that she could live with him for the rest of her life. On the nephew's bankruptcy, the aunt claimed an interest in the house. Although her claim succeeded on other grounds,[53] the argument that the loan gave rise to a resulting trust was rejected, *Hussey v Palmer* being distinguished as a case on "very special" facts.

E. Conditions and Charges

The distinction between a trust and a charge is that a trust pre- **2–012**
serves the beneficiary's ownership of property vested in the trustee, whereas a charge provides security over the chargor's own beneficial property. The usual role of a charge is to provide security for a commercial creditor, but a charge in favour of a beneficiary may be imposed by equity over a mixed fund where a trustee has wrongly mixed trust assets with his own.[54]

It is sometimes difficult to determine whether a gift of property is subject to a trust or whether it is conditional upon, or charged with, the duty of making certain payments. Thus a bequest to X "but he is

---

[49] [1972] 1 W.L.R. 1286.
[50] Below, para.12–043.
[51] This would not be within the principle of *Barclays Bank Ltd v Quistclose Investments Ltd*, above, fn.34, as the money *was* applied to the purpose for which it was paid. The trust was apparently of a proportionate share of the house.
[52] [1980] 1 W.L.R. 219. See also *Spence v Brown* (1988) 18 Fam.Law. 291; *Risch v McFee* (1991) 61 P. & C.R. 42.
[53] Below, para.27–016.
[54] Below, para.23–055.

to pay £50 to Y" could give rise to several possible constructions, each of them having different consequences.[55]

The bequest could be construed as a gift to X upon trust to pay Y £50.[56] In that situation, Y would immediately become entitled in equity to the £50, provided that the property bequeathed was of sufficient value; a trustee is not required to produce money of his own to make up deficiencies in the trust property.[57] If there is a surplus, a trustee is not, on principle, entitled to obtain any benefit from the trust and the surplus will usually be held upon a resulting trust.[58] But a possible construction is that, even if there was a trust of the £50, X was intended to take the surplus beneficially, the trust being applicable only to the £50.[59]

The bequest might also be construed as a gift to X conditional upon his performing the obligation. In that situation, Y obtains no interest in the £50; X has the choice of keeping the property and paying £50 or of declining both.[60] It could also be construed so as to impose a charge on the property. Here again, X will only be obliged to make the payment if he receives the property. His obligation will be limited to the value of the property,[61] and he will be entitled to retain any surplus.[62] Y will have an equitable right by virtue of the charge,[63] but this right is a different one from that of a beneficiary under a trust.

The House of Lords has held that equity will protect the right of an insurer to be subrogated to the insured person's rights against the wrongdoer by imposing an equitable lien or charge, although not a trust, in favour of the insurer on the damages payable by the wrong-doer.[64] The imposition of a trust would be onerous, commercially undesirable and unnecessary to the protection of the insurer.

F. Interest under a Will or Intestacy

2–013   The relationship between a personal representative and a legatee or devisee bears many similarities to that of trustee and beneficiary.

---

[55] T. Thomas (1952) 11 C.L.J. 240.

[56] *Re Frame* [1939] Ch. 700 (devise to housekeeper "on condition that she adopt my daughter Alma and also gives to my daughters Jessie and May the sum of £5 each, and a like sum to my son Alexander."); cf. *Re Brace* [1954] 1 W.L.R. 955.

[57] *Re Cowley* (1885) 53 L.T. 494.

[58] *King v Denison* (1813) 1 V. & B. 260 at 272; *Re West* [1900] 1 Ch. 84; *Re Rees' WT* [1950] Ch. 204; below, para.5–012.

[59] *Re Foord* [1922] 2 Ch. 519 ("To my sister, Margaret Juliet, absolutely on trust to pay my wife per annum" £300); distinguished in *Re Osoba* [1979] 1 W.L.R. 247.

[60] *Att Gen v The Cordwainers Co* (1833) 3 Myl. & K. 534.

[61] *Re Cowley* (1885) 53 L.T. 494.

[62] *Re Oliver* (1890) 62 L.T. 533.

[63] *Parker v Judkin* [1931] 1 Ch. 475.

[64] *Napier and Ettrick (Lord) v Hunter* [1993] A.C. 713.

The origins of the relationship, however, are quite distinct, the former originating in the Ecclesiastical Court and the latter in Chancery and their basic function is different. The trustee's duty is to manage the trust so long as it continues. The personal representative's duty is to liquidate the estate and distribute the assets; either to individual beneficiaries, or, if a trust is established by the will, to the trustees. Commonly, the executors and the trustees are the same persons, and, as we shall see,[65] in the case of personalty the transfer to themselves is notional; in the case of land an assent is required. Although the two relationships often coalesce or overlap, there are important distinctions between them.

i. Whether a Personal Representative is a Trustee. The defini- 2–014
tion of trustee in the Trustee Act 1925 includes a personal representative[66] where the context so admits; and the Act, except where otherwise expressly provided, applies to executorships and administratorships.[67] A personal representative is sometimes treated in Administration of Estates Act 1925 as a trustee.[68] A personal representative is under fiduciary duties which are very similar to those of a trustee. There are, however, a number of ways in which a personal representative has been held not to be a trustee.

(a) *Different Periods of Limitation Apply.* Generally, an action for 2–015
the recovery of trust property or for a breach of trust must be brought against a trustee within six years.[69] An action against a personal representative in respect of a claim to personal estate must be brought within 12 years, and an action for the recovery of arrears of interest on legacies within six years.[70] Where a personal representative completes the administration and continues as trustee of a will trust, any later breaches of his duty as trustee are governed by the six-year rule.[71]

(b) *Power of Disposition of Personalty.* The power of personal 2–016
representatives to dispose of pure personalty is *several*; that of trustees is *joint*.[72] This means that one of several executors can pass title to a chattel; but in a sale by trustees, all must combine. It thus

---

[65] Below, para.2–016.
[66] s.68(17); AEA 1925 s.33; Trustee Act 2000 s.35; *contra*, Income Tax Act 2007 s.463.
[67] s.69.
[68] AEA 1925 ss.33, 46, 49; Intestates' Estates Act 1952.
[69] Limitation Act 1980 s.21(3); for exceptions, see s.21(1) and (2).
[70] Limitation Act 1980 s.22.
[71] *Davies v Sharples* [2006] W.T.L.R. 839.
[72] *Attenborough v Solomon* [1913] A.C. 76.

becomes important to ascertain when a personal representative becomes a trustee. Where, of course, a will appoints certain persons as executors and other persons as trustees, the executors, on the completion of the administration, must assent to the vesting of the property subject to the trust in the trustees. In the case of personalty the assent may be oral, or even implied,[73] in the case of a legal estate in land however an assent must be in writing, and it becomes an essential document of title in the case of unregistered land.[74]

When however, the executors are appointed trustees also, or where no provision is made for the appointment of trustees in a will which provides for property to be held in trust after the completion of administration, the question arises of the way in which, and of the time at which, the executors become trustees. The principle is that the transition from executors to trustees occurs automatically after completion of the administration, but as far as powers of disposition of property are concerned, there must also have been a sufficient assent by the executors in their own favour as trustees.

In *Attenborough v Solomon*,[75] the House of Lords held that a pledge of silver plate by one of two executors, which was made 13 years after the completion of the administration of the estate, passed no title to the pledgee. The executors had long since become trustees; an assent in their own favour could be inferred from their conduct; and trustees must act jointly.

A similar view was taken in the cases allowing a personal representative to act as a trustee in the exercise of the statutory power of appointing new trustees.[76]

There is no distinction with regard to the power of disposition of land, the power being joint in both cases.[77] Formerly one of two or more personal representatives could enter into a contract to sell land, but this is no longer possible.[78] Where there is only a single personal representative, he may give a receipt for capital money arising on the sale,[79] while at least two trustees or a trust corporation are required in the case of a conveyance by a tenant for life or trustees of

---

[73] *Attenborough v Solomon* [1913] A.C. 76. See C. Stebbings [1990] Conv. 257.

[74] "An assent to the vesting of a legal estate shall be in writing, signed by the personal representative, and shall name the person in whose favour it is given and shall operate to vest in that person the legal estate to which it relates; and an assent not in writing or not in favour of a named person shall not be effectual to pass a legal estate." AEA 1925 s.36(4). This does not apply to the vesting of an equitable interest in land; *Re Edwards's WT* [1982] Ch. 30.

[75] [1913] A.C. 76.

[76] *Re Ponder* [1921] 2 Ch. 59; *Re Cockburn* [1957] Ch. 438. See also C. Stebbings [1984] Conv. 423.

[77] AEA 1925 s.2(2).

[78] Law of Property (Miscellaneous Provisions) Act 1994 s.16.

[79] LPA 1925 s.27(2).

land.[80] It is necessary for all personal representatives who are registered shareholders of a company to execute any transfer of the shares.[81]

(c) *Tenure of Office.* Formerly a personal representative held his   **2–017**
office for life (unless the grant was for a limited period) and could
not retire. Now, however, the court may discharge an executor or
administrator and appoint a substitute.[82] A trustee, on the other
hand, may retire without a court order.[83] Subject to the above, a
personal representative's duties terminate with the completion of the
administration of the estate, but his liabilities are limited only by the
passage of time. Thus solicitors who were sureties of an administrator
and who handed over the residue of the estate to the administrator
(who then absconded) were held liable on their bond.[84]

(d) *Duty to Estate: Duty to Beneficiaries.* Executors and trustees   **2–018**
are both subject to fiduciary duties. A trustee's duty is to the beneficiaries,
and he must "hold the balance evenly between the beneficiaries
to whom the property belongs."[85] With an unadministered
estate, no legatee, devisee or next of kin, has, as will be seen,[86]
beneficial ownership of the assets. The executor's duty is to the
estate as a whole.[87] In *Re Hayes' Will Trusts*,[88] a testator appointed
four persons, including his son, executors and trustees of his will,
and gave power to:

> "[M]y trustees . . . to sell . . . to any person . . . including my son
> despite his being a trustee and in his case at the value placed upon
> the same for purposes of estate duty."

In agreeing the estate duty valuation of the farm, it was held that the
executors were not obliged to consider the implications of the fact
that a low valuation benefited the son, a high one benefited the other
beneficiaries. They negotiated in the usual way with the District
Valuer and agreed as low a valuation for tax purposes as they could

---

[80] TA 1925 s.14; below, para.20–007.
[81] Companies Act 2006 s.773 (re-enacting earlier legislation). For electronic transfer, see below, para.4–008.
[82] Administration of Justice Act 1985 s.50. See *Re Steel* [2010] W.T.L.R. 531.
[83] TA 1925 ss.36, 39; below, para.17–036.
[84] *Harvell v Foster* [1954] 2 Q.B. 367.
[85] *Re Hayes' WT* [1971] 1 W.L.R. 758 at 764.
[86] Below, para.2–020.
[87] *Re Charteris* [1917] 2 Ch. 379, where a postponement of sale of some assets acted to the disadvantage of the life tenant, although it was in the interest of the estate.
[88] [1971] 1 W.L.R. 758; J. Mummery (1971) 36 Conv.(N.S.) 136.

obtain. This was the usual correct procedure, and they were right to sell to the son at that price.

2–019   (e) *Vesting of a Legal Estate.* A further question arises, however, with a legal estate in land. Where trustees under an existing trust make an appointment of a new trustee under a statutory power given to them by Trustee Act 1925 s.36,[89] the legal estate in the trust property vests in the new trustee under s.40.[90] Although personal representatives cannot appoint successors to their offices, they may, after they have become trustees following the completion of the administration of the estate,[91] appoint additional or successor trustees. But in *Re King's Will Trusts*,[92] Pennycuick J. held that Trustee Act 1925 s.40 did not apply to an appointment of a new trustee by the surviving executor and trustee of a will, who had not previously assented in writing to the vesting of the legal estate in himself in his capacity as trustee. We have seen that an assent in writing is necessary for the vesting of a legal estate in land, and that it constitutes an essential document of title.[93] The executor could have assented to the vesting of the legal estate in himself and the new trustee after the appointment; or he could have assented, before the appointment, to the vesting in himself as trustee; in which case s.40 would have applied.

This decision has been criticised,[94] but it is consistent with the principle of the 1925 legislation that every dealing with a legal estate in land should be supported by a document of title. An assent to the vesting of an equitable interest in land need not, however, be in writing, and may be inferred from conduct.[95]

2–020   **ii. The Nature of the Interest of a Legatee or Devisee.** A legatee or devisee does not, on the testator's death, become equitable owner of any part of the estate. The executor takes full title to the testator's property, not merely a bare legal estate.[96] He is, by virtue of his office, subjected to various fiduciary duties, which can be enforced against him by persons interested; and these duties are

---

[89] Below, para.17–020.

[90] Registration is necessary in the case of registered land.

[91] Above, fn.76.

[92] [1964] Ch. 542; Mellows, *The Law of Succession*, 5th edn, 1993, pp.326–327.

[93] Above, para.2–016.

[94] J. Garner (1964) 28 Conv.(N.S.) 298; R. Walker (1964) 80 L.Q.R. 328; E. Ryder (1976) 29 C.L.P. 60.

[95] *Re Edwards's WT* [1982] Ch. 30. But see P. Smith [1982] Conv. 4 for the view that only an executor, and not an administrator, can make such an implied assent.

[96] *Commissioner of Stamp Duties (Queensland) v Livingston* [1965] A.C. 694 at 707, 708, 712. But, for the purposes of inheritance tax, a person who would become entitled to a residuary estate (or part thereof) on the completion of the administration is treated as having become entitled at the death of the deceased. Inheritance Tax Act 1984 s.91.

inconsistent with his holding the property on trust for the legatee or devisee.[97] The equitable ownership is "in suspense".[98]

The fiduciary duties of the personal representatives are:

"[T]o preserve the assets, to deal properly with them, and to apply them in a due course of administration for the benefit of those interested according to that course, creditors, the death duty authorities, legatees of various sorts, and the residuary beneficiaries. They might just as well have been termed 'duties in respect of the assets' as trusts. What equity did *not* do was to recognise or create for residuary legatees a beneficial interest in the assets in the executor's hand during the course of administration."[99]

It may be, as with an insolvent estate, that nothing is left which can be applied for the beneficiaries. Even if the estate is solvent, the devisee or legatee is not the owner in equity of any asset in the estate. He has a chose in action, a right to compel the administration of the estate. In *Commissioner of Stamp Duties (Queensland) v Livingston*,[100] the question was whether succession duty was payable under a Queensland statute which applied to property situated in Queensland. A widow died domiciled in New South Wales, and was residuary legatee under her husband's will. The estate, which was not administered at the date of the widow's death, contained land in Queensland. The Privy Council held that succession duty was not payable on that property. The widow was not the owner of it. She was the owner of a chose in action, and that was situated in New South Wales, the state of her domicile. In *Eastbourne Mutual Building Society v Hastings Corp*,[101] a husband occupied a house on his wife's intestacy. He was unable to claim compensation for the value of the house on compulsory purchase, because the estate was not administered, and he had no interest in the house. Similarly, in *Lall v Lall*,[102] a widow wished to defend an action for possession of the matrimonial home, which had been owned by her deceased husband. No grant of administration of his estate had yet been made, and so she had no standing to defend the action. In *Re K (Deceased)*[103]

---

[97] *Sudeley (Lord) v Att Gen* [1897] A.C. 11; *Corbett v Commissioners of Inland Revenue* [1938] 1 K.B. 567 at 575–577; *Passant v Jackson (Inspector of Taxes)* [1986] S.T.C. 164; see also *Skinner v Att Gen* [1940] A.C. 350. For a full discussion of Commonwealth cases, see D. Waters (1967) 45 C.B.R. 219.

[98] *J Sainsbury Plc v O'Connor (Inspector of Taxes)* [1991] S.T.C. 318 at 326.

[99] per Lord Radcliffe [1965] A.C. 694 at 707; *Re Hayes' Will Trusts* [1971] 1 W.L.R. 758; C. Davis (2002) 61 C.L.J. 423 at 424.

[100] [1965] A.C. 694. See also *Crowden v Aldridge* [1993] 1 W.L.R. 433; J. Ross Martyn [1994] Conv. 446; *Marshall (Inspector of Taxes) v Kerr* [1995] 1 A.C. 148; *Maye v Director of Public Prosecutions, Northern Ireland, The Times*, February 11, 2008.

[101] [1965] 1 W.L.R. 861.

[102] [1965] 1 W.L.R. 1249; S. Bailey (1965) 23 C.L.J. 144.

[103] [1986] Ch. 180; below, para.12–042.

residuary beneficiaries under an unadministered estate had not acquired an "interest in property" within s.2(7) of the Forfeiture Act 1982 so as to preclude the court from giving relief under the Act from the forfeiture rule in favour of an applicant who had killed the testator. On the other hand, in *Re Leigh's Will Trust*,[104] a bequest by a widow of "all the shares which I hold and any other interest or assets which I may have" in a particular company was held to be wide enough to include a claim to her husband's unadministered estate which contained such shares; and her claim passed under her will. Following on from this, a beneficiary of an unadministered estate who has taken possession of the land is a person "entitled to a beneficial interest in the land or in the proceeds of sale" within the Limitation Act 1980[105] (with the result that he cannot acquire title against the other beneficiaries).[106] Similarly, where a person entitled under an unadministered estate is bankrupt, the chose in action and its fruits are property of the bankrupt capable of passing to his trustee in bankruptcy.[107] Property held by the personal representatives of an estate which has not been fully administered is property "held on trusts" for the purposes of s.1(1) of the Variation of Trusts Act 1958, as there is no good policy reason against this interpretation.[108]

While it is settled that a residuary legatee or devisee or an intestate successor has no equitable interest in any particular assets of an unadministered estate, the position of a specific legatee or devisee is less clear. While there is some authority that such a legatee or devisee does have an equitable interest in the property in question as from the testator's death,[109] some statements in the *Livingston* case cast doubt on this.[110] The view of the Law Commission is that a specific legatee or devisee has no equitable interest during the period of administration.[111] After all, the assets in question may need to be used for the discharge of debts even if the estate is solvent.

A devisee or legatee may be said to become the equitable owner of specific property once property has been allocated by the executor for the purpose.[112] In the case of a residuary gift or a claim on intestacy, the allocation cannot occur until the residuary accounts

---

[104] [1970] Ch. 277; PVB (1970) 86 L.Q.R. 20.

[105] Schedule 1, para.9.

[106] *Earnshaw v Hartley* [2000] Ch. 155.

[107] *Official Receiver in Bankruptcy v Schultz* (1990) 170 C.L.R. 306 (High Court of Australia); *Re Hemming (Deceased)* [2009] Ch. 313.

[108] *Re Bernstein* [2010] W.T.L.R. 559.

[109] See *Re Neeld* [1962] Ch. 643 at 688.

[110] [1965] A.C. 694 at 707, 708. See also *Official Receiver in Bankruptcy v Schultz*, above, fn.107, at 312.

[111] Law Com. No.188 (1989), para.2.16. Pending administration a specific devisee may make a valid contract to sell the land, which becomes specifically enforceable when his interest becomes proprietary; *Wu Koon Tai v Wu Yau Loi* [1997] A.C. 179.

[112] *Phillipo v Munnings* (1837) 2 Myl. & Cr. 309.

are prepared.[113] That is the time at which the executors are turning into trustees. The interest of the person entitled then becomes that of a beneficiary under a trust.

G. Powers[114]

i. Trusts Imperative; Powers Discretionary. The distinction **2–021** between trusts and powers is fundamental. Trusts are imperative; powers are discretionary. Trustees must perform the duties connected with their trusts. A donee of a power may exercise it, or not, at his choice. If the donee of a power created by will predeceases the testator then the power lapses, but it is otherwise in the case of a trust, which does not fail for lack of a trustee.[115]

Trustees are under a duty to hold the trust property for the beneficiaries in accordance with the terms of the trust. The beneficiaries under a trust are the owners in equity of the trust property. Objects of a power own nothing, unless and until the donee of the power makes an appointment in their favour.[116] They merely have a hope that the power will be exercised in their favour. Until the power is exercised, equitable ownership in such a case is in those who will take in default of an appointment, their interest being defeated by its exercise. Thus, if a testator by his will leaves property to his widow for life and after her death to his children in equal shares, the widow and the children obtain vested interests in the property. Compare this with a gift to the widow for life and after her death as she shall appoint among the children, and, in default of appointment, to charity. Then the children obtain nothing unless and until an appointment is made in their favour.

Whether a trust or a power has been created depends on the construction of the language of the instrument. A properly drafted instrument will leave no room for doubt.

The distinction is however complicated by the fact that a trust may give to the trustees considerable discretion. A trustee may be given a discretion to select beneficiaries from a specified class, or to determine the proportions in which specified beneficiaries are to take. This is the basis of a discretionary trust. Under such a trust no member of a class of the discretionary beneficiaries has an interest in a specific part of the trust property until the discretion of the trustees

---

[113] *Re Claremont* [1923] 2 K.B. 718.
[114] Thomas, *Powers*, 1998; Halsbury's *Laws of England*, 4th edn, Vol.36(2), p.127; J. Hopkins (1971) C.L.J. 68; J. Harris (1971) 87 L.Q.R. 31. For views on the changing nature of trusts and powers, see J. Davies [1970] A.S.C.L. 187; Y. Grbich (1974) 37 M.L.R. 643. Below, Ch.6.
[115] *Brown v Higgs* (1803) 8 Ves. 561.
[116] *Vestey v IRC* [1980] A.C. 1148.

has been exercised in his favour. The beneficiaries as a whole, however, are the owners of the trust property. If all are adult and under no disability, they may combine together to terminate the trust and demand a distribution of the property.[117] The trustees throughout are under an obligation to perform the trust; that is to say, in the context of a discretionary trust, to exercise their discretion; and so to make a selection after proper consideration. "If the trustees fail to exercise their discretion, the court can compel them to exercise the trust."[118] Thus a beneficiary under a discretionary trust cannot demand payment. He has, however, the right to demand that the trustees exercise their discretion in accordance with the trust. What happens if the trustees refuse to do so is one of the matters discussed in *McPhail v Doulton*.[119] The court could replace obstructive trustees with willing ones; and, if no suitable trustees would act, the court ultimately would need to make a selection. The point is that a discretionary trust puts the trustees under an obligation. Their duty is to make a selection. This is very different from a mere power to appoint; for in that case there is no duty to make a selection. It has been held, however, that the court has similar powers of intervention in the case of a fiduciary power where there is nobody to exercise it.[120]

2–022   Although the donee of a mere power of appointment is not obliged to exercise it, he does have certain duties. Thus he must consider periodically whether to exercise it, consider the range of objects, and the appropriateness of individual appointments. If he does decide to exercise the power, he must do so in a responsible manner according to its purpose and, of course, refrain from making any appointment which is not within the terms of the power.[121] This is the case where the power is given to a trustee as such; the duties described above are necessary to the performance of his fiduciary role. Where, however, the donee of the power is not a fiduciary, he is not subjected to these fiduciary duties, although he must, of course, keep within the terms of the power.

But it is difficult in borderline cases to draw a dividing line between discretionary trusts and powers,[122] and between fiduciary

---

[117] *Re Smith* [1928] Ch. 915; *Re Nelson* [1918] Ch. 926; *Vestey v IRC (Nos 1 and 2)* [1980] A.C. 1148.

[118] per Lord Guest in *McPhail v Doulton* [1971] A.C. 424 at 444; *Re Locker's ST* [1977] 1 W.L.R. 1323.

[119] [1971] A.C. 424; below, para.3–026.

[120] *Mettoy Pension Trustees Ltd v Evans* [1990] 1 W.L.R. 1587; below, para.6–007.

[121] *Re Hay's ST* [1982] 1 W.L.R. 202; A. Grubb [1982] Conv. 432; *Turner v Turner* [1984] Ch. 100.

[122] *Re Leek* [1969] 1 Ch. 563; *Re Gulbenkian's Settlements* [1970] A.C. 508 at 525, per Lord Upjohn; *McPhail v Doulton*, above, fn.119, at 448; *Vestey v IRC*, above, fn.117. See also, in the context of charity, *Re Cohen* [1973] 1 W.L.R. 415.

and personal powers. The decision turns on the proper construction of the language of the instrument.[123]

The matter is made more difficult by reason of the fact that a discretionary trust may be "exhaustive" or "non-exhaustive". An exhaustive discretionary trust is one where the trustees' duty to exercise their discretion can only be satisfied by making a distribution. A non-exhaustive discretionary trust, on the other hand, is one where the settlor has given the trustees power to decide not to distribute all of the income, for example, by giving them power to accumulate it for a certain period.[124] It must be admitted that the identification of the precise duty in the case of a non-exhaustive discretionary trust is a difficult task. The distinction from a power of appointment is a fine one, and the matter will be further discussed in Ch.8. For present purposes the position may be summarised as follows: whereas the donee of a fiduciary power of appointment need only consider exercising the power, the trustee of a discretionary trust must actually exercise it, although in the case of a non-exhaustive discretionary trust this duty may be satisfied by deciding to accumulate rather than to distribute.

ii. Terminology. Nor is the matter helped by the terminology. **2–023** Discretionary trusts have been referred to as a "power in the nature of a trust", or "a power coupled with a duty", or even as a "trust power". Terminology of this type adds to confusion. The situation is that if the words, on their proper construction, are held to impose a duty, then the words create a trust—though one in which the trustees have a power of selection.

iii. Significance of the Distinction. The question may be mate- **2–024** rial in a number of circumstances.

(a) *Whether the Class Takes if the Discretion is not Exercised.* If **2–025** there is a gift in favour of such members of a class as X shall select, and X fails to make a selection, will the gift take effect in favour of the class, or will it fail? If the power is construed as a mere power, the non-exercise of the power will cause it to fail,[125] and the property will then pass on default of appointment, or go on resulting trust for the grantor. But if the gift is construed as a gift to the class

---

[123] *Re Scarisbrick's WT* [1951] Ch. 622 at 635, per Lord Evershed M.R.; *Mettoy Pension Trustees Ltd v Evans* [1990] 1 W.L.R. 1507; *Gomez v Gomez-Monche Vives* [2009] Ch. 245.

[124] This led some commentators to take the view that there is no longer any analytical distinction between trusts and powers. See J. Davies [1970] A.S.C.L. 187; Y. Grbich (1974) 37 M.L.R. 643; M. Cullity (1976) 54 C.B.R. 229.

[125] Subject to *Mettoy Pension Trustees Ltd v Evans* [1990] 1 W.L.R. 1587; below, para.6–007.

subject to X's power of selection, the trust in favour of the class will take effect.

In *Burrough v Philcox*[126] a testator provided that the survivor of his children should have power, by will:

"[T]o dispose of all my real and personal estates amongst my nephews and nieces, or their children, either all to one of them or to as many of them as my surviving child shall think proper."

No appointments were made and the members of the class were held to take equally as a trust had been created. On the other hand in *Re Weekes' Settlement*,[127] a testatrix gave her husband a life interest and a power "to dispose of all such property by will amongst our children." He died intestate. There was held to be no trust, and so the children took nothing. In neither case was there a gift over in default.

The question is whether, on the proper construction of the words, it is possible to show an intention to benefit the objects in the event of no appointment being made.[128] It has been said that the courts are more inclined to such a construction when the objects are small in number, such as children under a marriage settlement.[129] But in *McPhail v Doulton*[130] a deed was held to create a trust which provided that the trustees "shall apply the net income in making at their absolute discretion" grants to employees, past and present, and their dependants. The principle to be applied was laid down by Lord Cottenham in *Burrough v Philcox*.[131]

"When there appears a general intention in favour of a class, and a particular intention in favour of individuals of a class to be selected by another person, and the particular intention fails, from that selection not being made, the Court will carry into effect the general intention in favour of the class."

The presence of a gift over in default of appointment destroys any such implication; the gift over shows that the settlor is providing for a situation where the donee does not appoint to the class; and this is

---

[126] (1840) 5 Myl. & Cr. 72. Such a trust, it is submitted, should be regarded as a fixed trust subject to defeasance by exercise of the power of selection, and thus unaffected by *McPhail v Doulton*, below, fn.130. See below, para.3–037.
[127] [1897] 1 Ch. 289.
[128] *Re Llewellyn's Settlement* [1921] 2 Ch. 281; *Re Arnold* [1947] Ch. 131.
[129] *Re Perowne* [1951] Ch. 785 at 790.
[130] [1971] A.C. 424.
[131] (1840) 5 Myl. & Cr. 72 at 92.

inconsistent with a trust in favour of the class.[132] But there is no hard and fast rule that a trust is intended if there is no gift over.[133]

Where the court finds that there is a trust, the question arises of the share which each of the beneficiaries will take. In the nineteenth-century cases, where the question usually arose in the context of division among a family group, the rule of equal division was applied, on the principle that equality was equity.[134] Such a solution would be particularly inappropriate in the context of modern trusts in favour of employees of companies and their dependants. In *McPhail v Doulton*[135] the House of Lords, as we have seen, was more courageous, and accepted the obligation, where necessary, of itself making a decision on division.

(b) *The Test of Certainty.* With both trusts and powers, it is necessary for the beneficiaries, or the objects, to be defined with sufficient certainty to enable the trustees or the donees to exercise their functions, and for the court to supervise them. Before the decision of the House of Lords in *McPhail v Doulton*,[136] it was necessary to draw a distinction between the requirement of certainty in the case of trusts (fixed and discretionary) and that required for mere powers. *McPhail v Doulton*, however, decided that the test was the same for discretionary trusts and mere powers. The test came from *Re Gulbenkian's Settlements*,[137] a case on a power, and is whether "it can be said with certainty that any given individual is or is not a member of the class".[138] This test will be discussed in detail in Ch.3. But it may be said here that the assimilation of the test of certainty for discretionary trusts and mere powers has greatly reduced the practical significance of the distinction between them. Prior to *McPhail v Doulton*,[139] most of the litigation on the distinction between discretionary trusts and mere powers concerned the question whether a class description had to comply only with the above test; or whether it was void for failure to comply with a stricter test which had earlier been applicable to all trusts.[140] That test was whether the description of the beneficiaries enabled the trustee to draw up a full list of the

2–026

---

[132] This is so even if the gift over is void; *Re Sprague* (1880) 43 L.T. 236. But it would not be so because of a residuary gift, or a gift over in default of there being any objects of the power; *Re Leek* [1969] 1 Ch. 563.

[133] *Re Weekes* [1879] 1 Ch. 289; *Re Combe* [1925] Ch. 210; *Re Perowne* [1951] Ch. 785; *McPhail v Doulton* [1971] A.C. 424.

[134] This will still be the result if such was the settlor's intention; below, para.3–037.

[135] [1971] A.C. 424. Equal division would not be possible in any event if the total membership of the class was not known. As will be seen, the certainty test propounded in *McPhail v Doulton* does not require all the objects to be ascertained.

[136] Above, fn.133.

[137] [1970] A.C. 508.

[138] per Lord Wilberforce in *McPhail v Doulton*, above, fn.135, at 456; *Re Baden's Deed Trusts (No.2)* [1973] Ch. 9, below, para.3–028.

[139] [1971] A.C. 424.

[140] *IRC v Broadway Cottages Trust Ltd* [1955] Ch. 20.

beneficiaries. That test still remains applicable to "fixed" as opposed to discretionary trusts; that is to say trusts which give a specific share to each beneficiary. Unless the court could make a complete list of all the beneficiaries, it would be impossible to make a division, or to supervise the trustees if they failed to distribute.

2–027   (c) *Terminating the Trust.* Where all the beneficiaries of a discretionary trust are adult and under no disability they may determine the trust and require the trust property to be shared out.[141] On the other hand, objects of a power can never claim any proprietary interest in the property until the power has been exercised in their favour.

2. CLASSIFICATION OF TRUSTS[142]

2–028   Trusts have been variously classified and subdivided. The categories are not exclusive; some trusts could appear in more than one category. The basic division is between private trusts, and public or charitable trusts.[143] Charitable trusts, which are dealt with in Ch.15, are trusts for certain purposes which are so beneficial to the community that the Attorney General undertakes responsibility for their enforcement. They are accorded special privileges in terms of non-liability to tax, and in terms of perpetual duration. Private trusts, on the other hand, are trusts for persons, the beneficiaries; and the beneficiaries can enforce the trust. It may also be noted here that there are a few anomalous cases in which trusts for non-charitable purposes, usually for the building of monuments or the upkeep of particular animals, have been upheld. Such trusts are usually called non-charitable purpose trusts, or trusts of imperfect obligation. The latter name indicates one of their main anomalies; who will enforce such a trust? These trusts are dealt with in Ch.14.

Private trusts are divided into express, constructive and resulting trusts[144]; and express trusts may be divided into executed and executory, and into completely constituted and incompletely constituted trusts. Sometimes implied trusts are included as a further category of private trusts.[145] This classification serves little purpose, and the examples commonly given might preferably be regarded as express, resulting or constructive trusts, as the case may be. Trusts have often

[141] *Re Smith* [1928] 1 Ch. 915.
[142] See C. Rickett (1999) 18 N.Z.U.L.R. 305.
[143] Historically "public trusts" were not synonymous with charitable trusts. The term referred to the protection of public money from unlawful application. See J. Barratt (2006) 69 M.L.R. 514.
[144] Chambers, *Resulting Trusts*, p.5, prefers a classification distinguishing trusts generated by consent or by responses to wrongs, unjust enrichment or other events.
[145] Such a classification at times appears in statutes, for example, LPA 1925 s.53(2).

been established although express words to that effect have not been used,[146] yet such trusts are "express" because the settlors intended to create them. Trusts based on the presumed intention of the settlor as, for example, in the case of a voluntary conveyance, are sometimes described as implied trusts, but will here be treated as resulting trusts. Mutual wills are also sometimes described as implied trusts, but will here be treated as constructive trusts. The term may be used as meaning any private trust which is not express, but the matter is purely one of terminology.

A. Express Trusts

An express trust is one intentionally declared by the creator of the   **2–029** trust, who is known as the settlor, or, if the trust is created by will, the testator. A trust is created by a manifestation of an intention to create a trust; though certain formalities, as will be seen, are required in the case of lifetime trusts of land and of all testamentary trusts.

Two subdivisions of express trusts should be mentioned.

(i) Executed and Executory. An executed trust is one in which   **2–030** the testator or settlor has marked out in appropriate technical expressions what interests are to be taken by all the beneficiaries. On the other hand, in an executory trust, the execution of some further instrument is required, in order to define the beneficial interests with precision. The property is immediately subject to a valid trust, but it remains executory until the further instrument is duly executed.

The practical significance of the distinction is that while the language of executed trusts is governed by strict rules of construction, executory trusts are construed more liberally. Where, in the case of an executed trust, the settlor has made use of technical expressions, as to the interpretation of which the law has laid down rules, equity will follow the law and give effect to such interpretation.[147] In the case of an executory trust, however, equity will attach less importance to the use or omission of technical words, but will seek to discover the settlor's true intention, and order the preparation of a final deed which gives effect to such intention. It is necessary, however, for the court to be able to ascertain, from the language of the instrument, the trusts which are intended to be imposed on the property.[148]

---

[146] See *Paul v Constance* [1977] 1 W.L.R. 527, and the cases discussed under the heading "Certainty of Intention", below, para.3–019.

[147] *Re Bostock's Settlement* [1921] 2 Ch. 469; see also LPA 1925 s.60(1); cf. *Re Arden* [1935] Ch. 326.

[148] *Re Flavel's Will Trusts* [1966] 1 W.L.R. 445 at 447 ("for formation of a superannuation and bonus fund for the employees").

Executory trusts appeared most commonly in marriage articles, which often provided that certain property belonging to one of the parties should be settled upon them and their children, and in wills. They are rarely met at the present day; due no doubt to the fact that many modern trusts have tax-saving implications, and it is necessary, for such purposes, to be precise and specific in drafting the trust. A rare recent example is *Pengelly v Pengelly*,[149] where a testator left property by will on a discretionary trust for a class of beneficiaries as his trustees should decide, to include some or all of his children, grandchildren and their spouses, widows and widowers. The will stated that the settlement was to be established by a deed executed by the trustees no later than two years after his death, and was to contain such powers and provisions as the trustees should decide. As it stood this was not a valid executory trust, as it failed sufficiently to define the class of beneficiaries. However, the court was able to rectify the will[150] by inserting the word "only" before "to include". As the class was thus confined to the specified relatives, the will created a valid immediate executory discretionary trust.

A pension fund trust provides another modern example. In *Davis v Richards & Wallington Industries Ltd*[151] the question arose as to entitlement to surplus funds. A pension scheme had been established by an interim trust deed, which provided for the execution of a definitive trust deed. This deed was later executed, and contained rules as to the entitlement to any surplus, but there was doubt as to its validity. In fact the definitive deed was upheld, but if it had not been, the court would have held the interim deed to be a valid executory trust. This could have been executed by a court order bringing into effect rules corresponding to those in the definitive deed, thereby resolving the issue as to the surplus.

2–031   **(ii) Completely and Incompletely Constituted Trusts.** There cannot be a trust unless the trust is completely constituted. This heading is therefore irrational; it is dealing, not with two different types of trust, but with a rule for distinguishing what is a trust from something that is void. Nevertheless, it is convenient to make the point here, and to deal in more detail with the matter below.[152]

A trust is only valid if the title to the property is in the trustee and if the trusts have been validly declared. A declaration that A holds on trust for B is ineffective if the property is not vested in A. The trust becomes constituted and valid when the property is vested in

---

[149] [2008] Ch. 375.
[150] Below, para.26–023.
[151] [1990] 1 W.L.R. 1511; disapproved on another point in *Air Jamaica Ltd v Charlton* [1999] 1 W.L.R. 1399.
[152] Below, Ch.4.

A. The form of transfer to A depends on the nature of the property
—land, chattel, money, shares in a company, copyrights, patents,
debts or other choses in action—and the appropriate method must of
course be used.[153] In the case of a trust of land there must also be
written evidence of the declaration of trust.[154] The settlor may of
course declare himself trustee, and there is then an automatic constitution, because title was in the settlor throughout. Testamentary
trusts are always completely constituted; for the executors, if not the
trustees themselves, are under a duty to transfer the trust property to
the nominated trustees.

Although no trust is created unless the trust is completely constituted, there are situations where intended beneficiaries under an
incompletely constituted trust may compel the transfer of the property to the trustees. In general, they can do so if they have given
consideration, but not if they are volunteers, for there is yet no trust
and "equity will not assist a volunteer".[155]

B. Resulting Trusts[156]

A resulting trust exists where property has been conveyed to **2–032**
another, but the beneficial interest returns, or "results" to the transferor. This may happen in various situations; the simplest one is
where the property is conveyed to trustees upon certain trusts which
fail or which do not exhaust the whole beneficial interest. The part
undisposed of results to the settlor. For example, if there is a gift on
trust for A for life and then on trust for X if X attains the age of 21,
but X dies under 21 in A's lifetime, the property will result on A's
death to the settlor.

Such a resulting trust has been described as "automatic",[157]
meaning that it arises by operation of law, without depending on the
intention of the settlor. Another view is that the so-called "automatic" resulting trust gives effect to the settlor's presumed intention.[158]

Another category, clearly based on the presumed intention of the
settlor, is the "presumed" resulting trust in favour of the transferor
where property is conveyed to a volunteer. The presumption is rebuttable by evidence of an intention to make a gift or, where the
volunteer is the transferor's wife or child, by the presumption of
advancement.[159] (The presumption of advancement was abolished

---

[153] Below, paras 4–008 et seq.
[154] LPA 1925 s.53; below, para.3–004.
[155] Below, Ch.4.
[156] Below, Ch.10.
[157] per Megarry J. in *Re Vandervell's Trust (No.2)* [1974] Ch. 269 at 291.
[158] *Westdeutsche Landesbank Girozentrale v Islington LBC* [1996] A.C. 669 at 708.
[159] Below, para.10–022.

by the Equality Act 2010,[160] but not retrospectively.) The modern analysis is that both kinds of resulting trust depend on the intention of the transferor. Such a trust arises in circumstances where the transferor did not intend the transferee to take beneficially.[161]

C. Constructive Trusts[162]

2–033   While express trusts arise from the act of the parties, constructive trusts arise by operation of law.[163] Equity says that in certain circumstances the legal owner of property must hold it on trust for others. The absence of the need for formalities in such circumstances is obvious. There is, however, much dispute and uncertainty as to the occasions on which constructive trusts arise, and also as to their nature.

The term has indeed been used in different senses. It can cover the duty of a trustee who has obtained benefits by fraud; the obligation of a transferee from an express trustee, unless he proves he was a bona fide purchaser for value without notice, to hold the transferred property on the trusts previously applicable; the obligation of a trustee who has made a profit, however innocently, through his office, to hold such profit for the benefit of his beneficiaries[164]; the position of a stranger to the trust who has dishonestly assisted in a breach of trust[165]; the relationship of vendor and purchaser between the contract and the execution of the conveyance[166]; and other relationships, such as licensees, and claimants to a matrimonial home, where the introduction of a constructive trust was considered to be necessary to enable the court to reach a just solution.[167] A controversial question is whether the "remedial" constructive trust, favoured in some commonwealth jurisdictions, is available to prevent unjust enrichment whenever the personal remedy is inadequate.

Lord Denning M.R. pioneered a constructive trust "of a new model",[168] to be imposed "whenever justice and good conscience required it ... " as an equitable remedy "by which the court can enable an aggrieved party to obtain restitution".[169] The implications of these developments will be discussed in Ch.12.

---

[160] s.199 (not in force at the time of writing).
[161] See Chambers, *Resulting Trusts*; cf W. Swadling (2008) 124 L.Q.R. 72.
[162] Below, Ch.12. Waters, *The Constructive Trust*, 1964; Oakley, *Constructive Trusts*, 3rd edn.
[163] cf. C. Rickett (1999) 18 N.Z.U.L.R. 305 taking the view that all trusts are founded on intention.
[164] *Keech v Sandford* (1726) Sel.Cas.t. King 61; *Boardman v Phipps* [1967] 2 A.C. 46.
[165] Below, para.12–011.
[166] Below, para.12–035.
[167] *Binions v Evans* [1972] Ch. 359 (licensee); *Eves v Eves* [1975] 1 W.L.R. 1338 (cohabitant); *Re Densham* [1975] 1 W.L.R. 1519 (wife). See below, para.12–043.
[168] *Eves v Eves* [1975] 1 W.L.R. 1338.
[169] *Hussey v Palmer* [1972] 1 W.L.R. 1286 at 1289.

D. Bare Trusts

A distinction is sometimes made between bare or simple trusts, on **2–034** the one hand, and "special" trusts on the other. There is said to be a bare trust when the trustee holds trust property in trust for an adult beneficiary absolutely. In such a situation the beneficiary may call for a conveyance of the legal estate at any time, and the trustee must comply.[170] In the meantime the trustee has no duties to perform and must deal with the trust property in accordance with the instructions of the beneficiary.[171]

It is said that all other trusts are "special" trusts. The description however, is not generally used except as a mode of contrast with a bare or simple trust.

A bare trust may arise at the outset, as where an absolute owner puts shares or other property into the name of trustees[172] or some other third party[173] to hold for himself. This may arise in a commercial context, as where a solicitor holds money for a client.[174] A trust which was not originally a bare trust may become one when an adult beneficiary becomes absolutely entitled, as on the death of A in a trust for A for life, remainder to B. A bare trust need not be express, but can take the form of a resulting or constructive trust, as where the settlor fails to declare the beneficial interests[175] or did not intend any beneficial interest to pass to the fraudulent transferee.[176]

A bare trustee into whose name an absolute owner transfers property is sometimes called a nominee.[177] This must be distinguished from the situation where the trustees vest securities in a nominee in order to facilitate share dealings. Such a person is in effect an agent of the trustees.[178]

E. Trusts in the Higher Sense and Trusts in the Lower Sense

The word "trust" is used in various contexts which have no **2–035** relationship to the legal meaning of the term.[179] The Crown may

---

[170] As, indeed, could a multiplicity of beneficiaries, all adult and under no disability; *Saunders v Vautier* (1841) 4 Beav. 115; below, para.22–001. See also *Clarence House Ltd v National Westminster Bank Plc* [2010] 1 W.L.R. 1216 ("virtual assignment" of lease whereby "virtual assignor" retained legal title did not create a bare trust for the "virtual assignee", who could not have called for a transfer of the legal estate as this was not permitted by the lease. It was an agency relationship.)

[171] *Re Cunningham and Fray* [1891] 2 Ch. 567; D Hayton (1992) 1 J.I.P. 3.

[172] *Grey v IRC* [1960] A.C. 1.

[173] *Hardoon v Belilios* [1901] A.C. 119; *Ingram v IRC* [2000] 1 A.C. 293.

[174] *Target Holdings Ltd v Redferns (A Firm)* [1996] 1 A.C. 421; below, para.23–007.

[175] *Vandervell v IRC* [1967] 2 A.C. 291.

[176] *Hodgson v Marks* [1971] Ch. 892.

[177] See *Ingram v IRC*, above (land conveyed by owner to solicitor as nominee as a step in a tax avoidance scheme).

[178] Below, para.20–012 (delegation of powers). See also custodian trustees; below, para.20–016.

[179] See R. Bartlett [1996] Conv. 186, discussing National Health Service Trusts.

entrust ministers or officials with property, perhaps providing that they shall hold it "in trust" for the benefit of some person or body of persons. While such a situation is capable of creating a trust in the legal or "lower" sense:

" '[T]rust' is not a term of art in public law and when used in relation to matters which lie within the field of public law, the words 'in trust' may do no more than indicate the existence of a duty owed to the Crown by the officer of state as servant of the Crown, to deal with the property for the benefit of the subject for whom it is expressed to be held in trust, such duty being enforced administratively or by disciplinary sanctions and not otherwise; *Kinlock v Secretary of State for India*.[180]" [181]

Similarly, where it is alleged that the Crown is trustee for members of the public. In *Tito v Waddell*[182] phosphate had been mined on Ocean Island by a British company until 1920, when the mining rights were acquired by the governments of the United Kingdom, Australia and New Zealand. The Ocean Islanders claimed that the Crown stood in a fiduciary position to them and was liable for various breaches of trust. The claim failed. Although the relevant documents used the word "trust", their wording was, as a matter of construction, consonant with the creation of a governmental obligation, for the breach of which the court was powerless to give relief. This governmental obligation, or "trust in the higher sense", was not a true trust in the conventional sense. It created no fiduciary obligation, and was not justiciable in the courts.

---

[180] (1882) 7 App.Cas. 619.
[181] per Lord Diplock in *Town Investments Ltd v Department of the Environment* [1978] A.C. 359 at 382. But the Crown can be a trustee in the "lower sense"; *Civilian War Claimants Association Ltd v R.* [1932] A.C. 14; *Lonrho Exports Ltd v Export Credits Guarantee Department* [1999] Ch. 158.
[182] (*No.2*) [1977] Ch. 106.

PART II

TRUSTS AND POWERS

CHAPTER 3

REQUIREMENTS OF A TRUST

1. CAPACITY TO CREATE A TRUST

CAPACITY to create a trust is, generally speaking, co-extensive with **3–001** the ability to hold and dispose of a legal or equitable interest in property, but there are two special situations to consider.

A. Children

A settlement made by a child is voidable; he may repudiate it **3–002** before or within a reasonable time after attaining the age of 18.[1]

---

[1] *Edwards v Carter* [1893] A.C. 360.

A child may not hold a legal estate in land.[2] If a child becomes entitled to a freehold or leasehold, the land is held in trust for him.[3]

B. Persons who Lack Mental Capacity

3–003   A person is presumed to have mental capacity unless the contrary is established.[4] Capacity issues may affect the ability of a person to make a will or a gift or to create a trust. In the case of a lifetime gift, it seems that the test varies according to the size of the gift and its relationship to the sum of the assets owned by the donor. In *Re Beaney*[5] a mother who was suffering from senile dementia made a gift of her house, the only substantial asset of her estate, to one daughter, Valerie, who had stayed at home to look after her mother for many years; but this had the effect of virtually disinheriting the other two (married) children. The position was summarised as follows[6]:

> "The degree or extent of understanding required in respect of any instrument is relative to the particular transaction which it is to effect. In the case of a will the degree required is always high. In the case of a contract, a deed made for consideration or a gift *inter vivos*, whether by deed or otherwise, the degree required varies with the circumstances of the transaction. Thus, at one extreme, if the subject-matter and value of a gift are trivial in relation to the donor's other assets a low degree of understanding will suffice. But, at the other, if its effect is to dispose of the donor's only assets of value and thus for practical purposes to pre-empt the devolution of his estate under his will or on his intestacy, then the degree of understanding required is as high as that required for a will, and the donor must understand the claims of all potential donees and the extent of the property to be disposed of."

It was held that Mrs Beaney's gift to Valerie was void, because she was not capable of understanding the conflicting claims of her other children. More recently the question whether such a gift is

---

[2] LPA 1925 s.1(6).

[3] Trusts of Land and Appointment of Trustees Act 1996 Sch.1, para.1.

[4] Mental Capacity Act 2005 s.1(2).

[5] [1978] 1 W.L.R. 770; F. Crane [1978] Conv. 387. See also *Simpson v Simpson* [1992] 1 F.L.R. 601 (lifetime gift which upset the balance of the will held void for want of mental capacity. Transferee of bank deposits held them on resulting trust); *Re Morris* [2001] W.T.L.R. 1137; *Pesticcio v Huet* [2003] W.T.L.R. 1327; *Williams v Williams* [2003] W.T.L.R. 1371; *Cattermole v Prisk* [2006] 1 F.L.R. 693.

[6] At 774.

void or voidable has been reconsidered and the position said to be "quite obscure".[7] The point remains unresolved.

In the case of wills, provided the testator had capacity when he gave instructions for the will to be drawn up, the will is valid even though he had lost testamentary capacity by the date he signed it, so long as he then understood that he was executing a will for which he had given instructions.[8] This principle was recently held to apply to lifetime dispositions in *Re Singellos*.[9] Mrs Singellos gave instruction for a complex gift of assets worth £4.5 million aimed at avoiding inheritance tax, which required her to sign 21 documents. She had capacity when giving the instructions and when signing the first 12 documents, but was losing capacity when she signed the last 9 at a later date shortly before her death. As she was still capable of understanding, and did understand, that the 9 documents gave effect to her earlier instructions, the gift was valid.

Where a person lacks capacity to make a disposition, an application may be made to the Court of Protection.

Under the Mental Capacity Act 2005 (replacing earlier legislation) the Court of Protection has wide powers of dealing with the property and affairs of a person who lacks capacity to make the decision in question.[10]

The guiding principle for the court is the best interests of the person who lacks capacity, which normally involves a consideration of what the person would be likely to do if he were not subject to the disability. Thus, in *Re TB*,[11] the court approved the creation of a revocable trust in favour of the settlor's illegitimate child; the property would otherwise have passed on intestacy to remoter relatives. If the matter had arisen after 1969, the court could have authorised the making of a will. Since that date,[12] the court has had power to make a will for an adult, if the judge has reason to believe that he lacks testamentary capacity. Before the Mental Capacity Act 2005, the court's aim was to make a will which the patient, acting reasonably, would have made if notionally restored to full mental capacity, memory and foresight.[13] Since that Act the paramount principle is that the court must do what is in the best interests of the person who lacks capacity. While giving effect to his wishes remains important,

---

[7] *Sutton v Sutton* [2010] W.T.L.R. 115 at 133. The point was not fully argued and did not affect the outcome.

[8] *Parker v Felgate* (1883) L.R. 8P.D. 171; applied in *Perrins v Holland* [2011] Ch. 270.

[9] [2011] Ch. 324.

[10] MCA 2005 ss.16, 18. A settlement may be ordered under s.18(1)(h) and a gift under s.18(1)(b).

[11] [1967] Ch. 247. See also *Re S (Gifts by Mental Patient)* [1997] 1 F.L.R. 96.

[12] AJA 1969, adding the provisions now found in MCA 2005 s.18(1)(i) and Sch.2, paras 1–4. See *Re Davey* [1981] 1 W.L.R. 164.

[13] *Re D (J)* [1982] Ch. 237.

the court must take in to account how the testator will be remembered after his death. For many people it is in their best interests that they be remembered with affection by their family and as having done "the right thing" by their will.[14]

Applications to the court for the approval of schemes affecting the property of a person who lacks capacity have commonly been brought in circumstances in which it was desirable in the interests of the family to reduce the tax liability of a rich person. The applicant must show that the scheme is for the benefit of the person who lacks capacity. It is sufficient that it is the sort of settlement which he would be likely to make in favour of other members of the family if he had not lacked capacity to do so.[15]

2. FORMALITIES

A. Lifetime

3–004   **i. Creation.** The basic rule is that a settlor may create a trust by manifesting an intention to create it. No formalities are required for the creation of a lifetime trust of personalty.[16] Evidence in writing is required for the creation of a trust of land, and all testamentary trusts must be in writing, signed by the testator and attested by two witnesses as required by the Wills Act 1837 s.9.[17]

It is necessary, however, to observe literally every word of the basic rule. The intention must be to *create a trust*; a general intention to benefit someone will not suffice.[18] The words or acts of the settlor must be sufficient to establish an intention that either another person (or persons), or the settlor himself, shall be trustee of property for the beneficiary. In practice lifetime trusts are created in writing and usually by deed. Such trusts usually have as one of their objects the saving of tax, and this can only be achieved where there is clear documentary proof of the date and terms of the trust.

With regard to trusts of land, the LPA 1925 s.53(1)(b), provides:

> "A declaration of trust respecting any land or any interest therein must be manifested and proved by some writing signed by some person who is able to declare such trust or by his will."[19]

---

[14] *Re P* [2010] Ch. 33; R. Kerridge All E.R. Rev 2009, p.467. See also *Re M* [2009] W.T.L.R. 1791.

[15] See *Re CWM* [1951] 2 K.B. 714; *Re C* [1960] 1 W.L.R. 92; *Re CEFD* [1963] 1 W.L.R. 329. For the variation of existing trusts, see Ch.22.

[16] *M'Fadden v Jenkyns* (1842) 1 Ph. 153; *Paul v Constance* [1977] 1 W.L.R. 521; *Re Kayford* [1975] 1 W.L.R. 279.

[17] Below, para.3–017.

[18] *Jones v Lock* (1865) L.R. 1 Ch.App. 25; below, para.4–013; *Paul v Constance* [1977] 1 W.L.R. 521.

[19] Replacing Statute of Frauds 1677 s.7.

The writing is required as evidence of intention; the declaration need not itself be in writing. Failure to comply with the requirements of s.53(1)(b) renders the trust unenforceable, and not void.[20] The signature will normally be that of the settlor, although there is authority that the transferee of the land may sign.[21]

These requirements apply to express trusts only, and not to resulting, implied or constructive trusts,[22] although, as will be seen from the case-law discussed below, dispositions of interests arising under such trusts are subject to the formality requirements.

ii. The Instrument of Fraud Principle. The question which **3–005** next arises concerns the effect, if any, of an oral declaration of a trust of land. What should be done if a transferee procures a conveyance of land to him on the strength of a oral agreement to hold on trust for the transferor or a third party, and then seeks to shelter behind the statute?

Equity, where possible, will not permit a statute to be a cloak for fraud. The question is whether equity can, by acting in personam against the fraudulent party, prevent the fraud without disregarding the statute.

In *Rochefoucauld v Boustead*,[23] the claimant was the mortgagor of some land. It was sold by the mortgagee to the defendant, who had orally agreed to hold the land on trust for the mortgagor subject to the repayment to the defendant of the purchase price, and expenses. The defendant sold the land at a profit, but did not account to the mortgagor. The defendant became bankrupt.

The mortgagor obtained an order for an account. The Court of Appeal refused to allow the Statute of Frauds to prevent the proof of fraud:

" ... [I]t is a fraud on the part of a person to whom land is conveyed as a trustee, and who knows it was so conveyed, to deny the trust and claim the land himself. Consequently, notwithstanding the statute, it is competent for a person claiming land conveyed to another to prove by parol evidence that it was so conveyed upon trust for the claimant, and that the grantee, knowing the facts, is denying the trust and relying upon the

---

[20] *Gardner v Rowe* (1828) 5 Russ. 258.
[21] *Gardner v Rowe* (1828) 5 Russ. 258.
[22] LPA 1925 s.53(2). They do not apply to trusts arising from co-ownership; *Roy v Roy* [1996] 1 F.L.R. 541.
[23] [1897] 1 Ch. 196. See also *Davies v Otty (No.2)* (1865) 35 Beav. 208; *McCormick v Grogan* (1869) L.R. 4 H.L. 82; *Bannister v Bannister* [1948] 2 All E.R. 133; *Hodgson v Marks* [1971] Ch. 892; *Binions v Evans* [1972] Ch. 359; *Lyus v Prowsa Ltd* [1982] 1 W.L.R. 1044; *Du Boulay v Raggett* (1989) 58 P. & C.R. 12; B. McFarlane (2004) 120 L.Q.R. 667.

form of conveyance and the statute, in order to keep the land himself."[24]

The principle of this decision is that in the case of fraud oral evidence is admissible to establish the trust in spite of the statute. On this basis the trust is express,[25] although modern cases have tended to treat trusts established in this way as constructive.[26]

Where the conveyance is by A to B on an oral trust for A, the effect of this doctrine is clearly that B holds on trust for A. The more difficult case is where the conveyance is by A to B on an oral trust for C. Should the beneficial interest be enjoyed by C, or held on resulting trust for A? The latter is all that is necessary to prevent B's unjust enrichment; to give the benefit to C looks like a disregard of the statute. It is a question of balancing the policy of the formality requirement against the injustice which may be caused by relying on the formality rule. If the trust is properly to be classified as express, it is easier to say that C should benefit, especially as the effect of s.53(1)(b) is that the trust is not void but merely unenforceable. There are authorities tending to support C's claim,[27] and some commentators favour this view.[28] More compelling is the view that B should hold on trust for A.[29] To go further leaves s.53(1)(b) applying only where A orally declares himself trustee. The fraud doctrine cannot be invoked here, and it has been held that the beneficiary cannot assert a constructive trust and thereby avoid s.53(1)(b) unless he has acted to his detriment in reliance on the declaration.[30]

A similar question arises where a prospective legatee or devisee agrees with the testator to hold the property on trust for C. Here the doctrine of secret trusts allows C to benefit in spite of the requirements of the Wills Act 1837. Here the resulting trust solution is less appropriate because it is too late for the testator to make other provision for C. This is discussed in Ch.5.

---

[24] per Lindley L.J. at p.206.

[25] So held in *Rochefoucauld v Boustead*, above, fn.23, but specifically in the context of the Limitation Act 1874. See W. Swadling in Mitchell (ed.), *Constructive and Resulting Trusts* (2009), Ch.3.

[26] *Bannister v Bannister*, above, fn.23; *Binions v Evans*, above, fn.23; *Re Densham* [1975] 1 W.L.R. 1519; *Neale v Willis* (1968) 19 P. & C.R. 839; *Ashburn Anstalt v Arnold* [1989] Ch. 1. See further Elias, *Explaining Constructive Trusts*, 2002, pp.106–113.

[27] *Taylor v Salmon* (1838) 4 Myl. & Cr. 134; *Binions v Evans*, above, fn.23; *Neale v Willis*, above, fn.26; *Lyus v Prowsa Ltd*, above, fn.23; *Rochefoucauld v Boustead* itself should not be regarded as such a case because effectively A arranged with B that B would buy from the mortgagee and hold on trust for A.

[28] G. Costigan (1915) 28 H.L.R. 237 at 366; T. Youdan (1984) 43 C.L.J. 306 and [1988] Conv. 267. See also Elias, *Explaining Constructive Trusts*, 2002, p.103 (supporting C's claim in the context of a wider view that formality rules should be abolished).

[29] J. Feltham [1987] Conv. 246. But as the oral declaration is not void, B may convey to C unless A has revoked his authority to do so.

[30] *Midland Bank Ltd v Dobson* [1986] 1 F.L.R. 171; cf. *Re Densham* [1975] 1 W.L.R. 1519.

iii. Disposition.[31] A disposition of an equitable interest is re- **3–006** quired to be in writing; otherwise, the disposition is void. Section 53(1)(c) provides[32]:

"A disposition of an equitable interest or trust subsisting at the time of the disposition must be in writing signed by the person disposing of the same, or by his agent thereunto lawfully authorised in writing or by will."

"The subsection . . . " said Lord Wilberforce,[33] "is certainly not easy to apply to the various transactions in equitable interests which now occur." Such transactions have included attempts to avoid stamp duty on share transfers, and the practice of putting shareholdings in nominees. A question which has more recently arisen is whether and how far the subsection applies to securities held in trust which are traded electronically.[34] A more general question is whether the subsection may be satisfied by electronic writing and signature. Statutes requiring transfers to be in signed writing may be modified by secondary legislation so as to permit electronic documents,[35] but it seems that requirements of writing and signing may in any event already be capable of being satisfied by an electronic document.[36] A signed email may, therefore, suffice.[37]

Modern litigation has established some fine, and not always logical, distinctions. Of course, it might be said that the equitable interest is disposed of whenever an absolute owner declares himself trustee of the property. Such a view would, however, make s.53(1)(b) meaningless. The word "subsisting" in s.53(1)(c) indicates that the subsection only applies where the equitable interest has already been separated from the legal estate.[38]

---

[31] G. Jones (1966) 24 C.L.J. 19; S. Spencer (1967) 31 Conv.(N.S.) 175; G. Battersby [1975] Ottawa L.R. 483 and [1979] Conv. 17; D. Sugarman and F. Webb (1978) 94 L.Q.R. 170. There is no disposition where a condition remains unfulfilled; *Chandler v Clark* (2003) 1 P. & C.R. 15.

[32] Re-enacting Statute of Frauds 1677 s.9, with some alterations, the most significant one being that s.9 applied to "all grants and assignments of any trust or confidence" while s.53(1)(c) applies to a "disposition of an equitable interest".

[33] In *Vandervell v IRC* [1967] 2 A.C. 291 at 329.

[34] The issue was examined by the Trust Law Committee on the basis of a paper by Joanna Benjamin. Further statutory disapplication of the subsection has since been effected, along the lines of the Stock Transfer Act 1982 s.1(2) (gilts) and Uncertificated Securities Regulations 1995 (SI 1995/3272) (CREST). See Unit Trusts (Electronic Communications) Order 2009 (SI 2009/555); *Mills v Sportsdirect.com Retail Ltd* [2010] 2 B.C.L.C. 143.

[35] Electronic Communications Act 2000 s.8. See Open-Ended Investment Companies (Amendment) Regulations 2009 (SI 2009/553).

[36] See Pt 3 of the Advice from the Law Commission, *Electronic Commerce: Formal Requirements in Commercial Transactions* (2001).

[37] *J Pereira Fernandes SA v Mehta* [2006] 1 W.L.R. 1543 (but the inclusion of the sender's email address is not a signature).

[38] See *Kinane v Mackie-Conteh* [2005] W.T.L.R. 345.

3–007   (a) *Assignment of Equitable Interest.* The simple case is where a beneficiary under a trust assigns his interest to another. This is a disposition of an equitable interest, and is void unless in writing. This is so, whether the beneficial interest is a limited interest, such as a life interest, or an absolute interest which is held on a bare trust by a nominee. The subsection applies to equitable interests in both land and personalty.[39] The disposition must actually be in writing, and not merely evidenced in writing,[40] but a number of connected documents can provide the necessary writing.[41]

3–008   (b) *Direction to Trustees to Hold on Trust for Another.* Where a beneficiary directs the trustee to hold his interest upon other trusts, there is a disposition of the beneficiary's interest. This is the basis of *Grey v IRC*,[42] which was concerned with an attempt by the settlor to save stamp duty on shares being put into the settlement. At that time ad valorem stamp duty (i.e. varying with the value of the interest transferred) was payable on deeds of gift, although this is no longer the position.[43] Where stamp duty is payable, it is payable upon instruments whereby property is transferred, and not upon transactions.[44]

> In *Grey v IRC*,[45] the settlor made six settlements of nominal sums in favour of his grandchildren. Later, he transferred shares of substantial value to the trustees, as his nominees, on trust for himself. That transfer attracted only nominal stamp duty. Then he orally instructed the trustees to hold that property upon the trusts of the six settlements. Finally, the trustees executed documents confirming that they held the shares upon the trusts of the settlements. The settlor, though not expressed to be a party, executed the documents.
>
> It was accepted that the trusts were validly declared. The question was whether they were declared by the settlor's oral declaration, in which case the subsequent documents were truly confirmatory, and passed no beneficial interest; or whether, as the Revenue argued, the documents effected a disposition of an existing equitable interest within s.53(1)(c), in which case they were subject to ad valorem duty.[46]

[39] See B. Green (1984) 47 M.L.R. 385 at 388, discussing LPA 1925 s.205(1)(x).
[40] cf. LPA 1925 s.53(1)(b). See further fn.46, below.
[41] *Re Danish Bacon Co Staff Pension Fund Trusts* [1971] 1 W.L.R. 248 at 255.
[42] [1960] A.C. 1; J. Thornley (1960) C.L.J. 31; G. Battersby [1979] Conv. 17; B. Green (1984) 47 M.L.R. 385. See also *Crowden v Aldridge* [1993] 1 W.L.R. 433.
[43] FA 1985 s.82. Stamp duty was abolished (subject to certain exceptions) by the Finance Act 2003, which introduced stamp duty land tax in relation to land.
[44] *IRC v Angus* (1889) 23 Q.B.D. 579; *Oughtred v IRC* [1960] A.C. 206 at 227.
[45] [1960] A.C. 1. See also *Halley v The Law Society* [2003] W.T.L.R. 845 (money held on trust in solicitor's client account).
[46] It was conceded that the documents should be regarded as dispositive in the event of the oral directions being held ineffective. See B. Green (1984) 47 M.L.R. 385 at 391.

In argument, Pennycuick QC posed the question thus[47]:

"If X holds property in trust for A as absolute owner and A then directs X to hold the property on the settlement trusts for the benefit of B, C, and D, and X accepts the trust, is that direction a 'disposition' of a subsisting equitable interest within the meaning of section 53?"

The House of Lords answered affirmatively. While the trustees held the shares as nominees for the settlor, the settlor owned the entire beneficial interest. When the trustees held them upon the trusts of the settlements, the beneficial interest passed from the settlor to the beneficiaries under the settlements. That, according to the natural meaning of the word, was a disposition. Ad valorem stamp duty was payable on the documents.

It seems that the settlor's objectives would have been achieved if he had orally declared himself trustee of the shares for the beneficiaries while still the legal owner; following the declaration with a confirmatory document; and retiring, when he wished, in favour of other trustees.

It appears that s.53(1)(c) is satisfied if the equitable owner writes to the trustee in terms which refer to prior oral instructions to hold on new trusts, even though the writing does not include the particulars of the new trusts.[48]

(c) *Conveyance of Legal Estate by Trustee.* The subsection does **3–009** not apply where the trustee or nominee conveys the legal estate to a third party with the consent or at the direction of a beneficiary absolutely entitled. In that situation "prima facie a transfer of the legal estate carries with it the absolute beneficial interest in the property transferred."[49]

In *Vandervell v IRC*,[50] Vandervell wished to give sufficient money to the Royal College of Surgeons to found a Chair of Pharmacology. He decided to do so by arranging for the transfer to the College of shares in Vandervell Products Ltd, subject to an option exercisable by Vandervell Trustees Ltd, a company which acted as trustee for various Vandervell family trusts, to repurchase

---

[47] [1960] A.C. 1 at 4.

[48] *Re Tyler* [1967] 1 W.L.R. 1269. *Grey v IRC*, fn.47, above, was cited in argument but not referred to in the judgment.

[49] per Diplock L.J. [1966] Ch. 261 at 287.

[50] [1967] 2 A.C. 291; G. Jones (1966) 24 C.L.J. 19; S. Spencer (1967) 31 Conv.(N.S.) 175; N. Strauss (1967) 30 M.L.R. 461; J. Harris (1975) 38 M.L.R. 557; R. Nolan (2002) 61 L.Q.R. 169, explaining the decision as an application of the doctrine of overreaching, above, para.1–047.

the shares for £5,000. The shares were held by the National Provincial Bank Ltd as nominee for Vandervell.

The Bank transferred the shares to the College subject to the option. Dividends amounting to £250,000 were declared on the shares and paid to the College, and the income in the hands of the College, being a charity, was not subject to income tax. But the Revenue claimed surtax from Vandervell on the ground that he had not completely divested himself of the beneficial interest in the property.[51] The Revenue succeeded on the ground that there had been no declaration of the trusts on which the option was held by Vandervell Trustees Ltd, and accordingly they held it on a resulting trust for Vandervell. This aspect of the case is considered in Ch.10 below.

A second argument of the Revenue was that, since the Bank had held the shares on trust for Vandervell, the transfer by the Bank to the College transferred only the bare legal estate; and the equitable interest could not leave Vandervell except by a disposition in writing signed by him. If A holds property on trust for B, and A transfers the legal title to X, a volunteer, the ordinary rule would suggest that X took subject to B's beneficial interest; that the beneficial interest, in short, did not pass on the transfer of the legal title by A. Certainly this would be the case if the transfer was in breach of trust, or was only the appointment of a new trustee. On the other hand, there could be no argument in favour of the application of the section in the case of a transfer by an absolute owner, at law and in equity[52]; and the House of Lords held that the section was similarly not applicable in the case of a transfer by a trustee on the directions of a beneficial owner of the whole interest. Lord Upjohn explained the object of the section as being to prevent hidden oral transactions relating to equitable interests.

> "But when the beneficial owner owns the whole beneficial estate and is in a position to give directions to his bare trustee with regard to the legal as well as the equitable estate there can be no possible ground for invoking the section where the beneficial owner wants to deal with the legal estate as well as the equitable estate."[53]

Presumably, however, the subsection would apply if the beneficial owner were to direct that the legal title should be transferred to X, who should hold on trust for Y. In such a case the equitable interest,

---

[51] The current legislation is Income Tax (Trading and Other Income) Act 2005 s.624.

[52] Such a transfer would include the equitable interest unless there is evidence that such was not intended, or where the presumption of resulting trust applies; below, para.10–020.

[53] [1967] 2 A.C. 291 at 311.

although passing at the same time as the legal title, would remain separated from it.[54]

(d) *Declaration of Trust with Consent of Beneficial Owner.* That **3–010** decision did not exhaust the subtleties of the section in its application to Mr Vandervell's affairs. Faced with the surtax claim in 1961 in respect of the dividends paid to the Royal College of Surgeons, he instructed Vandervell Trustees Ltd to exercise the option. They did so, in the same year, using £5,000 from the Vandervell children's settlement for the purpose, manifesting an intention with Vandervell's consent that the shares which they thereby acquired should be held on the trusts of the children's settlement, and so informing the Revenue. In 1965, Vandervell executed a deed formally assigning to Vandervell Trustees Ltd any right or interest he might still have in the option or the shares.

The Revenue assessed Vandervell to surtax in respect of the years 1961–65. Up to 1961, there was a resulting trust in his favour of the option. He had not, until 1965, they argued, disposed of that beneficial interest in writing, and therefore he must still have it; though now in the shares into which the option had been converted.

The executors of Vandervell's estate stepped in before the Revenue's claim was litigated, and claimed from Vandervell Trustees Ltd the dividends paid during 1961–1965.[55] They applied to join the Revenue as second defendants, but Vandervell Trustees Ltd successfully objected.[56] The executors' claim to the dividends succeeded before Megarry J. on the ground that the resulting trust which applied to the option applied also to the shares, and there had been no valid declaration of trust in favour of the children's settlement. This was reversed by the Court of Appeal, holding that the trustee company held the dividends on the trusts of the children's settlement. Four reasons were given[57]: first, that the trustees used funds of the children's settlement to exercise the option; secondly, that the trustees and Vandervell showed an intention that the shares should be held on the trusts of that settlement; thirdly, that there had been a perfect gift of the dividends to the children's settlement; and fourthly, that the resulting trust attached to the option and not to the shares, and the trust of the option came to an end with the exercise

---

[54] But compare the position in *Re Vandervell's Trusts (No.2)*, below, where the subsection did not apply to a transaction whereby the legal title passed to the trustees and the equitable interest to the children's settlement, having previously been united in the Royal College of Surgeons. On the latter point it is distinguishable from the example in the text, and is in fact the converse of *Vandervell v IRC.*

[55] *Re Vandervell's Trust (No.2)* [1974] Ch. 269; J. Harris (1975) 38 M.L.R. 557.

[56] *Vandervell Trustees Ltd v White* [1971] A.C. 912.

[57] Lord Denning also considered that Vandervell, having arranged for the exercise of the option and the payment of dividends to the children's settlement, was estopped from claiming any interest; [1974] Ch. 269 at 321.

of the option. Neither the extinction of the trust of the option nor the creation of the new trust of the shares, nor the two, viewed as a whole, amounted to a disposition by Vandervell of an interest within s.53(1)(c).

The subsection did not apply where a trustee, with the consent of the beneficiary, declared new trusts of what could be regarded as new property.

The decision of the Court of Appeal leaves many problems in its wake. Essential to the decision was the finding of a valid declaration of trust in favour of the children's settlement, but the three things relied on as constituting the declaration are unconvincing.[58] Surely an element of intention is necessary in the declaration of a trust, yet none of the parties had such an intention, but merely acted on the assumption that the children's settlement was entitled. It is difficult to accept the proposition that the use of the money from the settlement resulted in the acquisition of the beneficial ownership of the shares. Is not the owner of an option entitled to the fruits of it? The fact that it was exercised with X's money gives rights to X, but not equitable ownership.[59] Equally doubtful is the point that there was a "perfect gift" of the dividends to the children's settlement. A valid gift requires a donative intention and capacity to give. Here the dividends were paid to the children's settlement not with a donative intention but on the assumption that the children were already entitled to them.[60]

Other criticisms can be directed at the proposition that Vandervell had no interest in the shares but only in the option, so that when the option terminated (upon its exercise) there was no question of any interest in the shares passing from him to the children's settlement. Underlying the entire decision is the supposition that, if the children's claim failed, there would be a resulting trust of the shares to Vandervell. How could this be if he had no interest in them? Indeed, the House of Lords, in *Vandervell v IRC*,[61] had held that he had. He was liable to surtax on the dividends because his beneficial ownership of the option meant that he retained some interest in the *shares*. Certainly this was not the entire beneficial interest, but it cannot be said that he had no interest in the shares.

Even assuming a valid declaration of trust for the children, it would have to occur no later than the exercise of the option in order to avoid a resulting trust to Vandervell, whereby any subsequent declaration would be a disposition of his interest.[62] Yet two of

[58] Below, para.4–015.
[59] Para.4–015.
[60] See, however *Milroy v Lord* (1862) 4 De G.F. & J. 264 at 277 (dividends irrecoverable although gift of shares invalid).
[61] [1967] 2 A.C. 291.
[62] As in *Grey v IRC* [1960] A.C. 1, above.

the three acts relied on as constituting the declaration occurred after the exercise of the option. Finally, how did the equitable interest in the shares pass from the college to the children's settlement without satisfying the subsection?[63] As the college was at that time also the legal owner, presumably s.53(1)(c) did not apply.[64]

(e) *Declaration by Equitable Owner of Himself as Trustee.* A **3–011** further aspect of the matter which has not yet been worked out is the situation in which the beneficiary declares himself trustee of his equitable interest for another. On the one hand, it can be argued that this is, on its face, a declaration of trust, and not a disposition. It is a sub-trust, the subject-matter not being identical to that of the original trust.[65] On the other hand, it was said in *Grainge v Wilberforce*[66] that, "where A was trustee for B, who was trustee for C, A holds in trust for C, and must convey as C directed." Thus, B "disappears from the picture",[67] and C becomes the beneficiary. This looks like a disposition. It may be otherwise where B retains active duties, as where he declares a trust of his interest for such of a class as he shall select.[68]

The question whether B "disappears from the picture" was recently considered by the Court of Appeal in *Nelson v Greening & Sykes (Builders) Ltd.*[69] The case did not involve s.53(1)(c), nor was there any express declaration of trust by B. A was trustee of land for B under a constructive trust of land arising out of A's contract to sell the land to B.[70] B held his interest on resulting trust for C because C had provided the purchase money.[71] Following "regrettably pointless" litigation between the parties, a charging order was made against B's interest in the land "as trustee"[72] prior to the date on

---

[63] See J. Harris (1975) 38 M.L.R. 557.

[64] On the basis that there was no "subsisting" separate equitable interest. Compare the reasoning of *Vandervell v IRC*, above, fn.61. It might also be argued that the exercise of the option gave rise to a contract, which gave rise to a constructive trust, as in the *Oughtred* argument. Thus the equitable interest passed from the college, by virtue of s.53(2), without the need for a written disposition. But this would not solve the problem of where it went to. Presumably it would go to the beneficial owner of the option unless he had disposed of his interest elsewhere, which was the very issue.

[65] Compare the reasoning of *Re Vandervell's Trusts (No.2)*, above, fn.55.

[66] (1889) 5 T.L.R. 436 at 437; below, para.4–007; see also *Re Tout & Finch* [1954] 1 W.L.R. 178; *DHN Food Distributors Ltd v Tower Hamlets LBC* [1976] 1 W.L.R. 852; D. Sugarman and F. Webb (1977) 93 L.Q.R. 171; *Corin v Patton* (1990) A.L.J.R. 256 at 272.

[67] per Upjohn J. in *Grey v IRC* [1958] Ch. 375 at 382.

[68] *Re Lashmar* [1891] 1 Ch. 258 at 268; see PVB (1958) 74 L.Q.R. 180; B. Green (1984) 37 M.L.R. 385 at 396. This principle is confirmed in Law Com No.260, *Trustees' Powers and Duties* (1999), p.61, discussing the position where trustees vest the legal title to assets such as securities in a nominee. It is considered that the trustees would not "drop out of the picture" on losing legal title, because only limited functions would be delegated to the nominee.

[69] *The Times*, January 22, 2008.

[70] Below, para.12–035.

[71] Below, para.10–033.

[72] Under s.2(1)(b)(ii) of the Charging Orders Act 1979.

which the legal title was transferred to C. It was held that the charging order was valid because it was made at a time when A held on trust for B, who held on trust for C, and B had not "dropped out". The authorities[73] on "dropping out" were saying that the trustee (A) might decide as a matter of practicality that it was more convenient to deal directly with the beneficiary of the sub-trust (C), but this did not mean that, as a matter of law, the intermediate trustee (B) ceased to be a trustee. Nor did they apply to a case where the trust property was a purchaser's interest under a contract for sale.

3–012   (f) *Specifically Enforceable Oral Contracts for Sale. Oughtred v IRC*,[74] like *Grey*, concerned an attempt to avoid stamp duty on a share transfer.

Mrs Oughtred was the owner of 72,700 shares in a company and was also tenant for life under a settlement which contained 100,000 preference shares and 100,000 ordinary shares. Her son, Peter, was entitled in remainder. In order to reduce the estate duty which would be payable on Mrs Oughtred's death, an oral agreement was made in 1956 under which Peter would surrender his remainder interest in the settled shares in consideration for the transfer to him of his mother's 72,700 shares.

A deed was executed by Mrs Oughtred and Peter which recited that the settled shares were then held in trust for Mrs Oughtred absolutely. The trustees then transferred the shares to Mrs Oughtred; and she transferred the 72,700 shares to Peter. The question was whether ad valorem stamp duty was payable on the transfers. The document selected for the purpose of the claim was the transfer of the shares from the trustees to Mrs Oughtred.

The question depended on whether or not Mrs Oughtred was owner in equity of the shares before the legal transfer. Provided a contract is specifically enforceable, a constructive trust is said to arise as soon as the contract is entered into, whereby the equitable interest passes to the purchaser by virtue of his right to specific performance.[75] Contracts for the sale of land are normally specifically enforceable, provided they are in writing, as required by s.2 of the Law of Property (Miscellaneous Provisions) Act 1989. Contracts for the sale of personalty are specifically enforceable only if the remedy of damages would be inadequate. Thus contracts to sell shares in a public company are not normally specifically enforceable, but the position is otherwise in the case of shares in a private

---

[73] In particular *Grey v IRC* [1960] A.C. 1.
[74] [1960] A.C. 206. See P. Turner [2006] Conv. 390, discussing Australian decisions on equivalent legislation.
[75] Below, para.12–035.

company, which are not available for purchase on the market. Mrs Oughtred was accordingly able to claim that the equitable interest had passed to her by virtue of her right to specific performance of the contract; or, putting the same point another way, that Peter, after the agreement, held his interest as constructive trustee for her (constructive trusts being exempted from the writing requirement by s.53(2)). The later document would then be only a transfer of the bare legal estate.

The House of Lords, however, by three to two, held to the contrary. For the majority, Lord Jenkins, with whose speech Lord Keith expressed entire agreement, accepted that Mrs Oughtred's interest, after the agreement, was similar to that of a purchaser of land between contract and conveyance. The purchaser's interest:

> "[I]s no doubt a proprietary interest of a sort, which arises, so to speak, in anticipation of the execution of the transfer for which the purchaser is entitled to call. But its existence has never (so far as I know) been held to prevent a subsequent transfer, in performance of the contract, of the property contracted to be sold from constituting for stamp duty purposes a transfer on sale of the property in question."[76]

So here, the transfer of the legal estate was an instrument attracting duty.

Lord Radcliffe, dissenting, took the view that Mrs Oughtred became equitable owner of the reversionary interest in the settled shares by virtue of the specifically enforceable agreement to exchange. She became the absolute owner in equity. **3–013**

> "There was ... no equity to the shares that could be asserted against her, and it was open to her, if she so wished, to let the matter rest without calling for a written assignment, from her son. ... It follows that, in my view, this transfer cannot be treated as a conveyance of the son's equitable reversion at all."[77]

This argument is compelling, and it points out a number of questions relating to the nature of the interest which Mrs Oughtred held before the legal transfer from the trustees; the majority speeches leave these questions unanswered. It has always been held that stamp duty[78] is

---

[76] [1960] A.C. 206, at 240. See also *Henty and Constable (Brewers) Ltd v IRC* [1961] 1 W.L.R. 1504, at 1510. *Oughtred* was applied in *Parinv (Hatfield) Ltd v IRC* [1998] S.T.C. 305 (sub nom. *Bishop Square Ltd v IRC* (1999) 78 P. & C.R. 169), involving an unsuccessful attempt to avoid stamp duty by executing a declaration of trust for the purchaser prior to the transfer ("The appeal is as hopeless as any that I have heard").

[77] [1960] A.C. 206 at 228.

[78] Stamp duty was replaced by stamp duty land tax in relation to land transactions by the Finance Act 2003.

payable on a conveyance of land, even though the beneficial interest in the property passed on the signing of the contract; similarly with a purchase of shares. This factor may have influenced the court's approach to the application of s.53. *Oughtred* may thus be viewed as a policy decision.

Later decisions in varying contexts have tended to support the view that an equitable interest can pass under a contract without formality, although the point is rarely fully argued. In *Re Holt's Settlement*,[79] concerning the Variation of Trusts Act 1958, Megarry J., relying on the minority judgments in *Oughtred*, accepted the proposition that where there is a specifically enforceable agreement, the beneficial interest passes to the purchaser under a constructive trust without writing. Similarly in *DHN Food Distributors Ltd v Tower Hamlets LBC*,[80] concerning compulsory purchase, the Court of Appeal assumed that an equitable interest in land could pass without writing where the transaction was contractual.[81] In *Chinn v Collins*,[82] concerning a capital gains tax avoidance scheme, Lord Wilberforce said that:

> "The legal title to the shares was at all times vested in a nominee ... and dealings related to the equitable interest in these required no formality. As soon as there was an agreement for their sale accompanied or followed by payment of the price, the equitable title passed at once to the purchaser ... and all that was needed to perfect his title was notice to the trustees or the nominee ... "

The shares were in a public company, but Lord Wilberforce did not appear to consider a specifically enforceable contract to be essential to this proposition which, it should be noted, led to the establishment of capital gains tax liability. Neither *Oughtred* nor even s.53 itself was cited. Tax liability was not involved in *Neville v Wilson*,[83] where nominees held shares in U Ltd on trust for J Ltd, a family company. The shareholders of J Ltd agreed informally to liquidate the company and to divide its equitable interest in the U Ltd shares amongst themselves in proportion to their existing shareholdings. The question was whether s.53(1)(c) invalidated this agreement (in

---

[79] [1969] 1 Ch. 100 at 116.

[80] [1976] 1 W.L.R. 852 at 865, 867.

[81] This argument is no longer tenable in the case of land because the contract must be in writing; Law of Property (Miscellaneous Provisions) Act 1989 s.2. See *United Bank of Kuwait Plc v Sahib* [1997] Ch. 107.

[82] [1981] A.C. 533, at 548.

[83] [1997] Ch. 144; R. Nolan (1996) 55 C.L.J. 436; M. Thompson [1996] Conv. 368; P. Milne (1997) 113 L.Q.R.; cf. *United Bank of Kuwait Plc v Sahib* [1997] Ch. 107, where Chadwick J. held that a contract to assign an equitable interest by way of mortgage required writing to satisfy s.53(1)(c) and doubted whether s.53(2) could apply. The point was not argued on appeal.

which case the equitable interest would have passed to the Crown
when J Ltd was struck off the register). The Court of Appeal held
that each shareholder's agreement gave rise to an implied or constructive trust so that s.53(2)[84] applied. Thus the agreement was
effective to vest the equitable interest in the shareholders without
writing. The analysis of Lord Radcliffe in his dissent in *Oughtred v
IRC*[85] that a specifically enforceable agreement to assign passed the
equitable interest to the assignee was correct. It was noted that Lords
Jenkins and Keith had left the point open and that Lord Denning
(with whom Lord Cohen appeared to agree) had rejected the application of s.53(2) without giving reasons.

It is probable that s.53(2) was intended to embrace the kind of
constructive trust which is imposed to prevent fraud,[86] and did not
envisage the anomalous constructive trust arising on a specifically
enforceable contract for sale. The latter is in any event only a qualified trust (under which the vendor retains valuable rights until the
conveyance).[87] In favour of the *Oughtred* decision it might also be
said that in the case of a contract there is a transfer of the equitable
interest from the vendor to the purchaser, whereas in the case of
resulting trusts and constructive trusts imposed to prevent fraud,
contemplated by s.53(2), there is no *passing* of the equitable interest, which remains throughout in the true beneficial owner.[88] It
seems that the acceptance of the argument that a contract can shift
the equitable interest without formality under the constructive trust
principle depends very much on the context, and that it is more
likely to be accepted in the tax context where this would result in
liability.

(g) *Variation of Trusts Act 1958.* We shall see in Ch.22 that the   **3–014**
Variation of Trusts Act 1958 gave power to the court to approve, on
behalf of categories of persons unable to make the decision for
themselves, variations of the existing beneficial interests under
trusts where it is for the benefit of the beneficiaries to do so. Many
variations had been approved by the courts when suddenly, in *Re
Holt's Settlement*,[89] Megarry J. asked whether it was not necessary
for the disposition of each existing beneficial interest to be in writing under s.53. Megarry J. was able to satisfy himself that writing

---

[84] "This section does not effect the creation or operation of resulting, implied or constructive trusts."

[85] [1960] A.C.206.

[86] As in *Bannister v Bannister* [1948] 2 All E.R. 133; *Hodgson v Marks* [1971] Ch. 892. See
also *Midland Bank Ltd v Dobson* [1986] 1 F.L.R. 171, below, para.11–007.

[87] Below, para.12–035.

[88] Although Lord Browne-Wilkinson in *Westdeutsche Landesbank Girozentrale v Islington
LBC* [1996] A.C. 669 at 705–706 suggests otherwise; below, para.10–002.

[89] [1969] 1 Ch. 590.

was not necessary, and the threat of invalidity to most of the variations previously approved was removed. The details of the matter are best postponed until the Act is explained.[90]

3–015   (h) *Right of Nomination under Staff Pension Fund.* The rules of the pension fund of the *Danish Bacon Co Ltd* provided that employees could nominate a person to receive moneys due in the case of death in service. Such a nomination might arguably be regarded as a lifetime disposition of an equitable interest under the pension fund trust; or as a testamentary disposition in that it took effect only in the event of the employee's death. In *Re Danish Bacon Co Staff Pension Fund Trusts*,[91] Megarry J. held that it was not a testamentary disposition. He very much doubted "whether the nomination falls within section 53(1)(c)"[92]; but held that, even if it did, the necessary writing was supplied by two connecting documents.

3–016   (i) *Disclaimer; Surrender.* In *Re Paradise Motor Co Ltd*,[93] a stepfather made a gift of shares to his stepson. The transfer, though technically defective, was sufficient to make the stepson equitable owner of the shares. The stepson knew nothing of the transfer. When he became aware of the circumstances, he stated in unmistakable language that he wished to make no claim to the shares. But when the company was in liquidation, he changed his mind and claimed his share of the proceeds. On the question whether there could be a disclaimer of an equitable interest without compliance with s.53, it was held that "a disclaimer operates by way of avoidance and not by way of disposition."[94] The disclaimer was effective and the claim failed.

However, the position seems otherwise as far as tax matters are concerned,[95] where it has been found necessary to make express provision that a disclaimer shall not be treated as a disposition for inheritance tax purposes.[96]

A surrender, on the other hand, appears to be a "disposition".[97] The House of Lords in *Newlon Housing Trust v Alsulaimen*[98] considered that the surrender of a lease would be a "disposition" within

---

[90] Below, para.22–012.
[91] [1971] 1 W.L.R. 248. Followed by the Privy Council in *Baird v Baird* [1990] 2 A.C. 548 (application of Wills Act depends on each scheme); G. Kodilinye [1990] Conv. 458; *Gold v Hill* [1999] 1 F.L.R. 54 (nomination did not dispose of any equitable interest).
[92] [1971] 1 W.L.R. 248 at 256.
[93] [1968] 1 W.L.R. 1125.
[94] *Re Paradise Motor Co Ltd*, above, at fn.93, at 1143; *Dewar v Dewar* [1975] 1 W.L.R. 1532; *Allied Dunbar Assurance plc v Fowle* [1994] 1 E.G.L.R. 122; *Lohia v Lohia* [2001] W.T.L.R. 101 (affirmed on appeal unreported, October 25, 2001). But see LPA 1925 s.205(1)(ii).
[95] *Re Stratton's Disclaimer* [1958] Ch. 42 (estate duty).
[96] Inheritance Tax Act 1984 s.17.
[97] cf. J. Monroe [1960] B.T.R. 20.
[98] [1999] 1 A.C. 313.

s.37 of the Matrimonial Causes Act 1973, adding that the ordinary meaning of the term was an act by which someone ceased to be the owner of property at law or in equity and that, in some contexts, this might include a case where the property ceased to exist.

B. By Will

Additional formalities are required for the creation of a testamen- **3–017**
tary trust. The Wills Act 1837 s.9, as amended by the Administration of Justice Act 1982 s.17, provides:

> "No will shall be valid unless:
>
> (a) it is in writing, and signed by the testator, or by some other person in his presence and by his direction; and
> (b) it appears that the testator intended by his signature to give effect to the will; and
> (c) the signature is made or acknowledged by the testator in the presence of two or more witnesses present at the same time; and
> (d) each witness either—
>
> (i) attests and signs the will; or
> (ii) acknowledges his signature,
>
> in the presence of the testator (but not necessarily in the presence of any other witness),
>
> but no form of attestation shall be necessary."

No attempt will be made here to deal with the details of this enactment. The question of the validity of trusts taking effect on a testator's death which fail to comply with these provisions—the so-called "secret trusts"—will be discussed in Ch.5.

3. Certainty

A private express trust cannot be created unless the three certain- **3–018**
ties[99] are present; certainty of intention; certainty of subject-matter; and certainty of beneficiaries. Each of these heads will be considered below. Different considerations apply to each; yet they are inter-related.

---

[99] See Lord Langdale in *Knight v Knight* (1840) 3 Beav. 148 at 173. Extrinsic evidence is not generally admissible to aid the construction of a trust deed; *Rabin v Gerson Berger Association Ltd* [1986] 1 W.L.R. 526.

"Uncertainty in the subject of the gift has a reflex action upon the previous words, and shows doubt upon the intention of the testator, and seems to show that he could not possibly have intended his words of confidence, hope, or whatever they may be—his appeal to the conscience of the first taker—to be imperative words."[100]

Similar, but distinct, questions about certainty may arise in relation to a conditional gift; whether a condition precedent to taking,[101] or a condition of defeasance.[102] Further, the requirement of certainty of beneficiaries operates differently with discretionary as opposed to fixed trusts, and with trusts for purposes as opposed to trusts for people. A trust for a non-charitable purpose is normally invalid; but where such a trust has been upheld, the court has insisted that the purpose be described with sufficient certainty.[103] With charitable trusts, there is no need to specify in any way which charity is to be benefited; but the language of the gift must clearly establish that the gift is applicable for charitable purposes only.[104]

A. Certainty of Intention

3–019   We have already seen that a trustee is under an obligation, but that the obligation may be inferred from the nature of the gift, considered as a whole.[105] Technical words are not required. The question is whether, on the proper construction of the words used, the settlor or testator has shown an intention to create a trust. A trust may be created without using the word "trust", and, conversely, the use of the word "trust" does not conclusively indicate the existence of a trust.[106] The settlor's subjective intentions are irrelevant. If he enters into arrangements which have the effect of creating a trust, it is not necessary that he should appreciate that; it suffices that he intends to enter into them.[107] A "precatory" expression of hope or desire, or suggestion or request, is not sufficient. The words in each case must be examined to see whether the intention was to impose a trust upon the donee.

The Court of Chancery at one time leaned in favour of construing expressions of desire as intended to create a binding trust.[108] This

---

[100] *Mussourie Bank v Raynor* (1882) 7 App.Cas. 321 at 331.

[101] *Re Allen* [1953] Ch. 810; *Re Barlow's WT* [1979] 1 W.L.R. 278.

[102] *Clayton v Ramsden* [1943] A.C. 320; *Blathwayt v Lord Cawley* [1976] A.C. 397.

[103] *Re Astor's ST* [1952] Ch. 534; below, para.14–013.

[104] Below, para.15–003.

[105] Above, para.2–021. In the context of charity, see *Re Cohen* [1973] 1 W.L.R. 415.

[106] *Tito v Waddell (No.2)* [1977] Ch. 106, above, para.2–035; *Customs and Excise Commissioners v Richmond Theatre Management Ltd* [1995] S.T.C. 257, above, para.2–011.

[107] *Twinsectra Ltd v Yardley* [2002] 2 A.C. 164; N. Richardson (2002) 16 T.L.I. 165.

[108] See, however, *Cook v Fountain* (1676) 3 Swan. 585.

was because an executor who had administered an estate was entitled to keep for himself any surplus which was undisposed of by the will, and the court was ready to find that he took as trustee in order to prevent this. This approach then spread beyond executors. In 1830, however, the Executors Act provided that undisposed-of residue should be held on trust for the next-of-kin; and from about the middle of the 19th century, a stricter construction was placed upon these "precatory words". Where, however, an express trust is construed from precatory words, it is, of course, just as much a trust as any other.[109]

The older cases are therefore unhelpful as guides to construction. *Lambe v Eames*[110] is usually regarded as the case which marks the "turning of the tide". There the testator gave his estate to his widow, "to be at her disposal in any way she may think best, for the benefit of herself and her family." By her will she gave part of the estate outside the family; it was held that she had been absolutely entitled to the property and that the gift was valid. Similarly in *Re Adams and the Kensington Vestry*,[111] where a testator gave his estate:

> "[U]nto and to the absolute use of my dear wife, Harriet . . . in full confidence that she will do what is right as to the disposal thereof between my children, either in her lifetime or by will after her decease."

The Court of Appeal held that she took absolutely.

But a trust will be found from precatory words if on a proper construction of the language that was the intention of the testator. In *Comiskey v Bowring-Hanbury*,[112] a testator gave to his wife:　　**3–020**

> "[T]he whole of my real and personal estate . . . in full confidence that . . . at her death she will devise it to such one or more of my nieces as she may think fit and in default of any disposition by her thereof by her will . . . I hereby direct that all my estate and property acquired by her under this my will shall at her death be equally divided among the surviving said nieces."

A majority of the House of Lords held that the testator intended to make a gift to his wife, with a gift over of the whole property at her

---

[109] In *Re Williams* [1897] 2 Ch. 12 at 27 Rigby L.J. protested against the use of the term "precatory trust", calling it a "misleading nickname".

[110] (1871) L.R. 6 Ch. 597. See also *Re Hamilton* [1895] 2 Ch. 370 at 374.

[111] (1884) 27 Ch.D. 394; *Mussourie Bank v Raynor* (1882) 7 App.Cas. 321 ("feeling confident that she will act justly to our children in distributing the same"); *Re Diggles* (1888) 39 Ch.D. 253 ("it is my desire that she allows . . . an annuity of £25"); *Re Johnson* [1939] 2 All E.R. 458 ("I request that my mother will on her death leave the property or what remains of it . . . to my four sisters").

[112] [1905] A.C. 84.

death to such of her nieces as should survive her, shared according to the wife's will, and otherwise equally.

Where a form of words has once been held to create a trust, the testator's intention may be held to be such as to reach the same result, at any rate where the words have been used as a precedent, even though the words used, when subjected to the stricter modern construction, might be expected to produce a different result.[113]

Where the words used are held not to create a trust, the donee of the property takes beneficially.[114] This must be distinguished from the situation where there is certainty of intention to create a trust, but uncertainty as to the objects or the shares they are to take. In such cases, as we shall see, there is a resulting trust.

Where a testator leaves to his spouse (or civil partner) an interest in property which is in terms absolute but by the same instrument purports to give his issue an interest in the same property, s.22 of the Administration of Justice Act 1982 provides that the spouse takes absolutely, in the absence of a contrary intention. This presumption did not apply where a testator left a bungalow "in trust for my wife", and then provided that it should be sold on her death and the proceeds shared between his children. The gift to the wife was not in terms absolute, as it was clear on a fair reading of the will that she was intended to have a life interest only.[115]

The question of certainty of intention may also arise where there is no document to construe. The question then is whether the acts or words of the parties indicate an intention to create a trust; as where a man tells his cohabitant that she can share his bank account[116]; or where a mail order company puts money sent by customers into a separate bank account.[117] This aspect of the problem will be discussed in Ch.4, where the requirements of the declaration of trust are examined.[118]

Finally, the intention to create a trust must be genuine, and not a sham, as where the "settlor" did not intend the trust to be acted upon, but entered into it for some ulterior motive, such as deceiving

---

[113] *Re Steele's WT* [1948] Ch. 603; following *Shelley v Shelley* (1868) L.R. 6 Eq. 540; P. Langan (1968) 32 Conv.(N.S.) 361.

[114] *Lassence v Tierney* (1849) 1 Mac. & Cr. 551; *Hancock v Watson* [1902] A.C. 14; *Watson v Holland* [1985] 1 All E.R. 290; cf. *Re Pugh's WT* [1967] 1 W.L.R. 1261.

[115] *Harrison v Gibson* [2006] 1 W.L.R. 1212.

[116] *Paul v Constance* [1977] 1 W.L.R. 527. See also *Re Vandervell's Trusts (No.2)* [1974] Ch. 269; *Swain v The Law Society* [1983] 1 A.C. 598.

[117] *Re Kayford Ltd (In Liquidation)* [1975] 1 W.L.R. 279, above, para.2–010; cf. *Re Challoner Club (In Liquidation), The Times*, November 4, 1997 (no trust where members' money paid into separate account as terms of intended trust uncertain). See also *R. v Clowes (No.2)* [1994] 2 All E.R. 316 (terms of investment brochures indicated a trust); *Re Lewis's of Leicester Ltd* [1995] 1 B.C.L.C. 428 (company created trust by paying takings of concessionnaires into separate account, although its commission had not been deducted from the payments, thus the company was also a beneficiary).

[118] Below, para.4–013.

creditors or the tax authorities. In *Midland Bank Plc v Wyatt*[119] a declaration of trust was executed by a husband and wife in 1987 (when the husband was contemplating a new business) whereby the family home, their only real asset, was apparently settled on the wife and daughters. The document was kept in a safe and the couple continued to act as absolute owners of the property, in particular by mortgaging it. The husband's business failed and the bank obtained a charging order against the house. The husband then revealed the trust document. This was held to be a sham. The inference was that the husband had "kept it up his sleeve for a rainy day" in order to defeat future creditors and had not otherwise intended it to have any effect. This principle does not require a finding of fraud, and can apply if the transaction is the result of merely mistaken advice. Where the settlor and trustees are different persons, there will be no sham unless the trustees shared the settlor's intentions,[120] or at least did not care what they were signing.[121] A trust which was not a sham when created cannot later become one.[122] However, a sham trust can become genuine at a later stage, for example if new trustees (not knowing of the intentions of the settlor and the original trustees) exercised their powers and duties in accordance with its terms. The trust would be genuine as from their appointment.[123]

B. Certainty of Subject-matter

The subject-matter may be an interest in land; it may be chattels   **3–021** or money; it may be a chose in action, such as a covenant[124] or a debt owed to the settlor. Whatever form it takes, it must be specified with reasonable certainty. Testamentary gifts have failed where they concerned "the bulk of my estate",[125] or "such parts of my estate as she shall not have sold",[126] or "the remaining part of what is left"[127] or "all my other houses",[128] i.e. those remaining after a choice had

---

[119] [1995] 1 F.L.R. 696; below, para.13–020; J. Mowbray (1994) 8 T.L.I. 68; P. Matthews (1998) 4 *Trusts & Trustees* 11 and (2007) 21 T.L.I. 191. See also *Re Pfrimmer Estate* (1936) 2 D.L.R. 460; *Rahman v Chase Bank (CI) Trust Co Ltd* [1991] J.L.R. 103 (Jersey); *Official Assignee in Bankruptcy v Wilson* [2008] W.T.L.R. 1235 (NZCA).

[120] *Shalson v Russo* [2005] Ch. 281; *Re the Esteem Settlement* [2004] W.T.L.R. 1 (Jersey Royal Court).

[121] *A v A* [2007] 2 F.L.R. 467.

[122] *Shalson v Russo*, above, fn.120.

[123] *A v A*, above, fn.121. See generally M. Conaglen (2008) 67 C.L.J. 176; T. Tey (2009) T.L.I. 183 at 193–199.

[124] *Fletcher v Fletcher* (1844) 4 Hare 67; below, para.4–020. See also *Swift v Dairywise Farms Ltd* [2000] 1 W.L.R. 1177 (trust of milk quota).

[125] *Palmer v Simmonds* (1854) 2 Drew. 221. See also *Choithram (T) International SA v Pagarani* [2000] 1 W.L.R. 1 (left open whether trust of "all my wealth" void for uncertainty).

[126] *Re Jones* [1898] 1 Ch. 438; cf. *In the Estate of Last* [1958] P. 137 ("anything that is left" created valid remainder interest).

[127] *Sprange v Barnard* (1789) 2 Bro.C.C. 585.

[128] *Boyce v Boyce* (1849) 16 Sim. 476.

been made by another beneficiary who died before choosing. Similarly a direction that the testator's widow was to get "such minimal part of [the] estate as she might be entitled to under English law for maintenance purposes" was void for uncertainty, as no such entitlement could be identified.[129] These cases should be contrasted with one where the subject-matter of the gift is to be determined in the discretion of a trustee. In *Re Golay's Will Trusts*,[130] a gift directing the executors to allow a beneficiary to "enjoy one of my flats during her lifetime and to receive a reasonable income from my other properties" was upheld. The executors could select the flat. The words "reasonable income" were not intended to allow the trustees to make a subjective decision: but they provided a sufficient objective determinant to enable the court, if necessary, to quantify the amount. The problem, however, is that no objective determination of words such as "reasonable" can be made unless the context is known. In *Re Golay's Will Trusts*[131] it was assumed that the criterion was the beneficiary's previous standard of living. The word "reasonable" in isolation has little meaning. If a testator were to give "a reasonable legacy" to X, then no doubt the gift would fail, unless it was clear that the amount was to be fixed by the executors.

Where the subject-matter of the trust is uncertain, then no trust is created. There is nothing to form the subject-matter of a resulting trust. If the purported trust has been attached to an absolute gift, then the absolute gift takes effect. It may be, however, that the property itself is certain, but the beneficial shares are not. Unless the trustees have a discretion to determine the amounts, then the trust will fail, and the property will be held on a resulting trust for the settlor. This was the case in *Boyce v Boyce*,[132] where the determination was to be made by a beneficiary who died before choosing. Sometimes the problem will be solved by the principle that equity is equality,[133] or by the court determining what is the proper division according to the circumstances.[134]

Certainty of subject-matter has been an issue more recently not only in relation to express trusts but also in the commercial context of the sale of goods. Where purchasers have paid for goods but have not taken delivery prior to the seller's insolvency, they may seek to gain priority over general creditors by claiming a trust of the goods in their favour. Where the goods have not been segregated but form part of a bulk, these claims failed (prior to a legislative reform mentioned below) on the ground that there cannot be a trust of

---

[129] *Anthony v Donges* [1998] 2 F.L.R. 775.
[130] [1965] 1 W.L.R. 969.
[131] Above, fn.130.
[132] (1849) 6 Sim. 476.
[133] *Burrough v Philcox* (1840) 5 Myl. & Cr. 72; A Hawkins (1967) 31 Conv.(N.S.) 117.
[134] *McPhail v Doulton* [1971] A.C. 424 (selection of beneficiaries); below, para.3–026.

unidentified chattels. Thus in *Re London Wine Co*[135] the buyers of wine stored in a warehouse and not segregated from the general stock of similar wine could not establish a trust. It was otherwise where the wine had been segregated for a group of customers (even though not appropriated to each individual customer), as in *Re Stapylton Fletcher Ltd*,[136] although the judge warned that the court:

> "[M]ust be very cautious in devising equitable interests and remedies which erode the statutory scheme for distribution on insolvency. It cannot do it because of some perceived injustice arising as a consequence only of the insolvency."[137]

In that case the legal title had passed to the customers and there was no need to consider the trust argument.

The leading authority is *Re Goldcorp Exchange Ltd*,[138] where purchasers of bullion, who had paid but had not taken delivery, asserted proprietary rights on the insolvency of the company. Save for a group of customers whose bullion had been segregated, these claims were rejected by the Privy Council. Legal title had not passed, nor was there any trust, as there was no identifiable property to which any trust could attach. Thus the customers were unsecured creditors.

Although no doubt some chattels can be regarded as identical to **3–022** other chattels of the same description, the rationale of the rule that there cannot be a trust of chattels which have not been segregated from a mass of similar chattels is that they are not necessarily identical.[139] Even bottles of wine of the same label may not be identical; some may be "corked" and undrinkable. Now, however, the Sale of Goods (Amendment) Act 1995[140] provides that purchasers who have paid for unascertained goods forming part of an identified bulk (where the goods are interchangeable) acquire property rights as tenants in common of the bulk, subject to any contrary agreement. Thus they will prevail over general creditors in an insolvency. This provision will not, of course, apply to the creation of express trusts of chattels.

The chattels rule does not apply to money, shares and other choses in action because, in the nature of things, there is no difference between one pound and another pound, or one share and another

---

[135] (1986) Palmer's Company Cases 121.
[136] [1994] 1 W.L.R. 1181 (tenancy in common); considered "eminently sensible and fair" in A. Clarke (1995) 48 C.L.P. 117 at 131.
[137] [1994] 1 W.L.R. 1181 at 1203 (Paul Baker QC).
[138] [1995] 1 A.C. 74; L. Sealy (1994) 53 C.L.J. 443; below, para.23–056.
[139] cf. P. Clarke All E.R. Rev. 1994 250, doubting the distinction in an age of mass-produced goods.
[140] Amending the Sale of Goods Act 1979.

share of the same class in the same company.[141] Difficult problems do, however, arise.

In *Hunter v Moss*[142] the settlor owned 950 shares in M Co, which had an issued share capital of 1,000. He orally declared a trust of 5 per cent of the share capital, i.e. 50 shares. The Court of Appeal upheld the trust. Provided the shares were of the same class and in the same company, there was no need to segregate 50 shares before declaring the trust. *Re London Wine Co*[143] was distinguished as involving chattels. Cases upholding bequests[144] of part of a larger shareholding showed that the chattels rule did not apply to choses in action. Thus a declaration of trust of part of a larger shareholding or £50 out of a designated bank account with a larger balance would be valid. In fact the settlor had subsequently sold the shares to B Co in exchange for shares in B Co and cash, and the judgment was for 5 per cent of the consideration.

The decision has been criticised, but before considering the criticisms it is necessary to examine a different situation, where a settlor attempts to create a trust of money but (unlike in the bank account example above) does not designate the source of the money. In *MacJordan Construction Ltd v Brookmount Erostin Ltd*[145] a building contract provided that the employer would retain 3 per cent of the contract price as trustee for the builder (pending confirmation that the work was satisfactory). The retention fund was never set up. On the employer's insolvency the builder claimed entitlement to the retention money in priority to a bank which had a floating charge over all the assets. This claim failed because no identifiable assets had been impressed with a trust for the builder. There was merely a contractual right, which did not "carry with it any equitable interest of a security character in the assets for the time being of the employer."[146] This is clearly correct, being in effect no different from an attempt by X to declare himself trustee of £100 for Y without identifying the source of the money. Thus in *Hemmens v Wilson Browne (A Firm)*[147] a document purporting to give A the right to call on B for payment of £110,000 at any time did not create a trust (or

[141] Although they are distinguishable by serial number. See Smith, *The Law of Tracing*, 1997, p.224.

[142] [1994] 1 W.L.R. 452; J. Martin [1996] Conv. 223. The position is otherwise in Australia; see *Re Harvard Securities Ltd (In Liquidation)* [1997] 2 B.C.L.C. 369; below, para.3–023.

[143] Above, fn.135.

[144] *Re Cheadle* [1900] 2 Ch. 620; *Re Clifford* [1912] 1 Ch. 29. These are considered distinguishable in M. Ockelton (1994) 53 C.L.J. 448.

[145] [1992] B.C.L.C. 350.

[146] *MacJordan Construction Ltd v Brookmount Erostin Ltd* [1992] B.C.L.C. 350.

[147] [1995] Ch. 223 (a professional negligence action).

any other right) because there was no identifiable fund to form its subject-matter. Likewise there is no trust of money paid into an overdrawn account, as there is no identifiable subject-matter.[148]

Criticisms of *Hunter v Moss* point to the difficulties which could **3–023** arise on subsequent dealings with the shareholding or bank account of which an unsegregated part is subject to a trust. Before any such dealings, the beneficiary could call for a transfer of the money or shares. But what would happen if, after declaring a trust of 50 out of 950 shares, the settlor then sold 50 shares and invested the proceeds (disastrously or profitably)? Whose 50 shares were they? There seems no reason why the tracing rules relating to mixed assets should not apply.[149] Those rules normally deal with trust property which has subsequently become mixed with other property, but there seems no reason why they should be so confined. In any event, it could be said that a settlor who declares a trust of part of his shareholding or bank balance becomes under a duty to segregate the trust assets from his own. Tracing will not work, on the other hand, in a case like *MacJordan*[150] because there is no identifiable mixed fund; the employer there had only one bank account in credit at the insolvency but had never assumed an obligation to set up the retention fund out of that account.[151] It may be that the tracing rules will not always work in a case like *Hunter v Moss*,[152] but inability to trace need not mean that there was no valid trust in the first place.

It has been said that the approval of *MacJordan*[153] by the Privy Council in *Re Goldcorp Exchange Ltd*[154] shows by inference that *Hunter v Moss* is incorrect.[155] This would be so only if *Hunter* and *MacJordan* were indistinguishable, but the discussion above sought to establish that *Hunter* may be distinguished on the basis that the larger asset from which the trust was carved was identified. It is submitted that the *Hunter v Moss* solution is fair, sensible and workable.[156] Unlike the other cases, it did not involve a claim by unsecured creditors to gain priority in insolvency. It is an example of the court's policy of preventing a clearly intended trust from failing for uncertainty.[157]

---

[148] *Fortex Group Ltd v MacIntosh* [1998] 3 N.Z.L.R. 171.

[149] Below, para.23–054.

[150] See fn.145.

[151] To claim a charge over the general assets would go beyond even the unorthodox dicta in *Space Investments Ltd v Canadian Imperial Bank of Commerce Trust Co (Bahamas)* [1986] 1 W.L.R. 1072; below, para.23–056.

[152] See criticisms in P. Clarke All E.R. Rev. 1994 p.250.

[153] Above fn.145.

[154] [1995] 1 A.C. 74; above.

[155] D. Hayton (1994) 110 L.Q.R. 335; P. Birks (1995) 9 T.L.I. 43 at 45.

[156] See A. Clarke (1995) 48 C.L.P. 117; P. Parkinson (2002) 61 C.L.J. 657 at 663–676.

[157] See *Re Golay's WT* [1965] 1 W.L.R. 969; above, para.3–021; *Re Tepper's WT* [1987] Ch. 358; below, para.3–030.

The academic criticisms of *Hunter v Moss* were noted with some sympathy by the High Court in the context of an insolvency in *Re Harvard Securities Ltd (In Liquidation)*,[158] but the decision was regarded as binding and not effectively overruled by *Re Goldcorp*. It was noted that, after the latter decision, the House of Lords had refused the defendant in *Hunter* leave to appeal.[159] *Hunter* was recently referred to without disapproval in the Court of Appeal, where Arden L.J. said that "the shareholding was in existence, the shares were fungible [interchangeable] and thus the trust property could be identified".[160] It was also applied in the High Court in a family dispute, where a declaration of trust of 4,000 shares out of a 12,500 holding was held to have been made. The decision was upheld on appeal, but this aspect was not in issue.[161] *Hunter* has been followed in New South Wales after a full review of the academic opinions and of decisions in various jurisdictions. A declaration of trust of shares which formed part of a larger holding was upheld:

> "Given the nature of shares in a company, it is perfectly sensible to talk about an individual having a beneficial interest in 220,000 shares out of a parcel of 1.5 million, even if it is not possible to identify individual shares that are held on trust."[162]

Of course, there is no difficulty in a trust of a co-owned share, but that solution was rejected in *Hunter v Moss*[163]: the claimant was held to be equitable owner of 50 shares, and not to have a tenancy in common interest in the whole holding. Professor Goode has cogently argued that intangible assets such as shares of the same issue or a bank deposit can only be held (if not by a sole owner) in co-ownership.[164] Shares of the same issue are no more than fractions of a single asset, the share capital. A bank deposit (a debt owed by the bank) is a single asset. Thus a declaration of trust (or transfer) of a number of shares of the same issue or part of a bank balance must create co-ownership of the single asset and cannot be attacked for uncertainty of subject-matter on grounds of failure to segregate. As there is a single asset, segregation is not necessary (or indeed possible) for the creation of a co-owned share.

---

[158] [1997] 2 B.C.L.C. 369; T. Villiers (1998–9) 9 K.C.L.J. 112.

[159] [1994] 1 W.L.R. 614.

[160] *Lehman Brothers International (Europe) (in administration) v CRC Credit Fund Ltd* [2011] Bus. L.R. 277 at 323.

[161] *Shah v Shah* [2011] W.T.L.R. 519.

[162] *White v Shortall* [2006] NSWSC 1379 (Supreme Court).

[163] [1994] 1 W.L.R. 452.

[164] [2003] L.M.C.L.Q. 379. See also P. Oliver (1994-95) 5 K.C.L.J. 139. Co-ownership is the legislative solution for goods; Sale of Goods (Amendment) Act 1995, above.

Before leaving the question of certainty of subject-matter, it might be said that uncertainty as to the precise scope of property subjected to a secret trust,[165] a trust arising under mutual wills,[166] a constructive trust of a family home,[167] or a proprietary estoppel claim,[168] has not proved fatal to its validity. Insistence on strict rules in these contexts could facilitate fraud or unjust enrichment.

C. Certainty of Objects: The Beneficiaries[169]

3-024
"It is clear law that a trust (other than a charitable trust) must be for ascertainable beneficiaries."[170] In the case of future interests, the beneficiaries must be ascertainable within the period of perpetuity.[171] The test to be applied to determine certainty of objects depends upon the nature of the trust. With a "fixed" trust, it is, and always has been, that a trust is void unless it is possible to ascertain every beneficiary. With a discretionary trust, the House of Lords decided in *McPhail v Doulton*[172] that the test was: can it be said with certainty that any individual is or is not a member of the class?[173] That is the same test as was established for certainty of objects of a mere power in *Re Gulbenkian's Settlements*.[174] This assimilation of the tests for powers and discretionary trusts destroys what used to be one of the most important reasons for distinguishing between trusts and powers.[175]

3-025
i. Fixed Trusts. A fixed trust is one in which the share or interest of the beneficiaries is specified in the instrument. The beneficiary is the owner of the equitable interest allocated to him. This situation is contrasted with a discretionary trust; where the trustees hold the trust property on trust for such member or members of a class of beneficiaries as they shall in their absolute discretion determine. In that situation, no beneficiary owns any part of the trust fund unless

---

[165] *Ottaway v Norman* [1972] Ch. 698, below, para.5–008.

[166] *Re Cleaver* [1981] 1 W.L.R. 939, below, para.12–032.

[167] *Gissing v Gissing* [1971] A.C. 886 at 909; *Stokes v Anderson* [1991] 1 F.L.R. 391; below, para.11–014. Likewise remedial constructive trusts, where they are recognised; *Fortex Group Ltd v MacIntosh* [1998] 3 N.Z.L.R. 171.

[168] *Thorner v Major* [2009] 1 W.L.R. 776; below, para.27–022.

[169] H. Cohen (1971) 24 C.L.P. 133; J. Harris (1971) 87 L.Q.R. 31; J. Hopkins (1971) 29 C.L.J. 68; (1973) 5 N.Z.U.L.R. 348; Y. Grbich (1974) 37 M.L.R. 643; L. McKay (1973) 7 V.U.W.L.R. 258; S. Fradley (1975) 4 Anglo-American L.R. 442; C. Emery (1982) 98 L.Q.R. 551; Law Com. No.58 para.63. For the position in Australia, see P. Creighton (2000) 22 Sydney Law Review 93.

[170] per Lord Denning in *Re Vandervell's Trusts (No.2)* [1974] Ch. 269 at 319; *Re Wood* [1949] Ch. 498.

[171] *Re Flavel's WT* [1969] 1 W.L.R. 444 at 446–447.

[172] [1971] A.C. 424.

[173] per Lord Wilberforce [1971] A.C. 424 at 454, 456.

[174] [1970] A.C. 508; below, para.3–026.

[175] *Re Gestetner Settlement* [1953] Ch. 672.

and until the trustees have exercised their discretion in his favour.[176]

Commonly, but not necessarily, there is a fixed trust where there are successive interests in favour of individual beneficiaries; such as a trust for A for life and then for B absolutely. Where there is a gift for a class, it is necessary in the case of a fixed trust to lay down what share each beneficiary is to take; a discretionary trust will provide for the trustees to exercise a discretion in the selection of a beneficiary. The requirement of certainty in discretionary trusts is considered in (ii) below. The point here is that if trust property is to be divided among a class of beneficiaries in equal (or in any other fixed) shares, the trust cannot, in the nature of things, be administered unless the number and identify of beneficiaries are known. Some of the language in *McPhail v Doulton*[177] might suggest the decision applied to all trusts. But it concerned a discretionary trust and the cases which it examines are cases of discretionary trusts.[178] Although the rule of certainty should be the minimum necessary to make the trust workable, a stricter rule is needed for fixed trusts. How could the trustee or the court administer a trust for "my employees, ex-employees and their relatives and dependants in equal shares"?[179] It has now been confirmed that, in the case of a fixed trust, it must be possible to identify each member of the class of beneficiaries.[180]

To summarise the position, what is required of a fixed trust is that the description of beneficiaries should involve neither conceptual nor evidential uncertainty.[181] But the court will strive to uphold the trust and a common-sense approach will be taken.[182] Furthermore, provided the identity of the beneficiaries is known, it is no objection that their whereabouts or continued existence is not discoverable, as their shares can be paid into court.[183] The requirement is that a list will be able to be drawn, which is on balance of probabilities complete, as to the maximum number of shares, at the time for distribution.

3–026   **ii. Discretionary Trusts.** The rule of certainty should be no stricter than is necessary to permit trustees to perform their duties.

---

[176] Below, para.8–015.

[177] [1971] A.C. 424.

[178] *Re Ogden* [1933] Ch. 678; *IRC v Broadway Cottages Trust* [1955] Ch. 678.

[179] *McPhail v Doulton*, above fn.134. See P. Matthews [1984] Conv. 22 and (2006) 122 L.Q.R. 268 at 276, suggesting that complete ascertainment is not necessary in the case of fixed trusts. This is doubted at J. Martin [1984] Conv. 304 and D. Hayton 307.

[180] *OT Computers Ltd v First National Tricity Finance Ltd* [2007] W.T.L.R. 165 at 174 (decided 2003).

[181] Below, para.3–028.

[182] See *Gold v Hill* [1999] 1 F.L.R. 54 (oral direction to recipient to "look after Carol and the kids" sufficiently certain although it could be interpreted in various ways).

[183] C. Emery (1982) 98 L.Q.R. 551; cf. P. Matthews [1984] Conv. 22.

We have seen that, where the trust property is to be divided into specific shares, it is necessary for the trustees to know exactly how many beneficiaries there are. Until 1971, the same rule applied to discretionary trusts[184] (sometimes confusingly called "trust powers"[185]). If the trustees should fail or refuse to carry out their duty to select the beneficiaries and distribute, the court must be able to do so; and, it was argued, the court would necessarily distribute equally on the basis that equality is equity and, for that purpose, the beneficiaries must be identifiable.[186] The fallacy of this argument was shown in *McPhail v Doulton*.[187]

Bertram Baden executed a deed establishing a fund to provide benefits for the staff of a company and their relatives and dependants.

Clause 9(a) provided as follows:

"The trustees shall apply the net income of the fund in making at their absolute discretion grants to or for the benefit of any of the officers and employees or ex-officers or ex-employees of the company or to any relatives or dependants of any such persons in such amounts at such times and on such conditions (if any) as they think fit."

The trustees were not obliged to exhaust the income of any year. Capital could be realised for the purpose of making grants if the income was insufficient.

The deed created a discretionary trust not a mere power. It was not possible to make a list of all the members of the class of beneficiaries. The House of Lords, however, held that the test for certainty in discretionary trusts was that applied to fiduciary powers in *Re Gulbenkian's Settlements*.[188] "Can it be said with certainty that any given individual is or is not a member of the class?"[189] The case was referred to the Chancery Division to determine whether the test was satisfied. The Court of Appeal held that it was.[190]

In reaching a decision on the question of the test to be applied, it was necessary to deal with two main arguments in favour of the stricter test. First, that a trustee's duty to distribute could only be performed if he was able to consider every possible claimant; and

---

[184] *IRC v Broadway Cottages Trust* [1955] Ch. 678.

[185] For a possible distinction between these two terms, see below, para.3–037.

[186] [1971] A.C. 424 at 442, per Lord Hodson.

[187] Above fn.134; F. Crane (1970) 34 Conv.(N.S.) 287. One result of the decision is to confirm that a trust may be valid although it is impossible to state who is entitled to the equitable interest. See A. Everton [1982] Conv. 118.

[188] [1970] A.C. 508.

[189] per Lord Wilberforce [1971] A.C. 424 at 454, 456.

[190] [1973] Ch. 9; below, para.3–028.

secondly, that the court could only execute the trust, on failure of the trustees to do so, by equal division of the fund. If these arguments could be answered, there was much to be said for assimilating the test with that for powers; for, although the distinction between trust and power is, in some contexts, basic to a lawyer, it is often difficult to ascertain which exists in any particular case. Thus a relaxation of the test was needed to save many trusts from failure.

3–027   A trustee's duty to distribute requires a consideration of the claims of possible recipients.

"If [a trustee] has to distribute the whole of a fund's income, he must necessarily make a wider and more systematic survey than if his duty is expressed in terms of a power to make grants"[191];

and "a wider and more comprehensive range of inquiry is called for in the case of a trust power than in the case of a power."[192] But the difference is only one of degree; there is no need for a trustee of a discretionary trust to "require the preparation of a complete list of names".[193] The difference does not justify a stricter rule for certainty in discretionary trusts.

The main question is whether the court can execute the trust upon the failure of the trustees to do so. This is primarily a theoretical problem. In the reported cases there have been no examples of trustees refusing to execute a discretionary trust; if a trustee did so, he could be removed and replaced. Secondly, "it does not follow that execution is impossible unless there can be equal division."[194] There are a number of cases, prior to 1801,[195] in which the court exercised a discretion in relation to distribution, deciding in accordance with guidance given by the circumstances of the case.[196] In many of these situations equal division would have been inappropriate. As indeed it would be in modern forms of discretionary trusts for the benefit of employees and their dependants. It would have been paradoxical if the trust in *McPhail v Doulton*[197] had failed because of the court's inability to divide equally; for equal division would have been a nonsensical solution. Thus, the court, if called upon to execute a discretionary trust, will do so in the manner best calculated to give effect to the testator's intentions.

---

[191] [1971] A.C. 424 at 449, 457; (1971) 87 L.Q.R. 31 at 61–62.
[192] [1973] Ch. 9 at 27.
[193] [1971] A.C. 424 at 449.
[194] [1971] A.C. 424 at 451.
[195] *Kemp v Kemp* (1801) 5 Ves.Jr. 849.
[196] *Mosely v Mosely* (1673) Fin. 53; *Clarke v Turner* (1694) Free Ch. 198; *Warburton v Warburton* (1702) 4 Bro.P.C. 1; *Richardson v Chapman* (1760) 7 Bro.P.C. 318.
[197] [1971] A.C. 424.

"It may do so by appointing new trustees, or by authorising or directing representative persons of the classes of beneficiaries to prepare a scheme of distribution, or even, should the proper basis for distribution appear, by itself directing the trustees so to distribute."[198]

In cases where the trustees have failed to exercise their discretion within a reasonable time, the court may direct them to do so, provided there is no evidence of bias or obstinacy.[199] There is no need therefore to require a stricter rule for discretionary trusts than that accepted in *Gulbenkian*[200] as applicable to powers.

It is thought that this less stringent test will also apply to purpose trusts upheld on the principle of *Re Denley's Trust Deed*[201] as being for the benefit of ascertainable individuals. It has been held that the strict test does not apply to *Quistclose* trusts.[202] Lord Millett has analysed such a trust as a resulting trust for the lender, subject to a power or mandate to apply the property for a specified purpose. Provided the power is sufficiently certain to enable the court to determine whether it is capable of being carried out or if the money has been misapplied, it is valid. If the power is uncertain, there is simply a resulting trust for the lender.[203]

iii. Conceptual Uncertainty[204] and Evidential Difficulties. In 3–028
Re Baden's Deed Trusts (No.2), Brightman J.,[205] and then the Court of Appeal,[206] had to apply the test laid down by the House of Lords, and consider in particular whether the words "dependants" and "relatives" were too uncertain. In applying the test, "it is essential to bear in mind the difference between conceptual uncertainty and evidential difficulties."[207] The test is concerned with the former;

---

[198] [1971] A.C. 424 at 457, per Lord Wilberforce. See also *Mettoy Pension Trustees Ltd v Evans* [1990] 1 W.L.R. 1587, holding that the court has similar powers of intervention in the case of fiduciary powers.

[199] *Re Locker's Settlement* [1977] 1 W.L.R. 1323; (1978) 94 L.Q.R. 177. The distribution must be in favour of those who were objects at the time the discretion should have been exercised. It is otherwise in the case of a mere power, where the default gift will operate if the power is not exercised within the proper time limits.

[200] [1970] A.C. 508.

[201] [1969] 1 Ch. 373, below, para.14–002. See *R. v District Auditor Ex p. West Yorkshire Metropolitan County Council* (1986) 26 R.V.R. 24, holding that "administrative unworkability" (below) was fatal to a *Re Denley* type of purpose trust.

[202] Above, para.2–009.

[203] *Twinsectra Ltd v Yardley* [2002] 2 A.C. 164 (power to apply in acquisition of property).

[204] Sometimes called linguistic or semantic uncertainty.

[205] [1972] Ch. 607.

[206] [1973] Ch. 9; D. Hayton (1973) 36 Conv.(N.S.) 351.

[207] per Sachs L.J. [1973] Ch. 9 at 19; see also, per Lord Wilberforce [1971] A.C. 424 at 457.

"the court is never defeated by evidential uncertainty."[208] The illustration given of a conceptual question is that of the contrasting cases "someone under a moral obligation", which is conceptually uncertain and "first cousins", which is conceptually certain.[209] It would be possible in the latter case, but not in the former, to say with certainty "that any given individual is or is not a member of the class".[210] It is no objection that it may be difficult to establish whether or not any given person satisfies the description, so long as the description is conceptually clear.[211] In each case the precise words must of course be examined to see whether the test is satisfied. Once the class is determined as being conceptually certain the question of inclusion is an issue of fact. "Relatives" and "dependants" were both sufficiently certain.

Provided the class is certain in the above sense, it does not matter that the whereabouts or continued existence of an object is not known.[212]

3–029   **iv. Problems with the Test.** The test is not without its difficulties, theoretical and practical.

3–030   (a) *What is Conceptually Certain?* Different minds may take different views on the question of whether a particular description is conceptually certain or not. Indeed, the illustrations referred to in the previous paragraph, which were selected to make the point, are not wholly persuasive. The problem is that few descriptions of the kind likely to be encountered in trusts and powers are so clear as to admit of no borderline cases. Most fall between those which are indisputably certain, for example "Nobel prize winners", and those which are conceptually unclear, for example "friends". To insist on complete certainty would be to defeat most gifts. Dispositions ought if possible to be upheld and "should not be held void on a peradventure".[213] Words such as "relatives" may cause difficulties[214] but trustees can be expected to act sensibly and not to select a remote kinsman.[215] The best solution, it is submitted, is to regard such words as conceptually certain, leaving it to the claimant to establish his case, as discussed below. Words such as "friends", on the other

---

[208] [1973] Ch. 9 at 20; in *Re Tuck's ST* [1978] Ch. 49 at 59, Lord Denning M.R. in the context of a condition precedent, confessed that he found "the dichotomy most unfortunate".

[209] [1973] Ch. 9.

[210] Above, para.3–026.

[211] This is discussed further below. Such evidential difficulties would, however, invalidate a fixed trust; above, para.3–025.

[212] *Re Gulbenkian's Settlement Trusts* [1970] A.C. 508; C. Emery (1982) 98 L.Q.R. 551. This point is more significant in the case of fixed trusts.

[213] *Re Hay's Settlement Trusts* [1982] 1 W.L.R. 202 at 212.

[214] Below.

[215] *Re Baden's Deed Trusts (No.2)* [1973] Ch. 9.

hand, must fall on the wrong side of the line. Although "old friends" was upheld in *Re Gibbard*,[216] this was the result of applying a test which has not survived later decisions,[217] namely that it was sufficient that there was some person who could be shown to be within the class. Browne-Wilkinson J., in *Re Barlow's Will Trusts*,[218] attempted to clarify who a "friend" was. But that was in the context of a gift subject to a condition precedent, which, as we shall see,[219] is governed by a less strict test.

Conceptual uncertainty may in some cases be cured by a provision that the opinion of a third party (the trustees or another person) is to settle the matter. The provision is more likely to be upheld where the settlor (or testator) leaves the definition of a term to the third party as opposed to leaving it to the third party to determine the meaning the settlor himself intended it to have. In the former case the settlor in effect adopts the meaning ascribed by the third party.[220] In *Re Coxen*[221] it was held that the testator could validly make the trustees' opinion the criterion provided he had sufficiently defined the state of affairs on which they were to form their opinion. The question whether the testator's wife had "ceased permanently to reside" at a property passed this test, whereas in *Re Jones*[222] the question whether X should at any time have a "social or other relationship" with Y in the "uncontrolled opinion" of the trustees was insufficiently defined to enable the trustees to come to a proper decision. A gift to persons "having a moral claim" on the donor would be conceptually uncertain, but a gift to "such persons as the company may consider to have a moral claim" on the donor would satisfy the test.[223] Similarly, any uncertainty in the requirement of being of the Jewish faith and married to an "approved wife" could be cured by a provision that disputes were to be decided by a chief rabbi.[224] The settlor or testator cannot, however, purport to oust the jurisdiction of the court by giving the trustees conclusive power to

---

[216] [1967] 1 W.L.R. 42. See also *Re Byron's Settlement* [1891] 3 Ch. 474 (bare power).

[217] See *Gulbenkian's Settlement Trusts (No.1)* [1970] A.C. 508.

[218] [1979] 1 W.L.R. 278. It was said that a trust or power in favour of "friends" would probably fail. See also *Re Byron's Settlement* [1891] 3 Ch. 474.

[219] Below, para.3–038.

[220] Thomas, *Powers*, pp.133–138.

[221] [1948] Ch. 747 at 761–762 (condition subsequent).

[222] [1953] Ch. 125 (condition subsequent).

[223] *Re Leek* [1969] 1 Ch. 563; cf. *Re Wright's WT* (1981) 78 L.S.Gaz. 841 (Gift to trustees "for such people and institutions as they think have helped me or my late husband" uncertain. There was an appeal on the issue of severance; below, para.3–035). See also *Re Coates* [1955] Ch. 495 (for any friends the testator's wife might feel he had forgotten). In the case of a discretionary trust, difficulties might arise if the court is called upon to execute it.

[224] *Re Tuck's Settlement Trusts* [1978] Ch. 49 (in fact the condition was held certain). For a contrary view, see Underhill and Hayton, 18th edn, p.135 (taking the view that only evidential uncertainty may be cured in this way). See also *Re Tepper's Will Trusts* [1987] Ch. 358, holding that the meaning of "Jewish faith" could be elucidated by extrinsic evidence of the faith as practised by the testator; P. Clarke and C. Sherrin All E.R. Rev. 1987, at 159 and 260 respectively; D. Cooper and D. Herman (1999) 19 L.S. 339. cf. AJA 1982 s.21.

construe the words used.[225] Such a clause will be void as contrary to
public policy. Assuming the power to resolve an uncertainty has
been validly given to trustees, the court may intervene if it is exercised in bad faith and possibly on other grounds.[226]

3–031   (b) *Proof of Inclusion and Exclusion; Proving Negatives.* Read
strictly, the test means that it must be possible to show either that
any person is within the class or that he is not within it. But, how
could you show that a person is, for example, not your relative?
Sachs L.J.[227] said that the claimant needs to show that he is within
the class; if he cannot do that, he is not within it. His Lordship was
here referring to evidential uncertainty. Clearly conceptual uncertainty cannot be cured by casting the onus of proof on to the claimant, because the matter would not be susceptible of proof.[228] Megaw
L.J. said that the test was satisfied[229]:

> "[I]f, as regards at least a substantial number of objects, it can be
> said with certainty that they fall within the trust; even though, as
> regards a substantial number of other persons . . . the answer
> would have to be, not 'they are outside the trust,' but 'it is not
> proven whether they are in or out'. "

His Lordship suggested that to require proof that any given person
was or was not within the class would return to the old rule requiring
the making of a list. This seems doubtful. To be in a position to
accept or reject the claim of any given person does not require
ascertainment of the whole class. The "substantial number" test
might be thought to be a return to the *Gibbard*[230] test which was
rejected in *Gulbenkian*.[231] This is not so, as the *Gibbard*[232] test
allowed a degree of conceptual uncertainty, while the statement of
Megaw L.J. quoted above concerns evidential uncertainty. It is submitted that the majority view is to be preferred to the somewhat
stricter test laid down by Stamp L.J., which seems to require that the
trustees be in a position to say affirmatively whether any given
person is within or outside the class. His Lordship considered that
the validity or invalidity of a discretionary trust depended on[233]:

> "[W]hether you can say of any individual—and the accent must
> be on that word 'any' for it is not simply the individual whose

---

[225] *Re Wynn* [1952] Ch. 271; *Re Raven* [1915] 1 Ch. 673.
[226] Below, para.17–047.
[227] [1973] Ch. 9; and see J. Hopkins (1973) 32 C.L.J. 36.
[228] cf. *Re Barlow's Will Trusts* [1979] 1 W.L.R. 278, Below, para.3–038.
[229] [1973] Ch. 9 at 24.
[230] [1967] 1 W.L.R. 42.
[231] [1970] A.C. 508.
[232] Above, fn.230.
[233] [1973] Ch. 9 at 28.

claim you are considering who is spoken of—[that he] 'is or is not a member of the class,' for only thus can you make a survey of the range of objects or possible beneficiaries."

If Stamp L.J. had not been able to construe "relatives" as meaning "next-of-kin" or "nearest blood relations" he would have held the trust void for uncertainty.[234]

(c) *Width of the Class; Administrative Unworkability.*[235] Lord **3–032** Wilberforce in *McPhail v Doulton*[236] indicated that there might be a difference in one situation between the test to be applied to discretionary trusts and that for mere powers. A description of beneficiaries which might comply with the certainty test laid down might be "so hopelessly wide as not to form 'anything like a class,' so that the trust is administratively unworkable,"[237] and he hesitatingly gave as an example a class consisting of "all the residents of Greater London". This was said in the context of a discretionary trust. The question has arisen whether this concept applies also to mere powers. Buckley L.J. assumed obiter that it did in *Blausten v IRC*[238] This was doubted in *Re Manisty's Settlement*,[239] where Templeman J. held that a mere power could not be invalid on the ground of width of numbers, preferring the view that its validity should depend on whether or not it was capricious. This point is discussed below. *Manisty* was preferred to *Blausten* by Megarry V.C. in *Re Hay's Settlement Trusts*.[240] A mere power, whether or not fiduciary, was not invalid on the ground of the size of the class. Mere numbers could not prevent the trustee from considering whether to exercise the power nor from performing his other duties,[241] nor prevent the court from controlling him. But it was suggested that a discretionary trust in favour of the same wide class[242] as the mere power would have been void as administratively unworkable, as the duties of a

[234] The view of the majority was that it meant "descendants from a common ancestor". It has long been established that "relatives" should be confined to next of kin only if this is necessary to save the gift, e.g. where the "list test" applies. See *Re Shield's WT* [1974] 2 W.L.R. 885; *Re Barlow's WT* [1979] 1 W.L.R. 278; *Re Poulton's WT* [1987] 1 W.L.R. 795.

[235] See S. Gardner (1991) 107 L.Q.R. 214 at 218: "it is not easy to see just what difficulty it is aimed at pre-empting".

[236] [1971] A.C. 424; criticised on this point in L. McKay (1974) 38 Conv.(N.S.) 269; Y. Grbich (1974) 37 M.L.R. 643.

[237] *McPhail v Doulton* [1971] A.C. 424 at 427.

[238] [1972] Ch. 256. The power was upheld because the trustees' power to include any other person as an object was subject to the settlor's consent. The settlor had, therefore, put "metes and bounds" on the otherwise unrestricted class.

[239] [1974] Ch. 17. In *Re Beatty's WT* [1990] 1 W.L.R. 1503; J. Martin [1991] Conv. 138, a fiduciary power given to trustees in favour of "such person or persons as they think fit" was upheld without mention of the concept of administrative unworkability.

[240] [1982] 1 W.L.R. 202.

[241] i.e. to make no unauthorised appointment; to consider the range of objects; to consider the appropriateness of any individual appointment.

[242] Any person except the settlor, settlor's spouse or trustees.

discretionary trustee were more stringent, and the objects of a discretionary trust had rights of enforcement which objects of a mere power lacked. A similar view was taken in *R. v District Auditor Ex p. West Yorkshire Metropolitan County Council*,[243] where a local authority, purporting to act under statutory powers, resolved to set up a trust "for the benefit of any or all or some of the inhabitants of the County of West Yorkshire".[244] There were 2,500,000 potential beneficiaries. The court was prepared to assume that "inhabitant" was sufficiently certain, but held the trust void for administrative unworkability as the class was far too large, applying Lord Wilberforce's dictum in *McPhail v Doulton*.[245] *Re Manisty's Settlement*[246] was distinguished as concerning a power, where the function of the court was more restricted. The weight of authority, therefore, supports the view that "administrative unworkability" can invalidate discretionary trusts but not mere powers.[247]

3–033   (d) *Capriciousness.* There is no general principle of English law that a capricious disposition is invalid. Wigram V.C. in *Bird v Luckie*[248] said:

> "No man is bound to make a will in such a manner as to deserve approbation from the prudent, the wise, or the good. A testator is permitted to be capricious and improvident, and moreover is at liberty to conceal the circumstances and the motives by which he has been actuated in his dispositions."

But while a capricious legacy may be valid, the position may be otherwise in a discretionary trust or power. Unlike an outright gift, discretionary trusts and powers involve fiduciary obligations, the performance of which may be rendered impossible if their terms are capricious. In upholding a power of great width in *Re Manisty's Settlement*[249] Templeman J. held that the terms of the power need not provide guidance to the trustees; an absolute discretion did not preclude a sensible consideration of whether and how to exercise the

---

[243] (1986) 26 R.V.R. 24 (QBD); C. Harpum (1986) 45 C.L.J. 391.

[244] The details of the trust, which was not charitable, are given in Ch.14, Below, para.14–003.

[245] Above, fn.237.

[246] Above, fn.239.

[247] cf. A. Grubb [1982] Conv. 432 at 434; C. Emery (1982) 98 L.Q.R. 551; I. Hardcastle [1990] Conv. 24, taking the view that it applies also to powers, and Riddall, *The Law of Trusts*, 6th edn, 2002, p.36, taking the view that it applies also to fixed trusts. It has been suggested that one result of *Mettoy Pension Trustees Ltd v Evans* [1990] 1 W.L.R. 1587, which adapts discretionary trust remedies to fiduciary powers, may be to make the concept of administrative unworkability applicable to powers; S. Gardner (1991) 107 L.Q.R. 214.

[248] (1850) 8 Hare 301. See also *Re James's Will Trusts* [1962] Ch. 226; *Nathan v Leonard* [2003] 1 W.L.R. 827 at 831: "a testator may dispose of his property as he wishes, however capriciously".

[249] [1974] Ch. 17.

power. The example of a class comprising "residents of Greater London" would be capricious and void, not on the basis of numbers, but on the ground that the terms of the power negatived any sensible intention on the settlor's part and any sensible consideration by the trustees. The objects must either be unlimited, in which case the trustees can perform their obligations sensibly, or limited to a "sensible" class. The disposition would be void if membership of the class of objects was accidental and irrelevant to any purpose or to any method of limiting or selecting beneficiaries.[250]

Is "capriciousness" the same notion as "administrative unworkability"?[251] The latter, as we have seen, has been held inapplicable to mere powers, while the former has been held applicable to both mere powers and discretionary trusts.[252] In *R. v District Auditor Ex p. West Yorkshire Metropolitan County Council*[253] a trust for the benefit of 2,500,000 inhabitants of West Yorkshire was held void for administrative unworkability (as being too large a class) even though it was not capricious because the local authority (the settlor) had every reason to wish to benefit the inhabitants in the ways specified. Thus it appears that the two concepts are distinct, although the same example may give rise to invalidity on both grounds. Capriciousness has no necessary connection with width of numbers, which is the characteristic of administrative unworkability.

It might also be mentioned that the capricious exercise of a fiduciary power or trust, as where objects are chosen by height or complexion, will be invalid even though the power or trust is valid.[254]

(e) *Duty to Survey the Field.* Clearly the trustees of a discretionary trust are not obliged to consider every object, as the trust may be valid although the identity of all the objects is not known. But as we have seen, Lord Wilberforce in *McPhail v Doulton*[255] considered that the trustees ought to make such a survey of the range of objects as would enable them to carry out their fiduciary duty, and that a wider or more comprehensive range of enquiry was called for in the case of discretionary trusts than in the case of powers. In the case of a wide-ranging discretionary trust, where the number of objects may run to hundreds of thousands, the trustees' duty is to assess in a

3–034

[250] [1974] Ch. 17 at 26. See A. Grubb [1982] Conv. 432 at 435 explaining that the "appointment criteria", necessary to avoid invalidity on the ground of capriciousness, need not be apparent from the power itself.
[251] See C. Emery (1982) 98 L.Q.R. 551 for the view that they are the same.
[252] See *Re Manisty's Settlement*, above, fn.239; *Re Hay's Settlement Trusts* [1982] 1 W.L.R. 202.
[253] (1986) 26 R.V.R. 24; C. Harpum (1986) 45 C.L.J. 391; above, para.3–032. See also *Re Harding* [2008] Ch. 235, where a trust for so large a class as the black community in four London boroughs would have been void as unworkable had it not been held charitable.
[254] *Re Manisty's Settlement*, above, fn.239; *Re Hay's Settlement Trusts*, above, fn.252.
[255] [1971] A.C. 424; criticised in Y. Grbich (1974) 37 M.L.R. 643.

businesslike way "the size of the problem".[256] Megarry V.C. in *Re Hay's Settlement Trusts*,[257] said:

> "The trustee must not simply proceed to exercise the power in favour of such of the objects as happen to be at hand or claim his attention. He must first consider what persons or classes of persons are objects of the power . . . there is no need to compile a complete list of the objects, or even to make an accurate assessment of the number of them: what is needed is an appreciation of the width of the field, and thus whether a selection is to be made merely from a dozen or, instead, from thousands or millions. . . . Only when the trustee has applied his mind to the 'size of the problem' should he then consider in individual cases whether, in relation to other possible claimants, a particular grant is appropriate. In doing this, no doubt he should not prefer the undeserving to the deserving; but he is not required to make an exact calculation whether, as between deserving claimants, A is more deserving than B."

This was the duty which had emerged from cases concerning discretionary trusts, but "plainly the requirements for a mere power cannot be more stringent than those for a discretionary trust."[258] The duties of a trustee of a discretionary trust are more stringent than those of the donee of a fiduciary power because of the obligation to distribute. The precise scope of the less onerous duty to survey in the case of a power awaits clarification.[259]

3–035   (f) *Many Certain Categories; One Uncertain.* Further difficulties could arise with a definition of a class of beneficiaries which contained a long series of categories which complied with the *McPhail v Doulton* test, but to which there was added one category which did not. What, for example, would the court say to a trust in the same language as that in *McPhail v Doulton* but to which there was added "any other person to whom I may be under a moral obligation and any of my old friends"? . . . which is, let it be assumed, conceptually uncertain. The same problem could arise in a case of power.

---

[256] *Re Baden's Deed Trusts (No.2)* [1973] Ch. 9 at 20 (per Sachs L.J.)

[257] [1982] 1 W.L.R. 202 at 209–210.

[258] [1982] 1 W.L.R. 202 at 209–210. This may be contrasted with the view of Harman J. in *Re Gestetner* [1953] Ch. 672 at 688: " . . . there is no obligation on the trustees to do more than consider from time to time the merits of such persons of the specified class as are known to them. . . . " See also Templeman J. in *Re Manisty's Settlement* [1974] Ch. 14 at 25.

[259] See A. Grubb [1982] Conv. 432 at 437, suggesting that the duty is merely to consider those who press claims and present themselves for inspection; there is no need to "go forth and search out worthy candidates". Presumably this duty arises only if the donee has decided to exercise the power.

In this situation, the class as the whole does not satisfy the test. It would however be unfortunate to declare the whole trust void because of the final addition. After all, the trust is workable as it is. Such a trust, however, may be held void unless it is possible to excise the offending phrase by severance: this suggestion has sometimes been made,[260] but the severance principle has yet to be established. Thus in *Re Wright's Will Trusts*,[261] where the class consisted of identifiable named charities and other bodies which could not be identified, the Court of Appeal refused to give effect to the gift in favour of the named charities only.

v. Effect of Certainty Test on Rights of Objects. When, prior to 3–036 *McPhail v Doulton*,[262] complete ascertainment of objects was required in the case of a discretionary trust, it was thought that each object had a right to be considered, and to share in the fund if the trustees failed in their duty to exercise their discretion. Clearly this is no longer accurate, now that the trust may be valid without the necessity of ascertaining the full membership of the class. The question of equal division in default of exercise has already been dealt with.[263] Any right to be considered must be confined to the situation where the claim is brought to the attention of the trustees. The right of the object is simply to require that the trustees perform their obligation to allocate the fund after surveying the range of objects, as described above.[264] If the unknown or unascertainable object is not considered by the trustees, at any rate he is no worse off than he would have been prior to *McPhail v Doulton*,[265] when the possibility of his existence would have caused the discretionary trust to fail.

vi. Trust Powers in the Old Sense; Trusts with a Power of 3–037 **Selection.** If, as a matter of construction, it can be inferred that the settlor's intention was that the entire class should take if the trustee failed to make a selection, then no doubt equal division is still appropriate, in which case the "complete ascertainment" test must still be satisfied. This is more likely to be the case in a family trust, where the objects are not large in number, as in *Burrough v Philcox*.[266] It may be that the minority and the majority in *McPhail v*

---

[260] per Sachs L.J. in *Re Leek* [1969] 1 Ch. 563 at 586 (assuming, however, that legislation would be required); and in the case of a power (Winn L.J.) in *Re Gulbenkian's Settlements* [1968] Ch. 126 at 138 CA. cf. decisions on trusts which are not exclusively charitable; below, para.15–060.

[261] (1999) 13 T.L.I. 48 (decided 1982); above, para.3–030.

[262] [1971] A.C. 424.

[263] Above, para.3–026.

[264] See generally *Re Hay's Settlement Trusts*, above, fn.252; *Turner v Turner* [1984] Ch. 100; *Murphy v Murphy* [1999] 1 W.L.R. 282 (undesirable for trustees to be "badgered" with claims by many beneficiaries).

[265] Above, fn.237.

[266] (1840) 5 Myl. & Cr. 72; above, para.2–025.

Doulton[267] were talking at cross-purposes, the former having in mind the more old-fashioned "trust power" as described above, while the latter analysed the modern discretionary trust in favour of a large class, where the settlor could not have contemplated equal division.[268]

3–038   **vii. Gifts Subject to a Condition Precedent.** A less strict test applies where there is a gift subject to a condition precedent as opposed to a discretionary trust or power. A degree of conceptual uncertainty does not invalidate such a gift.[269] The test, as laid down in *Re Allen*,[270] is that the gift is valid if it is possible to say that one or more persons qualify, even though there may be difficulty as to others. This test may also apply to personal (non-fiduciary) powers.[271]

This test was considered by Browne-Wilkinson J. in *Re Barlow's Will Trust*,[272] where the testatrix left a valuable collection of paintings, directing her executor to sell those not specifically bequeathed, subject to a proviso that "any friends of mine who may wish to do so" be allowed to purchase any of them at a price below the market value. This disposition was held sufficiently certain. Total ascertainment of the testatrix's friends was not required. A "friend" was a person who had a relationship of long standing with the testatrix, which was a social as opposed to a business or professional relationship; and who had met her frequently when circumstances permitted.[273] The effect of the gift was to confer on her friends a series of options to purchase. There was no legal necessity to inform them of their rights, although this would be desirable. The claimant must prove "by any reasonable test" that he qualified.[274] In case of doubt, the executors could apply to the court for directions. The justification for this less strict test was that in the case of individual gifts, unlike trusts and powers, uncertainty as to some beneficiaries did not affect the quantum of the gift in respect of those who clearly

---

[267] Above, fn.237.

[268] See Y. Grbich (1974) 37 M.L.R. 643; C. Emery (1982) 98 L.Q.R. 551. For the proper meaning of "trust power", see R. Bartlett and C. Stebbings [1984] Conv. 227.

[269] A stricter test applies to a condition subsequent. The distinction, though criticised by Lord Denning M.R. in *Re Tuck's Settlement Trusts* [1978] Ch. 49, was acknowledged by the House of Lords in *Blaithwayt v Lord Cawley* [1976] A.C. 397 at 425; below, para.13–004. See also *Re Tepper's Will Trusts* [1987] Ch. 358; *Ellis v Chief Adjudication Officer* [1998] 1 F.L.R. 184.

[270] [1953] Ch. 810.

[271] C. Emery (1982) 98 L.Q.R. 551; *Re Byron's Settlement* [1891] 3 Ch. 474.

[272] [1979] 1 W.L.R. 278; criticised by L. McKay [1980] Conv. 263. C. Emery (1982) 98 L.Q.R. 551. See also Underhill and Hayton, 18th edn, pp.149–151.

[273] [1979] 1 W.L.R. 278 at 282.

[274] cf. *Re Baden's Deed Trusts (No.2)* [1973] Ch. 9, where the onus of proof on the claimant concerns evidential, and not conceptual, uncertainty.

qualified. To uphold the gift in the case of the latter gave effect, at least in part, to the donor's intention.[275]

Although the "condition precedent" test is now settled, this decision illustrates the difficulties inherent in it. The trustees could be in real difficulty in giving effect to such a disposition. The solution that trustees could apply to court in cases of doubt is unsatisfactory. How can the court be in any better position than the trustees to pronounce on the question whether X is a "friend" of Y?[276]

---

[275] This has not been regarded as sufficient to justify a less strict test in the case of trusts and powers.

[276] See, however, s.58 of the Safeguarding Vulnerable Groups Act 2006, which refers to "friends" without attempting any definition.

CHAPTER 4

CONSTITUTION OF TRUSTS
EQUITY WILL NOT ASSIST A VOLUNTEER

1. THE GENERAL PROBLEM

A. Requirements of Conveyance and Declaration

WE have seen that the interest of the beneficiary under a trust is a **4–001** proprietary interest. The legal title is in the trustee; the equitable and beneficial title is in the beneficiary. The trust may be of any form of property—land, chattels, money, choses in action—and for any interest known to the law, whether legal or equitable, in possession, remainder[1] or reversion. An intention to create a trust is, as we have seen, one of the requirements for the creation of an express trust,[2] but it is not sufficient in itself. To declare that A is to hold Blackacre

---

[1] *Re Ralli's WT* [1964] Ch. 288.
[2] Above, para.3–019.

on trust for B does not create a trust unless Blackacre is conveyed to
A. Similarly, a conveyance to A does not create a trust of Blackacre
for B unless the trust is properly declared. In short, it is necessary
both to declare the trust *and* to convey the property to the trustee.
The principle is that, "although equity will not aid a volunteer, it
will not strive officiously to defeat a gift".[3]

Many difficulties have been caused by failure to observe these
basic propositions. Even where they are observed, complications
can arise, and a number of questions are left open. Is it necessary
that the conveyance and the declaration be contemporaneous? If X
conveys Blackacre to A to hold upon trust for B, a trust is created in
favour of B; also if X conveys to A upon trust and later declares the
trusts.[4] If X conveys Blackacre to A, he cannot then tell A to hold on
trust for B, because after the conveyance A became the absolute
owner. May the declaration precede the conveyance? May X create
a trust for B by declaring that A is to hold on trust for B; and later
convey Blackacre to A? This question raises a number of difficulties
as we will see; they will be discussed in this chapter and also in
Ch.5.

B. Methods of Benefiting an Intended Donee

4–002   If X is the owner at law and in equity, he can make B the beneficial owner in any one of three ways:

4–003   **i. Outright Transfer.** He can transfer legal and equitable ownership to B. In the case of land, this transaction is called a conveyance.
With a chattel, it is called a sale or gift; with a chose in action, it is
called an assignment; with shares it is usually called a transfer.
Whatever type of transaction, X, by following the correct procedure
appropriate to the type of property, can transfer his absolute interest,
legal and equitable, to B. Obviously if X does not follow the correct
procedure, he will not transfer the legal or beneficial interest to B.
This self-evident proposition is stated here because arguments have
unsuccessfully been raised that an unsuccessful transfer to B might
be construed as a declaration of trust for B. It is not.[5]

4–004   **ii. Transfer to Trustee.** X may transfer the property to A to hold
on trust for B. Provided that the legal title is correctly transferred to
A, according to the type of property concerned, A will become legal
owner; and provided that an intention to create a trust in favour of B

---

[3] *Choithram (T) International SA v Pagarani* [2001] 1 W.L.R. 1 at 11, per Lord Browne-
Wilkinson; applied in *Pennington v Waine* [2002] 1 W.L.R. 2075.
[4] *Re Tyler* [1967] 1 W.L.R. 1269; *Grey v IRC* [1960] A.C. 1; above, para.3–008.
[5] Below, para.4–013.

is sufficiently manifested, B will become equitable and beneficial owner. A holds on trust for B.

iii. Declaration of Self as Trustee. X may declare that he holds **4–005** the property on trust for B. In this situation all that is necessary is a declaration of trust in favour of B. There is no problem of the legal estate being vested in the trustee. It was, and remains, in X, who is the trustee, holding on trust for B. These three situations should be borne in mind in the discussion which follows.

C. Contracts to Convey or to Create a Trust

Situations (ii) and (iii) above concern the creation of trusts in the **4–006** strict sense. B in each case will obtain an equitable proprietary interest. In such a situation, it is immaterial whether B gave consideration or not. A gift confers title just as effectively as a sale.

If, however, the transaction in question had been *in*effective to transfer the legal title from X to B in situation (i), what is B's position? If B gave no consideration there is nothing more that he can do; the gift fails, just as it would fail if a Christmas present were promised and not given. Equity will not assist a volunteer. If B gave consideration, the position is different. B could either sue X for damages for breach of contract, or, in appropriate circumstances, obtain specific performance of the contract.[6] If, in situation (ii), B gave consideration for any contract by X to convey to A on trust for B, or—more realistically, for this question usually arose in connection with marriage settlements—if B is treated as being within the marriage consideration,[7] B can compel A to take proceedings against X, either to obtain the property or damages for breach, and to hold the property or the damages on the trusts declared. Thus B, not being a volunteer, is entitled to enforce the contract; and, in accordance with the principle that equity considers as done that which ought to be done, may be treated as entitled in equity to the property which was the subject of the contract.[8] Even if B is a volunteer, he may now enforce the contract between X and A in his own right in certain circumstances under the Contracts (Rights of Third Parties) Act 1999.[9]

D. Beneficial Owner under a Trust

Reference should also be made here to the way in which an **4–007** equitable owner (the legal title being in trustees) may create interests in favour of other persons out of his equitable interest.

[6] Below, Ch.24.
[7] Below, para.4–017.
[8] See *Pullan v Koe* [1913] 1 Ch. 9; below, para.4–017.
[9] Below, para.4–016.

In *Timpson's Executors v Yerbury*,[10] Romer L.J. said:

"Now the equitable interest in property in the hands of a trustee can be disposed of by the person entitled to it in favour of a third party in any one of four . . . ways. The person entitled to it (1) can assign it to the third party directly; (2) can direct the trustees to hold the property in trust for the third party (see per Sargant J. in *Re Chrimes*[11]); (3) can contract for valuable consideration to assign the equitable interest to him; or (4) can declare himself to be a trustee for him of such interest."

Category (2), as Lord Evershed pointed out in *Grey v IRC*[12]:

"[A]ppears . . . to have been regarded as distinct from both an assignment, on the one hand, and a declaration of trust of the interest in the beneficial owner's hands, on the other."

We know however that such a direction is a "disposition" within Law of Property Act 1925 s.53, according to the wide construction put upon that word by the House of Lords,[13] and required therefore to be in writing. If the beneficial owner authorises the trustees to transfer the legal estate to donees, then the beneficial interest passes to the donees without express mention.[14]

It should also be noted that category (4) creates what is usually called a sub-trust; a situation in which A holds property on trust for B, and B declares himself to be trustee of his interest for C. Unless B has specific duties to perform, he is a bare trustee and apparently drops out, the original trustee A holding on trust for C.[15] Where, however, V contracted to sell land to P, X having provided P with the purchase money, it was held that P did not "drop out".[16] V held on trust for P under a constructive trust arising on a contract for the sale of land,[17] and P held on resulting trust for X as provider of the purchase price.[18] P remained a trustee within the Charging Orders Act 1979,[19] so that a charging order made against his interest in the land as trustee was valid.

---

[10] [1936] 1 K.B. 645 at 664; *Zeital v Kaye* [2010] W.T.L.R. 913.
[11] [1917] 1 Ch. 30.
[12] [1958] Ch. 690 at 709 CA.
[13] *Grey v IRC* [1960] A.C. 1; above, para.3–008.
[14] *Vandervell v IRC* [1967] 2 A.C. 291; above, para.3–009.
[15] *Grainge v Wilberforce* (1889) 5 T.L.R. 436; above, para.3–011.
[16] *Nelson v Greening & Sykes (Builders) Ltd, The Times*, January 22, 2008; above, para.3–008.
[17] Below, para.12–035.
[18] Below, para.10–033.
[19] s.2(1)(b)(ii).

2. TRANSFER OF THE PROPERTY TO TRUSTEES UPON TRUST

A. Legal Interests

The classic statement of the law relating to the requirement of a **4–008** transfer of the property to trustees is that of Turner L.J. in *Milroy v Lord*[20]:

> "I take the law of this Court to be well settled, that, in order to render a voluntary settlement valid and effectual, the settlor must have done everything which, according to the nature of the property comprised in the settlement, was necessary to be done in order to transfer the property and render the settlement binding upon him. He may, of course, do this by actually transferring the property to the persons for whom he intends to provide, and the provision will then be effectual, and it will be equally effectual if he transfers the property to a trustee for the purposes of the settlement, or declares that he himself holds it in trust for those purposes; and if the property be personal, the trust may, as I apprehend, be declared either in writing or by parol; but, in order to render the settlement binding, one or other of these modes must, as I understand the law of this court, be resorted to, for there is no equity in this court to perfect an imperfect gift. The cases, I think, go further to this extent, that if the settlement is intended to be effectuated by one of the modes to which I have referred, the Court will not give effect to it by applying another of those modes. If it is intended to take effect by transfer, the court will not hold the intended transfer to operate as a declaration of trust, for then every imperfect instrument would be made effectual by being converted into a perfect trust."

The transfer to the trustees must accord with the rules applicable to the property concerned. Legal estates in land must be transferred by deed,[21] equitable interests[22] and copyright[23] by writing (which may include an electronic document[24]), chattels by deed of gift[25] or by an intention to give coupled with a delivery of possession,[26] a bill

---

[20] (1862) 4 De G.F. & J. 264 at 274–275. For the position where the trustee disclaims, see *Mallott v Wilson* [1903] 2 Ch. 494; P. Matthews [1981] Conv. 141.

[21] LPA 1925 s.52(1). Registration of freeholds and leases of over seven years is necessary under the registered title system; LRA 2002. See *Mascall v Mascall* (1985) 49 P. & C.R. 119, below, para.4–012.

[22] LPA 1925 s.53(1).

[23] Copyright Designs and Patents Act 1988 s.90(3).

[24] Above, para.3–006.

[25] Thus it has been held that a trust of a painting was validly constituted without physical delivery to the trustees (one of whom was in Ireland) on the ground that the formal declaration of trust transferred the property in the painting to the trustees, each of whom had a copy of the document and agreed to act; *Jaffa v Taylor Gallery Ltd, The Times*, March 21, 1990.

[26] *Kilpin v Raltey* [1892] 1 Q.B. 582; *Re Cole* [1964] Ch. 175; *Thomas v Times Book Co Ltd* [1966] 1 W.L.R. 911; J. Thornely (1953) 12 C.L.J. 355; A. Diamond (1964) 27 M.L.R. 357.

of exchange by endorsement,[27] and shares by the appropriate form of transfer followed by registration.[28] Since July 1996 it has been possible to transfer shares in most quoted companies electronically, thereby avoiding the need for transfer forms and share certificates, but this does not detract from the principle that legal title passes only on registration.[29]

In *Milroy v Lord*,[30] a settlor executed a voluntary deed purporting to transfer shares in the Bank of Louisiana to Samuel Lord to be held on trust for the claimant. The shares, however, could only be transferred by the appropriate transfer form followed by registration of the name of the transferee in the books of the Bank. Lord held a power of attorney to act on behalf of the settlor, and it would have enabled him to take all necessary further steps to obtain registration. But this was not done. The Court of Appeal in Chancery held that there was no trust, although the intention clearly was to benefit the intended beneficiary.

4–009	On the other hand, once the property has been vested in the trustees, and the trusts declared, the trust is constituted, and the settlor is unable to reclaim the property, even though the beneficiaries may be volunteers.[31] It has been held that the trust may be constituted where the property is vested in the trustees, even though it reached them in a capacity distinct from their office as trustees of the trust in question.

In *Re Ralli's Will Trusts*,[32] a testator left his residuary estate on trust for his widow for life and then for his two daughters Irene and Helen. Helen's marriage settlement included a covenant to settle existing and after-acquired property in favour of (in the events which happened) volunteers. Helen predeceased her mother and so never transferred her remainder interest pursuant to her covenant. The claimant was the trustee both of the testator's will and also of Helen's marriage settlement. Buckley J. had to

[27] Bills of Exchange Act 1882 s.31; see, however, Cheques Act 1957 ss.1, 2.
[28] See Companies Act 2006 ss.770–772 (re-enacting earlier legislation); Stock Transfer Act 1963 s.1.
[29] This is the CREST system. It is not compulsory for companies or investors to use it. It is designed for speedy and economic transfer. Gilts were taken into CREST in 2000. See also Open-Ended Investment Companies (Amendment) Regulations 2009 (SI 2009/553); Unit Trusts (Electronic Communications) Order 2009 (SI 2009/555).
[30] (1862) 4 De G.F. & J. 264.
[31] *Paul v Paul* (1882) 20 Ch.D. 742; *Jefferys v Jefferys* (1841) Cr. & Ph. 138; *Re Ellenborough* [1903] 1 Ch. 697 (the assets received under her sister's will); *Re Bowden* [1936] Ch. 71; similarly for voluntary covenants to settle: *Re Adlard* [1954] Ch. 29. For the current position with regard to the enforcement of the covenant, see Contracts (Rights of Third Parties) Act 1999, below, para.4–016.
[32] [1964] Ch. 288.

decide on what trusts the residue was held. He concluded, as one ground for his decision, that the vesting of the property in the trustee was sufficient to constitute the trusts of the remainder interest even though the property came to him in his other capacity as trustee of the will.

> "The circumstance that the [claimant] holds the fund because he was appointed a trustee of the will is irrelevant. He is at law the owner of the fund, and the means by which he became so have no effect upon the quality of his legal ownership."[33]

This may be contrasted with *Re Brooks' Settlement Trusts*,[34] where a settlor made a voluntary settlement under which he purported to assign after-acquired property to the trustee, Lloyds Bank. Subsequently a power of appointment under another settlement of which Lloyds Bank was also trustee was exercised in the settlor's favour. It was held that the settlor was entitled to be paid the appointed sum by the Bank because the assignment of a mere expectancy was ineffective. Thus the beneficiaries had no claim.

B. Equitable Interests

The same general principle applies where the settlor's interest is equitable. A correct transfer of the equitable interest to a trustee upon properly declared trusts is necessary to create a trust of that equitable interest. A disposition of an equitable interest must, as has been seen, be in writing.[35] In *Kekewich v Manning*,[36] shares were held on trust for A for life and then for B. B assigned his equitable interest in remainder to trustees to hold on certain trusts, and this was held to create a trust of the equitable interest in remainder.

4–010

C. Act of Third Party Required to Perfect Title

Difficulties can arise where the act of a third party is necessary to perfect the transfer of legal title. The problem commonly involves shares, the legal title to which is transferable by the execution of the form of transfer required by the company's articles, followed by registration in the share register of the company.[37] If the transaction is for consideration, the purchaser becomes equitable owner of the shares from the date of the execution of the document of transfer, and is entitled to dividends declared after that date.[38] The position is

4–011

---

[33] [1964] Ch. 288 at 301.
[34] [1939] 1 Ch. 993, not cited in *Re Ralli's WT*.
[35] LPA s.53(1)(c); above, para.3–006.
[36] (1851) 1 De G.M. & G. 176; *Gilbert v Overton* (1864) 22 H. & M. 110.
[37] See Companies Act 2006 ss.770–772; Stock Transfer Act 1963 s.1.
[38] *Black v Homersham* (1878) 4 Ex.D. 24; *Re Wimbush* [1940] Ch. 92.

the same where shares are transferred electronically.[39] The purchaser becomes equitable owner on generation of the instruction to the registrar and legal owner on registration.

The transfer of shares in a private company is restricted, and the Articles usually provide that the directors may refuse to register the transfer. A difficult situation arises where a settlor makes a voluntary settlement of such shares, executing a transfer which purports to transfer the shares to trustees to be held on the trusts of the settlement. The expectation is that the registration of the transfer will follow and the trust become constituted. The directors however may refuse to register the transfer. In that case, under the strict rule of *Milroy v Lord*,[40] the trust would be incompletely constituted. The validity of the trust would be dependent upon the uncontrollable discretion of the directors. Even if they do register it, the date on which this happens may be crucial in determining whether the transfer is liable to inheritance tax at the full death rate applicable to gifts made within three years of death or at the lower rates for gifts made three to seven years before death.[41]

In *Re Rose*,[42] a settlor by voluntary deed transferred shares in a private company to trustees to be held on certain trusts. The directors, who had power to refuse to register transfers, registered this transfer some two months later. The settlor died at a time at which the shares would be treated as part of his estate for tax purposes if the date of the transfer were the date of registration; but would not be so treated if the date was the date of the deed. The Court of Appeal held that the relevant date was that of the deed; for the settlor had at that time done everything possible to divest himself of the property by executing the instrument and delivering it to the transferees. All that was needed in addition was the formal act of registration by the third party.

Evershed M.R. went so far as to say that after the execution of the transfer, the settlor held the shares as trustee for the beneficiaries.[43] He did not however give any convincing answer to the Crown's argument that, consistently with *Milroy v Lord*,[44] the transfer was

---

[39] Above, para.4–008.

[40] (1862) 4 De. G.F. & J. 264. There, however, the correct transfer form was not used.

[41] IHTA 1984 s.7; below, para.9–009.

[42] [1952] Ch. 499; *Re Fry* [1946] Ch. 312; *Re Rose* [1949] Ch. 78; *Re Paradise Motor Co Ltd* [1968] 1 W.L.R. 1125; *Vandervell v IRC* [1967] 2 A.C. 291 at 330.

[43] "If a man executes a document transferring all his equitable interest, say, in shares, that document, operating, and intended to operate, as a transfer, will give rise to and take effect as a trust; for the assignor will then be a trustee of the legal estate in the shares for the person in whose favour he has made an assignment of his beneficial interest." [1952] Ch. 499 at p.510. See Oakley, *Constructive Trusts*, 3rd edn, p.318, suggesting that a constructive trust arises in these circumstances.

[44] (1862) 4 De G.F. & J. 264.

either a valid transfer at law; or a declaration of trust; or it was ineffective. The settlor clearly did not intend to declare himself a trustee,[45] and would have been surprised to have been told that, if the directors had refused to register, he was unable to withdraw from the transfer because he was a trustee; or that he was required to exercise the voting powers conferred by the shares in the interests of the beneficiaries.[46] *Re Rose* thus creates a number of theoretical difficulties,[47] although one rationalisation may be that it is possible for legal and equitable title to be separated without all the incidents of trusteeship.[48] It is submitted, however, that it is an eminently sensible decision in a context in which the liability to tax may be affected by the date on which the transfer is treated as being effective. *Re Rose* can be contrasted with *Re Fry*,[49] where the donor was domiciled abroad, and had not, at the critical time, done everything that was needed of him, as he had not obtained Treasury consent to the transfer.

The *Re Rose* principle was applied to a transfer of registered land **4–012** in *Mascall v Mascall*,[50] where a father executed a transfer of a house to his son, a volunteer, and handed over the land certificate. After the transfer had been sent to the Inland Revenue for stamping, and returned, the father (having fallen out with the son), sought a declaration that the transfer was ineffective. The son had not yet sent the documents to the Land Registry in order to become registered proprietor and had, therefore, not acquired legal title.[51] It was held that the gift was complete. The father had done all that he could, as the application to the Land Registry could be made by the son, from whom the father had no right to recover the transfer and land certificate. In the case of the assignment of a lease which has not been completed by registration, the *Re Rose* principle would apply as between assignor and assignee, but has been held not to affect the legal position as between the assignor and the landlord.[52] Thus the assignor retained the right to exercise an option to terminate conferred by the lease. The issue was not the ownership of the equitable interest, which would be resolved by *Re Rose*, but the location of the

---

[45] See *Jones v Lock* (1865) L.R. 1 Ch.App. 25.

[46] *Butt v Kelsen* [1952] Ch. 197; cf. *Re George Whichelow Ltd* [1954] 1 W.L.R. 5.

[47] L. McKay (1976) 40 Conv.(N.S.) 139, criticising the reasoning. *Re Rose* was described in *Rowlandson v National Westminster Bank Ltd* [1978] 1 W.L.R. 798 at 802 as a "gloss" on the principle of perfect gifts.

[48] S. Lowrie and P. Todd (1998) 57 C.L.J. 46, relying on *Westdeutsche Landesbank Girozentrale v Islington LBC* [1996] A.C. 669 at 706–707.

[49] [1946] Ch. 312 (he had applied for consent, but further information might have been required); *Re Transatlantic Life Assurance Co Ltd* [1980] 1 W.L.R. 79.

[50] (1985) 49 P. & C.R. 119. cf. *Corin v Patton* (1990) 169 C.L.R. 540 (gift incomplete where transferor had not requested mortgagee to produce land certificate, without which transferee could not be registered).

[51] The current provision is LRA 2002 s.6.

[52] *Brown & Root Technology Ltd v Sun Alliance and London Assurance Co Ltd* (1998) 75 P. & C.R. 223.

legal estate, from which derived the legal rights and duties of the
landlord and tenant.

The principle that "the donor has done everything he can" is not
absolute: it is always possible to find something more that he could
have done. The Court of Appeal reviewed the authorities in *Pennington v Waine*,[53] where the donor had executed a share transfer
form concerning shares in a private company in favour of her
nephew, with the intention that he should become director of the
company (which position required him to own shares). The share
transfer form was not delivered to the nephew, nor had he been
registered as shareholder by the date of her death a few weeks later.
The donor had sent the transfer form to her agent, the company
auditor, who told the nephew that he need take no further steps with
regard to the shares. The nephew signed a form of consent to act as
director and was duly appointed. It was held that the shares did not
form part of the donor's estate on her death, as there had been an
equitable assignment in favour of the nephew.

The Court of Appeal did not seek to detract from the principle that
equity will not assist a volunteer to perfect an imperfect gift. The
execution of the share transfer form took effect as an equitable
assignment in circumstances where it was clear that the donor intended it to have immediate effect. Clarke L.J. reached his decision
primarily by relying on s.1(1) of the Stock Transfer Act 1963, which
provides that shares may be transferred by an instrument in writing,
with no reference to any requirement of delivery of the instrument to
the transferee. Arden L.J., with whom Schiemann L.J. agreed,
placed more emphasis on the principle that a gift is complete in
equity if the stage has been reached where it would be unconscionable to retract. In the present case it would have been unconscionable
as the donor had told the donee of the transfer and he had been
appointed director on the strength of it. In these circumstances delivery of the form to the transferee was not prerequisite to the validity
of the transfer as an equitable assignment.

This decision may be viewed as a hard case making bad law. It
has been rightly criticised as leading to uncertainty as to whether a
failed absolute gift will be treated as a perfect gift of the beneficial
interest. The "unconscionable" test creates uncertainty as to
whether and when (essential for tax and other purposes) the beneficial interest passes.[54] It is difficult to disagree with the view that the
court has given itself an unfettered discretion to give effect to ineffective transactions if it would be unconscionable not to do so.[55] The

[53] [2002] 1 W.L.R. 2075.
[54] H. Tjio and T. Yeo [2002] L.M.C.L.Q. 296; D. Ladds (2003) 17 T.L.I. 35. See also P.
Clarke All E. R. Rev. 2002, p.229; A. Doggett (2003) 62 C.L.J. 263; H. Delany and D. Ryan
[2008] Conv. 401 at 430. The decision is given a cautious welcome in J. Garton [2003] Conv.
364. See also C. Tham [2006] Conv. 411 suggesting a contractual analysis.
[55] M. Halliwell [2003] Conv. 192.

case is not easy to distinguish from *Jones v Lock*,[56] but is clearly distinguishable from *Choithram (T) International SA v Pagarini*,[57] with which Arden L.J. drew an analogy. However, *Pennington v Waine*[58] was recently distinguished in *Zeital v Kaye*,[59] where the Court of Appeal took a more orthodox approach. A held a share in a company on trust for B, and the question was whether B had transferred his equitable interest to C, a woman with whom he had a relationship after separating from his wife some twenty years previously. B had given her a stock transfer form (which A had signed, leaving the date and transferee blank), but without adding her name as transferee. This was not effective to transfer B's equitable interest, as it was neither an assignment nor a declaration of trust.[60] C relied on the *Re Rose*[61] principle, but it did not apply because B had not done all he could. Although C could have completed the blank transfer form, B had not given her the share certificate, which was necessary for registration as a shareholder. (It was lost, but B had not asked A to obtain a replacement.) The share certificate had not been handed over in *Pennington*, but in that case the certificates were held by the company, and so no question arose as to the donor's failure to deliver the certificate to the donee. Thus B's widow and daughters were entitled to the share on B's death intestate. The case may be contrasted with *Shah v Shah*,[62] where X sent a letter to Y, stating that: "I am as from today holding 4,000 shares in the above company for you". X enclosed a signed undated stock transfer form but no share certificate. The letter was held to be a declaration of trust, so it was not necessary to consider the other aspects. In a recent review of these decisions Briggs J. doubted whether the existing rules about the circumstances in which equity will or will not perfect an apparently imperfect gift of shares serve any clearly identifiable or rational policy objective.[63]

3. DECLARATION OF SELF AS TRUSTEE

There is no difficulty if a settlor wishes to declare himself trustee of   **4–013**
some or all of his property. All that is needed is a manifestation of an intention to declare a trust; and, if the property is land, evidence in writing of such intent. The settlor:

---

[56] (1865) L.R. 1 Ch. App. 25; below.
[57] [2001] 1 W.L.R. 1; below, para.4–014.
[58] [2002] 1 W.L.R. 2075.
[59] [2010] W.T.L.R. 913; G. Griffiths [2010] Conv. 321.
[60] Above; para.4–007.
[61] [1952] Ch. 499; above, para.4–011.
[62] [2011] W.T.L.R. 519.
[63] *Curtis v Pulbrook* [2011] 1 B.C.L.C. 638.

"[N]eed not use the words, 'I declare myself a trustee,' but he must do something which is equivalent to it, and use expressions which have that meaning; for, however anxious the Court may be to carry out a man's intention, it is not at liberty to construe words otherwise than according to their proper meaning."[64]

It is necessary to show, not only an intention to benefit someone; but an intention to be trustee for that person.

"Men often mean to give things to their kinsfolk, they do not often mean to constitute themselves trustees. An imperfect gift is no declaration of trust."[65]

The issues which arise in this section are quite different from those discussed in Pt 2. There, the question was whether the property was vested in the trustee. Here, there is no such problem; if there is a trust the settlor is trustee (or may be one of co-trustees, as mentioned below[66]). The question here is whether a trust has properly been declared. The problems usually arise in cases where the settlor's intention was to make a gift to a donee but the gift failed, and the question is whether the intent to benefit the donee can be construed as a declaration of trust in his favour.

The rule is that equity will not construe a void gift as a declaration of trust. What is needed is a manifestation of an intention to declare a trust.

In *Jones v Lock*,[67] a father, being chided for failing to bring a present from Birmingham for his baby son, produced a £900 cheque payable to himself, saying: "Look you here, I give this to baby; it is for himself." He gave it to the child, who was about to tear it up, and the father took it away and put it in a safe. The father died and the cheque was found among his effects.

The question was whether the child was entitled to the cheque or whether it formed part of the father's estate. It would belong to the father unless he gave it to the child, or declared himself trustee of it. Clearly, he had not given it to the child, because a gift of a

---

[64] *Richards v Delbridge* (1874) L.R. 18 Eq. 11 at 14, per Jessel M.R.

[65] Maitland, p.72.

[66] *Choithram (T) International SA v Pagarani* [2001] 1 W.L.R. 1 (PC); below, para.4–014. See also *Wallbank and Wallbank v Price* [2008] 2 F.L.R. 501; J. Brown [2008] Conv. 336; *Stablewood Properties Ltd v Amrit Virdi* [2011] W.T.L.R. 723 (declaration of trust subject to security interest).

[67] (1865) L.R. 1 Ch.App. 25. See also *Pappadakis v Pappadakis, The Times*, January 19, 2000 (invalid assignment failing to identify assignee who would hold on trust could not operate as declaration of trust).

non-bearer cheque requires endorsement.[68] Had he declared himself trustee? No. He intended to give it to the child. There was no evidence that he intended to declare himself trustee of it, and to burden himself with a trustee's duties, including that of investing it and being personally liable for failure to do so. There was no such intention here; nor was there an effective gift. The child took nothing.

Similarly, in *Richards v Delbridge*,[69] a grandfather who was entitled to leasehold premises endorsed on the lease a memorandum as follows: "This deed and all thereto belonging I give to [my grandson] from this time forth, with all the stock-in-trade." He delivered the document to the grandson's mother, and then died, making no mention of the property in his will. Jessel M.R. held that no interest passed; not at law, because the endorsement was ineffective to assign a lease; and not in equity, for the words were inappropriate for the declaration of a trust.

These cases may be contrasted with the situation where the legal owner has not attempted to transfer the property to the third party, but has shown that he considers himself to hold the property as trustee for the third party. Whether or not, in any case, the evidence is sufficient will depend on the facts; it has been held that the intent can be implied from conduct where the evidence is clear.[70]

So in *Paul v Constance*[71] the conduct of the parties was suffi- **4–014**
cient to establish an intention to declare a trust. Mr Constance was separated from his wife, and lived with the claimant, Mrs Paul. He received, as damages for an injury suffered at work, a cheque for £950 and he and Mrs Paul decided to put it into a deposit account at Lloyds Bank. The account was opened in the name of Mr Constance only; because he and Mrs Paul felt an embarrassment in opening a joint account in different names. Mr Constance indicated on many occasions that the money was as much Mrs Paul's as his. On his death, the widow claimed the money in the account as part of her husband's estate. The question was whether the account was owned beneficially by Mr Constance, or whether, on the particular facts, he had shown an intention to hold the

---

[68] Under the Cheques Act 1992 s.1, cheques are no longer transferable if they are crossed and the words "account payee" appear.

[69] (1874) L.R. 18 Eq. 11.

[70] *New, Prance and Garrard's Trustee v Hunting* [1897] 2 Q.B. 19. See also *Re Kayford Ltd* [1975] 1 W.L.R. 279; *Re Chelsea Cloisters Ltd* (1981) 41 P. & C.R. 98; above, para.2–010.

[71] [1977] 1 W.L.R. 54; convincingly criticised in Heydon, Gummow and Austin, *Cases and Materials on Equity and Trusts*, 4th edn, p.142: "The law of express trusts normally requires an intention to benefit the *cestui que trust* specifically by way of trust—a mere intention to benefit him in some way is insufficient." See also *Choithram (T) International SA v Pagarani* [2001] 1 W.L.R. 1, where words indicating an outright gift were construed in the context as words of a gift to be held on the trusts of a settlement created by the donor.

property as trustee for Mrs Paul, or as trustee for the two of them in equal shares. The Court of Appeal found that the evidence was sufficient to support an intention in Mr Constance to declare himself a trustee; although it was not easy to pinpoint a specific moment of declaration.[72] Mrs Paul was thus able to recover half of the proceeds of the account.

This decision was applied in *Rowe v Prance*,[73] where the defendant, a wealthy man who was conducting an extra-marital relationship with the claimant, Mrs Rowe, acquired an ocean-going boat which was registered in his sole name. After the relationship broke down, Mrs Rowe succeeded in her claim to a half share. The defendant had repeatedly referred to the boat as "our boat", had assured Mrs Rowe that her interest in the boat was her security, and had felt bound to give an explanation (although absurd[74]) as to why he alone could be registered as owner. As no formalities were required in the case of personalty, the trust had been sufficiently declared. On the other hand, where a house in the joint names of a mother and father was transferred, pursuant to a consent order, to the mother "for the benefit of the child", no trust was created for the child, who had since fallen out with her mother and left home.[75]

An unusual situation arose in *Choithram (T) International SA v Pagarani*,[76] where a wealthy man who had just executed a trust deed establishing a charitable foundation made an oral statement along the lines of "I now give all my wealth to the foundation". He instructed his accountant to transfer his assets to the trustees, of whom he was one, but he died before this was done. The Privy Council held that, as the settlor was one of the co-trustees, the trust was constituted by his declaration of trust of property vested in him, even though the property had not yet been vested in the co-trustees. In such a case the settlor was obliged to give effect to the trust by transferring the property into the names of all the trustees. While the words used in the present case were normally appropriate to an outright gift, in the context they could only mean that the settlor was giving his wealth to the trustees of the foundation, to be held on the trusts set out in the trust deed. His words, therefore, amounted to a declaration of trust.

---

[72] This could cause problems. See Heydon, Gummow and Austin, at p.142.

[73] [1999] 2 F.L.R. 787.

[74] He stated that the claimant could not be registered as she did not possess a master's certificate.

[75] *Re B (Child: Property Transfer)* [1999] 2 F.L.R. 418.

[76] [2001] 1 W.L.R. 1; J. Hopkins (2001) 60 C.L.J. 483; C. Rickett [2001] Conv. 515; P. Clarke All E.R. Rev. 2001, p.265. See also *Shah v Shah* [2011] W.T.L.R. 519; above para.4–012.

A lenient view of the requirements of a declaration of trust was **4–015** taken by the Court of Appeal in *Re Vandervell's Trusts (No.2)*.[77] An option to purchase certain shares was held by trustees on a resulting trust for Vandervell. The trustees exercised the option, using money from Vandervell's children's settlement. It was held that the shares were henceforth held on trust for the children's settlement. There was no declaration of trust by Vandervell, but such a declaration could be inferred from certain acts of the trustees[78]: first, the use of the money from the children's settlement; secondly, the subsequent payment of the dividends to that settlement; and thirdly, the trustees' notification to the Revenue that they now held the shares on trust for that settlement. The inadequacy of these three acts as establishing a declaration of trust lies in the fact that the second and third merely indicate what the trustees thought the position to be, while the first ignores Vandervell's beneficial ownership of the option. This has already been examined.[79]

It will be noted that it is not necessary that the beneficiary should be aware of the declaration of trust.[80] The beneficiary becomes equitable owner just as he would become legal owner if the property had been conveyed to him.

4. COVENANTS TO SETTLE

If a settlor has neither conveyed the property to trustees nor declared himself a trustee, no trust is created. If he has covenanted by deed to settle the property, the crucial question is whether or not the intended beneficiary can compel him to carry out the covenant and settle it.

A. Contracts (Rights of Third Parties) Act 1999

Formerly the general rule was that a third party could not enforce **4–016** a contract purporting to benefit him. The position was changed by the Contracts (Rights of Third Parties) Act 1999. Section 1 of the Act, which does not affect any right or remedy of a third party that exists apart from the Act,[81] provides that a third party may in his own right enforce a term of the contract if the contract expressly provides that he may, or if the term purports to confer a benefit on him, unless on a proper construction of the contract it appears that

---

[77] [1974] Ch. 269.
[78] Trustees cannot normally declare a trust, but here it was accepted that the option was held on such trusts as might thereafter be declared by Vandervell or the trustees.
[79] Above, para.3–010.
[80] *Middleton v Pollock* (1876) 2 Ch.D. 104; *Standing v Bowring* (1885) 31 Ch.D. 282.
[81] Contracts (Rights of Third Parties) Act 1999 s.7. For transitional provisions, see s.10. The Act implements Law Com. No.242 (1996).

the parties did not intend the term to be enforceable by the third party. The section further provides that the third party must be expressly identified by name, as a member of a class, or as answering a particular description, but need not be in existence when the contract is entered into.[82] Thus a third party could now enforce a covenant to convey property to trustees for his benefit.

Clearly s.1 enables a third party who falls within it to enforce the contract by an action for damages. So far as specific performance is concerned, s.1(5) provides that:

> "[T]here shall be available to the third party any remedy that would have been available to him in an action for breach of contract if he had been a party to the contract (and the rules relating to damages, injunctions, specific performance and other relief shall apply accordingly)."

This might be interpreted as meaning that the third party may obtain specific performance if the subject-matter is such that the remedy of damages would be inadequate.[83] On the other hand, it is established that a volunteer may not obtain specific performance.[84] In *Cannon v Hartley*[85] a volunteer beneficiary who was a party to a deed was able to sue upon it for damages, but would not have been able to obtain specific performance. It is difficult to see why a third party, who has not given consideration, should be in a better position under the 1999 Act.

The law relating to covenants to settle which were entered into prior to the 1999 Act will be considered in the remainder of this part and in Pt 5 of this chapter.

B. Covenants to Settle prior to the Contracts (Rights of Third Parties) Act 1999

4–017   A beneficiary who has given consideration can enforce the covenant by obtaining specific performance; one who has not given consideration cannot do so. Equity will not assist a volunteer.

---

[82] See *Avraamides v Colwill*, *The Times*, December 8, 2006.

[83] Consider the Explanatory Notes to s.1, to the effect that subs.(5) "makes it clear that the courts may award all the remedies which are available to a person bringing a claim for breach of contract to a third party seeking to enforce his rights under subs(1). The normal rules of law applicable to those remedies ... apply to the third party's claim."

[84] Below, para.24–019. See N. Andrews (2001) 60 C.L.J. 353 at 361 for the view that s.1(5) is an exception to the volunteer rule.

[85] [1949] Ch. 213; below, para.4–017. On the distinction between a deed poll and a deed inter partes, and the question whether a non-executing party may enforce, see *Moody v Condor Insurance Ltd* [2006] 1 W.L.R. 1847.

For this purpose, "consideration" has a wider meaning than at common law, in that equity also treats as having given consideration, in the case of a covenant in a marriage settlement, the husband and wife and issue of the marriage.[86] Illegitimate children, children by a former marriage, and children to whom one of the parties stands in loco parentis, cannot normally be included.[87]

In *Pullan v Koe*,[88] a marriage settlement of 1859 settled property on the husband and wife and prospective children, and also contained a covenant by the wife to settle on the same trusts any property she later acquired of the value of £100 and upwards. In 1879 the wife received £285, part of which was invested in bearer bonds, which remained at the bank in the husband's name until his death in 1909. The question was whether the trustees could then take steps to obtain the bonds from his executors and hold them on the trusts of the settlement. It was held that it was their duty to do so.

Indeed, the beneficiaries could have taken action themselves if the trustees had refused to do so. Here, however, the common law action on the covenant was barred by the lapse of time; but the court held that the £285 was impressed with the trust at the moment the wife received it, and that the trust could be enforced against the bonds.

Such a covenant would not however be enforceable in favour of next-of-kin, for they are volunteers.[89] Thus, if there had been no children of the marriage, the next-of-kin would not have been able to enforce the covenant.

Where the covenant is enforced by persons within the marriage consideration, the court may order the covenantor to settle the property in accordance with the covenant[90]; or, as in *Pullan v Koe*,[91] declare that the property is subject to the trusts of the settlement. However where one of the intended beneficiaries is a party[92] to the covenant, even though a volunteer, he may sue for damages, although the equitable remedy of specific performance would not lie.

[86] *Att Gen v Jacobs-Smith* [1895] 2 Q.B. 341. "Issue" includes remoter issue; *MacDonald v Scott* [1893] A.C. 642.

[87] See *Att Gen v Jacobs-Smith* [1895] 2 Q.B. 341; *Rennell v IRC* [1962] Ch. 329 at 341, affirmed [1964] A.C. 173; *Re Cook's ST* [1965] Ch. 902 at 914.

[88] [1913] 1 Ch. 9. See C Rickett (1979) 32 C.L.P. 1 at 4–5.

[89] *Re D'Angibau* (1880) 15 Ch.D. 228; *Re Plumptre's Marriage Settlement* [1901] 1 Ch. 609; *Re Cook's ST* [1965] Ch. 902.

[90] This may have the effect of benefiting volunteers, as in *Davenport v Bishopp* (1843) 2 Y. & C.C.C. 451 (life interest to husband, remainder to volunteers).

[91] [1913] 1 Ch. 9, above.

[92] For the meaning of which, see *Beswick v Beswick* [1968] A.C. 58 at 102.

In *Cannon v Hartley*,[93] a settlement upon a separation, to which the spouses and a daughter were parties, provided that the father should pay to the daughter any sum exceeding £1,000 which he might inherit from his parents. Having inherited, he failed to make the payment. The daughter was a volunteer. She could however sue upon her father's covenant, and recover damages for breach of covenant at common law.

5. ACTION FOR DAMAGES BY THE TRUSTEES. TRUSTS OF CHOSES IN ACTION

4–018 There is no difficulty in enforcing a completely constituted trust of a chose in action.[94] Where a contractual right is held by A on trust for B, A may sue and obtain damages or specific performance on behalf of B[95]; or B may obtain such relief on his own account if A refuses to act, joining A as a co-defendant in the action.[96]

The question is whether this principle can assist a volunteer in the case of a covenant to settle existing or after-acquired property.[97] Such a volunteer may now be able to enforce the covenant directly under the Contracts (Rights of Third Parties) Act 1999.[98] The remainder of this section deals with the position where the covenant was entered into prior to that Act and is unaffected by it. In such a case could not the trustees sue, recover damages, and hold them on trust for the volunteer? Or could not the volunteer argue that there is already a completely constituted trust of the benefit of the covenant, a trust of a chose in action for which they are the beneficiaries, and thus entitled to enforce?

The courts have given volunteers no comfort in this respect. In *Re Pryce*,[99] Eve J. held that the trustees should not be compelled to pursue whatever remedy they may have at law on the covenant, and in *Re Kay's Settlement*,[100] Simonds J. decided that they should be

---

[93] [1949] Ch. 213. See generally M. Macnair (1988) 8 L.S. 172, suggesting that there is some historical support for allowing specific performance of covenants in favour of volunteers.

[94] Below, para.4–020.

[95] *Lloyd's v Harper* (1880) 16 Ch.D. 290.

[96] *Les Affréteurs Réunis Société Anonyme v Leopold Walford Ltd* [1919] A.C. 801; *Parker-Tweedale v Dunbar Bank Plc* [1991] Ch. 12. This exception to the privity rule is less important after the Contracts (Rights of Third Parties) Act 1999. For problems where a trust is declared of a non-assignable contract, see *Barbados Trust Company v Bank of Zambia* [2007] 1 Lloyd's Rep 495; A. Trukhtanov (2007) 70 M.L.R. 848; P. Turner (2008) 67 C.L.J. 23; M. Smith (2008) 124 LQ.R. 517 and [2008] 22 T.L.I. 140; R. Goode [2009] L.M.C.L.Q. 300 at 313–315.

[97] i.e. property which might come subsequently to the settlor. It was common in a marriage settlement for the spouses to covenant to add to the settlement any such property.

[98] Above, para.4–016.

[99] [1917] 1 Ch. 234.

[100] [1939] Ch. 329.

instructed not to do so. In *Re Cook's Settlement Trusts*,[101] Buckley J. refused to allow volunteers to enforce a covenant even though another person had given consideration. These however are all decisions of courts of first instance, and the matter should be analysed more closely.

A. Action by the Trustees

There are certain difficulties which lie in the way of the proposition that the trustees, as parties to the covenant, can sue to recover damages with a view to holding the money received on trust for the (volunteer) beneficiaries. One question is whether the trustee would recover substantial damages in an action at law on the covenant. If he can recover only nominal damages, the action will be of no help to the beneficiary. The general rule is that the claimant may recover in an action for breach of contract damages sufficient to compensate him for his loss. Damages suffered by third parties are not recoverable by the claimant unless, as explained below, the claimant contracted as trustee for the third parties.

4–019

The real question, however, is this: what does the common law regard as the claimant's own loss? In the context of a voluntary covenant to settle, it has been said that:

"[F]or breach of a covenant to pay a certain sum the measure of damages (if that is the appropriate expression) is the certain sum; and for breach of a covenant to transfer property worth a certain sum, it is the value of the property".[102]

There is no doubt that this is the usual rule, as shown by the cases where the volunteer beneficiary is a party to the covenant.[103] Applying this rule, substantial damages should be recoverable at law by B where A covenants to pay a certain sum (or to transfer Blackacre) to B to be held on trust for C. It is no answer at common law to say that B suffers no loss by the breach of such a covenant. At law the position is no different from that of a trustee of a completely constituted trust, who may recover substantial damages for the breach of any contract he may make as trustee even though he personally suffers no loss.

---

[101] [1965] Ch. 902.
[102] D. Elliott (1960) 76 L.Q.R. 100 at 112; J. Barton (1975) 91 L.Q.R. 236 at 238; D. Goddard [1988] Conv. 19 at 21. See also M. Friend [1982] Conv. 280 at 281, agreeing that substantial damages are available on the basis of debt in the case of a voluntary covenant to pay money, but suggesting that this is less clear in the case of specific property other than money.
[103] *Cannon v Hartley* [1949] Ch. 213.

In *Re Cavendish-Browne's Settlement Trusts*[104] the covenantor
was absolutely entitled under two wills to land in Canada, which
he entered into a voluntary covenant to settle. The trustees sued
for damages and were awarded a sum equivalent to the value of
the property which would have come into their hands if the covenant had been performed, to be held on the trusts of the settlement.

This, then, supports the view that a covenantee may recover substantial damages at law for breach of a covenant to settle, although
he has suffered no loss personally. We saw, however, that it was held
in *Re Kay's Settlement*[105] that the covenantee should not sue.

B. Trust of the Benefit of the Covenant

4–020   If there is a completely constituted trust of the benefit of the
covenant, there is no difficulty, as has been seen,[106] in enforcing it,
either by the trustees on behalf of the beneficiaries, or by the beneficiaries themselves. It was said, however, in *Re Cook's Settlement
Trusts*,[107] that a covenant to settle future property cannot be the
subject-matter of a trust, because it does not "create a debt enforceable at law . . . that is to say, a property right."[108] It is submitted that
this restriction is not supportable. Of course, future property itself,
or unascertained property, or a mere hope of acquisition, cannot be
the subject-matter of a trust.[109] But a covenant to pay a sum to be
ascertained in the future is just as good a chose in action as a
covenant to pay a specified sum, and it creates legal property of
value. The subject-matter of the trust is the benefit of the covenant,
the chose in action; not the property which will be obtained by its
performance.[110] There is no difficulty in a trust of a bank account,
which is a chose in action, its value varying with the state of the
account from day to day; nor in a trust of an insurance policy under
which the obligation is to pay an undetermined sum on a future
event which may not happen. The decision in *Re Cook's Settlement
Trusts*[111] is justifiable, however, on the basis that there was no
manifestation of an intention to create a trust of the benefit of the
covenant.

---

[104] [1916] W.N. 341; (1916) 61 S.J. 27. See Underhill and Hayton, *Law of Trusts and Trustees*, 18th edn, p.249 for the view that any damages should be held on resulting trust for the covenantor.

[105] [1939] Ch. 329.

[106] Above, para.4–018.

[107] [1965] Ch. 902.

[108] [1965] Ch. 902 at 913.

[109] Below, para.4–023.

[110] *Williamson v Codrington* (1750) 1 Ves.Sen. 511; *Lloyd's v Harper* (1880) 16 Ch.D. 290.

[111] [1965] Ch. 902.

On the assumption that there is no difficulty in the concept of a trust of the benefit of a covenant, there is nevertheless considerable difficulty in any particular case in deciding whether or not there was an intention to create one.[112] The critical case is *Fletcher v Fletcher*,[113] a decision which presents certain difficulties.

Ellis Fletcher entered into a voluntary covenant with trustees to pay to them £60,000 to be held on trust, in the events which happened, for his illegitimate son Jacob. The trustees did not wish to accept the trust or to receive the money unless they were required to do so. Vice-Chancellor Wigram held that Jacob was able to claim the money, saying that equity would either allow Jacob to use the name of the trustees to sue at law, or to recover in his own name in a court of equity.

Wigram V.C. explained the matter thus:

"I cannot, I admit, do anything to perfect the liability of the author of the trust, if it is not already perfect. This covenant, however, is already perfect. The covenantor is liable at law, and the Court is not called upon to do any act to perfect it. One question made in argument has been whether there can be a trust of a covenant the benefit of which shall belong to a third party; but I cannot think that there is any difficulty in that. . . . the real question is whether the relation of trustee and *cestui que trust* is established in the present case."[114]

There was, then, a trust of the benefit of the covenant, and the beneficiary could enforce it. The crucial question in such a case is whether or not there has been a manifestation of an intention to declare a trust of a chose in action, and this is a matter in which the courts have not, over the years, maintained a consistent approach. There are some difficulties in holding that there was a trust of the chose in action on the facts of *Fletcher v Fletcher*.[115] In the first place, positive evidence of intention is lacking. Ellis Fletcher covenanted that he would pay the £60,000 to trustees "to be held on the following trusts". There is clearly a trust which will affect the money once it is received by the trustee, but no evidence of an intention by either party to create a trust of a chose in action. It cannot be assumed from the fact that the property itself is to be subjected to a trust that an immediate trust of the benefit of the covenant was also intended.

---

[112] *Vandepitte v Preferred Accident Insurance Corp of New York* [1933] A.C. 70; *Re Schebsman* [1944] Ch. 83; *Scruttons Ltd v Midland Silicones Ltd* [1962] A.C. 446.
[113] (1844) 4 Hare 67.
[114] (1844) 4 Hare 67 at 74.
[115] Above, fn.113.

Another question is whether the relevant intention is that of the covenantor (settlor) or the covenantee (trustee). Certainly there was no intention to create a trust of the chose in action on the part of the trustees, if that is the requirement, in *Fletcher v Fletcher*[116]: they did not know about the arrangement, and wished to decline the trust upon hearing of it. A trust of tangible property is declared by the owner of the property, whether he declares himself trustee or transfers it to another on trust. As a general rule, a trust of a debt is declared by the creditor. Thus in *Paul v Constance*[117] the question whether a trust of a bank account had been created was determined by examining the intention of the account-holder (creditor), Mr Constance. It is submitted, however, that a distinction must be drawn between covenants supported by valuable consideration and those which are not. Where there is consideration, the relevant intention to create a trust of the chose in action is that of the covenantee.[118] This will usually be proved by showing that the latter covenanted as trustee for the persons nominated by the covenantor. Where, on the other hand, the covenant is voluntary, as in *Fletcher v Fletcher*[119] the covenantor is the creator of the trust, and if he manifests an intention that the covenantee's rights under the promise shall be held in trust, the covenantee immediately becomes trustee of his rights under the covenant.

C. Specific Performance at the Suit of the Contracting Party

4–021   *Beswick v Beswick*[120] suggests the possibility of another approach to this problem. If the administratrix of old Mr Beswick could in that case obtain specific performance against young Mr Beswick and compel him to perform his promise to make payments to the widow Beswick (a volunteer), can it not be argued that the trustee-covenantees should be able to obtain specific performance of the promise to settle property in favour of volunteers?

It is submitted however that the principle of *Beswick v Beswick*[121] does not apply to the case of voluntary covenants. In that case, old Mr Beswick gave consideration for the promise of young Mr Beswick and had a right of action for damages against him. When the loss was shown to be nil, and the damages therefore nominal, specific performance became available instead. That remedy is available where the legal remedy of damages is inadequate.[122] Where

---

[116] (1844) 4 Hare 67.

[117] [1977] 1 W.L.R. 54; above, para.4–014.

[118] See the insurance cases: *Vandepitte v Preferred Accident Insurance Corp of New York* [1933] A.C. 70; *Swain v The Law Society* [1983] 1 A.C. 598. The question in these cases is whether the policy-holder intended to hold the company's obligation on trust.

[119] Above, fn.113.

[120] [1968] A.C. 58; below, paras 24–047–24–050.

[121] [1968] A.C. 58.

[122] Below, para.24–003.

valuable consideration has been given, the remedy of nominal damages is inadequate, although there is no loss to the contracting party, because the result is the unjust enrichment of the defendant. In the case of a voluntary covenant to pay to trustees the situation (assuming that damages would be nominal[123]) is different. There is no unjust enrichment of the covenantor; nominal damages are therefore adequate. Specific performance in any event is not available to a volunteer, and most trustees are volunteers. Furthermore, the availability of specific performance in *Beswick v Beswick*[124] was not hampered by the principle that trustees are not allowed to sue,[125] because the claimant there was not a trustee.[126]

We have seen that it made no difference in *Re Cook's Settlement Trusts*[127] that one of the parties had given consideration.

In *Re Cook's Settlement Trusts*, property including a Rembrandt was settled on H for life, remainder to his son, F. Under the terms of a resettlement the property became F's absolutely and he covenanted to pay to the trustees the proceeds of sale of the Rembrandt (and other pictures) if sold in H's lifetime, to be held on trust for F's children (volunteers). F gave the Rembrandt to his wife, who wished to sell it. Buckley J. held that the trustees could not enforce the covenant if the Rembrandt were sold.

The decision preceded *Beswick v Beswick*,[128] in which it was **4–022** apparently not cited. A similarity between the two cases appears on close analysis. H entered into a contract for consideration with F, one of the terms of which was that F would confer a benefit on X. If H had sued F, could he succeed, as in *Beswick v Beswick*, by saying that the damages awardable for the breach were inadequate, and that specific performance of the covenant to pay should be decreed in favour of X? The covenant was not in terms to pay to the volunteers, but to the trustees, who would hold the money in trust for them; but this seems immaterial. It is H who, on this reasoning, could sue (although he would not be obliged to) and not the trustees; but the action should not be dependent upon H's physical survival, for his estate, on the reasoning of *Beswick v Beswick*,[129] should be able to do so. It is submitted, however, that *Beswick* will not enable trustees to enforce voluntary covenants to settle.

---

[123] Which may not be correct; above, para.4–019. See, however, *Staden v Jones* [2008] 2 F.L.R. 1931 at 1938.

[124] [1968] A.C. 58.

[125] Above, para.4–018.

[126] She was a personal representative, but the position was exactly the same as if Mr Beswick senior had been in a position to bring the action himself. There was no trust.

[127] [1965] Ch. 902; above, para.4–018.

[128] [1968] A.C. 58.

[129] See also *Coulls v Bagot's Trustee* (1967) 40 A.L.J.R. 471.

That line of reasoning is wholly separate from the question of the enforcement of a covenant in the *Fletcher v Fletcher* type of situation.[130] There, no consideration was given. The covenant was voluntary. It would be enforceable by, or on behalf of the beneficiaries if, and only if, there was found to be a trust of the chose in action. That brings us back to the most basic question of all in relation to the creation of trusts: whether the settlor has manifested an intention to create a trust.

The question whether such an intention can be found has been the subject of much litigation since the privity rule was established. It is well known that the courts have been inconsistent in their decisions, and that, since *Walford's* case,[131] they have been more reluctant to find such an intention. It is doubtful whether it would be found today in a case like *Fletcher v Fletcher*.

All this is of reduced importance now that the Contracts (Rights of Third Parties) Act 1999[132] permits third parties in certain cases to enforce contracts in their own right. The old learning, however, remains relevant in relation to covenants entered into before the Act.

6. TRUSTS OF FUTURE PROPERTY

4–023　A contract for consideration to convey future property to trustees upon trust is valid[133] and, in most cases, specifically enforceable.[134] A voluntary covenant to convey future property to trustees is actionable at law by a beneficiary who is a party to the covenant.[135] If the beneficiary is not a party he may now have rights of enforcement under the Contracts (Rights of Third Parties) Act 1999. A purported assignment of an expectancy[136] cannot be a conveyance because there is nothing to convey. Nor can there be a valid declaration of trust of property not yet existing.[137] If consideration is given for a

---

[130] (1844) 4 Hare 67.

[131] *Les Affréteurs Réunis Société Anonyme v Leopold Walford (London) Ltd* [1919] A.C. 801. See *Swain v The Law Society* [1983] 1 A.C. 598 (the Law Society did not contract as trustee by using words "on behalf of all solicitors" in insurance contract). Outside the contract area, however, an intention to create a trust has been upheld without strong evidence; see *Paul v Constance* [1977] 1 W.L.R. 54, above, para.4–014.

[132] Above, para.4–016. The ambiguous drafting of s.1(5) in relation to the availability of specific performance to the third party has been noted.

[133] *Re Lind* [1915] 2 Ch. 345; *Re Gillott's Settlements* [1934] Ch. 97; *Re Haynes' WT* [1949] Ch. 5.

[134] *Pullan v Koe* [1913] 1 Ch. 9.

[135] *Cannon v Hartley* [1949] Ch. 213; above, para.4–017.

[136] *Williams v CIR* [1965] N.Z.L.R. 345; ("the first £500 of the net income which shall accrue to the assignor... from the Trust."). An assignment of the assignor's life interest under the trust would, of course, have been valid.

[137] cf. *Re Ralli's WT* [1964] Ch. 288 (valid declaration of trust of remainder interest, which is not future property). See also *Simpson v Simpson* [1992] 1 F.L.R. 601 (share of proceeds of sale of cottage which was not yet sold).

purported conveyance, it will be construed as a contract to assign and enforceable as such.[138] But if it is made gratuitously it is a nullity.[139]

In *Re Ellenborough*,[140] the sister of Lord Ellenborough purported to convey by voluntary settlement the property which she would receive under her brother's will. On his death she declined to transfer the property to the trustees, and Buckley J. held that the trustees could not compel her to do so.

A further question is whether such a gratuitous covenant, assignment or declaration in respect of future property can subsequently be treated as an effective declaration of trust if the property does later vest in the trustee. The situation can arise if the property, on materialising, is transferred to trustees without a further declaration of the trusts, or where the property vests in the settlor after he has declared the trusts on which he is to hold it.

We have seen that, prior to the Contracts (Rights of Third Parties) Act 1999, a covenant in a marriage settlement to settle after-acquired property is not enforceable at the suit of the next-of-kin because they are volunteers[141]; and that a deed purporting to convey future property upon trust is ineffective.[142] But if, in either of these cases, the property found its way into the hands of the trustees, it would presumably be held upon the trusts declared in the relevant documents.[143] If the settlor, in either case, conveyed the property to the trustees, that action could be construed as a further declaration of the trusts; but if the property reached the trustees by another route, being conveyed perhaps by the executors of the testator from whom the property came,[144] or coming into the hands of the trustee in a different capacity,[145] the possibility of finding that there was a further declaration of trust is less strong. There appear to be three possible solutions to such a case: that the trustees take beneficially, that they hold on trust for the settlor, or that they hold on the trusts

---

[138] *Re Burton's Settlement* [1955] Ch. 82. See also *Don King Productions Inc v Warren* [2000] Ch. 291 (agreement for value to assign non-assignable contracts took effect as declaration of trust of benefit of contracts). For criticisms, see A. Tettenborn [1999] L.M.C.L.Q. 353; A. Trukhtanov (2007) 70 M.L.R. 848.

[139] *Meek v Kettlewell* (1842) 1 Hare 464; *Re Brooks' ST* [1939] Ch. 993; *Williams v CIR* [1965] N.Z.L.R. 345.

[140] [1903] 1 Ch. 697; cf. *Re Bowden* [1936] Ch. 71; *Re Adlard* [1954] Ch. 29. A purported disclaimer of rights under the will or intestacy of a living person for no consideration is a nullity; *Re Smith* [2001] 1 W.L.R. 1937.

[141] *Re D'Angibau* (1880) 15 Ch.D. 228; *Re Plumptre's Settlement* [1910] 1 Ch. 609.

[142] *Re Ellenborough* [1903] 1 Ch. 697; *Re Brooks' ST* [1939] Ch. 993.

[143] *Re Ellenborough*, above, fn.142. Miss Emily Towry Law had already handed over to the trustees the property which she received under her sister's will; and no attempt was made to recover it; *Re Adlard* [1954] Ch. 29; *Re Ralli's WT* [1964] Ch. 228.

[144] *Re Adlard* [1954] Ch. 29.

[145] *Re Ralli's WT* [1964] Ch. 288.

declared in the previous document. The first is obviously untenable.
The second involves the proposition that the settlor could claim
back in equity property which he had covenanted or purported to
settle.[146] The third avoids the necessity of making the ultimate destination of the property depend upon the route by which it reached the
trustees; it is consistent with the expressed intention of the parties
and appears to be the most satisfactory solution.[147]

Where the property comes to the settlor himself, it is possible for
the court to hold that a previous declaration of trust,[148] followed by
the vesting of the property in him, constitutes the trust. It is clear
that a previous declaration is not of itself sufficient[149]; subsequent
confirmation of a previous declaration is sufficient.[150] In less obvious cases it is no doubt a question of construction to determine
whether or not the settlor is to be taken to have made a subsequent
declaration or to have affirmed a previous one. If he made the
declaration every day, the last declaration being made the moment
before he received the property, this would no doubt be sufficient.
But in the absence of authority, it is unsafe to predict to what extent
an argument on these lines might be acceptable. What is clear in
these cases is that the beneficiaries must show that the trust was
properly declared and properly constituted. There appears to be
nothing intrinsically wrong in holding that the declaration of a trust
may precede its constitution, as in the secret trusts cases.[151]

7. EXCEPTIONS TO THE RULE THAT EQUITY WILL NOT ASSIST A VOLUNTEER

A. The Rule in *Strong v Bird*[152]

4–024   Where an incomplete gift is made during the donor's lifetime, and
the donor appointed the donee as executor,[153] or, in the case of an
intestacy, the donee is appointed administrator,[154] the vesting of the
property in the donee in his capacity as executor or administrator

---

[146] Dicta in *Re Ralli's WT* [1964] Ch. 288, indicate that this could be regarded as unconscionable. cf. *Re Brooks' ST* [1939] Ch. 993.

[147] So held in *Re Ralli's WT*, above, discussed above, para.4–009.

[148] As opposed to a mere covenant to settle or purported assignment; *Re Ellenborough*, above, fn.142.

[149] *Brennan v Morphett* (1908) 6 C.L.R. 22; *Williams v CIR* [1965] N.Z.L.R. 345.

[150] *Re Northcliffe* [1925] Ch. 651.

[151] Ch.5.

[152] See G. Kodilinye [1982] Conv. 14; J. Jaconelli [2006] Conv. 432.

[153] (1874) L.R. 18 Eq. 315. It is sufficient if he is appointed one of the executors; *Re Stewart* [1908] 2 Ch. 251. See also *Blackett v Darcy* [2006] W.T.L.R. 581 (New South Wales Supreme Court held that the rule applied where an imperfect gift was made to joint donees, only one of whom was appointed executor).

[154] *Re James* [1935] Ch. 449; *Re Gonin* [1979] Ch. 16 (where, however, doubts were expressed by Walton J.); (1977) 93 L.Q.R. 485. In *Strong v Bird* itself, the rule was said only to apply to an executor.

may be treated as the completion of the gift, overriding the claims of the beneficiaries under the will or intestacy. Similarly with the release of a debt owed to the donor. At common law the appointment of the debtor as executor released the debt. In equity such a debtor had to account to the estate unless the testator intended in his lifetime to release the debt, such intention continuing until death.

In *Strong v Bird*,[155] B borrowed £1,100 from A, his stepmother, who lived in his house, paying £212 10s. a quarter for board, and it was agreed that the debt should be paid off by a deduction of £100 from each quarter's payment. Deductions of this amount were made for two quarters; but on the third quarter-day and thereafter, A paid the full amount. Thus on her death, some four years later, £900 remained owing. B was appointed her sole executor, and proved the will. Later A's next-of-kin claimed for the balance of the debt. It was held that the appointment of B as executor released the debt.

It is necessary to show that the donor intended to make an immediate lifetime gift[156] (or to release a debt, as the case may be), and also that he had a continuing intention until the date of his death. Thus, an intention to make a testamentary gift is not sufficient.[157] The intention must relate to a specific item of property. It is not sufficient that there was a vague desire to provide something for the donee. In *Re Gonin*[158] a mother wished to leave her house to her daughter, who had given up a career to look after her parents, but thought for some reason that she could not do so because the daughter was illegitimate. Instead, she wrote a cheque for £33,000 in the daughter's favour, which was found after her death. (The cheque could not be cashed, as the bank's mandate to pay is terminated by notice of death.[159]) The daughter became administratrix, but failed in her claim to the house. There was no evidence of a continuing intention that the daughter should have an immediate gift of the house. The drawing of the cheque, as a substitute, pointed the other way. Nor will the rule apply if the testator, subsequently to the act on which the executor relies as establishing the intention to give a chattel, acted inconsistently with that intention by giving or lending the chattel to someone else,[160] nor if the testator, having once had an

---

[155] (1874) L.R. 18 Eq. 315; *Re James* [1935] Ch. 449 (a gift of realty).
[156] cf. *Re Ralli's WT* [1964] Ch. 288, above, para.4–009 (covenant to settle in the future). See also *Simpson v Simpson* [1992] 1 F.L.R. 601 (future gift of proceeds of sale of cottage which was not yet sold).
[157] *Re Stewart* [1908] 2 Ch. 251; *Re Innes* [1910] Ch. 188.
[158] [1979] Ch. 16; (1977) 93 L.Q.R. 488.
[159] Bills of Exchange Act 1882 s.75.
[160] *Re Freeland* [1952] Ch. 110.

intention to give, forgot the gift, and treated the property as his own.[161]

B. *Donatio Mortis Causa*[162]

4–025   **i. The Principle.** A *donatio mortis causa* is a lifetime gift which is conditional upon, and which takes effect upon, death. It must be distinguished on the one hand from a normal lifetime gift, under which title passes immediately to the transferee; and, on the other hand, from a testamentary gift which takes effect under the provisions of a will.[163] It may therefore be regarded as an exception either to the rules governing lifetime gifts, or to the rules governing testamentary gifts. In the present context, we are concerned with the former aspect. But the assistance of equity will not be required by the donee in all cases. Where the subject-matter is a chattel which has been delivered to the donee, the donee's title is complete on the donor's death, no further act being necessary. In the case of a chose in action or land, on the other hand, the donee's title is not complete on the donor's death as the legal title vests in the donor's personal representatives. The donee can seek the assistance of equity to compel the personal representatives to do whatever is necessary to perfect the donee's title.[164] It is in this latter situation that the doctrine of *donatio mortis causa* can be seen as an exception to the rule that equity will not assist a volunteer to perfect an imperfect gift.

The three essentials for a valid *donatio mortis causa* were laid down by Lord Russell C.J. in *Cain v Moon*.[165]

(a) The gift must have been in contemplation, though not necessarily in the expectation, of death[166];

(b) the subject-matter of the gift must have been delivered to the donee[167];

(c) the gift must have been made under such circumstances as to show that the property is to revert to the donor if he should recover.[168]

---

[161] *Re Wale* [1956] 1 W.L.R. 1346.

[162] See Borkowski, *Deathbed Gifts—The Law of Donatio Mortis Causa*, 1999.

[163] See generally Snell, para.24–016. As to availability to meet deceased donor's debts, see S. Warnock-Smith [1978] Conv. 130.

[164] *Duffield v Elwes* (1827) 1 Bli.(N.S.) 497; *Re Lillingston* [1952] 2 All E.R. 184.

[165] [1896] 2 Q.B. 283; *Re Craven's Estate* [1937] Ch. 423 at 426; *Delgoffe v Fader* [1939] Ch. 922. The requirements should be stringent as claims are often made without independent evidence; *Wilson v Paniani* [1996] 3 N.Z.L.R. 378.

[166] *Wilkes v Allington* [1931] 2 Ch. 104.

[167] *Cain v Moon* [1896] 2 Q.B. 283.

[168] *Re Lillingston* [1952] 2 All E.R. 184.

ii. Contemplation of Death. The donor must have been contem- **4–026**
plating death more particularly than by merely reflecting that we
must all die some day. Commonly, *donationes mortis causa* are
made in reference to a particular illness, but the principle applies
equally to other causes such as a hazardous journey,[169] or possibly
even to the contemplation of active service in war.[170] If death occurs, the *donatio* may still be valid even though it comes from a
cause different from that contemplated.

In *Wilkes v Allington*[171] the donor was suffering from an incurable
disease, and made a gift in the knowledge that he had not long to
live; as things turned out, he had an even shorter time than he
imagined, for he died two months later of pneumonia. It was held
that the gift remained valid.

iii. Delivery of Subject-matter. A *donatio mortis causa* will not **4–027**
be valid without a delivery of the property to the donee[172] with the
intention of parting with the "dominion" over it. It will not suffice if
the property is handed over merely for safe custody.[173]

(a) *Chattels.* The donor must hand over either the chattel itself or **4–028**
the means of getting control over it such as, for example, a key to the
box or place where the subject-matter is located.[174] In the case of a
car, it is not necessary that the log book be handed over.[175]

(b) *Choses in Action.* The position is more difficult if the title to **4–029**
the chose in action does not pass by mere delivery of any document.
The donor must hand over such documents as constitute "the essential indicia or evidence of title, possession or production of which
entitles the possessor to the money or property purported to be
given".[176] Thus the delivery of a bank deposit pass-book,[177] a Post
Office Savings Bank-book,[178] national savings certificates[179] or a

---

[169] cf. *Thompson v Mechan* [1958] O.R. 357: the ordinary risks of air travel do not
suffice.

[170] *Agnew v Belfast Banking Co* [1896] 2 I.R. 204 at 221.

[171] [1931] 2 Ch. 104. A valid *donatio mortis causa* cannot be made in contemplation of
suicide; *Re Dudman* [1925] 1 Ch. 553. This is probably not affected by the Suicide Act 1961,
whereby suicide is no longer a crime.

[172] *Ward v Turner* (1752) 2 Ves.Sen. 431.

[173] *Hawkins v Blewitt* (1798) 2 Esp. 663.

[174] *Re Lillingston* [1952] 2 All E.R. 184; *Re Cole* [1964] Ch. 175. It may not suffice if the
donor retains a duplicate key; *Re Craven's Estate* [1937] Ch. 423 at 428. cf. *Woodard v
Woodard* [1995] 3 All E.R. 980 (possible retention of second set of car keys by donor who was
too ill to use them held insignificant).

[175] *Woodard v Woodard*, above, fn.174; J. Martin [1992] Conv. 53.

[176] *Birch v Treasury Solicitor* [1951] Ch. 298 at 311. cf. *Re Weston* [1902] 1 Ch. 680;
Delgoffe v Fader [1939] Ch. 922.

[177] *Birch v Treasury Solicitor* [1951] Ch. 298.

[178] *Re Weston* [1902] 1 Ch. 608. It is otherwise if withdrawals may be made without
producing the book; *Delgoffe v Fader* [1939] Ch. 922.

[179] *Darlow v Sparks* [1938] 2 All E.R. 235.

cheque or promissory note payable to the donor[180] have been held to
create a *donatio mortis causa* of the chose in action represented by
the document in question, so that, on the death of the donor, the
donee can compel the personal representatives to perfect his legal
title.

4–030   (c) *Land*. It had long been considered that land could not be the
subject-matter of a *donatio mortis causa*. Although there was no
English authority directly in point, Lord Eldon had doubted the
possibility.[181] The reason may have been the supposed difficulty of
parting with the "dominion" over land. The matter was reviewed by
the Court of Appeal in *Sen v Headley*.[182]

> The claimant and the deceased, who was separated from his
> wife, had lived together for 10 years until 1964, after which they
> remained on close terms. When the deceased was terminally ill in
> hospital he said to the claimant, "The house is yours, Margaret.
> You have the keys. They are in your bag. The deeds are in the
> steel box." The claimant had always had a set of keys to the
> house. After the deceased died (intestate), she found the box in a
> cupboard, used the key (which the deceased had slipped into her
> bag) and took possession of the deeds.

> The claimant's entitlement to the house was upheld. The title
> deeds were essential indicia of title to the house (which had an
> unregistered title[183]), and had been constructively delivered to her.
> As in the case of a chose in action, parting with dominion over the
> essential indicia of title sufficed. The donor's continuing theoretical
> ability to deal with the property, and his retention of keys to the
> house to which he knew he would not return, did not amount to a
> retention of dominion. Every *donatio mortis causa*, whether or not
> of land, circumvented the Wills Act. The additional statutory for-
> malities for lifetime transfers of land provided no greater obstacle
> than the Wills Act, as the trust on the donor's death was implied or
> constructive. The exception to the formality rule now contained in
> s.53(2) of the Law of Property Act 1925 was not as well developed

---

[180] Even though unendorsed and therefore not transferable by delivery. See *Re Mead* (1880)
15 Ch.D. 651; *Wilson v Paniani* [1996] 3 N.Z.L.R. 378 (where the claim failed because there
was no delivery).

[181] *Duffield v Elwes* (1827) 1 Bli.(N.S.) 497 (where a *donatio mortis causa* of a mortgage of
land was upheld).

[182] [1991] Ch. 425; M. Halliwell [1991] Conv. 307; J. Thornely (1991) 50 C.L.J. 404; P.
Clarke All E.R. Rev. 1991 at 207; G. Kodilinye (1991) 1 Carib.L.R. 100; P. Baker (1993) 109
L.Q.R. 19; M. Pawlowski (1994) 144 N.L.J. 48.

[183] The result would be the same if the land certificate of registered land had been delivered.
However, there is no role for a land certificate under the Land Registration Act 2002. There
are no indicia of title outside the register, and it is doubtful whether handing over the keys to
the property would suffice.

in Lord Eldon's day as now. The policy of the law that formalities were required for the transfer of land should be upheld, but it should be acknowledged that that policy had been substantially modified by the developments in estoppel and constructive trusts.[184] The doctrine of *donatio mortis causa* was anomalous, but to except land from it would be a further anomaly.

iv. The Intention of the Donor. The donor's intention must be to make a gift which is conditional upon death, and revocable upon recovery by the donor. Thus, there is no *donatio mortis causa* if the intention is to make an immediate unconditional gift, even though the gift may fail,[185] nor where the intention is to make a future gift.[186] The conditional nature of the gift need not be expressed, but may be implied from the circumstances.[187]   **4–031**

v. Revocation. In addition to automatic revocation upon the donor's recovery,[188] the donor may revoke expressly, or by recovering dominion over the subject-matter,[189] but he cannot revoke by will, the reason being that the donee's title is complete before the will takes effect.[190] It might be added that the gift fails if the donee predeceases the donor.[191]   **4–032**

vi. Exceptions. It has been held that a *donatio mortis causa* cannot be made of the donor's own cheque[192] or promissory note.[193] The former is merely a revocable mandate to the bank,[194] while a gift of the latter is merely a gratuitous promise, thus they are not the "property" of the donor at all. It may be otherwise if the cheque is actually paid in the donor's lifetime, or before the bank has been informed of his death, or if it has been negotiated for value.[195]   **4–033**

There is some authority that stocks and shares cannot form the subject-matter of a *donatio mortis causa*. It was held in *Ward v Turner*[196] that South Sea annuities could not be the subject-matter of such a gift. The decision may have been based on the inadequacy of the transfer on the facts, but it has been applied in cases concerning

---

[184] See generally M. Howard and J. Hill (1995) 15 L.S. 356.
[185] *Edwards v Jones* (1836) 1 My. & Cr. 226.
[186] *Solicitor to the Treasury v Lewis* [1900] 2 Ch. 812.
[187] *Re Lillingston* [1952] 2 All E.R. 184.
[188] *Staniland v Willott* (1852) 3 Mac. & G. 664.
[189] *Bunn v Markham* (1816) 7 Taunt. 224.
[190] *Jones v Selby* (1710) Prec.Ch. 300 at 303.
[191] *Tate v Hilbert* (1793) 2 Ves. 111 at 120.
[192] *Re Beaumont* [1902] 1 Ch. 886.
[193] *Re Leaper* [1916] 1 Ch. 579.
[194] Only a holder for value can sue.
[195] *Tate v Hilbert* (1793) 2 Ves. 111. See also *Blackett v Darcy* [2006] W.T.L.R. 581 (New South Wales Supreme Court).
[196] (1752) 2 Ves.Sen. 431.

railway stock[197] and building society shares.[198] On the other hand, it has been held that shares in a public company can be the subject-matter of a *donatio mortis causa*.[199] This exception is, therefore, a doubtful one.

C. Statutory Exception; Conveyance to Child

4–034   For the sake of completeness, the position concerning a conveyance to a child is mentioned, although the exception arises from statute and not from the rules of equity.

A conveyance (whether it is for value or not) which purports to convey a legal estate to a child[200] operates as a declaration that the land is held in trust for the child.[201]

D. Proprietary Estoppel

4–035   It has long been settled that promissory estoppel works as a shield and not as a sword.[202] In other words, where one person has been led to act upon the statement of another, he can prevent that other person from acting inconsistently with his statement.

There is another doctrine of long standing, which received its modern formulation in the dissenting speech of Lord Kingsdown in *Ramsden v Dyson*,[203] and a more precise formulation by Fry J. in *Willmott v Barber*,[204] and which can have the effect of creating a proprietary interest in a volunteer although there was no valid gift or trust in his favour. The doctrine is based on acquiescence and has in modern times acquired the name of Proprietary Estoppel.

Most of the modern applications of this doctrine have been in the context of licences to occupy land, and the matter will be fully discussed in Ch.27. It will there be seen that, in applying the doctrine, the court exercises a wide discretion in reaching a solution which is appropriate to the facts of a particular case. Solutions will be seen to vary from finding, in some cases, that a volunteer has acquired a proprietary interest; in others that a mere licence is appropriate, with many variations in between.

---

[197] *Moore v Moore* (1874) L.R. 18 Eq. 474.
[198] *Re Weston* [1902] 1 Ch. 680.
[199] *Staniland v Willott* (1852) 3 Mac. & G. 664.
[200] Who is incapable of holding a legal estate; LPA 1925 s.1(6).
[201] Trusts of Land and Appointment of Trustees Act 1996 Sch.1, para.1 (replacing earlier legislation).
[202] *Combe v Combe* [1951] 2 K.B. 215; Denning L.J. (1952) 15 M.L.R. 1.
[203] (1866) L.R. 1 H.L. 129 at 170.
[204] (1880) 15 Ch.D. 96 at p.105. The current approach was reformulated by the House of Lords in *Thorner v Major* [2009] 1 W.L.R. 776.

CHAPTER 5

TESTAMENTARY GIFTS NOT COMPLYING
WITH THE WILLS ACT 1837, SECRET TRUSTS

1. GENERAL[1]

WE have seen that certain formalities are necessary for the creation   **5–001**
of lifetime trusts of land and for testamentary dispositions. A trust of
land must be evidenced in writing,[2] and all testamentary dispositions
must be in writing and signed by the testator, in the presence of two
or more attesting witnesses present at the same time.[3] We now have
to consider the effect of intended dispositions which fail to comply
with the necessary formalities.

The problem over the enforcement of secret trusts is the fact that
the terms of the trusts are not expressed in a form which complies
with the Wills Act; though, in cases in which the testator's intention
is clear and there is no possibility of doubt or fraud, there is a real
compulsion to enforce the secret trust. The question is whether the
enforcement of the secret trust infringes the Wills Act; or whether
there is recognised doctrine which allows secret trusts to be enforced
in spite of the Wills Act. What should be done, for example, where a
legatee or devisee persuades the testator to make a will in his favour

---

[1] L. Sheridan (1951) 67 L.Q.R. 314; J. Andrews (1963) 27 Conv.(N.S.) 92; R. Burgess
(1972) 36 Conv.(N.S.) 113; P. Critchley (1999) 115 L.Q.R. 631; D. Kincaid [2000]
Conv. 420.

[2] LPA 1925 s.53(1)(b); above para.3–004.

[3] Wills Act 1837 s.9; above, para.3–017.

in reliance on an oral promise to hold on trust for a third party? Or an intestate successor similarly persuades the intending testator not to make a will at all?

We saw in Ch.3 that there is an established principle that equity will not allow a statute to be used as an instrument of fraud. It was there suggested, in the context of formalities for the creation of a lifetime trust, that the better solution was to require the trustee to hold on resulting trust for the settlor where land had been conveyed to the trustee pursuant to an oral declaration of trust for a third party.[4] In the case of wills, it is more complicated; for the solution of a resulting trust for the settlor is less satisfactory; in the case of a living settlor he can think again; with a will he is dead, and a resulting trust for the residuary estate is often what the testator most wished to avoid.

There may be many reasons why a testator wishes to be secret about his testamentary dispositions. In many of the older cases, the reason was that he wished to make a gift to support an illegitimate child and its mother. To include the gift in the will would give unwanted publicity; either among members of the family when its provisions are disclosed, or to any person who makes official application to examine the will. At the present day, the usual reason is that the testator cannot make up his mind upon all the details of the disposition of his estate.[5] By using a secret trust, he is able to escape from the policy of the Wills Act, and to retain for himself a power to make future gifts which do not comply with the Act. There seems to be no good reason why he should be able to do so. It is also common to make a lifetime settlement and then, by will, to add further property to the settlement. The details of the disposition do not in that case appear in the will; but this is not a proper case of a secret trust, but of incorporating the other document into the will by reference.

To create a secret trust the testator will usually arrange to leave a legacy to a trusted friend (often his solicitor) who undertakes to hold it upon certain trusts; or the will may give it to him "to be held upon such trusts as I have declared to him." The question in the former case is whether the friend could keep the legacy for himself; if not, and clearly in the latter case he cannot, who can claim it: the intended beneficiaries, or the estate?

Different considerations apply to these two situations, as will be seen. The former case is known as a fully secret trust; the latter a half-secret trust. Before attempting to answer these questions in the context of secret trusts, it is necessary to mention other ways in

---

[4] Above, para.3–005.
[5] This has been described as an abuse of the doctrine, as secrecy is irrelevant; T. Watkin [1981] Conv. 335. See *Re Snowden* [1979] Ch. 528. A survey of modern levels of usage is discussed in R. Meager [2003] Conv. 203.

which a trust or gift may be created by will although the will does not spell out the precise terms. First, the details may be supplied by extrinsic evidence, the admissibility of which is governed by the principles relating to the construction of wills. Thus if the testator creates a trust in favour of "my grandchildren" or "my partners" their identity can be established by extrinsic evidence. The trust is an ordinary testamentary trust, not a secret trust. What the testator cannot do is to make a gift in favour of persons named in an unattested document, unless that document is incorporated into the will. This leads us to the second way of creating a trust, the details of which do not appear in the will itself. This is the doctrine of incorporation by reference, which bears superficial similarity to the doctrine of half-secret trusts, but which must be distinguished from it.

2. INCORPORATION BY REFERENCE

" . . . [I]f a testator, in a testamentary paper duly executed, refers **5–002** to an existing unattested testamentary paper, the instrument so referred to becomes part of his will; in other words it is incorporated into it; but it is clear that, in order that the informal document should be incorporated in the validly executed document, the latter must refer to the former as a written instrument then existing—that is at the time of execution—in such terms that it may be ascertained."[6]

It is not sufficient that the document was in existence; it must be *referred to as an existing document.* Where the doctrine of incorporation applies, the incorporated document is admitted to probate, and the advantage of secrecy is lost. We will see that this doctrine appears to be in the minds of some judges when they are dealing with cases of secret trusts, and that the rules applicable to this doctrine have sometimes been applied to secret trust cases.[7]

It is common practice to make a bequest to trustees of an existing settlement to be held by them upon the trusts of that settlement. There is no difficulty in doing so if the existing settlement is incorporated by reference in the will.

However, the requirement that only an existing document may be incorporated causes difficulty where a settlement is amended after

---

[6] per Gorell-Barnes J. in *In bonis Smart* [1902] P. 238 at 240. For an unusual example, see *Re Berger (Deceased)* [1990] Ch. 118.

[7] For differing views as to whether this doctrine is the basis of half-secret trusts, see P. Matthews [1979] Conv. 360; D. Hodge [1980] Conv. 341; T. Watkin [1981] Conv. 335; P. Critchley (1999) 115 L.Q.R. 631.

the date of the will. In *Re Jones*,[8] a testamentary gift which attempted to include future alterations of the settlement was held void even though no alterations were made. The testator was there attempting to reserve for himself a power to dispose of his property by future unattested document.[9] Is this so whenever there is a testamentary addition to a settlement which includes a power of revocation or amendment? A strict application of the rules of incorporation by reference would suggest that it is; but the courts have been willing, where possible, to find a construction which will allow the testamentary gift to be upheld.[10]

In *Re Schintz's Will Trusts*,[11] a settlor made a settlement in which he expressly reserved a power to amend or to revoke. His will provided that the residuary estate should be held on the trusts of the settlement and those which might be created by future deeds executed under the power of amendment or revocation, "or as near thereto as the situation will admit." No new trusts were declared. Wynn-Parry J. upheld the gift, finding, as a matter of construction, that the words referring to the future deeds were "otiose and . . . really no more than descriptive of the terms of the settlement."[12] *Re Jones*[13] was distinguished on that ground.

It is not common for a settlor to reserve a power of revocation and amendment, for tax reasons. But the point is important because it is common to include in settlements a provision for the trustees to have power to amend the trusts, or to appoint upon new trusts, or to terminate the settlement; and it is necessary to know the effect of these factors upon a testamentary addition to the settlement.

If the settlement has not been changed at the date of the testator's death, the question is whether the testamentary addition is valid or not. Where the settlement has been altered, there are three possible solutions; first, that the testamentary addition is void; secondly, that it takes effect upon the settlement in its original form; thirdly, that it takes effect upon the settlement as amended. The testator's intention would in most cases be the third choice. He will know of the amendment of the trust made before his death, and which may have been made for tax or for family reasons. But clearly the doctrine of incorporation by reference is incapable of incorporating an amendment made after the date of the will. We have seen that the courts

---

[8] [1942] Ch. 328.
[9] The gift was to the trustees of the settlement, "or any substitution thereof or modification thereof or addition thereto which I may hereafter execute."
[10] *Re Edwards'* WT [1948] Ch. 440.
[11] [1951] Ch. 870.
[12] [1951] Ch. 870 at 877.
[13] [1942] Ch. 328.

can sometimes escape the necessity of holding the gift void. But the second solution is not satisfactory on any argument.

The third solution could be achieved by legislation, such as the Uniform Testamentary Additions to Trusts Act 1960 in the United States, which enables the testamentary gift to be held on the trusts of the settlement in accordance with any amendments made to those trusts prior to the testator's death. In England the matter must be resolved by applying the doctrine of incorporation by reference, with all its limitations.[14]

3. FULLY SECRET TRUSTS

A. Informal Disclosure of the Existence and the Terms of the Trust

Where an absolute gift has taken effect in favour of the donee, it **5–003** is too late to impose a trust. This is so whether the disposition is a lifetime transfer or a gift by will, which takes effect on the testator's death. Thus in *Wallgrave v Tebbs*[15] no secret trust was established where the testator's instructions were not communicated to the legatees, who took absolutely on the face of the will, but were found among his papers after his death. Where, however, a testator makes a gift by will to a legatee in reliance upon the legatee's express or implied[16] undertaking to hold the property upon certain trusts, or to dispose of it in a certain way by his will,[17] it would not be satisfactory to permit the legatee to take advantage of the requirement of testamentary formality and to keep the property for himself.[18] The doctrine applies also where the deceased failed to revoke an existing gift,[19] or where an intestate, in reliance on the undertaking of those entitled on intestacy, failed to make a will.[20] "It is altogether immaterial whether the promise is made before or after the execution of the will, that being a revocable instrument."[21]

If the legatee or intestate successor is not allowed to take the property beneficially, the next question is whether the oral trust

---

[14] For other possibilities, see *Re Playfair* [1951] Ch. 4.

[15] (1855) 2 K. & J. 313; *McCormick v Grogan* (1869) L.R. 4 H.L. 82; *Re Boyes* (1884) 26 Ch.D. 531; *Re Hawkesley's Settlement* [1934] Ch. 384.

[16] "Acquiescence either by words of consent or by silence": per Wood V.C. in *Moss v Cooper* (1861) 1 J. & H. 352 at 366. The communication may be by the testator or by his agent.

[17] *Re Gardner* [1920] 2 Ch. 523; *Re Young* [1951] Ch. 344; *Ottaway v Norman* [1972] Ch. 698.

[18] *Stickland v Aldridge* (1804) 9 Ves.Jr. 516; *Wallgrave v Tebbs* (1855) 2 K. & J. 313 at 320. For the position where the trustee revokes his acceptance during the testator's lifetime, see Underhill and Hayton, *Law of Trusts and Trustees*, 18th edn, p.359.

[19] *Moss v Cooper*, above, fn.16.

[20] *Stickland v Aldridge*, above, fn.18, at 519; J. Fleming (1948) 12 Conv.(N.S.) 28.

[21] per Wood V.C. in *Moss v Cooper* (1861) 1 J. & H. 352 at 367.

should be enforced, or whether the legatee or intestate successor should hold on resulting trust for the estate. The rule in these cases is that the secret trust is enforced in favour of the beneficiary.[22]

This result is justifiable if it is correct to say, as explained below,[23] that a secret trust is enforced because the testator validly declared a trust during his lifetime, and the trust became constituted by the vesting of the property on his death in the trustee. That, as will be seen below, is the modern theoretical explanation of the enforcement of secret trusts. That is not, however, the reason which has been relied on historically to enforce fully secret trusts. Without that theory, the courts were in real difficulty in that the Wills Act laid down the requirements for the creation of a testamentary trust, and those requirements were not met. If, therefore, the trusts were enforced, was not the Wills Act being disregarded? Or, as they said, did the courts not "give the go-by" to it?[24] The courts searched for a justification in not observing the terms of the Wills Act, and found it in the doctrine of fraud: it would be fraudulent if the legatee were to take beneficially in the circumstances. The fraud theory was laid down in the clearest terms by Lord Hatherley L.C. and Lord Westbury in *McCormick v Grogan*,[25] although the House of Lords held in that case that the testator had not intended to impose an obligation on Grogan, the sole executor, and that, therefore, no trust existed on the facts of the case. To base the court's intervention on the ground of fraud could well be a sufficient justification for not applying the Wills Act; but the next step was not so obvious. It would be wrong for the legatee to keep the property, but it was difficult to see how the prevention of fraud would justify the projection forward of the beneficial interest to the beneficiary. As we will see, this matter became all the more clear when the courts were dealing with the question of half-secret trusts, where the testator requires the legatee to take the property as trustee, without saying in the will who the beneficiaries are. In that situation, there was no possibility of the legatee being fraudulent, in the sense of enriching himself, because he was expressed to take as trustee. In *Blackwell v Blackwell*,[26] the leading case on half-secret trusts, the enforcement of the half-secret trust was justified by saying that the intention of the testator was clear, and that it was communicated to and acquiesced in by the legatee. As explained above, the modern view is to justify the enforcement of secret trusts upon the theory that a life-

---

[22] *Thynn v Thynn* (1684) 1 Vern. 296.
[23] Below, para.5–013.
[24] *Re Pitt-Rivers* [1902] 1 Ch. 403 at 407; *Blackwell v Blackwell* [1929] A.C. 318 at 337.
[25] (1869) L.R. 4 H.L. 82.
[26] [1929] A.C. 318.

time trust has been declared and that it is constituted by the testamentary gift to the legatee. There are, as will be seen, some theoretical difficulties in this view also.[27]

B. Proof

Related to the question whether the doctrine is based upon fraud **5–004** is the question of the standard of proof required to establish a secret trust. A high standard of proof is required to prove fraud, and there are dicta in many cases indicating that a secret trust can only be proved where there is "clear evidence",[28] and suggesting that the standard is the same as that required to support the rectification of a written instrument.[29] In *Re Snowden*,[30] however, Megarry V.C. disregarded the historical connection of the doctrine of secret trusts and the requirement of fraud, and laid down that the standard required to prove communication and acceptance is the ordinary civil standard of proof required to establish an ordinary trust.[31] The evidence may, of course, establish an intention to create a trust, and its acceptance by the legatee, without establishing who the beneficiaries were. The legatee would then hold on resulting trust.[32] If questions of fraud or other special factors arose, the standard required would rise. The onus is on the person contending that the trust exists.[33]

C. Disclosure to the Legatee of the Existence of the Trust but not its Terms

If the testator discloses to the legatee the fact that he is to hold the **5–005** legacy on trust, but does not disclose the terms of the trust before his death, the legatee will hold on resulting trust for the estate.[34] The intended trust, not being declared before the death, cannot be enforced. The imposition of the resulting trust will prevent the unjust enrichment of the legatee.

---

[27] Below, para.5–013.

[28] See *McCormick v Grogan* (1869) L.R. 4 H.L. 82 at 87, per Lord Westbury; *Ottaway v Norman* [1972] Ch. 698 at 699.

[29] *Fowler v Fowler* (1859) 4 De G. & J. 250 at 264; *Crane v Hegeman-Harris Co Inc* [1939] 4 All E.R. 68 at 71; *Joscelyne v Nissen* [1970] 2 Q.B. 86 at 98; *Ottaway v Norman*, above, fn 28.

[30] [1979] Ch. 528; C. Rickett (1979) 38 C.L.J. 260; B. Robertson (1991) 107 L.Q.R. 194.

[31] [1979] Ch. 528 at 537.

[32] *Re Boyes* (1884) 26 Ch.D. 531.

[33] *Jones v Badley* (1868) L.R. 3 Ch.App. 362.

[34] Similarly if the terms, although disclosed, are unlawful or uncertain. See *Re Pugh's WT* [1967] 1 W.L.R. 1262; *Brown v Pourau* [1995] 1 N.Z.L.R. 352; *Gold v Hill* [1999] 1 F.L.R. 54 ("Look after Carol and the kids" sufficiently certain).

In *Re Boyes*,[35] a legacy was given to the testator's solicitor, who had undertaken to hold the property according to directions which he would receive by letter. The letter was found only after the death. The solicitor accepted that he held as trustee, and wished to carry out the trust. Kay J. held that there was a resulting trust in favour of the next-of-kin, and explained the rule by saying:

> "The essence of all these decisions is that the devisee or legatee accepts a particular trust which thereupon becomes binding upon him, and which it would be a fraud in him not to carry into effect.[36]

This situation is similar to that of half-secret trusts in that the legatee takes as a trustee. But there is an important difference. In *Re Boyes*,[37] the gift was absolute on its face; the trust could have been enforced if the terms had been declared before death.[38] Where the existence of a trust is disclosed on the face of the will, the communication, as we shall see, must be prior to or contemporaneous with the execution of the will.[39]

D. Methods of Communication

5–006   We have seen that the trust must be communicated before the testator's death. The communication may be made orally or in writing, and must be sufficiently imperative.[40] It appears that, just as "a ship which sails under sealed orders, is sailing under orders though the exact terms are not ascertained by the captain till later,"[41] a testator may, during his lifetime, give to the legatee a sealed envelope which is not to be opened until the testator's death. This is sufficient provided the legatee knows that it contains details of the trust.

E. Additions to the Secret Trust

5–007   A testator must communicate not only the trust and the terms, but also the identity of the property to be held on trust.

In *Re Colin Cooper*,[42] the testator left £5,000 to two persons as trustees, and informally communicated to them the terms of the

---

[35] (1884) 26 Ch.D. 531; *Re Hawkesley's Settlement* [1934] Ch. 384.
[36] (1884) 26 Ch.D. 531 at 536.
[37] (1884) 26 Ch.D. 531.
[38] *Re Gardner* [1920] 2 Ch. 523.
[39] Below, para.5–010.
[40] *Margulies v Margulies* [2008] W.T.L.R. 1853.
[41] per Lord Wright in *Re Keen* [1937] Ch. 236 at 242; *Re Boyes*, above, fn.35 at 536.
[42] [1939] Ch. 811; criticised in D. Kincaid [2000] Conv. 420 at 428–430.

trust. By a later codicil he purported to increase the sum to be devoted to the secret trust to £10,000, they "knowing my wishes regarding that sum." This addition was not communicated to the trustees. It was held that the first instalment could be devoted to the secret trusts; but the later instalment went on a resulting trust.[43]

F. Undertaking to Leave by Will

A secret trust may impose an obligation not only to hold on trust   **5–008**
for a beneficiary on the testator's death; but also an obligation to make provision for an intended beneficiary after the legatee's death.

In *Re Gardner (No.1)*,[44] a wife left her estate to her husband for life, and there was an agreement that the property should be divided among certain beneficiaries on his death. The husband died intestate, and the Court of Appeal decided that he held the property, after his life interest, on trust for the beneficiaries.

Ottaway v Norman[45] took the matter a stage further. The testator agreed with his housekeeper that she should have a bungalow after his death, and she agreed to leave it to the testator's son by her will. The testator left the bungalow (plus its contents and some money) to her absolutely. She first made a will in favour of the testator's son; but she then changed that will, and left the bungalow to the defendant. Brightman J. held that the son was entitled to the bungalow and its contents, although not to the money.

The enforcement of a secret trust in this situation creates a number of problems concerning the status of the trust during the housekeeper's lifetime, and the theoretical basis on which secret trusts are enforced. This question is discussed in s.6 below, but some of the questions arising from *Ottaway v Norman*[46] are more conveniently considered in Ch.12.

G. Tenants in Common and Joint Tenants

Where a testamentary gift is made to two or more persons as   **5–009**
tenants in common, and secret trusts are communicated to some but not all of the tenants in common, those to whom the communication

---

[43] Had it been a fully secret trust, the legatees would have been beneficially entitled to the addition.

[44] [1920] 2 Ch. 523; *Re Young* [1951] Ch. 344; below, para.5–013.

[45] [1972] Ch. 698; D. Hayton (1972) 36 Conv.(N.S.) 129.

[46] Above, fn.45.

was made are bound, the others taking beneficially.[47] "To hold otherwise would enable one beneficiary to deprive the rest of their benefits by setting up a secret trust."[48]

But where a gift is made to them as joint tenants, a distinction is made between the case where the trust is communicated before the making of the will, and where the communication is between the will and the death. In the former case, all joint tenants are bound.[49] In the latter, only those who have accepted the trust are bound by it,[50] "the reason being that the gift is not tainted with any fraud in procuring the execution of the will."[51]

Farwell J. was dissatisfied with his own explanation. He confessed that he was "unable to see any difference between a gift made on the faith of an antecedent promise and a gift left unrevoked on the faith of a subsequent promise."[52] It has been suggested that gifts upon secret trusts to joint tenants and tenants in common should be decided on the principle of *Huguenin v Baseley*,[53] that "no man may profit by the fraud of another".[54] Thus if A induces B to make or leave unrevoked a will leaving property to A and C whether as joint tenants or tenants in common, C will be bound if the testator would not have made any gift to C unless A had promised. If the testator would still have left property to C even if A had not promised, C is not bound. Whether A and C are joint tenants or tenants in common, and whether A's promise was before or after the making of the will are matters of evidence that may help to determine whether or not there was such an inducement, but of themselves both matters are inconclusive.[55] The argument is persuasive; but the cases say otherwise. The wrong turning was taken in *Rowbotham v Dunnett*.[56]

The principles discussed above have emerged from cases concerning fully secret trusts. Of course, in the case of half-secret trusts there could be no question of the legatees taking beneficially. The issue would be whether a valid half-secret trust could be created by communication to fewer than the whole number of trustees. It seems that the principles applicable to fully secret trusts would be applied by analogy, bearing in mind that half-secret trustees will invariably be joint tenants, and that communication after the will is ineffective

---

[47] *Tee v Ferri* (1856) 2 K. & J. 357.
[48] *Re Stead* [1900] 1 Ch. 237 at 241.
[49] *Jones v Badley* (1868) L.R. 3 Ch.App. 362; *Re Gardom* [1914] 1 Ch. 662; *Re Young* [1951] Ch. 344.
[50] *Moss v Cooper* (1861) 1 J. & H. 352.
[51] per Farwell J. in *Re Stead* [1900] 1 Ch. 237 at 241.
[52] [1900] 1 Ch. 237.
[53] (1807) 14 Ves. 273.
[54] B. Perrins (1972) 88 L.Q.R. 225 at 226.
[55] B. Perrins (1972) 88 L.Q.R. 225 at 226.
[56] (1878) 8 Ch.D. 430.

in the case of half-secret trusts, as explained below. Hence communication to one of the trustees prior to the making of the will is effective.[57]

4. HALF-SECRET TRUSTS

Where the will gives property to a legatee *upon trust*, without, however, saying what the intended trusts are, the question of the enforcement of a secret trust communicated to the legatee has been treated very differently from the case where the property was given to the legatee *absolutely* in the will. The courts have found it more difficult to enforce a secret trust in the former case—where the legatee takes expressly as trustee—than in the latter case. It is difficult to see any sense, however, in a rule which allows a secret trust to be enforced if the trust is nowhere mentioned in the will; but holds it void if the testamentary gift discloses the fact that the legatee takes as trustee. If it is right that secret trusts are express trusts operating wholly outside the scope of the Wills Act, it is difficult to see why the two situations should not be treated alike.

5–010

But there is a historical explanation. We saw that the nineteenth-century judges said that secret trusts were enforced to prevent fraud[58]; to prevent the legatee taking for himself what he had promised the testator to hold upon trust. The element of fraud, however, was not present in the case of the gift to a legatee as trustee. As he took in a fiduciary capacity, he could in no circumstances take the property for himself. There was no possibility of fraud, and no justification, so the argument ran, for not applying the Wills Act. And it was at one time held that the mention of the existence of a trust did prevent the operation of the doctrine of secret trusts.[59] The validity of half-secret trusts was not finally established until the House of Lords decision in *Blackwell v Blackwell*[60] in 1929.

The testator by a codicil gave a legacy of £12,000 to legatees upon trust to apply the income "for the purposes indicated by me to them." The trust had been accepted prior to the execution of the codicil. The House of Lords enforced the trust. They were assisted by *Re Fleetwood*[61] and *Re Huxtable*[62] where it was held

[57] See *Re Gardom* [1914] 1 Ch. 662.
[58] Above, para.5–003.
[59] *Moss v Cooper* (1861) 1 J. & H. 352 at 367; *Le Page v Gardom* (1915) 84 L.J.Ch. 749 at 752; W. Holdsworth (1937) 53 L.Q.R. 501.
[60] [1929] A.C. 318. If the words in the will are insufficient to impose a trust, any secret trust will be fully secret; *Jankowski v Petek Estate* (1995) 131 D.L.R. (4th) 717 (gift to executor "to deal with as he may in his discretion decide upon").
[61] (1880) 15 Ch.D. 594.
[62] [1902] 2 Ch. 793.

that the secret trust doctrine applied although the gift was in terms
a gift upon trust, and where therefore there was no question of
fraud in the legatee. Lord Sumner concluded that:

> "[I]t is communication of the purpose to the legatee, coupled
> with acquiescence or promise on his part, that removes the
> matter from the provision of the Wills Act and brings it within
> the law of trusts, as applied in this instance to trustees, who
> happen also to be legatees."[63]

The effect of the bequest "remains to be decided by the law as
laid down by the Courts before and since the [Wills] Act, and
does not depend on the Act itself."[64] Thus the trust operated
outside the Act and could be enforced without proof of fraud.

In *Blackwell v Blackwell*[65] the trusts were communicated before
the will and were stated to have been so communicated. Will the
same rule apply where the trusts are or may be declared in the
future? On the one hand, there is logically no difference between
declarations of trusts before and after the will; for the will is ambula-
tory and of no effect until the death.[66] The distinction is not made, as
we have seen, with fully secret trusts.[67] If the trust operates independently of the Wills Act, the date of the will should be immaterial.
On the other hand, it is more difficult to *assume* acquiescence where
the communication is after the will; in the absence of proof of
express agreement, the fact of non-revocation may be the only basis
on which to presume acquiescence. More importantly:

> "[A] testator cannot reserve to himself a power of making future
> unwitnessed dispositions by merely naming a trustee and leaving
> the purposes of the trust to be supplied afterwards. . . . "[68]

To allow that to be done by half-secret trust would be to give a wider
rule for secret trusts (which might be oral) than that which as we
have seen is applied in the case of incorporation of documents by
reference.[69] It would be surprising if the law of wills permitted this;
but, if the proper explanation of the enforcement of secret trusts is
that they operate outside the will and independently of the Wills Act,
then the rules relating to incorporation by reference are, as has been
pointed out, quite irrelevant.[70] And what Lord Sumner feared can
always be achieved by a fully secret trust.

---

[63] [1929] A.C. 318 at 339–340; *Ottaway v Norman* [1972] Ch. 698 at 711.
[64] [1929] A.C. 318 at 339.
[65] [1929] A.C. 318.
[66] W. Holdsworth (1937) 53 L.Q.R. 501.
[67] Above, para.5–003; *Re Gardner* [1920] 2 Ch. 523.
[68] per Lord Sumner in *Blackwell v Blackwell* [1929] A.C. 318 at 339.
[69] *In bonis Smart* [1902] P. 238; P. Matthews [1979] Conv. 360.
[70] W. Holdsworth (1937) 53 L.Q.R. 501; *Moss v Cooper* (1861) 1 J. & K. 352 at 367.

With half-secret trusts however the distinction appears to be **5–011** made.

In *Re Keen*[71] the testator gave a sum of money to trustees:

"[T]o be held upon trust and disposed of by them among such person, persons or charities as may be notified by me to them or either of them during my lifetime. . . . "

Previously, one of the trustees had been given a sealed envelope containing the name of the beneficiary of the intended trust. In deciding in favour of the residuary legatees, the Court of Appeal held that the handing over of the sealed envelope was a communication of the trust, but that this, being *prior* to the date of the will,[72] was inconsistent with the terms of the will which provided for "a future definition . . . of the trust subsequent to the date of the will," while "the sealed letter relied on as notifying the trust was communicated . . . before the date of the will."[73]

The trust would, however, have failed independently of the question of inconsistency. The disposition contained a power to declare trusts in the future. This was void, for it "would involve a power to change a testamentary disposition by an unexecuted codicil and would violate section 9 of the Wills Act."[74]

The criticisms of this rule have been discussed. The contrary rule exists in Ireland,[75] New South Wales[76] and in most of the American jurisdictions.[77] The matter is still open to the House of Lords; it may be that the true ratio of *Re Keen*[78] is the narrow point of inconsistency; but it was followed in *Re Bateman's Will Trusts*,[79] where, it seems, the rule was not challenged. The present position is unsatisfactory; there is no sense in a rule which (in the case of communication between the will and the death) enforces a trust in a bequest "to X" but disregards the trust in a bequest "to X upon trust".[80]

---

[71] [1937] Ch. 236; *Johnson v Ball* (1851) 5 De G. & Sm. 85; R Burgess (1972) 23 N.I.L.Q. 263.

[72] *Re Huxtable* [1902] 2 Ch. 793.

[73] *Re Keen*, above, fn.71 at 248; *Re Rees' WT* [1950] Ch. 204.

[74] *Re Keen*, above, fn.71 at 247; *Johnson v Ball* (1851) 5 De G. & Sm. 85; *Re Hetley* [1902] 2 Ch. 866.

[75] *Riordan v Banon* (1876) 10 Ir.R.Eq. 469; contra *Balfe v Halfpenny* [1904] 1 Ir.R. 486; *Re Browne* [1944] Ir.R. 90; L. Sheridan (1951) 67 L.Q.R. 413; J. Mee [1992] Conv. 202; P. Coughlan (1991) 5 T.L.I. 69.

[76] *Ledgerwood v Perpetual Trustee Co Ltd* (1997) 41 N.S.W.L.R. 532, following *Re Browne*, above, fn.75.

[77] American Law Institute, *Restatement of Trusts*, § 18, 3rd edn, 2003, comment (c).

[78] [1937] Ch. 236.

[79] [1970] 1 W.L.R. 1463.

[80] But see B. Perrins [1985] Conv. 248, supporting the communication rules as being based on the extrinsic evidence rule.

Other views are that the distinction is justified because wills creating half-secret trusts are invariably drawn up by solicitors, and so stricter rules are appropriate[81]; or that consistency should be achieved by requiring the communication to be before the will even in the case of a fully secret trust. If the trusteeship was accepted after the will, the legatee would hold on trust for the residuary legatee or next-of-kin. This would have the advantage of preventing reliance on the doctrine of secret trusts by testators who are merely indecisive[82] and thus not within the rationale of the doctrine.[83]

We have seen that the doubts concerning the effectiveness of a communication after the will in the case of a half-secret trust derive from the testamentary formality rules. These rules do not apply to the analogous situation of a trust of a life policy nomination. In *Gold v Hill*[84] the insured nominated X and referred to him (erroneously) as executor on the nomination form. Later he informed X of the nomination and asked him to use the proceeds to "look after" his common law wife and children and to make sure that his widow got nothing. It was held that a trust analogous to a half-secret trust was validly created even though the communication was after the nomination.

5. CAN THE SECRET TRUSTEE TAKE A BENEFIT?

5–012 The legatee may claim that the testator intended him to take some benefit from the gift, perhaps, for example, a specific sum, or possibly any surplus after performing the trust. Two separate questions arise here; first, was this the testator's intention? Secondly, how far is evidence of such an intention admissible in favour of the trustee?

To consider first the question of intention, it is necessary to construe the language of the will to determine whether the testator's intention was to make the legatee a trustee of the whole of the property given, or to make a beneficial gift to him subject to his performing certain obligations.[85] In the former case, any surplus left

---

[81] D. Wilde [1995] Conv. 366.

[82] As in *Re Snowden* [1979] Ch. 528.

[83] T. Watkin [1981] Conv. 335. See also the discussion of how the suggested reform would operate in the case of a person who refrains from making a will in reliance upon the acceptance of a trust by the next-of-kin.

[84] [1999] 1 F.L.R. 54. It was doubted in *Kasperbauer v Griffith* [2000] W.T.L.R. 333, whether a secret trust or any trust could be made of a pension scheme death benefit, as it was not owned by the testator: at most he could require it to be paid to his estate rather than to his widow under the rules of the pension scheme.

[85] Above, para.2–012. This construction is more likely where the legatee is a relative for whom the testator may be supposed to have been intending to provide. See *Irvine v Sullivan* (1869) L.R. 8 Eq. 673 (fiancée).

after carrying out the trusts is held upon resulting trusts[86]; in the latter, the legatee may keep it.[87] There is thus no difficulty in a case where the will itself makes it clear that the trust does not extend to the whole of the legacy, but the will may be silent on the matter, and the only evidence extrinsic. This leads us to the second question, namely whether the trustee may be permitted to prove his claim to benefit by relying on documentary or even oral evidence.

The difficulty, whether the trust be fully or half-secret, is the danger of fraud by the secret trustee. A further problem in the case of a half-secret trust is that the evidence would contradict the terms of the will, which impose a trust on the entire legacy.[88]

In *Re Rees' WT*[89] the testator by will appointed a friend and his solicitor (thereinafter called his trustees) to be executors and trustees. He left the whole estate "unto my trustees absolutely they well knowing my wishes concerning the same."

The testator had told the trustees that he wished them to make certain payments and to retain any surplus for themselves. A substantial surplus remained. It was held that the trustees were not entitled to the surplus, which passed as on intestacy. The will, on its true construction, imposed a trust on the whole, and evidence was not admissible to show that the trustees were to take a benefit. It was not without significance that the trustee was the testator's solicitor. As Evershed M.R. said:

> "In the general public interest it seems to me desirable that, if a testator wishes his property to go to his solicitor and the solicitor prepares the will, that intention on the part of the testator should appear plainly in the will and should not be arrived at by the more oblique method of what is sometimes called a secret trust."[90]

In *Re Tyler*,[91] however, there are suggestions that evidence is admissible as to all the terms of a trust, including any in favour of the trustee himself, although such evidence will not lightly be admitted. Pennycuick J. found difficulty in the reasoning of *Re Rees*. But

---

[86] Above, para.2–012.

[87] Above, para.2–012; *Irvine v Sullivan* (1869) L.R. 8 Eq. 673.

[88] We have seen, in the context of communication, that evidence inconsistent with the will is not admissible; *Re Keen* [1937] Ch. 236, above, para.5–011.

[89] [1950] Ch. 204. See also *Re Pugh's WT* [1967] 1 W.L.R. 1262, suggesting that it is easier to infer an intention that a sole trustee should take beneficially than that two or more trustees should do so.

[90] [1950] Ch. 204 at 211.

[91] [1967] 1 W.L.R. 1269 (concerning a lifetime trust). See also *Ottaway v Norman* [1972] Ch. 698, above, para.5–008, where the secret trustee took a benefit in the form of a life interest. This was clearly the testator's intention and the point was not discussed. In any event, the interest had already been enjoyed.

evidence contained in the (now deceased) trustee's own written memorandum did not suffice.[92]

Finally, we have seen that if a secret trust fails for non-compliance with the communication rules, or for uncertainty, the secret trustee holds on trust for the residuary legatee or next-of-kin. He could not claim the legacy for himself if the trust was half-secret, or, although fully secret, if he had accepted trusteeship. A question might arise as to whether the secret trustee could take the property if he himself was the residuary legatee or next-of-kin. There is no reason in principle why he should not, as he would be claiming in a different capacity, but the court might intervene if he disclaimed the legacy in order to benefit.[93]

6. THEORETICAL BASIS OF SECRET TRUSTS

A. Lifetime Trust Outside the Will

5–013   The formal requirements for a will, contained in the Wills Act 1837, are based upon a sound policy. It is important to avoid doubt, fraud and uncertainty in connection with testamentary dispositions; and it is essential to rely upon written formalities as there is no other way of ascertaining the intention of the testator. If secret trusts, which effectively create dispositions of property on death, are to be allowed, it is important to justify the failure to apply the provisions of the Wills Act. In terms of policy, it is easy to favour an exception in cases in which the intention of the testator is clear, and is opposed only by the formalities which were set up in the hope of establishing it. But further justification is needed. The Wills Act is a statute, and not merely an expression of policy. The question is whether some theory can be found to justify the enforcement of secret trusts.

We have seen that the early cases were explained on the ground of fraud[94]; the fear that the legatee would otherwise keep the property for himself. There is substantial authority for a refusal to allow a statute to be used as an instrument of fraud, but the fraud theory appears not to justify the enforcement of half-secret trusts, because the legatee, being named as a trustee, cannot claim. On the other hand, it may be said that a secret trustee who relies on the Wills Act to defeat the testator's expectation commits a fraud against the testator and the secret beneficiary even in the absence of personal

---

[92] Although generally such a memorandum is *admissible* under the Civil Evidence Act 1995 to prove the terms of the trust.

[93] See *Blackwell v Blackwell* [1929] A.C. 318 at 341. Disclaimer might in any event not cause a half-secret trust to fail, by reliance on the maxim that a trust does not fail for want of a trustee; but it has been said that a fully secret trust will fail if the trustee disclaims; *Re Maddock* [1902] 2 Ch. 220 at 231; cf. *Blackwell v Blackwell*, above; Oakley, *Constructive Trusts*, 3rd edn, p.252. See also D. Kincaid [2000] Conv. 420 at 440.

[94] Above, para.5–003; doubted in Oakley, *Constructive Trusts*, 3rd edn, pp.252–253.

benefit, and recent authority on mutual wills has confirmed that fraud can be perpetrated without gain.[95] On this view the fraud theory can explain both kinds of secret trust. What is clear, however, is that it is not sufficient to say as did Lord Sumner in *Blackwell v Blackwell*[96] that secret trusts are based upon the essential elements of intention, communication and acquiescence, for this assumes a new basis for the enforcement of testamentary dispositions which is wholly inconsistent with the Wills Act, and suggests that a testator could "contract out of" the Wills Act, and create testamentary dispositions by a different method. The modern view is that secret trusts can be enforced because they are not trusts created by will; but are trusts arising outside and independently of the will[97]; that they arise by reason of the personal obligation accepted by the legatee.[98]

In *Re Young*,[99] the testator made a bequest to his wife with a direction that on her death she should leave the property for the purposes which he had communicated to her. One of the purposes was that she would leave a legacy of £2,000 to the chauffeur. The chauffeur had witnessed the will. A witness may not normally take a legacy, and the question was whether he had thereby forfeited his interest.[100] Danckwerts J. held that he had not; the trust in his favour was not a trust contained in the will but one created separately and imposed upon the legatee.[101]

It is one thing to say that the trust operates outside the will, but it is another to say just how and when the trust takes effect. If some of

---

[95] *Re Dale (Deceased)* [1994] Ch. 31; A Brierley (1995) 58 M.L.R. 95; below, para.12–030. See generally D. Hodge [1980] Conv. 341, supporting the fraud theory as the basis of half-secret trusts. This is doubted in Oakley, p.248.

[96] [1929] A.C. 318 at 340.

[97] *Cullen v Att Gen for Northern Ireland* (1866) L.R. 1 H.L. 190 at 198; *Blackwell v Blackwell* [1929] A.C. 318 at 340; Oakley, *Constructive Trusts*, 3rd edn, p.253. The theory is rejected in P. Critchley (1999) 115 L.Q.R. 631. See also B. McFarlane (2004) 120 L.Q.R. 667.

[98] "I think the solution is to be found by bearing in mind that what is enforced is not a trust imposed by the will, but one arising from the acceptance by the legatee of a trust communicated to him by the testator, on the faith of which acceptance the will was made or left revoked, as the case might be": *Blackwell v Blackwell* [1929] A.C. 318 at 342. For New Zealand views, see *Brown v Pourau* [1995] 1 N.Z.L.R. 352.

[99] [1951] Ch. 344; *Cullen v Att Gen for Northern Ireland* (1866) L.R. 1 H.L. 190.

[100] Wills Act 1837 s.15. cf. *Re Fleetwood* (1880) 15 Ch.D. 594; *O'Brien v Condon* [1905] Ir.R. 51. If it is the secret trustee who attests there should be no difficulty if it is a half-secret trust, as he takes no beneficial interest on the face of the will. If it is fully secret, the position is less clear. For the view that it would fail, see Oakley, *Constructive Trusts*, 3rd edn, p.250.

[101] To the contrary is *Re Maddock* [1902] 2 Ch. 220, where the property subject to a fully secret trust was treated as being subject to a specific bequest for the purpose of the payment of debts out of the estate. No doubt the legacy would be treated as part of the estate for tax purposes and for the purposes of the Inheritance (Provision for Family and Dependants) Act 1975, rather than as property disposed of prior to the death.

the propositions discussed in Ch.4[102] are sound, the most natural way for this to occur is to treat the communication to the trustee as the declaration of trust, and the vesting of the property in the trustee by the will as the constitution of the trust. If this is so, it is a lifetime declaration, and the Wills Act has no effect upon it; the only statutory formalities that are relevant are Law of Property Act 1925 s.53(1)(b),[103] which requires that declarations of trusts of land should be evidenced in writing; but this would not affect the rule requiring a fraudulent trustee in a fully secret trust of land to hold on a constructive trust.[104] There would be no awkward distinction between declarations prior to and subsequent to the will in half-secret trusts[105]; the sole question would be whether or not a trust was declared of the property before the death, and whether that trust became properly constituted by the vesting of the property in the trustee.

5–014   We have seen that the usual rule in the case of property coming to a person who had previously declared himself trustee of it was that the trust did not become constituted without a further manifestation of intention.[106] It was submitted that where a third person accepted an instruction to hold the property on certain trusts and the settlor subsequently transferred the property to him without further declaration, the trust would be constituted. It should make no difference whether the property passed to the trustee by a conveyance or by a will.[107] It will probably fail however if the trustee predeceases the testator, at any rate in the case of a fully secret trust.[108] Assuming its terms were known, it may be that a half-secret trust could be saved by the maxim "a trust does not fail for want of a trustee".[109]

Ottaway v Norman[110] raises a further complication. There the secret trust was upheld as to the bungalow (and its contents). Assuming that it is correct to say that the testator made a lifetime declaration that the bungalow was to be held on trust for his son

---

[102] Above, para.4–001.

[103] Above, para.3–004. *Re Baillie* (1886) 2 T.L.R. 660 at 661; but there was no writing in *Ottaway v Norman* [1972] Ch. 698; below.

[104] LPA 1925 s.53(2). As to whether he should hold on trust for the secret beneficiaries, see below, para.5–015.

[105] *Re Keen* [1937] Ch. 236; above, para.5–011.

[106] Above, para.4–023.

[107] As with the property received by Miss Towry Law from her sister and conveyed to the trustees: *Re Ellenborough* [1903] 1 Ch. 697; *Re Adlard* [1954] Ch. 29; *Re Ralli's WT* [1964] Ch. 288.

[108] *Re Maddock* [1902] 2 Ch. 220 at 251; Oakley, *Constructive Trusts*, 3rd edn, p.250; cf. D. Kincaid [2000] Conv. 420 at 439.

[109] Unless the particular trustee is regarded as essential to the trust. For the view that a half-secret trust would also fail, see D. Wilde [1995] Conv. 366 at 373; cf. Oakley, *Constructive Trusts*, 3rd edn, p.250. The question of disclaimer by the secret trustee has already been considered; above, para.5–012.

[110] [1972] Ch. 698; D. Hayton (1972) 36 Conv.(N.S.) 129; R. Burgess (1972) 36 Conv.(N.S.) at 115; J. Hackney [1971] A.S.C.L. 375 at 384.

after the housekeeper's death, and that the trust was constituted by the vesting of the property in the housekeeper as trustee, then the trust of the bungalow arose on the testator's death, the housekeeper's interest effectively being a life interest. But the son also claimed entitlement to so much of the money left to the housekeeper as remained at her death. This claim failed. The testator had not intended to impose an obligation on the housekeeper as to *all* her money, nor had he intended to impose an obligation as to the money derived from his will, because this would be unworkable unless this money was to be kept separately, which was not envisaged. But Brightman J. was content to assume, without deciding, that if property was given on the understanding that the primary donee would dispose of such assets, if any, as he may still have at his death in favour of a secondary donee, there would be a valid trust, "in suspense"[111] during the lifetime of the primary donee but attaching to the estate of the primary donee on the latter's death. This would be a "floating trust",[112] such as was recognised by the High Court of Australia in *Birmingham v Renfrew*[113] but which can hardly be said to be a recognised legal concept. The situation during the primary donee's lifetime would be similar to that existing during the lifetime of the survivor of makers of mutual wills. But the origin of the trust is of course quite different. In the former case it is based upon the declaration of the trust, followed by communication and acquiescence and the vesting of the property in the trustee; in the case of mutual wills, it is based on the contract between the parties followed by the death of the first testator in reliance upon non-revocation by the survivor. Once the trust has attached, however, the problems are similar, and will be discussed in Ch.12.

Until the property has so vested, there is no completely constituted trust; the declaration can have no effect, and cannot create property rights. The will can be revoked or altered, or the property may be disposed of during the testator's lifetime. The testator can revoke his instructions to the secret trustee at any time,[114] and if he acts as if he had forgotten the declaration or assumed it to be no longer existent, no doubt it will be treated as having expired. No rational theory, it is suggested, can be found which will justify the remarkable decision in *Re Gardner (No.2)*.[115] We have seen that a wife left her estate to her husband for life,[116] and that after his death

---

[111] [1972] Ch. 698 at 713.

[112] D. Hayton (1972) 36 Conv.(N.S.) at 132.

[113] (1937) 57 C.L.R. 666. Applied in *Re Cleaver* [1981] 1 W.L.R. 939.

[114] But any substituted instructions given after the will is executed will be invalid in the case of a half-secret trust. See also M. Pawlowski and J. Brown [2000] Conv. 388.

[115] [1923] 2 Ch. 230. See Oakley, *Constructive Trusts*, 3rd edn, p.251, suggesting that there is no clear rule against a non-testamentary trust for a dead person. This is doubtful, as such a beneficiary has no legal personality, unless it is clear that his estate is intended to take.

[116] *Re Gardner (No.1)* [1920] 2 Ch. 523; above, para.5–008.

it was to be held on secret trust for five named beneficiaries. One of the beneficiaries predeceased the wife. The representatives of the deceased beneficiary successfully claimed the share.

A gift by will normally lapses if the donee predeceases the testator,[117] and the estate of the donee can only claim if the donee acquired some interest in the property before he died. No such interest could exist in this case; and the theory which suggests that a secret trust can be treated as a lifetime declaration of trust does not suggest that any interest is obtained by any beneficiary prior to the constitution of the trust by vesting of the legal estate in the trustee.

B. Express or Constructive Trust

5–015   Closely connected with the theoretical basis of secret trusts is the question whether a secret trust is properly categorised as an express or constructive trust.[118] The question is not merely academic, for, as we have seen,[119] constructive trusts of land are excepted from the requirement of written evidence. Is an oral secret trust of land valid?

An express trust is one declared by the settlor; a constructive trust is one imposed by the law.[120] The analysis of secret trusts as being declarations outside the will categorises them as express trusts, whether they are fully or half-secret. In the case of a half-secret trust the will itself expressly declares a trust. While this element is absent with a fully secret trust, such a trust may claim to be express on the basis of the testator's express declaration to the secret trustee. There is authority that a half-secret trust of land is not enforceable without written evidence.[121] In *Ottaway v Norman*,[122] however, a fully secret trust of land was upheld without written evidence, but the point was not discussed.

Fully secret trusts however have, as it were, another string to their bow. They were enforced long before secret trusts were thought of as taking effect outside the will. We have seen that they have been said on high authority to be enforceable on the ground of fraud,[123]

---

[117] A special exception is made in the case of children of the testator who predecease him, leaving issue: Wills Act 1837 s.33. Such a gift takes effect in favour of the issue.

[118] One view is that the attempt to classify as express or constructive is misguided because the secret trust doctrine is concerned with the procedural question of admitting evidence of a trust and not with the nature of the trust itself; B. Perrins [1985] Conv. 248, at 253.

[119] Above, para.3–004.

[120] Below, para.12–001.

[121] *Re Baillie* (1886) 2 T.L.R. 660 at 661.

[122] [1972] Ch. 698. See also *Strickland v Aldridge* (1804) 9 Ves.Jr. 516; *Brown v Pourau* [1995] 1 N.Z.L.R. 352; C. Rickett [1996] Conv. 302. Similarly with lifetime transfers; *Rochefoucauld v Boustead* [1897] 1 Ch. 196.

[123] *McCormick v Grogan* (1869) L.R. 4 H.L. 82; above, para.5–003.

and they can claim also to be constructive trusts.[124] It is submitted that fully secret trusts can be enforced under either head.

If it becomes established that even a fully secret trust is express, it does not follow that the secret trustee would take beneficially if the trust fails for lack of compliance with the formality requirements. The result in such a case would be that, having accepted trusteeship, he would hold on trust for the residuary beneficiary or next-of-kin.[125]

C. Conclusion

Ultimately, the enforcement of secret trusts is a matter of policy **5–016** relating to testamentary dispositions. The rules of the Wills Act 1837 are intended to achieve a reasonable degree of certainty in respect of testamentary dispositions. Secret trusts have, in effect, created a wide gap in the law relating to testamentary formalities. It is possible to take the view that secret trusts should not be enforced beyond preventing the unjust enrichment of the fraudulent legatee; or, on the other hand, to hold that the testator's intention should be upheld in every case. This is really a matter for the Legislature, and it is submitted that it would be more satisfactory to review the whole matter and to incorporate into the statutory scheme as much of the secret trust doctrine as it is desired to retain.[126]

---

[124] This is assumed obiter in *Re Cleaver* [1981] 1 W.L.R. 939 at 947.

[125] B. Perrins [1985] Conv. 248; M. Thompson (1986) 36 N.I.L.Q. 358. Another view is that both fully and half-secret trusts are constructive, as both are imposed to prevent fraud on the testator, which may occur without any benefit to the secret trustee; D. Hodge [1980] Conv. 341. cf. L. Sheridan (1951) 67 L.Q.R. 413; Oakley, *Constructive Trusts*, 3rd edn, p.258.

[126] See E. Challinor [2005] Conv. 492, favouring abolition.

CHAPTER 6

POWERS

1. Powers[1] and Trusts

A Power is an authorisation to do certain things which affect prop-   **6–001**
erty to which the appointor is not solely entitled, and in which he
may have no beneficial interest at all. A person may hold a power in
a personal or an official capacity, a distinction relevant to the question whether he has fiduciary obligations. The source of the power
may be express grant or a statute. Thus trustees have by statute
powers of investment, sale, and so on. They may also be given other
powers by the terms of the trust instrument, such as a power of
appointment which enables those holding the power to effect the
disposal of the settlor's property by "appointing" it to other people.
It is with "powers" in the latter sense that this chapter is concerned.

---

[1] See *Farwell on Powers*, 3rd edn, 1916; Thomas, *Powers*; Halsbury, 4th edn, Vol.36(2),
p.123.

It has been seen that there are important points of distinction between powers and trusts.[2] Essentially a trust is imperative and a power discretionary. The dividing line is not always clear; for many trusts contain discretionary elements; and many powers are given to trustees who are governed by fiduciary duties in the exercise of their powers.

The practical importance of the distinction lies in the extent of the obligations imposed on a trustee as compared with the donee of a power, for example, the question how far he is obliged to consider the claims of possible recipients,[3] also the extent of the rights of objects of a trust as compared with a mere power, including the question of entitlement to the property in default of exercise and the question whether the beneficiaries, all being adult and under no disability, can terminate the trust and either divide the trust property[4] or dispose of it.[5]

Whether a particular disposition creates a mere power or a discretionary trust is a question of construction. This has already been discussed.[6]

2. BARE POWERS AND FIDUCIARY POWERS

6–002 A distinction must also be made between a bare power (sometimes called a personal power) and a power to which some fiduciary obligation is attached, such as a power given to trustees of property exercisable in relation to that property. Several aspects of this distinction will be explained in connection with powers of appointment. Of general application however is the rule that a bare power given to an individual can only be exercised by him,[7] and a bare power given to two or more by name cannot (subject to any contrary intent in the instrument creating it) be executed by the survivor.[8] But a power given to trustees is prima facie given to them by virtue of their office, and may be exercised by the survivor,[9] or by their successors in office,[10] and powers given to two or more trustees jointly may be exercised by the survivor or survivors of them, or by

---

[2] Above, paras 2–021–2–027.

[3] *McPhail v Doulton* [1971] A.C. 424; especially at 456; above, para.3–026.

[4] *Saunders v Vautier* (1841) 4 Beav. 115; *Re Brockbank* [1948] Ch. 206; above, para.2–027, below, para.22–001.

[5] *Re Smith* [1928] Ch. 915; *Re Nelson* (1918) [1928] Ch. 920 n.

[6] See above, para.2–025.

[7] *Re Harding* [1923] 1 Ch. 182; *Re Lysaght* [1966] Ch. 191.

[8] Thomas, *Powers*, p.26; *Re Beesly's WT* [1966] Ch. 223 (contrary intention).

[9] *Re Bacon* [1907] 1 Ch. 475; *Bersel Manufacturing Co Ltd v Berry* [1968] 2 All E.R. 552; TA 1925, s.18(1).

[10] *Re Smith* [1904] 1 Ch. 139; *Re De Sommery* [1912] 2 Ch. 622.

the personal representatives of the last of them, pending the appointment of new trustees.[11]

3. POWERS OF APPOINTMENT

A power of appointment is one given by the donor of the power to **6–003** the donee of the power (the appointor) to appoint property to some person (the appointee). Such powers are useful in that they make it possible for the donee of the power to take into consideration circumstances existing at the date of the appointment which the settlor or testator could not have foreseen. Thus, a husband may give his estate to his widow for her life, and after her death to their children. He may leave his widow to decide upon the shares which each child is to receive by giving to her a power to appoint among the children in such shares as she shall in her absolute discretion select, with a gift in default of appointment to the children in equal shares. Powers feature in trusts of all sorts, and modern trusts commonly give various powers of appointment to the trustees in addition to imposing the obligation to hold the property upon trust. In such situations the property is owned by the beneficiaries who are entitled in default of appointment, subject to defeasance upon the exercise of the power.[12]

A. General, Special and Intermediate (or Hybrid) Powers

A gift to A for life with remainder to whomsoever he shall ap- **6–004** point is a general power; A may appoint to himself and become absolute owner. A general power is in most cases equivalent to ownership.[13] If, however, in the illustration given above, the power were exercisable only by will, it would still be a general power even though A would then be unable to appoint to himself. A special power is one in which the choice of appointees is restricted by the terms of the power: for example a power to appoint in favour of one's own children, or of the employees of a company and their families and dependants.[14] The power is special even though the appointor is himself a member of the restricted group.[15] A power which does not fit neatly into these categories is one where the

---

[11] TA 1925 s.18, and see also s.36(7); *Re Wills' Trust Deeds* [1964] Ch. 219, below, para.6–029.

[12] *Re Brooks' ST* [1939] Ch. 993 at 997; Thomas, *Powers*, p.21.

[13] See, for example, Inheritance Tax Act 1984 s.5(2); *Melville v IRC* [2002] 1 W.L.R. 407 (effect reversed by Finance Act 2002 s.119); Inheritance (Provision for Family and Dependants) Act 1975 s.25(1).

[14] *Re Gestetner* [1953] Ch. 672; *Re Sayer* [1957] Ch. 423.

[15] *Re Penrose* [1933] Ch. 793. See, however, Perpetuities and Accumulations Act 2009 s.11.

donee is given power to appoint to anyone except certain people or groups of people, for instance himself,[16] or all persons except the settlor and his wife,[17] or to all persons living at the death of the donee[18]; such powers are called intermediate or hybrid powers,[19] and they may be treated as general powers for some purposes, and special for others.[20] Intermediate powers are classified as special powers for the purpose of the Wills Act 1837, s.27.[21] For the purposes of the rule against perpetuities[22] a power is special unless it is exercisable by one person only and he could at all times transfer the interest to himself or his personal representatives.

A power may be exercisable in the donee's lifetime, or by will, or by either method. A power which is exercisable by will only is called a testamentary power; and may be general or special.

B. The Requirement of Certainty; Wide Powers; Capricious Powers

6–005   These matters have been dealt with in Ch.3, where the requirements of trusts and powers are compared.[23]

C. Duties of Donee of Power; Rights of Objects

6–006   A donee of a power is not, as such, under any fiduciary duties. In the example given above of the power given to the wife to determine the shares in which the children shall receive the property from their father's estate, the widow is under no obligation to exercise the power or even to consider its exercise, although if she does exercise it, then she owes a duty to the default beneficiaries to keep within the terms of the power.[24] This is a bare, or personal, power of appointment. This must be contrasted with a fiduciary power held by a trustee by virtue of his office, which in turn must be distinguished from the obligation of a trustee of a discretionary trust.

---

[16] *Re Park* [1932] 1 Ch. 580; *Re Byron's Settlement* [1891] 3 Ch. 475 (except "her husband or any friend or relative of his.") *Re Abraham's WT* [1969] 1 Ch. 463 at 474; *Re Lawrence's WT* [1972] Ch. 418 (except his "wife's relatives").

[17] To avoid aggregation of the income of the trust with that of the settlor; Income Tax (Trading and Other Income) Act 2005 ss.619–648 (replacing earlier provisions). Also to avoid "reservation of benefit" under the inheritance tax system.

[18] *Re Jones* [1945] Ch. 105.

[19] *Re Lawrence's WT* [1972] Ch. 418; *Re Manisty's Settlement* [1974] Ch. 17; *Re Hay's ST* [1982] 1 W.L.R. 202; *Re Beatty's WT* [1990] 1 W.L.R. 1503.

[20] "This division (i.e. of powers into general and special) is neither precise nor exhaustive, for there are some powers which may be general for some purposes and not for others." (Halsbury, 4th edn, Vol.36(2), § 205.)

[21] Below, para.6–010.

[22] PAA 2009 s.11.

[23] See also Ch.2, para.2–026.

[24] *Re Hay's ST* [1982] 1 W.L.R. 202.

A discretionary trust is a trust in which the property is held by the trustees on trust, not for named beneficiaries in fixed proportions, but on trust for such members of a class of beneficiaries as the trustees shall in their absolute discretion select. That situation has many points of similarity with a power of appointment held by trustees to appoint among a group of objects. The distinction however remains that a trust is obligatory, a power permissive. In many aspects the distinction is theoretical only. We have seen that the test for certainty of objects has been assimilated, but clear distinctions remain in the area of the rights and duties of the parties.

Although a power is discretionary and permissive, a trustee who is the donee of a power must act in accordance with his fiduciary duty. The duties in the case of a fiduciary power arise, as it were, not from the power, but those inherent in the office of trustee. Thus, a trustee may not disregard a power, or forget about it, or release it. His fiduciary duty requires him to give consideration to the exercise of the power, and particularly to any application made to him by an object of the power requesting an exercise in his favour.[25] "Trustees of a power must consider from time to time whether and how to exercise the power."[26]

> "A settlor or testator who entrusts a power to his trustees must be relying on them in their fiduciary capacity so they cannot simply push aside the power and refuse to consider whether it ought in their judgment to be exercised."[27]

The duties of the donee of a fiduciary power were analysed by Megarry V.C. in *Re Hay's Settlement Trusts*.[28] He must make no unauthorised appointment; he must consider periodically whether to exercise the power; he must consider the range of objects[29]; and he must consider the appropriateness of individual appointments. These duties, which were not intended to be exhaustive,[30] were further explained as follows: the donee, if he exercises the power, must do so:

> "[I]n a responsible manner according to its purpose. It is not enough for him to refrain from acting capriciously; he must do more. He must 'make such survey of the range of objects or

---

[25] *Re Gestetner* [1953] Ch. 672 at 688; *Re Manisty's Settlement* [1974] Ch. 17 at 25.

[26] [1974] Ch. 17 at 22, per Templeman J.; *Re Gestetner* (above, fn.25); *Re Abraham's WT* [1969] 1 Ch. 463 at 474; *Re Gulbenkian's Settlements* [1970] A.C. 508 at 518; *McPhail v Doulton* [1972] A.C. 424 at 456.

[27] *Re Gulbenkian's Settlements*, fn.26, at 518.

[28] [1982] 1 W.L.R. 202.

[29] Further discussed in Ch.3.

[30] For the duty not to delegate, and to appoint in good faith, see below, paras 6–017, 6–018.

possible beneficiaries' as will enable him to carry out his fiduciary duties."[31]

He must not simply exercise the power in favour of those objects who happen to be at hand or to claim his attention. He must first consider who the objects are. He need not compile a list or assess the number:

" . . . [W]hat is needed is an appreciation of the width of the field, and thus whether a selection is to be made merely from a dozen or, instead, from thousands or millions. . . . Only when the trustee has applied his mind to 'the size of the problem' should he then consider in individual cases whether, in relation to other possible claimants, a particular grant is appropriate. In doing this, no doubt he should not prefer the undeserving to the deserving; but he is not required to make an exact calculation whether, as between deserving claimants, A is more deserving than B."[32]

6–007 The question arises of what the court will do if the trustees fail in their duty to consider the exercise of the power.

"Normally the trustee is not bound to exercise it, and the court will not compel him to do so. That, however, does not mean that he can simply fold his hands and ignore it, for normally he must from time to time consider whether or not to exercise the power, and the court may direct him to do this."[33]

A recalcitrant trustee may be removed. Where the power has been exercised, the court "will intervene if the trustees exceed their power, and possibly if they are proved to have exercised it capriciously."[34] The court will also intervene if the trustees have failed in any other respect to discharge the duties described above. Thus, in *Turner v Turner*,[35] the exercise of a power of appointment was invalid when the trustees, who were not professional trustees, failed to appreciate their powers and duties and left all the decision-making to the settlor (who was not a trustee). They executed documents of appointment on his direction without reading them, and without understanding that they had a discretion. The settlor "held the reins", and the trustees acted as a "rubber-stamp". This was a breach of their duty to consider the exercise of the power and the

---

[31] [1982] 1 W.L.R. 202 at 209, quoting from *McPhail v Doulton* [1971] A.C. 424 at 449.
[32] *Re Hay's Settlement Trusts* [1982] 1 W.L.R. 202 at 210.
[33] [1982] 1 W.L.R. 202 at p.209.
[34] [1971] A.C. 424 at 456, per Lord Wilberforce.
[35] [1984] Ch. 100. See also *Re Hastings-Bass* [1975] Ch. 25.

appropriateness of the appointments made. There was no effective exercise at all, and the appointments accordingly were null and void, save to the extent that one appointment concerned land and was effective to transfer the legal title, which was held on trust by the appointee for the trustees of the settlement.

The principles on which the court will declare the exercise (or purported exercise) of a fiduciary power such as a power of appointment to be either void or voidable are more fully discussed below.[36]

A further question is whether the court may intervene in a more positive way than merely removing a trustee or setting aside an appointment made in breach of duty. It was held in *Mettoy Pension Trustees Ltd v Evans*[37] that where the court was called upon to intervene (because of breach of duty or where there was nobody left to exercise a fiduciary power),[38] it could adopt any of the methods suggested by Lord Wilberforce in *McPhail v Doulton*[39] in the context of discretionary trusts. Thus it could appoint new trustees, authorise the beneficiaries to prepare a scheme of distribution, or itself order a distribution.[40]

Whatever the form of the court's intervention, it is based upon the breach by the trustee of his fiduciary duty, and not upon any property right or entitlement among the objects of the power to compel a payment to them. Thus, in appropriate cases, an object of a power may seek the intervention of the court to compel disclosure of documents by the trustees.[41] The right of an object is not to compel an exercise of the power, in his own favour or at all, but merely to insist that the trustees consider the exercise of the power, to restrain any invalid exercise of the power, and, of course, to retain any property duly appointed to him.[42]

D. Power to Apply for Purposes

There seems to be no reason why a power should not permit the application of money for specific purposes, as opposed to being paid to persons. The purposes must be sufficiently certain to enable a court to determine whether any particular application is within the

6–008

---

[36] See *Pitt v Holt* [2011] 3 W.L.R. 19; below, para.17–045.

[37] [1990] 1 W.L.R. 1587; S. Gardner (1991) 107 L.Q.R. 214; J. Martin [1991] Conv. 364; R. Ellison K.C.L.J. 2 (1991–92), p.127; Vinelott J. (1994) 8 T.L.I. 35 at 36.

[38] See now Pensions Act 1995 s.25(2) (fiduciary powers exercisable by independent trustee of pension fund on employer's insolvency); below, para.16–010.

[39] [1972] A.C. 424, above para.3–026.

[40] Reliance was placed on *Klug v Klug* [1918] 2 Ch. 67, below, para.17–046, which was not cited in *Re Manisty's Settlement* [1974] Ch. 17, where the appointment of new trustees is said to be the only remedy. The *Mettoy* approach was followed in *Thrells Ltd v Lomas* [1993] 1 W.L.R. 456 and *Re William Makin & Sons Ltd* [1993] O.P.L.R. 171 (pension trust cases).

[41] *Schmidt v Rosewood Trust Ltd* [2003] 2 A.C. 709.

[42] *Vestey v IRC (No.2)* [1979] Ch. 198 (Walton J.); affirmed [1980] A.C. 1148.

terms of the power or not. Such a power may be useful as a means of permitting the application of money to non-charitable purposes; a trust for non-charitable purposes lacks a means of enforcement and is void. That is a problem which is not faced by a power. The matter is discussed in Ch.14.

4. Exercise of Powers of Appointment

A. General Rule

6–009   **i. Lifetime.** No technical words are required for the exercise of a power. All that is required is an intention on the part of the donee that the fund shall pass to some one who is an object of the power.[43] If the appointment relates to land, it must comply with Law of Property Act 1925 s.53(1)(b), and be evidenced in writing, signed by the donee of the power; an appointment of personalty may be made orally.[44] The terms of the power may require certain further formalities[45] for its exercise, or specific reference to the power or to the property subject to it,[46] and such requirements must be strictly complied with. Thus, if a power is to be executed by deed, it cannot be validly exercised by will,[47] and a power to be executed by will cannot be validly exercised by any instrument to take effect in the lifetime of the donee of the power.[48]

6–010   **ii. By Will.** The Wills Act 1837 s.27, provides, in relation to both realty and personalty, and subject to a contrary intention, that, where a testator has a "power to appoint in any manner he may think proper", a general devise[49] or bequest shall operate as an execution of the power. This clearly excludes special powers, and also intermediate or hybrid powers, which in any way restrict the donee's freedom of choice.[50] The section applies even though the will was executed before the power was created.[51]

Any power to which the section does not apply is only exercised by will if "there is an indication of intention to exercise the power",

---

[43] *Re Ackerley* [1913] 1 Ch. 510; *Re Lawrence's WT* [1972] Ch. 418; Thomas, *Powers*, pp.236–237.

[44] Halsbury, 4th edn, Vol.36(2), para.265.

[45] *Hawkins v Kemp* (1803) 3 East 410; subject to LPA 1925 s.159, below, para.6–014.

[46] *Re Lane* [1908] 2 Ch. 581; *Re Priestley's WT* [1971] Ch. 562, 858; *Re Lawrence's WT* [1972] Ch. 418; C. Sherrin (1971) 121 N.L.J. 41, 597, 808.

[47] *Re Phillips* (1889) 41 Ch.D. 417 at 419; Thomas, *Powers*, p.222.

[48] *Reid v Shergold* (1805) 10 Ves.Jr. 370; *Re Evered* [1910] 2 Ch. 147 at 156.

[49] e.g. a devise which refers generally to realty and not specifically to separate pieces; e.g. "all my realty".

[50] *Re Ackerley* [1913] 1 Ch. 510; *Re Byron's Settlement* [1893] 3 Ch. 474 (death of excluded persons would make the power general).

[51] *Boyes v Cook* (1880) 14 Ch.D. 53.

a sufficient indication being "either a reference to the power or a sufficient reference to the property subject to the power."[52] Whether or not this is so in any particular case is often a question of great difficulty.[53]

B. Excessive Execution[54]

The donee has only the power which is given to him by the instrument. Thus he may not exercise it in favour of non-objects; nor in breach of the perpetuity rule; nor impose unauthorised conditions.[55] Any such purported exercise will be void. Difficult questions can arise when an appointment is partly good and partly bad, as where there is an appointment of a sum greater than that authorised; or where some of the appointees are objects and some are not. The rule is that the court will sever the good from the bad where possible: **6–011**

> "If there is a complete execution of the power with the addition of something improper, the execution is good and the excess bad, whereas if there is no complete execution, or if the boundaries between the excess and the execution are not distinguishable, the whole appointment fails. In order to be valid, the appointment must be distinct and absolute."[56]

It is believed that this rule will apply where the exercise of a power makes an appointment and contains a release; if the release is invalid, the rest of the appointment may stand.[57]

C. Defective Execution

The donee of a power should exercise it in accordance with the provisions of the instrument creating it. Thus the necessary formalities should be observed, and the required consents obtained. Failure to comply will usually render the exercise void, but there is a jurisdiction in equity and under statute to validate certain cases of defective execution.   **6–012**

[52] *Re Ackerley*, fn.50, at 513; *Re Priestley's WT* [1971] Ch. 858.

[53] *Re Ackerley*, fn.50; *Re Priestley's WT* [1971] Ch. 562, 858; *Re Lawrence's WT* [1972] Ch. 418; C. Sherrin (1971) 121 N.L.J. 41 at 597, 808.

[54] See Halsbury, 4th edn, Vol.36(2), para.353; Thomas, *Powers*, Ch.8.

[55] See *Re Hay's ST* [1982] 1 W.L.R. 202, below, para.6–017.

[56] Halsbury, 4th edn, Vol.36(2), para.353; *Re Holland* [1914] 2 Ch. 595; see also Halsbury, paras 354–358, for illustrations. The rule applies also where part of the appointment is void under the doctrine of "fraud on a power", below, para.6–018.

[57] Below, para.6–027.

6–013   **i. In Equity.** Where the donee "shows an intention to execute the power in discharge of some moral or natural obligations"[58] equity will act upon the conscience of those entitled in default to compel them to make good the defect in the execution. Relief may be obtained in favour of purchasers for value, creditors, charities, and persons to whom the donee is under a natural or moral obligation to provide.[59]

The essential features of the intended execution must be proved; these are the intention to dispose of the property to the persons to be benefited and the amount of the benefit. Also, the defects must not go to the essence of the power.[60] There will not normally be relief against the non-execution of a power,[61] except perhaps in the case of fraud by the person entitled in default.[62] The doctrine, which is falling into disuse, applies to defects in the form of the execution of the power, but not to the situation where the trustees have purported to exercise the power after it has expired.[63]

The jurisdiction applies to the execution of express powers generally, but not to defective execution of statutory powers; for:

"[I]t is difficult to see how the court can give validity to any such act if done otherwise than in accordance with the statutory requirements; to give relief in such a case would be to legislate afresh."[64]

ii. By Statute.

6–014   (a) *Lifetime Appointment.* Law of Property Act 1925 s.159, provides that the execution of a deed of appointment will be valid if executed in the presence of and attested by two or more witnesses, even though it does not comply with additional formalities stipulated in the instrument. This provision does not however dispense with any necessary consents, nor does it apply to any acts required to be performed which have no relation to the mode of executing and attesting the document. Nor does it require a power to be exercised by deed where another method of exercise complies with the terms of the power.

---

[58] Thomas, *Powers*, p.495; *Chapman v Gibson* (1791) 3 Bro.C.C. 229 at 230.

[59] Halsbury, 4th edn, Vol.36(2), para.362.

[60] *Kennard v Kennard* (1872) L.R. 8 Ch.App. 227; Thomas, *Powers*, pp.496–507.

[61] *Holmes v Coghill* (1806) 12 Ves.Jr. 206. cf. *Mettoy Pension Trustees v Evans* [1990] 1 W.L.R. 1587; above, para.6–007.

[62] *Vane v Fletcher* (1717) 1 P.Wms. 352 at 355.

[63] *Breadner v Granville-Grossman* [2001] Ch. 523.

[64] *Farwell on Powers*, 3rd edn, 1916, p.394. This is criticised in Thomas, *Powers*, pp.500–501, where it is suggested that relief might be given if the defective execution was procured by fraud, accident or mistake, or where the statutory provision was ambiguous.

(b) *Appointment by Will.* Similarly, an appointment by will is **6–015** valid as regards execution and attestation if the provisions of the Wills Acts relating to the formalities of wills are complied with.[65]

D. Contract to Exercise

A valid contract to exercise a general power, if capable of specific **6–016** performance, operates as a valid exercise of the power in equity; but there can never be specific performance of a contract to exercise a testamentary power, and the only remedy for breach is an action for damages against the estate.[66] A contract to exercise a special testamentary power is not enforceable[67]; but a release, in appropriate circumstances,[68] can be effective, as can a contract not to exercise the power[69]; the property will then go in default of appointment.

5. DELEGATION OF POWERS

In general, a person to whom a discretion has been given, whether **6–017** personally or by virtue of his being in a fiduciary relationship, may not delegate his discretion to others. *Delegatus non potest delegare.*[70] A donee may delegate the performance of merely ministerial acts[71]; and the donee of a general power equivalent to absolute ownership may appoint to a class in such proportions as another shall select.[72] But many powers involve a personal discretion and this prevents delegation.[73] There is no objection however to a testator or settlor giving a power of appointment to a trustee.[74] Such a power given by a testator is not to be impugned as a delegation of testamentary disposition. In *Re Beatty's Will Trusts*[75] the testatrix gave her personal estate and £1.5 million to trustees to allocate "to or among such person or persons as they think fit." Hoffmann J.

[65] Wills Act 1837 s.10; Wills Act 1963 s.2; *Taylor v Meads* (1865) 4 De G.J. & S. 597 at 601.

[66] *Re Parkin* [1892] 3 Ch. 510; below, para.24–026.

[67] *Re Bradshaw* [1902] 1 Ch. 436; *Re Cooke* [1922] 1 Ch. 292.

[68] Below, para.6–025.

[69] *Re Evered* [1910] 2 Ch. 147.

[70] Below, para.20–012.

[71] *Re Hetling and Merton's Contract* [1893] 3 Ch. 269; *Farwell on Powers*, 3rd edn, 1916, pp.503–504.

[72] Thomas, *Powers*, p.392; *Re Triffitt's Settlement* [1958] Ch. 852 (explained in *Re Hay's ST* [1982] 1 W.L.R. 202 as showing that the rule does not apply to bare powers). See also *Fonu v Merrill Lynch Bank and Trust Co (Cayman) Ltd* [2011] W.T.L.R. 1249 (non-fiduciary power to revoke settlement could be delegated).

[73] *De Bussche v Alt* (1878) 8 Ch.D. 286; *Re Morris' Settlement* [1951] 2 All E.R. 528; *Re Hunter's WT* [1963] Ch. 372.

[74] *Houston v Burns* [1918] A.C. 337; *Att Gen v National Provincial Bank* [1924] A.C. 262; *Re Manisty's Settlement* [1974] Ch. 17 at 26; *Re Park* [1932] 1 Ch. 580; *Re Abraham's WT* [1969] 1 Ch. 463 at 475.

[75] [1990] 1 W.L.R. 1503; J Davies (1991) 107 L.Q.R. 211; J Martin [1991] Conv. 138.

upheld the power, rejecting the supposed "anti-delegation" rule: there was no doubt as to the validity of testamentary powers, whether special, general or intermediate.

In the absence of express provision in the instrument creating a special power, the donee may not appoint on discretionary trust.[76] This question arose in *Re Hay's Settlement Trusts*.[77]

> Trustees had a power to appoint to "such persons or purposes" as they should in their discretion select, except the settlor, her husband, or the trustees. Prior to the appointment, the income was to be applied, at the trustees' discretion, for the settlor's nephews and nieces or for charity. The trustees exercised the power of appointment by appointing the property to themselves on a discretionary trust for similar purposes. Prior to the distribution, the income was to be applied to any person or charity. Megarry V.C. held that the exercise of the power was void, so that the property vested in the persons entitled in default of appointment (the period during which the power was exercisable having expired). The appointment did not designate the persons appointed, as the settlement required. It merely provided a mechanism whereby the appointees might be ascertained. The power was to appoint persons, and not to nominate persons to make an appointment. Intermediate powers were subject to the rule against unauthorised delegation, and it was immaterial that the donees of the power were the same persons as the trustees of the discretionary trust.

If the donee appoints on protective trusts,[78] the determinable life interests will be valid, but the discretionary trusts due to take effect on forfeiture of the life interest are void and the trusts in default take effect.[79] There is no objection, however, to the inclusion in an appointment of a power of advancement.[80] Generally, where it is desired that the donee should be able to make an appointment which itself includes a power of appointment or involves any other delegation of discretion, express provision should be made in the instrument creating the power.

6. FRAUD ON A POWER

6–018   An appointor, in the typical case of a special power of appointment with a gift over in default, is under no duty to exercise the power;

---

[76] *Re Morris' Settlement* [1951] 2 All E.R. 528.
[77] [1982] 1 W.L.R. 202.
[78] Below, Ch.7.
[79] *Re Boulton's ST* [1928] Ch. 703; *Re Morris' Settlement*, above, fn.76; *Re Hunter* [1963] Ch. 372.
[80] *Re Mewburn's Settlement* [1934] Ch. 112; *Re Morris' Settlement* [1951] 2 All E.R. 528; *Re Wills' WT* [1959] Ch. 1; *Pilkington v IRC* [1964] A.C. 612; below, para.20–042.

but if he chooses to exercise the power, he must exercise it honestly.[81] Unless he is a fiduciary,[82] he need not weigh the merits of the
possible beneficiaries; he may appoint all the available assets to any
one beneficiary, who may indeed be himself.[83] But he must exercise
it within the limits imposed by the donor or testator who created it.[84]
If, of course, he expressly exceeds those limits the exercise of the
power will be void unless it can be cut down by severing the invalid
excess.[85] But the doctrine of fraudulent exercise of a power goes
further than this, for it extends to the intent with which a power is
exercised. The theory is that, in the case of a special power, the
property is vested in those entitled in default of its exercise subject
to its being divested by a proper exercise of the power,[86] and that an
exercise of the power for any "sinister object" is not proper, is a
fraud on those entitled in default, and void.[87] It should be appreciated that the term "fraud" is used here in a special sense: "The
equitable doctrine of 'fraud on a power' has little, if anything, to do
with fraud".[88] It signifies "in more modern parlance an improper
use of the power for a collateral purpose".[89]

A. Prior Agreement

The first type of case in which an apparently valid exercise of a		**6–019**
power will be void for what in this context is termed fraud[90] is
where the appointment is made as the result of a prior agreement
with the appointee as to what he will do with the proceeds. Such an
exercise of a power will be wholly void save when the appointor is
the person entitled in default, or where the person entitled in default
is a party to it.[91]

B. Benefit to Appointor

A second type of case is where the power is exercised so as to		**6–020**
benefit the appointor. The benefit is usually financial in character, as
where an appointment is made to an ailing child by its father, who

---

[81] *Cloutte v Storey* [1911] 1 Ch. 18.
[82] In which case, see *Re Hay's ST* [1982] 1 W.L.R. 202, above, para.6–017.
[83] *Re Penrose* [1933] Ch. 793.
[84] Y. Grbich (1977) 3 Monash L.R. 210, describing the doctrine of fraud on a power as an
"*ultra vires* appointments" doctrine. See also R. Nolan (2009) 68 C.L.J. 293 at 297–304.
[85] *Churchill v Churchill* (1867) L.R. 5 Eq. 44; *Re Oliphant* (1917) 86 L.J.Ch. 452.
[86] *Re Brook's ST* [1939] Ch. 993.
[87] *Vatcher v Paull* [1915] A.C. 372; *Pitt v Holt* [2011] 3 W.L.R. 19 at 49–50; below,
para.17–045.
[88] *Medforth v Blake* [2000] Ch. 86 at 103.
[89] *Hillsdown Holdings plc v Pensions Ombudsman* [1997] 1 All E.R. 862 at 883.
[90] Above. See the classification in Thomas, *Powers*, p.460, and also Sheridan, *Fraud in
Equity*, 1957, p.116.
[91] See generally *Vatcher v Paull* [1915] A.C. 372.

will benefit on the child's death,[92] but it is not restricted to financial benefit.[93] For the exercise of the power to be void, there must be more than a hope of benefit. Thus an appointment to a healthy child by a father will be valid.[94] For fraud to operate, the appointment must have been made with intent to benefit the appointor. An appointment is sometimes made, however, which in fact benefits the appointor, but which is clearly intended to, and does, benefit the appointees; this is true of many an appointment that forms part of the variation of a trust, for the tax savings achieved will often be a benefit to the appointor. Thus in *Re Merton*,[95] Wynn-Parry J. decided that there was no inflexible rule that forced him to declare such an exercise of a power to be void. The intent that renders an appointment void is a matter "of fact or of inference rather than of law",[96] and must be ascertained as a single fact after consideration of all the relevant evidence.[97] In the context of variation of trusts however, modern cases have shown a reluctance to apply this benevolent view.[98]

Pension trusts provide further scope for the application of the doctrine, as in *Hillsdown Holdings Plc v Pensions Ombudsman*.[99] In that case the pension scheme had a substantial actuarial surplus. Its rules did not permit payment of surplus to the employer, but did permit the transfer of funds to another scheme provided the transfer did not seriously prejudice the members. The trustees transferred the entire fund to another pension scheme, of which the rules could be amended to permit the payment of surplus to the employer. This was done pursuant to an agreement with the employer whereby the benefit to the members would be increased and the surplus (over £11 million) paid to the employer. Although the trustees acted under legal advice and considered the arrangement to be beneficial to the members, it was a breach of trust in the nature of a fraud on a power. The power to transfer the funds had been exercised improperly for the collateral purpose of paying the surplus to the employer.

C. Non-objects

6–021   An appointment is sometimes drafted so that the intent appears to be to benefit objects of the power, but the real intent is to benefit non-objects. It will then be void, even though the appointee was in

---

[92] *Lady Wellesley v Earl Mornington* (1855) 2 K. & J. 143.

[93] *Cochrane v Cochrane* [1922] 2 Ch. 230.

[94] *Henty v Wrey* (1882) 21 Ch.D. 332.

[95] [1953] 1 W.L.R. 1096 at 1100; *Re Robertson's WT* [1960] 1 W.L.R. 1050.

[96] *Re Holland* [1914] 2 Ch. 595 at 601, per Sargant J.

[97] *Re Crawshay* [1948] Ch. 123.

[98] *Re Wallace's Settlements* [1968] 1 W.L.R. 711; *Re Brook's Settlement* [1968] 1 W.L.R. 1661; below, para.22–020, JGM [1968] B.T.R. 199; S Cretney (1969) 32 M.L.R. 317.

[99] [1997] 1 All E.R. 862.

no sense a party, and might not even have known of the appointment or its intent.[100] Thus, in *Re Dick*[101]:

A widow had a power to appoint amongst her brothers and sisters and their issue, but she wished to provide for a family who were looking after her. She had inadequate free capital to do so. She appointed by will to her favourite sister, but coupling the appointment with a request "without imposing any trust or legal obligation" that the sister should provide an annuity for the family concerned. The Court of Appeal held that the absence of obligation on the appointee was not crucial; but rather that the whole intent in making the appointment was to secure a benefit to non-objects by subjecting the appointee to "strong moral suasion to benefit a non-object, which suasion the [appointee] would in the appointor's opinion, be unable to resist."[102] This intent was enough to constitute the exercise of the power as fraudulent.

Difficulties arise from this rule as to real intent, for it is not easy to distinguish cases such as *Re Dick* from cases where there was a real intent to benefit the appointee but coupled with a hope that the appointee would benefit a non-object, which cases are of course not within the doctrine of fraud on a power. But the intent in many cases is simply dual—genuinely to benefit the appointee but also to subject him to strong moral persuasion as to part of the benefit appointed. It may therefore be relevant in *Re Dick*[103] that a substantial proportion of the sum appointed would have been absorbed by the annuity and that a great deal of planning and discussion had gone into the making of the appointment coupled with the expression of the request in formal memoranda. For the danger inherent in extending the doctrine too far is that, if the appointment is void, the appointee loses all benefit unless the appointor is alive to re-appoint,[104] a loss to the appointee which is not justified if intent to benefit him was a substantial element in the exercise of the power.

[100] *Re Nicholson's Settlement* [1939] Ch. 11. This case decided that the doctrine as to the real intent behind an appointment did not apply to a power exercisable only in favour of one person and so exercised. But see the criticism in Sheridan, *Fraud in Equity*, 1957, p.122.

[101] [1953] Ch. 343; *Re Kirwan* (1884) 25 Ch.D. 373 cf. *Re Marsden's Trusts* (1859) 4 Drew. 594.

[102] The matter was put in this way by Cohen L.J. in *Re Crawshay* [1948] Ch. 123 at 135, a case which contained the additional vitiating factor of a covenant by the appointee assigning to non-objects any benefits received by the exercise of the power; H. Hanbury (1948) 64 L.Q.R. 221.

[103] Above, fn.101.

[104] There can be no severance in these cases as there is nothing to sever. But *Re Chadwick's Trusts* [1939] 1 All E.R. 850 shows that a fresh appointment is valid if free from the element that vitiated a prior one.

D. Excessive Exercise; Severance

6–022   If there is a genuine intent to benefit the appointee, something expressly superadded so as to benefit a non-object can be severed, leaving the appointment valid.[105] But severance will not occur in the absence of such a genuine intent.[106] Again if, in a will by which he exercises a power, a testator makes a gift of *his own* property conditional on the appointee resettling the *appointed* property, this is a valid condition on his own gift and the exercise of the power also is valid, provided there was a genuine intent to benefit the appointee.[107] This would be difficult to reconcile with strict emphasis on the intent with which a power was exercised as being "entire and single".[108]

E. Releases

6–023   The doctrine of fraud on a power does not apply to releases, for releases simply benefit those entitled in default. It is irrelevant that the appointor, in releasing his power, is intended to benefit thereby, as he has no duty in respect of the disappointed objects.[109] Nor does the doctrine apply to the revocation of the exercise of a power.[110] An appointment may only be revoked where such right of revocation has been reserved. Where such right exists, it seems that the appointor is under no duty to the appointees. It has even been said that, in revoking, he may stipulate for a benefit, but it would be strange if, by first exercising a power and then revoking it, an appointor could obtain a benefit rightly denied him on an appointment, and it is significant that, in the leading case,[111] the revocation was followed by a release.[112]

F. Position of Third Parties

6–024   The position of a bona fide purchaser, for instance a mortgagee, of an interest appointed to his vendor in such a manner as to amount to a fraud on the power is complicated. Those entitled in default of

---

[105] *Re Kerr's WT* (1878) 4 Ch.D. 600; *Re Holland* [1914] 2 Ch. 595; *Re Burton's Settlements* [1955] Ch. 82; *Price v Williams-Wynn* [2006] W.T.L.R. 1633.

[106] *Re Cohen* [1911] 1 Ch. 37. Severance will not of course occur when there has been a prior agreement with the appointee.

[107] *Re Burton's Settlements* [1955] Ch. 82.

[108] In *Re Simpson* [1952] Ch. 412, Vaisey J. had held that *Re Crawshay* and *Re Dick* impelled him to take this strict view on facts analogous to those in *Re Burton's Settlements* in which case, however, Upjohn J. rightly refused to follow the lead.

[109] *Re Somes* [1896] 1 Ch. 250. Releases may be an important element in the variation of a trust; *Re Ball's Settlement Trusts* [1968] 1 W.L.R. 899, below, para.22–019.

[110] *Re Greaves* [1954] Ch. 434.

[111] [1954] Ch. 434.

[112] cf. Evershed M.R. in *Re Greaves*, above, at 448.

appointment who can challenge the exercise of the power as fraudulent have an interest in the property appointed which in principle prevails over the interest of its bona fide purchasers for value,[113] because no legal title passes under the ordinary power of appointment. The Law of Property Act 1925 s.157, protects such purchasers, but only if the vendor-appointee was at least 25 years of age at the time of sale, and only to the extent to which he was presumptively entitled in default of appointment. Apart from this curious and limited protection, a fraudulent appointment is void even against a bona fide purchaser.

7. RELEASE OF POWERS

A. Why Release?

As a power is discretionary, it may be asked why it becomes **6–025** advantageous to release it as opposed merely to not exercising it. This may be for various reasons; for example, to create indefeasible interests in those entitled in default,[114] to make a gift charitable by releasing a power to appoint to anyone else,[115] to avoid the "reservation of benefit" rules under the inheritance tax system by excluding the settlor from the class of objects,[116] and especially to avoid the effect of the income tax legislation which provides for the income of a settlement to be treated as that of the settlor where, for example, the settlor or his wife may benefit from the exercise of a power of appointment. Until 1958, it had been common to include the wife of the settlor as a member of the discretionary class; and it thus became important to exclude her.[117] This was usually done by exercising the trustees' power to appoint on new trusts which were identical with the old ones except that the wife was omitted. This is in effect a partial release of the earlier power, and is treated as such.[118] As we will see, many of the releases which have been made in this way are of doubtful validity.

---

[113] *Cloutte v Storey* [1911] 1 Ch. 18. See also *Turner v Turner* [1984] Ch. 100, above, para.6–007, on the effect of appointments made in breach of the duty to consider; and *Re Hay's ST* [1982] 1 W.L.R. 202, above, para.6–017, on the effect of an appointment in breach of the duty not to delegate.

[114] *Re Mills* [1930] 1 Ch. 654; *Mettoy Pension Trustees Ltd v Evans* [1990] 1 W.L.R. 1587 (where default beneficiary insolvent).

[115] *Re Wills* [1964] Ch. 219.

[116] Below, para.9–012.

[117] FA 1958 s.22, now Income Tax (Trading and Other Income) Act 2005 ss.624, 625; *Blausten v IRC* [1972] Ch. 256; D Hayton (1972) 36 Conv.(N.S.) 127.

[118] *Re Wills*, above, fn.115; *Muir v IRC* [1966] 1 W.L.R. 251 and 1269; *Blausten v IRC* (above, fn.117).

B. How to Effect a Release

6–026   Trustees may in effect surrender their trusts and powers by paying the money into court under the Trustee Act 1925 s.63[119]; or they may apply to the court for an administration order; or they may ask the court for directions as to the way in which they should act on questions arising in the administration of the trust. Usually, however, the court will not give general directions concerning the exercise of discretionary powers in the future.[120]

They may also effect a release of a power, in appropriate circumstances, by executing a deed of release, or by a contract not to exercise the power.[121] A power may also be extinguished by implication by any dealing with the property by the donee which is inconsistent with its further exercise[122]; or by obtaining the approval of the court to an arrangement which is so inconsistent. There is much uncertainty concerning the validity of releases in some circumstances, and it is important that express provision should be made in the instrument creating the power which expressly authorises the donees of the power to release it.[123]

C. Validity of Release

6–027   It is not possible to lay down with confidence what are the circumstances in which, in the absence of express provision, a release will be valid. The Law of Property Act 1925 s.155, provides that: "A person to whom any power, whether coupled with an interest or not, is given may by deed release, or contract not to exercise, the power."[124]

The question arose whether this provision applied to a situation where the donees of the power were trustees who held the power in a fiduciary capacity. Admittedly they cannot be compelled to exercise it; but can they be allowed to release it? The courts answered this question in the negative[125]; the problem is how to determine which are the cases to which the statute does not apply.

6–028   **i. Trusts.** The first category is that discussed above where the situation is not really a power but a discretionary trust. Here the

---

[119] Below, para.18–026; this is now rare; A. Hawkins (1968) 84 L.Q.R. 67. See also *Thrells Ltd v Lomas* [1993] 1 W.L.R. 456 (exercise of fiduciary power properly surrendered to court to avoid conflict of duties).

[120] *Re Allen-Meyrick's WT* [1966] 1 W.L.R. 499; A. Hawkins (1967) 31 Conv.(N.S.) 117; below, para.18–025.

[121] LPA 1925 ss.155, 160.

[122] *Re Christie-Miller's Settlement* [1961] 1 W.L.R. 462; *Re Wills* [1964] Ch. 219; *Muir v IRC* [1966] 1 W.L.R. 251, 1269; *Re Courtauld's Settlement* [1965] 2 All E.R. 544; *Blausten v IRC* [1972] Ch. 256; A Hawkins (1968) 84 L.Q.R. 92–93.

[123] *Muir v IRC* [1966] 1 W.L.R. 1269; *Blausten v IRC*, above, fn.122.

[124] Replacing earlier legislation.

[125] *Re Eyre* (1883) 49 L.T. 259; *Saul v Pattinson* (1886) 55 L.J.Ch. 831.

trustees are under a duty to appoint; if they fail to do so, the court will declare the property to be held on trust for the possible appointees.[126] There is no question of release here.

ii. Fiduciary Powers. Where a power is conferred upon a person   **6–029** by virtue of his office, he may not release it "*In the absence of words in the trust deed authorising [him] so to do.*"[127] Here there may be a gift over in default, either to the class of appointees or to a different class. This is a power proper, and not a trust. But the power is one given to the trustees to be exercised in a fiduciary capacity. They cannot discard it; they are, as has been seen,[128] under a duty to consider from time to time whether and how to exercise the power. This is so whether it is given to them as trustees, or whether it is given to persons by name if on the true view of the facts, they were selected as donee of the power because they were trustees.[129] Conversely, persons selected as individuals may be described as trustees. In *Re Wills' Trust Deeds*[130] a power of appointment in respect of property which was the subject of a *settlement* was given to the trustees of the settlor's *will*; this was not given by virtue of their office. Modern pension fund cases provide illustrations of the rules as to the release of powers. In *Re Courage Group's Pension Schemes*[131] fiduciary powers were vested in a committee set up to manage a pension scheme. It was held that even if existing members of the committee could release, fetter, or agree not to exercise their powers (which was not decided),[132] they could not deprive their successors of the right to exercise their powers. In *Mettoy Pension Trustees Ltd v Evans*[133] there was a power in favour of the pension fund beneficiaries, with the employer company taking in default. On the company's insolvency, the liquidator sought to release the power in the interests of the creditors. This could not be done because the power was fiduciary. The liquidator could not exercise the power because of a conflict of duties,[134] and so the court could intervene to protect the objects.[135]

---

[126] Equal division is not necessary in the case of the modern discretionary trust; above, para.3–026.

[127] *Muir v IRC* [1966] 1 W.L.R. 1269 at 1283, per Harman L.J.; the italics are original; *Blausten v IRC* [1972] Ch. 256.

[128] Above, para.6–006.

[129] *Re Cookes' Contract* (1877) 4 Ch.D. 454.

[130] [1964] Ch. 219. (The actual decision probably does not survive that of the Court of Appeal in *Muir v IRC* [1966] 1 W.L.R. 1269).

[131] [1987] 1 W.L.R. 495.

[132] See H. Arthur (1993) 7 T.L.I. 69.

[133] [1990] 1 W.L.R. 1587.

[134] See now Pensions Act 1995 s.25(2).

[135] Above, para.6–007.

6–030   **iii. Bare Powers.** Where the power is given to a person in his private capacity, the donee is prima facie able to release it,[136] even if the release operates in favour of the donee, as where a father releases a power so that the shares of his sons (who are entitled in default) become absolute, and that of a deceased son passes to the donee.[137] A release, or a covenant not to exercise it, (which will be equivalent to a release)[138] may be effective if it refers only to part of the property,[139] or if it relates only to one or more of several objects.[140]

6–031   **iv. Variation of Trusts Act 1958.** Section 1 of the Variation of Trusts Act 1958 makes no express reference to powers. Many powers are vested in trustees, as in the case of discretionary or protective trusts; and a variation of such powers will no doubt be covered by the provisions of the Act. It appears that an arrangement under the Act which recites the release of a power,[141] or one which is inconsistent with the future exercise of the power,[142] will effectively release it.

---

[136] This is Buckley J.'s fifth category in *Re Wills' Trust Deeds* [1964] Ch. 219.
[137] *Re Radcliffe* [1892] 1 Ch. 227; an appointment in favour of the estate of the deceased son would have been a fraud on the power.
[138] per Buckley L.J. in *Re Evered* [1910] 2 Ch. 147 at 161.
[139] *Re Evered*, above, fn.138.
[140] *Re Brown's Settlement* [1939] Ch. 944; Thomas, *Powers*, p.614.
[141] [1961] 1 W.L.R. 462.
[142] *Re Courtauld's Settlement* [1965] 2 All E.R. 544; *Re Ball's ST* [1968] 1 W.L.R. 899.

CHAPTER 7

PROTECTIVE TRUSTS

1. THE GENERAL PROBLEM

A DEBTOR'S property is in principle available for the satisfaction of **7–001** his creditors and, if he becomes bankrupt, it will pass to his trustee in bankruptcy; but it is possible, by making use of a protective trust, to obtain a measure of protection against such an event.

In the development of protective trusts the courts have been torn between two conflicting pressures. On the one hand, nobody should have the power of defeating his creditors by putting his property beyond their grasp; on the other, a settlor should be able to create a trust in any form, so long as it is not unlawful; and there is much to be said for allowing some means of protecting a person's dependants from the ill-effects of his extravagance. The technique of protective trusts involves the giving of a determinable life interest with a gift over upon the happening of certain events. Originally, the gift over was usually in favour of other members of the family[1]; but the modern practice is to provide for a gift over to trustees to hold on discretionary trusts in favour of a class which includes the life tenant and members of his family; and this pattern is provided for by the Trustee Act 1925 s.33.[2] Protective trust clauses are commonly used today in occupational pension schemes, to prevent alienation of

---

[1] e.g. *Re Detmold* (1889) 40 Ch.D. 585.
[2] Below, para.7–005.

pension rights.[3] A similar result was achieved in *Re Scientific Pension Plan Trusts*,[4] where a forfeiture clause operating on the bankruptcy of a member prevented the benefits passing to the trustee in bankruptcy. Instead they passed to the pension scheme trustees, who had power to apply them for the benefit of the member's dependants.

2. DETERMINABLE AND CONDITIONAL INTERESTS

7–002   A distinction is made in law between an interest subject to a condition subsequent and a determinable interest.[5] The former exists where there is a gift of an absolute interest which is then cut down by the application of a condition; such as a gift to X absolutely, but if he should change his nationality, then over to Y. A determinable interest exists where something less than an absolute interest is given in the first place; as a gift to X until he changes (or so long as he retains) his nationality. The distinction is subtle[6]; it depends entirely upon the language of the gift; but it is a distinction that has importance in several contexts. The relevance in the present context is twofold: first, that a condition against alienation is void[7]; secondly, that a condition subsequent, being one which effects a forfeiture of an existing interest, is strictly construed[8]; if the condition is held void, the interest becomes absolute.[9] The determining event, however, in the case of a determinable interest is less strictly construed; and if it should be held invalid, the whole interest fails.[10]

Thus it is clear that a *condition* so drafted as to terminate an interest upon alienation[11] or bankruptcy[12] is void and the prior interest is absolute. But an interest *determinable* on alienation or bank-

---

[3] Below, para.16–026.

[4] [1999] Ch. 53. See now Welfare Reform and Pensions Act 1999 s.14(3).

[5] *Brandon v Robinson* (1811) 18 Ves.Jr. 429 at 433 (Lord Eldon); M. & W., p.65; Cheshire and Burn, Ch.17. The clue to the existence of a determinable limitation is the use of words such as "until", "so long as", "whilst", as distinct from phraseology such as "but if" and "when, if ever".

[6] "Little short of disgraceful to our jurisprudence," per Porter M.R. in *Re King's Trusts* (1892) 29 L.R.Ir. 401 at 410; "The distinction is not a particularly attractive one, being based on form rather than substance", per Rattee J. in *Re Scientific Investment Pension Plan Trusts* [1999] Ch. 53 at 59.

[7] *Re Brown* [1954] Ch. 39.

[8] *Clavering v Ellison* (1859) 7 H.L.Cas. 707; *Sifton v Sifton* [1938] A.C. 656.

[9] *Re Greenwood* [1903] 1 Ch. 749.

[10] *Re Moore* (1888) 39 Ch.D. 116. (Gift of a weekly sum to T's sister "whilst . . . living apart from her husband" construed as a gift determinable upon returning to her husband, and held void); *Re Tuck's ST* [1978] Ch. 49.

[11] *Brandon v Robinson* (1811) 18 Ves.Jr. 429; *Re Dugdale* (1888) 38 Ch.D. 176; *Re Brown* [1954] Ch. 39; Glanville Williams (1943) 59 L.Q.R. 343.

[12] *Re Sanderson's Trust* (1857) 3 K. & J. 497; *Re Scientific Investment Pension Plan Trusts*, above, fn.6.

ruptcy is valid.[13] The basis of protective trusts is therefore a determinable life interest.

3. SELF-PROTECTION

A settlor cannot make a settlement which will protect himself **7–003** against his own bankruptcy.[14]

In *Re Burroughs-Fowler*,[15] the settlor, by ante-nuptial settlement, settled property upon trust to pay the income to himself for life or until one of certain events should occur, including his bankruptcy, after which event the income was to be paid to his wife. The settlor was adjudicated bankrupt during the wife's lifetime. It was held that the life interest vested indefeasibly in his trustee in bankruptcy, who could validly dispose of it.

A settlor may however protect himself against other forms of alienation, voluntary or involuntary. And if the limitation, as is usual, provides for the termination of his interest upon any one of such events *or* upon his bankruptcy, the gift over, as we have seen, is void in the event of bankruptcy, but valid in all other cases.[16] If the gift over has taken effect upon, for example, an attempt to charge the life interest, the subsequent bankruptcy of the settlor has no effect upon it.

In *Re Detmold*,[17] a marriage settlement of the settlor's own property provided for the payment of the income to the settlor for life or "till he shall become bankrupt or shall . . . suffer something whereby the same . . . would . . . by operation of law . . . become . . . payable to some other person . . . " and, after such determination, on trust to pay the income to his wife. In July 1888, an order was made appointing a judgment creditor to be receiver of the income; and in September 1888 the settlor was adjudicated bankrupt. It was held that the forfeiture took place upon the involuntary alienation of the income by process of law.

---

[13] Below, para.7–004; see also the earlier authorities relied on by Turner V.C. in *Rochford v Hackman* (1852) 9 Hare 475. For a modern application of these principles, see *Money Markets International Stockbrokers Ltd (In Liquidation) v London Stock Exchange Ltd* [2002] 1 W.L.R. 1150.

[14] *Mackintosh v Pogose* [1895] 1 Ch. 505. This rule is preserved by TA 1925 s.33(3). Nor may he settle his property on a third party to prejudice his own creditors; below, paras 13–017–13–029.

[15] [1916] 2 Ch. 251; *Official Assignee v NZI Life Superannuation Nominees Ltd* [1995] 1 N.Z.L.R. 684.

[16] *Re Detmold* (1889) 40 Ch.D. 585; *Re Brewer's Settlement* [1896] 2 Ch. 503; *Re Johnson* [1904] 1 K.B. 134.

[17] (1889) 40 Ch.D. 585.

The wife then became entitled to the income, and she did not lose the right on the subsequent bankruptcy.

4. PROTECTED LIFE INTERESTS IN PERSONS OTHER THAN THE SETTLOR

7–004 Though a person cannot make a settlement of his own property upon himself until bankruptcy, and then over, a trust created by A to pay the income to B until B dies or becomes bankrupt alienates or charges his life interest and then over to C is good in the event of the occurrence of any of those events, including B's bankruptcy.[18] The essence of the device of protected life interests[19] is that, on the occurrence of a determining event, such as alienation or bankruptcy, the interest of the life tenant determines, and the trustees then hold the property on discretionary trusts for the benefit of the life tenant and his family.

Some early attempts to reach this result failed, owing to the absence of any clear gift over of the income.[20] Eventually, however, discretionary trusts became accepted,[21] and in modern times quite independently of protective trusts.

The court may exercise its jurisdiction to vary trusts so as to convert a beneficial interest into a protected life interest where it is feared that the beneficiary cannot manage his affairs in a responsible manner.[22]

5. TRUSTEE ACT 1925 SECTION 33

7–005 Before 1926 it was necessary to set out expressly the terms of the trusts; and a settlor may still do so if he wishes.[23] In relation, however, to trusts coming into operation after 1925, the Trustee Act 1925 s.33, "provides a shorthand arrangement whereby a settlor may establish a trust without setting forth in detail all the terms upon

---

[18] *Re Ashby* [1892] 1 Q.B. 872; *Re Scientific Investment Pension Plan Trusts* [1999] Ch. 53.

[19] L. Sheridan (1957) 21 Conv.(N.S.) 110.

[20] The point is discussed in *Rochford v Hackman* (1852) 9 Hare 475.

[21] And may take effect where the forfeiture precedes the settlement; as where the bankruptcy began before the testator died: *Metcalfe v Metcalfe* [1891] 3 Ch. 1. See also *Re Forder* [1927] 2 Ch. 291; *Re Walker* [1939] Ch. 974.

[22] *Hambro v Duke of Marlborough* [1994] Ch. 158; below, para.22–008 (unsuitability of Marquess of Blandford to manage Blenheim). See also *Re Abram (Deceased)* [1996] 2 F.L.R. 379 (protected life interest ordered under Inheritance (Provision for Family and Dependants) Act 1975, where any capital sum would have gone to applicant's creditors).

[23] *Re Shaw's Settlement* [1951] Ch. 833; *Re Rees (Deceased)* [1954] Ch. 202; *Re Munro's ST* [1963] 1 W.L.R. 145.

which the property is to be held."[24] The section applies although the statutory formula "on protective trusts" may not be used, so long as the intention is clear.[25] The section then applies subject to any modification contained in the instrument creating the trust.[26]

Section 33(1)[27] provides:

"Where any income, including an annuity or other periodical income payment, is directed to be held on protective trusts for the benefit of any person (in this section called 'the principal beneficiary') for the period of his life or for any less period, then, during that period (in this section called the 'trust period') the said income shall, without prejudice to any prior interest, be held on the following trusts, namely:—

(i) Upon trust for the principal beneficiary during the trust period or until he . . . does or attempts to do or suffers any act or thing, or until any event happens, other than an advance under any statutory or express power, whereby, if the said income were payable during the trust period to the principal beneficiary absolutely during that period, he would be deprived of the right to receive the same or any part thereof,[28] in any of which cases . . . this trust of the said income shall fail or determine;

(ii) [and during the remainder of the trust period] . . . upon trust for the application thereof for the maintenance or support, or otherwise for the benefit, of all or any one or more exclusively of the other or others of the following persons[29] (that is to say)—

(a) the principal beneficiary and his or her spouse or civil partner, if any, and his or her children or more remote issue, if any; or

(b) if there is no spouse or civil partner or issue of the principal beneficiary in existence, the principal beneficiary and the persons who would, if he were actually dead, be entitled to the trust property or the income thereof or the annuity fund, if any, or arrears of the annuity, as the case may be;

as the trustees in their absolute discretion, without being liable to account for the exercise of such discretion, think fit."

---

[24] Griswold, *Spendthrift Trusts*, 1936, p.375.

[25] *Re Wittke* [1944] Ch. 166 ("under protective trusts for the benefit of my sister").

[26] TA 1925 s.33(2).

[27] As amended by the Civil Partnership Act 2004.

[28] See *Re Smith's Will Trusts* (1981) 131 N.L.J. 292.

[29] Relationships are to be construed in accordance with s.1 of the Family Law Reform Act 1987 (i.e. without regard to legitimacy); FLRA 1987 Sch.2, para.2.

6. Forfeiture of the Life Tenant's Interest

7–006   It is necessary in each case to decide whether or not the event which has occurred is sufficient to determine the interest of the life tenant, and thus to bring the discretionary trusts into operation.[30] The question usually arises under trusts governed by the Trustee Act 1925, s.33. Where the question arises in respect of an express protective trust, the question will depend on the construction of the particular trust under consideration.[31] The principles applicable will however be the same.

It will be appreciated that a forfeiture is not in the bankruptcy cases a disaster. The forfeiture deprives the life tenant of his life interest, which would otherwise have become available to his creditors. The effect of the forfeiture is to allow the protective provisions to come into effect, and to keep the principal beneficiary's interest from his trustee in bankruptcy.[32]

A. Determining Events

7–007   If the principal beneficiary alienates his interest,[33] or goes bankrupt, a forfeiture obviously occurs. In other circumstances, it is often difficult to draw a clear dividing line between those which will and those which will not effect a forfeiture. The matter is best explained by illustrations. The first three are cases of express protective trusts in which the instrument provided that the life interest should be determinable upon the happening of some event whereby some or all of the income became payable to another person.

In *Re Balfour's Settlement Trusts*,[34] the trustees had, at the life tenant's request, and in breach of trust, advanced parts of the capital to him. They then asserted their right to retain the income of the fund in order to make good the breach. Subsequently, the life tenant became bankrupt. Farwell J. held that the life tenant's interest had determined because the trustees became entitled to the income.[35] The life interest was thus saved from the bankruptcy.

[30] *Re Brewer's Settlement* [1896] 2 Ch. 503.
[31] [1896] 2 Ch. 503 at 507; *Re Dennis' ST* [1942] Ch. 283 at 286; *Re Hall* [1944] Ch. 46.
[32] See *Re Scientific Investment Pension Plan Trusts* [1999] Ch. 53.
[33] *Gibbon v Mitchell* [1990] 1 W.L.R. 1304, below, para.26–002 (surrender of protected life interest to remaindermen for tax purposes caused forfeiture, but deed set aside for mistake).
[34] [1938] Ch. 928; *Re Gordon* [1978] Ch. 145.
[35] Distinguishing *Re Brewer's Settlement* [1896] 2 Ch. 503, where bankruptcy took place before the trustees exercised their right.

In *Re Baring's Settlement Trusts*,[36] a sequestration order was made against the property of a mother who failed to obey a court order to return her children to the jurisdiction. Morton J. held that the order effected a forfeiture, although the mother's loss of income was only temporary.

In *Re Dennis' Settlement Trusts*,[37] the settlor's son was entitled to a protective life interest under a family settlement. A rearrangement took place on his attaining the age of 21, and provided that for the next six years the trustees should pay to him only part of the income and should accumulate the rest for him. The rearrangement caused a forfeiture.

In *Re Gourju's Will Trusts*,[38] the protective trust was one governed by the Trustee Act 1925 s.33. The life tenant ceased to be entitled to receive the income of the trust because she lived in Nice, which became enemy occupied country during the Second World War. This caused a forfeiture. The Custodian of Enemy Property had no claim; nor could the trustees treat the tenant for life as still entitled, and retain income for her until the end of the war. The discretionary trusts came into effect, and the income was payable to one or more members of the class of beneficiaries.

On the other hand, residence in enemy occupied territory did not cause a forfeiture in *Re Hall*,[39] where forfeiture was to take place if the annuitant should "do or suffer any act" whereby the annuity should be payable elsewhere. The annuity could no longer be paid to the annuitant; but this was not due to anything that she had done or permitted; the Custodian of Enemy Property was entitled. Nor was there a forfeiture where a life tenant under a protective trust (terminable if the income became "payable to . . . some other person") assigned his interest to the trustees of his marriage settlement (of which he was tenant for life), authorised the trustees to charge their expenses to the fund and appointed them his attorneys to receive the income.[40] Again there was no forfeiture where the life tenant lacked mental capacity and a receiver was appointed.[41] Nor does the fact that a receiver's (or now a deputy's) fees become payable out of the

---

[36] [1940] Ch. 737.

[37] [1942] Ch. 283.

[38] [1943] Ch. 24; *Re Wittke* [1944] Ch. 166; *Re Allen-Meyrick's Will Trusts* [1966] 1 W.L.R. 499. See also Trading with the Enemy (Custodian) (No.2) Order, 1945 (S.R. & O. 1945 No.887) providing that vesting in the Custodian should not take place if it would cause a forfeiture.

[39] [1944] Ch. 46; *Re Harris* [1945] Ch. 316; *Re Pozot's ST* [1952] Ch. 427.

[40] *Re Tancred's Settlement* [1903] 1 Ch. 715. Similarly an assignment of income already accrued; *Re Greenwood* [1901] 1 Ch. 887.

[41] *Re Oppenheimer's WT* [1950] Ch. 633; *Re Marshall* [1920] 1 Ch. 284. Receivers are replaced by deputies under the Mental Capacity Act 2005.

estate of such a person effect a forfeiture.[42] An authority to pay to creditors the dividends due from a company for a period of time during which the company declared no dividend did not cause a forfeiture.[43]

B. Order of the Court under the Trustee Act 1925
Section 57[44]

7–008　　The court may make an order under the Trustee Act 1925 s.57, which may affect the operation of a trust. If an order is made authorising the trustees to raise money to pay the debts of a life tenant under a protective trust, there is no forfeiture; for the power must be treated as if it had been "inserted in the trust instrument as an over-riding power."[45] If the order provides that the life tenant effects an insurance policy to secure a like amount of money at his death, and that the trustees shall pay the premiums out of the income if the life tenant fails to do so, there is no forfeiture so long as the life tenant makes the payments; but if the life tenant fails to pay and they become payable by the trustees from the income, there would be a forfeiture.[46]

C. Order of the Court under the Matrimonial Causes Acts
1859–1973

7–009　　It is not clear whether a forfeiture is effected when a court order is made which alters a protected life interest under a marriage settlement.[47] In *Re Richardson's Will Trusts*,[48] the court ordered that the principal beneficiary should charge his interest with an annual payment of £50 in favour of his divorced wife. The charge was held to create a forfeiture. On the other hand, in *General Accident Fire and Life Assurance Corp Ltd v IRC*[49] an order diverting part of the income from the life tenant in favour of a former wife was held not to effect a forfeiture.

---

[42] *Re Westby's Settlement* [1950] Ch. 296; Mental Capacity Act 2005 s.56(2), re-enacting earlier legislation.

[43] *Re Longman* [1955] 1 W.L.R. 197.

[44] Below, para.22–007.

[45] *Re Mair* [1935] Ch. 562 at 565, per Farwell J.

[46] *Re Salting* [1932] 2 Ch. 57 at 65.

[47] Which the court has power to do under Matrimonial Causes Act 1973 s.24(1).

[48] [1958] Ch. 504, illustrating the advantage of establishing a series of protective trusts, "one set until the beneficiary is twenty-five, another from twenty-five to thirty-five, a third from thirty-five to forty-five, and another for the rest of his life." A forfeiture of, or a charge upon, the principal beneficiary's interest in one of the trusts would not affect his interest in subsequent trusts. He would get a fresh start. REM (1958) 74 L.Q.R. 182.

[49] [1963] 1 W.L.R. 1207.

These cases are distinguishable on a narrow ground of construction of s.33.[50] But the broader ground of the decision, that this situation has no relevance to the real purpose of protective trusts, would seem to apply to the charge in *Re Richardson's Will Trusts*[51] as much as to the diversion of part of the income in the *General Accident* case.[52] It is submitted that the principle of the *General Accident* case is sound. As Donovan L.J. said[53]:

" . . . [T]he section is intended as a protection to spendthrift or improvident or weak life tenants. But it can give . . . no protection against the effect of a court order such as was made here. Furthermore, if such an order involves a forfeiture much injustice could be done."

Perhaps the problem can be rationalised with the cases on s.57 by saying with Russell L.J., who made clear, however, that he did not rest his decision on this approach: "the settlement throughout was potentially subject in all its trusts to such an order as was made."[54] *Re Richardson's Will Trusts*[55] was not mentioned; but an earlier case on the Matrimonial Causes Act 1859 in favour of forfeiture, *Re Carew*,[56] was overruled. It is tempting to say that *Re Richardson's Will Trusts* is wrong; but it should be noted that in that case, as in *Re Carew*, the decision in favour of forfeiture forwarded the broad policy of s.33; for the forfeiture in those cases allowed the discretionary trusts to operate when otherwise the trustee in bankruptcy would have claimed the interest.

7. ADVANCEMENTS

Section 33(1) expressly exempts, as a cause of forfeiture, an advancement under any statutory[57] or express power. Thus the fact that the life tenant no longer receives the income of the part of the capital which has been advanced does not effect a forfeiture.[58] It appears that the same rule applies in the case of an express protective trust.[59]

7–010

---

[50] [1963] 1 W.L.R. 1207. See Donovan L.J. at 1217 and Russell L.J. at 1221; F. Crane (1963) 27 Conv.(N.S.) 517.

[51] [1958] Ch. 504.

[52] [1963] 1 W.L.R. 1207.

[53] [1963] 1 W.L.R. 1207 per Donovan L.J. at 1218.

[54] [1963] 1 W.L.R. 1207 at 1222.

[55] [1958] Ch. 504.

[56] (1910) 103 L.T. 658.

[57] TA 1925 s.32; below, para.20–038.

[58] See however *General Accident Fire and Life Assurance Corp Ltd v IRC* [1963] 1 W.L.R. 1207 which suggests that an advancement does not effect a forfeiture and that the proviso to s.33 is for the avoidance of doubt.

[59] *Re Hodgson* [1913] 1 Ch. 34; *Re Shaw's Settlement* [1951] Ch. 833; *Re Rees (Deceased)* [1954] Ch. 202.

Re Stimpson[60] is to the contrary, but is regarded as of doubtful authority.

8. EFFECT OF FORFEITURE

7–011 When a forfeiture has taken place, the life interest of the principal beneficiary is terminated, and the trusts in s.33(1)(ii), or those expressly contained in the instrument, as the case may be, come into play.[61] The termination is not usually, however, an occasion of charge to inheritance tax,[62] although this rule is subject to certain restrictions where the protective trust arises on or after March 22, 2006.[63] Under s.33 there are discretionary trusts in favour of the principal beneficiary and other persons, depending on whether or not a spouse or civil partner or issue of the principal beneficiary is in existence. The trustees may apply the income for the remainder of the trust period for any member of the discretionary class. The principal beneficiary is not entitled to any income; but the trustees may, if they wish, pay it to him. They must pay the income to one or more of the members.[64] If the trustees decide to pay some income to the principal beneficiary, they face the problem that the money may be claimed by the trustee in bankruptcy as the assignee of his "interest" under the discretionary trust,[65] or perhaps only the surplus above that needed for his "mere support".[66] They may, however, in their absolute discretion, apply the money for his use and benefit.[67] Thus:

> "[I]f the trustees were to pay an hotel-keeper to give him a dinner he would get nothing but the right to eat a dinner, and that is not property which could pass by assignment or bankruptcy."[68]

It is safer to pay the money to third persons in satisfaction of services provided for the bankrupt.

---

[60] [1931] 2 Ch. 77.

[61] See also the forfeiture clause in *Re Scientific Investment Pension Plan Trusts* [1999] Ch. 53 (interest passed to pension scheme trustees with power to apply to member's dependants).

[62] Inheritance Tax Act 1984 s.88; below, para.9–027.

[63] Finance Act 2006 Sch.20, para.24.

[64] *Re Gourju's WT* [1943] Ch. 24.

[65] *Re Coleman* (1888) 39 Ch.D. 443; *Re Bullock* (1891) 64 L.T. 736 at 738.

[66] *Re Ashby* [1892] 1 Q.B. 872 at 877.

[67] *Re Bullock* (above, fn.65); *Re Coleman* (above, fn.65); *Re Smith* [1928] Ch. 915 at 919; *Public Trustee v Ferguson* [1947] N.Z.L.R. 746.

[68] *Re Coleman*, above, fn.65, at 451.

CHAPTER 8

DISCRETIONARY TRUSTS

1. GENERAL

IT has been seen that discretionary trusts were used as a means of **8–001** dealing with the income of a protective trust after the interest of the principal beneficiary had ended. Other advantages which discretionary trusts could offer came to be appreciated, especially in the context of estate duty saving, and they developed into one of the principal tools of estate and tax planners. Estate duty was replaced by capital transfer tax (now inheritance tax) in the Finance Act 1975. An explanation of the current tax position will be delayed until the next chapter, so that the fiscal situation of different types of trusts may be considered together. It will then be seen that discretionary trusts suffered substantially upon the introduction of capital transfer tax, and became at a disadvantage in relation to other trusts.[1] The disadvantage was increased when the discretionary trust became the only form of trust to be initially chargeable to inheritance tax upon its lifetime creation. However, as we will see in the next chapter, the Finance Act 2006 withdrew many inheritance tax advantages from non-discretionary trusts. Outright gifts and some non-discretionary trusts are potentially exempt (i.e. chargeable only if the transferor dies within seven years).[2] The importance of discretionary trusts has been to some extent reduced because of their current inheritance tax treatment, but they need to be examined because they retain many advantages outside the fiscal field; also because they raise a number of interesting and important theoretical questions in the law of trusts.

2. Uses of Discretionary Trusts

8–002   There are various reasons why a settlor may prefer to establish discretionary trusts rather than fixed trusts. As previously indicated, the most important reason used to be the saving of estate duty, and this will be referred to in Ch.9. The emphasis is now on the other advantages.

A. To Protect the Beneficiary Against Creditors
8–003   If one member of a class of beneficiaries under a discretionary trust goes bankrupt, the trustee in bankruptcy is not entitled to claim any part of the fund.[3] The trustee in bankruptcy is however entitled to goods and money paid over by the trustees to the beneficiary in the exercise of their discretion[4]; or perhaps only to the amount in excess of that needed for the maintenance of the beneficiary.[5] The trustee in bankruptcy is however excluded if the trustees make the maintenance payments to third parties, such as a hotel keeper[6] or tradesman.[7]

We have already seen that discretionary trusts are employed under protective trusts as a means whereby a protected life tenant may

---

[1] Although the rules applicable to discretionary trusts were substantially amended and rationalised by the Finance Act 1982.

[2] Below, para.9–009.

[3] *Re Ashby* [1892] 1 Q.B. 872 at p.877; *Re Bullock* (1891) 64 L.T. 736. If the bankrupt is the sole member of the discretionary class, the interest passes to the trustee in bankruptcy: *Green v Spicer* (1830) 1 Russ. & M. 395. See also *Re Trafford's Settlement* [1985] Ch. 32, below, para.8–015.

[4] *Re Coleman* (1888) 39 Ch.D. 443.

[5] *Re Ashby*, above, fn.3, at 877; *Page v Way* (1840) 3 Beav. 20, above, para.7–011.

[6] *Re Coleman*, above, fn.4, at 451; above, para.7–011.

[7] *Godden v Crowhurst* (1842) 10 Sim. 642 at 656.

continue to receive some benefit from settled funds after his bankruptcy.[8] Indeed, this was their earliest use.

B. To Continue to Exercise Control over Young or Improvident Beneficiaries

Many take the view that it is unwise to put large sums of money at **8–004** the disposal of beneficiaries if they are young or extravagant. This is due not only to the fear of the loss of family capital in case of insolvency; but also because a rich young beneficiary may be encouraged to develop habits of idleness and extravagance, and waste the inheritance; older beneficiaries may already have done so. While the discretionary trust is in operation, each member of the class of beneficiaries is entitled only to the money which the trustees see fit to allocate to him in the exercise of their discretion. The settlor may, whether or not he is a trustee, be able to influence the selection so as to exercise some element of control over the beneficiaries.[9]

C. To React to Changes in Circumstances

The trustees can exercise their discretion in relation to distribution **8–005** of income and capital according to the circumstances existing at the time. When the trust is set up, there is no way of knowing how the beneficiaries will fare in the future; which of them will be most in need; which will be deserving, which spendthrift, which inebriate; which will marry millionaires, and which missionaries. The trustees can take all these factors into consideration in making their decisions; and will be much influenced by the wishes of the settlor. In making these decisions, they will also take tax factors into consideration; it is more economical to give income to those with smaller incomes; and capital given to rich beneficiaries may bear inheritance tax not only on the distribution but also when disposed of by them. Decisions by trustees which favour one beneficiary over another may of course give rise to criticism and resentment by disappointed beneficiaries.[10] All these factors need to be taken into consideration. It might be added that a discretionary trust may be used where the settlor wishes to provide for a beneficiary without making him ineligible for means-tested state benefits, as he has no entitlement to capital or income.

---

[8] Ch.7.

[9] But if he influences the trustees to such an extent that they fail to exercise their discretion independently, the appointment will be void; *Turner v Turner* [1984] Ch. 100, below, para.8–021.

[10] The trustees need not disclose the reasons for their decisions; *Re Beloved Wilkes's Charity* (1851) 3 Mac. & G. 440, below, para.17–043.

3. Usual Form of Discretionary Trusts

A. Trustees' Discretion

8–006   The essential feature of a discretionary trust is that the property is conveyed to trustees to be held by them on trust to apply the income or the capital or both for the benefit of the members of a class of beneficiaries in such proportions as the trustees shall, in their absolute discretion, think fit. Most discretionary trusts are concerned with distribution of income; the distribution of capital is commonly effected under a power to appoint. It used to be common to include a wider class of beneficiaries as objects of the power of appointment, and a narrower, more specific class of beneficiaries of the discretionary trusts.[11] But, since *McPhail v Doulton*,[12] the test of certainty of beneficiaries of a discretionary trust has been assimilated to that of objects of a mere power, and the wider class can now be employed for both purposes. During the period of the trust, no individual beneficiary is entitled to any share of the property, income or capital; he receives what the trustees see fit to give him and no more.

B. The Trust Period

8–007   Provision will be made for the discretionary trust to continue for the trust period; which can be any desired period which is not in excess of the perpetuity period. Discretionary trusts provide a special situation for the application of the perpetuity rule. Since no individual beneficiary has any interest under the trust, property only vests in a beneficiary upon the exercise of the trustees' discretion in his favour; and such a vesting is void unless it takes place within the perpetuity period.[13] A discretionary trust can only exist, therefore, for the duration of the perpetuity period.

A discretionary trust will therefore be designed to terminate before the end of the period. This is normally done by postulating the "trust period" at the conclusion of which the discretionary trust will terminate, and providing for a gift over on fixed trusts which will themselves vest within the perpetuity period. Since 1964, a period of years not exceeding 80 years could be specified.[14] For instruments made on or after April 6, 2010 the perpetuity period is 125 years.[15]

C. Power to Accumulate

8–008   In many cases the income beneficiaries will not need the trust income each year. Until quite recently it was possible to save tax by

---

[11] *Re Gestetner* [1953] Ch. 672.
[12] [1971] A.C. 424; above, para.3–026.
[13] *Re Coleman* [1936] Ch. 521.
[14] PAA 1964 s.1.
[15] PAA 2009 s.5. No other perpetuity period may be specified.

retaining income in the trust because the rate applicable to the trust was lower than that of a beneficiary who paid higher rate income tax, but this is no longer the case.[16] The trustees are commonly given a power to accumulate. Without such a power, they will be obliged to distribute the income[17]; not to any particular beneficiary, but among the beneficiaries. It was noted above[18] that such a power makes the distinction between exhaustive and non-exhaustive discretionary trusts. The trust is non-exhaustive as to the income if the income is not required to be distributed each year; and non-exhaustive as to the capital if the trustees are not obliged to distribute all the capital during the currency of the trust.

For instruments made before April 6, 2010[19] there are statutory restrictions upon powers of accumulation. The permitted periods are (by the Law of Property Act 1925 s.164 as amended by the Perpetuities and Accumulations Act 1964 s.13):

(a) the life of the grantor or settlor; or
(b) a term of 21 years from the death of the grantor, settlor or testator; or
(c) the duration of the minority or respective minorities of any person or persons living or *en ventre sa mère* at the death of the grantor, settlor or testator; or
(d) the duration of the minority or respective minorities only of any person or persons who under the limitations of the instrument directing the accumulations would, for the time being, if of full age be entitled to the income directed to be accumulated; or
(e) a term of 21 years from the date of the making of the disposition; or
(f) the duration of the minority or respective minorities of any person or persons in being at that date.

The settlor could select whichever period he wished. If he selected a period in excess of those permitted, the accumulation would be invalid only as to the excess. The court selects whichever period is the most appropriate to the settlor's intent.[20] At the conclusion of the period of accumulation, the income must be distributed. The rule against excessive accumulations was abolished by the Perpetuities and Accumulations Act 2009 in relation to instruments made on or

---

[16] This is because the rate applicable to trusts now found in s.9 of the Income Tax Act 2007 has been increased from 34 to 50%. Discretionary trusts now have their own income tax rates on dividends; below, para.9–003.

[17] *Re Gourju's WT* [1943] Ch. 24; *Re Locker's ST* [1977] 1 W.L.R. 1323; subject to TA 1925 s.31, below, para.20–023.

[18] Above, para.2–022.

[19] The date on which PAA 2009 came into operation.

[20] Maudsley, *The Modern Law of Perpetuities*, p.208; Morris & Leach, p.272.

after April 6, 2010,[21] with the exception of charitable trusts.[22] The former restrictions still apply to a will made before that date even though the testator dies after the commencement of the Act of 2009, and they also apply to an instrument made in the exercise of a special power of appointment if the instrument creating the power took effect before that date.[23] Thus, in the case of instruments to which the Act of 2009 applies, the income may be accumulated for the whole of the perpetuity period of 125 years,[24] although of course this is subject to any contrary provision in the instrument. The Law Commission had proposed that the rule against excessive accumulations should be abolished on the ground that it was too complex and no longer fulfilled any policy objective.[25] The Act of 2009 implemented those proposals.

D. Power to Add to, or to Exclude from, the Class of Beneficiaries

8–009   The trustees may be given a power to add new members to the class of beneficiaries, or to exclude existing members.[26] The power to exclude members became important when Finance Act 1958[27] provided that a settlor should be liable to income tax upon the income of a settlement if the settlor or the spouse of the settlor might benefit from the income or property of the settlement. Many settlements in existence at that date included the spouse of the settlor as a member of the class of beneficiaries, and the Act provided that the settlor should not be so liable if, amongst other conditions, the power to make the payments was not exercisable after April 9, 1959. Similar situations may arise in the future. A difficulty could arise if the trustees decided to exclude a member of the class for no good reason. Arbitrary exclusion will be inconsistent with the trustees' fiduciary duties.[28] It might also be construed as an improper release of a power held in a fiduciary capacity.[29] Yet it is difficult to see how the excluded member could establish loss; because, as a member of a class of beneficiaries under a discretionary trust, he was not entitled to any interest under the trust, and would be deprived of nothing except the hope or expectation of favourable consideration by the trustees.

[21] s.13.

[22] s.14.

[23] s.15.

[24] This is the period laid down by s.5.

[25] Law Com. No.251, *The Rules Against Perpetuities and Excessive Accumulations* (1998).

[26] *Re Manisty's Settlement* [1974] Ch. 17; *Blausten v IRC* [1972] 1 Ch. 256.

[27] s.22; now Income Tax (Trading and Other Income) Act 2005 ss.624, 625; *Watson v Holland* [1985] 1 All E.R. 290.

[28] Below, paras 8–020–8–021.

[29] Above, para.6–027.

It may be useful also to give power to the trustees to add new members to the class. Care has to be taken to ensure that the trustees cannot include persons, such as the settlor or his spouse, whose inclusion would have damaging tax consequences.[30] The power to add new members to the class is usually done by defining a class of excepted persons, and giving to the trustees a power to include in the class of beneficiaries any person who was not a member of the excepted class. Such a provision was upheld in *Re Manisty's Settlement*,[31] concerning a power of appointment; the settlor's mother, and any person who should become his widow, were added to the class of beneficiaries. The validity of trusts and powers in favour of very large classes was discussed in Ch.3.

E. Power to Appoint Upon New Trusts

It is common to give to trustees power to appoint on further trusts,   **8–010**
including discretionary and protective trusts, and also in favour of trustees of a foreign settlement[32] and to give them full power of delegation. This makes possible a resettlement on new trusts at the end of any specified accumulation period, or at any time at which it becomes advantageous for fiscal or other reasons, to do so. Such an appointment must keep within the perpetuity period as measured from the date of the original settlement,[33] and it may not provide for accumulation for any period beyond that which was available to the original settlor.[34] Time starts to run afresh only if appointments are made to a beneficiary who resettles; but such a course would result in a double transfer of the capital, which may have damaging inheritance tax consequences.

F. Miscellaneous Administrative Provisions

Trustees of every trust need to be given the powers necessary to   **8–011**
enable them to perform their duties. Obvious powers which they need are the power to sell, to invest, to apply income for the maintenance of child beneficiaries, to make advancements, to make payments to, and accept receipts from, guardians of children, etc. It was at one time necessary to include all such powers in the settlement. But now the basic necessary powers are given to trustees by the

---

[30] Inclusion of the settlor (but probably not the settlor's spouse) would, for example, attract the "reservation of benefit" rules of inheritance tax; below, para.9–012.

[31] [1974] Ch. 17; the power was described as an "intermediate" power; above, para.6–004: *Re Park* [1932] 1 Ch. 580; *Re Abraham's WT* [1969] 1 Ch. 463. See also *Re Hay's ST* [1982] 1 W.L.R. 202.

[32] Below, para.17–033.

[33] *Pilkington v IRC* [1964] A.C. 612.

[34] Because the appointors cannot be given powers in excess of those available to the settlor. For the available accumulation period, see above, para.8–008.

Trustee Acts 1925 and 2000, discussed in detail below.[35] The statutory powers can be added to, or restricted, by the terms of the trust instrument. It is usual, in the case of a discretionary trust, to give to the trustees the widest and most extensive powers. They may also be given a power to amend the trust. In terms of bulk, these administrative provisions will form the greater part of the trust instrument.

4. THE SELECTION OF TRUSTEES

8–012 The selection of the right trustees is important in the case of any trust; but particularly so in the case of a discretionary trust, where the trustees are given such extensive discretionary powers. The technical aspects of the matter are postponed to Ch.17; but it may be useful here to anticipate some of that discussion. The settlor, in confiding such broad discretion, will wish to select individuals whose judgment and co-operation he respects. He can select his most trusted friends, but they may have no expertise in investment, accounting or law or taxes.[36] He may thus favour the inclusion of some professionals; who should do the job more efficiently; but they will need to be paid for their work. In a case of executorships or trusts generally, it is common to appoint a corporate trustee, usually the Executor and Trustee Company of a bank, but there may be reluctance to appoint a corporate trustee in a case of a discretionary trust, because it may be felt that the trust officer will not be in as good a position as a personal friend to exercise the broad discretions contained in a discretionary trust. It is common to select a mixture of professionals and non-professionals; and there is no legal reason why a corporation and an individual should not be trustees.

As the disposition of the property is dependent upon the discretion of the trustees, the settlor may wish to be appointed trustee in order to be able to participate in decisions on distribution. Such an appointment has, in the past, been considered unadvisable because it might be possible for him to obtain a benefit under the settlement, and, under the estate duty system, this would have had the effect of treating the trust property as being part of the settlor's estate for estate duty purposes.[37] Under the system of inheritance tax the old estate duty concept of "reservation of benefit" has been reintroduced.[38] In the context of the discretionary trust, this means that the property is treated as remaining part of the settlor's estate if he is within the class of objects. If the settlor is merely a trustee it is

---

[35] Below, Ch.20.

[36] For an illustration of the dangers of appointing such persons without the inclusion of professionals, see *Turner v Turner* [1984] Ch. 100, below, para.8–021.

[37] *Oakes v Stamp Duty Commissioner for NSW* [1954] A.C. 51.

[38] FA 1986 s.102 and Sch.20.

unlikely that the "reservation of benefit" rules will apply, but it will be otherwise if he can in fact derive benefit from his trusteeship, for example by way of remuneration. In view of these uncertainties, the appointment of the settlor as trustee is best avoided.

Even if he is not a trustee, it is possible for the settlor to exert some influence upon the trustees in the way in which they exercise their discretion.[39] However, if the settlor effectively dictates the distribution of the property in such a way that the trustees exercise no independent discretion, any appointments so made will be void.[40]

5. THE NATURE OF THE INTEREST OF THE BENEFICIARIES UNDER A DISCRETIONARY TRUST

The nature of the interest of beneficiaries under a discretionary trust raises some important theoretical and practical questions. The discussion will tie in with some of the points made earlier in the distinction between trusts and powers.[41] In that context, the present discussion will justify the recognition of the basic difference between trusts and powers as being one of obligation or discretion. But it will be clear that the "duty" concept in the case of discretionary trusts is a very different duty from that recognised in the case of fixed trusts.[42]

8–013

A. Exhaustive and Non-exhaustive Discretionary Trusts

If the trustees are required to distribute the whole of the income, the discretionary trust is exhaustive. Where, as in the case of most modern discretionary trusts, the trustees may apply the income for some purposes other than distribution among the beneficiaries, as where there is a power to accumulate income not so applied, there is a non-exhaustive discretionary trust. The rights of the beneficiaries are more complex in the case of a non-exhaustive discretionary trust. For the income beneficiaries cannot argue that they are, as a group, *entitled* to the income. The income may be accumulated in whole or in part and added to the capital.

8–014

B. The Nature of the Interest of the Beneficiaries

i. Individual Beneficiaries. In the case of a fixed trust, we saw that the beneficiary's interest is regarded as proprietary. He is the

8–015

---

[39] For example, by a "letter of wishes".
[40] *Turner v Turner*, above, fn.36.
[41] Above, para.2–021.
[42] M. Cullity (1976) 54 C.B.R. 229; J. Davies [1970] A.S.C.L. 187; Y. Grbich (1974) 37 M.L.R. 643.

owner of an equitable interest under the trust. This is not so in the
case of a beneficiary under a discretionary trust. He is dependent
upon the exercise by the trustees of their power of selection in his
favour.[43] This point was crucial to the success of discretionary trusts
in the estate duty days; because estate duty was payable when property "passed" on a death,[44] as on the death of a life tenant.[45] A
discretionary beneficiary could not be said to be entitled to any
quantifiable share. He therefore owned no part of the property and
no property passed on his death. The position is similar under the
inheritance tax system. As we will see, the death of a discretionary
beneficiary is not an event upon which the trust fund is taxable.
Inheritance tax is, however, payable on a payment to a beneficiary
and on certain other occasions.[46]

A sole member of a class of discretionary beneficiaries cannot
claim entitlement to the income so long as there is a possibility that
another member could come into existence.[47] The trust fund may be
regarded as financial resources of a sole beneficiary (or in other
appropriate circumstances[48]) for the purpose of an order for financial provision (in favour of or against the beneficiary) under s.25 of
the Matrimonial Causes Act 1973, provided the order would not put
improper pressure on the trustees in the exercise of their discretion.[49]

8–016   **ii. The Class.** Whether or not the class of beneficiaries is properly regarded as the owner is a different matter. We have seen that a
sole beneficiary of a discretionary trust and the beneficiaries entitled
upon the determination of the trust on his death, may, if all are adult
and under no disability, call for the capital to be paid over to them,
or may validly assign to a third party who will become the beneficiary.[50]

Cases on estate duty have indicated that a class of beneficiaries
may not hold a proprietary interest which "passes" for estate duty
purposes. "Two or more persons," said Lord Reid:

---

[43] He can renounce his position as class member; *Re Gulbenkian's Settlement (No.2)* [1970]
Ch. 408.

[44] FA 1894 s.2.

[45] *Earl Cowley v IRC* [1899] A.C. 198.

[46] Below, Ch.9.

[47] *Re Trafford's Settlement* [1985] Ch. 32 (capital transfer tax). See also *Figg v Clarke
(Inspector of Taxes)* [1997] 1 W.L.R. 603 (capital gains tax).

[48] See *Charman v Charman* [2007] W.T.L.R. 1151 (discretionary trust founded by husband
treated as his resources); G. Kleiner and P. Munro (2007) 21 T.L.I. 117; cf. *A v A* [2007] 2
F.L.R. 467. See also *SR v CR (Ancillary Relief: Family Trusts)* [2009] 2 F.L.R. 1083; *B v B
(Ancillary Relief)* [2010] 2 F.L.R. 887; *M v W (Ancillary Relief)* [2010] 2 F.L.R. 1484; *Whaley
v Whaley* [2011] W.T.L.R. 1267.

[49] *Browne v Browne* [1989] 1 F.L.R. 291 (order against wife who was sole beneficiary); *J v
J (C Intervening) (Minors: Financial Provision)* [1989] Fam. 29 (maintenance of two children, the only beneficiaries, who would become absolutely entitled at majority).

[50] *Green v Spicer* (1830) 1 Russ. & My. 395; *Re Smith* [1928] Ch. 915.

"[C]annot have a single right unless they hold it jointly or in common. But clearly objects of a discretionary trust do not have that: they have individual rights, they are in competition with each other and what the trustees give to one is his alone."

This was said in *Gartside v IRC*[51] which was a case of a non-exhaustive discretionary trust, but in *Re Weir's Settlement*[52] and *Sainsbury v IRC*[53] the same analysis was applied to exhaustive discretionary trusts. Lord Reid's rejection of the "group or class" interest concept "seems equally applicable, whether the trust is exhaustive or not exhaustive."[54] The question has ceased to be of significance in relation to estate duty, but is relevant to determine where the beneficial interest is in a discretionary trust; and whether the class of beneficiaries, all being adult and under no disability, is able to call for a transfer of the legal title and to terminate the trust. It is submitted that the beneficial ownership should be in all those persons in whose favour the discretion may be exercised, including the beneficiaries of an accumulation provision under a non-exhaustive trust; and that, on the principle of *Re Smith*,[55] they should be able to terminate the trust in appropriate circumstances, if all adult and under no disability.[56]

C. Powers and Duties

It may be useful at this stage to recapitulate some of the points, **8–017** discussed above,[57] in connection with the nature of rights, duties and discretions in the context of trusts and powers. It will be seen that the basic distinction between trusts and powers continues to be that between obligations and discretions; but it is important to be able to identify what the trustees' duty is in the case of a discretionary trust. There are various contexts in which the question of the distinction between trusts and powers arises.

i. Fixed Trust. At one end of the spectrum is the case of trustees **8–018** of a fixed trust. This is clearly an obligation upon the trustees. Having once accepted the trusteeship, they have no choice of whether or not to perform the trust. They are obliged to do so; they

---

[51] [1968] A.C. 553 at 605–606.
[52] [1969] 1 Ch. 657, reversed on a different point [1971] Ch. 145.
[53] [1970] Ch. 712.
[54] [1970] Ch. 712 at 724, per Ungoed-Thomas J.
[55] [1928] Ch. 915; above; *Saunders v Vautier* (1841) 4 Beav. 115, affirmed Cr. & Ph. 240. This was accepted by the Privy Council in *Schmidt v Rosewood Trust Ltd* [2003] 2 A.C. 709.
[56] This will not be possible unless all members are ascertainable, which may not be the case since *McPhail v Doulton* [1971] A.C. 424.
[57] Above, para.2–021.

can be required by the court to perform, and are personally liable for breach. Some of the trustees' duties will require the exercise of a discretion in their performance. Thus, trustees are under a duty to invest[58]; but, they will of course exercise a discretion in the selection of investments. The trustees' duty may be seen as a correlative of the beneficiaries' rights. The position is wholly different from that at the other end of the spectrum; that of the donee of a power held in a non-fiduciary capacity. As will be seen, the question whether to exercise such a power is wholly a matter of the donee's discretion.

8–019   **ii. Trust with a Power of Selection.** We have seen that there are cases in which the trustees hold property upon trust for a specified group of persons, subject to a power to select the shares and proportions in which those persons shall take. Thus in *Burrough v Philcox*[59] the disposition was "among my nephews and nieces, or their children, either all to one or to as many of them as my surviving child shall think proper." We saw that, in the absence of an appointment being made, the nieces and nephews took in equal shares. The nieces and nephews thus held a vested interest under the trust, subject to divestment upon an appointment being made. Their situation is exactly the same as it would have been if the testamentary provisions had given to a donee a power to appoint, and in default of appointment to my nephews and nieces in equal shares. Those entitled in default are treated as owners in equity subject to divestment on the exercise of the power.[60] The trust in their favour is a fixed trust.[61] The division into equal shares makes it necessary to identify each member, and to know how many there are. This case is the same as that of a fixed trust; but the beneficiaries' interests are subject to defeasance. The trustee's duty to the beneficiaries is clear. It is a question of construction whether the instrument creates such a trust or creates a discretionary trust, discussed below.

8–020   **iii. Discretionary Trusts: Exhaustive and Non-exhaustive.** A discretionary trust may require the trustees to distribute all the income; or it may give to the trustees a power to accumulate it.[62] Similarly, it may require the trustees to dispose of the capital during the trust period, or it may provide for a gift over of the assets of the trust at the end of the trust period. Whether the trust is exhaustive or non-exhaustive, an individual beneficiary is not regarded as having

---

[58] Below, para.18–005.
[59] (1840) 5 My. & Cr. 72.
[60] *Re Brooks' ST* [1939] Ch. 993 at 997.
[61] And thus not affected by the decision in *McPhail v Doulton* [1971] A.C. 424, above, para.3–026. See C. Emery (1982) 98 L.Q.R. 551.
[62] Above, para.8–008.

any proprietary interest in the trust property.[63] If the trust is exhaustive, there is authority to say the class as a whole, if adult and under no disability, can terminate the trust.[64]

This raises the question: what is the trustee's duty? Clearly, it is different from the case of a fixed trust. Where are the beneficiary's correlative rights? This situation does not fit neatly into the right-duty correlation. The beneficiary has no proprietary rights. Is it correct to describe the situation as a trust; which, by definition, involves a duty? The answer, it is submitted, is: yes; this is a trust, and it involves a duty, although different from that in the case of a fixed trust.

The duty here is to exercise the discretion. In the case of an exhaustive discretionary trust, a selection must be made; whereas if the discretionary trust is non-exhaustive, the discretion may be exercised by deciding to accumulate. As Harris argued[65] persuasively, "the discretionary trust in fact depends on a rule-concept of duty, with no such necessity for correlative rights." Herein is the trustee's duty in a discretionary trust; and here is the point of distinction between a discretionary trust and a mere power. Each member of the class of beneficiaries under a discretionary trust has standing to sue in order to have the trustees' duty performed. Not that such a beneficiary will necessarily benefit by the performance of the trustees' duty; as it is a duty, not to pay to that beneficiary, but to exercise their discretion as described above.

In *Re Locker's Settlement*,[66] the terms of an exhaustive discretionary trust required the trustees to pay, divide and apply the income for charitable purposes or among the class of beneficiaries as the trustees "shall in their absolute discretion determine". Because of subsequent expressions of wishes by the settlor, the trustees failed to make distributions of income from 1965 to 1968. The question arose in 1975 what should be done with that income, and particularly whether the trustees' discretion had expired.

Goulding J. held that the discretion still continued, and that the trustees should apply their discretion in the distribution of the money among those who were members of the class of beneficiaries in the relevant years. In discussing the question of the trustees' duty and the court's power to enforce the exercise of the discretion, he said[67]:

---

[63] Above, para.8–015.

[64] *Re Smith* [1928] Ch. 915; *Re Nelson* [1928] Ch. 920n.; above, para.8–016.

[65] (1971) 87 L.Q.R. 231.

[66] [1977] 1 W.L.R. 1323; *Re Gourju's WT* [1943] Ch. 241; *McPhail v Doulton* [1971] A.C. 424.

[67] [1977] 1 W.L.R. 1323 at 1325.

> "[I]t is common ground that it was the duty of the trustees to distribute the trust income within a reasonable time. ... A court of equity, where the trustees have failed to discharge their duty of prompt discretionary distribution of income, is concerned to make them, as owners of the trust assets at law, dispose of them in accordance with the requirements of conscience. ... "

If the trustees refuse to perform their duty, the court can itself execute the trust:

> "[B]y appointing new trustees, or by authorising or directing representative persons of the classes of beneficiaries to prepare a scheme for distribution, or even, should the proper basis for distribution appear, by itself directing the trustees so to distribute."[68]

The trustees in *Locker*,[69] as is usual in these cases,[70] were ready and willing to perform, and did so.

The point is that the trustees under these circumstances are under a duty to distribute. That is an obligation which is subject to enforcement by the court in one of the ways stated. *Locker*[71] was a case of an exhaustive discretionary trust; though the individuals in the class of beneficiaries were not, as a class, entitled to the whole of the income, because the trustees could make payments to charity. The duty and obligation of the trustees, however, is the same in the case of a non-exhaustive discretionary trust as in *McPhail v Doulton*[72] itself. The difference is that in a non-exhaustive trust the duty to exercise the discretion can be satisfied by deciding to accumulate.

8–021   **iv. Powers Held as Trustee; Fiduciary Powers.**[73] The situation is quite different where the trustees, as one of the terms of the trust instrument, are given a power of appointment. Here there is no duty to exercise; and the court will not order the trustee to exercise the discretion. Typical is *Re Allen Meyrick's Trust*[74] where:

> A will gave property to trustees to hold:

> "[U]pon trust that they may apply the income thereof in their absolute discretion for the maintenance of my said husband and

---

[68] [1977] 1 W.L.R. 1323 at 1325, quoting Lord Wilberforce in *McPhail v Doulton* [1971] A.C. 424 at 457.
[69] Above, fn.66.
[70] As pointed out by Lord Wilberforce in *Locker*, fn.66, at 449.
[71] Above, fn.66.
[72] Above, fn.68.
[73] See Ch.6.
[74] [1966] 1 W.L.R. 499.

> subject to the exercise of their discretion on trust for my two godchildren . . . in equal shares absolutely."

Various difficulties arose. The husband was an undischarged bankrupt. Some of the money was applied in paying the rent and certain debts. The trustees could not agree on the disposal of other income, and attempted to surrender their discretion to the court.

The court refused to accept, and was willing only to hear applications for directions in particular circumstances as they arose. Nor were the trustees ordered to exercise their discretion. The trust here was in favour of the godchildren, subject to the overriding power. If the trustees could not reach unanimity as to the exercise of the power, the godchildren became entitled.

This is not, of course, to say that the trustees in this situation are not subject to duties in relation to the exercise of the power. They hold the power in a fiduciary capacity, and are subject to the highest fiduciary duties in the way in which they make their decision. They must do more than refrain from acting capriciously. Their duty is to consider periodically whether to exercise the power, and to consider the range of objects in such manner as will enable them to carry out their fiduciary duties. If they decide to exercise the power they must, of course, keep within its terms; they must exercise it in a responsible manner according to its purpose and consider the appropriateness of individual appointments.[75] The court will intervene if they exceed their powers or act capriciously.[76] Furthermore, they must not release the power, nor delegate it without authority.[77] They must appreciate that the discretion is theirs and not that of the settlor. If they merely obey the settlor's instructions without any independent consideration, they will be in breach of the duties described above, and any appointment made in such circumstances will be void.[78] These duties stem from the fact that the power is fiduciary; not from any duty to exercise the power. If they decide not to do so, the court will not interfere. It has been held, however, that the court must step in where a fiduciary power is left with no-one to exercise it.[79] In such a case the court can adopt any of the methods indicated by Lord

---

[75] *Re Hay's ST* [1982] 1 W.L.R. 202; A Grubb [1982] Conv. 432. These duties, which were laid down in *McPhail v Doulton* [1971] A.C. 424, *Re Gestetner* [1953] Ch. 672, and *Re Gulbenkian's ST* [1970] A.C. 508, are not necessarily exhaustive.

[76] *McPhail v Doulton* [1971] A.C. 424 at 456–457. See also *Pitt v Holt* [2011] 3 W.L.R. 19; below, para.17–045.

[77] *Re Hay's ST*, above, fn.75.

[78] *Turner v Turner* [1984] Ch. 100.

[79] *Mettoy Pension Trustees Ltd v Evans* [1990] 1 W.L.R. 1587 (fiduciary powers of company directors ceased on appointment of liquidator, but could not be exercised by liquidator or receiver because of conflict of duties); S. Gardner (1991) 107 L.Q.R. 214; J. Martin [1991] Conv. 364.

Wilberforce in *McPhail v Doulton*[80] in the context of discretionary trusts, i.e. it may appoint new trustees, direct the beneficiaries to prepare a scheme of distribution, or itself direct a distribution.[81]

8–022   v. Powers Held in a Non-fiduciary Capacity. As is seen in Ch.6, no duty is imposed upon a donee who holds a power in a non-fiduciary capacity. If a grandparent leaves property on trust for his grandchildren, and gives his son a power to appoint in favour of charity, the son is under no duty to appoint or even to consider the rival claims of charity or the grandchildren. He is, of course, if he makes an appointment, required to keep within the terms of the power, and to avoid exercising the power for an improper purpose.

8–023   vi. The Rule of Certainty in Ascertaining Beneficiaries or Objects. Reference should be made to Ch.3, where this aspect of discretionary trusts is fully discussed.

8–024   vii. Discretionary Trusts and Inheritance Tax. Because of the change in tax policy, discretionary trusts of this type became unpopular in tax planning circles. Such trusts created after March 1974 suffer higher rates of tax than those existing before the capital transfer tax legislation came into operation.[82] Since the introduction of inheritance tax, discretionary trusts have suffered further by reason of their exclusion from the "potentially exempt transfer" regime.[83] The lifetime creation of such trusts is, therefore, taxable even if the settlor survives a further seven years. For this reason few discretionary trusts of substantial size (other than "offshore" trusts) are likely to be created under the present tax system, although more modest discretionary trusts falling within the settlor's inheritance tax "nil rate band"[84] are still attractive. However, as we will see in the following chapter, the inheritance tax disadvantages of discretionary trusts have been extended to most other kinds of trusts by the Finance Act 2006.

---

[80] Above, fn.76.

[81] *Mettoy Pension Trustees Ltd v Evans*, above, fn.79. *Re Manisty's Settlement* [1974] Ch. 17, suggested that the only remedy was the appointment of new trustees, but *Klug v Klug* [1918] 2 Ch. 67, below, para.17–046, was not there cited.

[82] Capital Transfer Tax was introduced by FA 1975, with effect from March 26, 1974.

[83] Below, para.9–009.

[84] Below, para.9–023. The reduction of the maximum lifetime rate to 20% by FA 1988 alleviates the position to some extent.

CHAPTER 9

TAXATION AND TRUSTS

1. ESTATE AND TAX PLANNING

THE most significant factor in the lifetime creation of trusts has been **9–001** the avoidance of taxation. A wealthy person may benefit the family by making gifts to them, and then leave property to them by will. But tax legislation imposes higher rates on larger accumulations of property, and this wealthy person will seek ways of conferring benefits on the family and at the same time reducing tax liability. The tax payable by 10 people on incomes of £10,000 each is less in total than that payable by one person with an income of £100,000. Similarly, tax on capital is at its highest in large concentrations. More details of the income, and especially of the capital tax system, will be given below. The point here is that a wealthy person can best preserve the family fortune by sharing out, and that this has commonly been done by creating lifetime trusts. This tax planning of an estate is one of the most important and sophisticated functions of trust lawyers.

In earlier times the courts in determining the effectiveness of any scheme of tax avoidance applied the principle laid down by Lord Tomlin in *IRC v Duke of Westminster*[1]: "every man is entitled if he

[1] [1936] A.C. 1; described as "no more than a ghost from a different age" by Lord Walker in (2004) 120 L.Q.R. 412 at 427.

can to order his affairs so that the tax attaching under the appropriate Acts is less than it otherwise would be."[2] But starting in *W T Ramsay v IRC*,[3] the House of Lords began to elaborate a new and much more restrictive principle to apply in dealing with questions of the effectiveness of complex tax avoidance schemes. Where there occurs a pre-ordained series of transactions (or a single composite transaction) designed to reduce tax payable by a particular taxpayer the court is free to disregard any of those transactions if they are inserted for no good commercial purposes other than the reduction of tax. The transactions will be treated as a single composite whole and taxed accordingly. This principle is "founded on a broad purposive interpretation, giving effect to the intention of Parliament".[4] It is, however, "no more than a useful aid".[5] It applies to the creation and manipulation of trusts as well as to commercial and corporate dealings.[6]

As the circumstances of each individual differ, so each situation needs individual treatment. The estate- or tax-planner, with the assistance of accountants and other specialists, will present to the client various possible solutions, indicating the tax implications of each. The client must then decide how much to give away immediately and irrevocably, and to whom; and how much to keep; and, in days of inflation, many people will hesitate before making gifts, and thereby running the risk of leaving themselves short of capital in their old age. What is kept will be disposed of by will, and a testamentary trust may be created. Those whose fortunes are insufficient to create tax problems will not be concerned with lifetime tax planning; but may, again, create testamentary trusts on their deaths.

2. THE TAX STRUCTURE

9–002 To explain how best to minimise liability to tax, it is essential to explain the tax system in detail. There is no room to do that here,

---

[2] [1936] A.C. 1 at 19. But these observations "have ceased to be canonical as to the consequence of a tax avoidance scheme"; *IRC v McGuckian* [1997] 1 W.L.R. 991 at 1000.

[3] [1982] A.C. 300. See also *IRC v Burmah Oil Co Ltd* (1981) 54 T.C. 200; *Furness v Dawson* [1984] A.C. 474; *Craven (Inspector of Taxes) v White* [1989] A.C. 398 (where the House of Lords refused to extend this principle); *Ensign Tankers (Leasing) Ltd v Stokes* [1992] 1 A.C. 655; *Moodie v IRC* [1993] 1 W.L.R. 266; *IRC v McGuckian* [1997] 1 W.L.R. 991.

[4] *IRC v McGuckian*, above, fn.3, at 1000.

[5] *MacNiven (HM Inspector of Taxes) v Westmoreland Investments Ltd* [2003] 1 A.C. 311 at 320; *Barclays Mercantile Business Finance Ltd v Mawson (Inspector of Taxes)* [2005] 1 A.C. 684. See Lord Templeman (2001) 117 L.Q.R. 575; Lord Walker (2004) 120 L.Q.R. 412; J. Freedman (2007) 123 L.Q.R. 53.

[6] *IRC v Fitzwilliam* [1993] 1 W.L.R. 1189 (but *Ramsay* principle did not apply on facts, Lord Templeman dissenting); J. Kirkbride [1994] Conv. 67.

and only a few highlights can be given. It is in any case dangerous, in a book of this nature, to include too much detail; for each annual Budget may be expected to make some changes in the rates; and, if there is a change of Government, the policy behind the tax system also changes. Tax policy is often dictated more by political philosophy than by the search for a system which is rational and just.

The greatest revenue raiser is income tax. The net receipts from capital taxes have been disappointingly small. In 2010/2011 the yield from income tax was over £153,000 million while the combined yield from inheritance tax and capital gains tax was nearly £6,000 million.[7] A Government in need of money has therefore an interest in keeping income tax rates high; though the logic of the matter would seem to be that you should pay lower taxes on the money that you work for, than on inheritances. There was a substantial argument to the effect that income tax rates, reaching up to 83 per cent,[8] resulted in the stifling of initiative and enterprise. The Conservative Government in 1979[9] heeded that argument and reduced the top rate to 60 per cent, and it has since been reduced further. More recently, reductions have been made to the basic rate rather than the top rate. The tax system has hitherto been regarded not only as a revenue raiser, but also as a means of promoting the social, economic and political philosophy of the Government.

So far as trusts are concerned, the Government recognised that the tax laws had become too complex and were in need of modernisation and simplification. The Finance Act 2006 addressed the problem to some extent by harmonising the income tax and capital gains tax rules on the definition of "settlor" and "settled property", and the test for deciding whether the trustees are to be treated as resident in the UK.[10]

A. Income Tax

Tax is chargeable upon an individual's taxable income[11] at the rates laid down annually in the Finance Act. Currently the first £35,000 of taxable income is subject to the basic rate of 20 per cent, after which the higher rate of 40 per cent is payable.[12] An additional rate of 50 per cent on income above £150,000 became payable from

9–003

---

[7] HMRC website.

[8] On incomes over £21,000 in 1979.

[9] F (No.2) A. 1979 s.5.

[10] FA 2006 ss.88, 89 and Schs 12 and 13.

[11] The provisions relating to income other than employment income are now found in the Income Tax (Trading and Other Income) Act 2005, as part of the "tax rewrite" project. Employment income is now dealt with by the Income Tax (Earnings and Pensions) Act 2003.

[12] FA 2011 ss.1 and 2.

April 6, 2010.[13] The Finance Act 2008 controversially abolished the starting rate of 10 per cent, but a starting rate of 10 per cent for savings is payable on the first £2,560 of taxable savings income.[14] A special rate of 10 per cent, or 32.5 per cent in the case of higher-rate taxpayers, is payable on UK dividends.[15] The dividend additional rate of 42.5 per cent applies to those who pay income tax at the additional rate of 50 per cent.[16] There are a number of allowances and reliefs to which individuals are entitled.

We are concerned, however, with the taxation of trusts. Trustees are not individuals for income tax purposes. Trusts as such therefore enjoy no personal allowances. The income of a trust (other than a discretionary trust) is chargeable at the basic rate, and the trustees are assessable.[17] In a wide range of circumstances the income arising under a trust may be treated as the settlor's income.[18] The trustees need take no action in respect of dividend income from most stock exchange investments which is paid net of the ordinary rate payable on UK dividends (currently 10 per cent). The beneficiary who is entitled to the income is responsible for the payment of any dividend upper rate tax (currently 32.5 or 42.5 per cent) which may be due; and it is often convenient to arrange for the dividends to be paid direct to him. The trustees will, however, need to deduct and account for income tax which is due on any income of the trust which has been received without deduction of tax, such as income from land or profits if they carry on a trade.

Trustees must also deduct and account for the rate applicable to trusts (currently 50 per cent) which becomes due in the case of the income of a trust where there is no person currently entitled to the income.[19] With such a trust, the income may either be paid out at the discretion of the trustees or, if the trust contains such a power, it may be accumulated. If it is accumulated, it is taxed at the rate applicable to trusts (50 per cent). Where the income is paid to or for the benefit of a beneficiary, the ultimate tax liability is dependent upon the

---

[13] FA 2009 s.6 and Sch.2. The tax free personal allowance was reduced or removed for individuals with income above £100,000; s.4.

[14] FA 2008 s.5 and Sch.1, amending Income Tax Act 2007. The amount is indexed.

[15] Income Tax Act 2007 s.8.

[16] FA 2009 s.6 (from April 6, 2010).

[17] There is no specific statutory provision. The higher rates do not apply to trustees because they are not "individuals".

[18] Income Tax (Trading and Other Income) Act 2005 ss.619–648, replacing earlier provisions. See *Watson v Holland* [1985] 1 All E.R. 290. These provisions are intended to prevent and penalise tax avoidance.

[19] Income Tax Act 2007 s.9. The trust rate on dividends is 42.5%. This includes income of a discretionary trust or an accumulation and maintenance trust; below, para.9–021. The tax is charged on the whole income of the trust, after deducting expenses properly chargeable to income under the general law; *Carver v Duncan (Inspector of Taxes)* [1985] A.C. 1082; *Revenue and Customs Commissioners v Trustees of the Peter Clay Discretionary Trust* [2009] Ch. 296; below, para.19–001.

beneficiary's tax situation.[20] He is treated as having received the value of the payment grossed up to reflect the rate applicable to trusts.[21] If the beneficiary's taxable income is already in excess of £150,000, he will have no further liability as the tax already paid (50 per cent) and the tax due at his personal rate on income above £150,000 (50 per cent) are the same. On the other hand, if his other income does not exhaust his allowances and reliefs and the basic or higher rate, he may claim a repayment of an appropriate amount on producing to the Revenue the trustees' certificate of deduction of tax. It will thus be seen that income tax may be saved if the trustees have a discretion as to the distribution of income, and use it to make payments to those on low incomes whose tax rate is lower than the trust's. Thus, if £50 of trust income after tax at 50 per cent, is paid to a child beneficiary with no income, the child would get a rebate of £50.[22] There is, of course, no choice where the beneficiaries are entitled to the income or a specified share. Moreover none of the above consequences apply if the sum as received by the beneficiary is capital in his hands, for example where it is paid pursuant to a power of appointment restricted to capital or out of accumulated income.[23]

Reforms were introduced by the Finance Act 2005 to reduce the tax payable by discretionary trusts and to reduce compliance burdens on small trusts of this kind. Where a trust is subject to the rate applicable to trusts (50 per cent) or the dividend trust rate (42.5 per cent), the first £1,000 of annual income is charged at the basic rate (20 per cent) instead of the rate applicable to trusts. Dividends within this first slice of income are taxed at the ordinary rate of 10 per cent and bank and building society interest at the starting rate for savings of 10 per cent.[24]

9–004

The Finance Act 2005 also introduced reforms to reduce the income tax and capital gains tax burdens on trusts with "vulnerable beneficiaries", with retrospective effect from April 6, 2004. "Vulnerable beneficiaries" are of two kinds. The first kind is disabled beneficiaries, which (broadly) means those who lack mental capacity to manage their affairs and those in receipt of certain disability-related benefits. The second is minors where at least one of their parents has died.[25] In these cases the trustees and the "vulnerable

---

[20] But where the payment is in favour of the unmarried child under 18 of the settlor, the income is treated as that of the settlor: Income Tax (Trading and Other Income) Act 2005 s.629 (similarly where the income is retained in a bare trust for the settlor's child); below, para.9–024.

[21] Income Tax Act 2007 s.494.

[22] The child is entitled to the personal allowance (currently £7,475; FA 2011 s.3). It is no longer possible to obtain a rebate in respect of the 10% dividend rate.

[23] See *Stevenson (Inspector of Taxes) v Wishart* [1987] 1 W.L.R. 1204.

[24] Now Income Tax Act 2007 s.491. Section 491(4) sets out the way in which types of income are to be allocated to the first £1,000 slice.

[25] Income Tax Act 2007 ss.38 (disabled) and 39 (minors).

beneficiary" (or person acting on his behalf) may jointly elect to adopt a special tax treatment, whereby the trustees' liability will be what the beneficiary's liability would have been if he had received the income directly.[26] This will normally result in a lower tax bill because the trustees can use the beneficiary's personal allowances and the basic rate band. The trust must be a "qualifying trust".[27] In the case of a disabled beneficiary, no property (i.e. capital) may be applied for the benefit of any other beneficiary during the lifetime of the disabled beneficiary (or until the trust terminates if that occurs before his death), nor may any income be applied for the benefit of any other person.[28] In the case of minors, the trust qualifies if it is a "statutory trust" arising on the parent's death intestate, a trust arising under the will of the deceased parent, or a trust established under the Criminal Injuries Compensation Scheme. In the last two cases, the minor must become absolutely entitled at 18 and the property and income must not be applied for the benefit of any other person before that time. In the case of a will, this condition is quite restrictive, as many parents prefer to stipulate in their wills that their child will not become entitled until the age of 21 (or even 25).

These rules are not confined to trusts solely for the benefit of vulnerable beneficiaries, provided an identifiable part of the settled property is held on a qualifying trust.[29] They do not, however, apply to trusts where the income is treated as the settlor's.[30]

Income tax on "pre-owned" assets, introduced by the Finance Act 2004, is discussed below.[31]

B. Capital Gains Tax

9–005   Capital gains tax was introduced by the Finance Act 1965, and originally imposed at a rate of 30 per cent upon the gains accruing upon the disposal of an asset. The Finance Act 1988 wrought significant changes in the tax. The position is now governed by the consolidating Taxation of Chargeable Gains Act 1992. The tax on individuals was until quite recently charged at income tax rates on savings (20 and 40 per cent) and the rate for trusts was 40 per cent. The position was radically changed by the Finance Act 2008, which reduced the rate for the tax year 2008/2009 and subsequent years to a flat rate of 18 per cent in all cases.[32] This was controversial

---

[26] Income Tax Act 2007 ss.25–29. It seems that the election made under s.37 may not be confined to income tax or capital gains tax but must apply to both.

[27] Income Tax Act 2007 ss.34, 35.

[28] The existence of a power of advancement under s.32 of the Trustee Act 1925 does not prevent the trust from qualifying.

[29] FA 2005 s.36.

[30] FA 2005 s.25(3). See above, para.9–003, fn.20.

[31] Below, paras 9–013, 9–014.

[32] FA 2008 s.8, amending TCGA 1992 s.4.

because, although the rate was reduced, the Act of 2008 also abolished taper relief, which in some situations had operated to reduce the rate to as little as 10 per cent. The rate has since been increased to 28 per cent for higher rate income tax payers, trustees and personal representatives.[33]

In many cases the gain accruing on a disposal of an asset is computed as though the disposer's acquisition cost had been the market value of the asset on March 31, 1982.[34] Thus gains attributable to a period of ownership prior to the 1982 date escape tax.[35] Capital gains tax is payable upon a sale, exchange or gift.[36] The tax is not payable on death, though the deceased's property is deemed to be acquired by his personal representatives on his death at a consideration equal to its then market value.[37] This generally involves a "tax-free uplift" in the notional acquisition cost of the assets in question, since their market value at death is usually greater than the acquisition cost enjoyed by the deceased. When the personal representatives pass the assets to the legatee[38] no disposal is deemed to occur and the legatee acquires the assets with an acquisition cost equal to that of the personal representatives. Finally, capital gains tax is payable where disposals are deemed to occur, as where a capital sum is derived from an asset.[39]

There are many exemptions from liability to capital gains tax, the most important being an annual exemption of gains of £10,600 for individuals and £5,300 for a trust,[40] the taxpayer's main or only residence,[41] a chattel worth less than £6,000[42] and dated gilt-edged securities.[43]

The settlor will be liable to capital gains tax on making the settlement since this is a disposal even where the settlor declares himself trustee.[44] Under the settlement, the trustees will be affected in two quite different ways. First, in relation to the disposition of assets of the trust. On a disposal, the trustees are liable to tax on gains, as individuals would be. This situation normally arises where

---

[33] F(No.2)A 2010 s.2 and Sch.1, for gains accruing on or after June 23, 2010.

[34] TCGA 1992 s.35. The date is that of the introduction of indexation allowance (which has since been abolished).

[35] This is not so in all cases; s.35(3).

[36] Relief on gifts was withdrawn (with exceptions) by FA 1989 s.124.

[37] TCGA 1992 s.62.

[38] TCGA 1992 s.62. Defined in s.64(2) to include "any person taking under a testamentary disposition or on an intestacy or partial intestacy, whether he takes beneficially or as trustee . . . "

[39] TCGA 1992 ss.22–24. See also *Zim Properties v Proctor* [1985] S.T.C. 90.

[40] TCGA 1992 s.3, Sch.1; Capital Gains Tax (Annual Exempt Amount) Order 2011 (SI 2011/899). The exemptions are index-linked.

[41] TCGA 1992 s.222.

[42] TCGA 1992 s.262. An increase to £12,000 is recommended by the Office of Tax Simplification, *Review of Tax Reliefs, Final Report* (March 2011).

[43] TCGA 1992 s.115.

[44] TCGA 1992 s.70. The rules relating to offshore trusts cannot be dealt with here.

trustees sell investments in the ordinary course of administration of the trust.

Secondly, there are certain occasions on which a disposal is deemed to have been made. Disposals are deemed to be made on various occasions, but the only one in this context on which tax may be chargeable is that on which a person becomes absolutely entitled against the trustee[45] as, for example, where the beneficiary becomes absolutely entitled upon fulfilling a condition, such as majority, or where an advancement is made to a beneficiary. As originally enacted, tax was chargeable on the death of a life tenant, but that was changed by the Finance Act 1971[46] to bring the settlement provisions in line with the death rule for free estates.

The Finance Act 2005 provides for special treatment of trusts with "vulnerable beneficiaries".[47] One advantage of these trusts was that capital gains tax was calculated in accordance with the beneficiary's tax rate, which was likely to be lower than the trust rate (now 28 per cent). The beneficiary's higher annual exemption may also be used in the calculation, thus reducing the tax bill for qualifying trusts.

C. Inheritance Tax

9–006   Inheritance tax is a modified version of its predecessor, capital transfer tax. Estate duty was replaced by capital transfer tax by the Finance Act 1975,[48] with effect from March 26, 1974. This was part of a complete reorganisation of the structure of the taxation of capital, which was extended to lifetime gifts. A wealth tax, in the form of an annual tax on ownership of assets, was planned in 1974, but was never introduced. The application of capital transfer tax to lifetime gifts was largely removed by the Finance Act 1986, in which the tax was renamed as inheritance tax.

9–007   **i. Estate Duty.** Before March 26, 1974, estate duty was the only tax on private capital. It was a death tax only, and payable upon property passing on a death.[49] It could therefore be avoided by disposing of property before death; save that transfers made within seven years before death were subject to the tax.[50]

---

[45] TCGA 1992 s.71. See *Jenkins (Inspector of Taxes) v Brown* [1989] 1 W.L.R. 1163; *Swires (Inspector of Taxes) v Renton* [1991] S.T.C. 490; *Figg v Clarke (Inspector of Taxes)* [1997] 1 W.L.R. 603 (beneficiaries not absolutely entitled if birth of further class member possible, however unlikely). A deemed disposal, whether or not tax is charged, has the effect of establishing the acquisition value in the hands of the recipient.

[46] See now TCGA 1992 s.72, as amended by FA 2006 Sch.20, para.30.

[47] FA 2005 ss.30–32, as amended by FA 2008. See above, para.9–004.

[48] The provisions are now consolidated by the Inheritance Tax Act 1984, hereafter referred to as IHTA 1984.

[49] FA 1894 ss.1, 2.

[50] FA 1968 s.35.

The disposal would often be by the lifetime creation of a trust. The settlor would wish to avoid estate duty, not only on his death, but also upon the deaths of the beneficiaries. It was held that estate duty was payable upon the whole capital of a trust upon the death of a life tenant, or of the holder of some other limited interest.[51] The members of a class of beneficiaries of a discretionary trust owned no interest, however, in the fund[52]; they had no more than a hope that the trustees' discretion would be exercised in their favour. It was possible, therefore, to avoid liability to estate duty, until 1969, on the death of the settlor and of any of the beneficiaries by creating a discretionary trust at least seven years before the death of the settlor.[53] No wonder that the tax was called a "voluntary tax". The Finance Act 1969 imposed a charge upon the death of any beneficiary who had received payments of income in the past seven years.[54] The charge was on a portion of the capital equivalent to the share of the income received by the deceased during the "relevant" period. This system had little time to work, and would not in any case have been very effective because the trustees of a discretionary trust could pay the income to those whom they judged least likely to die in the near future; and so long as the income was thus disposed of, there was no objection to making capital payments to the old and sick beneficiaries.[55]

ii. Capital Transfer Tax. In a White Paper on Capital Transfer **9–008**
Tax[56] and a Green Paper on Wealth Tax,[57] the Labour Government in 1974 announced its intention of imposing both taxes. The policy was to effect a levelling of wealth[58]; estate duty, with all its loopholes, had conspicuously failed to do so. Capital transfer tax was a tax on capital transfers, whether during life or on death, and was planned to tax family capital, whether or not settled, at least once a generation. The Wealth Tax would go further, and impose a tax annually on capital. The imposition of a wealth tax would take some time, and the Government appreciated that it needed to be preceded by capital transfer tax.

Capital transfer tax in its original form was a cumulative tax applying to all transfers of value made by an individual after March 26, 1974 until the final transfer on death. Rates were progressive,

---

[51] *Cowley (Earl) v IRC* [1899] A.C. 198.
[52] Eventually so decided in *Gartside v IRC* [1968] A.C. 553; above, para.8–016.
[53] See *Pearson v IRC* [1980] Ch. 1, per Templeman L.J. at 25.
[54] ss.36, 37.
[55] See FA 1969 s.37(3)(b).
[56] Cmnd. No.5705 of 1974.
[57] Cmnd. No.5705 of 1974.
[58] "The Government is committed to use the taxation system to promote greater social and economic equality. This requires a redistribution of wealth as well as income." Preface to Green Paper.

and those chargeable on death (or on transfers within three years of death) were double those chargeable on lifetime transfers. The tax was modified by subsequent Conservative Governments, in particular by alleviating the cumulation principle. Instead of cumulating all transfers (made after March 26, 1974), only those made within the previous 10 years had to be cumulated, the figure finally being reduced to seven years.[59] The rates of tax being progressive, these amendments were beneficial to the transferor. Further substantial modifications were made by the Finance Act 1986, which renamed the tax as inheritance tax, to which we now turn.

9–009   **ii. Inheritance Tax.** The most significant changes brought about by the 1986 Act were the introduction of the "potentially exempt transfer" and the reintroduction of the estate duty principle of "reservation of benefit". These are explained in the outline of inheritance tax which follows. As we will see, the rules on the taxation of trusts were significantly changed by the Finance Act 2006.

The central concept of inheritance tax is the transfer of value, which may be chargeable, exempt or potentially exempt.[60] There is a transfer of value where a person makes a disposition as a result of which the value of his estate immediately after the disposition is less than it would have been but for the transfer, and the value transferred is the amount by which the estate is the less.[61] On a death, the deceased is treated as making a transfer of value of the whole of his estate immediately before the death.[62] There are special rules relating to settled property,[63] which will be examined below, and a number of exemptions and reliefs. The most important exemptions relate to transfers of any amount between spouses, whether in the lifetime or on death,[64] certain foreign property,[65] and certain personal exemptions.[66] Other reliefs and exemptions relate to situations which were familiar with estate duty, and include gifts to charities, works of art, agricultural or business property, and woodlands. They cannot be examined here.

---

[59] FA 1986 s.101.

[60] IHTA 1984 ss.1, 2.

[61] IHTA 1984 s.3. It may include an omission to claim an entitlement: s.3(3).

[62] IHTA 1984 s.4.

[63] IHTA 1984 Pt III.

[64] IHTA 1984 s.18. The exemption applies to same-sex couples who have registered under the Civil Partnership Act 2004, by regulations made under the FA 2005 s.103.

[65] IHTA 1984 s.6, not strictly an exemption; but effectively so.

[66] IHTA 1984 ss.19–28. These include £3,000 per donor per year; £250 per donee per year; normal expenditure out of income; gifts in consideration of marriage of various permitted amounts up to £5,000; and payments for the maintenance of dependants. (s.11). They give considerable scope for tax saving, though the amounts need uprating; Office of Tax Simplification, *Review of Tax Reliefs, Final Report*, para.2.29 (March 2011). It is obviously important for a donor to start giving early, especially since the introduction of the potentially exempt transfer.

The spouse exemption has quite recently been enhanced by permitting a surviving spouse or civil partner who dies on or after October 9, 2007 to utilise on death any unused part of the nil-rate band available to the first of the couple to die, however long ago that death may have been.[67] The amount transferred is calculated in accordance with the nil-rate band as at the date of the survivor's death. So, for example, if a husband died leaving everything to his wife, the wife's estate would have the benefit of a double nil-rate band.

The exemptions referred to above may be described as substantive exemptions, to distinguish them from the potentially exempt transfer, introduced by the Finance Act 1986.[68] A lifetime transfer by an individual made on or after March 18, 1986 is potentially exempt. As in the days of estate duty, it becomes chargeable if the transferor does not survive for seven years. If he dies within three years, the rates are those chargeable on a death. If he dies between three and seven years from the transfer, there is a taper relief on a sliding scale.[69] In certain exceptional cases, in particular the creation of certain types of trust, a lifetime disposition is *immediately* chargeable,[70] although at half the rates applicable on death.[71] If the settlor dies within seven years, the rates are increased as described above.

In the case of a lifetime transfer which is either initially chargeable or which becomes so by reason of death within seven years, and in the case of a transfer on death, the rates of tax are affected by any chargeable transfers within the previous seven years, which must be cumulated.[72] No tax will, however, be payable if the transfer falls within the "nil rate band", which stands at £325,000 at the time of writing.[73] Thereafter the rate is 40 per cent if the transfer was on death or within three years of death, and 20 per cent in the case of an initially chargeable lifetime transfer. As mentioned above, there is a sliding scale applicable to a potentially exempt transfer which becomes chargeable.[74] To encourage charitable giving, it was announced in the 2011 Budget that the 40 per cent rate would be reduced to 36 per cent for deaths on or after April 6, 2012 where at least 10 per cent of the net estate is left to charity.[75]

---

[67] FA 2008 s.10 and Sch.4, introducing IHTA 1984 ss.8A, 8B and 8C.

[68] IHTA 1984 s.3A, introduced by FA 1986 s.101 and Sch.19.

[69] IHTA 1984 s.7, as amended.

[70] IHTA 1984 s.3A.

[71] IHTA 1984 s.2.

[72] IHTA 1984 s.7.

[73] FA 2006 s.155 (for the tax year 2009–2010). It was announced in the 2011 Budget that the nil rate band would be frozen at £325,000 until April 2015. Inheritance tax yielded over £2.7 billion in 2010/2011 (HMRC website).

[74] IHTA 1984 s.7(4).

[75] See HMRC Consultation Paper, *A new incentive for charitable legacies*, June 10, 2011.

9–010   In the case of an initially chargeable lifetime transfer, the tax may be paid by the transferor or the transferee. If it is paid by the transferor, the value of the chargeable transfer is the amount by which his estate is reduced, therefore the amount of the transfer for tax purposes must include the tax. It will be necessary to "gross up" the sum transferred. The amount of tax payable on any sum varies, not only with the size of the sum, but also with the total of prior chargeable transfers within the previous seven years. The calculations in any particular case can be formidable, and will be worked out in each case from grossing up tables. On the other hand, if the transferee pays the tax, the actual amount of the transfer is treated as the gross gift, and added to the transferor's total gifts. The amount of tax payable will be less; but the amount received by the transferee will also be less.

The last transfer which a person makes is that of the estate on death. The rates applicable are those which begin at the total value of any taxable lifetime gifts within the previous seven years, grossed up as necessary. There is no question of grossing up the estate at death. Any tax is deducted prior to distribution. The incidence of tax as between specific and residuary beneficiaries is another problem.[76]

It is thus necessary to keep a "score" of taxable lifetime gifts, pay tax on them if due, and apply the seven-year cumulation rule when calculating the tax liability on subsequent chargeable gifts, and ultimately on death. The tax planner's job is to enable the client to make the best use of available exemptions and reliefs, and of the potentially exempt transfer. The adviser's dilemma is that the calculations have to be made on a number of assumptions about future events and tax liabilities.

9–011   Before examining the special rules relating to trusts, mention must be made of the principle of reservation of benefit. Although familiar under the estate duty regime, this concept was not relevant to capital transfer tax. It was reintroduced by the Finance Act 1986 and is a fundamental feature of inheritance tax. The object of this principle is that the donor should not be permitted to take advantage of the potentially exempt transfer rule by making gifts where he effectively retains an interest. As Lord Hoffmann has put it:

"Not only may you not have your cake and eat it, but if you eat more than a few *de minimis* crumbs of what was given, you are deemed for tax purposes to have eaten the lot".[77]

---

[76] IHTA 1984 ss.38, 39.
[77] *Ingram v IRC* [2000] 1 A.C. 293 at 304.

Where an individual makes a gift on or after March 18, 1986 the property is treated as subject to a reservation in two cases (amendments added by the Finance Acts 1999 and 2003 are dealt with below). First, where possession and enjoyment of the property is not bona fide assumed by the donee prior to the seven-year period ending with the donor's death (or, if the donor died within seven years of the gift, at the date of the gift). Secondly, where the property is not enjoyed "to the entire exclusion, or virtually to the entire exclusion, of the donor and of any benefit to him by contract or otherwise" at any time during the seven years ending with his death (or, if the donor died within seven years of the gift, at any time after the gift[78]). There are certain exceptions, for example where the donor occupies the property for full consideration in money or money's worth.[79] Nor does the principle apply where the gift falls within certain of the substantive exemptions, for example (subject to exceptions) the spouse exemption.[80]

The effect of a gift with reservation of benefit is that the property is treated as remaining in the estate of the donor. Hence the making of a gift with reservation normally has no immediate inheritance tax consequence, but the property will be treated as part of the donor's estate on death (at its value at that time) and taxed accordingly.[81] If during his lifetime there is a change of circumstances so that there is no longer a reservation of benefit, for example where the donor renounces any benefit retained, a potentially exempt transfer is treated as made at that time, so that the donor must survive a further seven years if tax is to be avoided.[82] If he dies within seven years, the property is taxed on its value at the date of the release of benefit, not of the prior gift. In the case where the lifetime gift is initially chargeable, as in the case of the creation of certain trusts, the property subject to a reservation will be treated as part of the settlor's estate on his death and taxed again, but relief is given against this double charge.[83]

Cases on estate duty and comparable Commonwealth legislation **9–012** afford guidance as to what is a reservation of benefit.[84] In the context of trusts, the settlor will be treated as reserving a benefit if he is

---

[78] FA 1986 s.102. See also s.102ZA, introduced by FA 2006 Sch.20, para.33 (beneficiary who continues to occupy after termination of interest in possession deemed to have made gift with reservation of benefit).

[79] FA 1986 Sch.20, para.6.

[80] FA 1986 s.102(5). The exceptions are discussed below, para.9–012.

[81] FA 1986 s.102(3).

[82] FA 1986 s.102(4).

[83] FA 1986 s.104; Inheritance Tax (Double Charges Relief) Regulations 1987 (SI 1987/1130).

[84] See *Chick v Commissioner of Stamp Duties of New South Wales* [1958] A.C. 435; *Nichols v IRC* [1975] 1 W.L.R. 534; *Munro v Commissioner of Stamp Duties of New South Wales* [1934] A.C. 61; *St Aubyn v Att Gen* [1952] A.C. 11. See also (1986) 83 L.S.Gaz 3728.

among the class of objects of a discretionary trust,[85] even though he receives nothing. Similarly if the settlor is a remunerated trustee of the settlement.[86] The settlor does not, however, reserve a benefit by reason of being an unpaid trustee,[87] nor if he has a reversionary interest in the settled property, because the subject-matter of the gift does not include the reversion.[88]

One way of attempting to reduce the value of property without losing the right to occupy it is for the owner to arrange for the grant to himself of a non-assignable lease at a low rent and to give away the freehold reversion. The value of the latter is much reduced by the lease, and the lease itself is of little value on the owner's death because it is not assignable. The efficacy of such a scheme was the issue in *Ingram v IRC*.[89] Lady Ingram transferred her property to a nominee for herself who then granted her a rent-free 20-year lease which prohibited assignment and subletting (the transfer to the nominee being necessary because a freeholder cannot grant a lease to himself). The nominee then transferred the freehold reversion, subject to the lease, to trustees on certain trusts. The object was thus to "carve out" the lease before making the gift. The House of Lords held that this scheme did not amount to a gift with reservation. When Lady Ingram died, only the then-valueless lease was part of her estate.[90]

Such a scheme is no longer effective in relation to disposals by way of gift on or after March 9, 1999.[91] While the original provisions continue to operate, gifts not within them may now be caught by ss.102A or 102B of the Finance Act 1986. Under s.102A a lifetime gift of an interest in land is a gift with reservation in the following circumstances: during the period of seven years ending on the donor's death the donor or the donor's spouse enjoys a significant right or interest, or is party to a significant arrangement, in relation to the land, which entitles or enables the donor to occupy all or part of the land otherwise than for full consideration in money or money's worth. This would cover a case such as *Ingram*. A right, interest or arrangement is not "significant" if it does not and cannot prevent enjoyment of the land to the entire exclusion (or virtually to

---

[85] *Att Gen v Heywood* (1887) 19 Q.B.D. 326; *IRC v Eversden* [2003] W.T.L.R. 893. It does not seem that the inclusion of his spouse would have this effect; (1986) 83 L.S.Gaz. 3728.

[86] *Oakes v Commissioner of Stamp Duties of New South Wales* [1954] A.C. 57.

[87] *Commissioner of Stamp Duties of New South Wales v Perpetual Trustee Co Ltd* [1943] A.C. 425; (1986) 83 L.S.Gaz. 3728.

[88] *Commissioner of Stamp Duties of New South Wales v Perpetual Trustee Co Ltd* [1943] A.C. 425.

[89] [2000] 1 A.C. 293; R. Kerridge (1999) 115 L.Q.R. 351.

[90] Because Lady Ingram died within three years of the gift of the freehold reversion, it was a chargeable transfer. However, it was valued as at the date of the gift. Land values had increased sharply by the date of her death. Had the reservation rule applied, the reversion would have been treated as part of her estate at its higher value at the date of death.

[91] FA 1999 s.104.

the entire exclusion) of the donor, or does not entitle him to occupy all or part of the land immediately after the disposal, but would do so but for the interest disposed of. Thus there is no gift with reservation where the donor gives a leasehold interest and retains the reversion.

By s.102B, a gift of an undivided share in land (an interest under a tenancy in common) is not a gift with reservation, provided: (a) the donor does not occupy (other than for full consideration) to the exclusion of the donee, or (b) the donor and donee both occupy and the donor does not receive any benefit at the expense of the donee in connection with the gift.[92] This provision reflects pre-existing Revenue practice.

Exemptions applicable to the original provisions of the 1986 Act,   **9–013** such as a gift to a spouse or to charity, apply also to the provisions introduced in 1999.[93]

When the reservation of benefit principle was introduced, it did not apply to gifts between spouses.[94] This gave rise to a loophole whereby a gift by a married person could be routed through a trust for his or her spouse, as illustrated by *IRC v Eversden*.[95] In that case a settlement was created in 1988 in which the settlor's spouse had a life interest, followed by a discretionary trust which included the settlor as a beneficiary. The spouse died in 1992. It was held that no inheritance tax was payable on the settlor's death in 1998 because the reservation of benefit rule (which would otherwise have applied because the settlor was a beneficiary of the discretionary trust) was excluded by the spouse exemption. The effect of s.102(5) was that the spouse exemption applied once and for all when the settlement was created, and was not confined to the period during which the spouse's life interest continued.

This avoidance scheme was closed by the Finance Act 2003, in relation to gifts made on or after June 20, 2003. This amendment applies to the creation of a settlement in which the settlor's spouse has an interest in possession, such as a life interest, so that the spouse exemption applies on the creation of the settlement. If the spouse's interest terminates before the settlor's death and the spouse does not on the termination become entitled to the settled property or another interest in possession in it, the original settlement will be treated as having been made on the termination of the spouse's interest in possession.[96] The effect of this is that the spouse exemption will no longer exclude the application of the reservation of

---

[92] This section operates to the exclusion of ss.102 and 102A, thus a gift satisfying s.102B will not be a gift with reservation under the other sections.

[93] FA 1986 s.102C.

[94] FA 1986 s.102(5).

[95] [2003] W.T.L.R. 893.

[96] FA 1986 s.102(5A) and (5B), inserted by FA 2003 s.185.

benefit principle where the settlor has an interest in the settled property during the period following the termination of the spouse's interest.

9–014   Concerns as to the scale of inheritance tax avoidance by the use of schemes which were not caught by the reservation of benefit rule led the Government to levy income tax on "pre-owned" assets. This controversial rule, introduced by the Finance Act 2004,[97] applies from April 6, 2005. Income tax is payable by a person resident in the UK[98] who has disposed of assets of any kind after March 18, 1986 but retained some benefit in circumstances where the reservation of benefit rule does not apply. The income tax charge applies also if the taxpayer provided the funds to enable another person to buy property in which the taxpayer enjoys some benefit.[99] Only an outline can be given here.

Where income tax is chargeable under this rule, the former owner is treated as receiving the market rent in the case of land (less any lower rent actually received) or a prescribed percentage of the capital value of property other than land.

As mentioned above, income tax is not chargeable where the asset is treated as part of the donor's estate for inheritance tax purposes under the reservation of benefit rule (or otherwise). Nor is it chargeable where the reservation of benefit rule would have applied but for the spouse exemption or but for the provision relating to a gift of a share of property where the donor and donee both occupy it after the gift.[100] Thus in these cases inheritance tax and income tax will be avoided.

The main exemptions from this income tax rule (most of which apply only to chattels and land) are as follows:

- a transfer to a spouse, or to a former spouse pursuant to a court order;
- a transfer whereby the asset became settled property in which the settlor's spouse (or former spouse pursuant to a court order) has an interest in possession;
- where the transferor disposed of his whole interest except for an expressly reserved right over the property and the transaction was at arm's length with an unconnected person or was such as might be expected to be made at arm's length with an unconnected person;

[97] s.84 and Sch.15. The rules have limited application to intangible property.
[98] If the resident is not domiciled in the UK, the income tax charge is confined to "pre-owned" property in the UK. If he is domiciled in the UK, the charge applies to "pre-owned" property worldwide.
[99] This rule is excluded where a gift of money was made at least seven years before the taxpayer enjoyed a benefit in the property bought with the money.
[100] Above, para.9–012.

- where the transferor disposed of part of his interest and the transaction was at arm's length with an unconnected person or was such as might be expected to be made at arm's length with an unconnected person[101];
- the value of the benefit enjoyed by the transferor does not exceed £5,000 in the tax year in question[102];
- the disposal was exempt for inheritance tax purposes as being for the maintenance of the family;
- the disposal was exempt for inheritance tax purposes under the annual £3,000 or small gifts exemptions;
- where the transferor became owner by inheriting the property but it was later diverted to another beneficiary by a deed of variation.[103]

The person who would otherwise be subject to the income tax charge for pre-owned assets may elect to have the asset treated as part of his estate for inheritance tax purposes.[104] If such an election is made, the taxpayer avoids income tax, but in effect his inheritance tax planning is reversed: property which he no longer owns and which escaped the reservation of benefit rule is treated as part of his estate for inheritance tax purposes.

3. INHERITANCE TAX AND SETTLEMENTS[105]

Family trusts have been used for many years as ways of avoiding **9–015** tax. Not surprisingly, trusts in general, and discretionary trusts in particular, were treated harshly by the capital transfer and inheritance tax legislation. There were originally, for inheritance tax purposes, two broad categories of settlements; those in which there was an interest in possession and those in which there was not, these being primarily discretionary trusts. The rules relating to reservation of benefit, discussed above,[106] must be borne in mind in relation to both categories.

---

[101] This exemption was introduced by the Charge to Income Tax by Reference to Enjoyment of Formerly Owned Property Regulations 2005 (SI 2005/724) in order to exempt commercial equity release schemes.

[102] This could catch a transaction concerning a house worth £100,000 in an estate falling within the nil-rate band, where inheritance tax avoidance would not have been the motive.

[103] Below, para.22–002. This exemption and that in the 5th bullet point above extend to intangible property.

[104] See FA 2007 s.66, for the date by which the election must be made.

[105] IHTA 1984 Pt III. "Settlement" is defined in s.43(2). A bare trust is not included. The rules relating to foreign elements cannot be dealt with here.

[106] Above, para.9–011.

When the Finance Act 1986 introduced the potentially exempt transfer, the only type of trust to benefit from it was the accumulation and maintenance trust.[107] The lifetime creation of other settlements was initially chargeable irrespective of seven-year survival. This position was subsequently modified so that the lifetime creation of an interest in possession settlement became potentially exempt.[108] The lifetime creation of a discretionary trust (other than an accumulation and maintenance trust) remained initially chargeable.

However, the Finance Act 2006 (without any prior consultation) introduced new rules which severely restrict the inheritance tax advantages of interest in possession and accumulation and maintenance settlements. In effect the discretionary trust regime now applies to other kinds of settlement, subject to certain narrow exceptions. This means that the creation of most trusts is initially chargeable and also subject to the charging regime (called the "relevant property" regime) applicable to discretionary trusts after their creation. Thus the current classification is based on whether or not the trust is of "relevant property".

In the account which follows it will be necessary to consider the treatment of interest in possession settlements both before and after the Finance Act 2006.

A. Settlements in which there is an Interest in Possession

9–016   This category deals with the standard form situation of a fixed trust for successive beneficiaries, whose interests are specified in the trust instrument; as a trust for Mrs X for her life, and after her death for her children in equal shares. A beneficiary has an interest in possession if he is entitled to the income as it arises. He is so entitled even though the trustees have a power to revoke or to appoint elsewhere, but not if they have a power to accumulate the income, even if unexercised.[109]

9–017   **i. Before the Finance Act 2006.** The following account deals with interest in possession trusts created before March 22, 2006. These trusts are unaffected by the Finance Act 2006 while the interest in possession continues. If the interest in possession terminates on or after March 22, 2006, the tax treatment depends on whether the settlement then ends, as will be further explained below.

---

[107] Below, para.9–024.
[108] F(No.2)A 1987 s.96 and Sch.7.
[109] See *Pearson v IRC* [1981] A.C. 753; W. Murphy (1980) 43 M.L.R. 712; J. Tiley (1980) 39 C.L.J. 246; (1981) 97 L.Q.R. 1; *Re Trafford's Settlement* [1985] Ch. 32; *Swales v IRC* [1984] 3 All E.R. 16; *Miller v IRC* [1987] S.T.C. 108.

A person entitled to an interest in possession is treated for the purposes of inheritance tax as being beneficially entitled to the property in which his interest subsists.[110] Mrs X would thus be regarded, for purposes of inheritance tax, not merely as the owner of a life interest in the trust property, but as the owner of the property itself. There are special provisions to deal with cases where there is a shared entitlement to the income,[111] or where the beneficiary is entitled to a fixed amount,[112] and also for the beneficiary who is entitled to the use and enjoyment of property which does not produce income.[113]

When an interest in possession comes to an end, the person enti- **9–018** tled to the interest is treated as having at that time made a transfer of value of his interest. His interest is regarded as coming to an end on his disposing of or surrendering his interest, or on its termination in whole or in part by an appointment being made of the property in which his interest subsisted.[114] Where the interest in possession terminates during the lifetime of the person entitled to it, the transfer is potentially exempt.[115] If the disposal is for a consideration in money or money's worth, the value of the property is treated as reduced by the amount of the consideration,[116] but in determining that amount, the value of a reversionary interest in the property (which the tenant for life may acquire on a partition) must be left out of account.[117] Additionally, depreciatory transactions between the trustees and the persons interested under the settlement (as where the value of the trust property is reduced by granting a long lease of the property at a low rent) are treated as transfers of value.[118] Where a person dies entitled to an interest in possession, he is treated as having made a transfer of value immediately before his death of the property in which the interest subsisted.[119]

As the coming to an end of an interest in possession is treated as a transfer of value by the person beneficially entitled to that interest, the *rate* of any tax chargeable is determined by his personal scorecard.[120] There is, however, no question of grossing up; for the value

---

[110] IHTA 1984 s.49. Accordingly, reversionary interests are "excluded property" (s.48); but there are exceptions.

[111] IHTA 1984 s.50(1).

[112] IHTA 1984 s.50(2).

[113] IHTA 1984 s.50(5).

[114] IHTA 1984 ss.51, 52.

[115] F(No.2)A 1987 s.96. A different rule applies if the interest terminates on or after March 22, 2006 and the settlement does not then end; below, para.9–019.

[116] Which will be less than the value of the property in which the interest subsisted. See IHTA 1984 s.49(2), dealing with the case where more than the actuarial value is paid.

[117] IHTA 1984 s.52(2).

[118] IHTA 1984 s.52(3).

[119] IHTA 1984 s.4. See *IRC v Lloyds Private Banking Ltd* [1998] S.T.C. 560 (right to reside for life gave interest in possession so that capital value taxed on death).

[120] IHTA 1984 s.52(1). But the tax is payable out of the settled property, and the trustees are responsible for it, concurrently with the beneficiary; s.201.

of the transfer is not the loss to the transferor, but the value of the property in which the interest subsisted.[121]

There are certain reliefs and exemptions.[122] No tax is payable where an interest in possession comes to an end and (subject to certain qualifications) it reverts to the settlor,[123] or to the spouse, widow or widower of the settlor.[124]

There is total or partial relief where the person whose interest comes to an end becomes on the same occasion entitled either to the property or to another interest in possession in the property; there is a potentially exempt transfer only to the extent that the value of the property to which he becomes entitled is less than the value of the property in which his interest subsisted.[125] If, however, the life tenant becomes absolutely entitled by purchasing the reversion, he makes a potentially exempt transfer of the amount of the purchase price.[126] The result of these rules in the case of partition is that there is a potentially exempt transfer of that part of the fund to which the remainderman becomes absolutely entitled.

Some of the general exemptions which apply to transfers of non-settled property apply also to termination of interests in possession, for example, transfers to a spouse or to charity, the annual exemption (£3,000) and marriage consideration[127]; and also transfers for family maintenance.[128] Finally, quick succession relief reduces the rate of tax where tax is payable on the termination of an interest in possession in settled property within five years of a previous chargeable transfer.[129]

9–019   **ii. After the Finance Act 2006.**[130] The general position is that the creation of a lifetime trust with an interest in possession is immediately chargeable at the rate of 20 per cent so far as the assets exceed the settlor's nil-rate band. The trust is subject to the "relevant property" regime applicable to discretionary trusts.[131] This means that a "periodic charge" of up to 6 per cent of the value of the

---

[121] IHTA 1984 s.52(1).

[122] Terminations under protective trusts are dealt with below, (para.9–027). See also IHTA 1984 s.90 (trustees' annuities).

[123] IHTA 1984 s.54(1).

[124] IHTA 1984 s.54(2).

[125] IHTA 1984 s.53(2). This relief is restricted by s.53(2A), as substituted by FA 2008 s.140, where the person becomes entitled to another interest in possession on or after March 12, 2008.

[126] Otherwise the life tenant could reduce the value of his taxable estate, as his free estate is reduced by the payment, while the value of the trust property in his estate is unaffected. See IHTA 1984 ss.10, 55.

[127] IHTA 1984 s.57. But the small gifts exemption (£250) does not apply. Valuation reliefs on business and agricultural property are also available to settlements.

[128] IHTA 1984 s.11.

[129] IHTA 1984 s.141.

[130] The provisions are found in FA 2006 s.156 and Sch.20.

[131] Below, para.9–020.

trust assets will be levied on every tenth anniversary, and that an "exit charge" will be payable on capital leaving the trust, as where the trustees advance or appoint capital. The life tenant is no longer treated as owning the property for inheritance tax purposes, which means that the spouse exemption does not apply where a settlor gives an interest in possession to his spouse. It also means that the value of the trust property is no longer aggregated with the life tenant's free estate on his death. The only situation in which the lifetime creation of an interest in possession trust is favourably treated is in the case of a trust for a disabled person, which is subject to the rules applying to the creation of an interest in possession trust before the Finance Act 2006.[132]

Where an interest in possession trust arises on or after March 22, 2006 under a will or intestacy, the old rules apply.[133] The spouse exemption will, therefore, apply where the interest in possession is in favour of the spouse of the deceased. However, the old rules do not apply indefinitely. When the interest in possession ends (either in the lifetime or on the death of the life tenant), the discretionary trusts "relevant property" regime takes over if the settlement continues.[134]

We saw that an interest in possession created before March 22, 2006 was not affected by the Finance Act 2006 while the interest continued, or if it terminated before that date.[135] Where such an interest in possession terminates (in the lifetime or on the death of the life tenant) on or after March 22, 2006, the transitional provisions of the Finance Act 2006 apply. Where the settlement itself comes to an end on the termination of the life interest (as where there is a partition or the remainder beneficiary becomes absolutely entitled on the life tenant's death), the old rules apply. This means that a lifetime termination is a potentially exempt transfer, and that, where the interest in possession ends on death, the value of the settled property is aggregated for inheritance tax purposes with the life tenant's free estate.[136]

Where the settlement continues after the termination of the interest in possession, the general rule is that the settlement then becomes subject to the "relevant property" regime applicable to

---

[132] IHTA 1984 ss.49(1A), 89A and 89B, inserted by FA 2006 Sch.20, paras 4 and 6. This is in addition to the preferential rules for disabled trusts which previously existed; below, para.9–027. Preferential treatment is also given to interest in possession trusts arising under life policies created before March 22, 2006; FA 2006 Sch.20, para.11.

[133] IHTA 1984 ss.49(1A) and 49A, inserted by FA 2006 Sch.20, paras 4 and 5.

[134] Unless it continues in favour of a disabled beneficiary, a bereaved minor (below, para.9–025) or an "age 18 to 25 trust" (below, para.9–026).

[135] Above, para.9–017.

[136] IHTA 1984 s.3A(1A), introduced by FA 2006 Sch.20, para.9. The old rules also apply if the property passes into a disabled trust on termination of the interest in possession.

discretionary trusts.[137] Two exceptions arise under the transitional provisions.[138] The old rules continue to apply where, on termination of the interest in possession on or after March 22, 2006, a further interest in possession arose before October 6, 2008. Secondly, the old rules continue where, on the death of the life tenant on or after October 6, 2008, the life tenant's spouse or civil partner takes an interest in possession. In these two cases (known as "transitional serial interests") the old rules apply so that a lifetime termination by the successor is a potentially exempt transfer and termination on death results in the aggregation of the trust property with the life tenant's free estate. However, if the settlement continues after termination of the successor's interest in possession, the "relevant property" regime applicable to discretionary trusts will then take over.

B. Settlements in which there is No Interest in Possession

9–020   **i. Discretionary Trusts.** In the context of inheritance tax, a discretionary trust means a settlement in which there is no interest in possession. Such trusts were hard hit by the original provisions of the 1975 Act, but the position was somewhat rationalised and ameliorated by the modifications of the Finance Act 1982.[139] The present code applies to "relevant property".[140] This used to mean settled property in which there was no interest in possession, other than certain types of settlements which were preferentially treated.[141] As explained above, the Finance Act 2006 has brought most interest in possession trusts into the "relevant property" regime. The lifetime creation of a trust of "relevant property" is initially chargeable, although at half the rate applicable on death.[142]

9–021   (a) *The "Exit" Charge.* Tax is chargeable on any part of the funds which ceases to be "relevant property".[143] This covers not only the simple case of a payment of capital to a beneficiary, including the winding-up of the trust, but also (before the changes made by the Finance Act 2006) the situation where the trustees converted the

---

[137] Similarly where property is added to a pre-existing interest in possession trust on or after March 22, 2006: the addition is subject to the "relevant property" regime.

[138] IHTA 1984 ss.49B, C and D, introduced by FA 2006 Sch.20, para.5. The transitional period was extended from April to October 2008 by FA 2008 s.141.

[139] It has also been mitigated by the reduction in rates; below, para.9–023.

[140] IHTA 1984 s.58, as amended by FA 2006.

[141] IHTA 1984. The exceptions include accumulation and maintenance trusts (as amended by FA 2006), discussed below, and the special trusts mentioned in Pt C, below.

[142] Above, para.9–009.

[143] IHTA 1984 s.65(1)(a). Tax is also chargeable where the trustees make a disposition resulting in the reduction in the value of the property; s.65(1)(b). See *IRC v Macpherson* [1989] A.C. 159.

trust into an accumulation and maintenance settlement.[144] There are certain exceptions to this rule; for example, no tax is payable in respect of a payment of costs or expenses, nor where the payment is income for income tax purposes in the hands of the recipient.[145] Only a limited number of the general exemptions, such as distributions to charity, are available.[146]

(b) *The Decennial Charge.* The "exit" charge alone is not suffi- **9–022** cient, for the capital may not be distributed until the end of the trust period, which, as has been seen, may not occur until just before the end of the perpetuity period.[147] It is provided, therefore, that tax is payable on the whole of the settled funds every 10 years, although only at 30 per cent of the "effective rate", as described below.[148] Thus the capital is fully taxed broadly once a generation, whether the capital is distributed or retained, or the trust is converted into another form.

(c) *Rates of Tax.* Different rules apply to the "exit" charge and **9–023** the decennial charge, although in both cases the rates applicable to lifetime transfers are used. Only an outline can be given here.

In the case of the decennial charge, tax is charged on the value of the "relevant property" on the day before the 10-year anniversary, at 30 per cent of the "effective rate" which would have been charged on a hypothetical transfer at that time, on the assumption that the hypothetical transferor's cumulative total to be taken into account includes the settlor's chargeable transfers during the seven years preceding the creation of the settlement, plus the amounts, if any, subjected to an "exit charge" in the 10 years before the 10-year anniversary in question.[149]

In the case of the "exit" charge, the rate depends on whether the charge is payable before or after the first 10-year anniversary. In both cases the amount on which tax is payable is the amount by which the value of the "relevant property" is diminished by the event in question.[150] The rate before the first 10-year anniversary is the "appropriate fraction" of the rate payable on an assumed chargeable transfer made at the time of the "exit" charge, where the

---

[144] Below, para.9–024; *Inglewood (Lord) v IRC* [1983] 1 W.L.R. 366.
[145] IHTA 1984 s.65(5); *Stevenson (Inspector of Taxes) v Wishart* [1987] 1 W.L.R. 1204. See also s.65(4), (6)–(8).
[146] The annual exemption (£3,000) is not available, nor does quick succession relief apply. The valuation reliefs, however, available for business and agricultural property, do apply.
[147] Above, para.8–007.
[148] IHTA 1984 ss.64, 66.
[149] IHTA 1984 s.66.
[150] "Grossing-up" occurs; IHTA 1984 s.65(2).

amount is the value of the settled property at the date of the settlement, and the hypothetical cumulative total is the settlor's chargeable transfers during the seven years prior to the creation of the
settlement. The "appropriate fraction" is $3/10 \times N/40$, where N is
the number of completed quarters (i.e. three-month periods) between the creation of the settlement and the chargeable event.[151]
Different rules apply to settlements made before March 27,
1974.[152]

Where an "exit" charge arises after a 10-year anniversary, tax is
charged at the "appropriate fraction" of the rate at which it was
charged on the last 10-year anniversary. The "appropriate fraction"
is $N/40$, where N is the number of completed quarters between the
last 10-year anniversary and the chargeable event.[153] This rule applies also to settlements made before March 27, 1974.

Although discretionary trusts were, prior to the Finance Act 2006,
treated more harshly than other settlements, the rates outlined above
are not high. Now that the maximum lifetime rate is 20 per cent,[154]
the rate of the decennial charge cannot exceed 6 per cent (being 30
per cent of the rate applicable to an actual transfer, as explained
above). Furthermore, a discretionary trust within the nil-rate band[155]
retains considerable attraction. Indeed, now that the "relevant property" regime has been imposed on many non-discretionary trusts by
the Finance Act 2006, the flexibility of the discretionary trust gives
it some advantages.

9–024   **ii. Accumulation and Maintenance Settlements.** An accumulation and maintenance settlement is one in which no interest in possession exists, but one or more beneficiaries will, on attaining a
specified age not exceeding 25 years, become entitled to an interest
in possession.[156] In this area also the Finance Act 2006 has made
considerable changes.

It has long been common practice to create accumulation and
maintenance settlements in favour of children in the family, and to
give to the trustees power to apply the income at their discretion for
the maintenance and education of the children, and to accumulate
any income not so applied; and power to advance some or all of the
capital for the advancement or benefit of the beneficiaries. The
powers are now statutory,[157] subject to the expression of a contrary
intention, and are discussed in more detail in Ch.20.

[151] IHTA 1984 s.68.
[152] IHTA 1984 s.68(6).
[153] IHTA 1984 s.69.
[154] FA 1988 s.136.
[155] Above, para.9–009.
[156] IHTA 1984 s.71. There are other conditions. See *Inglewood (Lord) v IRC* [1983] 1
W.L.R. 366.
[157] TA 1925 s.31; below, para.20–023.

The income of the trust will be taxed at the rate applicable to trusts (currently 50 per cent).[158] Where income is paid to or applied for the maintenance or education of a beneficiary, the income is taxed according to the tax status of the beneficiary. But there is one important limitation. If the beneficiary is an unmarried child under 18 *of the settlor*,[159] any income paid to or applied for his maintenance or education is aggregated for tax purposes with the income of the settlor.[160] There is no aggregation, however, if such income is accumulated.

Before the Finance Act 2006 accumulation and maintenance trusts were very favourably treated. However, that Act withdrew the inheritance tax advantages for the future. Where such a trust is created on or after March 22, 2006 it is subject to the "relevant property" regime applicable to discretionary trusts in general.[161] This means that the lifetime creation of such a trust is not potentially exempt but attracts an immediate charge at the rate of 20 per cent (so far as the nil-rate band is exceeded). It is also subject to the decennial charge and to exit charges on distributions of capital.

The favourable rules applying to accumulation and maintenance trusts created before March 22, 2006 were as follows. Lifetime creation was a potentially exempt transfer.[162] The usual rules governing discretionary trusts did not apply,[163] so that there was no decennial charge nor any exit charge on a distribution of capital to the beneficiary (on an advancement or when his interest vested), nor on the death of a beneficiary before becoming entitled to the capital.[164] The advantages just described continue to apply after March 22, 2006 to a trust created before that date only if the beneficiaries become entitled to capital at the age of 18. Few such trusts meet this condition, as the usual age of vesting is 21 or 25. In recognition of that fact, the Finance Act 2006 provided a transitional period ending on April 5, 2008 during which the terms of the trust could be varied (if the terms of the trust permitted this or by application to court[165]) to reduce the age of vesting to 18, in which case the favourable treatment continues to apply.[166] In cases where the capital vests between the ages of 18 and 25, exit charges are payable on distributions of capital as from April 6, 2008.[167] The rate of the exit charge

---

[158] Above, para.9–003.
[159] cf. grandchildren of the settlor.
[160] Income Tax (Trading and Other Income) Act 2005 ss.629, 631, above, para.9–003, fn.20. Similarly in the case of income retained in a bare trust for the settlor's child.
[161] IHTA 1984 s.71, as amended by FA 2006 Sch.20, para.2.
[162] IHTA 1984 s.3A.
[163] IHTA 1984 s.58(1)(b).
[164] IHTA 1984 s.71(4). The beneficiary would normally be entitled to income from the age of 18; TA 1925 s.31(1)(ii).
[165] Below, para.22–003.
[166] IHTA 1984 s.71, as amended by FA 2006 Sch.20, para.3.
[167] IHTA 1984 s.71D(3), (4), inserted by FA 2006 Sch.20, para.1.

cannot exceed 4.2 per cent,[168] and there is no decennial charge. Where the capital vests at an age greater than 25, the full "relevant property" regime applies.

These changes were criticised on the ground that most settlors do not think it advisable to give large amounts of capital to beneficiaries at the age of 18. Now they must weigh the disadvantages of giving capital to a beneficiary at a young age or incurring inheritance tax.

The effect of the Finance Act 2006 is that it is no longer possible to create favourably treated trusts for children or grandchildren by lifetime disposition. However, the Act provides two situations where a trust for children (but not grandchildren) may be created on death without attracting the "relevant property" rules.

9–025   **iii. Trusts for Bereaved Minors.** Such a trust is one created (before or after March 22, 2006) by the will (or intestacy) of a parent for the benefit of a minor, at least one of whose parents has died.[169] The minor must become entitled to the capital absolutely no later than the age of 18. It must not be possible for the trustees to apply income or capital other than for the minor's benefit. Although inheritance tax may be payable on the parent's death, none will be payable while the trust exists or when the capital vests (nor if the minor dies under the age of 18). In view of the requirement of vesting by the age of 18, this type of trust is unlikely to be widely used.

9–026   **iv. Age 18 to 25 Trusts.** These are similar to trusts for bereaved minors save that a later vesting age is permitted. However, exit charges are payable if the capital vests after the age of 18. The 18 to 25 trust is one arising (before or after March 22, 2006) under the will of a parent for the benefit of a minor who will become entitled to the capital at an age no greater than 25.[170] Inheritance tax may be payable on the parent's death, but none is payable before the minor reaches 18. The trustees must not have power to apply capital or income elsewhere. An exit charge will be payable when capital is paid to the beneficiary (by advancement or when the interest vests) at an age from 18 to 25. The maximum exit charge rate is 4.2 per cent and the decennial charge does not apply.

These exceptions from the full "relevant property" regime are narrow, in that they can only arise on the death of a parent of the

---

[168] IHTA 1984 s.71F.

[169] IHTA 1984 s.71A, inserted by FA 2006 Sch.20, para.1. "Parent" includes step-parent. The provisions apply also to trusts created under the Criminal Injuries Compensation Scheme.

[170] IHTA 1984 s.71D. "Parent" includes step-parent, and trusts created by the Criminal Injuries Compensation Scheme are included.

minor. Other relatives may create life interests, bare trusts or absolute gifts in favour of minors in their wills, but other trusts for
minors attract no favourable treatment.

C. Protective and Other Trusts

Other forms of trusts which are entitled to special treatment are **9–027**
protective trusts,[171] superannuation schemes,[172] trusts for the benefit
of employees[173] and for disabled persons,[174] charitable trusts,[175]
newspaper trusts,[176] maintenance funds for historic buildings,[177] and
various special compensation funds, such as those maintained by
Lloyd's and the Law Society.[178]

A protective trust does not fit neatly into the two categories into
which trusts are divided for inheritance tax purposes; for there is an
interest in possession during the currency of the interest of the
principal beneficiary, but a discretionary trust after the forfeiture.
There is a charge to inheritance tax upon the death of the principal
beneficiary; but not usually on the forfeiture of his interest, which,
for the purpose of inheritance tax, is deemed to continue during the
currency of the discretionary trusts which then arise.[179]

D. Reform

The Office of Tax Simplification has proposed a review of inheri- **9–028**
tance tax, which would consider its scope and operation with reference to the original and desired policy rationale. This would be a
long term project and would include a review of the taxation of
trusts.[180]

---

[171] IHTA 1984 s.88; above, Ch.7.
[172] IHTA 1984 ss.58(1)(d), 151.
[173] IHTA 1984 s.86.
[174] IHTA 1984 s.89; *Barclays Bank Trust Co. Ltd v Commissioners for HM Revenue and Customs* [2011] W.T.L.R. 1489. The lifetime creation of a trust for a disabled person is favourably treated by FA 2006; above, para.9–019.
[175] IHTA 1984 s.58(1)(a). As to temporary charitable trusts, see s.70.
[176] IHTA 1984 s.87.
[177] IHTA 1984 s.58(1)(c) and Sch.4.
[178] IHTA 1984 s.58(1)(e).
[179] IHTA 1984 s.88, as amended by FA 2006 Sch.20, para.24. The rule is modified where the protective trust arises on or after March 22, 2006.
[180] *Review of Tax Relief, Final Report*, para.2.30 (March 2011).

CHAPTER 10

RESULTING TRUSTS

1. GENERAL

A RESULTING trust is a situation in which a transferee is required by **10–001**
equity to hold property on trust for the transferor; or for the person
who provided the purchase money for the transfer. The beneficial
interest results, or comes back to the transferor or to the party who
makes the payment. In effect the resulting trust is the basis of a
claim to recover one's own property.[1] This situation can arise in a
wide variety of circumstances, and it has been seen that resulting
trusts overlap with other categories.[2]

---

[1] See *MacMillan Inc v Bishopsgate Investments Trust Plc (No.3)* [1995] 1 W.L.R. 978
at 989.
[2] Above, para.2–028.

Resulting trusts are not subject to all the rules of express trusts. Their creation is not dependent on compliance with formalities[3]; and a child may be a resulting trustee.[4]

The true nature of the resulting trust has been much scrutinised in recent years. The main points for debate have been the role of intention, the question of whether the beneficial interest remains in the transferor or is returned to him, and the linked question of whether the trust comes into effect only when the conscience of the transferee is affected by notice.

It used to be said that resulting trusts fell into two categories: presumed and automatic.[5] Under this classification the presumed resulting trust, arising in the case of transfers to volunteers, depended on the presumed intent of the transferor, whereas automatic resulting trusts, arising on failure to dispose of the beneficial interest, were imposed by operation of law without regard to intention. This classification is no longer favoured by the judiciary,[6] although it retains some academic support.[7] The most widely held view is that all resulting trusts are based on the absence of any intention by the transferor to pass a beneficial interest to the transferee.[8] In the case of transfers to volunteers, this absence of intention is rebuttably presumed:

> "Like a constructive trust, a resulting trust arises by operation of law, though unlike a constructive trust it gives effect to intention. But it arises whether or not the transferor intended to retain a beneficial interest—he almost always does not—since it responds to the absence of any intention on his part to pass a beneficial interest to the recipient".[9]

10–002   On one view it might be supposed that where a transferor fails to dispose of the beneficial interest, he must still have it. In other words, the effect of the resulting trust is that the beneficial interest remains in the transferor throughout. Lord Reid put it thus:

> "[T]he beneficial interest must belong to or be held for some-

---

[3] LPA 1925 s.53(2).

[4] *Re Vinogradoff* [1936] W.N. 68.

[5] *Re Vandervell's Trust (No.2)* [1974] Ch. 269 (Megarry J.).

[6] *Westdeutsche Landesbank Girozentrale v Islington LBC* [1996] A.C. 669 at 708 (Lord Browne-Wilkinson). See generally P. Birks [1996] R.L.R. 3.

[7] W. Swadling (2008) 124 L.Q.R. 72 at 98.

[8] Chambers, *Resulting Trusts*; R. Chambers (2001) 15 T.L.I. 2. R. Chambers in Mitchell (ed.), *Constructive and Resulting Trusts* (2009), Ch.9. See also C. Rickett (1999) 18 N.Z.U.L.R. 305, preferring the term "presumed trusts".

[9] *Air Jamaica Ltd v Charlton* [1999] 1 W.L.R. 1399 at 1412 (Lord Millett), giving the advice of the Privy Council. See also Lord Millett's judgment in *Twinsectra v Yardley* [2002] 2 A.C. 164 (dissenting on another issue).

body: so if it was not to belong to the donee or to be held by him in trust for somebody it must remain with the donor".[10]

This view has a firm historical foundation.[11] The modern analysis, however, is that the transferor's absolute beneficial interest is not to be regarded as comprising separate legal and equitable interests, so that only the legal interest passes to the transferee in situations where resulting trusts arise. In such cases the transferee takes the absolute title but holds on trust for the transferor, who acquires for the first time a separate equitable interest.[12] This view is crucial to the theory that resulting trusts effect restitution to the transferor and are thus part of the law of unjust enrichment.[13]

Building on this point, Lord Browne-Wilkinson has sought to establish that the resulting trust (or indeed any other trust) will take effect only when the conscience of the transferee is affected by his becoming aware that he has received property which was not intended for his benefit.[14] His Lordship regarded this theory as "uncontroversial", but it appears problematic and unsupported by authority. It has been much criticised.[15] Who would be entitled to the beneficial interest, for example dividends on shares, pending the acquisition of knowledge by the trustee? To link the creation of a resulting trust with the conscience of the trustee "would be a difficult and dangerous departure from existing law. There is little to be gained by such a move and much to be lost".[16] A preferable view is that the resulting trust arises as soon as the property is transferred, but the transferee does not become subject to fiduciary duties and liability for breach of trust until he is aware of the position.[17] Indeed, the duties of a resulting trustee have not been fully worked out.[18] Lord Browne-Wilkinson's theory is not borne out by the cases on

[10] *Vandervell v IRC* [1967] 2 A.C. 291 at 308. See also 313, 329. See further W. Swadling (2008) 124 L.Q.R. 72 at 100, criticising the reasoning but supporting the result.

[11] J. Mee in Mitchell (ed.), *Constructive and Resulting Trusts* (2009), Ch.7. See also J. Penner in Ch.8 of the same work, favouring the "retention" analysis.

[12] *Westdeutsche Landesbank Girozentrale v Islington LBC*, above, fn.6, at 706 (Lord Browne-Wilkinson).

[13] Chambers, *Resulting Trusts*; Sir Peter Millett (1998) 114 L.Q.R. 399; P. Birks and F. Rose (eds) *Restitution and Equity, Volume One: Resulting Trusts and Equitable Compensation*; R. Chambers (2002) 16 T.L.I. 104 and 138; R. Chambers in Burrows and Rodger (eds) *Mapping the Law*, Ch.13; cf. W. Swadling (2008) 124 L.Q.R. 72.

[14] *Westdeutsche Landesbank Girozentrale v Islington LBC*, above, fn.6.

[15] P. Birks [1996] 4 R.L.R. 3 at 20; G. Jones (1996) 55 C.L.J. 432; Sir Peter Millett (1998) 114 L.Q.R. 399 and [1998] 6 R.L.R. 283 and (2008) 124 L.Q.R. 72; W. Swadling (1998) 12 T.L.I. 228; P. Oliver (1997–98) 8 K.C.L.J. 147; N. McBride (1998) 57 C.L.J. 33 at 35–36.

[16] Chambers, *Resulting Trusts*, p.208, highlighting problems with taxation, insurance, priorities and so forth. See also R. Chambers (2010) 63 C.L.P. 631 at 648.

[17] Chambers, *Resulting Trusts*; Sir Peter Millett (1998) 114 L.Q.R. 399 at 404; N. McBride (1998) 57 C.L.J. 33 at 35–36.

[18] Chambers, *Resulting Trusts*, Ch.9.

presumed resulting trusts,[19] and is not necessary to the view that
resulting trusts effect restitution.

The situations in which resulting trusts arise will now be examined. The main examples, discussed below, involve incomplete disposal of the beneficial interest and transfers of property to volunteers. There are other cases where resulting trusts have been held to arise in circumstances where the transferor intended the property to revert to him unless used for a particular purpose. Such trusts might be regarded as express. An example is *Barclays Bank Ltd v Quistclose Investments Ltd*,[20] where the parties intended that the Bank transferee should hold the funds on trust for the transferor if they could not be used to pay the Rolls Razor dividend; but there was no formal declaration. Lord Millett's analysis is that the money is held on resulting trust for the lender as soon as it is transferred, but subject to the borrower's power or duty to apply it to the specified purpose.[21] This situation has already been considered.[22]

A. Incomplete Disposal

10–003   Where property is conveyed to a person in the capacity of a trustee, there will be a resulting trust for the grantor of any part of the beneficial interest which is not disposed of. This result arises by operation of law. As discussed above, it is based on the absence of any intention to benefit the transferee. It will be discussed in more detail in Pt 2.

B. Voluntary Conveyance

10–004   A conveyance to a third party will in some circumstances give rise to a resulting trust for the transferor. The trust will be raised by a presumption of a resulting trust. The presumption may of course be rebutted. In the case of a conveyance to the transferor's wife or child or to a person to whom the transferor is in loco parentis, the presumption was reversed by the presumption of advancement prior to its abolition by the Equality Act 2010. These matters are discussed in Pt 3.

---

[19] In particular *Re Vinogradoff* [1935] W.N. 68, below, para.10–021, where a young child was held to be a resulting trustee.

[20] [1970] A.C. 567; above para.2–009. See also *Carreras Rothmans Ltd v Freeman Mathews Treasure Ltd* [1985] Ch. 207 (contractual arrangement whereby money paid into a special bank account for a specific purpose created a trust); cf. *Re Multi Guarantee Co Ltd* [1987] B.C.L.C. 257; *Re EVTR Ltd* [1987] B.C.L.C. 647 (*Quistclose* principle applied to loan for specific purpose which partially failed).

[21] *Twinsectra v Yardley* [2002] 2 A.C. 164.

[22] Above, para.2–009.

C. Purchase Money Resulting Trust

Closely related to the previous category are conveyances to trans-   **10–005**
ferees who provide none or only part of the purchase price. This
category includes cases where the conveyance is made to A, but
some or all of the purchase price is provided by B, or where the
conveyance is to persons jointly, but the purchase price is provided
unequally. The latter situation is significantly affected by the decision of the House of Lords in *Stack v Dowden*, discussed below.[23]
The complex questions of the division of property ownership between spouses or cohabitants, where the contribution to the family
may be in ways other than the payment of money, will be dealt with
in Ch.11.

2. CONVEYANCE TO TRUSTEES

A. Where a Trust Fails

A resulting trust may arise on the failure, for a variety of reasons,   **10–006**
of an express trust. In *Morice v Bishop of Durham*,[24] the trusts were
void; so also in *Re Diplock*,[25] where a large sum of money was left
to be applied for purposes which the executors thought to be charitable, and was distributed among a number of charitable institutions.
The trusts were void. The next-of-kin were entitled under a resulting
trust; and they were able to recover the bulk of the money from the
charities. In *Essery v Cowlard*,[26] an intending wife executed a pre-
nuptial settlement in which she conveyed the trust property to trustees upon trust for herself, the intended husband and the issue of the
marriage. The marriage never took place, but the parties cohabited
and children were born. Six years later, the woman successfully
reclaimed the property. The trusts failed as the "contract to marry
had been definitely and absolutely put an end to".

In *Re Ames' Settlement*[27] property had been settled by the husband's father upon the trusts of a marriage settlement, and the marriage took place. Eighteen years later the wife obtained a decree of
nullity (which then had the effect of declaring the marriage void

---

[23] [2007] 2 A.C. 432; below, paras 10–035, 11–004.

[24] (1804) 8 Ves. 399; (1805) 10 Ves. 522; below, para.14–005. See also *Simpson v Simpson*
[1992] 1 F.L.R. 601 (transferee of bank deposit held on resulting trust for transferor where the
latter lacked mental capacity to make a gift).

[25] [1941] Ch. 253; [1944] A.C. 341; sub nom. *Chichester Diocesan Fund and Board of
Finance (Inc) v Simpson*; [1948] Ch. 465; [1951] A.C. 251; sub. nom. *Ministry of Health v
Simpson*; below, para.23–048.

[26] (1884) 26 Ch.D. 191; *Burgess v Rawnsley* [1975] Ch. 429 (if conveyance taken jointly for
a purpose which fails, resulting trust to each party of his share. Majority view that must be a
common purpose).

[27] [1946] Ch. 217.

from the outset).[28] Vaisey J. decided, after the husband's death, that
the property was held on a resulting trust for the executors of the
settlor.

Difficult questions arise as to the effect of void transactions. In the
rare case where the vitiating factor prevents title passing,[29] there is
no need for a resulting trust. Where, however, the title passes and,
notwithstanding the vitiating factor, the transferor intended the
transferee to become absolute owner, there is no resulting trust but
merely personal restitutionary liability. Thus in *Westdeutsche Landesbank Girozentrale v Islington LBC*,[30] where the bank paid money
to the local authority under a transaction which was ultra vires the
local authority, the latter was subject only to personal liability as the
bank had intended the authority to become absolute owner in spite
of its mistaken belief as to the validity of the transaction. Where a
transaction is merely voidable, as in the case of misrepresentation or
undue influence, title passes although the transferor may elect to set
aside the transaction. Chambers once argued that a resulting trust
arose on such a voidable transfer,[31] but he subsequently revised this
opinion.[32] The better view is that the beneficial title revests in the
transferor on rescission, but that the transferee is the absolute owner
pending that event.[33] While this is the position in relation to a
voidable contract, it appears to be otherwise in the case of a non-
consensual transfer of land procured by fraudulent misrepresentation, where the beneficial interest remains in the transferor.[34]

B. Incomplete Disposal of Beneficial Interest

10–007   Unskilful draftsmanship and the failure to foresee and provide for
future contingencies may leave the beneficial ownership incomplete.[35] A resulting trust will then arise, although, as will be seen,

---

[28] A decree of nullity in respect of a voidable marriage now operates to annul the marriage
only from the date of the decree absolute; Matrimonial Causes Act 1973 s.16. See also the
court's power to make property adjustments under s.24.

[29] See Sir Peter Millett (1998) 114 L.Q.R. 399 at 415–416.

[30] [1996] A.C. 669. The judgment in *Re Ames*, above, fn.27, was regarded as confused at
715. Title would not have passed if the transaction had been ultra vires the bank. It is
considered in Chambers, *Resulting Trusts*, pp.160–162, that the reasons for rejecting a resulting trust in *Westdeutsche* are unsatisfactory, and that such a trust should arise wherever vitiated
consent entitles the transferor to restitution.

[31] Chambers, *Resulting Trusts*, Ch.7.

[32] R. Chambers (2001) 15 T.L.I. 2 at 7. See also P. Birks and F. Rose (eds) *Restitution and
Equity—Volume 1: Resulting Trusts and Equitable Compensation* (2000).

[33] See Sir Peter Millett (1998) 114 L.Q.R. 399 at 416 and [1998] 6 R.L.R. 283; S. Worthington [2002] 10 R.L.R. 28; *Shalson v Russo* [2005] Ch. 281.

[34] *Collings v Lee* [2001] 2 All E.R. 332 (agent procuring transfer to himself for no consideration and in breach of fiduciary duty); below, para.23–052.

[35] See *Re Cochrane* [1955] Ch. 309; *John v George* [1995] 1 E.G.L.R. 9 (conveyance to
trustees on trust for daughter at 18 gave rise to resulting trust until she reached 18).

some sets of circumstances can render this result so inconvenient that other solutions are sought.

The fact that an equitable interest is not fully disposed of may not become apparent until some time has elapsed since the constitution of the trust.

In *Re Trusts of the Abbott Fund*[36] a sum of money was collected, to be used for the maintenance of two deaf and dumb ladies. It was held by Stirling J. that the ladies had no enforceable interests in the capital sum and that on their death, the sum remaining went on resulting trust to the subscribers.

The consequent problem of distribution on resulting trust among subscribers becomes acute when the number of subscribers is great, and the gifts are mostly anonymous, as in *Re Gillingham Bus Disaster Fund.*[37]

A number of marine cadets were injured or killed when a bus was driven into the rear of a marching column. The mayors of three towns appealed for subscriptions to a fund that would initially care for the disabled and thereafter be available for "worthy causes" in memory of those killed. More money was contributed than could be used for the object (liability at common law for the accident having been accepted) and the second object failed as it had not been confined within the limit of legal charity.[38] Harman J. held that, despite the manifest inconvenience of such a decision, a resulting trust arose. All subscribers, large or small, intended to contribute to a specific purpose; on that purpose being attained or no longer attainable, each donor had an interest by way of resulting trust. There was no evidence on which to arrive at any other conclusion. The suggestion that the money should be treated as bona vacantia was regarded by Harman J. as taking the line of least resistance in a manner unauthorised by law.

"The resulting trust arises where [the donor's] expectation is for some unforeseen reason cheated of fruition and is an inference of law based on after-knowledge of the event."[39]

---

[36] [1900] 2 Ch. 326, below, para.14–002.

[37] [1958] Ch. 300, below, para.14–002.

[38] Charities Act 2011 s.63 (below, para.15–076) provides the most convenient solution to this type of case, but it applies only when the gift is charitable. The fund was finally wound up in 1965, when the remainder of the money was paid into court. It was announced on April 5, 1993, that the money (£7,300) was to be paid out and used for a memorial to the victims. For a different solution, see *Re West Sussex Constabulary's Widows, Children and Benevolent Fund Trust* [1971] Ch.1, below.

[39] [1958] Ch. 300 at 310.

C. Methods of Disposal of Surplus Funds

10–008   A resulting trust is not, however, the most appropriate solution in
many situations; and, although something of a digression, it will be
convenient here to examine other solutions. The question arises
particularly in two contexts: First, that of gifts to persons for stated
purposes, without specifying what is to be done when the purposes
are completed; and, secondly, in the context of the dissolution of
unincorporated associations.

In determining the correct solution in each of these contexts, two
points will be of particular significance. First, did the transferor
intend to dispose of his whole interest; or did he intend to transfer
for a particular purpose only? Secondly, was the transfer made to a
person in a capacity of trustee? If so, a resulting trust may be
expected of the surplus.

10–009   **i. Transfer to Persons for Particular Purposes.** If property is
given for the care and maintenance of certain persons, what is to
happen to the property when the period of maintenance comes to an
end? Do the intended beneficiaries (or their estates) keep the property, or does it return on a resulting trust to the donor? The answer
will depend on the intention of the donor, which has to be ascertained from all the surrounding circumstances. The construction of
the gift in *Re Trusts of the Abbott Fund*[40] may be regarded as
unusual. It will be noted that the beneficiaries in that case had died.
More commonly, the gift is regarded as absolute. The principle of
construction was laid down in *Re Sanderson's Trust*[41] as follows:

> "If a gross sum be given, or if the whole income of the property
> be given, and a special purpose be assigned for that gift, the court
> always regards the gift as absolute, and the purpose merely as the
> motive of the gift, and therefore holds that the gift takes effect as
> to the whole sum or the whole income, as the case may be."

This principle is illustrated by the decisions below.

> In *Re Andrew's Trust*,[42] a fund was subscribed for the children
> of a deceased clergyman. An accompanying letter showed that the
> contributions were made "for or towards their education; . . . as
> being necessary to defray the expenses of all, and that solely in
> the matter of education." After their formal education was com-
> pleted, the question arose of the disposal of the surplus. Kekewich
> J. decided that the children were entitled in equal shares.

---

[40] [1900] 2 Ch. 326.
[41] per Page Wood V.C. (1857) 3 K. & J. 497 at 503; *Barlow v Grant* (1684) 1
Vern. 255.
[42] [1905] 2 Ch. 48.

In *Re Osoba*[43] there was a gift by will of a residuary estate, consisting, for present purposes, of a freehold house in London, to the testator's widow on trust to be used "for her maintenance and for the training of my daughter up to University grade and for the maintenance of my aged mother..." The mother predeceased the testator; the widow died in 1970, and the daughter's education up to university grade was completed in 1975. The children under an earlier marriage claimed the residue on intestacy.

The Court of Appeal found that the testator's intention was to provide absolute gifts for the beneficiaries, the references to maintenance and to education being expressions of motive. In the absence of words of severance, the beneficiaries took as joint tenants, with the daughter becoming entitled, on her mother's death, to the whole. The result would have been the same if the daughter had not gone to university.

ii. Surplus Funds on Dissolution of Unincorporated Association.[44]

(a) *Trust or Contract.* As will be seen in Ch.14, funds of such an association will sometimes be held by trustees on an express trust for the members and sometimes by the treasurer or committee on a bare trust; in either case the property rights in the assets of the society are likely to be governed by the rules of the society which operate as a contract between the members. The question whether the property is held upon the terms of any trust created by the donor, or whether it is held by the members absolutely according to their contractual rights is relevant here also. The question commonly arises on a dissolution. It will be seen in the analysis which follows that the distinction between rights governed by a trust and those governed by a contract has not always been kept clear. In the case of a failure of a trust, the most appropriate solution is by way of resulting trust. In a case of dissolution of a society where the rights of the members are governed by a contract (i.e. by the rules of the society) the likely solution is in accordance with the terms of the contract; and if the contract is silent; by equal division among the members. The Crown might claim the fund as bona vacantia. It may also have to be considered whether any third party contributors may have a claim to participate in the distribution along with the members. Whether the matter is regarded as one of trust or contract affects the question of who is entitled and the calculation of the share. All these solutions will be demonstrated here, although the

10–010

---

[43] [1979] 1 W.L.R. 247.

[44] See generally Warburton, *Unincorporated Associations: Law & Practice*, 2nd edn; S. Gardner [1992] Conv. 41. For the meaning of "unincorporated association" see *Conservative and Unionist Central Office v Burrell* [1982] 1 W.L.R. 522, below, para.14–020.

analysis in the earlier cases was subject to criticism by Walton J. in *Re Bucks Constabulary Fund (No.2)*.[45]

10–011   (b) *Meaning of Dissolution.* An association may be wound up in a formal manner, but in the absence of a formal dissolution, the question arises as to the circumstances which will justify a finding that the body has ceased to exist. In *Re GKN Bolts and Nuts Ltd (Automotive Division) Birmingham Works, Sports and Social Club*,[46] the trustees of a social club had purchased a sports ground for £2,200 in 1946. In 1975, membership cards ceased to be issued and the last annual general meeting was held. No further accounts were taken, the stock of drinks was sold and the steward dismissed. A special meeting was convened on December 18, 1975 to deal with an offer to buy the land. Resolutions were passed that the land be sold, but no sale then took place. In 1978, the trustees sold the land for £253,000. One question which arose was the date the club ceased to exist.[47] It was held that mere inactivity did not suffice, unless it was so prolonged or so circumstanced that the only reasonable inference was spontaneous dissolution, in which case the court must select a date. On the facts, it ceased to exist on December 18, 1975, on the basis of inactivity coupled with positive acts to wind it up. This would be so even if the resolution to sell the land was invalid, as by that date the club's activities had ceased and it had become incapable of carrying out its objects.

10–012   (c) *Resulting Trust for Members.* In *Re Printers' and Transferrers' Society*,[48] a society was founded to raise funds by weekly contributions to defend and support its members in maintaining reasonable remuneration for their labour, and to provide strike and lock-out benefits for members. The scale of payments varied according to the length of time a claimant had been a member of the society, and different conditions applied to printers and transferrers respectively. No provision was made by the rules for the distribution of the funds of the society on a dissolution. At the time of its dissolution the society consisted of 201 members, and its funds amounted to £1,000. The question arose as to how the sum was to be distributed. The Attorney General made no claim to the fund as bona vacantia. It was held that there was a resulting trust in favour of those who had subscribed to the fund, and that the money was

---

[45] [1979] 1 W.L.R. 936; below, para.10–014.
[46] [1982] 1 W.L.R. 774; R. Griffith [1983] Conv. 315. See also *Re William Denby & Sons Ltd Sick and Benevolent Fund* [1971] 1 W.L.R. 973; *Re Bucks Constabulary Widows' and Orphans' Fund Friendly Society (No.2)* [1979] 1 W.L.R. 936.
[47] The question of entitlement to the money is dealt with below, para.10–016.
[48] [1899] 2 Ch. 184.

divisible amongst the existing members at the time of the dissolution, in proportion to the amount contributed by each member to the funds of the society irrespective of fines, or payments made to members in accordance with the rules.

In *Re Hobourn Aero Components Air Raid Distress Fund*,[49] a fund was established during the Second World War for employees of a company who were on war service or who sustained loss in air raids. The fund was financed by voluntary subscriptions among the employees, but it was not charitable. The Crown made no claim to the fund as bona vacantia. After the war, the fund was found to have a surplus. It was held that each contributor, past or present, had an interest in the surplus by way of resulting trust in proportion to the amount he had contributed, but subject to adjustment in relation to any benefit he had received from the fund.

This conclusion, although logically consistent with the resulting trust analysis, is less convenient than the decision in *Re Printers' and Transferrers' Society*,[50] in that it concentrates attention on all the contributors to a society, however remote in time past, and not on those who have retained a connection with it. There is much to be said for the simpler solution of the earlier case, which, however, Cohen J. in the present case thought defensible only in cases where the ascertainment of the true entitlements would be too difficult. A more recent example is provided by *Air Jamaica Ltd v Charlton*,[51] where, however, the surplus arose in the context of a pension trust rather than an association. That part of the surplus which derived from the members' contributions resulted to them and was divided pro rata between the members and the estates of deceased members in proportion to their contributions, irrespective of benefits received and the dates of the contributions.

(d) *Contractual Basis.* In *Cunnack v Edwards*,[52] a society governed by the Friendly Societies Act 1829[53] had been established in 1810 to raise a fund, by the subscriptions of its members, to provide annuities for the widows of its deceased members. By 1879 all the members had died. The last widow-annuitant died in 1892, the society then having a surplus of £1,250. A claim to the assets was **10–013**

---

[49] [1946] Ch. 86 (affirmed at 194), see especially 97–98; following *Re British Red Cross Balkan Fund* [1914] 2 Ch. 419, (which is doubted in Tudor, *Charities*, 9th edn, at p.397, fn.77).

[50] [1899] 2 Ch. 184.

[51] [1999] 1 W.L.R. 1399, PC; C. Harpum [2000] Conv. 170; C. Rickett and R. Grantham (2000) 116 L.Q.R. 15. The bona vacantia solution of *Davis v Richards & Wallington Industries Ltd* [1990] 1 W.L.R. 1511, below, para.10–015, was considered wrong.

[52] [1896] 2 Ch. 679; H. Hickling (1966) 30 Conv.(N.S.) 117; B. Green (1980) 43 M.L.R. 626. The decision was distinguished in *Re Bucks Constabulary Fund (No.2)*, below, fn.60 as turning upon the combined effect of the rules and the 1829 Act.

[53] For the special position of Friendly Societies, see Warburton, *Unincorporated Associations: Law & Practice*, 2nd edn, pp.5–6.

made by the personal representatives of the last surviving members. It was held that there was no resulting trust in favour of the personal representatives of the members of the society. Each member had paid away his money in return for the protection given to his widow, if he left one. "Except as to this he abandoned and gave up the money for ever."[54] The assets went to the Crown as bona vacantia.

In *Re West Sussex Constabulary's Widows, Children and Benevolent (1930) Fund Trust*,[55] a fund had been established to provide benefits to widows and certain dependants of members who died. The income of the fund came from members' subscriptions, the proceeds of entertainments, sweepstakes, raffles and collecting boxes and various donations and legacies. On the amalgamation of the West Sussex Constabulary with other police forces in 1968, the question arose of the distribution of the fund.

Goff J. held that the surviving members had no claim because first, the members had received all that they had contracted for, and secondly, the money was paid on the basis of contract, and not of trust. The funds went as bona vacantia to the Crown. The possibility that living members may have a contractual claim on the basis of frustration of the contract or failure of consideration was met by the Crown giving an indemnity to the trustees.

Contributions from outside sources were divided into three categories. The first two, proceeds of entertainments, etc. and collecting boxes, could not be the subject of a resulting trust,[56] they were out-and-out payments.[57] Identifiable donations, however, and legacies were in a different position. The object of the gift had failed, and the property was held on resulting trust. On the latter point, it is difficult to see why third party contributors, even if identifiable, should have any claim in such circumstances. The validity of the initial gift is usually explained on the basis that it is an absolute gift to the members of the association.[58] If that is so, such contributions should be dealt with on the same basis as the rest of the funds. It is submitted that there is no room here for a resulting trust for third parties.

10–014　　　The more acceptable modern solution to the distribution of assets of an unincorporated society is among the members. The matter is regarded as one of contract between the members, express or implied. On this analysis, the resulting trust solution is no longer appropriate. This is so, even though the assets of the society may be

---

[54] [1896] 2 Ch. 679 at 683.

[55] [1971] Ch. 1; M. Albery (1971) 87 L.Q.R. 464.

[56] Not following *Re Gillingham Bus Disaster Fund* [1958] Ch. 300, above, para.10–007.

[57] *Re Welsh Hospital (Netley) Fund* [1921] 1 Ch. 655; *Re Hillier's Trusts* [1954] 1 W.L.R. 9; *Re Ulverston and District New Hospital Building Trust* [1956] Ch. 672.

[58] Below, para.14–019.

vested in trustees; as is indeed required in the case of unincorporated Friendly Societies.[59] The trustees then hold the assets on trust for the members according to the rules of the society. The rules may provide for the distribution upon dissolution. Otherwise, the assets will be divided among the members at the time of the dissolution.

Re Bucks Constabulary Fund (No.2)[60] was another case of the distribution of a fund established to provide benefits for the widows and orphans of deceased police officers and the provision of payments on the death of a member or during sickness. The Bucks Constabulary amalgamated with other constabularies and in 1968 the fund was wound up.

The question of the proper method of distribution came before Walton J., who held that the assets should be divided equally among members alive at the date of dissolution. He emphasised the distinction between property held under the terms of the trust, and that governed by contract. In such a case, quoting Brightman J.[61]

"The right of the member of the fund to receive benefits is a contractual right and the member ceases to have any interest in the fund if and when he has received the totality of the benefits to which he was contractually entitled. In other words, there is no possible claim by any member founded on a resulting trust. . . . If it has been dissolved or terminated, the members entitled to participate would *prima facie* be those persons who were members at the date of dissolution or termination."[62]

The *West Sussex*[63] decision, although distinguishable on the ground that it did not involve a Friendly Society, was criticised by Walton J. on the basis that the principle of law applicable to the members' club cases should have governed the distribution. It made no difference whether or not the association was for the benefit of the members themselves. They controlled the assets, which were theirs all along. Thus bona vacantia was not an appropriate solution in that case.

Walton J. suggested that, if there was only one member left, the property would be ownerless and would pass to the Crown. Lewison J. recently disagreed, holding that the sole surviving member

---

[59] Friendly Societies Act 1974 s.49(1). The Friendly Societies Act 1992 provides for the incorporation of Friendly Societies carrying on mutual insurance business for the members and their families.

[60] [1979] 1 W.L.R. 936; C. Rickett (1980) 39 C.L.J. 88; B. Green (1980) 43 M.L.R. 626.

[61] *Re William Denby and Sons Ltd Sick and Benevolent Fund* [1971] 1 W.L.R. 973 at 978.

[62] [1979] 1 W.L.R. 936 at 948.

[63] Above, fn.55.

of a non-charitable unincorporated association was entitled to the assets on the basis that the members were the joint tenants in equity, subject to any contractual restrictions.[64] The property accrued to the last member by the doctrine of survivorship, and neither the Crown nor any former members or their estates had any entitlement. This, it is submitted, is the correct analysis. As Lewison J. pointed out, diverting the property from the last surviving member to the Crown would be a breach of art.1 of the First Protocol to the European Convention on Human Rights (right to peaceful enjoyment of possessions).

10–015   Similar problems may arise in the context of surplus pension funds. As this situation involves a trust rather than an unincorporated association, it may be expected (in the absence of rules in the pension scheme to deal with it) that the surplus would be held on resulting trust for the contributors. In *Davis v Richards & Wallington Industries Ltd*,[65] however, Scott J. considered that any resulting trust to the members would be excluded by implication, partly because of the difficulty of calculating their shares in view of the different benefits received, and partly because tax relief would be lost if the members received under a resulting trust any sums in excess of the maximum benefits permitted by the relevant legislation. Thus the bona vacantia solution was preferred. This analysis was considered to be wrong by the Privy Council in *Air Jamaica Ltd v Charlton*[66] on the basis that a resulting trust cannot be avoided simply because the transferor does not intend to retain the beneficial interest: it may arise even where the transferor positively wished to part with the beneficial interest.[67] The two reasons given by Scott J. should not have excluded a resulting trust, which arose by operation of the general law and outside the scope of the tax legislation. The alleged difficulty of calculating the shares rested on the erroneous assumption that the benefits received by each member had to be taken into account. In the present case the proper solution was a resulting trust for the employer[68] and the members. The members' share was divided pro rata between the members and the estates of

---

[64] *Hanchett-Stamford v Att Gen* [2009] Ch. 173. *Cunnack v Edwards*, above, fn.52, para.10–013, was distinguished as all members there had disappeared or their claims had been satisfied. The grounds for distinguishing *Cunnack* are criticised by S. Baughen [2010] Conv. 216 at 228.

[65] [1990] 1 W.L.R. 1511; J. Martin [1991] Conv. 366; S. Gardner [1992] Conv. 41; Chambers, *Resulting Trusts*, p.66.

[66] [1999] 1 W.L.R. 1399.

[67] As in *Vandervell v Inland Revenue Commissioners* [1967] 2 A.C. 291, below, para.10–018.

[68] A clause in the deed excluding any repayment to the employer was to preclude any amendment to the scheme allowing such repayment and did not rebut a resulting trust arising outside the scheme.

deceased members in proportion to their contributions, irrespective of benefits received and the dates of the contributions.

(e) *Methods of Distribution Among the Members.* If entitlement **10–016** is on the basis of a resulting trust, the distribution will be made amongst all members, past and present, including personal representatives of deceased members, in shares proportionate to their contributions. Past members may be excluded if the calculation would prove too difficult.[69] We have seen, however, that the resulting trust analysis is not usually favoured today in cases of unincorporated associations. It is also unlikely, in view of *Re Bucks Constabulary Fund (No.2)*,[70] that the Crown will establish a claim to the assets as bona vacantia in many cases, or, as submitted above,[71] that outside contributors will have any claim. Assuming that the contractual basis is adopted, only those members existing at the date of dissolution will be entitled. Unless the rules provide otherwise, the distribution will be on a per capita basis, prima facie in equal shares, and ignoring actual contributions.

In *Re Sick and Funeral Society of St John's Sunday School, Golcar*,[72] a society was formed in 1866 to provide sickness and death benefits for its members. Those under 13 paid $\frac{1}{2}$d per week, and the others paid 1d. The benefits for those paying the whole subscription were twice those of the smaller subscribers. Upon the winding up of the society, the surplus funds were held distributable among the members as at that date on a per capita basis, but as the benefits and burdens differed among the two classes of members, the proper basis for distribution was full shares for full members and half shares for the children. The per capita basis did not favour new members at the expense of older ones, as each got what he paid for: the newer members had had the benefits of membership for a short time and the older members for a longer time. The latter could not complain if they did not receive more in the winding up.

In *Re Bucks Constabulary Fund (No.2)*,[73] Walton J. held that the prima facie rule of equal division applied also to Friendly Society cases, although in the past some of those cases had favoured a distribution in proportion to contributions.[74] This approach was also adopted in *Re GKN Bolts & Nuts Ltd (Automotive Division) Birmingham Works, Sports and Social Club*,[75] where those entitled to

[69] *Re Hobourn Aero Components Air Raid Distress Fund* [1946] Ch. 86 at 97.
[70] [1979] 1 W.L.R. 936.
[71] Above, para.10–013.
[72] [1973] Ch. 51.
[73] Above, fn.70. See also *Elvidge v Coulson, The Times,* August 27, 2003.
[74] *Re Printers' and Transferrers' Society* [1899] 2 Ch. 184; *Re Lead Workmens Fund Society* [1904] 2 Ch. 196.
[75] [1982] 1 W.L.R. 774. The facts have been given, above, para.10–011. See also *Re St Andrew's Allotment Association* [1969] 1 W.L.R. 229; *Re Horley Town Football Club* [2006] W.T.L.R. 1817; P. Luxton [2007] Conv. 274.

share the assets on a per capita basis were the full members and the ordinary members. Honorary, temporary and associate members, who neither paid subscriptions nor had voting rights, were excluded.

10–017   **iii. Trust and Charge.** Here also the distinction between a trust and a charge is important.[76] A distinction was drawn by Lord Eldon in *King v Denison*[77] between devises *charged with payment* of debts, and devises *on trust to pay* debts. In the former case it is assumed that the testator intended a beneficial interest for the devisee, subject to the payment of debts; in the latter case it is assumed that he intended merely to use the devisee as a vehicle for payment of the debts, and not to confer any benefit upon him. In the latter case there will, therefore, be a resulting trust of any surplus for the residuary devisee, or those entitled on intestacy; but there will be no resulting trust in the former case. In construing the language of a gift, it must be remembered that equity will not allow trustees themselves to give evidence that what was intended was a conditional gift.[78]

D. No Declaration of Trust

10–018   Where property is conveyed to persons in circumstances in which they are intended to take as trustees, then, if no beneficial interests are declared, they will hold on resulting trust for the grantor; as where a transfer is made to a nominee.[79] We have seen this principle in operation in the case of testamentary gifts to legatees as trustees, without the trusts upon which they are to hold being declared prior to the testator's death.[80]

The *Vandervell* litigation serves as a warning of the crucial importance of attention to detail in tax planning. There were two visits to the House of Lords and three to the Court of Appeal. The problem was caused by the fact that Mr Vandervell's advisers overlooked the possibility of the existence of a resulting trust; when all that Mr Vandervell was doing was trying to give away a large sum of money to charity.

In 1958 Vandervell decided to found a Chair of Pharmacology at the Royal College of Surgeons with a gift of £250,000. This

---

[76] Above, para.2–012.

[77] (1813) 1 Ves. & Bea. 260; *Smith v Cooke* [1891] A.C. 297; *Re West* [1900] 1 Ch. 84; *Re Foord* [1922] 2 Ch. 519, distinguished in *Re Osoba* [1979] 1 W.L.R. 247, above, para.10–009.

[78] *Re Rees* [1950] Ch. 204; *Re Pugh* [1967] 1 W.L.R. 1262; *Re Tyler* [1967] 1 W.L.R. 1269; above, para.5–012, cf. *Smith v Cooke*, above, fn.77.

[79] *Hodgson v Marks* [1971] Ch. 892; *Vandervell v IRC* [1967] 2 A.C. 291.

[80] *Re Boyes* (1884) 26 Ch.D. 531; above, para.5–005; *Re Pugh's WT* [1967] 1 W.L.R. 1262.

was to be effected by a scheme under which a block of shares in Vandervell Products Ltd would be transferred to the College, and the necessary dividends subsequently declared on them. Such dividends, in the hands of the College, would be free of liability to income tax and surtax.[81] The shares were to be transferred subject to an option to repurchase for £5,000 in favour of Vandervell Trustees Ltd, a private company whose only function was to act as trustee for various trusts connected with the Vandervell family and business. It was trustee of the Vandervell children's trust.

The transfer of the shares was made in 1958, and between then and 1961 the necessary dividends were paid to the College. The Revenue assessed Vandervell for surtax on the dividends on the ground that he had not entirely disposed of all his interest in the property,[82] because, in the absence of a declaration of trust of the option, it was held on resulting trust for Vandervell. The Revenue succeeded. That was *Vandervell v IRC*.[83] Before discussing the reasoning, it will be best to complete the story.

On receiving the Revenue's claim in 1961, Vandervell ordered Vandervell Trustees Ltd to exercise the option, and they did so, taking £5,000 from the children's settlement to finance it. All the dividends since that date were paid to Vandervell Trustees Ltd, who applied them to the children's settlement. They so informed the Revenue.

The Revenue assessed Vandervell to surtax in respect of the years 1961–65 on the footing that the shares were held on trust for him during that period. In 1965 he at last executed a deed which transferred all or any interest which he may have in the shares in favour of the children's settlement. In 1967 he died.

Before this claim of the Revenue was litigated, Vandervell's estate stepped in and claimed the dividends from Vandervell Trustees Ltd. If the estate succeeded, the Revenue's claim was clearly good; and the Revenue attempted to join the litigation in support. The defendants successfully excluded them.[84] In *Re Vandervell's Trusts (No.2)* the estate succeeded before Megarry J., but failed before the Court of Appeal.[85]

In the first case, *Vandervell v IRC*,[86] the Revenue succeeded by a **10–019** majority of three to two. The option was held on trust for Vandervell. He was effectively the grantor of the option, although it was in

---

[81] Because the College is a charity.
[82] ITA 1952 s.415(2). Now Income Tax (Trading and Other Income) Act 2005 s.624.
[83] [1967] 2 A.C. 291; G. Jones (1966) 24 C.L.J. 19; S. Spencer (1967) 31 Conv.(N.S.) 175; N. Strauss (1967) 30 M.L.R. 461.
[84] *Re Vandervell's Trusts (No.1)* [1971] A.C. 912.
[85] [1974] Ch. 269.
[86] [1967] 2 A.C. 291.

form granted by the Royal College. It was taken by Vandervell
Trustees Ltd upon trust, but no effective trusts of the option were
declared, "and so the defendant company held the option on an
automatic trust for Mr Vandervell."[87] In this situation, there was, as
Lord Wilberforce said:

> "[N]o need, or room to invoke a presumption. The conclusion, on
> the facts found, is simply that the option was vested in the trustee
> company as a trustee on trusts, not defined at the time, possibly to
> be defined later. But the equitable, or beneficial interest, cannot
> remain in the air: the consequence in law must be that it remains
> in the settlor."[88]

An indication of the parties' intention, as opposed to what they
might be supposed to have desired, would of course have changed
the whole situation. But the donor's mere intention not to have the
beneficial interest cannot prevent a resulting trust.[89]

In *Re Vandervell's Trusts (No.2)*,[90] the Court of Appeal, reversing
Megarry J., found that the resulting trust of the option in favour of
Vandervell terminated with the exercise of the option; and that a
trust of the shares had been declared in favour of the children's
settlements. Criticisms of the finding of a declaration of trust have
already been made.[91] Another difficulty is that even if the acts of the
trustees were sufficient to manifest an intention to create a new trust,
how could the option and the shares be separated? Is it right
to say:

> "Before the option was exercised, there was a gap in the benefi-
> cial ownership. So there was a resulting trust for Mr. Vandervell.
> But, as soon as the option was exercised and the shares registered
> in the trustees' name, there was created a valid trust of the shares
> in favour of the children's settlement"?[92]

Other problems relating to the formality requirements of Law of
Property Act 1925 s.53(1)(c) were discussed in Ch.4.

---

[87] [1974] Ch. 269 at 296, per Megarry J.

[88] [1967] 2 A.C. 291 at 329.

[89] [1974] Ch. 269 at 298, per Megarry J.; *Air Jamaica Ltd v Charlton* [1999] 1 W.L.R.
1399.

[90] [1974] Ch. 269; P. Clarke (1974) 38 Conv.(N.S.) 405; J. Harris (1975) 38 M.L.R. 557; G.
Battersby (1975) 7 D.L.R. 483.

[91] Above, paras 3–010, 4–015.

[92] [1974] Ch. 269 per Lord Denning M.R. at 320; Lawton L.J. made the same point: "There
could not be a resulting trust of a chose in action which was no more" at 325.

3. VOLUNTARY CONVEYANCE AND THE PRESUMPTIONS

A. Presumption of Resulting Trust: Conveyance to a Third Party

i. Land. One of the effects of the Statute of Uses was to prevent   **10–020**
the operation of resulting uses. Previously, a resulting use arose on a
voluntary conveyance which did not declare a use; the beneficial
interest reverted to the grantor. After the Statute of Uses, the use was
executed, and the grantor retained the legal estate; the conveyance
was thus ineffectual. When equitable interests returned under the
name of trusts, the beneficial interest might again result to the grantor in cases both of realty and personalty, where the grantee was not
intended to take beneficially. A number of problems remain in the
ascertainment of the intention to be ascribed to the grantor.

The Law of Property Act 1925 s.60(3), helps in solving these
problems in relation to land.[93] While before 1926 it was necessary,
in a voluntary conveyance, to insert a use in favour of the grantee in
order to prevent a resulting trust arising, s.60(3) makes this no
longer essential. Section 60(3) however, only prevents the implication of a resulting trust *merely* by reason that the conveyance is not
expressed to be for the benefit of the grantee. If it is intended to take
effect as a gift, it is still preferable to make this clear in the conveyance, as s.60(3) does not preclude the implication of a resulting trust
on general equitable principles.[94] Where the transferor establishes
that no gift was intended, s.60(3) does not prevent the finding of a
resulting trust.

In *Hodgson v Marks*,[95] Mrs Hodgson was an old lady who was
the registered owner of a house. A lodger, Evans, lived there. Mrs
Hodgson developed an affection for Evans, and trusted him to
look after all her affairs. Her nephew disapproved of Evans, and
tried to persuade Mrs Hodgson to turn him out. To protect Evans,
she transferred the house to him, under an oral agreement that she
would continue to be beneficial owner. Evans, as registered
owner, sold it to a bona fide purchaser, Marks, and the question
was whether Mrs Hodgson was protected against Marks.

---

[93] "In a voluntary conveyance a resulting trust for the grantor shall not be implied merely
by reason that the property is not expressed to be conveyed for the use or benefit of the
grantee."

[94] This was accepted by the Court of Appeal in *Lohia v Lohia* (2002) 16 T.L.I. 231,
although the question whether the presumption had been abolished did not need to be decided
in the circumstances of that case. See also *Ali v Khan* [2009] W.T.L.R. 197 (decided
2002).

[95] [1971] Ch. 892.

The Court of Appeal held that she remained beneficial owner in equity, and that this was an overriding interest.[96] The express oral agreement in her favour was unenforceable under the Law of Property Act 1925, s.53(1)(b). Evidence of her intention was however admissible, and this gave rise to a resulting trust of the beneficial interest, which was not affected by s.53(1). Section 60(3) was not discussed.

10–021   **ii. Personalty.** In relation to personalty, the initial presumption remains that a voluntary transfer to a third party gives rise to a resulting trust.

In *Re Vinogradoff*,[97] the testatrix had transferred a sum of £800 War Loan, then standing in her name, into the joint names of herself and her granddaughter, then four years old. The testatrix continued to receive the dividends until her death.

Farwell J. held that, even though a child may not be appointed a trustee, the presumption of resulting trust applied, and the grand-daughter held that property on resulting trust for the estate of the testatrix.

It is questionable whether such a result coincides with the real intention of the transferor. If, however, as would be one possible construction, her intention was to keep the property as her own during her lifetime and to give it to the granddaughter upon her death, such an attempted disposition would be testamentary, and void for failure to comply with the formal requirements of the Wills Act. A valid gift could be effected if intended to be held by the transferor for her life and after her death for the donee, or if a beneficial joint tenancy with a right of survivorship was created.[98]

It is even more doubtful whether the presumption accords with the transferor's intention in the case of a transfer to the grantee alone. The majority of such transfers must be intended as gifts. Although it seems correct to say that the presumption of a resulting trust exist in such cases,[99] it gives way to the slightest contrary evidence. The common sense of the transaction frequently prevails, and the rules of evidence do not prevent the sense of the transaction being deduced.

---

[96] Because she was in actual occupation. The provision is now found in LRA 2002 s.29 and Sch.3, para.2.

[97] [1935] W.N. 68; *Standing v Bowring* (1885) 16 Ch.D. 282 at 287; *Fowkes v Pascoe* (1875) L.R. 10 Ch.App. 343; *Thavorn v Bank of Credit & Commerce International SA* [1985] 1 Lloyd's Rep. 259 (resulting trust where aunt opened bank account in name of 15-year-old nephew).

[98] *Fowkes v Pascoe* (1875) L.R. 10 Ch.App. 343; below, para.10–033. See *Thavorn v Bank of Credit & Commerce International SA*, above, fn.97, at 262.

[99] *George v Havard* (1819) 7 Price 646 at 651, per Richards C.B.

Lord Browne-Wilkinson has suggested that the resulting trust in such cases does not arise at the date of the transfer if the transferee was then ignorant of the facts, but arises only when the transferee's conscience becomes affected.[100] It is difficult to see how *Re Vinogradoff* supports this analysis, in view of the age of the transferee at all relevant times. This point has already been discussed.[101]

B. Presumption of Advancement

The presumption of advancement is a presumption working in the opposite direction. It arises where certain relationships exist, where the donor or purchaser is under an obligation recognised in equity, to support or provide for the transferee.[102] It arises if the person to whom a voluntary conveyance is made is the wife or child of the donor, or someone to whom he stands in loco parentis. It is clear from the cases, however, that adult children are within the presumption. Like the presumption of resulting trust, it is rebuttable by evidence that the donor intended to keep the beneficial interest for himself. The Law Commission called it "archaic and discriminatory."[103] The gender bias of the presumption was thought likely to contravene the European Convention on Human Rights.[104] This led to the abolition of the presumption in s.199(1) of the Equality Act 2010.[105] However, the abolition of the presumption has no effect in relation to:

10–022

(a) anything done before the commencement of this section, or
(b) anything done pursuant to any obligation incurred before the commencement of this section.[106]

This means that it will remain necessary for years to come to consider the effect of the presumption in relation to transactions taking place before its abolition which are the subject of a later dispute.

---

[100] *Westdeutsche Landesbank Girozentrale v Islington LBC* [1996] A.C. 669 at 705–706.

[101] Above, para.10–002.

[102] See *Cavalier v Cavalier* (1971) 19 F.L.R. 199, (SCNSW) at 205, where Carmichael J. considered this statement too narrow; J. Hackney [1974] A.S.C.L. 527.

[103] Law Com. No.320 (2010), *The Illegality Defence*, para.1.26.

[104] Article 5 of the Seventh Protocol. See the Law Commission Discussion Paper, *Sharing Homes* (2002), para.2.60; cf. J. Glister (2010) 73 M.L.R. 807. The UK has not yet ratified the Seventh Protocol.

[105] The section is not in force at the time of writing. The common law rule that a husband must maintain his wife was abolished by s.198.

[106] s.199(2). See J. Glister (2010) 73 M.L.R. 808, criticising ambiguities in the drafting of this provision.

i. Husband and wife.

10–023   (a) *Gift by Husband.* The presumption of advancement applies
where a husband makes a transfer to his wife. Even before its
abolition the strength of the presumption was much diminished in
modern times.[107] "It would in my view," said Lord Diplock in
Pettitt v Pettitt[108]:

> "[B]e an abuse of the legal technique for ascertaining or imputing
> intention to apply to transactions between the post-war generation
> of married couples 'presumptions' which are based upon infer-
> ences of fact which an earlier generation of judges drew as the
> most likely intentions of earlier generations of spouses belonging
> to the propertied classes of a different social era."

Pettitt v Pettitt was a case of a claim to a share in the ownership of a
matrimonial home, as to which special considerations apply, and
will be discussed in Ch.11.

In *Re Eykyn's Trusts*[109] in 1877, Malins V.C. said:

> "The law of this court is perfectly settled that where a husband
> transfers money or other property into the name of his wife
> only, then the presumption is, that it is intended as a gift or
> advancement to the wife absolutely at once . . . "

Transfers of chattels to a wife are within the presumption; and so
is the matrimonial home which is conveyed to the wife although
paid for by the husband. In *Tinker v Tinker*,[110] the presumption was
readily applied, in spite of the comments upon the presumption in
Pettitt v Pettitt; but there was ample evidence to show that the wife
was intended to benefit.

The presumption also applies where the gift is made before marriage, but with a specific marriage (which in fact takes place) in
mind.[111] There is no presumption of advancement where a man puts

---

[107] *Pettitt v Pettitt* [1970] A.C. 777; *Gissing v Gissing* [1971] A.C. 886; *Falconer v Falconer* [1970] 1 W.L.R. 1333.

[108] Above, fn.107, at 824. See also *Simpson v Simpson* [1992] 1 F.L.R. 601; *Harwood v
Harwood* [1991] 2 F.L.R. 274.

[109] (1877) 6 Ch.D. 115 at 118; quoted in *Pettitt v Pettitt* above, fn.107, at 815.

[110] [1970] P. 136.

[111] *Moate v Moate* [1948] 2 All E.R. 486; *Ulrich v Ulrich* [1968] 1 W.L.R. 180; E. Ellis
(1975) 119 S.J. 108. A void marriage is not included. As to engaged couples, see Law Reform
(Miscellaneous Provisions) Act 1970 s.2(1). One effect of s.2(1) is that the presumption of
advancement applies to resolve disputes between couples whose engagement has ended;
Mossop v Mossop [1989] Fam. 77; JEM [1988] Conv. 284; cf. *Bernard v Josephs* [1982] Ch.
391 at 400.

property into the name of his unmarried partner,[112] nor is there such a presumption where a wife puts property into the name of her husband.[113] With a matrimonial home, at least, very little evidence will suffice to establish a sharing of the beneficial interest.[114]

(b) *Rebuttal.* The presumption can be rebutted by evidence **10–024** which tends to show that no gift was intended. Thus, in *Anson v Anson*,[115] a husband guaranteed his wife's banking account, and eventually the guarantee was called and he was obliged to pay a sum of money to the bank as a result. Pearson J. held that the husband could recover that sum from the wife, as the transaction was not in the nature of an advancement. There will be no advancement if, for example, a joint account was opened for the purposes of making it easier for the wife to draw money from an account, the husband being ill.[116] A joint account, though funded by the husband, will frequently lead to the inference of a joint tenancy in law and equity.[117] A special statutory rule applies to money and property derived from a housekeeping allowance. Section 1 of the Married Women's Property Act 1964 provided that, where the allowance was made by the husband, it was to be treated as belonging to the husband and wife equally. This provision has been amended by the Equality Act 2010 in order to make it human rights compliant.[118] Section 1 of the 1964 Act, which has been renamed as the Matrimonial Property Act 1964, now applies to housekeeping allowances made by either spouse to the other, and applies similarly to civil partners.

ii. Father and Child. There is a presumption of advancement **10–025** between a father and his legitimate child. The presumption here is stronger, and, "should not ... give way to slight circumstances."[119]

---

[112] *Diwell v Farnes* [1959] 1 W.L.R. 624; but the other rules for ascertaining the ownership of the home apply; below, paras 11–002–11–012.

[113] *Mercier v Mercier* [1903] 2 Ch. 98; *Heseltine v Heseltine* [1971] 1 W.L.R. 342. The Law Commission recommended otherwise; Law Com. No.175 (1988), *Matrimonial Property*, para.4.19. This was not implemented.

[114] per Lord Upjohn in *Pettitt v Pettitt* [1970] A.C. 777 at 815.

[115] [1953] 1 Q.B. 636. Similarly where the husband lacked mental capacity to make a gift; *Simpson v Simpson* [1992] 1 F.L.R. 601.

[116] *Marshal v Crutwell* (1875) L.R. 20 Eq. 328; *Simpson v Simpson*, above, fn.115; *Sillett v Meek* [2009] W.T.L.R. 1065.

[117] *Re Bishop* [1965] Ch. 450; *Re Figgis* [1969] Ch. 123; M. Cullity (1969) 85 L.Q.R. 530; *McHardy and Sons (A Firm) v Warren* (1994) 2 F.L.R. 338; cf. *Heseltine v Heseltine* [1971] 1 W.L.R. 342 (husband had no interest where money provided by wife).

[118] Equality Act 2010 ss.200, 201.

[119] per Viscount Simonds in *Shephard v Cartwright*, below, fn.129; cf. Lord Upjohn in *Pettitt v Pettitt*, above, fn.107, at 815; *McGrath v Wallis* [1995] 2 F.L.R. 114; below, para.10–035.

In *Re Roberts*,[120] a father took out an insurance policy on the life of his son and paid the premiums on it. It was contended after the father's death that the amounts paid by way of premium (by the father in his lifetime and by his estate until the son's death) were recoverable by his estate by means of a lien over the policy moneys. Evershed J. held that the presumption of advancement prevailed, and that each premium paid by the father during his lifetime was a separate advancement to the son. The premiums paid after the father's death by his estate were, however, recoverable as the relationship of father and son no longer existed.

It has been held in some Commonwealth jurisdictions that the presumption does not apply in favour of a child who is legally an adult, because it is based on the obligation to support, which applies only to minor children.[121] This is not yet established in England and Wales.

10–026   **iii. Other Relationships.** But the moment one passes from this type of case to transfers from a mother to a child (subject to what is said below), from a father to an illegitimate child,[122] from grandparents, aunts and uncles, then the presumptions fade. Whether or not the presumption is technically in favour of a resulting trust, or technically in favour of advancement, the important consideration is whether or not there is evidence that the donor or purchaser regarded himself or herself as being in loco parentis, and the donee as being someone for whom an obligation to provide is felt.[123] The issue is treated as one of fact in the modern cases, and it is only in the absence of any evidence that the technical presumptions prevail.[124] Although, therefore, in cases other than that of father and legitimate child, the presumption may technically be in favour of a resulting trust, this is not, for the vast majority of cases, a decisive factor. The point is well brought out by the cases dealing with widowed mothers and their children.[125] In this situation, equity did not recognise in the

---

[120] [1946] Ch. 1. The policy itself was held on express trust for the son. A case where the presumption was rebutted is *Re Gooch* (1890) 62 L.T. 384 (father purchased shares to qualify son as director, and son handed over dividends to his father). See also *McEvoy v Belfast Banking Co* [1935] A.C. 24.

[121] *Pecore v Pecore* [2007] W.T.L.R. 1591, Canadian Supreme Court; M. McInnes (2007) 123 L.Q.R. 582; J. Glister [2007] Conv. 370. See also K. Low (2008) 124 L.Q.R. 369, discussing the position in Singapore.

[122] This principle seems unaffected by the Family Law Reform Act 1987, which in general removes the property law disadvantages of children of unmarried parents.

[123] See, per Page-Wood V.C. in *Tucker v Burrow* (1865) 2 H. & M. 515 at 525–527; *Re Paradise Motor Co Ltd* [1968] 1 W.L.R. 1125.

[124] *Re Vinogradoff* [1935] W.N. 68.

[125] *Bennet v Bennet* (1879) 10 Ch.D. 474, discussing *Sayre v Hughes* (1868) L.R. 5 Eq. 376. Commonwealth authorities favour extending the presumption of advancement to the mother/ child relationship; see *Nelson v Nelson* (1995) 132 A.L.R. 133; *Pecore v Pecore* [2007] W.T.L.R. 1591; cf. *Sekhon v Alissa* [1989] 2 F.L.R. 94. See J. Glister in Mitchell (ed.), *Constructive and Resulting Trusts* (2009), Ch.10.

mother, as it would have done in the father, an obligation to provide, hence there was technically no presumption of advancement. But the strangeness of this conclusion was wholly mitigated by the ease with which, on very little evidence, the courts would find the intent to advance.[126] In the analogous sphere of the presumption against "double portions" (whereby substantial lifetime provision for a child may be taken to adeem, or cancel, a legacy to that child), it has been held that this entirely judge-made law should move with the times. Thus the presumption should apply to gifts made by mothers, although traditionally only a father or person in loco parentis could make a "portion": "both parents should nowadays be taken to be in loco parentis unless the contrary is proved".[127] Indeed, the Court of Appeal recently accepted that the presumption of advancement could apply to a transfer from mother to child, but would be easily rebutted where the child was living independently and the mother had other children.[128]

iv. Admissibility of Transferor's Statements. In *Shephard v Cartwright*,[129] C caused shares in companies he was promoting to be allotted to himself, his wife and his three children in 1929. The companies made considerable profits and in 1934 a public company was formed; the original shareholders received partly new shares and partly cash for their old shares. C, in fact, controlled the whole family wealth, and the shares and money were divided between his wife and children for tax reasons. The wife and children at all times acquiesced in C's activities, and signed powers of attorney and powers to withdraw money at his wish.

By 1936, the cash had all been withdrawn by C and spent. Dividends on the shares allotted to the children were, however, treated as the income of the children, not the income of C. The House of Lords upheld a claim by the children against C's estate to recover the cash drawn by him on their bank accounts. The onus of rebutting the presumption of advancement lay on C's executors, and there was nothing in C's conduct that was truly inconsistent with the presumption. The House of Lords also applied the rule that evidence of declarations and conduct subsequent to the original transaction is admissible only against the party making them, though those made at the time of the original transaction are admissible for or against him. However, it has been doubted whether this principle, which was based on the law of evidence at that time, has any further role.

10–027

---

[126] See especially Jessel M.R. in *Bennet v Bennet*, above, fn.125.

[127] *Re Cameron (Deceased)* [1999] Ch. 386 at 405.

[128] *Laskar v Laskar* [2008] 1 W.L.R. 2695; *Musson v Bonner* [2010] W.T.L.R. 1369. See also *Silverwood (Geoffrey) v Silverwood (Arnold)* (1997) 74 P.&C.R. 453 at 458 (presumption assumed in mother/son case).

[129] [1955] A.C. 431. Mellish L.J.'s judgment in *Fowkes v Pascoe* (1875) L.R. 10 Ch.App. 343, emphasising the sense of the transaction, was expressly approved.

The modern tendency is to admit all relevant evidence, although self-serving statements carry little or no weight.[130] There is, therefore, a strong argument that "The rule in *Shephard v Cartwright*[131] is an anomalous relic of the common law of former times and should be recognised as such."[132] However, the rule was recently applied by the Privy Council without criticism.[133]

10–028   **v. Transfers for Unlawful Purposes.** A further question is whether a transferor who has put property in the name of the transferee to achieve an unlawful purpose may rebut the presumption of advancement by proving his real intention. If the relevant presumption is that of resulting trust, the question is whether he may rely on it in spite of the illegality.

The matter was reviewed by the House of Lords in *Tinsley v Milligan*.[134]

> Two women agreed to put a house which they owned jointly into the name of one of them (the claimant) in order to facilitate fraudulent claims to housing benefit by the other (the defendant). Both were parties to the fraud, which was perpetrated over several years, but had now ceased. Eventually the claimant sought to evict the defendant.

It was held by a bare majority,[135] that the defendant could assert ownership of her equitable interest. The principle that a litigant cannot rely on his own fraud or illegality to rebut the presumption of advancement was confirmed.[136] Here, however, the operative presumption was that of a resulting trust. The defendant merely had to found her claim on that presumption and not on any illegality. Nor was she seeking to enforce executory provisions of an unlawful contract, in which the court would not assist. This result, according to the majority, promoted harmony between the approaches of equity and the common law to illegality. Policy did not require a wider application of the "clean hands" principle, which would not deter fraudulent conduct. The nineteenth-century authorities supported

---

[130] *Lavelle v Lavelle*, *The Times*, March 9, 2004. See also *Musson v Bonner* [2010] W.T.L.R. 1369.

[131] Above, fn.129.

[132] E. Fung (2006) 122 L.Q.R. 651 at 688.

[133] *Antoni v Antoni* [2007] W.T.L.R. 1335.

[134] [1994] 1 A.C. 340. See generally Enonchong, *Illegal Transactions*, 1998; D. Sheehan (2009) L.M.C.L.Q. 319.

[135] Lords Jauncey, Lowry and Browne-Wilkinson.

[136] Discussed below. The presumption may be rebutted by evidence of illegality where the dispute is between the transferee and a third party; *R. v London Borough of Harrow Ex p. Coker*, *The Times*, March 14, 1989. See also *Halley v The Law Society* [2003] W.T.L.R. 845.

the claimant, but, although the wide "clean hands" approach favoured by Lord Eldon[137] had never been overruled, the law on
illegality had continued to develop. The reason why the property
had been conveyed to the claimant was irrelevant to the defendant's
claim, to which the presumption of resulting trust was crucial. The
illegality only emerged because the claimant raised it; it was not
necessary to the defendant's case.[138]

Lords Goff and Keith dissented on the ground that the "clean
hands" principle espoused by Lord Eldon had been consistently
followed. Subject only to the "repentance" exception,[139] once it had
come to the attention of the court that the claimant did not have
clean hands, the court would refuse assistance even though the claim
could be established without relying on the illegality. Both the majority and the minority agreed, however, that the "public conscience" test adopted by the Court of Appeal[140] (whereby a claim
would succeed in spite of the illegality if the public conscience
would not be offended) was too vague and discretionary, and not
based on authority. Only Parliament could introduce such a
reform.[141]

A solution which discourages illegality and also prevents the
unjust enrichment of the transferee is not easy to find. It is unfortunate that the majority decision is based on the old presumptions,
which (even before the recent abolition of the presumption of advancement[142]) were generally regarded as outmoded.[143] The result
of *Tinsley v Milligan* was that if a husband transferred to his wife or
a father to his daughter for an unlawful purpose, he would be unable
to assert any claim after carrying out the purpose,[144] whereas a wife
who transferred to her husband, or a mother to her daughter, or a
brother to his sister, would be successful. There seemed little merit
in this distinction, and in any event even a wife, mother or brother
could be unsuccessful in the case of a voluntary conveyance of land,
because s.60(3) of the Law of Property Act 1925[145] removes the
presumption of a resulting trust, so that the onus of proof of entitlement is on the transferor.

---

[137] In *Muckleston v Brown* (1801) 6 Ves. 52.
[138] See also *Haigh v Kaye* (1872) 7 Ch.App. 469.
[139] Discussed below.
[140] [1992] Ch. 310.
[141] See Illegal Contracts Act 1970 (New Zealand), ss.6, 7, permitting restitution of property
at the court's discretion; *Duncan v McDonald* [1997] 3 N.Z.L.R. 669. *Tinsley* has been
rejected in Australia in favour of a more flexible public policy approach; *Nelson v Nelson*
(1995) 132 A.L.R. 133; P. Creighton (1997) 60 M.L.R. 102.
[142] Above, para.10–023.
[143] See *Pettitt v Pettitt* [1970] A.C. 777; above, para.10–023; *McGrath v Wallis* [1995] 2
F.L.R. 114; below, para.10–035.
[144] It is otherwise if the purpose has not been carried out; *Tribe v Tribe* [1996] Ch. 107;
below.
[145] Above, para.10–020.

10–029   The decision of the House of Lords has been much criticised.[146] Its effect has been said to be that "He who comes to equity should keep unclean hands in his pockets."[147] The decision was subsequently applied by the Court of Appeal, although not without adverse comment. In *Silverwood (Geoffrey) (Executor of the Estate of Daisy Silverwood) v Silverwood (Arnold)*[148] Daisy (aged 87) authorised the withdrawal from her account of over £21,000 at the request of her son, A, who put the money in another account in the names of his two children. Daisy then applied for and received income support, which would not have been available if she had kept the money or divested herself of it in order to qualify. It was not shown, however, that Daisy was knowingly a party to any illegal purpose. On her death her son G, the executor, claimed that the children held the money on a resulting trust for Daisy. Applying *Tinsley v Milligan*,[149] his claim was upheld, although if the money had been put in the son's name, the estate would have been unable to rebut the presumption of advancement.[150] Nourse L.J. criticised the *Tinsley* principle as a "straightjacket",[151] and preferred the approach of the Court of Appeal in that case, although on the present facts the outcome would have been the same. His Lordship expressed the rule as being that the claimant "is entitled to recover if he is not forced to plead or rely on the illegality. It is immaterial that he may give evidence of it. . . ".[152] The matter arose again in *Lowson v Coombes*,[153] where elderly cohabitants both contributed to the purchase of a house, intending to share the beneficial interest. The house was put in the sole name of the woman in order to prevent the man's wife having any claim on it. This could be viewed as an illegal transaction under s.37 of the Matrimonial Causes Act 1973. When the elderly couple separated, the man sought a declaration that the woman held on resulting trust for him as to a half share. His claim was upheld, as it did not require reliance on illegality, although Robert Walker L.J. criticised the artificiality of the *Tinsley* principle.[154]

---

[146] R. Thornton (1993) 52 C.L.J. 394; M. Lunney (1993) 7 T.L.I. 114; M. Halliwell [1994] Conv. 62 and [2004] Conv. 439; H. Stowe (1994) 57 M.L.R. 441; R. Buckley (1994) 110 L.Q.R. 3. For a different analysis, see N. Enonchong (1995) 111 L.Q.R. 135.

[147] B. Council (1993) 143 N.L.J. 1577.

[148] (1997) 74 P. & C.R. 453. The report does not state the ages of the children. See also *Mortgage Express v Robson* [2001] 2 All E.R. (Comm.) 886 (property acquired with fraudulently obtained funds).

[149] [1994] 1 A.C. 340.

[150] This assumed that the presumption of advancement applied between mother and son.

[151] (1997) 74 P. & C.R. 453 at 458.

[152] (1997) 74 P. & C.R. 453 at 459.

[153] Ch. 373; M. Thompson [1999] Conv. 242; I. Cotterill [1999] L.M.C.L.Q. 465. *Tinker v Tinker* [1970] P. 136, below, para.10–031, was distinguished. See also *Slater v Simm* [2007] W.T.L.R. 1043; *Ledger-Beadell v Peach* [2007] 2 F.L.R. 210; *Knowlden v Tehrani* [2008] EWHC 54 (Ch.); *Barrett v Barrett* [2008] 2 P. & C.R. 17; S. Evans [2008] Conv. 534.

[154] Above at 385.

It has long been established and, as mentioned above, was con- **10–030**
firmed by the House of Lords, that the presumption of advancement
could not be rebutted by evidence of the transferor's illegal purpose.
Thus where a husband transferred property to his wife in order to
evade tax[155] or to defeat his creditors[156] the property belonged to the
wife even if she was a party to the scheme.[157] Similarly where a
father transferred property to his son for an unlawful purpose.[158] In
these cases it appears that the unlawful purpose had been carried
out. The question which arose in *Tribe v Tribe*[159] was whether the
presumption of advancement could be rebutted by evidence of an
illegal purpose where that purpose has not been carried out.

A landlord served repair notices on the tenant of two properties. The required works were substantial. If the tenant were to be
held responsible, he would need to raise funds by selling his
shares in his family company which occupied the premises. He
transferred his shares to his son for a stated consideration which
was not paid, in order to deceive the landlord as to his assets and
thereby safeguard them. In fact the matter of the repairs was
resolved without resort to deception, as the landlord agreed to
the surrender of one lease and sold the reversion of the other to
the tenant. When the son claimed to be entitled to the shares, the
Court of Appeal held that the presumption of advancement was
rebutted by evidence of the father's intentions, which were not
consistent with a gift to the son. Although his purpose was illegal,
the illegality had not been carried out.[160]

Tinsley v Milligan did not decide that there was no exception to
the rule that a claim could not be founded on an illegal act. Earlier
cases established that the transferor could succeed where he "re-
pented" and withdrew from the illegal transaction, although they
were inconsistent as to whether genuine repentance was necessary.[161] In *Sekhon v Alissa*,[162] for example, a mother who had a

[155] *Re Emery's Investment Trusts* [1959] Ch. 410.
[156] *Gascoigne v Gascoigne* [1918] 1 K.B. 223.
[157] [1918] 1 K.B. 223.
[158] *Chettiar v Chettiar* [1962] A.C. 294; *Collier v Collier* [2003] W.T.L.R. 617 (intention to
deceive creditors and Inland Revenue). It was suggested in *Muckleston v Brown* (1801) 6 Ves.
52 at 68 that where the transferor could not recover, an innocent person claiming through him
could do so, but this seems contrary to principle: *Ayerst v Jenkins* (1873) L.R. 16 Eq. 274
at 281.
[159] [1996] Ch. 107; criticised S. Cretney (1996) 26 Fam.Law 30; G. Virgo (1996) 55 C.L.J.
23; F. Rose (1996) 112 L.Q.R. 386; P. Pettit (1996) 10 T.L.I. 51; N. Enonchong [1996]
R.L.R. 78.
[160] *Perpetual Executors and Trustees Association of Australia Ltd v Wright* (1917) 23
C.L.R. 185 was applied.
[161] See generally I. Samet in Mitchell (ed.), *Constructive and Resulting Trusts* (2009),
Ch.12.
[162] [1989] 2 F.L.R. 94. The presumption was of resulting trust but the case predated *Tinsley
v Milligan* [1994] 1 A.C. 340.

house conveyed into her daughter's name was able to establish beneficial ownership where her alleged purpose of capital gains tax evasion had not been carried out simply because the house had not yet been sold. In *Tribe v Tribe* there was no "repentance" because the father did not seek to recover the shares until the danger had passed. As the authorities on repentance were conflicting, it was held that a transferor could succeed if he withdrew from the transaction only because it was no longer necessary. The exception (i.e. that recovery is permitted where the illegal purpose has not been wholly or partly[163] carried out) mitigates the harshness of the general rule, which could otherwise lead to injustice, and is designed to encourage withdrawal from fraud. The fact that "repentance" is not necessary does not further this policy, but it was felt that a stricter requirement could lead to bizarre results. The result, it will be noted, enabled the father to keep his assets out of reach until the danger passed.

10–031   The Court of Appeal noted the arbitrary aspects of the principles laid down in *Tinsley v Milligan*,[164] where so much depended on the relationship of the parties. As the presumption of advancement had fallen into disfavour, "there seems to be some perversity in its elevation to a decisive status in the context of illegality."[165] Miss Milligan had recovered although she had defrauded. There would be cause for concern if a claimant who had not done so could not recover simply because the transferee was his son.

Millett L.J. sought to eliminate these arbitrary aspects by saying that the transferor would not invariably succeed where the presumption of resulting trust applied.[166] The presumption would be rebutted where the transferee led evidence that the transferor's subsequent conduct was inconsistent with any intention to retain a beneficial interest. An example would be where an uncle transferred assets to his nephew to conceal them from creditors and then settled with his creditors on the footing that he did not own the assets. He could not recover as his own conduct would be inconsistent with the retention of any interest. The problem with this is that the example is difficult to distinguish from *Tinsley v Milligan* itself.

Of course, evidence that property was transferred to protect it from creditors does not alone rebut the presumption of advancement. Rather, it reinforces it, because the only way of protecting the property is for the transferor to divest himself of his interest. *Tinker*

---

[163] See *Q v Q* [2009] 1 F.L.R. 935; M. Pawlowski [2009] Conv. 145 (purpose partly carried out by making false statements in tax returns).

[164] [1994] 1 A.C. 340.

[165] [1996] Ch. 107 at 118, per Nourse L.J. See also the criticisms of Mance L.J. in *Collier v Collier* [2003] W.T.L.R. 617 at 654–655.

[166] His Lordship considered that *Re Great Berlin Steamboat Co* (1884) 26 Ch.Div. 616 (no recovery in resulting trust case where illegality carried out) had not been impliedly overruled.

v Tinker,[167] where a husband put a house in his wife's name to protect it from creditors if his new business should fail, was such a case. In fact there were no creditors and the husband in any event was not dishonest as his solicitors had advised the transfer. The evidence strengthened rather than rebutted the presumption of advancement. In order to rebut the presumption, a dishonest transferor must show that he intended to retain an interest and conceal it from his creditors. As Millett L.J. explained, compelling evidence of such an intention would be required. The court would be unlikely to reach such a conclusion where there was no imminent threat from known creditors at the transfer.

This area has recently been reviewed by the Law Commission.[168] **10–032** The recommendations focus on the treatment of trusts which have been used to conceal the true ownership of property for a criminal[169] purpose, leaving other aspects of illegality in trusts, contracts and other areas to develop incrementally. The Commission considers that the arbitrariness of *Tinsley v Milligan*[170] is impossible to defend, leaving the law in a very unsatisfactory state. The proposals take into account the fact that the House of Lords in *Stack v Dowden*[171] has discarded the presumption of a resulting trust from disputes concerning the ownership of family property. The Law Commission considered that this had introduced further uncertainty into the law, as it was unclear whether a party trying to rebut the presumption that equity follows the law by establishing a common intention constructive trust would be able to bring evidence of illegal conduct.[172] The Law Commission report predates the abolition of the presumption of advancement by the Equality Act 2010,[173] but anticipated it. While the abolition of that presumption removes one unsatisfactory aspect of the illegality rule,[174] further reform remains necessary in order to achieve a coherent doctrine. In cases involving jointly owned family homes, the effect of *Stack v Dowden*[175] is that neither party may rely on a resulting trust and the abolition of the presumption of advancement would not have any impact on these cases.[176]

---

[167] [1970] P. 136; cf. *Heseltine v Heseltine* [1971] 1 W.L.R. 342 (presumption of resulting trust not rebutted where wife transferred assets to husband to save estate duty and qualify him as a Lloyd's "name", although these purposes would not be achieved unless the husband took beneficially).

[168] Law Com. No.320 (2010), *The Illegality Defence*; P. Davies [2010] Conv. 282; D. Sheehan [2010] L.M.C.L.Q. 543.

[169] As widened by the Fraud Act 2006; below, para.23–024.

[170] [1994] 1 A.C. 340. Likewise *Tribe v Tribe* [1996] Ch. 107.

[171] [2007] 2 A.C. 432; below, para.11–004.

[172] Law Com. No.320 (2010), *The Illegality Defence*, paras 1.27, 1.28 and 2.4.

[173] Above, para.10–022.

[174] As illustrated by *Tribe v Tribe* [1996] Ch. 107; above, para.10–030.

[175] [2007] 2 A.C. 432.

[176] Law Com. No.320 (2010), *The Illegality Defence*, para.2.18.

The Commission proposes that the courts should have a statutory discretion to decide whether the illegality in question should have any effect. The proposed legislation would also provide for the consequences (in terms of who should own the property) of a decision not to recognise a beneficial interest on the ground of illegality, and would give guidance on the exercise of the discretion, which is recommended to include the following:

   (i) the conduct and intention of all of the relevant parties;
  (ii) the value of the equitable interest at stake;
 (iii) the effect of allowing the claim on the criminal purpose;
 (iv) whether refusing the claim would act as a deterrent; and
  (v) the possibility that the person from whom the equitable interest was being concealed may have an interest in the value of the assets of the beneficiary.[177]

It was emphasised that the circumstances would have to be exceptional for the court to decide that the beneficiary should not be allowed to enforce the equitable interest. There would have to be strong public policy reasons to justify this decision, not just a "run of the mill" case.[178]

The discretion would not be exercisable if a statute making the conduct illegal expressly provided for the effect of the illegality.

In cases outside the scope of the proposal, the existing "reliance" principle will apply: a person who needs to rely on his own illegal conduct to establish his claim will not succeed.

4. Purchase Money Resulting Trusts

A. Purchase in the Name of Another

10–033   **i. Presumptions in Favour of the Purchaser.** Where a purchaser of realty or personalty takes a conveyance in the name of a third party, but there is nothing to indicate an intention on his part of not having the beneficial interest, then there is a presumption that he intended to obtain the beneficial interest for himself, and a resulting trust will be decreed in his favour. In the words of Eyre C.B.: "The trust of a legal estate ... results to the man who advances the purchase-money".[179]

The presumption arises when a purchase is made in the joint names of a purchaser and a third party, and where a purchase is

---

[177] Law Com. No.320 (2010), *The Illegality Defence*, paras 2.79 and 2.80. Further details may be found in paras 2.66–2.78.
[178] paras 2.58–2.61.
[179] *Dyer v Dyer* (1788) 2 Cox 92 at 93.

made in the name of third party alone; also where property purchased with the contributions of more than one person is conveyed into the name of only one of them, or where unequal contributors become joint legal owners. It no longer applies, however, in the context of ownership of the family home.[180]
The classic case is *Fowkes v Pascoe*.[181]

Mrs B purchased stock in the names of herself and the son of her widowed daughter-in-law. The son was outside the relationships where the presumption of advancement would arise, hence he would prima facie be presumed to hold on resulting trust for Mrs B. But the Court of Appeal in Chancery held that the strength of the presumption varied according to the circumstances and that, once there is some evidence to rebut it, the court must look at the facts from a common-sense point of view. In the present case, the only rational inference was that Mrs B intended the purchase as a gift, so that the presumption of resulting trust was rebutted, though the effect of the gift would not be apparent until Mrs B's death, for the court also held that any income declared on the stock during Mrs B's lifetime would belong beneficially to her. Such a gift does not infringe the Wills Act 1837, as the legal title passes by the transfer; the legal title carries with it the right of survivorship, and all that happens on the death of Mrs B is that her equitable right ceases to be outstanding.[182] There is thus no *testamentary* gift provided the lifetime transfer is complete and not revocable.[183]
It was more recently held that there was nothing to rebut the presumption of a resulting trust where, in addition to paying for her own share, a wife paid £1 to a lottery syndicate in relation to a share which was in her estranged husband's name. Thus the wife was entitled to the winnings attributable to both shares.[184]

ii. Presumption of Advancement. We saw that the presumption **10–034** of advancement was abolished by the Equality Act 2010, but remains applicable to transactions before the commencement of the

---

[180] *Stack v Dowden* [2007] 2 A.C. 432; below, para.10–035.
[181] (1875) L.R. 10 Ch.App. 343; see also *Pettitt v Pettitt* [1970] A.C. 777; *Hoare v Hoare* (1983) 13 Fam.Law 142.
[182] *Young v Sealey* [1949] Ch. 278. The argument is not an easy one, but Romer J. preferred to take this view as no previous English case had taken this point under the Wills Act, and gifts of this sort had not previously been thought to raise difficulties. See J. Miller (1992) 6 T.L.I. 57.
[183] But in the case of a joint bank account opened by a husband in the name of himself and his wife so that either can draw on it (the account being kept in credit by the husband), there is a gift to the wife of what happens to be in the account at the date of the husband's death. The difficulties of this reasoning are discussed by Megarry J. in *Re Figgis* [1969] Ch. 123, where however *Young v Sealey*, above, fn.182 was followed; M. Cullity (1969) 85 L.Q.R. 530.
[184] *Abrahams v Trustee in Bankruptcy of Abrahams*, *The Times*, July 26, 1999.

legislation.[185] In relation to such transactions, a purchase in the name of a wife or child or other person to whom the purchaser stands in loco parentis is presumed to be an advancement. As Lord Eldon said in *Marlees v Franklin*[186]:

> "The general rule that on a purchase by one man in the name of another, the nominee is trustee for the purchaser is subject to exception where the purchaser is under a species of natural obligation to provide for the nominee."

The presumption was weak in the case of husband and wife. It was stronger with a parent and child, at any rate where the house was for the sole occupation of the child,[187] but could be rebutted.

In *Warren v Gurney*[188] a father bought a house for his daughter, who was shortly to get married, to live in. The conveyance was taken in the name of the daughter, but the father retained the title deeds. On his death 15 years later, the daughter claimed to be the beneficial owner of the house. The Court of Appeal held that there was a presumption of advancement in her favour, but that it had been rebutted by the fact of the retention of the title deeds, accompanied by evidence contemporaneous with the purchase in 1929. Retention of the deeds by itself is probably insufficient evidence, however.

10–035   **iii. Family Home Held in Joint Names.** For many years it has been common practice for the family home to be held in joint names. In the case of a married couple it is not normally necessary to establish exactly how the beneficial interest is held if the relationship breaks down, in view of the court's wide powers under the Matrimonial Causes Act 1973. In the case of an unmarried couple, their shares were traditionally established by applying the presumption of a resulting trust, so that beneficial ownership was proportionate to their contributions. This approach was firmly rejected by a majority of the House of Lords in *Stack v Dowden*.[189] It was there held that the beneficial interest would normally follow the legal (in other words, the parties would be equally entitled irrespective of their contributions). The burden of proving unequal shares was on the person claiming that the beneficial interest differed from the legal interest, and such a claim would only be successful if the facts were very unusual. In cases of this kind, the presumption is of

---

[185] Above, para.10–023.
[186] (1818) 1 Swans. 13 at 17.
[187] cf. *McGrath v Wallis*; below, fn.198.
[188] [1944] 2 All E.R. 472; see also *Pettitt v Pettitt* [1970] A.C. 777.
[189] [2007] 2 A.C. 432. Lord Neuberger alone favoured the resulting trust approach.

equality. It may be rebutted by establishing a constructive trust arising from the shared intentions of the parties in the light of their whole course of conduct, but not by a mathematical resulting trust based on contributions. This decision is more fully discussed below.[190]

However, the traditional resulting trust approach continues to govern disputes as to commercial property and property bought as an investment, even where the purchasers are family members.[191]

B. Purchase by Several in the Name of One

The general principle (which applies to land and other assets[192]) is that the legal title is held on trust for the purchasers in the proportions in which they contributed to the purchase price,[193] although in some circumstances the court may be able to infer an agreement (giving rise to a constructive trust) to hold in shares which are not proportionate to the contributions.[194] The purchasers thus have a concurrent interest and can claim the due proportion of the proceeds on any eventual sale of the property to include a proportion of any increase in the value of the property.[195]

10–036

Many cases under this head are concerned with the question of the ownership of a family home, and are dealt with in Ch.11. We will see there that, whether the home is in the name of one party or both, property disputes between cohabiting couples are these days resolved by constructive trust principles rather than resulting trusts.[196]

Where two people contributed to the purchase of a property which was conveyed into the name of one, the presumption of advancement,[197] which arose if the legal owner was the wife or child of the other party, was a last resort, and was rebuttable by comparatively slight evidence in both cases.

---

[190] Below, para.11–004. See also *Jones v Kernott* [2011] 3 W.L.R. 1121; below, para. 11–006.

[191] *Laskar v Laskar* [2008] 1 W.L.R. 2695 (property bought for letting by mother and daughter held in shares proportionate to contributions); N. Piska [2008] Conv. 441.

[192] See *Parrott v Parkin* [2007] 2 F.L.R. 444 (boat in A's name held on resulting trust for A and B in proportion to their contributions).

[193] *Wray v Steele* (1814) 2 v & B. 388. The trust is traditionally regarded as resulting, but Lord Bridge described it as constructive in *Lloyds Bank Plc v Rosset* [1991] 1 A.C. 107 at 133.

[194] *Midland Bank Plc v Cooke* [1995] 4 All E.R. 562; *Drake v Whipp* [1996] 1 F.L.R. 826; *Oxley v Hiscock* [2005] Fam. 211; S. Gardener (2004) 120 L.Q.R. 541; below, para.11–008.

[195] *Diwell v Farnes* [1959] 1 W.L.R. 624. See further, below, para.11–015.

[196] Below, paras 11–004–11–015.

[197] The presumption was abolished, but not retrospectively, by the Equality Act 2010; above, para.10–023.

In *McGrath v Wallis*[198] a house was acquired for the occupation of a family (parents, son and daughter) but was put in the adult son's name to enable a mortgage loan to be obtained (the father being unemployed). The father contributed £34,500 towards the price of £42,995, the balance being raised by the mortgage. The father's solicitors drew up a declaration of trust whereby the beneficial interest was to be held as to 80 per cent for the father and 20 per cent for the son, but, for reasons which were not established, it was never executed. After the death of the parents, the son claimed absolute entitlement, but the Court of Appeal held that the presumption of advancement was rebutted. The parties' intentions were to hold in shares proportionate to their contributions.

The decisive features were that the son alone was acceptable as mortgagor (which alone was probably enough to rebut the presumption); there was no evidence that the father had instructed the solicitors not to proceed with the declaration; and there was no reason why the father, who was only 63 at the time and not ill, should wish to give the house to the son. The observations in *Pettitt v Pettitt*[199] and elsewhere as to the weakness of the presumption of advancement between husband and wife applied equally to father and child.

---

[198] [1995] 2 F.L.R. 114; criticised in J. Dewar (1995) 25 Fam.Law 552.
[199] [1970] A.C. 777.

CHAPTER 11

TRUSTS OF THE FAMILY HOME

1. INTRODUCTION

IN the last chapter we saw the part played by the doctrine of result-   **11–001**
ing trusts in the acquisition of property interests. Most of the modern
cases involve disputes between married or unmarried couples over
ownership of the home. In this chapter we will examine the special
considerations which apply to the matrimonial or family home. The
first part of the chapter will deal with the establishment of a proprietary interest in the home. The second part will examine some of the
problems of co-ownership of land. To complete the picture, reference should also be made to Ch.27, where it will be seen that those
who cannot establish an interest under a trust of the family home
might nevertheless acquire rights as licensees or under the doctrine
of estoppel.

2. ACQUISITION OF INTERESTS IN THE HOME

A. Background to the Problem
In the case of a married couple, one problem which arises is that   **11–002**
the older rules of property law, which became established at a time
when the wife was less likely to be earning her living than is the case
today, do not properly recognise her contribution to the relationship:

287

"Until little more than a century ago the common law did not permit married women to own any property whatsoever. It became the property of her husband. When a measure of reform was proposed in 1856 one Member of Parliament protested, 'If a woman had not full confidence in a man, let her refrain from marrying him' ".[1]

The modern view is that marriage is a partnership between equals, in which the wife has an economic contribution to make. But she does not always insist on the matrimonial home being conveyed to the spouses jointly; or on a declaration of trust of a share of the house in favour of herself. Nor is justice done to her by the presumption of a resulting trust, based on payment of the purchase money; first, because childcare and housework are not money-producing, and secondly, because if she has a job, her earnings may be spent on household expenses and not in contributing to the purchase price of the house. "The cock can feather the nest because he does not have to spend most of his time sitting on it."[2]

Another problem stems from the fact that today a significant and increasing proportion of couples cohabit outside marriage. The 2001 census recorded over two million cohabiting couples in England and Wales.[3] Should their relationship break down, the court has no statutory power to adjust their property interests save in the case of registered civil partnerships.[4] Divorcing couples, on the other hand, can invoke the court's discretionary powers to order a distribution of the property of the spouses.[5] This statutory jurisdiction will not be discussed here, but its significance must be emphasised. The following account deals only with the general law, which applies, subject to minor exceptions, equally to married and unmarried couples. A difficulty frequently encountered, as will be seen, is that the parties do not formulate their intention at the time the property is acquired, but consider the matter only when their relationship breaks down.[6]

---

[1] *Rooney v Cardona* [1999] 1 F.L.R. 1236 at 1240, per Robert Walker L.J.

[2] per Sir Jocelyn Simon, extrajudicially quoted by Lord Hodson in *Pettitt v Pettitt* [1970] A.C. 777 at 811.

[3] Statistics from the 2011 census are not available at the time of writing.

[4] Below, para.11–003.

[5] Matrimonial Causes Act 1973, as amended by Family Law Act 1996; *Wachtel v Wachtel* [1973] Fam. 72. Property disputes between spouses are best settled under this jurisdiction; *Williams v Williams* [1976] Ch. 278 at 286; *Suttill v Graham* [1977] 1 W.L.R. 819 at 824. The statutory jurisdiction does not apply to engaged couples by reason of Law Reform (Miscellaneous Provisions) Act 1970, s.2(1); *Mossop v Mossop* [1989] Fam. 77; JEM [1988] Conv. 286.

[6] See *Carlton v Goodman* [2002] 2 F.L.R. 259 at 273 (Ward L.J.): "I will try one more time: always try to agree on and then record how the beneficial interest is to be held. It is not very difficult to do."

The question then is how to ensure that the ownership of the home   **11–003**
is fairly shared. The possibility of giving the court, in the case of
married couples, a wide discretionary power to declare what are the
appropriate shares to be held by disputing spouses in any particular
case has been rejected[7]; likewise the concept of community of property.[8] A proposal[9] that the matrimonial home should be shared
equally was not implemented.

After a lengthy review, the Law Commission in 2002 was unable
to propose any scheme based on property law principles which
could apply satisfactorily to the diverse kinds of relationships it
would need to cover.[10] The current law was considered complicated,
difficult to apply and unsuited to the informality of home sharers.
The Commission subsequently made proposals relating to cohabiting couples.[11]

There is one area, however, in which the property rights of unmarried couples have been reformed by Parliament. Same-sex couples may register their relationship under the Civil Partnership Act
2004. If that is done, their property and financial rights are broadly
similar to those of married couples, and their tax position corresponds to that of spouses.[12] One partner may acquire a share or
enhanced share by making a substantial improvement to property in
which either or both have an interest.[13] Either party may refer to
court any question relating to the title to or possession of property
(whether or not it is still in the possession or control of the other
party), and the court may make such order as it thinks fit.[14] The
registered partners are put in the same position as married couples in
relation to wills, intestacy and the administration of estates.[15] If the
partnership is terminated by breakdown, the court may make the
same kind of orders for financial relief as in the case of married
couples, for example property adjustment orders and orders for sale
or pension-sharing.[16]

The new legislation attracted criticism for putting same-sex couples in a more favourable position than heterosexual unmarried

[7] *Gissing v Gissing* [1971] A.C. 886.
[8] Law Com. No.52, para.59. See also Law Com. No.90, para.5.20.
[9] Third Report on Family Property (Law Com. No.86). These proposals were flawed by
registration requirements.
[10] Law Commission Discussion Paper: *Sharing Homes* (July 2002), para.3.100; criticised
R. Probert (2002) 32 Fam. Law 834; C. Rotherham [2004] Conv. 268. See also S. Bridge and
Lord Justice Thorpe (2002) 32 Fam. Law 743 and 891 respectively; Baroness Hale (2004) 34
Fam. Law 419; A. Barlow and G. James (2004) 67 M.L.R. 143.
[11] Below, para.11–016.
[12] As a result of regulations made under FA 2005, s.103.
[13] s.65. For the provisions relating to married couples, see below, para.11–014.
[14] ss.66, 67. Such applications may be made within three years of the termination of the
civil partnership; s.68.
[15] s.71 and Sch.4. This includes applications under the Inheritance (Provision for Family
and Dependants) Act 1975.
[16] s.72 and Schs 5–7.

couples, to which the Government's answer was that heterosexual couples have the option of marriage, although this may be unrealistic in some cases.[17]

Where the parties are neither married nor registered civil partners, their rights are determined according to the principles of property law, making whatever use is appropriate of evidence of agreement, declarations of trust (which comply with the necessary formalities applicable to trusts of land) and of inferences and presumptions.

The first question to determine is whether each party owns some share. If so, there is co-ownership, and the house is held upon trust, even though it may be vested only in one.[18] The next question is to determine what is the share of each party. A number of other problems can arise, such as a decision on sale if one party wishes to sell and the other to retain; questions as to the right to possession and the payment of rent; and the protection of an occupying co-owner if the sole legal owner sells to a third party.

B. Legal Title in Both Parties

11–004   Where the legal title is in both parties, the beneficial interest will prima facie also be shared.[19] Any express declaration of the beneficial interests in the title documents will be conclusive.[20] The Land Registry transfer form in use since April 1998 indicates whether transferees hold as beneficial joint tenants or tenants in common or on other trusts, but the transfer is valid even if the boxes are not completed.[21] It remains possible, therefore, to have a transfer into joint names but with no express declaration of the beneficial interests, either where the title was unregistered, or where a transfer of registered land occurred before 1998, or where the current form was used but the boxes were not completed.

The principles which apply to ascertain the beneficial interests of parties who are co-owners of the legal title was examined by the House of Lords in *Stack v Dowden*.[22]

An unmarried couple, M and W, purchased a house in joint names as a family home. W paid 65 per cent of the purchase price

---

[17] Law Com. No.307 (2007); *Cohabitation: The Financial Consequences of Relationship Breakdown*, paras 2.56, 2.57.

[18] Below, para.11–017.

[19] *Pettit v Pettit* [1970] A.C. 777 at 813–814. See also *Crossley v Crossley* [2006] 2 F.L.R. 813.

[20] See *Goodman v Gallant* [1986] Fam. 106; S. Juss (1986) 45 C.L.J. 205; J. Martin [1986] Conv. 355. (Severance of beneficial joint tenancy must result in equal shares even though unequal contributions.) For the position where the declaration contains inconsistent provisions, see *Martin v Martin* (1987) 54 P. & C.R. 238.

[21] *Stack v Dowden* [2007] 2 A.C. 432; cf. A. Moran [2007] Conv. 364. A proposal for mandatory completion was not implemented; E. Cooke (2011) 41 Fam. Law 1142.

[22] Above, fn.21.

from an account in her name and funded by her. The balance was provided by a loan secured by a joint mortgage and two endowment policies, one in joint names and one in W's name. M paid the mortgage interest and the premiums on the joint policy. The loan was repaid by lump sums, to which W contributed about 60 per cent. M and W had four children and lived together for nearly 20 years, but had separate bank accounts and investments. After they separated, it was held that W was entitled to 65 per cent of the net proceeds of sale.

The House of Lords confirmed that the normal assumption was that, as equity followed the law, the beneficial interests of legal joint owners would also be joint. Similarly in the case of sole legal ownership, where the starting point was an assumption of sole beneficial ownership. In both cases the burden of establishing otherwise was on the person claiming that the beneficial ownership did not follow the legal ownership. In order to succeed in such a claim, the facts would have to be "very unusual", and the fact that the contributions were unequal would not suffice.

In the case of a domestic property, the strict resulting trust approach based on financial contributions to the purchase was no longer appropriate.[23] To rebut the presumption of equal shares, the search was for shared intentions in the light of the whole course of conduct. Relevant factors would include any advice or discussions at the time of the purchase, why the property was in joint names, the nature of the relationship, whether they had any children for whom both were responsible for providing a home, how the purchase was financed, how the parties arranged their finances, and how they discharged the outgoings and expenses. An arithmetical calculation would be unlikely to be important, as it would be easier to infer that the parties intended that each should contribute as much to the household as they reasonably could and that they would share the eventual benefit or burden equally. In the present case W had contributed more, and they did not pool their resources. Everything apart from the house itself was kept strictly separate. This was considered very unusual,[24] as they had lived together for a long time and had children. W had, therefore, discharged the burden of establishing that she was entitled to more than half, and her share was 65 per cent.

---

[23] Cases such as *Springette v Defoe* [1992] 2 F.L.R. 388 and *Huntingford v Hobbs* [1993] 1 F.L.R. 736 were disapproved. The resulting trust approach is still appropriate in the case of a property purchased as an investment, even if there is a family relationship; *Laskar v Laskar* [2008] 1 W.L.R. 2695 (mother and daughter); N. Piska [2008] Conv. 441.

[24] Research indicates that such arrangements are more common than their Lordships thought; R. Probert (2007) 37 Fam. Law 924; N. Piska (2008) 71 M.L.R. 120; G. Douglas, J. Pearce and H. Woodward (2009) 72 M.L.R. 24.

Lord Neuberger agreed with the result, but not the reasoning. He favoured the resulting trust approach, which on the facts led to the same result, and considered that the majority had crossed the line between inferring the parties' intentions and imputing them.[25] An inferred intention is one which is objectively deduced to be the subjective actual intention of the parties, while an imputed intention is attributed to the parties even though they had no such intention. His Lordship considered the "whole course of dealing" concept to be too vague, and that "fairness" was not the yardstick. In his view, beneficial ownership is normally judged at the time of acquisition. It could change, for example if one party funded a major improvement, but not on the basis of their subsequent course of conduct. There is much force in Lord Neuberger's comment that the rejection of the resulting trust solution where the contributions were unequal amounted to:

"[A] resurrection of the 'family assets' hypothesis disposed of in *Pettit v Pettit*.[26] It involves invoking a presumption of advancement between unmarried cohabitants, where such a presumption has never applied, and at a time when, as I have mentioned, the court is increasingly unenthusiastic about the presumption, even in relationships where it does apply."[27]

Applying these principles, the Court of Appeal held in *Fowler v Barron*[28] that a man who had paid the deposit, all the mortgage repayments and all direct outgoings was unable to rebut the presumption that the beneficial interest was held jointly with his unmarried partner.

11–005   Some commentators welcomed the majority decision in *Stack v Dowden*,[29] regarding it as a legitimate extension of the law to satisfy social justice.[30] However, it is perceived by many as having created uncertainty as to the circumstances necessary to establish unequal shares, and thus to have done little to reduce litigation.[31] It is "likely

---

[25] See now *Jones v Kernott* [2011] UKSC 53; [2011] 3 W.L.R. 1121; below, para.11–006. See also *Abbott v Abbott* [2008] 1 F.L.R. 1451, where the Privy Council did not shrink from imputing intentions.

[26] [1970] A.C. 777 at 795, 809–810, 816–817.

[27] [2007] 2 A.C. 432 at 469.

[28] [2008] W.T.L.R. 819; N. Piska [2008] Conv. 451; *Gibson v Revenue and Customs Prosecutions Office* [2009] Q.B. 348.

[29] Above, fn.21.

[30] T. Etherton (2008) 67 C.L.J. 265 at 279; cf. T. Etherton [2009] Conv. 104. See also M. Pawlowski [2007] Conv. 352; M. Harding [2009] Conv. 309. For a full analysis see S. Gardner (2008) 124 L.Q.R. 422.

[31] A. Cloherty and D. Fox (2007) 66 C.L.J. 517; M. Dixon [2007] Conv. 352; G. Douglas (2008) 38 Fam. Law 639.

to prove a recipe for injustice",[32] offers an "unprincipled solution",[33] and fails to lay down clear principles or to explain why the resulting trust doctrine is no longer applicable to the family home.[34] The rejection of resulting trusts was "an act of abolition . . . with the benefit of almost no reasoning, and even a mistaken view of their nature".[35] Much criticism has centred on the imputation of intentions to the parties (although we will see that the Supreme Court has since gone further[36]). The approach:

"[S]eems little different from that of Lord Denning M.R. in the 1960s, where he asserted a jurisdiction in the court to create trusts, not on the basis of any bargain or expressed intention, but because it was 'reasonable and fair in the circumstances'".[37]

Without a fundamental analysis, we are "doomed to continue lurching from one seemingly arbitrary precedent to another".[38] The majority "clothe fairness in the language of intention without providing explicit guidance for determining the content of either".[39] One critic has said:

"I have, incidentally, no doubt in my mind that had the bigger contributor in this case been Mr Stack, the court would have found that the joint ownership in the registration was conclusive—another case of paternalism."[40]

As the Law Commission has pointed out, the decision in *Stack v Dowden*[41] does not purport to offer a comprehensive solution to the hardships arising when cohabitants separate.[42] The Commission advocates a statutory solution.[43] *Stack v Dowden* "exemplifies the limitations of judicial law reform", and property law "is a blunt instrument with which to deal fairly with the financial consequences of the ending of personal relationships."[44]

---

[32] G. Lightman (2008) 22 T.L.I. 11.
[33] R. Lee (2008) 124 L.Q.R. 209.
[34] P. Wee [2007] L.M.C.L.Q. 455.
[35] W. Swadling (2007) 123 L.Q.R. 511 at 518; P. Sparkes [2011] Conv. 156.
[36] *Jones v Kernott* [2011] UKSC 53; [2011] 3 W.L.R. 1121; below, para.11–006.
[37] (2007) 123 L.Q.R. 511 at 515. See also (2008) 124 L.Q.R. 72 at 96, by the same author.
[38] (2007) 123 L.Q.R. 511 at 518.
[39] N. Piska (2008) 71 M.L.R. 120 at 128.
[40] R. Deech (2010) 40 Fam. Law 39.
[41] Above, fn.21.
[42] Law Com. No.307 (2007); *Cohabitation; The Financial Consequences of Relationship Breakdown*; para.2.14.
[43] Below, para.11–016.
[44] S. Bridge (2007) 37 Fam. Law 911 at 915.

11–006   The question before the Supreme Court in *Jones v Kernott*[45] was whether the shares of beneficial joint tenants of a property had changed over time since their separation.

> A property was bought in the joint names of an unmarried couple in 1985. Both contributed financially and it was common ground that they originally held in equal shares. When the man left in 1993 he stopped contributing to the mortgage and outgoings. Around 1995 they agreed to cash in a joint life insurance policy and to divide the proceeds. The man then bought another property for himself. The county court ruled (on the woman's application) that her share had increased to 90 per cent because she had paid over 80 per cent of the mortgage interest. This ruling was upheld by the High Court, but on the man's appeal to the Court of Appeal it was held (by a majority) that an intention to vary their shares could not be spelled out from the fact that one party alone lived there, paying the outgoings and supporting their children, and so their shares remained equal. The Supreme Court allowed the woman's appeal and restored the original ruling, so that her share was 90 per cent.

The starting point was that they were joint tenants at law and in equity, but this could be displaced by showing that they later formed a common intention that their shares should change. Their common intention (if not express) was to be deduced objectively from their conduct. If it was clear that the parties had changed their original intention but it was not possible to ascertain, either by direct evidence or inference, what shares they intended to have, each was entitled to such share as the court considered fair, having regard to their conduct and whole course of dealing in relation to the property.

Although the decision of the Supreme Court was unanimous, there were differences in the reasoning. Lord Walker and Lady Hale delivered a joint judgment. They noted that *Stack v Dowden*[46] had attracted much comment, some of it adverse, and sought to clarify that decision by reiterating its principles and confirming that the presumption of a resulting trust no longer applied to a purchase in joint names for joint occupation by a married or unmarried couple whose contributions were unequal. They discussed the difference between inference and imputation, accepting that the search was primarily to ascertain the parties' actual intentions, whether expressed or inferred from conduct. If the parties' actual intentions

---

[45] [2011] UKSC 53; [2011] 3 W.L.R. 1121; J. West (2011) N.L.J. 1571; R. Bailey-Harris (2011) 41 Fam.Law 1339.
[46] [2007] 2 A.C. 432.

could be discovered, it was not open to the court to impose a different solution on them just because the court considered it fair. However, if it was impossible to ascertain their common intention as to the size of their shares, the court would be driven to impute an intention which they may never have had. Lord Walker and Lady Hale considered that the conceptual difference between inferring and imputing was clear, but "the difference in practice may not be so great".[47] In the present case there was no need to impute an intention that the parties shares would change because the county court judge had made a finding that their intentions had in fact changed. When the parties cashed in the life policy and the man purchased a home, the "logical inference" was that they intended that the man's interest in the property should crystallise then. He would have the sole benefit of any capital gain in his own home and the woman would have the sole benefit of any capital gain in the other property. This intention could be inferred from their conduct. Lord Walker and Lady Hale concluded that the "whole course of dealing", which the court would take into account, should be given a broad meaning and that each case would turn on its own facts. Financial contributions would be relevant but so would many other factors. They added that, if the shares had remained the same, it would have been necessary to consider matters such as equitable accounting[48] in relation to the man's share of the mortgage interest and whether he could claim an occupation rent (though this was unlikely while the house was needed for the children).

Lord Collins agreed that, if it was impossible to ascertain or infer what shares were intended, each would be entitled to a fair share in the light of the whole course of dealing. He considered that "the difference between inference and imputation will hardly ever matter" and that "what is one person's inference will be another person's imputation".[49] Lord Kerr agreed that the appeal should be allowed but highlighted the differences in the reasoning of the members of the court. These were: (a) whether there was sufficient evidence in the present case from which the parties' intentions could be inferred, and (b) whether the difference between inferring and imputing an intention was likely to be great in practice. He considered that, if the parties' intentions could not be inferred, the court should not be reluctant to impute an intention. Unlike Lord Walker and Lady Hale, he found it difficult to infer that the man intended his interest in the property to crystallise when he bought his own home. He preferred to allow the appeal on the basis that it was impossible to infer that the parties intended their shares to be 90 per cent and 10 per cent, but that such an intention should be imputed to them.

---

[47] [2011] 3 W.L.R. 1121 at 1132.
[48] Below, para.11–015.
[49] [2011] 3 W.L.R. 1121 at 1140.

Lord Wilson welcomed the development that a common intention as to the size of their shares could be imputed to the parties, though he left open the question (which did not arise) whether the court could impute an intention that one party should have a share at all if it was not otherwise identifiable. However, he considered that Lord Walker and Lady Hale might have gone too far in suggesting that the difference between inferring and imputing a common intention may not be great. He found it impossible to infer that the parties intended their shares to be 90 per cent and 10 per cent, but was prepared to impute such an intention.

Opinions will differ as to whether the shares allocated to the parties were in fact "fair", and whether it is right for the court to impute intentions to the parties which they never had. The alternative would be that, if the parties have not expressed their intentions, and they cannot be inferred, their shares must remain as they were. What seems clear is that a fact-sensitive principle requiring the court to examine the "whole course of dealing" over many years in order to decide on their fair shares is a recipe for litigation.

The Supreme Court in *Jones v Kernott*[50] emphasised that, in cases where the property was not in joint names, the starting point was different, the first issue being whether the party whose name was not on the title was intended to have any interest at all. Their common intention on that issue (if not express) would need to be deduced objectively from their conduct. If the evidence showed a common intention to share but did not show what shares were intended, the court would proceed to decide their shares in the same way as in the joint names cases.

We turn now to the cases where the property is in the name of one party only.

C. Conveyance to One Party Only

11–007   If the house is conveyed to one party only, to the man, let us assume, for that is the usual case, then he will prima facie be the owner of the whole beneficial interest as well.[51] If the documents of title expressly declare the beneficial interests, that, in the absence of fraud or mistake, is conclusive,[52] although those who were not parties to the deed cannot be prejudiced by such a declaration if they have contributed.[53] Failing that, the woman may claim a share of the beneficial interest in various ways. First, there may be an express

---

[50] [2011] UKSC 53; [2011] 3 W.L.R. 1121.
[51] *Gissing v Gissing* [1971] A.C. 886 at 900, 901, 910; *Burns v Burns* [1984] Ch. 317.
[52] *Pettitt v Pettitt* [1970] A.C. 777 at 813; *Goodman v Gallant* [1986] Fam. 106.
[53] See *City of London Building Society v Flegg* [1988] A.C. 54.

contract in writing,[54] or a trust in her favour which is evidenced in writing.[55] Subject to estoppel arguments, an oral contract for the disposition of an interest in land is void. An oral declaration of a trust of land which is not evidenced in writing is unenforceable unless it has been acted upon so as to give rise to a constructive trust.[56] This is discussed below. If there is no express agreement or declaration, direct contributions in money or money's worth have traditionally been regarded as giving rise to a resulting trust, but the House of Lords and Supreme Court no longer favour this approach.[57] Finally, a trust has been imposed in some cases simply in the interests of justice.[58]

i. Express Agreement or Declaration. If the declaration is con- **11–008** tained in the documents of title, then it will be conclusive, as stated above. If it is not contained in the documents of title but is nevertheless evidenced in writing, it is enforceable under s.53(1)(b) of the Law of Property Act 1925. These formality requirements do not apply to resulting or constructive trusts.[59] In the present context, the question arises as to the circumstances necessary for the imposition of a constructive trust where there is an express oral declaration or agreement.

The first point to consider is what constitutes an express oral declaration or agreement. The question is whether prior to the acquisition, or exceptionally at some later date,[60] the parties had an agreement to share (whether or not it dealt with the size of the shares), based on evidence of express discussions, however imperfectly remembered and however imprecise the terms.[61] A common intention to renovate a house as a joint venture or to share it as a family home does not amount to a common intention to share the beneficial ownership.[62] An excuse as to why the property is in the man's name

---

[54] Law of Property (Miscellaneous Provisions) Act 1989, s.2. See L. Bently and P. Coughlan (1990) 10 L.S. 325.

[55] LPA 1925, s.53(1)(b).

[56] *Midland Bank Ltd v Dobson* [1986] 1 F.L.R. 171; *Grant v Edwards* [1986] Ch. 638.

[57] *Stack v Dowden* [2007] 2 A.C. 432; above, para.11–004; *Jones v Kernott* [2011] UKPC 53; [2011] 3 W.L.R. 1121; above, para.11–006.

[58] *Cooke v Head* [1972] 1 W.L.R. 518; A. Oakley (1973) C.L.P. 17 at 25; *Eves v Eves* [1975] 1 W.L.R. 1338.

[59] LPA 1925, s.53(2); Law of Property (Miscellaneous Provisions) Act 1989, s.2(5); *Yaxley v Gotts* [2000] Ch. 162.

[60] *Bernard v Josephs* [1982] Ch. 391; *Burns v Burns* [1984] Ch. 317; *Austin v Keele* (1987) 61 A.L.J.R. 605; *Lloyds Bank plc v Rosset* [1991] 1 A.C. 107; *Stokes v Anderson* [1991] 1 F.L.R. 391.

[61] *Lloyds Bank plc v Rosset*, above, fn.60. But see N. Glover and P. Todd (1996) 16 L.S. 325.

[62] *Lloyds Bank plc v Rosset*, fn.60, above. See also *Otway v Gibbs* [2001] W.T.L.R. 467 (using words such as "our home" does not suffice); *Mollo v Mollo* [2000] W.T.L.R. 227 (accommodation "for the boys" gave them no interest).

will, however, be treated as an express declaration of an intention to share the beneficial ownership.[63]

Assuming that an express common intention is established, the claimant must also show that she has acted upon it to her detriment if a constructive trust (or estoppel) is to arise.[64] An oral agreement alone cannot suffice, as this would infringe the formality rules and could prejudice the legal owner's creditors.[65] It is clear that significant contributions in money or money's worth, even though indirect, will satisfy the requirements of detrimental reliance. Thus in *Grant v Edwards*[66] a woman was entitled to a half share where, pursuant to an express oral declaration, she had made substantial indirect contributions to the mortgage by applying her earnings to the joint household expenses in addition to keeping house and bringing up the children. The Court of Appeal considered that any detrimental act relating to the joint lives of the parties would have sufficed. Such a view provides an opportunity for a sympathetic treatment of a woman who has made no financial contribution.[67] In similar vein, the Privy Council has said that once a common intention has been established it may not be difficult to find conduct on the part of the woman which is referable to the creation of her beneficial interest.[68]

The House of Lords reviewed these principles in *Lloyds Bank plc v Rosset*.[69] In that case there was no express common intention. If there had been, the wife's acts of decorating and supervising renovation works would not have constituted detrimental reliance, as they were acts which any wife would do.[70] Acts which have been considered sufficient include refraining from seeking repayment of a loan

---

[63] *Eves v Eves*, above, fn.58 (excuse that woman under 21); *Grant v Edwards* [1986] Ch. 638 (excuse that joint names might prejudice her divorce proceedings); criticised B. Sufrin (1987) 50 M.L.R. 94; S. Gardner (1993) 109 L.Q.R. 263 at 265 and 282; cf. R. Smith (1993) 3 Carib.L.R. 96; P. Milne (1995) 145 N.L.J. 423, 456. See also *Rowe v Prance* [1999] 2 F.L.R. 787 (woman entitled to half share of boat registered in man's name; "absurd" excuse that she did not possess a master's certificate); S. Baughen [2000] Conv. 58; *Van Laethem v Brooker* [2006] 2 F.L.R. 495 (excuse about capital gains tax). Estoppel may be a preferable analysis in these cases.

[64] The onus is on the legal owner to prove that any detrimental act was not done in reliance upon the common intention; *Greasley v Cooke* [1980] 1 W.L.R. 1306; *Maharaj v Chand* [1986] A.C. 898.

[65] *Midland Bank Ltd v Dobson* [1986] 1 F.L.R. 171; cf. *Re Densham* [1975] 1 W.L.R. 1519. See also *Supperstone v Hurst* [2006] 1 F.L.R. 1245.

[66] Above, fn.63. See also *Eves v Eves*, above, fn.58; *Chan Pui Chun v Leung Kam Ho* [2003] 1 F.L.R. 23.

[67] B. Sufrin (1987) 50 M.L.R. 94; J. Montgomery [1987] Conv. 16; A. Lawson (1996) 16 L.S. 218; cf. *Coombes v Smith* [1986] 1 W.L.R. 808, below, para.27–013.

[68] *Austin v Keele* (1987) 61 A.L.J.R. 605 at 610.

[69] [1991] 1 A.C. 107; J. Davies (1990) 106 L.Q.R. 539; M. Thompson [1990] Conv. 314; S. Cretney All E.R.Rev. 1990, p.138; M. Dixon (1991) 50 C.L.J. 38; S. Gardner (1991) 54 M.L.R. 126.

[70] cf. *Ungurian v Lesnoff* [1990] Ch. 206; M. Oldham (1990) 49 C.L.J. 25 (common intention to create life interest sufficiently acted upon by decorating and refurbishment).

or interest upon it,[71] and a payment of £12,000 to the man so that he could buy out his estranged wife's share and pay the mortgage on her new house.[72] In *Hammond v Mitchell*[73] a woman was held entitled to a half share of a bungalow when, pursuant to an oral agreement, she acted as the man's unpaid business assistant and supported him in his business ventures as well as looking after the home and children. The judge also classified her act of agreeing to subordinate her rights to those of a mortgagee as one of detrimental reliance, but this seems inadequate. "Can consent to the possible loss of property one does not own make one an owner of that very property?"[74]

ii. Direct Contributions. The traditional approach used to be **11–009** that there would be a purchase money resulting trust in favour of a person who contributed to the purchase price. Beneficial ownership would then be enjoyed in the proportion in which the purchase money was provided.[75] If the purchase money was provided equally, the parties would be beneficial joint tenants. If the contributions were unequal, they would be tenants in common. Payment of, or substantial contributions to the mortgage instalments, would usually suffice[76]; however, such payments did not give rise to a resulting trust unless the payer had assumed liability to make them when the property was purchased (although they could found a constructive trust).[77] For a resulting trust to arise, any payments had to be in money or money's worth.[78] Where property was put into a person's name (solely or jointly) in order to facilitate a mortgage advance, he or she would not normally acquire an interest where the understanding was that another person would make all the repayments.[79]

---

[71] *Risch v McFee* (1991) 61 P. & C.R. 42.

[72] *Stokes v Anderson* [1991] 1 F.L.R. 391. The woman had also spent £2,500 on decorating. The parties had drawn up a promissory note, but it was held that the £12,000 was not in fact a loan.

[73] [1991] 1 W.L.R. 1127; L. Clarke and R. Edmunds (1992) 22 Fam. Law 523.

[74] A. Lawson [1992] Conv. 218 at 222; P. Clarke All E.R.Rev. 1992, p.210; P. O'Hagan (1993) 56 M.L.R. 224.

[75] *Re Roger's Question* [1948] 1 All E.R. 328; *Bull v Bull* [1955] 1 Q.B. 234. A strict view was taken in *Winkworth v Edward Baron Development Co Ltd* [1986] 1 W.L.R. 1512, where, however, the protection of creditors was a significant factor. See J. Warburton [1987] Conv. 217.

[76] *Springette v Defoe* (1993) 65 P. & C.R. 1. The share of a party who contributed capital via a mortgage will be debited with any outstanding principal; *Savill v Goodall* [1993] 1 F.L.R. 755.

[77] P. Matthews (1994) 8 T.L.I. 43; Law Com. No.307 (2007); *Cohabitation: The Financial Consequences of Relationship Breakdown*; A.28, A.29; *Barrett v Barrett* [2008] 2 P. & C.R. 17.

[78] *Muetzel v Muetzel* [1970] 1 W.L.R. 188; *Wachtel v Wachtel* [1973] Fam. 72. A council tenant's discount in exercising a right to buy is usually treated as a financial contribution; *Ashe v Mumford* (2001) 33 H.L.R. 67.

[79] *Re Share (Lorraine)* [2002] 2 F.L.R. 88; *Carlton v Goodman* [2002] 2 F.L.R. 259.

The presumption of advancement once arose in a case where a husband has transferred or arranged for the transfer of the legal estate to his wife; but, as has been seen, statements in *Pettitt v Pettitt*[80] show that the influence of the presumptions has been much reduced. The presumption of advancement was abolished by the Equality Act 2010.[81] There was no presumption of advancement where a wife was transferred to her husband[82]; nor in the case of an unmarried couple.[83]

Doubt was cast on the resulting trust approach by the House of Lords in *Lloyds Bank plc v Rosset*,[84] where direct contributions were regarded as giving rise to a constructive trust rather than a resulting trust. Many subsequent cases adopted the constructive trust approach, and the House of Lords and Supreme Court firmly rejected the resulting trust analysis in *Stack v Dowden*[85] and *Jones v Kernott*[86] in the context of the family home. Both cases involved a property in joint names, but the rejection of the resulting trust was not intended to be confined to that situation. The presumption of a resulting trust still applies, however, in the context of commercial property or property bought as an investment, even where the purchasers are family members.[87]

The remainder of this section deals with interests arising under a constructive trust where the person claiming a share of the property held in the name of the other party has made a direct contribution. Modern cases display a broad approach.

11–010   In *McHardy and Sons (A Firm) v Warren*[88] the Court of Appeal held that where a parent pays a deposit on a house as a wedding present, the irresistible conclusion is that all three intended the couple to have equal shares in the house and not shares measured by reference to the percentage which the deposit bore to the price. In *Midland Bank plc v Cooke*[89] a house was bought in the husband's

---

[80] 1970 A.C. 777. See also *Simpson v Simpson* [1992] 1 F.L.R. 601.

[81] Above, para.10–022. The relevant provisions are not in force at the time of writing.

[82] *Heseltine v Heseltine* [1971] 1 W.L.R. 342 (personalty).

[83] Unless they had agreed to marry; Law Reform (Miscellaneous Provisions) Act 1970, s.2(1); *Mossop v Mossop* [1989] Fam. 77. As to "agreement to marry," see *Shaw v Fitzgerald* [1992] 1 F.L.R. 357.

[84] [1991] 1 A.C. 107.

[85] [2007] 2 A.C. 432; above, para.11–004. Lord Neuberger's minority view favoured the resulting trust approach. See Law Com. No.307 (2007); *Cohabitation: The Financial Consequences of Relationship Breakdown*, A.25.

[86] [2011] UKSC 53; [2011] 3 W.L.R. 1121; above, para.11–006.

[87] *Laskar v Laskar* [2008] 1 W.L.R. 2695 (property bought by mother and daughter for letting).

[88] [1994] 2 F.L.R. 338, questioned in J. Dewar (1994) 24 Fam. Law 567. See also *Halifax Building Society v Brown* [1996] 1 F.L.R. 103 (loan from mother-in-law for deposit).

[89] [1995] 4 All E.R. 562, applying *Gissing v Gissing* [1971] A.C. 886. See S. Cretney and P. Clarke All E.R.Rev. 1995, pp.286 and 312 respectively; S. Gardner (1996) 112 L.Q.R. 378; M. Oldham (1996) 55 C.L.J. 194; D. Wragg and M. Pawlowski (1996) 26 Fam. Law 298 and 484 respectively; G. Battersby [1996] 8 C.F.L.Q. 261; N. Glover and P. Todd (1996) 16 L.S. 325 at 340; M. Dixon [1997] Conv. 66.

name with a mortgage loan of £6,450, his savings of £950 and a gift of £1,100 from his parents to the couple. The wife did not pay the mortgage directly but paid other outgoings from her earnings. Both stated that they never discussed their shares. In possession proceedings relating to a later mortgage, the Court of Appeal held that if an equitable interest has been acquired by direct contribution (the money derived from the gift) and there is no express evidence of intention, the court will assess the proportions the parties are assumed to have intended by surveying the course of dealing between them, their sharing of the burdens and benefits of the property, and all conduct throwing light on the question. On that basis (which seems over generous to the wife) the parties took in equal shares, as they agreed to share everything equally: the profits of the husband's business and the risks of indebtedness if it failed, the upbringing of the children, and the home (which had been put into joint names after the date of the claimant's mortgage) which the wife had helped to maintain and improve, coupled with the added commitment of marriage. However, "it seems illogical to enable factors which cannot create beneficial entitlement to determine the extent of an interest".[90] Further, it is "nothing less than the re-emergence of the doctrine of family assets."[91] A similar example is *Drake v Whipp*,[92] where the woman made a direct contribution of about one-fifth to the purchase and conversion of a barn. The parties had a common intention that she should have a beneficial interest, which the Court of Appeal determined as one-third, adopting a "broad brush" approach, and taking into account her work on the conversion and contribution to household expenses. The need to distinguish constructive and resulting trust principles was emphasised. Thus the finding of a common intention now enables the court to fix a fair share which differs from the proportionate resulting trust.

The question next arose in *Oxley v Hiscock*,[93] where the Court of Appeal reviewed the authorities. In that case an unmarried couple both made direct contributions to the acquisition of a house which was in the man's name. There was evidence of an express common intention to share, but no evidence of intention as to the size of their respective shares. Chadwick L.J., with whom the other members of the court agreed, considered that the law had moved on from the mathematical resulting trust approach of cases like *Springette v*

---

[90] Hopkins, *The Informal Acquisition of Rights in Land*, 2000, p.122.

[91] P. O'Hagan (1997) 60 M.L.R. 420 at 427.

[92] [1996] 1 F.L.R. 826; A. Dunn [1997] Conv. 467. See also *Le Foe v Le Foe* [2001] 2 F.L.R. 970 (direct contributions of about 10% combined with indirect contributions gave wife a half share); *Mollo v Mollo* [2000] W.T.L.R. 227.

[93] [2005] Fam. 211; P. Clarke All E.R. Rev. 2004, p.274; R. Bailey-Harris (2004) 34 Fam. Law 571; S. Gardner [2004] 120 L.Q.R. 541; M. Thompson [2004] Conv. 496. See also *Cox v Jones* [2004] 2 F.L.R. 1010; R. Probert [2005] Conv. 168.

Defoe.[94] In cases involving the family home, where the parties had an express common intention to share but had not discussed the size of their shares, or where their common intention was inferred from their direct contributions, there is no necessary inference that their shares should be proportionate to their contributions. Thus in effect the constructive trust overrides the resulting trust in this type of case. The court will "supply or impute" a common intention as to what their shares should be, on the basis of what is fair in the circumstances, including later acts and conduct (such as paying outgoings or housekeeping). On that basis the woman was held entitled to 40 per cent, which modestly exceeded her financial contributions. His Lordship considered that, in cases of this kind, proprietary estoppel principles would lead to the same outcome.[95]

The *Oxley v Hiscock*[96] line of cases was discussed by the House of Lords in *Stack v Dowden*,[97] and the majority of their Lordships confirmed that a wide view should be taken of what counts as a contribution in cases of this kind. The *Oxley* approach, requiring the court to have regard to the "whole course of dealing" between the parties, was endorsed. Likewise in *Jones v Kernott*,[98] where Lord Collins described the judgment of Chadwick L.J. in *Oxley* as "magisterial".[99] Although *Jones* involved a property in joint names, the Supreme Court indicated that the court should apply the same principles in a case where the property was in one name only when deciding on the extent of the parties' shares, once it had been established that they had a common intention to share the beneficial interest.[100]

The difficulty with this approach is that the width of discretion leads to uncertainty and litigation. Indeed, the Law Commission[101] considered that this "broad brush" approach is an arbitrary method of quantifying shares, and that the cases are difficult to reconcile: Mrs Drake made a larger contribution than Mrs Cooke but obtained a smaller share.

The next question is whether, in the absence of a direct contribution or express agreement, a common intention to share may be inferred solely from indirect contributions or other conduct.

---

[94] (1992) 65 P. & C.R. 1. The House of Lords in *Stack v Dowden* [2007] 2 A.C. 432 has confirmed that *Springette* should not be followed.

[95] Below, para.11–013.

[96] Above, fn.93. See also *Lightfoot v Lightfoot-Brown* [2005] W.T.L.R. 1031 (communication of common intention); *Supperstone v Hurst* [2006] 1 F.L.R. 1245 ("fairness" can include fairness to creditors); *Holman v Howes* [2007] W.T.L.R. 1539.

[97] [2007] 2 A.C. 432; above, para.11–004.

[98] [2011] UKSC 53; [2011] 3 W.L.R. 1121; above, para.11–006.

[99] [2011] 3 W.L.R. 1121 at 1139.

[100] [2011] 3 W.L.R. 1121 at 1137.

[101] Law Com. Discussion Paper, *Sharing Homes* (2002), paras 2.87, 2.109.

iii. Indirect Contributions. It is important to appreciate at the **11–011**
outset that, since *Gissing v Gissing*,[102] the court does not decide how
the parties might have ordered their affairs; it only finds how they
did. "The court cannot devise agreements which the parties never
made. The court cannot ascribe intentions which the parties in fact
never had".[103] In that case the House of Lords rejected the claim of
a wife who had paid £220 for furnishings and for laying a lawn, plus
some household expenses, because she had made no contribution to
the purchase price. It was, however, accepted that a wife who contributed indirectly by relieving her husband of household expenses
and thereby enabling him to pay the mortgage would be entitled to
an interest.[104]

Later decisions in the Court of Appeal, primarily in Lord Denning's time, supported the view that substantial financial contributions, even though indirect, would suffice for the acquisition of a
share.[105] Thus interests were acquired by the contribution of physical labour on the property,[106] or by unpaid work in the family
business which enabled the husband to put the money saved towards
the purchase of property.[107] Domestic duties in the home, on the
other hand, have never sufficed. In *Burns v Burns*[108] the woman's
housework, childcare, decorating and the purchase of chattels for the
home over a period of 17 years gave her no share. If this was unjust,
it was suggested that the remedy lay with Parliament. The position is
otherwise in some other Commonwealth jurisdictions, where the
view that domestic services do not suffice is now considered untenable. Thus in *Peter v Beblow*[109] a woman who cared for her own
children and those of her partner for some years, did the housework,
and contributed to the housekeeping with earnings from a part-time
job was held entitled to the house under a constructive trust on the
basis that her partner (who was entitled to keep a van and a house-
boat acquired during the cohabitation) would otherwise be unjustly
enriched by her services, which enhanced his ability to pay off the
mortgage and acquire other assets. The free accommodation she had
enjoyed was not sufficient compensation.

In English law it appears that, in the absence of an express com- **11–012**
mon intention, indirect contributions alone may not suffice. In

---

[102] [1971] A.C. 886.
[103] [1971] A.C. 866 per Lord Morris of Borth-y-Gest at 898; cf. *Jones v Kernott* [2011]
UKSC 53; [2011] 3 W.L.R. 1121; above, para.11–006.
[104] [1971] A.C. 886 at 903, 907–908.
[105] *Falconer v Falconer* [1970] 1 W.L.R. 1333; *Hargrave v Newton* [1971] 1 W.L.R. 1611;
Wachtel v Wachtel [1973] Fam. 72.
[106] *Cooke v Head* [1972] 1 W.L.R. 518. For improvements, see below, para.11–014.
[107] *Nixon v Nixon* [1969] 1 W.L.R. 1676.
[108] [1984] Ch. 317 (unmarried couple). See also *Richards v Dove* [1974] 1 All E.R. 888;
Layton v Martin (1986) 16 Fam. Law 212; *Windeler v Whitehall* [1990] 2 F.L.R. 505 (housework and business entertaining insufficient).
[109] (1993) 101 D.L.R. (4th) 621; below, para.11–013.

Lloyds Bank plc v Rosset,[110] where the wife had made no substantial contribution, direct or indirect, Lord Bridge took the opportunity to state that direct contributions (whether initially or by payment of the mortgage) were necessary, and that "it is at least extremely doubtful whether anything less will do."[111] The earlier cases of *Eves v Eves*[112] (extensive decorative work and heavy gardening) and *Grant v Edwards*[113] (substantial indirect contributions to the mortgage by applying earnings to household expenses, plus running the home) were correctly decided because both involved an express common intention. In the absence of the latter, neither claimant would have succeeded, because the conduct in each case "fell far short" of conduct which would by itself have supported a claim to a share. Applying this principle, it has been held that a woman who acted as the man's unpaid business assistant, supported him in his speculative ventures and looked after the home and children, could not acquire a share in the property in the absence of an express common intention.[114] Likewise where a daughter worked full-time in her mother's public house for pocket money only, assisting her mother to make a profit which facilitated the purchase of a house. The daughter had no interest in the house as there was neither direct contribution nor express agreement.[115]

However, Lord Bridge's view in *Rosset*[116] has long been considered too restrictive, and the House of Lords in *Stack v Dowden*[117] subsequently expressed the view (obiter, as the case involved direct contributions and a property in joint names) that Lord Bridge's well-known comment that it was "extremely doubtful if anything less will do" (i.e. anything less than direct contributions in the absence of an express common intention) failed to take full account of the views expressed in *Gissing v Gissing*.[118] Their Lordships, sitting as the Privy Council in *Abbott v Abbott*,[119] again doubted the need for direct contributions, saying that the law had "moved on" since *Rosset*. However, this approach cannot yet be said to be firmly established, and it remains unclear how a party who has made only

---

[110] [1991] 1 A.C. 107.
[111] [1991] 1 A.C. 107 at 133.
[112] [1975] 1 W.L.R. 1338.
[113] [1986] Ch. 638.
[114] *Hammond v Mitchell* [1991] 1 W.L.R. 1127 (the Spanish house); above, para.11–008.
[115] *Ivin v Blake* (1994) 67 P. & C.R. 263; criticised A. Lawson [1996] Conv. 462. See also *Thomson v Humphrey* [2010] 2 F.L.R. 107.
[116] Above, fn.110.
[117] [2007] 2 A.C. 432; above, para.11–004.
[118] [1971] A.C. 886.
[119] [2008] 1 F.L.R. 1451; criticised M. Dixon [2007] Conv. 456; R. Lee (2008) 124 L.Q.R. 209. The Privy Council repeated that the constructive trust has replaced the resulting trust in cases on the family home, and appeared to accept the propriety of imputing intentions to the parties. On the latter point see *Jones v Kernott* [2011] 3 W.L.R. 1121, discussed further below and above, para.11–006.

domestic contributions will fare.[120] Indeed, the Court of Appeal recently ruled that a woman who worked unpaid in the man's business, eventually becoming a partner in it, acquired no interest in the home which the man owned before their cohabitation, even though income from the business was used to pay all the outgoings and to fund renovations. She was, however, entitled to share in the partnership assets.[121] As has been said, the concept of unjust enrichment was not meant, and is ill-equipped, to deal with dashed expectations of a long term domestic relationship.[122]

While the claim of a party who cannot establish an express common intention and whose only contributions are indirect remains in doubt, although greatly strengthened by the comments in *Stack v Dowden* and *Abbott v Abbott*, we have seen that, where a party has made direct contributions, any indirect contributions may also be taken into account in assessing the shares the parties are assumed to have intended.[123] In *Le Foe v Le Foe*[124] the wife contributed indirectly in the early years by paying for general outgoings while her husband made the mortgage payments. After inheriting some money she made direct contributions of about 10 per cent of the value of the house, primarily by way of mortgage payments. The husband claimed that her direct contributions led to the inference of a common intention that she should have a 10 per cent share. The judge referred to *Gissing v Gissing*[125] and *Burns v Burns*[126] and held that her indirect contributions justified the inference of a common intention to share, and that her share should be quantified at 50 per cent. This approach reduces any remaining impact of *Lloyds Bank plc v Rosset*.[127] Finally, we saw that the Supreme Court in *Jones v Kernott*[128] did not shrink from imputing intentions to the parties in order to arrive at their "fair shares". However, Lord Collins left open the question whether the court could impute an intention that one party should have a share at all if no such common intention had been expressed or could be inferred: "That question will merit careful thought."[129]

---

[120] Law Com. No.307 (2007); *Cohabitation: The Financial Consequences of Relationship Breakdown*; para.2.13.

[121] *James v Thomas* [2008] 1 F.L.R. 1598; criticised R. Probert (2009) 62 C.L.P. 316 at 334–6. See also *Morris v Morris* [2008] Fam. Law 521.

[122] *Walsh v Singh* [2010] 1 F.L.R. 1658 (no claim where woman gave up Bar career and helped in man's business, expecting marriage).

[123] *Midland Bank plc v Cooke* [1995] 4 All E.R. 562; *Oxley v Hiscock* [2005] Fam. 211.

[124] [2001] 2 F.L.R. 970 (High Court); M. Pawlowski (2002) 32 Fam. Law 190; M. Thompson [2002] Conv. 273.

[125] [1971] A.C. 886.

[126] [1984] Ch. 317.

[127] Above, fn.110. See R. Probert (2009) 62 C.L.P. 316 at 342.

[128] [2011] UKSC 53; [2011] 3 W.L.R. 1121; above, para.11–006.

[129] [2011] 3 W.L.R. 1121 at 1145.

11–013   Another solution might be to base such claims on the doctrine of
proprietary estoppel, where the act of detrimental reliance need not
take the form of financial contributions, and which does not require
a search for an artificial common intention,[130] although estoppel
itself has elements of artificiality.[131] Modern cases have tended to
assimilate the doctrines of constructive trusts and proprietary estoppel,[132] although the process is not yet complete.[133] It appears that
interests under constructive trusts crystallise as soon as a sufficient
act of detrimental reliance has occurred, prior to their vindication by
the court, so that they can affect third parties.[134] It is now established
that proprietary estoppel interests may take effect before the court
order.[135] The Court of Appeal has expressed the view not only that
constructive trusts in the context of the family home are "almost
interchangeable" with proprietary estoppel, but also that estoppel
interests of a family nature are overreachable in the same way as
interests under trusts by payment to two trustees.[136]

However, Lord Walker in *Stack v Dowden* retreated from his
previous support of the "assimilation" approach, saying:

> "I am now rather less enthusiastic about the notion that proprie-
> tary estoppel and 'common intention' constructive trusts can or
> should be completely assimilated. Proprietary estoppel typically
> consists of asserting an equitable claim against the conscience of
> the 'true' owner. The claim is a 'mere equity'. It is to be satisfied
> by the minimum award necessary to do justice ... A 'common
> intention' constructive trust, by contrast, is identifying the true
> beneficial owner or owners, and the size of their beneficial in-
> terests."[137]

[130] *Gillies v Keogh* [1989] 2 N.Z.L.R. 327; M. Bryan (1990) 106 L.Q.R. 213. See also J.
Eekelaar [1987] Conv. 93; M. Thompson and D. Hayton [1990] Conv. 314 and 370 respectively; cf. P. Ferguson (1993) 109 L.Q.R. 114; D. Hayton (1993) 109 L.Q.R. 485; Law Com.
Discussion Paper, *Sharing Homes* (2002), para.2.104.
[131] *Phillips v Phillips* [1993] 3 N.Z.L.R. 159, doubting estoppel as the way forward.
[132] *Grant v Edwards* [1986] Ch. 638; *Austin v Keele* (1987) 61 A.L.J.R 605; *Lloyds Bank
plc v Rosset*, above, fn.110 (but see S. Gardner (1991) 54 M.L.R. 126 and (1993) 109 L.Q.R.
263); *Hammond v Mitchell* [1991] 1 W.L.R. 1127; *Lloyds Bank plc v Carrick* [1996] 4 All
E.R. 630; P. Ferguson (1996) 112 L.Q.R. 549; *Yaxley v Gotts* [2000] Ch. 162 at 176–177;
Chan Pui Chun v Leung Kam Ho [2003] 1 F.L.R. 23; *Oxley v Hiscock* [2005] Fam. 211;
Supperstone v Hurst [2006] 1 F.L.R. 1245; *Van Laethem v Brooker* [2006] 2 F.L.R. 495.
[133] *Stokes v Anderson* [1991] 1 F.L.R. 391; *Hyett v Stanley* [2004] 1 F.L.R. 394.
[134] Implicit in *Lloyds Bank plc v Rosset*, above, fn.110. See D. Hayton [1990] Conv. 370; J.
Warburton (1991) 5 T.L.I. 9; P. Evans [1991] Conv. 155; Presidential Address to the Holdsworth Club, Birmingham University (1991) (Sir Nicolas Browne-Wilkinson), published in
(1996) 10 T.L.I. 98; P. Matthews in Mitchell (ed.), *Constructive and Resulting Trusts* (2009),
pp.50–60.
[135] Below, para.27–031.
[136] *Birmingham Midshires Mortgage Services Ltd v Sabherwal* (2000) 80 P. & C.R. 256;
below, para.27–032. For the distinction between trusts and estoppel concerning onus of proof,
see P. Ferguson (1993) 109 L.Q.R. 114.
[137] [2007] 2 A.C. 432 at 448 (retreating from his view in *Yaxley v Gotts* [2000] Ch. 162 at
177).

Other solutions have been found in Commonwealth jurisdictions.[138] In Australia the property rights of unmarried couples, including same-sex couples, have been recognised by legislation.[139] Similarly in New Zealand.[140] More recently a statutory scheme dealing with the property rights of cohabiting couples has been introduced in Scotland.[141] The principles of unjust enrichment have been utilised in Australia, New Zealand and Canada,[142] although "unconscionability is not a notion which makes hard cases easier to decide".[143] The majority of the Canadian Supreme Court in *Peter v Beblow*[144] considered that a constructive trust should be imposed on the basis of unjust enrichment where there was a direct link between substantial indirect contributions and the acquisition or improvement of property; otherwise compensation could be available on a quantum meruit basis. The decision also reflects the "reasonable expectation" principle applied in New Zealand in *Lankow v Rose*,[145] that where a claimant has contributed in more than a minor way, either directly or indirectly, to the acquisition, preservation or enhancement of the defendant's assets, a constructive trust will be imposed on the basis that the parties must reasonably have expected the claimant to have an interest. The contribution need not be financial, but must be causally related to the acquisition, preservation or enhancement. This objective test thus replaces the search for an artificial common intention, and gives effect to indirect contributions which, although giving rise to difficulties of proof and quantification, are just as real as direct contributions.[146]

iv. Substantial Improvements. Some of the problems of indirect contributions arose where one of the parties had made a substantial contribution in time or money to the improvement of the property subsequent to the purchase. The Matrimonial Proceedings **11–014**

---

[138] See S. Wong (1998) 18 L.S. 369; Law Com. Discussion Paper, *Sharing Homes* (2002), Pt IV. For the position in Ireland, see J. Mee [1993] Conv. 359.

[139] Family Law Amendment (De Facto Financial Matters and Other Measures) Act 2008, amending the Family Law Act 1975; H. Baker (2009) 39 Fam. Law 1201; S. Leigh and D. Barry (2011) 41 Fam. Law 404; Law Com. Discussion Paper, *Sharing Homes* (2002), paras 5.20–5.22; M. Pawlowski (2003) 33 Fam. Law 336; K. Kiernan, A. Barlow and R. Merlo [2006] 36 Fam. Law 1074.

[140] New Zealand Property (Relationships) Amendment Act 2001.

[141] Family Law (Scotland) Act 2006; E. Hess (2009) 39 Fam. Law 405.

[142] *Baumgartner v Baumgartner* (1988) 62 A.L.J. 29; *Gillies v Keogh* [1989] 2 N.Z.L.R. 327; *Peter v Beblow* (1993) 101 D.L.R. (4th) 621. See generally R. Chambers [2006] 14 R.L.R. 146; M. McInnes (2011) 127 L.Q.R. 339; M. Lower [2011] Conv. 515.

[143] M. Bryan (1990) 106 L.Q.R. 25 at 28; M. Bryan (1994) 8 T.L.I. 74; Halliwell, *Equity and Good Conscience in a Contemporary Context*, 1997, Ch.4. See also S. Gardner (1993) 109 L.Q.R. 263, advocating the "communality" approach based on the relationship itself, with less emphasis on intention or contribution.

[144] Above, fn.142, para.11–011.

[145] [1995] 1 N.Z.L.R. 277; *McMahon v McMahon* [1996] 3 N.Z.L.R. 334. See also J. Eekelaar *The Frontiers of Liability*, 1994, Vol.2, p.204.

[146] [1995] 1 N.Z.L.R. 277 at 295.

and Property Act 1970, s.37, which applies only to married couples,[147] provides that:

"[W]here a husband or wife contributes in money or money's worth to the improvement of real or personal property in which . . . either or both of them has or have a beneficial interest, the husband or wife so contributing shall, if the contribution is of a substantial nature and subject to any agreement between them to the contrary express or implied, be treated as having then acquired by virtue of his or her contribution a share or an enlarged share, as the case may be, in that beneficial interest of such an extent as may have been then agreed or, in default of such agreement, as may seem in all the circumstances just . . . ".[148]

Lord Denning said that this provision was declaratory of the previous law,[149] indeed the language of the statute is declaratory. As far as unmarried couples are concerned, substantial improvements may give rise to an interest on the basis of common intention or estoppel, even though s.37 does not apply.[150]

11–015   **v. Date for Valuation of the Share.** If it is established that a person is entitled to a share of the home under a trust (express or constructive), and in the absence of any intention of the parties to change their respective shares,[151] it follows that he or she is entitled to share proportionately in any increase (or decrease) in its value, although occurring after separation, until such time as the property is sold.[152] This principle has been firmly upheld by the Court of Appeal.[153] Credit will be given by way of "equitable accounting" for expenditure such as mortgage payments and repairs incurred by the occupying co-owner after separation.[154]

---

[147] And to engaged couples by reason of Law Reform (Miscellaneous Provisions) Act 1970, s.2(1); *Dibble v Pfluger* [2011] 1 F.L.R. 659. A similar provision now applies to civil partnerships; above, para.11–003.

[148] *Griffiths v Griffiths* [1973] 1 W.L.R. 1454; *Re Nicholson (Deceased)* [1974] 1 W.L.R. 476.

[149] *Davis v Vale* [1971] 1 W.L.R. 1021; *Jansen v Jansen* [1965] P. 478.

[150] *Thomas v Fuller-Brown* [1988] 1 F.L.R. 237 (where the claim failed because the inference was that the expenditure was in return for rent-free accommodation); *Passee v Passee* [1988] 1 F.L.R. 263; J. Warburton [1988] Conv. 361. It is otherwise if the money was advanced as a loan; *Spence v Brown* (1988) 18 Fam. Law 291; cf. *Hussey v Palmer* [1972] 1 W.L.R. 1286; above, para.2–011. See generally M. Pawlowski (2009) 39 Fam. Law 680.

[151] *Jones v Kernott* [2011] UKSC 53; [2011] 3 W.L.R. 1121; above, para.11–006.

[152] Or the co-ownership ends in another way, e.g. if one buys the other out. See *Young v Lauretani* [2007] 2 F.L.R. 1211.

[153] *Turton v Turton* [1988] Ch. 542; J. Warburton [1987] Conv. 378; (1987) 103 L.Q.R. 500; J. Montgomery (1988) 18 Fam. Law 72; I. Hardcastle (1989) 86/31 L.S.Gaz. 31; *Gordon v Douce* [1983] 1 W.L.R. 563; *Passee v Passee* [1988] 1 F.L.R. 263. See also *Cousins v Dzosens* (1984) 81 L.S.Gaz. 2855; *Bernard v Josephs* [1982] Ch. 391.

[154] *Wilcox v Tait* [2007] 2 F.L.R. 871; G. Lightman (2008) 22 T.L.I. 11.

D. Reform

We saw that the Law Commission in 2002 was unable to make **11–016** proposals which could apply generally to those who share homes without formalising their property rights.[155] Proposals have since been published which apply only to cohabiting couples.[156]

The proposed statutory scheme will apply to cohabitants who are neither married to each other nor civil partners. Unless they have a child together, they will be eligible only if they lived as a couple in a joint household for a continuous minimum period before separation. The Law Commission did not select the minimum period, but recommended that it should be between two and five years.

The next condition is that the applicant must have made a "qualifying contribution", which means any contribution, whether or not financial, to the shared lives of the parties or to the welfare of members of their families. Financial relief will be available where, as a result of this contribution, the respondent has retained a benefit or the applicant has an economic disadvantage. A retained benefit could be either capital (for example from the other party's contribution to the acquisition of the home), income, or related to earning capacity. An economic disadvantage means a present or future loss, for example by reduced earning capacity through childcare. Claims must be brought within two years of the separation.

Where these conditions are satisfied, the court may direct the payment of capital (by way of a lump sum or instalments), pension sharing, or a transfer of property. It will not order maintenance by way of periodical payments. Discretionary factors, in particular the welfare of minor children, may be taken into account in deciding the form of relief.

Cohabitants will be free to opt out of the statutory scheme by written agreement signed by both parties. Where they have not opted out, claims will be regulated by the statutory scheme, to the exclusion of the general law of trusts, estoppel and contract.

Where separation occurs on death, the proposal is to enhance existing rights under the Inheritance (Provision for Family and Dependants) Act 1975 if the survivor would have been eligible under the statutory scheme.

It was announced on March 6, 2008 that the Government proposed to take no action pending the outcome of research by the

---

[155] Above, para.11–003.

[156] Law Com. No.307 (2007); *Cohabitation: The Financial Consequences of Relationship Breakdown*. The report contains no draft Bill. See generally S. Bridge (2007) 37 Fam. Law 998 and 1076 and (2008) *Trusts and Estates Law & Tax Journal* 26. The proposals are criticised by D. Hughes, M. Davis and L. Jacklin [2008] Conv. 197, where an opt-in system or the extension of civil partnerships to heterosexual couples are preferred. See also G. Douglas, J. Pearce and H. Woodward [2008] Conv. 365 and (2009) 72 M.L.R. 24; S. Singer (2009) 39 Fam. Law 234; R. Probert (2009) 62 C.L.P. 316; Baroness Hale of Richmond (2011) 41 Fam. Law 1341 at 1342.

Scottish Executive into the cost and efficacy of provisions in the Family Law (Scotland) Act 2006, which are similar in many ways to the proposals of the Law Commission. A Private Members' Bill, the Cohabitation Bill, was introduced in the House of Lords in 2008 but was not enacted. In September 2011 it was announced that reform would not be implemented during the current Parliament.

3. Consequences of Co-Ownership

A. The Trust of Land

11–017   The two forms of co-ownership existing under the modern law are the joint tenancy and the tenancy in common. Here only a brief outline will be given, as the details may be found in the land law books.[157] Under the Law of Property Act 1925 a trust for sale was imposed on both forms of co-ownership, while successive interests came within the Settled Land Act 1925. This system operated for many years, but was subject to criticism partly because the dual system was perceived as unnecessary and partly because the duty to sell which arose under the trust for sale was not readily understood by co-owners. Furthermore, this duty to sell brought into play the doctrine of conversion, often with inconvenient and artificial results. The effect of this doctrine was that the interests of the co-owners were treated as personalty, which gave rise to difficulties, particularly in the interpretation of many legislative provisions.

Following Law Commission proposals,[158] the dual system of the trust for sale and the strict settlement was replaced by the "trust of land" under the Trusts of Land and Appointment of Trustees Act 1996, which applies to both concurrent and successive interests. While pre-existing settlements under the Settled Land Act 1925 (other than those relating to charity land) are preserved, no new settlements may be created.[159] The definition of "trust of land"[160] is "any trust of property which consists of or includes land", whether the trust is express, implied, resulting or constructive, including a trust for sale and a bare trust. With the exception of pre-existing strict settlements, the 1996 Act applies to trusts of land created before and after its commencement (January 1, 1997).

Under the trust of land, the trustees have a power of sale, but no duty to sell. (Other powers and duties will be mentioned where relevant in the following sections). The interests of the beneficiaries are overreached on sale (provided there are at least two trustees), as

---

[157] M. & W., p.452; Cheshire and Burn, Ch.14.

[158] No.181 (1989), *Trusts of Land*. On the 1996 Act see N. Hopkins [1996] Conv. 411; Smith, *Plural Ownership*, 2005, Part III.

[159] Trusts of Land and Appointment of Trustees Act 1996, s.2. Entailed interests may no longer be created; Sch.1, para.5. See, however, E. Bennett Histed (2000) 116 L.Q.R. 445; S. Pascoe [2001] Conv. 396.

[160] TLATA 1996, s.1.

under the previous legislation.[161] Trusts for sale may still be expressly created,[162] but, as already mentioned, fall within the definition of a "trust of land". All express trusts for sale of land, whenever created, include (despite any provision to the contrary) a power to postpone the sale, and the trustees are not liable in any way for postponing sale for an indefinite period in the exercise of their discretion.[163] Although the duty to sell remains in such a case, the doctrine of conversion is abolished in respect of all trusts for sale of land whenever created, save for those created by the will of a testator dying before the commencement of the 1996 Act.[164] Thus the interests of the beneficiaries are no longer interests in personalty, but are recognised as interests in the land itself.

As already mentioned, the 1925 legislation imposed a trust for sale on co-owned land (and in various other circumstances, such as intestacy). Under the current regime the statutory trust for sale is replaced by the trust of land. While the legal estate, if vested in more than one person, must be held jointly, the beneficial interest may be held either on a joint tenancy or on a tenancy in common. The relevant legislation is Law of Property Act 1925, s.34 (tenancies in common) and s.36 (joint tenancies), as amended by the 1996 Act to reflect the replacement of the trust for sale by the trust of land.[165] To facilitate conveyancing, the legal joint tenancy cannot be severed, but severance of any equitable joint tenancy can be effected by any of the means applicable before 1926[166]; and also by notice in writing to the other joint tenants.[167] The purpose of severance is to convert the joint tenancy into a tenancy in common and thereby prevent the application of the doctrine of survivorship (whereby the survivor of joint tenants takes the whole).

B. Occupation Rights

Difficulties arose in the past concerning the occupation rights of **11–018** beneficiaries under a trust for sale, whether imposed expressly or, more commonly, by statute, as in the case of co-ownership. The difficulty stemmed from the old doctrine of conversion, whereby the interests of the beneficiaries were regarded as in the proceeds of sale, not the land. Although the situation was somewhat obscure, modern decisions upheld the occupation rights of the beneficiaries,

---

[161] Above, para.1–047.
[162] See P. Pettit (1997) 113 L.Q.R. 207; R. Mitchell [1999] Conv. 84.
[163] TLATA 1996, s.4.
[164] TLATA 1996, s.3.
[165] TLATA 1996, Sch.2.
[166] M. & W., p.504; Cheshire and Burn, p.457.
[167] LPA 1925, s.36(2); *Re Draper's Conveyance* [1969] 1 Ch. 486; *Harris v Goddard* [1983] 1 W.L.R. 1203.

regarding the doctrine of conversion as artificial.[168] Thus it was held in the leading case of *Bull v Bull*[169] that a son, who held the legal estate on trust for sale for himself and his mother as equitable tenants in common, was not entitled to evict his mother.

The occupation rights of beneficiaries are now governed by the Trusts of Land and Appointment of Trustees Act 1996, whenever the trust of land arose. The Act abolished the doctrine of conversion.[170] Section 12 provides that a beneficiary beneficially entitled to an interest in possession is entitled to occupy at any time if at that time (a) the purposes of the trust include making the land available for his occupation (or for the occupation of beneficiaries of a class of which he is a member or of beneficiaries in general) or (b) the land is held by the trustees so as to be so available. The section does not confer a right to occupy land if it is either unavailable or unsuitable for occupation by him,[171] and is subject to s.13, discussed below. When considering whether the property is suitable for occupation, the court looks at the nature of the property and the characteristics, circumstances and requirements of the particular beneficiary. If it is suitable for occupation by a couple, it will not be considered unsuitable for the sole occupation of the partner remaining after the relationship breaks down.[172] Thus a beneficiary will normally be entitled to occupy unless, for example, the land has been let, or it is clear that the purpose of the trust is the sale of the property and division of the proceeds among the beneficiaries.[173]

11–019   Section 13(1) of the 1996 Act provides that where two or more beneficiaries are entitled to occupy under s.12, the trustees may, provided they do not act unreasonably, exclude or restrict the entitlement of any one or more (but not all) of them. If a building lends itself to physical partition, the trustees may restrict one beneficiary to a particular part and the other to the other part.[174] They may also impose reasonable conditions from time to time on any beneficiary in relation to his occupation.[175] The matters to which the trustees must have regard in exercising these powers include (a) the intention of the person or persons (if any) who created the trust, (b) the purposes for which the land is held, and (c) the circumstances and wishes of each of the beneficiaries who is (or apart from any previous exercise by the trustees of those powers would be) entitled to

---

[168] *Williams & Glyn's Bank Ltd v Boland* [1981] A.C. 487; *City of London Building Society v Flegg* [1988] A.C. 54.

[169] [1955] 1 Q.B. 234; cf. *Barclay v Barclay* [1970] 2 Q.B. 677 (express testamentary trust for sale).

[170] s.3.

[171] s.12(2). See J. Ross Martyn [1997] Conv. 254 at 260.

[172] *Chan Pui Chun v Leung Kam Ho* [2003] 1 F.L.R. 23.

[173] As in the testamentary trust for sale in *Barclay v Barclay*, above, fn.169.

[174] *Rodway v Landy* [2001] Ch. 703 (doctor's surgery).

[175] s.13(3). See *Rodway v Landy*, above, fn.174, (contribution to costs of adapting building).

occupy the land under s.12.[176] The conditions which they may impose include the payment of outgoings or expenses in respect of the land, or the assumption of any other obligation in relation to the land or to any activity which is or is proposed to be conducted there.[177] If the entitlement of any beneficiary has been excluded or restricted under the section, conditions may be imposed on any other beneficiary requiring him to compensate the beneficiary whose rights have been excluded or restricted, or to forgo a benefit under the trust so as to benefit the other beneficiary.[178] The trustees may not exercise their powers so as to prevent any person in occupation (whether or not by reason of any entitlement under s.12) from continuing to occupy, or in a manner likely to have that result, unless he consents or the court gives approval.[179] Disputes concerning the exercise of the trustees' powers under s.13 may be resolved by an application to court under s.14, where the circumstances and wishes of each beneficiary with occupation rights will be considered.[180]

Prior to the 1996 Act occupying co-owners were in certain cases obliged to pay rent to non-occupying co-owners, as where the latter had been "ousted" by the occupier,[181] or where the occupier had presented a divorce petition against the non-occupier,[182] or as a condition of postponing a sale.[183] As a general principle, however, no rent was payable to a beneficiary who chose not to occupy.[184] The position was somewhat uncertain, but the matter now falls within s.13 which, as mentioned above, permits the imposition of conditions by the trustees including the compensation of a non-occupying beneficiary by an occupier.[185] The court may direct the payment of rent in any case where it is necessary in order to do broad justice between co-owners, and "ouster" is not required.[186] It has been held that ss.12 to 15 of the 1996 Act do not provide an exhaustive regime for compensation for exclusion of a beneficiary from occupation. In cases not expressly covered by the Act, the old principles of equitable accounting may still apply. Thus a co-owner in sole occupation may be ordered to pay rent to the trustee in

---

[176] s.13(4).
[177] s.13(5).
[178] s.13(6).
[179] s.13(7). The court will have regard to the matters set out in s.13(4).
[180] See s.15(2); below, para.11–024.
[181] See *Dennis v McDonald* [1982] Fam. 63.
[182] *Re Pavlou (A Bankrupt)* [1993] 1 W.L.R. 1047 (discussing also the question of set-off against mortgage interest paid by the occupier).
[183] *Harvey v Harvey* [1982] Fam. 83.
[184] *Jones (AE) v Jones (FW)* [1977] 1 W.L.R. 438.
[185] See also Family Law Act 1996, s.40(1)(b) (periodical payments while occupation order in force).
[186] *Murphy v Gooch* [2007] 2 F.L.R. 934.

bankruptcy of the other co-owner on the basis of equitable accounting.[187]

One problem with ss.12 and 13 is that they are ill-suited to trusts arising out of co-ownership, where the trustees and beneficiaries are frequently the same persons. Indeed, it has been said that these sections contain a "cross-fertilisation of ideas implemented without concrete policy considerations",[188] and that the Act has unintentionally curtailed the occupation rights of co-owners by eroding the concept of unity of possession, and that beneficiaries should be able to resort to their general law rights where these are superior to those conferred by the Act.[189]

Finally, a spouse who is not a legal owner may assert occupation rights under the Family Law Act 1996 (replacing Matrimonial Homes Act 1983) whether or not he or she has an equitable interest in the home.[190] This right is registrable, but failure to register will not affect enforcement against the other spouse, or enforcement of any rights arising independently by reason of an equitable interest in the home.

C. Sale by Sole Trustee

11–020 Under the trust of land and its predecessor, the trust for sale, at least two trustees are necessary if the overreaching machinery is to operate.[191] While there are likely to be at least two trustees in the case of an expressly created trust of land, the difficulty which arises in many cases of co-ownership is that the land is vested in one person only. That person holds on trust for all those who are beneficially entitled, but the overreaching machinery will not operate. As we saw in the earlier parts of this chapter, the question whether a person other than the legal owner has acquired an interest is often difficult, so that the existence of the trust may not be appreciated, either by the parties or the purchaser (or mortgagee).

Where there are two trustees, the interests of the beneficiaries will be overreached whether or not they are occupying[192] and whether the title is registered or unregistered. Where there is a sole trustee,

---

[187] *French v Barcham* [2009] 1 W.L.R. 1124; B. McFarlane All E.R. Rev. 2009, 318. See also *Re Byford* (2004) 1 P. & C.R. 12; H. Conway [2003] Conv. 533; N. Berry (2005) 155 N.L.J. 486.

[188] S. Pascoe [2006] Conv. 54. See also S. Bright [2009] Conv. 378.

[189] D. Barnsley (1998) 57 C.L.J. 123; cf. S. Pascoe [2006] Conv. 54.

[190] Former spouses, cohabitants and former cohabitants may in certain cases obtain occupation orders whether or not they have an equitable interest. These are not registrable. The "spouse" provisions apply also to civil partners; Civil Partnership Act 2004, s.82 and Sch.9.

[191] LPA 1925, s.2.

[192] *City of London Building Society v Flegg* [1988] A.C. 54; cf. Law Com. No.188, *Transfer of Land; Overreaching; Beneficiaries in Occupation.* This Report will not be implemented; [1998] Conv. 349.

the principles applicable to registered and unregistered titles must be considered separately.

If the title is unregistered,[193] the question whether the transferee, typically a mortgagee, is bound by the equitable interests depends on whether the mortgagee had notice, actual or constructive, of the interest of the beneficiary. The equitable co-ownership usually arises by virtue of one party having contributed to the purchase price, or to the mortgage payments; and there will be nothing in the documents of title to indicate this. The question is whether the beneficiary's occupation gives constructive notice. It was at one time held that a bank mortgagee dealing with the husband as sole legal owner did not have constructive notice of the wife's equitable interest by contribution, even though the bank knew that the parties lived together in the house.[194] This view soon became untenable.[195] So many wives have a share in the home that a reasonable mortgagee should consider the possibility. If it made insufficient inquiries, the fact of the wife's (or other beneficiary's) occupation gives constructive notice of her rights. The question whether sufficient inquiries had been made arose in *Kingsnorth Finance Co v Tizard*,[196] where a wife had a half share in a house which was vested in her husband alone. When the marriage broke down she slept elsewhere but came to the house every day to look after the children and kept her possessions there. The husband mortgaged the property, falsely stating that he was single. The mortgagee's surveyor inspected the house at a time when the husband had arranged for the wife to be out. He saw evidence of the children's occupation and was told that the wife had left. The husband later emigrated, leaving the loan of £66,000 unpaid. It was held that the wife was in occupation for the purpose of constructive notice. In order for physical presence to amount to occupation, it did not need to be exclusive, continuous or uninterrupted, nor was it negatived by regular absences. When the surveyor discovered that the mortgagor was married, he was put on enquiry as to the wife's rights. As no further enquiries were made, the mortgagee had constructive notice of her rights.

It should be added that where spouses occupy a matrimonial **11–021** home, a spouse who has no legal title may protect his or her statutory rights of occupation under the Family Law Act 1996 (replacing Matrimonial Homes Act 1983) by registration, whether or not that

---

[193] i.e. not subject to the provisions of the Land Registration Act (now the Act of 2002) at the time of the transaction. Many titles remain unregistered even though the registration system applies in all areas. Sale is a transaction which triggers a duty to register. Likewise, various other transactions including the grant of a first legal mortgage; Land Registration Act 2002, s.4. Priority disputes, however, commonly arise some years after the mortgage and may still be governed by unregistered land principles.

[194] *Caunce v Caunce* [1969] 1 W.L.R. 286.

[195] *Williams & Glyn's Bank Ltd v Boland* [1981] A.C. 487.

[196] [1986] 1 W.L.R. 783.

spouse has any equitable interest in the home. But there is no possibility of protecting a substantive equitable interest by registration in cases of unregistered title.

In the case of registered land, the doctrine of notice does not apply. Equitable interests are binding on a purchaser only if proper steps have been taken to protect them by entering a notice or a restriction; or if the interest is an "overriding interest"; which is binding although not protected by entry on the register. The issue came to a head in *Williams & Glyn's Bank Ltd v Boland*.[197]

> Mr and Mrs Boland each contributed towards the purchase of, and to the mortgage payments due upon, a matrimonial home. Title was taken in the sole name of Mr Boland, and he was registered as sole proprietor.
>
> Later, Mr Boland mortgaged the house to the Bank. On default being made in the mortgage payments, the Bank started proceedings for possession. The wife resisted this claim on the ground that she was entitled to an equitable interest in the house which the Bank could not override.

It was accepted that the wife had, by virtue of her financial contribution, an equitable interest in the house. The question whether this interest was valid against the Bank depended on whether it was an overriding interest under the provision then in force: Land Registration Act 1925, s.70(1)(g)[198]; it could not otherwise be binding, because the wife had taken no steps to protect it by entry on the register. Nor could it be overreached by the payment to a sole trustee.

The House of Lords unanimously held that the wife's interest was an overriding interest as she was "in actual occupation" at the execution of the mortgage.[199] Lord Scarman emphasised the importance of construing the legislation in the light of current social policy, and of protecting the "beneficial interest which English law now recognizes that a married woman has in the matrimonial home."[200] It is thus necessary to make inquiries of all persons in occupation, whether spouse, cohabitant, or other persons; for their interests are capable of being binding as overriding interests on the

---

[197] [1981] A.C. 487; J. Martin [1980] Conv. 361; S. Freeman (1980) 43 M.L.R. 692; M. Prichard (1980) 39 C.L.J. 243; R. Smith (1981) 97 L.Q.R. 12. See also D. Wilde [1999] Conv. 382; P. Omar [2006] Conv. 509; M. Conaglen (2006) 69 M.L.R. 582; N. Jackson (2006) 69 M.L.R. 214 and [2007] Conv. 120.

[198] s.70(1)(g) protected "The rights of every person in actual occupation of the land or in receipt of the rents and profits thereof, save where enquiry is made of such person and the rights are not disclosed; ... ".

[199] This is the relevant date, rather than the later date of registration of the legal charge; *Abbey National BS v Cann* [1991] 1 A.C. 56.

[200] [1981] A.C. 487 at p.510.

purchaser or mortgagee. It should be appreciated however, that a wife (or other person) with an overriding interest cannot necessarily prevent a sale by the mortgagee, although she will still have a prior claim to her share of the proceeds.[201]

The provisions on overriding interests have been modified by the Land Registration Act 2002. Although the interest of a person "in actual occupation" may still override a registered disposition, an exception is made in the case of: **11–022**

"[A]n interest

(i) which belongs to a person whose occupation would not have been obvious on a reasonably careful inspection of the land at the time of the disposition; and
(ii) of which the person to whom the disposition is made does not have actual knowledge at that time".[202]

The principles discussed above are subject to an important proviso. An equitable co-owner in occupation can rely neither on constructive notice (in unregistered land) nor on an overriding interest by reason of occupation (in registered land) where he or she was aware of the mortgage transaction and did not bring the equitable interest to the attention of the mortgagee.[203] This seems to be a version of the doctrine of estoppel. The principle is that in such circumstances it is impossible to infer any common intention other than that the equitable owner authorised the legal owner to raise money by mortgage which would have priority to any beneficial interest. Apparently it is not relevant that the mortgagee failed to make the inquiries which might have revealed the interest. As has been said, this seems to be a reversal of the doctrine of notice; the onus has shifted to the occupier to declare his rights to a purchaser (mortgagee) of whom he has notice, or be deemed to concede priority.[204] In the case of an acquisition mortgage, the House of Lords has taken the principle further by holding that a purchaser who depends on a mortgage in order to buy the property acquires on completion only an equity of redemption, (i.e. the property already subject to the

---

[201] *Bank of Baroda v Dhillon* [1998] 1 F.L.R. 524; R. Wells (1998) 28 Fam. Law 208; S. Pascoe [1998] Conv. 415; *Halifax Mortgage Services Ltd v Muirhead* (1998) 76 P. & C.R. 418.

[202] LRA 2002, ss.29, 30 and Sch.3, para.2; N. Jackson (2003) 119 L.Q.R. 660; B. Bogusz [2011] Conv. 268. This modification would not have affected the decision in *Boland*. The Act of 2002 preserves the exception in the previous legislation to the effect that the interest of an occupier of whom enquiry was made and who failed to disclose his rights is not overriding.

[203] *Bristol and West Building Society v Henning* [1985] 1 W.L.R. 778; *Paddington Building Society v Mendelsohn* (1985) 50 P. & C.R. 244; criticised P. Todd [1985] Conv. 361; [1986] Conv. 57; M. Thompson (1986) 49 M.L.R. 255 and (1986) 6 L.S. 140.

[204] M. Welstead (1985) 44 C.L.J. 354.

mortgage). Thus a third party claiming a beneficial interest as against the purchaser can assert no rights against the mortgagee, whether or not the third party was aware of the mortgage.[205] The effect of these principles is to restrict the application of *Williams & Glyn's Bank Ltd v Boland*[206] and *Kingsnorth Finance Co v Tizard*[207] to subsequent mortgages of which the co-owner was unaware.

D. Disputes over Sale

11–023   Disputes commonly arise, primarily on the breakdown of a relationship, as to whether the property should be sold or not. The question may also arise on the death of a co-owner, if his or her share devolves on a third party. Where the legal estate is vested in all the co-owners, they (being trustees) must act unanimously in the exercise of any power.[208] Since the commencement of the Trusts of Land and Appointment of Trustees Act 1996, trustees of land have a power of sale instead of the duty to sell which formerly existed under the statutory trust for sale imposed in cases of co-ownership. Thus the power of sale cannot be exercised unless all agree. In cases of dispute, as explained below, they can apply to court under s.14 of the 1996 Act, replacing s.30 of the Law of Property Act 1925.

It may be that the legal estate is vested in one co-owner only, as where a husband holds the legal estate on trust for himself and his wife as co-owners in equity. In the last section we saw the effect of a sale or mortgage by a sole trustee. Here we will consider the position prior to any such disposition. The question of unanimity does not arise, because there is only one trustee. In the event of a dispute, the wife (or other equitable co-owner) may apply to court under s.14 if she has the opportunity to act in time. In any event, sale will be hampered if she has registered her statutory right of occupation[209] or (in the case of registered land) has protected her equitable interest by the entry of a restriction or a notice. Even if she has not done so, her interest is likely to prevail against the purchaser or mortgagee if she is in occupation.[210] She may also seek an injunction to prevent sale

---

[205] *Abbey National BS v Cann* [1991] 1 A.C. 56; S. Baughen and P. Evans [1991] Conv. 116 and 155 respectively. As to remortgages, see *Equity & Law Home Loans Ltd v Prestidge* [1992] 1 W.L.R. 137; R. Smith (1992) 108 L.Q.R. 372; M. Lunney (1993) 56 M.L.R. 87; J. Dewar (1993) 23 Fam. Law 231.

[206] Above, fn.197.

[207] [1986] 1 W.L.R. 783, above, para.11–020.

[208] *Re Mayo* [1943] Ch. 302; below, para.17–007. The parties may have made express provisions for sale or for one to buy the other out; *Miller v Lakefield Estates Ltd* (1989) 57 P. & C.R. 104.

[209] Family Law Act 1996, re-enacting Matrimonial Homes Act 1983; *Wroth v Tyler* [1974] Ch. 30.

[210] As an overriding interest (registered land) or under the doctrine of notice (unregistered land); above, para.11–020.

without the appointment of a second trustee to safeguard the proceeds of sale, or to restrain the husband from disregarding his statutory duty to consult the beneficiaries.[211] Section 11 of the Trusts of Land and Appointment of Trustees Act 1996 (re-enacting the previous legislation) provides that the trustees, in the exercise of any function relating to the land, shall (so far as practicable) consult the beneficiaries of full age and beneficially entitled to an interest in possession, and, so far as consistent with the general interest of the trust, give effect to the wishes of those beneficiaries or of the majority of them, according to the value of their combined interests.[212] Clearly this section is of limited assistance to a beneficiary with a minority interest, and will result in a stalemate if there are two disputing co-owners who are equally entitled. In certain cases, however, it will resolve the situation. A purchaser (or mortgagee) is not concerned to see that the trustees' duties to consult the beneficiaries and to have regard to their rights have been complied with, whether the title to the land is unregistered[213] or registered.[214]

Assuming that the dispute cannot otherwise be resolved, application may be made to court under s.14 of the 1996 Act. The application may be made by a trustee or any person having an interest in the property.[215] Thus the trustee in bankruptcy of a beneficiary (whose position is discussed below) or chargee of a beneficial interest may apply, as under the previous law. The court may make such order as it thinks fit (a) relating to the exercise by the trustees of any of their functions (including an order relieving them of any obligation to obtain the consent of, or to consult, any person in connection with the exercise of any of their functions),[216] or (b) declaring the nature or extent of a person's interest in the property[217]; but may not appoint or remove trustees under this section.[218]

11–024

The matters to which the court is to have regard include (a) the intentions of the person or persons (if any) who created the trust,[219]

---

[211] *Waller v Waller* [1967] 1 W.L.R. 451. See also *Lee v Lee* [1952] 2 Q.B. 489n. (jurisdiction under Married Women's Property Act 1882, s.17).

[212] This duty may be excluded in an express trust. Also, the trustees must have regard to the rights of the beneficiaries when exercising the powers of an absolute owner conferred by s.6 of the 1996 Act; s.6(5); G. Ferris and G. Battersby [2009] Conv. 39. Section 11 does not apply to one of joint lessees who serves a notice to quit; *Notting Hill Housing Trust v Brackley, The Times*, June 15, 2001.

[213] Trusts of Land and Appointment of Trustees Act 1996, s.16(1).

[214] LRA 2002, s.26; E. Cooke [2002] Conv. 11 at 23–25; G. Ferris and G. Battersby (2003) 119 L.Q.R. 94; S. Pascoe [2005] Conv. 140.

[215] s.14(1). See generally N. Hopkins (2009) 125 L.Q.R. 310.

[216] See *Page v West* [2010] W.T.L.R. 1811.

[217] See *Lowson v Coombes* [1999] Ch. 373.

[218] Trusts of Land and Appointment of Trustees Act 1996, s.14(2), (3).

[219] This refers to intentions at the time the trust was created; *W v W (Joinder of Trusts of Land Act and Children Act Applications)* [2004] 2 F.L.R. 321 (holding also that related applications under the Children Act 1989 should be heard with the application under the 1996 Act). In contested divorce cases ancillary relief proceedings are preferable to proceedings under the 1996 Act; *Smith v Smith* [2010] W.T.L.R. 519.

(b) the purposes for which the property subject to the trust is held,[220] (c) the welfare of any child who occupies or might reasonably be expected to occupy any land subject to the trust as his home, and (d) the interests of any secured creditor of any beneficiary.[221] So far as applications relating to the exercise of the trustees' powers under s.13 to exclude or restrict occupation rights are concerned, the court will also consider the circumstances and wishes of each of the beneficiaries who is (or apart from any previous exercise by the trustees of those powers would be) entitled to occupy the land under s.12.[222] In the case of any other application, the court will also consider the circumstances and wishes of any beneficiaries of full age and entitled to an interest in possession or (in case of dispute) of the majority (according to the value of their combined interests).[223] Different considerations apply to applications by a trustee in bankruptcy, which are discussed below.

Decisions on the predecessor legislation (s.30 of the Law of Property Act 1925) may afford some guidance, bearing in mind, however, that those decisions were influenced by the primacy of the duty to sell which then arose under the statutory trust for sale in cases of co-ownership. Another distinction is that s.30, unlike s.15 of the 1996 Act, did not spell out the factors to be taken into account by the court. As under the previous law, the provision of a home for the parties' children will continue to be a significant, although not paramount, consideration in family cases.[224] The width of s.15, however, makes it unlikely that much resort will need to be made to the previous authorities, which must be treated with caution. It has been held that s.15 gives the court a wider discretion than under the previous law to refuse an order for sale of the family home, and that it is no longer the position that applications by chargees and trustees in bankruptcy are to be similarly treated.[225] Thus a chargee may be less likely to secure an order for sale than under the previous law, although whether the creditor is receiving proper recompense for being kept out of his money is still a powerful consideration.[226] The

---

[220] This means the purposes at the time the court deals with the matter; *Rodway v Landy* [2001] Ch. 703; *Holman v Howes* [2006] 1 F.L.R. 1003.

[221] TLATA 1996, s.15(1). See *The Mortgage Corp v Shaire* [2001] Ch. 743, above.

[222] TLATA 1996, s.15(2). For ss.12 and 13, see above, para.11–018.

[223] TLATA 1996, s.15(3). This does not apply to applications relating to s.6(2) (power to convey to adult beneficiaries absolutely entitled without request).

[224] See *Williams v Williams* [1976] Ch. 278; *Re Evers' Trust* [1980] 1 W.L.R. 1327 (unmarried couple); *Harris v Harris* (1996) 72 P. & C.R. 408 (no sale on father's death where deed of family arrangement had provided for retention as family home for father and son, who still occupied). For property other than the family home, see *Re Buchanan-Wollaston's Conveyance* [1939] Ch. 738.

[225] *The Mortgage Corp v Shaire* [2001] Ch. 743; S. Pascoe and M. Thompson [2000] Conv. 315 and 329 respectively; M. Oldham (2001) 60 C.L.J. 43; P. Clarke All E.R. Rev. 2001, p.258. See generally M. Dixon (2011) 70 C.L.J. 579.

[226] *Bank of Ireland Home Mortgages Ltd v Bell* [2001] 2 F.L.R. 809; R. Probert [2002] Conv. 61. For the position where both co-owners are the debtors, see *Close Invoice Finance Ltd v Pile* [2009] 1 F.L.R. 873.

court must exercise its discretion compatibly with the European Convention on Human Rights, but a due consideration of the factors set out in s.15 ordinarily enables the court to balance the respective rights of the creditor and of the debtor's family.[227]

Where, however, the sale is requested by the trustee in bankruptcy **11–025** of one party, different considerations arise: "Bankruptcy has, in relation to the matrimonial home, its own claim to protection".[228] The rights of the creditors are in competition with the interests of all the beneficiaries. They do not automatically defeat the interests of the family; but the reported cases indicate that it is only in exceptional circumstances that the trustee in bankruptcy will not succeed,[229] although sale may be deferred for a short time if the spouse has some prospect of buying the bankrupt's share.[230] The fact that the bankrupt's family will be unable to buy a comparable home and that his children's schooling may be disrupted are not exceptional circumstances justifying refusal of an order for sale; they are the "melancholy consequences of debt and improvidence".[231]

The law in this area was amended by the Insolvency Act 1986, following an examination by the Review Committee on Insolvency Law and Practice.[232] The 1986 provisions have in turn been amended by the Trusts of Land and Appointment of Trustees Act 1996. Where an application for sale is made under s.14 of the 1996 Act by the trustee in bankruptcy of a co-owner, the position is governed by s.335A of the Insolvency Act 1986. On such an application the court shall make such order as it thinks just and reasonable, having regard to:

(a) the interests of the bankrupt's creditors;
(b) where the application is made in respect of land which includes a dwelling-house which is or has been the home of the bankrupt or the bankrupt's spouse[233] or former spouse,

---

[227] *National Westminster Bank Plc v Rushmer* [2010] 2 F.L.R. 362. See below, para.11–026.

[228] *Re Bailey* [1977] 1 W.L.R. 278 at p.279, per Megarry V.C.

[229] *Re Solomon* [1967] Ch. 573; *Re Turner* [1974] 1 W.L.R. 1556; *Re McCarthy* [1975] 1 W.L.R. 807; *Re Lowrie* [1981] 3 All E.R. 353; *Re Densham* [1975] 1 W.L.R. 1519, cf. *Re Holliday* [1981] Ch. 405 (no order until 1985, where no creditors pressing, more assets than debts, and debtor bankrupt on his own petition); C. Hand (1981) 97 L.Q.R. 200; A. Sydenham [1982] Conv. 74; C. Hand [1983] Conv. 219; I. Goldrein (2011) 41 Fam. Law 1227. For the equity of exoneration, see *Re Pittortou* [1985] 1 W.L.R. 58.

[230] *Re Gorman* [1990] 1 W.L.R. 616.

[231] *Re Citro* [1991] Ch. 142 at 157 (bankruptcy prior to Insolvency Act 1986). See also *Barclays Bank plc v Hendricks* [1996] 1 F.L.R. 258.

[232] 1982, Cmnd. 8558. Some jurisdictions offer greater protection by "homestead legislation". See Joint Family Homes Act 1964 (New Zealand); Gray, *Elements of Land Law*, 5th edn, 2009, p.1016; P. Omar [2006] Conv. 157.

[233] "Spouse" now includes a registered civil partner; s.335A as amended by the Civil Partnership Act 2004.

(i) the conduct of the spouse or former spouse, so far as contributing to the bankruptcy,
(ii) the needs and financial resources of the spouse or former spouse, and
(iii) the needs of any children; and

(c) all the circumstances of the case other than the needs of the bankrupt.[234]

11–026   Where, however, the application is made after a year from the vesting in the trustee in bankruptcy, the court must assume that the interests of the creditors outweigh all other considerations save in exceptional circumstances. These do not include the needs of the bankrupt.[235] It has been said that "exceptional circumstances" reflects the same test as has been applied in the case law prior to the 1986 Act.[236] This provision, therefore, gives some protection to the family by delaying the sale, but the trustee will normally succeed after a year. Some recent decisions, however, reveal a more "humanitarian" approach.[237] There are similar provisions relating to occupation orders under s.33 of the Family Law Act 1996 in cases of bankruptcy.[238]

The trustee in bankruptcy may apply under s.14 of the 1996 Act for the sale of a jointly owned home even where the bankrupt's spouse is entitled to occupy under an order of the divorce court postponing sale until her remarriage or some other future event.[239] Such an order does not give the spouse an absolute right to occupy until one of the specified events happens. Whether the trustee will succeed depends on the application of s.335A of the 1986 Act.

A question which has been aired in recent cases is whether s.335A is compatible with art.8 of the European Convention on

---

[234] The "needs" of the bankrupt include his financial, medical, emotional and mental needs; *Everitt v Budhram (A Bankrupt)* [2010] Ch. 170.

[235] *Everitt v Budhram (A Bankrupt)* [2010] Ch. 170.

[236] *Re Citro* [1991] Ch. 142 (in the context of s.336); J. Hall (1991) 50 C.L.J. 45; S. Cretney (1991) 107 L.Q.R. 177; A. Lawson [1991] Conv. 302; D. Brown (1992) 55 M.L.R. 284.

[237] *Judd v Brown, Bankrupts* [1998] 2 F.L.R. 360 (no order for sale where bankrupt's wife being treated for cancer); *Re Raval (A Bankrupt)* [1998] 2 F.L.R. 718 (order suspended for a year where bankrupt's wife mentally ill); *Claughton v Charalamabous* [1999] 1 F.L.R. 740 (order suspended until bankrupt's wife, who was chronically ill and had reduced life expectancy, vacated the house or died); *Re Haghighat (A Bankrupt)* [2009] 1 F.L.R. 1271 (order suspended for 3 years as wife cared for vulnerable adult child at home). The appeal was dismissed at [2010] EWCA Civ 1521. See also *Re Bremner (A Bankrupt)* [1999] 1 F.L.R. 912 (where bankrupt husband terminally ill, elderly wife's need to care for him at home was an "exceptional circumstance").

[238] Insolvency Act 1986, ss.336, 337, as amended. See *Re Bremner (A Bankrupt)*, above, fn.237. These provisions now apply to civil partners; Civil Partnership Act 2004, s.82 and Sch.9.

[239] *Avis v Turner* [2008] Ch. 218. An order for sale was granted; *Turner v Avis* [2009] 1 F.L.R. 74.

Human Rights, which protects the right to respect for the home.[240] In *Barca v Mears*[241] it was suggested that the interpretation of the section might need to be reconsidered in the light of art.8, but the point was left open. The question was further debated in *Nicholls v Lan*,[242] where the wife's schizophrenia was an "exceptional" circumstance, but she co-owned another house. It was held that s.335A was not inconsistent with the qualified rights protected by art.8. It was added that the interests of creditors should not be dismissed just because there was no specific evidence of their identities or concerns. It appears, therefore, that the right to respect for the home is a consideration to be weighed in the balance, but that arguments based on art.8 are unlikely to prevail. Indeed, "it is difficult to escape the conclusion that little more than a nod has been accorded to the effect of the [Human Rights] Act upon the meaning of 'exceptional circumstances'."[243]

The Enterprise Act 2002[244] affords some relief to the bankrupt in relation to property which was the residence of the bankrupt or his spouse or former spouse at the date of the bankruptcy. If the trustee in bankruptcy has not sold the property or applied for an order for possession or sale within three years of that date, the property revests in the bankrupt and ceases to be available to creditors.

---

[240] Article 8 is set out in Sch.1 of the Human Rights Act 1998.

[241] [2005] 2 F.L.R. 1; M. Dixon [2005] Conv. 161; A. Baker [2010] Conv. 352. See also *Donohoe v Ingram* [2006] 2 F.L.R. 1084; *Holtham v Kelmanson* [2007] W.T.L.R. 285.

[242] [2007] 1 F.L.R. 744; M. Pawlowski [2007] Conv. 78. Sale was ordered but postponed for 18 months. See also *National Westminster Bank Plc v Rushmer* [2010] 2 F.L.R. 362.

[243] *Official Receiver for Northern Ireland v Rooney* [2009] 2 F.L.R. 1437 at 1449 (on the equivalent legislation in N. Ireland).

[244] s.261, inserting s.283A into the Insolvency Act 1986, with effect from April 1, 2004. "Spouse" includes a registered civil partner.

CONSTRUCTIVE TRUSTS

1. GENERAL

A CONSTRUCTIVE trust is one which arises by operation of law, and **12–001** not by reason of the intention of the parties, express or implied.[1]

"English law provides no clear and all-embracing definition of a constructive trust. Its boundaries have been left perhaps deliberately vague, so as not to restrict the court by technicalities in deciding what the justice of a particular case may demand".[2]

[1] For a different view, see C. Rickett (1999) 18 N.Z.U.L.R. 305.
[2] *Carl Zeiss Stiftung v Herbert Smith & Co* [1969] 2 Ch. 276 at 300, per Edmund Davies L.J.

"It is impossible to prescribe exhaustively the circumstances sufficient to create a constructive trust but it is possible to recognise
particular factual circumstances that will do so and also to recognise other factual circumstances that will not."[3]

It has been "a ready means of developing our property law in
modern times."[4] The principle is that where a person who holds
property in circumstances in which in equity and good conscience it
should be held or enjoyed by another, he will be compelled to hold
the property on trust for that other.[5] Such a statement can be criticised as being too general to be helpful. It used to be said that equity
had developed pragmatically in this field, relying on the precedents
and paying too little attention to the general principle. Subsequently
the pendulum swung the other way, and a constructive trust was
used as a means of reaching a desired result over a wide variety of
cases; constructive trusts of a "new model",[6] "wherever justice and
good conscience require it".[7] The "new model" is now consigned to
history.[8] Modern developments have caused Lord Millett to say that
"At present the language of constructive trust has become such a
fertile source of confusion that it would be better if it were abandoned".[9] The confusion could be avoided if the term were to be
confined to "a situation in which it would be unconscionable for one
party to deny the other's beneficial proprietary interest in a particular and identified property".[10] Finally, the court will not impose a
constructive trust if it would be inconsistent with an express trust
whose terms cover the situation.[11]

A. Overlap in Classification

12–002   We saw, in discussing the classification of trusts,[12] that there is an
overlap between resulting and constructive trusts. Normally it
makes little practical difference whether a trust is described as constructive or resulting. The formality rules, for example, apply to

---

[3] *Yeoman's Row Management Ltd v Cobbe* [2008] 1 W.L.R. 1752 at 1769 (Lord Scott).
[4] *Sen v Headley* [1991] Ch. 425 at 440 (Nourse L.J.).
[5] See *Beatty v Guggenheim Exploration Co* 225 N.Y. 380 at 386 (1919); *Soar v Ashwell*
[1893] 2 Q.B. 390; Lord Millett [1999] 14 *Amicus Curiae* 4; Waters, *The Constructive Trust*,
1964; Oakley, *Constructive Trusts*; Elias, *Explaining Constructive Trusts*, 2002; Mitchell
(ed.), *Constructive and Resulting Trusts*, 2009.
[6] *Eves v Eves* [1975] 1 W.L.R. 1338 at 1341.
[7] *Hussey v Palmer* [1972] 1 W.L.R. 1286 at 1290, per Lord Denning M.R.
[8] Below, para.12–043.
[9] (1995) 9 T.L.I. 35 at 38.
[10] (1995) 9 T.L.I. 35 at 39. See also *Paragon Finance Plc v DB Thakerar & Co (A Firm)*
[1999] 1 All E.R. 401 at 409.
[11] *McGuane v Welch* [2009] W.T.L.R. 1201.
[12] Above, para.2–028.

neither type.[13] But the tendency to merge the two categories makes any definition of a constructive trust even harder to formulate.

> "It has been suggested that nomenclature in this context is unimportant. There is, however, some risk that confusion of terminology may lead to confusion of thought".[14]

Distinctions have been emphasised in the context of the conflict of laws, where it has been said that a resulting trust involves the claim of an equitable owner to assert a continuing proprietary interest in his own property, while a constructive trust may be imposed in appropriate circumstances where a breach of fiduciary obligation has given rise to an equity between the parties.[15] Similarly in the context of family property, where a common intention may found a constructive trust which is quantified differently from the proportionate shares arising under a resulting trust.[16]

The constructive trust is usually regarded as a residual category; one which is called into play where the court desires to impose a trust and no other suitable category is available.[17]

B. Establishing the Existence or the Terms of the Trust

The imposition of a constructive trust is often a determination that **12–003** previously declared trusts are enforceable against someone other than the original trustee, or extend to additional property.[18] Thus, a recipient of trust property, not being a bona fide purchaser without notice from a trustee, takes the property subject to the existing trusts. A trustee who makes an improper profit holds the profit on the trusts

---

[13] LPA 1925 s.53, above, para.3–004.
[14] The Child & Co Oxford Lecture (1984) "The Informal Creation of Interests in Land," at p.4 (Sir Christopher Slade); cf. F. Bates [1982] Conv. 424 at 431.
[15] *Macmillan Inc v Bishopsgate Investment Trust plc (No.3)* [1995] 1 W.L.R. 978; affirmed on other grounds (to which the distinction was not relevant) at [1996] 1 W.L.R. 387. See also *Westdeutsche Landesbank Girozentrale v Islington LBC* [1996] A.C. 669 at 707.
[16] *Drake v Whipp* [1996] 1 F.L.R. 826; above, para.11–008 (lax terminology a "potent source of confusion"); *Stack v Dowden* [2007] 2 A.C. 432.
[17] Recent examples include *James v Williams* [2000] Ch. 1 (intestacy beneficiary who took possession of land was constructive trustee for co-beneficiaries so that no limitation period applied); cf. *Nolan v Nolan* [2004] W.T.L.R. 1261; *Ord v Upton* [2000] Ch. 352 (cause of action vesting in claimant's trustee in bankruptcy held on constructive trust for claimant so far as it related to damages for pain and suffering as opposed to financial loss); *Banner Homes Group Plc v Luff Developments Ltd* [2000] Ch. 372 (if A and B informally agree that A shall acquire specific property for joint benefit and B in reliance thereon refrains from attempting to acquire it, A cannot retain the whole benefit and is constructive trustee of a share for B); M. Thompson [2001] Conv. 265; B. McFarlane (2004) 120 L.Q.R. 667. For criticisms, see P. Clarke All E.R. Rev. 2000, p.245; N. Hopkins [2002] Conv. 35. See also *Hughes v Lloyd* [2008] W.T.L.R. 485 (constructive trust for carer of past care element of damages award); *De Bruyne v De Bruyne* [2010] W.T.L.R. 1525).
[18] Bowen L.J. in *Soar v Ashwell* [1893] 2 Q.B. 390 at 396.

which had previously been declared of the property out of which the profit was made.[19]

It may be, however, that the constructive trust doctrine will determine the trusts on which a person, admittedly a trustee, will hold the property. Thus, in a case of mutual wills, the executor of the second party to die needs to know whether he holds on the trusts of that party's will, or under the agreement which was the basis of the mutual wills.[20] Thus the constructive trust covers situations in which either the existence of the trusteeship or the terms of the trust or both are determined by operation of law.

C. The Duties of a Constructive Trustee

12–004   The duties and liabilities of a constructive trustee are not necessarily the same as those of an express trustee. A decision that X holds as constructive trustee does not necessarily subject him to the usual trustees' duties in respect of investments, etc.[21] If a person purchases property with constructive but not actual notice of a trust, the beneficiaries may enforce the trust against him; but if he is not informed of their claims for some time, it seems that he will not be subjected also to liability for failure to invest in trustee investments and to the usual standard of care which is required of express trustees in the performance of their duties.[22] The duties of a constructive trustee have not been made clear; they probably vary with the circumstances and will be greater for a fraudulent trustee than for others.

D. Distinction Between Constructive Trusts, Accountability and Proprietary Remedies

12–005   Circumstances giving rise to a constructive trust may give rise to other remedies also. Strictly speaking a person can only be a trustee, express or constructive, if there is vested in him certain property which he holds upon trust.[23] Constructive trusteeship should be distinguished from the equitable proprietary remedy of tracing, and a personal action in equity against a fiduciary for an account. They are considered in more detail below.[24]

Where a trustee (express or constructive) has had trust property vested in him but has wrongfully disposed of it, he will commonly

---

[19] Below, para.12–009.

[20] Below, para.12–026.

[21] See *Lonrho plc v Fayed (No.2)* [1992] 1 W.L.R. 1 at 12. See also *Jasmine Trustees Ltd v Wells & Hind (A Firm)* [2007] 1 All E.R. 1142, discussing the liabilities of a "trustee de son tort."

[22] For examples of where the duty to invest arises, see C. Mitchell and S. Watterson in C. Mitchell (ed.), *Constructive and Resulting Trusts*, pp.138–140.

[23] *Re Barney* [1892] 2 Ch. 265 at 272; *Westdeutsche Landesbank Girozentrale v Islington LBC* [1996] A.C. 669.

[24] Below, Chs 21, 23.

be regarded as retaining his status as trustee. Subject to what is said below concerning tracing, the absence of trust property means that the remedy against him is personal only. Where, however, no trust property has ever been vested in the defendant (as where liability arises from dishonestly assisting the trustees in a breach of trust),[25] he cannot properly be called a trustee, constructive or otherwise. As in the previous example, the remedy against him is personal only. The defendant is *accountable*; he is not a constructive trustee of any property. If he has insufficient assets, the claimant will be unable to obtain compensation in full.

There is, however, another possibility. It may be possible to show that the property, wrongly obtained and disposed of, is now represented by money or by some other property in the trustee's or a third party's hands; and, by use of the equitable proprietary remedy, to "follow" the original property into that for which it has been exchanged. This is done by the technique of "tracing".[26]

The advantages of "tracing" the money (or other property) in this way are twofold. First, if the defendant should become insolvent, the claimant takes in priority to the general creditors, for the money "traced" is trust money, and is kept out of the defendant's insolvency.[27] Secondly, if the money has been invested successfully by the defendant, the claimant is entitled to a share of the investments which is proportionate to the share which the trust money contributed to the invested fund.[28] A distinction between constructive trusteeship and liability to the "tracing" process is that the latter may be available against a person who is not liable as constructive trustee. For example, where trust property is transferred to an innocent volunteer, i.e. a person who is not a purchaser and who thus takes subject to the trust but who has neither actual nor constructive knowledge of it, the volunteer is apparently not liable as constructive trustee,[29] but the "tracing" remedy lies against him while he still has the property or its identifiable proceeds.[30]

There are thus three separate matters to consider: constructive trusts, proprietary remedies, and personal actions. They are all interrelated, but each is distinct. Many decisions fail to make these distinctions, and fail to make clear whether the issue is one of accountability or one of trust,[31] although the matter has recently

---

[25] Below, para.12–011.

[26] Below, para.23–042.

[27] *Re Hallett's Estate* (1880) 13 Ch.D. 696.

[28] *Re Tilley's WT* [1967] Ch. 1179.

[29] Below, para.12–016. The view that the innocent volunteer is personally liable is discussed below, para.12–021.

[30] *Re Diplock* [1948] Ch. 465, below, para.23–066.

[31] *Reading v Att Gen* [1951] A.C. 507; *Boardman v Phipps* [1967] 2 A.C. 46.

been clarified by the Court of Appeal.[32] This chapter will examine constructive trusts properly so called and also certain cases of personal liability which have traditionally (but inappropriately) been treated as constructive trusteeship. Accountability for profits and the question of liability to proprietary remedies are considered later.[33]

E. The Remedial Constructive Trust

12–006 We saw that the duties of a constructive trustee differ from those of an ordinary trustee, although the extent of the difference is unclear. If the claimant merely wishes to have the property returned, the question is whether a constructive trust need be considered as anything beyond a means of demanding the return of the property to which he is entitled in equity.[34]

Such a constructive trust is regarded as a "remedial rather than substantive" institution.[35] The constructive trust is imposed under this doctrine whenever it is needed to prevent unjust enrichment. Like other equitable remedies, it is available where the legal remedy is inadequate. Thus, in a case of unjust enrichment the claimant will bring a common law personal action; but if the defendant still has the property, and either the claimant wants specific recovery, or the defendant is insolvent, or the property has increased in value, the claimant will be able to assert a constructive trust.[36] The English cases have however, traditionally regarded the constructive trust as a substantive institution,[37] vindicating a pre-existing proprietary right.

The existence of such a doctrine has been left open by the Privy Council.[38] Millett J., however, warned that, while equity must be flexible, "its intervention must be based on principle; there must be some relationship between the relief granted and the circumstances which give rise to it".[39] To which his Lordship has added:

[32] *Sinclair Investments (UK) Ltd v Versailles Trade Finance Ltd (in administrative receivership)* [2011] 3 W.L.R. 1153; D. Hayton (2011) 127 L.Q.R. 487 and (2011) 25 T.L.I. 3; cf. R. Goode (2011) 127 L.Q.R. 493; G. Virgo (2011) 70 C.L.J. 502; below, para.21–028.
[33] Below, Chs 21, 23.
[34] See A. Scott (1955) 71 L.Q.R. 71; *Carl Zeiss Stiftung v Herbert Smith & Co* [1969] 2 Ch. 276 at 300.
[35] R. Pound (1920) 33 Harv.L.R. 420. See also R. Goode (1983) 3 L.S. 283 at 292; D. Hayton [1988] Conv. 259; C. Rickett (1991) 107 L.Q.R. 608; Elias, *Explaining Constructive Trusts*, 2002, pp.159–163; Wright, *The Remedial Constructive Trust*, 1998.
[36] See *Lac Minerals Ltd v International Corona Resources Ltd* (1989) 61 D.L.R. (4th) 14.
[37] See *Re Sharpe* [1980] 1 W.L.R. 219, where the notion of imposing a constructive trust as a remedy was described as a novel concept in English law.
[38] *Re Goldcorp Exchange Ltd (In Receivership)* [1995] 1 A.C. 74; cf. *Metall und Rohstoff AG v Donaldson Lufkin & Jenrette Inc* [1990] 1 Q.B. 391 at 479 (overruled on another point by *Lonrho Plc v Fayed* [1992] 1 A.C. 448).
[39] *Lonrho Plc v Fayed (No.2)* [1992] 1 W.L.R. 1 at 9 (no constructive trust where claim had no proprietary base). See also Sir Peter Millett (1991) 107 L.Q.R. 71 at 85.

"[T]here is neither room nor need for the remedial constructive trust. In my view it is a counsel of despair which too readily concedes the impossibility of propounding a general rationale for the availability of proprietary remedies. We need to be more ready to categorise wrongdoers as fiduciaries and to extend the situations in which proprietary remedies are made available, but we can do all this while adhering to established principles".[40]

Similarly, "the remedial constructive trust is a judicial discretion to vary property rights and, as such, an object of suspicion".[41] Lord Browne-Wilkinson, on the other hand, suggested that the introduction of the remedial constructive trust may provide a satisfactory basis for developing proprietary restitutionary remedies.[42]

The question arose in *Halifax Building Society v Thomas*,[43] where **12–007** the defendant obtained a mortgage loan to buy a flat by fraudulent misrepresentation. When he fell into arrears the mortgagee sold the flat. After the repayment of the debt a surplus remained, to which the mortgagee claimed entitlement under a constructive trust in its favour, to prevent the defendant profiting from his fraud. In rejecting this claim the Court of Appeal noted that English law had not followed other jurisdictions where the constructive trust had become a remedy for unjust enrichment. There was no universal principle that there must be restitution of a benefit derived from wrongdoing. The relationship was not fiduciary but was merely one of debtor and secured creditor. The mortgagee had recovered all it was contractually entitled to, and the surplus belonged to the defendant. It was thus available for confiscation under Pt VI of the Criminal Justice Act 1988, the enactment of which indicated that the profits of crime did not belong to the victim. This was also the approach of the Court of Appeal in *Re Polly Peck International Plc (In Administration) (No.2)*,[44] where it was said that there was no prospect of the imposition of a remedial constructive trust[45] on the assets of an insolvent company so as to give the claimants a proprietary interest, to the detriment of creditors. To do so would confer a priority not accorded by the insolvency legislation. Although the law moves, it:

---

[40] (1995) 9 T.L.I. 35 at 40. See also *Paragon Finance Plc v DB Thakerar & Co (A Firm)* [1999] 1 All E.R. 401 at 413: the distinction between institutional trusts and the remedial formula is the distinction "between a trust and a catch-phrase".

[41] *The Frontiers of Liability*, Vol.2, p.24, P. Birks; cf. at 165, D. Waters and 186, S. Gardner. See also P. Birks [1996] R.L.R. 3; Oakley, *Constructive Trusts*, 3rd edn, p.26; Goff and Jones, 7th edn, p.89. The remedial constructive trust is considered unavailable in Jersey; *Re the Esteem Settlement* [2004] W.T.L.R. 1.

[42] *Westdeutsche Landesbank Girozentrale v Islington LBC* [1996] A.C. 669 at 716.

[43] [1996] Ch. 217; P. Birks (1996) 10 T.L.I. 2; P. Watts (1996) 112 L.Q.R. 219; P. Jaffey [1996] R.L.R. 92.

[44] [1998] 3 All E.R. 812. See also *Fortex Group Ltd v MacIntosh* [1998] 3 N.Z.L.R. 171.

[45] Defined by Nourse L.J. at 830 as the grant of a proprietary right, as a remedy, to someone who, beforehand, had no such right.

"[C]annot be legitimately moved by judicial decision down a road signed 'No Entry' by Parliament. The insolvency road is blocked off to remedial constructive trusts, at least when judge-driven in a vehicle of discretion".[46]

Nourse L.J. emphasised that his conclusions were not confined to insolvency, because property rights could only be varied by statute.[47] The decision has been said to be "the end of the remedial constructive trust"[48]; similarly, "It bangs the door shut on the 'remedial constructive trust' in this jurisdiction".[49] Recent decisions appear to have left the door closed.[50] The Court of Appeal has confirmed that the remedial constructive trust is not recognised in this jurisdiction because the existence of a proprietary interest is a matter of property law, not a matter of discretion.[51] On the other hand, Lord Scott has suggested that cases involving representations about inheritance prospects should be treated as giving rise to a remedial constructive trust rather than proprietary estoppel, but the other members of the House of Lords based their decision firmly on proprietary estoppel.[52] It may also be noted that one commentator considers that the constructive trust deployed in *Stack v Dowden*[53] was a radical departure from the institutional constructive trust giving rise to an identifiable property right before judgment, and was in fact a discretionary remedial constructive trust giving proprietary restitutionary relief for unjust enrichment, although the decision of the House of Lords was not couched in those terms.[54]

The remedial constructive trust has been accepted in Australia,[55] New Zealand[56] and Canada[57] (although the Canadian courts have

[46] [1998] 3 All E.R. 812 at 827, per Mummery L.J.

[47] [1998] 3 All E.R. 812 at 831.

[48] P. Birks (1998) 12 T.L.I. 202. See also Sir Peter Millett (1998) 114 L.Q.R. 399; P. Matthews (1998) 4 *Trusts & Trustees* 14; C. Rickett and R. Grantham [1999] L.M.C.L.Q. 111.

[49] P. Birks and W. Swadling All E.R. Rev. 1998 at 415; cf. D. Wright [1999] R.L.R. 128. See also Law Com. Discussion Paper, *Sharing Homes* (2002), p.25, fn.92: "there has been a relatively steadfast refusal to develop constructive trusts as a purely remedial device."

[50] *Ultraframe (UK) Ltd v Fielding* [2007] W.T.L.R. 835 at 881; *Turner v Jacob* [2008] W.T.L.R. 307 at 332; *De Bruyne v De Bruyne* [2010] W.T.L.R. 1525 at 1541.

[51] *Sinclair Investments (UK) Ltd v Versailles Trade Finance Ltd (in administrative receivership)* [2011] 3 W.L.R. 1153 at 1165, applying *Foskett v McKeown* [2001] A.C. 102 at 109.

[52] *Thorner v Major* [2009] 1 W.L.R. 776; below, para.27–022.

[53] [2007] 2 A.C. 432; above, para.11–004.

[54] T. Etherton (2008) 67 C.L.J. 265 and [2009] Conv. 104.

[55] *Muschinski v Dodds* (1985) 160 C.L.R. 583; K. Mason [2007] 15 R.L.R. 1.

[56] *Powell v Thompson* [1991] 1 N.Z.L.R. 579 at 615 ("a broad equitable remedy for reversing that which is inequitable or unconscionable"); *Equiticorp Industries Group Ltd v Hawkins* [1991] 3 N.Z.L.R. 700. But caution is needed in insolvency cases; *Fortex Group Ltd v MacIntosh*, above, fn.44.

[57] *Pettkus v Becker* (1980) 117 D.L.R. (3d) 257; *Sorochan v Sorochan* (1986) 29 D.L.R. (4th) 1; *Lac Minerals Ltd v International Corona Resources Ltd* (1989) 61 D.L.R. (4th) 14; G. Hammond (1990) 106 L.Q.R. 207; *Rawluk v Rawluk* (1990) 65 D.L.R. (4th) 161; C. Rickett [1991] Conv. 125; G. Fridman (1991) 11 L.S. 304; *Peter v Beblow* (1993) 101 D.L.R. (4th) 621; N. Richardson (2002) 16 T.L.I. 53.

recognised it more in the case of property disputes between cohabitees than in the commercial context[58]). It has not replaced the traditional institutional constructive trust, but exists alongside it.[59]

One distinction between institutional and remedial constructive trusts may lie in the date from which the claimant may assert proprietary rights. This question has significance for third parties acquiring interests in the property before the court makes its order. It seems clear that the traditional institutional constructive trust vindicates a pre-existing proprietary interest which is operative before the date of the court order.[60] The effect of a remedial constructive trust, on the other hand, may be to confer a new proprietary interest on the claimant.[61] In such a case it will have prospective effect only, operating from the date of the court order which creates it.[62]

We will now examine the circumstances in which a constructive trust has been held to exist.

2. WHEN A CONSTRUCTIVE TRUST ARISES

Constructive trusts can arise over a wide variety of situations. No claim is made that those discussed in this section cover the whole field; they are merely illustrations. It will be seen that some of the selected categories lay down specific rules; others rely on general principles, which have been stated in the widest terms. **12–008**

A. Unauthorised Profit by a Trustee or Fiduciary

The principle is that a fiduciary may not make use of his position to gain a benefit for himself. Trustees, personal representatives and agents[63] are by their position "debarred from keeping a personal advantage derived directly or indirectly out of his fiduciary or quasi-fiduciary position."[64] With other fiduciaries, such as company directors[65] and partners,[66] the question is one of fact whether the benefit **12–009**

---

[58] L. Smith [2003] 11 R.L.R. 163. For an overview, see R. Chambers [2006] 14 R.L.R. 146; H. Delany and D. Ryan [2008] Conv. 401 at pp.415–424.

[59] *Muschinski v Dodds*, above, fn.55 at 613–615.

[60] This is assumed in the English cases such as *Lloyds Bank Plc v Rosset* [1991] 1 A.C. 107; above, para.11–008. See *Westdeutsche Landesbank Girozentrale v Islington LBC*, above, fn.42, at 716.

[61] *Lac Minerals Ltd v International Corona Resources Ltd*, above, fn.57, at 50. The term "imposed proprietary remedy" is preferred in C. Rickett (1999) 18 N.Z.U.L.R. 305 at 331.

[62] *Muschinski v Dodds* (1985) 160 C.L.R. 583 at 615; cf. *Rawluk v Rawluk*, above, fn.57. A similar question arises as to the date on which an estoppel interest takes effect, below, para.27–031. The claim in *Polly Peck*, above, fn.44 was that the remedial constructive trust should be imposed retrospectively.

[63] *De Bussche v Alt* (1878) 8 Ch.D. 286 at 310; *Boardman v Phipps* [1967] 2 A.C. 67.

[64] *Re Biss* [1903] 2 Ch. 40 at 56.

[65] Below, paras 21–019–21–021.

[66] *Clegg v Fishwick* (1849) 1 Mac. & G. 294.

was obtained by reason or independently of, the fiduciary relationship. The category of fiduciaries is not closed.[67]

These matters are dealt with in Ch.21. We will there see that a trustee must not renew in his own favour any lease held on trust; nor may he purchase the reversion on any such lease; nor may he purchase the trust property. He must not make any incidental profits out of his trusteeship. In the present context, one example must suffice.

> In *Boardman v Phipps*,[68] the trustees held a minority shareholding in a private company which was not being efficiently managed. Boardman had acted as solicitor to the trust, and was therefore a fiduciary. He decided that the beneficiaries would be in a better position if the trustees had control of the company, but no trust money was available to buy the extra shares. Boardman and one of the beneficiaries therefore bought the necessary shares themselves and reorganised the company. All this was done in good faith and with the object of enhancing the trust holding. Both the personal and the trust holdings increased in value. A majority of the House of Lords held that Boardman was constructive trustee of the profit made on his personal shareholding. The opportunity to make the profit arose out of his fiduciary relationship with the trust and certain confidential information had been used in the process. However, compensation was ordered from the trust in recognition of the work and skill involved.

B. Liability of Third Parties

12–010   Third parties may incur personal liability (in addition to the trustees' liability) in certain circumstances, in particular where they dishonestly assist the trustee (or other fiduciary) in a breach of duty, or where they receive trust property transferred in breach of trust. Such persons are commonly called constructive trustees,[69] although this is misleading because the liability is personal only. The two categories were until recently known as "knowing assistance" and "knowing receipt".[70] As explained below, the terminology in the first case is no longer appropriate. The terms "accessory liability" and "recipient liability" may be preferable. Whatever the heading of liability, the existence of the trust must be established.[71] Knowledge

[67] *English v Dedham Vale Properties Ltd* [1978] 1 W.L.R. 93.
[68] [1967] 2 A.C. 67, below, para.21–022.
[69] Lord Millett considers the "receipt" cases to be examples of resulting trusts; (1995) 9 T.L.I. 35 at 39; *Macmillan Inc v Bishopsgate Investment Trust Plc (No.3)* [1995] 1 W.L.R. 978. Similarly Chambers, *Resulting Trusts* (Ch.8).
[70] The categories were based on Lord Selborne's speech in *Barnes v Addy* (1874) L.R. 9 Ch. App. 244 at 251–252.
[71] See *Box v Barclays Bank Plc* [1998] Lloyd's Rep. Bank. 185.

of a "doubtful equity" does not suffice; hence a solicitor was not accountable for moneys received in payment of costs and expenses paid by a client for work done in defending an action in which the claimant was asserting that the client was a trustee of the whole of its assets.[72] It would be otherwise if he knew that the claim was well-founded. A defendant may be liable even though he does not know what a trust means.[73]

i. Dishonest Assistance

(a) *Terminology.* An agent or other third party may be liable to **12–011** make good the loss to a trust without the trust property ever vesting in him and without his purporting to act as trustee; as where an agent dishonestly participates with a trustee in a breach of trust. Thus liability does not depend on unjust enrichment.

It is submitted that, as no trust property is or has been vested in him, he should not be called a constructive, or any other kind of trustee.[74] The question at issue is one of personal liability. The matter will nevertheless be dealt with in this chapter because the constructive trust terminology has been used in much of the case law,[75] although Lord Millett has said that the words "accountable as constructive trustee" should be discarded in favour of "accountable in equity".[76] One explanation is that the constructive trustee label has been used to overcome the supposed difficulty in a beneficiary being able to sue anybody but the trustee.[77] It might be added that, if it should become established that an innocent volunteer is strictly liable for receipt of trust property on a restitutionary

---

[72] *Carl Zeiss Stiftung v Herbert Smith & Co (No.2)* [1969] 2 Ch. 276; PVB (1969) 85 L.Q.R. 160; C. Harpum (1986) 102 L.Q.R. 267 at 287. See also *Williams v Williams* (1881) 17 Ch.D. 437; *Competitive Insurance Co Ltd v Davies Investments Ltd* [1975] 1 W.L.R. 1240. A solicitor in doubt as to possible liability should apply to court for directions; *Finers v Miro* [1991] 1 W.L.R. 35. See also *United Mizrahi Bank Ltd v Doherty* [1998] 1 W.L.R. 435; *Bank of Scotland (Governor and Company) v A Ltd* [2001] 1 W.L.R. 751 (where bank suspects client).

[73] *Barlow Clowes International Ltd (In Liquidation) v Eurotrust International Ltd* [2006] 1 W.L.R. 1476.

[74] See P. Birks in McKendrick's *Commercial Aspects of Trusts and Fiduciary Obligations*, 1992, Ch.8; cf. S. Elliott and C. Mitchell (2004) 67 M.L.R. 16. A person who dishonestly assists in a breach of trust is not a trustee within s.21(1)(a) of the Limitation Act 1980 (below, para.23–036), and so the six-year rule applies; *Cattley v Pollard* [2007] Ch. 353; cf. *Statek Corp v Alford* [2008] W.T.L.R. 1089; C. Mitchell [2008] Conv. 226; D. Hayton (2008) 22 T.L.I. 81.

[75] See *Westdeutsche Landesbank Girozentrale v Islington LBC* [1996] A.C. 669 at 705; *Ghana Commercial Bank v C, The Times*, March 3, 1997.

[76] *Dubai Aluminium Co Ltd v Salaam* [2003] 2 A.C. 366 at 404. See also *Paragon Finance Plc v DB Thakerar & Co (A Firm)* [1999] 1 All E.R. 401 at 412; *Peconic Industrial Developments Ltd v Lau* [2009] W.T.L.R. 999.

[77] L. Smith (1999) 58 C.L.J. 294 at 299, 301. The term "remedial constructive trust" is used in *Coulthard v Disco Mix Club Ltd* [2000] 1 W.L.R. 707 at 731, but that term normally implies a proprietary remedy.

basis,[78] the term "constructive trustee" could usefully be employed to indicate the more onerous personal liability which results from receipt with knowledge.[79]

12–012   (b) *Nature of Trustee's Breach.* In *Barnes v Addy*,[80] Lord Selborne laid down the test of liability as that of as assisting "with knowledge in a dishonest and fraudulent design on the part of the trustees." This statement was obiter, but the principle that the third party could not be liable under this heading unless the breach of trust in which he assisted was dishonest on the part of the trustee became entrenched in the law until clarified by the Privy Council in *Royal Brunei Airlines Sdn Bhd v Tan*.[81]

> The claimant appointed a company (BLT) to act as its travel agent and to account for the proceeds of ticket sales. It was conceded that BLT committed a breach of trust by using the money in its business. BLT fell into arrears in accounting and the contract was terminated. As BLT was insolvent, the claimant sued Tan, the principal shareholder and director. It was conceded that Tan had assisted in the breach with actual knowledge. The Brunei Court of Appeal found for Tan, holding that the breach in which he had assisted had not been shown to be fraudulent on the part of BLT. The appeal to the Privy Council centred upon the question whether accessory liability requires the breach of trust itself to be fraudulent. Tan was held personally liable for dishonestly assisting BLT's breach. There was no further requirement of dishonesty by BLT.[82]

Lord Nicholls of Birkenhead reviewed the authorities prior to *Barnes v Addy*.[83] Those authorities did not require dishonesty on the part of the trustee whether the third party had procured the breach[84] or merely assisted in it. The law had taken a wrong turning in

[78] Below, para.12–021.
[79] See J. Martin [1998] Conv. 13. See also C. Mitchell and S. Watterson in C. Mitchell (ed.), *Constructive and Resulting Trusts*, p.130, defending the terminology in receipt cases.
[80] (1874) L.R. 9 Ch.App. 255 at 251, 252.
[81] [1995] 2 A.C. 378; M. Halliwell [1995] Conv. 339; C. Harpum (1995) 111 L.Q.R. 545; R. Nolan (1995) 54 C.L.J. 505; J. Stevens (1995) 3 R.L.R. 105; S. Gardner (1996) 112 L.Q.R. 56; M. Tugendhat in F. Rose (ed.) *Restitution and Banking Law*, Ch.9; C. Mitchell in Birks and Pretto (eds) *Breach of Trust*, Ch.6. For criticisms, see P. Birks (1996) L.M.C.L.Q. 1; A. Berg (1996) 59 M.L.R. 443.
[82] In fact BLT's breach was dishonest because Tan's state of mind could be imputed to it. See *El Ajou v Dollar Land Holdings Plc* [1994] 2 All E.R. 685 ("directing mind and will").
[83] Above, fn.80.
[84] See *Eaves v Hickson* (1861) Beav. 136 (trustees innocently deceived by forgery made wrongful distribution which the party responsible for the deceit was liable to restore). A modern authority not requiring dishonesty by the trustees is *Powell v Thompson* [1991] 1 N.Z.L.R. 597. See also *Hurstanger Ltd v Wilson* [2007] 1 W.L.R. 2351 (third party who procured a breach of fiduciary duty must pay "equitable compensation").

reliance on Lord Selborne's dictum in *Barnes v Addy*. The trustee would be liable whether or not the breach was dishonest, but it would make no sense for a dishonest accessory, whose liability is fault-based, to escape simply because the trustee did not also act dishonestly. Although cases where the accessory is dishonest but the trustee is not will be rare, especially where the trustee is a company of which the accessories are directors,[85] this is a welcome clarification of the law.

Provided it is established that the breach caused the loss, there is no need to prove a causal link between the assistance and the loss.[86] It has been held that a dishonest assistant is jointly and severally liable with the trustee for any loss but is accountable only for his own share of any profit from the breach.[87]

(c) *Dishonesty of Third Party.* The next question is whether the **12–013** accessory must be shown to have acted dishonestly, or whether constructive knowledge of the breach (i.e. negligence) suffices. This is a matter of great importance, because frauds and other breaches of duty in the commercial context are complex, and can involve participants who are unaware of the wrongdoing.

Opinions have differed as to whether dishonesty is required on the part of the accessory or whether it suffices that he ought to have known of the breach. The weight of modern authority supports the view that dishonesty is required, and the matter has now been put beyond doubt by the Privy Council in *Royal Brunei Airlines Sdn Bhd v Tan*.[88] Although the main issue, as we have seen, was whether the breach must be dishonest on the part of the trustee, their Lordships considered also the question whether the accessory must have acted dishonestly. In confirming that requirement, Lord Nicholls rejected the label "knowing assistance" because "knowledge" has too many shades of meaning. The five categories of knowledge elaborated by Peter Gibson J. in the *Baden* case[89] were "best forgotten". The word "dishonesty" was also to be preferred to "unconscionable conduct", a term little used save by equity lawyers. Lord Nicholls summarily rejected the view that an accessory could never be directly liable to the beneficiaries, because they are entitled to expect that others will refrain from intentionally intruding in the trustee-beneficiary relationship. Similarly rejected was the view that

---

[85] See fn.82, above.

[86] *Grupo Torras SA v Al-Sabah* [2001] Lloyd's Rep. Bank. 36; J. Garton (2001) 15 T.L.I. 93. See also *Gencor ACP Ltd v Dalby* [2001] W.T.L.R. 825.

[87] *Ultraframe (UK) Ltd v Fielding* [2007] W.T.L.R. 835; S. Baughen [2007] L.M.C.L.Q. 545; A. Goymour [2008] 16 R.L.R. 113. See generally P. Ridge (2008) 124 L.Q.R. 445.

[88] [1995] 2 A.C. 378; above.

[89] *Baden, Delvaux and Lecuit v Société Générale pour Favoriser le Développement du Commerce et de l'Industrie en France SA* [1983] B.C.L.C. 325. The Court of Appeal in *Heinl v Jyske Bank (Gibraltar) Ltd* [1999] Lloyd's Rep. Bank. 511, considered that *Baden* might still be helpful.

even an innocent third party could be liable, as that would make commerce impossible. In rejecting the view that negligence was a sufficient basis for liability, Lord Nicholls observed that in the commercial context persons such as bankers, advisers and many other agents would be liable to the trustees if they acted negligently. There was no reason why they should also be liable to the beneficiaries.[90] Thus the conclusion was that dishonesty is the basis of accessory liability.

12–014   It remains to consider what is meant by dishonesty. Lord Nicholls explained that it combines the objective standard of not acting as an honest person would in the circumstances with a strong subjective element: the court will assess the conduct in the light of what the defendant actually knew, not what a reasonable person would have known, and will have regard to the defendant's experience, intelligence and reasons for acting as he did. The broad meaning is conscious impropriety.[91] The House of Lords revisited the issue in *Twinsectra Ltd v Yardley*,[92] where the words of Lord Nicholls in *Royal Brunei Airlines Sdn Bhd v Tan*[93] were closely analysed. Their Lordships described three tests of dishonesty:

   (i) the purely subjective "Robin Hood test", which the courts have rejected;

  (ii) the purely objective test; and

 (iii) the "combined test" favoured by Lord Nicholls, whereby the conduct is dishonest by ordinary standards and the defendant realised that, by those standards, his conduct was dishonest.

The majority of their Lordships held[94] that dishonesty required an awareness that the conduct was dishonest by the ordinary standards of reasonable and honest people. Lord Millett, in a dissenting speech which attracted academic support,[95] considered that the only subjective elements allowed by Lord Nicholls in *Royal Brunei Airlines* were the defendant's experience, intelligence and actual state of knowledge. There was no requirement that he must have realised he was acting dishonestly. Lord Millett preferred an objective approach, adding that, so far as the defendant's state of knowledge was

---

[90] cf. G. McCormack (1995) 9 T.L.I. 102, suggesting that an accessory to fraud should be liable if negligent.

[91] See also *Heinl v Jyske Bank (Gibraltar) Ltd*, above, fn 86 (high standard of proof of dishonesty required); *Walker v Stones* [2001] Q.B. 902; below, para.17–005.

[92] [2002] A.C. 164; T. Yeo and H. Tjio (2002) 118 L.Q.R. 502; P Clarke All E.R. Rev. 2002, p.231. See also *Papamichael v National Westminster Bank plc* [2003] 1 Lloyd's Rep. 341.

[93] Above, fn.88.

[94] Subject to a "reinterpretation" by the Privy Council, below.

[95] C. Rickett [2002] 10 R.L.R. 112; J. Penner (2002) 16 T.L.I. 165 at 174; R. Thornton (2002) 61 C.L.J. 524; P. Kenny and M. Thompson [2002] Conv. 303 and 387 respectively.

concerned, he did not need to know the details of the trust. It sufficed if he knew that the money was not at the free disposal of the person whose breach he assisted.

The meaning of dishonesty was re-examined by the Privy Council in *Barlow Clowes International Ltd (In Liquidation) v Eurotrust International Ltd.*[96] Lord Hoffmann confirmed that the test laid down in *Royal Brunei Airlines Sdn Bhd v Tan*[97] is that the defendant must either have known that the transaction was not one in which he could honestly participate or have suspected this and decided not to make enquiries. Although a dishonest state of mind is subjective, the standard by which it is judged is objective: if, by ordinary standards, it would be considered dishonest, it is irrelevant that the defendant's standards are different.

Lord Hoffmann sought to interpret *Twinsectra Ltd v Yardley*[98] as not introducing a different test from *Royal Brunei Airlines*. He considered that Lord Hutton's remarks in that case (and indeed some of his own), although ambiguous, had been misinterpreted by academic writers. In his Lordship's view, Lord Hutton had not meant that, in order to be dishonest, the defendant must have thought about what normally accepted standards were. Lord Hoffmann in *Barlow Clowes* was thus able to conclude that the principles laid down by the House of Lords in *Twinsectra Ltd v Yardley* were in fact no different from those laid down by the Privy Council in *Royal Brunei Airlines*. The subjective element is what the defendant knew. The objective element is that his conduct was dishonest by the ordinary standards of honest people. It is not necessary for him to have formed a view on the propriety of his conduct. While appearing to support the conclusions of the majority in *Twinsectra Ltd v Yardley*,[99] the decision in *Barlow Clowes* is more in accordance with Lord Millett's dissent.

While the decision in *Barlow Clowes* has been welcomed, the reasoning has been criticised: it is a "volte face" by the Privy Council,[100] an unconvincing clarification,[101] an "implausible interpretation",[102] a "sleight of hand",[103] "brazen",[104] and "taking judicial re-interpretation to new heights".[105]

---

[96] [2006] 1 W.L.R. 1476.

[97] [1995] 2 A.C. 378; above.

[98] [2002] A.C. 164; above.

[99] Above, fn.98. The *Twinsectra* test still applies in disciplinary proceedings; *Bryant v The Law Society* [2009] 1 W.L.R. 163.

[100] D. Ryan [2006] Conv. 188; cf. M. Halliwell and E. Prochaska [2006] Conv 465.

[101] T. Yeo (2006) 122 L.Q.R. 171.

[102] J. Penner (2006) 20 T.L.I. 122.

[103] M. Conaglen and A. Goymour (2006) 65 C.L.J. 18.

[104] T. Akkouh (2005) 149 N.L.J. 1475.

[105] G. Virgo in Burrows and Rodger (eds), *Mapping the Law, Essays in memory of Peter Birks*, 2006, p.86. See also P. Clarke All E.R. Rev. 2006, p.255.

The Court of Appeal has subsequently described the test for dishonesty as "predominantly objective": the elements are the defendant's knowledge of the facts and that he acted contrary to normal standards of honest conduct, but he need not have been conscious of his own wrongdoing.[106] It was considered that the law laid down by the House of Lords in *Twinsectra Ltd v Yardley*, as interpreted by the Privy Council in *Barlow Clowes*, now represented the law of England and Wales.

12–015 Clearly dishonesty includes deliberately closing one's eyes or deliberately not asking questions, of which an example is *Agip (Africa) Ltd v Jackson*:

> Payment orders from Agip to third parties were fraudulently altered by Agip's accountant, Z, who changed the name of the payees to that of B Co and other companies. B Co (and the other companies) had been formed by the defendants, who were two accountants in partnership (Jackson & Co) and their employee. Two of the defendants were the sole directors and shareholders of B Co. The money was transferred to the account of B Co and thence to Jackson's client account in the Isle of Man. It was then paid to various recipients abroad who had no connection with Agip. B Co was then put into liquidation. Agip sought to recover from the defendants, who had throughout followed the instructions of their client, a French lawyer acting for unidentified principals.

The claim based on assistance in the breach was successful before Millett J.[107] Z had committed a fraudulent breach of his duty to Agip, which the defendants must have realised was going on. They obviously knew they were "laundering" money, and were consciously helping Z to conceal the fraud. At best, they had been indifferent to it, which amounted to dishonesty. One partner and the employee were liable for assisting the breach, and the other partner was vicariously liable for their acts.[108] The judgment of Millett J. was upheld on appeal[109]: the defendants were liable because they did not act honestly.

The issue arose also in *Lipkin Gorman v Karpnale Ltd.*

---

[106] *Abou-Rahmah v Abacha* [2007] W.T.L.R. 1; D. Ryan [2007] Conv. 168; G. Virgo (2007) 66 C.L.J. 22. See also *Starglade Properties Ltd v Nash* [2011] Lloyd's Rep. F.C. 102 (deliberate removal of assets of insolvent company to frustrate claim of creditor was dishonest).

[107] [1990] Ch. 265; Sir Peter Millett (1991) 107 L.Q.R. 71. See also *Finers v Miro* [1991] 1 W.L.R. 35.

[108] Below, para.12–025.

[109] [1991] Ch. 547; S. Goulding [1992] Conv. 367; H. Norman (1992) 12 L.S. 332; P. Oliver (1993–94) 4 K.C.L.J. 82.

A solicitor, C, wrongly withdrew £200,000 from his firm's client account at the bank and spent it on gambling at the Playboy Club. C's firm sued the bank and the Club. In the present context, we are concerned only with the action against the bank. The bank manager had known that C was a gambler, but made no enquiries about the withdrawals.[110]

The Court of Appeal[111] held that the bank was not liable. It was conceded that the bank could not be liable as accessory if it was not in breach of its contract with the claimant firm. There was no breach of contract because the bank had no reason to believe that C was drawing money for his own purposes.

The beneficiary may also have a remedy against those who have received the property, whose position will now be examined.

ii. Liability for Receipt

(a) *Personal and Proprietary Remedies.* A basic principle of **12–016** property law is that any person who receives trust property,[112] not being a purchaser for value without notice (actual or constructive), takes subject to the trust. So long as he retains the property he is bound to return it, and the tracing process[113] is available to identify the property or its proceeds. However, this is different from the question whether the recipient should be under a *personal* liability to account. The distinction is important if he no longer has the property. If he is liable to account, his liability remains. If he is not so accountable, his liability is confined to the return of the property or its proceeds while still in his possession. Not every transferee who fails to prove that he was a bona fide purchaser of the legal estate without notice is subjected to the additional personal liability. An "innocent volunteer",[114] for example, who took without notice that the property was trust property transferred in breach of trust cannot take free of the trust, but, on the present state of the authorities, does not incur personal liability.[115] Whether the defendant has received the trust property will depend on the application of the

---

[110] Any allegation of dishonesty was insufficiently pleaded.

[111] [1989] 1 W.L.R. 1340. The House of Lords dealt only with the Club's position; [1992] A.C. 548; below, para.12–020.

[112] For receipt of confidential information, see *Satnam Investments Ltd v Dunlop Heywood & Co Ltd* [1999] 3 All E.R. 652.

[113] Below, Ch.23. See also R. Nolan (2006) 122 L.Q.R. 232 at 259, explaining that a trustee's positive duties of management are not imposed on the recipient. See generally C. Mitchell and S. Watterson in C. Mitchell (ed.), *Constructive and Resulting Trusts*, Ch.4.

[114] *Re Diplock* [1948] Ch. 465 at 478–479; above, para.12–005, below, para.23–066.

[115] For the view that liability should be strict, see below, para.12–021. See M. Conaglen and A. Goymour in C. Mitchell (ed.), *Constructive and Resulting Trusts*, Ch.5, for the view that the personal action does not lie against a purchaser of registered land. See also E. Bant [2011] Conv. 309.

tracing rules discussed in Ch.23.[116] Where a company has been used as a device for receiving property transferred in breach of fiduciary duty, the court will treat the director who is the company's "controlling mind" as having personally received the property.[117] It has been held that the Civil Liability (Contribution) Act 1978 may enable recipients to recover a contribution from other persons responsible for the loss to the trust.[118]

12–017   (b) *Degree of Knowledge.* While constructive knowledge clearly suffices where the question is whether the recipient took the property subject to the trust, it does not follow that the same applies where the question is whether he has incurred the personal liability to account. Opinions have differed as to whether liability is based on actual knowledge, or constructive knowledge, or whether it is strict, so that even an innocent volunteer is liable. Formerly it appeared established that constructive notice sufficed.[119] Thus in *Belmont Finance Corp v Williams Furniture Ltd (No.2)*[120] company directors who participated in an unlawful share purchase scheme were liable because they had knowledge of all the facts which established the improper use of the funds, and knew or ought to have known that the money which they received was impressed with a trust. It was immaterial that, as the judge found, the directors did not act fraudulently.

A different view was taken in *Re Montagu's ST.*[121]

> Trustees transferred certain settled chattels to the beneficiary (the tenth Duke) absolutely, in breach of trust. The situation resulted from an "honest muddle" by all concerned. The Duke's solicitor had at an earlier stage been aware of the terms of the settlement. The Duke disposed of a number of the chattels during his lifetime. After his death, the eleventh Duke claimed that his predecessor had become a constructive trustee of them. Megarry V.C. held that, while the tenth Duke's estate must return any remaining chattels or their traceable proceeds, the Duke was not

---

[116] See *El Ajou v Dollar Land Holdings plc (No.2)* [1995] 2 All E.R. 213; below, para.23–058.

[117] *Trustor AB v Smallbone (No.3)* [2001] 1 W.L.R. 1177; S. Watson (2003) 119 L.Q.R. 13.

[118] *Charter Plc v City Index Ltd* [2008] Ch. 313; G. Virgo (2008) 67 C.L.J. 254; A. Goymour [2008] 16 R.L.R. 113; J. Edelman and C. Mitchell All E.R. Rev. 2008, 398; S. Gardner (2009) 125 L.Q.R. 20.

[119] *Karak Rubber Co Ltd v Burden (No.2)* [1972] 1 W.L.R. 602.

[120] [1980] 1 All E.R. 393; see also *(No.1)* [1979] Ch. 250; *International Sales and Agencies Ltd v Marcus* [1982] 3 All E.R. 551 at 558. It is also assumed in *Re Diplock* [1948] Ch. 465 at 477–479 that constructive knowledge would suffice.

[121] [1987] Ch. 264 (decided 1985); C. Harpum (1986) 102 L.Q.R. 267 and (1987) 50 M.L.R. 217. See also *Hillsdown Holdings Plc v Pensions Ombudsman* [1997] 1 All E.R. 862; *Sinclair Investments (UK) Ltd v Versailles Trade Finance Ltd (in administrative receivership)* [2011] 3 W.L.R. 1153.

liable as constructive trustee because he had no actual knowledge that the chattels were trust property transferred in breach of trust. Even if he had once understood the terms of the settlement, there was nothing to suggest that he remembered them so as to be aware at the date of receipt that the chattels were trust property. Nor was there any reason to impute the solicitor's knowledge to the Duke, by analogy with the doctrine of imputed notice.

The V.C. emphasised that the relevant question was whether the recipient had *knowledge*, not whether he had *notice* according to the rules established under the doctrine of notice which dealt with the question whether an equitable interest was binding on a transferee. The question in the present context was whether a person was to have imposed on him the burdens of trusteeship. His Lordship held that liability should not be imposed unless the conscience of the recipient was affected; this required "want of probity", which includes actual knowledge, shutting one's eyes to the obvious, or wilfully and recklessly failing to make such enquiries as a reasonable and honest person would make; it does not include knowledge of circumstances which would indicate the facts to an honest and reasonable person or would put the latter on enquiry.

The question was more recently examined by the Court of Appeal **12–018** in *Bank of Credit and Commerce International (Overseas) Ltd v Akindele*,[122] where the defendant had received \$6.68 million in 1988 as a return on \$10 million he had paid to the bank in 1985 under an artificial loan agreement. The transaction involved a fraudulent breach of the fiduciary duties owed to the bank by certain parties, but the defendant knew nothing of the frauds within the BCCI group at that time nor of the fraudulent aspect of the particular agreement. Nourse L.J. reviewed the authorities (including Commonwealth decisions) and academic commentaries on the degree of knowledge required to found recipient liability. First, his Lordship confirmed that dishonesty had never been required. There was considerable authority supporting the view that constructive notice sufficed,[123] although in much of it the question had not been examined in depth because the defendant had actual knowledge, or the decisions were based on assistance rather than receipt. Other authorities favoured the view that constructive notice did not suffice, at any rate in the case of commercial transactions, where (in cases not involving title to land) there was no duty to investigate. In such cases purchasers

[122] [2001] Ch. 437; R. Nolan (2000) 59 C.L.J. 447; J. Penner (2000) 14 T.L.I. 229; P. Birks and W. Swadling All E.R. Rev. 2000, p.319; J. Stevens [2001] 9 R.L.R. 99.
[123] *Belmont Finance Corp v Williams Furniture Ltd (No.2)* [1980] 1 All E.R. 393; above, para.12-017; *Agip (Africa) Ltd v Jackson* [1990] Ch. 265 (not dealt with on appeal at [1991] Ch. 547); *Polly Peck International Plc v Nadir (No.2)* [1992] 4 All E.R. 769; *Houghton v Fayers* [2000] 1 B.C.L.C. 511.

have been held not liable unless they had actual knowledge of the impropriety or acted with wilful or reckless disregard,[124] although Commonwealth courts had taken a different view.[125]

Nourse L.J. regarded *Re Montagu's ST*,[126] where Megarry V.C. had laid down the "want of probity" test, as the "seminal judgment". So far as the five categories of knowledge elaborated in the *Baden*[127] case were concerned, they had been formulated with "assistance" rather than "receipt" in mind. There were grave doubts as to the utility of this categorisation in receipt cases. The purpose of such a categorisation could only be to enable the court to determine whether the defendant's conscience was sufficiently affected to bind him as constructive trustee. There was, therefore, no need for the categorisation. There was a single test of dishonesty for assistance liability, and there should be a single test of knowledge for recipient liability: "The recipient's state of knowledge must be such as to make it unconscionable for him to retain the benefit of the receipt".[128] His Lordship considered that this test would enable the court to give common sense decisions in the commercial context. Applying the test in the present case, the defendant's knowledge was not such as to make it unconscionable for him to enter into the agreement in 1985, when the integrity of BCCI was not doubted. At the time of the receipt of $6.68 million in 1988 he had suspicions, but his state of knowledge was not such as to make it unconscionable for him to retain the money. His knowledge in 1988 concerned the general reputation of the BCCI group from late 1987 onwards, and not the particular transaction entered into in 1985. If his Lordship had thought that it was still the appropriate test, he would have held that the defendant did not have actual or constructive knowledge that his receipt was traceable to a breach of fiduciary duty.

12–019 It remains to be clarified by later cases what the distinction is between dishonesty (not required) and the degree of knowledge making it unconscionable for the defendant to retain the benefit of his receipt.[129] As the defendant was held not even to have had constructive knowledge, the point remains unclear. However, the authority of this case has been seriously weakened by the decision in

---

[124] See *Eagle Trust Plc v SBC Securities Ltd* [1993] 1 W.L.R. 484; *Cowan de Groot Properties Ltd v Eagle Trust Plc* [1992] 4 All E.R. 700; *El Ajou v Dollar Land Holdings Plc* [1993] 3 All E.R. 717 (reversed on another point at [1994] 2 All E.R. 685). Banks and other financial institutions must, however, satisfy the money laundering regulations.

[125] *Powell v Thompson* [1991] 1 N.Z.L.R. 597; *Equiticorp Industries Group Ltd v Hawkins* [1991] 3 N.Z.L.R. 700; *Citadel General Assurance Co v Lloyds Bank Canada* (1997) 152 D.L.R. (4th) 411.

[126] [1987] Ch. 264; above, para.12–017.

[127] Above, para.12–013.

[128] [2001] Ch. 437 at 455.

[129] Compare *Niru Battery Manufacturing Company v Milestone Trading Ltd* [2004] Q.B. 985 (similar distinction in relation to "change of position" defence); P. Birks (2004) 120 L.Q.R. 373; below, para.23–070.

Criterion Properties Plc v Stratford UK Properties LLC.[130] The House of Lords there explained that the equitable principles governing liability for receipt of trust property do not apply to liability for receipt of property under a contract which is set aside (which was the situation in *Akindele*). In such a case there is no trust property, and the general rules of restitution apply. As explained below, liability under these rules does not depend on knowledge. Thus the case was considered to have been decided on the wrong basis.

Nourse L.J. in *Akindele*[131] took the opportunity to comment on the debate as to whether innocent volunteers should be strictly liable to account on the ground of unjust enrichment, subject to the defence of change of position. Before examining this, the position at common law must be considered.

(c) *Common Law Remedy.* A discussion of the equitable principles alone would be misleading, because the circumstances giving rise to a receipt claim may also found the common law personal action for money had and received. It is clear that the common law personal action lies against an innocent volunteer who had no knowledge, actual or constructive, of the fact that the money belonged not to the transferor but to the claimant. The claimant must, however, show title at common law to the money which, by applying the tracing rules, the defendant can be shown to have received. It is not necessary that the money should remain identifiable in the recipient's hands (in which case a proprietary claim might be considered).[132] A recipient of the money in good faith and for value has a defence.

12–020

These issues came before the House of Lords in *Lipkin Gorman v Karpnale Ltd*,[133] where a firm of solicitors sought to recover money paid to the Playboy Club by a member of the firm, Cass, who had withdrawn it from the firm's client account and spent it on gambling. The Club had no knowledge of the source of the money, but had not given consideration: the gaming contract was not legally enforceable, and so the Club had incurred no obligation to honour

---

[130] [2004] 1 W.L.R. 1846; R. Stevens (2004) L.M.C.L.Q. 421; J. Yap (2011) 127 L.Q.R. 350. The Court of Appeal in *Charter Plc v City Index Ltd* [2008] Ch. 313 accepted *Akindele* as correct on the test for recipient liability, but the point was not argued as the defendant was liable on any view. See also *Law Society of England and Wales v Isaac and Isaac International Holdings Ltd* [2011] W.T.L.R. 425.

[131] Above, fn.122.

[132] It is doubtful whether any personal action lies against a transferee from the recipient. See *Agip (Africa) Ltd v Jackson* [1990] Ch. 265 at 287–288; A. Burrows (1990) 106 L.Q.R. 20; Sir Peter Millett (1991) 107 L.Q.R. 71; A. Tettenborn [1997] 5 R.L.R. 1; D. Sheehan [2002] 10 R.L.R. 69; Goff and Jones, pp.103–104 (exceptional cases where transferee liable). See also B. McFarlane (2009) 17 R.L.R. 37.

[133] [1991] 2 A.C. 548; above, para.12–015. The claimants were content to bring a personal action as the defendant was not insolvent.

the bets. The solicitors were held entitled to recover in the common law action, subject to the defence of change of position.

The decision has been criticised on the ground that the claimant firm did not have legal title to the money after it was withdrawn from the bank, because the legal title vested in Cass.[134] Lord Goff avoided this difficulty by holding that the firm had a legal chose in action (the debt owed to them by the bank holding their client account) which they could follow into the money drawn by Cass and thence into the hands of the Club (the Club surprisingly conceded that this legal title was not defeated by reason of any mixing of the money by Cass with his own).

Of great significance was the unqualified acceptance by the House of Lords of the defence of change of position, widely recognised in the common law world, which should be left to develop on a case by case basis.[135] The defence is available to an innocent defendant[136] (but not to a wrongdoer) who has so changed his position that it would be inequitable to require restitution or restitution in full. Of course, it will not be available where the recipient has applied the money to normal expenses which would have been incurred in any event. In the present case the Club could invoke the defence to the extent that it had paid out winnings to Cass. These sums could be set off against the total sums received from him.

12–021   (d) *Unjust Enrichment Theory.* A question which has been much debated, primarily by academic commentators, is whether an innocent volunteer who has received trust property transferred in breach of trust should be strictly liable to account, subject to the defence of change of position, even though he took without notice. As we have seen, this is the position with regard to the common law personal action, discussed above. It is also the position with regard to the action in equity against an innocent volunteer who has received property to which he is not entitled in the administration of an estate.[137] This view is based on the principle that restitutionary liability is receipt-based, not fault-based: the volunteer is unjustly enriched if he is not accountable.[138] Of course, there is no room for strict liability in the case of a bona fide purchaser, either at common law or in equity. Lord Browne-Wilkinson stated in *Westdeutsche*

---

[134] M. Halliwell [1992] Conv. 124; E. McKendrick (1992) 55 M.L.R. 377.

[135] Below, para.23–070. The defence existed in limited form, as discussed by the House of Lords.

[136] See Goff and Jones, pp.864–866.

[137] *Ministry of Health v Simpson* [1951] A.C. 251 (subject to requirement of suing personal representative first); below, para.23–077. The volunteers were not, however, liable *as constructive trustees* because they were entitled to assume that the executors were acting properly; [1948] Ch. 465 at 477–479.

[138] Goff and Jones, pp.759–762.

Landesbank Girozentrale v Islington LBC[139] (which involved a common law action) that an innocent volunteer is not personally liable to account as constructive trustee because he lacks the necessary knowledge. This does not preclude the strict liability argument because, as shown by *Re Diplock*[140] itself, personal liability to account in equity can arise in the absence of constructive trusteeship. It is right that an innocent volunteer should not be a constructive trustee, with consequent liability to repay with interest,[141] but it does not follow that there should be no restitutionary liability in equity in the absence of change of position, in order to prevent unjust enrichment.[142] That recipient liability is restitution-based has been emphasised by the Privy Council.[143] It has been said, however, that the law does not recognise any personal unjust enrichment claim founded on equitable title, and that this is a further illustration of the principle that a beneficiary's interest does not have the same incidents as the title of a legal owner.[144]

Nourse L.J. in *Bank of Credit and Commerce International (Overseas) Ltd v Akindele*[145] took the opportunity to discuss the issue, although it did not arise for decision because the defendant was not a volunteer. His Lordship referred to a paper in which Lord Nicholls had advocated the strict liability approach.[146] Nourse L.J. doubted whether strict liability coupled with the change of position defence would be preferable to fault-based liability in many commercial transactions. In his Lordship's view, it would appear commercially unworkable, on proof of misapplication, that the burden should shift to the recipient to defend the receipt by change of position or in some other way, and there would be obvious difficulty in saying that it would be equitable for change of position to afford a defence if the circumstances were such that it would be unconscionable to retain the benefit. It must be emphasised, however, that the advocates of the strict liability principle have never sought to apply it to commercial purchasers nor to argue that the defence of change of position, which applies only to innocent recipients,[147] should be available in

---

[139] [1996] A.C. 669 at 707.

[140] [1948] Ch. 465. Liability based on constructive trusteeship was rejected at 478.

[141] Liability to pay compound interest was the issue in the *Westdeutsche* case.

[142] See Goff and Jones, pp.759–762; J Martin [1998] Conv. 13; cf. *Hillsdown Holdings Plc v Pensions Ombudsman* [1997] 1 All E.R. 862 at 904 (doubting whether lower courts could give effect to a claim in restitution where no constructive trust).

[143] *Royal Brunei Airlines Sdn Bhd v Tan* [1995] 2 A.C. 378 (a case of dishonest assistance). The receipt-based restitutionary claim was described by Auld L.J. as an "equitable newcomer" in *Macmillan Inc v Bishopgate Investment Trust Plc (No.3)* [1996] 1 W.L.R. 387 at 407.

[144] L. Smith (2000) 116 L.Q.R. 412. See also L. Smith (2009) 125 L.Q.R. 338 at 347, fn.43.

[145] [2001] Ch. 437. His Lordship's views are criticised in Goff and Jones, p.761.

[146] "Knowing Receipt: the Need for a New Landmark", published in *Restitution: Past, Present and Future-Essays in Honour of Gareth Jones* (1998).

[147] Below, para.23–070.

circumstances where it would be unconscionable to retain the benefit. Lord Millett has given some support to the strict liability theory by confirming the restitutionary basis of liability for receipt:

"Constructive notice is sufficient, and may not even be necessary. There is powerful academic support for the proposition that the liability of the recipient is the same as in other cases of restitution, that is to say strict but subject to a change of position defence."[148]

His Lordship has given further support in his extra-judicial writings.[149]

12–022   It may be that legislation will be required to achieve coherence in this area.[150] It is indeed difficult to discern any convincing policy reason why an innocent recipient of misapplied property should be vulnerable to the claims of a legal owner (including a trustee) and of underpaid beneficiaries of estates but not to the claims of other equitable owners.[151] Case law goes the other way, but:

"[A]uthority cannot militate indefinitely against reason, and there is no rational argument for depriving the equitable owner of the claim in unjust enrichment based on strict liability".[152]

Although most recipient claims arise in the context of commercial fraud, it may nevertheless be said that the debate as to whether the innocent volunteer should be strictly liable in equity has lost some of its significance now that the common law remedy has been extended to recovery of money paid by mistake of law.[153] Trustees as

---

[148] *Twinsectra Ltd v Yardley* [2002] A.C. 164 at 194 (obiter, as the issue was dishonest assistance).

[149] (2007) 123 L.Q.R. 159 at 164–165: "All recipient liability should be strict, whether at law or in equity." See also Lord Millett and M. Bryan in Degeling and Edelman (eds), *Equity in Commercial Law*, 2005, Ch.12 and Ch.13; P. Millett in Burrows and Rodger (eds), *Mapping the Law*, 2006, p.267.

[150] See C. Harpum (1995) 111 L.Q.R. 545.

[151] A beneficiary may sue a third party on behalf of the trust where the trustee unreasonably refuses to sue or has disabled himself from doing so: *Parker-Tweedale v Dunbar Bank Plc* [1991] Ch. 12.

[152] P. Birks in Birks and Pretto (eds), *Breach of Trust*, 2002, p.239. See also Chambers, *Resulting Trusts*, Ch.8; A. Burrows (1997) 50 C.L.P. 95 at 103, 112; P. Birks (2004) 120 L.Q.R. 373 at 377, describing the law on knowing receipt as "in a very poor state". For contrary views, see Halliwell, *Equity and Good Conscience in a Contemporary Context*, 1997, pp.121, 134; P. Jaffey (2001) 15 T.L.I. 151; J. Stevens [2001] 9 R.L.R. 99; C. Rotherham [2003] 11 R.L.R. 57 at pp.76–77; D. Hayton (2007) 21 T.L.I. 55; M. Conaglen and R. Nolan (2007) 66 C.L.J. 515; P. Ridge and J. Dietrich (2008) 124 L.Q.R. 26; D. Sheehan and K. Low [2008] 16 R.L.R. 41 and 96 respectively; H. Delany and D. Ryan [2008] Conv. 401 at pp.425–430; C. Mitchell and S. Watterson in C. Mitchell (ed.), *Constructive and Resulting Trusts*, pp.155–158.

[153] *Kleinwort Benson Ltd v Lincoln City Council* [1999] 2 A.C. 349. There is no defence of "honest receipt".

legal owners may now succeed on this basis against innocent volunteers.

(e) *Ministerial Receipt.* Recipient liability cannot arise where **12–023** the third party has received the trust property merely in his capacity as agent and has dealt with it according to his principal's instructions. In other words, the "receipt" category is confined to third parties who have received the property for their own benefit.[154] Thus in *Agip (Africa) Ltd v Jackson*[155] the defendants were not liable on the basis of receipt because they had merely received the money as agents and passed it on to third parties according to their principal's instructions. As we have seen, they were liable for dishonest assistance.

Where money is paid to a bank it does not receive the money as agent for the payer. The money becomes the property of the bank, and the defence of purchaser without notice will normally apply.[156]

iii. Agent Assuming Trustee's Duties.[157] An agent of the trus- **12–024** tees may, as we have seen, incur liability under the above rules if he has been dishonest or has received trust property for his own benefit. There will normally be no such liability where trust property is transferred to an agent in the ordinary process of delegation,[158] as his receipt is ministerial and there is no breach of trust. In such a case he will only be subjected to a trustee's liability if he receives the property into his hands in connection with his assumption of the trustee's office and duties. In *Williams-Ashman v Price and Williams*,[159] Bennett J. treated *Mara v Browne*[160] as authority for the proposition that:

> "[A]n agent in possession of money which he knows to be trust money, so long as he acts honestly, is not accountable to the beneficiaries interested in the trust money unless he intermeddles in the trust by doing acts characteristic of a trustee and outside the duties of an agent."

[154] Birks, *Introduction to the Law of Restitution*, 1985, p.445; C. Harpum (1986) 102 L.Q.R. 114; P. Birks (1989) 105 L.Q.R. 528; Sir Peter Millett (1991) 107 L.Q.R. 71.
[155] [1990] Ch. 265, affirmed [1991] Ch. 547. The facts have been given, above, para.12–014. See also *Twinsectra Ltd v Yardley* [2002] 2 A.C. 164.
[156] *Agip (Africa) Ltd v Jackson*, above, fn.155 at p.292; *Polly Peck International Plc v Nadir (No.2)* [1992] 4 All E.R. 769; *Sinclair Investments (UK) Ltd v Versailles Trade Finance Ltd (in administrative receivership)* [2011] 3 W.L.R. 1153.
[157] See C. Harpum (1986) 102 L.Q.R. 114 at p.130.
[158] Below, para.20–012.
[159] [1942] Ch. 219 at 228.
[160] [1896] 1 Ch. 199.

Thus, where a solicitor received trust money through his own account, and invested it in unauthorised mortgages on the instructions of the trustees, the solicitor was held to be acting in his capacity as a solicitor, and not liable as a constructive trustee.[161] A stockbroker would not incur such liability for receiving trust money and investing it on the trustee's instructions in an unauthorised investment. The remedy is against the trustees.

If the agent does not know that the property is trust property, he is not liable if he acts honestly and within the scope of his agency, even if the facts were such as to put him on enquiry.[162]

12–025   **iv. Liability of Partner of Constructive Trustee.** The circumstances in which a firm will be vicariously liable for the acts of a partner who has dishonestly assisted in a breach of trust were quite recently clarified by the House of Lords in *Dubai Aluminium Co Ltd v Salaam*.[163] In that case a dishonest partner had planned, drafted and signed sham agreements giving effect to a scheme involving over $50 million which he knew to be fraudulent. The question was whether s.10 of the Partnership Act 1890 applied, under which a firm is liable for any wrongful act or omission of a partner acting in the ordinary course of the business of the firm, or with the authority of his partners. The firm was held vicariously liable on the ground that, although the wrongful acts had not been authorised, the fraudulent scheme was so closely connected with the acts the dishonest partner was authorised to do that he could be said to have been acting in the ordinary course of the firm's business when he committed them. It is not within the ordinary course of a solicitor's practice to act as an express trustee,[164] nor to act as a trustee when not appointed as such and so incur liability as a constructive trustee in the sense of a de facto trustee.[165] The present case was not of that kind, as the dishonest partner was not a trustee, nor had he assumed the position of a trustee. Given that a solicitor may be guilty of dishonest conduct while acting within the ordinary scope of his practice, there was no reason why his firm should not incur vicarious

---

[161] *Mara v Browne* [1896] 1 Ch. 199 (any negligence action would have been statute-barred); *Williams-Ashman v Price and Williams* [1942] Ch. 219.

[162] *Williams v Williams* (1881) 17 Ch.D. 437; *Competitive Insurance Co Ltd v Davies Investments Ltd* [1975] 1 W.L.R. 1240.

[163] [2003] 2 A.C. 366; C. Mitchell (2003) 119 L.Q.R. 364. *Re Bell's Indenture* [1980] 1 W.L.R. 1217 was overruled in part. See also *Agip (Africa) Ltd v Jackson* [1991] Ch. 547. For vicarious liability to account for a profit, see J. Edelman (2008) 124 L.Q.R. 21.

[164] See *Walker v Stones* [2001] Q.B. 902.

[165] This was the sense in which the term "constructive trustee" was used in *Mara v Browne* [1896] 1 Ch. 199, where Lord Herschell said that it was not within a partner's implied authority to make himself a constructive trustee and thereby subject his partners to the same liability.

liability for loss caused by conduct which constituted him a "constructive trustee" in the sense of a person who was personally accountable for dishonest assistance in a breach of trust.

Another question is whether a firm is vicariously liable for an act of dishonest assistance in a breach of trust committed by its employee (as opposed to a partner). The firm will be liable where the victim of the employee's dishonesty was the firm's own client, but not where the victim was not its client.[166]

C. Mutual Wills[167]

Two persons (often husband and wife)[168] may agree that, on the death of the first to die, all their property shall be enjoyed by the survivor, and after his (her) death by nominated beneficiaries (for example, children of a previous marriage); and may make mutual wills to that effect. The survivor may be given a life interest,[169] an absolute interest[170] or no interest at all.[171] The question is whether, and to what extent, such an agreement controls the devolution of their property.

12–026

i. **Agreement Necessary.** Before any remedy can be obtained, an agreement to make wills and not to revoke them[172] between the parties must be proved. The agreement must indicate that the wills are to be mutually binding, whether or not expressed in the language of revocation.[173] The standard of proof is the ordinary civil standard (i.e. on balance of probabilities); the evidence must be "clear and satisfactory" and may be extrinsic, as where the agreement is substantiated by family conversations.[174] The mere fact that the wills were made simultaneously and in the same form is not, of itself, proof of an agreement although it is a relevant circumstance to be

12–027

---

[166] *Balfron Trustees Ltd v Peterson* [2002] W.T.L.R. 157; S. Baughen [2007] L.M.C.L.Q. 545.

[167] G. Graham (1951) 15 Conv.(N.S.) 28; J. Mitchell (1951) 14 M.L.R. 140; R. Burgess (1970) 34 Conv.(N.S.) 230; C. Rickett (1989) 105 L.Q.R. 534; Oakley, *Constructive Trusts*, 3rd edn, pp.263–274; Cassidy, *Mutual Wills*, 2000.

[168] *Walpole v Lord Orford* (1797) 3 Ves.Jr. 402.

[169] *Dufour v Pereira* (1769) Dick. 419.

[170] *Re Green* [1951] 148.

[171] *Re Dale (Deceased)* [1994] Ch. 31.

[172] *In the Goods of Heys* [1914] p.192.

[173] *Re Goodchild (Deceased)* [1997] 1 W.L.R. 1216 (mistaken belief of first testator that wills mutually binding may enable intended beneficiary to claim under the Inheritance (Provision for Family and Dependants) Act 1975 on death of survivor). See also *Re Walters* [2009] Ch. 212.

[174] *Re Cleaver* [1981] 1 W.L.R. 939; *Re Newey* [1994] 2 N.Z.L.R. 590; C. Rickett [1996] Conv. 136; *Charles v Fraser* [2010] W.T.L.R. 1489; *Fry v Densham-Smith* [2011] W.T.L.R. 387.

taken into account.[175] The agreement must amount to a clear contract at law, not a mere common understanding.[176] But the court may
infer an agreement from the conduct of the parties, the circumstances and the terms of the wills.[177] Preferably the agreement, if
there was one, should be recited in the will.

In *Re Oldham*,[178] a husband and wife made mutual wills in
similar form; each spouse left his (or her) property to the other
absolutely with the same provisions in the event of the other
predeceasing. There was no evidence of an agreement that they
should be irrevocable. After the husband's death, the wife married
again, and made a new will which was quite different from the
earlier one. The second will was upheld; Astbury J. saying:

> "The fact that the two wills were made in identical terms does
> not necessarily connote any agreement beyond that of so mak-
> ing them ... there is no evidence ... that there was an agree-
> ment that the trust in the mutual will should in all
> circumstances be irrevocable by the survivor who took the
> benefit."

The parties had left their estates to each other "absolutely".
They:

> "[M]ay have thought it quite safe to trust the other. . . . But that
> is a very different thing from saying that they bound them-
> selves by a trust that should be operative in all circumstances
> and in all cases".[179]

In *Re Cleaver*,[180] on the other hand, the evidence of mutual
wills was sufficient. An elderly couple married in 1967. The
husband had three children. They made wills in each other's
favour absolutely, and in default to the three children. In 1974,
each of them reduced the share of one daughter, Martha, to a life
interest. After the husband's death the wife made a new will
consistent with the earlier one. Thereafter she made a further will
enlarging Martha's share from a life interest to an absolute interest; and by her last will she left her residue to Martha and her
husband, and nothing to the other two children. It was held that
the wife's executors held the estate on the trusts of the 1974 will.

---

[175] [1981] 1 W.L.R. 939. Where mirror wills are not intended to be mutual wills, it is
desirable for the will to include such a statement.

[176] *Re Goodchild (Deceased)*, above, fn.173; *Birch v Curtis* [2002] 2 F.L.R. 1158; D.
Rowell (2003) 43 *Trusts and Estates* 14.

[177] *Dufour v Pereira* (1769) Dick. 419; *Stone v Hoskins* [1905] p.194; *Re Hagger* [1930] 2
Ch. 190; *Re Green* [1951] Ch. 148.

[178] [1925] Ch. 75.

[179] [1925] Ch. 75 at 88–89; *Gray v Perpetual Trustee Co* [1928] A.C. 391.

[180] Above, fn.174.

Sufficient evidence of an agreement to make mutual wills was shown by the simultaneity and similarity of the original wills; the pattern of successive wills made together; the fact that both parties reduced Martha's interest; the faithful terms of the first will made after the husband's death; and the fact that, in family conversations, the wife had regarded herself as under an obligation to leave her estate to the children.

ii. Remedies on the Contract. The agreement is binding between the parties. If it is broken by the first party to die, his estate will be liable in damages to the survivor.[181] If the breach is by the second party to die, as by revocation or alteration of his will, it has always been assumed that no remedy could be obtained against him or his estate under the contract. The law which has developed on the subject is based upon a trust which arises in appropriate cases in favour of the beneficiaries.

12–028

It is arguable that the principle of *Beswick v Beswick*[182] could apply in this situation. The estate of the first to die is in a similar position to Mrs Beswick, the administratrix. It seems that an action for specific performance of the contract would lie by the estate against the survivor or his estate. An examination of the problems which have arisen in treating the interests of the beneficiaries as trusts, as will be seen, makes a contractual solution attractive.[183] The court in *Re Dale (Deceased)*[184] rejected the argument that the second testator could be ordered to make a will in accordance with the contract, or restrained from revoking it. It may remain arguable that specific performance could be obtained to enforce a conveyance of the property.[185]

Until quite recently there could have been no question of the beneficiary suing in contract because of the privity doctrine. It may now be possible for the beneficiary to enforce the contract in his own right under the Contracts (Rights of Third Parties) Act 1999, in the case of contracts between testators made after the Act.[186] The Act does not affect rights or remedies of third parties which are otherwise available, thus the trust solution remains.[187]

---

[181] *Robinson v Ommanney* (1883) 23 Ch.D. 285; but not where the revocation of the first will is by the subsequent marriage of the covenantor. See further C. Rickett (1991) 54 M.L.R. 581.

[182] [1968] A.C. 58.

[183] See T. Youdan (1979) 29 U. of Toronto L.J. 390. The executor must be willing to sue. See K. Hodkinson [1982] Conv. 228, suggesting that the ultimate beneficiary should be the executor; C. Rickett (1989) 105 L.Q.R. 534.

[184] [1994] Ch. 31; A. Brierley (1995) 58 M.L.R. 95. *Beswick v Beswick* was not discussed.

[185] Below, para.24–026.

[186] See s.10; C. Davis (2002) 61 C.L.J. 423 at 430. The Act is outlined at para.4–016, above.

[187] s.7(1).

12–029   **iii. Trusts Created by Mutual Wills.** A will is always revocable; an agreement not to revoke it does not make it irrevocable.[188] Thus, if the survivor of an agreement to make mutual wills revokes his will, he will die intestate: and if he makes a new will, that later one will be admitted to probate.[189] But the disposition of his property on his death will be affected by the agreement. For the principle is established that the agreement between the parties, followed by the death of the first party, relying on the undertaking of the other party to observe the agreement, creates trusts in favour of the intended beneficiaries, which are enforceable against the property of the survivor.[190] Of the leading case of *Dufour v Pereira*,[191] Clauson J. said[192]:

> "*Dufour v Pereira* decides that where there is a joint will ... on the death of the first testator the position as regards that part of the property which belongs to the survivor is that the survivor will be treated ... as holding the property on trust to apply it so as to carry out the effect of the joint will".

A number of difficulties arise concerning the operation of such trusts.[193]

12–030   (a) *When Does the Trust Arise?* It has been said that there are three possibilities.[194] When the agreement was made; when the first testator dies; or when the survivor dies. It is clear that no trust exists from the date of the agreement. For either party can revoke or alter his will[195] before either dies, on giving notice to the other[196]; and even notice is not necessary in the case of the first to die, for the survivor has notice on the first death and will not be prejudiced.[197] The survivor in such circumstances is unable to establish any trust in his favour against the estate of the first to die.[198] Nor can the death of the survivor be the correct time. For where a beneficiary died

---

[188] *Vynior's Case* (1609) 8 Co.Rep. 81b.

[189] *Charles v Fraser* [2010] W.T.L.R. 1489 (all non-dispositive parts of the new will are valid).

[190] *In the Goods of Heys* [1914] p.192; *Stone v Hoskins* [1905] p.194 (later will of first to die).

[191] (1769) Dick 419; interpreted in *Re Dale (Deceased)*, above, fn.184, as not requiring any benefit to pass to the survivor.

[192] *Re Hagger* [1930] 2 Ch. 190 at 195.

[193] These difficulties are discussed in T. Youdan (1979) 29 U. of Toronto L.J. at 411–419.

[194] J. Mitchell (1951) 14 M.L.R. 137.

[195] See *Re Hobley (Deceased)*, *The Times*, June 16, 1997 (effect of mutual wills destroyed where first to die had altered his will in a minor but not insignificant way).

[196] *Dufour v Pereira* (1769) Dick. 419 at 420.

[197] (1769) Dick. 419. See also *Re Hobley* [2006] W.T.L.R. 467.

[198] *Stone v Hoskins* [1905] p.194.

between the date of the death of the first to die and the survivor, the estate of that beneficiary was able to claim its share on the ground that the interest was vested and there was no lapse.[199] Of these three possibilities, it seems therefore that the trust arises on the death (without having revoked his will) of the first to die.[200]

Until quite recently a fourth possibility was arguable: that the trust arises when the survivor receives a benefit under the first will. On this question there were dicta both ways. Most of the dicta favoured the view that the trust is imposed only where the survivor takes a benefit.[201] Clauson J., however, in *Re Hagger*[202] said obiter that the trust would arise "even though the survivor did not signify his election to give effect to the will by taking benefits under it".

It was held by Morritt J. in *Re Dale (Deceased)*,[203] after a full review of all the authorities, that the doctrine of mutual wills applies even where the survivor does not benefit from the will of the first testator. A husband and wife agreed that each would leave his or her whole estate to their son and daughter equally. The husband died first, leaving his estate of £18,500 in this way. The wife later made a new will leaving her daughter £300 and the rest of her estate of £19,000 to her son. It was held that the son, as executor, held the estate on trust for himself and the daughter equally. Benefit by the survivor was a sufficient but not a necessary requirement for the operation of the doctrine. The survivor committed a fraud on the first testator who died in reliance upon their bargain even if he or she did not benefit from the will. That this was the true basis of the doctrine appeared from *Dufour v Pereira*[204]:

> "[H]e, that dies first, does by his death carry the agreement on his part into execution. If the other then refuses, he is guilty of a fraud, can never unbind himself, and becomes a trustee of course. For no man shall deceive another to his prejudice".[205]

Morritt J. considered that the imposition of the trust was consistent with all the authorities, supported by some of them and was in furtherance of equity's original jurisdiction to intervene in cases of fraud.

---

[199] *Re Hagger* [1930] 2 Ch. 190; cf. *Re Gardner (No.2)* [1923] Ch. 230.

[200] *Thomas and Agnes Carvel Foundation v Carvel* [2008] Ch. 395.

[201] *Dufour v Pereira* (1769) Dick. 419 at 421; *Stone v Hoskins* [1905] p.194 at 197; *Re Oldham* [1925] Ch. 75 at 87. See also *Re Cleaver* [1981] 1 W.L.R. 939.

[202] [1930] 2 Ch. 190 at p.195. See R. Burgess (1970) 34 Conv.(N.S.) 230; K. Hodkinson [1982] Conv. 228 at 230.

[203] [1994] Ch. 31; D. Brown (1993) 7 T.L.I. 18; C. Sherrin All E.R.Rev. 1993, 415.

[204] As more fully reported in *Hargrave's Juridical Arguments*, 1797, Vol.2, p.304.

[205] *Hargrave's Juridical Arguments*, Vol.2, 1797, p.304 at 310 (Lord Camden).

12–031   (b) *To what Property Does the Trust Attach?*[206] This may be clear from the express terms of the will.[207] Failing that, and subject always to a contrary intention, there are four possibilities; that the trust attaches to the property, if any, which the survivor receives from the estate of the first to die: or to all the property that the survivor owned at that time: or to all the property which the survivor owned at his death: or to all property which the survivor owned at any time since the first death.

Clearly the trust must include any property received from the first to die. If the will gave only a life interest, there is no scope for the trust in respect of that property. If the gift is absolute, the imposition of a trust in favour of ultimate beneficiaries will in effect reduce the survivor's interest to a life interest.

The position is more complex in relation to the property of the survivor. *Re Hagger*,[208] suggests that the trust attaches at least to all the property which the survivor had at the time of the first death. Morritt J. held that the trust embraced the survivor's whole estate at his or her death.[209] This means that a lifetime disposition by the survivor would be a breach of trust; indeed it would make nonsense of the trust if he could so dispose of the property.[210] This raises the question of acquisitions by the survivor by his own efforts after the first death. After all, the property acquired after the date of the wills by the first to die was included in his estate; and the agreement, in the absence of a contrary provision, would apply to all property. The agreement thus acts like a covenant to settle after-acquired property, and the property becomes subject to the trust on its becoming vested in the trustee.[211] If this is correct, the effect of mutual wills is to reduce the survivor to the position of a life tenant in respect of all his property. He may use the income, but the capital is held on trust for the ultimate beneficiaries. It was held, however, in *Healey v Brown*[212] that where the mutual wills related to land, the effect of the Law of Property (Miscellaneous Provisions) Act 1989 was that the constructive trust which could arise in spite of the absence of a contract in writing could not affect the survivor's own share in the land. The constructive trust arising under the mutual wills doctrine affected only the share acquired from the first to die. This seems

---

[206] See L. Sheridan (1977) 15 Alberta L.Rev. 211.

[207] As in *Re Green* [1951] Ch. 148, where the wills provided that if the other spouse predeceased, the residue was to be divided into halves, one half being considered as the testator's personal property and the other as the benefit received from the other spouse. It was held that the trust attached only to the latter.

[208] [1930] 2 Ch. 190. (Interest of beneficiary vested before death of survivor.)

[209] *Re Dale (Deceased)* [1994] Ch. 31; cf. *Re Walters* [2009] Ch. 212 at 222, where the claim related only to the property of the deceased (the survivor was alive).

[210] See however Astbury J. in *Re Oldham* [1925] Ch. 75 at 87, 88; suggesting that the trust attaches only to property held by the survivor at death.

[211] *Paul v Paul* (1882) 20 Ch.D. 742; *Re Ralli's WT* [1964] Ch. 288.

[212] [2002] W.T.L.R. 849; C Davis [2003] Conv. 238.

contrary to principle, all the more so as the mutual wills were intended to govern the inheritance of land owned by the testators at the date of their wills.

In *Re Cleaver*[213] Nourse J., relying on the Australian decision   **12–032** *Birmingham v Renfrew*,[214] adopted the view there expressed that the survivor could enjoy the property as an absolute owner in his lifetime, "subject to a fiduciary duty which, so to speak, crystallised on his death and disabled him only from voluntary dispositions *inter vivos*".[215] This meant dispositions calculated to defeat the agreement. There was no objection to ordinary gifts of small value. The difficulty however, is that any such duty not to dissipate the assets in the survivor's lifetime will be unenforceable if the beneficiary does not discover his rights until the survivor's death. Although Nourse J. affirmed the requirement of certainty of subject-matter, this is not fully consistent with his formulation of the rights and duties of the parties.[216] If, on the other hand, the survivor's obligation is merely not to dispose of the property *by will* inconsistently with the agreement,[217] then the difficulties are all the greater; for the trust property would be indefinite until his death. These problems were not examined in *Re Dale (Deceased)*.[218]

(c) *The Survivor as Trustee.* If it is correct that the survivor be-   **12–033** comes a trustee of all the property he owns or acquires before his death, the consequences of the doctrine could be draconian for the survivor, for example if he acquires new dependants after the death of the first testator, or wins the lottery; similarly if the agreed beneficiary acquires a fortune elsewhere or is guilty of misconduct.[219] As far as the beneficiaries are concerned, there is very little opportunity to ensure that proper control over the survivor is maintained. Purchasers have no notice of the trusts, and the trust property may be lost on alienation to them.[220] Also, the survivor may have no idea that he is a trustee. If land is included in the trusts the lack of knowledge of all parties concerned may result in disputes and uncertainties as to title if it is alienated without observing the proper procedures. And, as noted above, further problems arise if the trust is treated as attaching only on the death of the survivor; and as

---

[213] [1981] 1 W.L.R. 939. Similarly in *Goodchild v Goodchild* [1997] 1 W.L.R. 1216.
[214] (1936) 57 C.L.R. 666.
[215] (1936) 57 C.L.R. at 690. cf. *Palmer v Bank of NSW* (1975) 7 A.L.R. 671. See also *Healey v Brown*, above, fn.212 (duty "crystallises" at moment of lifetime disposition in breach).
[216] See K. Hodkinson [1982] Conv. 228.
[217] See *Palmer v Bank of NSW*, above, fn.215.
[218] [1994] Ch. 31; above.
[219] See P. O'Hagan (1994) 144 N.L.J. 1272.
[220] *Pilcher v Rawlins* (1872) L.R. 7 Ch.App. 259.

"floating"[221] or as being "in suspense"[222] in the meantime. This is the problem, it should be noted, created in the field of secret trusts by dicta in *Ottaway v Norman*.[223] The possibilities of trouble are unlimited; they have not yet been finally worked out.

12–034   **iv. Conclusion.** It is clear that the imposition by law of a trust in cases of mutual wills is a clumsy and inadequate way of dealing with a complicated problem. A contractual solution under the *Beswick* principle would be much more satisfactory; but this has not been accepted.[224] The impact of the Contracts (Rights of Third Parties) Act 1999 in this area remains to be seen. A solution based on the idea of a floating charge has also been suggested.[225] A legislative solution is possible.[226] For the present, persons who wish to leave property by way of mutual wills should be advised to consider most carefully the trusts on which they wish the property to be held; what property is to be included; the position during the survivor's lifetime; who they wish to be trustees; what administrative powers the trustees should have; and how best the scheme desired can be carried out from an inheritance tax point of view. It is the duty of a solicitor acting for testators making mirror wills to ascertain the intentions of both as to revocation, to advise on the effect of mutual wills, and to ensure that any agreement is clearly and accurately recorded.[227]

The law in this context, as in most other areas of constructive trusts, imposes a trust in an attempt to prevent one party from committing a fraud on the other. It is a kind of salvage operation; a salvage of a wreck which competent legal advice would have avoided in the first place.[228] The recently expressed view of the Court of Appeal is that the mutual wills doctrine:

> "[C]ontinues to be a source of contention for the families of those who have invoked it. The likelihood is that in future even fewer people will opt for such an arrangement and even more will be warned against the risks involved."[229]

---

[221] Above, para.12–032; D. Hayton (1972) 36 Conv.(N.S.) 129 at 132; C. Davis (2002) 61 C.L.J. 423 at 427.

[222] per Brightman J. [1972] Ch. 698 at 713; *Re Cleaver*, above, fn.213.

[223] [1972] Ch. 698 at 713 ("suspended trust" where donee obliged to bequeath to X whatever remains at the donee's death), above, para.5–008.

[224] *Re Dale (Deceased)* [1994] Ch. 31.

[225] K. Hodkinson [1982] Conv. 228, at 231. This does not solve the problem that the "beneficiaries" are often unaware of the situation.

[226] See New Zealand Wills Act 2007, applying only where both testators have died; N. Richardson (2010) 24 T.L.I. 99.

[227] *Charles v Fraser* [2010] W.T.L.R. 1489; G. Griffiths [2011] Conv. 511.

[228] For a different view, see F. Sunnucks (1988) 138 N.L.J. 351.

[229] *Re Walters* [2009] Ch. 212 at 215; P. Luxton [2009] Conv. 498.

D. The Vendor under a Specifically Enforceable Contract for Sale

A contract for sale is specifically enforceable where the remedy of **12–035** damages would be inadequate.[230] Contracts relating to personalty are rarely specifically enforceable, as the property may be purchased elsewhere. If this is not so, as in the case of shares in a private company, then the contract will be specifically enforceable.[231] In the present context, however, we are mainly concerned with contracts relating to land. The availability of specific performance means that, in equity, the purchaser is regarded as already the owner. Thus it has many times been said by high authority that a vendor of land, on the conclusion of the contract of sale, becomes a trustee of the land for the purchaser.[232] He must take reasonable care to preserve the property pending completion.[233] Any changes in the nature of the property between contract and completion, for example by fire or flooding, if they occur without the fault of the vendor, are at the purchaser's risk.[234] If the vendor sells to another, he holds the purchase money on trust for the purchaser.[235] Beyond that, however, there is little agreement.[236] It is clear at least that this is not an ordinary trusteeship. Cotton L.J. said that the vendor was trustee only in a qualified sense[237]; Lord Greene M.R. called him a quasi-trustee,[238] and Stamp L.J. a "constructive trustee or a trustee *sub modo*"[239]; and Lord Cairns[240] explained that the trustee was entitled to protect his own interest in the property. Similarly, the vendor is entitled to keep for himself the rents and profits of the land (or dividends in the case of shares[241]) until the date of the completion of the sale,[242] and to retain possession against the purchaser until the purchase price has been paid; and he retains a lien on the land for the

---

[230] Below, Ch.24.

[231] See *Oughtred v IRC* [1960] A.C. 206; *Neville v Wilson* [1997] Ch. 144; *Michaels v Harley House (Marylebone) Ltd* [2000] Ch. 104.

[232] *Lysaght v Edwards* (1876) 2 Ch.D. 499 at 507; V. Wellings (1959) 23 Conv.(N.S.) 173; Waters, *The Constructive Trust*, 1964, Ch.2; Oakley, *Constructive Trusts*, Ch.6. See further *Nelson v Greening & Sykes (Builders) Ltd*, *The Times*, January 22, 2008.

[233] *Englewood Properties Ltd v Patel* [2005] 1 W.L.R. 1961.

[234] *Paine v Meller* (1801) 6 Ves.Jr. 349. As to insurance, see LPA 1925 s.47. For the view that the risk does not pass to the purchaser see M. Thompson [1984] Conv. 43. See further Law Com. No.191 (1990), *Transfer of Land; Risk of Damage after Contract for Sale*, para.2.25, suggesting that the risk should pass only on completion.

[235] *Lake v Bayliss* [1974] 1 W.L.R. 1073; *Shaw v Foster* (1872) 5 H.L. 321 at 327; F. Crane (1974) 38 Conv.(N.S.) 357.

[236] Cotton, Brett and James L.JJ. in *Rayner v Preston* (1881) Ch.D. 1 expressed different views on the situation.

[237] *Rayner v Preston*, above, fn.236, at p.6; *Lysaght v Edwards* (1876) 2 Ch.D. 499 at 506; *Royal Bristol Permanent Building Society v Bomash* (1887) 35 Ch.D. 390 at 397 ("a modified sense"); *Re Hamilton-Snowball's Conveyance* [1959] Ch. 308.

[238] *Cumberland Consolidated Holdings Ltd v Ireland* [1946] K.B. 264 at 269.

[239] *Berkley v Poulett* (1977) 242 E.G. 39 at 43.

[240] *Shaw v Foster* (1872) L.R. 5 H.L. 321 at 338.

[241] *J. Sainsbury Plc v O'Connor (Inspector of Taxes)* [1991] S.T.C. 318.

[242] *Cuddon v Tite* (1858) 1 Giff 395.

price if the land is conveyed before the price is paid,[243] and time runs under the Limitation Act 1980 against the vendor in respect of possession of the land.[244] The relationship between the parties contains a number of aspects in which they are hostile and the vendor self-interested.

Once the date for completion has arrived and the price is paid in full, the vendor must immediately convey. This is an example of a trusteeship arising because the bare legal estate is in one person, and the entire beneficial ownership in another.[245] Until that situation has arisen, it does not seem that any useful purpose is served by stating that the relationship between the parties is one of trustee and beneficiary. The position at law is that they are parties to a contract and no more. In equity additional rights arise by reason of the fact that specific performance is available as a remedy in favour of an innocent party. Equity then treats as done that which ought to be done, and considers the purchaser as being the owner in equity. Hence, where a receiver was appointed upon the vendor company's insolvency before completion, the contract remained specifically enforceable against the receiver as opposed to merely sounding in damages.[246] This is not attributable to any trust, but to the characteristics of a specifically enforceable contract for sale, whereby the equitable interest passes to the purchaser and is not destroyed by the subsequent insolvency of the vendor. The trust cannot be enforced against a purchaser if the contract, being unregistered, does not bind him.[247] In many other respects the contractual nature of the relationship is apparent; each party is continuing to guard his own interests against the other in a way which is quite inconsistent with the existence of the relationship of trustee and beneficiary.

A further question is whether the vendor becomes trustee for a sub-purchaser, if the purchaser has entered into a contract to sell to the sub-purchaser. In such a case, the sub-purchaser, by virtue of his contract with the purchaser, is entitled to specific performance and is treated as the owner in equity. In *Berkley v Earl Poulett*[248] the vendor, with the concurrence of the purchaser, had allegedly allowed certain fixtures to be taken away. The sub-purchaser claimed that the vendor was in breach of the trustee's duty to take proper care of the property. A majority of the Court of Appeal considered

---

[243] *Mackreth v Symmons* (1808) 15 Ves.Jr. 329. See further S. Worthington (1994) 53 C.L.J. 263.

[244] *Bridges v Mees* [1957] Ch. 475; cf. *Hyde v Pearce* [1982] 1 All E.R. 1029.

[245] *Lloyds Bank Plc v Carrick* [1996] 4 All E.R. 630; M. Thompson [1996] Conv. 295; S. Cretney (1997) 27 Fam. Law 95; N. Hopkins (1998) 61 M.L.R. 486.

[246] *Freevale Ltd v Metrostore (Holdings) Ltd* [1984] 1 All E.R. 495 (a receiver, unlike a liquidator, has no statutory right to disclaim contracts); D. Milman and S. Coneys [1984] Conv. 446; *Re Coregrange Ltd* [1984] B.C.L.C. 453.

[247] *Lloyds Bank Plc v Carrick*, above, fn.245.

[248] (1977) 242 E.G. 39.

that no fiduciary duty was owed to the sub-purchaser. It was not that the vendor was a trustee and therefore had fiduciary duties; rather that the vendor owed duties to the purchaser and was labelled a trustee. A sub-purchaser's right is to have the purchaser enforce the contract against the vendor.

No doubt it is too late now to say that the relationship between vendor and purchaser is not that of trustee and beneficiary.[249] The terminology must, however, be received with reserve. Unlike other cases of constructive trusts, the element of improper conduct is absent and the situation must, at best, be treated as anomalous.[250]

E. Secret Trusts

It is unsettled whether secret trusts, and more particularly half-secret trusts, are to be regarded as express or constructive. The practical significance of the distinction is that, in the case of land, s.53 of the Law of Property Act 1925 requires written evidence in the case of express trusts, but not in the case of constructive trusts. The matter is examined in detail in Ch.5.

12–036

F. Conveyance by Fraud

Where property has been obtained by the fraud of the defendant, he may be compelled to hold it as a constructive trustee. The trust is not imposed in every case.[251] While it is difficult to define the circumstances in which the trust will be imposed, some broad principles are in practice clear. In the case of a conveyance of land, the transferee may be prevented, by the imposition of a constructive trust, from setting up the apparently absolute nature of the conveyance in order to defeat a beneficial interest which, by oral agreement, was intended to remain in the transferor,[252] or in some third party.[253] Where owners of land appointed an agent to sell their property, but the agent instead procured a transfer into his own name by fraudulent misrepresentation, for no consideration and in breach

12–037

---

[249] cf. Hopkins, *The Informal Acquisition of Rights in Land*, 2000, p.64, relying on *Westdeutsche Landesbank Girozentrale v Islington LBC* [1996] A.C. 669.

[250] See W. Swadling, Degeling and Edelman (eds), *Equity in Commercial Law*, Ch.18. We have seen that it is not treated as a constructive trust for the purpose of LPA 1925 s.53(2); *Oughtred v IRC* [1960] A.C. 206, above, para.3–012.

[251] For example, if the claimant had acquiesced in the fraud; *Lonrho Plc v Fayed (No.2)* [1992] 1 W.L.R. 1. See *Halifax Building Society v Thomas* [1996] Ch. 217; above, para.12–007.

[252] *Rochefoucauld v Boustead* [1897] 1 Ch. 196; *Bannister v Bannister* [1948] 2 All E.R. 133; *Hodgson v Marks* [1972] Ch. 892; above, para.3–005.

[253] *Binions v Evans* [1972] Ch. 359; *Peffer v Rigg* [1977] 1 W.L.R. 285; *Lyus v Prowsa Developments Ltd* [1982] 1 W.L.R. 1044; *Staden v Jones* [2008] 2 F.L.R. 1931. See also J. Feltham [1987] Conv. 246; E. Cooke and P. O'Connor (2004) 120 L.Q.R. 640, discussing these cases in the context of the Land Registration Act 2002.

of fiduciary duty, he held the property on trust for the transferors. The Court of Appeal considered it to be immaterial whether the trust was labelled implied, resulting or constructive.[254]

Similarly, situations in which a will is fraudulently revoked, or where the testator is fraudulently prevented from making a will, or fraudulently induced to leave property to a legatee or devisee, are all appropriate for the imposition of a constructive trust. These situations are discussed under the heading of secret trusts.[255]

G. Acquisition of Property by Killing[256]

12–038   Where a beneficiary kills the testator, or next of kin kills an intestate, there is good reason to prevent him from benefiting from his crime.[257] The English courts have established a rule to this effect, but they:

> "[H]ave worked out no rational theory for their actions in depriving killers[258] . . . there has been little discussion of the theoretical basis for a deprivation . . . and generally they have considered that the killer does not gain legal title".[259]

Such a result is contrary to the enactments relating to succession, testate or intestate, but clearly a rule of public policy can override statutory provisions.[260] If the killer does not acquire any title to the property in question, as in the pension and insurance cases, then there is no need for the imposition of a constructive trust. If, on the other hand, the killer acquires legal title, for example if it has been vested in him before the killing was discovered,[261] then he will be subjected to a constructive trust which is imposed to prevent unjust enrichment. A bona fide purchaser from the wrongdoer would then be protected.[262]

Whichever solution is reached, a number of problems remain, on which there is little authority.

---

[254] *Collings v Lee* [2001] 2 All E.R. 332.

[255] Above. For a fuller discussion, see Ch.5.

[256] Goff and Jones, Ch.38; T. Youdan (1973) 89 L.Q.R. 235, which has been used as the basis of this account; American Law Institute, *Third Restatement of the Law of Restitution and Unjust Enrichment*, 2011, para.45; G. Virgo [1998] 6 R.L.R. 34 at 46–61; P. Smith (2004) 18 T.L.I. 194.

[257] *In the Estate of Crippen* [1911] P. 108.

[258] (1973) 89 L.Q.R. 235.

[259] (1973) 89 L.Q.R. 235 at 251.

[260] See, for example, *R. v Chief National Insurance Commissioner, Ex p. Connor*, fn.270.

[261] Law Com. No.295 (2005), *The Forfeiture Rule and the Law of Succession*, para.3.23.

[262] *Re Cash* (1911) 30 N.Z.L.R. 571; *Beresford v Royal Insurance Ltd* [1938] A.C. 586 at 600.

i. Type of Killing. Killing may be effected by any means from **12–039**
murder to accident. The deprivation principle only applies to criminal killing. The rule has not in the past been applied to all cases of
manslaughter.[263] However, formulations based on whether the act
was deliberate or violent have not proved satisfactory, and the position now appears to be that the rule applies to all types of manslaughter.[264] In *Dunbar v Plant*[265] the public policy rule was applied
to the survivor of a suicide pact, who had aided and abetted the
other's suicide, but full relief was granted under the Forfeiture Act
1982 (discussed below).

ii. Means of Acquisition. The principle applies when the killer **12–040**
benefits by testamentary gift,[266] or under the victim's intestacy,[267]
and also under a life insurance policy on the victim's life[268]; and, in
the days when suicide was a crime, the estate of a suicide was held
to be unable to claim the benefits of an insurance policy.[269] Similarly, a woman who kills her husband cannot claim a widow's
pension.[270] More complicated questions arise where one joint tenant
kills another, or a remainderman kills the life tenant. In the case of a
joint tenancy, the killing effects a severance, so that the joint tenant
does not profit under the doctrine of survivorship. Thus he holds the
legal estate on trust for himself and the victim's estate in equal
shares.[271] In the case of the remainderman killing the life tenant, the
best course would be to postpone the killer's enjoyment until the
time at which the victim's life expectation would terminate.[272]

iii. Destination of Property. To deprive the wrongdoer does not **12–041**
solve all the problems. One question is whether persons claiming
through the wrongdoer should benefit from the crime. In *Re DWS*
(Deceased)[273] X murdered his parents, who died intestate, leaving

---

[263] *Gray v Barr* [1971] 2 Q.B. 544; *Re K (Deceased)* [1986] Ch. 180; cf. *Re Hall* [1914] P.
1; *Re Giles* [1972] Ch. 544; *Jones v Roberts* [1995] 2 F.L.R. 422; R. Buckley (1995) 111
L.Q.R. 196; *Re S (Deceased)* [1996] 1 W.L.R. 235.
[264] *Re Land* [2007] 1 W.L.R. 1009 (manslaughter by gross negligence).
[265] [1998] Ch. 412; M. Thompson [1998] Conv. 45; S. Bridge (1998) 57 C.L.J. 31.
[266] *Re Pollock* [1941] Ch. 219.
[267] *Re Sigsworth* [1935] Ch. 89.
[268] *Cleaver v Mutual Reserve Fund Life Association Ltd* [1892] 1 Q.B. 147; *Davitt v
Titcumb* [1990] Ch. 110; J. Martin [1991] Conv. 50 (mortgage protection policy).
[269] *Beresford v Royal Insurance Ltd* [1938] A.C. 586.
[270] *R. v Chief National Commissioner, Ex p. Connor* [1981] 1 Q.B. 758 (manslaughter); St J
Robilliard (1981) 44 M.L.R. 718. See also J. Shand (1972) 31 C.L.J. 144. As submitted above,
this is not a case of constructive trust, as the claimant acquires no title to any property.
[271] *Dunbar v Plant* [1998] Ch. 412.
[272] (1973) 89 L.Q.R. 235 at 250.
[273] [2001] Ch. 568. It is understood that a settlement was reached after Y applied to the
European Court of Human Rights.

no other children. X's only child, Y, claimed his grandparents' estates under s.47 of the Administration of Estates Act 1925, which provides that a grandchild is entitled to the share of a child who has predeceased the intestate. Y's claim failed on the basis that the public policy rule did not require the court to treat the murderer as having predeceased the victim. Thus the property devolved on the class of next-of-kin ranking after the issue of the intestate. However, this result was generally considered unfair, and it has now been reversed by the Estates of Deceased Persons (Forfeiture Rule and Law of Succession) Act 2011.[274] In other cases, the proper solution will be for the property to go to the victim's residuary legatee, or as on his intestacy,[275] or to the other members of a class of which the wrongdoer was one[276]; or, where there are special circumstances to show what the victim's intention was, as where it was shown that the killing took place in order to prevent the victim from changing his will in favour of another, then the flexibility introduced by the concept of the constructive trust should allow the property to be claimed by "the person who, in the eyes of equity, has the best right to it."[277]

12–042   **iv. Statutory Relief.** It is provided by the Forfeiture Act 1982[278] that the court may grant relief from the forfeiture of inheritance and other rights to persons guilty of unlawful killing[279] other than murder,[280] where the court is satisfied that the justice of the case so requires.[281] A convicted person must bring proceedings for this purpose within three months of any conviction.[282] The Act applies to benefits under a will or upon intestacy; nominations; a *donatio mortis causa*; and property held on trust before the death which would devolve on the offender as a result of the death.[283] The Court may grant relief as to all or part of the property.[284] In the case of social security benefits, such as a widow's pension, the Act confers

---

[274] s.1 (intestacy) and s.2 (wills). The Act applies to deaths after its commencement on February 1, 2012.

[275] See *Re Jones (Deceased)* [1998] 1 F.L.R. 246 (court cannot rewrite contingencies attached to residuary gift).

[276] *Re Peacock* [1957] Ch. 310.

[277] (1973) 89 L.Q.R. 235 at 257.

[278] P. Kenny (1983) 46 M.L.R. 66; A. Mithani and A. Wilton (1983) 80 L.S.Gaz. 910.

[279] Including aiding, abetting, counselling or procuring the death; s.1(2). The survivor of a suicide pact will usually obtain relief; *Dunbar v Plant* [1998] Ch. 412.

[280] s.5.

[281] s.2(2). Degree of moral blame is significant; *Re K (Deceased)* [1986] Ch. 180; *Re Murphy* [2003] W.T.L.R. 687.

[282] s.2(3); *Re Land* [2007] 1 W.L.R. 1009. But the Act and the doctrine may apply even in the case of acquittal, because the civil standard of proof is lower; *Gray v Barr* [1971] 2 Q.B. 544.

[283] s.2(4). See *Re S (Deceased)* [1996] 1 W.L.R. 235 (joint life insurance).

[284] s.2(1) and (5); *Re K (Deceased)*, above, fn.281.

the discretion not on the court but on the Social Security Commissioner.[285] Finally, it is provided that the forfeiture principle does not preclude an application under the Family Provision legislation.[286]

H. Constructive Trusts of a New Model: Justice and Good Conscience

Some cases indicated a wide extension of the operation of con- **12–043** structive trusts by the introduction of what Lord Denning M.R. called "a constructive trust of a new model".[287] The broad principle was that a constructive trust may be imposed, regardless of established legal rules, in order to reach the result required by equity, justice and good conscience. The principle was thus articulated in *Hussey v Palmer*[288]:

"It is a trust imposed by law wherever justice and good conscience require it. It is a liberal process, founded on large principles of equity. . . . It is an equitable remedy by which the court can enable an aggrieved party to obtain restitution."

Such a principle, if it survived, would effect a complete swing on the pendulum so far as the principles of English law concerning constructive trusts are concerned. The law in this field was once criticised as being too restricted[289]; in that the older cases would find a constructive trust only where the facts brought the case within one of the limited and established categories of constructive trust, usually requiring a fiduciary relationship. The new model opened up the possibility of finding a constructive trust in any situation in which the established rules lead to a result which would appear to be inconsistent with equity, justice and good conscience.[290]

Not surprisingly, this doctrine was applied in cases where satisfactory solutions under established doctrines proved particularly difficult to find. Illustrations came from the plight of the deserted wife or cohabitant and the problem of the licensee of land whose expectations had been disappointed. In Ch.11 we saw that, in the context of claims to an interest in the family home, some decisions were difficult to reconcile with the principles of *Pettitt v Pettitt*[291] and *Gissing v Gissing*,[292] to the effect that the interests of the parties

---

[285] s.4, as amended. See (1984) 81 L.S.Gaz. 288; (1988) 85 L.S.Gaz. 37 (sequel to *Re K (Deceased)*, above).
[286] s.3. See *Re Land*, above, fn.282.
[287] *Eves v Eves* [1975] 1 W.L.R. 1338.
[288] [1972] 1 W.L.R. 1286 at 1289.
[289] Waters, *The Constructive Trust*, 1964.
[290] R. Maudsley (1977) 28 N.I.L.Q. 123.
[291] [1970] A.C. 777.
[292] [1971] A.C. 886.

must be determined according to the principles of property law and not to what the court thinks would be "fair". In *Eves v Eves*,[293] involving an unmarried couple, the man bought a house as a joint home. He had it conveyed into his sole name, giving as an excuse the fact that the woman was under 21 years old. She did a great deal of heavy work in the house and garden, beyond ordinary housework. After they separated, the court held that she was entitled to a quarter share of the house.

> "In strict law she has no claim upon him whatever. She is not his wife. He is not bound to provide a roof over her head. He can turn her into the street. . . . And a few years ago even equity would not have helped her. But things are altered now. . . . "

It would be:

> "[M]ost inequitable for him to deny her any share in the house. The law will impute or impose a constructive trust by which he was to hold it in trust for both of them."[294]

12–044   The courts were thus "invoking the constructive trust as an equitable remedy to do justice inter partes."[295] While a liberalisation of the application of equitable remedies is generally to be welcomed, it is important to appreciate that the "new model" constructive trust left a number of problems in its wake. The concept of justice alone is too vague to be used as the basis for determining property rights, and, inevitably, the imposition of the constructive trust on this basis would be impossible to forecast. Further, a trust creates equitable proprietary rights, and these can operate more widely than the dispute between the parties. The question of the rights of third parties arises: whether, in particular, a purchaser or mortgagee is bound by a licensee's right of occupation, or by a cohabitant's claim to share in the home.

It is important also to appreciate that the "new model" constructive trust went far beyond the principle of the remedial constructive trust to prevent unjust enrichment,[296] although some examples of the remedial constructive trust differ little from Lord Denning's formulation.[297] The provision of a remedy for unjust enrichment does not require an unlimited free-wheeling discretion as to the imposition of a constructive trust. There must at least be general guide-lines for the exercise of the discretion. The law of unjust enrichment lays

---

[293] [1975] 1 W.L.R. 1338, above, para.11–012.
[294] [1975] 1 W.L.R. 1338 at 1341.
[295] A. Oakley (1973) 26 C.L.P. 17 at 35.
[296] Above, para.12–006.
[297] See M. Bryan (1994) 8 T.L.I. 74 at 79, discussing Australian decisions.

down with reasonable clarity when an action will lie. Some of the English cases seemed to treat a constructive trust as a magic formula to reach a just result between the parties, regardless of existing proprietary rights in them, or of the interests of persons who were not parties to the dispute.

Present indications, however, are that the "new model" constructive trust, which declined after the retirement of Lord Denning M.R., will not revive. Although the House of Lords and Supreme Court favour a broad approach to ascertaining the parties' intentions concerning their shares in the family home, this does not go as far as deciding a case on the basis of what the court itself considers a fair result.[298] Similarly in the Commonwealth, where, although the remedial constructive trust is accepted, it has been said that "the legitimacy of the new model is at least suspect; at best it is a mutant from which further breeding should be discouraged."[299]

---

[298] *Stack v Dowden* [2007] 2 A.C. 432 at 456; above, para.11–004; *Jones v Kernott* [2011] 3 W.L.R. 1121; above, para.11–006. See generally T. Etherton (2008) 67 C.L.J. 265.

[299] *Allen v Snyder* [1977] 2 N.S.W.L.R. 685 at 701. The "new model" was also rejected in *Carly v Farrelly* [1975] 1 N.Z.L.R. 356; G. Samuels (1978) 94 L.Q.R. 347; *Muschinski v Dodds* (1985) 160 C.L.R. 583. The "new model" was accepted in a modified form in *Pettkus v Becker* (1980) 17 D.L.R. (3rd) 257; M. Bryan (1982) 12 Fam. Law 21. See further W. Gummow (1978) 94 L.Q.R. 351; D. Waters (1975) 53 C.B.R. 366; F. Bates [1982] Conv. 424; K. Hodkinson [1983] Conv. 420.

TRUSTS WHICH CONTRAVENE THE LAW

A TRUST, though otherwise valid, may fail because it contains an element of unlawfulness or immorality, or is contrary to public policy. It is impossible to categorise all the possible grounds of unlawfulness, and only some of the more important ones can be mentioned here.

1. TRUSTS CONTRARY TO THE GENERAL POLICY OF THE LAW

A. Purposes Contrary to Law, Public Policy or Morality

It will be appreciated that such trusts are likely to fail in any **13–001** event, apart from any question of unlawfulness, on the ground that they are non-charitable purpose trusts.[1] There are, perhaps for this reason, few examples of cases decided on the basis of illegality, but one such is *Thrupp v Collett*,[2] where a testator attempted to provide for paying the fines of convicted poachers. Sir John Romilly M.R. held the trust void on the ground that it was against public policy. It was held in *Bowman v Secular Society*[3] that the denial of Christianity was not of itself an illegal purpose, but it was suggested in *Thornton v Howe*[4] that a trust whose purpose was adverse to all religion or subversive of morality would be void. It need hardly be added that trusts for the furtherance of illegal or immoral activities, such as, for example, terrorism or prostitution,[5] would fail. Likewise a trust for a fraudulent purpose, such as placing money with a company in order to give it the false appearance of a credit balance.[6] The Law Commission[7] regarded an "illegal trust" as comprising the following: a trust which it would be legally wrongful to create or impose; a trust which is created to facilitate fraud or some other legal wrong or which arises as a result of a transaction or arrangement with that objective; a trust which is created in return for the commission of a legal wrong or the promise to commit a legal wrong; a trust which expressly or necessarily requires a trustee or beneficiary to commit a legal wrong or which tends or is intended to do so; and a trust which is otherwise contrary to public policy at common law. However, this aspect was not included in the final report, which was confined to a different aspect of illegality in the law of trusts.[8]

It was at one time established that gifts by deed or will for future illegitimate children were void on the ground that they would tend to encourage immorality.[9] The position was changed by s.15(7) of the Family Law Reform Act 1969 (now replaced by the Family Law Reform Act 1987 s.19).[10]

---

[1] Below, Ch.14. See, for example, *Brown v Burdett* (1882) 21 Ch.D. 667, where a "useless" trust to seal up a house for 20 years failed.

[2] (1858) 26 Beav. 125.

[3] [1917] A.C. 406 (Lord Finlay L.C. dissenting).

[4] (1862) 31 Beav. 14.

[5] See Harman L.J.'s example of a "school for prostitutes or pickpockets" in *Re Pinion* [1965] Ch. 85. See also *Sutton v Mishcon de Reya (A Firm)* [2004] 1 F.L.R. 774 (contract for cohabitation).

[6] *Re Great Berlin Steamboat Co* (1884) 26 Ch.D. 616.

[7] Law Com. C.P. No.154 (1999), *Illegal Transactions: The Effect of Illegality on Contracts and Trusts*, para.8.22; below, para.13–011. See also *Re the Esteem Settlement* [2004] W.T.L.R. 1 at 45 (Jersey Royal Court), accepting that, in exceptional circumstances, an initially valid trust could become void as being contrary to public policy.

[8] Law Com. No.320, *The Illegality Defence* (2010); above, para.10–032.

[9] *Occleston v Fullalove* (1874) L.R. 9 Ch.App. 147; cf. *Re Hyde* [1932] 1 Ch. 95. The claim of an illegitimate beneficiary might have failed in any event on the ground that gifts were generally construed as confined to legitimate relatives. This is no longer the position: Family Law Reform Act 1987 s.19 (replacing FLRA 1969 s.15).

[10] This Act replaces the concept of the illegitimate child with that of the unmarried parent.

B. Statutory Provisions Against Discrimination

i. Background. It has been unlawful for many years to discrimi-   **13–002**
nate against persons with particular characteristics in areas such as
employment, the provisions of goods and services and the disposal
of property. Thus the Sex Discrimination Act 1975 made discrimination on grounds of sex unlawful in these areas, and the Race
Relations Act 1976 (replacing earlier legislation) did likewise in the
case of racial discrimination. Discrimination on the grounds of religion or belief was prohibited in the employment field by regulations,
and the prohibition was extended to other areas by the Equality Act
2006. That Act also enabled regulations to be made to prohibit
discrimination on the ground of sexual orientation. Age discrimination was also prohibited by regulations in the field of employment
and training.

ii. Equality Act 2010. The statutory provisions mentioned above   **13–003**
have now been replaced and in some respects extended by the
Equality Act 2010. The Act prohibits discrimination against persons
who share "protected characteristics", which are: age, disability,
gender reassignment, marriage and civil partnership, pregnancy and
maternity, race, religion or belief, sex and sexual orientation.[11]
"Race" is defined as including colour, nationality, ethnic or national
origins.[12] "Religion" means any religion or lack of religion (for
example atheism), and "belief" means any religious or philosophical belief or a lack of belief.[13]

The areas in which discrimination is made unlawful by the Act of
2010 include employment, public sector services, education, occupational pension schemes and the disposal of property. Subject to
what is said below about charitable trusts, the legislation does not
extend to discrimination in the making of a gift or trust. But trustees,
just as any other individuals, are bound by the provisions relating to
employment, disposal of property and so on. This is especially
significant in the administration of charitable trusts.

iii. Charitable Trusts. The Equality Act 2010 contains special   **13–004**
provisions relating to charitable trusts, which replace and harmonise
the separate exceptions in the previous legislation. There is no
breach of the Act if benefits are conferred on persons who share a
"protected characteristic" (for example race, age or sex), provided
this is a proportionate means of achieving a legitimate aim or is to

---

[11] Equality Act 2010 s.4.
[12] Equality Act 2010 s.9.
[13] Equality Act 2010 s.10.

prevent or compensate for a disadvantage linked to the characteristic.[14] In other words, it is lawful to discriminate in favour of such
groups of persons, but not against them.[15] Thus there is nothing
unlawful in single sex charities, such as the YMCA, as long as the
provisions of the Act are satisfied. In the case of educational charities, however, the single sex restriction may be removed or modified
by ministerial order.[16] So far as religion and belief are concerned, it
is not unlawful for a charity to require members and persons wishing
to become members to accept a particular religion or belief, and to
restrict the benefits and facilities accordingly.[17]

Special rules apply to discrimination on the basis of colour. While
the general position is that the Equality Act 2010 does not affect a
provision in a charitable instrument which provides for conferring
benefits on persons who share "protected characteristics", including
race, it is not permissible to discriminate even in favour of a class
defined by reference to colour.[18] Any such provision is to take effect
as if it provided for conferring the benefits in question on persons of
the class which results if the colour qualification is disregarded.

Finally, it should be noted that even where discrimination in a
charitable trust is not made unlawful by the legislation, the removal
of discriminatory provisions is possible under the cy-près doctrine.[19]

C. Conditions Precedent and Subsequent; Determinable Interests

13–005   Questions involving illegality often arise in connection with the
validity of conditions imposed upon otherwise valid gifts.[20] A condition precedent is one which must be satisfied before the gift can
vest, whereas a condition subsequent operates to defeat an already
vested gift by forfeiture. A determinable interest, on the other hand,
is one which will automatically determine on the occurrence of the
determining event, no question of forfeiture being involved.[21] It is

---

[14] s.193(1), (2).

[15] Thus the provisions contained in *Re Dominion Students' Hall Trust* [1947] Ch. 183
would now be unlawful (as was also the case under previous legislation). See also *Re Gwyon*
[1930] 1 Ch. 255.

[16] Equality Act 2010 Sch.14.

[17] Equality Act 2010 s.193(5).

[18] s.193(4). See *Re Harding* [2008] Ch. 235 (gift to "black community" of four London
boroughs was charitable but took effect without the colour qualification).

[19] Below, para.15–063. See *Re Lysaght* [1966] Ch. 191; *Re Dominion Students' Hall Trust*,
above, fn.15; *Canada Trust Company v Ontario Human Rights Commission* (1990) 69 D.L.R.
(4th) 321. The promotion of racial harmony is now a charitable purpose; Charities Act 2011
s.3(1)(h), replacing previous legislation.

[20] Where several conditions are attached to one gift, the valid conditions may be severed
from any which are invalid: *Re Hepplewhite Will Trusts*, *The Times*, January 21, 1977.

[21] Above, para.7–002. For a detailed account of the distinctions and their significance, see
Cheshire and Burn's *Modern Law of Real Property*, 18th edn, Ch.17.

not always easy, as a matter of construction, to decide whether a condition is intended to operate as a condition precedent or subsequent, or to distinguish conditional and determinable interests.[22] It seems that the latter are less susceptible to, although not immune from, attack on the ground of public policy.[23]

Apart from any question of illegality, conditions have frequently failed on the ground of uncertainty. A distinction has been drawn between conditions precedent and subsequent. A stricter test of certainty applies to a condition subsequent, which must be so framed that at the outset the beneficiary knows the exact event which will divest his interest.[24] Lord Denning M.R., has described this distinction as a "deplorable dichotomy", serving only to defeat the settlor's intention.[25] Even in the case of a condition subsequent, however, the court is reluctant to pronounce the condition void for uncertainty. So in *Re Tepper's Will Trusts*,[26] where a condition subsequent required the beneficiaries to remain within the Jewish faith and not to marry outside it, the court regarded as admissible extrinsic evidence of the Jewish faith as practised by the testator, to elucidate the meaning of his words.[27]

Assuming that the condition does not fail for uncertainty, the next question is whether it will be void as being illegal or otherwise contrary to public policy. The matter was recently discussed in *Nathan v Leonard*,[28] where a condition subsequent to the effect that if any beneficiary challenged the will, all dispositions would be forfeited and the estate would devolve to others was not contrary to public policy on the ground that it might deter an application under the Inheritance (Provision for Family and Dependants) Act 1975, nor because of its arbitrary nature. The categories discussed below involve the types of condition which have been most frequently

---

[22] See, for example, *Re Tuck's Settlement Trusts* [1978] Ch. 49; *Re Johnson's Will Trusts* [1967] Ch. 387; *Re Tepper's Will Trusts* [1987] Ch. 358.

[23] See *Re Johnson's Will Trusts*, above, fn.22, at 396; *Re Moore* (1888) 39 Ch.D. 116; Megarry and Wade, *The Law of Real Property*, 7th edn, p.69.

[24] *Re Tepper's Will Trusts*, above, fn.22. The test applying to conditions precedent is that laid down in *Re Allen* [1953] Ch. 810: conceptual uncertainty may not defeat such conditions. A modern example is *Re Barlow's Will Trusts* [1979] 1 W.L.R. 278, above, para.3–038. See generally Underhill and Hayton, 18th edn, pp.149–152; L. McKay [1980] Conv. 263.

[25] *Re Tuck's Settlement Trusts* [1978] Ch. 49 at p.60. But the distinction was acknowledged by the House of Lords in *Blathwayt v Lord Cawley* [1976] A.C. 397 at 425.

[26] Above, fn.22. See also *Ellis v Chief Adjudication Officer* [1998] 1 F.L.R. 184 (gift of house to daughter subject to condition subsequent that she should care for her mother in the house upheld). A condition which is impossible to fulfil is spent and the gift absolute; *Re Chambers* [2001] W.T.L.R. 1375 (condition relating to pet animals which had died).

[27] Relying on *Re Tuck's Settlement Trusts*, above, fn.25, where, however, the will expressly provided that the Chief Rabbi could determine the meaning of "Jewish faith" and "approved wife". cf. AJA 1982 s.21. See P. Clarke and C. Sherrin All E.R. Rev. 1987 at 159 and 260 respectively.

[28] [2003] 1 W.L.R. 827. The condition failed for uncertainty, however.

encountered. The validity of conditions relating to bankruptcy has already been discussed.[29]

13–006   **i. Marriage, Separation and Divorce.** Where property is given by way of a determinable gift until marriage, and then to other beneficiaries, the limitation is unobjectionable.[30] Conditions, on the other hand, will be void if they are designed to prevent marriage or to encourage divorce or separation.

As far as conditions restraining marriage are concerned, a distinction is drawn between total and partial restraints. A condition subsequent, operating to divest the property on marriage, is void if its object is to restrain marriage altogether.[31] But conditions operating only in the event of a second or subsequent marriage, or merely requiring consent to marriage,[32] are not void.[33] Nor is there any objection to a condition in restraint of marriage with certain persons, or a certain class.[34] The rules relating to partial restraints on marriage differ according to whether the gift is of realty or personalty, the reason being that the personalty rules evolved in the ecclesiastical courts, whereas the realty rules were developed by the common law. The result of this historical distinction is as follows: in the case of personalty a condition imposing a partial restraint on marriage is invalid as being merely *"in terrorem"* if there is no express gift over on the occurrence of the marriage[35] whereas in the case of realty, a partial restraint is never invalid, whether or not there is a gift over.[36]

Conditions designed to induce the separation or divorce of a husband and wife are void as being contrary to public policy.[37] But if the parties have already decided upon a separation, the trusts in any deed of separation are not invalid,[38] nor is a post-nuptial agreement providing for the consequences of a future separation.[39] Thus

[29] Above, para.7–003.

[30] *Re Lovell* [1920] 1 Ch. 122.

[31] *Lloyd v Lloyd* (1852) 2 Sim.(N.S.) 255. This includes a condition which in practice amounts to a general restraint: *Re Lanyon* [1927] 2 Ch. 264. (Condition against marriage with any blood relation). It seems that similar rules would apply to a condition precedent. See *Re Wallace* [1920] Ch. 274.

[32] *Re Whiting's Settlement* [1905] 1 Ch. 96.

[33] *Allen v Jackson* (1875) 1 Ch.D. 399.

[34] *Jenner v Turner* (1880) 16 Ch.D. 188; *Perrin v Lyon* (1807) 9 East. 170; condition against marrying a person born in Scotland or of Scottish parents upheld. See also the cases on religion, discussed below.

[35] *Leong v Lim Beng Chye* [1955] A.C. 648 (A residuary gift is not a gift over).

[36] Another possible distinction is that in the case of realty, but not personalty, even a general restraint is valid if intended merely to provide for the beneficiary while unmarried, rather than to promote celibacy: *Jones v Jones* (1876) 1 Q.B.D. 279.

[37] *Re Johnson's Will Trusts* [1967] Ch. 387; *Re Caborne* [1943] Ch. 224. See also *Re Hepplewhite Will Trusts, The Times*, January 21, 1977.

[38] *Wilson v Wilson* (1848) 1 H.L.C. 538. It is otherwise if the provision is designed to discourage reconciliation.

[39] *MacLeod v MacLeod* [2010] 1 A.C. 298. See also *Egerton v Egerton* [1949] 2 All E.R. 238 at 242.

there is no objection where the true object of a disposition is merely to make provision for a party during the separation.[40]

It will be seen that most of these cases were decided at a time when the sanctity of marriage was perhaps regarded more highly than it is today. A stricter view was taken of relationships outside marriage than is now the case. Thus in the past trusts or covenants to create trusts have been held void if created in consideration of a future immoral association.[41] The modern tendency might be to discover some other form of consideration from the beneficiary.[42]

ii. Parental Duties. A condition calculated to bring about the separation of parent and child is void as being contrary to public policy,[43] even where the parents are divorced.[44] Similarly, a condition designed to interfere with the exercise of parental duties.[45] In *Blathwayt v Lord Cawley*[46] a settlement provided for the forfeiture of the interest of any child who became a Roman Catholic. It was argued that the condition was void on the ground that it would hamper parental duties in religious instruction. The House of Lords rejected this argument: **13–007**

"To say that any condition which in any way might affect or influence the way in which a child is brought up, or in which parental duties are exercised, seems to me to state far too wide a rule."[47]

iii. Religion. It has already been noted that prohibitions on discrimination on grounds of religion or belief do not apply to private trusts.[48] Conditions restricting freedom of religion have long been popular with settlors and testators. While such conditions have sometimes failed for uncertainty, especially in the case of conditions   **13–008**

---

[40] *Re Lovell* [1920] 1 Ch. 122. As to the admissibility of any evidence of the settlor's motive, see *Re Johnson's Will Trusts* [1967] Ch. 387.

[41] See *Re Vallance* (1884) 26 Ch.D. 353; *Ayerst v Jenkins* (1873) L.R. 16 Eq. 275. See also *Re Jones* [1953] Ch. 125, where a condition prohibiting a "social or other relationship" with X failed for uncertainty.

[42] See, for example, *Tanner v Tanner* [1975] 1 W.L.R. 1346 where a contract was inferred between a man and his mistress in consideration of her looking after the house and family; cf. *Coombes v Smith* [1986] 1 W.L.R. 808.

[43] *Re Boulter* [1922] 1 Ch. 75.

[44] *Re Piper* [1946] 2 All E.R. 503.

[45] *Re Borwick* [1933] Ch. 657; *Re Sandbrook* [1912] 2 Ch. 471. These two decisions must now be read in the light of the comments made in *Blathwayt v Lord Cawley* [1976] A.C. 397, discussed below.

[46] [1976] A.C. 397.

[47] [1976] A.C. 397 at 426 (per Lord Wilberforce).

[48] Above, para.13–003.

subsequent,[49] it has never been held that such provisions are contrary to public policy, even in the case of charitable trusts.[50] In *Blathwayt v Lord Cawley*,[51] of which the facts have already been given, Lord Cross said that while it may be wrong for the Government to discriminate on religion, it does not follow that it is against public policy for an adherent of one religion to distinguish in disposing of his property; any other view amounts to saying that:

> "[I]t is disreputable for him to be convinced of the importance of holding true religious beliefs and of the fact that his religious beliefs are the true ones."[52]

It had been argued that the Race Relations Acts and the European Convention on Human Rights[53] showed that the law was now against discrimination. Lord Wilberforce said:

> "I do not doubt that conceptions of public policy should move with the times and that widely accepted treaties and statutes may point the direction in which such conceptions, as applied by the courts, ought to move. It may well be that conditions such as this are, or at least are becoming, inconsistent with standards now widely accepted."[54]

But this did not justify the introduction of a new rule, for to do so would reduce another freedom, that of testamentary disposition.

> "Discrimination is not the same thing as choice: it operates over a larger and less personal area, and neither by express provision nor by implication has private selection yet become a matter of public policy."[55]

13–009   **iv. Race.** We have already seen that discrimination on the grounds of race or colour is made unlawful by the Equality Act 2010

---

[49] *Clayton v Ramsden* [1943] A.C. 320 (forfeiture on marriage to person not of Jewish parentage and faith); *Re Abraham's Will Trusts* [1969] 1 Ch. 463; *Re Tepper's Will Trusts* [1987] Ch. 358. A condition precedent is less likely to fail on this ground: see *Re Allen* [1953] Ch. 810; *Re Selby's Will Trusts* [1966] 1 W.L.R. 43; *Re Tuck's Settlement Trusts* [1978] Ch. 49 (marriage to "approved wife" of Jewish blood and faith not uncertain); D. Cooper and D. Herman (1999) 19 L.S. 339. See also *Re Evans* [1940] Ch. 629.

[50] See *Re Lysaght* [1966] Ch. 191; cf. *Canada Trust Company v Ontario Human Rights Commission* (1990) 69 D.L.R. (4th) 321. See also Equality Act 2010 s.193(5); above, para.13–004.

[51] [1976] A.C. 397. See also *Re Remnant's Settlement Trusts* [1970] 1 Ch. 560; *Clayton v Ramsden*, above, fn.49. The heir to the throne may not be, or marry, a Roman Catholic: Act of Settlement 1701.

[52] [1976] A.C. 397 at 429.

[53] Article 9. There is nothing in the Human Rights Act 1998 to affect the dispositions of settlors or testators.

[54] [1976] A.C. 397 at 426.

[55] [1976] A.C. 397.

(replacing earlier legislation), and that, apart from special provisions relating to charities, the Act has no application to private trusts. It seems that it is not contrary to public policy for a settlor to discriminate on these grounds, although the point is not unarguable.[56] There is little authority on the point, which has arisen mainly in connection with charitable trusts.[57] Many of the comments made by the House of Lords in *Blathwayt v Lord Cawley*[58] in the context of religion would apply equally to racial discrimination, save that the dictum of Lord Cross[59] loses all conviction if race is substituted for religious beliefs.

v. Alienation. Conditions operating as a complete restraint on the alienation of property are void as being contrary to public policy.   **13–010**

In *Re Brown*,[60] a testator devised land among his four sons subject to a condition which would have produced forfeiture of his interest by any son who mortgaged or sold his interest other than among his brothers. The condition was held to be equivalent to a general restraint on alienation, and therefore void, since the class of permitted alienees was small and bound to get smaller.

A partial restraint on alienation is valid.[61] Discrimination in the disposal of property is unlawful, subject to exceptions, under the Equality Act 2010 (replacing earlier legislation).[62]

Restraints even of a general nature may be valid if they take the form of a determinable interest.[63] Section 33 of the Trustee Act 1925 itself provides such an example.[64]

D. The Consequence of Illegality

The general position appears to be that if an express trust fails on   **13–011** the ground of unlawfulness, a resulting trust to the settlor or his

---

[56] See Underhill and Hayton, at p.306.

[57] See *Re Gwyon* [1930] 1 Ch. 255; *Re Dominion Students' Hall Trust* [1947] Ch. 183. In neither case was public policy discussed.

[58] [1976] A.C. 397.

[59] [1976] A.C. 397 at 429; above.

[60] [1954] Ch. 39; cf. *Caldy Manor Estate Ltd v Farrell* [1974] 1 W.L.R. 1303 (covenant against alienation not unlawful).

[61] See *Re MacLeay* (1875) L.R. 20 Eq. 186. (Doubted in *Re Rosher* [1884] 25 Ch. 801). It is arguable that even partial restraints should be invalid as repugnant to ownership.

[62] Part 4.

[63] *Re Dugdale* (1883) 38 Ch.D. 176 at 178–181, per Kay J.; *Re Leach* [1912] 2 Ch. 422.

[64] Above, para.7–005 (the protective trust).

estate ensues.[65] This is so even if the trust was designed to encourage an offence prohibited by statute.[66] Where the trust is only partly unlawful, the whole fails if the proportion to be devoted to the unlawful purpose is unascertainable,[67] whereas if that proportion is ascertainable, only that part fails.[68] Where property has been transferred to a volunteer for an unlawful purpose, the question arises whether the court will assist the transferor to recover the property. The principle, which was discussed in Ch.10, is that the transferor may recover if he does not have to rely on his own illegality,[69] or if the illegality has not been carried out.[70]

This area has recently been reviewed by the Law Commission.[71] It is considered that the present law is unclear as to what happens when an express trust fails for illegality. While the appropriate response will normally be that the property results to the settlor, there may be cases where the settlor's illegal motivation has been so grave that a resulting trust in his favour should be excluded. It is proposed that the court should have a discretion to decide who should be entitled to the property, for example to declare that the trustee is the legal and beneficial owner. This statutory discretion should be based on factors such as the gravity of the illegal conduct, deterrence and proportionality as discussed above.[72]

Where a condition subsequent is unlawful, the gift takes effect as an absolute interest: the condition alone is void.[73] In the case of a condition precedent, a distinction is drawn between realty and personalty. As far as realty is concerned, the gift itself fails if the condition is bad.[74] Where the gift is of personalty, however, it takes effect free of the condition where the illegality is only a *malum prohibitum*.[75] But where the illegality is a *malum in se*, the gift fails. The Law Commission previously proposed the abolition of this distinction,[76] but this aspect of illegality was not included in the

[65] Above, para.10–006. cf. *Ayerst v Jenkins* (1873) L.R. 16 Eq. 275 (described as a "difficult case" in Law Com. C.P. No.154 (1999), *Illegal Transactions: The Effect of Illegality on Contracts and Trusts*, at 69).

[66] *Thrupp v Collett* (1858) 26 Beav. 125.

[67] *Chapman v Brown* (1801) 6 Ves. 404.

[68] *Mitford v Reynolds* (1842) 1 Ph. 185. There is some authority that in such a case the whole can go to the lawful part: *Fisk v Att Gen* (1867) L.R. 4 Eq. 521.

[69] *Tinsley v Milligan* [1994] 1 A.C. 340.

[70] *Tribe v Tribe* [1996] Ch. 107.

[71] Law Com. No.320, *The Illegality Defence* (2010). See paras 2.87–2.102.

[72] Above, para.10–032.

[73] *Re Beard* [1908] 1 Ch. 383. This is so whether the gift is realty or personalty.

[74] *Re Elliott* [1952] Ch. 217.

[75] i.e. something made unlawful only by statute. See *Re Piper* [1946] 2 All E.R. 503. The distinction was apparently not discussed in *Re Hepplewhite Will Trusts*, *The Times*, January 21, 1977.

[76] Law Com. C.P. No.154 (1999), *Illegal Transactions: The Effect of Illegality on Contracts and Trusts*, p.170.

final report.[77] In the case of a determinable interest, the gift fails if the determining event is unlawful.[78]

2. PERPETUITY, DURATION AND INALIENABILITY

A. General

One of the most common causes over the years of invalidity of interests under a trust has been the failure to comply with the Rule Against Perpetuities. The hazard was much reduced, and the law simplified by the Perpetuities and Accumulations Act 1964, which applies to dispositions coming into effect after July 15, 1964. Following recommendations of the Law Commission,[79] further simplifications were introduced by the Perpetuities and Accumulations Act 2009. As the new legislation applies only to instruments taking effect after its commencement date (April 6, 2010),[80] the Act of 1964 will continue in operation for many years to come.   **13–012**

The rule grew up in connection with settlements of land, but now applies mainly to trusts of personalty. The subject is one which has caused much confusion, not least in connection with the Act of 1964; and a few general comments may be helpful.

B. Tying Up Land

The perpetuity rule is based on a policy against the tying up of lands for an undue length of time. The struggle began in the earliest years of common law. Conditions against alienation were held void. Entails were by statute inalienable, but by 1472 it was recognised that an entail could be barred, turned into a fee simple and alienated.[81] The Old Rule Against Perpetuities prevented a series of contingent life estates. Alienability was successfully being maintained. But once it was decided that executory interests were valid and indestructible,[82] it was possible to create interests limited to vest at an indefinite time in the future. The Rule Against Perpetuities was designed to restrict the extent to which future vesting could be postponed.   **13–013**

---

[77] Law Com. No.320, *The Illegality Defence* (2010), para.2.114.

[78] *Re Moore* (1888) 39 Ch.D. 116. For the application of the perpetuity rule to conditional and determinable interests, see Perpetuities and Accumulations Act 1964, s.12: the interest becomes absolute if the determining event or breach of condition does not occur within the perpetuity period.

[79] Law Com. No.251, *The Rules against Perpetuities and Excessive Accumulations* (1998).

[80] PAA 2009 s.15. The new rules do not apply to wills made before the commencement date if the testator died on or after that date.

[81] *Taltarum's Case YB* 12 Edw. 4, 19.

[82] *Pells v Brown* (1620) Cro. Jac. 590.

C. Remote Vesting. Life in Being Plus 21 Years

13–014   The permitted period at common law was a life in being plus 21 years; permitting in effect, a grant to the first son of A to attain the age of 21 years. For A's son must attain the age of 21 years, if he ever does, within 21 years of A's death.[83] A period of gestation was also allowed in the case of posthumous children.

One could not wait and see whether the gift vested in time or not. The common law rule was that the interest was void if it *might* vest outside the period; even if in fact it vested the next day.

Thus, a gift to the first son of A to attain the age of 22 years was void at common law if A was still alive; even if A had a son of $21\frac{1}{2}$ at the time. For that son might die, another son be born, and A die; and A's first son to attain the age of 22 might do so more than 21 years after the death of any persons alive at the date of the gift. A long series of bizarre situations showing the ruthless operation of the rule has often been catalogued, and need not be repeated. The one simple example makes the point.

D. Wait and See

13–015   The Perpetuities and Accumulations Act 1964 dealt with this situation in three ways; first, by permitting a settlor to specify as the perpetuity period for the purpose of the disposition a period of years not exceeding 80[84]; secondly, by a number of specific reforms on individual points which had caused difficulty, and thirdly, by introducing a system of wait and see.[85] If the law was unrealistic because it made void an interest which vested in fact within the period merely because it might have vested outside it, an obvious solution would be to make its validity depend on whether or not it does in fact vest within it. That is the theory of wait and see.

There was much disagreement as to the identity of the lives in being at common law.[86] The 1964 Act, however, laid down, in s.3, its own list of statutory lives in being, to be used where the wait and see rule is invoked. Although certain common law lives in being, such as "royal lives", are not included, the statutory class is generally wider than the class of common law lives in being.

One would have thought it obvious that, on enacting wait and see, the common law rule should be abolished. It no longer has any part

---

[83] Scientific advances in reproduction have made this statement untrue, but if sperm or embryos are used after a man's death, he is not treated as the father; Human Fertilisation and Embryology Act 1990.

[84] s.1.

[85] s.3.

[86] J. Morris and H. Wade (1964) 80 L.Q.R. 486 at 495–508; D. Allan (1965) 81 L.Q.R. 106 at 108; R. Maudsley (1970) 86 L.Q.R. 357 and (1975) 60 Cornell L.R. 355; Maudsley, *The Modern Law of Perpetuities*; R. Deech (1981) 97 L.Q.R. 593; J. Dukeminier (1986) 102 L.Q.R. 251.

to play. If a disposition must vest, if at all, within the period, then it will vest, if at all, within the period. Thus, the common law test is contained within the wait and see test. There is no advantage in knowing that an interest complies with the common law test. The interest remains contingent, and its value is dependent, not on compliance with the common law rule, but upon its likelihood of vesting. Compliance with the common law rule is irrelevant in a system of wait and see.[87]

Nevertheless, the Act of 1964 retained the common law rule. Wait and see only applies to "void" limitations.[88] So it is necessary to apply the common law rule to test validity, and to apply wait and see, if it fails to comply with the common law rule. It is tempting to ignore the common law rule. Every limitation which was valid at common law would also be valid under wait and see: unless, however, there could be some situation in which a gift was validated by a common law life who is not in the statutory list, and the interest does not in fact vest within 21 years of the death of the survivor of the statutory lives. Because the class of statutory lives does not coincide exactly with the common law lives, that is theoretically possible.[89] But it is absurd to retain all the common law learning in order to save such a rare gift. The common law rule should have been abolished.[90]

If it had been, the application of the wait and see rule would have been simple. In the case of any gift, all that would be necessary would be the writing down of the measuring lives, the recording of their deaths, and the addition of 21 years. The interests which had then vested would be valid; those which had not vested would be void.

The Perpetuities and Accumulations Act 2009 has now introduced a simpler rule in relation to instruments taking effect on or after its commencement, primarily by imposing a mandatory perpetuity period of 125 years.[91] If a settlor or testator specifies any other perpetuity period, it will be overridden by the statutory period. A further consequence of this provision is that the old common law rule has no relevance to instruments governed by the 2009 Act. The "wait and see" rule applies, just as under the Act of 1964.[92]

Although the Act of 2009 does not in general apply to trusts created before its commencement, trustees of such trusts may by deed "opt in" to a perpetuity period of 100 years if it would be

---

[87] R. Maudsley (1970) 86 L.Q.R. 357 at 372 and (1975) 60 Cornell L.R. 355; Maudsley, *The Modern Law of Perpetuities*.

[88] s.3.

[89] As in the case of dispositions governed by a royal lives clause.

[90] R. Maudsley (1975) 60 Cornell L.R. 355 at 370.

[91] s.5.

[92] PAA 2009 s.7.

difficult or not reasonably practicable to ascertain whether the lives in being had ended.[93]

E. Duration and Inalienability

13–016   Separate from the perpetuity rule governing remoteness of vesting, but a further manifestation of the same policy, is the rule which declares void trusts which might continue for too long a period; longer, that is, than the perpetuity period. The rule is not affected by the Perpetuities and Accumulations Act 2009.[94]

The matter will be discussed in connection with non-charitable purpose trusts.[95] In so far as they are permitted, they must be limited to the perpetuity period. The restriction upon duration does not apply to charitable trusts, nor to most pension trusts.[96]

It should be added that this rule is not in any way inconsistent with the ownership of property in fee simple by a person or a corporation. Those owners may alienate at any time. They may of course keep the property forever; but the property is not tied up in any way. Thus in *Bowman v Secular Society*,[97] a gift to the "Secular Society", a society devoted to furthering anti-Christian beliefs, having survived an attack on the grounds of public policy, had nothing to fear on the score of perpetuity, as the Society was a limited company, and able to deal freely with its property.

3. ATTEMPTS TO KEEP PROPERTY FROM CREDITORS

A. General

13–017   A creditor can demand payment from his debtor out of the debtor's property. If the debtor's property is insufficient to pay his debts, he is insolvent, and it will not be possible to pay all the creditors in full. Generally speaking, before bankruptcy the debtor may choose which creditors he pays first[98]; but after bankruptcy the bankruptcy law provides for a fair sharing out of his property.

When a person foresees the danger of his own[99] future insolvency—as where he is entering upon a business venture—there is the temptation to put property out of the reach of creditors, by, for

---

[93] s.12.
[94] P.A.A. 2009 s.18.
[95] Below, para.14–022; cf. *Re Dean* (1889) 41 Ch.D. 552. For difficulties arising with unincorporated associations, see *Re Grant's Will Trusts* [1980] 1 W.L.R. 360, below, para.14–018.
[96] Below, paras 15–004, 16–027.
[97] [1917] A.C. 406.
[98] *Middleton v Pollock* (1876) 2 Ch.D. 104.
[99] Where he foresees his beneficiary's insolvency, the protective trust may be employed; above, Ch.7.

example, creating a settlement in favour of the family, in this or other jurisdictions.[100] If the business venture succeeds the profits will flow in; if it fails, the creditors will be unpaid; but the family will be cared for.[101] It may also be that a settlement is made for other reasons, such as the reduction of tax liability,[102] but insolvency subsequently occurs. The question for consideration here is the extent to which a creditor can upset dispositions made by debtors of property which would otherwise be available for the creditors, whether or not there is a bankruptcy.

B. Insolvency Act 1986

i. Transactions Defrauding Creditors. Section 423[103] of the   **13–018**
Insolvency Act 1986, replacing s.172 of the Law of Property Act 1925, provides that a transaction at an undervalue may be set aside if the court is satisfied that the person entering into the transaction (the debtor) did so for the purpose:

(a) of putting assets beyond the reach of a person who is making, or may at some time make, a claim against him; or
(b) of otherwise prejudicing the interests of such a person in relation to the claim which he is making or may make.

The court may make such order as it thinks fit for

(a) restoring the position to what it would have been if the transaction had not been entered into; and
(b) protecting the interests of persons who are victims of the transaction (defined as a person who is, or is capable of being, prejudiced by the transaction).[104]

The section applies equally to transactions entered into by individuals and by corporate bodies.[105]

(a) *Transactions at an Undervalue.* By s.423(1), a person enters   **13–019**
into a transaction with another person at an undervalue if

---

[100] For offshore asset protection trusts, see B. Marrache and G. Davis (1993) 143 N.L.J. 721; P. Matthews (1995–96) 6 K.C.L.J. 62.
[101] "If I succeed in business, I make a fortune for myself. If I fail, I leave my creditors unpaid. They will pay the loss", per Jessel M.R. in *Re Butterworth, Ex p. Russell* (1882) 19 Ch.D. 588 at 598. See also *Midland Bank Plc v Wyatt* [1995] 1 F.L.R. 696.
[102] Above, para.9–001.
[103] See generally G. Miller [1998] Conv. 362. For the application of the Limitation Act 1980, see *Giles v Rhind* [2008] 3 W.L.R. 1233.
[104] See *Hill v Spread Trustee Co Ltd* [2007] 1 W.L.R. 2404 (intention to deceive Inland Revenue).
[105] See also IA 1986 s.207.

(a) he makes a gift to the other person or he otherwise enters into a transaction with the other on terms that provide for him to receive no consideration; or

(b) he enters into a transaction with the other in consideration of marriage; or

(c) he enters into a transaction with the other for a consideration the value of which, in money or money's worth, is significantly less than the value, in money or money's worth, of the consideration provided by himself.

Thus the section applies where a husband makes a gift of money to his wife, transfers his interest in the matrimonial home to her,[106] or purchases property in the joint names of himself and his wife without any contribution from her.[107] Similarly where a married couple declare a trust of the family home for the wife and children.[108]

When assessing "undervalue" the court will view the transaction as a whole. In *Agricultural Mortgage Corp Plc v Woodward*[109] an insolvent farmer, whose land was mortgaged for £700,000, granted a tenancy at the full market rent of £37,250 to his wife, to ensure that the mortgagee could not get vacant possession. It was argued that the full rent prevented the application of s.423. The Court of Appeal set aside the tenancy on the ground that the wife received benefits beyond those granted by the tenancy agreement, namely the safeguarding of her home, the ability to carry on the family business freed from the claims of creditors, and the surrender value of the tenancy, which gave her a "ransom" position against the mortgagee. She had paid nothing for these extra benefits, which were significantly more valuable than the rent. It was argued that such benefits could not be valued in money or money's worth and so should be left out of account. However, the surrender value alone was significantly greater than the rent. It was unnecessary to decide whether a detriment to the husband which gave no corresponding benefit to the wife (i.e. the diminution by at least 50 per cent of the £1 million freehold value caused by the letting) could be treated as consideration provided by the husband.

13–020   (b) *Intention.* As stated above, the court must be satisfied that the person entering into the transaction did so for the purpose of putting assets beyond the reach of, or of otherwise prejudicing, an existing

---

[106] *Re Kumar (A Bankrupt)* [1993] 1 W.L.R. 224 (assumption of sole liability for the mortgage by the wife was worth significantly less than value of share transferred).

[107] *Moon v Franklin, The Independent*, June 22, 1990.

[108] *Midland Bank Plc v Wyatt* [1995] 1 F.L.R. 696 (the trust was in any event a sham; above, para.3–020).

[109] (1995) 70 P. & C.R. 53.

or potential claimant.[110] The court was so satisfied where a husband who was threatened with legal actions and who knew there was doubt as to his insurance cover made substantial gifts to his wife upon receiving a large sum from the sale of his practice.[111] Indeed, where a debtor transfers assets to his family at an undervalue when an action by creditors is expected, the retained assets being insufficient, there is a strong prima facie case of intention to prejudice the creditor.[112] It is not necessary, however, to establish dishonesty. Thus the section may apply where the transfer was considered proper by legal advisers.[113] Putting the assets beyond the reach of creditors must be a substantial purpose of the transaction but need not be the sole or dominant motive.[114]

As under the previous law, it is not necessary that there should be existing creditors at the time of the transaction. The section preserves the effect of *Re Butterworth, Ex p. Russell*,[115] where the court set aside a settlement made by a prosperous baker immediately before purchasing a grocer's business, a trade in which he had no experience. It makes no difference whether the anticipated creditors are those of the settlor himself or of a company he plans to set up.[116] Nor is it necessary that the person seeking to set aside the transaction should be technically a "creditor".[117]

(c) *Persons who may Apply to Court.* Where the debtor, being an **13–021** individual, is now bankrupt, or, being a body corporate, is being wound up or is the subject of an administration order under the 1986 Act, the application may only be made by the official receiver, the trustee of the bankrupt's estate or the liquidator or administrator of the body corporate. The victim of the transaction, as defined above,[118] may apply with the leave of the court, but this is in effect a class action, giving no priority to the applicant.[119] Where a voluntary arrangement has been approved under the 1986 Act, the application may be made by the supervisor of the voluntary arrangement or the victim of the transaction. In any other case, for example where

---

[110] See, on the previous law, *Lloyds Bank Ltd v Marcan* [1973] 1 W.L.R. 1387 (sufficient to show intent to deprive creditors of timely recourse to property otherwise applicable for their benefit).

[111] *Moon v Franklin, The Independent*, June 22, 1990.

[112] *Barclays Bank Plc v Eustice* [1995] 1 W.L.R. 1238.

[113] *Arbuthnot Leasing International Ltd v Havalet Leasing (No.2)* [1990] BCC 636. It should be added that legal professional privilege will be overridden on the ground of "iniquity" if a client seeks legal advice as to how to structure a transaction to defeat creditors; *Barclays Bank Plc v Eustice*, above, fn.112.

[114] *Moon v Franklin, The Independent*, June 22, 1990; *Midland Bank Plc v Wyatt* [1995] 1 F.L.R. 696; *IRC v Hashmi* [2002] W.T.L.R. 1027; A Keay [2003] Conv. 272.

[115] (1882) 19 Ch.D. 588; *Mackay v Douglas* (1872) L.R. 14 Eq. 106.

[116] *Midland Bank Plc v Wyatt* [1995] 1 F.L.R. 696.

[117] See *Cadogan v Cadogan* [1977] 1 W.L.R. 1041.

[118] Above, para.13–018.

[119] *Dora v Simper* [2000] 2 B.C.L.C. 561.

there is no insolvency, the application may be made by the victim of
the transaction. These provisions are found in s.424 of the 1986 Act,
which further provides that any application made under the section
is treated as made on behalf of every victim of the transaction.

13–022   (d) *Orders to be made.* Sections 423(2) and 425 of the 1986 Act
set out the orders which may be made by the court.[120] These include
orders:

> (a) requiring any property transferred by the impugned transac-
> tion to be vested in any person, either absolutely or for the
> benefit of all the persons on whose behalf the application is
> treated as made; or
> (b) requiring any property representing the application of the
> proceeds of sale of property transferred by the impugned
> transaction or of money transferred by it to be so
> vested; or
> (c) requiring any person to pay to any other person in respect of
> benefits received from the debtor such sums as the court may
> direct.

13–023   (e) *Third Parties.* Section 425(2) provides that any order made
may affect the property of, or impose an obligation on, any person
whether or not he was a party to the transaction, but the order shall
not prejudice any interest in property[121] acquired from a person
other than the debtor which was acquired in good faith, for value
and without notice of the circumstances making s.423 applicable, or
prejudice any interest deriving from such an interest. Nor shall the
order require a person who received a benefit from the transaction in
good faith, for value and without notice of the circumstances to pay
any sum unless he was a party to the transaction. "Value" here bears
its ordinary meaning.

13–024   **ii. Bankruptcy Provisions.** The Insolvency Act 1986 replaced
s.42 of the Bankruptcy Act 1914 with provisions dealing with transactions at an undervalue and preferences by individuals or corporate
bodies[122] within a certain time limit prior to insolvency.

13–025   (a) *Transactions at an Undervalue.* In the case of the insolvency
of an individual, s.339 permits the trustee of the bankrupt's estate to
apply to court for an order where the individual entered into a
transaction at an undervalue within certain time limits discussed

---

[120] See *Moon v Franklin*, *The Independent*, June 22, 1990 (order compelling return of
unspent portion of gift and restraining dealing with land).
[121] See *Chohan v Saggar* [1994] B.C.L.C. 706 (mortgage).
[122] The provisions relating to companies will not be dealt with here.

below. The court may make such order as it thinks fit for restoring the position to what it would have been but for the transaction. "Undervalue" here bears the same meaning as under s.423.[123] Thus, as under the previous law, the trustee may obtain the wife's share in the matrimonial home to the extent that she has not contributed to its acquisition.[124] The Court of Appeal recently re-examined the question whether a property adjustment order on divorce may be set aside under these provisions.[125] It was held that such an order, whether made at a contested hearing or by consent, is not made without consideration and cannot normally be set aside under s.339 on the subsequent bankruptcy of the transferor spouse. It was noted that the court had jurisdiction to set aside a property adjustment order under the bankruptcy provisions,[126] but this would be done only in rare cases, as where the order had been obtained by collusion, fraud, mistake or misrepresentation. The transfer by one spouse to the other is not regarded as a transaction at an undervalue because the spouse's ability to seek an ancillary relief order is a right recognised by the law. The value of the right may be quantified by reference to the value of the property ordered to be transferred. Thus a fair balance is maintained between protecting creditors against collusive orders and protecting the bankrupt's spouse and children.

(b) *Preference of Creditors.* Where an individual is adjudged **13–026** bankrupt and has given a preference to any person within time limits discussed below, the trustee of the bankrupt's estate may apply to court for an order under s.340. The court may make such order as it thinks fit for restoring the position to what it would have been if that individual had not given that preference. An individual gives a preference to a person if that person is a creditor,[127] surety or guarantor, and the effect is to put that person into a better position than he would otherwise have been in in the event of the individual's bankruptcy. An order may only be made if the individual was influenced by a desire to produce the effect mentioned above, but this is presumed where the other person was an associate.[128]

---

[123] Above, para.13–019.

[124] *Re Densham* [1975] 1 W.L.R. 1519; *Claughton v Charalamabous* [1999] 1 F.L.R. 740. See also *Re Windle* [1975] 1 W.L.R. 1628.

[125] *Hill v Haines* [2008] Ch. 412; D. Capper (2008) 124 L.Q.R. 361; *Re Jones (A Bankrupt)* [2008] 2 F.L.R. 1969. See also *Re Abbott (A Bankrupt)* [1983] Ch. 45.

[126] MCA 1973 s.39; *Wright v Wright* [2011] 1 F.L.R. 387.

[127] This result could be avoided if the apparent "creditor" was in reality a beneficiary under a trust who never became a creditor. See *Re Kayford* [1975] 1 W.L.R. 279, above, para.2–010.

[128] As defined by s.435. The definition includes relatives of the individual or of his spouse, partners, employers, employees and related companies. It also includes a civil partner where the partnership is registered under the Civil Partnership Act 2004.

13–027   (c) *Time Limits.* Section 341 provides a five-year time limit, ending with the day of the presentation of the bankruptcy petition, in the case of a transaction at an undervalue. In the case of a preference which is not an undervalue, the period is six months save in the case of an associate, where the period is two years.

Except in the case of a transaction at an undervalue made within two years[129] before the bankruptcy, no order may be made with respect to a transaction entered into within the above time limits unless the individual was insolvent at the time or became insolvent in consequence of the transaction or preference. In the case of a transaction at an undervalue entered into with an associate, there is a rebuttable presumption that the individual was or became insolvent at the time of the transaction. A person is insolvent for this purpose if he cannot pay his debts as they fall due, or if the value of his assets is less than his liabilities.

13–028   (d) *Orders to be made.* Section 342 sets out the orders which the court may make for the benefit of the bankrupt's estate. These are similar to the orders which may be made under s.425.[130] Exceptionally, the court may decide to make no order, where justice so requires.[131]

13–029   (e) *Third Parties.* No order may prejudice any interest in property acquired from a person other than the bankrupt and acquired in good faith and for value. A purchaser is rebuttably presumed not to be in good faith in two situations.[132] The first is where he had notice at the time he acquired his interest of the fact that the earlier transaction was at an undervalue (or was a preference) and of the fact that the earlier transferor had been adjudged bankrupt or that the petition on which he was later adjudged bankrupt had been presented. The second situation is where the purchaser was an associate of, or was connected with, the bankrupt or the person with whom the bankrupt entered into the transaction at an undervalue (or to whom preference was given). Thus mere notice of the fact that the previous transaction was at an undervalue does not suffice. Similar rules apply to a person who has received a benefit from the transaction or preference in good faith and for value. Such a person shall not be required to pay any sum to the trustee unless he was a party to the transaction or was given a preference at a time when he was a creditor of the bankrupt.

---

[129] The exercise of a power of appointment within this period is not caught by the rule if the settlement was made outside the period; *Clarkson v Clarkson* [1994] BCC 921.

[130] Above, para.13–022.

[131] *Singla v Brown* [2008] Ch. 357 (no order made to disturb transaction whereby bankrupt's half share reduced to 1% as the parties had never intended him to have more than a nominal interest).

[132] s.342, as amended by the Insolvency (No.2) Act 1994.

C. Protection of the Spouse and Family

The previous sections dealt with attempts by a debtor to deprive **13–030**
his creditors of satisfaction by transferring property by way of voluntary settlement to other persons, usually members of his family,
whom the debtor wishes to protect. We now deal with what is in
effect the converse of that problem; cases where the defendant is
trying to deprive his spouse or family of assets which should properly be available to them. This occurs in matrimonial proceedings,
and also in relation to the rights of dependants upon a death.

i. Matrimonial Causes Act 1973 Section 37. Section 37 protects **13–031**
a spouse[133] from activities of the other spouse which may diminish
the assets available for the purposes of financial relief under the Act.
If the court is satisfied that one spouse is about to make a disposition[134] or transfer with the intention of depriving the applicant of
financial relief, it may make such order as it thinks fit for the purpose of protecting the applicant's claim.[135] Where the defendant
spouse has made a disposition of property, other than one made for
valuable consideration to a bona fide purchaser without notice of
any intention to defeat the applicant's claim,[136] the disposition may
be set aside.[137]

The intention to defeat the applicant's claim must be affirmatively
proved, except in cases where the disposition was made within three
years before the date of the application, in which case there is a
statutory presumption[138] that the intention is to defeat the applicant's claim for financial relief.

ii. Inheritance (Provision for Family and Dependants) Act **13–032**
1975. A similar problem arises in connection with statutory
schemes which restrict a person's powers of free disposal of his
property by will, in order to provide for the surviving spouse and
children and other dependants. This is an old problem; originally
answered by the surviving spouse's right to dower or curtesy, and
now governed by a wide variety of provisions (such as "forced
heirship") in various parts of the world. A common solution is to
give to the surviving spouse, and sometimes to children, a fractional
share of the estate. The system in England and Wales is to give to
the court a discretionary power to make an award to a surviving
spouse and other dependants on the ground that the disposition of
the deceased's estate (whether by will or intestacy) is not such as to

---

[133] Similar provisions relating to civil partners are found in the Civil Partnership Act 2004
Sch.5, para.74.
[134] The wide definition in s.37(6) includes a trust, but not any provision made in a will.
[135] s.37(2)(a).
[136] Called a "reviewable disposition" and defined in s.37(4).
[137] See also *Lowson v Coombes* [1999] Ch. 373; above, para.10–029.
[138] s.37(5); rebuttable, of course.

make reasonable financial provision for the applicant.[139] But these schemes could be thwarted if a person who wished to deprive a widow and dependants could give away all his property before death.[140]

Provisions to deal with this problem are contained in ss.10–13 of the Act. In short, the court is given power to require a donee from the deceased to provide sums of money,[141] up to, but not in excess of, the value of the gift,[142] if the gift was made within six years before the death of the donor, and was made "with the intention of defeating an application for financial provision under this Act."[143] Protection is given to persons who gave full valuable consideration for a transfer. The intention is to be determined on a balance of probabilities,[144] and need not be the sole intention of the donor in making the gift. Similar provisions in s.11 deal with contracts to leave property by will; and transfers to trustees in s.13.

---

[139] s.2.

[140] See *Schaefer v Schuhmann* [1972] A.C. 572. It is possible that such transfers could be set aside independently of any statutory provisions in a case of fraud. See *Cadogan v Cadogan* [1977] 1 W.L.R. 1041.

[141] s.10(2); see also s.10(6), giving the factors which the court shall take into consideration.

[142] Valued, in the case of gifts other than cash, at the date of death of the deceased, or, if the property was disposed of by the donee, the value at the date of disposal.

[143] s.10(2).

[144] s.12.

CHAPTER 14

NON-CHARITABLE PURPOSE TRUSTS

1. THE GENERAL PROBLEM

A. Private Trusts, Purpose Trusts, Charitable Trusts

A private trust is essentially a trust in favour of ascertainable **14–001** individuals. A charitable trust is a trust for purposes which are treated in law as charitable. The question for consideration in this chapter is whether or not it is possible to establish a trust for non-charitable purposes.

We have considered in earlier chapters questions relating to the setting up of trusts for individuals. Charitable trusts are dealt with in Ch.15. For the present purpose, it will be sufficient to state that charitable purposes consist of trusts for the relief of poverty, trusts for the advancement of religion, trusts for the advancement of education, and trusts for a variety of other purposes beneficial to the community. The purpose trusts at present under consideration are those which do not come within these categories. A trust, for example, to feed the testator's horses and hounds,[1] to set up a monument,[2] or to be applied for useful or benevolent purposes.[3] There is no question of any such trusts having any privilege in relation to taxation or to perpetuity, such as is allowed in the case of charitable trusts. The question is whether they are valid or void.[4]

B. Trusts for Persons and Purposes

14–002   With any particular trust, there may be a question of construction to determine whether the trust is for persons or for purposes. Most purposes affect persons, and there is no reason why a trust should not be treated as a trust for persons where the beneficiaries are to be benefited in some way other than by payment of money. Thus, a trust for the education of the children of X can be construed as a trust of which the children of X are the beneficiaries.[5] A trust for the promotion of fox-hunting (before it became illegal) would be treated as a trust for a purpose, although it might be said that the individual sportsman might benefit from it.[6]

There are various examples of trusts in which the beneficiaries enjoy only a limited proprietary interest. Where, for example, a debtor assigns an asset to trustees for the payment of his debts, his creditors do not, unless there has been an absolute assignment, take any surplus.[7] In *Re the Trusts of Abbott Fund*[8] it was accepted that a trust for the maintenance of two old ladies was valid although it seems that they did not become owners of any proprietary interest. In *Re Gillingham Bus Disaster Fund*[9] a fund collected for the benefit of injured cadets was not invalid although there was no suggestion that the cadets could ever have claimed the assets of the fund. It may be possible to support these latter decisions as examples of discretionary trusts for the benefit of individuals; but they were not so drafted, and it may be preferable to regard them as examples of trusts for persons to be benefited in a particular way. The proper

---

[1] *Re Dean* (1889) 41 Ch.D. 554.

[2] *Mussett v Bingle* [1876] W.N. 170; *Re Endacott* [1960] Ch. 232.

[3] *Morice v Bishop of Durham* (1804) 9 Ves.Jr. 399.

[4] See generally L. Sheridan (1953) 17 Conv.(N.S.) 46; O. Marshall (1953) 6 C.L.P. 151; Morris and Leach, Ch.12; Maudsley, *The Modern Law of Perpetuities*, pp.166–178; P. Lovell (1970) 34 Conv.(N.S.) 77; J. Harris (1971) 87 L.Q.R. 31; L. McKay (1973) 37 Conv.(N.S.) 420; N. Gravells (1977) 40 M.L.R. 397; K. Widdows (1977) 41 Conv.(N.S.) 179; P. Matthews in A. Oakley (ed.), *Trends in Contemporary Trust Law*, Ch.1.

[5] See J. Davies [1968] A.S.C.L. at 439. See also *Re Osoba* [1979] 1 W.L.R. 247, above para.10–009.

[6] *Re Thompson* [1934] Ch. 342, below, para.14–012.

[7] *Re Rissik* [1936] Ch. 68.

[8] [1900] 2 Ch. 326, above, para.10–007; contrast *Re Andrew's Trust* [1905] 2 Ch. 48; *Re Foord* [1922] 2 Ch. 599; above, paras 2–012, 10–007.

[9] [1959] Ch. 62, above, para.10–007. The residue for "worthy causes" was void for uncertainty.

analysis of trusts of this kind was little discussed until the decision of Goff J. in *Re Denley's Trust Deed* in 1969.[10]

A plot of land was conveyed to trustees to hold, for a period determined by lives:

> "[F]or the purpose of a recreation or sports ground primarily for the benefit of the employees of the company and secondarily for the benefit of such other person or persons (if any) as the trustees may allow."

Goff J. upheld the trust as one for the benefit of the employees. They were ascertainable, and the trust was one which the court could control. If it had been construed as a trust for non-charitable purposes, it would have been void.

> "The objection [to non-charitable purpose trusts] is not that the trust is for a purpose or an object per se, but that there is no beneficiary or cestui que trust."[11]

Here, however, "the trust deed expressly states that . . . the employees of the company shall be entitled to the use and enjoyment of the land."[12] He contrasted this situation with:

> "[A] purpose . . . trust, the carrying out of which would benefit an individual or individuals, where that benefit is so indirect or intangible or which is otherwise so framed as not to give those persons any *locus standi* to apply to the court to enforce the trust"[13];

in which case the trust would have been a non-charitable purpose trust, and void.

The same line of reasoning was applied in *Re Lipinski's Will Trusts*,[14] a case of a gift to an unincorporated association.

The testator bequeathed his residuary estate to trustees in trust as to one-half for the Hull Judeans (Maccabi) Association:

> "[I]n memory of my late wife to be used solely in the work of constructing the new buildings for the association and/or improvements to the said buildings."

---

[10] [1969] 1 Ch. 373. See also *Wicks v Firth* [1983] A.C. 214 (non-charitable trust to award scholarships assumed valid).

[11] [1969] 1 Ch. 373 at 383.

[12] [1969] 1 Ch. 373 at 383.

[13] [1969] 1 Ch. 373 at 382. For discussion of *locus standi* to enforce the *Re Denley* type of trust, see A. Everton [1982] Conv. 118, at 124.

[14] [1976] Ch. 235; (1977) 93 L.Q.R. 167; K. Widdows (1977) 41 Conv.(N.S.) 179; N. Gravells (1977) 40 M.L.R. 231; *Re Turkington* [1937] 4 All E.R. 501.

14–003   At first sight, this would appear to be a gift to an unincorporated association to be applied for its (non-charitable) purposes.[15] We will see,[16] however, that gifts to unincorporated associations are normally upheld as gifts to the members rather than invalidated as purpose trusts. To the extent that the testator's superadded purpose hindered this construction, *Re Denley's Trust Deed*[17] came to the rescue.

The beneficiaries, the members of the association, were ascertainable; there was no problem of perpetuity,[18] because they could, according to the rules of the association, terminate the trust for their own benefit.[19] The implication of these factors will be discussed later in the chapter.

These cases show a more liberal judicial tendency in connection with the construction of gifts of this type.[20] *Re Denley*, however, could not save the trust in *R. v District Auditor, Ex p. West Yorkshire MCC*,[21] where a local authority, purporting to act under statutory powers, resolved to create a trust "for the benefit of any or all or some of the inhabitants of the County of West Yorkshire" in any of four ways: (i) to assist economic development in the county in order to relieve unemployment and poverty; (ii) to assist bodies concerned with youth and community problems in West Yorkshire; (iii) to assist and encourage ethnic and minority groups in West Yorkshire; and (iv) to inform all interested and influential persons of the consequences of the abolition (proposed by the Government) of the Council and other metropolitan county councils and of other proposals affecting local government in the county. The capital and income were to be applied within a short period, avoiding any perpetuity problems, but the trust was void as a non-charitable purpose trust. It was not within the purpose trust exceptions illustrated by *Re Denley* and *Re Lipinski* because there were no "ascertained or ascertainable beneficiaries". Even if "inhabitant" was sufficiently certain, the class of 2,500,000 potential beneficiaries was so large that the trust was unworkable. It has never been established what certainty test applies to a *Re Denley* trust,[22] but this decision suggests that the

---

[15] In favour of this construction, counsel relied on the reference to the testator's late wife's memory as indicating an intention to create an endowment; and on a requirement that the money was to be used "solely" for the stated purposes.

[16] Below, para.14–019.

[17] [1969] 1 Ch. 373.

[18] Below, para.14–022. cf. *Re Grant's WT* [1980] 1 W.L.R. 360, below, para.14–018.

[19] By altering the constitution of the association. The beneficiaries in *Re Denley*, on the other hand, would seem to have no right to divide up the assets under the *Saunders v Vautier* principle (below, para.22–001), but no perpetuity problem arose because the trust was expressly confined to the perpetuity period.

[20] P. Lovell (1970) 34 Conv.(n.s.) 77; J. Harris (1972) 87 L.Q.R. 31.

[21] [1986] R.V.R. 24; C. Harpum (1986) 45 C.L.J. 391. The certainty aspects are discussed in Ch.3, above, para.3–033.

[22] Above, para.14–002.

class of beneficiaries, even if conceptually certain and not capricious, must not be too wide. A private trust which fails for "administrative unworkability"[23] cannot be rescued by the *Re Denley* principle.

It is necessary now to consider the objections to non-charitable purpose trusts.

2. OBJECTIONS TO PURPOSE TRUSTS

If a disposition is construed as a trust for non-charitable purposes, there are various objections which may be made to it. The first of these objections denies the possibility of existence of non-charitable purpose trusts. It has not however been consistently applied; and purpose trusts for the building of graves and monuments and the care of specific animals, which succeeded in the 19th century[24] are now regarded as anomalous exceptions to the rule.[25] The other objections accept the possibility of the existence of non-charitable purpose trusts, but impose restrictions upon them. **14–004**

Before examining the objections, it should be said that a case may be made out that English law does not prohibit non-charitable purpose trusts.[26] Such trusts were regularly permitted before the 20th century, but a wrong turning was taken in cases such as *Re Endacott*,[27] where the supposed rule was "invented". Many of the cases commonly cited as supporting the invalidity of purpose trusts were in fact based on uncertainty, perpetuity or some other defect. Indeed, the trust in *Morice v Bishop of Durham*[28] failed for uncertainty. Trusts for beneficiaries do not fail if there is no current beneficiary (for example, where they are unborn); the real point is that the trustees are accountable not to the beneficiaries but to the court. Nevertheless, the rule against non-charitable purpose trusts has become so entrenched that it is unlikely that the contrary view will prevail unless legislation intervenes.

A. The Beneficiary Principle; Enforceability

The first objection may be seen in a celebrated dictum of Sir William Grant M.R. in *Morice v Bishop of Durham*.[29] "Every other [i.e. non-charitable] trust must have a definite object. There must be **14–005**

---

[23] Above, para.3–032.
[24] Below, para.14–009.
[25] per Roxburgh J. in *Re Astor's ST* [1952] Ch. 534 at 547.
[26] Baxendale-Walker, *Purpose Trusts*, 2nd edn, 2009.
[27] [1960] Ch. 232; below, para.14–010.
[28] Below.
[29] (1804) 9 Ves.Jr. 399.

somebody in whose favour the court can decree performance."[30] A trust, as we have seen, is an obligation. The objection is that there cannot be an obligation upon the trustees unless there is a correlative right in someone else to enforce it. With charitable trusts, the Attorney General and the Charity Commission are charged with the duty of enforcement.[31] With private trusts, no public official is involved. The trust is void unless there are human beneficiaries capable of enforcing the trust. In effect the objection is that there is no beneficial owner of the property. Acceptance of this principle renders non-charitable purpose trusts totally void.

B. Uncertainty

14–006   If non-charitable purpose trusts are recognised at all by the law, they are only valid if the purposes are expressed with sufficient certainty to enable the court to control the performance of the trust. The point commonly arises in the cases where incompetent draftsmanship has failed to create a charitable trust; where, for example, the property is to be applied for charitable or benevolent purposes,[32] or, as in *Morice v Bishop of Durham*[33] for, "such objects of benevolence and liberality as the Bishop of Durham in his own discretion shall most approve of." "Benevolence" and "liberality" are wider concepts than "charity", and the trust was not therefore applicable for charitable purposes only. The purposes were uncertain and the trust void. Indeed, this reason was more clearly emphasised by Sir William Grant M.R. than was the earlier objection. Having established that the trust was not for charitable purposes, and that the Bishop did not claim any personal benefit for himself, he said[34]:

> "That it is a trust, unless it be of a charitable nature, too indefinite to be executed by this Court, has not been, and cannot be denied. There can be no trust, over the exercise of which this Court will not assume a control; for an uncontrollable power of disposition would be ownership and not trust. If there be a clear trust, but for uncertain objects, the property, that is the subject of the trust, is indisposed of; and the benefit of such trust must result to those, to whom the law gives the ownership in default of disposition by the former owner. But this doctrine does not hold good with regard to trusts for charity. Every other trust must have a definite object.

---

[30] (1804) 9 Ves.Jr. 399 at 404.

[31] There is evidence that historically charitable trusts were enforced by individuals; Baxendale-Walker, *Purpose Trusts*, 2nd edn, 2009.

[32] *Blair v Duncan* [1902] A.C. 37; *Houston v Burns* [1918] A.C. 337; *Chichester Diocesan Fund and Board of Finance v Simpson* [1944] A.C. 341; *Re Atkinson's Will Trusts* [1978] 1 W.L.R. 586.

[33] (1804) 9 Ves.Jr. 399.

[34] (1804) 9 Ves.Jr. 399 at 404–405.

There must be somebody, in whose favour the Court can decree performance."

This objection can be met by specifying in sufficient detail the purposes to which the property is to be applied. Trusts for specific purposes like feeding the testator's animals, or maintaining a tomb or monument, usually pass this test. But general projects, even carefully drafted, are likely to be held void. The point only becomes significant, of course, if the problem of the beneficiary principle has been surmounted.

C. Excessive Delegation of Testamentary Power

There have been judicial statements to the effect that purpose **14–007** trusts created by will are void because, in the absence of anyone to enforce the trust, the trustees are left to determine the application of the property; thus "the testator has imperfectly exercised his testamentary power; he has delegated it, for the disposal of his property lies with them, not with him."[35] The objection is not relevant to non-testamentary trusts. Of the trust in *Re Denley's Trust Deed*, Goff J. said[36]:

> "If this were a will, a question might arise whether this provision might be open to attack as a delegation of the testamentary power. I do not say that would be so, but in any case it cannot be said of a settlement inter vivos."

The status of the objection was, however, not established, even with wills. Special, general and intermediate powers are permitted in wills[37]; and, "an anti-delegation rule is really an anti-power rule."[38]

In *Re Beatty's Will Trusts*[39] Hoffmann J., upholding a testamentary disposition to trustees to allocate, "to or among such person or persons as they think fit", rejected the supposed "anti-delegation" rule. Thus there is no objection on this basis to the validity of purpose trusts. Moreover, the acceptance of the validity of testamentary powers is significant. For one way, as will be seen,[40] of effecting a non-charitable purpose where there are willing trustees, may

[35] *Leahy v Att Gen for New South Wales* [1959] A.C. 457 at 484; *Re Wood* [1949] Ch. 498 at 501.
[36] [1969] 1 Ch. 373 at 387.
[37] *Re Park* [1932] 1 Ch. 580; *Re Abraham's WT* [1969] 1 Ch. 463; *Re Gulbenkian's Settlements* [1970] A.C. 508; *Re Manisty's Settlement* [1974] Ch. 17; *Re Hay's Settlement Trusts* [1982] 1 W.L.R. 202.
[38] D. Gordon (1953) 69 L.Q.R. 334 at 342.
[39] [1990] 1 W.L.R. 503; J. Martin [1991] Conv. 138.
[40] Below, para.14–031.

be to give them *power* to perform, and not attempt to require them to do so.

D. Perpetuity

14–008   A charitable trust may last for ever; a non-charitable trust is void if it is to continue beyond the perpetuity period.[41] The reason is that perpetual non-charitable purpose trusts would conflict with the *policy* of the perpetuity rule, which is the prevention of the tying up of property for too long a period.

In its more usual context the rule against perpetuities deals with the limit of time to which the vesting of future interests may be postponed. An outline of this has already been given.[42] In the present context, however, we are not concerned with future vesting. We are concerned with a situation in which the property is vested in the trustees to be applied by them for certain non-charitable purposes for a period which may exceed that of perpetuity. This situation will arise if either the capital or the income of the fund is to be so applied. If the trust relates to income, then the capital must be maintained in order to produce the income. It is no answer to say that, since the trustees may sell the present investments and purchase others, the capital is not inalienable. The objection relates, not only to alienability, but to duration. Whatever happens to individual investments, an obligation to retain the capital as a fund for an excessive period violates the rule. Accordingly, a non-charitable purpose trust is valid, if at all, only if it is confined to the perpetuity period. The matter is examined below.[43]

3. EXCEPTIONAL CASES UPHOLDING PURPOSE TRUSTS[44]

14–009   Until *Re Astor's Settlement Trusts*[45] in 1952, it was arguable that it was possible to establish a trust for a non-charitable purpose for the period of perpetuity. The authorities cover a narrow field, being nearly all concerned with trusts for building or maintaining monuments or tombs, or for caring for the testator's animals.[46] But the language of the judgments is general, and there are occasional cases outside those fields. As will be seen, *Re Astor's Settlement Trusts*[47]

---

[41] Most pension trusts are exempted; below, para.16–027.

[42] Above, Ch.13.

[43] Below, para.14–022.

[44] Morris and Leach, pp.310–319; Maudsley, *The Modern Law of Perpetuities*, pp.168–176.

[45] [1952] Ch. 534; below, para.14–013.

[46] A survey of practitioners in 2006 concluded that such trusts are still in use, mainly for animals; J. Brown [2007] Conv. 148.

[47] Above, fn.45.

underlined the beneficiary principle; and it is clear now that trusts for non-charitable purposes will fail unless they are kept strictly within the narrow confines of these exceptional cases.

A. Tombs and Monuments

Reasonable provision for the building of a tomb or a gravestone **14–010** for a testator may be regarded as a funeral expense, and valid independently of any doctrine relating to purpose trusts.[48] But bequests for family burial enclosures have been upheld as purpose trusts[49]; as have bequests for monuments to other people, such as the testator's wife's first husband.[50] Such a gift may be for the building of the monument which, it seems, may be assumed to be done within the period of perpetuity[51]; or for the care or the maintenance of the graves for a period limited to the period of perpetuity. An example is *Re Hooper.*[52]

A testator gave a sum of money to trustees for the care and upkeep of certain family graves and monuments, and a tablet in a window in a church so far as the trustees could legally do so. Maugham J. upheld the gift for a period of 21 years.[53]

Similarly, in *Mussett v Bingle*,[54] Hall V.C. held that since the executors were ready to carry out a bequest of £300 to erect a monument to the testator's wife's first husband, "it must be performed accordingly." But he held void for perpetuity a further gift for its upkeep.

Such trusts must of course comply with the requirement of certainty. In *Re Endacott*,[55] the Court of Appeal held void a residuary gift amounting to some £20,000 "to the North Tawton Devon Parish Council for the purpose of providing some useful memorial to myself." Such a trust, though specific in the sense that it indicated a purpose capable of expression, was "of far too wide and uncertain a nature to qualify within the class of cases cited."[56] No doubt was cast upon *Re Hooper*[57] and the early cases. Yet *Re Endacott*[58] may illustrate the stricter modern approach to purpose trusts; or perhaps

[48] *Trimmer v Danby* (1856) 25 L.J.Ch. 424. Gray thought that it was the only justification for upholding such trusts: *The Rule Against Perpetuities*, 4th edn, 1942, pp.310–311.
[49] *Pirbright v Salwey* [1896] W.N. 86; *Re Hooper* [1932] 1 Ch. 38.
[50] *Mussett v Bingle* [1876] W.N. 170.
[51] Below, para.14–022.
[52] [1932] 1 Ch. 38.
[53] Relying on *Pirbright v Salwey* [1896] W.N. 86.
[54] [1876] W.N. 170. See also *Trimmer v Danby* (1856) 25 L.J.Ch. 424.
[55] [1960] Ch. 232.
[56] [1960] Ch. 232 at 247.
[57] [1932] 1 Ch. 38.
[58] [1960] Ch. 232.

it indicates the willingness of the court to allow reasonable sums to be spent upon these purposes, and a reluctance to uphold such grandiose schemes. This policy, as will be seen, is articulated in *Re Astor*.[59] The Parish Councils and Burial Authorities (Miscellaneous Provisions) Act 1970 s.1, provides that a burial authority or a local authority may agree by contract to maintain a grave, or memorial or monument for a period not exceeding 99 years.

B. Animals

14–011   Gifts for the care of specific animals, though not charitable, have also been upheld. There was no argument on the point in *Pettingall v Pettingall*[60] where an annuity of £50 to be applied in maintaining the testator's favourite black mare was held valid. In *Re Dean*,[61] the leading case, North J., relying on *Mitford v Reynolds*[62] and the monument cases, upheld a gift of £750 per annum for the period of 50 years for the maintenance of the testator's horses and hounds if they should so long live. He met head-on the argument that the court will not recognise a trust unless it is capable of being enforced by someone, by pronouncing: "I do not assent to that view."[63] There was no objection to such a provision, "provided, of course, that it is not to last for too long a period."[64] It is difficult to see how the gift could be upheld for a 50-year period; for the horses and hounds could not be the measuring lives for the period of perpetuity. This aspect of the matter is discussed below.[65] The case has been accepted as authority for the proposition that trusts for the upkeep of specific animals are valid for the perpetuity period; and it is believed that this exception to the general rule has been relied on in countless cases since *Re Dean*.[66]

A possible difficulty, it has been suggested,[67] is that the fund might be claimed by the person who now owns the animal (e.g. as specific or residuary legatee). A fund to maintain another's property can be claimed by that other without applying it to the purpose.[68] Another solution might be to give the fund to the person acquiring the animal on the testator's death, determinable on the death of the

---

[59] [1952] Ch. 534.
[60] (1842) 11 L.J.Ch. 176.
[61] (1889) 41 Ch.D. 552.
[62] (1848) 16 Sim. 105.
[63] (1889) 41 Ch.D. 552 at 556.
[64] (1889) 41 Ch.D. 552 at 557.
[65] Below, para.14–023.
[66] (1889) 41 Ch.D. 552.
[67] P. Matthews (1983) 80 L.S.Gaz. 2451.
[68] *Re Bowes* [1896] 1 Ch. 507 (money directed to be laid out in planting trees on an estate belonged to the owners of the estate absolutely.) See also *Re Lipinski's Will Trusts* [1976] Ch. 235.

animal or on the trustee's decision that it is improperly maintained.[69]

C. Other Purposes

Trusts for other purposes have on occasion been upheld; and **14–012** others which have failed have been refused on the ground of perpetuity, without any indication that they would not have been valid if confined to the permitted period.

Trusts for the saying of masses for the benefit of private individuals have been considered to come into this category. Until the House of Lords decision in *Bourne v Keane* in 1919,[70] such trusts were regarded as being trusts for superstitious uses and void. *Bourne v Keane* held them valid. Such trusts have since been upheld as charitable in *Re Hetherington*[71] where the masses are said in public. Even where the masses are said in private, the trust is arguably charitable on the basis that public benefit can be found in the endowment of the priesthood. The acceptance of such trusts as charitable makes it unnecessary to consider them in the category of private purpose trusts.

One possible member of this category of miscellaneous purpose trusts is a trust for non-Christian private ceremonies. In *Re Khoo Cheng Teow*,[72] the Supreme Court of the Straits Settlements held valid a gift to be applied for the period of perpetuity in the performance of ceremonies called Sin Chew to perpetuate the testator's memory. The gift was not charitable; but the Court held that it was valid for a period measured by royal lives plus 21 years.

A decision which has perhaps been elevated to a position of importance which it does not merit is *Re Thompson*[73]:

> An alumnus of Trinity Hall, Cambridge, bequeathed a legacy to one Lloyd, an old friend, to be applied in such manner as he should think fit towards the promotion and furtherance of fox-hunting, and gave the residuary estate to Trinity Hall. Lloyd made no claim to any beneficial interest, but desired to carry out the testator's wishes if he should be permitted to do so. Trinity Hall also was anxious that the trust should be performed; but felt it its duty, as a charity, to submit that the trust was void for lack of a beneficiary. There was no problem of perpetuity, and Clauson J. held that the purpose was sufficiently certain. He upheld the gift

---

[69] See Matthews, above, fn.67, discussing other possibilities.

[70] [1919] A.C. 815.

[71] [1990] Ch. 1; N. Parry [1989] Conv. 453; below, para.15–045. See also *Re Caus* [1934] Ch. 162.

[72] [1932] Straits Settlements L.R. 226.

[73] [1934] Ch. 342. Fox-hunting with hounds is now illegal in England and Wales.

by ordering the money to be paid to Lloyd upon his giving an undertaking to apply it for these stated objects, and gave to Trinity Hall liberty to apply if the money should be used for other purposes.

The case is one of very limited significance. It does not, as some have claimed,[74] provide a solution to the beneficiary problem, by holding that the party entitled in default can enforce a purpose trust. Enforcement is contrary to the interest of the party entitled in default; he is interested to restrain misapplication, which is a very different matter. In *Re Thompson*,[75] there was no contest, as all parties desired enforcement. The case was only litigated because Trinity Hall, as a charity, could not, without the court's approval, forgo its strict legal claim to the property.

4. THE FAILURE OF THE ASTOR TRUST[76]

14–013 Subsequent decisions have made clear that this line of cases will not be extended.[77] They are regarded as "concessions to human weakness or sentiment",[78] "troublesome, anomalous and aberrant,"[79] and as "occasions when Homer has nodded."[80] Purpose trusts generally have failed under the beneficiary principle, and on the ground of uncertainty. In these circumstances, compliance with the perpetuity rule is no escape.

In *Re Astor's Settlement Trusts*,[81] a lifetime settlement was made in 1945, expressly limited to a period of lives in being plus 21 years, under which the trustees were to hold a fund upon various trusts for non-charitable purposes, including "the maintenance of good relations between nations ... the preservation of the independence of the newspapers", and other similar purposes in favour of independent newspapers. Roxburgh J. held the trust void; both because there was no one who could enforce the trust, and also on the ground of uncertainty.

---

[74] See Roxburgh J. in *Re Astor's ST* [1952] Ch. 534 at 543.
[75] Above, fn.73.
[76] O. Marshall (1953) 6 C.L.P. 151; L. Sheridan (1953) 17 Conv.(N.S.) 46; L. Leigh (1955) 18 M.L.R. 120.
[77] *Re Endacott* [1960] 2 Ch. 232 at 246.
[78] *Re Astor's ST* [1952] Ch. 534 at 547.
[79] *Re Endacott*, above, fn.77, at 251.
[80] [1960] 2 Ch. 232 at 250.
[81] [1952] Ch. 534.

Re Shaw[82] concerned the will of George Bernard Shaw, which provided that the residue of the estate should be applied to research the utility of the development of a 40-letter British alphabet in the place of the present one, and for the translation of his play "Androcles and the Lion" into the new alphabet. Harman J. held that the trust was not charitable, and that it failed on the beneficiary principle. The trustees were willing to carry out the testator's wishes if they were permitted to do so. But the judge concluded: "I am not at liberty to validate this trust by treating it as a power. A valid power is not to be spelled out of an invalid trust."[83]

These cases show the current trend in situations where the gift is construed as a gift for purposes. The insistence upon an ascertained beneficiary reflects the analysis of the law of trusts before the days when discretionary trusts became common. We have seen that a beneficiary under a discretionary trust is not entitled to specific property; only to a limited right to be considered. It has been argued that *McPhail v Doulton*[84] manifests a basic change in the conceptual development of the law of trusts.

"It has broken the stranglehold imposed on the development of trusts . . . by a rigid conception of a framework of fixed equitable interests and correlatively narrow obligations . . . it does not take much crystal-ball gazing to see the impact this extension will have on all the old sterile purpose trust and unincorporated association debates."[85]

5. UNINCORPORATED ASSOCIATIONS

An unincorporated association exists where two or more persons are bound together for one or more common purposes by mutual undertakings, each having mutual duties and obligations, in an organisation which has rules identifying in whom control of the organisation and its funds is vested, and which can be joined or left at will.[86]

14–014

---

[82] [1957] 1 W.L.R. 729.

[83] [1957] 1 W.L.R. 729 at 731, relying on *IRC v Broadway Cottages Trust* [1955] Ch. 20 at 36.

[84] [1971] A.C. 424; above, para.3–026.

[85] Y. Grbich (1974) 37 M.L.R. 643 at 655–656; J. Harris (1972) 89 L.Q.R. 31; J. Davies [1970] A.S.C.L. 189.

[86] *Conservative and Unionist Central Office v Burrell (Inspector of Taxes)* [1982] 1 W.L.R. 522. (The definition was for tax purposes, but seems to be of general application). See P. Creighton [1983] Conv. 150, doubting the last requirements; R. Rideout (1996) 49 C.L.P. 187.

Special problems arise in connection with the holding of property by unincorporated associations.[87] An unincorporated association is not a legal person, and, with the exception of trade unions,[88] cannot be the owner of property or the subject of legal rights and duties.[89] The question we will consider here is the effect of gifts to such associations, and the various ways in which their property is held. The latter is determined by the terms of the gift or by the constitution or rules of the association. The question of entitlement to the funds on the dissolution of the association is dealt with elsewhere.[90]

A. Charitable Purposes

14–015   The assets of an unincorporated association may be held upon charitable trusts. For example, a society for the relief of the poor. A charitable trust is valid even though it is a purpose trust; the usual rules of certainty of objects do not apply; it may continue forever; and it enjoys a number of tax privileges.

B. Non-Charitable Purposes

14–016   We have seen that, generally speaking, trusts for the promotion of non-charitable purposes are void. Hence gifts to non-charitable unincorporated associations will fail if construed as purpose trusts. But such a result may be avoided if it is possible to regard the gift as in favour of the members, as described below. Such a construction may be adopted even where the donor has expressly stated that his gift is for particular non-charitable purposes.[91]

C. Property Held on Trust for the Members

14–017   The property of an unincorporated association may be held on trust for the members of the association, and not for its purposes. Such a trust must comply with the usual rules for the creation of a trust. There must be an intention to create a trust, and there must be ascertainable beneficiaries. This will often be made clear by the terms of the constitution of the society; or, in the case of societies governed by statute, such as friendly societies, by the terms of the

---

[87] See Warburton, *Unincorporated Associations: Law and Practice*, 2nd edn, 1990, Ch.5.

[88] Trade Union and Labour Relations (Consolidation) Act 1992 s.10.

[89] Halsbury, 4th edn, Vol.9(2), para.1101. It is otherwise in the context of tax; *Worthing Rugby Football Club Trustees v IRC* [1987] 1 W.L.R. 1057.

[90] Above, paras 10–010–10–016.

[91] *Re Lipinski's Will Trusts* [1976] Ch. 235, above, para.14–002; *Re Horley Town Football Club* [2006] W.T.L.R. 1817 (land settled on trust "for the primary purpose of securing a permanent ground for the Horley Football Club").

statute governing them. The Friendly Societies Act 1974 s.54(1) provides that the property of an unincorporated friendly society shall vest in the trustees for the time being of the society, for the use and benefit of the society and its members.[92] It was at one time thought that there was no need to identify the beneficiaries of property held by unincorporated associations; and that a gift to persons holding the property as trustees was good so long as the trustees had power to spend the capital. A society could then dispose of any of its assets at any time; there would be no more tendency to inalienability than in the case of an individual holding property, and, it was argued, no reason for invalidating it. Thus, in *Re Drummond*,[93] a gift was made to the Old Bradfordians Club, London, to be utilised as the committee should think best in the interests of the club or school. Eve J. upheld the gift. It was not, he said, a gift to the members, but the committee was free to spend the money as it thought fit on the specified objects. It did not tend to a perpetuity, and was valid.

If the trustees could spend only the income however—if, in other words, the capital was tied up as an endowment—the trusts on which the assets were held would be perpetual and void. This view, which appeared to have been approved by the House of Lords,[94] dealt, however, only with the perpetuity aspect of the problem. It ignored the necessity to analyse the property interests which were created.

In *Leahy v Att Gen for New South Wales*,[95] a testator provided that Elmslea, a sheep station of some 730 acres, should be held upon trust for "such order of nuns of the Catholic Church or the Christian Brothers as my executors and trustees shall select." The gift was not valid as a charitable trust because some of the orders were purely contemplative orders which are not charitable in law.[96]

Nor was it valid as a private trust. In view of the nature of the property and the fact that the members of the selected orders might be very numerous and spread across the world, there was no intention to create a trust in favour of the individual members

---

[92] See *Re Bucks Constabulary Fund (No.2)* [1979] 1 W.L.R. 937. The Friendly Societies Act 1992 provides for the incorporation of such societies carrying on mutual insurance business.

[93] [1914] 2 Ch. 90; *Re Price* [1943] Ch. 422 ("To the Anthroposophical Society of Great Britain to be used at the discretion of the Chairman and Executive Council of the Society for carrying out the teaching of the founder Dr. Rudolf Steiner."); W. Hart (1937) 53 L.Q.R. 24 at 46.

[94] *Macaulay v O'Donnell*, July 10, 1933; reported at [1943] Ch. 435n.; *Carne v Long* (1860) 2 De G.F. & J. 75.

[95] [1959] A.C. 457.

[96] *Gilmour v Coats* [1949] A.C. 426; below, para.15–041.

of selected orders.[97] The testator's intention clearly was to establish an endowment. The gift would have failed if it had not been rescued by a statute of New South Wales which permitted partly charitable trusts to be applied wholly in favour of those parts which were charitable. The trustees' power of selection did not therefore extend to contemplative orders.

14–018   Other modern cases, however, have shown a "retreat from *Leahy*"[98] and have found a different construction, enabling the gift to be held valid as being a trust for the members of the association.[99] This has even proved possible, applying the principle of *Re Denley's Trust Deed*,[100] where the donor has stated that his gift is to be applied for specific non-charitable purposes.[101] The position was analysed in *Neville Estates v Madden*,[102] where Cross J. held that the property interests of the members of an association would fall into one of three categories. There might be a gift to the members at the relevant date as joint tenants, giving each a right of severance of his part; or a gift subject to the contractual rights and liabilities of the members towards each other, which prevent severance and cause a member's interest, on his death or resignation, to accrue to the remaining members; or a gift to present and future members, in which case the gift, unless confined to the perpetuity period, would be void. A fourth possibility is that this situation creates a specialised form of co-ownership, whose rules should be worked out separately, and independently of the law of trusts,[103] but this has recently been rejected.[104] All these possible solutions fail to explain how the equitable interest of a member passes on his resignation without compliance with Law of Property Act 1925 s.53(1)(c).[105]

Gifts to unincorporated associations can involve perpetuity problems of two distinct kinds, relating to remoteness of vesting and perpetual duration. To avoid both problems, the trust must be for the

---

[97] [1959] A.C. 457 at p.486; cf. *Re Smith* [1914] 1 Ch. 937, where a bequest to the Society of Franciscan Friars of Clevedon County, Somerset was construed as a gift to the members of the community at the date of the testator's death; *Cocks v Manners* (1871) L.R. 12 Eq. 574 (a share of residue to the "Dominican Convent of Carisbrooke payable to the Superior for the time being").

[98] F. Crane (1977) 41 Conv.(N.S.) 139.

[99] K. Widdows (1977) 41 Conv.(N.S.) 179; C. Rickett (1980) 39 C.L.J. 88; J. Warburton [1985] Conv. 318. See generally P. Kohler (2000) 53 C.L.P. 236 at 259–266.

[100] [1969] 1 Ch. 373, above, para.14–002. This did not involve an unincorporated association, but the reasoning is applicable to gifts to such associations.

[101] *Re Lipinski's Will Trusts* [1976] Ch. 235, above, para.14–002.

[102] [1962] Ch. 832 at 849; *Re Recher's WT* [1972] Ch. 526 at 538, below, para.14–019.

[103] Ford, *Unincorporated Non-Profit Associations*, 1959, Pt 1, especially at pp.5–8, 21–23.

[104] *Hanchett-Stamford v Att Gen* [2009] Ch. 173; below, para.14–019.

[105] Morris and Leach, pp.313–318; J. Hackney [1971] A.S.C.L. at 379. The *Re Denley* approach (above, para.14–002), whereby the beneficiary has no proprietary interest, does not encounter these difficulties. See further S. Baughen [2010] Conv. 216 at 225.

benefit of members who are both ascertainable during the perpetuity period and also able to claim a division of the funds before that period expires. If the members are not so ascertainable, the trust will fail, subject to what is said below, for remoteness of vesting. If the capital is to be retained as an endowment, the trust will be void as a perpetual trust.[106]

Cross J. in *Neville Estates v Madden*[107] referred to the problem of remoteness of vesting in his third category (gift to present and future members). This problem was resolved by the Perpetuities and Accumulations Act 1964, which excluded from the gift any members not ascertainable within the perpetuity period.[108] The 1964 Act did not remove the problem of perpetual duration (inalienability). The gift will fail if:

> "[T]here is something in its terms or circumstances or in the rules of the association which precludes the members at any time from dividing the subject of the gift between them on the footing that they are solely entitled in equity".[109]

This aspect of the perpetuity rule caused the gift to fail in *Re Grant's Will Trusts*.[110] The trust was for the purposes of the Chertsey Labour Party Headquarters, which were not charitable. The members of this local association did not control the property, nor could they change the rules of the association and thereby gain control, because the rules were subject to the approval of, and capable of alteration by, an outside body (the National Executive Committee). Although it seems that a way around this problem could have been found,[111] the trust was held void for perpetuity, even though the restriction on disposing of the capital was not one imposed by the testator. The decision has been described as one which "has shed more darkness than light".[112]

---

[106] *Carne v Long* (1860) 2 De G.F. & J. 75.

[107] Above, fn.102.

[108] s.4(4). This provision is repeated in s.8 of the Perpetuities and Accumulations Act 2009 in relation to instruments taking effect after its commencement.

[109] *Re Lipinski's Will Trusts*, above, fn.101, at p.244, quoting the summary of Cross J.'s categories in *Tudor on Charities*, 6th edn, 1967, p.150.

[110] [1980] 1 W.L.R. 360; B Green (1980) 43 M.L.R. 459; G. Shindler [1980] Conv. 80; cf. *Re Horley Town Football Club* [2006] W.T.L.R. 1817 (fact that rules conferred voting rights on non-member did not bring the *Re Grant* principle into play).

[111] See Heydon, Gummow and Austin, *Cases and Materials on Equity and Trusts*, 4th edn, p.595, suggesting that control by the outside body was not as significant as the case suggests. The beneficiaries could be treated as including the members of that body also. Another possibility is that the members could disaffiliate from the national body. See also *News Group Newspapers Ltd v SOGAT 82* [1986] I.C.R. 716, where *Re Grant* was distinguished because the members of a local branch of a trade union had control over the branch assets and could in theory secede from the union and divide the assets.

[112] P. Luxton [2007] Conv. 274 at 280.

D. Ownership by Members on Contractual Basis

14–019   The contractual analysis provides a method by which unincorporated associations can validly hold property without the necessity of discovering an intention to create a trust, and by which gifts to the association, in order to escape invalidity as purpose trusts, need not be regarded as taking effect as immediate distributive shares in favour of the members, which is unlikely to have been the donor's intention. Members of an association can:

> "[B]and themselves together as an association or society, pay subscriptions and validly devote their funds in pursuit of some lawful non-charitable purpose. An obvious example is a members' social club"[113]

—where it would in most cases be difficult to find an intention to create a trust. Their assets, whether donations or members' subscriptions, are held by the trustees or by the committee or officers of the club on the terms of the constitution or rules of the club, which are themselves a contract by the members with each other. A trust is interposed simply because it is normally inconvenient (and impossible in the case of land) for the assets to be vested in all the members. This is a bare trust and does not detract from the contractual analysis.

This solution avoids some of the difficulties which arise from an analysis which regards the members as beneficiaries under a private trust. The members' rights are contractual, and of course they depend upon the rules of the association. A member will not usually be able to claim his share at any time; but the members as a whole control the committee's activities in accordance with the rules, and can usually take the decision to wind up the association and share out the proceeds. A member's rights terminate on death or resignation, and a new member obtains rights in relation to the assets during his period of membership. As the members are joint tenants, the last surviving member is entitled to the property under the doctrine of survivorship.[114] Questions concerning the contractual rights of members usually arise on the termination of an association, as we have seen.[115]

The fact that the assets are held by the members on a contractual basis of course does not prejudge the construction of a gift by a third party to the association. But the court will lean in favour of validity, and is likely to regard such a gift as an accretion to the funds of the

---

[113] *Re Recher's WT* [1972] Ch. 526 at 538, per Brightman J.
[114] *Hanchett-Stamford v Att-Gen* [2009] Ch. 173; P. Clarke All E.R. Rev. 2008, p.302; G. Griffiths [2009] Conv. 428; S. Baughen [2010] Conv. 216.
[115] Above, para.10–013.

association. In *Re Recher's Will Trust*[116] there was a gift in trust for "The London and Provincial Anti-Vivisection Society". Brightman J. held that the assets of the society were owned by the members in accordance with the rules. "There is no private trust or trust for charitable purposes or other trust to hinder the process."[117] If it was correct that a gift to such an association must be construed as a (void) purpose trust or as distributive shares in favour of the members, then it would be difficult to make a donation in favour of the body, which would be contrary to common sense. The solution was that the gift could be construed as a beneficial gift in favour of the members, not so as to entitle them to an immediate distributive share, but as an accretion to the funds of the society subject to the contract of the members as set out in the rules. Such a construction was equally available whether the society existed to promote the interest of its members ("inward-looking") or, as in the present case, to promote some outside purpose ("outward-looking"). If the society had remained in existence, the gift would have been good. In fact, however, it had been dissolved before the date of the gift.

As has been pointed out,[118] the question whether a gift to an association is subject to any restriction on its use depends on the intention of the members as expressed in their contract with each other. Thus whether the gift is one to the members in severable shares or subject to the purposes of the association normally depends not on the donor's intention but on the rules of the association. To be valid, any restrictions imposed by the donor must infringe neither the beneficiary principle nor the perpetuity rule.[119]

6. MANDATE OR AGENCY

The principles described above apply to unincorporated associations, which have already been defined.[120] It may be that an organisation (which is not incorporated) fails to satisfy the requirements of an unincorporated association. This was the case in *Conservative and Unionist Central Office v Burrell (Inspector of Taxes)*,[121] where the Crown claimed that the Conservative Party was an unincorporated association. If this were so, Central Office would be assessable

14–020

---

[116] [1972] Ch. 526; (1972) 35 Conv.(N.S.) 381; P. Hogg (1971) 8 M.U.L.R. 1; (1973) 47 A.L.J. 305. The "accretion to funds" solution is adopted by the Queensland Succession Act 1981 s.63. See also *Artistic Upholstery Ltd v Art Forma (Furniture) Ltd* [1999] 4 All E.R. 277; *Re Horley Town Football Club* [2006] W.T.L.R. 1817; P. Luxton [2007] Conv. 274.

[117] [1972] Ch. 526 at 539; *Re Bucks Constabulary Fund (No.2)* [1979] 1 W.L.R. 937.

[118] P. Matthews [1995] Conv. 302. See also S. Gardner [1998] Conv. 8.

[119] See *Re Lipinski's Will Trusts* [1976] Ch. 235.

[120] Above, para.14–014.

[121] [1982] 1 W.L.R. 522. See generally P. Smart [1987] Conv. 415.

to corporation tax, as opposed to income tax, on certain income. The Court of Appeal rejected the Crown's claim. The Party was an amorphous combination of various elements, but not an unincorporated association, because the members had no mutual rights and obligations, there were no rules governing control (which lay in the party leader), and no event in history could be identified as marking the creation of the party as an association.[122]

Of interest in the present context was the analysis of the legal effect of a contribution to such a body. Where the body was not an unincorporated association, the *Re Recher*[123] analysis could not apply. The legal basis was mandate or agency. The contributor gives the recipient (e.g. the treasurer) a mandate to use the gift in a particular way. He can demand its return unless the mandate becomes irrevocable, as when the gift is added to a mixed fund with the authority of the contributor. There is no trust, only the fiduciary element inherent in the relationship of principal and agent. Once the mandate has become irrevocable, the contributor's rights are to an account of expenditure, and to restrain a misapplication. Difficulties might arise where there was a change of the office-holder to whom the mandate was given. More seriously, the mandate theory could not explain the validity of bequests to such organisations, as agency cannot be set up at death. No solution to this problem was offered, the Court of Appeal being content to suggest that the answer was "not difficult to find".[124]

14–021 It remains to be seen whether the mandate theory will be applied in other situations.[125] In view of its limitations, especially with regard to testamentary gifts, this is perhaps doubtful.

Another possibility, which is related to the mandate idea, is to utilise the type of trust upheld by the House of Lords in *Barclays Bank Ltd v Quistclose Investments Ltd*[126] as a means of achieving an abstract purpose trust.[127] In that case money was lent for a specific purpose (the payment of dividends), on the basis that it would be held for the lender if not applied to the purpose. It was held that the debtor took the money on trust to apply it for the purpose. As the

---

[122] Convincingly criticised in P. Creighton [1983] Conv. 150; "It may be as misleading to deny the organisation its status as an unincorporated association because its origins are obscure as it would be to deny the existence of a living human being on the ground that his birth certificate could not be found."

[123] Above, para.14–019.

[124] Perhaps referring to the principle of *Re Denley's Deed Trust* [1969] 1 Ch. 373, above, para.14–002, or to the fact that the testator may authorise his executors to give a mandate. See also P. Creighton [1983] Conv. 150; P. Smart [1987] Conv. 415.

[125] It was referred to in connection with members' subscriptions in *Re Recher's Will Trusts* [1972] Ch. 526 at 539. The reasoning might apply to cases such as *Re Gillingham Bus Disaster Fund* [1959] Ch. 62, above, para.14–002, involving public donations to non-charitable purposes.

[126] [1970] A.C. 567; above, para.2–009.

[127] Chambers, *Resulting Trusts*, p.90. See also C. Rickett (1991) 107 L.Q.R. 608.

purpose could no longer be carried out (because of the debtor's insolvency), the money was held on trust for the lender. Lord Millett's analysis is that the borrower holds on resulting trust for the lender but with a power (or, in some cases, a duty) to carry out the lender's revocable mandate. It is not a purpose trust, but simply a trust subject to a power to apply the money for a purpose.[128] It seems that the same reasoning would apply if the money was not a loan. So long as the mandate or power is not uncertain or contrary to public policy, this is a means of achieving the application of money to an abstract purpose.

7. PERPETUITY

A. Excessive Duration[129]

It has been said that a non-charitable purpose trust, even though otherwise valid, is void if it may last beyond the period of perpetuity; this being a rule designed to produce an effect analogous to the rule controlling remoteness of vesting, and applying the same general policy. If, therefore, a purpose trust survives an attack under the beneficiary principle, it must be restricted to the period of perpetuity: "The rule against inalienability is, in reality, just one of the devices that is employed to keep the development of such trusts in check."[130]

14–022

In applying the rule against excessive duration, the courts have been more generous than in other aspects of perpetuity law. First, they have assumed that a monument will be erected within the period.

In *Mussett v Bingle*,[131] a testator gave £300 to be applied in the erection of a monument to his wife's first husband, and £200 the interest on which was to be applied in maintaining it. The latter gift was perpetual and void. The former was upheld. In the absence of any objection on the ground of perpetuity, the court must have assumed that the monument would be erected within the period.

Secondly a trust will be upheld if the instrument provides that it is to continue "so long as the law allows" or some similar period. The gift is good for 21 years.[132] If no such saving phrase is included, the

---

[128] *Twinsectra v Yardley* [2002] 2 A.C. 164.
[129] Morris and Leach, pp.321–327; Maudsley, *The Modern Law of Perpetuities*, pp.166–178.
[130] Law Com No.251 (1998), *The Rules Against Perpetuities and Excessive Accumulations*, para.1.14.
[131] [1876] W.N. 170.
[132] *Pirbright v Salwey* [1896] W.N. 86; *Re Hooper* [1932] 1 Ch. 38.

trust is wholly void.[133] The court will not supply the necessary words to meet the testator's obvious intention. The wait and see principle has never applied to purpose trusts.[134] If it did, it would at least have solved this problem.

Thirdly, the courts have on various occasions taken judicial notice of the fact that an animal's lifespan is limited to 21 years. If the animal could not live that long, the trust could not endure beyond the period. Danckwerts J. in *Re Haines*[135] took judicial notice of the fact that a cat could not live for more than 21 years. Biologists have corrected him, showing that a cat may live for 25 years.[136] It seems that, if the courts are willing to take judicial notice of longevity, it should be permissible to take evidence of the age of the cats in question; for if the youngest cat is over four, the particular trust would not last for more than 21 years.

B. Human Lives Only

14–023   Perhaps North J. in *Re Dean*[137] should be taken to have applied some such doctrine. He upheld a gift of an annual sum for the period of 50 years if any of the testator's horses and hounds should so long live. The perpetuity point was not dealt with, and it seems almost as if the learned judge assumed that the life of an animal could be used as a measuring life for the purposes of the rule. The better doctrine however was provided by Meredith J. in *Re Kelly*[138]:

> "If the lives of dogs or other animals could be taken into account in reckoning the maximum period of 'lives in being and twenty-one years afterwards' any contingent or executory interest might be properly limited, so as only to vest within the lives of specified carp, or tortoises, or other animals that might live for over a hundred years, and for twenty-one years afterwards, which, of course, is absurd. 'Lives' means human lives. It was suggested that the last of the dogs could in fact not outlive the testator by more than twenty-one years. I know nothing of that. The court does not enter into the question of a dog's expectation of life. In point of fact neighbours' dogs and cats are unpleasantly long-lived; but I have no knowledge of their precise expectation of life.

---

[133] contra, *Re Budge* [1942] N.Z.L.R. 356, where a trust to apply the income in keeping a grave neat and tidy was held valid for 21 years. Morris and Leach, p.322.

[134] PAA 1964 s.15(4); PAA 2009 s.18; below, para.14–024; cf. New Zealand Perpetuities Act 1964; Maudsley, *The Modern Law of Perpetuities*, App. D.

[135] *The Times*, November 7, 1952.

[136] Morris and Leach, p.323; Maudsley, p.170.

[137] (1889) 41 Ch.D. 552.

[138] [1932] I.R. 255 at 260–261.

Anyway the maximum period is exceeded by the lives of specified butterflies and twenty-one years afterwards. And even, according to my decision—and, I confess, it displays this weakness
on being pressed to a logical conclusion—the expiration of the
life of a single butterfly, even without the twenty-one years,
would be too remote, despite all the world of poetry that may be
thereby destroyed . . . there can be no doubt that 'lives' means
lives of human beings, not of animals or trees in California."

Re Dean[139] is unsupportable on this point. All other purpose trusts
which may last beyond the period of perpetuity have been held
void.

C. A Fixed Number of Years

As we are dealing here with a question of duration and not one of **14–024**
remoteness of vesting of beneficial interests, it would be much more
convenient to have a perpetuity period which was gauged by a
number of years, rather than one measured by lives. It is possible to
argue that a court should hold that purpose trusts can last for 21
years only; for no purpose trust, with the exception of *Re Howard*,[140] when a parrot was to be fed during the lives of the survivor
of two servants, has been upheld for any other or longer period. Yet
a royal lives clause was not challenged in *Re Astor's Trusts*.[141] In *Re
Moore*,[142] the objection was to the excessive number of lives chosen
and not to the fact that lives were chosen, and in *Re Khoo Cheng
Teow*,[143] the Supreme Court of the Straits Settlements has upheld a
non-charitable purpose trust for the period of royal lives plus 21
years.

It was reasonable therefore to hope that the Perpetuities and Accumulations Act 1964 would have provided for a fixed period of
years. A restriction to a period of 21 years would have been welcome. The 80-year period would have been an improvement.[144] In
fact the Act left the period at lives plus 21 years.

Section 15(4) provides:

"Nothing in this Act shall affect the operation of the rule of law
rendering void for remoteness certain dispositions under which

---

[139] (1889) 41 Ch.D. 552.
[140] *The Times*, October 30, 1908. Law Com No.251 (1998), *The Rules Against Perpetuities
and Excessive Accumulations*, para.8.35, confirms that the period is lives (if any) plus 21
years.
[141] [1952] Ch. 534.
[142] [1901] 1 Ch. 936.
[143] [1932] Straits Settlements Report 226.
[144] See Trusts (Guernsey) Law 2007 (unlimited duration, replacing previous limit of 100
years); F. Noseda (2008) 22 T.L.I. 117; Belize Trusts Act 1992 (120 years). For the position in
the United States, see L. Waggoner (2011) 127 L.Q.R. 423.

property is limited to be applied for purposes other than the benefit of any person or class of persons in cases where the property may be so applied after the end of the perpetuity period."

Although the contrary is not unarguable,[145] it appears that the effect of this provision was that neither the 80-year period permitted by s.1 of the Act nor the "wait and see" rule of s.3 applied to purpose trusts.[146]

Law Commission proposals on the reform of the perpetuity rule did not affect the rule against excessive duration. This was excluded from the scope of the Report on the ground that it belonged more properly in a review of non-charitable purpose trusts and unincorporated associations.[147] The Law Commission proposals have been implemented by the Perpetuities and Accumulations Act 2009, the general effect of which is to replace the common law perpetuity period with a fixed period of 125 years. However, this does not apply to purpose trusts, as s.18 provides:

"This Act does not affect the rule of law which limits the duration of non-charitable purpose trusts."

Thus the period remains lives in being plus 21 years, or 21 years if there are no relevant lives in being.

8. Useless or Capricious Purposes

14–025   One question which has to be faced when considering whether, as a matter of policy, purpose trusts should be enforced is that of excluding trusts which are useless, wasteful, capricious, or even harmful or illegal. This aspect of the matter was in the mind of Roxburgh J. in *Re Astor's Trusts* when he said[148]:

" . . . [I]t is not possible to contemplate with equanimity the creation of large funds directed to non-charitable purposes which no court and no department of state can control, or in the case of maladministration reform."

---

[145] See Maudsley, *The Modern Law of Perpetuities*, p.177; J. Andrews (1965) 29 Conv.(N.S.) 165. For the view that s.15(4) does not apply to purpose trusts within the principle of *Re Denley's Trust Deed* [1969] 1 Ch. 373, see P. Matthews in A. Oakley (ed.) *Trends in Contemporary Trust Law*, 1996, pp.12, 18.

[146] Law Com No.251 (1998), *The Rules against Perpetuities and Excessive Accumulations*, para.8.35.

[147] Law Com No.251 para.1.14.

[148] [1952] Ch. at p.542.

The question ultimately is that of the extent to which one person, usually deceased, should be allowed to deprive the community or individuals within it, of the beneficial use of capital. The larger the amount, and the longer the period of application, the greater the problem. No attempt has been made to draw a precise line between those which are acceptable and those which are not. We will see that the greatest difficulty has been experienced in trying to draw a line between charitable and other trusts.[149] This does not augur well for the creation of a recognisable line between acceptable and non-acceptable non-charitable purpose trusts; but it is no reason for insisting on holding all non-charitable purpose trusts void. "The answer, of course, is that the courts will have to strike down the silly purposes and uphold the sensible ones."[150]

In *Brown v Burdett*,[151] the testator devised a freehold house to trustees upon trust to block up almost all the rooms of the house for a period of 20 years, and, subject thereto, to a devisee. Bacon V.C. decided that he must "unseal" this "useless, undisposed of property," and declared that there was an intestacy as to the period of 20 years.

Scottish judges have been forthright in their disapproval of the waste of money on useless projects:

"I consider that, if it is not unlawful, it ought to be unlawful, to dedicate by testamentary disposition, for all time, or for a length of time, the whole income of a large estate ... to objects of no utility, private or public, objects which benefit nobody, and which have no other purpose or use than that of perpetuating at great cost, and in an absurd manner, the idiosyncrasies of an eccentric testator."[152]

"The prospect of Scotland being dotted with monuments to obscure persons cumbered with trusts for the purpose of maintaining these monuments in all time coming, appears to me to be little less than appalling. ... "[153]

---

[149] Below, Ch.15.
[150] L. Sheridan (1959) 4 U. of W.A.L.R. at 239.
[151] (1882) 21 Ch.D. 667; see also *McCaig v University of Glasgow*, 1907 S.C. 231; *McCaig's Trustees v Kirk-Session of United Free Church of Lismore*, 1915 S.C. 426 (bronze statues at £1,000 each); *Aitken v Aitken*, 1927 S.C. 374 (massive bronze equestrian statue); *Mackintosh's Judicial Factor v Lord Advocate*, 1935 S.C. 406 (erection of vault).
[152] *McCaig v University of Glasgow*, above, fn.151, at 242.
[153] *McCaig's Trustees v Kirk-Session of United Free Church of Lismore*, above, fn.151, at 434.

9. ALTERNATIVE SOLUTIONS

14–026   It seems therefore that non-charitable purpose trusts are void under the beneficiary principle; that there are recognised exceptions in trusts for animals and monuments, which, to be valid, must be certain, not useless or capricious, and confined to the period of perpetuity; and that a trust may be upheld if, although expressed as a purpose trust, it is directly for the benefit of ascertainable individuals. Some take the view that this is too restricted a position. We now consider in what ways the effecting of a non-charitable purpose can be achieved.

A. By the Draftsman

14–027   **i. Incorporation.** A society may be incorporated to advance such purposes. The matter then leaves the law of trusts, and the problem here discussed disappears. This is the simplest practical solution.

14–028   **ii. Mandate or Agency.** Consideration should also be given to the possibility of utilising the mandate or agency theory expounded in *Conservative and Unionist Central Office v Burrell (Inspector of Taxes)*,[154] discussed in Pt 6, above. The principle could also be invoked in the case of gifts to unincorporated associations, although it is doubtful whether it has much to offer here, not least because it cannot be the basis of a testamentary gift.[155] Where this principle can be utilised, the matter then leaves the law of trusts, as in the case of incorporation. The problem of purpose trusts disappears, but other problems, as we have seen, take its place.

14–029   **iii. Gift to Members of an Association and Not for Purposes Only.** In *Re Lipinski's Will Trusts*,[156] Oliver J. emphasised the distinction between:

> "[T]he case where a purpose is prescribed which is clearly intended for the benefit of ascertained or ascertainable beneficiaries . . . and the case where no beneficiary at all is intended . . . or where the beneficiaries are unascertainable."

This distinction is crucial. A gift to provide recreational facilities may be a gift for beneficiaries if those persons are intended to be

---

[154] [1982] 1 W.L.R. 522; also the *Quistclose* trust, above, para.2–009.
[155] Above, para.14–020.
[156] [1976] Ch. 235, at 246.

benefited[157]; and similarly a gift to an association where it is construed as a gift for the members as an accretion to their funds.[158] The problem of construction was substantial in the cases discussed; but there is no need for any difficulty to arise if the draftsman is aware of the possibilities and the difficulties and drafts the gift accordingly.

iv. Conveyancing Devices. A gift over from one charity to another may validly take place at any time in the future; the rule against perpetuities does not apply.[159] Advantage was taken of this rule in *Re Tyler*,[160] to achieve a non-charitable purpose. **14–030**

A gift was made to the London Missionary Society, committing to their care the family vault, and if they failed to comply with the request the money was to go to the Bluecoat School. The gift was upheld. It could last perpetually if the value of the gift was sufficient to encourage the London Missionary Society to perform the task. If the task became unprofitable, as no doubt it would do by the progress of inflation, the gift over would take effect. The Bluecoat School would be under no obligation to perform the task. Indeed, if an attempt was made to impose an obligation on either donee by requiring any part of the income to be applied for the non-charitable purpose, the gift would have been void as not exclusively charitable.[161]

The Law Commission recommended no change to the exception from the perpetuity rule of gifts over from one charity to another, although noting that the exception has been employed as a means of enforcing non-charitable purpose trusts in perpetuity.[162] The exception is confirmed in the Perpetuities and Accumulations Act 2009.[163]

v. Draft as a Power; not as a Trust. The beneficiary principle applies to trusts. There must be someone who can enforce the trust. With a power, there is no question of enforcement; although questions of certainty and perpetuity arise. Assuming however that these are overcome, could not the purpose be achieved by giving the property, not to a trustee upon trust, but to the ultimate beneficiary **14–031**

---

[157] *Re Denley's Trust Deed* [1969] 1 Ch. 373.
[158] *Re Recher's WT* [1972] Ch. 526; *Re Lipinski's WT* [1976] Ch. 235.
[159] *Christ's Hospital (Governors) v Grainger* (1849) 1 Mac & G. 460.
[160] [1891] 3 Ch. 252.
[161] *Re Dalziel* [1943] Ch. 277. See further P. Smart [1987] Conv. 415.
[162] Law Com No.251 (1998), *The Rules against Perpetuities and Excessive Accumulations*, paras 7.34, 7.37.
[163] s.2(2).

subject to a power in a third party to apply the property for the stated purpose for the perpetuity period?

There is little authority on the validity of such a power. Clearly, a power can be something other than a general or special power to appoint to persons.[164] Lord Millett has analysed the *"Quistclose* trust"[165] as involving a resulting trust for the lender, subject to a power or mandate to apply the money to the designated purpose (in that case the acquisition of property). The power was valid provided it was sufficiently certain to allow the court to determine if it was capable of being carried out or if the money had been misapplied.[166] It may be, then, that a power to apply the income for the improvement of land,[167] or for research into the advantages of the 40-letter alphabet,[168] could, if limited to the period of perpetuity, be valid. It seems that the same rule should apply to repairing monuments or feeding animals. The person entitled in default could restrain misapplication.

There seems to be nothing contrary to policy in allowing the purpose to be effected in this way. Policy questions will arise, of course, where an eccentric testator provides for large sums to be applied for useless, capricious or harmful purposes for a substantial period.[169] The problem here is the same as that discussed in Pt 8 above.

Arguments have been put forward to the effect that an instrument which purports to create a purpose trust should be construed as a power so as to allow the purpose to be carried out.[170] Supporters of this view argued that this is a way of achieving the testator's or settlor's intention without conflicting with any rules of policy. In *Re Shaw,*[171] Harman J. appeared to find some attraction in the argument; but he rejected it, following what Jenkins L.J. had said in *Commissioners of Inland Revenue v Broadway Cottages Trust*[172]; "We do not think that a valid power is to be spelt out of an invalid trust."

B. By the Legislature

14–032 If reform is to come, it will come best from the Legislature. The basic question is whether gifts for non-charitable purposes should be

---

[164] See *Re Douglas* (1887) 35 Ch.D. 472; J. Gray (1902) 15 H.L.R. 67; L. Sheridan (1959) 4 U. of W.A.L.R. at 260. See also *Re Clarke* [1923] 2 Ch. 407, where a power to appoint to *uncertain* non-charitable objects failed.

[165] Above, para.2–009.

[166] *Twinsectra v Yardley* [2002] 2 A.C. 164.

[167] *Re Aberconway's ST* [1953] Ch. 647.

[168] *Re Shaw* [1957] 1 W.L.R. 729.

[169] See Morris and Leach, 2nd edn, p.320.

[170] D. Potter (1949) 13 Conv.(N.S.) 418 at 424; A. Kiralfy (1950) 14 Conv.(N.S.) 374; L. Sheridan (1959) 4 U. of W.A.L.R. at 240–244; (1953) 17 Conv.(N.S.) 46 at 59.

[171] [1957] 1 W.L.R. 729 at 746.

[172] [1955] Ch. 20 at 36.

upheld. If so, it is necessary to find a means of overcoming the beneficiary principle, and this would most conveniently be done by enacting that trusts for non-charitable purposes (if sufficiently certain) should be construed as powers.[173] The purpose could then be carried out by the trustees if they elected to do so. If they did not, the purpose would fail and the property would go to those entitled in default. The power would be valid only if it was sufficiently certain. It may be thought appropriate to limit such trusts to a period of 21 years.[174] The danger of maladministration would be no greater than that already encountered in the case of the permitted purpose trusts discussed in Pt 3 above.

To the statutory solution, it may be objected that it does not answer the anxiety expressed by Roxburgh J. in *Re Astor's Settlement Trusts*[175] that it was not in the general interest that large sums of money should be applied for non-charitable purposes for long periods of time. The period of perpetuity can be about 100 years, and non-charitable purposes include all those which at one end are nearly charitable and those which are so useless as to be capricious. In validating gifts for purposes, it is important to ensure that funds are made available for purposes which are useful to the public rather than for the satisfaction of the private interests of a settlor or testator. Resources are scarce, and need to be put to good use. The problem is one which exists also in the case of gifts which are drafted in the form of powers. No doubt, the amount of money involved, and the duration of the trust will be factors which will be relevant to a decision. The line is difficult to draw. But capricious trusts are the rare ones. The fact that they exist is no reason for failing to establish a rational method of validating the useful ones.

C. Offshore Jurisdictions

Purpose trusts are now permitted by statute in many jurisdictions **14–033** to facilitate estate planning and asset protection schemes, by exploiting the point that neither the settlor nor any other person is the beneficial owner of the property.[176] This has been done in the interests of attracting lucrative trusts business to the jurisdiction in question. Typically such legislation permits non-charitable purpose trusts

---

[173] See Ontario Perpetuities Act 1966. Alternatively, legislation could validate a purpose trust where the trust deed requires the appointment of an "enforcer"; D. Hayton (ed.), *Modern International Developments in Trust Law*, 1999, at p.282. Indeed, a purpose trust with an "enforcer" appointed under the terms of the trust may be valid without legislation; D. Hayton (2001) 117 L.Q.R. 96. See also J. Langbein (2001) 15 T.L.I. 66, discussing the US Uniform Trust Code, which permits purpose trusts for 21 years.

[174] New Zealand Perpetuities Act 1964 s.20.

[175] [1952] Ch. 534.

[176] See P. Matthews in A. Oakley (ed.), *Trends in Contemporary Trusts Law*, 1996, Ch.1; Baxendale-Walker, *Purpose Trusts*, 1999; (1999) 5 *Trusts & Trustees*, pp.5–92.

to last for long periods such as 120 years, and provides for enforcement by the "protector" of the settlement or by an "enforcer".[177] Of particular interest is the Cayman Islands Special Trusts (Alternative Regime) Law 1997.[178] This permits non-charitable purpose trusts (commonly known as STAR trusts) which are exempt from the perpetuity rule, which are enforceable by "enforcers" and which do not fail for uncertainty (any uncertainty may be resolved by the court settling a scheme).[179] Such trusts may also include human beneficiaries, but they have no standing to enforce the trust. This has given rise to a debate as to whether a "STAR trust" is really a trust at all, because the fundamental obligations owed by trustees to beneficiaries are absent,[180] or, to put it more strongly, that the fiduciary obligations of trustees have become "nothing more than a farce."[181] The danger is that a resulting trust might then arise in favour of the settlor, thus defeating his objectives. A settlor may seek to take advantage of these offshore enactments by including a provision in the trust instrument that the trust is to be governed by the law of a specified jurisdiction.[182] The attraction is that the beneficial ownership appears to be in abeyance, which is useful for confidentiality and secrecy, with possible adverse effects on dependants, creditors and tax authorities. Thus the suspicion is that "purpose trust legislation simply encourages hidden ownership by putting assets into a no-man's land".[183] The purpose trust vehicle can be used for "off balance sheet" transactions, as where a company is set up to acquire an asset from another company and thus take it off the latter's balance sheet, to be held on a purpose trust. There is no plan to introduce such legislation in the United Kingdom, because "there is a feeling that pure purpose trusts may be hijacked for shady dealings involving hiding beneficial ownership".[184]

---

[177] See, for example, the Belize Trusts Act 1992; Trusts (Amendment No.4) (Jersey) Law 2006 (unlimited duration); Trustee Act 2001 (Mauritius); T. Tey (2009) 23 T.L.I. 151.

[178] Now substantially incorporated into Pt VIII of the Trusts Law (2001) Revision.

[179] See Thomas and Hudson, *The Law of Trusts*, Ch.40.

[180] P. Matthews (1997) 11 T.L.I. 67; A. Duckworth (1998) 12 T.L.I. 16; P. Matthews (1997) 11 T.L.I. 67, at 98; A. Duckworth (1999) 13 T.L.I. 158; J. Hilliard (2003) 17 T.L.I. 144.

[181] T. Tey (2009) 23 T.L.I. 183 at 193.

[182] See the Hague Convention art.6. Under art.18, effect will not be given to this if it would be manifestly incompatible with public policy. See also art.2, defining a trust, for the purpose of the Convention, as being "for the benefit of a beneficiary or for a specific purpose."

[183] D. Hayton (ed.), *Modern International Developments in Trust Law*, p.12.

[184] Hayton (above, fn.183) at 305. For a more positive view by the same author, see D. Hayton (2001) 117 L.Q.R. 96 and D Hayton in Birks and Pretto (eds.), *Breach of Trust*, 2002, pp.382–383. Legislation is advocated in M. Pawlowski and J. Summers [2007] Conv. 440.

CHAPTER 15

CHARITABLE TRUSTS

1. Introduction[1]

15–001 CHARITABLE purposes are those which are considered to be of such value and importance to the community that they receive especially favourable treatment. Charity law was modernised by the Charities Act 2006 (now consolidated with other charity legislation by the Charities Act 2011), but much of the old law on charitable purposes is preserved in the new legislation. Prior to the Act of 2006 the definition of charity derived from the old Preamble to the Charitable Uses Act of 1601, an Act which was passed for the purpose of remedying abuses which had grown up in the administration of charitable trusts. The Preamble contained a general catalogue of the purposes then regarded as charitable. Since that time, purposes which were regarded as being within the "spirit and intendment"[2] or

---

[1] See generally *Tudor on Charities*, 9th edn, 2003; Picarda, *The Law and Practice Relating to Charities*, 4th edn, 2011.

[2] *Morice v Bishop of Durham* (1805) 9 Ves. 399 at 405.

"within the equity"[3] of the statute were accepted as being charitable. In 1891, Lord Macnaghten summarised these purposes into four categories. These were the relief of poverty, the advancement of education, the advancement of religion, and other purposes beneficial to the community.[4] The Preamble was repealed by the Charities Act 1960.[5] As no definition replaced it, Lord Macnaghten's classification continued until replaced by a new statutory definition in the Act of 2006, which was based on existing case law and decisions of the Charity Commissioners on the registration of charities.[6]

The Charities Act 2006 was enacted after extensive public consultation. It updated the list of charitable purposes, with clearer emphasis on delivering a public benefit; facilitated the more efficient administration of charities; introduced a new legal form of charitable body (the charitable incorporated organisation); increased accountability for charities which are not required to be registered; improved the regulation of charity fundraising; and replaced the Charity Commissioners with a new corporate body, the Charity Commission, with modernised functions.

We will see that charitable trusts are accorded a number of concessions over other trusts in terms of enforcement, perpetuity, certainty and taxation.[7] To earn these concessions, especially in relation to taxation, a trust must be of benefit to the public, and not merely to private individuals. The policy in question behind most litigation concerning charitable trusts is an examination of whether the purposes are so useful to the public as to earn the concessions. This has to be carried out against a background of cases decided in earlier times when the condition of society was very different. In the days when the State made little or no provision for the poor and uneducated or for other general welfare purposes, and at a time when religious observance was unchallenged, trusts for these categories were clearly for the public benefit. At the present time, however, many of the welfare and educational needs of society are provided from public sources, and purposes reflecting other needs have been recognised and are now included in the new statutory definition. Judicial attitudes to gifts for charitable purposes have varied. In 1908 Lord Loreburn said, "now there is no better rule than that a benignant construction will be placed upon charitable bequests."[8] But since the 1940s when taxation became higher the courts have been astute to restrict the scope of charity especially by emphasising

---

[3] See *Incorporated Council of Law Reporting v Att Gen* [1972] Ch. 73 at 87–88.
[4] *Commissioners for Special Purposes of Income Tax v Pemsel* [1891] A.C. 531.
[5] s.38. See Charities Act 2011 Sch.7, para.1.
[6] These are found in the Annual Reports of the Charity Commissioners. Annual Reports continue to be provided by the newly constituted Charity Commission.
[7] per Lord Cross in *Dingle v Turner* [1972] A.C. 601 at 624.
[8] *Weir v Crum-Brown* [1908] A.C. 162 at 167.

the requirement of public benefit. However, Lord Hailsham of St. Marylebone said:

> "In construing trust deeds the intention of which is to set up a charitable trust, and in others too, where it can be claimed that there is an ambiguity, a benignant construction should be given if possible."[9]

In similar vein, the intention of the Legislature is to encourage charitable giving (by tax incentives), and the development of the voluntary sector as a whole.

As mentioned above, one of the reforms of the Charities Act 2006 was the introduction of a new legal entity, the charitable incorporated organisation (CIO).[10] This is a new corporate vehicle for charities, which is designed to reduce the administrative burdens on corporate charities. It is not obligatory for charities to operate in this way, but conversion to the new form is likely to be considered advantageous. The details cannot be given here.

2. ADVANTAGES ENJOYED BY CHARITABLE TRUSTS

A. Purpose Trusts

15–002   Charitable trusts are purpose trusts. But there is no need for human beneficiaries to enforce them, as there is in the case of non-charitable purpose trusts.[11] Individuals who may benefit from a charitable trust have no standing to enforce them.[12] Charitable trusts are enforced by the Attorney General in the name of the Crown,[13] although the general administration of charitable trusts is overseen by the Charity Commission.[14] There must of course be an obligation upon the trustees; a mere power to apply to charitable purposes cannot be a trust.[15] It should be emphasised that this chapter deals with charitable *trusts*. The legal position differs in many ways where the charity is incorporated.[16]

---

[9] *IRC v McMullen* [1981] A.C. 1 at 14; *Re Koeppler's WT* [1986] Ch. 423; *Re Hetherington (Deceased)* [1990] Ch. 1; *Guild v IRC* [1992] 2 A.C. 310. The "benignant" approach applies only where a disposition would otherwise be void; *IRC v Oldham Training and Enterprise Council* [1996] S.T.C. 1218.

[10] Now Charities Act 2011, Part 11.

[11] Above, Ch.14.

[12] *Hauxwell v Barton-on-Humber UDC* [1974] Ch. 432; Charities Act 2011 s.115.

[13] See *Att Gen v Wright* [1988] 1 W.L.R. 164; *Att Gen v Cocke* [1988] Ch. 414. The Commission may exercise these powers with the consent of the Attorney-General; Charities Act 2011 s.114.

[14] Charities Act 2011 ss.13–20.

[15] *Re Cohen* [1973] 1 W.L.R. 415, where a gift to trustees to apply to a charitable purpose "the whole or any part" of the fund "in such manner and at such time or times as my trustees shall in their absolute and uncontrolled discretion think fit", was held to create a trust.

[16] For the distinctions, see J. Hill (1993–94) 2 *Charity Law and Practice Review* 133. The new charitable incorporated organisation (CIO) was mentioned above, para.15–001.

B. Objects Need Not be Certain

There is no requirement, as with other trusts, that the objects of **15–003** the trust must be certain. Thus, a trust for "charitable purposes" will be valid. The court and the Charity Commission[17] have jurisdiction to establish a scheme for the application of the funds for specific charitable purposes. There must, of course, be no doubt that the objects of the trust are exclusively charitable, and the purpose expressed must not be so vague and uncertain that the court could not control the application of the assets.[18] The relaxation of the certainty rule is only in respect of the particular form of charitable purpose intended.[19]

Where no trust has been created, but only a general intention expressed that the property should go to charity, the court has no jurisdiction. In such a case the Crown disposes of the gifts by sign manual.[20] But the Crown acts on principles very similar to those by which the court is governed.

C. May be Perpetual

Statements have often been made by judges to the effect that the **15–004** Rule against Perpetuities does not apply to charities.[21] That is not so. With the exception of the rule in *Christ's Hospital v Grainger*,[22] explained below, the rule governs the remoteness of vesting in the case of gifts to charities in the same way that it governs remoteness in the case of other gifts.[23]

Charitable trusts, however, may be perpetual. Indeed, the purpose of many charitable trusts could be said never to be capable of final achievement.[24] Many charitable trusts have existed for centuries. If a perpetual gift of income only is made to a charity, the charity cannot claim the capital, as an individual could do in such circumstances.[25] But where property is given absolutely to a charity with a direction to accumulate the income for a period of time, a charity

---

[17] Charities Act 2011 s.69; below, para.15–086.

[18] *Re Koeppler's Will Trusts* [1986] Ch. 423, where the formation of an informed international public opinion and the promotion of greater co-operation in Europe and the West were held too vague and uncertain to be charitable in themselves, but these aims did not destroy the charitable nature of the gift, which was to further the work of an educational project.

[19] See *Moggridge v Thackwell* (1792) 1 Ves.Jr. 464; (1803) 7 Ves.Jr. 36; (1807) 13 Ves.Jr. 416.

[20] *Moggridge v Thackwell*, above, fn.19; *Re Smith* [1932] 1 Ch. 53; *Re Bennett* [1960] Ch. 18; *Re Hetherington* [1990] Ch. 1.

[21] *Goodman v Mayor of Saltash* (1882) 7 App.Cas. 633 at 642; *Commissioners for Special Purposes of Income Tax v Pemsel* [1891] A.C. 531 at 580–581; *Att-Gen v National Provincial and Union Bank Ltd* [1924] A.C. 262 at 266.

[22] (1849) 1 Mac. & G. 460; *Re Tyler* [1891] 3 Ch. 252; *Royal College of Surgeons v National Provincial Bank Ltd* [1952] A.C. 631.

[23] *Re Wightwick's WT* [1950] Ch. 260; *Re Green's WT* [1985] 3 All E.R. 455.

[24] *Re Delius* [1957] Ch. 299.

[25] *Re Levy* [1960] Ch. 346.

may terminate the accumulation, and claim the principal forthwith.[26]

The exception to the rule regulating remoteness of vesting is that a gift over from one charity to *another charity* is not subject to the rule.[27] The gift over to the second charity is valid even if it takes effect outside the perpetuity period.[28]

The reason for the exception is that "there is no more perpetuity created by giving to two charities rather than by giving to one."[29] The explanation looks to the vesting for charitable purposes, rather than vesting in one specific charity. Once vested in charity, then, subject to express provision to the contrary, a trust will continue, even if the purposes become impossible of fulfilment; the property will be applied cy-près.[30] All that is done by the provision for vesting in another charity is to make expressly the selection of the charity to be benefited when the first gift terminates.

This rule therefore seems logical; and also reasonable when the gift over is to take effect upon the happening of some event related to the carrying out of the purposes of the charity, as was the case in *Christ's Hospital v Grainger*,[31] and *Royal College of Surgeons v National Provincial Bank*.[32] In the hands of conveyancers, however as has been seen,[33] it can be used to produce, in effect, a perpetual non-charitable trust by making a gift to one charity conditional upon carrying out a non-charitable purpose, and terminable in favour of another charity upon its failure to do so. This is not a satisfactory use of charity privilege: but this loophole was not questioned in the *Royal College of Surgeons* case. The rule is confirmed by the Perpetuities and Accumulations Act 2009 in spite of these opportunities for exploitation.[34]

The Law Commission recommended that the rule against excessive accumulations of income should in general be abolished, but should still apply to charitable trusts.[35] Otherwise income could be tied up for many years, during which there would be no public benefit. The Perpetuities and Accumulations Act 2009 now provides

[26] *Wharton v Masterman* [1895] A.C. 186; *Re Knapp* [1929] 1 Ch. 341.
[27] A gift from non-charity to a charity is caught: *Re Bowen* [1893] 2 Ch. 291. So also a gift from a charity to a non-charity; *Re Bowen* (above); *Re Peel's Release* [1921] 2 Ch. 218; *Re Engels* [1943] 1 All E.R. 506.
[28] *Christ's Hospital v Grainger* (1849) 1 Mac. & G. 460.
[29] per Shadwell V.C. in the court below (1848) 16 Sim. 83 at 100. See also *Royal College of Surgeons v National Provincial Bank Ltd* [1952] A.C. 631 at 650.
[30] Below, para.15–063.
[31] Above, fn.22.
[32] [1952] A.C. 631.
[33] Above, para.14–030, *Re Tyler* [1891] 3 Ch. 252.
[34] s.2(2).
[35] Law Com. No.251 (1998), *The Rules against Perpetuities and Excessive Accumulations*, para.10.21.

that any power or duty to accumulate charitable income must cease after 21 years.[36]

D. Fiscal Advantages

As explained below, charities enjoy tax advantages of two broad **15–005** kinds. First, the organisation itself may be exempt from paying a particular tax on its capital or income. Secondly, a person who makes a charitable gift may be eligible for tax relief on their own capital or income. Until recently, there was no relief if the gift was to a charity in another jurisdiction. This was changed by the Finance Act 2010, so that gifts made by a donor in this jurisdiction to charities in the European Union[37] may attract tax relief. However, the Act went further by imposing new requirements on domestic charitable bodies for the purposes of eligibility for tax relief. The four conditions to be satisfied for this purpose by charities in this jurisdiction and in the European Union are as follows.[38] First, the body must be established for charitable purposes only within the meaning of s.2 of the Charities Act 2011.[39] In other words, it must be carrying out activities which English law would recognise as exclusively charitable. Secondly, the body must be subject to the control of a court in the United Kingdom in the exercise of its charity jurisdiction, or of a court in the European Union[40] exercising a corresponding jurisdiction. Thirdly, the body must have complied with registration requirements in England and Wales[41] or any corresponding requirement in the European jurisdiction. Fourthly, its managers must be fit and proper persons. While the first three conditions are not controversial, the fourth one is, as the arbiter of whether this condition is met is HMRC, not the Charity Commission. We will now examine the reliefs available to charitable bodies and donors where these conditions are satisfied.

Charities are exempt from income tax, provided that the income is **15–006** applied for charitable purposes only.[42] They may recover from the Revenue income tax paid or credited prior to the payment of interest. Relief is also available with respect to "Gift Aid" donations.[43] Alternatively, donors who are employees may utilise the payroll

---

[36] s.14. The new rule relates only to instruments taking effect after commencement.

[37] The Taxes (Definition of Charity) (Relevant Territories) Regulations 2010 (SI 2010/1904). The Regulations apply also to charities in Iceland and Norway.

[38] FA 2010 s.30 and Sch.6. The conditions will apply to all charity tax reliefs and exemptions from April 2012. The new rules apply also to Community Amateur Sports Clubs.

[39] Below, para.15–008. The definition applies for this purpose regardless of where the body is established.

[40] Or Iceland or Norway.

[41] Below, para.15–083.

[42] Now Income Tax Act 2007 s.527. See *IRC v Educational Grants Association Ltd* [1967] Ch. 993; *IRC v Helen Slater Charitable Trust Ltd* [1982] Ch. 49.

[43] Income Tax Act 2007 ss.413–430 and 520–522; FA 2007 s.60.

deduction scheme.[44] Further, no income tax is chargeable in respect of profits of any trade carried on by the charity, if the profits are applied solely to the purposes of the charity and either the trade is exercised in the course of the carrying out of a primary purpose of the charity, or the work in connection with the trade is mainly carried out by beneficiaries of the charity.[45] Again the profits must be applied solely to the purposes of the charity. Similarly, charitable corporations are exempt from paying corporation tax.[46]

Gifts of any amount in favour of charity are exempt from inheritance tax if made by way of payment from a discretionary trust,[47] or by way of gift by an individual during his lifetime or on death.[48] Similarly, transfers from a charitable trust are exempt from inheritance tax.[49] To encourage charitable giving, it was announced in the 2011 Budget that the 40 per cent rate would be reduced to 36 per cent for deaths on or after April 6, 2012 where at least 10 per cent of the net estate is left to charity.[50]

No capital gains tax arises where a gain accrues to a charity and the gain is applicable and is applied for charitable purposes.[51] Nor will a donor be under any such liability in respect of a disposal to charity.[52] Charities may also claim relief from stamp duty and tax on conveyances,[53] and from National Insurance Surcharge.[54]

Charities, however, do have to bear Value Added Tax on goods and services which they purchase.[55] This liability will be particularly burdensome for many charities in respect of the maintenance and repair of buildings. Also, VAT may be chargeable in respect of goods and services provided, on payment, by some charities.[56]

All charities are entitled to exemption in respect of 80 per cent of the non-domestic rates of the properties which they occupy,[57] wholly or mainly used for charitable purposes. This includes premises used wholly or mainly for the sale of goods donated to a charity

---

[44] Income Tax (Earnings and Pensions) Act 2003 Pt 12 (replacing earlier legislation); D. Morris [1989] Conv. 175.
[45] Income Tax Act 2007 ss.524–526; J. Hill and J. de Souza (1989) 3 *Trust Law & Practice* 98.
[46] Corporation Tax Act 2010 s.481.
[47] Inheritance Tax Act 1984 s.76.
[48] IHTA s.23. See also ss.25, 26.
[49] IHTA s.58(1)(a).
[50] See HMRC Consultation Paper, *A new incentive for charitable legacies*, June 10, 2011. This will be included in the Finance Bill 2012.
[51] Taxation of Chargeable Gains Act 1992 s.256.
[52] TCGA 1992 s.257.
[53] FA 2003 s.68.
[54] FA 1977 s.57.
[55] For specific exemptions, see the consolidating Value Added Tax Act 1994 Sch.9.
[56] See *Customs and Excise Commissioners v Automobile Association* [1974] 1 W.L.R. 1447; Annual Report 1974 paras 17–21; J. Warburton (1995/96) 3 *Charity Law and Practice Review* 37. However, some goods supplied to or by charities are zero-rated under Sch.8 of the 1994 Act.
[57] Local Government Finance Act 1988 s.43(5), (6).

and applied for the purposes of a charity.[58] Relief can also be granted at the discretion of the rating authority up to the whole amount of the rates.[59] Churches, church halls and similar premises used for religious purposes are entitled to relief in respect of the whole of the rates,[60] as are those providing facilities for the disabled.[61]

In view of the extent of income and other assets thus exempted, this is a formidable list of fiscal advantages,[62] and explains the prominence of Revenue cases in charity litigation.

Measures have been taken to prevent abuse of these tax advantages, for example by requiring charities to take reasonable steps to ensure that payments made to overseas bodies will be applied to genuine charitable purposes and requiring them to justify certain loans or investments as being for the benefit of charity and not for tax avoidance.[63] These provisions restrict tax relief where funds are applied for non-charitable purposes and prevent manipulation of charity tax advantages by individuals.

3. THE DEFINITION OF CHARITY

A. The Statutory Definition

i. Position Before the Charities Act 2006. A claim to charitable   **15–007**
status was determined by considering whether the purpose came within Lord Macnaghten's classification as exemplified by the cases decided in accordance with it. Lord Macnaghten said:

"Charity in its legal sense comprises four principal divisions: trusts for the relief of poverty; trusts for the advancement of education; trusts for the advancement of religion; and trusts for other purposes beneficial to the community."[64]

It is obvious that these heads provided no precise definition. Charity law has always adapted to social changes, and, as has been explained, the significance of tax exemption, and also the development

---

[58] LGFA 1988 s.64(10); Hansard, HL, Vol.499, col.874, July 13, 1988.

[59] LGFA 1988 s.47.

[60] LGFA 1988 Sch.5, para.11. In *Gallagher (Valuation Officer) v Church of Jesus Christ of Latter-Day Saints* [2008] 1 W.L.R. 1852, a Mormon Temple failed to obtain exemption in respect of premises to which only approved members of the faith were admitted. Similarly, the Exclusive Brethren in *Broxtowe BC v Birch* [1983] 1 W.L.R. 314.

[61] LGFA 1988 Sch.5, para.16.

[62] The gross income of registered charities was over £55 billion in 2010/2011; Annual Report 2010/2011.

[63] See Income Tax Act 2007 s.547; Corporation Tax Act 2010 s.500 (replacing earlier legislation).

[64] *Commissioners for Special Purposes of Income Tax v Pemsel* [1891] A.C. 531 at 583.

of State agencies to provide education, relief from poverty, and other purposes needed by society transformed the concept of charity. It should be appreciated that the Charity Commissioners (now the Commission) had a major role in the development of this concept.[65]

Over the years more purposes were recognised by the courts and the Commissioners. They could not have been contemplated by the Charitable Uses Act 1601 nor by Lord Macnaghten. They were accepted by applying the principle that purposes analogous to, or within the spirit of, purposes already recognised as charitable should also be recognised as charitable. As we will see, this approach was preserved by the Charities Act 2006 (now Charities Act 2011).

15–008   **ii. The Charities Acts 2006 and 2011.** The Act of 2006 took the radical step of defining a charitable purpose, but did so by reference to purposes already recognised by the courts and the Commissioners. Lord Macnaghten's first three categories were retained, but the fourth ("other purposes beneficial to the community") was replaced by a list of specific purposes which reflect those which had been recognised under the old fourth category. Reference will, therefore, continue to be made to much of the previous case law. In 2011 the Charities Act was passed to consolidate the Charities Act 2006 with other charity legislation. The Act of 2011 provides that "charity" means an institution which is established for charitable purposes only, and is subject to the control of the High Court in the exercise of its jurisdiction with respect to charities.[66] Section 2 of the Act of 2011 defines a "charitable purpose" as one which is for the public benefit[67] and which falls within any of the following descriptions,[68] which are set out in s.3(1):

> (a) the prevention or relief of poverty;
> (b) the advancement of education;
> (c) the advancement of religion;
> (d) the advancement of health or the saving of lives;
> (e) the advancement of citizenship or community development;
> (f) the advancement of the arts, culture, heritage or science;
> (g) the advancement of amateur sport;
> (h) the advancement of human rights, conflict resolution or reconciliation or the promotion of religious or racial harmony or equality and diversity;

---

[65] Below, para.15–084.

[66] Charities Act 2011 s.1. "Institution" includes incorporated bodies, trusts and undertakings; s.9(3).

[67] Below, para.15–040.

[68] For an overview of the scope of each description, see the Charity Commission's *Commentary on the Descriptions of Charitable Purposes in the Charities Act 2006.*

(i) the advancement of environmental protection or improvement;

(j) the relief of those in need by reason of youth, age, ill-health,
disability; financial hardship or other disadvantage;

(k) the advancement of animal welfare;

(l) the promotion of the efficiency of the armed forces of the
Crown, or of the efficiency of the police, fire and rescue
services or ambulance services;

(m) any other purposes—

(i) that are not within paragraphs (a) to (l) but are recognised as charitable purposes by virtue of section 5 (recreational and similar trusts, etc.) or under the old
law,[69]

(ii) that may reasonably be regarded as analogous to, or
within the spirit of, any purposes falling within any of
paragraphs (a) to (l) or sub-paragraph (i), or

(iii) that may reasonably be regarded as analogous to, or
within the spirit of, any purposes which have been recognised, under the law relating to charities in England
and Wales, as falling within sub-paragraph (ii) or this
sub-paragraph.

This, therefore, preserved the charitable status of purposes already recognised as charitable, whether or not included in the statutory list, and retains the flexibility of the previous law by allowing
further development to meet changing social need.

iii. Public Benefit. It should also be noted at this stage that each   **15–009**
head involves two elements; the purpose must be beneficial, such as
the advancement of education, and there must be an element of
public benefit, that is to say, education being advanced in a way that
will benefit the whole community, or a sufficiently substantial part
of it.[70]

Before the Charities Act 2006 there was a presumption that the
relief of poverty and the advancement of religion and education
were for the public benefit, whereas this had to be established in the
case of purposes within the old fourth category ("other purposes
beneficial to the community"). One of the most significant features
of the Act of 2006 is that it removed any presumption. This is now
found in s.4(2) of the Charities Act 2011, which provides that, in
determining whether the public benefit requirement is satisfied, "it
is not to be presumed that a purpose of a particular description is for
the public benefit". It must, therefore, be demonstrated in all
cases.

---

[69] Below, para.15–036. The "old law" means that in force immediately before April 1,
2008; s.3(4).

[70] See generally J. Hackney (2008) 124 L.Q.R. 347.

This change was most likely to affect independent fee-paying schools, whose charitable status had long been the subject of debate.[71] It could also affect religious sects with few adherents. The requirement applies to all charities, including those registered before the implementation of the Charities Act 2006.

Before the Act of 2006 it was established that the requirement of benefit to a sufficient section of the community varied according to the category of charity in question. The Act does not expressly deal with this point, and it appears that this principle will continue.

The Charity Commission must issue guidance as to the operation of the public benefit requirement, to promote awareness and understanding of it.[72] It must carry out checks on organisations which have already been registered, as well as assess whether any organisation applying for registration satisfies the requirement. The public benefit requirement is examined in detail below.[73]

15–010   **iv. Exclusively Charitable.** A trust will not fail to be charitable because it may in its operation incidentally benefit the rich, or other non-objects of charity.[74] But if a non-charitable purpose is an object, the trust cannot be charitable, for it is not wholly and exclusively "for charitable purposes only".[75] A statement of objects which includes non-charitable purposes is not saved by adding, "in so far as they are of a charitable nature".[76]

15–011   **v. Charitable Purposes Overseas.** Special problems arise where the benefits arising from charitable trusts are to be enjoyed abroad. There is no rule requiring the benefits to be retained in this country.[77] But, how can the court or the (English) trustees control the application of the funds? Should tax privileges be given by HMRC for the benefit of communities abroad?[78] We have seen that tax privileges may now be available to charities established in other (primarily European Union) jurisdictions,[79] but the point under discussion here is whether organisations established in England and Wales to provide benefits abroad may be charitable.

---

[71] See below, para.15–049.

[72] Charities Act 2011 s.17.

[73] Below, para.15–040.

[74] *Verge v Somerville* [1924] A.C. 496; *Re Resch's WT* [1969] 1 A.C. 514; sub nom. *Le Cras v Perpetual Trustee Co* [1967] 1 All E.R. 915. But a trust for the relief of poverty will fail if it may benefit persons who are not poor; *Re Gwyon* [1903] 1 Ch. 255.

[75] Charities Act 2011 s.1(1)(a), restating the previous law.

[76] *McGovern v Att Gen* [1982] Ch. 321.

[77] *Re Robinson* [1931] 2 Ch. 122 at 126 (gift to German Government for the benefit of its soldiers disabled in the late war held charitable).

[78] Annual Report 1963, paras 69–76.

[79] Finance Act 2010 s.30 and Sch.6; above, para.15–005.

The Charity Commissioners stated[80] in 1992 that the relief of poverty[81] and the advancement of education and religion are presumed beneficial wherever they occur, but this predated the removal of the presumption in favour of those purposes in the Charities Act 2006.

The test of public benefit is the same whether the activity is at home or abroad, as our courts cannot judge what is for the benefit of the public in a foreign country. This does not mean that there must be a benefit to the public in this country. The courts should first consider if the activity would be charitable if it operated at home. If so, it is charitable even though operated abroad unless it would be contrary to public policy to recognise it.[82] For example, our courts would not consider an institution operating abroad whose object was contrary to the law of the state in question to be charitable. As mentioned above,[83] the jurisdiction of the court and the Charity Commission over charities may be exercised only in respect of charities established in England and Wales according to English law, and not over bodies established and administered abroad.[84]

It has been said that the court would be bound to take account of the probable results of the execution of the trust on the inhabitants of the country concerned, which would doubtless have a history and social structure quite different from that of the UK. So in *McGovern v Att Gen*,[85] a trust to procure the abolition of torture or inhuman or degrading treatment or punishment[86] in all parts of the world was not charitable, one reason being that the court would have no satisfactory means of judging the probable effects of, say, legislation to abolish the death penalty on the local community. If the purpose of a trust was to secure abolition of the death penalty for adultery in Islamic countries, the court would not be competent to deal with it because it would either have to apply English standards as to public benefit, which might not be appropriate in the local conditions, or attempt to apply local standards of which it knew little or nothing.

In *Re Jacobs* in 1970[87] a trust for the purpose of "planting a grove of trees in Israel to perpetuate my name on the eternal soil of the

---

[80] Annual Report 1992, paras 74, 75; Decisions, Vol.1 (1993), 16. See *Camille and Henry Dreyfus Foundation Inc v IRC* [1954] Ch. 672 at 684.

[81] See *Re Niyazi's Will Trusts* [1978] 1 W.L.R. 910 (trust for construction of working men's hostel in Cyprus charitable). The work overseas of organisations like Oxfam is well known.

[82] See *Re Carapiet's Trusts* [2002] W.T.L.R. 989 (advancement in life of Armenian children charitable).

[83] Charities Act 2011 s.1; above, para.15–008.

[84] *Gaudiya Mission v Brahmachary* [1998] Ch. 341.

[85] [1982] Ch. 321, below, para.15–038.

[86] Including punishment inflicted by process of law.

[87] Annual Report 1970 para.78.

Holy Land" was upheld. Soil conservation is of crucial importance in Israel. It was the benefit to the community abroad which was significant. Several organisations concerned with the preservation of the environment outside the UK have been registered.[88]

B. The Prevention or Relief of Poverty

15–012   **i. Meaning of Poverty.** The relief of poverty has always been one of the main categories of charity. The Charities Act 2006 added "prevention" to "relief".[89] There is no definition of poverty. Its meaning can only be understood by examining the cases on the subject.

> "It is quite clearly established that poverty does not mean destitution; . . . it may not unfairly be paraphrased as meaning persons who have to 'go short' in the ordinary acceptance of that term . . . "[90]

It is thus a matter of degree. Most of the cases come from a time before welfare payments were available from public funds. Such payments are intended to relieve poverty and hardship, and it could be argued that eligibility for such payments should be the test of poverty. But, if that were so, charity in this area would duplicate the work of a good welfare programme. If relief of poverty is the duty of the State, what scope is there for private charity? This is a problem which is met in many of the areas of charity today, especially in connection with trusts for the relief of poverty and for education and health. Private charity is useful to fill the gaps which the welfare state programme leaves uncovered.

15–013   **ii. Illustrations.** Gifts for the benefit of the poor are clearly charitable.[91] Also "needy" persons,[92] or "indigent"[93] persons. Often a group of poor is confined to a particular location,[94] or religion,[95] or

---

[88] Annual Report 1989 para.29.

[89] Now Charities Act 2011 s.3(1)(a). See also s.3(1)(j), dealing with the relief of those in need by reason of (amongst other things) financial hardship.

[90] *Re Coulthurst* [1951] Ch. 661 at 665–666. See generally A. Dunn (2000) 20 L.S. 222.

[91] *Re Darling* [1896] 1 Ch. 56: "to the poor and the service of God."

[92] *Re Scarisbrick* [1951] Ch. 622; *Re Cohen* [1973] 1 W.L.R. 415.

[93] *Weir v Crum-Brown* [1908] A.C. 162: "indigent bachelors and widowers who have shown sympathy with science."

[94] *Re Lucas* [1922] 2 Ch. 52 (oldest respectable inhabitants in Gunville).

[95] *Re Wall* (1889) 52 Ch.D. 570.

to a group which is assumed to be in need of help,[96] or victims of a disaster.[97] Persons of "limited means"[98] are included, and trusts for gentlewomen and distressed gentlefolk.[99] On the other hand, in *Re-Sanders' Will Trusts*,[100] a gift for the provision of housing for the working classes was not charitable. A gift which includes persons who are not in need will be excluded. In *Re Gwyon*,[101] a fund providing for a gift of clothing to boys in Farnham and district failed on the ground that the conditions for qualification, precise though they were in many ways, failed to exclude affluent children.[102] It is no objection, however, that the scheme operates by way of bargain rather than bounty, i.e. that the beneficiaries are required to contribute to the cost of the benefits they receive.[103]

There is no need for the trust to be an endowment. A trust may be charitable although the trustees may distribute the capital. A trust was upheld in *Re Scarisbrick*[104]:

"[F]or such relations of my . . . son and daughters as in the opinion of the survivor of my . . . son and daughters shall be in needy circumstances . . . as the survivor . . . shall by deed or will appoint."

This was a trust for "poor relations", and such trusts are excepted from the general rule that the beneficiaries must not be defined by a personal connection.[105] But there can be no charitable trust, even in the poverty category, where the persons to be benefited are specified individuals; and such a construction is more likely where the capital of a trust may be immediately distributed. But it is not decisive.

---

[96] *Att Gen v Ironmongers Co* (1834) 2 My. & K. 526 (debtors); *Biscoe v Jackson* (1887) 35 Ch.D. 460 (soup kitchen for the parish of Shoreditch); *Re Coulthurst* [1951] Ch. 661 (widows and orphaned children of employees); *Cawdron v Merchant Taylors' School* [2010] W.T.L.R. 775 (sons or dependants of "old boys" killed or disabled in the Great War).

[97] *Re North Devon and West Somerset Relief Fund Trust* [1953] 1 W.L.R. 1260 (flood disaster).

[98] *Re Gardom* [1914] 1 Ch. 664; *Re De Carteret* [1933] Ch. 103.

[99] *Mary Clark Home Trustees v Anderson* [1904] 2 K.B. 745; *Re Gardom* (above, fn.98); *Re Young* [1951] Ch. 344.

[100] [1954] Ch. 265. cf. *Re Niyazi's WT* [1978] 1 W.L.R. 910 (gift for "the construction of a working men's hostel" in Famagusta, Cyprus held charitable by Megarry V.C. "although it was desperately near the border-line".). But some homes for working classes have been registered as charities where there were other factors which indicated a requirement of poverty. Annual Report 1965, App.C, para.I.A.9.

[101] [1930] 1 Ch. 255.

[102] They also excluded black boys. This caused no comment at the time; but would no doubt do so today, above, para.13–002. See further T. Watkin [1981] Conv. 131; Annual Report 1983 para.19; Annual Report 1987 para.14.

[103] *Re Cottam's WT* [1955] 1 W.L.R. 1299; *Le Cras v Perpetual Trustee Co Ltd* [1969] 1 A.C. 514; *Joseph Rowntree Memorial Trust Housing Association Ltd v Att Gen* [1983] Ch. 159 (dwellings for sale to elderly at 70% cost).

[104] [1951] Ch. 622; *Re Cohen* [1973] 1 W.L.R. 415.

[105] *Dingle v Turner* [1972] A.C. 601; below, para.15–046.

C. The Advancement of Education[106]

15–014   **i. Meaning of Education.** This head had its origin in the phrases in the Preamble which spoke of "the maintenance of schools of learning, free schools and scholars in universities" and "the education and preferment of orphans". The endowments, some of course very ancient, of many schools and colleges and universities are based on this provision. Education in school and university is now however accepted as being within the responsibility of the State; and it is not surprising that modern cases have substantially widened the concept of educational charity. It can now cover almost any form of worthwhile instruction or cultural advancement, except for purely professional or career courses.

The following trusts have been held charitable under this head: education in the art of government,[107] the production of a dictionary,[108] the support of London Zoological Society,[109] the establishment and maintenance of museums,[110] the support of learned literary, scientific and cultural societies,[111] a search for the Shakespeare manuscript,[112] choral singing in London,[113] the promotion of the music of Delius,[114] classical drama and acting,[115] the publication of the Law Reports,[116] the study and dissemination of ethical principles and cultivation of a rational religious sentiment[117] and even a "sort of finishing school for the Irish people" where "self-control, oratory, deportment and the art of personal contact" were to be taught.[118]

The Charities Act 2006 recognised as a separate head "the advancement of the arts, culture, heritage or science".[119] Some of the examples just given could be regarded as involving either or both

[106] This was one of the main categories of charity before the Charities Act 2006 and is now found in s.3(1)(b) of the Charities Act 2011.

[107] *Re McDougall* [1957] 1 W.L.R. 81. But not for the promotion of political causes; below, para.15–020. The holding of conferences with a "political flavour" but not of a party political nature was upheld in *Re Koeppler's WT* [1986] Ch. 423.

[108] *Re Stanford* [1924] 1 Ch. 73.

[109] *Re Lopes* [1931] 2 Ch. 130.

[110] *British Museum Trustees v White* (1826) 2 Sm. & St. 594; *Re Pinion* [1965] Ch. 85 at 105.

[111] *Royal College of Surgeons v National Provincial Bank Ltd* [1952] A.C. 631; *Re Shakespeare Memorial Trust* [1923] 2 Ch. 398; *Re British School of Egyptian Archaeology* [1954] 1 W.L.R. 546.

[112] *Re Hopkins' WT* [1965] Ch. 669.

[113] *Royal Choral Society v IRC* [1943] 2 All E.R. 101.

[114] *Re Delius* [1957] Ch. 299.

[115] *Re Shakespeare Memorial Trust* (above, fn.111).

[116] *Incorporated Council of Law Reporting for England and Wales v Att Gen* [1972] Ch. 73.

[117] *Re South Place Ethical Society* [1980] 1 W.L.R. 1565. The Society was also charitable under the old fourth heading.

[118] *Re Shaw's WT* [1952] Ch. 163.

[119] Now Charities Act 2011 s.3(1)(f).

the advancement of education and the advancement of the arts, culture, heritage or science. Clearly there is a potential for overlap in the list of charitable purposes set out in the Act of 2011, just as in the case of the four heads of charity previously recognised.

ii. Research. Education requires something more than the mere **15–015** accumulation of knowledge. There must be some sharing, or teaching or dissemination, some way of showing that the public will benefit. This is all the more so since the Charities Act 2006 removed the presumption of public benefit which previously applied to education.[120] There is no difficulty in the case of research which is likely to produce material benefit to the community, such as medical or scientific research.[121] Such purposes would in any case come under other heads. On literary, cultural and scholarly subjects Wilberforce J. considered in *Re Hopkins*[122]:

> "[T]hat the word 'education' ... must be used in a wide sense, certainly extending beyond teaching, and that the requirement is that, in order to be charitable, research must either be of educational value to the researcher or must be so directed as to lead to something which will pass into the store of educational material, or so as to improve the sum of communicable knowledge in an area which education may cover—education in this last context extending to the formation of literary taste and appreciation."

In *Re Hopkins*,[123] there was a testamentary gift to the Francis Bacon Society, "to be earmarked and applied towards finding the Bacon-Shakespeare manuscripts." Wilberforce J. concluded that a:

> "[S]earch, or research, for the original manuscripts of England's greatest dramatist (whoever he was) would be well within the law's conception of charitable purposes. The discovery would be of the highest value to history and to literature."[124]

The gift was held to be a valid charitable trust under this head and under what was then the fourth head ("other purposes beneficial to the community").

---

[120] Now Charities Act 2011 s.4(2).
[121] *Royal College of Surgeons v National Provincial Bank Ltd* (above, fn.111). See also Annual Report 1987 para.12.
[122] [1965] Ch. 669 at 680.
[123] [1965] Ch. 669. See also *McGovern v Att Gen* [1982] Ch. 321, where research into human rights and dissemination of the results would have been charitable. The trust failed for other reasons.
[124] [1965] Ch. 669 at 679.

Re Shaw[125] was distinguished.

> George Bernard Shaw, by his will, directed that his residuary
> estate should be devoted to researching the advantages of a pro-
> posed British alphabet of 40 letters, in which each letter would
> indicate a single sound; and to translate his play "Androcles and
> the Lion" into the new alphabet. Harman J. held that the gift was
> not charitable "if the object be merely the increase of knowledge,
> that is not in itself a charitable object unless it be combined with
> teaching or education."[126]

This is thought to be too narrow a view of education. Whether the
trust in this case would be held charitable under Wilberforce J.'s test
depends on the usefulness of the research, and that is a matter of
judgment. Not every type of knowledge, whether researched, disseminated or taught is capable of being education. Not schools for
prostitutes or pickpockets,[127] nor guides to computer-hacking or
effective money-laundering, for example, as the public benefit requirement would not be met.[128]

15–016   **iii. Artistic and Aesthetic Education.** In *Royal Choral Society v
IRC*,[129] the Court of Appeal upheld as charitable a trust to promote
the practice and performance of choral works. Lord Greene said of
the view that education meant a master teaching a class[130]:

> "I protest against that narrow conception of education when one
> is dealing with aesthetic education. In my opinion, a body of
> persons established for the purpose of raising the artistic state of
> the country ... is established for educational purposes."

In *Re British School of Egyptian Archaeology*[131] a trust to exca-
vate and discover Egyptian antiquities, to hold exhibitions and to
promote the training and assistance of students in the field of Egyptian history was held charitable. In *Re Delius*,[132] a gift to increase
the general appreciation of the musical work of the composer was
for the advancement of education. The last three examples would
now also fall within the separate head "the advancement of the arts,

---

[125] [1957] 1 W.L.R. 729.
[126] [1957] 1 W.L.R. 729 at 737, referring to Rigby L.J. in *Re Macduff* [1896] 2 Ch. 451.
[127] per Harman J. [1957] 1 W.L.R. 729 at 737; and in *Re Pinion* [1965] Ch. 85 at 105.
[128] See the Charity Commission's supplementary guidance on *The Advancement of Education for the Public Benefit*, December 2008.
[129] [1943] 2 All E.R. 101.
[130] [1943] 2 All E.R. 101 at 104.
[131] [1954] 1 W.L.R. 540.
[132] [1957] Ch. 299.

culture, heritage or science".[133] But it seems that a trust for "artistic" purposes is too vague to be charitable.[134]

iv. Subjective Evaluation. The question whether a purpose is **15–017** educational or not will depend in many cases upon the evaluation of its quality and usefulness for that purpose. Music, drama, literature, archaeology, museums; these and many more are included. But not bad music, ham acting, pornography, useless digging or collections of rubbish, as the public benefit requirement would not be satisfied. In *Re Delius*,[135] Roxburgh J. recognised that there would be difficulty if a manifestly inadequate composer had been chosen. A judge may be assisted by expert evidence. But that may not be conclusive, and artistic evaluation changes with the times. It is clear that the court will require to be satisfied of the merit of artistic work.[136] The opinion of the donor that the gift is for the public benefit does not make it so.

In *Re Pinion*,[137] a testator gave his studio and its contents to trustees to enable it to be used as a museum for the display of his collection of furniture and objets d'art, and paintings, some of which were by the testator himself.
Expert opinion was unanimous that the collection had no artistic merit. One expert expressed his surprise that "so voracious a collector should not by hazard have picked up even one meritorious object."[138] The Court of Appeal held the trust void. "I can conceive," said Harman L.J., "of no useful object to be served in foisting upon the public this mass of junk. It has neither public utility nor educational value."[139]

v. Youth. Sports at School and University. Education is **15–018** specially concerned with the young. In many situations a provision for the young will be held charitable although the same provision for older people might fail.
In *Re Mariette*,[140] there was a gift to provide Eton fives courts and squash rackets courts at Aldenham School. Eve J. upheld this, on the principle that learning to play games at a boarding school was as important as learning from the books.

---

[133] Charities Act 2011 s.3(1)(f).
[134] *Associated Artists Ltd v IRC* [1956] 1 W.L.R. 752 at 758; see also *Royal Choral Society v IRC* [1943] 2 All E.R. 101 at 107.
[135] [1957] Ch. 299.
[136] The same problem arises with many situations under the fourth head.
[137] [1965] Ch. 85.
[138] [1965] Ch. 85 at 107.
[139] [1965] Ch. 85.
[140] [1915] 2 Ch. 284. For sport outside universities and schools, see below, para.15–028.

The sporting facilities need not be limited to a particular school or institution. In *IRC v McMullen*,[141] a trust to provide facilities for pupils at schools and universities in the United Kingdom to play association football or other games or sports was held valid by the House of Lords. Lord Hailsham said[142]:

"The picture of education when applied to the young . . . is complex and varied . . . It is the picture of a balanced and systematic process of instruction, training and practice containing both spiritual, moral, mental and physical elements . . . I reject any idea which would cramp the education of the young within the school or university campus, limit it to formal instruction, or render it devoid of pleasure in the exercise of skill."

But this wide definition of education is not without its limits. Lord Hailsham stated that the mere playing of games or enjoyment or amusement or competition was not per se charitable nor necessarily educational; and that a trust for physical education per se and not associated with persons of school age or just above was not necessarily a good charitable gift.

Trusts for sport outside educational facilities and the services were formerly considered not charitable[143] unless they came within the scope of the Recreational Charities Act 1958.[144] The Charities Act 2006, following decisions of the Charity Commissioners, recognised the advancement of amateur sport as a charitable purpose.[145] This is discussed below.[146] Intelligent games like chess are educational for young people,[147] and the definition of sport now found in the Charities Act 2011 includes games which promote health by involving mental skill.[148] We can say that purposeful activities for the young receive favourable treatment. The Boy Scout Movement[149] and the National Association of Toy Libraries[150] are charities, and a gift for an annual treat or field day for school children at Turton has been upheld as encouraging a study of natural history.[151]

15–019 **vi. Professional Bodies.** Professional bodies may be charitable if their object is the advancement of education. The object of the

---

[141] [1981] A.C. 1; J. Warburton [1980] Conv. 173, 225; D. Evans (1986) 1 *Trust Law & Practice* 22.

[142] [1981] A.C. 1 at 18.

[143] *Re Nottage* [1895] 2 Ch. 649 (a prize for a yacht race).

[144] Below, para.15–036.

[145] Now Charities Act 2011 s.3(1)(g).

[146] Below, para.15–028.

[147] *Re Dupree's Deed Trusts* [1945] Ch. 16.

[148] s.3(2)(d).

[149] *Re Webber* [1954] 1 W.L.R. 1500.

[150] Annual Report 1973, para.41.

[151] *Re Mellody* [1918] 1 Ch. 228.

Royal College of Surgeons[152] was stated in the royal charter of 1800 to be: "the due promotion and encouragement of the study and practice of the . . . art and science of surgery".

The fact that the College gives assistance and protection to its members is ancillary only; and the College was held to be a charity. Similarly, the Royal College of Nursing,[153] as the advance of nursing as a profession in all or any of its branches was a charitable purpose. The Construction Industry Training Board was held to be charitable,[154] and subsequently most of the Industrial Training Boards have been registered as charities.[155]

But if the object or one of the objects of the society is to promote the status of the profession or the welfare of its members, it will not be charitable. The General Medical Council was formerly held not to be charitable for this reason, but changes in its constitution led the Charity Commissioners to recognise it as charitable as promoting public health, the benefit to doctors being incidental.[156] Such a purpose now also falls within the separate head of the advancement of health.[157]

vii. Political Propaganda Masquerading as Education.[158] Political purposes are not charitable. They may be for the public benefit, but they are partisan. The court cannot determine whether any particular programme is for the public benefit.[159] Nor can such a trust be charitable even where the testator's project has subsequently been endorsed by Parliament.[160] A trust for political purposes will fail. Attempts have been made to foster the doctrines of a political party under the guise of a trust for education by providing for the advancement of adult education on the lines of the principles of that party.[161] In *Re Hopkinson*,[162] Vaisey J. explained the principle as follows:

15–020

---

[152] *Royal College of Surgeons v National Provincial Bank Ltd* [1952] A.C. 631.

[153] *Royal College of Nursing v St Marylebone BC* [1959] 1 W.L.R. 1077; *Institute of Civil Engineers v IRC* [1932] 1 K.B. 149.

[154] *Construction Industry Training Board v Att Gen* [1973] Ch. 173.

[155] Annual Report 1973 para.39; cf. *IRC v Oldham Training and Enterprise Council* [1996] S.T.C. 1218 (not exclusively charitable because promotion of commerce conferred private benefits).

[156] Annual Report 2001/02 p.19.

[157] Now Charities Act 2011 s.3(1)(d); below, para.15–025.

[158] Annual Report 1966 para.38 (warning the overworking of the word "education"); 1969, para.11; 1971, paras 7–10; 1981, para.54.

[159] *Bowman v Secular Society* [1917] A.C. 406 at 421.

[160] *Re Bushnell* [1975] 1 W.L.R. 1596 (national health system introduced after testator's death but before the litigation); R. Cotterrell (1975) 38 M.L.R. 471.

[161] *Bonar Law Memorial Trust v IRC* (1933) 49 T.L.R. 220 (Conservative); *Re Hopkinson* [1949] 1 All E.R. 346 (Socialist); cf. *McDougall* [1957] 1 W.L.R. 81. See also *Re Ogden* [1933] Ch. 678, where, however, a trust for Liberal institutions was upheld on other grounds.

[162] [1949] 1 All E.R. 346. See also *McGovern v Att Gen* [1982] Ch. 321 and *Southwood v Att Gen, The Times*, July 18, 2000, below, para.15–038, where essentially political trusts were not saved by educational elements.

"Political propaganda masquerading . . . I do not use the word in any sinister sense . . . as education is not education within the statute of Elizabeth . . . In other words it is not charitable."[163]

But there is no doubt that the prospects of success are greater if purposes are presented in the form of education. In *Re Scowcroft*,[164] the gift was of income to be applied "for the furtherance of Conservative principles and religious and mental improvement", and this succeeded. Similarly in *Re Koeppler's Will Trusts*[165] a gift to further the work of an educational project was held charitable even though the testator's express aspirations (the formation of informed international public opinion and the promotion of greater co-operation in Europe and the West) were not regarded as charitable. The project involved conferences with a "political flavour", but did not further the interests of a particular political party, nor seek to change the law or government policies.

While a students' union is a charitable body, as being ancillary to the educational purposes of the college or university,[166] the donation of union funds for political, or indeed for charitable purposes which are not educational, is not permitted. So in *Baldry v Feintuck*[167] the use of union funds to campaign for the restoration of free school milk was restrained as political, although the fact that a students' union has political clubs is not inconsistent with its charitable status.[168]

15–021   **viii. Private and Independent Schools.** An educational institution cannot be charitable if it is operated for profit.[169] The modern practice is to operate fee-paying schools as non-profit-making bodies which can then obtain the fiscal benefits available to educational charities.[170] The Charities Act 2006 removed the presumption of

---

[163] [1949] 1 All E.R. 346 at 350.

[164] [1898] 2 Ch. 638; cf. in the field of religion, *Re Hood* [1931] 1 Ch. 240 (spreading Christian principles by extinguishing "the drink traffic").

[165] [1986] Ch. 423; T. Watkin [1985] Conv. 412.

[166] *London Hospital Medical College v IRC* [1976] 1 W.L.R. 613. The National Union of Students is not a charity; see *Att Gen v Ross*, below, fn.168.

[167] [1972] 1 W.L.R. 552. A donation to the charity War on Want was also restrained, as it was not an educational charity. See Annual Report 1983 paras 95 and 96 and App.A; J Warburton (1986) 1 *Trust Law & Practice* 47. In *Webb v O'Doherty, The Times*, February 11, 1991, expenditure on a campaign to end the Gulf War was restrained.

[168] *Att Gen v Ross* [1986] 1 W.L.R. 252; P. Clarke All E.R. Rev. 1985 at 320. (Preliminary issue as to whether Attorney General had standing to seek injunction to restrain donation of union funds to striking miners and famine aid in Ethiopia). By similar reasoning, a charity cannot guarantee the liabilities of a non-charity; *Rosemary Simmons Memorial Housing Association Ltd v United Dominions Trust Ltd* [1986] 1 W.L.R. 1440. See further J. Warburton [1988] Conv. 275.

[169] *Re Girls' Public Day School Trust* [1951] Ch. 400.

[170] *Abbey, Malvern Wells Ltd v Minister of Local Government and Housing* [1951] Ch. 728.

public benefit, which must now be actively demonstrated by private schools.[171]

D. The Advancement of Religion

i. Meaning of Religion. The advancement of religion was one of the four heads of charity prior to the Charities Act 2006, and is now part of the statutory definition.[172] The promotion of religious harmony is a separate head.[173] Under the previous law it was presumed that the advancement of religion was for the public benefit, but the presumption has now been removed, so that public benefit must be demonstrated in every case.[174]

15–022

It was at one time considered that, for the purposes of charity law, a religion had to be "monotheistic".[175] The emphasis was on belief in one god, or a god.[176] This aspect was resolved by the Charities Act 2006, which provided that "religion" includes a religion which involves belief in more than one god, and a religion which does not involve belief in a god.[177] However, the legislation provides no guidance as to whether a system of belief constitutes a religion. The Charity Commission stated that belief in a "Supreme Being" rather than a god was required,[178] but this was subsequently modified in supplementary guidance.[179] It was there stated that the characteristics of a religious belief are:

- "[B]elief in a god (or gods) or goddess (or goddesses), or supreme being, or divine or transcendental being or entity or spiritual principle, which is the object or focus of the religion;

- a relationship between the believer and the supreme being or entity by showing worship of, reverence for or veneration of the supreme being or entity;

- a degree of cogency, cohesion, seriousness and importance;

- an identifiable positive, beneficial, moral or ethical framework."

[171] Below, para.15–049.
[172] Now Charities Act 2011 s.3(1)(c).
[173] Now Charities Act 2011 s.3(1)(h).
[174] Charities Act 2011 s.4(2).
[175] *Bowman v Secular Society* [1917] A.C. 406.
[176] *Re South Place Ethical Society* [1980] 1 W.L.R. 1565. The position of Buddhism was left open, but this was resolved by the Act of 2006.
[177] Now Charities Act 2011 s.3(2)(a).
[178] *Commentary on the Descriptions of Charitable Purposes in the Charities Act 2006* para.10.
[179] *The Advancement of Religion for the Public Benefit*, December 2008.

Some of the decisions preceding the Act of 2006 are still of assistance on this point. They laid down that religion involves a spiritual belief going beyond morality or a recommended way of life. In *Re South Place Ethical Society*,[180] one question was whether the Society's objects, which were the "study and dissemination of ethical principles and the cultivation of a rational religious sentiment", were charitable under this heading. Dillon J. held that they were not. Similarly, the objects of a body such as the Freemasons, whose rules demand the highest personal, social and domestic standards, do not constitute a religion, even though they insist upon a belief in a divine spirit.[181] In any event, to be charitable, a trust must be for the *advancement* of religion; and this means:

> "[T]he promotion of spiritual teaching in a wide sense and the maintenance of the doctrines on which this rests, and the observances that serve to promote and manifest it—not merely a foundation or cause to which it can be related."[182]

15–023   So far as Christianity is concerned, no distinction is drawn between the various churches.[183] Thus, trusts for Roman Catholics,[184] Quakers,[185] Baptists,[186] Methodists,[187] and the Exclusive Brethren,[188] have been upheld. So also small groups, promoting minority religions. In *Thornton v Howe*,[189] Romilly M.R. went so far as to hold as charitable a trust for the publication of the sacred writings of Joanna Southcott, who claimed that she was with child by the Holy Ghost and would give birth to a new Messiah. In *Re Watson*,[190] Plowman J. upheld a trust for "the continuation of the work of God . . . in propagating the truth as given in the Holy Bible" by financing the continued publication of the books and tracts of one Hobbs who, with the testator, was the leading member of a very

---

[180] [1980] 1 W.L.R. 1565. The Society was charitable under other headings; above, para.15–014.

[181] *United Grand Lodge of Ancient Free and Accepted Masons of England and Wales v Holborn BC* [1957] 1 W.L.R. 1080. See also *Berry v St Marylebone BC* [1958] Ch. 406. (Theosophy held to be a philosophical or metaphysical conception, rather than the advancement of religion). The promotion of spiritualism was held to advance religion in *Re Sacred Hands Spiritual Centre* [2006] W.T.L.R. 873. The Druid Foundation has been accepted by the Charity Commission; P. Luxton [2011] Conv. 144.

[182] *Keren Kayemeth le Jisroel v IRC* [1932] A.C. 650.

[183] *Dunne v Byrne* [1912] A.C. 407; *Re Flynn* [1948] Ch. 24.

[184] *Dunn v Byrne*, above, fn.183.

[185] *Re Manser* [1905] 1 Ch. 68.

[186] *Re Strickland's WT* [1936] 3 All E.R. 1027.

[187] "The Voice of Methodism" was registered in 1965; Annual Report App.C, para.1.

[188] *Holmes v Att Gen, The Times*, February 12, 1981.

[189] (1862) 31 Beav. 14. As this gift was to take effect out of land, it was void as infringing the Statutes of Mortmain, now repealed. See C. Stebbings (1997) 18 *Legal History* 1.

[190] [1973] 1 W.L.R. 1472. See also *Funnell v Stewart* [1996] 1 W.L.R. 288 (faith healing upheld); R. Fletcher (1996) 112 L.Q.R. 557.

small group of undenominational Christians. Expert evidence regarded the intrinsic value of the work as nil; but it confirmed the genuineness of the belief of the adherents of that small group. Now that public benefit must be demonstrated, the result would be different in these two cases.[191]

Non-Christian religions were recognised before the advent of the Charities Act 2006, as: "The law of charity does not now favour one religion to another."[192] A gift for the promotion of the Jewish religion has been upheld.[193] Likewise the promotion of the faith of a Hindu sect.[194] There seems little doubt that all non-Christian religions will be treated equally, although there can be difficult questions if charitable status is claimed for some mystical oriental and other cults.[195]

ii. Related Purposes. A large number of purposes have been **15–024** accepted as charitable, although indirectly connected with the advancement of religion. Again, only a few illustrations can be selected. Many of these relate to the erection of churches or the maintenance of the fabric of religious buildings; which includes a window,[196] a tomb in the church,[197] and bells.[198] A trust for a graveyard, even though restricted to one denomination, is charitable,[199] but not a trust for individual tombs in the churchyard.[200]

Similarly, a trust for the benefit of the clergy,[201] or for the church choir,[202] and also for retired missionaries.[203] Where the testator uses phrases like "for God's work",[204] or "for his work in the parish",[205]

---

[191] Charities Act 2011 s.4(2). See M. Harding (2008) 71 M.L.R. 159.

[192] *Varsani v Jesani* [1999] Ch. 219 at 235. See also *Neville Estates Ltd v Madden* [1962] Ch. 832; *Gilmour v Coats* [1949] A.C. 457–458.

[193] *Neville Estates Ltd v Madden* [1962] Ch. 832.

[194] *Varsani v Jesani* [1999] Ch. 219.

[195] On "fringe" religious organisations, see Annual Report 1976 paras 103–108; and on exorcism, paras 65–67. The Unification Church (the "Moonies") has also been registered; Annual Report 1982 paras 36–38, App.C. The Attorney General announced on February 3, 1988, that a High Court action to deprive the "Moonies" of charitable status was being dropped. As to Scientology, see *Re Church of Scientology (England and Wales)* [2005] W.T.L.R. 1151. It does not have charitable status. On Rastafarianism, see D. O'Brien (2001) 151 N.L.J. 509.

[196] *Re King* [1923] 1 Ch. 243; *Re Raine* [1956] Ch. 417.

[197] *Hoare v Osborne* (1866) L.R. 1 Eq. 585.

[198] *Re Pardoe* [1906] 2 Ch. 184; an extreme case, as the purpose was to commemorate the restoration of the Monarchy.

[199] *Re Manser* [1905] 1 Ch. 68; *Re Eighmie* [1935] Ch. 524.

[200] *Lloyd v Lloyd* (1852) 2 Sim.(N.S.) 225.

[201] *Middleton v Clitheroe* (1798) 3 Ves. 734 (stipends); *Re Williams* [1927] 2 Ch. 283 (education of candidates for Ministry); *Re Forster* [1939] Ch. 22.

[202] *Re Royce* [1940] Ch. 514.

[203] *Re Mylne* [1941] Ch. 204; *Re Moon's WT* [1948] 1 All E.R. 300.

[204] *Re Barker's WT* (1948) 64 T.L.R. 273. See also *Re Darling* [1896] 1 Ch. 50.

[205] *Re Simson* [1946] Ch. 299; below, para.15–054.

the court will often find circumstances to indicate that the purposes are intended to be limited to charitable religious purposes.[206]

E. The Advancement of Health; Saving Lives[207]

15–025   This head originates from the old Preamble to the Charitable Uses Act of 1601, which included in the list of charitable purposes "the relief of aged, impotent and poor people". "Impotent" meant sick or disabled. The new statutory head of "the advancement of health and the saving of lives" overlaps to some extent with other heads, such as education and the relief of those in need by reason of (amongst other things) ill-health.[208] It is notable also that the advancement of amateur sport has a link to health, as "sport" is defined as meaning sports or games which promote health by involving physical or mental skill or exertion.[209]

The advancement of health includes "the prevention or relief of sickness, disease or human suffering".[210] We have seen that the advancement of education has been held to include medical research,[211] and that bodies such as the Royal College of Nursing and the General Medical Council have been held charitable under that head. Those examples may now be regarded as falling under both heads.

The advancement of health category will now include examples previously upheld under the old fourth category ("other purposes beneficial to the community"). Trusts for the support of hospitals have long been recognised.[212] Indeed, prior to the introduction of the National Health Service in 1946, hospitals were amongst the greatest beneficiaries of charitable gifts. Ancillary purposes are included if their object is to improve the quality of the service.[213] A private hospital run for profit is not a charity.[214]

The saving of lives was already recognised as charitable, and the charitable status of bodies such as the Royal National Lifeboat Institution is well known. Disaster funds may be charitable, and the special issues affecting disaster appeals are discussed below.[215]

---

[206] *Re Moon's WT* [1948] 1 All E.R. 300.

[207] Charities Act 2011 s.3(1)(d).

[208] Charities Act 2011 s.3(1)(b) and (j).

[209] Charities Act 2011 s.3(1)(g) and 3(2)(d).

[210] Charities Act 2011 s.3(2)(b).

[211] *Royal College of Surgeons v National Provincial Bank Ltd* [1952] A.C. 631; above, para.15–015.

[212] *Re Smith's WT* [1962] 2 All E.R. 563. Faith healing has more recently been recognised; *Funnell v Stewart* [1996] 1 W.L.R. 288.

[213] *Re White's WT* [1951] 1 All E.R. 520 (benefits for nurses); *Re Dean's WT* [1950] 1 All E.R. 882 (accommodation for relatives).

[214] *Re Resch's WT* [1969] 1 A.C. 514 at 540.

[215] Below, para.15–062.

F. The Advancement of Citizenship

This purpose, which incorporates the advancement of community **15–026** development,[216] has been recognised in recent years in the decisions of the Charity Commissioners.[217] It includes rural or urban regeneration, and the promotion of civic responsibility, volunteering, the voluntary sector or the effectiveness or efficiency of charities.[218]

The Charity Commissioners considered that an appeal to fund a public memorial to a respected national figure of historical importance, such as Earl Mountbatten of Burma, could be charitable as being likely to foster patriotism and good citizenship.[219]

G. The Advancement of the Arts, Culture, Heritage or Science[220]

We have seen that, prior to the Charities Act 2006, this purpose **15–027** was accepted as an aspect of the advancement of education.[221] The examples given under that head may now be regarded as falling within either of these overlapping categories.

The Charity Commissioners recently recognised as charitable an appeal to fund a statue of the "Fine Lady Upon a White Horse" in Banbury.[222] This may considered as being for the advancement of heritage.

H. The Advancement of Amateur Sport

In *Re Nottage*[223] it was held that a trust to fund a prize for a yacht **15–028** race was not charitable, because the promotion of sport was not a charitable purpose. However, we saw that the provision of sporting facilities for children and young people has long been accepted as charitable as being for the advancement of education.[224] Sporting and other recreational activities could be charitable under the Recreational Charities Act 1958 (which has been consolidated in the Charities Act 2011).[225] Before the Charities Act 2006 the Commissioners had accepted that the promotion of community participation in healthy sport was a charitable purpose, as opposed to the promotion of a particular sport for its own sake.[226]

---

[216] Charities Act 2011 s.3(1)(e).

[217] Annual Report 2003/2004, p.8.

[218] Charities Act 2011 s.3(2)(c).

[219] Annual Report 1981 paras. 68–70. Scout and Guide groups would be included as promoting good citizenship.

[220] Charities Act 2011 s.3(1)(f).

[221] Above, paras 15–015 and 15–016.

[222] *Re The Fine Lady Upon a White Horse Appeal* [2006] W.T.L.R. 59.

[223] [1895] 2 Ch. 649.

[224] Above, para.15–018.

[225] Below, para.15–036.

[226] Annual Report 2003/2004 p.8.

The Charities Act 2006 provided that the advancement of amateur sport is a charitable purpose.[227] "Sport" means sports or games which promote health by involving physical or mental skill or exertion.[228] This overlaps to some extent with the advancement of health.[229] We saw that the promotion of chess for young people was upheld as a charitable purpose as being educational.[230] This would now be charitable without any restriction to young people as promoting health by involving mental skill.

I. The Advancement of Human Rights; Conflict Resolution; Promotion of Religious or Racial Harmony; Equality and Diversity

15–029   This head gathers together various related purposes which had been recognised by the Charity Commissioners. Research into human rights is charitable as being for the advancement of education,[231] and the promotion of human rights was subsequently recognised as charitable, along with the promotion of equality and diversity and the promotion of religious harmony.[232]

The Charities Act 2006 incorporated into one heading "the advancement of human rights, conflict resolution or reconciliation or the promotion of religious or racial harmony or equality and diversity".[233]

The promotion of peace had been recognised some 70 years before the Act of 2006,[234] provided the purpose was not political.[235]

More recently the Commissioners registered an organisation whose aim was to eliminate discrimination against lesbian, gay and bisexual parents and their children, as promoting equality and diversity.[236]

J. The Advancement of Environmental Protection or Improvement

15–030   Protection of the environment, both within and outside the UK, has been recognised as a charitable purpose for many years.[237] It is

---

[227] Now Charities Act 2011 s.3(1)(g). A registered sports club is not charitable; below, para.15–036, fn.276. The Charity Commission published a consultation paper on the advancement of amateur sport in 2011.

[228] Charities Act 2011 s.3(2)(d).

[229] Charities Act 2011 s.3(1)(d).

[230] *Re Dupree's Deed Trusts* [1945] Ch. 16; above, para.15–018.

[231] *McGovern v Att Gen* [1982] Ch. 321 (the Amnesty International Trust, which was not charitable because other objects were political).

[232] Annual Report 2003/2004 p.8.

[233] Now Charities Act 2011 s.3(1)(h).

[234] *Re Harwood* [1936] Ch. 285; below, para.15–069.

[235] Below, para.15–038.

[236] Annual Report 2003/2004 p.25 (Pink Parents (UK)).

[237] Above, para.15–011. See also Annual Report 2003/2004 p.8.

now a separate head within the statutory definition.[238] Gifts for the preservation of natural amenities have been held charitable,[239] and the charitable status of the National Trust is well known.

K. Youth, Age, Ill-health, Disability, Financial Hardship

The Charities Act 2006 included in its list of charitable purposes **15–031** "the relief of those in need by reason of youth, age, ill-health, disability, financial hardship or other disadvantage".[240] This includes relief given by the provision of accommodation or care to the persons just mentioned.[241] Parts of this broad category originate from the old Preamble to the Charitable Uses Act of 1601, which included as charitable "the relief of aged, impotent and poor people". We have seen that the relief of poverty is a separate head under what is now the Charities Act 2011,[242] but it overlaps with those in need by reason of financial hardship. There is also some overlap between the advancement of health category[243] and the relief of those in need by reason of ill-health or disability.

Charities such as Barnardo's (children) and Help the Aged are well known. An example of the relief of the disabled is *Re Lewis*,[244] where a gift of £100 each to 10 blind girls and 10 blind boys in Tottenham was charitable. A gift to found a children's home is charitable,[245] and this may be viewed as for the relief of those in need by reason of youth. Examples of relief of the aged abound. In *Re Robinson*[246] a gift for old people over 60 years of age was upheld. Trusts for the provision of housing for the aged are charitable.[247] While there is no requirement that the aged (or sick or disabled) persons who are being relieved should be poor, the word "relief" implies a need attributable to their condition as aged (or sick or disabled) persons which they may be unable to alleviate from their own resources. It is not synonymous with "benefit". Thus "a gift of money to the aged millionaires of Mayfair would not relieve a need of theirs as aged persons".[248]

---

[238] Charities Act 2011 s.3(1)(i).

[239] *Re Granstown* [1932] 1 Ch. 537; *Re Corelli* [1943] Ch. 332.

[240] Now Charities Act 2011 s.3(1)(j). On financial hardship, see *Re AITC Foundation* [2005] W.T.L.R. 1265 (hardship through investment losses).

[241] Charities Act 2011 s.3(2)(e).

[242] Above, para.15–012.

[243] Above, para.15–025.

[244] [1955] Ch. 104.

[245] *Re Sahal's WT* [1958] 1 W.L.R. 1243.

[246] [1951] Ch. 198; *Re Gosling* (1900) W.R. 300 ("old and worn-out clerks" of the bank).

[247] *Joseph Rowntree Memorial Trust Housing Association Ltd v Att Gen* [1983] Ch. 159; *Re Cottam* [1955] 1 W.L.R. 1299.

[248] [1983] Ch. 159, at 171.

L. The Advancement of Animal Welfare

15–032   While gifts for specified animals are not charitable,[249] it has long been accepted that trusts for the welfare of animals generally are charitable, and this was recognised in the Charities Act 2006.[250] Originally charitable status was limited to the welfare of animals useful to humans,[251] but this utilitarian approach was replaced by the principle that kindness to animals tends to "promote feelings of humanity and morality generally, repress brutality, and thus elevate the human race".[252] Thus a home for lost dogs,[253] a trust for cats needing care and attention,[254] and animal hospitals[255] have been held charitable.

However, not all purposes for the benefit of animals are charitable. In *National Anti-Vivisection Society v Inland Revenue Commissioners*[256] the Society, whose purpose was the total suppression of vivisection, was not charitable, because vivisection was considered a necessary part of medical research. The court had to weigh conflicting moral and material benefits, and held that, on balance, the purpose of the Society was not beneficial to the public, but was in fact detrimental. In *Re Grove-Grady*[257] a trust to set up an animal refuge where the animals would be safe from molestation by humans was held not charitable on the ground that a sanctuary which deprived humans of all involvement was not for the public benefit. However, animal sanctuaries generally are charitable, and some purposes connected with animals may be charitable as being for the advancement of education,[258] or for environmental preservation.[259]

M. The Promotion of the Efficiency of the Armed Forces, Police and Rescue Services

15–033   These purposes were recognised before the Charities Act 2006 as falling within the residual category of "other purposes beneficial to the community". The legislation now provides that "the promotion of the efficiency of the armed forces of the Crown, or of the efficiency of the police, fire and rescue services or ambulance services"

---

[249] Above, para.14–011.
[250] Now Charities Act 2011 s.3(1)(k).
[251] *London University v Yarrow* (1857) 1 De G. & J. 72.
[252] *Re Wedgwood* [1915] 1 Ch. 113 at 122. See also *Re Green's WT* [1985] 3 All E.R. 455.
[253] *Re Douglas* (1887) 35 Ch.D. 472.
[254] *Re Moss* [1949] 1 All E.R. 495.
[255] *London University v Yarrow*, above, fn.251.
[256] [1948] A.C. 31.
[257] [1929] 1 Ch. 557 (compromised on appeal; *Att Gen v Plowden* [1931] W.N. 89).
[258] *Re Lopes* [1931] 2 Ch. 130.
[259] Above, para.15–030.

is a charitable purpose.[260] So, for example, the promotion of sport in the Army is charitable as encouraging efficiency,[261] and a gift to a voluntary fire brigade has been held charitable.[262]

While the promotion of the efficiency of the police is a charitable purpose, the provision of mere recreational facilities will not suffice. In *IRC v Glasgow Police Athletic Association*[263] the Association, whose object was to promote "all forms of athletic sport and general pastimes" was held not charitable. While the improvement of the efficiency of the police and the encouragement of recruiting were charitable purposes, the provision of mere recreation for the police was not. As the provision of recreation was not merely incidental, the Association's purposes were not exclusively charitable.

N. Other Purposes

We have seen that s.3 of the Charities Act 2011 sets out a list of **15–034** specific purposes which are charitable. This is followed by the residual category of other purposes.[264] These are any other purposes:

"(i) that are not within paragraphs (a) to (l) but are recognised as charitable purposes by virtue of section 5 (recreational and similar trusts, etc.) or under the old law,[265]
    (ii) that may reasonably be regarded as analogous to, or within the spirit of, any purposes falling within any of paragraphs (a) to (l) or sub-paragraph (i) or,
    (iii) that may reasonably be regarded as analogous to, or within the spirit of, any purposes which have been recognised, under the law relating to charities in England and Wales, as falling within sub-paragraph (ii) or this sub-paragraph."

This provision ensures that purposes already recognised as charitable continue to have that status (subject to the public benefit requirement) even though not expressly mentioned in the statutory list, and also provides the flexibility to allow further development by preserving the "analogy" approach adopted by the courts and the Commissioners before the 2006 Act.

---

[260] Charities Act 2011 s.3(1)(l). Fire and rescue services are defined in s.3(2)(f) as meaning services provided by fire and rescue authorities under Pt 2 of the Fire and Rescue Services Act 2004.
[261] *Re Gray* [1925] Ch. 362. See also *Re Good* [1905] 2 Ch. 60 (gift to officers' mess held charitable).
[262] *Re Wokingham Fire Brigade Trusts* [1951] Ch. 373.
[263] [1953] A.C. 380. See also Annual Report 1984, para.17 (Police Memorial Trust to commemorate officers killed on duty held charitable).
[264] Charities Act 2011 s.3(1)(m).
[265] Below, para.15–036.

15–035   **i. Purposes Recognised under the Previous Law.** Most of the purposes which previously fell within the old fourth category of "other purposes beneficial to the community" are now expressly mentioned in the statutory definition. Examples of charitable purposes not expressly mentioned and consequently falling within this residual category include the publication of the law reports,[266] the protection of the country against enemy attack,[267] the promotion of agriculture,[268] and a gift "unto my country England".[269]

Also falling under this heading are the old "locality cases". A principle developed whereby the conferring of benefits which were restricted to a precise locality was regarded as charitable, as a way of saving a gift which would otherwise fail.[270] These cases are treated as anomalous and are not to be extended,[271] but they will be followed in cases directly similar.[272]

15–036   **ii. Recreational Charities.** Although gifts for the provision of recreation grounds for the general public have been held charitable,[273] recreation as such was not regarded as charitable prior to the Recreational Charities Act 1958. Thus in *Williams' Trustees v IRC*[274] a trust for promoting the interests of the Welsh community in London by various means, most of which were charitable, failed because they involved a social and recreational element. In *IRC v Baddeley*[275] land was conveyed to a Methodist Mission:

> "[F]or the promotion of the religious, social and physical well-being of persons resident in . . . West Ham and Leyton . . . by the provision of facilities for religious services and instruction; and for the social and physical training and recreation"

of persons likely to become members of the church. The House of Lords held that these purposes were not exclusively charitable because of the inclusion of purely social purposes.

The Recreational Charities Act 1958 (which has been consolidated in the Charities Act 2011) attempted to remove the uncertainties caused by these decisions by recognising as charitable certain

---

[266] *Incorporated Council of Law Reporting for England and Wales v Att Gen* [1972] Ch. 73; (1972) 88 L.Q.R. 171 (also held to be for the advancement of education).

[267] *Re Driffill* [1950] Ch. 92.

[268] *IRC v Yorkshire Agricultural Society* [1928] 1 K.B. 611; *Brisbane CC v Att Gen for Queensland* [1979] A.C. 411.

[269] *Re Smith* [1932] 1 Ch. 153.

[270] The leading case is *Goodman v Saltash Corp* (1882) 7 App. Cas. 633.

[271] *Houston v Burns* [1918] A.C. 337.

[272] See *Peggs v Lamb* [1994] Ch. 172; *Re Harding* [2008] Ch. 235; above, para. 13–004.

[273] *Re Hadden* [1932] Ch. 133; *Oldham BC v Att Gen* [1993] Ch. 210.

[274] [1947] A.C. 447. The trust was later validated under the Charitable Trusts (Validation) Act 1954, para.15–061, below; Annual Report 1977 paras 71–80.

[275] [1955] A.C. 572.

recreational facilities provided in the interests of social welfare. However, the drafting of the legislation was obscure in certain respects. Minor amendments were made by the Charities Act 2006. Section 5 of the Charities Act 2011[276] provides as follows:

"(1) It is charitable (and is to be treated as always having been charitable) to provide, or assist in the provision of, facilities for—

(a) recreation, or
(b) other leisure-time occupation,

if the facilities are provided in the interests of social welfare.

(2) The requirement that the facilities are provided in the interests of social welfare cannot be satisfied if the basic conditions are not met.

(3) The basic conditions are—

(a) that the facilities are provided with the object of improving the conditions of life for the persons for whom the facilities are primarily intended,[277] and
(b) that—

(i) those persons have need of the facilities because of their youth, age, infirmity or disability, poverty, or social and economic circumstances, or
(ii) the facilities are to be available to members of the public at large or to male, or to female, members of the public at large.

(4) Subsection (1) applies in particular to—

(a) the provision of facilities at village halls, community centres and women's institutes, and
(b) the provision and maintenance of grounds and buildings to be used for purposes of recreation or leisure-time occupation,

and extends to the provision of facilities for those purposes by the organising of any activity.

But this is subject to the requirement that the facilities are provided in the interests of social welfare.

(5) Nothing in this section is to be treated as derogating from the public benefit requirement."

---

[276] See also Charities Act 2011 s.6: a registered sports club, as defined in s.6(2), is not charitable.

[277] See *Cuppage v Lawson* [2011] W.T.L.R. 975 (working men's club).

Before the 2006 amendment facilities restricted to male members of the public were not included, and it was considered that this was incompatible with the European Convention on Human Rights.

The 1958 Act would not have affected the outcome of the cases previously discussed,[278] as the facilities in those cases were for the benefit of restricted classes who would not appear to have been in need of them in the way required by the Act.

The provision now found in section 5(3)(a) of the Charities Act 2011 refers to the object of "improving the conditions of life" of the intended users, and the question arose as to whether this impliedly confined the operation of the Act to facilities for "the deprived". The House of Lords in *Guild v IRC*[279] held that this was not so: the Act applied where the object was to improve the conditions of life of the community generally.

The social welfare element requires something more than a group of individuals combining together, as a club or society, to benefit themselves. The Charity Commissioners considered that there were two characteristics: an ethical element (meeting needs which ought to be met by society, otherwise the conditions of life of the class concerned would be inadequate), and altruism (seeking to improve the conditions of life of others).[280] Facilities for entertainment alone are unlikely to qualify.

15–037　　　**iii. Analogous Purposes.** No list, however long, can capture all the purposes which may be considered charitable as society changes. Before the Charities Act 2006 it had long been established that purposes which were "within the spirit" of, or analogous to, purposes already established as charitable were themselves charitable. The legislation retained this principle, thereby ensuring adequate flexibility to meet future developments.

When a new purpose arises, it is not sufficient to show that it is beneficial. It must be beneficial in the same sense as established charitable purposes. Cases decided before the Act of 2006 illustrate this principle. In *Scottish Burial Reform and Cremation Society v Glasgow City Corp*[281] a non-profit-making cremation society was held charitable by analogy with cases holding burial grounds to be so, although neither facility was mentioned in the old Preamble to the Charitable Uses Act of 1601 which was then the source of charitable purposes. On the other hand, we have seen from the cases

---

[278] *Williams v IRC* [1947] A.C. 447 (Welsh people in London); *IRC v Baddeley* [1955] A.C. 572 (Methodists in West Ham and Leyton): *IRC v Glasgow Police Athletic Association* [1953] A.C. 380.

[279] [1992] 2 A.C. 310 (public sports centre held charitable); H. Norman [1992] Conv. 361; J. Hopkins (1992) 51 C.L.J. 429.

[280] Decisions, Vol.5 (1997), p.7. The provision of internet facilities in a deprived area has been recognised; Annual Report 2003/2004 p.27.

[281] [1968] A.C. 138.

decided before the Recreational Charities Act 1958[282] that the provision of recreational facilities, although beneficial to the community, was nevertheless not beneficial in the way which the law regarded as charitable.

The Charity Commissioners expressed the view that a strict interpretation of the analogy requirement is undesirable,[283] and it is likely that this flexible approach will continue.

O. Political Trusts are not Charitable

Trusts whose object, direct or indirect, is the support of one political party are clearly not charitable.[284] The borderline between such trusts and trusts where political propaganda was "masquerading as education" has been discussed.[285] **15–038**

The general principle is that political trusts are not charitable. This principle is not affected by the Charities Acts 2006 and 2011. In *Re Bushnell*,[286] the testator left money for "the advancement and propagation of the teaching of socialised medicine." The trust was neither an educational charity nor charitable under any other heading. The testator had died in 1941, and at that time legislation would have been required to achieve the purpose. The desirability of such legislation was a political matter. It made no difference that a national health service had subsequently been introduced, as the relevant time for judging the matter was the testator's death.

A second reason for the failure of the Anti-Vivisection trust[287] was that the objects of the Society required a change in the law. The majority treated this as necessarily being a political purpose. Lord Normand stressed that this should only be so where, as here, the change in the law was a *predominant object*,[288] while Lord Porter, who dissented, would have excluded only trusts which were purely political,[289] that is to say, where the object is to be attained *only* by a

---

[282] Above, para.15–036.

[283] Annual Report 1985 paras 24–27.

[284] *Bonar Law Memorial Trust v IRC* (1933) 49 T.L.R. 220 (Conservative); *Re Ogden* [1933] Ch. 678 (Liberal); *Re Hopkinson* [1949] 1 All E.R. 346 (Socialist: the whole tenor of the gift was to mask political propaganda as education). It is doubtful whether *Re Scowcroft* [1898] 2 Ch. 638 would now be followed; the case itself might have been differently decided had the gift been only for the furtherance of Conservative principles. See also Annual Report 1982 paras 45–51 (refusal to register Youth Training, whose purpose was to assist the Workers' Revolutionary Party); Annual Report 1991 para.75 (Margaret Thatcher Foundation was political).

[285] Above, para.15–020.

[286] [1975] 1 W.L.R. 1596.

[287] *National Anti-Vivisection Society v IRC* [1948] A.C. 31; above, para.15–032.

[288] [1948] A.C. 31 at 77–78. See *Re Collier* [1998] 1 N.Z.L.R. 81 (promotion of euthanasia); *Hanchett-Stamford v Att Gen* [2009] Ch. 173 ("Performing and Captive Animals Defence League"); G. Griffiths [2009] Conv. 428.

[289] [1948] A.C. 31, at 56.

change in the law. Ultimately "It is a question of degree of a sort well known to the courts."[290]

The treatment as political of any trust whose object is to change the law has been criticised. But whether the proposed change is for the public benefit "is not for the court to judge, and the court has no means of judging."[291] The Legislature decides on changes in the law. The judges' duty is to apply it. The judges should not be put in a position of being asked to hold that a controversial object, often a minority object, is so obviously for the public good that it should be pursued perpetually and tax-free.

The matter arose in *McGovern v Att Gen*,[292] where a non-charitable body, Amnesty International, sought to obtain charitable status for part of its activities by setting up the Amnesty International Trust, to which were transferred those aspects of its work which were thought to be charitable. The objects were: (i) the relief of needy persons who were, or were likely to become, prisoners of conscience, and their relatives; (ii) attempting to secure the release of prisoners of conscience; (iii) the abolition of torture or inhuman or degrading treatment or punishment; and (iv) research into human rights and disseminating the results of the research.[293] These objects were to be carried out in all parts of the world. Purposes (i) and (iv), if standing alone, would have been charitable, but the inclusion of the other objects caused the trust to fail on the ground that it was political.[294] A trust could not be charitable if its direct and main object was to secure a change in the law of the United Kingdom or of foreign countries, for example by repealing legislation authorising capital or corporal punishment. The court could not judge whether this would be for the public benefit, locally or internationally. Nor could a trust be charitable if a direct and principal purpose was to procure the reversal of government policy or of governmental decisions at home or abroad.[295] Object (ii) was not simply for the

---

[290] *National Anti-Vivisection Society v IRC* [1948] A.C. 31 at 77.

[291] per Lord Simonds [1948] A.C. 31 at 62.

[292] [1982] Ch. 321; T. Watkin [1982] Conv. 387; R. Nobles (1982) 45 M.L.R. 704; F. Weiss (1983) 46 M.L.R. 385; C. Forder [1984] Conv. 263; G. Santow (1999) 52 C.L.P. 255. See also *Re Koeppler's WT* [1986] Ch. 423; where the formation of an informed international public opinion and the promotion of greater co-operation in Europe and the West were not regarded as charitable, although the gift was upheld as being for the furtherance of the work of a charitable educational project.

[293] The promotion of human rights is charitable; above, para.15–029. See, however, *R. v Radio Authority Ex p. Bull* [1998] Q.B. 294 (promotion of awareness of human rights with object of bringing pressure to bear on a government is political); J. Stevens and D. Feldman [1997] P.L. 615.

[294] It was not saved by a proviso restricting it to charitable purposes; below, para.15–052.

[295] The decision was distinguised in *Re Koeppler's WT*, above, fn.292, where an educational project involving conferences with a "political flavour" was held charitable. The project was not concerned with party politics nor did it seek to change laws or government policies.

"relief or redemption of prisoners or captives",[296] but involved putting pressure on foreign governments and authorities. To ascribe charitable status to such a trust could prejudice the relations of this country with the foreign country concerned. This public policy consideration could not be ignored.

Trusts for the promotion of peace have run into difficulties. While **15–039** the desirability of peace as an objective is not a matter of political controversy, and indeed the advancement of conflict resolution or reconciliation is a charitable purpose,[297] the promotion of peace will be political if designed to challenge government policies. So in *Southwood v Att Gen*[298] the "advancement of the education of the public in the subject of militarism and disarmament" was not charitable as the dominant purpose was to promote pacifism and to challenge the policies of Western governments. Likewise in *Re Collier*[299] a trust to promote world peace was political and indeed unlawful where the testator was encouraging soldiers to "down arms".

The question arises whether an existing charity my become involved in pursuing "causes" relating to the work with which it is concerned. It was suggested in *McGovern v Att Gen*[300] that if the objects had been charitable, it would not have mattered that the trustees had incidental powers to employ political means to further these objects. The Charity Commission publishes guidance to charity trustees, including the following points (with the emphasis on what charities can properly do)[301]:

(i) While political activity must not be the sole activity, charities may undertake it provided it is done only in the context of supporting the delivery of their charitable purposes.

(ii) Campaigning, advocacy and political activity are all legitimate and valuable activities for charities.

(iii) While charities cannot exist for a political purpose (any purpose directed at furthering the interests of a political party, or securing or opposing a change in the law, policy or decisions in this country or abroad), charities can campaign for a change in the law, policy or decisions if this would support their charitable purpose.

(iv) Although charities may not support a political party, they may support specific policies advocated by political parties

---

[296] Preamble to the Charitable Uses Act 1601.
[297] Charities Act 2011 s.3(1)(h).
[298] *The Times*, July 18, 2000; J. Garton (2000) 14 T.L.I. 233.
[299] [1998] 1 N.Z.L.R. 81.
[300] Above, fn.292.
[301] *Guidance on Campaigning and Political Activity by Charities* (March 2008 version).

if the policy would help to achieve their charitable purpose.

(v) Charities may respond to legislative initiatives, support or oppose Bills during their passage through Parliament, lobby Members of Parliament, and so forth.

(vi) When considering campaigning, charities must weigh up the possible benefits against the costs and risks in deciding whether it is likely to be effective for the achievement of their charitable purposes. They may use emotive or controversial material if it is lawful and justifiable.

(vii) The above principles apply equally to campaigning and political activity overseas.

4. PUBLIC BENEFIT

A. Preliminary Points

15–040   A gift can only be charitable if it is for the public benefit. There are two aspects to the public benefit requirement. First, the purpose in question must be for the public benefit; secondly, the benefit must be available to the public at large or a sufficient section of the community. On the first point, we saw that the Charities Act 2006 removed the presumption that the relief of poverty and the advancement of religion and education were for the public benefit, so that it must be demonstrated in all cases.[302] On the second point, it was established before the Act of 2006 that the requirement of benefit to a sufficient section of the community varied according to the charitable purpose in question.

The legislation requires the Charity Commission to issue guidance on the operation of the public benefit requirement, to promote awareness and understanding of it.[303] Guidance entitled *Charities and Public Benefit* was published in January 2008, along with the Commission's legal analysis of existing case law.[304] Supplementary guidance will be published from time to time, relating to particular types of charity. The guidance does not create new public benefit law, nor does it create a new legal definition of public benefit. It sets out a framework of factors to consider when assessing public benefit in the light of modern conditions, based on the principles contained in the existing case law. It applies to existing registered charities

---

[302] Now Charities Act 2011 s.4(2); above, para.15–009.

[303] Now Charities Act 2011 s.17.

[304] *Analysis of the Law underpinning Charities and Public Benefit.* Supplementary guidance on poverty, religion, education and fee-charging was published in December 2008. Part of the guidance was withdrawn in December 2011; below, para.15–049.

(whose trustees must take steps to address the position if the principles are not satisfied[305]), and to applications to register. The decisions of the Commission may be challenged by an appeal to the First-tier and the Upper Tribunal and then to court.[306]

Charity trustees are under a duty to carry out their charity's aims for the public benefit, to have regard to the Commission's guidance, and to report on their charity's public benefit in their Annual Reports.[307]

The guidance sets out two key principles, with subheadings within each, as follows:

Principle 1: There must be an identifiable benefit or benefits.

(a) It must be clear what the benefits are.
(b) The benefits must be related to the aims.
(c) Benefits must be balanced against any detriment or harm.

Principle 2: Benefit must be to the public, or a section of the public.

(a) The beneficiaries must be appropriate to the aims.
(b) Where benefit is to a section of the public, the opportunity to benefit must not be unreasonably restricted by geographical or other restrictions, or by ability to pay any fees charged.
(c) People in poverty must not be excluded from the opportunity to benefit.
(d) Any private benefits must be incidental.

B. The First Principle: There must be an Identifiable Benefit or Benefits

i. It must be Clear what the Benefits are. Different charitable aims involve different kinds of benefit. It must be possible to recognise and identify the benefit, even though it may not be quantifiable. For example, the benefit of viewing works of art can be identified although it cannot be measured. In some cases the benefit will be obvious, for example aiding the victims of a hurricane, while in other cases evidence may be needed, for example as to the merits of a collection of paintings.[308] Even where the benefit to the public of

15–041

---

[305] They cannot simply "opt out" of charitable status. The assets of an organisation which ceases to be charitable must be applied under the cy-près doctrine; below, para.15–075.

[306] The Charity Tribunal was abolished by regulations under the Tribunals, Courts and Enforcement Act 2007 and its functions transferred. See now Charities Act 2011 Part 17.

[307] Below, para.15–089.

[308] *Re Pinion* [1965] Ch. 85; above, para.15–017.

an organisation's purpose is clear, for example, conducting cancer research, it would have to show that its research was properly conducted.

If the benefit is not capable of proof, it will not be recognised. For example, the courts have held that they cannot assess the benefit of a "political" purpose.[309] Nor can they assess the value of intercessory prayers of a religious order.

> In *Gilmour v Coats*[310] a gift of £500 was made to a Carmelite Priory "if the purposes of [the Priory] are charitable". The Priory consisted of a community of about 20 cloistered nuns, who devoted their lives to prayer, contemplation and self-sanctification, and engaged in no external work.
>
> The House of Lords held that the purposes were not charitable because they lacked public benefit. This could not be found in the benefits conferred upon the public by the prayers of the nuns according to Roman Catholic doctrine, because such benefit was "manifestly not susceptible of proof"[311] in a court of law. Nor could it be found in the edification of the public by the example of the spiritual life followed by the nuns, as that was too vague and intangible; nor by the availability of the religious life being open to all women of the Roman Catholic faith.

This decision cast doubt on the charitable status of gifts for the saying of masses. Such gifts had been held charitable in *Re Caus*,[312] but this was doubted in *Gilmour*. The charitable nature of such a gift has since been upheld in *Re Hetherington (Deceased)*,[313] where the testatrix left £2,000 to the Roman Catholic Bishop of Westminster for masses for the souls of her husband, parents, sisters and herself. One reason was that the celebration of a religious rite in public conferred a sufficient public benefit in the edifying effect it had on those attending. Celebration of the rite in private would not suffice because the benefit conferred by prayer was incapable of proof and the edification of the private class attending was not a public benefit.[314] There was no express term that the masses should be said in

---

[309] *McGovern v Att Gen* [1982] Ch. 321; above, para.15–038.

[310] [1949] A.C. 426. Sufficient public benefit was found in *Holmes v Att Gen*, *The Times*, February 12, 1981 (Exclusive Brethren). The Charity Commission published guidance on public benefit and the advancement of religion in December 2008.

[311] [1949] A.C. 426 at 446. See C. Rickett [1990] Conv. 35. The problem can be overcome if the convent does external work. See Decisions, Vol.3 (1995), 11 (Society of the Precious Blood).

[312] [1934] Ch. 162.

[313] [1990] Ch. 1; N. Parry [1989] Conv. 453; J. Hopkins (1989) 48 C.L.J. 373; C. Sherrin All E.R. Rev. 1989, 307. The second reason for upholding the gift was that it provided stipends for the priests saying the masses, and thereby assisted in the endowment of the priesthood.

[314] *Gilmour v Coats*, above, fn.310; *Hoare v Hoare* (1886) 56 L.T. 147. Trusts for private masses may be valid as anomalous non-charitable purpose trusts; above, para.14–012.

public, but in practice they would be and the gift was so construed.

ii. The Benefits must be Related to the Aims. Benefits arising   **15–042**
from an organisation's work which are not related to its aims will
not be taken into account. If it has more than one aim, each aim must
satisfy the public benefit requirement.

For example, if a charity whose aim is to preserve a historic
building provides a skating rink in the grounds to attract visitors, the
health benefits from skating will not count in the assessment of
public benefit.

General benefits to the public at large which are not connected to
the aim are too remote. So, in *Oppenheim v Tobacco Securities Trust
Co Ltd*,[315] the fact that society generally may benefit from an educated person could not justify treating as charitable the provision of
education to a restricted class of beneficiaries.

**iii. The Benefits must be Balanced Against any Detriment or   15–043
Harm.** The public benefit requirement will not be satisfied where
the achievement of the aim, although of some benefit, is outweighed
by significant harmful effects. We saw that in *National Anti-Vivisection Society v Inland Revenue Commissioners*[316] the moral benefit to
mankind in suppressing vivisection was outweighed by the material
benefit of the medical research it assisted, and so the Society was not
charitable. An inconsequential detriment would not tilt the balance.
For example, the benefits of providing motorised transport for
the disabled would not be outweighed by the possible harm to the
environment.

C. The Second Principle: Benefit must be to the Public, or a Sufficient Section of the Public

i. The Beneficiaries must be Appropriate to the Aims. The   **15–044**
aims may be intended to benefit the public at large or a section of it.
The beneficiaries may be restricted to a locality or to those who have
need of the services, for example the elderly or people with a particular disease. So long as the numbers are not negligible, it does not
matter that the class is small, so long as it is a "public class". These
principles are explained in more detail in the following sections.

**ii. Where Benefit is to a Section of the Public, the Opportunity
to Benefit must not be Unreasonably Restricted by Geographical**

---

[315] [1951] A.C. 297; below, para.15–047.
[316] [1948] A.C. 31; above, para.15–032.

or Other Restrictions, or by Ability to Pay any Fees Charged.

15–045   (a) *Geographical or Other Restrictions.* Where the benefit is not to the public generally, any restrictions must be legitimate, proportionate, rational and justifiable. Where the restrictions are reasonable, it is accepted that society as a whole benefits indirectly by the help given to the sections of the community who benefit directly. There is no difficulty in providing benefits in a particular geographical area (at home or overseas), so long as there are no inappropriate restrictions on the persons in the area who may benefit. For example, it could be charitable to provide public gardens in a particular area, but not if they were restricted to use by persons of a particular faith. As Lord Simonds said in *IRC v Baddeley*[317]:

> "A bridge which is available for all the public may undoubtedly be a charity and it is indifferent how many people use it. But confine its use to a selected number of persons, however numerous and important, it is then clearly not a charity. It is not of general public utility: for it does not serve the public purpose which its nature qualifies it to serve."

It is necessary to distinguish between:

> "[R]elief extended to the whole community yet by its very nature advantageous only to the few and a form of relief accorded to a selected few out of a larger number equally willing to take advantage of it . . . Who has ever heard of a bridge to be crossed only by impecunious Methodists?"[318]

Trusts for the advancement of religion provide further examples. We saw that charity law does not distinguish between one religion and another.[319] Advancing a particular religion provides sufficient public benefit even though adherents are a small minority. However, if their number is negligible, the public benefit test is unlikely to be satisfied.[320] Subject to that point, a gift to a Church will be charitable even though the congregation is small. A trust is charitable if it makes a religious activity available to the public if they wish to take advantage of it. Another aspect is that it may be a sufficient benefit to society to have amongst it persons who have enjoyed the benefit

---

[317] [1955] A.C. 527 at 592.
[318] [1955] A.C. 527 at 592.
[319] Above, para.15–023.
[320] See *Re Watson* [1973] 1 W.L.R. 1472; above, para.15–023.

of religious experience. *Gilmour v Coats*,[321] where a closed order was not charitable, may be contrasted with *Neville Estates Ltd v Madden*,[322] where a trust for the advancement of religion among the members of a particular synagogue was held charitable because the court was:

> "[E]ntitled to assume that some benefit accrues to the public from the attendance at places of worship of persons who live in this world and mix with their fellow citizens."[323]

In other cases the restrictions may lie in beneficiaries being confined to those who have a need, such as ill-health, which it is charitable to relieve. It may be that the class in need is a sufficient section of the public but, in any event, it is for the benefit of society as a whole that assistance is given to those in need of it. Other restrictions may be of a personal nature, as where funds are devoted to those of a particular faith, gender or race.[324] Such restrictions are reasonable only if they are linked to the aims, as demonstrated by the "bridge for Methodists" example.[325]

Where benefits are confined to members of an organisation, restrictions on membership must be reasonable and justifiable. However, in some cases, such as learned societies, the public at large benefits from the work of the society.[326]

(b) *Classes Defined by a Personal Connection: Family Relationships or Common Employment* The general rule is that the beneficiaries must not be defined by a personal connection (called a "personal nexus" in some of the cases), such as a family relationship or being employees of a common employer. There is an exception relating to charities for the relief of poverty, where gifts to the "poor relations" of X or the "poor employees" of X have been upheld. **15–046**

It is necessary, however, to distinguish between a gift to a class or group of poor persons, and a gift to specified poor individuals. The former will be charitable, even if the group is small, and personally connected with the donor; gifts to poor relations have been upheld

---

[321] Above, para.15–041.
[322] [1962] Ch. 832.
[323] [1962] Ch. 832 at 853.
[324] Above, paras 13–002 to 13–004. See also recreational charities; above, para.15–036.
[325] *IRC v Baddeley* [1955] A.C. 527, above.
[326] See *Re South Place Ethical Society* [1980] 1 W.L.R. 1565; *Re Koeppler's WT* [1986] Ch. 423.

since the middle of the 18th century,[327] although the Charity Commission has expressed doubts as to their survival.[328] Jenkins L.J. explained them as follows:

> "I think that the true question in each case has really been whether the gift was for the relief of poverty amongst a class of persons . . . or was merely a gift to individuals, albeit with relief of poverty amongst those individuals as the motive of the gift . . .
> "[329]

Thus, a gift to such of the testator's relatives as shall be poor or "in special need"[330] or "in needy circumstances"[331] is charitable. Similarly a gift to "poor and needy" members of a class of six named relatives of the testator and their issue, there being 26 members at the testator's death and a likelihood of a substantial increase in future.[332] It does not matter that the distribution of capital can be made so as to exhaust the principal.[333] This relaxation in favour of poverty trusts applies also in connection with trusts for the relief of poverty among members of a friendly society,[334] or a professional association,[335] or employees of a company.

In *Dingle v Turner*,[336] a testator created a trust for paying pensions to:

> "[P]oor employees of E. Dingle and Co Ltd who are of the age of 60 years at least or who being of the age of 45 years at least are incapacitated from earning their living by reason of some physical or mental infirmity."

At the date of the testator's death, the company employed over 600 persons, and there was a substantial number of ex-employees. The House of Lords upheld the gift as a charitable trust.

---

[327] *Isaac v Defriez* (1754) Amb. 595. They are discussed at length in *Re Compton* [1945] Ch. 123, and in *Re Scarisbrick* [1951] Ch. 622. See also *Dingle v Turner* [1972] A.C. 601; below.

[328] *Analysis of the Law underpinning the Prevention or Relief of Poverty for the Public Benefit*, December 2008, paras 48, 58, 59; cf. A. Rahmatian [2009] Conv. 12. See further below (Attorney General's reference).

[329] In *Re Scarisbrick* [1951] Ch. 622 at 655; see also at 650–651; *Re Cohen* [1973] 1 W.L.R. 415 at 426; *Dingle v Turner* [1972] A.C. 601 at 617.

[330] *Re Cohen* [1973] 1 W.L.R. 415.

[331] *Re Scarisbrick* [1951] Ch. 622.

[332] *Re Segelman* [1996] Ch. 171; E. Histed [1996] Conv. 379. The inclusion of named persons as objects of charity may be an extension of the rule.

[333] *Re Scarisbrick*, above, fn.331; *Dingle v Turner*, above, fn.329.

[334] *Re Buck* [1896] 2 Ch. 727.

[335] *Spiller v Maude* (1886) 32 Ch.D. 158n. (aged and decayed actors).

[336] [1972] A.C. 601; *Re Gosling* (1900) 48 W.R. 300 (old and worn-out clerks in a banking firm); *Gibson v South American Stores (Gath & Chaves) Ltd* [1950] Ch. 177 ("necessitous and deserving employees, ex-employes and their dependants").

The poor relations cases had been recognised for 200 years, and, even if anomalous, should not be overruled. It would be illogical to draw a distinction between poor relations, and poor employees or poor members.[337] All forms of trusts for the relief of poverty should be treated the same, and there was no need to introduce into the poverty cases the stricter requirements of public benefit applicable to other forms of charitable trusts. Lord Cross suggested that one reason for the different treatment of poverty trusts—a practical justification but not the historical explanation—is that there is for a settlor a "temptation to enlist the assistance of the law of charity in private endeavours"[338] in order to gain the tax benefits, though the danger is not so great in the field of relief of poverty. Three Law Lords[339] doubted whether the fiscal considerations should be given any relevance in deciding whether a gift was charitable. There seems little doubt, however, that they often have done so.[340]

The Attorney General, at the request of the Charity Commission, made a reference[341] in January 2011 for a ruling on the question whether the "poor relations" and "poor employees" cases had survived the provisions of the Charities Act 2006 on public benefit. The reference was heard in November 2011 and a decision is expected in early 2012.

A trust which is not for the relief of poverty cannot be charitable **15–047** if the beneficiaries are selected on the basis of a personal connection, either with the donor or between themselves. Thus, a trust for the education of named persons or for descendants of named persons[342] is not charitable. But a trust for the education of children of members of a particular profession[343] is charitable, as are trusts for specified schools and colleges, and even "closed" scholarships from a specified school to a college at Oxford or Cambridge[344]; unless, of course, the number of possible beneficiaries was derisory.

In *Oppenheim v Tobacco Securities Trust Co*,[345] income was to be applied in "providing for . . . the education of children of

---

[337] The Charity Commission in its *Analysis of the Law underpinning the Prevention or Relief of Poverty for the Public Benefit*, December 2008, considered the poor relations and poor employees cases now to be in doubt; para.58.

[338] *Dingle v Turner* [1972] A.C. 601 at 625.

[339] Lords Dilhorne, McDermott and Hodson.

[340] Above, para.15–001.

[341] To the First-tier Tribunal (Charity).

[342] *Re Compton* [1945] Ch. 123. "A trust established by a father for the education of his sons is not a charity"; per Lord Simonds in *Oppenheim v Tobacco Securities Trust Ltd* [1951] A.C. 297 at 306.

[343] *Hall v Derby Sanitary Authority* (1885) 16 Q.B.D. 163.

[344] It is difficult to see how some of these trusts satisfy the *Oppenheim* rule; see Lord McDermott in *Oppenheim*, fn.342, at 318. See also the anomalous "founder's kin" cases; *Re Christ's Hospital* (1889) 15 App. Cas. 172. These are now doubtful. See Law Commission, *Analysis of the Law underpinning the Advancement of Education for the Public Benefit*, paras 3.9, 3.10, 3.20.

[345] [1951] A.C. 297.

employees or former employees of the British-American Tobacco Company Ltd . . . or any of its subsidiary or allied companies" and there was power also to apply capital. The number of employees of the company and the subsidiary and allied companies exceeded 100,000. The House of Lords held that there was a personal connection between the members of the class of beneficiaries and they did not constitute a section of the public. The trust failed.

In the leading majority speech, Lord Simonds said that to constitute a section of the community for these purposes the:

> "[P]ossible (I emphasize the word 'possible') beneficiaries must be not numerically negligible, and, secondly, that the quality which distinguishes them from members of the community . . . must be a quality which does not depend on their relationship to a particular individual . . . A group of persons may be numerous but, if the nexus between them is their personal relationship to a single propositus or to several propositi, they are neither the community nor a section of the community for charitable purposes."[346]

Lord McDermott, dissenting, pointed out the difficulties which arise in trying to lay down a positive rule in such a situation[347]:

> "[I]f the bond between those employed by a particular railway is purely personal, why should the bond between those who are employed as railwaymen be so essentially different? Is a distinction to be drawn in this respect between those who are employed in a particular industry before it is nationalised and those who are employed therein after that process has been completed and one employer has taken the place of many? . . . Is the relationship between those in the service of the Crown to be distinguished from that obtaining between those in the service of some other employer? Or, if not, are the children of, say, soldiers or civil servants to be regarded as not constituting a sufficient section of the public to make a trust for their education charitable?"[348]

The question, he thought, should be one of degree, depending upon the facts of each particular case. All five Law Lords, sitting in *Dingle v Turner*,[349] supported this view. This does not necessarily mean that *Oppenheim* would be decided differently. Taking

---

[346] [1951] A.C. 297 at 306.
[347] See also Cross J. in *Re Mead's Trust Deed* [1961] 1 W.L.R. 1244 at 1249; and Lord Denning M.R. in *IRC v Educational Grants Association Ltd* [1967] Ch. 993 at 1009; "There is no logic in it."
[348] [1951] A.C. 297 at 317–318.
[349] [1972] A.C. 601.

all factors into account, these educational trusts for employees are attempts to use charity's fiscal privileges for the benefit of the company by providing a tax-free fringe benefit for the employees.[350] Such trusts should fail, not on the ground that the employees, however numerous, can never constitute a class of the public, but because the *purpose* of the trust, being a company purpose, is not charitable.[351] A trust for the advancement of religion among employees might be different[352]; as might an "entirely altruistic educational trust . . . if the size of the company is sufficiently large."[353] It is obvious that it is easier to criticise the personal connection test than it is to improve upon it; and "it may well be that Lord Cross's half-way house creates more problems than it solves."[354] The view of the Charity Commission is that it should be "both cautious and flexible" in the application of the personal connection principle.[355]

A related question arises as to whether a donor can effectively obtain benefits for a group of private individuals by means of a charitable trust. He cannot do so by setting up a charitable trust in favour of the public and relying on the trustees to make grants in favour of a narrow group.

15–048

In *IRC v Educational Grants Association Ltd*[356] the defendant was a charitable corporation established for the advancement of education in general terms. It was financially supported by payments under a deed of covenant by the Metal Box Co Ltd, and by senior executives of the company. The Association claimed the repayment of tax due in respect of payment under the covenant. Between 76 per cent and 85 per cent of the income of the relevant year had been paid towards the education of children of persons connected with the Metal Box Co Ltd, and the Court of Appeal held that the tax was not recoverable, because the money had not been applied for charitable purposes only.[357]

---

[350] "It is an admirable thing that the children of employees should have a higher education, but I do not see why that should be at the expense of the taxpayer", per Harman L.J. in *IRC v Educational Grants Association Ltd* [1967] Ch. 993, at 1013.

[351] *Dingle v Turner*, above, fn.349.

[352] G. Jones (1974) 33 C.L.J. 63 at 66; *Dingle v Turner*, above, fn.349.

[353] Annual Report 1971 para.21.

[354] G. Jones (1974) 33 C.L.J. 63.

[355] See *Analysis of the law underpinning Charities and Public Benefit*, December 2008, para.3.45. Further supplementary guidance on *The Advancement of Education for the Public Benefit* was published in December 2008.

[356] [1967] Ch. 993.

[357] The current legislation is Income Tax Act 2007 s.527 and Corporation Tax Act 2010 s.481 (above, fn.42), which permit exemption for a charitable body *so far as the income is applied to charitable purposes only*. In the *Educational Grants* case the non-charitable payments were ultra vires. If the objects permit such payments, the body is not charitable (subject to *Re Koettgen*) and there will be no tax exemption.

It is impossible to say what percentage of a trust for charity could properly be spent in favour of a private group. In *Re Koettgen's Will Trusts*,[358] there was a trust for the promotion of commercial education among members of the public unable to acquire it at their own expense; and a direction that preference be given to the families of employees of a named company in respect of a maximum of 75 per cent of the income. This was charitable. Lord Radcliffe in *Caffoor v Income Tax Commissioner, Colombo*,[359] thought that *Re Koettgen* "edged very near to being inconsistent with" *Oppenheim*.[360] If a preference in favour of a private group is desired, it is essential to make it subsidiary to the trust in favour of the public; and the 75 per cent which succeeded in *Koettgen* should be regarded as the maximum.[361] If, however, there is an absolute right in favour of a private group, and not merely a preference, then the trust cannot be charitable. It is a matter of construction into which category the gift falls.[362]

15–049   (c) *Ability to Pay any Fees Charged.*[363] It is not unusual for charities to charge for their services, whether they be museums, independent schools, private hospitals, universities, sports centres or other organisations.[364] An organisation cannot be charitable if operated for private profit. Assuming this is not the case, if the practical effect of charging is that those who cannot afford to pay are excluded, the public benefit test will not be satisfied.

The organisation may be able to establish sufficient public benefit if it makes provision for exemption from charges or if it offers other benefits to those who cannot afford them. For example, it has long been the case that fee-paying independent schools have offered free or subsidised places, or have made their facilities available to state school pupils. These arrangements came under particular scrutiny by the Charity Commission.

It may be argued that an organisation (such as a fee-paying school or private hospital) which provides services which the State would otherwise have to provide benefits the public at large by relieving public funds. It appears that this remoter benefit does not suffice if it is the only benefit available to those who cannot afford the fees. A leading case is *Re Resch's WT*,[365] a case involving a private hospital

---

[358] [1954] Ch. 252.

[359] [1961] A.C. 584.

[360] [1961] A.C. 584 at 604.

[361] See Annual Report 1978 paras 86–89.

[362] *Re Martin, The Times*, November 19, 1980.

[363] The Commission's supplementary guidance, *Public Benefit and Fee-charging*, was withdrawn in December 2011, as mentioned below.

[364] See *Joseph Rowntree Memorial Trust Housing Association Ltd v Att-Gen* [1983] Ch. 159; above, para.15–013 (housing for the elderly).

[365] [1969] 1 A.C. 514 (Privy Council).

for paying patients which was held to be charitable. Nobody was expressly excluded, but in practice many could not afford to pay. The decision appears to hold that both direct and indirect benefits (relief of pressure on beds and staff at the public general hospital) may be taken into account, but that the indirect benefits alone would not be sufficient, as in practice this would make the public benefit requirement ineffectual.

The Independent Schools Council recently applied for judicial review of the Charity Commission's public benefit guidance in relation to independent charitable schools. The Attorney General also made a reference in relation to the guidance on fee-charging charities.[366] The Upper Tribunal held that it was up to the charity trustees of the school to assess how their obligations might best be fulfilled in the context of their school's own circumstances and that there were no objective benchmarks applicable to every case. However, the ruling has otherwise done little to clarify the law in this area. The tribunal required some corrections to the Charity Commission guidance. As a result the Commission withdrew its guidance on public benefit and fee charging in December 2011, and revised guidance is due in summer 2012.

iii. People in Poverty[367] must not be Excluded. This is related **15–050** to the principle that the opportunity to benefit must not be unduly restricted by ability to pay any fees charged.[368] If a charity which charged high fees, for example an independent school, made only a small reduction for those who could not afford the fees, people in poverty would be excluded and so the public benefit requirement would not be satisfied unless other benefits were provided for those who could not afford even the reduced fees.

As Lindley L.J. said:

"I am quite aware that a trust may be charitable though not confined to the poor, but I doubt very much whether a trust would be declared charitable which excluded the poor."[369]

iv. Any Private Benefit must be Incidental. This means that **15–051** any private benefits must be a "by-product" of carrying out the charity's aims. For example, the publication of the law reports is for the benefit of the community but incidentally benefits members of the legal profession by assisting them in their practice.[370] If the

---

[366] *Independent Schools Council v Charity Commission* [2012] 1 All E.R. 127. Further directions were given at [2011] UKUT B27 (TCC).

[367] For the meaning of "poverty", see above, para.15–012.

[368] Above, para.15–049.

[369] *Re Macduff* [1896] 2 Ch. 451 at 464.

[370] *Incorporated Council of Law Reporting for England and Wales v Att Gen* [1972] Ch. 73.

private benefits go beyond that, it is doubtful whether the aims would be exclusively charitable. This is discussed elsewhere.[371]

5. THE INTERPRETATION OF CHARITABLE GIFTS AND PURPOSES

15–052 A number of special questions arise in connection with the construction of instruments which are claimed to create charitable trusts. The problems here discussed provide a further reminder of the importance of proper draftsmanship when setting up a charitable trust. The Charity Commission will help with advice,[372] and they will give reasons for the refusal to register, and make it possible for the trusts to be redrafted. The Commission warns draftsmen not to draft object clauses in unnecessarily wide terms, for this may allow non-charitable purposes to be included.[373] In *McGovern v Att Gen*,[374] a trust included political objects, but the deed provided that the objects were "restricted to those which are charitable according to the law of the United Kingdom but subject thereto they may be carried out in all parts of the world." This proviso did not have the "blue-pencil" effect of cancelling out the non-charitable parts, and hence the trust was not charitable. The restriction was merely intended to make it clear that the trustees, when operating outside the United Kingdom, should be restricted to purposes charitable by United Kingdom law. In so far as the purposes of the trust included political and thus non-charitable objects, the proviso could not save it.

A. The Motive of the Donor

15–053 The charitable motive of the donor, even if expressed, is not of major significance. The rule cuts both ways. In *Re King*,[375] a will provided for the erection of a stained-glass window in a church in memory of her parents, her sister and the testatrix herself. This was held to be a valid charitable gift. The fact that the intention was "not to beautify the church or benefit the parishioners, but to perpetuate the memory of the testatrix and her relations"[376] was immaterial. Conversely, a non-charitable gift, such as a gift for the suppression of vivisection, cannot be made charitable by the donor's charitable

---

[371] Below, para.15–055. See also para.15–019 (professional bodies); para.15–096 (payments to trustees).
[372] Now Charities Act 2011 s.110.
[373] Annual Report 1971 paras 70–71.
[374] [1982] Ch. 321, above, para.15–038.
[375] [1923] 1 Ch. 243, following *Hoare v Osborne* (1866) L.R. 1 Eq. 585.
[376] [1923] 1 Ch. 243, at 245.

motive.[377] But a clear charitable intent may help to turn an ambiguity in favour of charity; especially, as has been seen, where it is possible to find an intention to benefit the poor.[378]

B. The Charitable Status of the Trustee[379]

The charitable nature of a trust is determined by the terms of the **15–054** trust and not by the status of the trustee. Non-charitable trustees may hold property on charitable trusts, and charity trustees may, subject, in the case of a corporation, to the terms of their incorporation, hold property on non-charitable trusts. But the charitable status of the trustee can in some cases, where the terms of the trust are not spelled out, lead the court to construe the terms of the trust as charitable. A gift to a bishop or vicar, without the purposes being specified, may be charitable. In *Re Flinn*,[380] a gift to:

> "His Eminence the Archbishop of Westminster Cathedral for the time being to be used by him for such purposes as he shall in his absolute discretion think fit"

was upheld. So, also, gifts to such officers for their work, for this is treated as being wholly charitable. In *Re Rumball*[381] a gift "to the bishop for the time being of the diocese of the Windward Islands to be used by him as he thinks fit in his diocese" was upheld.

But there is a danger in saying too much; where the terms of the gift specify the purposes and allow any part of the fund to be used for non-charitable purposes, the gift is void. The cases turn on the finest points of construction. "Parish work", for example, includes some non-charitable activities, and in *Farley v Westminster Bank*[382] a gift to a vicar "for parish work" was held invalid. But in *Re Simson*,[383] a gift to a vicar "for his work in the parish" was held valid. The former phrase is held to be dispositive, thus enlarging the ambit of the gift and producing the result that a charitable trustee holds on non-charitable trusts, while the latter phrase is held to be merely descriptive of the vicar's responsibilities. The many pages in the reports dealing with these refinements bring no credit to our jurisprudence.

---

[377] *National Anti-Vivisection Society v IRC* [1948] A.C. 31.
[378] *Biscoe v Jackson* (1887) 35 Ch.D. 460; *Re Coulthurst's WT* [1951] Ch. 193; *Re Cottam* [1955] 1 W.L.R. 1299; above, para.15–013.
[379] V. Delaney (1960) 25 Conv. (N.S.) 306.
[380] [1948] Ch. 241.
[381] [1956] Ch. 105.
[382] [1939] A.C. 430.
[383] [1946] Ch. 299.

C. The Objects Must be Exclusively Charitable

15–055   To be charitable, the funds of a trust must be applicable for charitable purposes only.[384]

15–056   **i. Main and Subsidiary Objects.** A trust may be charitable, however, even if some expenditure is permitted on non-charitable purposes, but only if those non-charitable purposes are entirely subsidiary to the main charitable purposes. The question is whether:

> "The main purpose of the body . . . is charitable and the only elements in its constitution and operation which are non-charitable are merely incidental to that purpose."[385]

Failure of a trust for this reason is fairly obvious in cases such as *Morice v Bishop of Durham*,[386] and *IRC v Baddeley*[387] where the purposes are patently too widely expressed but it is less obvious in cases where the non-charitable element is latent. In *Ellis v IRC*,[388] land was conveyed to trustees for use:

> "[G]enerally in such manner for the promotion and aiding of the work of the Roman Catholic Church in the district as the Trustees with the consent of the Bishop may prescribe."

The Court of Appeal held that assets could be spent on subsidiary objects which were not necessarily conducive to the main (and undoubtedly charitable) object; such subsidiary objects existed in their own right and prevented the gift from being "for charitable purposes *only*".

An acute form of this problem occurs where the furtherance of a charitable purpose also benefits particular groups of persons. For instance in *IRC v City of Glasgow Police Athletic Association*,[389] the House of Lords held that a police athletic association, intended to benefit policemen in Glasgow, was not wholly ancillary to increasing the efficiency of the Glasgow police force and therefore not charitable. On the other hand, the benefits to the medical profession in the constitution of the General Medical Council are ancillary to the promotion of public health[390]; similarly in the case of surgeons

---

[384] This principle is now found in Charities Act 2011 s.1(1)(a).

[385] per Lord Cohen in *IRC v City of Glasgow Police Athletic Association* [1953] A.C. 380 at 405. See N. Gravells [1978] Conv. 92.

[386] (1804) 9 Ves.Jr. 399; (1805) 10 Ves.Jr. 522 ("objects of benevolence and liberality").

[387] [1955] A.C. 572; above, para.15–036.

[388] (1949) 31 T.C. 178, following *Dunne v Byrne* [1912] A.C. 407. See also *IRC v Educational Grants Association Ltd* [1967] Ch. 993 at 1010 and 1015; *Oxford Group v IRC* [1949] 2 All E.R. 537, at 539–540.

[389] [1953] A.C. 380.

[390] Above, para.15–019.

in relation to the advancement of surgery in the constitution of the Royal College of Surgeons.[391] In *Re Coxen*[392] a substantial gift to a charity included provision for an annual dinner for the trustees; and this was held charitable as being ancillary to the better administration of the charity. And in *London Hospital Medical College v IRC*,[393] a students' union was held to be a charitable trust where its predominant object was to further the purposes of the college, even though one of its objects was to confer private and personal benefits on union members.

ii. And/Or Cases. Nowhere is the draftsman's error more obvious than in this group of cases. If a purpose is described as "charitable and benevolent"—philanthropic, useful, or any other such adjective—the purposes are wholly charitable. For the purposes, to qualify, must be, amongst other things, charitable; and that is enough. But if the draftsman says charitable *or* benevolent, there is prima facie an alternative; and the funds could be applied for purposes which are benevolent, but not charitable. But this is an oversimplification, and the question is one of construction in each case. Is the word conjunctive or disjunctive?   **15–057**

(a) *Cases of "or"*. In *Blair v Duncan*[394] the words were: "such charitable or public purposes as my trustee thinks proper"; in *Houston v Burns*,[395] "public, benevolent, or charitable purposes"; in *Chichester Diocesan Fund and Board of Finance v Simpson*[396] "charitable or benevolent"; in each of these cases the gift was held not to be charitable, in that the words were wide enough to justify the trustees in disposing of the fund, or an unascertainable part of it, to non-charitable objects.   **15–058**

In *Re Macduff*,[397] a bequest of money "for some one or more purposes, charitable, philanthropic or—" was held to be bad, not by reason of the blank, but because there may be philanthropic purposes that are not charitable.

---

[391] *Royal College of Surgeons v National Provincial Bank Ltd* [1952] A.C. 631; see also *Incorporated Council of Law Reporting v Att Gen* [1972] Ch. 73.

[392] [1948] Ch. 747.

[393] [1976] 1 W.L.R. 613. See also *Re South Place Ethical Society* [1980] 1 W.L.R. 1565 (social activities held to be ancillary to the objects of ethical humanist society); *Funnell v Stewart* [1996] 1 W.L.R. 288.

[394] [1902] A.C. 37. See also *Att Gen of the Cayman Islands v Wahr-Hansen* [2001] 1 A.C. 75 (trust for "religious, charitable or educational institutions or organisations or institutions operating for the public good" invalid).

[395] [1918] A.C. 337.

[396] [1944] A.C. 341; the trustees of the will paid the sums over to various charities, not anticipating the litigation by the next-of-kin which, in the event, occurred and the sequel was *Ministry of Health v Simpson* [1951] A.C. 251.

[397] [1896] 2 Ch. 451.

But in *Re Bennett*[398] the words were: "for the benefit of the schools, and charitable institutions, and poor, and other objects of charity, or *any other* public objects," and Eve J. held that the addition of the word "other" entitled him to apply the *ejusdem generis* rule of interpretation and dispensed him from the necessity of reading the word "or" disjunctively; the gift was, therefore, upheld as a charitable gift of the whole.

15–059   (b) *Cases of "and"*. Lord Davey in *Blair v Duncan*[399] said that if the words had been "charitable *and* public" effect might be given to them, because they could be construed to mean charitable purposes of a public character. Some cases support this view, the word "and" being regarded as having the power to draw the other word into the orbit of the charitable. This view is borne out by *Re Sutton*[400] and *Re Best*,[401] where gifts to "charitable and deserving objects" and "charitable and benevolent" objects respectively were upheld. In *Att Gen of the Bahamas v Royal Trust Co*,[402] on the other hand, a gift for the "education and welfare" of Bahamian children and young people was held void on a disjunctive construction. To construe the words conjunctively would result in a single purpose of educational welfare, but the word "welfare" was regarded as too wide to permit such a construction. The addition of a third word, "without any conjunction, copulative or disjunctive,"[403] was in *Williams v Kershaw*[404] held fatal to a gift to "benevolent, charitable and religious" purposes, and in *Re Eades*[405] Sargant J. refused to uphold a gift for "such religious, charitable and philanthropic objects" as three named persons should jointly appoint.

In *Att Gen v National Provincial and Union Bank of England*[406] there was a gift "for such patriotic purposes or objects and such charitable institution or institutions or charitable object or objects in the British Empire" as the trustees should select. The House of Lords interpreted this as a gift for any or all of four categories, two of which might not be charitable, and so held the whole gift void.

---

[398] [1920] 1 Ch. 305. See also *Guild v IRC* [1992] 2 A.C. 310 (gift to specified recreational charitable purpose "or some similar purpose in connection with sport" upheld).

[399] [1902] A.C. 37 at 4.

[400] (1885) 28 Ch.D. 464.

[401] [1904] 2 Ch. 354.

[402] [1986] 1 W.L.R. 1001; cf. *Re Carapiet's Trusts* [2002] W.T.L.R. 989 (education and advancement in life of Armenian children).

[403] per Pearson J. in *Re Sutton* (1885) 28 Ch.D. 464 at 466.

[404] (1835) 5 Cl. & F. 111n.

[405] [1920] 2 Ch. 353.

[406] [1924] A.C. 262.

So we cannot say more than that prima facie the word "or" causes the words to be read disjunctively; the word "and" causes them to be read conjunctively.

iii. Severance. Where the language permits funds to be applied **15–060** partly for charitable and partly for non-charitable purposes, the court will, in some cases, apply a doctrine of severance, separating the charitable from the non-charitable, and allow the former to stand although the latter may fail.

In *Salusbury v Denton*[407] a testator bequeathed a fund to his widow to be applied by her in her will, in part towards the foundation of a charity school, and as to the rest towards the benefit of the testator's relatives. The widow died without making any apportionment, but it was held, relying on the maxim "Equality is Equity", that the court would divide the fund into halves.

The distinction between this and the "charitable or benevolent" cases is well brought out by Page-Wood V.C.[408]:

"It is one thing to direct a trustee to give *a part* of a fund to one set of objects, and the *remainder* to another, and it is a distinct thing to direct him to give 'either' to one set of objects 'or' to another... This is a case of the former description. Here the trustee was bound to give a part to each."

The crux of the matter is that the whole of a fund cannot be devoted to non-charity; once this is established, the court will endeavour to quantify what proportion of the capital assets is needed to support the non-charitable part,[409] and then hold the remaining part to be validly devoted to charity. In the absence of factors requiring a different division, the court will divide equally.[410] But there may be good reasons for making an unequal division.

In *Re Coxen*,[411] a testator gave the residue of his estate, amounting to more than £200,000, to the Court of Aldermen of the City of London for charitable purposes, providing however that one guinea should be paid to each of the six aldermen chosen to administer the trust on the occasion of his attending any meeting to administer the trust, and that £100 p.a. be used for an annual dinner for the Court of Aldermen when it should meet to discuss the business of the trust. On the assumption that these administrative provisions were not

---

[407] (1857) 3 K. & J. 529.
[408] (1857) 3 K. & J. 529 at 539; the italics are the V.C.'s.
[409] In most cases this will produce partial invalidity.
[410] *Hoare v Osborne* (1866) L.R. 1 Eq. 585.
[411] [1948] Ch. 747.

charitable,[412] quantification was desirable, for a division into equal parts would be absurd. Jenkins J. held that the court would find the necessary means to quantify the maximum slice of capital that would be needed to support them.

15–061   **iv. Charitable Trusts (Validation) Act 1954.** If the terms of a trust coming into operation before December 16, 1952,[413] are such that the property could be applied exclusively for charitable purposes, but could also be applied for non-charitable purposes (called in the Act an "imperfect trust provision") then as from July 30, 1954, the terms shall be treated as if they permitted application for charitable purposes only.[414]

The simple case covered by this provision would be a gift, prior to December 16, 1952, for "charitable or benevolent purposes". It would have saved the trusts of the *Diplock* will,[415] and was applied in the case of a trust deed some of whose purposes were charitable and others not.[416] The difficulty arises where there is no express mention of any charitable purposes, but where the purposes are capable of including charitable purposes.[417] It was said in *Re Gillingham Bus Disaster Fund*[418] that a trust for "worthy causes" was covered, and in *Re Wykes' Will Trust*,[419] a trust for welfare purposes was upheld as those purposes are akin to the relief of poverty. The Act was recently held to apply to a trust for the "benefit" of employees of a company and their widows and children which was intended as a hardship fund, although no charitable purpose was expressly stated.[420] On the other hand, a trust for division among institutions and associations, some of which were not charitable, was not validated[421]; nor was a trust providing various benefits for employees which was not intended as a hardship fund, because it was essentially a private discretionary trust and contained no indication of an

---

[412] Jenkins J. later decided that they were charitable; above, para.15–056.

[413] The date of publication of the Committee on the Law and Practice relating to Charitable Trusts (1952) Cmnd. 8710 (the Nathan Report).

[414] s.1(2); *Re Chitty's WT* [1970] Ch. 254. The Act does not apply to assets already distributed; s.2.

[415] *Chichester Diocesan Fund and Board of Finance v Simpson* [1944] A.C. 341; above, para.15–058.

[416] *Re Mead's Trust Deed* [1961] 1 W.L.R. 1244; *Re South Place Ethical Society* [1980] 1 W.L.R. 1565 ("purposes either religious or civil"). The trust in *Williams Trustees v IRC* [1947] A.C. 447, para.15–036, above, was eventually saved by the Act; Annual Report 1977, paras 71–80.

[417] *Re Gillingham Bus Disaster Fund* [1959] Ch. 62; *Re Wykes* [1961] Ch. 229; *Re Mead's Trust Deed* (fn.416).

[418] [1959] Ch. 62 at 80.

[419] fn.417. Apart from the 1954 Act, such a trust fails: *Re Atkinson's WT* [1978] 1 W.L.R. 586.

[420] *Ulrich v Treasury Solicitor* [2006] 1 W.L.R. 33, where a fund worth £3,000 in 1927 was now worth £600,000. See also *Cawdron v Merchant Taylors' School* [2010] W.T.L.R. 775.

[421] *Re Harpur's WT* [1962] Ch. 78.

intention to benefit the public.[422] The principle seems to be that where there is a clear flavour of charity present, "a quasi-charitable trust" as Cross J. has put it,[423] the donor of such a gift would not feel that his intentions were being distorted by the whole of his gift being made available to charity. Or, to put it another way, the test is whether anyone could have complained if the whole fund had been applied to charity from the start.[424] It would thus cover "worthy causes," but not a case involving the mere possibility of charitable benefit.[425] It has recently been said that the Act contains "beneficial and salutary provisions, despite the denigration of the legislation, soon after the passage of the Act, by an earlier generation of Chancery judges".[426]

Commonwealth legislation[427] goes much further, and gives the courts a "blue pencil" power. Where non-charitable purposes are, or are deemed to be, within the ambit of a trust obviously intended to be charitable,[428] the trust is carried out as if the non-charitable elements were not present.

D. Disaster Appeals

Problems can arise when public appeals for donations are made **15–062** after some accident or disaster, if insufficient thought has been given to the question whether the fund is to be charitable or not. Such was the case with the loss of Penlee Lifeboat in Cornwall in 1982, when over £2 million was donated by the public to the dependants of the lost crew, numbering eight families. If charitable, the fund would attract tax relief but, contrary to the expectations of some donors, it could not be simply divided amongst the families, as charitable funds, being essentially public in nature, cannot be used to give benefits to individuals exceeding those appropriate to their needs. Any surplus would, under the cy-près doctrine, be applied to related charities.[429] If, on the other hand, the fund was not charitable, it would not attract tax relief, but could be distributed entirely among the dependants if, upon construing the terms of the appeal, that was the intention of the donors. If that was not their intention, the surplus

---

[422] *Re Saxone Shoe Co Ltd's Trust Deed* [1962] 1 W.L.R. 943.

[423] [1962] 1 W.L.R. 943 at 957–958.

[424] *Ulrich v Treasury Solicitor*, fn.420.

[425] cf. *Re Mead's Trust Deed*, above, fn.416, which goes rather far in restricting a trust to "poor" members of a union. The decision was doubted in *Ulrich v Treasury Solicitor*, above, fn.420.

[426] *Cuppage v Lawson* [2011] W.T.L.R. 975 (Act applied to trusts for working men's club and for welfare of the working population of East Grinstead).

[427] (New South Wales) Conveyancing Act 1919–1969; s.37D; (New Zealand) Charitable Trusts Act 1957 s.61B; (Victoria) Property Law Act 1958 s.131; (Western Australia) Trustees Act 1962 s.102. See also Charities Act (Northern Ireland) 1964 s.24.

[428] *Leahy v Att Gen for New South Wales* [1959] A.C. 457.

[429] Below, para.15–063.

would not be applicable cy-près, but would result to the subscribers or perhaps devolve upon the Crown as bona vacantia.[430] Similar problems can arise if the appeal is on behalf of one specific person, such as a sick child. In the Penlee case[431] it was decided, after negotiations with the Attorney General and the Charity Commissioners, to forgo tax relief and to treat the fund as private, so that the money could be divided among the families.[432]

The terms of the appeal are all-important in determining the status of the fund, and the consequences flowing from that status. The Attorney General has issued guidelines for consideration by persons planning to launch a public appeal of this sort.[433] It appears that non-charitable status has most often been chosen.[434]

6. CY-PRÈS

A. The Cy-Près Doctrine Prior to 1960

15–063 Where property is given for charitable purposes and the purposes cannot be carried out in the precise manner intended by the donor, the question is whether the trust should fail, or whether the property should be applied for other charitable purposes. The cy-près doctrine, where it applies, enables the court (or the Commission) to make a scheme for the application of the property for other charitable purposes as near as possible to those intended by the donor, and thus to increase the resources available to the charity sector.[435] This is judicial cy-près. If a gift is to charity but not upon trust, it is disposed of by the Crown under prerogative cy-près.[436] The distinction is not however always observed.

---

[430] *Re Gillingham Bus Disaster Fund* [1959] Ch. 62; *Re West Sussex Constabulary's Widows, Children and Benevolent* (1930) *Fund Trust* [1971] Ch. 1; above, para.10–013.

[431] Which was not litigated. See Annual Report 1981, paras 4–8; H Picarda (1982) 132 N.L.J. 223.

[432] The Charity Commissioners stated that the fund was not charitable; Annual Report 1981 para.6. If it had been charitable, as being for the relief of victims of a disaster (*Re North Devon and West Somerset Relief Fund Trusts* [1953] 1 W.L.R. 1260), presumably it would not be possible to forgo that status.

[433] See Annual Report 1981, App.A. The guidelines were updated in 2002. See also Annual Report 1982 paras 31–35 (South Atlantic Fund); Annual Report 1985 para.19 (Bradford City Disaster Charitable Trust); Annual Report 1988 para.25 (Armenian earthquake and Philippines Ferry); Annual Report 1989 paras 36, 37 (Clapham Junction and Hillsborough); Annual Report 2001/02 p.8 (World Trade Centre Disaster Fund).

[434] Annual Report 1988 para.25; 1989 para.36. See I. McLean and M. Johnes (1999) 19 L.S. 380.

[435] See J. Garton (2007) 21 T.L.I. 134.

[436] Above, para.15–003 (sign manual). But even if there is no trust, the court has jurisdiction if there is an analogous legally binding restriction; *Liverpool and District Hospital for Diseases of the Heart v Att Gen* [1981] Ch. 193 (charitable corporation); J. Warburton [1984] Conv. 112.

The cy-près jurisdiction was very narrow until the reforms of the Charities Act 1960, and was available only where it was "impossible" or "impracticable" to carry out the purposes of the trust.[437] Thus, trusts for the distribution of loaves of bread to the poor or of stockings for poor maidservants continued until modern times. Their performance was cumbersome, uneconomical, inconvenient, but not impossible nor impracticable. But it had at least, by the turn of the 19th century, become impracticable to apply money for the advancement and propagation of the Christian religion among the infidels of Virginia,[438] or for "the redemption of British slaves in Turkey or Barbary."[439] *Re Dominion Students' Hall Trust*[440] showed the furthest development of the doctrine by the courts.

One of the objects of a charity was to promote community of citizenship, culture and tradition among all members of the British Community of Nations; and it maintained a hostel for students in Bloomsbury. But the benefits of the charity were restricted to students of European origin. The cy-près power was used to remove the "colour bar". It could not be said that it was "absolutely impracticable" to carry on the charity in its present state; but, by 1947:

"[T]o retain the condition, so far from furthering the charity's main object, might defeat it and would be liable to antagonize those students, both white and coloured, whose support and goodwill it is the purpose of the charity to sustain. The case, therefore, can be said to fall within the broad description of impossibility . . . "[441]

More recently, in *Re J W Laing Trust*,[442] concerning a settlement of shares worth £15,000 in 1922, the question was whether the court could delete a term imposed by the settlor that the capital and income should be distributed no later than 10 years after his death. The investment was now worth £24 million. The trust was for Christian evangelical causes, and the individuals and bodies who would be the recipients were unsuited to receive large capital sums. The

[437] See *Re Weir Hospital* [1910] 2 Ch. 124.

[438] *Att Gen v City of London* (1790) 3 Bro.C.C. 121. Annual Report (1971) paras 65–69; see also *Re Robinson* [1921] 2 Ch. 332. (The wearing of a black gown by the preacher was impracticable because it was likely to offend the congregation and defeat the main object.).

[439] *Ironmongers' Co v Att Gen* (1844) 10 Cl. & F. 908.

[440] [1947] Ch. 183; see Equality Act 2010 s.193 (replacing earlier legislation); above, para.13–004; *Canada Trust Company v Ontario Human Rights Commission* (1990) 69 D.L.R. (4th) 321.

[441] [1947] Ch. 183 at 186, per Evershed J.

[442] [1984] Ch. 143; J. Warburton [1984] Conv. 319; P. Luxton [1985] Conv. 313. Section 13 of the Charities Act 1960 (now the Act of 2011) did not apply; below, para.15–074.

deletion of this term was approved under the court's inherent jurisdiction, as it had become inexpedient in the very altered circumstances of the charity.

It is convenient also at this stage to note that a distinction is made
between the initial failure of a charitable trust, and a failure after the
time when the trust has been in operation. Application cy-près is
much easier in the latter case; for, after application to charity, there
is no resulting trust for the donor.[443] If the donor wants the property
to pass to a third party, or to return to himself or his estate, he must
expressly so provide by a gift over to take effect within the perpetuity period.[444] In the case of initial failure, the gift will lapse unless
there is, on the proper construction of the instrument, a paramount
intention to benefit charity. These situations will now be examined.

B. Initial Failure. Paramount Charitable Intent

15–064   **i. Width of Charitable Intent.** Where a charitable trust fails as
being ineffective at the date of the gift, the gift will either lapse and
fall into residue, or the property will be applied cy-près. The decision depends on the width of charitable intent shown by the donor. If
the intention was that the property should be applied for a specified
purpose, which cannot be carried out, or for one specific charitable
institution which no longer exists, the gift will lapse. But if the court
finds a wider intent, a paramount or general charitable intention, the
property may be applied cy-près.

> In *Re Rymer*,[445] there was a legacy of £5,000 "to the rector for
> the time being of St Thomas's Seminary for the education of
> priests for the diocese of Westminster." At the time of the testa-
> tor's death, the Seminary had ceased to exist, and the students had
> been transferred to another Seminary in Birmingham. The Court
> of Appeal held that the gift failed. It was a gift "to a particular
> seminary for the purposes thereof." There was no wider intent.

This may be contrasted with *Re Lysaght*,[446] where the testatrix
gave funds to the Royal College of Surgeons to found medical
studentships. The gift was subject to restrictions, in that the students
were to be male, the sons of qualified British-born medical men,
themselves British-born, and not of the Jewish or Roman Catholic

---

[443] *Re Wright* [1954] Ch. 347 at 362–363. But see P. Luxton [1983] Conv. 107.
[444] Below, para.15–072.
[445] [1895] 1 Ch. 19; *Re Spence* [1979] Ch. 483; *Kings v Bultitude* [2010] W.T.L.R. 1571; J.
Picton [2011] Conv. 69.
[446] [1966] Ch. 191. See particularly at 201–202.

faith. The Royal College of Surgeons declined to accept the gift on these terms. As it was held that the particular trustee was essential to the gift, the refusal of the College would cause the gift to fail. Buckley J. held that there was a paramount charitable intention. The particularity of the testatrix's directions was not fatal to such a construction, as the directions were not an essential part of her true intention. A scheme was ordered whereby the money was payable to the College on the trusts of the will, but omitting the religious disqualification.

This liberal approach was followed in *Re Woodhams (Deceased)*,[447] where the testator left money to two music colleges to found annual scholarships for:

> "[T]he complete musical education of a promising boy who is an absolute orphan and only of British Nationality and Birth from any one of Dr. Barnardo's Homes or the Church of England Children's Society Homes."

The two colleges declined the gifts because it would be impractical to restrict the scholarships as required by the testator, but were prepared to accept them if available for boys of British nationality and birth generally. The gift failed for impracticability, but a paramount charitable intention to further musical education was found. The restriction to orphans from the named homes was not essential to the testator's purpose. Thus the gift was applicable cy-près under a scheme whereby the restriction was deleted.

ii. Has the Gift Failed? Continuation in Another Form. A gift **15–065** to a defunct charity may be regarded as not having failed at all, on the basis that it is continuing in another form. It may have been amalgamated with a similar charity by scheme, or have been reconstituted under more effective trusts. In such a case the gift may take effect in favour of the body now administering the assets of the old charity.[448] Or the court may construe the gift as being for the purposes of the named charity, so that the nomination of a defunct charity does not cause the gift to fail. Provided the purposes still exist the gift takes effect in favour of a body furthering those purposes. It will be appreciated that the significance of holding that such a gift has not failed is that it is not necessary to find a general charitable intention. A scheme will be ordered to give effect to the gift, but it will not be a cy-près scheme.

---

[447] [1981] 1 W.L.R. 493.
[448] A gift to a charity which has merged with another will usually be effective under what is now Charities Act 2011 s.311.

15–066   (a) *Gift in Augmentation of Funds of Defunct Charity.*

In *Re Faraker*,[449] there was a gift to "Mrs Bayley's Charity, Rotherhithe". A charity had been founded by a Mrs Hannah Bayly in 1756 for the benefit of poor widows in Rotherhithe. This, with a number of other local charities, had been consolidated under a scheme by the Charity Commissioners in 1905, and the funds were held in various trusts for the benefit of the poor in Rotherhithe. The Court of Appeal held that the Bayly trusts had not been destroyed by the scheme, and that the consolidated charities were entitled to the legacy. The gift had not failed, because a perpetual charity cannot die.[450]

15–067   (b) *Gifts for Purposes. Unincorporated Associations and Charitable Corporations.* In considering whether a gift is effectively for the purposes of the named institution, a distinction is drawn between gifts to unincorporated societies and to corporations.

"Every bequest to an unincorporated charity by name without more must take effect as a gift for a charitable purpose ... a bequest which is in terms made for a charitable purpose will not fail for lack of a trustee but will be carried into effect either under the Sign Manual or by means of a scheme"[451];

unless the testator's intention was to the contrary. On the other hand:

"[A] bequest to a corporate body ... takes effect simply as a gift to that body beneficially, unless there are circumstances which show that the recipient is to take the gift as a trustee. There is no need in such a case to infer a trust for any particular purpose."[452]

---

[449] [1912] 2 Ch. 488; *Re Lucas* [1948] Ch. 424; *Re Broadbent* [2001] W.T.L.R. 967; cf. *Re Slatter's WT* [1964] Ch. 512; J. Farrand (1964) 28 Conv.(N.S.) 313.

[450] Distinguished in *Re Stemson's WT* [1970] Ch. 16 (involving a terminable corporate charity), and *Re Roberts* [1963] 1 W.L.R. 406, below.

[451] per Buckley J. in *Re Vernon's WT* [1972] Ch. 300n; *Re Finger's WT* [1972] Ch. 286; R. Cotterell (1972) 36 Conv.(N.S.) 198; J. Martin (1974) 38 Conv.(N.S.) 187. See also *Liverpool and District Hospital for Diseases of the Heart v Att Gen* [1982] Ch. 193 (charitable corporation does not hold as trustee, but court has cy-près jurisdiction on winding-up). See Charities Act 2011 ss.197, 198, for the position where a charitable corporation ceases to be charitable or otherwise alters its objects.

[452] *Re Vernon's WT* [1972] Ch. 300n. See J. Warburton [1984] Conv. 112 and [1990] Conv. 95. See also *Re ARMS (Multiple Sclerosis Research) Ltd* [1997] 1 W.L.R. 877 (no failure where incorporated charity existed at testator's death although insolvent, thus legacy available to its creditors).

Thus a gift to a defunct charitable corporation lapses and fails,[453] and cy-près application is possible only if there was a general charitable intention. In *Re Finger's Will Trusts*,[454] there was a gift to the National Radium Commission (unincorporated) and to the National Council for Maternity and Child Welfare (incorporated). Both had ceased to exist by the testatrix's death. The gift to the unincorporated charity was construed as a gift to charitable purposes. As those purposes still existed there was no failure, as a trust does not fail for lack of a trustee. A scheme was ordered to settle the destination of the gift, but this was not a cy-près scheme and no general charitable intention was necessary.[455] In the case of the incorporated charity, on the other hand, it was a gift to a legal person which had ceased to exist, and was not a purpose trust. The gift therefore failed, but was saved from lapse by the finding of a general charitable intention, and was accordingly applied cy-près.

This is a technical distinction which might not be appreciated by the testator, but it has a certain logic. One difficulty which remains is that the same facts may allow either the *Re Faraker* construction or that adopted in *Re Finger's Will Trusts* in the case of the unincorporated charity, although the results are different. While both constructions avoid the finding of a failure and the need for a general charitable intention, the result of the *Re Faraker* construction is that the gift goes to the body now administering the funds of the defunct charity, even if its purposes are different. In *Re Faraker*[456] itself, the defunct charity was specifically for widows, while the new consolidated charity was for the poor generally, so that it "was not bound to give one penny to a widow,"[457] thus defeating the testator's intention to some extent. The result in *Re Finger's Will Trusts*[458] is that the gift is devoted, by means of a scheme, to the testator's purpose. It may be that the court would decline to apply *Re Faraker* where the purposes of the new body were widely different. Thus in *Re Roberts*,[459] a gift was made to the Sheffield Boys' Working Home, which had wound up and transferred most of its assets to the Sheffield Town Trust. The claim of the latter body was rejected as an undesirable extension of the *Re Faraker* principle, as it purposes were different. The money was applied, by means of an ordinary

---

[453] Unless the testator has indicated that the corporation was to take as trustee for its purposes.

[454] [1972] Ch. 286; applied by the Court of Appeal in *Re Koeppler's WT* [1986] Ch. 423. If the purposes had ceased to exist, the gift to the unincorporated charity would fail, but could be applied cy-près if there was a general charitable intention.

[455] It would be otherwise if the donor intended the particular institution and no other, as in *Re Rymer* [1895] 1 Ch. 19.

[456] [1912] 2 Ch. 488.

[457] [1912] 2 Ch. 488 at 496.

[458] [1972] Ch. 286.

[459] [1963] 1 W.L.R. 406. See J. Martin (1974) 38 Conv.(N.S.) 187.

scheme, to the purposes to which the defunct Home had been dedicated.

Both constructions, however, were rejected in *Re Spence*,[460] where money was left to a specified Old Folks Home "for the benefit of the patients." The home was no longer in use at the testatrix's death. Megarry V.C. held that the gift failed and could not be applied cy-près. It was not a general gift to the old people of the district. Following *Re Harwood*,[461] it was said that if a particular institution is correctly identified, then it is that institution and no other which is intended:

> "It is difficult to envisage a testator as being suffused with a general glow of broad charity when he is labouring, and labouring successfully, to identify some particular specified institution or purpose as the object of his bounty."[462]

This, with respect, is a very narrow view of the cy-près doctrine. A testator should always be careful to identify his beneficiary correctly. It is difficult to see why this should automatically negative a general charitable intention.

15–068   **iii. Projects.** The cases so far discussed have dealt with gifts to institutions, corporate or unincorporated. The same rules apply in principle also to cases where there is a gift for a purpose or project such as, for example, the payment of a schoolmaster at a school to be built,[463] or the establishment of a soup kitchen and cottage hospital.[464] In such cases, the question is whether the project is on the balance of probabilities capable or incapable of being implemented. If it is incapable, then, in the absence of wider intent, the gift will fail and will fall into residue. There is no "wait and see" provision.[465]

15–069   **iv. Non-existent Charity.** In *Re Harwood*,[466] it was said that, where there was a gift for a non-existent charity, it was easier to find a general charitable intent in a case where the institution had never existed than it was in the case where an identifiable institution had ceased to exist.

In that case, a testatrix, who died in 1934, left £200 to the Wisbech Peace Society and £300 to the Peace Society in Belfast.

---

[460] [1979] Ch. 483.
[461] [1936] Ch. 285, below. *Re Rymer* [1895] 1 Ch. 19 was also relied on.
[462] [1979] Ch. 483 at 493.
[463] *Re Wilson* [1913] 1 Ch. 314.
[464] *Biscoe v Jackson* (1887) 35 Ch.D. 460.
[465] *Re White's WT* [1955] Ch. 188; *Re Tacon* [1958] Ch. 447 at 453–455.
[466] [1936] Ch. 285; cf. *Re Goldschmidt* [1957] 1 W.L.R. 524, where a gift to a non-existent charity was not applied cy-près, but fell into residue, which was also given to charity.

The Wisbech Society had existed prior to 1934, but had ceased by that date to exist. There was no evidence that the Peace Society of Belfast had ever existed. The former failed, but in respect of the latter Farwell J. was able to find an intention to "benefit societies whose object was the promotion of peace",[467] and the £300 was applied cy-près.

Similarly, in *Re Satterthwaite's Will Trusts*,[468] where a testatrix, who hated the whole human race, left her residuary estate to a number of institutions concerned with animal welfare. Most of them were charitable, but a dispute arose over the share left to the London Animal Hospital. There was no charity of that name, but the claimant, a veterinary surgeon, carried on a practice under that trade name at a time prior to the date of the will and death. The Court of Appeal considered the gift as being to a non-existent charitable institution, and not to the claimant. A sufficiently wide charitable intent was discerned from the nature of the other shares (notwithstanding that one share was to a non-charity), and thus cy-près application was ordered.

v. A Group of Donees; Mostly Charitable. It may be that the testator has made a number of gifts, all of which are charitable except one. It can be argued that the intention clearly was to apply all the money for charitable purposes. On the other hand, "if you meet seven men with black hair and one with red hair, you are not entitled to say that here are eight men with black hair."[469] A gift for a non-charitable purpose is not made charitable by being included in a list of other gifts which are charitable. So held Buckley J. in *Re Jenkins' Will Trusts*[470] where a gift for the abolition of vivisection failed and could not be applied cy-près. This may be contrasted with *Re Satterthwaite's Will Trusts*,[471] where the gift in question was construed as charitable, and hence the cy-près doctrine could apply.

15–070

C. Subsequent Failure

Once assets are effectively dedicated to charity, there can be no question of a lapse or a resulting trust save where the gift effectively provides for it. Width of charitable intent is irrelevant. All that is necessary is that the property has been given "out and out" to

15–071

---

[467] [1936] Ch. 285 at 288. But the decision was doubted by the High Court in *Re Koeppler's Will Trusts* [1984] Ch. 243, on the basis that the purpose was political and not charitable. It was not cited in the Court of Appeal [1986] Ch. 423.

[468] [1966] 1 W.L.R. 277.

[469] per Buckley J. in *Re Jenkins' WT* [1966] Ch. 249.

[470] Above, fn.469.

[471] Above, fn.468.

charity, in the sense that the donor did not envisage its return in any circumstances.

In *Re Wright*,[472] a testatrix who died in 1933 provided for the foundation, on the death of a tenant for life, of a convalescent home for impecunious gentlewomen. The scheme was practicable in 1933, but not in 1942 when the tenant for life died. The Court of Appeal held that 1933 was the crucial date; at that date the scheme was practicable, dedication to charity occurred, and the possibility of a lapse or resulting trust was excluded. Cy-près was available in 1942 irrespective of width of charitable intent.

This rule is now firmly established,[473] but it was not always so, and it is not possible to reconcile some earlier cases on the subject, in particular the "surplus" cases.

In *Re King*,[474] £1,500 was bequeathed for one stained-glass window in a church. The cost of the window could not exceed £800. Romer J. held that the whole of £1,500 had been dedicated to charity with the necessary consequences that any surplus would be applied cy-près (in fact for a second window) irrespective of width of intent.

But in *Re Stanford*,[475] where £5,000 was bequeathed for the purpose of completing and publishing an etymological dictionary and over £1,500 remained unspent when the task was complete, Eve J. held that the surplus fell into residue.

Such a result is only justifiable if the surplus can be regarded as a case of initial impossibility pro tanto.[476] Similar confusion can be seen in the cases where the surplus has arisen in the circumstances of a public appeal. In *Re Welsh Hospital (Netley) Fund*[477] and *Re North Devon and West Somerset Relief Fund Trusts*[478] money was collected for purposes which were fulfilled, leaving surplus. The surplus was held applicable cy-près on the basis that there was a general charitable intention. If these cases are to be regarded as involving subsequent failure, it is difficult to see why such an intention is necessary. All that is required is an "out and out" gift to

---

[472] [1954] Ch. 347; *Re Slevin* [1891] 2 Ch. 236, where an orphanage was in existence at the testator's death, but came to an end before the money was paid over. Cy-près application was ordered; *Re Moon's WT* [1948] 1 All E.R. 300.

[473] *Re Tacon* [1958] Ch. 447, a case of a contingent gift; cf. *Re J W Laing Trust* [1984] Ch. 143, J. Warburton [1984] Conv. 319.

[474] [1923] 1 Ch. 243.

[475] [1924] 1 Ch. 73.

[476] See *Tudor on Charities*, 9th edn, p.480 (preferring view that subsequent impossibility).

[477] [1921] 1 Ch. 655; cf. *Re British Red Cross Balkan Fund* [1914] 2 Ch. 419.

[478] [1953] 1 W.L.R. 1260.

charity. Thus in *Re Wokingham Fire Brigade Trusts*[479] a surplus was applicable cy-près without the need to discover a general charitable intention. It is submitted that this approach, which was approved obiter by the Court of Appeal in *Re Ulverston and District New Hospital Building Trusts*[480] (involving initial failure as insufficient funds were collected) is to be preferred.

D. Termination in Favour of Non-charity

It was seen that a donor could, if he wished, make express provi- **15–072** sion for a gift over to a third party or to himself or to his estate upon the failure of a charitable gift within the period of perpetuity.[481] Before the Perpetuities and Accumulations Act 1964, a resulting trust after a determinable interest was immune from the perpetuity rule, although any express gift over was subject to it. Thus a determinable charitable gift could terminate at a remote time and result to the settlor. It could not be applied cy-près because, although a subsequent failure, there was no "out and out" gift to charity.[482] However, in the case of a charitable gift subject to a condition subsequent, the gift took effect as absolute if the gift over was void for perpetuity. The cy-près doctrine would then apply in the usual way on any subsequent failure, to the exclusion of a resulting trust.[483]

Under s.12 of the 1964 Act, the perpetuity rule became applicable to resulting trusts, but the Act also introduced the "wait and see" rule.[484] Similar provisions apply under the Perpetuities and Accumulations Act 2009.[485] Thus in the case of a determinable charitable gift, a gift over or resulting trust will operate to the exclusion of the cy-près doctrine if the determining event occurs within the perpetuity period. If it does not, the gift becomes absolute, so that cy-près will apply on any subsequent failure. Likewise if the charitable gift is subject to a condition subsequent. On breach of condition within the perpetuity period, the gift over (or resulting trust in default) will take effect. If, however, the condition is not broken within that period, the charitable gift becomes absolute. Thus the cy-près doctrine is available because, whatever the donor's intention, the gift is by statute an "out and out" gift to charity.

---

[479] [1951] Ch. 373.

[480] [1956] Ch. 622. The case illustrates the difficulties since resolved by provisions now found in Charities Act 2011 s.63, below, para.15–076. S.63 does not apply to the surplus cases unless it becomes established that a general charitable intention is necessary, contrary to the view expressed in the text.

[481] Above, para.15–063.

[482] *Re Randell* (1888) 39 Ch.D. 213.

[483] *Re Peel's Release* [1921] 2 Ch. 218; *Bath and Wells Diocesan Board of Finance v Jenkinson* [2001] W.T.L.R. 353.

[484] s.3(1).

[485] ss.1(4), 7, 10.

E. The Widening of Cy-Près Jurisdiction. Charities Act 2011 Section 62

15–073   **i. General.** As part of the policy of modernising charitable trusts, the Charities Act 1960 introduced far-reaching reforms (now found in the Charities Act 2011) in the application of the cy-près doctrine. Before examining these reforms it must be emphasised that it is the trustees' duty, where some or all of the property may be applied cy-près, to take steps to have the property so applied.[486] This situation will arise where there is an existing trust for outdated objects; for purposes which were once useful, but are now unnecessary, or overtaken by statutory services; or where the income of the trust has during the years become inadequate for the purpose, or, perhaps so large that there is a surplus. In short, the policy is to enable the trustees, with the help of the Charity Commission, to make the best use, in modern conditions, of funds dedicated to charity.

15–074   **ii. Section 62.**[487] Section 62 provides for application cy-près in five situations:

(1) Subject to subsection (3), the circumstances in which the original purposes of a charitable gift can be altered to allow the property given or part of it to be applied cy-près are—

(a) where the original purposes, in whole or in part,—

(i) have been as far as may be fulfilled, or
(ii) cannot be carried out, or not according to the directions given and to the spirit of the gift,

(b) where the original purposes provide a use for part only of the property available by virtue of the gift,
(c) where—

(i) the property available by virtue of the gift, and
(ii) other property applicable for similar purposes, can be more effectively used in conjunction, and to that end can suitably, regard being had to the appropriate considerations, be made applicable to common purposes,

(d) where the original purposes were laid down by reference to—

(i) an area which then was but has since ceased to be a unit for some other purpose, or

---

[486] Charities Act 2011 s.61.
[487] Re-enacting previous legislation.

> (ii) a class of persons or an area which has for any reason since ceased to be suitable, regard being had to the appropriate considerations, or to be practical in administering the gift, or

(e) where the original purposes, in whole or in part, have, since they were laid down—

> (i) been adequately provided by other means,
> (ii) ceased, as being useless or harmful to the community or for other reasons, to be in law charitable, or
> (iii) ceased in any other way to provide a suitable and effective method of using the property available by virtue of the gift, regard being had to the appropriate considerations.

(2) In subsection (1) "the appropriate considerations" means—

(a) (on the one hand) the spirit of the gift concerned, and
(b) (on the other) the social and economic circumstances prevailing at the time of the proposed alteration of the original purposes.

(3) Subsection (1) does not affect the conditions which must be satisfied in order that property given for charitable purposes may be applied cy-près, except in so far as those conditions require a failure of the original purposes.

In the case of subsequent failure, width of charitable intent is of no significance, but the Commission endeavours to follow the spirit of the original gift, so far as this is consistent with proper application of the funds. Before the Charities Act 2006 the legislation provided that regard must be had to the spirit of the gift. The Act of 2006 added that that regard must also be had to the social and economic circumstances prevailing at the time of the proposed alteration. The case law illustrations below predate the Act of 2006, but it appears that they would be decided the same way now. Nothing in the legislation requires a cy-près scheme where such a scheme was not required before the 1960 Act.[488]

Many schemes have been made under this jurisdiction.[489] The first occasion on which the original provision was litigated was *Re Lepton's Charity*.[490] **15–075**

A will dating from 1715 instructed trustees to pay £3 per annum to the Minister, and the "overplus of the profits" to the poor.

---

[488] *Oldham BC v Att Gen* [1993] Ch. 210.
[489] Annual Report 1970 para.43.
[490] [1972] Ch. 276.

At that time, the income was £5 per annum, and in 1970 the income from the proceeds of sale of the land was nearly £800. Pennycuick V.C. raised the payment to £100 per annum. This was consistent with the spirit of the gift. Subsection (1)(a) applied because "the original purposes" covered the purposes as a whole; it was not necessary to consider separately the gift of the annuity and that of the surplus. In any case (1)(e)(iii) would have applied.

In *Re J W Laing Trust*,[491] the question which arose was whether what is now s.62 could be utilised in order to dispense with the donor's requirement that the capital and income be distributed no later than 10 years after his death. It was held that the provision could not be deleted under subsection (1), as the "original purposes"[492] which the court could there review meant the objects of the trust, whereas the settlor's direction was merely administrative. The provision was, however, deleted under the court's inherent jurisdiction. In *Peggs v Lamb*[493] a trust was created in the Middle Ages for the freemen of Huntingdon and their widows. It was charitable on the basis of the anomalous "locality" cases.[494] In the past the freemen were a substantial section of the public and a suitable class of charitable objects. At present there were only 15 members, and they claimed equal division of the annual income, irrespective of need, which would give them over £30,000 each. A cy-près scheme was ordered to enable the money to be distributed amongst the inhabitants of the borough as a whole, in accordance with the spirit of the gift. The case fell within what is now s.62(1)(d), on the basis that the class had ceased to be suitable recipients of charitable funds. It was not necessary to decide whether what is now s.62(1)(e)(ii) also applied, on the basis that they were no longer a section of the public. What is now s.62(1)(e)(iii) was satisfied in *Varsani v Jesani*,[495] where a Hindu sect split into two groups. The groups could not resolve their differences, as each thought that it alone professed the faith. To give the sect's assets to one group would have been contrary to the spirit of the gift, which was the desire to provide facilities for followers of the sect. The solution was to divide the assets between the two groups.

Subsection (1)(e)(ii) will apply to the endowments of any bodies which were once charitable but lose that status as a result of the stricter "public benefit" requirement of the Charities Acts 2006 and

---

[491] [1984] Ch. 143. The facts were given at para.15–063, above.

[492] See further *Oldham BC v Att Gen* [1993] Ch. 210.

[493] [1994] Ch. 172.

[494] Above, para.15–035.

[495] [1999] Ch. 219. See also *White v Williams* [2010] W.T.L.R. 1083 (schism in Bibleway Church UK).

2011.[496] Perhaps also the section would, if then available, have applied to anti-vivisection trusts, for these had been held charitable in *Re Foveaux*,[497] but non-charitable in *National Anti-Vivisection Society v IRC*[498] in 1948. The same would seem to apply to charities which have been removed from the Register on the ground that they have ceased to be charitable.

iii. Section 63.[499] Charity Collections. Finally, it is necessary to refer to s.63. This provides that property given for specific charitable purposes which fail is applicable cy-près as if given for charitable purposes generally, where it belongs—   **15–076**

    (a) to a donor who after—

        (i) the prescribed[500] advertisements and inquiries have been published and made, and

        (ii) the prescribed period beginning with the publication of those advertisements has ended,[501]

    cannot be identified or cannot be found,[502] or

    (b) to a donor who has executed a disclaimer in the prescribed form of the right to have the property returned.

In the case of the proceeds of cash collections by means of collecting boxes or other means not adapted for distinguishing one gift from another, or the proceeds of lotteries and similar money-raising activities, the property is conclusively presumed to belong to unidentifiable donors, without any advertisement or inquiry. In other cases the court or the Commission may direct the property to be treated as belonging to unidentifiable donors, without any advertisement or inquiry, if it appears that it would not be reasonable, having regard to the amounts or the lapse of time since the gifts, to return it.[503]

Section 63 applies only to cases of initial failure. Section 66 provides that charitable purposes are deemed to fail, for the purposes of the section, where any difficulty in applying the property to

---

[496] Above, para.15–040.

[497] [1895] 2 Ch. 501.

[498] [1948] A.C. 31. Lord Simonds suggested at 64–65 that application cy-près would have been possible before the 1960 Act.

[499] Re-enacting previous legislation.

[500] The Charities (Cy-près Advertisements, Inquiries and Disclaimer) Regulations 1993.

[501] The trustees are not liable to any person in respect of the property if no claim is received before expiry of this period; s.63(2).

[502] Such donors may claim from the cy-près recipient within six months of the scheme; s.63(5). For an example of the operation of these provisions see *Re Henry Wood Memorial Trust* [1966] 1 W.L.R. 1601 (failure of Mile End Memorial Hall Fund through lack of financial support); Annual Report 1965 paras 19–21.

[503] Charities Act 2011 s.64.

those purposes makes it available for return to the donors.[504] In the case of subsequent failure, the property is not so available.

This solution is much more sensible than any attempt to solve the problem by applying the usual cy-près doctrine, involving either the imputation of an artificial general charitable intent, or, failing that, a search for the many donors of tiny gifts, with the possibility of a claim by the Crown to the property as bona vacantia.

Section 65 assists further by providing that a solicitation for char-itable gifts (such as an appeal) may include a statement to the effect that unless, at the time of the gift, the donor makes a declaration giving him the opportunity to reclaim his gift if the charitable pur-pose should fail, it will be applied cy-près. Where the donor makes such a declaration and the purpose does fail, the section sets out a process to be followed to return the donation or to apply it cy-près if the donor cannot be traced.

F. The Cy-Près Scheme

15–077   Section 67 of the Charities Act 2011[505] sets out how the power of the court or the Commission to make a cy-près scheme is to be exercised. The court or the Commission must have regard to three matters: (a) the spirit of the original gift; (b) the desirability of securing that the property is applied for charitable purposes which are close to the original purposes; and (c) the need for the charity which will apply the property under the scheme to have purposes which are suitable and effective in the light of current social and economic circumstances. If the scheme provides for the property to be transferred to another charity, the scheme may require the trus-tees of that charity to ensure that the property is applied for purposes which are, so far as is reasonably practicable, similar in character to the original purposes.

The section applies to cy-près schemes generally, whether or not involving charity collections.

G. Small Charities; Spending Capital; Mergers

15–078   The Charities Act 1985 introduced a principle enabling trustees of certain small charities in effect to determine their own cy-près appli-cation with the concurrence of the Charity Commissioners. The

---

[504] See D. Wilson [1983] Conv. 40, arguing that this is never the case where the gift is anonymous and indistinguishable, because the property either goes cy-près by the imputation of a general charitable intent (see *Re Hillier* [1954] 1 W.L.R. 700) or to the Crown as bona vacantia.

[505] Re-enacting previous legislation.

response from trustees was disappointing,[506] and so the Act was repealed and replaced by provisions now found in the Charities Act 2011.

Under s.267[507] of the 2011 Act, trustees of an unincorporated charity may resolve (if at least two-thirds of them agree) to pass all of its property to another charity if its gross income in the last financial year did not exceed £10,000 and it does not hold any land on trusts which stipulate that it is to be used for the purposes of the charity. The trustees must be satisfied that this would further the purposes of their charity and that the purposes of the charity receiving the property are substantially similar. There are various safeguards, including a duty to notify the Commission, which may direct the trustees to give a public notice, so that representations may be made.

Alternatively, the trustees of an unincorporated charity may resolve (if at least two-thirds of them agree) to replace the purposes of the charity. This may be done under s.275[508] of the 2011 Act, which sets out the same conditions as mentioned above in relation to annual income and land. The trusts may be modified by replacing all or any of the purposes of the charity with other charitable purposes, provided the trustees are satisfied that it is expedient in the interests of the charity to do so and that the new purposes are similar in character so far as is reasonably possible. Similar safeguards apply as in the case of transfer of property mentioned above.

Sections 281 to 314 of the 2011 Act[509] make further provision for the optimum use of charity funds by permitting the expenditure of capital (which would not otherwise be allowed) and facilitating the merger of charities. Broadly, trustees of an unincorporated charity may resolve that all or part of the permanent endowment may be spent if this would enable the purposes of the charity to be carried out more effectively than if only the income could be spent.[510] Where the capital was given by a particular individual or institution and the endowment fund exceeds £10,000 and the income in the last financial year exceeded £1,000, the Commission must be notified of the trustees' resolution and concur with it.[511]

Provision is made for the merger of two or more charities in circumstances where, for example, one charity transfers its property

---

[506] For statistics, see Annual Report 1986 para.14; 1987, para.49; 1988, para.95; 1989 para.105; 1990, para.91; 1991 para.30.

[507] Some of the conditions are set out in s.268. See also s.271, dealing with objections to the resolution by the Commission. Section 273 modifies the provisions where the charity has a permanent endowment.

[508] See also s.280, which enables the trusts of an unincorporated charity to be modified in relation to administrative powers and procedures.

[509] Re-enacting previous legislation.

[510] s.281.

[511] s.282.

to another and ceases to exist, or where two charities transfer their property to a new charity and then cease to exist. The Commission must maintain a register of such mergers.[512]

7. THE ADMINISTRATION OF CHARITIES

A. Reform

15–079   Reform of the law of charities was long overdue when the Charities Act was passed in 1960. The major problems were: the narrow limits of the cy-près doctrine; the gap and the competition which existed between the established charities and the statutory services of the welfare state; the haphazard state of existing charities and the lack of information about them. The Charities Act 1960 contained reforms on these matters.

Reform has subsequently been directed towards increasing the supervision of charities by the Charity Commissioners (now the Commission) in order to minimise abuse and maladministration by charity trustees. To this end the powers of the Commissioners were increased by the Charities Act 1992, following the Woodfield Report.[513] The reforms were mainly directed to increasing the duty of trustees to prepare annual accounts, to disqualifying certain persons from trusteeship, to controlling fundraising and public charitable collections, and to providing effective means of enforcement. The provisions were formerly in the Charities Act 1993 and are now found in the Charities Act 2011.[514]

B. The Authorities

15–080   **i. The Charity Commission.** Prior to the Charities Act 2006 charities were overseen by the Charity Commissioners. One of the reforms of the Act of 2006 was to establish the Charity Commission for England and Wales as a corporate body, with statutory objectives, functions, powers and duties.[515] The aim of this reform was to improve accountability and transparency.

The objectives of the Commission are: (i) the public confidence objective, to increase public trust and confidence in charities, (ii) the public benefit objective, to promote awareness and understanding of the operation of the public benefit requirement of charities, (iii) the

[512] s.305. A gift to a charity which has ceased to exist under a merger will normally take effect as a gift to the charity which still exists; s.311.

[513] Efficiency Scrutiny of the Supervision of Charities, 1987; National Audit Office Report, House of Commons Paper 380, 1986–87; Annual Report 1987; J. Hill (1993) 7 T.L.I. 9.

[514] For the territorial limits of the legislation, see *Gaudiya Mission v Brahmachary* [1998] Ch. 341 (no jurisdiction over charity established in India, operating in India and London).

[515] Now Charities Act 2011 s.13.

compliance objective, to promote compliance by charity trustees with their legal obligations, (iv) the charitable resources objective, to promote the effective use of charitable resources, and (v) the accountability objective, to enhance the accountability of charities to donors, beneficiaries and the public.[516]

The general functions of the Commission include, in particular, to determine whether institutions are charities or not; to encourage and facilitate the better administration of charities; and to identify, investigate and deal with mismanagement of charities or misconduct.[517]

The Commission must also publish an Annual Report.[518] This was previously done by the Commissioners, whose reports gave an excellent picture of the administration of the law of charities, and of the problems of the day.

ii. The Official Custodian for Charities. The Commission is required to appoint an Official Custodian for Charities,[519] a corporation sole. The original object was that charity trustees could vest trust property in the custodian and thereby avoid "the necessity for periodical transfers of land and securities upon the appointment of new trustees",[520] and the necessity to reclaim income tax on investments, as dividends are remitted without deduction. The role of the Official Custodian has been reduced, in order to increase the responsibility of the trustees. The Official Custodian now rarely holds property other than land.[521] **15–081**

iii. The Visitor. Ecclesiastical[522] and eleemosynary[523] corporations are subject to the jurisdiction of the visitor in relation to their internal affairs. The visitor once had an important role to play in the universities, but the Education Reform Act 1988 abolished the visitor's jurisdiction in relation to the appointment, employment and dismissal of university staff, and most student complaints are now dealt with by the Office of the Independent Adjudicator for Higher **15–082**

---

[516] Charities Act 2011 s.14.

[517] Charities Act 2011 s.15. See also s.16 (general duties) and s.20 (incidental powers). The Commission may charge fees in some cases; s.19.

[518] Charities Act 2011 Sch.1, para.11.

[519] Charities Act 2011 s.21, re-enacting previous legislation. See Annual Report 1974 para.107. The Custodian has no management powers; *Muman v Nagasena* [2000] 1 W.L.R. 299.

[520] Annual Report 1970 para.75.

[521] For the provisions as to land, see Charities Act 2011 ss.90–95.

[522] Corporations existing for the furtherance of religion and the perpetuation of the rites of the Church.

[523] The original meaning was corporations whose object was the distribution of free alms, or the relief of individual distress; *Re Armitage's WT* [1972] Ch. 438. But for the purpose of visitatorial powers, corporate schools and most universities became included. Similarly the Inns of Court; see *R. v Visitors to the Inns of Court, Ex Calder* [1994] Q.B. 1.

Education.[524] Ecclesiastical corporations are visitable by the ordinary. In the case of eleemosynary corporations, the founder may appoint a visitor. If none is appointed, the founder (or his heirs) is the visitor by operation of law.[525] A similar principle applies where the Crown is the founder.

The visitor's jurisdiction stems from the power recognised by the common law in the founder of an eleemosynary corporation to provide the law under which it was to be governed and to be sole judge of the interpretation and application of those laws, either himself or via the person appointed as visitor.

C. The Register

15–083   Section 29[526] of the 2011 Act requires the Commission to maintain a public register on which all charities are to be included except for (a) exempt charities,[527] (b) any charity excepted by order or regulation and whose gross income does not exceed £100,000 a year, and (c) any charity whose gross income does not exceed £5,000. The purpose of the register, now computerised and on the internet, is to obtain information about charities. Those which are excepted are those which are national institutions (exempt charities), small ones, and others such as ecclesiastical charities and some armed forces charities where provision for obtaining the necessary information already exists.

D. Decisions on Registration

15–084   It is the duty of trustees of charities to register,[528] enforceable by order of the Commission.[529] Registration is much to the advantage of the trustees, for it raises a conclusive presumption of being a charity,[530] and of being entitled therefore to the privileges accorded to charity. However, this is subject to an important exception. In order to be eligible for tax relief, the organisation must also satisfy the further requirements imposed by the Finance Act 2010.[531]

The decision to register an applicant is that of the Charity Commission, and an account of recent decisions is given in the Annual Reports. In this way, the development of charity law is greatly

---

[524] The complaints scheme is governed by the Higher Education Act 2004.

[525] *Phillips v Bury* (1694) Skinn. 447. If the heirs die out or cannot act, the Crown is the visitor.

[526] Re-enacting previous legislation.

[527] s.30. Exempt charities are regulated by other bodies, such as the Higher Education Funding Council.

[528] Charities Act 2011 s.35.

[529] s.335.

[530] s.37.

[531] s.30 and Sch.6; above, para.15–005.

influenced by the Commission. Any person who may be affected by registration may object to registration, or apply for removal.[532] Nearly all these matters are finally disposed of by the Commission, but there is an appeal system. Prior to the Charities Act 2006 appeal lay to the High Court. The Act of 2006 established the Charity Tribunal to hear appeals from decisions or orders of the Commission.[533] It has since been abolished and its functions transferred to the First-tier and Upper Tribunals.[534] An appeal from the Tribunal's decision lies to the High Court. The Attorney General may appeal to the Tribunal from a decision of the Commission, and may intervene in proceedings before the Tribunal or High Court.

In making its decision, the Commission is aware of the need for flexibility, and for keeping the law of charities in tune with changing circumstances. By the end of March 2011, nearly 180,000 charities had been registered, and during 2010/2011 8,600 charities were removed from the Register,[535] mainly because they had ceased to operate. On the matter of removal, the Commissioners are not bound by the view of the Attorney General.[536]

E. Advice

The Commission may also give to any charity trustee an opinion **15–085** or advice on any matter affecting the performance of his duties or the proper administration of the charity, and a trustee acting upon it is deemed to have acted in accordance with the trust.[537] The Commission's advice is also available where an application is made to register a new charity. If the application is refused, the reason will be given so that the language may be amended. It is not of course possible to alter the terms of established trusts which fail to be registered.

F. Other Powers of the Charity Commission

i. Schemes. The Charity Commission has concurrent jurisdic- **15–086** tion with the High Court in establishing schemes for the administration of a charity.[538] This helps the trustees of charities to administer

---

[532] Charities Act 2011 s.36; Annual Report 1978 para.84.
[533] See now Charities Act 2011 Part 17.
[534] Above, para.15–040, fn.306.
[535] Annual Report 2010/2011. In that year 5,776 were registered.
[536] See Annual Report 1982 paras 36–38, App.C, for the Commissioners' refusal to accede to the request of the Attorney General to remove the Church of Unification (the "Moonies") from the register. (The Attorney General's action was subsequently dropped).
[537] Charities Act 2011 s.110.
[538] Charities Act 2011 s.69; The exercise of the Commission's power to make cy-près schemes was discussed above, para.15–063.

them more efficiently and to make better use of their funds and property. Schemes may cover the appointment of new bodies of trustees, the vesting of property in new trustees, the provision of new cy-près objects in place of objects which have become impracticable, the extension of the trustees' investment powers, and the grouping or amalgamation of charities. Schemes are usually made by the Commission on the application of a charity, or where the court, on directing a scheme, orders that the Commission shall settle the scheme.[539] It is the duty of charity trustees to secure the effective use of charity property.[540] If they unreasonably refuse or neglect to apply for a scheme in circumstances in which they ought, in the interest of the charity, to do so, the Commission may proceed as if an application for a scheme had been made in the case of a charity at least 40 years old.[541]

15–087   **ii. Consent to Proceedings.** By s.115 of the Charities Act 2011, no court proceedings relating to the administration of a charity (other than an exempt charity) shall be entertained unless authorised by the Commission. This is to prevent the dissipation of charitable funds in legal proceedings over matters which the Commission could resolve.

15–088   **iii. Dealings with Charity Property.** Charity trustees are subject to various statutory restrictions on dealings in charity property. Of particular importance is s.117 of the Charities Act 2011,[542] restricting the trustees' powers[543] to sell, lease or otherwise dispose of charity land.[544] The trustees require an order of the court or of the Commission unless the following conditions are satisfied: (a) the trustees have obtained and considered a written report on the proposed disposition from a qualified surveyor; (b) they have advertised the proposed disposition as advised by the surveyor; and (c) they are satisfied that the terms are the best reasonably obtainable.[545] Where the trustees hold land on trusts which stipulate that it is to be used for the purposes (or any particular purpose) of the charity, they must

---

[539] Charities Act 2011 s.69. As to the right of appeal, see *Childs v Att Gen* [1973] 1 W.L.R. 497.

[540] Charities Act 2011 s.61.

[541] Charities Act 2011 s.70(5). The restriction to charities 40 years old was introduced in order to protect donors against official intervention to alter the terms of trusts within the donor's lifetime.

[542] See also s.124 (mortgages).

[543] Which derive from the Trusts of Land and Appointment of Trustees Act 1996 s.6 (which cannot be excluded by the settlor; s.8(3)), or under the founding instrument or statute.

[544] Such land is no longer settled land but is held on a trust of land; Trusts of Land and Appointment of Trustees Act 1996 s.2(5).

[545] s.119. Neither s.117 nor s.124 (mortgages) applies to exempt charities. A disposition not complying with s.117 is valid in favour of a purchaser in good faith; s.122(6). See *Bayoumi v Women's Total Abstinence Educational Union Ltd* [2004] Ch. 46; D Dennis [2006] Conv. 219.

also give public notice and invite and consider representations.[546] Such land could be sold in certain circumstances under the previous law.[547]

Under s.105 of the Act of 2011 the Commission has a general power to authorise dealings with charity property which the trustees would otherwise have no power to do.

iv. Accounts; Inquiries. The Commission oversees the trustees' **15–089** duty to provide accounts,[548] and, if dissatisfied in any way, may institute inquiries.[549] Ultimately, they may remove trustees from office.[550] The Commission may be alerted by HMRC and other public authorities to the possible misapplication of charity funds.[551]

It was in the area of accounts and audit that much disquiet was felt over the possibility of abuse and maladministration by charity trustees. Provisions now found in the Charities Act 2011 impose more rigorous duties on trustees of unincorporated charities[552] to keep accounting records and to prepare annual accounts, which must be audited.[553] The trustees must prepare and (in some case) send annual reports to the Commission of their activities, with a statement of accounts and the auditor's report.[554] The Commission may grant a unifying order enabling two or more charities with the same trustees to file consolidated accounts.[555]

G. Investment

i. Investment Powers.[556] The wide powers of investment con- **15–090** ferred by the Trustee Act 2000 (discussed in Ch.18) apply to charity

---

[546] s.121.

[547] See *Oldham BC v Att Gen* [1993] Ch. 210.

[548] Charities Act 2011 Part 8.

[549] Charities Act 2011 s.46. Examples may be found in most of the Annual Reports.

[550] Charities Act 2011 s.79, below, para.15–095. See also *Att Gen v Schonfeld* [1980] 1 W.L.R. 1182.

[551] Charities Act 2011 ss.54, 55. Disclosure of information by the Commission to other public authorities is dealt with by s.56.

[552] Companies Act 2006 Pt 15, applies to corporate charities. Charities Act 2011 Part 11, governs Charitable Incorporated Organisations. The rules do not apply to exempt charities, but s.136 of the 2011 Act imposes a duty to keep accounts on them.

[553] ss.130–132, 144.

[554] ss.162–164. The reports are subject to public inspection; s.170. The trustees must also send annual returns in prescribed form to the Commission; s.169. Persistent default in these duties is an offence; s.173.

[555] s.12(2). The order may apply to all or any of the purposes of the Act.

[556] See Charity Commission guidance CC14 (2011). As to ethical investment by charity trustees, see *Harries v Church Commissioners for England* [1992] 1 W.L.R. 1241; below, para.18–020. See also Law Com. No.315 (2009), *Capital and Income in Trusts: Classification and Apportionment*, paras 8.80–8.81, proposing that charity trustees should have a statutory power to invest on a "total return" basis, without needing express authorisation by the Charity Commission.

trustees. As mentioned below, this legislation also permits them to delegate their investment powers.

15–091   **ii. Pooling. COIF Common Deposit Scheme.** Without statutory authority, different bodies of trustees could not pool their funds for investment purposes, for this would involve a delegation of the trustees' investment powers, which was not permitted prior to the Trustee Act 2000. Section 96 of the 2011 Act (re-enacting earlier provisions) gives power to the court or the Commission to create common investment schemes under which the investment of property transferred to the fund is invested by trustees appointed to manage the fund, and the participating charities are entitled to shares related to their contributions.[557] The predecessor legislation established the Charities Official Investment Fund, which is open to all charities.

The Charities Act 2011 also authorises the creation of common deposit schemes,[558] whereby money can be deposited at interest.

H. Delegation

15–092   The Trustee Act 2000 widened trustees' delegation powers, as discussed in Ch.20. Special rules, however, apply to delegation by charity trustees. They may delegate:

(a) any function consisting of carrying out a decision that the trustees have taken;

(b) any function relating to the investment of trust assets (including the management of land held as an investment); and

(c) any function relating to the raising of funds otherwise than by means of profits of a trade which is an integral part of carrying out the trust's charitable purpose.[559]

Charity trustees may exercise the statutory powers of appointing nominees and custodians,[560] save in relation to assets vested in the official custodian for charities.[561]

I. Trustees

15–093   **i. Capacity.** One of the means by which the Charities Act 2011 aims to prevent fraud and maladministration is by the disqualifica-

---

[557] Annual Report 1970 paras 68–74; 1971 para.90; *Re London University's Charitable Trust* [1964] Ch. 284. For ethical investment opportunities, see Annual Report 1996 paras 54–55.

[558] s.100. See also Trustee Act 2000 s.38.

[559] Trustee Act 2000 s.11(3). Other functions may be added by statutory instrument.

[560] Trustee Act 2000 ss.16, 17. The Charity Commission has provided guidance.

[561] Above, para.15–081.

tion of certain persons from holding the office of trustee of a charity.[562] Those disqualified include persons convicted of an offence involving dishonesty or deception, undischarged bankrupts and persons previously removed from charity trusteeship on the grounds of misconduct or mismanagement.[563] Also a Local Authority may not be trustee of an eleemosynary charity.[564] We have seen that the appointment of a charity as trustee may colour the construction which a court will place upon the language of the trust, but does not ensure that a trust is charitable.[565]

ii. Number. Majority Vote. There is no limit upon the number **15–094** of persons who may be trustees of a charity.[566] Too great a number of trustees is an obvious inconvenience. But decisions of trustees of a charity may be taken by majority vote and need not be unanimous.[567]

iii. Retirement, Removal and Suspension. Charity trustees **15–095** may retire in the same way as trustees of private trusts.[568] The Commission may suspend a trustee on being satisfied as a result of inquiries[569] that (a) there has been misconduct or mismanagement or (b) that it is necessary or desirable for the purpose of protecting the property of the charity,[570] or it may appoint additional trustees or make orders for the protection of the property, such as the appointment of a receiver and manager. Where it is satisfied that both conditions (a) and (b) are fulfilled, it may order the removal of a trustee or other officer who has been responsible for or privy to the misconduct or mismanagement or has contributed to or facilitated it.[571] It may also (or instead) order a scheme for the administration of the charity. The Commission may also, by order made of its own motion, remove a charity trustee who has been discharged from bankruptcy within the last five years, who is a corporation in liquidation, lacks mental capacity to act, has failed to act, or is abroad or cannot be found.[572] In such cases it may appoint a replacement or additional trustee. These provisions do not apply to exempt charities. It can thus be seen that extensive powers have been given to the

---

[562] s.178, re-enacting previous legislation. By s.183, it is an offence to act while disqualified. The disqualification may be waived by the Commission; Charities Act 2011 s.181.
[563] There is a public register of persons so removed.
[564] *Re Armitage* [1972] Ch. 438.
[565] Above, para.15–054.
[566] TA 1925 s.34.
[567] *Re Whiteley* [1910] 1 Ch. 600 at 608.
[568] Below, para.17–036.
[569] Under Charities Act 2011 s.46. *Jones v Att Gen* [1974] Ch. 148.
[570] s.76.
[571] See *Weth v Att Gen* [1999] 1 W.L.R. 686.
[572] Charities Act 2011 s.80.

Commission for the protection of charities in the circumstances described above.[573]

15–096   **iv. Remuneration.** The Trustee Act 2000 extends trustees' powers to charge for their services, as discussed in Ch.21. The Law Commission recommended that charity trustees should be excluded, on the ground that public confidence in the sector might otherwise be undermined.[574] The provisions of the Act of 2000 whereby trust corporations may receive remuneration although the trust instrument confers no such entitlement do not apply to charity trustees, but the Secretary of State may by regulations make provision for the remuneration of charity trustees who are trust corporations or who act in a professional capacity.[575] Now the Charities Act 2011[576] permits a charity trustee (or a person connected with the trustee, such as a spouse) to be remunerated from charity funds by a written agreement made with the charity or its trustees (as the case may be). Various conditions apply, including that the remuneration must not exceed a reasonable amount, and it is in the best interests of the charity for the services to be provided by the trustee (or connected person).

A related question is whether charity trustees should be prohibited from supplying goods and services to a charity on the ground that this might create a conflict of interest and duty.[577] This is permitted in certain circumstances.[578]

15–097   **v. Misapplication or other Breach.** An application by the trustee for purposes not covered by the terms of the trust is a misapplication of charity funds, which may give rise to personal liability on the trustee, and may be restrained by injunction,[579] or may be the subject of an inquiry by the Charity Commission.[580] A charity trustee (or auditor) may be relieved from liability (wholly or partly) by order of the Charity Commission if it considers that he is or may be personally liable for breach of duty but has acted honestly and reasonably and ought fairly to be excused.[581] This is in addition to the similar powers of the court to grant relief under s.61 of the Trustee Act 1925.[582]

---

[573] Charities Act 2011 ss.76–85.
[574] Law Com. No.260 (1999); *Trustees' Powers and Duties*, para.7.22.
[575] Trustee Act 2000 ss.29, 30.
[576] s.185.
[577] Below, Ch.21.
[578] Annual Report 1971 para.93.
[579] *Baldry v Feintuck* [1972] 1 W.L.R. 552. (Resolution to apply Students' Union funds for political purposes). See Annual Report 1983 paras 95 and 96 and App.A.
[580] Above, para.15–089.
[581] Charities Act 2011 s.191.
[582] Below, para.23–033.

TRUSTS OF PENSION FUNDS

1. INTRODUCTION

PENSION fund trusts have received much public scrutiny in recent **16–001** years, primarily as a result of the misappropriation of about £453 million from the pension funds of the employees of Mirror Group Newspapers and the Maxwell Communications Corporation by the late Robert Maxwell.[1] The focus of the ensuing debate was the question whether pension schemes should continue to be governed by the law of trusts, and how the scheme members (the beneficiaries) could be better safeguarded against fraud, mismanagement and insolvency. The matter was referred to the Pension Law Review Committee, chaired by Professor Roy Goode. The Goode Report[2] favoured retaining the law of trusts as the most suitable mechanism for dealing with pension funds, primarily because of the well-established principles concerning the fiduciary responsibilities of trustees

---

[1] Most of the money was recovered; *The Times*, February 20, 1996.
[2] *Pension Law Reform: Pension Law Review Committee Report* (1993), Cmnd. 2342; D. Chatterton (1993) 7 T.L.I. 91. See also D. Hayton [1993] Conv. 283.

and the proprietary rights of beneficiaries, conferring protection from the employer's insolvency. Of course, no legal mechanism can prevent deliberate wrongdoing.

The Committee recommended various ways in which the rights of pension beneficiaries might be enhanced and safeguarded by the enactment of special rules going beyond the protection afforded to beneficiaries of traditional trusts under the general law. In particular, they recommended the introduction of a regulatory body, a compensation scheme to apply in cases of misappropriation, a minimum funding requirement to prevent a shortfall of funds in the case of funded schemes, restrictions on employers' rights to surplus funds, and reforms relating to the appointment, removal and disqualification of trustees. Most of their recommendations, some in modified form, were implemented by the Pensions Act 1995. Since that Act the pensions legislation has again been overhauled by the Pensions Act 2004. While parts of the 1995 Act remain in force, the Act of 2004 introduced new rules on pension scheme funding, a new Pensions Regulator and a new Pension Protection Fund.

The special treatment of pension fund beneficiaries reflects the fact that their entitlements arise from their contracts of employment. Unlike traditional beneficiaries, they are not volunteers. In many ways, however, pension trusts are subject to the same principles as any other trusts, and the pension trust case law has contributed much to the development of the general law of trusts.[3]

A long-term European goal is cross-border membership of pension schemes through the establishment of European pension funds covering workers in several member states, to reflect the principle of free movement of workers.[4]

The purpose of this chapter is to examine pension funds as an important modern illustration of the law of trusts in operation and to consider the ways in which pension fund trusts are treated differently from traditional trusts. Before doing so it is necessary to appreciate the different types of pension schemes available and to understand the terminology.

A. Types of Pension Scheme

16–002   Pension provision falls into three broad categories: the state pension, a personal pension (a form of investment made by an individual with an insurance company, to which the employer may contribute) and an occupational pension scheme, which is organised

---

[3] See G. Moffat (1993) 56 M.L.R. 471, examining whether a separate pensions law is developing, or whether the developments in modern pensions cases are applicable generally. See also Vinelott J. (1994) 8 T.L.I. 35; M. Milner [1997] Conv. 89; D. Hayton [2005] Conv. 229. For the "property" rights of pension beneficiaries, see R. Nobles (1994) 14 L.S. 345.
[4] See Pensions Act 2004 Pt 7.

by an employer to provide pensions and other benefits for employees (and usually for their dependants) on leaving employment (by retirement or otherwise) or on death. The latter category is the subject of this chapter. Occupational pension schemes themselves take various forms, but in essence trust law will apply where assets are segregated and invested to provide pension benefits. Many public sector schemes (such as those for teachers and the civil service) are established by legislation and are unfunded in the sense that there is no trust fund set aside to provide benefits. The employees' security is founded on the statute rather than on the segregation of assets. State pensions are also unfunded, benefits being paid from current contributions. A non-statutory scheme is unfunded where the employer does not set aside and accumulate assets in a separate trust fund in advance of the benefits commencing to be paid. Most private schemes, however, are funded. We are concerned with funded schemes, where a fund is held on trust to make provision in advance for future liabilities to members by accumulating assets. The assets are invested and the investments held by the trustees. This may be contrasted with an insured scheme, where the trustees have effected an insurance contract for each member which guarantees benefits corresponding to those promised under the scheme rules. In other words, this is an investment through the medium of an insurance company, the trustees using the contributions to pay the premiums. The insurance is the only significant asset of the scheme. If the sums payable by the insurer are sufficient at all times to cover all benefits, the scheme is said to be fully insured. Most small schemes are run through insurers.

The benefits to which an employee is entitled depend on whether **16–003** the scheme is earnings-related (a defined *benefit* scheme) or whether it is a "money purchase" scheme (a defined *contribution* scheme). An earnings-related scheme (sometimes called a final salary scheme) is where the benefit is calculated by reference to the member's pensionable earnings for a period of pensionable service ending at or before normal pension date or leaving service. There is normally a restriction on the number of years (e.g. 40) which qualify as pensionable service, and not all earnings (e.g. a bonus or allowance) are pensionable. The scheme may require contributions from employees (a contributory scheme) or may not (non-contributory). The benefits are usually based on a fraction of the final salary for each year of pensionable service.[5] The cost of providing these defined benefits cannot be accurately predicted, so the employer in a contributory scheme undertakes to pay whatever sum is needed to

---

[5] In 2007 the civil service pension was changed for new entrants from a final salary scheme to one based on the member's average salary during service.

top up employee contributions. If the fund is in surplus, the employer may be able to take a "contributions holiday", by temporarily suspending its contributions.[6] It follows that the risk of poor investment performance falls on the employer in an earnings-related scheme.

A "money purchase" scheme is where the benefits of an individual member are determined by reference to the contributions paid into the scheme by or on behalf of that member, usually increased by an amount based on the investment return of those contributions.[7] The contributions are fixed (normally a percentage of salary) by the scheme, and the benefits vary according to investment performance. Thus the employee takes the risk of poor investments, but also takes the benefit of a good performance.[8] The fund is either used to purchase an annuity to provide the pension, or a pension may be paid from the fund according to the size of the member's account in the fund.

Money purchase schemes have become increasingly popular with employers in recent years, and most new schemes are of that type. Earnings-related schemes have become too onerous and expensive for employers as a result of poorly performing stock markets worldwide, increasing life expectancy and the burden of regulation. This has led to the closure of large numbers of earnings-related schemes, which have either been wound up and replaced by money purchase schemes or closed to new members.[9] The Hutton Report[10] in March 2011 recommended that public sector final salary schemes should be replaced by schemes based on the employee's average salary over the period of employment, to reduce costs to the taxpayer.

The Pensions Act 2008 (as amended by the Pensions Act 2011) aims to address the lack of pension provision by requiring employers to enrol eligible employees with low to moderate earnings into a personal or occupational pension scheme (money purchase or defined benefit) chosen by the employer, who must make contributions to it. A trust-based pension scheme which can be chosen by employers has been set up under the Act. It is called the National Employment Savings Trust ("NEST"), and is an occupational pension

---

[6] A thirty-year "holiday" was a breach of trust by the trustees of the British Airways pension fund; (1996) 10 T.L.I. 26. See also *National Grid Co Plc v Mayes* [2001] 1 W.L.R. 864.

[7] For the definition of a "money purchase" scheme and distinctions from defined benefit schemes, see *Bridge Trustees Ltd v Yates* [2011] 1 W.L.R. 1912.

[8] The trustees are subject to the usual standard of prudence with regard to the investments; see N. Moore (1999) 13 T.L.I. 2.

[9] In 2011 the Association of Consulting Actuaries reported that 91% of final salary schemes had been closed to new employees and that 37% had been closed as to further contributions by current members.

[10] *Independent Public Service Pensions Commission: Final Report.*

scheme for tax purposes.[11] The scheme will be run by the National Employment Savings Trust Corporation in consultation with panels of members and participating employers. The scheme is due to start operating in 2012.

When a funded scheme is being set up, the trust deeds are lengthy **16–004** and take time to prepare. It is, therefore, usual to have an interim trust deed with outline rules, which appoints the first trustees. This enables the scheme to be started without delay, and provisional tax relief to be secured.[12] In due course this is replaced by the final (or definitive) trust deed.

Much of the case law deals with entitlement to surplus funds, the contest normally involving beneficiaries, employers, creditors of an insolvent employer, or companies which have taken over the employer company and wish to syphon off the surplus ("takeover raiders" or "predators"). At present a deficit is much more likely than a surplus. Of course, a surplus cannot arise in the case of a money purchase scheme or an unfunded scheme. In the case of a funded earnings-related scheme, any surplus is notional if the scheme is ongoing. A surplus is said to exist whenever, according to actuarial calculations, the value of the assets exceeds the estimated liabilities. There will be an actual surplus only if the scheme is wound up, leaving an excess after discharge of liabilities. Where a pension scheme is terminated by winding-up, the assets will usually be applied to the purchase of annuities to provide pensions for members, or the assets and liabilities may be transferred to another pension scheme.

B. Beneficiaries not Volunteers

The fact that pension trust beneficiaries are not volunteers puts **16–005** them in certain respects in a different position from the beneficiaries of traditional family trusts. The consideration arises from the fact that the pension benefits are a form of deferred remuneration for their services[13] and from their contributions (if any) to the fund. In *Mettoy Pension Trustees Ltd v Evans*[14] the scheme contained a power of appointment in favour of the members, any surplus not so appointed going to the employer, which was in liquidation. The fact

[11] Pensions Act 2008 s.67 and Sch.1; National Employment Savings Trust Order (SI 2010/917).

[12] For the fiscal benefits, see below, para.16–028.

[13] See *Brooks v Brooks* [1996] 1 A.C. 375. This meant that the husband (the employee) and not the employer was regarded as settlor of the marriage settlement constituted by the pension scheme.

[14] [1990] 1 W.L.R. 1587; above, para.6–007. See also *Thrells Ltd v Lomas* [1993] 1 W.L.R. 456; *In Re Makin (William) & Sons Ltd* [1993] B.C.C. 453; *Air Jamaica Ltd v Charlton* [1999] 1 W.L.R. 1399 at 1407. As to whether the employer is to be regarded as a beneficiary, see D. Pollard (2006) 20 T.L.I. 21; J. Hilliard (2009) 23 T.L.I. 119 at 122–124; D. Fox (2010) 69 C.L.J. 240.

that the members were not volunteers was influential in classifying the power as fiduciary rather than personal. Had it been only personal (i.e. a bare power), the unpalatable conclusion would have been that the entire surplus would have gone to the creditors, the power proving to be of illusory benefit to the members. The classification of the power as fiduciary meant that it could not be released[15] (in the interests of the creditors), and, further, that the court could intervene to secure the exercise of the power.[16]

In *Davis v Richards & Wallington Industries Ltd*[17] there were doubts whether the definitive (final) trust deed had been validly executed. This deed provided that any surplus should belong to the employers after increasing the pension benefits to the statutory maximum. If the deed was invalid the trust would be incompletely constituted. However, as the beneficiaries were not volunteers they could compel the execution of a valid deed and their rights (by applying the maxim that equity regards as done that which ought to be done) were as if such a deed had already been executed. In fact the deed was held valid.

In a pension trust the trustee/beneficiary relationship exists in parallel with the contractual employer/employee relationship and the pension scheme must be interpreted against this background. In *Imperial Group Pension Trust Ltd v Imperial Tobacco Ltd*[18] the company had power under the scheme to consent to an increase in benefits. The issue was whether it was under a duty to consider the interests of the members and not just its own interests when granting or withholding consent. It was held that the implied contractual obligation of good faith between employer and employee (meaning that the employer would not act in a manner calculated or likely to destroy or damage the relationship of confidence and trust between employer and employee) applied to the exercise of the employer's rights and powers under the pension scheme just as it applied to its other rights and powers. The power to give or withhold consent was accordingly subject to a restriction that it could not be validly exercised in breach of the obligation of good faith. Thus the pension trust "lies at the interface between trust and employment law".[19]

The fact that pension trust beneficiaries are not volunteers may allow them to be more favourably treated than other beneficiaries in

---

[15] See also *Re Courage Group's Pension Schemes* [1987] 1 W.L.R. 495; above, para.6–029.

[16] This controversial aspect of the decision was discussed at para.6–007, above. See now Pensions Act 1995 s.25 (fiduciary powers exercisable by independent trustee on insolvency); below, para.16–010.

[17] [1990] 1 W.L.R. 1511; above, para.10–015. The decision was disapproved on another point in *Air Jamaica Ltd v Charlton*, above, fn.14.

[18] [1991] 1 W.L.R. 589. On the good faith requirement, see M. Thomas and B. Dowrick [2007] Conv. 495.

[19] Vinelott J. (1994) 8 T.L.I. 35.

the matter of costs. In *McDonald v Horn*[20] it was held that, contrary to the usual rule, pension beneficiaries may obtain a "pre-emptive costs order" where there are serious allegations of impropriety and breach of trust against the employers and trustees. Thus the beneficiaries would obtain their costs, and any costs which they might be ordered to pay to the defendants, out of the fund whether or not their action ultimately proved successful. The fact that the beneficiaries had given consideration made the action analogous to an action by a minority shareholder on behalf of a company, where such an order could be made. Similarly, the equitable jurisdiction to grant relief for a mistake in a voluntary disposition does not extend to a pension trust.[21]

As a general proposition, however, the ordinary principles of trust law apply to pension trusts as to other trusts. This was emphasised in *Wilson v Law Debenture Trust Corp Plc*,[22] where it was held that the principle of *Re Londonderry's Settlement*,[23] whereby trustees are not obliged to give reasons for the exercise of their discretions to the beneficiaries, applied equally to pension fund trusts.[24] Although the court must have regard to the fact that the beneficiaries are not volunteers when construing the trust deed, effect must be given to settled principles of trust law in determining the effect of the deed on its true construction.

2. SPECIAL RULES APPLICABLE TO PENSION TRUSTS

In view of the special nature of pension fund trusts in terms of the size of the funds, their quasi-public nature, the opportunities for misappropriation by the employer, the non-volunteer status of the beneficiaries, and the public interest in the encouragement of such trusts, there are many statutory provisions which apply special rules to pension trusts. Most of these are contained in the Pensions Acts 1995 and 2004, but others, relating in particular to taxation and the application of the perpetuity rule, are found elsewhere.

16–006

A. Pensions Acts 1995 and 2004

As discussed at the beginning of this chapter, the main objective of the Act of 1995 was to protect the beneficiaries from the effects of

16–007

---

[20] [1995] 1 All E.R. 961; *Chessels v British Telecommunications Plc* [2002] W.T.L.R. 719.

[21] *Smithson v Hamilton* [2008] 1 All E.R. 1216.

[22] [1995] 2 All E.R. 337; P. O'Hagan (1995) 145 N.L.J. 1414. Member trustees will have access to reasons.

[23] [1965] Ch. 198; below, para.17–043.

[24] A contrary view is taken by Lord Browne-Wilkinson (1992) 6 T.L.I. 119 at 125; D. Schaffer (1994) 8 T.L.I. 27 and 118, Sir Robert Walker [1996] P.L.R. 107 and D. Hayton [2005] Conv. 229 at 234–237. Pension scheme trustees must record their decisions but not the reasons for them. See D. Pollard (1997) 11 T.L.I. 11 and 42.

maladministration, fraud and insolvency. Illustrations of this objective include the provision that the trustees must keep proper books and records and must keep any money received by them in a separate account at an institution authorised under the Banking Act 1987,[25] and that an employer who fails to pay over any contributions deducted from members within a certain period commits an offence.[26] The 1995 Act sought also to strike a fair balance between the interests of current employees, pensioners and employers. To the extent that any of the statutory provisions discussed below conflict with the terms of a pension scheme, such terms are overridden by the Act.[27] Provision is also made for modifying pension schemes in order to implement the requirements of the Act.[28]

The provisions of the 1995 Act mentioned above (and others) remain in force. However, major changes to other aspects of pension fund regulation were introduced by the Pensions Act 2004, most of which came into force on or before April 6, 2005. The minimum funding rules of the 1995 Act were perceived to be unsatisfactory and have been replaced. Other major features of the Pensions Act 2004 were the introduction of the new Pensions Regulator and the Pension Protection Fund. These will be considered below.

16–008　　　**i. Pensions Regulator.** Following the recommendations of the Goode Report, the 1995 Act set up the Occupational Pensions Regulatory Authority (replacing the Occupational Pensions Board) to supervise pension trusts and thereby reduce the likelihood of maladministration and fraud. The powers of the Regulatory Authority proved inadequate to achieve its objectives, and it was replaced by the Pensions Regulator in the Pensions Act 2004.[29] The Pensions Regulator (a corporate body) has wider powers, designed to promote good administration (for example by issuing codes of practice[30]) and to reduce the risk of under-funding and fraud.

The following functions of the Regulatory Authority under the Pensions Act 1995 have been transferred to the Pensions Regulator. It may, by an order under s.3 of the 1995 Act,[31] prohibit a person from being a trustee of a particular pension scheme, a particular kind of pension scheme or pension schemes in general if satisfied that he is not a fit and proper person to be a trustee of the scheme or schemes in question. Such an order, which is revocable, operates to

---

[25] Pensions Act 1995 s.49.

[26] s.49(8).

[27] s.117.

[28] ss.68, 69 as amended by Pensions Act 2004. Schemes often contain express modification powers, the exercise of which is restricted by s.67.

[29] Part I and Schs 1–3. For the Pensions Regulator Tribunal, see ss.102–106 and Sch.4.

[30] Pensions Act 2004 s.90.

[31] As substituted by Pensions Act 2004 s.33. The Regulator must keep a register of prohibited trustees for inspection; Pensions Act 2004 ss.66, 67.

remove the trustee. Section 4[32] of the 1995 Act enables the Pensions Regulator to make an order suspending a trustee in various circumstances, as where a bankruptcy petition has been presented against him or proceedings commenced for an offence involving dishonesty or deception, and such proceedings have not been concluded. While the order is in force, the person is prohibited from exercising any functions as trustee of the scheme or schemes in question. A person who purports to act as trustee while prohibited or suspended is guilty of an offence, but things done by him while purporting to act are not invalid merely because of the prohibition or suspension.[33] The 1995 Act contains further provisions which disqualify certain persons from acting as trustee of any occupational pension scheme. This is dealt with below.[34] Section 7 of the 1995 Act permits the Pensions Regulator to appoint a new trustee in place of one who has been removed or disqualified, or where the appointment is necessary to secure that the number of trustees is sufficient or that the trustees as a whole have the necessary skills.

In addition to the powers discussed above, the Pensions Regulator has jurisdiction under s.10 of the 1995 Act to impose financial penalties on trustees and other persons, such as the director of a corporate trustee, in respect of various breaches of their statutory duties.[35] It may also seek injunctions to restrain misuse or misappropriation of assets, and apply to court for the restitution of assets which have been misused or misappropriated.[36]

The Pensions Regulator may order an occupational pension scheme to be wound up in order to protect the interests of the members or if the scheme is no longer required or should be replaced by a different scheme.[37] The winding-up powers have been strengthened by enabling the Pensions Regulator to make a freezing order to prevent an immediate risk to the interests of scheme members.[38] Other powers of the Pensions Regulator include the power to recover any unpaid employer's contributions,[39] to issue an improvement notice to any person considered to be contravening the pensions legislation,[40] and to enter and inspect business premises.[41]

In addition to the Pensions Regulator, the Pensions Ombudsman has jurisdiction over occupational and personal pension schemes.

---

[32] As amended by Pensions Act 2004 s.34.

[33] Pensions Act 1995 s.6.

[34] Below, para.16–011.

[35] Trustees may not be indemnified out of the trust assets for financial penalties; Pensions Act 2004 s.256.

[36] Pensions Act 2004 s.15 (injunctions) and 16 (restitution). For information gathering by the Regulator, see Pensions Act 2004 ss.72–79.

[37] Pensions Act 1995 s.11, as amended.

[38] Pensions Act 2004 ss.23–32.

[39] Pensions Act 2004 s.17.

[40] Pensions Act 2004 s.13.

[41] Pensions Act 2004 ss.73–76.

He may investigate and determine various complaints and disputes relating primarily to maladministration.[42] A breach of trust does not automatically constitute maladministration.[43] The Ombudsman may not direct steps to be taken (such as the repayment of money to the fund or the setting aside of a deed) unless the court could do so.[44] It appears that he may direct the payment of damages for distress,[45] although this remains to be confirmed by the higher courts.

16–009   **ii. Trustees.** The supervisory powers of the Pensions Regulator over trustees, including the powers of removal, suspension and appointment, were noted above. The 1995 and 2004 Acts contain further important provisions concerning trustees, which are designed primarily to ensure good administration and to dilute the influence of the employer.

16–010   (a) *Constitution.* The constitution of the trustee body requires that representatives of the scheme members must be included, and that a trustee who is independent of the employer must be appointed on the employer's insolvency.

The trustees must make and implement arrangements for the selection of "member-nominated trustees".[46] They must constitute at least one-third of the total number of trustees. A greater number cannot be appointed without the employer's approval. Where the trustee is a company, the requirement is for "member-nominated directors".[47] Failure to comply may result in a civil penalty under s.10 of the 1995 Act. The provisions relating to member-nominated trustees were introduced by the Pensions Act 1995, but were criticised because the employer could opt out of the requirement. The replacement provisions in the Pensions Act 2004 remove this possibility, and also permit the proportion of one-third to be increased to half by regulations.[48]

Where a person is both a trustee and a beneficiary, as in the case of member-nominated trustees, difficult problems of conflict of interest and duty might arise. Where, for example, trustees have a discretion to use a surplus to augment the benefits of the members, any balance going to the employer, the question arises whether they can validly exercise their discretion in such a way as to benefit

---

[42] Pension Schemes Act 1993 ss.145–151, as amended by Pensions Acts 1995 and 2004. On the resolution of pension disputes, see J. Clifford (1998) 12 T.L.I. 26.

[43] *Law Debenture Trust Corp Plc v Pensions Ombudsman* [1998] 1 W.L.R. 1329.

[44] *Hillsdown Holdings Plc v Pensions Ombudsman* [1997] 1 All E.R. 862; *Edge v Pensions Ombudsman* [2000] Ch. 602.

[45] *City and County of Swansea v Johnson* [1999] Ch 189. The point was left open in *East Sussex County Council v Jacobs, The Times*, January 23, 2004.

[46] Pensions Act 2004 s.241.

[47] Pensions Act 2004 s.242.

[48] Pensions Act 2004 s.243.

themselves in their capacity as members.[49] This has been resolved by s.39 of the 1995 Act, which provides that:

> "[N]o rule of law that a trustee may not exercise the powers vested in him so as to give rise to a conflict between his personal interest and his duties to the beneficiaries shall apply to a trustee of a trust scheme, who is also a member of the scheme, exercising the powers vested in him in any manner, merely because their exercise in that manner benefits, or may benefit, him as a member of the scheme."[50]

An independent trustee must be appointed in circumstances connected with the insolvency of the employer, as where an insolvency practitioner begins to act in relation to the employer or if the official receiver becomes the liquidator of the employer company or the receiver and manager or trustee in bankruptcy of an individual employer.[51] The appointment is made by order of the Pensions Regulator.[52] Once appointed, and so long as the circumstances requiring the appointment continue, only the independent trustee may exercise any discretionary powers of the trustees under the scheme and any fiduciary powers of the employer.[53]

(b) *Disqualification.* Certain categories of persons are disquali- **16–011** fied by s.29 from being trustee of any occupational pension scheme. Broadly, the disqualification applies to a person convicted of any offence involving dishonesty or deception; an undischarged bankrupt; a company of which any director is disqualified under the section; a person who has made a composition with creditors and has not been discharged; and a person disqualified from acting as a company director.

A trustee who becomes disqualified ceases to be a trustee and commits an offence if he subsequently purports to act,[54] although things done by him while purporting to act as trustee are not invalid merely because of the disqualification.[55]

---

[49] See *In re Makin (William) & Sons Ltd* [1993] B.C.C. 453; M. Milner (1996) 10 T.L.I. 15; *Re Drexel Burnham Lambert UK Pension Plan* [1995] 1 W.L.R. 32; *Edge v Pensions Ombudsman* [2000] Ch. 602.

[50] See generally M. Fitzsimons (2006) 20 T.L.I. 211.

[51] Pensions Act 1995 s.22; (ss.22–25 have been amended by Pensions Act 2004 s.36). "Independent" is defined in s.23(3). He may be paid fees by the employer or from the trust fund; s.25(6). An independent trustee was already required in such circumstances under previous legislation.

[52] s.23.

[53] s.25. The employer, if previously sole trustee, ceases to be trustee on the appointment of the independent trustee.

[54] s.30(3).

[55] s.30(5).

16–012   (c) *Majority Decisions.* Under the general law, trustees (other than charity trustees) must act unanimously, unless the trust instrument provides otherwise.[56] Section 32 of the 1995 Act provides an exception for trustees of an occupational pension scheme, who may, unless the trust scheme provides otherwise, make decisions by majority. As a safeguard, the trustees must give notice of occasions at which decisions may be taken to each trustee, so far as reasonably practicable.[57]

16–013   (d) *Knowledge and Understanding.* The Pensions Act 2004 introduced a new requirement for trustees to be more professional. They must be conversant with the trust deed and scheme rules, the scheme's statements of investment and funding principles, and any documents recording policy adopted by the trustees relating to the administration of the scheme. They must have knowledge and understanding of the law relating to pensions and trusts, and the principles of scheme funding and investment. The degree of knowledge and understanding required is that appropriate for enabling the trustee to exercise his functions as trustee of the scheme.[58] These provisions do not affect any rule of law requiring a trustee to have knowledge of, or expertise in, any matter.[59]

16–014   **iii. Professional Advisers.** The trustees or managers of every occupational pension scheme must appoint an individual or a firm as auditor and an individual as actuary.[60] Where the trust assets include investments, an individual or firm must be appointed as fund manager.[61]

The trustees of the pension scheme (and any connected persons and associates) are ineligible to act as auditor or actuary of the scheme.[62]

16–015   **iv. Investment.** Under the general law, pension trusts have been governed by the same investment principles as traditional trusts,[63] although the courts, recognising the need for the trustees of large pension funds to have wide investment powers, have been ready to exercise their jurisdiction to vary trusts by extending these powers.[64]

---

[56] Below, para.17–007.
[57] s.32(2)(b).
[58] Pensions Act 2004 ss.247, 248.
[59] Pensions Act 2004 s.249.
[60] Pensions Act 1995 s.47. The duty to obtain audited accounts is imposed by regulations, the present source of which is s.41.
[61] Pensions Act 1995 s.47. For delegation of investment powers to the fund manager, see below.
[62] Pensions Act 1995 s.27. Contravention is an offence under s.28.
[63] See *Cowan v Scargill* [1985] Ch. 270; below, para.18–019.
[64] See *Mason v Farbrother* [1983] 2 All E.R. 1078; below, para.18–023.

It is now recognised, since the Pensions Act 1995, that the special nature of pension trusts requires special treatment.

(a) *General Principles.* The trustees of an occupational pension **16–016** scheme have, subject to the provisions of the 1995 Act on choosing investments[65] and to any restriction in the scheme, the same power to make an investment of any kind as if they were absolutely entitled to the assets.[66] They must ensure that a written statement in prescribed form of the principles governing investment decisions is prepared, maintained and revised from time to time.[67] Neither the trust scheme nor the statement may restrict the investment power by reference to the employer's consent.

The exercise of the power of investment by the trustees is governed by s.36 of the Pensions Act 1995 and regulations made under it.[68] Regulations may specify criteria to be applied in choosing investments and may require diversification. Before investing and at suitable intervals thereafter, the trustees must obtain and consider proper advice[69] on the question whether the investment is satisfactory having regard to the principles contained in their policy statement and the requirements of the regulations so far as they relate to the suitability of investments.[70] The trustees or fund manager must exercise their powers with a view to giving effect to the principles of their policy statement, so far as reasonably practicable.[71] Failure to comply with these investment duties may result in the imposition of a financial penalty under s.10 of the 1995 Act, but the statutory duty of care under the Trustee Act 2000 does not apply to investment powers under occupational pension schemes.[72]

Finally, regulations may prohibit trustees from borrowing money or acting as guarantor.[73]

(b) *Delegation to Fund Manager.* Under the general law a trustee **16–017** may not delegate the exercise of his discretions without authority, and this led to inconvenient problems over the delegation of investment decisions to fund managers prior to the Trustee Act 2000.[74]

[65] Pensions Act 1995 s.36(1), below.
[66] Pensions Act 1995 s.34(1). "Investment" is not defined. The wide investment powers conferred by the Trustee Act 2000 do not apply as there is no need for them; TA 2000 s.36.
[67] s.35, as substituted by Pensions Act 2004 s.244.
[68] s.36 was amended by Pensions Act 2004 s.245, introducing the power to make regulations governing investment by trustees. Where investment discretions have been delegated to a fund manager, as discussed below, the fund manager must exercise his discretion in accordance with the regulations.
[69] Defined in s.36(6).
[70] s.36(3), (4).
[71] s.36(5).
[72] TA 2000 s.36.
[73] Pensions Act 1995, s.36A, introduced by Pensions Act 2004 s.246.
[74] Below, para.20–012.

The Pensions Act 1995 already provided that trustees of occupational pension funds could delegate investment decisions to a fund manager authorised to conduct investment business under the financial services legislation (now the Financial Services and Markets Act 2000).[75] The trustees are not responsible for the act or default of such a fund manager if they have taken all reasonable steps to satisfy themselves that the manager has appropriate knowledge and experience and is carrying out his work competently and in accordance with statutory duties.[76] Alternatively, the trustees may delegate investment decisions by power of attorney under s.25 of the Trustee Act 1925,[77] or, subject to any restriction in the trust scheme, to a fund manager not authorised to conduct investment business under the Financial Services and Markets Act 2000, or may authorise two or more of their number to make investment decisions on their behalf.[78] In these three cases, however, the trustees as a whole remain liable for any breaches resulting from any acts or defaults in the exercise of the discretion.[79]

As the Pensions Act 1995 provides for delegation of investment decisions by trustees of occupational pension schemes, the power to delegate such decisions under the Trustee Act 2000 is inapplicable, as is the power under that Act to appoint nominees and custodians.[80] Other powers of delegation under the Trustee Act 2000 do apply to pension scheme trustees, although subject to certain restrictions.[81] The statutory duty of care under the Act of 2000 does not apply to pension scheme trustees when delegating investment decisions or appointing nominees or custodians pursuant to their powers under the 1995 Act or under the pension scheme provisions.[82]

16–018   (c) *Exclusion of Liability.* Liability for failure to take care or to exercise skill in the performance of investment functions exercisable by the trustees or the fund manager cannot be excluded or restricted by an instrument or agreement.[83] On the question whether the trustees may be exempted from responsibility for the acts and defaults of fund managers, we have seen that the trustees are not liable for the acts of fund managers who are authorised to conduct investment business under the Financial Services and Markets Act 2000, and so the point does not arise in such a case. In the case of delegation to

---

[75] Pensions Act 1995 s.34(2).
[76] s.34(4).
[77] Below, para.20–019.
[78] s.34(5).
[79] s.34(5); Trustee Act 1925 s.25(5).
[80] TA 2000 s.36.
[81] TA 2000 s.36.
[82] TA 2000 s.36.
[83] Pensions Act 1995 s.33. On trustee exemption clauses generally, see para.17–005, below.

fund managers who are not authorised to conduct investment business, where such delegation is permitted by s.34(5) of the 1995 Act, the trustees are normally liable for the acts and defaults of such a person, as mentioned above. In this case, however, the liability may be validly excluded or restricted provided the trustees have taken all reasonable steps to satisfy themselves that the fund manager has appropriate knowledge and experience and is carrying out his work competently and in accordance with statutory duties.[84]

(d) *Employer-related Investments.* Investments of pension fund **16–019** assets in the employer's business, such as the purchase of shares in the employer company or loans to the employer, are subject to restrictions[85] because of the danger they present on the employer's insolvency. If a substantial proportion of the fund could be invested in the employer company, the losses would be great if the employer went into liquidation. Section 40 of the Pensions Act 1995 obliges the trustees or managers of an occupational pension scheme to ensure that current restrictions on employer-related investments are complied with. Failure to do so may result in the imposition of a financial penalty under s.10, and a trustee or manager who agrees to invest in contravention of the restrictions commits an offence.

v. Scheme Funding. The scheme funding requirements are de- **16–020** signed to ensure that any inadequacies of funding will be revealed by a regular monitoring process and remedied in various ways, usually by an increase in contributions by the members or by the employer. The provisions apply to occupational pension schemes other than money purchase schemes.

The Pensions Act 1995 laid down the "minimum funding rule", but this proved unsatisfactory and was replaced with new scheme funding rules by the Pensions Act 2004. The new rules, although stricter, are more flexible in that they are "scheme specific". The statutory funding objective is that each scheme must have sufficient assets to cover its liabilities.[86] The trustees must prepare a statement of funding principles which sets out their policy for ensuring that the scheme meets its funding objectives.[87] They must obtain an actuary's valuation of the assets and liabilities at regular intervals.[88] They must also prepare and keep under review a schedule of employer's and members' contributions, to be certified by the actuary.[89]

---

[84] s.34(6).
[85] By regulations under Pension Schemes Act 1993 s.112. See I. Greenstreet (1994) 8 T.L.I. 56; D. Pollard and D. Heath (2010) 24 T.L.I. 13.
[86] Pensions Act 2004 s.222.
[87] Pensions Act 2004 s.223.
[88] Pensions Act 2004 s.224.
[89] Pensions Act 2004 s.227.

The actuary must inform the Pensions Regulator if his valuation of the fund shows that the trustees are failing to meet their funding objectives, or if he is unable to certify the schedule of contributions.[90] A recovery plan must then be drawn up, setting out the steps to be taken to meet the statutory funding objective.[91] A copy must be sent to the Regulator. The plan must be agreed between the trustees and the employer. The trustees must report any failure to reach agreement to the Regulator, which will exercise various powers to remedy the situation, such as directing increased contributions.[92] If the situation cannot be remedied, the scheme will be wound up, as discussed below.[93]

Trustees or actuaries who fail to comply with the obligations described above may incur a financial penalty under s.10 of the Pensions Act 1995.

16–021   **vi. Surplus.** Much of the pension trust litigation has involved entitlement to surplus funds.[94] Surpluses arose primarily in the 1980s because of the huge growth in the value of investments at that time. The opposite is the case at the present time. Where the scheme is ongoing, any surplus is notional, and means that the actuarial estimation of the assets at a given time exceeds the actuarial estimation of the liabilities. Such a calculation involves many projections and assumptions. There will be an actual surplus only if the scheme is wound up and all liabilities discharged. Surplus on a winding up is dealt with in the following section. Where the scheme is ongoing, the question is one of rights and duties in the application of the surplus rather than ownership as such.

16–022   The application of a surplus (actual or notional) will be crucial where the employer is insolvent,[95] or where the employer company is taken over by a company which proposes to "raid" the surplus,[96] or where, on a partial sale of the employer company, the employees are transferred to the purchaser's pension scheme and dispute the decision of the trustees of the original scheme not to transfer any of the substantial surplus to the purchaser's scheme.[97]

As explained below, the tax regime requires the taxation of any payments to the employer from the surplus, to avoid exploitation of pension fund tax reliefs.[98]

[90] Pensions Act 2004 ss.225, 227.
[91] Pensions Act 2004 s.226.
[92] Pensions Act 2004 ss.229, 231.
[93] Below, para.16–023.
[94] See generally D. Pollard (2003) T.L.I. 2.
[95] See *Mettoy Pension Trustees Ltd v Evans* [1990] 1 W.L.R. 1587; above, para.6–007; *Thrells Ltd v Lomas* [1993] 1 W.L.R. 456.
[96] See *Re Courage Group's Pension Scheme* [1987] 1 W.L.R. 495.
[97] *Wilson v Law Debenture Trust Corp Plc* [1995] 2 All E.R. 337; above, para.16–005; below, para.17–044.
[98] Below, para.16–031.

The Pensions Act 1995 (as amended) imposes further restrictions on payments of surplus to the employer from a scheme which is ongoing.[99] Where the scheme confers power on any person (including the employer) other than the trustees to make payments to the employer, it can be exercised only by the trustees.[100] The power can be exercised only on complying with strict conditions, including that the trustees are satisfied that it is in the interest of members to exercise it in the manner proposed.[101]

vii. Winding Up. On this event, which may occur on the employer's insolvency and in other circumstances specified in the scheme rules,[102] the members' rights crystallise. Liabilities to them must be discharged and any surplus assets distributed. The trustees may be able to rely on s.27 of the Trustee Act 1925 if they had no notice of a member's claim, but in practice it will be difficult for them to show that they had no notice.[103] It has already been noted that a pension scheme may be wound up by the order of the Pensions Regulator in certain circumstances.[104] The 1995 Act (as amended) contains other provisions dealing with the discharge of liabilities and distribution of surplus on the winding up of an earnings-related scheme. (The question of insufficient or excess assets will not arise with a money purchase scheme, where the level of benefits is not defined and depends on the performance of the investments). The assets must be applied to discharge liabilities to members and others in a specified order.[105] Liabilities may be discharged in various ways, such as by transferring credits to another scheme, by transfer to certain personal pension schemes, by the purchase of annuities or by cash payments.[106] If the assets are insufficient to discharge the liabilities, the deficit is treated as a debt from the employer to the trustees, without prejudice to any other right or remedy of the trustees.[107]

16–023

Where there are surplus assets, the scheme will normally provide for their allocation, often by requiring payment to the employer after augmenting benefits. In the rare case where the scheme makes no effective provision for surplus, the general law applies. Such a case

---

[99] See generally *National Grid Co Plc v Mayes* [2001] 1 W.L.R. 864.

[100] s.37(2), as amended by Pensions Act 2004 s.250. See also s.251, as amended by Pensions Act 2011 s.25.

[101] s.7(3), (4), as amended.

[102] For example, a solvent employer may wish to wind up an earnings-related scheme in order to replace it with a money purchase scheme.

[103] Below, para.18–028; *MCP Pension Trustees Ltd v Aon Pension Trustees Ltd* [2011] 3 W.L.R. 455.

[104] s.11; above, para.16–008. See also Pensions Act 2004 s.154 (winding up of failing scheme where rescue not possible).

[105] s.73, as substituted by Pensions Act 2004 s.270.

[106] s.74, as amended by Pensions Act 2004 s.270.

[107] s.75, as amended by Pensions Act 2004 s.271.

came before the Privy Council in *Air Jamaica Ltd v Charlton*,[108] where the pension scheme had been discontinued. An amendment to the scheme purporting to permit the payment of surplus to the employer was invalid because the power to amend was void for perpetuity. The surplus was held on a resulting trust as to half for the employer and half for the members (including the estates of deceased members) in proportion to their contributions. The decision of Scott J. in *Davis v Richards & Wallington Industries Ltd*,[109] to the effect that any share of the members would go to the Crown as bona vacantia on the basis (primarily for tax reasons) that the members must have intended to exclude a resulting trust, was wrong, having been based on an incorrect analysis of the role of intention. The fact that the extra benefits under a resulting trust would exceed the limits for tax relief was not a proper ground for rejecting a resulting trust for members.

As stated above, on insolvency of the employer any fiduciary powers, including powers relating to the allocation of surplus, are exercisable only by the independent trustee.[110] The 1995 Act (as amended) makes further provisions for the allocation of surplus assets on the winding up of an approved scheme, of which the rules either permit or prohibit distribution to the employer. If the scheme confers power on the employer or trustees to distribute assets to the employer, the power can only be exercised where all liabilities have been fully discharged and notice has been given to the members.[111]

Where a surplus remains after the discharge of all liabilities and the scheme prohibits distribution to the employer, permitted additional benefits must be provided, after which the trustees may distribute any surplus to the employer.[112] Sanctions for failure to comply with these provisions include the imposition of a financial penalty under s.10.

16–024   **viii. Information to Members.** As explained in Ch.19, trustees are under a general law duty to provide information and accounts to the beneficiaries. In addition, s.41 of the 1995 Act[113] provides for regulations requiring the trustees to make copies of various documents available to the members and prospective members and their spouses (and to certain other persons). The documents in question include the trustees' statement of funding principles, audited accounts, actuarial valuations of assets and liabilities of the scheme,

---

[108] [1999] 1 W.L.R. 1399; above, para.10–012.
[109] [1990] 1 W.L.R. 1511.
[110] Pensions Act 1995 s.25(2); above, para.16–010.
[111] s.76, as amended.
[112] s.77, as amended.
[113] As amended by the Pensions Act 2004. See also s.203 of the Act of 2004 (information to members concerning involvement of the Board of the Pension Protection Fund).

certificates relating to the scheme funding requirement and reports (required by the Act) concerning any failure to meet that requirement.

ix. Compensation. Although the aim of the pensions legislation **16–025** is to prevent the misappropriation of pension funds, no statutory mechanism can provide totally effective safeguards. The legislation, therefore, provides a compensation scheme to diminish hardships such as those suffered by the victims of Robert Maxwell's fraud. More recently, the plight of employees who have lost their pensions on the employer's insolvency has been publicised. The Pensions Compensation Board, set up by the Pensions Act 1995, was replaced in the Pensions Act 2004 by the Board of the Pension Protection Fund.[114]

The Board intervenes where the insolvency of an employer (of which it must be notified) leaves a defined benefit (final salary) scheme in deficit, so that members will lose some or all of their benefits.[115] If the scheme cannot be rescued, the Board is responsible for ensuring that compensation is paid to the members, whereupon the scheme is wound up.[116] It may direct legal proceedings to be taken, for example to recover misappropriated assets.[117]

The Pension Protection Fund[118] does not provide a full guarantee of benefits, because payments are standardised and subject to capping.[119] It derives its funds from a levy (which is partly risk-based) payable by defined benefit occupational pension schemes.[120] This may further discourage employers from setting up or continuing with such schemes.

The statutory compensation scheme was not retrospective, and so provided no help to some 85,000 people who had lost their pensions through the employer's insolvency before the commencement of the scheme. In 2006 the Parliamentary Commissioner (Ombudsman) upheld a complaint against the Government for misleading people over the safety of occupational pension schemes. The Government rejected the Ombudsman's findings but, following judicial review proceedings by the pensioners, finally agreed a compensation package.[121]

---

[114] Pensions Act 2004 Pt 2.

[115] This would not have helped the Maxwell pensioners, as the employer companies did not go into liquidation.

[116] Pensions Act 2004 s.161.

[117] Pensions Act 2004 s.134.

[118] Pensions Act 2004 s.173. See also ss.182, 188 (the Fraud Compensation Fund).

[119] The detailed provisions are contained in Sch.7 as amended by Pensions Act 2008, Sch.8 and Pensions Act 2011 Sch.4. The amount is set by Statutory Instrument, and is £33,219 as from April 1, 2011.

[120] Pensions Act 2004 s.174. See also s.189 (levy for the Fraud Compensation Fund).

[121] *R. (on the application of Bradley) v Secretary of State for Work and Pensions* [2009] Q.B. 114; J. Varuhas (2009) 72 M.L.R. 102.

The prospective availability of compensation from the fund is not a relevant factor for the trustees to take into account when exercising any power under the pension scheme rules, as this would be contrary to public policy.[122]

16–026   **x. Alienability; Bankruptcy.** Other provisions of the Pensions Act 1995 deal with the alienability of pension rights and the position on the bankruptcy of a scheme member. The object of a pension scheme is not to provide members with a disposable asset but to ensure an income on retirement. Accrued rights under an occupational pension scheme cannot be assigned, surrendered, charged or subjected to any right of set-off.[123] This general prohibition, which reflects the provisions normally found in pension schemes,[124] does not apply to assignments to or surrenders for the benefit of the member's widow, widower or dependant, and there are limited exceptions permitting a charge or set-off by the employer.

Where a member of an approved occupational or personal pension scheme is made bankrupt, his pension rights are excluded from his estate for the purposes of the Insolvency Act 1986 and are thus unavailable to creditors.[125] The provisions of the 1986 Act relating to the setting aside of certain dispositions made prior to bankruptcy[126] are extended so that contributions to an occupational or personal pension scheme may be ordered by the court to be recovered by the trustee in bankruptcy to the extent that the contributions were excessive and have unfairly prejudiced the creditors.[127] The court will consider in particular whether the contributions were made for the purpose of putting assets beyond the reach of creditors.

B. Other Statutory Provisions

16–027   **i. Rule Against Perpetuities.** As explained in Ch.14, the perpetuity rule prevents the vesting of property at a remote date beyond the perpetuity period (lives in being plus 21 years, a specified period not exceeding 80 years under the Perpetuities and Accumulations Act 1964, or 125 years under the Perpetuities and Accumulations Act 2009) and also invalidates non-charitable purpose trusts which

---

[122] *Independent Trustee Services Ltd v Hope* [2010] I.C.R. 553; D. Fox (2010) 69 C.L.J. 240.
[123] Pensions Act 1995 s.91. Forfeiture, meaning any manner of deprivation or suspension (e.g. for misconduct), is prohibited by s.92.
[124] See *Re Scientific Investment Pension Plan Trusts* [1999] Ch. 53, above, para.7–001.
[125] Welfare Reform and Pensions Act 1999, s.11.
[126] Above, para.13–018.
[127] s.342 A, B and C of the Insolvency Act 1986, inserted by Pensions Act 1995, and amended by Welfare Reform and Pensions Act 1999 s.15.

are not confined in duration to the perpetuity period. It will be appreciated that the perpetuity rule could prove troublesome if applied to occupational pension schemes.[128] The perpetuity rule is based on public policy, namely that it is undesirable for economic and other reasons to have property tied up for long periods of time save for charitable purposes (to which the rule does not apply). In the case of pension funds there is a countervailing public interest in encouraging the provision of retirement pensions. The Perpetuities and Accumulations Act 2009[129] provides, therefore, that occupational, personal and public service pension schemes are exempted from the perpetuity rule. However, the rule applies to nominations of benefits by scheme members and instruments exercising powers of advancement under pension schemes.[130]

ii. Tax Relief. The public interest in the provision of retirement **16–028** benefits beyond the state pension results in significant tax relief for occupational pension schemes. Previously tax relief depended on the scheme being an "exempt approved scheme", but that regime was replaced by the Finance Act 2004 (with effect from April 6, 2006) by a registration requirement. In order to obtain tax relief, the pension scheme must be registered under s.153 of the Act.[131] Registration may be withdrawn by decision of HMRC on certain grounds, for example failure to pay a substantial amount of tax due, or where a false declaration was made to secure registration.[132] A scheme may be registered whether it is earnings-related or money purchase, and whether the investments are held by the trustees or through the medium of an insurer. The Act of 2004 sets out a framework of principles for the payment of pensions in the context of tax relief.[133] The details cannot be given here, but examples include the rule that a pension may not be paid before the minimum pension age[134] save in cases of ill-health, and that death benefits may not be paid other than to a dependant of the member.

The court will not vary a pension trust in a manner which could put at risk its tax exempt status.[135] The effect of loss of eligibility for tax relief is severe, but this does not justify the exclusion of a resulting trust of surplus funds in favour of the members which

---

[128] See *Air Jamaica Ltd v Charlton* [1999] 1 W.L.R. 1399 (no exemption in Jamaica).
[129] s.2(4), replacing earlier legislation.
[130] PAA 2009 s.2(5).
[131] FA 2004 ss.186 to 203.
[132] FA 2004 ss.157, 158. The decision may be appealed; s.159. De-registration leads to a tax charge; below, para.16–031.
[133] FA 2004 ss.165 to 168.
[134] This is 50 before April 6, 2010 and 55 on and after that date; FA 2004 s.279.
[135] *Brooks v Brooks* [1996] 1 A.C. 375.

would put their benefits above the statutory limits for tax exemption.[136]

16–029   (a) *Tax Relief for Contributions.* Provided the scheme is registered, tax relief is given to both employer and employee contributions. Contributions by the employer are treated as trading expenses and thus deductible from income and corporation tax liability.[137] Contributions by the employee are deductible from taxable income, subject to certain conditions.[138] A further benefit is that the employer's contributions are not taxable as remuneration of the employee.[139] Ultimately the pension itself will be subject to income tax whether or not the scheme is registered,[140] although lump sums payable on retirement are tax free.[141]

16–030   (b) *Tax Relief for the Pension Fund.* Provided the scheme is registered, the fund itself attracts significant relief. Neither income tax[142] nor capital gains tax[143] is payable on the investments.

16–031   (c) *Overfunding.* In view of the above reliefs there might be a temptation to put more money than is required into the pension fund, which could either be used to pay excessive benefits or retrieved by the employer as surplus. The exploitation of tax relief is prevented in various ways. We have seen that the statutory framework for tax relief now contained in the Finance Act 2004 lays down conditions which must be satisfied in order for payments from pension funds to be authorised.[144] If unauthorised payments are made to the members or the employer, a tax charge of 40 per cent is levied.[145] Unauthorised payments can lead to the scheme being de-registered, whereupon tax is charged at 40 per cent on the assets of the scheme.[146] If a surplus (which has had the benefit of tax relief) has built up, it cannot be used as a tax shelter. An unauthorised payment of surplus to the employer will be taxed at 40 per cent, as just mentioned. The first call on a surplus is the increase of benefits, after which contributions may be reduced or suspended. Where a payment of surplus

---

[136] *Air Jamaica Ltd v Charlton* [1999] 1 W.L.R. 1399, disapproving *Davis v Richards & Wallington Industries Ltd* [1990] 1 W.L.R. 1511; above, para.10–015.

[137] FA 2004 s.196.

[138] FA 2004 s.188.

[139] Income Tax (Earnings and Pensions) Act 2003 s.307.

[140] Income Tax (Earnings and Pensions) Act 2003 s.393 and Pt 9.

[141] Income Tax (Earnings and Pensions) Act 2003 s.637.

[142] FA 2004 s.186.

[143] Taxation of Chargeable Gains Act 1992 s.271, as amended by FA 2004 s.187. For inheritance tax relief, see IHTA 1984 s.86 (employee trusts).

[144] Above, para.16–028.

[145] FA 2004 s.208. See also s.209 (unauthorised payments surcharge) and s.239 (scheme sanction surcharge).

[146] FA 2004 s.242.

to the employer is authorised by the scheme rules and the tax legislation, it is taxed at 35 per cent.[147]

3. EQUAL TREATMENT

Article 119 of the Treaty of Rome embodies the principle that men **16–032** and women should receive equal pay for equal work. Clearly this has no scope for application to traditional trusts conferring benefits by way of bounty, but it does apply to occupational pension schemes because, as we have seen, pension entitlements are a form of deferred remuneration for services. Thus it was held by the European Court of Justice in *Barber v Guardian Royal Exchange Assurance Group*[148] that pension rights fell within art.119, with the result that the common practice of conferring pension entitlements on women employees at an earlier age than their male counterparts was no longer permissible. There were doubts as to the precise scope of the *Barber* decision, and so the matter was tested again in the European Court of Justice in *Coloroll Pension Trustees Ltd v Russell*.[149] It was there held that trustees are bound to do everything within the scope of their powers to ensure compliance with the equal pay principle. Thus the trustees are bound, in the exercise of the powers and the performance of the duties laid down in the trust deed, to observe the principle of equal pay and treatment.

The Equality Act 2010, replacing a provision in the Pensions Act 1995, provides that an occupational pension scheme which does not contain a sex equality rule shall be treated as including one.[150]

4. PENSIONS ON DIVORCE

Another matter of current concern, which will be dealt with only in **16–033** outline here, is the extent to which the pension entitlement of one spouse (usually the husband) must be shared with the other spouse on divorce. A wife who has brought up a family instead of working may have no pension provision of her own and may be reduced to penury in old age if her former husband's pension (often the most valuable family asset after the matrimonial home) is not available to her. The question whether and how pension benefits should be shared is a matter of government policy. One way is to take the husband's pension into account by giving a greater share of other

---

[147] FA 2004 ss.177, 207. See also Pensions Act 1995 s.37, above (restrictions on exercise of power to make payments to employer).

[148] [1991] 1 Q.B. 344.

[149] [1995] I.C.R. 179.

[150] s.67. See also Pensions Act 2004 s.171.

assets to the wife on divorce. Alternatively, the pension itself may be split or earmarked as a source of payments to the spouse, either on divorce or later, when it comes to be paid. Pension sharing on divorce may now be ordered under the Matrimonial Causes Act 1973, as amended by the Welfare Reform and Pensions Act 1999 and the Pensions Act 2008. An alternative possibility is "earmarking", whereby an order made on divorce takes effect when the pension benefits under an occupational or personal pension scheme become payable to the scheme member. At that stage all or part of the benefits may be diverted to the former spouse.[151] The rules relating to spouses apply also to registered civil partners.[152] The details of pension sharing and earmarking are outside the scope of this book.

---

[151] MCA 1973, ss.25B, C, D and E. See also Pensions Act 2004 s.220.
[152] Civil Partnership Act 2004, as amended by Pensions Act 2008.

PART III

TRUSTEES

CHAPTER 17

GENERAL PRINCIPLES: CAPACITY; APPOINTMENT; REMOVAL; RETIREMENT; CONTROL

1. ONEROUS NATURE OF OFFICE

THE office of trustee is an onerous one. We will discuss in some **17–001** detail a trustee's duties, powers and liability; there is little to be said as to his rights. In the performance of his office a trustee must act exclusively in the interest of the trust. He stands to gain nothing from his work in the absence of a clause authorising remuneration, although professional trustees now have charging powers under the Trustee Act 2000.[1] He is required to observe the highest standards of integrity,[2] and a reasonable standard of care and skill in the management of the affairs of the trust; and he is subjected to onerous personal liability if he fails to reach the standards set. Nor may he compete in business with the trust; or be in a position in which his personal interests conflict with those of the trust. He may thus be forced to forgo opportunities which would be available to him if he were not a trustee.[3]

It may well be asked why people consent to become trustees. To this there are two answers. First, professional trustees undertake the work only where they are entitled to be paid. Solicitors, banks (Executor and Trustee Departments) and insurance companies come into this category. Most trusts of any size will have a professional trustee. There may be non-professional trustees also; but in any case the bulk of the work of administration—investment, distribution, accounting, tax payments, etc.—will in fact be done by professionals, either the trustees or others employed by them. Secondly, members of the family of the settlor or testator will often consent to be trustees out of feelings of duty to the settlor or testator. Where there is no professional trustee, the non-professionals will, as will be seen,[4] usually employ professional agents such as a solicitor, investment manager and accountant to perform the technical duties of the trust. It may well be better to have such experts appointed as trustees in the first place, so that technical matters will not be overlooked.[5] It is usual and common to appoint a mixture of professional trustees and non-professional. There is much to be said for appointing a corporation such as a bank which may be expected to have unrivalled facilities, dependability and permanence.

The settlor (typically in the case of an offshore trust) may also provide for the appointment of a "protector", an independent fiduciary to oversee the exercise of the trustees' powers.[6]

2. STANDARDS APPLICABLE TO TRUSTEES

A. Duties and Discretions

17–002   A distinction must be made between a trustee's duties and his powers or discretions. A duty is an obligation which *must* be carried

---

[1] Below, para.21–003. Charity trustees may be paid in certain cases; above, para.15–096.

[2] Below, para.17–002.

[3] *Boardman v Phipps* [1967] 2 A.C. 46; below, Ch.21.

[4] Below, para.20–012.

[5] For the dangers inherent in appointing no professional trustees, see *Turner v Turner* [1984] Ch. 100, above, para.6–007. See generally C. Bell (1988) 2 *Trust Law & Practice* 86.

[6] See A. Penney [1995] 4 J.Int.P. 31; P. Matthews (1995) 9 T.L.I. 108; P. Hobson (1996) 2 *Trusts & Trustees* 6; D. Waters in A. Oakley (ed.) *Trends in Contemporary Trust Law*, p.63; Underhill and Hayton, 18th edn, pp.47–54; J. Hilliard (2003) 17 T.L.I. 144; A. Duckworth (2006) 20 T.L.I. 180 and 235; T. Tey (2010) 24 T.L.I. 110.

out. The rules of equity require strict and diligent performance of a trustee's duties. On the other hand, a power is discretionary; it may be exercised, or it may not. This is so whether the power is one given to trustees by statute, or is a power or discretion contained in the instrument creating the trust, or relates to the general management of the affairs of the trust.

Trustees must act honestly; and must take, in managing trust affairs, "all those precautions which an ordinary prudent man of business would take in managing similar affairs of his own."[7] This formula has now been largely overtaken by the statutory duty of care discussed in the next section. If the trustee properly performs his duties, powers and discretions, he is not liable for loss[8] to or depreciation[9] of the trust property arising from factors beyond his control.

We will see that many of the rules relating to trustees' duties are more strict in their terms than in their practical application. The past 100 years have brought a great alleviation in the lot of the honest trustee. We saw that much of the work of administration of a trust is necessarily done by professionals. This development has led to great relaxation, first by the courts[10] and then by statute,[11] of the requirement that the trustee should act personally. Further, exemption clauses (discussed below) which exclude the trustees' personal liability in certain circumstances have become widespread; and the Trustee Act 1925 s.61, gives the court a discretion to excuse a trustee who has acted honestly and reasonably and ought fairly to be excused.[12]

B. The Statutory Duty of Care

The standard of conduct required of trustees has been put on a statutory basis by the Trustee Act 2000. It was previously laid down in *Speight v Gaunt*[13] that in the management of trust affairs the trustee must act as an ordinary prudent business person would act in managing similar affairs of his own. It had been established by the courts prior to the Trustee Act 2000 that a higher standard was expected of paid trustees.

17–003

---

[7] per Lord Blackburn in *Speight v Gaunt* (1883) 9 App.Cas. 1 at 19; in similar terms, Lord Watson in *Learoyd v Whiteley* (1887) 12 App.Cas. 727 at 733.

[8] *Morley v Morley* (1678) 2 Ch.Cas. 2.

[9] *Re Chapman* [1896] 2 Ch. 763.

[10] *Speight v Gaunt* (1883) 9 App.Cas. 1: below, para.20–012; *Learoyd v Whiteley*, above, fn.7; *Shaw v Cates* [1909] 1 Ch. 389.

[11] TA 2000 Pt IV, replacing the more limited provisions of TA 1925; below, para. 20–013–20–018.

[12] Below, para.23–033.

[13] (1883) 9 App.Cas. 1. See generally J. Getzler in Birks and Pretto (eds), *Breach of Trust*, 2002, Ch.2.

In *Re Waterman's Will Trusts*[14] Harman J. said:

"I do not forget that a paid trustee is expected to exercise a higher standard of diligence and knowledge than an unpaid trustee and that a bank which advertises itself largely in the public press as taking charge of administrations is under a special duty."

Subsequently, in *Bartlett v Barclays Bank Trust Co Ltd (No.1)*[15] Brightman J. said:

"I am of opinion that a higher duty of care is plainly due from someone like a trust corporation which carries on a specialised business of trust management. A trust corporation holds itself out in its advertising literature as being above ordinary mortals. With a specialist staff of trained trust officers and managers ... the trust corporation holds itself out, and rightly, as capable of providing an expertise which it would be unrealistic to expect and unjust to demand from the ordinary prudent man or woman who accepts, probably unpaid and sometimes reluctantly from a sense of family duty, the burdens of a trusteeship ... so I think that a professional corporate trustee is liable for breach of trust if loss is caused to the trust fund because it neglects to exercise the special care and skill which it professes to have."

The distinction between lay and professional trustees is maintained in s.1 of the Trustee Act 2000, which provides that a trustee:

"[M]ust exercise such care and skill as is reasonable in the circumstances, having regard in particular (a) to any special knowledge or experience that he has or holds himself out as having, and (b) if he acts as trustee in the course of a business or profession, to any special knowledge or experience that it is reasonable to expect of a person acting in the course of that kind of business or profession."

17–004   The duty of care, which may be excluded by the trust instrument,[16] applies to various functions of trustees listed in Sch.1 of the Act, whether arising by statute or by corresponding express provision in the trust instrument. The relevant functions are as follows: investment[17]; the acquisition of land[18]; the appointment of agents,

---

[14] [1952] 2 All E.R. 1054 at 1055; cf. *Jobson v Palmer* [1893] 1 Ch. 71; M. Davies (1969) 33 Conv.(N.S.) 179; D. Paling (1973) 37 Conv.(N.S.) 48.
[15] [1980] Ch. 515 at 534. See also *Re Rosenthal* [1972] 1 W.L.R. 1373.
[16] TA 2000 Sch.1, para.7.
[17] Below, paras 18–005–18–016.
[18] Below, para.18–011.

nominees and custodians[19]; compounding liabilities[20]; insurance[21]; and powers relating to reversionary interests, valuations and audit.[22] It does not apply to dispositive powers of trustees, such as the power to select from a class of beneficiaries. Nor does it apply to the powers of maintenance and advancement which (as will be seen in Ch.20) are in essence dispositive. The duty of care is primarily concerned with powers, and applies to the manner of their exercise, not to the trustee's decision whether to exercise them or not. So far as duties are concerned, the question is simply whether the duty has been performed or not. If it has not, as where a distribution has been made to the wrong beneficiary, a breach has been committed however careful the trustee was, although he may be relieved under s.61 of the Trustee Act 1925 if he acted honestly and reasonably.

A further distinction between paid and unpaid trustees is maintained through the application of s.61, under which an unpaid family trustee is more likely to be relieved from liability than a professional trustee.[23] Further, a paid trustee will be expected to do more of the work himself and to delegate less; and a paid trustee will be given less opportunity to rely upon the fact that he acted upon legal advice.[24]

C. Trustee Exemption Clauses[25]

A question which has attracted much attention in recent years is whether and how far the settlor may effectively exempt a trustee from liability. Before considering the construction of express clauses, it should be noted that the Trustee Act 2000 does not deal specifically with trustee exemption clauses, but, as noted above, it does provide that the statutory duty of care is inapplicable "if or in so far as it appears from the trust instrument that the duty is not meant to apply".[26] Further, as will be seen below, an exemption clause may be more strictly construed against a solicitor trustee than against a lay trustee.[27]

17–005

---

[19] Below, paras 20–012–20–018.
[20] Below, para.20–010.
[21] Below, para.20–008.
[22] Below, para.20–011.
[23] *National Trustee Co of Australasia Ltd v General Finance Co of Australasia* [1905] A.C. 373; *Re Pauling's ST* [1964] Ch. 303 at 338, 339.
[24] *Re Windsor Steam Co (1901) Ltd* [1929] 1 Ch. 151. See also *Steel v Wellcome Custodian Trustees Ltd* [1988] 1 W.L.R. 167, at 174.
[25] See J. Getzler in Birks and Pretto (eds), *Breach of Trust*, 2002, Ch.2.
[26] TA 2000 Sch.1, para.7.
[27] *Walker v Stones* [2001] Q.B. 902; below, (test of honesty depended on role and calling of trustee). See also *Breadner v Granville-Grossman (costs)* [2006] W.T.L.R. 411 at 420 (exemption clause does not protect a trustee against a court order that he should pay costs personally).

19th-century English[28] and Scottish[29] authorities indicated that exemption clauses, which are strictly construed against trustees,[30] would not protect them in cases of bad faith, recklessness or deliberate breach of duty.[31] To allow protection in cases of fraud would be contrary to public policy. It is, however, possible to confer protection against liability for gross negligence if the clause is unambiguous.[32] In *Armitage v Nurse*[33] the clause provided that the trustees should not be liable for loss or damage unless "caused by his own actual fraud". This, it was held, would protect the trustees so long as they did not act dishonestly, no matter how indolent, imprudent or negligent they were. As Millett L.J. explained, the "irreducible core of obligations" owed by trustees included the duty to act honestly and in good faith but did not include any duty of skill or care, thus it was not repugnant to their duties, nor contrary to public policy, to allow exemption from liability for gross negligence, which differed only in degree from ordinary negligence.[34] The expression "actual fraud" excluded notions of constructive or equitable fraud, arising for example under the doctrine of "fraud on a power".[35] Older cases appearing to suggest that it was not possible to exclude liability for gross negligence turned on the wording of particular clauses. Reference was made, however, to the prevailing view that exemption clauses had gone too far. It has since been held that an exemption clause covering defaults other than dishonesty could not be relied on, at least in the case of a solicitor trustee, where he had committed a deliberate breach of trust which no reasonable solicitor trustee could have thought was for the benefit of the beneficiaries, even if he genuinely believed that it was.[36]

There is a distinction between clauses which exempt from breach and those which prevent the duty from arising. Such a clause as the latter may be effective where there was no pre-existing fiduciary

---

[28] *Wilkins v Hogg* (1861) 31 L.J. Ch. 41; *Pass v Dundas* (1880) 43 L.T. 665. See also *Rehden v Wesley* (1861) 29 Beav. 213.

[29] *Knox v Mackinnon* (1888) 13 App.Cas. 753; *Rae v Meek* (1889) 14 App.Cas. 558. See generally P. Matthews [1989] Conv. 42; P. Clifton (2001) 15 T.L.I. 194.

[30] This principle does not prevent a solicitor trustee who drafted the clause from relying on it; *Bogg v Raper, The Times*, April 22, 1998. See also *Wight v Olswang, The Times*, May 18, 1999.

[31] See *Walker v Stones* [2001] Q.B. 902, below.

[32] This was recently confirmed obiter by the Privy Council in *Spread Trustee Co Ltd v Hutcheson* [2011] UKPC 13; L. Aitken (2011) 127 L.Q.R. 503; K. Loi [2011] Conv. 521.

[33] [1998] Ch. 241; G. McCormack [1998] Conv. 100; N. McBride (1998) 57 C.L.J. 33. Leave to appeal to the House of Lords was refused; [1998] 1 W.L.R. 270. See also D. Pollard (1997) 11 T.L.I. 93; I. Greenstreet (2004) 18 T.L.I. 132; Law Com. No.301 (2006) at 2.15 and *Spread Trustee Co Ltd v Hutcheson* [2011] UKPC 13 (casting doubt on the views of Millett L.J. on the Scottish cases).

[34] His Lordship, writing extra-judicially, doubted the *propriety* of exemption clauses covering gross negligence; (1998) 114 L.Q.R. 214.

[35] Above, para.6–018.

[36] *Walker v Stones* [2001] Q.B. 902.

relationship between the parties, especially in the context of a commercial agreement between parties of equal status.[37]

It should be added that special rules apply to pension trusts,[38] unit trusts[39] and debenture trusts.[40]

The Law Commission reviewed the matter and decided against recommending legislation, which had attracted little support during consultation and would restrict settlor autonomy. Instead it proposed that trustee exemption clauses should be regulated by professional bodies in order to ensure that settlors and testators were aware of the clauses.[41] It recommended that the regulatory and professional bodies should make and enforce regulations in accordance with their code of conduct, so that:

> "Any paid trustee who causes a settlor to include a clause in a trust instrument which has the effect of excluding or limiting liability for negligence must, before the creation of the trust, take such steps as are reasonable to ensure that the settlor is aware of the meaning and effect of the clause."[42]

A breach of the good practice rule, which of course applies only to new trusts, would not of itself render the trustee liable to damages, but would expose him to disciplinary measures. The Law Commission anticipated that "best practice will seep into the consciousness of the trust industry".[43] However, the Law Commission's conclusion has been criticised as not going beyond existing good practice and doing nothing to address the wrongfulness of the continued existence of exemption clauses protecting paid trustees.[44]

3. Liability to Third Parties

Persons entering into a contractual relationship with trustees, for **17–006** example by supplying goods or by lending money, can enforce their

---

[37] Law Com. No.236 (1995), *Fiduciary Duties and Regulatory Rules*. See also *Kelly v Cooper* [1993] A.C. 205; *Citibank NA v MBIA Assurance SA* [2007] 1 All E.R. (Comm) 475; A. Trukhlanov (2007) 123 L.Q.R. 342.

[38] Pensions Act 1995 ss.33, 34(6) (investment functions); I. Greenstreet (2004) 18 T.L.I. 132; M. Howard (2011) 25 T.L.I. 99 (liability insurance); above, para.16–018.

[39] Financial Services and Markets Act 2000 s.253 (exemption for negligence not permitted for manager or trustee).

[40] Companies Act 2006 s.750, re-enacting earlier legislation (exemption for negligence not permitted for trustee of debenture deed).

[41] Law Com. No.301 (2006); *Trustee Exemption Clauses*. Guidance for members has been published by the Law Society, the Society of Trust and Estate Practitioners (STEP) and the Institute of Chartered Accountants. The Government accepted the Report's recommendations (*Hansard*, September 14, 2010).

[42] Law Com. No.301 (2006), para.7.2.

[43] Law Com. No.301 (2006), para.6.117.

[44] A. Kenny [2007] Conv. 103; H. Delaney (2009) 23 T.L.I. 89 (contrasting the proposals of the Irish Law Reform Commission).

rights against the trustees personally, but have no direct right to payment out of the trust assets. From the point of view of the trustees, they are entitled to an indemnity out of the trust fund for liabilities properly incurred, but this leaves them exposed to personal risk if the trust fund is insufficient,[45] unless they have limited their liability to the amount of the trust assets when dealing with the third party. From the point of view of third parties, although they may be subrogated to the trustees' right to an indemnity out of the trust fund, the difficulty is that the creditor cannot make any claim against the trust fund which the trustees could not have made.[46] If the trustees have committed a breach of trust, then of course they are not entitled to an indemnity,[47] and the creditor can be in no better position.

The absence of direct rights against the trust assets may cause difficulties with large commercial trusts, such as pension funds, wishing to borrow money on a large scale. Reform has been proposed by the Trust Law Committee,[48] to protect creditors by giving them a primary right of action against the trust assets. This will be taken forward by the Law Commission after completion of other projects.[49]

4. Unanimity[50]

17–007 Each trustee should be active in the administration of the trust. Equity does not recognise a "sleeping" trustee. A trustee who concurs with his co-trustees has, in so agreeing, as much "acted" as those others, and thus will be equally liable with them to beneficiaries who suffer loss if a breach results.[51] Nor will the concurring trustee necessarily escape liability when his co-trustee was a solicitor, unless he reasonably deferred to what could legitimately be regarded as superior knowledge.[52] But blind trust cannot safely be

---

[45] See *Perring v Draper* [1997] E.G.C.S. 109 (trustees personally liable for £96,000 rent arrears on termination of lease vested in them as trustees); *Marston Thompson & Evershed Plc v Benn* [2007] W.T.L.R. 315 (£185,000 loan to fund development of rugby club clubhouse).

[46] See *Re Johnson* (1880) 15 Ch.D. 548; *Re Oxley* [1914] 1 Ch. 604.

[47] See *Holding & Management Ltd v Property Holding & Investment Trust Plc* [1989] 1 W.L.R. 1313; *White v Williams* [2011] W.T.L.R. 899.

[48] *Rights of Creditors Against Trustees and Trust Funds* (1999); D. Hayton (1997) 11 T.L.I. 58; H. Tjio (2005) 19 T.L.I. 75. See also D. Wingfield (2003) 119 L.Q.R. 44, discussing charity trustees.

[49] Law Com. No.323; *Annual Report 2009/10* para.2.76.

[50] See J. Jaconelli [1991] Conv. 30.

[51] *Bahin v Hughes* (1886) 31 Ch.D. 390; *Re Turner* [1897] 1 Ch. 536; *Wynne v Tempest* (1897) 13 T.L.R. 360. But the co-trustee who concurs may be able to obtain an indemnity from the active trustee; below, para.23–018.

[52] See *Head v Gould* [1898] 2 Ch. 250; *Bahin v Hughes*, above, fn.51.

placed in a co-trustee. For although there is no rule that trustees are vicariously liable for the acts of co-trustees, a non-active trustee may himself be liable for neglecting to take the steps necessary to have prevented the breach.[53]

Trustees (other than trustees of charities and pension trusts[54]) cannot act by a majority, unless expressly authorised in the trust instrument.[55] A majority binds neither a dissenting minority nor the trust estate.[56] The consequences of this rule need to be appreciated.

In *Re Mayo*,[57] for instance, one trustee of a trust for sale wished to sell, two to postpone. The trustees were by virtue of the trust to sell, under a *duty* to sell, but possessed *power* to postpone. Simonds J. held that their duty to sell prevailed unless they were unanimous in exercising their power to postpone. They were not unanimous on this point; the view of the single trustee who wished to sell prevailed, and the other two were directed to join in the sale.

5. Who may be a Trustee

In principle, any person who is able to hold property may be a trustee. Special rules apply to charity and pension trustees,[58] and other categories need special consideration.

17–008

i. Children. A child cannot hold a legal estate in land[59]; and the Law of Property Act 1925 s.20, provides that the appointment of a child to be a trustee in relation to any trust shall be void. A child of four years old was, however, held to be able to hold personalty on resulting trust.[60] As will be seen,[61] if a child is a trustee of personalty, he may be replaced, whether or not he consents.

17–009

---

[53] *Bahin v Hughes*, above, fn.51.

[54] Above, paras 15–094, 16–012.

[55] *Re Butlin's WT* [1976] Ch. 251; *Re Whiteley* [1910] 1 Ch. 600 at 608. See also TA 1925 s.63(3).

[56] *Luke v South Kensington Hotel Ltd* (1879) 11 Ch.D. 121.

[57] [1943] Ch. 302; cf. *Tempest v Lord Camoys* (1882) 21 Ch.D. 571; but the unanimity rule did not affect the validity of a notice to quit served by only one of two joint tenants holding on trust for sale, because the characteristic of a periodic tenancy is that all parties must concur in its continuance; *Hammersmith and Fulham LBC v Monk* [1992] 1 A.C. 478.

[58] Above, paras 15–093, 16–009.

[59] LPA 1925 s.1(6).

[60] *Re Vinogradoff* [1935] W.N. 68; above, para.10–021.

[61] Below, para.17–020.

17–010   **ii. The Crown.** It is usually said that the Crown may be a trustee[62] "if it chooses deliberately to do so",[63] but attempts to claim
funds in the hands of the Crown on the ground that the Crown
should be treated as a trustee have not been successful.[64] The circumstances in which the Crown will accept a trusteeship must be
rare indeed, and there would be substantial difficulties in enforcing
the trust if it did.[65]

17–011   **iii. Judicial Trustees.** The High Court may, on the application of
a person creating or intending to create a trust, or by or on behalf of
a trustee or beneficiary, appoint a person to be a judicial trustee of
that trust.[66] The court may appoint any fit and proper person,[67] and,
in the absence of the nomination of such person, may appoint an
official of the court.[68] Remuneration may be paid,[69] and the court
may direct an inquiry into the administration of the trust by a judicial trustee.[70] The court may give a judicial trustee any general or
special directions in regard to the trust or to the administration
thereof,[71] not, however, so as to:

> "[R]educe the administration of an estate by a judicial trustee to
> very much the same position as where an estate is being adminis-
> tered by the court and every step has to be taken in pursuance of
> the court's directions. . . . The object of the Judicial Trustees Act
> 1896 . . . was to provide a middle course in cases where the
> administration of the estate by the ordinary trustees had broken
> down, and it was not desired to put the estate to the expense of a
> full administration . . . a solution was found in the appointment of
> a judicial trustee, who acts in close concert with the court and

---

[62] *Penn v Lord Baltimore* (1750) 1 Ves.Sen. 444, per Lord Hardwicke at 453; *Burgess v Wheate* (1757–59) 1 Eden 177.

[63] *Civilian War Claimants Association Ltd v R.* [1932] A.C. 14, per Lord Atkin at 27 (a claim by the Association for payment by the Crown of reparations money received from Germany: "There is nothing so far as I know, to prevent the Crown acting as agent or trustee if it chooses deliberately to do so.").

[64] *Re Mason* [1929] 1 Ch. 1; *Civilian War Claimants Association Ltd v R.*, above, fn.63; *Tito v Waddell (No.2)* [1977] Ch. 106; above, para.2–035.

[65] Hanbury, *Essays in Equity*, 1934, pp.87–89; Holdsworth H.E.L., Vol.IX, pp.30–32.

[66] Judicial Trustees Act 1896 s.1(1); Judicial Trustee Rules 1983 (SI 1983/370). The procedure has not been much used in practice, but was recently applied to a trust arising under
mutual wills in *Thomas and Agnes Carvel Foundation v Carvel* [2008] Ch. 395.

[67] Judicial Trustees Act 1896 s.1(3); Public Trustee Act 1906 s.2(I)(d).

[68] Judicial Trustees Act 1896 s.1(3); usually the Official Solicitor of the court; Judicial
Trustees Act 1896 s.5.

[69] Judicial Trustees Act 1896 s.1(5); Practice Direction (Judicial Trustees: Remuneration)
[2003] 1 W.L.R. 1653.

[70] Judicial Trustees Act 1896 s.1(6), as amended by AJA 1982 s.57(1). On the auditing of
accounts, see Judicial Trustees Act 1896 s.4(1), as amended by AJA 1982 s.57(2). See also
Judicial Trustee Rules 1983 rr.2, 13.

[71] Judicial Trustees Act 1896 s.1(4); Judicial Trustee Rules 1983 r.8.

under conditions enabling the court to supervise his transactions."[72]

A judicial trustee may also be appointed in respect of the administration of an estate.[73] At the time when there was no machinery whereby a personal representative could retire, this provided a method of replacing one who could no longer act. Now, however, the court may appoint a substitute executor or administrator under s.50 of the Administration of Justice Act 1985. In an application under the 1896 Act for the appointment of a judicial trustee, the court may proceed as if it was an application under the 1985 Act, and vice versa.[74]

iv. The Public Trustee. The Public Trustee, established by the **17–012** Public Trustee Act 1906, could be appointed as trustee alone or jointly with another or others, and could act as a custodian trustee[75] or an ordinary trustee or as a judicial trustee. The Public Trustee is a corporation sole,[76] and is entitled to charge fees on a scale fixed by the Lord Chancellor.[77] One special function was the administration of small estates and, although he could decline to accept any trust, he could not do so on the ground "only of the small value of the trust property."[78] Another role of the Public Trustee is the holding of the property of a person who has died intestate, pending the appointment of an administrator.[79] Government policy in recent years has been to wind down the work of the Public Trustee, and in 2006 the Lord Chancellor approved a proposal that the Public Trustee should retire in bulk from his current caseload in favour of an approved private sector corporate trustee.

v. Custodian Trustees.[80] The Public Trustee,[81] the Official Cus- **17–013** todian for Charities[82] and a large number of other corporations[83] are authorised by statute to act as custodian trustees, and they may all

---

[72] *Re Ridsdel* [1947] Ch. 597 at 605.
[73] Judicial Trustees Act 1896 s.1(2).
[74] AJA 1985 s.50(4); Judicial Trustees Act 1896 s.1(7), added by the 1985 Act.
[75] s.4, below.
[76] Public Trustee Act 1906 s.1.
[77] Public Trustee Act 1906 s.9; Public Trustee (Fees) Act 1957; Public Trustee (Liability and Fees) Act 2002.
[78] Public Trustee Act 1906 s.2(3).
[79] Law of Property (Miscellaneous Provisions) Act 1994 s.14, amending AEA 1925 s.9.
[80] S. Maurice (1960) 24 Conv.(N.S.) 196.
[81] Public Trustee Act 1906 s.4(3).
[82] Above, para.15–081.
[83] Public Trustee Rules 1912 r.30, as substituted by the Public Trustee (Custodian Trustee) Rules 1975 (SI 1975/1189) r.2. See also Public Trustee (Custodian Trustee) Rules 1976 (SI 1976/836), 1981 (SI 1981/358) and 1994 (SI 1994/2519). Qualifying corporations include those of EU States which comply with the requirements and have a place of business in the UK carrying on trust business.

charge fees not exceeding those chargeable by the Public Trustee.[84] Others may act under the terms of the trust instrument, outside the statutory schemes. The custodian trustee holds property and the documents relating thereto while leaving to the managing trustee the day-to-day administration of the trust.[85]

The advantage of the scheme of custodian trusteeship is that new managing trustees can be appointed without the necessity of undergoing the trouble and expense—which can be considerable in the case of a large trust—of vesting all the trust investments in new trustees whenever there is a death, retirement or new appointment. It should be noted that this advantage cannot be gained by appointing the holder of an office as trustee, as the investments must be transferred to the names of the new holders of the office when a change is made. This can be avoided if the trustee is a corporation sole.[86]

In determining a number of trustees for the purpose of the Trustee Act 1925, the custodian trustee is not included.[87]

17–014   **vi. Trust Corporations.** Trust corporations play a large part in the administration of trusts. Their size, stability, dependability and expertise give them advantages over individual trustees.[88]

They enjoy a special status in that they can often act alone in circumstances in which at least two trustees would otherwise be necessary.[89] A trust corporation can give a valid receipt for capital money arising from the sale of land[90]; and a trust of land has greater overreaching powers if a trust corporation is trustee.[91] Further, trustees may retire and leave a sole trustee only if that trustee is a trust corporation.[92]

In most private trusts, a trust corporation is typically a bank. The legal definition is:

> "Trust corporation means the Public Trustee or a corporation either appointed by the court in a particular case to be a trustee, or entitled by rules made under subs.(3) of s.4 of the Public Trustee Act 1906, to act as custodian trustee."[93]

---

[84] Public Trustee Act 1906 s.4(3).

[85] For the relationship between custodian trustees and managing trustees, see Public Trustee Act 1906 s.4(2); *Forster v Williams Deacon's Bank Ltd* [1935] Ch. 359; *Re Brooke Bond and Co Ltd's Trust Deed* [1963] Ch. 357.

[86] *Bankes v Salisbury Diocesan Council of Education* [1960] Ch. 631 at 647–649.

[87] Public Trustee Act 1906 s.4(2)(g).

[88] See, however, N. Johnson (1997/98) 4 *Trusts & Trustees* 6, as to the advantages of a private company as trustee.

[89] See *In re Duxbury's ST* [1995] 1 W.L.R. 425; above, para.17–012 (Public Trustee).

[90] TA 1925 s.14; LPA 1925 s.27(2).

[91] LPA 1925 s.2(2).

[92] TA 1925 s.39; below, para.17–037.

[93] TA 1925 s.68(18); see also LPA 1925 s.205(1)(xxviii); AEA 1925 s.55(1)(xxvi); Senior Courts Act 1981 s.128.

The qualifications are contained in the Public Trustee (Custodian Trustee) Rules 1975.[94] The Law of Property (Amendment) Act 1926 s.3 added, amongst others, a trustee in bankruptcy, the Treasury Solicitor, and the Official Solicitor. Some solicitors' practices satisfy the definition. A trust corporation now has power to charge remuneration under the Trustee Act 2000, but express powers will normally be given for a fee to be charged for the service.

6. DISCLAIMER

Nobody can be compelled to accept the office of trustee against his will.[95] A person appointed as trustee who wishes to disclaim should do so by deed,[96] as this provides clear evidence of the disclaimer. However, a disclaimer may be implied; apathy will be evidence of an intention to disclaim, provided the apathy is consistent.[97] But if the trustee meddles with the estate, his conduct will be construed as an acceptance. Once he has disclaimed, he can no longer accept. Once he has accepted he can no longer disclaim[98] but as we will see, he may retire.[99]

17–015

7. NUMBER OF TRUSTEES

There is no restriction upon the number of trustees of personalty. It is inconvenient to have too many; and rare to have more than four, save in the case of charity and pension trustees, who can act by majority.[100] Where additional trustees are appointed under the statutory power, appointments may only be made up to a total of four.[101] A sole trustee is most unsatisfactory because of the opportunities for maladministration and fraud which then arise.

17–016

---

[94] SI 1975/1189. They include any corporation which (i) is constituted under the law of the UK or of another Member State of the EU; and (ii) is empowered by its constitution to undertake trust business in England and Wales; (iii) has one or more places of business in the UK; and (iv) being a registered company has a capital (in stock or shares) for the time being issued of not less than £250,000 (or its equivalent in the currency of the state of registration), of which not less than £100,000 (or its equivalent) has been paid up in cash. See also the Public Trustee (Custodian Trustee) Rules 1976 (SI 1976/8836) and 1981 (SI 1981/358). Companies Act 2006 s.31 permits other companies to act as trustees but they will not be trust corporations.

[95] A person can, of course, become a constructive or resulting trustee against his will.

[96] *Re Schär* [1951] Ch. 280; *Holder v Holder* [1968] Ch. 353 (an executor).

[97] *Re Clout and Frewer's Contract* [1924] 2 Ch. 230.

[98] *Re Sharman's WT* [1942] Ch. 311; *Holder v Holder*, above, fn.96.

[99] Below, para.17–035.

[100] Above, para.17–007. The special rules for the constitution of the trustees of pension funds are explained in Ch.16.

[101] TA 1925 s.36(6), below, para.17–023.

In trusts of land, the Trustee Act 1925 s.34, restricts the number of trustees to four. There are exceptions, the most important of which is that of land vested in trustees for charitable, ecclesiastical or public purposes.[102]

While a sole trustee of land is not forbidden,[103] the Trustee Act 1925 s.14(2), makes it impossible for a sole trustee (not being a trust corporation) to give a valid receipt for the proceeds of sale or other capital money arising under a trust of land, or capital money arising under the Settled Land Act 1925.[104]

8. Appointment of Trustees

A. The First Trustees

17–017   The first trustees will ordinarily be appointed by the settlor or testator in the deed or will creating the trust. In the case of a trust created by a settlor, the trustees will ordinarily be parties to the deed, and the trust is constituted upon the conveyance of the trust property to them. In a will, the same persons may be appointed executors and trustees. Where they are different persons, the trust is constituted upon the testator's death, for the title of the executors relates back to the death, and they hold on trust pending transfer to the persons appointed trustees in the will.

Trustees hold as joint tenants, and if one of several trustees dies, the survivors are the trustees, and they, and their successors, retain the same powers and duties as the original trustees.[105] On the death of a sole trustee, his personal representatives become trustees.[106] If he dies intestate, the trust estate will vest, pending the grant of administration, in the Public Trustee.[107] A trust does not normally fail for lack of a trustee; hence if the trustees disclaim, the trust still subsists, save in the rare cases where the settlor or testator has himself made the validity of the trust dependent upon the acceptance of office by particular trustees.[108] If all the nominated trustees predecease the testator in the case of a testamentary trust, the personal representatives of the testator will hold until such time as trustees are appointed.[109]

---

[102] TA 1925 s.34(3)(a).

[103] *Re Myhill* [1928] Ch. 100.

[104] Also LPA 1925 s.27(2); LP(A)A 1926 Sch.

[105] TA 1925 s.18; it is otherwise with a bare power given to two persons in their individual capacity: *Re Smith* [1904] 1 Ch. 139; *Re de Sommery* [1912] 2 Ch. 622; *Re Harding* [1923] 1 Ch. 182; above, para.6–002.

[106] AEA 1925 ss.1–3; TA 1925 s.18(2).

[107] Law of Property (Miscellaneous Provisions) Act 1994 s.14. Previously such property vested in the President of the Family Division.

[108] *Re Lysaght* [1966] Ch. 191; *Re Woodhams (Deceased)* [1981] 1 W.L.R. 493.

[109] *Re Smirthwaite's Trust* (1871) L.R. 11 Eq. 251.

B. Who May Appoint New Trustees

i. Express Power. The trust instrument may include an express **17–018** power to appoint new trustees, although it is normally sufficient to rely on the statutory power. Where an express power is given, it is often reserved to the settlor. The statutory power will be available in addition, unless a contrary intention appears in the instrument.[110]

ii. The Statutory Power: Trustee Act 1925 Section 36(1) **17–019** (2).[111]

(1) Where a trustee, either original or substituted, and whether appointed by the court or otherwise, is dead,[112] or remains out of the United Kingdom for more than 12 months,[113] or desires to be discharged from all or any of the trusts or powers reposed in or conferred on him,[114] or refuses[115] or is unfit to act therein, or is incapable of acting therein,[116] or is an infant,[117] then, subject to the restrictions imposed by this Act on the number of trustees,—

(a) the person or persons nominated for the purpose of appointing new trustees by the instrument, if any, creating the trust; or

(b) if there is no such person, or no such person able and willing to act, then the surviving or continuing trustees or trustee for the time being, or the personal representatives of the last surviving or continuing trustee;

---

[110] TA 1925 s.69(2). See *Re Wheeler and De Rochow* [1896] 1 Ch. 315; *Re Sichel's Settlements* [1916] 1 Ch. 358.

[111] The statutory power does not apply to personal representatives; *Re King's WT* [1964] Ch. 542; above, para.2–019. The court, however, may appoint a substitute personal representative under Administration of Justice Act 1985 s.50. Special rules for the appointment of pension trustees are dealt with in Ch.16.

[112] Which includes the case of a person nominated trustee in a will but dying before the testator: TA 1925 s.36(8), and above, para.17–017.

[113] The period must be continuous: *Re Walker* [1901] 1 Ch. 259; see also *Re Stoneham ST* [1953] Ch. 59. TA 1925 s.25, permits a trustee in such a case to delegate his duties by power of attorney for a period not exceeding 12 months; below, para.20–019.

[114] For retirement of a trustee, see below, para.17–035.

[115] This includes disclaimer.

[116] "Unfit" has a wider meaning than "incapable". "Incapable" refers to personal incapacity, such as illness or mental incapacity; see TA 1925 s.36(9). "Unfit" is more general and an absconding bankrupt has been held to be "unfit" but not "incapable": *Re Roche* (1842) 2 Dr. & War. 287. See s.36(3), providing that a corporation is "incapable" from the date of dissolution. LPA s.22(2) requires a mentally incapacitated trustee of land to be discharged before the legal estate is dealt with. This is not required where a donee of an enduring power of attorney is entitled to act for the incapable trustee; s.22(3), inserted by the Trustee Delegation Act 1999. This provision was further amended by the Mental Capacity Act 2005 to include the donee of a lasting power of attorney. See also Trusts of Land and Appointment of Trustees Act 1996 s.20; below, para.17–023.

[117] LPA 1925 ss.1(6), 20; *Re Parsons* [1940] Ch. 764.

may, by writing,[118] appoint one or more other persons (whether or not being the persons exercising the power) to be a trustee or trustees in the place of the trustee so deceased, remaining out of the United Kingdom, desiring to be discharged, refusing, or being unfit or being incapable, or being an infant, as aforesaid.

(2) Where a trustee has been removed under a power contained in the instrument creating the trust, a new trustee or new trustees may be appointed in the place of the trustee who is removed, as if he were dead, or, in the case of a corporation, as if the corporation desired to be discharged from the trust, and the provisions of this section shall apply accordingly, but subject to the restrictions imposed by this Act on the number of trustees.

In favour of a purchaser of a legal estate in land, a statement in an instrument appointing a new trustee to the effect that a trustee is unfit, incapable or refuses to act, or has remained out of the United Kingdom for more than 12 months, is conclusive evidence of the matter. Similarly, any appointment of a new trustee depending on that statement, and the consequent vesting of the trust property in the new trustee, is valid in favour of such a purchaser.[119]

17–020   **iii. Exercise of the Statutory Power.** It is common to appoint someone to exercise the statutory power.

(a) *By Persons Appointed under Section 36(1)(a).* If two or more persons are given power to exercise it jointly, the power is not, in the absence of a contrary intention, exercisable by the survivor. This is consistent with the usual rule relating to bare powers given to individuals.[120]

Complications can arise if the power is subjected to conditions and limitations.

In *Re Wheeler and De Rochow*,[121] the settlor gave power to donees to appoint a new trustee if one of the existing trustees should be "incapable". One of the trustees was bankrupt, and absconded. This made him "unfit" but not "incapable".[122] The question was whether a new trustee should be appointed by the donees under s.36(1)(a) or by the continuing trustees under

---

[118] See below, para.17–027, and TA 1925 s.40.

[119] TA 1925 s.38.

[120] *Re Harding* [1923] 1 Ch. 182; *Bersel Manufacturing Co Ltd v Berry* [1968] 2 All E.R. 552; above, para.6–002; it is otherwise where the power is given to persons as trustees: TA 1925 s.18(1).

[121] [1896] 1 Ch. 315; followed reluctantly in *Re Sichel's Settlements* [1916] 1 Ch. 358; cf. *Re Brockbank* [1948] Ch. 206.

[122] *Re Roche* (1842) Dr. & War. 287, above, para.17–019.

s.36(1)(b). It was held that the situation was not within the terms of the power given to the donees and that s.36(1)(b) applied.

(b) *By the Surviving or Continuing Trustees under Section* **17–021**
36(1)(b). In the case of continuing trustees it is expressly provided by s.36(8) that the provisions of s.36 "relative to a continuing trustee include a refusing or retiring trustee, if willing to act in the execution of the provisions of this section." This provision enables a retiring sole trustee or a retiring group of trustees to appoint their successors.[123] It raises the question, however, whether their participation is essential; whether an appointment in which they did not participate would be void. Such an objection failed in *Re Coates to Parsons*[124]; the retiring trustee is only included if it is shown that he is competent and willing to act. The concurrence of a trustee who is removed on the ground that he remained outside the United Kingdom for more than 12 months[125] is not required.[126] It is advisable, in order to avoid these difficulties, that refusing or retiring trustees should participate in the appointment of new trustees if possible, and this is the usual practice.

Section 37(1)(c) requires the replacement of trustees who are being discharged unless there will be either a trust corporation or at least two persons[127] to act if the vacancy is not filled. The exception is where only one trustee was originally appointed and a sole trustee will be able to give a good receipt for capital money. It appears that the settlor may override this provision.[128]

The statutory power to appoint a new trustee can be exercised by the executor of a sole trustee appointed by will,[129] but not by the personal representative of the survivor of a body of trustees named in a will, who has died in the testator's lifetime, as the Act does not contemplate the case of all the trustees named in the will predeceasing the testator.[130] Nor can the sole surviving trustee exercise the power by his will, so as thereby to appoint new trustees in succession to himself.[131] The aim of the Act of 1925 is to ensure the making

---

[123] But two retiring trustees cannot be replaced by one, not being a trust corporation; *Adam and Company International Trustees Ltd v Theodore Goddard (A Firm)* [2000] W.T.L.R. 349; criticised in F. Barlow [2003] Conv. 15.

[124] (1886) 34 Ch.D. 370.

[125] Above, para.17–019.

[126] *Re Stoneham ST* [1953] Ch. 59.

[127] As amended by Trusts of Land and Appointment of Trustees Act 1996 Sch.3, para.3(12), substituting "persons" for "individuals". A corporate trustee (whether or not it is a "trust corporation") is a "person" but not an "individual". For problems arising before the amendment, see *Jasmine Trustees Ltd v Wells & Hind (A Firm)* [2008] Ch. 194.

[128] *LRT Pensions Fund Trustee Company Ltd v Hatt* [1993] O.P.L.R. 225 at p.260; *Adam and Company International Trustees Ltd v Theodore Goddard (A Firm)* [2000] W.T.L.R. 349.

[129] *Re Shafto's Trusts* (1885) 29 Ch.D. 247.

[130] *Nicholson v Field* (1893) 2 Ch. 511.

[131] *Re Parker's Trusts* [1894] 1 Ch. 707.

of an appointment in all events. The executors who have proved the will need not have the concurrence of those who have not proved or intend to renounce probate.[132] A sole or last surviving executor who intends to renounce probate can nevertheless fulfil this one function without thereby accepting the office of executor,[133] but the title of an executor to exercise the statutory power can only be proved by a proper grant of administration.[134]

17–022   (c) *Additional Trustees.* A broad power is given by s.36(6),[135] restricted only by the limitation to a total number of four trustees, and by the fact that the power is to appoint "another person or other persons" and that consequently (and unlike appointments under subs.(1)) the appointor may not appoint himself.[136] Section 36(6) reads:

> "Where, in the case of any trust, there are not more than three trustees—
>
> (a) the person or persons nominated for the purpose of appointing new trustees by the instrument, if any, creating the trust; or
> (b) if there is no such person, or no such person able and willing to act, then the trustee or trustees for the time being;
>
> may, by writing, appoint another person or other persons to be an additional trustee or additional trustees, but it shall not be obligatory to appoint any additional trustee, unless the instrument, if any, creating the trust, or any statutory enactment provides to the contrary, nor shall the number of trustees be increased beyond four by virtue of any such appointment."

Section 36(6) was amended by the Trustee Delegation Act 1999 in order to give a limited power of appointing additional trustees to the donee of an enduring or lasting[137] power of attorney, to whom trustee functions relating to land or its proceeds of sale have been delegated under the 1999 Act or under s.25 of the Trustee Act 1925.[138] This is to ensure that there are at least two trustees to act, as

---

[132] TA 1925 s.36(4).

[133] TA 1925 s.36(5).

[134] *Re Crowhurst Park* [1974] 1 W.L.R. 583.

[135] As amended by Trusts of Land and Appointment of Trustees Act 1996 Sch.3, para.3(11).

[136] *Re Power's ST* [1951] Ch. 1074.

[137] Lasting powers of attorney were added by the Mental Capacity Act 2005.

[138] Trustee Delegation Act 1999 s.8, inserting s.36(6A)–(6D) into the 1925 Act. For enduring powers of attorney, see below, para.20–020. The new provisions apply only to powers of attorney created after the commencement of the 1999 Act.

required for the purpose of giving a good receipt for capital money. The amendment deals primarily with the situation where one co-owner of land has, prior to losing capacity, delegated his trustee functions to the other co-owner by enduring or lasting power of attorney.

iv. By Direction of the Beneficiaries. A new power was given to **17–023** beneficiaries by s.19[139] of the Trusts of Land and Appointment of Trustees Act 1996, which applies to trusts of land and personalty, whenever created, unless excluded by the settlor.[140] Provided the beneficiaries are of full age and capacity and together absolutely entitled, and there is no person with an express power to appoint, the beneficiaries may direct the trustees in matters of retirement[141] and appointment. They may give directions of either or both of the following kinds:

(a) a written direction to a trustee or trustees to retire from the trust; and

(b) a written direction to the trustees or trustee for the time being (or, if there are none, to the personal representative of the last person who was a trustee) to appoint by writing to be a trustee or trustees the person or persons specified in the direction.

The beneficiaries may give joint or separate directions, but they must specify the same person for appointment or retirement.[142] Section 19 has effect subject to the restrictions imposed by the 1925 Act on the number of trustees. In the absence of the exercise of the new power by the beneficiaries, the trustees' power of appointment is exercisable in the usual way.

C. Appointment by the Court

i. Trustee Act 1925 Section 41.[143] Subsection (1) provides: **17–024**

The court[144] may, whenever it is expedient to appoint a new trustee or new trustees, and it is found inexpedient difficult or

---

[139] This in effect reverses *Re Brockbank* [1948] Ch. 206. See also s.20 (replacement by direction of beneficiaries where trustee mentally incapacitated and no person entitled, willing and able to act under TA 1925 s.36(1)). Section 20 (unlike s.19) contains no provisions on vesting or indemnity. See M. Keppel-Palmer (1996) 146 N.L.J. 1779; N Hopkins [1996] Conv. 411 at pp.428–430.

[140] s.21(5). Living settlors of trusts created before the 1996 Act may exclude the power by deed under s.21(6). The same applies to the power under s.20.

[141] Below, para.17–039.

[142] s.21(1), (2).

[143] The section does not apply to the appointment of personal representatives (s.41(4)).

[144] i.e. the High Court; or where the estate or trust fund does not exceed its financial jurisdiction, the county court.

impracticable so to do without the assistance of the court, make an order appointing a new trustee or new trustees either in substitution for or in addition to any existing trustee or trustees, or although there is no existing trustee.

In particular and without prejudice to the generality of the foregoing provision, the court may make an order appointing a new trustee in substitution for a trustee who lacks capacity to exercise his functions as trustee or is a bankrupt, or is a corporation which is in liquidation or has been dissolved.

17-025 **ii. Circumstances in which the Jurisdiction will be Exercised.** The section gives the court a discretion. Cases arise in a variety of circumstances, e.g. where a sole surviving trustee has died intestate, or where all the trustees of a testamentary trust predeceased the testator,[145] and difficulty is experienced in obtaining administration of his estate,[146] or where the donee is incapable of making an effective appointment by reason of being under age.[147] The court has power to replace a trustee against his will[148]; and also where the trustees were the life tenant and remainderman and there was friction between them; or where a trustee has, through age or infirmity,[149] become incapable of acting, or who permanently resides abroad.[150] The statutory power of beneficiaries to direct appointments reduces the need to apply to court.[151]

It was held not to be "expedient" to appoint a new trustee of a pension fund on terms that it would be paid out of the fund in circumstances where the administrator of the employer company had sufficient expertise to administer the pension fund and could be paid only out of the company's free assets.[152]

The court should not be asked to exercise its jurisdiction where a statutory power can be exercised.[153] It has no jurisdiction to appoint a new trustee against the wishes of the persons who have a statutory power to appoint, even in a case where an application has been made to it by a majority of the beneficiaries.[154] Where the beneficiaries are of full capacity, absolutely entitled and unanimous, they may exercise the statutory power referred to above.

---

[145] *Re Smirthwaite's Trust* (1871) L.R. 11 Eq. 251.
[146] *Re Matthews* (1859) 26 Beav. 463.
[147] *Re Parsons* [1940] Ch. 973; REM (1941) 57 L.Q.R. 25.
[148] *Re Henderson* [1940] Ch. 764.
[149] *Re Lemann's Trust* (1883) 22 Ch.D. 633.
[150] *Re Bignold's ST* (1872) L.R. 7 Ch.App. 223.
[151] Trusts of Land and Appointment of Trustees Act 1996 ss.19, 20; above, para.17-023.
[152] *Polly Peck International Plc (In Administration) v Henry* [1999] 1 B.C.L.C. 407.
[153] *Re Gibbon's Trusts* (1882) 30 W.R. 287 (where, however, such an appointment was made); cf. *Re May's WT* [1941] Ch. 109.
[154] *Re Higginbottom* [1892] 3 Ch. 132.

9. Vesting of the Trust Property in Trustees

A. Requirement of Vesting

The trust property must be vested in the trustees to enable them to deal with outside parties. Before and after the vesting, however, a trustee, whether appointed under s.36 or by the court under s.41, or by direction of the beneficiaries under ss.19 or 20 of the Trusts of Land and Appointment of Trustees Act 1996,[155] has: **17–026**

> "[T]he same powers, authorities, and discretions, and may in all respects act as if he had been originally appointed a trustee by the instrument, if any, creating the trust."[156]

B. Vesting Declaration under Section 40

i. Subsection (1). In order to avoid the necessity of a formal transfer of the trust property from the old trustees to the new, s.40 provides that the vesting may, with important exceptions, be effected automatically if the appointment of the trustees has been made by *deed*.[157] It does not apply, however, where the property is held by personal representatives and not by a trustee.[158] **17–027**

Subsection (1) of s.40 provides that the deed of appointment shall operate to vest any land, chattel or chose in action subject to the trust in the new trustee, unless the deed expressly provides to the contrary.

ii. Exceptions under Subsection (4). These in outline are: **17–028**

(a) a mortgage of land to secure a loan of trust money;
(b) land held under a lease which contains a covenant against assignment without consent, and the consent has not been obtained prior to the execution of the deed;
(c) stocks and shares.[159]

These exceptions are necessary. Where trust money is lent on mortgage, no mention is made in the mortgage deed of the existence of the trust, nor upon a transfer of the mortgage, such as would occur

---

[155] s.21(3).
[156] TA 1925 ss.36(7), 43.
[157] Above, para.17–019.
[158] *Re Cockburn's WT* [1957] Ch. 438; *Re King's WT* [1964] Ch. 542; above, para.2–019.
[159] "Any share, stock, annuity or property which is only transferable in books kept by a company or other body, or in manner directed by or under an Act of Parliament." This includes money in a bank account, for example, but not bearer bonds.

on the appointment of a new trustee. If s.40(1) applied, the mortgagor on redeeming would have to investigate the appointments of new trustees to make sure he was paying the right persons. The second exception is included in order to avoid an unintended breach of covenant, such as could occur in the appointment of a new trustee. The most serious exception in practice is the third; for this is the most important and valuable form of property in modern settlements. The provision, however, was necessary, because title to stocks and shares depends on the registration of the owners in the register of shareholders, and it is essential (unless the shares are held by a nominee) that the current trustees should be registered.[160]

It will be seen that vesting orders relating to registered land are not expressly excepted; however, the legal title cannot pass until effect is given on the register to any vesting order or vesting declaration made on the appointment or discharge of a trustee. The provisions of the Trustee Act 1925 relating to the appointment and discharge of trustees and the vesting of trust property apply to registered land subject to proper entry being made on the register.[161]

C. Vesting Orders under Sections 44 to 56

17–029   Sections 44 to 56 contain the rules as to vesting orders by the court. These overlap s.40, for vesting orders as to all kinds of property can be made not only where the appointment has been made by the court, but also where it has been made out of court under an express or statutory power. The court is given wide powers to make such orders in a variety of eventualities.

10. Selection of Trustees

A. On Appointment by the Court under Section 41

17–030   The factors which a court will take into account when exercising its jurisdiction to appoint a trustee were discussed by Turner L.J. in *Re Tempest*.[162] The court should always have regard to three prime requirements: the wishes of the person by whom the trust was created; the interests, which may be conflicting, of *all* the beneficiaries; the efficient administration of the trust. It is important that the trustees act harmoniously together; but Turner L.J. thought it would be going too far to say that the court should refuse to appoint a particular trustee on the ground that the continuing trustee refused to act with him. That would give the continuing trustee a veto; rather, the

---

[160] See M. Russell (1992) 142 N.L.J. 541. For electronic transfer, see above, para.4–008.
[161] See further R. Towns [1998] Conv. 380.
[162] (1866) L.R. 1 Ch.App. 485.

reasons for the refusal should be examined to see whether the objection is well founded.

The court is reluctant to appoint a person who, though not himself interested, is related to, or connected with, someone who is. Thus a relative of one of the beneficiaries is not a desirable appointment,[163] nor is one nominated by a relative of the testator with whom the testator was on bad terms.[164] Again, the solicitor to the trust,[165] or to one of the beneficiaries[166] or trustees, should not be appointed, as there might be a conflict of duties; unless, of course, no other person can be found to undertake the position. If the solicitor to the trust is a continuing trustee, his partner should not be appointed.[167] Persons out of the jurisdiction will not be appointed[168] except in a case where circumstances require it, or where the beneficiaries are resident outside the jurisdiction also.[169] Even where the trust can be more conveniently administered by trustees resident abroad, the court may exact an undertaking from them that they will consult the court before proceeding to the appointment of new trustees out of the jurisdiction.[170] Trusts administered abroad have enjoyed a number of fiscal advantages, and this has encouraged the movement of many trusts to other jurisdictions.

B. On Appointment under Express Power or under Section 36

i. Choice by Donee of Power. It is said that the above principles   **17–031**
should guide persons exercising their power to appoint under s.36. In practice, however, it is common for beneficiaries and other members of the beneficiaries' families, and for solicitors to the beneficiaries, to be appointed. A conflict of interest and duty or of two duties should of course be avoided. However, even if the trustee appointed is one whom the court itself would not have selected, it seems that the court will not rectify it.[171]

ii. Foreign Trusts. Problems have arisen in relation to the ap-   **17–032**
pointment of foreign trustees with the intention of enjoying the tax

---

[163] *Re Coode* (1913) 108 L.T. 94; *Re Parsons* [1940] Ch. 973 (where a child purported to appoint his mother).

[164] *Re Tempest* (1866) L.R. 1 Ch. 485.

[165] *Wheelwright v Walker* (1883) 23 Ch.D. 752; *Re Orde* (1883) 24 Ch.D. 271.

[166] *Re Earl of Stamford* [1896] 1 Ch. 288; *Re Spencer's SE* [1903] 1 Ch. 75; *Re Cotter* [1915] 1 Ch. 307.

[167] *Re Norris* (1884) 27 Ch.D. 333.

[168] *Re Weston's Settlements* [1969] 1 Ch. 223.

[169] *Re Liddiard* (1880) 14 Ch.D. 310; *Re Simpson* [1897] 1 Ch. 256; *Re Seale's Marriage ST* [1961] Ch. 574; *Re Windeatt's WT* [1969] 1 W.L.R. 692; *Re Whitehead's WT* [1971] 1 W.L.R. 833.

[170] *Re Freeman's ST* (1888) 37 Ch.D. 148.

[171] In *Re Norris* (1884) 27 Ch.D. 333, the funds were being administered by the court; *Re Higginbottom* [1892] 3 Ch. 132; *Re Parsons* [1940] Ch. 973; REM (1941) 57 L.Q.R. 25.

advantages of offshore trusts. The tax advantages are now minimal unless there are beneficiaries who are resident abroad, or the settlor was domiciled[172] abroad at the date of the creation of the settlement. We have seen that the court was unwilling to appoint trustees resident abroad unless the beneficiaries have made their homes in the country in question.[173] It was said in *Re Whitehead's Will Trusts*[174] that trustees or persons with an express power should only appoint foreign resident trustees in similar circumstances (although an appointment inconsistent with this rule would be a valid appointment[175]). More recently, however, Millett J. held that the *Whitehead* approach is outdated.[176] Where the trustees are exercising their own discretion and are merely seeking the authorisation of the court for their own protection, the test is simply whether the proposed transaction is not so inappropriate that no reasonable trustee could entertain it. Thus Bermudan trustees were sanctioned although the trust had no Bermuda connection. Where it is clear that this test is satisfied, there is no need to apply to court. It is might be added that many settlements now expressly authorise the appointment of non-resident trustees.

17–033   **iii. Direction by Beneficiaries.** We saw that in certain circumstances, beneficiaries may give directions as to the exercise of the statutory power of appointment.[177] It appears that the beneficiaries are under no restrictions in the choice of person they direct to be appointed.

C. On Appointment by the Settlor

17–034   The settlor is under no restrictions in the selection of the original trustees whether English or foreign. The question is not merely one of selecting efficient, businesslike and fair-minded trustees who will carry out their duties according to law. They are commonly given wide discretions. They therefore should be people who will be relied on to respect the wishes of the settlor on matters on which they are in law virtually uncontrolled; and in circumstances which may have greatly changed since the trust was created.

---

[172] Inheritance Tax Act 1984 s.267.

[173] *Re Weston's Settlements* [1969] 1 Ch. 223; cf. *Re Seale's Marriage ST* [1961] Ch. 574; *Re Windeatt's WT* [1969] 1 W.L.R. 692; *Re Whitehead's WT* [1971] 1 W.L.R. 833; T. Watkin (1976) 40 Conv.(N.S.) 295. See generally Parker and Mellows, *The Modern Law of Trusts*, 9th edn, pp.620–626.

[174] [1971] 1 W.L.R. 833 at 838.

[175] *Meinertzhagen v Davis* (1844) 1 Coll. 353; PVB (1969) 85 L.Q.R. 15; *Re Whitehead's WT*, above, fn.173, at 837.

[176] *Richard v The Hon. AB Mackay* (1997) 11 T.L.I. 22 (decided 1987); R. Bramwell, The Offshore Tax Planning Review (1990/91), Vol.1, p.1. See also *Re Beatty's WT (No.2)* (1997) 11 T.L.I. 77.

[177] Trusts of Land and Appointment of Trustees Act 1996 ss.19–22; above, para.17–023.

11. RETIREMENT

A trustee may retire from a subsisting trust in any one of the ways **17–035**
explained below.[178] Retirement means a discharge from further responsibility and liability under the trust. A trustee should not retire
when faced with disputes among beneficiaries and leave them to
settle their differences among themselves. If he retires in order to
facilitate a breach of trust by his successors, he will remain
liable.[179]

A. Under an Express Power in the Trust Instrument
This is rare, since (the predecessors of) ss.36 and 39 made express **17–036**
powers unnecessary.

B. Under Section 39
We saw that a trustee desiring to be discharged could be replaced **17–037**
by a newly appointed trustee.[180] He may retire, without being replaced, if he complies with s.39 of the Trustee Act 1925.

"(1) Where a trustee is desirous of being discharged from the
trust, and after his discharge there will be either a trust corporation or at least two persons[181] to act as trustees to perform the
trust, then, if such trustee as aforesaid by deed declares that he is
desirous of being discharged from the trust, and if his co-trustees
and such other person, if any, as is empowered to appoint trustees,
by deed consent to the discharge of the trustee, and to the vesting
in the co-trustees alone of the trust property, the trustee desirous
of being discharged shall be deemed to have retired from the trust,
and shall, by the deed, be discharged therefrom under this Act,
without any new trustee being appointed in his place."

A retirement not complying with the statutory provisions is invalid, hence the trustee remains in office.[182]

---

[178] A personal representative may be discharged by the court; Administration of Justice Act 1985 s.50.

[179] *Head v Gould* [1898] 2 Ch. 250.

[180] TA 1925 s.36(1); above, para.17–019. cf. Y. Tan (1989) 9 L.S. 323, suggesting that s.36 permits retirement without replacement.

[181] A sole trustee other than a trust corporation does not suffice even if he has power to give a valid receipt for capital money, in contrast with the position under TA 1925 s.37(1)(c). The word "persons" in s.39(1) was inserted by Trusts of Land and Appointment of Trustees Act 1996 Sch.3, para.3(13), in place of "individuals". A corporate trustee (whether or not a "trust corporation") is a "person" but not an "individual".

[182] *Mettoy Pension Trustees Ltd v Evans* [1990] 1 W.L.R. 1587; *Jasmine Trustees Ltd v Wells & Hind (A Firm)* [2008] Ch. 194. See also *Re Epona Trustees Ltd and Pentera Trustees Ltd* [2009] W.T.L.R. 87 (Jersey Royal Court).

C. Under an Order of the Court

17–038   The court will only discharge a trustee under its statutory jurisdiction where it replaces him by a new appointment under s.41. It has however an inherent power to discharge him without replacement in the case of an action to administer the trust. While it will not, in the exercise of this jurisdiction, encourage capricious retirement,[183] it will allow a trustee to retire where it is entirely proper for him to do so.[184]

D. By Direction of the Beneficiaries

17–039   We saw that s.19 of the Trusts of Land and Appointment of Trustees Act 1996 gives beneficiaries of full age and capacity and together absolutely entitled, the power to give directions to the trustees in matters of appointment and retirement.[185] Where a trustee has been given a direction to retire under s.19 and reasonable arrangements have been made for the protection of any rights of his in connection with the trust, he must execute a deed declaring his retirement, provided that after his retirement there will be either a trust corporation or at least two persons to act, and either another person is to be appointed in his place (by direction of the beneficiaries or otherwise) or the continuing trustees by deed consent to his retirement.[186]

12. REMOVAL

17–040   We have seen that the court[187] may, on the appointment of a new trustee, remove an existing trustee and that some appointments by a donee of a power will have this effect.[188] The power of beneficiaries to direct a trustee to retire was discussed above. The court has also an inherent jurisdiction in actions for the administration of trusts to remove a trustee compulsorily; but the principles on which this power is exercised are somewhat vague.[189]

---

[183] *Courtenay v Courtenay* (1846) 3 Jo. & La.T. 519, 533.

[184] *Re Chetwynd's Settlement* [1902] 1 Ch. 692.

[185] Above, para.17–023. The power may be excluded by the settlor under ss.21(5), (6). For potential problems, see L. Clements (1998) 61 M.L.R. 56 at 67.

[186] s.19(3). For vesting and divesting of the trust property, see s.19(4) of the 1996 Act and TA 1925 s.40(2), as amended.

[187] Normally the Chancery Division, but the Family Division has such jurisdiction; *E v E* [1990] 2 F.L.R. 233 (post-nuptial settlement).

[188] TA 1925 ss.36, 41, above, paras 17–019, 17–030; *Re Stoneham ST* [1953] Ch. 59; as to removal of a charitable trustee, see Charities Act 2011 s.79; above, para.15–095.

[189] *Letterstedt v Broers* (1884) 9 App.Cas. 371; *Re Wrightson* [1908] 1 Ch. 789; *Re Pauling's ST (No.2)* [1963] Ch. 576; *Jones v Att Gen* [1974] Ch. 148 (trustee of charitable trust); *Re Edwards' WT* [1982] Ch. 30.

Actual misconduct on the part of a trustee need not be shown, but the court must be satisfied that his continuance in office would be prejudicial to the due performance of the trust, and so to the interests of the beneficiaries.[190] The court has a clear ground for removal in cases where a trustee is ignoring one of his duties.[191] Thus, though it will not necessarily constitute a breach of trust for a trustee of a will carrying on the business of his testator to set up a rival business, yet it will be a ground for his removal,[192] as he has put himself in a position wherein his duty and interest are bound to be in conflict. Similarly if trustees were to persist in an investment policy based on considerations other than the best interests of the beneficiaries.[193] Harman J. has suggested that a member of a discretionary class could procure the removal of a trustee who "deliberately refused to consider any question" relating to the qualification of members to receive payments.[194] Friction or hostility between the trustee and the beneficiaries is not a reason for removing the trustee unless the court is satisfied that it was impeding the proper execution of the trust.[195]

In the case of a foreign settlement, the court has inherent jurisdiction to make *in personam* orders removing and replacing foreign trustees, whether or not the assets are in England, provided that the individual trustee is subject to the jurisdiction of the English courts.[196] However, where the applicable law of the trust is not English law, matters such as the appointment, resignation and removal of trustees are governed by the law of the relevant jurisdiction.[197]

In administration actions the powers of the court are very elastic.[198] The court can, at any time during such proceedings, remove the trustees, if it considers such removal necessary for the preservation of the trust estate or the welfare of the beneficiaries, notwithstanding that such removal has not been expressly asked for in the statement of case. But each case must be weighed carefully on its merits; and the court will sometimes find it necessary to place in one

---

[190] See *E v E*, above, fn.187; *Isaac v Isaac* [2009] W.T.L.R. 265 (decided 2005).

[191] See *Walker v Walker* [2010] W.T.L.R. 1617.

[192] *Moore v M'Glynn* [1894] 1 Ir.R. 74. The possibility of conflict may not suffice; *Isaac v Isaac* [2009] W.T.L.R. 265.

[193] *Cowan v Scargill* [1985] Ch. 270, below, para.18–019.

[194] *Re Gestetner Settlement* [1953] Ch. 672 at 688; see also per Lord Wilberforce in *McPhail v Doulton* [1971] A.C. 424 at 456; above, para.3–027.

[195] *Alkin v Raymond* [2010] W.T.L.R. 1117; *Kershaw v Micklethwaite* [2011] W.T.L.R. 413 (executor).

[196] By reason of service of the claim form in England, or because the trustee has submitted to the jurisdiction, or because the court has assumed jurisdiction under, CPR 1998, Pt 6.30–6.47.

[197] Recognition of Trusts Act 1987 Sch., art.8. For the applicable law, see arts 6, 7; above, para.1–052.

[198] *Re Harrison's Settlement Trusts* [1965] 1 W.L.R. 1492. On the removal of an executor, see *IRC v Stype Investments (Jersey) Ltd* [1982] Ch. 456.

scale a minor breach of trust, and in the other the certain expense to the trust estate of a change of trustees.[199]

Special rules relating to the suspension, removal, disqualification and replacement of pension trustees are discussed in Ch.16.

13. CONTROL OF TRUSTEES[200]

17–041   The basic principle governing trustees is that, while duties must be discharged, the exercise of discretions needs only to be considered. The trustee is not obliged to exercise them in any particular manner, or indeed at all. Thus in *Tempest v Lord Camoys*,[201] one trustee wished to take advantage of a power in a trust instrument to purchase land but his co-trustee would not agree. It could not be shown that he had failed to consider the matter, and the court refused to issue any directive to him.

Nor is there a general principle that trustees should consult beneficiaries, though they should inform them that they have certain rights.[202] Frequently consultation takes place as a matter of practice, but only occasionally does statute[203] impose an obligation on them to do so, and even then their wishes are not mandatory but must be related to the overall welfare of the trust.

But what is the position if trustees exercise a discretion in a manner that appears wholly unreasonable? Is it a satisfactory answer to state simply that the matter has been fully considered? The law on this subject is neither wholly clear not wholly satisfactory.

A. Giving of Reasons

17–042   There is a basic rule that trustees cannot be compelled to explain their reasons for exercising or not exercising a discretionary power.

In *Re Beloved Wilkes' Charity*,[204] trustees were directed to select a boy to be educated for Orders in the Church of England. Their freedom of choice was limited by a preference for certain parishes, if a fit and proper candidate from these parishes could be found.

The trustees selected Charles Joyce, a boy who did not come from one of these parishes. It appeared that Charles' brother was a

---

[199] *Re Wrightson* [1908] 1 Ch. 789.
[200] See generally R. Nolan (2009) 68 C.L.J. 293.
[201] (1882) 21 Ch.D. 571. The statutory duty of care under Trustee Act 2000 s.1 (above, para.17–003) does not apply to the discretion whether or not to exercise a power.
[202] *Hawkesley v May* [1956] 1 Q.B. 304; *X v A* [2000] 1 All E.R. 490.
[203] e.g. Trusts of Land and Appointment of Trustees Act 1996 s.11; above, para.11–023.
[204] (1851) 3 Mac. & G. 440.

minister who had sought assistance on his behalf from one of the trustees. The trustees gave no reasons for their choice, but asserted that they had considered the candidates impartially.

Lord Truro refused to set aside the trustees' selection, or to require the trustees to explain how they had arrived at their conclusion.[205] However, this does not exclude the possibility of challenge if it appears that the trustees acted in breach of their duties, for example by failing to give a fair consideration to the question.[206]

No distinction exists in this context between oral and documentary evidence, which is a matter of some importance in view of the large amount of trust business which is conducted by correspondence or at meetings with written agenda and minutes. In *Re Londonderry's Settlement*,[207] the court drew a sharp distinction between written material of this nature which related to management of the trust property (which should be disclosed to requesting beneficiaries) and material which related to the exercise of discretions (which need not be disclosed). But if trustees do give reasons, or if they may be inferred, then the courts will look into their adequacy.[208]

The principle that trustees need not give reasons for their decisions is based on the fact that trustees have a confidential role which, it is said, they cannot properly exercise if they are to be subjected to an investigation to see whether they have exercised it in the best possible manner.[209] Documents relating to the trust may contain confidential information, the disclosure of which could cause trouble in the family, out of all proportion to the benefit gained from inspecting them. Thus the principle is designed not to encourage secrecy but to avoid litigation and family disputes.[210]

Whether the principle is appropriate to pension trusts may be doubted,[211] but it was held to apply in *Wilson v Law Debenture Trust Corp Plc*,[212] even though pension trusts are in many ways treated differently from traditional trusts because the beneficiaries are not **17–043**

[205] For a discussion on policy grounds, see A. Samuels (1965) 28 M.L.R. 220; A. Hawkins and F. Taylor (1965) S.J. 239.

[206] *Pitt v Holt* [2011] 3 W.L.R. 19 at 53.

[207] [1965] 1 Ch. 918; the facts are given below, para.19–020; *Butt v Kelson* [1952] Ch. 197.

[208] *Klug v Klug* [1918] 2 Ch. 67.

[209] *Re Londonderry's Settlement* [1965] Ch. 918 at 935–936.

[210] *Hartigan Nominees Pty Ltd v Rydge* (1992) 29 N.S.W.L.R. 405, holding that *Londonderry* accorded with principle and common sense; J. Lehane [1994] 3 J.I.P. 60.

[211] Lord Browne-Wilkinson (1992) 6 T.L.I. 119 at 125; D. Schaffer (1994) 8 T.L.I. 27; Sir Robert Walker [1996] P.L.R. 107; D. Pollard (1997) 11 T.L.I. 11 and 42.

[212] [1995] 2 All E.R. 337; criticised D. Schaffer (1994) 8 T.L.I. 118; P. Clarke All E.R. Rev. 1995 at 321.

volunteers.[213] There the employees failed to obtain disclosure of the trustees' reasons for not transferring a surplus to another scheme to which the employees had been transferred. Any change, it was said, would require legislation.[214] The significance of member trustees (required by the Pensions Act 2004, replacing earlier provisions) in this context should not, however, be overlooked.[215]

It is otherwise where there is evidence of bad faith or other impropriety. The difficulty is that it may not be possible to establish impropriety without seeing the documents which the trustees are not obliged to disclose. The beneficiaries may obtain disclosure of documents to support their case, but may not use that process to ascertain if a case exists.[216] Indeed the order made in the *Londonderry* case was without prejudice to the beneficiary's right to disclosure in separate proceedings against the trustees.[217]

B. Intervention by the Court

17–044   The cases are not clear, however, on whether the courts will look into the exercise of a discretion that *appears* to be wholly unreasonable. The duty of care under s.1 of the Trustee Act 2000 does not apply to the exercise of dispositive powers. If there is an allegation of fraud or misconduct, the courts must investigate it; but the complainant is in a difficulty in that the evidence which he requires is the personal motivation of the trustees. If fraud is proved, or if the exercise of the discretion is shown to be "capricious",[218] or if the trustees have blindly followed the settlor's wishes,[219] the court will declare the trustees' decision void. Likewise if the trustees have improperly exercised a power for a collateral purpose, by analogy with the doctrine of "fraud on a power",[220] which can occur even though the trustees acted honestly in the sense that they thought their action was in the interests of the beneficiaries.[221] There is some authority that the court will not intervene in the absence of bad faith if the instrument provides that the trustees' discretion is "uncontrollable".[222] It is not clear how far the court has greater powers in the

[213] Above, para.16–005.

[214] Regulations under the Pensions Act 1995 require the decisions of the trustees to be recorded, but do not impose any general duty to give reasons. For the implications of the Data Protection Act 1998, see M. Shillingford, The TACT Review, April 2000, p.3.

[215] P. O'Hagan (1995) 145 N.L.J. 1414.

[216] *Hartigan Nominees Pty Ltd v Rydge* (1992) 29 N.S.W.L.R. 405.

[217] [1965] Ch. 918 at 939. See also *Scott v National Trust for Places of Historic Interest or Natural Beauty* [1998] 2 All E.R. 705; P. Clarke All E.R. Rev. 1998 at 276–277.

[218] *Re Manisty's Settlement* [1974] Ch. 17; above, para.3–033.

[219] *Turner v Turner* [1984] Ch. 100.

[220] Above, para.6–018.

[221] *Hillsdown Holdings Plc v Pensions Ombudsman* [1997] 1 All E.R. 862 (transfer of surplus funds to employer).

[222] *Gisborne v Gisborne* (1877) 2 App.Cas. 300.

absence of such a statement.[223] Although some 19th-century decisions[224] asserted a wide jurisdiction, it seems that the court will not
intervene simply on the ground that the trustees have exercised their
discretion in good faith but unreasonably. The House of Lords in a
Scottish appeal[225] (which has been said to reflect also the law of
England[226]) indicated that the court could intervene, whether or not
the trustees had given their reasons, if it was clear that they had not
applied their minds to the right question or had perversely shut their
eyes to the facts.

A question which has been prominent in recent years is whether **17–045**
the court may intervene where trustees exercise a discretionary dispositive power in good faith but their disposition does not have the
full effect they intended because they were under some misapprehension, for example as to the tax consequences. In the leading case
of *Re Hastings-Bass*[227] trustees exercised a power of advancement
by creating a sub-trust but the remainder interests in it were void for
perpetuity. This did not invalidate the exercise of the power as the
primary intention was to create a life interest, and this had been
achieved. The ratio was that trustees, when exercising a power of
advancement, must consider whether it will operate for the benefit
of the advancee. If one or more aspects cannot take effect, it does
not follow that those which can take effect should not do so. Thus a
misapprehension by the trustees as to the effect is not by itself fatal
to the effectiveness of the advancement. If the provisions which can
take effect cannot reasonably be regarded as for the benefit of the
advancee, the exercise fails as not being within the scope of the
power. Otherwise it takes effect to the extent that it can.

However, the case came to be regarded as authority for the principle (the so-called "rule in *Re Hastings-Bass*") which it did not
actually decide, namely that the court could set aside a disposition if
it was clear that the trustees would (or possibly might) not have
acted as they did had they not taken into account considerations
which they should not have taken into account or failed to take into
account considerations which they ought to have taken into account.
The question whether the disposition was void or voidable was not
resolved. The wrong turn was taken in *Mettoy Pension Trustees Ltd
v Evans*,[228] and other cases followed suit.[229]

---

[223] See N. Parry [1989] Conv. 244.

[224] *Re Hodges* (1878) 7 Ch.D. 754; *Re Roper's Trust* (1879) 11 Ch.D. 272.

[225] *Dundee General Hospitals v Walker* [1952] 1 All E.R. 896. The trustees accepted that
unreasonableness was the test, but this was doubted.

[226] *Scott v National Trust for Places of Historic Interest or Natural Beauty*, above,
fn.217.

[227] [1975] Ch. 25; below, para.20–043.

[228] [1990] 1 W.L.R. 1587.

[229] See *Edge v Pensions Ombudsman* [2000] Ch. 602; *Sieff v Fox* [2005] 1 W.L.R.
3811.

The principles were recently reviewed by the Court of Appeal in *Pitt v Holt*,[230] which was heard with the case of *Futter v Futter*. The Commissioners for HMRC were parties to the proceedings as these cases, like several others before them, involved the potential setting aside of a tax liability. *Pitt v Holt* was an unusual case as it did not involve a trustee. A receiver appointed to act for her husband by the Court of Protection under the Mental Health Act 1983[231] exercised a power (authorised by the court) to create a discretionary trust of a personal injury award for the benefit of her husband, but did not appreciate that it had adverse inheritance tax consequences. It was considered that, as she was a fiduciary, the principles relating to dispositions by trustees applied. In *Futter v Futter* trustees exercised a power of advancement on the wrong assumption that no capital gains tax would be payable. The question in both cases was whether the disposition could be set aside. This had been the result in the High Court, but the appeal by HMRC was successful in both cases.

The Court of Appeal analysed the cases before and after *Re Hastings-Bass*[232] and concluded that, while that decision was correct and binding, the so-called "rule in *Re Hastings-Bass*" which had been developed in later cases was not a correct statement of the law. The true principle is that the purported exercise of a discretionary power will be void if what is done is not within the scope of the power, for example if a necessary consent was not obtained or if the appointment was to a non-object.[233] Cases involving "fraud on a power" are of this kind.[234] If there is some defect under the general law, for example perpetuity, the result depends on the extent of the invalidity. In advancement cases it depends on whether what remains can be considered to be for the benefit of the advancee, as in *Re Hastings-Bass*[235] itself, otherwise it will be void. In contrast with these cases are those where the exercise of the power is within its terms but the trustees have in some way breached their duties in its exercise. In such a case the exercise is not void but may be voidable at the instance of the beneficiary as an incident of a beneficiary's right to have the trust duly administered. Where the exercise is voidable, it is subject to the usual equitable defences if a beneficiary seeks to set is aside, but remains valid if nobody with standing seeks to set it aside. The court added that the cases in which an act done by

---

[230] [2011] 3 W.L.R. 19; R. Chambers [2011] 25 T.L.I. 17; M. Conaglen (2011) 70 C.L.J. 301; R. Nolan and A. Cloherty (2011) 127 L.Q.R. 499; P. Davies [2011] Conv. 406. Leave to appeal to the Supreme Court was granted on August 1, 2011.

[231] Receivers have since been replaced by deputies under the current legislation, the Mental Capacity Act 2005.

[232] [1975] Ch. 25.

[233] See also *Breadner v Granville-Grossman* [2001] Ch. 523 (power of appointment expired at date of purported exercise).

[234] Above, para.6–018.

[235] [1975] Ch. 25.

trustees apparently within their powers could be held void should be kept to a minimum.

The Court of Appeal then considered what trustees should take into account when exercising their fiduciary powers. The cases gave little guidance, but tax consequences would be a relevant consideration. In most cases it would be the trustees' duty to seek professional advice on tax matters, but the advice might be wrong. If wrong advice caused them to act outside their powers, they would be in breach of trust (though they could sue their adviser), and the exercise would be void. However, they would not be in breach of trust if they proceeded to act within their powers on the basis of wrong advice, and so the disposition could not be set aside. Subject to that point, the trustees would be in breach of their fiduciary duty if they acted within the scope of their powers but failed to take relevant matters into account or took irrelevant matters into account. In such a case the disposition would be voidable at the instance of the beneficiary. Applying these principles to the cases before them, the trustees in *Futter v Futter*[236] had acted within the scope of their powers but on mistaken legal advice and so were not in breach of trust and the disposition was neither void nor voidable. In *Pitt v Holt*[237] the fiduciary, having been authorised to create the settlement by the Court of Protection, acted within her powers but her legal advisers had failed to appreciate the adverse inheritance tax consequences. Thus she was not in breach of fiduciary duty and the settlement was neither void nor voidable. The Court of Appeal then considered whether the settlement could be set aside under the principles governing the setting aside of voluntary dispositions, and held that it could not.[238]

It will be appreciated that the result of the Court of Appeal's decision is that dispositions made by trustees under a misapprehension will be harder to set aside than under the so-called "rule in *Re Hastings-Bass*", which had come to be regarded as some kind of "get out of jail free card". The remedy, if any, is against professional advisers.

The principles just discussed cannot be invoked to correct a mistake in the drafting of the rules of a pension trust, as they apply to things done by trustees, not to things done by the settlor of a private trust or by an employer setting up a pension trust.[239] In other words, the principles cannot be used to circumvent the strict conditions of the doctrine of rectification.

---

[236] Above, fn.230.

[237] Above, fn.230; T. Peacock (2011) 25 T.L.I. 125.

[238] Below, para.26–002.

[239] *Smithson v Hamilton* [2008] 1 W.L.R. 1453 (mistake enabling early retirement without reduction of benefits). P. Clarke and J. Edelman All E.R. Rev. 2008 at 300, 392.

Where the court does intervene, the result is normally negative: the decision of the trustees may be set aside, or a future course of action restrained. Usually the court makes no positive direction that a discretion must be exercised in a particular way. However, this can be done in an appropriate case, as in *Klug v Klug*,[240] where a trustee refused to exercise a power of advancement for an extraneous reason (because the beneficiary, her daughter, had married without her consent). The court directed the trustee to agree to the advancement. Alternatively, a trustee may be persuaded by the prospect of removal.

C. Power of Decision

17–046   A trust deed may give the trustees or a third party power to decide a particular matter. We saw in Ch.3 that this may be a means of curing conceptual uncertainty,[241] in which case the question arises whether the court may intervene if the decision appears unreasonable or wrong. Lord Denning in *Re Tuck's Settlement Trusts* would only have accepted the decision of the Chief Rabbi "so long as he does not misconduct himself or come to a decision which is wholly unreasonable."[242]

The trustees cannot be given power to decide legal issues in such manner as to oust the jurisdiction of the court, as this would be contrary to public policy.[243] They may be given power to decide limited issues, such as where the beneficiaries reside, or what is their ancestry or faith. The House of Lords in *Dundee General Hospitals v Walker*[244] thought it possible, as mentioned above, that the decisions of trustees in such cases could be attacked on the grounds of perversity or failure to appreciate the issue, as well as on grounds of bad faith. Where a clause in a trust of a pension fund provided that the determination of matters such as eligibility and the construction of the instrument adopted by the trustees in good faith should be binding on all parties and beneficiaries, the Canadian court held that its jurisdiction was not excluded where the trustees acted in breach of their duty of impartiality, although in good faith.[245]

---

[240] [1918] 2 Ch. 67. See also *Re Hodges* (1878) 7 Ch.D. 754; *Re Roper's Trust* (1879) 11 Ch.D. 272. The appointment of new trustees is considered preferable to positive intervention (i.e. the judicial exercise of fiduciary discretions) in (1990) 107 L.Q.R. 214 at 219–220 (S. Gardner), discussing *Mettoy Pension Trustees Ltd v Evans*, above, fn.228. See also D. Hayton [2005] Conv. 229, supporting positive intervention in pensions cases.

[241] Above, para.3–030.

[242] [1978] Ch. 49 at 62.

[243] *Re Wynn* [1952] Ch. 271. See also *Re Raven* [1915] 1 Ch. 673 (trustees cannot be given conclusive power to resolve doubts as to identity of beneficiary).

[244] [1952] 1 All E.R. 896 at p.905. This was a Scottish appeal, but "of the highest persuasive value": per Lord Denning M.R. in *Re Tuck's ST*, above, fn.242, at 61.

[245] *Boe v Alexander* (1988) 41 D.L.R. (4th) 520. See also *Jones v Shipping Federation of British Columbia* (1963) 37 D.L.R. (2d) 273.

The general principle that beneficiaries cannot control trustees in the manner in which they exercise their powers applies even though all the beneficiaries are ascertained and of full capacity and wish the power to be exercised in a particular way.[246] But in such a case the trust can of course be brought to an end.

---

[246] *Re Brockbank* [1948] Ch. 206; cf. *Re George Whichelow Ltd* [1954] 1 W.L.R. 5 at 8. See, however, s.19 of the Trusts of Land and Appointment of Trustees Act 1996; above, para.17–023.

CHAPTER 18

DUTIES OF TRUSTEES IN RELATION TO THE TRUST PROPERTY

1. DUTY TO COLLECT IN THE ASSETS

A. Duty on Accepting Office

Trustees must, on their appointment, make themselves familiar **18–001** with the terms of the trust and the state and the details of the trust property, check that the trust fund is invested in accordance with the provisions of the trust deed, and that the securities and any chattels are in proper custody.[1] They should not wait until the trust property is formally vested in them. The discharge of their duties will obviously depend upon circumstances. The trustees of a trust newly constituted, and with suitable assets, are in an easier situation than personal representatives who find, as part of the estate, assets which are highly speculative or precarious. In the latter case the duty is to

---

[1] *Re Miller's Deed Trust* (1978) 75 L.S.Gaz. 454.

consider the best method of protecting the value of the assets, and this may involve delaying a decision to dispose of them. Liability for loss will not be imposed on them if their decision to delay was reasonable, even though subsequent events show it to have been the less wise course.[2]

A replacement trustee must make all reasonable inquiries[3] to satisfy himself that nothing has been done by his predecessor and the continuing trustees which amounts to a breach of trust; and the continuing trustees must provide this information from trust documents.[4] Omission to inquire may render the new trustee liable, but he is not to be fixed with notice of matters that do not appear on any of the trust documents, though the matter may be known to the retiring trustee.[5] On a similar principle, if he is ignorant of the existence of some right forming part of the trust, he is not liable for loss of that right through non-enforcement unless he could have discovered its existence from materials at his disposal.[6]

B. Extent of Duty

18–002   The duty to safeguard trust assets is a stringent one; indeed, it has sometimes been almost too strictly applied.

In *Re Brogden*,[7] the trustees of a marriage settlement took what they considered to be all reasonable steps to ensure that a covenant to pay £10,000 to them at the end of a stated period of five years was carried out. They did not sue because the covenantor's estate was the basis of the family partnership, the stability of which might have been imperilled by an action at a time of trade depression. The trustees were held liable. They should have taken every possible step to insist on payment, irrespective of the claims of sentiment within a family.

In *Buttle v Saunders*,[8] trustees had orally agreed to sell a freehold reversion to the leaseholder. Then a beneficiary made a

---

[2] *Buxton v Buxton* (1835) 1 My. & Cr. 80.

[3] *Re Lucking's WT* [1968] 1 W.L.R. 866.

[4] *Tiger v Barclays Bank* [1951] 2 K.B. 556.

[5] *Hallows v Lloyd* (1888) 39 Ch.D. 686.

[6] *Youde v Cloud* (1874) L.R. 18 Eq. 634. A similarly reasonable rule governs the inquiries trustees should make in relation to covenants to settle after-acquired property: *Re Strahan* (1856) 8 De. G.M. & G. 291.

[7] (1888) 38 Ch.D. 546. See also *Harris v Black* (1983) 46 P. & C.R. 366 (duty to preserve assets did not require court to compel a trustee-beneficiary to seek the renewal of a business tenancy which he did not want, the partnership with the other trustee-beneficiary having been dissolved).

[8] [1950] 2 All E.R. 193; E. Bodkin (1950) 14 Conv.(n.s.) 228; A. Samuels (1975) 30 Conv.(n.s.) 177; G Lightman (2008) 22 T.L.I. 11. See also *Sergeant v National Westminster Bank* (1991) 61 P. & C.R. 518.

higher offer. The trustees declined to consider it, feeling themselves bound by commercial morality to complete the agreement.
Wynn-Parry J. held that, although there may be cases where a
trustee should accept a lower offer—as where that offer may be
lost if not honoured—and although the honourable course was to
stand by the earlier offer, the trustees had an overriding duty to
obtain the best price for their beneficiaries.

C. Litigation

In *Re Brogden*,[9] the Court of Appeal laid down that the only **18–003**
excuse for not taking action to enforce payment was a well-founded
belief on the part of the trustees that such action would be fruitless;
and the burden of proof was on the trustees. Now trustees have
extensive powers of compounding (settling) liabilities, allowing
time for the payment of debts, and compromising doubtful actions,
etc. given by the Trustee Act 1925 s.15.[10] Trustees are not liable for
loss caused by any acts done by them in good faith in exercise of
these powers, provided they have directed their minds to the problem and not just let the matter slide.[11] A trustee will be allowed the
costs of litigation from the trust assets if properly incurred,[12] but not
where the litigation results from an unreasonable withholding of
property from those entitled to it,[13] nor where the litigation is speculative and turns out to be unsuccessful,[14] nor where the trustee has
acted in a manner hostile to the beneficiaries.[15] A beneficiary may
sue a third party on behalf of the trust where the trustee unreasonably refuses to sue or has disabled himself from doing so.[16] (Where,
however, the trustees are able and willing to sue, the beneficiary will
be penalised in costs.[17]) Trustees who discontinue litigation against
third parties because the trust fund could be exhausted in indemnifying them for costs do not act unreasonably, and the beneficiaries
may not take over the action.[18]

[9] (1888) 38 Ch.D. 546.
[10] Below, para.20–010.
[11] *Re Greenwood* (1911) 105 L.T. 509. cf. *Re Ezekiel's Settlements* [1942] Ch. 230.
[12] See generally *Alsop Wilkinson v Neary* [1996] 1 W.L.R. 1220; Lightman. J. (2006) 20
T.L.I. 151; below, para.21–001; *Singh v Basin, The Times*, August 21, 1998; *Bonham v Blake
Lapthorn Linnell* [2007] W.T.L.R. 189. As to how the costs are borne between capital and
income, see *Close Trustees (Switzerland) SA v Vildosola* [2008] W.T.L.R. 1543.
[13] *Re Chapman* (1895) 72 L.T. 66.
[14] *Re Beddoe* [1893] 1 Ch. 547; *Re England's ST* [1918] 1 Ch. 24.
[15] *Holding and Management Ltd v Property Holding and Investment Trust Plc* [1989] 1
W.L.R. 1313; *Breadner v Granville-Grossman* [2006] W.T.L.R. 411; *Shovelar v Lane* [2011]
4 All E.R. 669.
[16] *Parker-Tweedale v Dunbar Bank Plc* [1991] Ch. 12; G. McCormack (1997) 11
T.L.I. 60.
[17] *D'Abo v Paget (No.2), The Times*, August 10, 2000. There is more flexibility as to costs
under the Civil Procedure Rules 1998.
[18] *Bradstock Trustee Services Ltd v Nabarro Nathanson (A Firm)* [1995] 1 W.L.R. 1405.

D. A Continuing Duty

18–004   Trustees must regard their duty of safeguarding trust assets as a continuing one. In regard to investment in securities, the point is dealt with below. In regard to land, there is a duty to consider the maintenance and general welfare of the property, and in regard to deeds and chattels, a duty to see that they are kept securely.[19] There is no duty to insure unless required by the trust deed, but trustees have a power to insure.[20]

2. Duty to Invest[21]

A. Meaning of Investment

18–005   A trustee is under a duty to invest trust money in his hands. To invest means "to employ money in the purchase of anything from which interest or profit is expected".[22] From the point of view of an individual investing his own money, he may not mind whether the profit comes from income earned by the investment or from capital appreciation. But trustees often have to consider the interests of a life tenant, who is entitled to the income, and also of the remaindermen who are interested in the capital. The trustees' duty is to act fairly between them. The investments should produce income, and maintain the capital, although the "portfolio theory" now permits more flexibility on this point.[23] Thus premium bonds and chattels, such as antiques or silver, are not investments for this purpose. For this reason a purchase of a house for occupation by a beneficiary, and which therefore produces no income, was held not to be an investment,[24] but this has been remedied by statute.[25] It remains the case that investments which yield a high rate of income because the capital is wasting away, or an unsecured loan,[26] should be avoided.

Mention should also be made of "total return" investment. This enables the selection of investments on the basis of the value of the returns they are expected to yield, without regard to the classification of these returns as capital or income. This gives more flexibility in the choice of investments, thereby enabling potentially higher

---

[19] *Jobson v Palmer* [1893] 1 Ch. 71.

[20] Below, para.20–008.

[21] Trustees conducting investment business are required by Financial Services and Markets Act 2000 s.19, to be authorised under the Act or exempted.

[22] *Shorter Oxford English Dictionary; Re Wragg* [1919] 2 Ch. 58 at 64, per P.O. Lawrence J. who added: "and which property is purchased in order to be held for the sake of the income which it will yield."

[23] A. Hicks (2001) 15 T.L.I. 203. For the "portfolio theory", see below, para.18–014.

[24] *Re Power* [1947] Ch. 572.

[25] Trusts of Land and Appointment of Trustees Act 1996 s.6(3); Trustee Act 2000 s.8; below, para.18–011.

[26] *Khoo Tek Keong v Ch'ng Joo Tuan Neoh* [1934] A.C. 529.

returns. Trusts with interests in succession are not generally drafted to enable total return investment, and the tax implications are uncertain. The Law Commission has recently recommended that HMRC and HM Treasury should enter discussions with the trust industry as to the feasibility and mechanics of total return investment.[27]

Part II of the Trustee Act 2000, which confers wide investment powers on trustees, retains the traditional terminology of "investment" without elaboration. The Law Commission considers that trustees may acquire assets for capital appreciation rather than income yield.[28] The Explanatory Notes (which accompany, but are not part of, the Act) state that the general power of investment permits the trustees to invest in a way which is expected to produce an income or capital return. The point remains somewhat uncertain, and it is to be expected that express clauses permitting the application of trust funds in a manner which may not strictly be an "investment" will continue to be used.

B. Types of Investment

In most general terms, there are basically two types of investment. The first is a loan at a rate of interest. The second is a participation in a profit-making activity; such as the purchase of ordinary shares in a company ("equities"). Ordinary shares were first included in the list of permitted investments for trustees by the Trustee Investments Act 1961. Mention should also be made of "derivatives", such as futures and options. A "future" obliges the holder to buy or sell (shares, currency, commodities, etc.) at a set price at a future date. An option gives the holder the right, but not the obligation, to buy or sell at a set price at a set date. Pension fund trustees and others with sufficiently wide powers may make use of derivatives in appropriate circumstances, but they are not within the traditional meaning of "investments".[29] Dealing in derivatives can be risky, as illustrated in extreme form by the collapse of Barings Bank in 1995.

18–006

i. **Loans at a Rate of Interest.** In the case of an investment such as a deposit account at a bank or a building society, the capital sum does not alter (save by additions or withdrawals). Interest is earned at a rate which is normally variable.

18–007

---

[27] Law Com. No.315 (2009), *Capital and Income in Trusts: Classification and Apportionment*, para.5.104. For charities, see above, para.15–090.

[28] No.260 (1999), *Trustees' Powers and Duties*, p.22; No.315 (2009), *Capital and Income in Trusts: Classification and Apportionment*, para.2.69. This view is supported in A. Hicks (2001) 15 T.L.I. 203 and in *Legal underpinning: Charities and Investment Matters* (Charity Commission, 2011).

[29] cf. Law Com. No.315 (2009), *Capital and Income in Trusts: Classification and Apportionment*, para.2.69.

Most fixed interest securities issued by the Government and local authorities are in the form of stock and pay a fixed rate of interest. The purchaser may sell the stock to other purchasers. The value of the stock is whatever a purchaser will give for it. That depends on many factors; essentially the current rate of interest chargeable on loans. Where interest rates have increased since the stock was issued, the value of the stock declines. A 3 per cent stock, paying £3 per annum on an investment of £100, needs to pay the current rate of interest (if higher) in order to be saleable, but the interest is fixed at a lower rate. If the current market rate of return was 10 per cent, a 3 per cent stock would be worth £30. £3 per annum on an outlay of £30 is a 10 per cent return.

Some stocks however are "dated"; that is, they will be repaid at "par" (100) at a stated date in the future. The nearer the date, the higher the price. Thus in December 2011, Treasury 5 per cent 2012 was priced at 101.24. Capital gains on certain government stocks are free of capital gains tax.[30] This and other factors contribute to the price.

A debenture is an acknowledgement of indebtedness by a company, supported in practice by a charge upon the undertaking and assets of a company. This is a floating, as opposed to a fixed, charge. The company is free to deal with any of its specific assets unaffected by the charge. The charge crystallises when the debenture holders take the necessary steps to enforce their security. The value of a debenture is dependent partly upon the ability of the assets and undertaking of the company to provide sufficient security for the loan, and it is therefore to some extent dependent upon the commercial stability of the company.

Preference shares are shares in a company which have a preference in relation to the payment of a fixed rate of dividend, and may have other preferential rights as well. Being dependent upon the earning by the company of sufficient profits to pay the dividends, they are less secure than government securities (gilts) or debentures, and consequently they normally carry a higher return. That does not mean that the rate of dividend rises. It is the price at which the shares can be purchased on the market which varies. If 5 per cent preference shares, paying £5 per annum on their par value were priced at 50, the dividend of £5 per annum on an outlay of £50 would put the shares on a return of 10 per cent.

ii. Equities.

18–008   (a) *Ordinary Shares.* A company must provide a statement of its capital and initial shareholdings when applying for registration.[31]

---

[30] Taxation of Chargeable Gains Act 1992 s.115; above, para.9–005.
[31] Companies Act 2006 s.9 (replacing earlier legislation).

Shares are divided into classes and normally include ordinary shares. Ownership of an ordinary share entitles the purchaser to vote at the general meeting, to participate in dividends when declared on the ordinary shares, and to participate in a winding up.

The Annual General Meeting will declare the dividend payable for the year, if any. The value of ordinary shares varies with the fortunes of the company. They necessarily contain an element of speculation, and it is for this reason that ordinary shares were not authorised investments for trustees until 1961.

(b) *Unit Trusts and Investment Trusts.*[32] The selection of ordinary shares for investment is a highly specialised matter. Further, it is important that the investment of a trust should be spread over a wide range of companies. But a small trust cannot provide a satisfactory spread. This can be achieved by participating in an investment fund which is managed by investment experts. There are basically two types. First the unit trust, in which the managers receive money from investors, and form a single fund, divided up into units which are owned by the investors. The investors have the advantage of investment expertise, and of the spread of investments. Units in a trust can be bought and sold. Secondly, the misleadingly named investment trust. This is a limited company in which shares can be bought and sold like other shares. The company buys shares in other companies, and the investors receive their return in the form of dividends from the investment trust.

18–009

C. Express Powers of Investment

A trustee may be given wide power by the trust instrument to select investments; or his selection may be left to investments authorised by the general law. Express clauses at one time were strictly construed, reflecting the court's fear of investment in ordinary shares in the 19th century. Thus it seemed to be established that words such as a "power to invest in such securities as they might think fit"[33] gave power merely to select among securities then authorised for trustee investment. This had changed by the time of *Re Harari's Settlement Trusts*,[34] where the words "in or upon such investments as to them may seem fit" permitted the trustees to invest in equities.

It is likely to remain the usual practice to include a clause giving trustees wide powers of investment even after the extension of investment powers by the Trustee Act 2000; and the trustees, or other persons, may be given authority to amend the power.[35]

18–010

---

[32] See A. Harris (1995) 92/09 L.S.Gaz. p.18.
[33] *Re Braithwaite* (1882) 21 Ch.D. 121; *Re Maryon-Wilson's Estate* [1912] 1 Ch. 55.
[34] [1949] 1 All E.R. 430.
[35] *Re Harari's ST*, above, fn.34, at 434.

D. The Purchase of Land

18–011   Until quite recently trustees could not purchase land unless the trust instrument so provided. Even where the instrument did authorise investment in land, we saw that the purchase of a house for the occupation of a beneficiary was not an "investment".[36] Statutory power to purchase land was first given to trustees of land by the Trusts of Land and Appointment of Trustees Act 1996.[37] The power has since been widened and extended to trustees in general by the Trustee Act 2000. Subject to any restriction or exclusion in the trust instrument, trustees may acquire freehold or leasehold land in the United Kingdom:

  (a) as an investment, or
  (b) for occupation by a beneficiary, or
  (c) for any other reason.[38]

There is no restriction as to the length of any lease which may be acquired. Trustees who acquire land under this provision have all the powers of an absolute owner in relation to the land for the purpose of exercising their functions as trustees.[39] The statutory duty of care applies to trustees in the exercise of their powers under the Act in relation to land and also to the exercise of express powers relating to land.[40] Land outside the United Kingdom is excluded from the statutory power because such a purchase could create problems in a jurisdiction which does not recognise trusts. Trustees may, however, be given express power to purchase such land.

Trustees' power to invest in a mortgage of land is dealt with below.[41]

E. Authorised Investments

18–012   **i. Traditional Rule.** The rules on investment by trustees have been governed by the principles, first that trustees must avoid all risk to the capital of the fund, and secondly, that the value of the £ will remain stable. Throughout the 19th century, the system worked well enough. At first, trustees were restricted to consols,[42] and were subsequently permitted to choose among a narrow range of fixed interest investments, known as trustee securities. Investment was

---

[36] *Re Power* [1947] Ch. 572, above, para.18–005.
[37] s.6(3).
[38] TA 2000 s.8. Only the acquisition of a legal estate in the land is permitted. The provision does not apply to settled land; s.10.
[39] TA 2000 s.8(3).
[40] TA 2000 Sch.1, para.2.
[41] Below, para.18–014.
[42] Fixed interest Government securities without redemption date.

not yet a technical or specialised matter. The income beneficiaries were assured of an income, and the capital was secure. But progressive inflation changed all that.

Much of the problem of the decline of the value of the currency should be solved by investment in equities. A purchaser of a share in a company owns a share of the operation. If the business prospers, its actual value may increase. Assume, however, that the actual value of the business remains the same; if the value of money is reduced to one-third, the value of the shares will treble, providing "a hedge against inflation".

But in times of recession, the prices of ordinary shares fall even faster than those of gilts. Prices on investment exchanges are established by buyers and sellers, and a number of irrational factors play their part in establishing and undermining confidence. The overall prices of shares are gauged by an index called the *Financial Times Index*.[43] The fluctuations in prices underline the dangers involved in investment in ordinary shares, and emphasise the need for expertise in selecting investments; and the avoidance of speculation.

ii. Trustee Investments Act 1961. Authorised investments were **18–013** extended by the Trustee Investments Act 1961. The object of the Act was to permit trustees to invest a proportion of trust funds in equities. The original permitted proportion was one-half, but the Treasury increased this to three-quarters, pending a more fundamental reform of trustee investments.[44]

The Act of 1961 had long been criticised as outdated, and it was invariably side-stepped in any well-drawn trust by the provision of wider powers. Nevertheless, the Act remained an obstacle in cases such as trusts arising on intestacy or under home-made wills. The criticisms were broadly twofold. First, the Act had not kept pace with the developments in the world of investments and thus did not permit trustees to utilise many advantageous investments. Secondly, its machinery was cumbersome as a result of the requirement of division of the fund before any investment in equities could be made.

iii. Trustee Act 2000. The expansion of investment powers was **18–014** one of the major purposes of the Trustee Act 2000. This legislation substantially widens investment powers so that trust income may be maximised without eroding the capital. The beneficiaries remain protected by the requirement of professional advice, the financial services legislation and the general law on investment duties.

Before examining the investment provisions of the Act in detail, mention should be made of the modern "portfolio theory", whereby

---

[43] This is now the FT30-share index. Since 1984 there is also the broader-based FT-SE 100 Index. See also the Dow Jones (USA), Hang Seng (Hong Kong) and Nikkei (Japan).

[44] Trustee Investments (Division of Trust Fund) Order (SI 1996/845).

trustees' investment decisions must be evaluated not in relation to individual assets in isolation but in the context of the trust portfolio as a whole and as part of an overall investment strategy.[45] This theory has been approved by the Law Commission.[46] Although not expressly dealt with in the Act of 2000, it may now be regarded as part of the general law.[47]

Section 3 of the Trustees Act 2000 provides that, subject to the other provisions of Pt II of the Act, "a trustee may make any kind of investment that he could make if he were absolutely entitled to the assets of the trust". This is called "the general power of investment", and it applies to trusts whenever created.[48] The general power is additional to any express powers, but may be restricted or excluded by the trust instrument or by other legislation.[49] For example, a settlor may wish to exclude investments he does not consider ethical.[50] The general power does not apply to trustees of pension funds or authorised unit trusts, nor to trustees managing common investment or common deposit schemes under what is now the Charities Act 2011.[51] Trustees in these categories are subject to their own statutory regimes.

Trustees' powers to acquire land have already been dealt with.[52] So far as mortgages are concerned, the limited powers contained in the Trustee Act 1925 and the Trustee Investments Act 1961 have been replaced by a power to invest by way of a loan secured on land.[53] It appears from the general power to acquire land contained in s.8, which is confined to legal estates, that any secured loan must take effect by way of a legal mortgage, as under the previous law, although the point is unclear. While the power to acquire land is restricted to land in the United Kingdom, there is no geographical limit on other investments.

F. The Standard Investment Criteria

18–015   Section 4 of the Trustee Act 2000 provides that trustees must have regard to the standard investment criteria when exercising any statutory or express power of investment. They must "from time to time

---

[45] See Lord Nicholls (1995) T.L.I. 71; E. Ford (1996) 10 T.L.I. 102; I. Legair (2000) 14 T.L.I. 75; R. Thornton (2008) 67 C.L.J. 396 at 399–401.

[46] No.260 (1999), *Trustees' Powers and Duties*, p.23. It was also adopted in a Treasury consultation paper; *Investment Powers of Trustees* (May 1996), paras 35(ii), 40(iii).

[47] See Law Com. No.315 (2009), *Capital and Income in Trusts: Classification and Apportionment*, para.3.7: "The Trustee Act 2000 enables but does not require trustees to follow modern portfolio theory."

[48] TA 2000 s.7. The Act of 1961 is substantially, although not entirely, repealed.

[49] TA 2000 s.6. No provision in a trust instrument made before August 3, 1961 is to be treated as a restriction or exclusion; s.7(2).

[50] Below, para.18–019.

[51] TA 2000 ss.36–38.

[52] Above, para.18–011.

[53] TA 2000 s.3(3), (4).

review the investments of the trust and consider whether, having regard to the standard investment criteria, they should be varied". The standard investment criteria are:

"(a) the suitability to the trust of investments of the same kind as any particular investment proposed to be made or retained and of that particular investment as an investment of that kind, and (b) the need for diversification of investments of the trust, in so far as is appropriate to the circumstances of the trust".

These criteria are based on similar provisions in the Trustee Investments Act 1961 and, in conjunction with the duty to review, are consistent with the "portfolio theory" discussed above.[54] Diversification is particularly important with large funds.[55] The duty to consider it arises in relation to investments held at the creation of the trust as well as to investments acquired later.[56] Thus trustees of a will trust were in breach of their duty to review investments where they decided to retain and refurbish a valuable but dilapidated property for six years without seeking professional advice, which would have been to sell it straight away in its unrepaired state.[57]

A small fund may achieve diversification by investing in unit trusts or shares in an investment trust company.[58]

G. Advice

Section 5 of the Trustee Act 2000, following similar provisions in **18–016** the previous legislation, requires trustees to obtain and consider proper advice about the way in which, having regard to the standard investment criteria, the power of investment (whether express or statutory) should be exercised. Similarly, when reviewing the investments, the trustees must obtain and consider proper advice as to whether the investments should be varied. "Proper advice" is the advice of a person who is reasonably believed by the trustees to be qualified to give it by his ability in and practical experience of financial and other matters relating to the proposed investment.[59] The advice need not be written. By way of exception, trustees need not obtain such advice if they reasonably conclude that, in all the

---

[54] Above, para.18–014.
[55] *Cowan v Scargill* [1985] Ch. 270; *Nestlé v National Westminster Bank Plc* [1993] 1 W.L.R. 1260.
[56] *Gregson v HAE Trustees Ltd* [2008] W.T.L.R. 999.
[57] *Jeffery v Gretton* [2011] W.T.L.R. 809. However, the breach caused no loss to the trust; below, para.23–012.
[58] Above, para.18–009.
[59] Persons acting as investment advisers must be authorised under Financial Services and Markets Act 2000 s.19.

circumstances, it is unnecessary or inappropriate to do so.[60] An example may be when they propose to make a small and secure investment.

The trustees must, of course, consider the advice and then make their own decision.[61] They must not repose blind faith in the adviser. They may, however, delegate investment decisions, as discussed below. In the case of a trust corporation, there seems no reason why the advice should not be that of a competent officer, as under the previous law.

H. Duty of Care

18–017   Prior to the Trustee Act 2000, the standard of conduct required of a trustee was that of the "prudent man of business".[62] This has been reformulated by s.1 of the Trustee Act 2000, which provides that a trustee must exercise such care and skill as is reasonable in all circumstances. What is reasonable will vary according to whether the trustee is a layman or a professional.[63] The duty of care applies to trustees in the exercise of statutory or express powers of investment, including their duty to have regard to the standard investment criteria and to obtain and consider proper advice.[64] It applies also in relation to their power to acquire land.[65] So, for example, trustees may be in breach of duty if they invest by way of a secured loan which equals the value of the property, leaving no margin for depreciation, even though the former restrictions on the amount of the loan have gone. As will be seen in the following section, trustees may delegate investment decisions and may appoint nominees and custodians to hold the trust investments. The duty of care applies also to the exercise of these powers.[66]

I. Delegation of Investment Powers

18–018   We have seen that investment normally needs expert advice. Trustees may wish to go further and delegate their investment powers to a professional such as an investment manager authorised under the financial services legislation. As this involves the delegation of a discretion, it could not be done prior to the Trustee Act 2000 unless permitted by the trust instrument. An exception existed in the case

---

[60] TA 2000 s.5(3).
[61] *Shaw v Cates* [1909] 1 Ch. 389; *Martin v City of Edinburgh District Council* [1988] S.L.T. 329; *Jones v AMP Perpetual Trustee Company NZ Ltd* [1994] 1 N.Z.L.R. 690.
[62] *Speight v Gaunt* (1883) 9 App. Cas. 1.
[63] Above, para.17–003.
[64] TA 2000 Sch.1, para.1.
[65] TA 2000 para.2.
[66] TA 2000 para.3.

of pension trustees,[67] but other trustees (in the absence of an express power) needed to apply to court for an extension of investment powers.[68] Alternatively, they could delegate by power of attorney under s.25 of the Trustees Act 1925.

Reform of this area was one of the major purposes of the Trustee Act 2000. Section 11 achieves this by listing functions which may *not* be delegated, investment powers being omitted from the list. Where investment powers are delegated, the agent must satisfy the requirements relating to the standard investment criteria and the duty to review the investments from time to time.[69] He does not, however, need to obtain advice if he is the kind of person from whom the trustees could properly have obtained advice.[70] The delegation of asset management functions[71] must be done by an agreement in writing or evidenced in writing.[72] Further, the trustees must prepare a "policy statement" giving guidance as to how these functions should be exercised in the best interests of the trust, and the agent must agree to comply with it.[73]

Section 16 of the Trustee Act 2000 confers on trustees the power to appoint a nominee (save in regard to settled land) and to vest the trust property in question in the nominee. Section 17 permits the appointment of a custodian, to undertake safe custody of the assets in question or of any documents or records concerning them. Neither power applies to a trust which has a custodian trustee.[74] There are various restrictions as to who may be appointed as a nominee or custodian.[75] Normally the agent will be a person who carries on a business including acting as a nominee or custodian. The trustees may appoint one of their number if that one is a trust corporation, or may appoint two (or more) of their number if they are to act as joint nominees or joint custodians.[76] Charity trustees must act in accordance with guidance given by the Charity Commission concerning the selection of a nominee or custodian.[77]

The trustees may pay the nominee or custodian from the trust fund, and, if reasonably necessary, may appoint him on terms which

---

[67] Pensions Act 1995 s.34. Thus the powers in the Trustee Act 2000 do not apply to pension trusts.

[68] See *Anker-Petersen v Anker-Petersen* (1998) 12 T.L.I. 166 (decided 1991).

[69] TA 2000 s.13(1).

[70] TA 2000 s.13(2).

[71] These are investment, the acquisition of property, the management of trust property and disposing of the property or of interests in it; s.15(5).

[72] TA 2000 s.15.

[73] TA 2000 s.15. This may refer to liquidity, the balance between capital and income, or ethical considerations.

[74] TA 2000 ss.16(3), 17(4). Nor do they apply to assets vested in the official custodian for charities. For bearer securities, see s.18.

[75] TA 2000 s.19.

[76] The trustee(s) so appointed must satisfy the conditions laid down in s.19, e.g. that he or they carry on a business including acting as a nominee or custodian.

[77] Current guidance may be found in the publication CC42.

permit him to appoint a substitute, restricting his liability, or permitting him to act in circumstances capable of giving rise to a conflict of interest.[78] This reflects the fact that persons acting as nominees or custodians may in practice insist on the inclusion of such terms.

Unless the trust instrument provides otherwise, trustees who delegate to investment managers, nominees or custodians must keep the arrangements under review, including the review of any policy statement.[79] Trustees are not liable for the default of such agents unless they have failed to comply with the statutory duty of care when making the appointment or reviewing the arrangements.[80] The duty of care applies to the exercise of statutory or express powers to appoint agents, nominees or custodians. It applies in particular to the selection of the person who is to act, the terms upon which he is to act, and the preparation of a policy statement where asset management functions are delegated.[81] If, however, the trustees fail to act within their statutory powers of delegation, the appointment of the agent, nominee or custodian is not thereby invalidated.[82]

As in the case of other powers conferred by the Trustee Act 2000, the power to delegate to investment managers, nominees and custodians applies to trusts whenever created, but is subject to any restriction or exclusion in the trust instrument or other legislation.[83] Further details of the general power of delegation will be found in Ch.20.

J. General Duty in Choosing Investments; Ethical Investments

18–019   We have seen that the Trustee Act 2000 provides a framework for the exercise of trustee investment powers. The traditional standard of the "prudent man of business"[84] has been reformulated by s.1 of the Act as a duty to exercise such care and skill as is reasonable in the circumstances. No doubt it remains true that trustees must avoid investments "which are attended with hazard".[85] Although a trustee now has statutory power to "make any kind of investment that he could make if he were absolutely entitled to the assets of the trust",[86] the fact that he is not absolutely entitled places him in a different position from an absolute owner, who may speculate as he

---

[78] TA 2000 s.20.
[79] TA 2000 ss.21, 22.
[80] TA 2000 s.23. See s.23(2) for liability for substitute agents.
[81] TA 2000 Sch.1, para.3.
[82] TA 2000 s.24.
[83] TA 2000 ss.26, 27.
[84] *Speight v Gaunt* (1883) 9 App.Cas. 1; cf. *Nestlé v National Westminster Bank Plc* [1993] 1 W.L.R. 1260 (standard of prudence regarded as "undemanding" and likely to result in complacency and inactivity). See generally P. Pearce and A. Samuels [1983] Conv. 127.
[85] *Learoyd v Whiteley* (1887) 12 App.Cas. 727 at 733.
[86] Trustee Act 2000 s.3.

pleases. He must also consider the competing interests of the life tenant and the remainderman, investing so as to provide a reasonable income, and to keep secure the capital.[87] We have seen that the modern "portfolio theory"[88] requires the investment decisions of trustees to be made and evaluated in the context of the portfolio as a whole rather than in relation to individual assets.

These general investment duties were reviewed in *Nestlé v National Westminster Bank Plc*,[89] where the remainder beneficiary complained that the fund of £270,000 would have been worth over £1m if properly invested. The claim failed because, although the trustees had failed to appreciate the scope of their investment power and to conduct regular reviews, the beneficiary had not proved that these failures had resulted in wrong investment decisions and loss. Although the investments fell "woefully short" of maintaining the real value of the fund, failure to maintain the value was not in itself a breach of trust, as to do so would require extraordinary skill and luck, and would at times be impossible.[90] Further, the trustees were entitled and bound to consider tax implications, which justified investment in government stock rather than equities where the life tenant was non-resident. In the absence of such special factors, however, it was accepted that trustees should invest at least half of the fund in equities. If the case had arisen after the Trustee Act 2000, no doubt the trustees would have been held to be in breach of the statutory duty of care, but the issue of establishing loss would remain. A trustee who commits a mere error of judgment is unlikely to be held in breach of the duty of care.[91]

The question whether trustees may adopt non-financial investment criteria arose in *Cowan v Scargill*.[92]

A mineworkers' pension fund with large assets and very wide powers of investment was managed by 10 trustees, of whom five, including the defendant, were appointed by the National Union of Mineworkers. They were assisted in investment decisions by an advisory panel of experts. An investment plan was submitted,

---

[87] Below, Ch.19.

[88] Above, para.18–014. This is reflected in Pensions Act 1995 s.35; above, para.16–016.

[89] [1993] 1 W.L.R. 1260; J. Martin (1992) 142 N.L.J. 1279; A. Kenny [1993] Conv. 63; G. Watt and M. Stauch [1998] Conv. 352. See also Law Com. No.315 (2009), *Capital and Income in Trusts, Classification and Apportionment*, para.5.25.

[90] See *Jones v AMP Perpetual Trustee Company NZ Ltd* [1994] 1 N.Z.L.R. 690 (trustee is neither insurer nor guarantor of fund).

[91] See *Jones v AMP Perpetual Trustee Company NZ Ltd*, above, fn.90 (not liable for mere error of judgment in retaining shares in a falling market).

[92] [1985] Ch. 270; S. Butler (1984) 81 L.S.Gaz. 2291; P. Clarke All E.R.Rev. 1984, 306. See also Uniform Prudent Investor Act 1994, s.5 (USA), requiring investment solely in the interest of the beneficiaries; J. Langbein in D. Hayton (ed.), *Modern International Developments in Trust Law*, 1999, Ch.11.

which the union trustees, on the basis of union policy, refused to accept unless it was amended so that there should be no increase in overseas investments; those already made should be withdrawn; and there should be no investment in energies in competition with coal. It was held that the trustees would be in breach of duty if they refused to adopt the investment strategy. They must exercise their powers in the best interests of present and future beneficiaries. If the purpose of the trust was the provision of financial benefit, the best interests of the beneficiaries normally meant their best *financial* interests. This duty to the beneficiaries was paramount. The trustees must exercise their investment powers so as to yield the best return, putting aside personal interests and social and political views. If investments in, for example, armaments or tobacco, were beneficial, they must not refrain because of their own views, however sincere. But financial benefit was not *inevitably* paramount. If all the beneficiaries were adults with strict views on, say, tobacco, it might not "benefit" them to make such investments. Here, however, there was no justification for reducing the benefit because the trustees had an investment policy intended to assist the union or the industry. The trustees were pursuing union policy, and the ultimate sanction was removal.[93]

18–020   It is difficult to see, however, why the trustees would be failing in their duties if they confined themselves to the investments proposed by the union trustees. In the case of a pension fund, maintenance of the prosperity of the industry must be in the financial interests of the beneficiaries, and to invest in a competing industry may be harmful.[94] Overseas investments may be risky, and there is an ample range of authorised investments at home: "no trust fund is so big as to exhaust the home market."[95] Perhaps the outcome would have been different if the union trustees had not argued their case on ideology rather than law.[96]

Presumably there would be no breach if trustees were to pursue an ethical investment policy only after satisfying themselves that their selected investments were at least as financially sound as those

---

[93] Damages would not be recoverable unless the policy was implemented and caused loss, which is unlikely.

[94] This argument was rejected by Megarry V.C. on the facts. The miners' pension fund is fully funded and is unusual in that its value even at that time far exceeded that of the declining coal industry, and there were many more pensioners than miners.

[95] P. Pearce and A. Samuels [1985] Conv. 52 at 53. Overseas investments are permitted by the Trustee Act 2000.

[96] J. Farrar and J. Maxton (1986) 102 L.Q.R. 32. See also J. Langbein and R. Posner (1980) 79 Mich. L.Rev. 72.

rejected on ethical grounds (a "socially sensitive" policy).[97] The point is that they must not fetter their discretion by adopting a policy which excludes any consideration of the financial merits of a particular class of investments (a "socially dictated" policy). Thus in *Martin v City of Edinburgh District Council*[98] the Scottish court granted a declaration that a policy to oppose apartheid by disinvesting in companies which had South African interests was a breach of duty, even though no loss was incurred. The trustees (the local authority) had failed to consider whether their policy was in the best financial interests of the beneficiaries. These principles should be adhered to whether the trustees have a negative investment policy (to avoid certain types of investments) or, less commonly, a positive investment policy (to make only certain types of investments). They must remember that their duty is the provision of financial benefits, "not the reform of the world".[99]

In the case of a charity, an additional factor is that the trust is pursuing an aim, so that the question arises whether the trustees can invest in undertakings which are incompatible with their objective. For example, can trustees of a cancer charity invest in the tobacco industry?[100] As we have seen, trustees (including charity trustees) must have regard to "the suitability to the trust of investments of the same kind as any particular investment proposed to be made or retained".[101] In *Harries v Church Commissioners for England*[102] the claim was that the Commissioners, whose purpose was to promote the Christian faith through the Church of England, should not invest in a manner incompatible with that purpose even if this involved a risk of significant financial detriment. It was held that they could take non-financial ethical considerations into account only in so far as they could do so without jeopardising the profitability of investments. Their charitable purpose would be best served by seeking the maximum financial return. There might be rare cases where certain investments would directly conflict with the objects of the charity (as in the cancer/tobacco example). In these cases the trustees

[97] See generally P. Docking and I. Pittaway (1990) 4 *Trust Law & Practice* 25; N. Convey (1990) 87/23 L.S.Gaz. 17; R. Ellison (1991) 5 T.L.I. 157; L. Irish and A. Kent (1994) 8 T.L.I. 10; Lord Nicholls (1995) 9 T.L.I. 71; P. Watchman, J. Anstee-Wedderburn and L. Shipway (2005) 19 T.L.I. 127 at 134; R. Thornton (2008) 67 C.L.J. 396.

[98] [1988] S.L.T. 329.

[99] (1991) 5 T.L.I. 157 at 165–166; *Harries v Church Commissioners for England*, below, fn.102 (trustees must not make moral statements at the expense of the trust).

[100] See BMA Report on Investment in the UK Tobacco Industry; H. Beynon (1982) 45 M.L.R. 268; J. Thurston (1987) 1 *Trust Law & Practice* 162; Annual Report of the Charity Commissioners, 1987, paras. 41–45; Annual Report 1996, paras. 54–55 (pooled funds set up to exclude incompatible investments). Charity Commission guidance is given in publication CC14 (revised 2011). See also *Legal underpinning: Charities and Investment Matters)* (Charity Commission, 2011).

[101] Trustee Act 2000 s.4(3)(a).

[102] [1992] 1 W.L.R. 1241; R. Nobles [1992] Conv. 115; P. Luxton (1992) 55 M.L.R. 587; Lord Browne-Wilkinson (1992) 6 T.L.I. 119 at 123.

should not make such investments even if this results in financial detriment, but this was unlikely to arise because of the width of other investments. There might also be rare cases where a particular investment might alienate potential donors or recipients. The Commissioners already had a policy which excluded investment in armaments, gambling, tobacco, newspapers and South Africa, considering that there was an adequate width of alternative investments, and the propriety of this was not doubted.[103]

A settlor may secure ethical investments by providing in the instrument that the trustees must or must not make certain kinds of investments.[104] Where the trustees have delegated their investment powers, any such direction by the settlor will be reflected in the policy statement which they must prepare for the agent.[105] Where the trust instrument is silent on the matter, trustees may include ethical considerations in the policy statement, subject to their general law duties discussed above. The guidance in the policy statement must be formulated "with a view to ensuring that the functions will be exercised in the best interests of the trust",[106] and the statutory duty of care applies to its preparation.[107]

The investment policy of pension trustees must now be explicit as to the extent (if any) of ethical considerations.[108]

K. Trustees Holding Controlling Interest in a Company

18–021   Difficult questions arise in relation to the trustees' duties where the trust owns a controlling interest in a company. The first question is whether the shareholding is a proper investment at all. If the company is a private company, as is the usual case in this situation, express authorisation was needed prior to the Trustee Act 2000 to purchase such shares. Now the issue is whether such a purchase satisfies the standard investment criteria laid down in s.4 of the Act.[109] Usually the question is one of retention. A provision expressly authorising retention is desirable (whether the holding is a majority or a minority), but the right to retain will be implied where the trust deed or will specifically refers to the property, as in the case

---

[103] The Commissioners appeared to have fettered their discretion, but this seems permissible where the excluded investments conflict with the charity's purpose, even if not directly incompatible.

[104] TA 2000 s.6(1)(b); *Harries v Church Commissioners for England*, above, fn.102.

[105] TA 2000 s.15(2).

[106] TA 2000 s.15(3).

[107] TA 2000 Sch.1, para.3.

[108] Pensions Act 1995 s.35. The investment provisions of the 1995 Act remain in force although much of the Act has been repealed by Pensions Act 2004.

[109] Above para.18–015.

of a specific bequest on trust.[110] A right to retain does not impliedly authorise a right to purchase more of the shares.[111]

But that is not the end of the matter. It is not sufficient for the trustees to determine that the investment is suitable, and leave it at that. For the company or its directors may engage in practices which are wholly unsuitable for a trust investment, such as speculative activities. Can the trustees shelter behind the directors, whose acts they are in a position to control?

In *Bartlett v Barclays Bank Trust Co Ltd*,[112] the bank was trustee of the Bartlett trust. The sole asset of the trust was a shareholding amounting to virtually all the shares in a family property company, which held some £500,000 worth of rent-producing properties.

Tax would need to be paid on the death of the life tenants, and a suggestion was made that cash would be more easily raised if the company went public; and merchant bankers advised that a public issue would be more successful if the company were not only a manager of existing property, but a developer of new properties also. The bank agreed to a policy of active development, so long as the income available to the income beneficiaries was not prejudiced.

The board then embarked upon speculative developments, one of which was a disaster, because planning permission for the intended office development could not be obtained. This resulted in a large loss to the trust shareholding.

The Bank was held liable. It was not sufficient that they believed **18–022** the directors to be competent and capable of running a profitable business. Their duty was "to conduct the business of the trust with the same care as an ordinary prudent man of business would extend to his own affairs."[113] To do that it was necessary, especially as the bank was aware that the company was moving into speculative development, to get the fullest information on the conduct of the business; and not merely to be content with the supply of information which they received as shareholders. Cross J. in *Re Lucking's Will Trusts*[114] held that a controlling shareholder should insist on being represented on the board; but Brightman J. treated this as one

---

[110] *Re Pugh* [1887] W.N. 143; *Re Van Straubenzee* [1902] 2 Ch. 779.

[111] *Re Pugh*, above, fn.110.

[112] [1980] Ch. 515; *Walker v Stones* [2001] Q.B. 902. See Lord Nicholls (1995) 9 T.L.I. 71 at 76.

[113] [1980] Ch. 515 at 531, quoting *Speight v Gaunt* (1883) 9 App.Cas. 1. Now the question would be whether the trustees had complied with the duty of care under Trustee Act 2000 s.1.

[114] [1968] 1 W.L.R. 866 at 874.

convenient way of ensuring that all the necessary information was available.[115]

So the controlling shareholder must obtain the necessary information, as a means of "enabling the trustee to safeguard the interests of the beneficiaries."[116] How do the trustees do that? Ultimately, of course, the majority shareholder will get its way; as by adopting "the draconian course of threatening to remove, or actually removing, the board in favour of compliant directors",[117] which is asking a lot of the trust department of a bank. Brightman J. was able to avoid the practical difficulties of such a course by finding that the members of the board were "reasonable persons, and would (as I find) have followed any reasonable policy desired by the bank had the bank's wishes been indicated to the board."[118] It is now common for the trust deed to contain a provision relieving the trustees of any duty to involve themselves in the affairs of the company in which they have a majority holding.

L. Extension of Investment Powers by the Court

18–023   Trustees may apply to court under s.57 of the Trustee Act 1925[119] or under the Variation of Trusts Act 1958[120] to widen investment powers. An application under s.57 is more convenient provided the beneficial interests are not affected.[121] Applications have been rare since the passing of the Trustee Investment Act 1961, the court taking the view (here described as the *Re Kolb* principle[122]), that special circumstances have to be shown to justify an extension beyond the powers conferred by a modern statute. The question arose in *Mason v Farbrother*,[123] concerning a pension fund which had limited investment powers. By 1982, as a result of inflation, the fund had vastly increased, and the trustees wished to have wider powers. They applied to court under s.57 of the Trustee Act 1925.[124]

[115] [1980] Ch. 515 at 533. "Other methods may be equally satisfactory and convenient depending upon the circumstances of the individual case. Alternatives which spring to mind are the receipt of copies of the agenda and minutes of board meetings if regularly held, the receipt of monthly management accounts in the case of a trading concern . . . the possibilities are endless. . . . " See *Re Miller's Trust Deed* (1978) 75 L.S.Gaz. 454, where one of the trustees was a member of a firm of accountants which acted as auditors for the company.

[116] [1980] Ch. 515 at 534.

[117] [1980] Ch. 515 at 530.

[118] [1980] Ch. 515. The Virgin Islands Special Trusts Act 2003 removes this duty in relation to "VISTA trusts."

[119] Below, para.22–007.

[120] Below, para.22–012.

[121] *Anker-Petersen v Anker-Petersen*; (1998) 12 T.L.I. 166 (decided 1991).

[122] *Re Kolb's Will Trusts* [1962] Ch. 531; *Re Cooper's Settlement* [1962] Ch. 826; *Re Clarke's Will Trusts* [1961] 1 W.L.R. 1471.

[123] [1983] 2 All E.R. 1078; H. Norman [1984] Conv. 373.

[124] The application under the 1958 Act did not proceed because of difficulties with the representative parties. The aspect concerning the court's inherent jurisdiction to approve a compromise is dealt with below, para.22–005.

It was held that there was no absolute rule that the court should not widen investment powers after the 1961 Act. The court approved a wide modern clause, as there were special circumstances, which included the effect of inflation and the fact that it was in the nature of a public fund.

A different approach was subsequently taken by Megarry V.C. in *Trustees of the British Museum v Att Gen*,[125] where the trustees were granted a relaxation of their existing scheme, made in 1960, as they needed a wider choice and a power to invest abroad. The trustees were eminent and responsible, and had highly skilled advice. The size of the fund (£5 million–£6 million) made it unlike a private trust and more like a pension fund or large institutional investor. Referring to *Mason v Farbrother*,[126] where, as we have seen, the court treated the *Re Kolb*[127] principle as still binding in the absence of special circumstances, Megarry V.C. disagreed that inflation could be called a special circumstance, and preferred to say that the *Re Kolb* principle had gone, although if the statutory powers were increased, the principle could apply again. Now, as we have seen, the Trustee Act 2000 has revolutionised investment powers, making it unlikely that trustees will have much need to apply to court for extended powers. Should they do so, for example if they should wish to purchase land abroad (which the Act of 2000 does not permit), the *Re Kolb* principle would again be relevant. It is more likely that applications to court after the commencement of the Act will involve attempts to lift specific restrictions and exclusions imposed by the settlor. In such cases the *Re Kolb* principle would not apply, as the trustees would not be seeking powers beyond those contained in the Trustee Act 2000. The issue for the court would be whether it would be justified in overturning the wishes of the settlor.

3. Duty to Distribute. Satisfaction of Claims

A. Liability for Wrongful Payments

A trustee is obliged to make payments of income and capital as **18–024** they become due, and to make them to the persons properly entitled. Failure to do so is a breach of trust, which the trustee must normally make good, such as for example, a payment based on a forged

---

[125] [1984] 1 W.L.R. 418. See also *Steel v Wellcome Custodian Trustees Ltd* [1988] 1 W.L.R. 167; B. Dale [1988] Conv. 380. (Trustees of large charity with funds of £3,200 million including share capital in W Ltd which could not be sold sought wider powers of beneficial owner. Variation approved, having regard to size of fund, eminence of trustees and provisions requiring advice).
[126] Above, fn.123.
[127] [1962] Ch. 531, above.

document,[128] or upon an erroneous construction of a document,[129] even if legal advice was taken,[130] or without regard to the entitlement of illegitimate beneficiaries.[131]

Where a trustee makes an overpayment of income or of instalments of capital, the error may be adjusted in later payments.[132] If the payment is to a person who is not entitled, the trustee's right of recovery is governed by the law of restitution, and the money will be recoverable if the mistake is one of fact or law.[133] An unpaid or underpaid beneficiary may, in addition to his right to sue the trustee, proceed against the property in the hands of the wrongly paid recipient not being a bona fide purchaser for value without notice.[134] A trustee-beneficiary who fails to pay himself in full has been held to have no remedy,[135] but this rule appears too extreme.[136]

B. Doubtful Claims

18–025   **i. Application to Court for Directions.** Where the trustees are in any doubt in relation to the claims of the beneficiaries, they may make an application to the court for directions; and will be protected if they obey the directions of the court.[137] This course can now be taken with a minimum of complication.[138] In this way problems of construction of the trust instrument and difficulties in administering the trust can be brought before the court, so that the trustees are not forced to take the risk of making decisions upon a false premise.[139] An application to the court can also be helpful in cases where the trustees are deadlocked or disabled by a conflict of interest in connection with the exercise of a discretion, for instance a discretionary power to make advancements. In such a case the trustees surrender their discretion to the court, and must put all relevant information before it to enable the discretion to be exercised.[140] Trustees cannot,

---

[128] *Eaves v Hickson* (1861) 30 Beav. 136.

[129] *Hilliard v Fulford* (1876) 4 Ch.D. 389.

[130] *National Trustees Company of Australasia Ltd v General Finance Company of Australasia Ltd* [1905] A.C. 373.

[131] Family Law Reform Act 1987 s.20, reversing the previous position under FLRA 1969 s.17.

[132] *Dibbs v Goren* (1849) 11 Beav. 483 (administration by the court); *Re Musgrave* [1916] 2 Ch. 417; P. Matthews [1994] 2 R.L.R. 44.

[133] *Kleinwort Benson Ltd v Lincoln City Council* [1999] 2 A.C. 349.

[134] *Re Diplock* [1948] Ch. 465.

[135] *Re Horne* [1905] 1 Ch. 76.

[136] It may have been overtaken by developments in the law of restitution.

[137] *Re Londonderry's Settlement* [1965] Ch. 918; *Finers v Miro* [1991] 1 W.L.R. 35.

[138] CPR 1998 Pts 8, 64.

[139] See also AJA 1985 s.48, giving the court power to authorise action to be taken in reliance on counsel's opinion respecting the contruction of a will or trust.

[140] *Royal Society for the Prevention of Cruelty to Animals v Att Gen* [2002] 1 W.L.R. 448 (court has unfettered discretion to decide what to do).

however, surrender the future exercise of discretions to the court.[141]
Where, on the other hand, the trustees merely wish to obtain the
blessing of the court for their proposed course of action, because it is
for some reason momentous, their act of applying to court for directions does not involve a surrender of discretion.[142] Trustees or beneficiaries may apply for the trust to be administered by the court, but
the court will only make an administration order if it considers that
the issues cannot properly be resolved in any other way.[143]

ii. Payment into Court. Where beneficiaries cannot be ascer-   **18–026**
tained, or where for some exceptional reason trustees cannot obtain
a good discharge from the trust, there is a residual power in trustees
to pay the trust moneys into court.[144] The residue of the fund in *Re
Gillingham Bus Disaster Fund*,[145] for instance, was eventually paid
into court.

But this will not be tolerated by the court as a means of trustees
evading their obligations when difficulties arise.[146] It is a last resort
when all other methods of dealing with the problem have proved
unsuccessful. Trustees who pay trust funds into court when a different course was preferable, may be liable for costs.[147]

iii. "Benjamin" Order. The court has a power to authorise dis-   **18–027**
tribution of the whole of the assets of an estate, although not all the
beneficiaries or creditors have made themselves known so as to be
able to receive their share. A typical situation is where the whereabouts or continued existence of a certain beneficiary is not known.
The procedure is sometimes known as a "Benjamin" order, and its
purpose is to protect those distributing the assets.[148] If those entitled
who have received nothing under the distribution eventually come
forward to establish their claim, they may still be able to proceed,
within the period of limitation, against the person wrongly paid,[149]
or against the property itself. Such an order will of course only be

---

[141] *Re Allen-Meyrick's WT* [1966] 1 W.L.R. 499.
[142] *Public Trustee v Cooper* [2001] W.T.L.R. 901, explaining *Marley v Mutual Security
Merchant Bank and Trust Co Ltd* [1991] 3 All E. R. 198. The court will sanction the proposed
exercise of discretion if the decision is one which a reasonable trustee could have reached and
is not vitiated by any conflict of interest. See also *X v A* [2006] W.T.L.R. 171.
[143] CPR 1998 Pt 64.
[144] Payment into court furnishes an exception to the rule that a majority of trustees cannot
defeat a dissentient minority, for TA 1925 s.63, provides that the payment may in certain
circumstances be made by a majority of the trustees.
[145] [1959] Ch. 62; above, para.10–007.
[146] See *Re Knight's Trust* (1859) 27 Beav. 45.
[147] *Re Cull's Trusts* (1875) L.R. 20 Eq. 561; A. Hawkins (1968) 84 L.Q.R. 64 at 65–67.
[148] *Re Benjamin* [1902] 1 Ch. 723; *Re Gess* [1942] Ch. 37; *Re Taylor* [1969] 2 Ch. 245.
[149] *Ministry of Health v Simpson* [1951] A.C. 251; *Re Lowe's WT* [1973] 1 W.L.R. 882 at
887. The overpaid beneficiary may be protected from this risk by "missing beneficiary"
insurance; *Re Evans* [1999] 2 All E.R. 777.

made after all practicable inquiries have been instituted. A modern example as *Re Green's Will Trusts*,[150] where the testatrix left her property to her son, providing that it should go to charity if he did not claim it by the year 2020. The son had disappeared on a bombing raid in 1943, and all but his mother were satisfied that he was dead. A "Benjamin" order was made, allowing distribution to the charity, it being no bar to such an order that it was contrary to the intention of the testatrix.[151] "Missing beneficiary" insurance may be a preferable course, especially in the case of a small estate.[152]

18–028   **iv. Distribution after Advertisement.** Under the Trustee Act 1925 .s.27, trustees have themselves the power to advertise for claimants[153] and, after compliance with certain formalities, the power to distribute the whole of their trust assets to claimants who have responded or of whom the trustees otherwise have notice. Those who subsequently demonstrate an entitlement are enabled to proceed against the property distributed, save when it is in the hands of a purchaser.[154] Section 27 applies to the trustees of pension funds, although in practice it will be more difficult for them to show that they did not have notice of a particular claim. If they once had notice but have forgotten, they still have notice.[155]

18–029   **v. Setting Aside a Fund.** The Trustee Act 1925 s.26,[156] provides a procedure whereby trustees can set aside out of trust assets a sum to meet any potential liabilities under a lease or rentcharge, and then to distribute the remainder of the trust assets to those entitled. Again, should the sum set aside prove insufficient, those entitled to the extra sums may still follow the distributed property. In the case of contingent liabilities outside s.26, the trustees can either retain a fund, distribute under a court order, obtain insurance cover if available, or obtain an indemnity from the beneficiaries and then distribute.[157]

---

[150] [1985] 3 All E.R. 455.

[151] Criticised on this point in P. Luxton [1986] Conv. 138.

[152] *Re Evans* [1999] 2 All E.R. 777.

[153] Normally creditors, but also beneficiaries, for example claimants under an intestacy. Advertising is not sufficient protection against contingent debts; *Re Yorke* [1997] 4 All E.R. 907.

[154] s.27(2)(a); and see *Re Aldhous* [1955] 1 W.L.R. 459.

[155] *MCP Pension Trustees Ltd v Aon Pension Trustees Ltd* [2011] 3 W.L.R. 455.

[156] As amended by Landlord and Tenant (Covenants) Act 1995 Sch.1.

[157] See Mellows, *The Law of Succession*, 5th edn, p.379; *Re Yorke* [1997] 4 All E.R. 907 (contingent liabilities of Lloyd's underwriter); *Re K* [2007] W.T.L.R. 1007 (estate distributed subject to retention of £50,000 for three years to fund defence of any proceedings by unpaid creditors whose claims were stale or disputed). See further Practice Note [2001] 3 All E.R. 765.

C. Relief under Section 61

A trustee who makes an erroneous distribution may be relieved **18–030**
from liability if he acted honestly and reasonably and ought fairly to
be excused.[158]

D. Discharge

On the termination of the trust, the trustees should present their **18–031**
final accounts and obtain a discharge from the beneficiaries. The
best protection is provided by a release by deed, for that places on a
complaining beneficiary the burden of proving fraud, concealment,
mistake or undue influence.[159] But a trustee is not entitled to a
release by deed.[160] If the beneficiaries are unwilling to give one, the
trustees may apply to the court for the accounts to be taken and
approved.[161]

---

[158] Below, para.23–033; *Re Evans*, above, fn.152.
[159] *Fowler v Wyatt* (1857) 24 Beav. 232.
[160] *King v Mullins* (1852) 1 Drew. at 311, per Kindersley V.C.
[161] Underhill and Hayton, 18th edn, p.1083.

CHAPTER 19

DUTIES OF TRUSTEES IN RELATION TO THE BENEFICIARIES

1. DUTY TO MAINTAIN EQUALITY BETWEEN THE BENEFICIARIES

A TRUSTEE is under a general duty to maintain equality between the **19–001** beneficiaries. This duty forms the basis of the specific rules of conversion and apportionment, discussed below, which apply as between life tenant and remainderman. It is not, however, confined to such cases. A modern example of the wider general duty is *Lloyds Bank Plc v Duker*,[1] where a testator's residuary estate included 999 company shares. He left 46/80 to his wife, and the rest to other beneficiaries. In spite of the general rule that a beneficiary is entitled in specie to his share of divisible personalty held on trust for sale, it was held that the wife could not claim 574 shares, as such a majority holding would be worth more than 46/80. The only fair solution was for the trustees to sell the shares and divide the proceeds in the specified proportions. Of course, where the trustees have a power to

---

[1] [1987] 1 W.L.R. 1324. See also *Nestlé v National Westminster Bank Plc* [1993] 1 W.L.R. 1261; *X v A* [2000] 1 All E.R. 490; *Pagliaro v Thomas* [2008] W.T.L.R. 1417.

choose between various classes of beneficiaries, the duty to act impartially has no application. In such a case the trustees are entitled to prefer some beneficiaries over others, provided they do not take irrelevant matters into account.[2] However, so far as trustees' expenditure is concerned, if it is incurred for the benefit of the whole estate, it must be allocated to capital for income tax purposes and thus does not reduce the amount of income subject to the higher rates of tax applicable to the income of a discretionary trust.[3] Only those expenses which can be shown to relate solely to the discharge of the trustees' duties to the income beneficiaries may be attributed to income.

A. The Rule in *Howe v Earl of Dartmouth*

19–002   **i. Life Tenant and Remainderman.** A trustee must act impartially between life tenant and remainderman. This duty applies to the selection of investments[4]; and the rules governing investment by trustees are an attempt to strike a balance between the provision of income for the life tenant and the preservation of the capital for the remainderman.[5] So long as those rules are observed, a trustee is usually under no duty to rearrange the investments so as to balance equally the interests of the life tenant and remainderman.[6] Nor, if there are investments in the fund which have ceased to be authorised, are the trustees under any immediate duty to convert them into authorised investments. However the fund is invested, the normal rule is that the tenant for life takes all the income; the remainderman's interest is in the capital. The capital is not of course available until the life tenant's death; but he may, if he wishes, deal with or dispose of his reversionary interest in the fund.

There are, as we will see, some situations in which there is a duty to convert into authorised investments; and this duty carries with it a duty to apportion the income earned before the conversion is effected.

---

[2] *Edge v Pensions Ombudsman* [2000] Ch. 602.

[3] *Revenue and Customs Commissioners v Trustees of the Peter Clay Discretionary Trust* [2009] Ch. 296. See also *Close Trustees (Switzerland) SA v Vildosola* [2008] W.T.L.R. 1543 (how costs of litigation allocated to capital and income).

[4] *Raby v Ridehalgh* (1855) 7 De G. M. & G. 104 at 109; *Re Dick* [1891] 1 Ch. 423 at 431.

[5] Above, para.18–005. There is no duty to preserve the real value of the capital; *Nestlé v National Westminster Bank Plc* [1993] 1 W.L.R. 1261 (suggesting also that trustees entitled to incline towards high income investments if rich remainderman and poor life tenant).

[6] "It is perhaps surprising that equity has not cast upon trustees, in every such case, a duty to convert the trust property as soon as practicable into something more likely to produce an equitable result", S. Bailey (1943) 7 Conv.(N.S.) 128 at 129; *Re Searle* [1900] 2 Ch. 829 at 834; cf. *Re Smith* (1971) 18 D.L.R. (3d) 405; M. Cullity (1972) 50 Can.B.R.116 (duty to reinvest where authorised shares producing low return because of company policy to pursue capital growth).

ii. The Duty to Convert. A duty to convert (i.e. sell) and re- **19–003**
invest in authorised investments may arise by reason of the existence of an express trust to sell, or, in the case of a bequest of
residuary personalty, under the rule in *Howe v Earl of Dartmouth*.[7]
Only an outline of the rule will be given, partly because it is almost
invariably excluded in a professionally drafted will, and partly because the investment powers of trustees are so wide after the Trustee
Act 2000 that the duty to sell unauthorised investments now has
little scope for application. Furthermore, the Law Commission has
proposed its abolition.[8]

Howe v Earl of Dartmouth establishes that, subject to a contrary
provision in the will, there is a duty to convert where residuary
personalty is settled by will in favour of persons in succession. The
trustees should convert all such parts of it as are of a wasting[9] or
future or reversionary[10] nature or consist of unauthorised securities,[11] into authorised investments.

Thus property such as royalties and copyrights[12] should be converted in the interest of the remainderman. For these may be of
reduced or of no value at the life tenant's death. On the other hand,
"future" property such as a remainder or reversionary interest, or
other property which at present produces no income, is of no immediate benefit to the tenant for life. In his interest therefore it
should be converted into income-bearing properties. And, as we
shall see, provision is made for apportionment between the life
tenant and remainderman of the value of such property when it falls
into possession.[13]

It will be seen that, on its terms, the rule is of limited application.
It does not apply to life-time settlements[14]; nor to specific as opposed to residuary bequests[15] (for the settlor's or testator's intention
in such cases is for the specific property settled to be enjoyed suc-
cessively). Nor has it applied to leaseholds since the property legislation of 1925.

iii. Apportionment. Where there is a duty to convert, there is, in **19–004**
the absence of an intention that the life tenant shall enjoy the income

---

[7] (1802) 7 Ves.Jr. 137. The duty to sell the assets of an intestate has been replaced by a
power of sale; AEA 1925 s.33, as amended by Trusts of Land and Appointment of Trustees
Act 1996 Sch.2.
[8] Below, para.19–010.
[9] Such as mines or ships which will eventually become worthless; or patents or copyrights
which expire.
[10] i.e. property which will only come into possession after the death of the life tenant.
[11] i.e. not authorised by the terms of the will, nor by Trustee Act 2000. cf. *Re Smith* (1971)
18 D.L.R. (3d) 405, above, para.19–002 (authorised securities).
[12] *Re Evans' WT* [1921] 2 Ch. 309; *Re Sullivan* [1930] 1 Ch. 84.
[13] *Re Earl of Chesterfield's Trust* (1883) 24 Ch.D. 643; below, para.19–006.
[14] *Re Van Straubenzee* [1901] 2 Ch. 779.
[15] [1901] 2 Ch. 779, at 782.

until sale, a duty also to apportion fairly between the life tenant and the remainderman the original property pending conversion.

19–005   (a) *Wasting, Hazardous or Unauthorised Investments.* It is assumed that wasting, hazardous and unauthorised securities produce income in excess of that which the life tenant should reasonably receive; and do so at the expense of the security of the capital. With such property therefore the object of the apportionment rule is to provide that the life tenant receives an income which represents the current yield on authorised investments,[16] and that the excess is added to capital.[17] If the interest received is less than 4 per cent, the balance should be made up out of subsequent income or from the proceeds of the unauthorised investments when sold.[18]

19–006   (b) *Future, Reversionary or other Non-income Producing Property.* Where personalty which is subject to a duty to convert includes reversionary property, it is necessary, in the interest of the life tenant, to provide for apportionment[19]; otherwise the life tenant would obtain no benefit from the property until it fell into possession. The reversion should be sold and the proceeds re-invested; until that is done there is no way of producing income for the life tenant. When it has been sold, there is still the problem of determining how much of the proceeds of sale should be apportioned to capital and how much to the life tenant. This is done by[20] ascertaining the sum:

> "[W]hich, put out at 4 per cent per annum . . . and accumulating at compound interest at that rate with yearly rests,[21] and deducting income tax at the standard rate, would, with the accumulation of interest, have produced, at the respective dates of receipt, the amounts actually received; and that the aggregate of the sums so ascertained ought to be treated as principal and be applied accordingly, and the residue should be treated as income."

In other words, the proceeds of sale of the reversion are part principal, part interest. The principal is the sum which, if invested at 4 per cent at the date of the testator's death, would have produced the sum now received. The balance goes to the tenant for life.

---

[16] The life tenant's income was fixed at 4% in *Re Baker* [1924] 2 Ch. 271. However, this became out of line with the return from gilt-edged investments, although interest rates are very low at the time of writing. Trustees who have to decide what income to pay may be well advised to take instructions from the court.

[17] The life tenant will of course receive the income from the capital as thus increased.

[18] *Re Fawcett* [1940] Ch. 402.

[19] A reversionary interest in land is not within the rule (*Re Woodhouse* [1941] Ch. 336).

[20] *Re Earl of Chesterfield's Trusts* (1883) 24 Ch.D. 643.

[21] i.e. the income is transferred to capital at the end of each year.

iv. *Howe v Earl of Dartmouth* Today. The rules relating to con-   **19–007**
version and apportionment demonstrate basic principles of equity.
But they should be understood in their proper perspective.

(a) *Exclusion of Duty to Apportion.* The duty to apportion is in   **19–008**
practice nearly always excluded, both in respect of income from
unauthorised securities and in respect of reversionary interests. The
duty to convert, where it exists, thus appears in the context of a duty
to change the investments.

(b) *Effect of Current Investment Situation.* The utility of the   **19–009**
rules of conversion and apportionment varies according to the current investment situation:

"The dividend yield on the shares in the most regarded index of
100 leading equities has for years been far less than the interest
yield obtainable on medium-dated fixed-interest government
stock. In present-day circumstances, retaining unauthorised equities therefore tends to depress the life tenant's income, whereas
when *Howe v Dartmouth* was decided the effect was the opposite.
It no longer makes sense to say that the income of a life tenant
from a fund of unauthorised equities ought to be limited to the
yield of government stocks, since that would usually be higher,
not lower".[22]

Thus the life tenant wants fixed interest investments when they
provide a high income; the remainderman wants unauthorised securities for the preservation of the real value of the capital. It is the life
tenant who would be pressing the trustees to convert urgently into
gilt-edged securities at times when they could bring an income in
excess of the 4 per cent allowed to the life tenant by the rule of
apportionment.

(c) *Reform.* The apportionment rules have recently been re-   **19–010**
viewed by the Law Commission.[23] It is proposed that all equitable
rules of apportionment (the rules in *Howe v Earl of Dartmouth* and
Re Earl of Chesterfield's Trusts and other equitable rules discussed
in the following section of this chapter) should be abolished.
It had previously been proposed that the apportionment rules
should be replaced by a statutory power of allocation, which would
be an administrative power enabling trustees to allocate trust receipts and expenses to capital or income, so far as necessary to

---

[22] Trust Law Committee Consultation Paper, *Capital and Income of Trusts* (1998).
[23] Law Com. No.315 (2009), *Capital and Income in Trusts: Classification and Apportionment.* For previous reviews, see Law Reform Committee 23rd Report (1982); Trust Law
Committee Consultation Paper, *Capital and Income of Trusts* (1998). For solutions in another
jurisdiction, see the Uniform Principal and Income Act of 1977 of the United States.

discharge their duty to maintain the balance between capital and income. Such a power would have given the trustees more freedom in choosing investments with a view to overall growth rather than capital and income returns, thus promoting a "total return" investment policy.[24] However, this power of allocation was not included in the Law Commission's final proposals because of adverse tax consequences.[25] It is, therefore, proposed that the equitable rules of apportionment should be abolished for future trusts (subject to any contrary provision in the trust instrument) without being replaced by any statutory power.[26] The proposals will be enacted when parliamentary time permits.[27]

The reform proposals include a new classification of company distributions to trustees.[28] No changes are proposed to the classification of other trustee receipts (or expenses).

Another way of maintaining the balance between beneficiaries is the "percentage trust", in which the settlor specifies that a percentage of the whole trust fund (valued annually after adding all receipts and deducting all outgoings) is to be given to the life tenant each year. The balance goes to the remainderman on termination of the life interest. It is not clear how the rules for the taxation of trusts apply to such a trust. The Law Commission would like more work to be done to develop percentage trusts, but this would be a task for the trust industry, in partnership with HM Treasury and HMRC.[29]

B. Other Methods of Apportionment

19–011   Apportionment is necessary in other situations, and these will be mentioned in outline only.

19–012   **i. Apportionment Act 1870.** When a testator or a life tenant dies, the question arises of the entitlement to periodical income, such as rents, interest and dividends, earned in whole or in part, but not paid, at the time of the death. That which is treated as being earned before the death will be added to the estate, and that earned afterwards is payable as income to the income beneficiary under the will or, in the case of the death of a life tenant, to the next life tenant, or to the capital.

The division is governed by the Apportionment Act s.2, which provides that:

---

[24] Above, para.18–005.
[25] Law Com. No.315 (2009), paras 5.67–5.83.
[26] Law Com. No.315 (2009), paras 6.54–6.65.
[27] Response to Ministry of Justice consultation on the draft Bill, January 17, 2011.
[28] Below, para.19–017.
[29] Law Com. No.315 (2009), para.5.23. See also paras 3.17–3.22, discussing USA models.

"[A]ll rents, annuities, dividends, and other periodical payments in the nature of income ... shall ... be considered as accruing from day to day, and shall be apportionable in respect of time accordingly."

It is necessary therefore to ascertain the proportion of the earning period which expired prior to the death, and to divide the payment, when received, in the same proportion.[30] When rent is due, or a dividend earned, but not paid prior to the death, the whole income is paid to the testator's estate or to that of the life tenant. The Act may be excluded by an expression of an intention to do so. This is now common in order to avoid the complications which are introduced into the administration of an estate. The Law Commission has proposed that the Act should no longer apply to trusts, so that income would accrue to the income beneficiary at the date it arises.[31]

ii. The Rule in *Allhusen v Whittell*. This rule attempts to strike   **19–013**
a fair balance between life tenant and remainderman in respect of the payment of the debts of an estate. The life tenant under a will is entitled to income earned after the testator's death. The debts of the testator must also be paid; and it may take some time to do so. In the meantime the assets of the estate are earning income for the life tenant. He should, in fairness, only have the income from the net estate. The rule in *Allhusen v Whittell*[32] provides that the life tenant shall make a contribution.

Romer L.J. in *Corbett v Commissioners of Inland Revenue*[33] explained the rule as follows:

"For the purposes of adjusting rights as between the tenant for life and the remainderman of a residuary estate, debts, legacies, estate duties, probate duties and so forth, are to be deemed to have been paid out of such capital of the testator's estate as will be sufficient for that purpose, when to that capital is added interest on that capital from the date of the testator's death to the date of the payment of the legacy or debt, or whatever it may have been, interest being calculated at the average rate of interest[34] earned by the testator's estate during the relevant period."

The rule may be excluded by an expression of contrary intent, or where its application would in the circumstances be inappropriate.[35]

---

[30] For class gifts, see *Re Joel* [1967] Ch. 14.
[31] Law Com. No.315 (2009), above, para.6.70.
[32] (1867) L.R. 4 Eq. 295.
[33] [1938] 1 K.B. 567.
[34] *Re Wills* [1915] 1 Ch. 769.
[35] *Re McEuen* [1913] 2 Ch. 704; *Re Darby* [1939] Ch. 905.

Witnesses to the Law Reform Committee in 1982 described the rule as "complex, fiddlesome and resulting in a disproportionate amount of work and expense," adding that where the rule was not excluded it was often simply ignored.[36] The Law Commission recently recommended that, as in the case of the rules in *Howe v Earl of Dartmouth* and *Re Earl of Chesterfield's Trusts*,[37] it should be abolished.[38]

19–014   **iii. The Rule in *Re Atkinson*.** Where an authorised mortgage security is sold by the trustee mortgagees and the proceeds are insufficient to satisfy the principal and interest in full, it is necessary to determine the way in which the loss is to be shared between life tenant and remainderman. The sum realised must be apportioned between the life tenant and the remainderman in the proportion which the amount due for the arrears of interest bears to the amount due in respect of the principal.[39] This rule would also be abolished under Law Commission proposals mentioned above.

19–015   **iv. Interest on Damages.** Where loss of the trust fund results in an award of compensation, interest will be payable on the sum awarded from the date of the claim form until judgment. The interest should be apportioned between life tenant and remainderman. In *Jaffray v Marshall*,[40] a fair apportionment was considered to be half and half, taking a broad view.

19–016   **v. Purchase or Sale of Shares Cum Dividend.** One of the factors which affects the price of shares is the date of payment of the next dividend. A share whose dividend will be paid tomorrow is worth more than it would be if the dividend has been paid yesterday. It would seem reasonable to require an apportionment when shares are bought or sold cum dividend (that is, with the dividend), but the general rule is that there is none.[41] In this respect, the beneficiaries take "the rough with the smooth".[42] This is probably more convenient overall than an insistence on an apportionment in every case. But an apportionment will be required if there would otherwise be "a glaring injustice".[43]

---

[36] 23rd Report, above. See para.3.31.

[37] Above, fn.20.

[38] Law. Com. No.315 (2009), para.6.65.

[39] *Re Atkinson* [1904] 2 Ch. 160.

[40] [1993] 1 W.L.R. 1285 (overruled as to the assessment of damages in *Target Holdings Ltd v Redferns (A Firm)* [1996] 1 A.C. 421).

[41] *Bulkeley v Stephens* [1896] 2 Ch. 241; *Re Ellerman's ST* (1984) 81 L.S.Gaz. 430, where the decision to the contrary in *Re Winterstoke's WT* [1938] Ch. 158 was regarded as wrong; I. Pittaway (1986) 1 *Trust Law & Practice* 62. See Law. Com. C.P. 175 (2004), paras 3.64–3.71.

[42] *Re Maclaren's ST* [1951] 2 All E.R. 414 at 420.

[43] [1951] 2 All E.R. 414.

vi. Company Distributions. Questions can also arise as to the **19–017** entitlements of life tenant and remainderman to certain distributions by companies. The question of entitlement and that of the liability of the distribution to income tax are related questions, but are not identical.[44] The tax aspect is the reason for the attraction to shareholders generally of distributions as capital. The question whether the life tenant or remainderman is entitled (or whether an apportionment must be made) will arise, for example, where the company has taken steps to capitalise profits,[45] or where shareholders are given the right to choose between a cash dividend and an allotment of shares. The problem is that the rules derive from company law concepts of capital and income, which are different from the trust law classification.[46] The modern context in which the question arises is the company demerger, where a company in effect splits into two, and shares in the new company are given to shareholders in the original company. The demerger may be "direct", where the original company allocates to its shareholders the shares in the new company, or "indirect", where the new company allocates its own shares to shareholders of the original company. Whether these shares are to be treated as income or capital is relevant to beneficial entitlement and, as mentioned above, to taxation. When ICI transferred its bioscience business to a new company, Zeneca, and shares in the latter were given to ICI shareholders (the ICI shares being reduced in value by the demerger) in satisfaction of a dividend, it was held in *Sinclair v Lee*[47] that the new shares were capital assets, and hence did not pass under a gift by will of income from the ICI shares. The effect of the reconstruction was that two capital assets replaced one. Investment philosophy had greatly changed since the older cases,[48] and any other result would not reflect reality. *Sinclair* involved an "indirect" demerger. However, shares distributed under a "direct" demerger are treated as income both for the purposes of entitlement and taxation. The Law Commission has proposed reform of the classification of company distributions. While no reform is needed in respect of the classification of other receipts (for example rental income from trust property), it is proposed that cash distributions by companies to trustee shareholders and distributions which the trustees could have taken in cash should be classified as income, and all other company distributions should be classified as

---

[44] *Re Bates* [1928] Ch. 682; *Re Doughty* [1947] Ch. 263; *Re Sechiari* [1950] 1 All E.R. 417; *Howell v Trippier (Inspector of Taxes)* [2004] W.T.L.R. 839; *Pierce v Wood* [2010] W.T.L.R. 253 (scrip dividend shares were income).

[45] *Bouch v Sproule* (1887) 12 App.Cas. 385.

[46] Law Com. No.315 (2009), *Capital and Income in Trusts: Classification and Apportionment*, para.2.36.

[47] [1993] Ch. 497. See D. Hayton, *Modern International Developments in Trust Law*, pp.288–291; P. Duffield (1995) 9 T.L.I. 55.

[48] Such as *Hill v Permanent Trustee Co of NSW* [1930] A.C. 720.

capital. This classification would be subject to a narrow power of adjustment by the trustees.[49]

2. Duty to Provide Accounts and Information

A. Accounts

19–018   **i. Extent of Duty.** A trustee must keep accounts and be constantly ready to produce them for the beneficiaries.[50] It seems that a beneficiary is entitled only to see and inspect the accounts; if he wants a copy himself, he must pay for it; but it is common practice to provide a copy for each of the beneficiaries.[51] An income beneficiary is entitled to full accounts, but a remainderman is entitled only to such information as relates to capital transactions. A member of a class of discretionary beneficiaries is entitled to accounts,[52] but a person who is merely a potential object of a discretionary trust has no such right, at any rate where there is a large number of possible beneficiaries.[53]

19–019   **ii. Audit.** Apart from the case of pension trusts and charitable trusts,[54] it is neither necessary nor, except in large and complicated trusts or where trouble with a beneficiary is foreseen, usual to have trust accounts audited. However, trustees may, in their absolute discretion, have the trust accounts examined and audited by an independent accountant, and may pay the costs out of income or capital. Audit should not be effected more than once in every three years, except in special cases.[55]

　　Any trustee or beneficiary may apply for the accounts of any trust to be investigated and audited by such solicitor or public accountant as may be agreed upon, or in default of agreement by the Public Trustee or by some person appointed by him.[56] The costs are usually

---

[49] Law Com. No.315 (2009), paras 5.53–5.66.

[50] *Pearse v Green* (1819) 1 Jac. & W. 135, per Plumer M.R. at 140.

[51] *Ottley v Gilby* (1845) 8 Beav. 602; *Kemp v Burn* (1863) 4 Giff. 348.

[52] *Chaine-Nickson v Bank of Ireland* [1976] I.R. 393; *Re Murphy's Settlements* [1999] 1 W.L.R. 282.

[53] *Hartigan Nominees Pty Ltd v Rydge* (1992) 29 N.S.W.L.R. 405. It has been held in the Cayman Islands that the right to see accounts is not absolute: *Lemos v Coutts & Co* [1992–93] Cayman I. L.R. 400 at 518–519.

[54] Pensions Act 1995 s.41 and regulations thereunder; above, para.16–014; Charities Act 2011 ss.144–161; above, para.15–089.

[55] TA 1925 s.22(4). For the audit by the court of the accounts of a judicial trustee, see Administration of Justice Act 1982 s.57; Judicial Trustee Rules 1983 (SI 1983/370). By r.2 there is to be no automatic audit by the court of the accounts of a "corporate trustee," meaning the Official Solicitor, Public Trustee or a corporation appointed by the court to be a trustee, or which is entitled to be a custodian trustee by the Public Trustee Act 1906 s.4(3).

[56] Public Trustee Act 1906 s.13. The Law Reform Committee recommended the repeal of s.13, which is very rarely used and is ineffective because there are no powers to enforce the findings of the Public Trustee. (23rd report, 1982, Cmnd. 8733, para.4.48).

borne by the trust, but the Public Trustee may order that the appellant or the trustees must pay them or share them.[57]

B. Information. Trust Documents

The beneficiaries are entitled to be informed about matters currently affecting the trust.[58] Beneficiaries of pension trusts have a statutory right to information.[59] A large trust will keep many documents, such as the minutes of trustees' meetings. Documents connected with the trust are trust documents, and prima facie the property of the beneficiaries, and as such open to their inspection.[60]   **19–020**

We saw, however, in Ch.17, that trustees are not bound to give reasons for the exercise of their discretions. The policy of that principle has already been discussed.[61] In the present context, the problem is to reconcile that principle with the principle that beneficiaries are entitled to see the trust documents. If reasons for the exercise of discretionary powers are recorded in documents relating to the trust, are the beneficiaries entitled to see the documents?

In *Re Londonderry's Settlement*,[62] the donees of a power under a discretionary trust decided to distribute the capital. One member of the discretionary class was dissatisfied with the sum which they intended to give her. She asked for copies of the minutes of trustees' meetings, documents prepared for the meetings, and correspondence between various interested persons. The trustees were willing only to show her documents giving the intended distributions and the annual trust accounts. They declined, in the general interest of the family, to disclose further documents, and brought a summons to determine the nature and extent of their duties in relation to disclosures.

The Court of Appeal found great difficulty in defining in general terms what were the "trust documents" which a beneficiary prima

---

[57] See *Re Oddy* [1911] 1 Ch. 532.

[58] But this does not go so far as to put the trustees "under any duty to proffer information to their beneficiary, or to see that he has proper advice merely because they are trustees for him and know that he is entering into a transaction with his beneficial interest with some person or body connected in some way with the trustees, such as a company in which the trustees own some shares beneficially.": *Tito v Waddell (No.2)* [1977] Ch. 106 at 243, per Megarry V.C.; questioned by F. Crane (1977) 41 Conv.(N.S.) 438.

[59] Pensions Act 1995 s.41 and regulations thereunder; above, para.16–024.

[60] *O'Rourke v Darbishire* [1920] A.C. 581 at 619, 626.

[61] Above, paras 17–042, 17–043.

[62] [1965] Ch. 918; REM (1965) 81 L.Q.R. 192. See further D. Hayton in A. Oakley (ed.), *Trends in Contemporary Trust Law*, 2 at 49; D. Hayton, *Modern International Developments in Trust Law*, 1999, pp.13–16, 325–327.

facie had a right to see. Salmon L.J. said that the category of trust documents could not be defined. They have however:

" . . . [T]hese characteristics in common: (1) they are documents in the possession of the trustees as trustees; (2) they contain information about the trust, which the beneficiaries are entitled to know; (3) the beneficiaries have a proprietary interest[63] in the documents and, accordingly, are entitled to see them. If any parts of a document contain information which the beneficiaries are not entitled to know, I doubt whether such parts can be truly said to be integral parts of a trust document."[64]

19–021   Applying this reasoning, it was held in *Hartigan Nominees Pty Ltd v Rydge*[65] that the beneficiaries were not entitled to see the settlor's confidential memorandum of wishes, a document of no legal force setting out how he wished the trustees to exercise their discretions. This was recently the issue in *Breakspear v Ackland*,[66] where the previous authorities (including those in the Commonwealth and Channel Isles) and academic commentaries were fully analysed. Briggs J. applied the *Londonderry*[67] principle and held that a beneficiary was not normally entitled to disclosure of a letter of wishes of the settlor of a family discretionary trust (leaving for another occasion the question whether the same applied to employee, pension and other commercial trusts). However, the trustees may disclose such a letter if they consider this to be in the interests of the sound administration of the trust, and their discretion to do so should not be fettered by the settlor.

Another question is whether a potential beneficiary of a discretionary trust has any right to information, at any rate if one of a large number of such persons. This was doubted in *Hartigan*.[68] The question of a discretionary beneficiary's right to information arose again in *Re Murphy's Settlements*,[69] where a member of a class of beneficiaries of a discretionary trust sought to compel the settlor to disclose the names and addresses of the trustees. It was held that the court could make such an order, as a discretionary beneficiary was entitled to enquire as to the nature and value of the trust property, its income

---

[63] The right to information does not, however, depend on the beneficiary having a proprietary right, as explained below.

[64] [1965] Ch. 918 at 938.

[65] (1992) 29 N.S.W.L.R. 405; J. Lehane [1994] 3 J.Int.P. 60. The court may order the disclosure of a letter of wishes if there is good reason in a particular case; *Re Rabaiotti Settlements* (2001) 31 Fam. Law 808 (Royal Court of Jersey); *Breakspear v Ackland*, below, fn.66.

[66] [2009] Ch. 32; D. Fox (2008) 67 C.L.J. 252; G. Griffiths [2008] Conv. 322; T. Tey (2008) 22 T.L.I. 126.

[67] Above, para.19–020.

[68] Above, fn.65.

[69] [1999] 1 W.L.R. 282; C. Mitchell (1999) 115 L.Q.R. 206.

and how the fund had been invested and distributed. The court would be unlikely, however, to exercise its discretion in favour of a "remote" potential beneficiary, as it would be undesirable for the trustees to be "badgered" with claims by numerous beneficiaries for information.

The matter has now been clarified by the Privy Council in *Schmidt v Rosewood Trust Ltd*,[70] where the question was whether (i) an unnamed discretionary beneficiary and (ii) the object of a power of appointment could require disclosure of trust documents. Lord Walker noted that trusts had changed radically, and it was often the case (for tax avoidance reasons) that the beneficiaries and their interests or expectations were not clearly identified.[71] It was fundamental to the law of trusts that the court had jurisdiction to supervise and intervene in the administration of trusts, including discretionary trusts. The right to disclosure was an aspect of this inherent supervisory jurisdiction and did not depend on entitlement to a fixed and transmissible beneficial interest. A proprietary right was not necessary nor, in some cases, would it be sufficient. A discretionary beneficiary or an object of a mere power of appointment might be entitled, although the nature of their protection would depend on the court's discretion. The court might need to make a judgment in three areas: (a) whether a discretionary beneficiary or a beneficiary with a remote or wholly defeasible interest should be granted any relief; (b) what classes of documents should be disclosed, either totally or partially; and (c) what safeguards should be imposed to limit the use to be made of them. Where issues of confidentiality arose, the court might have to balance the competing interests of the beneficiaries, the trustees and third parties. The case was remitted to the lower court to decide whether disclosure should be ordered.

Subject to the above, a trustee's duty is not merely one of answering questions; but also to provide beneficiaries with information concerning their interests under the trust; or, in the case of a child beneficiary, to inform him of his entitlement on coming of age.[72] There is, however, no duty to search out possible objects of a discretionary trust and inform them of their position.[73] Executors are under no positive duty, as a will is a public document.[74]

---

[70] [2003] 2 A.C. 709 (Isle of Man); J. Davies (2004) 120 L.Q.R. 1. The case does not deal with the position of objects of a personal (non-fiduciary) power. See also *Foreman v Kingstone* [2004] 1 N.Z.L.R. 841; G. Griffiths [2005] Conv. 93; *Charman v Charman* [2006] 2 F.L.R. 422 (disclosure of assets of Bermuda trust in connection with divorce proceedings).

[71] Indeed they were often barely perceptible behind "a web of camouflage" ([2003] 2 A.C. 709, at 724).

[72] *Hawkesley v May* [1956] 1 Q.B. 304; including, it seems, his rights under the rule in *Saunders v Vautier* (1841) Cr. & Ph. 240; below, para.22–001; A. Samuels (1970) 34 Conv.(N.S.) 29.

[73] *Hartigan Nominees Pty Ltd v Rydge* (1992) 29 N.S.W.L.R. 405.

[74] *Re Lewis* [1904] 2 Ch. 656; *Re Mackay* [1906] 1 Ch. 25; *Cancer Research Campaign v Ernest Brown & Co (A Firm)* [1997] S.T.C. 1425 (resulting in loss of opportunity to vary estate for inheritance tax purposes within statutory time limit).

CHAPTER 20

POWERS OF TRUSTEES

Trustees may exercise such powers as are given to them by the trust instrument or by statute. A power, as has been seen,[1] is to be distinguished from a duty, in that its exercise is not compulsory. In

20–001

---

[1] Above, para.2–021.

the absence of bad faith, the court will not interfere with the exercise of discretions. At most, the holder of a fiduciary power is under a duty to consider its exercise.[2]

Originally, it was necessary to spell out a trustee's powers in detail in the trust instrument. The Trustee Act 1925 (as amended) provided the basic powers needed by trustees. They may unless otherwise stated be excluded or amended as desired.[3] The 1925 Act became outdated in many respects, in particular with regard to delegation, insurance, remuneration, investment and the power to employ nominees and custodians. The powers were substantially modernised by the Trustee Act 2000, as will be explained in the relevant sections of this chapter. The Act came into force on February 1, 2001. No doubt practitioners will continue to insert detailed provisions into the trust instrument. It should be added that many modern trust instruments give the trustees a power to amend the trust.[4]

1. TRUSTEES OF LAND

20–002   Section 6(1) of the Trusts of Land and Appointment of Trustees Act 1996 provides that:

> "For the purpose of exercising their functions as trustees, the trustees of land have in relation to the land subject to the trust all the powers of an absolute owner."

Where the trust includes land and personalty, these powers are thus confined to the land. The width of the statutory powers is reduced by an important proviso: the powers conferred by s.6 "shall not be exercised in contravention of, or of any order made in pursuance of, any other enactment or any rule of law or equity."[5] The trustees, in exercising their powers under s.6, must also have regard to the rights of the beneficiaries,[6] and they have a general duty to consult adult beneficiaries with an interest in possession.[7] Thus trustees of land remain subject to the general duties imposed by equity on trustees and to restrictions on the statutory powers of trustees contained in

---

[2] As to whether trustees can fetter their powers by deciding in advance how to exercise them, see H. Arthur (1993) 7 T.L.I. 69.

[3] TA 1925 s.69(2).

[4] See *Society of Lloyd's v Robinson* [1999] 1 W.L.R. 756; below, para.22–002.

[5] s.6(6). See also s.6(7).

[6] s.6(5). A purchaser of unregistered land is not concerned to see that this duty has been complied with; s.16(1). For registered land, see LRA 2002 s.26; G. Ferris and G. Battersby (2003) 119 L.Q.R. 94 and [2009] Conv. 39; S. Pascoe [2005] Conv. 140.

[7] s.11(1). This duty may be excluded by the settlor.

other legislation or in other sections of the 1996 Act.[8] They are also subject to the statutory duty of care under s.1 of the Trustee Act 2000.[9]

Section 6 applies whether the trust of land is express, implied, resulting or constructive, and whether arising before or after the commencement of the 1996 Act; trusts for sale and bare trusts are also included.[10] In the case of an expressly created trust of land, however, s.6 may be excluded by the settlor or the powers made exercisable subject to consent.[11]

In addition to the general powers described above, the 1996 Act confers certain specific powers on trustees of land. Under the general law, beneficiaries who are of full age and capacity and together absolutely entitled may call for a transfer of the trust property.[12] In the case of land, s.6(2) gives the trustees power to convey to such beneficiaries provided each is absolutely entitled,[13] even though they have not required the trustees to do so. If the beneficiaries do not co-operate, the court may order them to do whatever is necessary to secure that the land vests in them.

Where beneficiaries of full age are absolutely entitled as tenants in common, the trustees may partition the land or any part of it, obtaining the consent of each beneficiary and providing (by mortgage or otherwise) for the payment of any equality money.[14] This power may be excluded or made subject to other consents in an expressly created trust of land.[15] The delegation powers of trustees of land are dealt with later in this chapter.

2. Power of Sale[16]

A. Land

Land is held either by an owner absolutely entitled or under a trust   **20–003**
of land or, in the case of a settlement created before the commencement of the Trusts of Land and Appointment of Trustees Act 1996,

---

[8] See s.6(8). If a conveyance of unregistered land by the trustees (other than charity trustees) contravenes s.6(6) or (8), it is not invalid if the purchaser had no actual notice of the contravention; s.16(2). For registered land, see LRA 2002 s.26, above.

[9] s.6(9), introduced by TA 2000.

[10] s.1. The Act came into force on January 1, 1997. For the application of the Act to personal representatives; see s.18.

[11] s.8. The settlor of a charitable trust may not exclude s.6. See G. Watt [1997] Conv. 263, discussing whether the power of sale may be excluded.

[12] *Saunders v Vautier* (1841) Cr. & Ph. 240; below, para.22–001.

[13] i.e. they are equitable co-owners. That their interests together add up to the whole does not otherwise suffice.

[14] Trusts of Land and Appointment of Trustees Act 1996 s.7. A purchaser of unregistered land is not concerned to see that the beneficiaries have consented; s.16(1). For registered land, see LRA 2002 s.26.

[15] Trusts of Land and Appointment of Trustees Act 1996 s.8.

[16] See generally R. Mitchell [1999] Conv. 84.

under a strict settlement. In the latter case the tenant for life has the legal estate and a power of sale.[17] In the case of a trust of land, the legal estate is vested in the trustees, and they have a power of sale.[18] Where an express trust for sale is created, the trustees have power to postpone the sale indefinitely in the exercise of their discretion, despite any provision to the contrary in the trust instrument.[19] The receipt of at least two trustees or of a trust corporation is required for all capital money arising under a trust of land or strict settlement,[20] and the same rule applies to the overreaching of the beneficial interests.[21]

B. Chattels

20–004   Where chattels or other personalty are held upon trust for sale, the position is the same as with land except that the receipt of a sole trustee is sufficient discharge to a purchaser.[22] The trust for sale may arise expressly or be implied, as we have seen, under the rule in *Howe v Earl of Dartmouth*.[23] Personal representatives have power to sell chattels (and other property) on intestacy.[24]

C. Other Property

20–005   In the case of many other forms of property, a power of sale, if not given expressly, will usually be implied. Unauthorised investments, investments which the trustees think are not suitable for the trust, and trust property which is not in a state of investment at all, should be sold and invested in accordance with the express terms of the relevant investment power, or with the provisions of the Trustee Act 2000.[25]

Whenever trustees are authorised to pay or apply capital money for any purpose or in any manner, they have power to raise such money by sale, mortgage, etc. of the trust property then in possession.[26] But this does not authorise trustees to raise money by charging existing investments in order to purchase others.[27]

---

[17] SLA 1925 s.38(1).
[18] Trusts of Land and Appointment of Trustees Act 1996 s.6(1); above. This includes bare trusts; s.1(2). See G Watt [1997] Conv. 263, as to whether the power of sale may be excluded. Personal representatives on intestacy have a power to sell land; AEA 1925 s.33, as amended by the 1996 Act.
[19] Trusts of Land and Appointment of Trustees Act 1996 s.4.
[20] TA 1925 s.14; LPA 1925 s.27(2); SLA 1925 s.94(1).
[21] LPA 1925 s.2.
[22] TA 1925 s.14; below, para.20–007.
[23] (1802) 7 Ves.Jr. 137; above, para.19–002.
[24] AEA 1925 s.33, as amended by Trusts of Land and Appointment of Trustees Act 1996 Sch.2.
[25] Above, paras 18–014–18–018.
[26] TA 1925 s.16(1).
[27] *Re Suenson-Taylor* [1974] 1 W.L.R. 1280 (land).

D. Sales by Trustees

The detailed provisions relating to sales by trustees are contained **20–006**
in the Trustee Act 1925 s.12.[28] Trustees may sell all or any part of
the property, by public auction or by private contract, subject to any
such conditions respecting title or other matter as the trustee
thinks fit.

As we have seen, trustees are under an overriding duty to obtain
the best price for the beneficiaries.[29] If they fail to do so, the beneficiaries may seek an injunction restraining the sale.[30] But if the sale
has taken place, it may not be impeached by a beneficiary on the
ground that any of the conditions of the sale were unduly depreciatory, unless it also appears that the consideration for the sale was
thereby rendered inadequate.[31] A purchaser will not be affected
unless he was acting in collusion with the trustees.[32]

3. POWER TO GIVE RECEIPTS: SECTION 14

By the Trustee Act 1925 s.14, the written receipt by a trustee for **20–007**
money, securities, investments, etc. is a sufficient discharge to the
person paying, and effectually exonerates him from being answer-
able for any loss or misapplication of the money. The section applies
notwithstanding anything to the contrary in the trust instrument,[33]
and applies to sole trustees, except in the case of proceeds of sale or
other capital money arising under a trust of land or under the Settled
Land Act where, unless the trustee is a trust corporation, the receipt
of at least two trustees is necessary.[34] Where there is more than one
trustee, all must sign, in accordance with the rule that they must act
together.[35]

4. POWER TO INSURE: SECTION 19

A. Insurance

At common law trustees have a power to insure the trust property, **20–008**
and possibly a duty to do so (of uncertain scope) in accordance with

---

[28] As amended by Trusts of Land and Appointment of Trustees Act 1996 Sch.3.

[29] *Buttle v Saunders* [1950] 2 All E.R. 193; above, para.18–002. See also *Sergeant v National Westminster Bank* (1991) 61 P. & C.R. 518. As to whether trustees can sell at a valuation to be determined by a third party, see G. Lightman [1985] Conv. 44.

[30] *Wheelwright v Walker* (1883) 23 Ch.D. 752.

[31] TA 1925 s.13(1); *Dance v Goldingham* (1873) L.R. 8 Ch.App. 902. The trustee may, of course, be liable.

[32] TA 1925 s.13(2).

[33] TA 1925 s.14(3).

[34] TA 1925 s.14(2) as amended by Trusts of Land and Appointment of Trustees Act 1996 Sch.3.

[35] Above, para.17–007; charitable and pension trustees may act by a majority.

their general duty of acting in the best interests of the trust.[36] As a general rule, however, they are not liable if the property is destroyed; and if the trustees differ on the question whether the property should be insured, it seems that nothing can be done to compel them.[37]

Section 19 of the Trustee Act 1925 provided a power to insure, but it was limited and unsatisfactory. A new s.19 was substituted by the Trustee Act 2000.[38] This provides that a trustee may insure any trust property against risks of loss or damage due to any event and pay the premiums out of income or capital. In the case of property held on a bare trust (i.e. where the beneficiary is of full age and capacity and absolutely entitled or, where there is more than one beneficiary, each of them is of full age and capacity and they are together absolutely entitled), the power is subject to their directions.[39] The statutory duty of care[40] applies to the exercise of the power to insure, whether under s.19 or under an express power.[41]

The policy moneys must be treated as capital and applied in accordance with the terms of the trust.[42]

B. Reinstatement

20–009   Trustees may apply the policy money relating to land or other property in reinstatement, subject to the consent of any person whose consent is required by the trust instrument,[43] and without prejudice to the statutory or other right of any person to require the money to be spent in reinstatement.[44] Persons interested under the trust can, therefore, insist on having the premises rebuilt if they wish; or, if they do not wish it, can prevent the trustees from using the money for that purpose, but in any case the money is capital money.

5. Power to Compound Liabilities: Section 15

20–010   Trustees are given a wide discretion in settling claims which may be made by third persons against the trust estate,[45] or by the trust estate

---

[36] Law Com No.260 (1999), *Trustees' Powers and Duties*, paras 6.7–6.8.
[37] *Re McEacharn* (1911) 103 L.T. 900.
[38] s.34. The substituted provision applies to trusts whenever created.
[39] TA 1925 s.19(2), (3).
[40] TA 2000 s.1; above, Ch.17.
[41] TA 2000 Sch.1, para.5.
[42] TA 1925 s.20.
[43] TA 1925 s.20(4).
[44] TA 1925 s.20(5).
[45] The section confers no power to make reasonable provision for satisfying contingent claims. See *Re Yorke (Deceased)* [1997] 4 All E.R. 907.

against third persons. Adult beneficiaries who are under no disability may, of course, make any arrangement that they wish among themselves. Until the Variation of Trusts Act 1958[46] was passed, the court had no general power to approve adjustments in the beneficial interests. But the dividing line is difficult to draw. The Court has inherent power to compromise a genuine dispute between beneficiaries[47] and s.15 has been held to authorise the settlement of a dispute with a person claiming to be a beneficiary,[48] and also litigation between the trustees and beneficiaries on the question whether certain property was subject to the trust or not.[49] It was no objection to the jurisdiction under s.15 that the proposed compromise involved an adjustment of interests among the beneficiaries.[50]

Personal representatives and trustees may accept compositions for debts; allow time for payment of debts; compromise, abandon, submit to arbitration or otherwise settle any claim; and may enter into such agreements and execute such instruments as may be necessary for the efficient performance of these duties.[51] A wide power of this nature is of great practical importance in enabling the trustee to make a reasonable compromise instead of being obliged to litigate in respect of every possible claim, or risk liability for breach of trust if he fails to do so.[52] Trustees are not liable for loss caused by any act done by them in the exercise of the powers conferred by this section as long as they have discharged the statutory duty of care under the Trustee Act 2000,[53] and they have reached their decision by exercising their discretion and not by failing to consider the matter.[54] They may apply to the court to sanction a compromise. The court must consider what is the best from the point of view of everybody concerned, paying especial attention to the interests of child beneficiaries.[55]

6. Power in Regard to Reversionary Interests: Section 22[56]

Where part of the trust property consists of choses in action or reversionary interests the trustees may, on such interests falling into possession, "agree or ascertain the amount or value thereof in such **20–011**

---

[46] Below, Ch.22.
[47] *Re Barbour's Settlement* [1974] 1 W.L.R. 1198; *Re Downshire SE* [1953] Ch. 218.
[48] *Eaton v Buchanan* [1911] A.C. 253; cf. *Abdallah v Rickards* (1888) 4 T.L.R. 622.
[49] *Re Earl of Strafford* [1980] Ch. 28.
[50] [1980] Ch. 28.
[51] See *Re Shenton* [1935] Ch. 651.
[52] *Re Brogden* [1948] Ch. 206; above, para.18–003. *Bradstock Group Pension Scheme Trustees Ltd v Bradstock Group Plc* [2002] I.C.R. 1427.
[53] s.15(1), as amended by TA 2000. For the duty of care, see Ch.17.
[54] *Re Greenwood* (1911) 105 L.T. 509.
[55] *Re Ezekiel's ST* [1942] Ch. 230; *Re Earl of Strafford* (above, fn.49).
[56] As amended by TA 2000.

manner as they think fit," without being responsible for any loss, if they have discharged the statutory duty of care under the Trustee Act 2000. But nothing in the section is to be construed as relieving trustees from the duty of getting in such interests as soon as possible after their falling into possession, for this is one of their primary duties.[57]

7. POWER TO DELEGATE

A. The Early Rule in Equity

20–012   The basic rule is that a person entrusted with a fiduciary duty does not fulfil it if he delegates it to someone else; he remains liable for the other person's default.[58] But this rule was never inflexible, even in the times when the most rigorous views were being taken of the standard of conduct required from a trustee. Indeed, there are certain things which a business person would always delegate to a skilled agent. Thus, the employment of solicitors for legal, and brokers and bankers for financial, business was sanctioned by the ordinary business practice. This was recognised as early as 1754, by Lord Hardwicke in *Ex p. Belchier*,[59] and the trend of judicial decision, fortified by occasional statutory provisions, grew more and more tolerant of delegation in cases of commercial necessity. Following the two famous decisions of the House of Lords in *Speight v Gaunt*[60] and *Learoyd v Whiteley*,[61] it could be said that delegation was permissible if the trustees could show that it was reasonably necessary in the circumstances or was in accordance with ordinary business practice. The trustees had to exercise proper care in the selection of the agent, employ him in his proper field,[62] and exercise general supervision.[63] Trustees who delegated without authority remained vicariously liable for any resulting loss.[64] They were not vicariously liable for the acts of authorised agents, but incurred personal liability for failing to act prudently in matters of supervision and so forth. A trustee's discretions could not, however, be delegated.[65] Further, exemption clauses expressly limiting his liability to cases of "wilful default" did not relieve him from the responsibility of acting as a prudent

---

[57] See above, para.18–001.
[58] *Turner v Corney* (1841) 5 Beav. 515 at 517, per Lord Langdale.
[59] (1754) Amb. 218.
[60] (1884) 9 App.Cas. 1.
[61] (1887) 12 App.Cas. 727.
[62] *Fry v Tapson* (1884) 28 Ch.D. 268.
[63] *Rowland v Witherden* (1851) 3 Mac. & G. 568.
[64] *Clough v Bond* (1838) 3 My. & Cr. 490 at 496–497; *Speight v Gaunt*, above, fn.60; *Target Holdings Ltd v Redferns (A Firm)* [1996] 1 A.C. 421 at 434.
[65] *Speight v Gaunt*, above, fn.60; below, para.20–019.

man of business.[66] Nor did the statutes of 1859 and 1893, the predecessors of the Trustee Act 1925 s.30(1) (now repealed), which restricted the liability of trustees to cases of wilful default, do more
than change the onus of proof; these statutes placed the onus on:

"[T]hose who seek to charge an executor or trustee with a loss
arising from the default of an agent, when the propriety of employing the agent has been established."[67]

The kind of delegation referred to above is sometimes termed
"collective delegation", meaning that all the trustees acting together
appoint an agent to carry out some function. This may be contrasted
with "individual delegation", where one trustee delegates all his
functions to another person, which may be done by power of attorney.[68]

B. Trustee Act 1925

Under the Trustee Act 1925 trustees were no longer required to **20–013**
show a need to delegate. Delegation as such was accepted as a
normal method of performing the duties incidental to trusteeship;
but the overall duties of trusteeship remained of course in the trustees. Section 23(1) of the 1925 Act provided that a trustee could
delegate acts (of an administrative nature) to agents, and that he
would not be responsible for the default of the agent "if employed in
good faith". Section 30(1) provided that a trustee was responsible
for his own acts and defaults but not for those of any co-trustee or
agent, nor for any other loss unless occasioned by "his own wilful
default". The proper interpretation of, and the relationship between,
these provisions remained a matter of doubt until their repeal by the
Trustee Act 2000. In *Re Vickery*[69] an executor employed a solicitor
to wind up the estate. He was unaware that the solicitor had twice
been suspended from practice. Eventually the solicitor absconded
with money belonging to the estate. Maugham J. considered that
s.23(1) had not removed the need to exercise care in the selection of
the agent. There was no suggestion that the executor had not done
so. He was not liable, because he was not guilty of "wilful default"
within s.30(1), which meant intentional or reckless breach of duty.
This interpretation was inconsistent with the settled construction of

---

[66] *Re Chapman* [1896] 2 Ch. 763; *Re Brier* (1884) 26 Ch.D. 238; cf. *Armitage v Nurse*
[1998] Ch. 241 at 252; below. Exemption clauses are discussed at para.17–005, above.
[67] per Lord Selborne in *Re Brier*, above, fn.66, at 243; *Re Chapman*, above, fn.66,
at 776.
[68] Below, para.20–019.
[69] [1931] 1 Ch. 572.

the expression in trustee exemption clauses, where it included imprudence.[70] Maugham J.'s interpretation of s.30(1) was long criticised, although Millett L.J. in *Armitage v Nurse*[71] rejected the criticisms. It was confirmed, however, in *Re Lucking's Will Trusts*[72] that the 1925 Act had not removed the duty to supervise the agent adequately. In that case the trustee was liable for a loss of £16,000 caused by his signing blank cheques in favour of the agent, an old and trusted friend, and failing to supervise his drawings on the funds after the time at which there was reason to suspect his honesty.

It was mentioned above that s.23(1) permitted the delegation of administrative acts. It did not permit the delegation of the exercise of discretions. That may be done by power of attorney under s.25 of the Trustee Act 1925,[73] but the trustee remains liable for the defaults of the attorney. The Law Commission concluded that:

"Far from promoting the more conscientious discharge of the obligations of trusteeship, the prohibition on the delegation of fiduciary discretions may force trustees to commit breaches of trust in order to achieve the most effective administration of the trust".[74]

A major purpose of the Trustee Act 2000 was to reform trustees' powers of delegation. First, it repealed the problematic ss.23 and 30 of the Act of 1925 and provided in their place a clearer framework for delegation. Secondly, it extended the circumstances in which discretionary functions may be delegated. This is particularly important in the context of investment, but is not confined to that. We will now consider the delegation provisions of the Trustee Act 2000. Other statutory provisions permitting the delegation of discretions are dealt with separately below.[75]

C. Trustee Act 2000

20–014   The wide powers of delegation introduced by the Act apply to trusts whenever created, but are subject to any restrictions or exclusions in the trust instrument or other legislation.[76] The powers apply to pension trusts, save that the trustees may not delegate investment functions nor appoint nominees and custodians under the new Act,

---

[70] Above, para.17–005.
[71] [1998] Ch. 241 at 252. See also *Woodland-Ferrari v UCL Group Retirement Benefits Scheme* [2003] Ch. 115.
[72] [1968] 1 W.L.R. 866.
[73] Below, para.20–019.
[74] Law Com. No.260 (1999), *Trustees' Powers and Duties*, para.4.6.
[75] Below, Sections D, E.
[76] TA 2000 ss.26, 27. For transitional provisions, see Sch.3.

as these matters should be dealt with under the pensions legislation.[77] The scope and effect of the power to delegate will now be considered.

i. General Power to Delegate. The approach taken in the Act of   **20–015**
2000 is that trustees may delegate any or all of their "delegable functions". Section 11 does not (save in the case of charitable trusts) provide a list of such functions, but instead lists those which may *not* be delegated. The delegable functions are those *other than*:

(a) any function relating to whether or in what way any assets of the trust should be distributed;

(b) any power to decide whether any fees or other payment due to be made out of the trust funds should be made out of income or capital;

(c) any power to appoint a person to be a trustee of the trust; or

(d) any power conferred by any other enactment or the trust instrument which permits the trustees to delegate any of their functions or to appoint a person to act as nominee or custodian.

Thus the trustees cannot delegate their power of selection amongst the beneficiaries of a discretionary trust. They may, however, delegate investment decision-making, and thereby obtain the benefit of the skilled professional service of an investment manager authorised under the financial services legislation. The detailed provisions of the Act in relation to the delegation of investment and other asset management functions were considered in Ch.18.[78] The new powers are additional to a trustee's power of individual delegation by power of attorney.[79] In the case of a charitable trust, s.11 lists the functions which may be delegated. Broadly, these are matters relating to income generation, including investment, but are otherwise administrative acts. These have already been mentioned.[80]

The trustees may delegate to one or more of their number, but not to a beneficiary, even if he is also a trustee.[81] If the same function is delegated to two or more persons, they must act jointly.

If it is reasonably necessary to do so, the trustees may delegate on terms permitting sub-delegation, restricting the liability of the agent, or permitting him to act in circumstances capable of giving rise to a

---

[77] TA 2000 s.36. The delegation provisions do not apply to trustees of unit trusts or those managing a fund under a common investment or common deposit scheme for charities; ss.37, 38.

[78] Above, para.18–018.

[79] Below, Sections D, E.

[80] Above, para.15–092.

[81] TA 2000 s.12.

conflict of interest.[82] It was doubtful under the previous law whether this could be done, thus the reform was needed in order to permit delegation to fund managers on their standard terms of business.

Whether the delegation is under the Act of 2000 or otherwise, the trustees may pay the agent from the trust funds if the terms of his appointment so provide, but the amount must not exceed what is reasonable for the services in question.[83] They may also reimburse him from the trust funds for expenses properly incurred.

Where the trustees have appointed an agent under the Act of 2000 or under the trust instrument or other legislation, they must keep the arrangement under review and must consider whether there is a need to revoke the appointment or to exercise any power they may have to give directions to the agent.[84]

20–016   **ii. Nominees and Custodians.** Prior to the Trustee Act 2000 it was doubtful whether trustees could appoint nominees or custodians in the absence of an express power. This is a convenient practice which reduces delays in completing share transactions. As trust property (such as shares) would be vested in the nominee, the practice appeared contrary to the rule (mentioned below) that trustees must have the trust property under their control.

In order to allow trustees to benefit from modern investment practices, s.16 of the Trustee Act 2000 permits trustees to appoint nominees and vest trust assets in them, while s.17 permits the appointment of a custodian to undertake safe custody of the assets or of any documents or records concerning them. Further details may be found in Ch.18.[85] The provisions already discussed concerning the terms of appointment of agents, remuneration and the duty to keep the arrangement under review apply also to nominees and custodians.

As mentioned above, a trustee may not vest trust assets in a third party unless authorised by the trust instrument or legislation. Thus under the general law investments must be in the joint names of the trustees. If two trustees divide investments or invest separately, and one commits a breach of trust, the other will be equally liable for any loss.[86]

It is convenient also to mention here the related rule that trust capital should be received by all the trustees unless the trust instrument or legislation provides otherwise.[87] However, it has always been possible to delegate the receipt of income to one of several

---

[82] TA 2000 s.14.

[83] TA 2000 ss.14, 32. See also s.29(6) (remuneration of co-trustee appointed as agent).

[84] TA 2000 ss.21, 22. This is subject to any contrary intention in the trust instrument or other legislation.

[85] Above, para.18–018.

[86] *Lewis v Nobbs* (1878) 8 Ch.D. 591.

[87] See *Lee v Sankey* (1873) L.R. 15 Eq. 204; TA 1925 s.14; above, para.20–007.

trustees,[88] although the co-trustees may be liable if they permit the payee to retain the money for longer than necessary.[89] In the case of company shares, the articles provide that trusts shall not be recognised.[90] In the case of joint ownership, the dividend is paid to the first named who can give a valid receipt.[91]

iii. Duty of Care. Prior to the Trustee Act 2000, the standard of conduct applicable to trustees was that expected of a "prudent man of business". However, as a result of the "good faith" terminology of s.23(1) of the Trustee Act 1925, there remained uncertainty as to exactly what standard applied in the context of delegation. The matter has now been put beyond doubt by the application of the statutory duty of care laid down in s.1 of the Trustee Act 2000. This duty applies to a trustee when exercising the power of delegation under the Act of 2000 or under any other power of delegation.[92] He is subject to the duty of care when appointing an agent, nominee or custodian and when carrying out the obligation to keep the arrangement under review. In particular, he must comply with the duty when selecting the person to act, determining the terms on which he is to act, and, where asset management functions are delegated, when preparing the policy statement under s.15 of the Trustee Act 2000.[93] It appears that the duty of care applies to the selection of a person to act under a power of attorney, even though the delegating trustee in any event remains liable for any defaults of the attorney.[94]

iv. Liability of Trustee. We saw that the provisions of the Trustee Act 1925 left room for doubt as to the circumstances in which a trustee would be liable for the defaults of an agent. The uncertainty has been removed by s.23 of the Trustee Act 2000, which provides that a trustee is not liable for any act or default of the agent, nominee or custodian unless he has failed to comply with the duty of care when entering into the arrangement or when keeping it under review. Where the arrangement permitted the agent to appoint a substitute, the trustee is not liable for the acts of the substitute unless he failed to comply with the duty of care when agreeing the term permitting substitution or when reviewing the arrangement. Section 23 applies whether the delegation was in the exercise of the power

20–017

20–018

---

[88] *Townley v Sherborne* (1634) J. Bridg. 35.
[89] *Carruthers v Carruthers* [1896] A.C. 659.
[90] Companies Act 2006 s.126.
[91] Companies (Tables A–F) Regulations 1985 (SI 1985/805), Table A, reg.106. Further regulations have been made under the Companies Act 2006; s.19; Companies (Model Articles) Regulations 2008 (SI 2008/3229).
[92] TA 2000 Sch.1, para.2.
[93] Above, para.18–018.
[94] See Section D, below.

under the Act of 2000 or under an express power or pursuant to other legislation, unless it would be inconsistent with the trust instrument or other legislation. So, for example, s.23 will not apply to the question whether a trustee is liable for the acts of a person to whom he has granted a power of attorney, because s.25(5) of the Trustee Act 1925 provides that the trustee remains liable (irrespective of fault) for the acts and defaults of the donee of the power.

D. Other Statutory Provisions Permitting Delegation of Discretions

20–019   We have seen that trustees cannot as a general rule delegate their discretions, for example the distribution of funds to beneficiaries of a discretionary trust. The delegation of discretions is permitted by Part IV of the Trustee Act 2000, s.25 of the 1925 Act, s.9 of the Trusts of Land and Appointment of Trustees Act 1996, and under s.1 of the Trustee Delegation Act 1999.

Section 25[95] enables a trustee to delegate by deed[96] to any person[97] by power of attorney for 12 months or any shorter specified period "all or any of the trusts, powers and discretions vested in him as trustee either alone or jointly with any other person or persons." Written notice must be given within seven days to each of the other trustees and to each person who has the power to appoint new trustees.[98] It was previously doubted whether a trustee who was not himself entitled to remuneration could pay the delegate out of the trust fund. This has now been alleviated by the provisions of the Trustee Act 2000 enabling professional trustees to charge even though the trust instrument does not so provide.[99] Delegation to a sole trustee is permitted, but this cannot circumvent the rule requiring payment of capital money to at least two trustees.[100] Following the Trustee Delegation Act 1999, a power of attorney under s.25 of the 1925 Act may be an enduring power or a lasting power of attorney under the Mental Capacity Act 2005. These powers survive the incapacity of the trustee.[101]

---

[95] As amended by Trustee Delegation Act 1999 s.5.

[96] In the case of delegation by a single donor, a prescribed form must be used; s.25(5), (6).

[97] Including a trust corporation; subs.(3).

[98] Subs.(4). But failure to give notice does not, in favour of a person dealing with the donee of the power, invalidate any act done by the donee.

[99] TA 2000 s.29.

[100] Trustee Delegation Act 1999 ss.7, 8. Previously delegation to a sole co-trustee was not permitted.

[101] Trustee Delegation Act 1999 s.6, repealing s.2(8) of the Enduring Powers of Attorney Act 1985. The 1985 Act has been repealed and re-enacted by the Mental Capacity Act 2005. For enduring and lasting powers, see section E, below.

These provisions should only be used when such delegation is essential, for the donor of the power of attorney remains liable for the acts and defaults of the donee.[102]

The position relating to trusts of land is now found in s.9 of the Trusts of Land and Appointment of Trustees Act 1996, which permits the trustees to delegate any of their functions as trustees relating to the land, including sale, to any beneficiary (or beneficiaries) of full age and beneficially entitled to an interest in possession.[103] The delegation may be for any period or indefinite,[104] and must be by power of attorney[105] given by all the trustees jointly. It is revocable by any one or more of them, and will also be revoked if another person is appointed trustee.[106] Where a beneficiary ceases to be beneficially entitled, the delegation is revoked so far as it relates to him, but the functions remain exercisable by the remaining beneficiaries in the case of joint delegation.[107]

Beneficiaries to whom functions have been delegated under s.9 are in the same position as the trustees in relation to the exercise of the functions, but are not regarded as trustees for any other purpose. In particular, they cannot sub-delegate or give a valid receipt for capital money.[108] The provisions of the 1996 Act dealing with the trustees' liability for any defaults of the beneficiary to whom they have delegated were changed by the Trustee Act 2000. The duty of care under s.1 of the Act of 2000 applies to trustees of land in entering into an arrangement to delegate their functions under s.9 of the 1996 Act. If the delegation is not irrevocable, they must keep the arrangement under review, including the need to exercise any power they have to revoke the delegation or to give directions to the beneficiary. The trustees are not liable for the acts or defaults of the beneficiary unless they have failed to comply with their duty of care in deciding to delegate or in reviewing the arrangement.[109]

A more general power of delegation applying to trustees of land who are also beneficiaries, in other words co-owners, is provided by s.1 of the Trustee Delegation Act 1999. Such a trustee may delegate all trustee functions, including discretions, relating to the land or to income arising from it or to its proceeds of sale by power of attorney, which may be an enduring power of attorney or a lasting power of attorney under the Mental Capacity Act 2005.[110] Trustees who are

---

[102] TA 1925 s.25(7).

[103] Where the trustees purport to delegate to a person who is not such a beneficiary, third parties dealing with that person in good faith are protected by s.9(2).

[104] s.9(5).

[105] s.9(6) provides that this cannot be an enduring power of attorney or a lasting power of attorney under the Mental Capacity Act 2005; below, para.20–020.

[106] s.9(3). It is not revoked if any grantor ceases to be a trustee.

[107] s.9(4).

[108] s.9(7).

[109] See s.9A of the 1996 Act, inserted by TA 2000 Sch.2.

[110] See section E, below, where the 1999 Act is more fully discussed.

not also beneficiaries do not fall within the scope of this provision. If they wish to delegate their discretions, they must do so under s.25 of the Trustee Act 1925, discussed above.

E. Delegation by Enduring or Lasting Power of Attorney

20–020 We have seen that s.25 of the Trustee Act 1925 permits a trustee to delegate all of his functions by power of attorney for a maximum of 12 months, subject to various procedural requirements.[111] This could be done, for example, if he was going abroad.

Until 1985 there was no possibility of a power of attorney which would continue in force after the donor had become mentally incapable, as such incapacity automatically revoked the power. The Enduring Powers of Attorney Act 1985 introduced a power of attorney which would survive the donor's subsequent incapacity. Unfortunately the 1985 Act inadvertently produced inconsistent but overlapping regimes for delegation by power of attorney by individual trustees under s.3(3) of the 1985 Act and under s.25 of the 1925 Act. Following recommendations of the Law Commission,[112] the problems were resolved by the Trustee Delegation Act 1999.

The Enduring Powers of Attorney Act 1985 was repealed and re-enacted by the Mental Capacity Act 2005.[113] Enduring powers of attorney created before October 1, 2007 remain valid and may be registered at any time, but no new enduring powers of attorney may be created as from October 1, 2007. The Act of 2005 introduced the lasting power of attorney, which may apply to property and financial affairs or to health and welfare matters. A lasting power of attorney which applies to property and financial affairs is similar to an enduring power of attorney. The main distinction is that a lasting power of attorney is not valid unless registered, whereas an enduring power of attorney needs to be registered only upon the onset of the donor's mental incapacity.

The Trustee Delegation Act 1999 draws a distinction between trustees who have a beneficial interest and those who do not. Its broad effect is first, to permit the delegation by power of attorney of all the functions of a trustee who also has a beneficial interest in the property. This is primarily directed to co-owners of land, who are normally both trustees and beneficiaries. Secondly, it ensures that a trustee who has no beneficial interest may only delegate trustee functions by power of attorney subject to the safeguards imposed by s.25 of the Trustee Act 1925. Thirdly, it ensures that the rule requiring capital money to be paid to at least two trustees cannot be circumvented by using a power of attorney.

---

[111] Above, para.20–019.
[112] Law Com. No.222 (1994), *Delegation by Individual Trustees*.
[113] The provisions of the 1985 Act are now found in Sch.4 of the Act of 2005.

In the case of a trustee who has a beneficial interest, s.1 of the 1999 Act permits the delegation by power of attorney of the trustee's powers and duties in relation to land, income from the land or its proceeds of sale. This may take the form of an enduring or lasting power of attorney.[114] The donor (the trustee) is liable for the acts and defaults of the attorney, although not for the act of delegation itself. Section 1 applies only to powers of attorney created after the Act, although, by way of exception, it applies to enduring powers of attorney created before the commencement of the Act at the end of a transitional period during which s.3(3) of the 1985 Act (which subsection was otherwise repealed) could continue to apply to such a power.[115] Thus there was no need for the donor of an enduring power to execute a fresh power after the Act of 1999, which indeed he may have been unable to do by reason of loss of capacity. In favour of a purchaser dealing with the donee of a power of attorney, a signed statement by the donee at the time of the transaction or within the following three months to the effect that the donor trustee had a beneficial interest in the property is conclusive evidence of that fact.[116]

A co-owner may, therefore, delegate his trustee functions by power of attorney without being subject to the restrictions contained in s.25 of the Trustee Act 1925, for example the 12-month time limit. An enduring or lasting power of attorney may be utilised to provide for the onset of mental incapacity. Where, however, one of two co-owners creates the power in favour of the co-trustee, the latter cannot give a good receipt for capital money.[117] In such a case another trustee must be appointed for the purpose,[118] but there is no need for the incapacitated trustee to be discharged.[119] **20–021**

Prior to the 1999 Act it was not possible to delegate by way of enduring power of attorney under s.25 of the Trustee Act 1925.[120] That restriction was removed by s.6 of the 1999 Act in relation to powers created after its commencement. A trustee who has no beneficial interest may now delegate his trustee functions by way of an enduring or lasting power, but this may be done only by complying with s.25 of the 1925 Act, which is subject to more restrictions and

---

[114] Such powers may not be created by trustees of land under s.9(1) of the Trusts of Land and Appointment of Trustees Act 1996; s.9(6), as amended by Sch.6 of the Mental Capacity Act 2005.

[115] Trustee Delegation Act 1999 s.4.

[116] Trustee Delegation Act 1999 s.2.

[117] Trustee Delegation Act 1999 s.7.

[118] Such an appointment may be made by the donee of the power under s.36 of the Trustee Act 1925 (above, para.17–022), as amended by s.8 of the 1999 Act.

[119] LPA 1925 s.22, as amended by s.9 of the 1999 Act and by Sch.6 of the Mental Capacity Act 2005.

[120] Enduring Powers of Attorney Act 1985 s.2(8).

safeguards than a co-owner's power of delegation under s.1 of the 1999 Act. As in the case of delegation by a trustee who is a co-owner, delegation under s.25 to a co-trustee cannot circumvent the rule requiring payment of capital money to at least two trustees.[121]

8. POWERS OF MAINTENANCE AND ADVANCEMENT

20–022 Where any person has a contingent interest in property the question arises as to the use which should be made of the income until the gift vests. Otherwise the income would not be put to any use during the period. The policy is to allow the gift to "carry the intermediate income" unless there are good reasons to the contrary. Generally speaking, all testamentary gifts except contingent pecuniary legacies carry the intermediate income unless it is otherwise disposed of.[122]

One of the most common contingencies is that of attaining the age of 21 or more. It is important to make provision for the use of the income for the maintenance and education of the beneficiary before the interest vests.

A similar question arises in the opposite case of children who have a vested interest in property; for it may then be desirable that they should not be entitled to draw the whole of the income. It is better that they should receive what is reasonably necessary for their maintenance and education, and that the balance should be invested for them. Again, it may be that capital sums may be needed to establish them in a profession or in business or on marriage.

These matters may be expressly provided for in the trust instrument. If not, the court has an inherent power to approve the use of income, or even of capital for the maintenance of children.[123] But the statutory powers of maintenance[124] and advancement[125] about to be discussed are sufficient to meet the needs of most situations, and they can be amended as required to meet the needs of a particular trust. Such powers have commonly been used, not only, or mainly, for their original purposes, but rather for the fiscal advantages which they have been able to offer.[126] The duty of care under s.1 of the Trustee Act 2000 does not apply to these powers.

---

[121] Trustee Delegation Act 1999 ss.7, 8.
[122] Below, para.20–029.
[123] Below, para.20–045.
[124] TA 1925 s.31.
[125] TA 1925 s.32.
[126] *Pilkington v IRC* [1964] A.C. 612. See J. Brown (1994) 8 T.L.I. 49.

A. Maintenance. Trustee Act 1925 Section 31

i. Subsection (1).

"Where any property is held by trustees in trust for any person **20–023** for any interest whatsoever, whether vested or contingent, then, subject to any prior interests or charges affecting that property—

(i) during the infancy of any such person, if his interest so long continues, the trustees may, at their sole discretion, pay to his parent or guardian, if any, or otherwise apply for or towards his maintenance, education, or benefit,[127] the whole or such part, if any, of the income of that property as may, in all the circumstances, be reasonable, whether or not there is—

    (a) any other fund applicable to the same purpose; or
    (b) any person bound by law to provide for his maintenance or education[128]; and

(ii) if such person attaining the age of [18][129] years has not a vested interest in such income, the trustees shall thenceforth pay the income of that property and of any accretion thereto under subsection (2) of this section to him, until he either attains a vested interest therein or dies, or until failure of his interest: ... "

(a) *Prior Interests.* The power of maintenance can only arise **20–024** where a person is entitled to the income, whether by virtue of a vested interest, or by virtue of a contingent interest which carries the intermediate income.[130] If the income is applicable in favour of a prior interest, no question of its use for maintenance can arise. Similarly, a member of a discretionary class is not entitled to any income and the section does not therefore apply to payments made by the trustees in the exercise of their discretion.[131]

(b) *Child Beneficiary.* The question of application of income for **20–025** the child's maintenance, education or benefit, whether his interest is vested or contingent, is a matter for the trustees' discretion. The decision to apply income for such maintenance must be taken as a

---

[127] See *Re Heyworth's Contingent Reversionary Interest* [1956] Ch. 364; *Pilkington v IRC* above, fn.126; *Re Pauling's ST* [1964] Ch. 303; D. Waters (1959) 23 Conv.(N.S.) 27.
[128] See *Fuller v Evans* [2000] 1 All E.R. 636.
[129] Reduced from 21 by Family Law Reform Act 1969. See *Begg-McBrearty (Inspector of Taxes) v Stilwell* [1996] 1 W.L.R. 951; *Walker v Walker* [2010] W.T.L.R. 1617.
[130] TA 1925 s.31(3); below, paras 20–029–20–032.
[131] *Re Vestey's Settlement* [1951] Ch. 209.

result of a conscious exercise of their discretion, and not automatically.[132] So long as the trustees have regard only to the interests of the children, it is no objection that the exercise of their discretion may incidentally benefit a parent.[133] The trustees should, so far as practicable, arrange for maintenance payments to be shared proportionately among various funds available for the purpose.[134] The payments are usually made to the parent or guardian whose receipt is a sufficient discharge for the trustees.

20–026   (c) *Adult Contingently Entitled.* A beneficiary contingently entitled to the principal becomes entitled under para.(ii) of subs.(1) to the income at majority.[135] His entitlement to the capital must, of course, await the happening of the contingency. The entitlement to income at majority is subject to a contrary intention; and this has been found to exist where there is a direction to accumulate.

> In *Re Turner's Will Trusts*,[136] a testator provided interests in favour of his grandchildren contingently on their attaining the age of 28, and expressly gave the trustees power to apply the income for their maintenance, education and benefit until that time, and instructed the trustees to accumulate the surplus.
> One grandchild, Geoffrey, was 21 when the testator died; and himself died three years later aged 24. No income had been paid to him, and some £3,000 had been accumulated since the testator's death. The question was whether s.31(1) applied. If it did, Geoffrey's estate would have become entitled to the income. The Court of Appeal held that, in spite of the imperative terms of s.31, it gave way to an expression of a contrary intention in accordance with the Trustee Act 1925 s.69(2).

ii. Subsection (2).[137]

20–027   (a) *Surplus Income to be Accumulated for Child Beneficiaries.* Subsection (2) provides that the residue of the income, not applied for maintenance, shall be accumulated by investment until the person contingently entitled reaches majority. Income from such investments becomes available for future maintenance; and the

---

[132] *Wilson v Turner* (1883) 22 Ch.D. 521.

[133] *Fuller v Evans*, above, fn 128.

[134] TA 1925 s.31(1), proviso. The Law Commission has proposed that this requirement should be removed; Law Com. No.331 (2011), *Intestacy and Family Provision Claims on Death*; para.4.95. Minor amendments to the wording of s.31(1) are also proposed.

[135] *Re Jones' WT* [1947] Ch. 48.

[136] [1937] Ch. 15; *Re Ransome* [1957] Ch. 348; J. Riddall [1979] Conv. 243; *Brotherton v IRC* [1978] 1 W.L.R. 610; *IRC v Bernstein* [1961] Ch. 399; *Re McGeorge* [1963] Ch. 544, where the contrary intention was shown by deferring the gift to a daughter until after the death of a widow; *Re Erskine's ST* [1971] 1 W.L.R. 162.

[137] TA 2000 Sch.2, para.25, has made minor amendments.

accumulations themselves may be applied, before the beneficiary reaches majority, as if they were income arising in the then current year.

(b) *Entitlement to Accumulations.* On the majority (or earlier **20–028** marriage) of a child, the question arises whether or not any accumulations should be given to him. As would be expected, he is entitled to the accumulations if he had a vested interest before reaching full age (for he was entitled all along to the income); or if, on attaining his majority, he "becomes entitled to the property from which the income arose in fee simple, absolute or determinable, or absolutely or for an entailed interest." In short, he is entitled to the accumulations on his majority (or earlier marriage) if he is then entitled to the capital.[138]

The question arose in *Re Sharp's Settlement Trusts*[139] whether the provision covered the case where the children of the settlor became entitled, subject to an overriding power of appointment, to the capital on attaining the age of 21. Were they then entitled absolutely? Pennycuick V.C. held that they were not: the fact that their interests could be defeated by the exercise of the power prevented their becoming entitled absolutely. It is anomalous that "a person having a determinable interest in realty should qualify to take accumulations at 21",[140] but "a person having a like interest in personalty should not equally so qualify".[141] "This is just another one of those curious instances where the 1925 legislation just did not go far enough in its expressed intention so far as possible to assimilate the rules relating to realty and personalty."[142] In all other cases, as for example the case of a contingent beneficiary whose interest never vests, or where the beneficiary, although having a vested interest, fails to reach majority, the accumulations are added to capital for all purposes.[143]

The provisions relating to the destination of accumulations in s.31(2) are also subject to a contrary intention in the trust instrument.[144] In *Re Delamere's Settlement Trusts*,[145] the trustees appointed income to beneficiaries "absolutely" in 1971. All the

---

[138] TA 1925 s.31(2)(i). Marriage includes civil partnership.
[139] [1973] Ch. 331; D. Hayton (1972) 36 Conv.(N.S.) 436. See also *Re Delamere's Settlement Trusts*, below, fn.145.
[140] The words "fee simple, absolute or determinable," applying only to realty.
[141] [1973] Ch. 331 at 346.
[142] (1972) 36 Conv.(N.S.) 436 at 438. The accumulations of income were added to the share of each child, subject to the exercise of the power: *Re King* [1928] Ch. 330; *Re Joel's WT* [1967] Ch. 14; below, para.20–034.
[143] TA 1925 s.31(2)(ii). On the distinction between contingent interests and interests subject to defeasance, see *Phipps v Ackers* (1842) 9 Cl. & F. 583; *Brotherton v IRC* [1978] 1 W.L.R. 610.
[144] TA 1925 s.69(2).
[145] [1984] 1 W.L.R. 813; R. Griffith [1985] Conv. 153.

beneficiaries were then children. By 1981, £122,000 had been accumulated. The question arose whether s.31(2) applied, so that the share of any beneficiary dying before majority would devolve with the capital, or whether there was a contrary intention, so that the accumulations were held indefeasibly for the appointees. It was held that the word "absolutely" in the 1971 appointment indicated indefeasibility, thus excluding s.31(2). Clearly the mere fact that the interest is vested is not sufficient to achieve this result.[146]

20–029   **iii. Gifts Carrying Intermediate Income.** Section 31 only applies to contingent interests which carry the intermediate income; that is to say, to gifts which entitle the donee to claim the income earned by, or interest upon, the subject-matter of the gift between the date of the gift and the date of payment. Whether or not a gift should do so is not self-evident, and there are some complex and technical rules which do not provide any conceptual unity. Some rules are based on case law, and some on statute. It is unfortunate that there is not a single comprehensive code.

Vested gifts carry the intermediate income unless a contrary intention appears, as where the income is given to someone other than the donee for a period. A direction to accumulate the surplus income until majority, on the other hand, does not indicate that the gift does not carry the income, but merely that the power of maintenance is excluded.

With contingent gifts, the rules, subject always to an expression of contrary intention, are as follows.[147]

20–030   (a) *Contingent Residuary Bequest.* A contingent bequest of residuary personalty carries all income earned from the testator's death.[148] The undisposed of income "becomes part of the residue".[149] But it seems that, if a residuary bequest of personalty (whether vested or contingent) is postponed "to a future date which must come sooner or later,"[150] the intermediate income is undisposed of and therefore not carried by the gift.[151]

20–031   (b) *Contingent or Future Specific Gifts of Personalty or Realty and Contingent Residuary Devises of Freehold Land.* The Law of Property Act 1925 s.175 provides that a contingent specific bequest of personalty or devise of realty and a contingent residuary devise of

---

[146] See TA 1925 s.31(2)(i)(a).
[147] B. Ker (1953) 17 Conv.(N.S.) 273; PVB (1963) 79 L.Q.R. 184.
[148] *Re Adams* [1893] 1 Ch. 329.
[149] [1893] 1 Ch. 329 at 334.
[150] per Cross J. in *Re McGeorge* [1963] Ch. 544 at 551; such as the death of an annuitant.
[151] *Re Oliver* [1947] 2 All E.R. 161; *Re Gillett's WT* [1950] Ch. 102; *Re Geering* [1964] Ch. 136; *Beard v Shadler* [2011] W.T.L.R. 1147.

freehold land, and a devise of freehold land to trustees on trust for persons whose interests are contingent or executory shall carry the intermediate income. It will be noticed that the section does not affect a residuary gift of a leasehold interest, which ranks as personalty.[152]

(c) *Contingent Pecuniary Legacy.* A contingent pecuniary legacy **20–032** does not carry the intermediate income.[153] To this rule there are three exceptions, in which cases the contingent pecuniary legacy will carry interest, and it will be available for the maintenance of a child.

First: where the legacy was given by the father of the child legatee, or by some person in loco parentis, so long as no other fund is provided for his maintenance,[154] and the contingency is the attainment of majority.[155]

Secondly: where the testator shows an intention to maintain.[156]

Thirdly: where the testator has set aside the legacy as a separate fund for the benefit of the legatee.[157]

Section 31, having laid down that the section applies only to a gift which carries the intermediate income, refers expressly to the first of these exceptions, and provides that the rate of interest shall (if the income available is sufficient, and subject to any rules of court to the contrary) be 5 per cent.[158] Thus, the subsection refers only to the first of the recognised exceptions, and the question arises whether that is an indication that the other two are not intended to apply. The better view is that they are unaffected by subs.(3), and that "the specific mention of the rule in [the first exception] is only for the purpose of establishing a suitable rate of interest".[159] The statute widens the exception by making it applicable in the case of either parent, and not only in the case of a father.

iv. Aggregation of Income of Children with that of their Par- **20–033** **ents.** It has been seen that an accumulation and maintenance settlement[160] giving contingent gifts to children with power to use the income for maintenance, and to accumulate that not so used, could offer tax advantages, both in the context of income tax and of inheritance tax, but that income so accumulated carries the income

---

[152] *Re Woodin* [1895] 2 Ch. 349.
[153] *Re Raine* [1929] 1 Ch. 716; *Re George* (1877) 5 Ch.D. 837.
[154] *Re George* (1877) 5 Ch.D. 837 at 843.
[155] *Re Abrahams* [1911] 1 Ch. 108.
[156] *Re Churchill* [1909] 2 Ch. 431.
[157] *Re Medlock* (1886) 54 L.T. 828.
[158] cf. CPR 1998 Pt 40, PD40A 15 (interest at basic rate payable on funds in court or at such other rate as the court shall direct or the will may specify where legacy ordered to be paid by the court. Basic rate is currently 0.3%).
[159] See (1953) 17 Conv.(N.S.) 273 at 279.
[160] Above, para.9–024.

tax disadvantage of liability to the rate applicable to trusts (currently 50 per cent).[161] This high rate of income tax, coupled with the restrictions imposed by the Finance Act 2006 in relation to inheritance tax, have made these settlements less attractive. Where income is paid to the unmarried child of the settlor, the income is treated as that of his parent.[162] In other cases, the income is treated as part of the child's total income.

20–034   **v. Gifts to Classes.** Where there is a gift to a class contingently on attaining the age of 21, the trustees may treat separately, for these purposes, each person's presumptive share. That is to say, that when one member of the class attains 21 and becomes entitled to his share, the trustees may continue to exercise their powers of maintenance in respect of the other members.[163] Similarly, income may only be used for the maintenance of any member of the class if that income was earned during the lifetime of that member,[164] but if a member of a class dies without obtaining a vested interest, the accumulation of income representing his contingent share is added to the capital under s.31(2)(ii), although this means that future born members will thus benefit from it.[165]

B. Advancement

20–035   **i. The Meaning of Advancement.** We saw that maintenance was concerned with the payment of income for the benefit of child beneficiaries. Advancement is concerned with the payment or application of capital sums to the beneficiary's advantage before the time comes when he is entitled to demand the fund. The scope of the power depends upon the terms of the instrument giving it,[166] and upon Trustee Act 1925 s.32.[167] Payments under the power have been made not only for the purpose of providing capital sums when needed, but also for the purpose of tax saving.

Thus, suppose a fund is held on trust for A, the capital being payable to him on attaining 25. If A marries, or sets up in business or in a profession before that time, a power of advancement makes possible the payment to him of some or all of the capital of the fund

---

[161] Above, para.9–003.
[162] Income Tax (Trading and Other Income) Act 2005 s.629, replacing earlier provisions. Similarly where income is retained in a bare trust for the settlor's child.
[163] *Re King* [1928] Ch. 330.
[164] *Re Joel's WT* [1967] Ch. 14. This decision is based on s.2 of the Apportionment Act 1870. The Law Commission recommends that s.2 should no longer apply; Law Com. No.315 (2009), *Capital and Income in Trusts: Classification and Apportionment*, para.6.70.
[165] [1967] Ch. 14; not following *Re King*, above, fn.163, on this point.
[166] See *Re Collard's WT* [1901] Ch. 293.
[167] Below, para.20–038.

to help with such a project. There is a similar but more complicated question if A's interest is subject to a prior life interest in X; for X's income will be affected by any payments out of the capital fund which produces it. Likewise if A's interest is contingent on his attaining 25; for if payments are made to A and A never attains 25 the capital payments will have been made to the wrong person.

The tax-saving question arises where trustees hold a large sum on trust for A for life and then to A's children equally at 21. Independently of the fund A is rich enough to provide the children with all they need. It may be advantageous to make transfers of capital from the trust for the children. Inheritance tax will be avoided in some cases if the advancement was made more than seven years before A's death,[168] but the operation of this principle has been restricted by the Finance Act 2006.[169] Such a payment is certainly not an "advancement" within the usual meaning of the word, but no one could deny that the saving of tax on the trust is a benefit to the children. A further question arises, whether such sums must be held in trust for the children absolutely, or whether they may themselves be settled by the creation of sub-trusts for the benefit of themselves and also for other persons such as future dependants. These questions are dealt with below.

ii. Original Meaning of Advancement.   20–036

"The word 'advancement' itself meant in this context the establishment in life of the beneficiary who was the object of the power or at any rate some step that would contribute to the furtherance of his establishment.[170] . . . Typical instances of expenditure for such purposes under the social conditions of the nineteenth century were an apprenticeship or the purchase of a commission in the Army or of an interest in business. In the case of a girl there could be advancement on marriage."[171]

iii. Express Powers. Until 1925 there was no statutory power of   20–037
advancement. Express powers of advancement were given narrow scope consistent with the established meaning of the word.[172] So:

"[T]o prevent uncertainties about the permitted range of objects for which moneys could be raised and made available, such words

---

[168] FA (No.2) 1987 s.96. This is because A was treated as owning the capital.

[169] Above, para.9–019.

[170] See per Jessel M.R. in *Taylor v Taylor* (1875) L.R. 20 Eq. 155; *Lowther v Bentinck* (1874) L.R. 19 Eq. 166 (payment of debts); *Roper-Curzon v Roper-Curzon* (1871) L.R. 11 Eq. 452 (starting a career at the Bar); *Re Long's Settlement* (1868) 38 L.J.Ch. 125 (passage money to go to a colony); *Re Williams' WT* [1953] Ch. 138 (purchase of a house as a surgery); *Hardy v Shaw* [1976] Ch. 82 (shares in family company).

[171] per Lord Radcliffe in *Pilkington v IRC* [1964] A.C. 612 at 634.

[172] per Kennedy L.J. in *Molyneux v Fletcher* [1898] 1 Q.B. 648 at 653.

as 'or otherwise for his or her benefit' were often added to the word 'advancement'. It was always recognised that these added words were 'large words'[173] and indeed in another case[174] the same judge spoke of preferment and advancement of being 'both large words' but of 'benefit' as being the 'largest of all.' "[175]

The combined phrase "advancement or benefit" is read disjunctively.[176] It now means "any use of the money which will improve the material situation of the beneficiary."[177] The scope of an express power depends of course upon its own language. The standard form of express power was incorporated in the Trustee Act 1925 s.32; and express provisions on the question of advancement are now usually confined to extensions of the statutory power by making the power applicable to the whole of the beneficiary's presumptive share,[178] or by giving express powers to the trustees to create sub-trusts.[179]

iv. The Statutory Power. Trustee Act 1925 Section 32.

20–038   Section 32—

(1) Trustees may at any time or times pay or apply any capital money subject to a trust, for the advancement or benefit, in such manner as they may, in their absolute discretion, think fit, of any person entitled to the capital of the trust property or of any share thereof, whether absolutely or contingently on his attaining any specified age or on the occurrence of any other event, or subject to a gift over on his death under any specified age or on the occurrence of any other event, and whether in possession or in remainder or reversion, and such payment or application may be made notwithstanding that the interest of such person is liable to be defeated by the exercise of a power of appointment or revocation, or to be diminished by the increase of the class to which he belongs:

Provided that—

(a) the money so paid or applied for the advancement or benefit of any person shall not exceed altogether in amount one-half of the presumptive or vested share or interest of that person in the trust property; and

---

[173] See Jessel M.R. in *Re Breed's Will* (1875) 1 Ch.D. 226 at 228.

[174] *Lowther v Bentinck* (1874) L.R. 19 Eq. 166 at 169.

[175] per Lord Radcliffe in *Pilkington v IRC* [1964] A.C. 612 at 634; *Re Halsted's WT* [1937] 2 All E.R. 570 at 571; *Re Moxon's WT* [1958] 1 W.L.R. 165 at 168.

[176] *Lowther v Bentinck* (1874) L.R. 19 Eq. 166; *Re Halsted's WT*, above, fn.175, at 571.

[177] per Lord Radcliffe in *Pilkington v IRC* [1964] A.C. 612 at 635.

[178] By proviso (a) to TA 1925 s.32, the statutory power extends only to one-half of the beneficiary's presumptive share; below.

[179] Below, para.20–042.

(b) if that person is or becomes absolutely and indefeasibly entitled to a share in the trust property the money so paid or applied shall be brought into account as part of such share; and

(c) no such payment or application shall be made so as to prejudice any person entitled to any prior life or other interest, whether vested or contingent, in the money paid or applied unless such person is in existence and of full age and consents in writing to such payment or application.

The section does not apply to capital money arising under the Settled Land Act 1925.[180] Its application is always subject to the expression of a contrary intention[181] and it has been held to be excluded by provision for accumulation.[182]

v. Problems in the Application of Section 32. *Pilkington v IRC.*[183] The wide construction of the phrase "advancement" or "benefit" must have been carried into the statutory power created by s.32, since it adopts without qualification the accustomed wording, "for the advancement or benefit in such manner as they may in their absolute discretion think fit."[184] But this leaves open a number of questions; can payments be made for the "benefit" of a person who is not in any way in need? To what extent can an advancement re-settle the money advanced, the re-settlement changing the original trust? Can trustees, exercising the statutory power of advancement, delegate their discretion by giving a dispositive discretion to the trustees of the re-settlement; i.e. can they make an advancement on protective or discretionary trusts? These questions were discussed and largely settled in the long litigation over the will of William Pilkington.

20–039

The testator left a share of his residuary estate on trust for his nephew Richard upon protective trusts during his life and after Richard's death upon trust for such of his children or remoter issue as he should by deed or will appoint and in default of appointment in trust for such of Richard's children as attained 21 (or, if female, married under that age) in equal shares. Richard had three children all born after the death of the testator of whom

---

[180] TA 1925 s.32(2), as substituted by Trusts of Land and Appointment of Trustees Act 1996 Sch.3, para.3(8).

[181] *Re Evans' Settlement* [1967] 1 W.L.R. 1294.

[182] *IRC v Bernstein* [1961] Ch. 399. This was so even if the direction for accumulation contravened statutory restrictions then in force; *Re Ransome* [1957] Ch. 348; *Brotherton v IRC* [1978] 1 W.L.R. 610.

[183] [1964] A.C. 612.

[184] per Lord Radcliffe in *Pilkington v IRC* [1964] A.C. 612 at 635; *Re Pauling's ST* [1964] Ch. 303.

a two-year-old daughter Penelope was one. Richard's father (brother of the testator and grandfather of Penelope) proposed to make a settlement in favour of Penelope, providing that the trustees hold the property on trust to pay the income to Penelope at 21, and the capital for her absolutely at 30 and if Penelope died under 30 leaving children, on trust for such children at 21 with further family trusts in default. The trustees had power to apply the income for Penelope's maintenance until she reached the age of 21, and were to accumulate the surplus income.

The trustees proposed to advance, with the consent of Richard, one-half of Penelope's expectant share under the testator's will, and pay it to the trustees of Richard's father's settlement.

The House of Lords held that this proposal was within the trustees' power under s.32. They held also that the exercise of the power of advancement was analogous to the exercise of a special power of appointment and that in the circumstances the advancement would be void for perpetuity.

20–040　　　(a) *Benefit.* On the question of the benefit to Penelope, Lord Radcliffe held that it was immaterial that other persons, such as her future dependants, would benefit also.

" . . . [I]f the disposition itself, by which I mean the whole provision made, is for her benefit, it is no objection to the exercise of the power that other persons benefit incidentally as a result of the exercise." [185]

The relief from anxiety about the future maintenance of a wife and a family has been held to be a sufficient benefit[186]; as has the payment from a wife's fund to her husband to enable him to set up in business in England and prevent separation of the family.[187] The performance of the moral obligation felt by a wealthy man to contribute to a charitable trust where it would be a great burden to do so out of taxed income has been held to benefit him.[188] In that case the beneficiary would otherwise have made the contribution from his own resources and so there was a material benefit to him in the advancement. Where a beneficiary wished to have an advancement of capital in order to make a large charitable gift which she could not make from her own resources, it was held that the trustees should not exercise their power of advancement in this way: trust money could

---

[185] per Lord Radcliffe in *Pilkington v IRC* [1964] A.C. 612 at 636; *Re Halsted's WT* [1937] 2 All E.R. 570.

[186] *Re Halsted's WT*, above, fn.185.

[187] *Re Kershaw's Trusts* (1868) L.R. 6 Eq. 322.

[188] *Re Clore's Settlement Trust* [1966] 1 W.L.R. 955. See also *Re Leigh's ST* [2006] W.T.L.R. 477 (decided 1980).

only be advanced to discharge a moral obligation if the beneficiary's material situation would be improved in some way.[189]

Where the purpose of the advancement is to mitigate inheritance tax (or formerly estate duty) on the beneficiary's death, there is no need to show a material benefit to the beneficiary. The tax saving is a sufficient benefit.[190]

(b) *Settlement of Funds Advanced. Sub-trusts.* Nor was it any **20–041** objection that the funds were being subjected to a settlement, and not paid for the sole benefit of Penelope; nor that her enjoyment was deferred. The settlement of advanced funds had many times been approved[191] and this inevitably meant that the trusts on which the funds would be held under the advancement were different from those laid down by the original settlor.

(c) *Delegation.* Closely connected with the question of resettle- **20–042** ment is that of the extent to which trustees, in making an advancement on new trusts, can give discretionary powers to the trustees of the new settlement. In general, *delegatus non potest delegare*.[192] However:

"[T]he law is not that trustees cannot delegate: it is that trustees cannot delegate unless they have authority to do so. If the power of advancement which they possess is so read as to allow them to raise money for the purpose of having it settled, then they do have the necessary authority to let the money pass out of the old settlement into the new trusts. No question of delegation of their powers or trusts arises. If, on the other hand, their power of advancement is read so as to exclude settled advances, cadit quaestio."[193]

This does not, however, solve all the problems. The statutory power allows trustees to advance money by paying it to other trustees to hold on new trusts. Such trusts may include a power of advancement[194]; and presumably s.32 applies to the new trustees.

---

[189] *X v A* [2006] 1 W.L.R. 741.

[190] " . . . if the advantage of preserving the funds of a beneficiary from the incidence of death duty is not an advantage personal to that beneficiary, I do not see what is"; per Lord Radcliffe in *Pilkington v IRC*, above, fn.185 at 640; see also Upjohn J. in *Re Wills WT* [1959] Ch. 1, 11–12; *Re Clore's ST* [1966] 1 W.L.R. 955.

[191] *Re Halsted's WT* [1937] 2 All E.R. 570; *Re Moxon's WT* [1958] 1 W.L.R. 165; *Re Wills' WT* [1959] Ch. 1; *Re Abrahams' WT* [1969] 1 Ch. 463; *Re Hastings-Bass* [1975] Ch. 25; F Crane (1974) 38 Conv.(N.S.) 293.

[192] *Re May* [1926] 1 Ch. 136; *Re Mewburn* [1934] Ch. 112; *Re Wills' WT*, above, fn.191.

[193] per Lord Radcliffe in *Pilkington v IRC* [1964] A.C. 612 at 639.

[194] *Re Mewburn* [1934] Ch. 112; *Re Morris* [1951] 2 All E.R. 528; *Re Hunter's WT* [1963] Ch. 372.

Further, acting on the analogy of cases on special powers of appointment, it seems that the new trusts may include a protective and
forfeitable life interest[195]; but that the discretionary trusts which
come into effect upon the determination of the life interest may be
invalid, because the duties of trustees of a discretionary trust involve
dispositive (as opposed to administrative) discretions,[196] and these
cannot be delegated without express authority.[197] This latter point is
unaffected by the Trustee Act 2000.[198]

If that is correct, s.32 appears to give trustees no power to make
an advancement upon a new settlement which takes the form of
discretionary trusts. Such a situation appears necessarily to raise
questions of delegation; and not to be covered by Lord Radcliffe's
dictum quoted above.[199] Whether a settlement on discretionary
trusts would satisfy the test of "benefit" is another matter; for under
such a trust no interest of course is technically given to the advanced
beneficiary.[200] The delegation problem can be met by expressly
empowering the trustees of the original settlement to delegate their
powers in that manner.[201]

20–043   (d) *Perpetuity.* For the purposes of the perpetuity rule, the exercise of a power of advancement is treated, as has been seen,[202] on
the analogy of a special power of appointment. Where a sub-trust is
created by an advancement, the limitation in the sub-trust is tested
for validity by being read back into the original instrument under
which the power was exercised.[203] The advancements made in *Re
Abrahams' Will Trusts*[204] and *Re Hastings-Bass*[205] failed, in part, to
comply; as the intended advancement would have done in
Pilkington v IRC.[206] In *Re Abrahams' Will Trusts*, the failure of the
void parts of the sub-trust wholly changed the character of the
benefit being conferred on the beneficiary, and the advancement was
held void: there never was a valid exercise of the power by the
trustees. In *Re Hastings-Bass*, however, the trustees' prime consideration was to create a life interest in the life tenant of the sub-trust

---

[195] *Re Boulton's ST* [1928] Ch. 703; *Re Hunter*, above, fn.194; *Re Morris*, above,
fn.194.
[196] See A. Kiralfy (1953) 17 Conv.(N.S.) 285 at 289.
[197] per Eve J. in *Re Boulton's ST* above, fn.195, at 709.
[198] See TA 2000 s.11(2)(a); above, para.20–015.
[199] Above, fn.193.
[200] *Gartside v IRC* [1968] A.C. 553. This is not per se an objection; *Re Clore's Settlement
Trust*, above, fn.190.
[201] For the view that *Pilkington v IRC* ([1964] A.C. 612) does authorise the creation of
discretionary trusts under the statutory power of advancement, see (1963) 27 Conv.(N.S.) 65;
Parker and Mellows, *The Modern Law of Trusts*, 9th edn, pp.804–805.
[202] *Pilkington v IRC* [1964] A.C. 612; above, para.20–039.
[203] *Re Paul* [1921] 2 Ch. 1.
[204] [1969] 1 Ch. 463.
[205] [1975] Ch. 25.
[206] [1964] A.C. 612.

in order to save estate duty on the death of his father, the life tenant of the original settlement. The fact that the interests in remainder in the sub-trust were void for perpetuity did not make the advancement itself void. The principles on which the exercise (or purported exercise) of a discretionary power such as the power of advancement may be held void or voidable have already been discussed.[207]

The Perpetuities and Accumulations Act 1964 introduced the "wait and see" rule, whereby the interests under the sub-trusts would be treated as valid until it became known that they would in fact vest outside the perpetuity period. This rule is preserved by the Perpetuities and Accumulations Act 2009.[208]

vi. The Provisos.[209] (a) Only half the presumptive share of each **20–044** beneficiary may be advanced under the statutory power.[210] The reason for this is that, if the contingent interest of the advanced beneficiary never vests, the fund in the hands of the person next entitled is reduced by the amount advanced. However, it may be advantageous to be able to advance the whole; and it is common to extend the statutory power so as to give the trustees power to advance the whole if they see fit.[211] The Law Commission has proposed that the statutory power should be extended to the whole of the beneficiary's share.[212] This would bring the power into line with standard practice in drafting trusts, and would reduce the need for court applications to permit advances of more than half.

(b) This attempts to effect an equality between the members of a class of beneficiaries, by requiring those who have received benefits in advance of other members of a class of beneficiaries to count the advancement against their ultimate share.[213] Of course it is otherwise if the share never vests.[214]

(c) By advancing some or all of the capital, the fund which provides the income of the tenant for life is reduced. The consent of the tenant for life is therefore required for the exercise of the power.

---

[207] *Pitt v Holt* [2011] 3 W.L.R. 19; above, para.17–045.

[208] s.7.

[209] Set out above, para.20–038.

[210] See *Re Marquess of Abergavenny's Estate Act Trusts* [1981] 1 W.L.R. 843; J. Price [1982] Conv. 158; (express power to pay life tenant any part or parts not exceeding one-half in value of the settled fund was exhausted by the advance of one-half, even though the remainder subsequently increased in value).

[211] In the absence of such an express power, the trust may be varied by the court to permit advancement of the whole in favour of a minor; *D (A Child) v O* [2004] 3 All E.R. 780; below, para.22–012.

[212] Law Com. No.331, *Intestacy and Family Provision Claims on Death*; para.4.72. See also para.4.76 (property other than capital money).

[213] The advance is brought into account at its value at the date of advancement. In times of inflation this can have capricious results. A form of indexation was therefore recommended by the Law Reform Committee, 23rd Report, *The Powers and Duties of Trustees* (1982 Cmnd. 8733), paras. 4.43–4.47.

[214] *Re Fox* [1904] 1 Ch. 480 (express power).

The court has no power to dispense with this consent.[215] A member of a discretionary class is not, however, a person whose consent is required.[216]

C. The Court's Inherent Power to Provide Maintenance and Advancement

20–045   The court has inherent power to order provision to be made for a child out of his property. This power is usually applied in respect of income,[217] but occasionally capital is used.[218] Also, the court has statutory power to make an order authorising a person to make use of a child's property with a view to the application of the capital or income for the child's maintenance, education or benefit.[219]

D. Responsibility of the Trustees to See to the Application of the Money Advanced

20–046   We have seen that the trustees must be satisfied that the proposed advancement is for the benefit of the beneficiary. The next question is whether the trustees, in making an advancement, are under an obligation to see that the money is applied towards the purposes for which the payment was made. In *Re Pauling's Settlement Trusts*[220] the Court of Appeal, dealing with an express power to advance one-half of an expected or presumptive share for the "absolute use" of a beneficiary, held that the power was fiduciary; the trustees could hand over a sum of capital quite generally to a beneficiary if they thought that he was the type of person who could be trusted with the money. Or, if the trustees made the advance for a particular purpose, which they stated, they could quite properly pay it over if they reasonably thought that he could be trusted to carry it out.

> "What they cannot do is prescribe a particular purpose, and then raise and pay the money over to the advancee leaving him or her entirely free, legally and morally, to apply it for that purpose or to spend it in any way he or she chooses without any responsibility on the trustees even to inquire as to its application."[221]

---

[215] *Re Forster's Settlement* [1942] Ch. 199. See also *Henley v Wardell, The Times*, January 29, 1988. (Power in will giving trustees "absolute and uncontrolled discretion" to advance whole capital did not give them power to dispense with the consent of the prior income beneficiary. The purpose of the clause was merely to enlarge the power as to the amount advanced).
[216] *Re Beckett's Settlement* [1940] Ch. 279.
[217] *Wellesley v Wellesley* (1828) 2 Bli.(N.S.) 124.
[218] *Barlow v Grant* (1684) 1 Vern. 255.
[219] Below, para.22–009; TA 1925 s.53.
[220] [1964] Ch. 303; below, para.23–025.
[221] [1964] Ch. 303 at 334.

CHAPTER 21

THE FIDUCIARY NATURE OF TRUSTEESHIP

1. REMUNERATION AND REIMBURSEMENT

THE basic principle of equity is that a trustee acts voluntarily and is **21–001** not paid for his services.[1] It does not matter whether his services are of a professional nature, as where he is a solicitor, or whether they are personal. It follows, therefore, that a trustee can only claim remuneration if he can show a specific entitlement to it. The discussion that follows is essentially an account of how that entitlement can arise.

It is also a basic principle that a trustee may recover, by means of a lien over the trust property, for his legitimate out-of-pocket expenses, which include the payment of agents' fees wherever their employment is permitted,[2] and the proper costs of litigation,[3] including the

---

[1] *Robinson v Pett* (1734) 3 P. Wms. 249; *Re Barber* (1886) 34 Ch.D. 77; *Dale v IRC* [1954] A.C. 11 at 27.

[2] This must be borne in mind when considering the principle that the trustee's office is gratuitous. His burden is alleviated to the extent that he can properly delegate the work to agents; above, para.20–012.

[3] Above, para.18–003. See *Re Spurling's Will Trusts* [1966] 1 W.L.R. 920; *Holding and Management Ltd v Property Holding and Investment Trust Plc* [1989] 1 W.L.R. 1313; *Breadner v Granville-Grossman (costs)* [2006] W.T.L.R. 411 (costs not recoverable where trustees had acted in a hostile or partisan manner).

costs of successfully (but not unsuccessfully) defending themselves from liability for breach of trust.[4] Trustees should seek the court's authorisation (a *Beddoe*[5] order) before suing or defending, to avoid the risk that their costs are found to have been improperly incurred,[6] but they may nevertheless recover their costs from the trust fund without such an order if the costs were properly incurred.[7] Where there is hostile litigation between rival claimants to the trust fund, the trustee should not become involved but should offer to submit to the court's direction; where the trustee is sued successfully by the beneficiaries, his costs will not come out of the trust fund; but where the dispute is with a third party, the trustee's duty is to protect the trust and he will be indemnified so long as the proceedings are properly brought or defended for the benefit of the trust, whether or not successfully.[8] Trustees do not fail in their duty where they discontinue litigation against a third party because the trust fund is likely to be exhausted in indemnifying them, leaving them personally exposed as to any insufficiency.[9] The trustee's lien over the fund extends to an indemnity against contingent liabilities.[10]

The right to reimbursement is statutory,[11] and prevails against trust property generally, both capital and income, and in some cases against the beneficiaries personally,[12] as in the case of a bare trust.[13]

A. Remuneration Authorised by the Trust Instrument

21–002   Express remuneration clauses are extremely common, and are frequently very widely drafted. Otherwise, prior to the reforms of the Trustee Act 2000 discussed in section B below, it would have been difficult to persuade professional people to act as trustees. While the principle of equity is that clauses authorising remuneration are to be strictly construed,[14] this has been relieved by s.28 of the Act of 2000. This provides that where there is an express clause permitting the trustee to be paid for his services, and the trustee is a

---

[4] *Armitage v Nurse* [1998] Ch. 241 at 262.
[5] [1893] 1 Ch. 547. See *Shovelar v Lane* [2011] 4 All E.R. 669.
[6] See *Singh v Basin, The Times*, August 21, 1998.
[7] *Bonham v Blake Lapthorn Linnell* [2007] W.T.L.R. 189. See also *Close Trustees (Switzerland) SA v Vildosa* [2008] W.T.L.R. 1543 (how litigation costs borne as between capital and income).
[8] *Alsop Wilkinson v Neary* [1996] 1 W.L.R. 1220; Lightman J. (2006) 20 T.L.I. 151. See also *McDonald v Horn* [1995] 1 All E.R. 961; *Chessels v British Telecommunications Plc* [2002] W.T.L.R. 719.
[9] *Bradstock Trustee Services Ltd v Nabarro Nathanson (A Firm)* [1995] 1 W.L.R. 1405.
[10] *X v A* [2000] 1 All E.R. 490; A. Kenny [2000] Conv. 560.
[11] Trustee Act 2000 s.31, replacing previous legislation. Interest is not payable; *Foster v Spencer* [1996] 2 All E.R. 672.
[12] See generally *Stott v Milne* (1884) 25 Ch.D. 710; *Re Grimthorpe* [1958] Ch. 615.
[13] *Hurst v Bryk* [2002] 1 A.C. 185 at pp.196–197 (partners holding lease on trust for partnership).
[14] *Re Chalinder & Herington* [1907] 1 Ch. 58; *Re Gee* [1948] Ch. 284.

trust corporation or is acting in a professional capacity, the trustee is entitled to be paid even if the services are capable of being provided by a lay trustee. The remuneration may take the form of the income from a part of the estate[15] or capital under a power of appointment,[16] or the trustee may be given power to make use of trust money in other ways.[17] A clause in a will authorising remuneration is no longer treated as a legacy.[18]

B. Trustee Act 2000

Part V of the Trustee Act 2000 facilitates the remuneration of **21–003** professional trustees in cases where neither the trust instrument nor any other legislation provides for it. Section 29 (which applies whenever the trust was created) provides that a trust corporation[19] is entitled to receive reasonable remuneration out of the trust fund for services provided. A professional trustee who is neither a trust corporation nor a sole trustee is similarly entitled if each other trustee has agreed in writing that he may be remunerated. A sole trustee is excluded because the safeguard of collective scrutiny would be absent. Section 29 extends to personal representatives acting professionally,[20] but does not apply to trustees of charitable trusts. The Secretary of State, however, may make provision by regulations for the remuneration of charity trustees.[21] The Charities Act 2011 permits remuneration for charity trustees in certain cases.[22]

C. Other Statutory Provisions

Other statutory provisions enable fees to be charged by the Public **21–004** Trustee,[23] by persons appointed to be Judicial Trustees,[24] and by corporations appointed as custodian trustees.[25] In this last case, the

---

[15] *Public Trustee v IRC* [1960] A.C. 398. See J Thurston (1988) 2 *Trust Law & Practice* 93.

[16] *Re Beatty's WT* [1990] 1 W.L.R. 1503.

[17] See *Space Investments Ltd v Canadian Imperial Bank of Commerce Trust Co (Bahamas) Ltd* [1986] 1 W.L.R. 1072 (settlement provided that bank trustee could deposit trust money with itself and use for own purposes, subject to normal obligation to repay).

[18] Trustee Act 2000 s.28.

[19] As defined in the Trustee Act 1925.

[20] Trustee Act 2000 s.35.

[21] TA 2000 s.30. It was considered that to apply the general provision to charity trustees might undermine public confidence in the sector; Law Com. No.260 (1999), para.7.22. See also s.32 (remuneration and reimbursement of agents, nominees and custodians).

[22] Above, para.15–096.

[23] Public Trustee Act 1906 s.9; Public Trustee (Fees) Act 1957; Public Trustee (Liability and Fees) Act 2002. He is paid such salary as the Lord Chancellor determines; Public Trustee Act 1906 s.8(1A).

[24] Judicial Trustees Act 1896 s.1.

[25] Public Trustee Act 1906 s.4.

corporation concerned cannot also be a managing trustee.[26] But where a corporation is appointed to be a trustee by the court, the court has full discretion as to its fees, and is not restricted by this distinction.[27]

D. Remuneration Authorised by the Court

21–005   The court has an inherent jurisdiction, which is exercisable retrospectively[28] and prospectively, but in exceptional cases only, to authorise remuneration for trustees and other fiduciaries. The power has even been exercised in favour of a fiduciary who was guilty of undue influence. In *O'Sullivan v Management Agency and Music Ltd*[29] a contract between a performer and his agent was set aside for undue influence and breach of fiduciary duty, but the agent was awarded remuneration (including a reasonable profit element) as he had contributed significantly to the claimant's success. The argument that the jurisdiction was exercisable only in favour of the morally blameless was rejected.

The jurisdiction extends to increasing the rate of remuneration authorised by the settlor.[30] The court in such a case would have regard to the nature of the trust, the experience and skill of the trustee, and the sums claimed in comparison with the charges of other trustees.

Factors in favour of the exercise of the court's discretion include the fact that the fiduciary's work has been of substantial benefit to the trust, as in *Boardman v Phipps*,[31] and that if the work had not been done by the fiduciary it would have had to be done by someone else at the expense of the trust.[32] A modern example is where trustees (a surveyor and a building contractor) used special skills over many years to bring about a sale of trust land at a profit. They had not appreciated the extent of the task when appointed, otherwise they would have declined to act gratuitously. Remuneration was

---

[26] *Forster v Williams Deacon's Bank Ltd* [1935] Ch. 359; *Arning v James* [1936] Ch. 158.

[27] Trustee Act 1925 s.42.

[28] *Re Worthington* [1954] 1 W.L.R. 526; *Re Jarvis* [1958] 1 W.L.R. 815; *Phipps v Boardman* [1967] 2 A.C. 46; *Foster v Spencer* [1996] 2 All E.R. 672.

[29] [1985] Q.B. 428; W. Bishop and D. Prentice (1986) 49 M.L.R. 118. See also *Warman International Ltd v Dwyer* (1995) 69 A.L.J.R. 362 (share of profits of business); R. Nolan (1996) 55 C.L.J. 201; *Cobbetts LLP v Hodge* [2010] 1 B.C.L.C. 30 (reimbursement of costs but no remuneration).

[30] *Re Duke of Norfolk's ST* [1982] Ch. 61; B. Green (1982) 45 M.L.R. 211; PVB (1982) 98 L.Q.R. 181; K. Hodkinson [1982] Conv. 231. See also *Re Barbour's Settlement* [1974] 1 W.L.R. 1198 (application for increase should be made directly and not included as a term of a compromise of an unconnected dispute); cf. *Re Codd's WT* [1975] 1 W.L.R. 1139. The court will not appoint a paid trustee unless in the best interests of the beneficiaries; *Polly Peck International Plc (In Administration) v Henry* [1999] 1 B.C.L.C. 407.

[31] [1967] 2 A.C. 46, below, para.21–022.

[32] *Re Berkeley Applegate (Investment Consultants) Ltd* [1989] Ch. 32 at 50–51.

awarded for the work done, but not for remaining tasks, which required no special expertise.[33] The House of Lords in *Guinness v Saunders*[34] refused a claim to remuneration by a company director who, it was assumed, had acted bona fide but in circumstances involving a clear conflict of interest and duty. It was doubted whether the jurisdiction would ever be exercised in favour of a director, as this would constitute interference by the court in the administration of the company's affairs. The company's articles gave the power to remunerate to the board of directors, to whom the claim should be addressed. Lord Goff considered that the jurisdiction could only be reconciled with the fundamental rule that a trustee is not entitled to remuneration to the extent that its exercise did not conflict with the policy underlying that rule. Such a conflict would only be avoided if the exercise of the jurisdiction was restricted to cases where it could not have the effect of encouraging trustees to put themselves in a position of conflict of interest and duty.[35] *Boardman v Phipps*[36] was such a case. There the merits of the claim were overwhelming, but the present case was very different: the director had put himself in a position where his interests were in stark conflict with his duty. Also, he had received money which belonged to the company.

E. Remuneration for Litigious Work by Solicitor-Trustees

Under the rule in *Cradock v Piper*,[37] a solicitor-trustee may **21–006** charge costs if he has acted for a *co-trustee as well as himself*[38] in respect of business done in an action or matter *in court*, provided that his activities have not increased the expenses. It is not necessary that the court action should be hostile in character, but it must be some form of litigious matter.[39] The rule will not be extended by analogies.

It may also be noted here that a solicitor-trustee may employ his *partner* in cases where it would be proper to employ an outside solicitor, provided that he himself will derive no benefit, direct *or* indirect, from such an employment.[40] There must be complete separation of the trust work from the firm's general work, so as to

---

[33] *Foster v Spencer*, above, fn.28.

[34] [1990] 2 A.C. 663; J. Beatson and D. Prentice (1990) 106 L.Q.R. 365; J. Hopkins (1990) 49 C.L.J. 220; Law Com. C.P. No.146 (1997), p.155. The facts are given at para.21–020, below.

[35] [1990] 2 A.C. 663, at 701; cf. *O'Sullivan v Management Agency and Music Ltd* [1985] Q.B. 428, above, which was not referred to.

[36] Above, fn.31.

[37] (1850) 1 Mac. & G. 664. See W. Bishop and D. Prentice (1983) 46 M.L.R. 289 at 306; C. Stebbings (1998) 19 Legal History 189.

[38] *Lyon v Baker* (1852) 5 De G. & Sm. 622.

[39] *Re Corsellis* (1887) 34 Ch.D. 675.

[40] *Clack v Carlon* (1861) 30 L.J.Ch. 639.

make it clear that the solicitor-trustee is not involved in the former. This power is not restricted to matters in court, but it does not enable a solicitor-trustee to employ his own *firm*.[41]

F. Authorisation by Contract

21–007   Trustees may contract for remuneration with those beneficiaries who are of full age and capacity.[42] But such agreements may somewhat easily be brought under the head of undue influence,[43] and are not encouraged. Nor, in fact, are they at all common.

2. TRUSTEES MUST NOT BE PURCHASERS

A. Purchase of the Trust Property

21–008   This rule and those which follow are based on the principle that a trustee may not place himself in a position where his duty and his interest may conflict.[44] This means that trustees are not to become the owners or lessees of trust property. This rule is independent of any question of inadequacy of price, or unfairness, or undue advantage; the sale may have been at auction[45] and the trustee may have taken the bidding well above the reserve price, but he is still caught by the rule, which derives from his status and position and not from his conduct in the particular case.[46] The fairness of the transaction is irrelevant in the absence of informed consent of the beneficiaries. Nor does it matter that he left the decision to sell and the manner of sale wholly to his co-trustee; nor that he retired from the trust before making an offer.[47] His responsibility as trustee is such that he must not contemplate the purchase at all.

The rule was somewhat relaxed in *Holder v Holder*,[48] involving an executor who had purported to renounce the executorship, but

---

[41] *Christophers v White* (1847) 10 Beav. 523; *Re Hill* [1934] Ch. 623.

[42] If the beneficiaries are not all of full age and capacity, application must be made to court, as in *Re Duke of Norfolk's ST*, above, fn.30, (living beneficiaries did not object, but some unborn).

[43] *Ayliffe v Murray* (1740) 2 Atk. 58; below, paras 26–007 et seq.

[44] *Boardman v Phipps* [1967] 2 A.C. 46 at 123. This principle does not apply if it is the settlor who has placed the trustees in such a position; *Sargeant v National Westminster Bank Plc* (1991) 61 P. & C.R. 518; *Breakspear v Ackland* [2009] Ch. 32. See generally M. Conaglen (2005) 121 L.Q.R. 452, (2006) 65 C.L.J. 366, (2009) 125 L.Q.R. 111 and (2010) 126 L.Q.R. 72.

[45] See *Newgate Stud Co v Penfold* [2008] 1 B.C.L.C. 46.

[46] *Campbell v Walker* (1800) 5 Ves.Jr. 678; *Ex p. Lacey* (1802) 6 Ves.Jr. 625; *Movitex Ltd v Bulfield* [1988] B.C.L.C. 104; *Re Peck* [2011] W.T.L.R. 605.

[47] *Wright v Morgan* [1926] A.C. 788; *Re Boles and British Land Co's Contract* [1902] 1 Ch. 244.

[48] [1968] Ch. 353. cf. *Re Mulholland's WT* [1949] 1 All E.R. 460 (option to purchase acquired before trusteeship).

invalidly, as he had already done some minor acts in the administration of the estate. After his purported renunciation, the executor took no further part in the administration. He later purchased at auction for a fair price some farmland belonging to the estate, of which he had previously been tenant. The Court of Appeal declined to set aside the purchase. The circumstances were special, because the executor had not interfered in the administration of the estate; nor had he taken part in organising the auction; nor was there any conflict of interest and duty, as the beneficiaries were not looking to him to protect their interests; and finally, any special knowledge he had about the property was acquired as tenant and not as executor. In any event, the claimant beneficiary had acquiesced in the sale. As a general rule, however, a trustee or executor who has once involved himself in his office is affected by the rule for a considerable period after retirement.

The effect of the rule is that the purchase is voidable at the option **21–009** of a beneficiary, who is allowed a generous time to discover the position.[49] The right to avoid the sale is effective against a purchaser with notice of the circumstances. The rule cannot be got around by sales to nominees,[50] for a repurchase by the trustee will be regarded as on behalf of the trust (unless the original sale was bona fide).[51] A sale to the trustee's spouse is looked upon with suspicion,[52] and likewise a sale to a company in which the trustee has a substantial interest.[53] The rule was applied by analogy in *Kane v Radley-Kane*,[54] where a widow who was sole administratrix appropriated unquoted shares worth £50,000 to herself in satisfaction of the statutory legacy to which she was entitled on her husband's intestacy. This was done without the consent of her stepsons, who were entitled on the intestacy subject to her rights. The estate at that time was worth only £93,000, thus it appeared that the widow was entitled to it all. She sold the shares two years later for over £1 million. It was

---

[49] For an illustration see *Re Sherman* [1954] Ch. 653. See also *Walker v Walker* [2010] W.T.L.R. 1617.

[50] *Silkstone & Haigh Moor Coal Co v Edey* [1900] 1 Ch. 167.

[51] *Re Postlethwaite* (1888) 60 L.T. 514.

[52] See *Burrell v Burrell's Trustees* 1915 S.C. 33, where the sale was upheld; *Tito v Waddell (No.2)* [1977] Ch. 106; *Newgate Stud Co v Penfold* [2008] 1 B.C.L.C. 46.

[53] See *Re Thompson's Settlement* [1986] Ch. 99; C. Sherrin (1986) 1 *Trust Law & Practice* 66 , where the contract for sale to a company of which the trustee was managing director and majority shareholder was held unenforceable; *Movitex Ltd v Bulfield* [1988] B.C.L.C. 104. A mortgagee is also debarred from selling the property to himself, but it has been held that he can sell to a company in which he has an interest if he acts in good faith and gets the best price reasonably obtainable; *Tse Kwong Lam v Wong Chit Sen* [1983] 1 W.L.R. 1349. See also *Farrar v Farrar's Ltd* (1889) 40 Ch.Div. 395.

[54] [1999] Ch. 274; C. Sherrin All E.R. Rev. 1998 at 463; S. Cretney (1998) 28 Fam. Law 526. The Law Commission invited views as to whether reform was needed in this context, but decided not to make any recommendation because the risks of reform outweighed the possible advantages; Law Com. No.331 (2011), *Intestacy and Family Provision Claims on Death*, para.5.67.

held that the appropriation of the shares breached the self-dealing rule and was equivalent to a purchase of trust property by a trustee. Thus the widow held the shares and their proceeds for the estate.

The court may in certain circumstances prefer to order a re-sale, and, if the price is higher than the previous sale price, the trustee must convey; otherwise he is held to his purchase. The trustee will not be allowed to bid at the new sale if this is objected to.[55]

The rule discussed above is subject to certain exceptions. The trust instrument may expressly permit the purchase by a trustee.[56] Secondly, the court has a discretion to allow such a purchase in a proper case,[57] or to permit the trustee to bid at an auction.[58] Finally, a tenant for life of settled land, which he holds on trust, is permitted by statute to purchase the property.[59]

B. Purchase of the Beneficial Interest

21–010   Equity's view is less stringent when dealing with a purchase by a trustee of the beneficial interest of a beneficiary.[60] This is a type of transaction which is carefully watched; the onus is on the trustee to show that he gave full value, and that the beneficiary gave informed consent.[61] The principles of undue influence apply; but it is open to a trustee in this type of case to show that the whole transaction was conducted at arm's length. This must however be very distinctly proved.[62]

3. INCIDENTAL PROFITS

A. Trustees

21–011   The rules discussed below apply in full force to trustees. Many of them apply also to other fiduciaries. Although we are mainly concerned here with trustees, it will be convenient to mention also, where relevant, the application of the rules to persons who are not strictly trustees.

---

[55] See Cross J. in *Holder v Holder* [1968] Ch. 353 at 371.

[56] See *Sargeant v National Westminster Bank Plc* (1991) 61 P. & C.R. 518.

[57] *Farmer v Dean* (1863) 32 Beav. 327. Or the beneficiaries, all being of full age and capacity, may agree to it.

[58] *Holder v Holder*, above, fn.55, at 398, 402.

[59] SLA 1925 s.68.

[60] *Tito v Waddell (No.2)* above, fn.52, at 241; *Re Thompson's Settlement* [1986] Ch. 99; M. Conaglen (2006) 65 C.L.J. 366.

[61] *Thomson v Eastwood* (1877) 2 App.Cas. 215 at 236; *Hill v Langley, The Times*, January 28, 1988.

[62] See generally *Coles v Trecothick* (1804) 9 Ves.Jr. 234; *Morse v Royal* (1806) 12 Ves.Jr. 355; cf. *Williams v Scott* [1900] A.C. 499.

i. Rule in *Keech v Sandford*.[63] This rule prevents a trustee from **21–012**
keeping for his own benefit a renewal of a lease which he was able
to obtain for himself by reason of his being the trustee of the original
lease; and even though the trustee had tried unsuccessfully to obtain
a renewal for the benefit of his beneficiary. In the leading case, from
which the rule takes its name, the defendant held a lease of the
profits of a market on trust for a child. Before the expiration of the
lease, the defendant asked the lessor to renew the lease in favour of
the child. The lessor refused to grant a lease to the child on the
grounds that, as the lease was of the profits of the market, he would
be unable to distrain, and would be unable to enforce the covenant
against the child. The trustee then took a lease for his own
benefit.

Lord Chancellor King held that the trustee must hold the lease on
trust for the child. He said[64]:

> "This may seem hard that the trustee is the only person of all
> mankind who might not have the lease; but it is very proper that
> the rule should be strictly pursued, and not in the least relaxed; for
> it is very obvious what would be the consequences of letting
> trustees have the lease, on refusal to renew to *cestui que use*."

A similar principle applies to the renewal of contracts.[65] It is otherwise, however, where there is no fiduciary relationship.

> In *Re Biss*,[66] a lessor had refused to renew a seven-year lease of
> premises, and the lessee remained in possession as tenant from
> year to year. He died, leaving a widow and three children. The
> widow, who was his administratrix, and two of the children con-
> tinued the business under the existing lease. The lessor terminated
> the lease, and then granted a three-year lease to one of the chil-
> dren. The Court of Appeal allowed him to keep the lease for his
> own benefit. Romer L.J. said that[67] "where the person renewing
> the lease does not clearly occupy a fiduciary position" he:
>
> > "[I]s only held to be a constructive trustee of the renewed lease
> > if, in respect of the old lease, he occupied some special position

---

[63] (1726) Sel. Cas. t. King 61; A. Hicks (2010) 69 C.L.J. 287 (describing the decision at 319 as a "poorly reported decision of a less than distinguished Chancellor"); *Re Edwards' WT* [1982] Ch. 30; *Chan v Zacharia* (1984) 154 C.L.R. 178; cf. *Harris v Black* (1983) 46 P. & C.R. 366.
[64] (1726) Sel. Cas. t. King 61 at 62.
[65] *Don King Productions Inc v Warren* [2000] Ch. 291.
[66] [1903] 2. Ch. 40; *Brenner v Rose* [1973] 1 W.L.R. 443. See also *Savage v Dunningham* [1974] Ch. 181.
[67] [1903] 2 Ch. 40 at 61.

and owed, by virtue of that position, a duty towards the other persons interested."

21–013   **ii. Purchase of the Reversion.** Where the trustee acquires the freehold reversion, the position is unclear.[68] The trustee is liable if he has in any way made use of his position to get a personal benefit: thus if the lessor makes an offer to all his lessees giving them the right to enfranchisement on favourable terms, or if the lessee had any statutory right of enfranchisement, there could be no doubt that the trustee who sought to take the reversion for his own benefit would be liable. The courts have, however, vacillated in deciding whether there is any *absolute* liability in the absence of such abuse.[69] In *Protheroe v Protheroe*[70] the Court of Appeal, without referring to the relevant authorities, held that the rule was applicable, without qualification, to purchases of the freehold. A husband held the lease of the matrimonial home on trust for his wife and himself in equal shares. After the wife had petitioned for divorce, he purchased the freehold reversion. When he sold, the wife was held to be entitled to a share of the proceeds.[71] In earlier cases the courts had limited the rule to cases where the lease, the reversion on which was being purchased, was renewable by law or custom.[72] The rationale of that limitation was that if the lease were normally renewed in practice,[73] the lessee would suffer if the lease passed to a third party who might not follow the custom (particularly if the lease, as was commonly the case with church leases, was generally renewed at less than the market rent). Thus it was wrong to allow the trustee, who ought to be protecting his beneficiary's interests, to damage them. Today, by statute, many lessees are given valuable rights of renewal or enfranchisement. It is submitted that the proper question in each case is: has the trustee taken advantage of his position to get a personal benefit? If so, he is liable, otherwise he is not. "It seems to me," said Pennycuick V.C. in *Thompson's Trustee in Bankruptcy v Heaton*[74]:

[68] The converse situation where a trustee of the reversion purchases the lease was left open in *Re Thompson's Settlement* [1986] Ch. 99.

[69] *Norris v Le Neve* (1743) 3 Atk. 26; *Randall v Russell* (1817) 3 Mer. 190; cf. *Phillips v Phillips* (1885) 29 Ch.D. 673.

[70] [1968] 1 W.L.R. 519; P. Jackson (1968) 31 M.L.R. 707; F. Crane (1968) 32 Conv.(N.S.) 220; *Thompson's Trustee v Heaton* [1974] 1 W.L.R. 605; (1974) 38 Conv.(N.S.) 288; P. Jackson (1975) 38 M.L.R. 226; *Popat v Shonchhatra* [1997] 1 W.L.R. 1367.

[71] "It may be that there were facts in the case which indicated that the husband obtained the freehold by virtue of his position as leaseholder, but they are not apparent from the report"; L. Megarry (1968) 84 L.Q.R. 309.

[72] *Bevan v Webb* [1905] 1 Ch. 620; cf. *Griffith v Owen* [1907] 1 Ch. 195; per Wilberforce J. in *Phipps v Boardman* [1964] 1 W.L.R. 993 at 1009.

[73] See generally S. Cretney (1969) 33 Conv.(N.S.) 161, where the history of the doctrine is traced.

[74] [1974] W.L.R. 605 at 606. See also *Don King Productions Inc v Warren* [2000] Ch. 291, favouring the *Protheroe* approach. Textbook criticisms of *Protheroe* were rejected.

"[T]hat apart from the fact that it binds me, this decision [*Protheroe v Protheroe*], like the rule in *Keech v Sandford*, is really in modern terms an application of the broad principle that the trustee must not make a profit out of the trust estate."

The onus would be on the trustee to satisfy the court, and it can be a very difficult one to discharge.

iii. Trustees as Company Directors. The question has arisen **21–014** several times in connection with the remuneration of directorships which trustees have obtained by virtue of their position as trustees.

In *Re Macadam*,[75] trustees had power under the articles by virtue of their office to appoint two directors of a company. They appointed themselves, and were held liable to account for the remuneration which they received because they had acquired it by the use of their powers as trustees.

On the other hand, the remuneration may be retained if the trustees were directors before they became trustees,[76] or if the trustees were appointed directors independently of the votes of the shares of the trust,[77] or if the trustee did not obtain the remuneration by the use of his position as a trustee, but by an independent bargain with the firm employing him.[78] Indeed, as Cohen J. said in *Re Macadam*,[79] " . . . the root of the matter really is: Did [the trustee] acquire the position in respect of which he drew the remuneration by virtue of his position as trustee?" Trustees will not be liable even within that test if the terms of the trust authorised them to appoint themselves and receive remuneration.[80]

iv. Other Profits by Trustees. Incidental profits come to trus- **21–015** tees in a variety of ways and must always be disgorged.

"Whenever it can be shewn that the trustee has so arranged matters as to obtain an advantage, whether in money or money's

---

[75] [1946] Ch. 73; *Re Francis* (1905) 92 L.T. 77; *Williams v Barton* [1927] 2 Ch. 9.
[76] *Re Dover Coalfield Extension Ltd* [1908] 1 Ch. 65. See also *Re Orwell's WT* [1982] 1 W.L.R. 1337.
[77] *Re Gee* [1948] Ch. 284.
[78] *Re Lewis* (1910) 103 L.T. 495, as explained in *Re Gee*, above, fn.77.
[79] [1946] Ch. 73 at 82. Harman J. accepted this test in *Re Gee*, above, fn.77.
[80] *Re Llewellin's WT* [1949] Ch. 225. The court may sanction the retention of the fees; *Re Keeler's ST* [1981] Ch. 156.

worth, to himself personally through the execution of his trust, he will not be permitted to retain, but will be compelled to make it over to his constituent."[81]

A few examples must suffice. A trustee who introduced business of the trust to a firm, of which he was a member, was compelled to account for the profit[82]; similarly, a trustee who received a sum of £75 to induce him to retire[83] and a trustee who used trust funds in his own business was required to account for the profits he received[84]; and a trustee may be liable for profits which he ought reasonably to have received.[85] There was some authority that trustees of pension funds who were also beneficiaries were excluded from benefit where they exercised a power to apply funds among a class of which they were members.[86] This over-strict interpretation of the principle, which has not been applied to trustee-beneficiaries of other trusts, has now been overturned by statute.[87]

21–016 **v. Trustee must not be in Competition with the Trust.** One possible area of conflict of interest and duty is where the trustee operates in business in competition with the trust. Such competition was inevitable in *Re Thompson*[88] where executors of a will were directed to carry on the business of the testator who had been a yacht broker. One of the executors was intending to set up on his own account as a yacht broker in competition. It was held that he must not set up in a competing business.

This rule applies to other fiduciaries who are not trustees. A partner is required by statute to "account for and pay over to the firm all profits made" by carrying on a business "of the same nature as and competing with that of the firm"[89] unless he has the consent of

---

[81] *Huntingdon Copper Co v Henderson* (1872) 4 R. (Court of Session) 294 at 308; cf. *Patel v Patel* [1981] 1 W.L.R. 1342 (no breach where trustees sought to live in the trust property where the beneficiaries were young children adopted by the trustees on the death of their parents).

[82] *Williams v Barton* [1927] 2 Ch. 9; cf. *Jones v AMP Perpetual Trustee Company NZ Ltd* [1994] 1 N.Z.L.R. 690 (no breach where subsidiary placed trust business with parent company).

[83] *Sugden v Crossland* (1856) 3 Sm. & G. 192; *Re Smith* [1896[1 Ch. 71.

[84] *Brown v IRC* [1965] A.C. 244 (a Scottish solicitor compelled to account for interest earned by deposits of clients' moneys).

[85] *Re Waterman's WT* [1952] 2 All E.R. 1054.

[86] Discussed in J. Mowbray (1996) 10 T.L.I. 49. See also, in the context of a family discretionary trust, *Breakspear v Ackland* [2009] Ch. 32.

[87] Pensions Act 1995 s.39; above, para.16–010. See *Edge v Pensions Ombudsman* [2000] Ch. 602.

[88] [1930] 1 Ch. 203; *Aberdeen Railway Co v Blaikie Bros* (1854) 1 Macq. 461; *Warman International Ltd v Dwyer* (1995) 69 A.L.J.R. 362.

[89] Partnership Act 1890 s.30.

the other partners. It is a question of fact in each case whether or not the activity is in conflict with the fiduciary duty.[90]

B. Other Fiduciaries[91]

i. The Principle. A similar rule applies to profits[92] made by other persons in breach of a fiduciary relation; indeed such persons are grouped with trustees in many formulations of the rule although there is no rule that they must act gratuitously.

> "It is an inflexible rule of a Court of Equity that a person in a fiduciary position, . . . is not, unless otherwise expressly provided, entitled to make a profit; he is not allowed to put himself in a position where his interest and duty conflict."[93]

But it is not safe to make the attractive over-simplification of saying that a fiduciary must always account for all gains which come to him by reason of his fiduciary position. Indeed, Lord Herschell in the paragraph containing the above quotation plainly recognised its limitations[94]:

> "But I am satisfied that it might be departed from in many cases, without any breach of morality, without any wrong being inflicted, and without any consciousness of wrong-doing. Indeed, it is obvious that it might sometimes be to the advantage of the beneficiaries that their trustee should act for them professionally rather than a stranger, even though the trustee were paid for his services."[95]

It is not always easy, however, to determine whether a particular relationship should be classified as fiduciary. While some examples

21–017

---

[90] *Moore v M'Glynn* [1894] 1 Ir.R. 74.

[91] Goff and Jones, Ch.33; G. Jones (1968) 84 L.Q.R. 472; R. Goode (1976) 92 L.Q.R. 360 at 372; Oakley, *Constructive Trusts*, 3rd edn, Ch.3; J. Shepherd (1981) 97 L.Q.R. 51; Shepherd, *The Law of Fiduciaries* (1981); Snell, para.7–004; L. Smith in Getzler (ed.), *Rationalizing Property, Equity and Trusts*, 2003, Ch.4; Conaglen. *Fiduciary Loyalty* (2010); J. Edelman (2010) 126 L.Q.R. 302. See Law Com. No.236 (1995), *Fiduciary Duties and Regulatory Rules*, examining the mismatch between general law obligations and regulatory rules.

[92] For losses caused by breach of the duty of loyalty, see *Item Software (UK) Ltd v Fassihi* [2005] 2 B.C.L.C. 91; A. Berg (2005) 121 L.Q.R. 213; J. Armour and M. Conaglen (2005) 64 C.L.J. 48; R. Lee [2009] Conv. 236; M. Conaglen (2010) 126 L.Q.R. 72.

[93] Lord Herschell in *Bray v Ford* [1896] A.C.44 at 51; see also Lord Cranworth in *Aberdeen Railway Co v Blaikie Bros* (1854) 1 Macq. 461 at 471; *Regal (Hastings) Ltd v Gulliver* [1942] 1 All E.R. 378; [1967] 2 A.C. 134n.

[94] Lord Upjohn in *Boardman v Phipps* [1967] 2 A.C. 46 at 123.

[95] *Bray v Ford* [1896] A.C. 44 at 52.

are well established, the boundaries of the category of fiduciary relationships are not clear, and the category is not closed.[96] The defining feature is the assumption of the duty of loyalty. It includes certain agents,[97] (including "self-appointed" agents[98]), solicitors,[99] company directors,[100] partners,[101] confidential employees,[102] a pawnbroker,[103] and certain bailees,[104] but not a vendor of goods to which title has not yet passed to the purchaser.[105]

21–018   Indeed, it may sometimes appear that the defendant may be classified as a fiduciary, or not, in order to achieve the desired result.

In *Reading v Attorney General*,[106] a staff-sergeant in the British Army stationed in Cairo was bribed by Egyptians to ride in their civilian lorries carrying contraband goods, enabling the lorries to pass check posts without difficulty. The British authorities seized £20,000 from Reading; later he petitioned to recover it. He had obtained the money wrongfully, but he argued that this fact did not mean that the British Government was entitled to claim it.

---

[96] *English v Dedham Vale Properties Ltd* [1978] 1 W.L.R. 93; A. Duggan (1997) 113 L.Q.R. 601 at 619–626; Sir Anthony Mason (1997–98) 8 K.C.L.J. 1 at 6; Sir Peter Millett (1998) 114 L.Q.R. 214; S Worthington (1999) 58 C.L.J. 500; Birks (ed.), *Privacy and Loyalty*, Chs 10, 11.

[97] *De Bussche v Alt* (1878) 8 Ch.D. 286; *NZ Netherlands Society v Kuys* [1973] 1 W.L.R. 1126 at 1129. Not all agents are fiduciaries, although there may be a presumption that they are; *Aluminium Industrie Vaasen BV v Romalpa Aluminium Ltd* [1976] 1 W.L.R. 676; below, para.23–073. See Goff and Jones, p.112, fn.93, suggesting that "much depends on whether the agent is under a duty to keep separate his own money from his principal's money."; cf. *Re Air Canada and M & L Travel Ltd* (1994) 108 D.L.R. (4th) 592.

[98] *English v Dedham Vale Properties Ltd*, above, fn.96 (where the intending purchaser obtained planning permission in the vendor's name); A. Nicol (1978) 41 M.L.R. 474; G. Samuel (1978) 94 L.Q.R. 347.

[99] *Brown v IRC* [1965] A.C. 244; (1964) 80 L.Q.R. 480; *Islamic Republic of Iran Shipping Lines v Denby* [1987] 1 Lloyd's Rep. 367; *Longstaff v Birtles* [2002] 1 W.L.R. 470; *Ratiu v Conway* [2006] W.T.L.R. 101. See also *Hanson v Lorenz* [1987] 1 F.T.L.R. 23 (no liability to account to client for his profits from a joint venture where client had understood the agreement).

[100] *Regal (Hastings) Ltd v Gulliver*, above, fn.93; *Industrial Development Consultants Ltd v Cooley* [1972] 1 W.L.R. 443; below, para.21–020. See also *Horcal Ltd v Gatland* [1984] B.C.L.C. 549.

[101] *Clegg v Fishwick* (1849) 1 Mac. & G. 294; *John Taylors (A Firm) v Masons* [2005] W.T.L.R. 1519; *Conlon v Simms* [2006] 2 All E.R. 1024.

[102] *Att Gen v Guardian Newspapers Ltd (No.2)* [1990] 1 A.C. 109 (The "Spycatcher" case; duty to account for profits). A former member of the security service does not owe a continuing fiduciary duty to the Crown in relation to information which is not confidential; *Att Gen v Blake* [2001] 1 A.C. 268; P. Jaffey [2000] R.L.R. 578. See also *Nottingham University v Fishel* [2000] I.R.L.R. 471; *Cobbetts LLP v Hodge* [2010] 1 B.C.L.C. 30. On the duty of "fidelity", see R. Flannigan (2008) 124 L.Q.R. 274.

[103] *Mathew v TM Sutton Ltd* [1994] 1 W.L.R. 1455; N. Palmer All E.R. Rev. 1994 p.26. (Surplus proceeds of sale held on trust for pawnor and interest payable).

[104] *Aluminium Industrie Vaasen BV v Romalpa Aluminium Ltd*, above, fn.97; *Re Andrabell Ltd (In Liquidation)* [1984] 3 All E.R. 407.

[105] *Re Goldcorp Exchange Ltd (In Receivership)* [1995] 1 A.C. 74.

[106] [1951] A.C. 507.

Reading failed, however, and one of the grounds for the decision in the House of Lords was that he, as a non-commissioned officer, was in a fiduciary relation to the Crown, and was therefore under a duty to account for the profit wrongfully made.

Illegal or secret commissions or bribes obtained by a confidential servant or agent are recoverable by the principal or employer regardless of any quantifiable loss to him.[107] If the fiduciary relationship in this case is accepted, the result merely follows the earlier cases on agents. The application of the rule to a policeman[108] and a staff-sergeant may be an extension; indeed it has been said that the speeches in the House of Lords in *Reading v Attorney General*[109] "confirm that the status of a fiduciary may... be easily acquired."[110]

Where a fiduciary agent has taken a secret commission, it has been held that he forfeits his contractual remuneration.[111] In addition to paying no further fees, the principal is entitled to recover fees already paid as well as an account of profits, and the agent is not entitled to an allowance for the value of any work done. This principle could operate inequitably if the breach occurred towards the end of an agency relationship. It may be that a distinction should be drawn between long term fiduciary relationships and those of a "single transaction" character.[112]

ii. Company Directors. Company directors are treated as fiduciaries[113] in so far as they are prohibited from making a profit out of their office[114] unless the articles permit it or the shareholders or (as now confirmed by the Companies Act 2006) the board of directors **21–019**

---

[107] *Att Gen for Hong Kong v Reid* [1994] 1 A.C. 324; below, para.21–026. See also *Brown v IRC* [1965] A.C. 244; *Logicrose Ltd v Southend United Football Club Ltd* [1988] 1 W.L.R. 1256 (principal can recover from agent whether he affirms or repudiates the transaction between the agent and the third party); G. Jones (1989) 48 C.L.J. 22; *Swindle v Harrison* [1997] 4 All E.R. 705 (undisclosed profit by solicitor from loan transaction arranged for client); *Murad v Al-Saraj* [2005] W.T.L.R. 1573.

[108] *Att Gen v Goddard* (1929) 98 L.J.K.B. 743 (bribes received when on duty).

[109] Above, fn.106.

[110] Goff and Jones, p.751. See also *Swain v The Law Society* [1983] A.C. 598 (no fiduciary relationship between Law Society and solicitors).

[111] *Imageview Management Ltd v Jack* [2009] Lloyd's Rep. 436 (agent hired to negotiate contract for professional footballer); P. Watts (2009) 125 L.Q.R. 369.

[112] S. Oram [2010] L.M.C.L.Q. 95.

[113] The duty is owed to the company, not to the shareholders; *Percival v Wright* [1902] 2 Ch. 421. This is made statutory by Companies Act 2006 s.170(1).

[114] The office of director should not, however, be equated with that of trustee. The assets of the company, unlike trust property, are not vested in the director but in the company which is a separate legal entity and, more importantly, directors "are ... commercial men managing a trading concern for the benefit of themselves and of all other shareholders in it ... ": per Jessell M.R. in *Re Forest of Dean Coal Mining Co Ltd* (1878) 10 Ch.D. 450, at 451–452.

consent. Following the recommendations of the Law Commission,[115] the fiduciary (and other) duties of directors have now been codified by the Companies Act 2006, in order to make the law more certain, accessible and comprehensible. The duties set out in the Act are based on and replace the previous common law rules and equitable principles governing the duties owed by directors to the company.[116] The statutory duties are to be interpreted and applied by having regard to the common law rules and equitable principles, thus preserving existing case law.[117] The consequences of, and remedies for, breach of the fiduciary duties have not been codified and are, therefore, those provided by the general law on breach of fiduciary duty.[118]

While the statutory provisions for the most part reflect the rules laid down by the general law, one of the most important and to some extent controversial provisions of the Act is the express duty of a director to act in a way he considers, in good faith, would be most likely to promote the success of the company for the benefit of its members as a whole.[119] This goes further than the law it replaces.[120] The duty to exercise reasonable care, skill and diligence is made statutory,[121] although the Act makes it clear that this is not a fiduciary duty.[122]

Fundamental to the codification of fiduciary duties is s.175 of the Act of 2006, which sets out the duty to avoid a situation in which the director has, or can have, a direct or indirect interest which conflicts, or possibly may conflict, with the interests of the company. A director must not exploit any property, information or opportunity, and it is immaterial whether the company could take advantage of it.[123] There is no breach of duty if the situation could not reasonably be regarded as likely to give rise to a conflict of interest.[124] Importantly, the Act confirms that there is no breach if the matter has been authorised by the directors, although the manner of authorisation is

---

[115] Law Com. No.261; *Company Directors: Regulating Conflicts of Interest and Formulating a Statement of Duties*. See generally D. Ahern (2012) 128 L.Q.R. 114.

[116] Companies Act 2006 s.170. The duties apply, with any necessary adaptations, to former directors.

[117] Companies Act 2006 s.170(4).

[118] Companies Act 2006 s.178. The Law Commission recommended otherwise.

[119] Companies Act 2006 s.172.

[120] J. Lowry (2009) 68 C.L.J. 607.

[121] Companies Act 2006 s.174.

[122] Companies Act 2006 s.178(2).

[123] Companies Act 2006 s.175(2). The reflects the strict rule of equity laid down in *Keech v Sandford* (1726) Sel. Cas. Ch. 61; above, para.21–012.

[124] Companies Act 2006 s.175(4)(a). This reflects Lord Upjohn's dissenting view in *Boardman v Phipps* [1967] 2 A.C. 46 at 124. It may also be regarded as lending support to the view that there is no breach where the board, being fully informed, has rejected the opportunity or venture; *Peso Silvermines Ltd v Cropper* (1966) 58 D.L.R. (2d) 1. See also *Foster Bryant Surveying Ltd v Bryant* [2007] B.C.L.C. 239; J. Payne All E.R. Rev. 2007, p.73.

subject to conditions.[125] The statutory no-conflict rule expresses in a single rule the previous distinct but overlapping no-conflict and no-profit rules.

The rule against taking bribes and secret commissions is made statutory,[126] likewise the duty to declare to the other directors any interest, direct or indirect, which a director has in a proposed transaction or arrangement with the company.[127]

The statutory rules may be illustrated by the case law based on the equitable principles which they codify. The leading case is the House of Lords decision in *Regal (Hastings) Ltd v Gulliver*.[128] **21–020**

> R Ltd set up a subsidiary, A Ltd, to acquire the leases of two cinemas. A Ltd had a share capital of 5,000 £1 shares. The owner of the cinemas was only willing to lease them if the share capital of A Ltd was completely subscribed for. However, R Ltd had resources to subscribe for only 2,000 of the 5,000 shares and it was therefore agreed that the directors of R Ltd should subscribe for the rest. When the business of R Ltd was transferred to new controllers the directors made a profit from their holdings in A Ltd. The new controllers of R Ltd caused the company to sue the ex-directors of R Ltd for an account of the profit. The directors were held liable. They had made the profit out of their position as directors and, in the absence of shareholder approval, they were obliged to account.

There are a number of noteworthy features of *Regal*. First, the directors were found by the court to have acted bona fide, but the liability of a fiduciary to account for a profit made from his office "in no way depends on fraud, or absence of bona fides."[129] Secondly, the new controllers obtained a windfall.[130] Thirdly, it was arguable that the directors, by purchasing the shares in A Ltd had enabled R Ltd to enter into a transaction which it was otherwise commercially impossible for the company to enter into. While there is some truth in this, the decision that R Ltd did not have the necessary financial resources to enter into the transaction was made by the directors who were the very persons who benefited from this decision. Because of this a compelling argument can be made that a "reasonable man looking at the relevant facts and circumstances of

---

[125] Companies Act 2006 s.175(4)(b). The conditions are laid down in subss.(5) to (7). See also s.180 (consent, approval or authorisation by members).

[126] Companies Act 2006 s.176 (duty not to accept benefits from third parties).

[127] Companies Act 2006 s.177. See *Newgate Stud Co v Penfold* [2008] 1 B.C.L.C. 46 (involvement of fiduciary's wife).

[128] [1967] 2 A.C. 134n. For a review of this line of cases, see *Ultraframe (UK) Ltd v Fielding* [2007] W.T.L.R. 881; D. Prentice and J. Payne (2006) 122 L.Q.R. 558.

[129] [1967] 2 A.C. 134n. at 144.

[130] See D. Prentice (1979) 42 M.L.R. 215.

the particular case would think that there was a real sensible possibility of conflict."[131]

A clear case of conflict of interest and duty arose in *Guinness Plc v Saunders*,[132] where a director (Ward) agreed to provide his services in connection with a proposed take-over of another company (Distillers), on terms that he would be paid a fee the size of which depended on the amount of the take-over bid if successful. The bid was successful, and the fee paid to Ward was £5.2 million. The claim by Guinness for summary judgment for the repayment of this sum was upheld in the House of Lords. Ward's interest in obtaining a fee calculated on the above basis conflicted with his duty as director, which was to give impartial advice concerning the take-over. The agreement for the fee, made with two other directors, but not the board of directors, was void for want of authority. Ward had no arguable defence to Guinness's claim that he had received the money, paid under a void contract, as a constructive trustee.

The courts have imposed liability on directors to account where the directors have made the profit out of an economic opportunity, or information, even though they acquired it in a personal capacity, if it was information which could have been exploited by their company.[133]

> In *Industrial Development Consultants Ltd v Cooley*,[134] the defendant was a director and general manager of the claimant company, which provided construction consultancy services. He attempted to interest a public Gas Board in a project, but was unsuccessful because the Gas Board's policy was not to employ development companies. The defendant was a distinguished architect who had worked in the gas industry for many years. For this reason the Gas Board decided to offer the contract to him personally, which he accepted, obtaining a release from the claimant by falsely representing that he was ill. He was held to be liable to account to the claimant for the profits of the contract.

The significance of the case is twofold. First, the court rejected Cooley's defence that the information concerning the Gas Board's

---

[131] *Boardman v Phipps* [1967] 2 A.C. 46 at 124, per Lord Upjohn.

[132] [1990] 2 A.C. 663; J. Beatson and D. Prentice (1990) 106 L.Q.R. 365; J. Hopkins (1990) 49 C.L.J. 220; S. Goulding [1990] Conv. 296.

[133] See *Canadian Aero Service Ltd v O'Malley* (1973) 40 D.L.R. (3d) 371 SCC.

[134] [1972] 1 W.L.R. 443; [1972] 2 All E.R. 162 (the reports on the case are not identical); A. Yoran (1973) 89 L.Q.R. 187; J. Collier (1972A) 30 C.L.J. 222; H. Rajak (1972) 35 M.L.R. 655; D. Prentice (1972) 50 C.B.R. 623. See also *CMS Dolphin Ltd v Simonet* [2001] 2 B.C.L.C. 704; *Re Bhullar Bros Ltd* [2003] 2 B.C.L.C. 241; D. Prentice and J. Payne (2004) 120 L.Q.R. 198; J. Armour (2004) 63 C.L.J. 33; *Kingsley IT Consulting Ltd v McIntosh* [2006] B.C.C. 875.

contract came to him in his private capacity, and not as director of the claimant company:

> "This is the first case in which it was decided that the prohibition on exploiting a corporate opportunity applies also to an opportunity which was presented to the director personally and not in his capacity with the company."[135]

Secondly, the decision whether or not the contract went to the company lay not with the fiduciary, Cooley, but with a third party, the Gas Board.[136] In *Cooley's* case there were special circumstances; this was exactly the type of opportunity which the company relied on Cooley to obtain; furthermore, the absence of bona fides was clear. Also, the imposition of liability will provide directors with an incentive to channel opportunities to their companies and not exploit them for their personal advantage. A director's duty of undivided loyalty means that he must inform the company of a relevant business opportunity. It is not for the director to decide that the company would not be interested and then to appropriate the opportunity for himself.[137]

There are other decisions which suggest a more benign attitude towards directors. **21-021**

In *Queensland Mines Ltd v Hudson*[138] the claimant company had been interested in developing a mining operation and the defendant, the managing director, was successful in obtaining for the company the licences necessary to enable it to do so. However, because of financial problems it could not proceed. Hudson resigned as managing director and, with the knowledge of the company's board, successfully developed the mines. The Privy Council held that Hudson was not liable to account, for either of two reasons: (a) the rejection of the opportunity by the company because of cash difficulties took the venture outside the scope of Hudson's fiduciary duties or (b) because Hudson had acted with

---

[135] (1973) 89 L.Q.R. 187 at 189.

[136] Roskill J. found that there was only a 10% chance that the Gas Board would have awarded the contract to the company. Thus the company only benefited because Cooley had breached his duty.

[137] *Re Allied Business and Financial Consultants Ltd* [2009] 2 B.C.L.C. 666; D. Ahern (2011) 74 M.L.R. 596.

[138] (1978) 18 A.L.R. 1; W. Braithwaite [1980] Conv. 200; applied in *Jones v AMP Perpetual Trustee Company NZ Ltd* [1994] 1 N.Z.L.R. 690. See also *Island Export Finance Ltd v Umunna* [1986] B.C.L.C. 460 (defendant not liable for developing a business opportunity after resigning as managing director because company was not actively pursuing the venture when he resigned, and his resignation was influenced not by any wish to acquire the business opportunity but by dissatisfaction with the company). See also *In Plus Group Ltd v Pyke* [2002] 2 B.C.L.C. 201; P. Koh (2003) 62 C.L.J. 42, 403.

the full knowledge of the company's board, they should be taken to have consented to his activities.[139]

This decision was considered controversial. However, it now appears to be endorsed by the Companies Act 2006.[140]

21–022   **iii. *Boardman v Phipps.*** Many of the difficulties relating to the application of the rule came to the fore in *Boardman v Phipps.*[141]

The Phipps trust owned a substantial minority holding of shares in a private company. John Phipps, the claimant, was one of the beneficiaries under the trust, and the defendants were Boardman, a solicitor, and Tom Phipps, also a beneficiary. The trustees were an elderly widow who died in 1958, her daughter and an accountant. Boardman acted as solicitor to the trust.

In 1956 the defendants were dissatisfied with the way in which the company was managed. They made various inquiries on behalf of the trust, and in that capacity obtained confidential information about the company. They realised that it would be advantageous to sell some of the non-profit-making assets. They obtained control of the company by purchasing the remainder of the company's shares, and carried out the desired sales and reorganisation. The transaction was highly profitable. The trust gained in respect of its holding and the defendants gained in respect of the shares which they had purchased for the purpose of obtaining control.

Boardman had informed the beneficiaries and the two active trustees (the widow having lost mental capacity and taking no part in the affairs of the trust) giving them an outline of the negotiations and asking them whether they had any objection to his taking a personal interest, bearing in mind that his initial inquiry had been on behalf of the trust. Boardman acted bona fide throughout and thought that he had made a full disclosure and had the beneficiaries' consent. Wilberforce J. however found that the claimant was justified in thinking that he had only been told half the truth. The trustees had been invited to consider whether the trust should find the money for the purchase of the shares; but the trustees were unable and unwilling to do so.

John Phipps then called upon the defendants to account for the profits which they had made. The House of Lords (3–2) held that

---

[139] (1978) 18 A.L.R. 1 at 10. Lord Upjohn's reasoning in *Boardman v Phipps* [1967] 2 A.C. 46 was adopted on the basis that he had "dissented on the facts, but not on the law." (at 3).

[140] See s.175(4)(a), (b); above, para.21–019.

[141] [1967] 2 A.C. 46; G. Jones (1968) 84 L.Q.R. 472; B. Rider [1978] Conv. 114. The case was distinguished in *Satnam Investments Ltd v Dunlop Heywood & Co Ltd* [1999] 3 All E.R. 652, where the defendant, who took advantage of an opportunity arising from another's breach of fiduciary duty, was not himself a fiduciary.

they must do so; but having acted bona fide, they were entitled to payment on a liberal scale for their work and skill.[142]

A number of points of importance arise from the case. First, Boardman was not a trustee. The fiduciary relation arose from his employment as solicitor by the trustees. He was not, however, employed to act for the trust in the dealings in question and he claimed, as he stated at the time, to have been acting in a private capacity. The members of the House of Lords took different views on this issue. In the early negotiations with the company, the defendants, who were not shareholders in their own right, purported to represent the trust, although strictly they did not do so. Lord Cohen, in the majority, said[143] "that information and that opportunity they owed to their representing themselves as agents for the holders of the 8,000 shares held by the trustees." Lord Upjohn, dissenting, said[144] "though they portrayed themselves as representing the Phipps Trust, it is quite clear the offer was made by these two personally."

Secondly, the liability of the defendants was unaffected by the fact that the trust had lost nothing; nor that the trust had greatly benefited; nor did it matter that the Phipps Trust could not have found the money; nor that the trustees would not have wished to use the money for that purpose even if they had it; nor that such user would have been in breach of trust, unless they had applied to the court and obtained consent to the investment.[145]

21–023

It is extremely difficult to determine the limits of this inflexible rule. Part of the difficulty stems from the lack of agreement as to whether the confidential information acquired by the appellants was trust property. The dissenting judges considered that it was not property. Of the majority, Lords Hodson and Guest considered that it was,[146] while Lord Cohen merely held that it was not property "in the strict sense of that word", so that liability to account for profits from its use depended on the facts of the case.[147] In *Aas v Benham*,[148] Lindley L.J. laid down that information obtained in the course of a partnership business must not be used by the partners for their own benefit within the scope of the partnership business; but that they may make use of it for:

---

[142] Above, para.21–005.

[143] [1967] 2 A.C. 46 at 103.

[144] [1967] 2 A.C. 46, at 120; see also Viscount Dilhorne at 91; and *NZ Netherlands Society v Kuys* [1973] 1 W.L.R. 1126, (1973) 37 Conv.(N.S.) 362.

[145] Lord Denning M.R. in the Court of Appeal mentioned this as a source of a potential conflict of interest and duty; [1965] Ch. 992, at 1020. The suggestion, however, seems unrealistic. See [1967] 2 A.C. 46 at 92, 124; cf. Lord Cohen at 103–104.

[146] Criticised G. Jones (1968) 84 L.Q.R. 472; Oakley, *Constructive Trusts*, 3rd edn, p.170; Sir Peter Millett (1998) 114 L.Q.R. 214 at 222.

[147] [1967] 2 A.C. 46 at 102. It was accepted in *Crown Dilmun Plc v Sutton* [2004] W.T.L.R. 497 that confidential information is not property. It may, however, be "sold in the market"; *Douglas v Hello! Ltd (No.3)* [2008] A.C. 1 (conjoined appeal with *OBG Ltd v Allan*).

[148] [1891] 2 Ch. 244.

"[P]urposes which are wholly without the scope of the firm's business . . . It is not the source of the information, but the use to which it is applied, which is important in such matters."[149]

This was not disapproved in *Boardman v Phipps*,[150] but it seems that a stricter view there prevailed; the defendants were held accountable because they had obtained the information by purporting to represent the trust; and although they were acting independently when they made the purchase. It is submitted that it is difficult to answer Lord Upjohn's argument in dissent[151]:

"I think, again, that some of the trouble that has arisen in this case, it being assumed rightly that throughout he was in such a [fiduciary] capacity, is that it has been assumed that it has necessarily followed that any profit made by him renders him accountable to the trustees. That is not so. . . . It is perfectly clear that a solicitor can if he so desires act against his clients in any matter in which he has not been retained by them provided, of course, that in acting for them generally he has not learnt information or placed himself in a position which would make it improper for him to act against them. This is an obvious application of the rule that he must not place himself in a position where his duty and his interest conflict. So, in general, a solicitor can deal in shares in a company in which the client is a shareholder, subject always to the general rule that the solicitor must never place himself in a position where his interest and his duty conflict; and in this connection it may be pointed out that the interest and duty may refer (and frequently do) to a conflict of interest and duty on behalf of different clients and have nothing to do with any conflict between the personal interest and duty of the solicitor, beyond his interest in earning his fees."

His Lordship concluded:

"To extend the doctrines of equity to make the [defendants] accountable in such circumstances, is, in my judgment, to make unreasonable and inequitable applications of such doctrines."[152]

21–024   Some 40 years later, the Court of Appeal suggested that the time has come to revisit the inflexibility of the rule in cases where the

---

[149] [1891] 2 Ch. 244, at 256.
[150] [1967] 2 A.C. 46.
[151] [1967] 2 A.C. 46, at 126.
[152] [1967] 2 A.C. 46 at 133–134, quoting Lord Selborne L.C. in *Barnes v Addy* (1874) 9 Ch.App. 244, at 251. See also *Chan v Zacharia* (1984) 154 C.L.R. 178 at 204, suggesting that there should be no liability if it would be unconscientious to assert it, or if there was no possible conflict of interest and duty and it was plainly in the interest of the beneficiary that the fiduciary obtain the rights for himself that he was absolutely precluded from seeking or obtaining for the beneficiary.

fiduciary has acted in good faith, with no concealment, and in the belief that he was acting in the best interests of the beneficiaries.[153]

Where the rule applies, the only escape of the fiduciary is that he made full disclosure, and obtained the consent of the other parties, and it is not open to him to argue that they would have consented if asked.[154] It is not, however, clear whether the "other parties" are the trustees or the beneficiaries. In the straightforward case of a profit made by a trustee, the relevant consent must be that of the beneficiaries, to whom the duty is owed. Difficulties will arise if any of the beneficiaries are children or unborn. *Boardman v Phipps*,[155] however, was not such a case. Boardman was a fiduciary agent, the principals being the trustees. To whom did he owe his fiduciary duties? Presumably consent must be obtained from those persons. If the trustees had not consented, they would, as principals, have a right of recovery against their agent, any money thus recovered being held by them on trust for the beneficiaries. If the trustees had consented, the agent would nevertheless be liable to the beneficiaries if he owed fiduciary duties to *them*.[156] The result of *Boardman v Phipps*[157] was that the beneficiary successfully sued the agent, but the basis of this is not clear. Their Lordships spoke, rather ambiguously, of his being a fiduciary "to the trust".[158] Lord Guest spoke of the "knowledge and assent of the trustees".[159] Lord Hodson held that the relevant consent was that of the beneficiary; Boardman "was in a fiduciary position vis-à-vis the trustees, and through them vis-à-vis the beneficiaries."[160] Viscount Dilhorne regarded the consent of the principals as necessary, but also referred to the fact that the beneficiary was not fully informed.[161] Lord Upjohn said that Boardman was:

"[I]n a fiduciary capacity at least to the trustees. Whether he was ever in a fiduciary capacity to the [claimant] was not debated before your Lordships and I do not think that it matters."[162]

[153] *Murad v Al-Saraj* [2005] W.T.L.R. 1573; J. Edelman and C. Mitchell All E.R. Rev. 2005, p.369; M. McInnes (2006) 122 L.Q.R. 11; M. Conaglen (2006) 65 C.L.J. 278; R. Cunnington (2008) 71 M.L.R. 559 at 583.

[154] [2005] W.T.L.R. 1573.

[155] Above, fn.152.

[156] Presumably the beneficiaries could sue the trustees in such circumstances even if they could not sue the agent.

[157] Above, fn.152.

[158] [1967] 2 A.C. 46 at 100, 104, 110.

[159] [1967] 2 A.C. 46 at 117.

[160] [1967] 2 A.C. 46 at 112. Lord Cohen also regarded the consent of the beneficiary as necessary, at 104. See further Law Com. C.P. No.146 (1997), *Trustees' Powers and Duties*, paras 3.29, 3.32, describing *Boardman v Phipps* as a "particularly difficult case in this regard".

[161] [1967] 2 A.C. 46 at 93.

[162] [1967] 2 A.C. 46 at 125–126.

This raises the question whether trustees can, if acting unanimously, give consent to dealings by their agent which would otherwise be a breach of his fiduciary obligations.[163] In the present case Boardman had obtained the consent of the two active trustees, but did not inform the third because she had lost mental capacity. Russell L.J. in the Court of Appeal[164] held that this was insufficient because two out of the three trustees:

> "[H]ad no authority to turn this aspect of the trust property [the exploitation of the shares] over to the defendants, unless to be used exclusively for the benefit of the trust",

and that the fiduciary could not "rid himself of the disqualification inherent in that position save with the informed consent of all three." It is submitted that the better view is that of Lord Upjohn, who replied that "not all the trustees acting together could do it for they cannot give away trust property."[165] On this view it is only the beneficiaries or the settlor (by express provision in the trust instrument) who can authorise such dealings. The Law Commission doubted whether trustees can authorise others to do what they themselves have no power to do.[166] However, it is now provided by s.14 of the Trustee Act 2000 that trustees may authorise their agent to act in circumstances capable of giving rise to a conflict of interest, provided it is reasonably necessary for the trustees to do so. This provision is primarily applicable to investment management functions.

Finally, it is important to determine what remedy was decreed in *Boardman v Phipps*.[167] This is discussed below.

21–025   **iv. The Extent of the Fiduciary Principle.** Essentially the problem is one of determining the limits of the rule.

> "Rules of equity have to be applied to such a great diversity of circumstances that they may be stated only in the most general terms and applied with particular attention to the exact circumstances of each case."[168]

---

[163] See D. Hayton (1990) 106 L.Q.R. 87 at 91–92, taking the view that prior specific (but not general) authority may be given if there is full disclosure by the agent and provided the "prudent businessman" test is satisfied.

[164] [1965] Ch. 992 at 1031.

[165] [1967] 2 A.C. 46 at 128.

[166] Law Com. CP. No.146 (1997), *Trustees' Powers and Duties*, paras 3.26–3.33; Law Com. No.260 (1999), para.4.27.

[167] [1967] 2 A.C. 46.

[168] *Boardman v Phipps* [1967] 2 A.C. 46 at 123. See generally E. Simpson in Birks and Pretto (eds), *Breach of Trust*, 2002, Ch.3.

If a fiduciary obtains a benefit for himself at the expense of his beneficiary, there is no difficulty. The case is one of unjust enrichment. The position is more difficult where the beneficiary loses nothing; where he did not wish to make the profitable purchase which the trustee makes; where the fiduciary acted honestly; or even where the fiduciary conferred by his activities every possible benefit on the beneficiary, but received an additional benefit for himself. A windfall has been received through the exertions of the fiduciary; the beneficiary has risked nothing, and lost nothing; should he be entitled to the profits?[169] *Boardman v Phipps* answers this question in the affirmative but the Court of Appeal has more recently suggested that the House of Lords might relax the severity of the inflexible rule in cases where it operates harshly and the remedy is disproportionate.[170]

The law as it now stands might be criticised on the ground that, although intended as a deterrent, it fails to draw any distinction between the honest and the dishonest fiduciary. Both are liable. However, it should be borne in mind that the honest fiduciary may be remunerated by order of the court, as in *Boardman v Phipps*.[171] A dishonest fiduciary, on the other hand, may be made to pay a higher rate of interest.[172]

But this still leaves open the question, to be determined on the facts of each case, whether the opportunity for profit arose by reason of the fiduciary position.[173] For example, a merchant banker, insurance broker, solicitor or company director learns through the proper course of his business information from a confidential source which may be of advantage to other clients in companies with which he is associated. Having satisfied the requirements of a particular client, is he precluded from making use of this information in respect of other trusts with which he is concerned or for himself? Similarly with the directors of several (non-competing) companies? Or, does his fiduciary duty to the second client place him under a duty to provide that client with the confidential information?[174] There is the danger that

---

[169] See generally G. Jones (1968) 84 L.Q.R. 472; Oakley, *Constructive Trusts*, 3rd edn, pp.168–179. A rigid application of the rule may lead to the unjust enrichment of the claimant; *Warman International Ltd v Dwyer* (1995) 69 A.L.J.R. 362 at 369.

[170] *Murad v Al-Saraj* [2005] W.T.L.R. 1573; criticised M. Conaglen (2011) 70 C.L.J. 548; above, para.21–024.

[171] Above, fn.167. A fiduciary guilty of undue influence has, however, been remunerated by the court; *O'Sullivan v Management Agency and Music Ltd* [1985] Q.B. 428, above, para.21–005.

[172] Below, para.23–016.

[173] G. Jones (1970) 86 L.Q.R. 463.

[174] See B. Rider [1978] Conv. 114; *North and South Trust Co v Berkeley* [1971] 1 W.L.R. 470; M. Kay and D. Yates (1972) 35 M.L.R. 78; *Movitex Ltd v Bulfield* [1988] B.C.L.C. 104 (fiduciary must not place himself in a position where his duty to X conflicts with his duty to Y); M. Conaglen (2010) 126 L.Q.R. 72.

the rule, if applied inflexibly, may impose an impossible burden. As Lord Cohen said in *Boardman v Phipps*[175]:

" . . . [I]t does not necessarily follow that because an agent acquired information and opportunity while acting in a fiduciary capacity he is accountable to his principals for any profit that comes his way as the result of the use he makes of that information and opportunity. His liability to account must depend on the facts of the case."

Viscount Dilhorne[176] quoted Lindley L.J. as saying "to hold that a partner can never derive any personal benefit from information which he obtains from a partner would be manifestly absurd."[177]

It is difficult to formulate any single test which may be applied to determine whether a fiduciary has incurred liability. It is submitted that liability will arise if any of the following factors is present:

(a) the fiduciary has used trust property;
(b) the profit has been made by use of or by reason of the fiduciary position or of an opportunity or knowledge resulting from it, even though no trust property was used;
(c) there was a conflict (or a significant possibility of a conflict) of interest and duty, even if no trust property was used, and the opportunity did not arise from the fiduciary relationship.[178]

C. Personal and Proprietary Remedies

21–026   It is often said that a fiduciary who is required to account for profits becomes a constructive trustee. But a duty to account is a personal liability; a constructive trust is a proprietary remedy; the significance of the distinction appears where the fiduciary is bankrupt, or where the assets in question have been profitably invested. A related question is whether tracing is available, which is discussed in Ch.23. Liability to account is not synonymous with constructive trusteeship, but the cases do not always maintain the distinction. Indeed, Lord Lane C.J. has said "We find it impossible to reconcile much of the language used in these decisions."[179] A recent analysis is that the 19th century decisions offer little support for the principle

---

[175] [1967] 2 A.C. 46 at 102–103; see also Lord Upjohn at 126.
[176] [1967] 2 A.C. 46 at 90.
[177] *Aas v Benham* [1891] 2 Ch. 244 at 255–256.
[178] *Chan v Zacharia* (1984) 154 C.L.R. 178 at 198; *Industrial Development Consultants Ltd v Cooley* [1972] 1 W.L.R. 443. See also Stephenson L.J. in *Swain v Law Society* [1982] 1 W.L.R. 17 at 31: there must be a possibility of a conflict of interest and duty, and a nexus between the fiduciary position and the profit made.
[179] *Re Att Gen's Reference (No.1 of 1985)* [1986] Q.B. 491 at 503.

that unauthorised profits are held on constructive trust, and that this principle was developed at that time by text writers rather than judges.[180]

In *Boardman v Phipps*, Wilberforce J. had held that the shares were held on constructive trust[181] for the beneficiaries; and that Boardman was accountable for profits he made, less a sum for his skill and effort. The House of Lords did not distinguish between accountability and constructive trust. Lord Guest concluded that the defendants held the shares as constructive trustees, and were bound to account to the claimant.[182] The other members spoke of accountability only.

As submitted above, there is a difference between a duty to hold specific property on trust and a duty to account. Could Boardman have satisfied the judgment by payment of the value of the shares at that time, keeping any subsequent increase? Would a purchaser (with notice) have taken the shares subject to the same obligation? What would have been the position if Boardman had been bankrupt? None of these matters arose, and it was not necessary to discuss them.

If the fiduciary has used or received trust property, then any profits made are held on constructive trust for the beneficiaries.[183] But what is the position if the disputed asset did not derive from the trust property but came from a third party, as in the case of a bribe or secret commission? It was laid down by the Court of Appeal in *Lister & Co v Stubbs*[184] that where an agent or other fiduciary took a bribe, the principal's remedy was personal. The fiduciary had to account for the bribe, but did not hold it on constructive trust. The result in that case was that the fiduciary could keep any profit made from investing the bribe money. This decision was long criticised[185] as contravening the principles of unjust enrichment and treating a dishonest fiduciary more leniently than an honest fiduciary such as Boardman in *Boardman v Phipps*.[186] It was, however, affirmed by the Court of Appeal in *Re Att Gen's Reference (No.1 of 1985)*,[187] although in a criminal law context, with the result that an employee

---

[180] A. Hicks (2010) 69 C.L.J. 287.

[181] [1964] 2 All E.R. 187; cf. [1964] 1 W.L.R. 993.

[182] [1967] 2 A.C. 46 at 117. See D. Hayton (1990) 106 L.Q.R. 87 at 102, suggesting that the liability was personal only. See also *Ultraframe (UK) Ltd v Fielding* [2007] W.T.L.R. 881 (remedy in *Boardman* was not proprietary); cf. *Att Gen for Hong Kong v Reid* [1994] 1 A.C. 324, below, where Lord Templeman clearly regarded Boardman as a constructive trustee.

[183] *Guinness Plc v Saunders* [1990] 2 A.C. 663, above, para.21–020; *Neptune (Vehicle Washing Equipment) Ltd v Fitzgerald* [1996] Ch. 274; *CMS Dolphin Ltd v Simonet* [2001] 2 B.C.L.C. 704 (business opportunity exploited by director treated as company property).

[184] (1890) 45 Ch.D. 1.

[185] Although supported in R. Goode (1987) 103 L.Q.R. 433; R. Goode in B. Rider (ed.), *Law at the Centre*, 1999, p.185; A. Burrows (2001) 117 L.Q.R. 412 at 427.

[186] [1967] 2 A.C. 46.

[187] [1986] Q.B. 491.

who made a secret profit was not guilty of theft of his employer's property.

Lister & Co v Stubbs was disapproved by the Privy Council in a decision which concerned bribes but which is very significant in the wider area of profits made by fiduciaries.

In *Att Gen for Hong Kong v Reid*[188] the defendant, a public prosecutor, took bribes of over $HK12 million to obstruct prosecutions, in breach of his fiduciary duty as a Crown servant. He failed to comply with an order to repay and was imprisoned. He had purchased three freehold properties with the money, which had since increased in value. The Privy Council decided that these properties were held on trust for the Crown.

21–027   Lord Templeman pointed out that bribes cause loss and damage to the principal, although it may not be quantifiable, as in the present case, where unquantifiable harm to the administration of justice had been done. A constructive trust of the bribe money arose because the fiduciary was under an immediate duty to pay it over to the principal. Applying the maxim "equity regards as done that which ought to be done", the money was the property of the principal in equity. The fiduciary's creditors should be in no better position than the fiduciary. If the bribe money was profitably invested, the profits belonged to the principal. If it decreased in value, the fiduciary was personally liable for the deficit. The constructive trust arose whether the fiduciary took property from the trust or from a third party in breach of duty. Any other result, it was said, would be inconsistent with the principle that a fiduciary must not profit from his office. There was no logic in treating a dishonest fiduciary more favourably than an honest fiduciary who had become liable as constructive trustee.

The decision was welcomed so far as it prevented the unjust enrichment of a dishonest fiduciary, but certain difficulties remained. Instead of dealing with the policy issue of when proprietary remedies should be available, the Privy Council based its decision more narrowly on the equitable maxim, the application of which is controversial in that it is founded on the availability of specific performance, but an obligation to pay money is not normally specifically enforceable.[189] It might also be doubted whether the claimant

---

[188] [1994] 1 A.C. 324. The person who bribed the agent is accountable to the principal for any resulting profit; *Fyffes Group Ltd v Templeman* [2000] 2 Lloyd's Rep. 643; A. Berg [2001] L.M.C.L.Q. 27 at 57. See also *Hurstanger v Wilson* [2007] 1 W.L.R. 2351; C. Miller All E.R. Rev 2007, p.98.

[189] Below, para.24–018; A. Oakley (1994) 53 C.L.J. 31; D. Crilley [1994] 2 R.L.R. 57; P. Clarke All E.R. Rev. 1994, at 252; S. Gardner (1995) 54 C.L.J. 60; cf. Sir Peter Millett (1998) 114 L.Q.R. 399 at 407; S. Worthington in Degeling and Edelman (eds), *Equity in Commercial Law*, 2005, Ch.5; P. Millett in Burrows and Rodger (eds), *Mapping the Law*, 2006, pp.274–275.

deserves priority over the defendant's unsecured creditors, who have not necessarily taken the risk of insolvency.[190] So far as the bribe has increased in value, the increase is a windfall to the claimant. To balance the interests of creditors and the prevention of unjust enrichment, a compromise solution was suggested of imposing only personal liability for any increase in value.[191] By allowing the claimant to assert ownership of the bribe money and any profits made from it, the decision amounts to "proprietary overkill".[192] As leading commentators have said, "By the light of nature it is not easy to see why bribery should trigger a proprietary response if other wrongs do not."[193]

As *Att Gen for Hong Kong v Reid*[194] was a decision of the Privy Council, the question arises as to how far it is binding as a precedent. Must the Court of Appeal follow its own decision in *Lister & Co v Stubbs*[195] even though that decision was disapproved by the Privy Council? The Court of Appeal recently answered that question in the affirmative in *Sinclair Investments (UK) Ltd v Versailles Trade Finance Ltd (In Administration)*.[196] A director made a secret profit of nearly £30 million on the sale of his own shares at the top of the market. He had breached his fiduciary duty by entering into fraudulent dealings to increase the value of his own holding, which was in reality worthless. The question was whether the fiduciary held the profit on constructive trust for the principal (the company) or whether he was personally accountable only, in which case the principal would be in competition with other unsecured creditors.

21–028

The director had not acquired the shares with company funds or money deriving from company funds, nor did he even acquire them as an indirect consequence of his misuse of those funds. Thus the claim was not to funds in respect of which the director owed fiduciary duties to the company, nor to any asset or proceeds of any asset purchased with those funds, nor to the proceeds of any right or opportunity belonging to the company. However, there was a close causal connection between the misuse of company funds and the money the director made on the sale of his shares. The profit derived

---

[190] Lawrence Collins J. in *Daraydan Holdings Ltd v Solland International Ltd* [2005] Ch. 119 considered, however, that insolvency of the fiduciary should make no difference, as there would be no injustice to creditors in their not sharing an asset which the fiduciary should not have had. This view is supported in M Halliwell [2005] Conv. 88 and P Clarke All E.R. Rev 2005, p.271.

[191] Birks, *An Introduction to the Law of Restitution* (revised edn, 1989), p.389; P. Watts (1994) 110 L.Q.R. 178; W. Swadling All E.R. Rev. 1994, 365; A. Jones [1994] Conv. 156; T. Allen (1995) 58 M.L.R. 87.

[192] D. Crilley [1994] 2 R.L.R. 57. See also G. Virgo in Getzler (ed), *Rationalizing Property, Equity and Trusts*, 2003, pp.96–98; R. Calnan [2004] 12 R.L.R. 1 at 21.

[193] P. Birks and W. Swadling All E.R. Rev. 1998 at 415; W. Swadling (1998) 12 T.L.I. 228.

[194] [1994] 1 A.C. 324.

[195] (1890) 45 Ch.D. 1.

[196] [2011] 3 W.L.R. 1153.

from his fiduciary position and its receipt was a plain breach of fiduciary duty. The Court of Appeal considered that an unauthorised secret profit of this kind was to be treated in the same way as a bribe.

Lord Neuberger M.R. examined the cases before *Att Gen for Hong Kong v Reid*.[197] He noted that the report in *Keech v Sandford*[198] was unreasoned and unsatisfactory, but it could be treated as an example of a trustee seizing for his own benefit an opportunity effectively owned by the trust. Amongst the earlier cases was a decision of the House of Lords[199] which was inconsistent with the notion that a fiduciary held a bribe on trust for the principal, but the decision had not been cited in many cases and had been misinterpreted in *Reid*. *Boardman v Phipps*[200] took the matter no further as the precise remedy was not in issue.

His Lordship held that the Court of Appeal should not follow a decision of the Privy Council in preference to its own decisions unless there were domestic authorities which showed that the Court of Appeal decisions were *per incuriam*, or at least of doubtful validity. It should follow its own decisions, leaving the Supreme Court to overrule them if appropriate, although it could follow a contrary Privy Council decision if it was a foregone conclusion that, if the matter were to go on appeal, the Supreme Court would follow the Privy Council decision.[201] Lord Neuberger was "far from satisfied" that the Supreme Court would follow *Reid*, adding that: "In any event it does not seem to me right to follow *Reid*."[202] He gave seven reasons why *Reid* should not be followed. First, there were five decisions of the Court of Appeal spread over 95 years all going the same way, coupled with the reasoning in a House of Lords case. Secondly, much of Lord Templeman's reasoning in *Reid* "seems to me to beg the question, or to assume what it asserts".[203] Thirdly, Lord Templeman's concern that the false fiduciary should not profit by keeping any increase in value of the bribe could be met by ordering an equitable account. Fourthly, *Reid* was unsound because there was a fundamental distinction between a fiduciary enriching himself by depriving the beneficiary of an asset (where the remedy would be proprietary), and enriching himself by doing a wrong to the beneficiary. Fifthly, there was more academic commentary in support of *Lister v Stubbs*[204] than *Reid*. Sixthly, Lord Templeman

---

[197] [1994] 1 A.C. 324.
[198] (1726) Sel. Cas. T. King 61; above, para.21–012.
[199] *Tyrell v Bank of London* (1862) 10 HL Cas. 26.
[200] [1967] 2 A.C. 46.
[201] As in *Abou-Rahma v Abacha* [2007] 1 Lloyd's Rep. 115.
[202] [2011] 3 W.L.R. 1153 at 1174.
[203] [2011] 3 W.L.R. 1153 at 1175.
[204] (1890) 45 Ch. D. 1.

may have given insufficient weight to the potentially unfair consequences to other creditors. Where the fiduciary is insolvent, there is nothing objectionable about proprietary claims if well established, but it is "a reason for not extending the reach of such claims beyond what is established by authority and accords with principle".[205] Seventhly, *Lister* had been followed in other post-*Reid* decisions.[206]

The Court of Appeal concluded that there was a consistent line of authority which established that a beneficiary cannot claim a proprietary interest in an asset or money acquired by the fiduciary in breach of duty unless the asset or money is or has been beneficially owned by the beneficiary or the fiduciary acquired the asset or money by taking advantage of an opportunity or right which was properly that of the beneficiary. The remedy is an equitable account. It was not yet established whether this personal remedy extends to the profit made on an asset purchased by the fiduciary with the bribe or secret commission, but Lord Neuberger considered that the policy question of preventing the false fiduciary from retaining the increase in value should be dealt with by extending the rules on equitable compensation, which were more flexible than the rules on proprietary interests. This would interfere less with the rights of other creditors than extending proprietary interests. It is submitted that this answers the criticisms of *Lister v Stubbs*[207] while providing a sounder analysis of the principles than the decision of the Privy Council in *Att Gen for Hong Kong v Reid*.[208]

Finally, a claimant cannot have an account of profits and also damages for what he would have received had he been able to use the property for the period in question. These remedies are alternative, not cumulative, and the claimant must elect between them at the time of judgment in his favour, by which time it will be clear which remedy is the more advantageous.[209]

---

[205] [2011] 3 W.L.R. 1153 at 1169.

[206] *Reid* was followed in *Daraydan Holdings Ltd v Solland International Ltd* [2005] Ch. 119, but that was before the guidance given in *Re Spectrum Plus Ltd (in liquidation)* [2005] 2 A.C. 680.

[207] (1890) 45 Ch. D. 1; R. Goode (2011) 127 L.Q.R. 493; G. Virgo (2011) 70 C.L.J. 502. A contrary view is taken by D. Hayton (2011) 127 L.Q.R. 487 and (2011) 25 T.L.I. 3, who considers that the ruling "undermines the integrity of the trust concept".

[208] [1994] 1 A.C. 324.

[209] *Tang Man Sit (Personal Representatives) v Capacious Investments Ltd* [1996] 1 A.C. 514 (secret profits from wrongful lettings of houses in breach of trust); P. Birks (1996) 112 L.Q.R. 375; J. Stevens [1996] R.L.R. 117.

CHAPTER 22

VARIATION OF TRUSTS

1. THE BACKGROUND

A TRUSTEE must administer the trust according to its terms. Any **22–001** deviation is a breach of trust for which the trustee will be personally liable.[1] However, any adult beneficiary who does not lack capacity may deal with his equitable interest under the trust in any way he wishes; and may consent to the trustee dealing with the trust funds in a way which affects his interest. Further, adult beneficiaries who together are absolutely entitled to the trust property may terminate the trust and demand that the fund be handed over to them[2]; but not if any interests are outstanding,[3] nor if the trustees have no power to transfer the property.[4]

[1] Above, para.17–001; below, Ch.23.
[2] *Saunders v Vautier* (1841) Cr. & Ph. 240; *Re Smith* [1928] Ch. 915; *Re Nelson* [1928] Ch. 920n; *Re Becket's Settlement* [1940] Ch. 279. See also Trusts of Land and Appointment of Trustees Act 1996 s.6(2); above, para.20–002.
[3] *Berry v Green* [1938] A.C. 575; *Re Robb* [1953] Ch. 459; *Re Wragg* [1959] 1 W.L.R. 922; *Law Debenture Trust Corp plc v Elektrim Finance NV* [2007] 1 P. & C.R. DG 6 (trustee's lien).
[4] *Don King Productions Inc v Warren* [2000] Ch. 291 (trust of benefit of non-assignable contracts). The point was not discussed on appeal.

They may wish to do this for various reasons. In *Saunders v Vautier*,[5] the beneficiary wished to terminate an accumulation which was to continue until he reached 25; he was able to claim the fund at 21 (then the age of majority). If property is given to A for life and then to B, and both A and B are adult, they may each wish to have capital immediately available, and may agree to partition the fund. This was often done in order to reduce tax liability and especially liability for inheritance tax on the death of A. Inheritance tax, an outline of which was given in Ch.9, is chargeable on transfers on or within seven years before death. It is also chargeable on certain lifetime transfers even if the transferor survives for seven years, for example the creation of most trusts, although in such a case the rate is lower.[6] In the case of a life interest trust, the advantage of partitioning the fund between life tenant and remainderman before the Finance Act 2006 was that, provided the life tenant survived for seven years (which could be covered by insurance), no tax would be payable on the partition, whereas the whole capital was taxable if the life interest terminated on death.[7] The inheritance tax treatment of life interest trusts created on or after March 22, 2006 was changed by the Finance Act 2006.[8] The Act phased out the rule that life tenants were treated for inheritance tax purposes as owing the capital.

It may be advantageous in terms of income tax liability to share out the entitlement to income. It appears that a variation is not a disposal for capital gains tax purposes.[9] As far as inheritance tax is concerned, trustees of a discretionary trust could formerly improve the tax position of the settlement by converting it to a trust with an interest in possession or to an accumulation and maintenance settlement, but the Finance Act 2006 removed the advantages of doing this.[10] The tax saving aspect of the matter is emphasised here because it was the motive force in the passing of the Variation of Trusts Act 1958, and in the variations which have been made under it. "Nearly every variation," said Lord Denning M.R., "that has come before the court has tax-avoidance for its principal object."[11]

---

[5] (1841) Cr. & Ph. 240; P. Matthews (2006) 122 L.Q.R. 266. For the meaning of "absolutely entitled" in a tax context, see *Figg v Clarke (Inspector of Taxes)* [1997] 1 W.L.R. 603 (class consisting of children of X not absolutely entitled for capital gains tax purposes until death of X, although X incapable of fathering more children); *Thorpe v Commissioners for HM Revenue and Customs* [2009] W.T.L.R. 1269.

[6] Inheritance Tax Act 1984 s.7.

[7] FA (No.2) 1987 s.96. See *Gibbon v Mitchell* [1990] 1 W.L.R. 1304.

[8] Above, para.9–019.

[9] *Wyndham v Egremont* [2009] W.T.L.R. 1473. There would be a disposal if the effect of the variation is to revoke the original settlement and to create a new one, but not if the original settlement continues as varied.

[10] Above, paras 9–019, 9–024.

[11] In *Re Weston's Settlements* [1969] 1 Ch. 234 at 245.

Variations have, of course, been made for other purposes, as will be seen.

One particular tax exemption should be noted. Where, not more **22–002** than two years after a death of a person, testate or intestate, the disposition of his property taking effect upon his death is varied by an instrument in writing, such a variation is not a transfer of value for inheritance tax purposes,[12] nor a disposal for capital gains tax purposes,[13] and the variation takes effect as if made by the deceased. These provisions used to be of great help where a wealthy testator wasted his nil-rate band by leaving everything to his wife.[14] They clearly apply to an agreed variation by adult beneficiaries and to a variation under the Variation of Trusts Act 1958. A similar principle applies to an order under the Family Provision legislation.[15]

It should be added that the trust instrument may give the trustees a power to amend the trust. Such a power must be exercised for the purpose for which it was granted.[16] It has been said (in the context of a commercial trust) that, although the power must not be exercised beyond the reasonable contemplation of the parties, it would be going too far to say that such a power may never be exercised to alter rights or to bring a new class of property within the scope of the trust.[17]

2. Variations which Need the Approval of the Court[18]

We have seen that children and persons lacking mental capacity are **22–003** not able to deal with their property. If a situation arose where variations needed to be made to a trust in the interests of such persons, nothing could be done which involved any negotiation with or compromise by the persons under disability, without the approval of the court. The person under disability could be benefited at the expense of the other parties. The life tenant may be willing to agree to an advancement by the trustees,[19] or to surrender his life interest. But if the life tenant wanted something in return from the person under disability, there was no way in which he could negotiate it.

Yet, especially in the tax context, it was in the interest of the remaindermen that the variation should be made. Adult remaindermen could agree to a variation; it was hard for children, persons

---

[12] Inheritance Tax Act 1984 ss.17, 142, as amended by FA 2002 s.120.

[13] Taxation of Chargeable Gains Act 1992 s.62(6).

[14] Unused nil-rate bands may now be transferred to the spouse's estate; above, para.9–009.

[15] Inheritance Tax Act 1984 s.146.

[16] *Hole v Garnsey* [1930] A.C. 472.

[17] *Society of Lloyd's v Robinson* [1999] 1 W.L.R. 756. See also Pensions Act 1995 ss.67–71.

[18] O. Marshall (1954) 17 M.L.R. 420; Harris, *Variation of Trusts*.

[19] *Pilkington v IRC* [1964] A.C. 612, above, para.20–039.

under a disability and unborn persons to be denied advantages which competent adults could obtain for themselves. The court, however, has no inherent jurisdiction to vary a trust in favour of children and unborn persons.[20] But there are cases where the court can intervene, and these have been substantially increased by several statutes.

A. Inherent Jurisdiction

22–004　　**i. Salvage and Emergency.** A court has inherent power in the case of absolute necessity to sanction the mortgage of a child's property in order to protect the property which he retains. The jurisdiction is very narrow and is usual where expenditure is necessary to save buildings from collapse.[21] An extension of this jurisdiction allows the court in an emergency, not foreseen or anticipated by the settlor, to authorise the trustees to perform certain acts which are beyond the powers given to them in the trust instrument, where this is in the best interests of the trust estate and where the consent of all the beneficiaries cannot be obtained because they are not in existence or are under a disability.

In *Re New*,[22] the court approved a scheme of capital reconstruction of a company, splitting the shares into different and smaller denominations, and authorised the trustees to take the new shares, subject to an undertaking to apply for further authorisation to retain the shares after one year. This decision was said in *Re Tollemache*[23] to be the "high water-mark" of the emergency jurisdiction. Kekewich J. and the Court of Appeal refused to sanction a widening of the trustees' investment powers merely because this would be for the advantage of the beneficiaries. There was no emergency. It is clear that the jurisdiction applies to administrative matters only, and does not cover schemes for the variation of beneficial interests.

22–005　　**ii. Compromise.**[24] Until the decision of the House of Lords in *Chapman v Chapman*[25] in 1954, the courts had accepted a wide definition of the word "compromise" as the basis of a useful jurisdiction to approve a variation from the terms of a trust although there was no dispute between the parties in any real sense of the term. The cases were more akin to bargains or exchanges approved by the court as being fair to children or remaindermen, than to

---

[20] *Chapman v Chapman* [1954] A.C. 429. See *CD v O* [2004] W.T.L.R. 751, discussing limited exceptions.

[21] *Re Jackson* (1882) 21 Ch.D. 786; *Conway v Fenton* (1888) 40 Ch.D. 512; *Re Montagu* [1897] 2 Ch. 8 at 11, per Lopes L.J.

[22] [1901] 2 Ch. 534. See also *Grender v Dresden* [2009] W.T.L.R. 379.

[23] [1903] 1 Ch. 457, affirmed at 955.

[24] O. Marshall (1954) 17 M.L.R. 427.

[25] [1954] A.C. 429.

compromised litigation. There was a question whether the jurisdiction effected a variation of beneficial interests as distinct from varying the property subject to the trusts,[26] and the jurisdiction did not extend to the redrafting of a settlement as such—there had to be some element of composition of rights.[27] But this distinction was of course paper-thin. Denning L.J., the minority judge in the Court of Appeal in the *Chapman* case, would have got round the difficulty by accepting for the courts a general jurisdiction to vary trusts on behalf of those unascertained or under disability, but the House of Lords preferred the other solution—that of limiting the jurisdiction to sanction compromises to cases where there was a genuine dispute. Nor could matters that did not genuinely contain an element of dispute be made to look as if they did.[28] Where there is a genuine dispute, the court of course has power to sanction a compromise, even if the compromise solution contains tax-saving advantages for the beneficiaries.

In *Allen v Distillers Co (Biochemicals) Ltd*[29] the question was whether the court, in approving a settlement of the action of the child victims of the thalidomide drug, had jurisdiction to postpone the vesting of the capital in the children to an age greater than 18. Eveleigh J. held that the court had no inherent jurisdiction to order a postponement; a beneficiary with a vested interest under a trust was entitled to demand possession on majority.[30] Nor was there a trust to which the Variation of Trusts Act 1958 applied; the payment out to trustees of sums paid into court did not give rise to the kind of trust contemplated by that Act. However, it was found that the terms of the settlement of the action were wide enough to authorise a postponement of payment.

An attempt to invoke the court's compromise jurisdiction occurred in *Mason v Farbrother*,[31] where trustees of a pension fund set up in 1929 for Co-operative Society employees had power to invest principally in the society itself and otherwise in authorised trustee securities. By 1982, as a result of inflation, the fund had increased to £127 million, and the trustees, who were anxious to have the wide powers of investment appropriate for modern pension funds, applied to the court for approval of an investment clause giving wider powers than those of the Trustee Investments Act 1961, which at that time governed trustee investments. The trustees were uncertain as to the proper construction of the original investment clause, one view

22–006

---

[26] *Re Downshire Settled Estates* [1953] Ch. 218.
[27] *Re Chapman's ST* [1953] Ch. 218.
[28] *Re Powell-Cotton's Resettlement* [1956] 1 W.L.R. 23. Nor should the trustees, in their application to court for the exercise of the compromise jurisdiction, insert an unrelated claim for increased remuneration; *Re Barbour's Settlement Trusts* [1974] 1 W.L.R. 1198.
[29] [1974] Q.B. 384.
[30] *Saunders v Vautier* (1841) 4 Beav. 115; above, para.22–001.
[31] [1983] 2 All E.R. 1078; P Clarke All E.R. Rev. 1984 at 308.

being that the whole fund should be invested in the society, and the
other that the whole should be invested under the 1961 Act. This
was sufficient to give the court jurisdiction, as genuine points of
difference existed. It was not necessary that there should be a contested dispute. While a compromise need not be something between
the two views, it was doubtful whether the court could substitute an
entirely new investment clause. Thus the variation was not permitted under the court's jurisdiction to approve a compromise. (It was,
however, authorised by s.57 of the Trustee Act 1925).[32]

B. Statutory Provisions (other than Variation of Trusts Act 1958)

22–007   ### i. Trustee Act 1925 Section 57(1).

"Where in the management or administration of any property
vested in trustees, any sale, lease, mortgage, surrender, release, or
other disposition, or any purchase, investment, acquisition, expenditure, or other transaction, is in the opinion of the court
expedient, but the same cannot be effected by reason of the absence of any power for that purpose vested in the trustees by the
trust instrument, if any, or by law, the court may by order confer
upon the trustees ... the necessary power ... on such terms ... as
the court may think fit ... "

This subsection overlaps the "emergency" jurisdiction discussed
above, and widens it by making the statutory jurisdiction available
in cases of expediency rather than emergency. It operates as if its
provisions were read into every settlement.[33] It is clear from the
opening words of the section that it is only available in questions
arising in the *management* or *administration* of property; it is not
therefore available for the purpose of remoulding beneficial interests
or for tax saving generally.[34] It is available, however, if the impact
of the proposal on the beneficial interests is only incidental.[35]

Applications are usually heard in private, and it is not possible to
learn from reported cases the full scope of the operation of the
subsection. It has however been effectively used to authorise the
sale of land where necessary consents had been refused[36]; to authorise borrowing and mortgaging[37]; and to authorise the purchase of a

---

[32] Below.
[33] *Re Mair* [1935] Ch. 562; see also *Re Salting* [1932] 2 Ch. 57.
[34] *Re Downshire SE* [1953] Ch. 218; cf. *Re Forster's Settlement* [1954] 3 All E.R. 714.
[35] *Southgate v Sutton* [2011] W.T.L.R. 1235 (partition authorised).
[36] *Re Beale's ST* [1932] 2 Ch. 15.
[37] *Page v West* [2010] W.T.L.R. 1811.

residence for the tenant for life,[38] the sale of a reversionary interest which under the terms of the trust instrument was not to be sold until it fell into possession,[39] and wider investment powers.[40] It has been held that s.57 should be used in preference to the Variation of Trusts Act 1958 where wider investment powers are sought, provided the beneficial interests are not affected.[41]

ii. Settled Land Act 1925 Section 64(1). 22–008

"Any transaction affecting or concerning the settled land, or any part thereof, or any other land ... which in the opinion of the court would be for the benefit of the settled land, or any part thereof, or the persons interested under the settlement, may, under an order of the court, be effected by a tenant for life, if it is one which could have been validly effected by an absolute owner."[42]

It will be seen that this subsection is wider than Trustee Act, s.57(1). "Transaction" is widely defined[43]; and there is no limitation restricting the court's powers to cases of management and administration.[44] The subsection enables the court to alter beneficial interests in such a way as to reduce tax liability[45] and was the most effective vehicle for this purpose before 1958. It applies however only to cases of settled land, and not to the ordinary case of a personalty settlement. In *Hambro v Duke of Marlborough*[46] the Duke and the trustees considered that the second defendant, the Marquess of Blandford, who was tenant in tail in remainder, would be incapable of managing the Blenheim estate on the death of the Duke because of his "unbusinesslike habits" and lack of responsibility. They proposed a scheme whereby the estate would be conveyed to trustees of a new trust, to pay the income to the Duke for life, and then to hold on protective trusts for the second defendant for life, thereafter on the trusts of the existing settlement. This was

---

[38] *Re Power* [1947] Ch. 572; (1947) 91 S.J. 541.

[39] *Re Cockerell's ST* [1956] Ch. 372.

[40] *Re Shipwrecked Fishermen and Mariners' Royal Benevolent Society* [1959] Ch. 220; cf. *Re Powell-Cotton's Resettlement* [1956] 1 W.L.R. 23; *Mason v Farbrother* [1983] 2 All E.R. 1078.

[41] *Anker-Petersen v Anker-Petersen* (1998) 12 T.L.I. 166 (decided 1991).

[42] Settlements of land cannot be created after the Trusts of Land and Appointment of Trustees Act 1996.

[43] SLA 1925 s.64(2). See *Raikes v Lygon* [1988] 1 W.L.R. 281; *Hambro v Duke of Marlborough* [1994] Ch. 158.

[44] It has been used for such purposes; *Re White-Popham's SE* [1936] Ch. 725; *Re Scarisbrick's Re-Settlement Estates* [1944] Ch. 229.

[45] *Re Downshire SE* [1953] Ch. 218; *Raikes v Lygon* [1988] 1 W.L.R. 281.

[46] Above, fn.43; E. Cooke [1994] Conv. 492.

held to be a "transaction" within s.64, which could vary the beneficial interests even where an ascertained adult beneficiary did not consent.[47]

22–009   **iii. Trustee Act 1925 Section 53.**[48] Under s.53 the court is given power to authorise certain dealings with a child's property "with a view to the application of the capital or income thereof for the maintenance, education, or benefit of the infant." As with s.57, the section overlaps and extends the inherent power to make provision for the maintenance of children. The word "benefit" has been widely construed, and the court has authorised transactions whose object was the reduction of estate duty for the child's benefit.[49] Thus, entails have been barred in order to exclude the interests of large numbers of remote beneficiaries with a view to raising money for the child's benefit[50] or to simplifying an application to the court under the Variation of Trusts Act 1958[51]; and reversionary interests have been sold to the tenant for life.[52] However, the proceeds of sale should be resettled; this will be an "application" for the child's benefit[53]; while an outright payment to him of the proceeds of sale will not be.[54]

22–010   **iv. Matrimonial Causes Act 1973.** The court has wide power to make orders affecting the property of parties to matrimonial proceedings. It may order capital provision to be made, by cash payment, or property transfer, or by the making of a settlement for the benefit of the other spouse and the children of the family.[55] It may also effect the variation of ante-nuptial or post-nuptial settlements,[56] and the variation of orders for settlements made under the Act.[57]

The jurisdiction to vary a "post-nuptial settlement" under s.24 of the 1973 Act enabled the provision of a pension for a wife on

---

[47] This was a preliminary issue. The scheme was subsequently approved; *The Times*, July 23, 1994.

[48] O. Marshall (1957) 21 Conv.(N.S.) 448.

[49] *Re Meux* [1958] Ch. 154.

[50] *Re Gower's Settlement* [1934] Ch. 365.

[51] *Re Bristol's SE* [1964] 3 All E.R. 939; *Re Lansdowne's WT* [1967] Ch. 603.

[52] *Re Meux*, above, fn.49, cf. *Re Heyworth's Contingent Reversionary Interest* [1956] Ch. 364.

[53] *Re Meux*, above, fn.49.

[54] *Re Heyworth's Contingent Reversionary Interest*, above, fn.52; criticised O. Marshall (1957) 21 Conv.(N.S.) 448 at 450–454.

[55] Matrimonial Causes Act 1973 ss.23 and 24. See also s.25, laying down the principles to be observed by the court in exercising its jurisdiction under ss.23, 24.

[56] s.24(1)(c), (d); M Bennett (2007) 37 Fam. Law 916. See *E v E* [1990] 2 F.L.R. 233; *C v C (Ancillary Relief: Nuptial Settlement)* [2005] Fam. 250; *N v N and F Trust* [2006] 1 F.L.R. 856. On the variation of Jersey trusts under the 1973 Act, see *Re B Trust* [2007] W.T.L.R. 1361; P. Matthews (2008) 22 T.L.I. 63; Trusts (Amendment No.4) (Jersey) Law 2006 art.9(4).

[57] s.31(2)(e). Further details must be obtained from the Family Law books.

divorce in *Brooks v Brooks*.[58] A company pension scheme of which the husband was the sole member provided that on retirement he could direct that part of his benefit should be used to make provision for his wife after his death, and that a lump sum would be payable at the discretion of the trustee to a class including the wife if he were to die prematurely. These factors made it a "marriage settlement", which had a wide meaning. The scheme could be varied so far as it constituted a settlement made by the husband. The trust was varied by directing that an immediate annuity and a deferred pension were to be provided in priority to and, if necessary, in diminution of the husband's pension. Had there been any other scheme members, the court would not have ordered a variation to their detriment, nor would it sanction a variation with adverse tax consequences.

This decision has been restricted by later legislation, and in any event it did not solve the problem of pension-splitting on divorce, which is dealt with by other legislation.[59]

v. Mental Capacity Act 2005. Mental Capacity Act 2005,   **22–011** s.18(1)(h), re-enacting earlier legislation, gives to the Court of Protection a power to make a settlement of the property of a person who lacks capacity; and also, if the settlement contains a provision for variation or revocation, or if any material fact was not disclosed when the settlement was made, or where there has been any substantial change in circumstances, to vary the settlement in such manner as the judge thinks fit.[60]

C. Variation of Trusts Act 1958[61]

The Variation of Trusts Act 1958 gives to the court a "very wide   **22–012** and, indeed, revolutionary discretion"[62] to approve on behalf of four groups of persons[63]:

> "[A]ny arrangement . . . varying or revoking all or any of the trusts, or enlarging the powers of the trustees of managing or administering any of the property subject to the trusts."[64]

---

[58] [1996] 1 A.C. 375; M. Rae (1995) 145 N.L.J. 1009; M. Thomas [1997] Conv. 52.

[59] Welfare Reform and Pensions Act 1999. See also Pensions Act 1995, above, para.16–033 (earmarking).

[60] MCA 2005 Sch.2, para.6.

[61] Harris: *Variation of Trusts*, Ch 3; M. Mowbray (1958) 22 Conv.(N.S.) 373; D. Evans (1963) 27 Conv.(N.S.) 6; A. Maclean (1965) 43 Can.B.R. 181. The jurisdiction given by the Act is independent of TA 1925 s.57, and SLA 1925 s.64, above. There may be technical reasons, e.g. difficulties as to representative parties, why it is not possible to invoke the 1958 Act. See *Mason v Farbrother* [1983] 2 All E.R. 1078.

[62] per Evershed M.R. in *Re Steed's WT* [1960] Ch. 407 at 420–421.

[63] Below para.22–013.

[64] VTA 1958 s.1(1). But see *Allen v Distillers Co (Biochemicals) Ltd* [1974] Q.B. 384, above, para.22–005.

On its terms, this provision covers not only administrative matters, but also variations in the beneficial interests; but the court may only approve such an arrangement if it would be for the benefit of the person on whose behalf the approval is given.[65] The Act applies to the statutory trusts arising on intestacy[66] and to property in the course of administration by a personal representative.[67]

The courts have approved a wide variety of variations, and, in addition to approving changes in the beneficial interests, have inserted a power of advancement,[68] terminated an accumulation,[69] inserted an accumulation period[70] and have widened the investment powers of trustees.[71] Investment clauses are rarely the subject of an application, for it became established that only in exceptional circumstances should a court give its approval to wider investment powers than those given to trustees in the Trustee Investments Act 1961.[72] The Act of 1961, however, became outdated, and the courts were prepared to sanction an extension of investment powers.[73] It was held that s.57 of the Trustee Act 1925 was more appropriate than the 1958 Act where wider investment powers were sought, provided the beneficial interests were not affected.[74] Under s.57 the court would consider the interests of the beneficiaries collectively in income and capital but would not need to consent on behalf of the various categories of beneficiaries as required by the 1958 Act, nor would it require the consent of adult beneficiaries. Such applications are less likely to be made now that investment powers have been widened by the Trustee Act 2000.

It is of course in connection with schemes which vary beneficial interests for tax saving purposes that the 1958 Act has been mainly applied.

---

[65] Except for persons in para.(d), below.

[66] *S v TI* [2006] W.T.L.R. 1461 (variation to prevent child of intestate father being disinherited by an adoption order).

[67] *Re Bernstein* [2010] W.T.L.R. 559; S. Evans [2011] Conv. 151.

[68] *Re Lister's WT* [1962] 1 W.L.R. 1441. See also *D (A Child) v O* [2004] 3 All E.R. 780 (extension of power of advancement).

[69] *Re Tinker's Settlement* [1960] 1 W.L.R. 1011.

[70] *Re Lansdowne's WT* [1967] Ch. 603; *Re Holt's Settlement* [1961] Ch. 100.

[71] *Re Coates' Trusts* [1959] 1 W.L.R. 375; *Re Burney's ST* [1961] 1 W.L.R. 545.

[72] *Re Kolb's WT* [1962] Ch. 531; *Re Cooper's Settlement* [1962] Ch. 826; *Re Clarke's WT* [1961] 1 W.L.R. 1471. See also *Re Rank's ST* [1979] 1 W.L.R. 1242, where an arrangement included a power of appointment in terms wide enough to permit the donee to give wider powers of investment to the trustees for the benefit of the appointees.

[73] In *Mason v Farbrother* [1983] 2 All E.R. 1078, above, para.18–023, concerning TA 1925 s.57, the effect of inflation and the fact that the trust was in the nature of a public fund were regarded as special circumstances; cf. *Trustees of the British Museum v Att Gen* [1984] 1 W.L.R. 418, H. Norman [1984] Conv. 373, where Megarry V.C. preferred the view that the *Re Kolb* principle, above, had gone. This was discussed in Ch.18. See also *Steel v Wellcome Custodian Trustees Ltd* [1988] 1 W.L.R. 167; B. Dale [1988] Conv. 380.

[74] *Anker-Petersen v Anker-Petersen* (1998) 12 T.L.I. 166 (decided 1991).

i. Persons on whose Behalf Approval may be Given. The prin- 22–013
ciple is that the court is not asked to approve on behalf of ascertainable adults who can consent for themselves. The classes (as set out
in Variation of Trusts Act 1958 s.1) are:

"(a) any person having, directly or indirectly, an interest,
whether vested or contingent, under the trusts who by reason of
infancy or other incapacity is incapable of assenting, or

(b) any person (whether ascertained or not) who may become
entitled, directly or indirectly, to an interest under the trusts as
being at a future date or on the happening of a future event a
person of any specified description or a member of any specified
class of persons, so however that this paragraph shall not include
any person[75] who would be of that description, or a member of
that class, as the case may be, if the said date had fallen or the said
event had happened at the date of the application to the
court, or

(c) any person unborn, or

(d) any person in respect of any discretionary interest of his
under protective trusts where the interest of the principal beneficiary has not failed or determined."[76]

Paragraph (b) may well of course include adults; but because the
class is ascertainable only at a future time, its members cannot yet
be known. Under the proviso, however, those who would qualify if
the future event happened at the date of the application to the court
must themselves consent. If however they are children, they come
within para.(a).

In *Re Suffert*,[77] income was given under protective trusts to an
unmarried woman for life, and, in the event of her having no
issue, and subject to a general testamentary power, in trust for
those who would become entitled under her intestacy. She had
three adult cousins, who would be entitled in equal shares to her
estate if she had died at the date of the application to the court.
One cousin was made a party, and consented, but the others were
not. In asking the court to approve the arrangement, it was argued
that the court should approve on behalf of those who would be
entitled on intestacy, as they came within para.(b). Buckley J.
however held that the proviso applied and that he could not approve on behalf of the two cousins. Otherwise he approved the
arrangement.

---

[75] This presumably means any ascertained person; Harris, *Variation of Trusts*, pp.39–40.
[76] See *Gibbon v Mitchell* [1990] 1 W.L.R. 1304.
[77] [1961] Ch. 1.

22–014   The meaning of the words "may become entitled" in para.(b) were examined in *Knocker v Youle*.[78]

> Property was held on trust for the settlor's daughter for life under a settlement in which her cousins had very remote contingent interests. It was not practicable to get the approval of the cousins to the proposed variation because they were very numerous, and some were in Australia.[79] Approval was therefore sought on their behalf under s.(1)(1)(b). The question was whether para.(b) included persons with an existing contingent interest, however remote. Warner J. held that it did not. A person having a contingent interest was not a person who "may become entitled" to an interest. Paragraph (b) covered the case of a person who had a mere *spes* (an expectation) such as the prospective next of kin of a living person in *Re Suffert*,[80] or a potential future spouse.[81] The adult cousins were in any event excluded by the proviso to para.(b).

22–015   **ii. Parties.** In general, the settlor, if living,[82] and all beneficiaries under the trusts, both adults and children, should be made parties. The children, unless their interests coincide with those of adult beneficiaries who consent, should be separately represented,[83] and a litigation friend must give full consideration to the way in which the proposed variation will affect the children's interests.[84] In the case of a class, those who are members of the class at the date of the application should be included[85]; but it is not necessary to join persons who may become members later[86]; nor persons who may become interested under discretionary trusts[87]; nor those who are possible objects of a power.[88] Persons unborn cannot of course be made parties, but their interests must be represented.[89] Where a

[78] [1986] 1 W.L.R. 934; criticised J. Riddall [1987] Conv. 144, also discussing persons who are objects of mere powers and discretionary trusts.

[79] The Act does not deal with the problem of the beneficiary who must consent on his own behalf but who is untraceable. In such a case a *Benjamin* order (above, para.18–027) could be used. See P. Luxton (1986) 136 N.L.J. 1057.

[80] Above, fn.77; *Re Moncrieff's ST* [1962] 1 W.L.R. 1344. But see J. Riddall [1987] Conv. 144 at p.146 for the view that such persons do have a contingent interest in the *settlement*, although not, of course, in the estate of their living relative.

[81] See *Re Clitheroe's ST* [1959] 1 W.L.R. 1159; *Re Lister's WT* [1962] 1 W.L.R. 1441.

[82] CPR, 1998 Pt 64.

[83] *Re Whigham's ST* [1971] 1 W.L.R. 831.

[84] *Re Whittall* [1973] 1 W.L.R. 1027. See CPR 1998 Pt 21.

[85] *Re Suffert's Settlement* [1961] Ch. 1.

[86] *Re Moncrieff's ST* [1962] 1 W.L.R. 1344.

[87] *Re Munro's ST* [1963] 1 W.L.R. 145.

[88] *Re Christie-Miller's Marriage Settlement* [1961] 1 W.L.R. 462; *Practice Direction* [1976] 1 W.L.R. 884.

[89] The court must consider the position of any individual who may be born and become a beneficiary, not merely the class of unborn beneficiaries as a whole; *Re Cohen's ST* [1965] 1 W.L.R. 1229.

person who lacks capacity is involved the Court of Protection decides whether the proposed variation would be for his benefit.[90]

iii. Applicants. The application should be made by a benefici-   **22–016**
ary, usually the person currently receiving the income. But the settlor may do so.[91] It is not usually satisfactory for the trustees to make the application because there might be an undesirable conflict of interest between their interest as an applicant, and as guardian of some of the beneficial interests for which they are responsible.[92] They may apply if no-one else will do so, and the variation is in the interests of the beneficiaries.[93]

iv. Foreign Trusts. The court will not approve an agreement   **22–017**
which provides for a settlement under the law of a foreign jurisdiction if the beneficiaries remain resident and domiciled in England; nor, as in *Re Weston's Settlement*,[94] where the connection with Jersey, the foreign jurisdiction, was recent and tenuous, and where the court doubted whether the living beneficiaries really intended to make Jersey their permanent home. Trusts have, however, been "exported" in favour of a settlement with foreign trustees and governed by foreign law where the beneficiaries have emigrated permanently to the foreign country[95]; and approval has been given for the transfer of funds from a trust governed by English law to one governed by the law of Guernsey where the primary beneficiaries were resident and domiciled in France and the remainderman in Indonesia.[96] The advantages of trust exporting have been much reduced since the introduction of inheritance tax.[97]

It should be added that the appointment of a foreign trustee may be made in a proper case without the intervention of the court.[98]

Where the question is not one of exporting a trust to another jurisdiction but of varying a foreign trust, such a variation is governed by the applicable law of the trust.[99] However, where the

[90] VTA 1958 s.1(3), as amended by the Mental Capacity Act 2005.
[91] *Re Clitheroe's ST* [1959] 1 W.L.R. 1159.
[92] *Re Druce's ST* [1962] 1 W.L.R. 363.
[93] [1962] 1 W.L.R. 363 at 370.
[94] [1969] 1 Ch. 223.
[95] *Re Seal's Marriage Settlement* [1961] Ch. 574 (Canada); *Re Windeatt's WT* [1969] 1 W.L.R. 692 (Jersey); see also *Re Whitehead's WT* [1971] 1 W.L.R. 833.
[96] *Re Chamberlain* (unreported) discussed in J Morcom (1976) 126 N.L.J. 1034; T Watkin (1976) 40 Conv.(N.S.) 295.
[97] See IHTA 1984, ss.48(3), 201(1)(d), 267.
[98] *Re Whitehead's WT*, above, fn.95. But application will often be made to the court, and a variation will be necessary if the form of the trust needs to be altered in order to comply with the foreign law, if there is no power in the trust instrument to do this. See Parker and Mellows, *The Modern Law of Trusts*, 9th edn, pp.620–626; R. Bramwell (1990/91) 1 *The Offshore Tax Planning Review*, p.1, discussing *Richard v The Hon, AB Mackay*, unreported, 1987, above, para.17–032.
[99] Recognition of Trusts Act 1987 Sch., art.8. The applicable law is determined by arts 6, 7; above, para.1–052.

English court has jurisdiction to deal with an application for ancillary relief following divorce, it has jurisdiction to vary a nuptial settlement by way of ancillary relief even though the applicable law of the settlement is not English law.[100]

22–018   **v. Effect of Approval by the Court.** It appears that the arrangement is effective from the time of the approval by the court. The reasons why this is so are not clear; and the result may be due to the practice established by *Re Viscount Hambledon's Will Trusts*.[101] Several, and in some cases conflicting, accounts have been given of the effect of approval by the court.

In *Re Joseph's Will Trusts*[102] Vaisey J. included in his order approving the variation a direction that the variation should be carried into effect. In *Re Viscount Hambleden's Will Trusts*,[103] Wynn-Parry J. thought that he had no jurisdiction to make such a direction. Nor was it required. "I hold that the effect of my approval is effective for all purposes to vary the trusts."[104] In *Re Holt's Settlement*,[105] Megarry J. was unconvinced. Before him it was argued that the Act gives the court power to approve only on behalf of the persons mentioned in s.1(1); and the consent of the adults to a change in their beneficial interests was a "disposition", and ineffective unless in writing, as required by s.53(1)(c) of the Law of Property Act 1925.[106] Megarry J. was reluctant to disturb what had become a very convenient practice based on *Re Viscount Hambleden*,[107] and searched for a theory to justify it. The suggestion that there was no "disposition" of the interests of the consenting adults, but a "species of estoppel"[108] operating against them was "unattractive". He was satisfied however that it could be explained on the ground that s.53(1)(c) was by necessary implication excluded; or that, where the variation was made for consideration, the consenting adults could be compelled to perform their contract and they held their original interests on constructive trusts, these being unaffected by s.53(1)(c).[109] The view that the variation obtains its effect by reason of the consent of the beneficiaries is supported by dicta in *IRC v*

---

[100] Recognition of Trusts Act 1987 art.15; *C v C (Ancillary Relief: Nuptial Settlement)* [2005] Fam. 250 (wife's claim under s.24(1)(c) of the Matrimonial Causes Act 1973); J. Harris (2005) 121 L.Q.R. 16.

[101] [1960] 1 W.L.R. 82; *Re Holt's Settlement* [1969] 1 Ch. 100 at 113.

[102] [1959] 1 W.L.R. 1019.

[103] [1960] 1 W.L.R. 82.

[104] [1960] 1 W.L.R. 82 at 86.

[105] [1969] 1 Ch. 100; PVB (1968) 84 L.Q.R. 162.

[106] Above, para.3–006; *Grey v IRC* [1960] A.C. 1.

[107] [1960] 1 W.L.R. 82.

[108] [1969] 1 Ch. 100 at 114; *Spens v IRC* [1970] 1 W.L.R. 1173.

[109] LPA 1925 s.53(2); *Oughtred v IRC* [1960] A.C. 206; *Re Holt's Settlement* [1969] 1 Ch. 100 at 115–116.

Holmden,[110] where however the question of s.53(1)(c) did not arise.

The arrangement coupled with the court's order is an "instrument" for the purposes of the Perpetuities and Accumulations Act 1964 s.15(5) and the Perpetuities and Accumulations Act 2009 s.15(1). This means that future interests permitted by the Acts may be provided for in an arrangement.[111] Because the variation does not owe its authority to the settlor, its provisions need not be such that the settlor could have created them.[112] In contrast with powers of appointment and advancement,[113] the perpetuity period does not relate back to the original settlement. A variation which is inconsistent with the continuous existence of a power operates as a release of a power.[114]

vi. Variation or Resettlement. The jurisdiction, as we have seen, is very wide. It is however a jurisdiction to "vary" and not to "resettle".[115] This is a difficult dividing line. In *Re Ball's Settlement*, Megarry J. laid down the general test as follows[116]:   **22–019**

> "If an arrangement changes the whole substratum of the trust, then it may well be that it cannot be regarded merely as varying the trust. But if an arrangement, while leaving the substratum, effectuates the purpose of the trust by other means, it may still be possible to regard that arrangement as merely varying the original trusts, even though the means employed are wholly different and even though the form is completely changed."

vii. Fraud on a Power. Nor will the court approve a variation which involves a fraud on a power, as for example where property is held on trust for A for life and to such of A's children as he shall appoint, and A, in order to avoid tax liability on his death, appoints in favour of his living children, and does so with a view to partitioning the fund, with the court's approval, between his children and himself. Such an appointment has been held to be fraudulent and   **22–020**

---

[110] [1968] A.C. 685; cf. TA 1925 s.57; *Re Mair* [1935] Ch. 562.

[111] *Re Lansdowne's WT* [1967] Ch. 603; *Re Holt's Settlement*, above, fn.109.

[112] *Re Holt's Settlement*, above, fn.109. See also *Wyndham v Egremont* [2009] W.T.L.R. 1437.

[113] *Pilkington v IRC* [1964] A.C. 612, above, para.20–039.

[114] *Re Christie-Miller's Marriage Settlement* [1961] 1 W.L.R. 462; *Re Courtauld's Settlement* [1965] 1 W.L.R. 1385; *Re Ball's ST* [1968] 1 W.L.R. 899; above, para.6–031.

[115] *Re T's ST* [1964] Ch. 158; *Re Ball's ST* [1968] 1 W.L.R. 899; criticised PVB (1968) 84 L.Q.R. 458; *Re Holt's Settlement* [1969] 1 Ch. 100 at 117; *Allen v Distillers Co (Biochemicals) Ltd* [1974] Q.B. 384; *Wyndham v Egremont* [2009] W.T.L.R. 1473.

[116] [1968] 1 W.L.R. 899 at 905.

void on the ground that it was made so that the appointor may obtain a benefit for himself under the variation.[117]

22–021   **viii. The Settlor's Intention.** In giving approval, the court must be satisfied about the arrangement as a whole.[118] One relevant factor is whether or not the arrangement is consistent with the general plan of the settlor or testator.

> In *Re Steed's Will Trusts*[119] a testator had left property to a faithful housekeeper for her life on protective trusts and after her death as she should appoint, the trustee having power to pay capital moneys to her as they should think fit. The property included a farm which was let to the housekeeper's brother. The terms of the will were designed to give the maximum benefit in the property to the housekeeper, without giving her an absolute interest, because of the danger which the testator "thought was real, of being, to use a common phrase, sponged upon by one of her brothers."[120]
>
> The trustees decided to sell the farm. The housekeeper started proceedings to stop them, exercised the power of appointment in favour of herself, and applied under the Variation of Trusts Act, s.1, for the elimination of the protective element in her life interest. The result would be that she would become absolutely entitled to the property, because she would then be the life tenant, having appointed to herself the reversion. The only persons who might be prejudiced by such a variation would be those who might benefit under the discretionary trusts which would arise if the protective life interests were forfeited[121]; and under para.(d), the court is not concerned to see that they benefit from a variation. Was there any reason why approval should not be given?

The Court of Appeal refused:

> "It is the *arrangement* which has to be approved not just the limited interest of the person on whose behalf the court's duty is to consider it . . . the court must regard the proposal as a whole, and so regarding it, then ask itself whether in the exercise of its jurisdiction it should approve that proposal on behalf of the per-

---

[117] *Re Robertson's WT* [1960] 1 W.L.R. 1050; *Re Brook's Settlement* [1968] 1 W.L.R. 1661; cf. *Re Wallace's Settlement* [1968] 1 W.L.R. 711.

[118] *Re Burney's ST* [1961] 1 All E.R. 856.

[119] [1960] Ch. 407; *Re Michelham's WT* [1964] Ch. 550.

[120] [1960] Ch. 407 at 415.

[121] Above, para.7–005; assuming that she would not now have children, this was only a prospective husband, described in the case of the "spectral spouse".

son who cannot give a consent . . . it was part of the testator's scheme . . . that this trust should be available for the [claimant] so that she should have proper provision made for her throughout her life, and would not be exposed to the risk that she might, if she had been handed the money, part with it in favour of another individual about whom the testator felt apprehension, which apprehension is plainly shared by the trustees."[122]

The question also arose in *Re Remnant's Settlement Trusts*,[123]   **22–022**
where the proposed variation was the deletion of a forfeiture clause whereby beneficiaries who practised Roman Catholicism or married a Roman Catholic would lose their entitlement. The fact that the variation would defeat the settlor's intention was regarded as a serious matter, but not conclusive. As the forfeiture clause was undesirable in the circumstances of the family (unlike the disputed provision in *Re Steed's Will Trusts*,[124] which was not cited), it was fair and proper to delete it, notwithstanding the settlor's intention.

In *Goulding v James*[125] the clear intention of the testatrix was that her daughter should have only a life interest and that her grandson should not have capital until aged 40 (because she mistrusted her son-in-law and her grandson had not "settled down"). A variation was sought whereby the daughter would have capital and the grandson would become entitled before the age of 40. As the proposed terms substantially increased the financial benefit to unborn beneficiaries, approval was given by the Court of Appeal, even though the proposal was contrary to the intention of the testatrix. Her wishes related only to the adult beneficiaries, and so carried little weight. *Re Steed's Will Trusts*,[126] which laid down no general rule, was distinguishable because there the testator's purpose was evidenced in the will itself, and no benefit needed to be established for the class of beneficiaries on whose behalf consent was sought. In the present case extrinsic evidence of the wishes of the testatrix could not be allowed to outweigh considerations of benefit to the class of unborns, to whom this evidence had no relevance. The role of the court is not to stand in for the settlor but to consent on behalf of the beneficiaries who are unable to consent.

ix. Benefit. It is necessary that the variation should be for the   **22–023**
benefit of the persons in categories (a) or (c) on whose behalf

---

[122] [1960] Ch. 407 at 421–422.
[123] [1970] Ch. 560; below, para.22–027.
[124] Above, fn.119.
[125] [1997] 2 All E.R. 239; criticised P. Luxton (1997) 60 M.L.R. 719.
[126] Above, fn.119.

approval is sought. There is no such requirement of benefit in re-spect of persons under category (d).[127]

22–024   (a) *Financial Benefit.* There is usually no difficulty in showing financial benefit. But evidence must be presented to show that there is an advantage to each person required to be benefited.[128] Variations have commonly been made to save estate duty or inheritance tax,[129] capital gains tax,[130] and income tax.[131] Any saving provides a larger sum for distribution, and remaindermen may also be benefited by the termination of an interest in possession as their interests will be accelerated. As stated above,[132] a partition of the settled fund be-tween tenant for life and remainderman had inheritance tax advan-tages subject to changes made by the Finance Act 2006.[133] Provided the tenant for life survived for seven years, no tax would be payable, whereas the whole capital would be taxable if a life interest termi-nated on death.

22–025   (b) *Moral and Social Benefit.* But benefit is not only financial. The court must also consider the general welfare of the persons on whose behalf approval is sought; this does not necessarily coincide with their financial interest.

In *Re Weston's Settlements*,[134] two settlements had been made in 1964, one in favour of each of the settlor's sons (both young men and one still under age) and their children. The settlor moved to Jersey in 1967, and the sons followed him. The application was for the appointment of new trustees under Trustee Act 1925 s.41,[135] and for the insertion into the settlement of a power for the trustees to discharge the trust of the settlements and to create almost identical Jersey settlements. The object was to take advantage of the favour-able fiscal situation in Jersey. The Court of Appeal refused. The variation would make the beneficiaries richer but would not be for their benefit:

> "The court should not consider merely the financial benefit to the infant and unborn children, but also their educational and social benefit. There are many things in life more worthwhile than

---

[127] VTA 1958 s.1, proviso. See *Re Van Gruisen's WT* [1964] 1 W.L.R. 449.
[128] *Re Clitheroe's ST* [1959] 1 W.L.R. 1159 at 1163.
[129] *Re Druce's ST* [1962] 1 W.L.R. 363; *Gibbon v Mitchell* [1990] 1 W.L.R. 1304.
[130] *Re Sainsbury's Settlement* [1967] 1 W.L.R. 476.
[131] *Re Clitheroe's ST* [1959] 1 W.L.R. 1159.
[132] Above, para.22–001.
[133] Broadly, the inheritance tax rules discussed in the text apply to life interests arising before March 22, 2006 and those arising under a will or intestacy on or after that date; above, paras 9–017, 9–019.
[134] [1969] 1 Ch. 233.
[135] Above, para.17–024.

money. One of these things is to be brought up in this our England, which is still 'the envy of less happier lands.' I do not believe that it is for the benefit of the children to be uprooted from England and transported to another country simply to avoid tax . . . many a child has been ruined by being given too much. The avoidance of tax may be lawful, but it is not yet a virtue. The Court of Chancery should not encourage or support it—it should not give its approval to it—if by so doing it would imperil the true welfare of the children, already born or yet to be born."[136]

Similarly, as has been seen, with the housekeeper who wished to become the absolute owner of a farm which would then have been at the mercy of her brother.[137] In *Re CL*[138] it was held to be for the benefit of a person who lacked capacity to consent to the surrender of a protected life interest and a contingent remainder interest in favour of her daughter. It was what she would have done if she had not lacked capacity. Such persons should not be denied the opportunity of taking proper steps to preserve the family fortune.

(c) *Postponing Vesting.* It may be for the benefit of a child that   **22–026**
the date of vesting of an interest in the capital should be postponed.

In *Re T's Settlement Trusts*,[139] a beneficiary who was irresponsible and immature was entitled to a vested interest on attaining her majority, which she would do a few months after the application. The proposal was that her interest should be varied to become a protected life interest. Wilberforce J. could not regard such protection as a "benefit in its own right"; but he made an order postponing the vesting of the capital until a specified age and providing that the property should be held on protective trusts in the meantime.

(d) *Trouble in the Family.* Where a trust treats members of the   **22–027**
family unequally, it may be for everyone's benefit, even for those who surrender a claim to property as a result, to vary the trust so as to treat each of them equally. Russell J. thought not in *Re Tinker's Settlement*,[140] where, owing to the draftsman's oversight, the settlement provided that the share of the settlor's son should accrue to his

---

[136] [1969] 1 Ch. 233 at 245.
[137] *Re Steed's WT* [1960] Ch. 407; above, para.22–021.
[138] [1969] 1 Ch. 587.
[139] [1964] Ch. 158; *Re Holt's Settlement* [1969] 1 Ch. 100; *Re RGST Settlement* [2008] W.T.L.R. 527; *Wyndham v Egremont* [2009] W.T.L.R. 1473. See also *Allen v Distillers Co (Biochemicals) Ltd* [1974] Q.B. 384; above, para.22–005. It was reported in *The Times*, February 16, 1999, that a trust had been varied so that the son of the Duke of Northumberland would receive £250,000 a year from the age of 25 instead of 18.
[140] [1960] 1 W.L.R. 1011.

sister's share if he died under the age of 30 years, even if he left children. It was not for the benefit of the sister's children to surrender their contingent interest.

A broader view was taken in *Re Remnant's Settlement Trusts*.[141]

> A trust fund gave contingent interests to the children of two sisters, Dawn and Merrial, and contained a forfeiture provision in respect of any of the children who practised Roman Catholicism or was married to a Roman Catholic at the time of vesting, with an accruer provision in favour of the children of the other. Dawn's children were Protestant, but Merrial's were Roman Catholic.

> Pennycuick J. approved the deletion of the forfeiture provision. This was clearly not for the financial benefit of Dawn's children, for they surrendered a very good chance of gaining by it. But it was overall for their benefit. "Obviously, a forfeiture provision of this kind might well cause very serious dissension between the families of the two sisters."[142] The forfeiture clause could also operate as a deterrent in the selection of a spouse. Freedom from such problems would be more important to the lives of the children than some more money.

22–028   (e) *Taking a Chance.* A difficulty arises where the proposed variation will almost certainly confer a benefit, but there may possibly be circumstances in which it will not. Thus, in *Re Cohen's Settlement Trust*,[143] an application was made to vary a settlement so as to make the interest of the grandchildren vest on a specified date, and not upon the death of a life tenant, in order to reduce estate duty. Although it was most unlikely (but not impossible) that the life tenant would live until the specified date, any children born after that date but before his death would lose their interests. Thus approval could not be given on behalf of unborn children. Where trustees wish to distribute on the footing that a middle-aged woman will not have further children, this may be sanctioned by court order (made in the exercise of its jurisdiction to secure the proper administration of a trust) without recourse to the 1958 Act.[144] Indeed, no application to court is needed where the woman is elderly.[145]

---

[141] [1970] Ch. 560; R. Cotterrell (1971) 34 M.L.R. 98.

[142] [1970] Ch. 560 at 566. Another benefit, of less weight, was to be freed from having to choose between one's religion and the entitlement under the will.

[143] [1965] 1 W.L.R. 1229.

[144] *Re Westminster Bank Limited's Declaration of Trust* [1963] 1 W.L.R. 820 (over 50). The order did not extinguish the rights of any future child.

[145] *Re Pettifor's ST* [1966] Ch. 257 (over 70); cf. *Figg v Clarke (Inspector of Taxes)* [1997] 1 W.L.R. 603 (presumption of fertility until death in context of capital gains tax, where a deemed disposal occurs when beneficiaries become absolutely entitled to the trust property). See also *Re Levy Estate Trust* [2000] 5 C.L.Y. 635.

The question is one of degree. The court will not give its approval where the benefit is a matter of chance, but it will not require absolute certainty of benefit,[146] if the risk is one which a "prudent and well advised adult would be prepared to take."[147] Most risks can be covered by insurance.

---

[146] *Re Holt's Settlement* [1969] 1 Ch. 100; *Re Robinson's ST* [1976] 1 W.L.R. 806.
[147] REM (1960) 76 L.Q.R. 22.

CHAPTER 23

BREACH OF TRUST

691

1. Personal Liability to Beneficiaries

A. General[1]

23–001　**i. Liability is Compensatory.** A trustee who fails to comply with his duties is liable to make good the loss to the trust estate. Even if there is no loss, the trustee is accountable for any profit made in breach of trust.[2] The object of the rule is not to punish the trustee, but to compensate the beneficiaries. However, the court will, on suitable occasions, authorise acts which are technical breaches of trust; a trustee will not be liable for a technical breach which the court would have authorised[3]; but there is no need to take the risk; he should obtain the directions of the court before acting.[4] The effect of exemption clauses was considered in Ch.17.[5]

23–002　**ii. Liability is Personal, not Vicarious.** The rule has always been that a trustee is liable for his own breaches and not for those of his co-trustees.[6] The dividing line however is extremely difficult to draw; for if there is a breach by a co-trustee, the trustee may himself be at fault by leaving the matter in the hands of a co-trustee without inquiry, or for standing by while a breach of trust is being committed,[7] or for allowing trust funds to remain in the sole control of a co-trustee, or for failing to take steps to obtain redress on becoming aware of a breach of trust.

23–003　**iii. Breaches before Appointment.** A trustee is not liable for breaches of trust committed before his appointment in the absence of evidence indicating a breach of trust.[8] On appointment, however, he should examine the books and documents relating to the trust, and should ensure that the trust property is vested in him. If in the course of his inquiries he discovers a breach of trust, he should take steps against the former trustees; unless for some reason he can show that such proceedings would have been useless.[9]

23–004　**iv. Breaches after Retirement.** A trustee remains liable after retirement for breaches committed by him during office; and similarly his estate remains liable after his death. He may on the other

---

[1] See Birks and Pretto (eds), *Breach of Trust*, 2002. As to costs, see *McDonald v Horn* [1995] 1 All E.R. 961; above, para.21–001. For the liability of a director for breach by a corporate trustee, see D. Pollard (1997) 11 T.L.I. 48.
[2] See Ch.21.
[3] *Brown v Smith* (1878) 10 Ch.D. 377.
[4] Above, para.18–025.
[5] Above, para.17–005.
[6] *Townley v Sherborne* (1643) J. Bridg. 35 at 37, 38.
[7] *Bahin v Hughes* (1886) 31 Ch.D. 390; below, para.23–019.
[8] *Re Strahan* (1856) 8 De G.M. & G. 291.
[9] *Re Forest of Dean Coal Co* (1878) 10 Ch.D. 450 at 452.

hand have been released by the other trustees, or by the beneficiaries being of full capacity and in possession of all the facts. He will not usually be liable in respect of breaches committed after his retirement; but he may be if he retired in order to facilitate a breach of trust.[10]

v. Trustee-Beneficiary. Where the trustee in breach is also a beneficiary, his beneficial interest bears the loss against the other beneficiaries,[11] and, as we will see,[12] against the trustees[13]; and this liability applies although the beneficial interest was acquired by him derivatively, even by purchase.[14]   **23–005**

B. Measure of Liability

i. General Principles. In the case of an unlawful profit, the trustee must account for the profit, which will normally be held on constructive trust. Thus any increase in value belongs to the trust, while the trustee remains personally liable for the deficit if there is a decrease in value.[15] Indeed, he may be liable to account for the highest value between the date of breach and the date of judgment.[16] Thus the principle that liability is measured as at the date of judgment, applicable to other breaches, does not apply to profits.[17] Where a profit has been made from the wrongful use of property, the claimant must elect at judgment between an account of profits and compensation for loss sustained by the deprivation of the use of the property.[18]   **23–006**

With other breaches of trust or fiduciary duty, the measure of liability is the loss caused to the trust estate, directly or indirectly,[19]

---

[10] *Head v Gould* [1898] 2 Ch. 250 at 272. This question came into prominence in the context of pressure upon English resident trustees to retire in favour of foreign resident trustees in order to allow a trust fund to escape liability for capital gains tax: *Re Whitehead's WT* [1971] 1 W.L.R. 833; above, para.17–032.

[11] *Re Dacre* [1915] 2 Ch. 480; [1916] 1 Ch. 344. Assignees are also bound, unless they took for value and without notice.

[12] Below, para.23–023.

[13] *Chillingworth v Chambers* [1896] 1 Ch. 685.

[14] *Re Dacre*, above, fn.11.

[15] *Att Gen for Hong Kong v Reid* [1994] 1 A.C. 324; above, para.21–026. (It has since been doubted whether the defendant held any trust property; *Sinclair Investments (UK) Ltd v Versailles Trade Finance Ltd (in administrative receivership)* [2011] 3 W.L.R. 1153.

[16] *Nant-y-glo and Blaina Ironworks Co v Grave* (1879) 12 Ch.D. 738 (liable to account for shares at previous value of £80 each although since fallen to £1 each).

[17] *Target Holdings Ltd v Redferns (A Firm)* [1996] 1 A.C. 421, below.

[18] *Tang Man Sit (Personal Representatives) v Capacious Investments Ltd* [1996] 1 A.C. 514; above, para.21–028.

[19] *Knott v Cottee* (1852) 16 Beav. 77; *Bartlett v Barclays Bank Trust Co Ltd (No.2)* [1980] Ch. 515.

and the onus is on the claimant to prove that there is a loss and that it would not have occurred but for the breach.[20]

The principles of equitable compensation have not yet been fully worked out.[21] Liability is restitutionary, and the principles are not identical to the common law rules for the assessment of damages.[22] Thus the rules of remoteness and foreseeability applicable in contract and tort are not relevant, but causal connection must be established. In *Canson Enterprises Ltd v Boughton & Co*[23] a solicitor committed a breach of fiduciary duty in a sale transaction in which he knew that the vendor made a secret profit. The purchaser (who would not have completed if aware of the facts) then built a warehouse which, due to the negligence of the builders, was defective. The purchaser's claim for compensation against the solicitor for the defective building was unanimously dismissed by the Canadian Supreme Court because there was insufficient causal connection between the breach and the loss, but different views were taken as to whether the common law rules of remoteness applied by analogy in equity.

23–007   The principles were reviewed in *Target Holdings Ltd v Redferns (A Firm)*[24]

Target agreed to advance £1,525,000 to C Ltd, to purchase property valued (allegedly negligently) at £2m, to be secured by a mortgage. The arrangement, unknown to Target, was that the vendor would sell to P Ltd for £775,000, which would sell to K Ltd for £1.25m, which in turn would sell to C Ltd for £2m. This appeared to be a mortgage fraud by the three related companies. The defendant solicitors acted for the three companies and for Target. Target transferred £1,525,000 to the solicitors, who held it

---

[20] *Re Miller's Trust Deed* (1978) L.S.Gaz. 454; *Nestlé v National Westminster Bank Plc* [1993] 1 W.L.R. 1260 (holding also that "loss" includes a gain which is less than the profit a prudent trustee would have made); *Target Holdings Ltd v Redferns (A Firm)* [1996] 1 A.C. 421 at 440.

[21] See D. Capper (1994) 14 L.S. 313. This is discussed in the context of "fusion"; above paras 1–022, 1–023. See also *Medforth v Blake* [2000] Ch. 86; L. Sealy (2000) 59 C.L.J. 31; P. Birks and F. Rose (eds), *Restitution and Equity*, 2000, Vol.1: *Resulting Trusts and Equitable Compensation*; J. Edelman and S. Elliott (2004) 18 T.L.I. 116.

[22] See *Re Bell's Indenture* [1980] 1 W.L.R. 1217 (trustee must restore trust property without deducting tax which would have been payable if it had not been misappropriated, in contrast with principles of assessing tort damages for loss of earnings). The decision was overruled on another point in *Dubai Aluminium Co Ltd v Salaam* [2003] 2 A.C. 366.

[23] (1991) 85 D.L.R. (4th) 129. See also *Mahoney v Purnell* [1996] 3 All E.R. 61; J. Heydon (1997) L.Q.R. 8.

[24] [1996] 1 A.C. 421; J. Ulph (1995) 9 T.L.I. 86; C. Rickett (1996) 112 L.Q.R. 27; R. Nolan [1996] L.M.C.L.Q. 161; D. Capper [1997] Conv. 14; Sir Anthony Mason and R. Davern (1997–98) 8 K.C.L.J. 1 and 86 respectively; G. Vos (2001) 60 C.L.J. 337; S. Elliott and J. Edelman (2003) 119 L.Q.R. 545; C. Mitchell (2006) 59 C.L.P. 267 at 284. The proceedings were interlocutory, as a result of which the defendants obtained leave to defend. See also *Bank of New Zealand v New Zealand Guardian Trust Co Ltd* [1999] 1 N.Z.L.R. 664 at 687–688; *Collins v Brebner* [2000] Lloyd's Rep. P.N. 587.

on a bare trust for Target. In breach of trust the solicitors paid away the money to P Ltd and K Ltd before completion of the purchase and the mortgage. The mortgage was in fact completed a few days later. On the insolvency of C Ltd the property was sold by Target as mortgagee, but, because of the property slump, raised only £500,000. Target sued the solicitors for breach of trust in paying away the £1,525,000 and claimed that sum less the proceeds of sale. The House of Lords found for the solicitors. Target was in the same position as it would have been if the money had not been transferred until the security was in place and had thus failed to establish that the loss would not have occurred but for the breach.

Lord Browne-Wilkinson considered that it was wrong to apply rules developed in the context of traditional trusts to trusts arising in commercial dealings. In the case of a traditional trust for A for life then for B, each beneficiary was entitled to a restoration of the fund.[25] The present case involved a bare trust of a commercial kind. Before the transaction had been completed the solicitors could have been required to restore the money wrongly paid away. But "the clock did not stop" when the money was paid away. Once the transaction had been completed, equity required a trustee to make good a loss suffered which, using hindsight and common sense, could be seen to have been caused by the breach. The quantum of liability was to be assessed not at the date of the breach but at the date of judgment.[26] Although the principles underlying the common law and equitable rules were similar, the detailed rules were different. If it could be shown that the loss would not have occurred but for the breach,[27] the trustee would be liable even if the immediate cause of the loss was the dishonesty or negligence of a third party, as the common law rules of remoteness and causation would not apply.[28]

It is important, however, to distinguish a breach of trust or fiduci- **23–008**
ary duty from other breaches of duty by a fiduciary. The special restitutionary principles of assessment of equitable compensation discussed above apply only where there is a breach of trust or

[25] See *Clough v Bond* (1838) 3 My. & Cr. 490; *Hillsdown Holdings Plc v Pensions Ombudsman* [1997] 1 All E.R. 862.

[26] *Jaffray v Marshall* [1993] 1 W.L.R. 1285, which measured the loss as the highest value of the property between breach and judgment, was overruled. See also *Re Dawson* [1966] 2 N.S.W.L.R. 211 (date of judgment equally applicable where this operates to the detriment of the trustees); *Hulbert v Avens, The Times*, February 7, 2003; *Jeffery v Gretton* [2011] W.T.L.R. 809.

[27] Target would be able to prove this at trial if it could show that P Ltd could not have purchased from the vendor (and then sold on) without the funds advanced in breach of trust. Thus leave to defend was conditional upon paying £1m into court.

[28] See S. Elliott (2002) 65 M.L.R. 588 at 597, proposing different foreseeability tests for intentional and unintentional breaches.

fiduciary duty. A breach of fiduciary duty means a breach of those proscriptive, i.e. negative, duties which are special to fiduciaries, whose core obligation is loyalty.[29] Where a fiduciary (such as a solicitor) commits some other breach, as where he acts incompetently, there is no reason why compensation in equity should be assessed differently from common law damages.[30]

The principle that equity does not require a trustee to compensate for a loss which would have occurred had there been no breach is surely correct. However, it is not clear exactly how the rules applicable to traditional trusts and commercial trusts differ. Sir Peter Millett said of the supposed distinction: "It is difficult to know what to make of this".[31] Would the result in *Target Holdings* have been any different if the trustees of a family trust investing on mortgage had committed a similar breach? Indeed, it has been said that *Target Holdings* "has not done a great deal to clarify the rules of causation employed in equity."[32] The distinction between traditional and commercial trusts in this context may prove illusory. A more useful distinction is that between breaches of fiduciary duty and other breaches by fiduciaries, as mentioned above.

23–009   Different considerations apply where the fiduciary has misrepresented or failed to disclose a material fact.[33] The Court of Appeal in *Swindle v Harrison*[34] emphasised that this special principle applies only where the fiduciary's breach was the equivalent of fraud. In that case a client of the solicitor claimants mortgaged her house in order to purchase an hotel, anticipating a loan from a brewery to provide the balance. When, after exchange of contracts, the brewery refused to lend, the solicitors lent the money, secured on the hotel. They failed to disclose that the firm was (by arrangement with the bank) making a hidden profit on the loan and that they had known that the brewery would not lend. The hotel business failed, so that the client defaulted on both mortgages and her house was repossessed. When the solicitors sought to enforce the charge over the hotel, the client claimed the value of the lost equity in her house as compensation for breach of fiduciary duty. Her claim failed because

---

[29] See R. Nolan (1997) 113 L.Q.R. 220 and (1997) 56 C.L.J. 39; S. Elliott (1999) 13 T.L.I. 74; *Bristol and West Building Society v Fancy & Jackson (A Firm)* [1997] 4 All E.R. 582; P. Birks (2002) 16 T.L.I. 34; R. Lee [2009] Conv. 236.

[30] *Bristol & West Building Society v Mothew* [1998] Ch. 1; *Hilton v Barker Booth & Eastwood (A Firm)* [2005] 1 W.L.R. 567 at 575; J. Getzler (2006) 122 L.Q.R. 1; cf. *Bristol & West Building Society v May May & Merrimans* [1996] 2 All E.R. 801, where the breach was considered to be of fiduciary duty, and *Target Holdings* itself, where breach of trust was conceded. The concession is criticised in D. Hayton in P. Birks (ed.), *Privacy and Loyalty*, p.288.

[31] (1998) 114 L.Q.R. 214 at 224.

[32] R. Nolan [1996] L.M.C.L.Q. 161 at 164.

[33] The principle derives from *Brickenden v London Loan and Savings Co* [1934] 3 D.L.R. 465. See P. Matthews (1997) 3 *Trusts & Trustees* 6.

[34] [1997] 4 All E.R. 705; L. Ho (1997) 11 T.L.I. 72 and (1998) 12 T.L.I. 66; S. Elliott [1998] 6 R.L.R. 135; H. Tjio and T. Yeo (1998) 114 L.Q.R. 181.

she could not prove that, but for the breach, she would not have accepted the loan and completed the purchase. Thus she would have lost her house in any event. In the absence of proof of fraud, *Target Holdings* applied, not the special principle relating to misrepresentation and non-disclosure. The remedy for the latter would have been rescission of the loan agreement and an account of profits.[35] It has since been emphasised that the application of the special principle depends on whether the victim of the misrepresentation or non-disclosure is seeking compensation for loss or rescission and an account of profits.[36] Where the claimant is seeking rescission and an account of profits as a remedy for misrepresentation or non-disclosure of material facts in breach of fiduciary duty, the defendant cannot maintain that the claimant would have acted in the same way if in possession of the true facts. If, however, the claimant is seeking compensation for loss (as in *Swindle v Harrison*[37]), the court must consider what would have happened if the claimant had known the material facts. If the loss would probably have occurred even if disclosure had been made, the defendant's conduct cannot be regarded as having caused the loss.

Subsidiary rules applicable to particular situations will now be considered.

ii. Purchase of Unauthorised Investments. When trustees 23–010
make an unauthorised investment, they will be liable for any loss incurred on the sale. This is so even if the sale is at a time chosen by the court, and if the investments would have shown a profit if they had been retained until the decision of the court holding them to be improper.[38] The beneficiaries may, if they are of full capacity and so wish, adopt the unauthorised investment[39]; if they do so, there is dispute whether that is the limit of their remedy,[40] or whether they may claim the difference between the value of the investment and the purchase price.[41] There is less scope for this principle now that most investments are authorised for trustees.

iii. Improper Retention of Investments.

(a) *Unauthorised Investments.* A trustee who improperly retains 23–011
an unauthorised investment is liable for the difference between the

---

[35] See further S. Moriarty (1998) 114 L.Q.R. 9; T. Akkouh (2002) 16 T.L.I. 151; V. Vann (2003) 17 T.L.I. 66; M. Conaglen (2003) 119 L.Q.R. 246 and (2010) 126 L.Q.R. 72.
[36] *Gwembe Valley Development Company Ltd v Koshy* [2004] W.T.L.R. 97.
[37] Above, fn.34.
[38] *Knott v Cottee* (1852) 16 Beav. 77.
[39] *Re Jenkin's and Randall's Contract* [1903] 2 Ch. 362; *Wright v Morgan* [1926] A.C. 788 at 799.
[40] *Thornton v Stokill* (1855) 1 Jur.(N.S.) 751.
[41] *Re Lake* [1903] 1 K.B. 439.

present value (or selling price) and the price which it would have raised if it had been sold at the proper time. How hard this can be on a trustee holding property in a falling market is shown by *Fry v Fry*[42] where trustees were liable for the difference between the price offered for a hotel in 1837 which they refused as inadequate, and the much lower price prevailing in 1859, the fall being largely due to the diversion of road traffic by the building of a railway.

23–012   (b) *Authorised Investments.* We have seen that the Trustee Act 2000 s.5, following the pattern of earlier legislation, requires advice to be taken on the question of retaining investments.[43] Failure to do so will constitute a breach of the statutory duty of care.[44] However, there will be no liability if the improper retention caused no loss to the trust. In *Jeffery v Gretton*[45] trustees of a will trust decided to retain and refurbish a valuable but dilapidated property without taking professional advice, but the repairs were sporadic and took nearly six years. Professional advice would have been to sell it in its unrepaired state in 2002, when it was worth £610,000. Although this was a breach of trust, the beneficiary's claim failed because her share of the proceeds after the eventual sale in 2008 for £885,000 was more than she would have received if the property had been sold in 2002 and her share invested. It was "a case of a thoughtless breach of trust that happens to have turned out well".[46]

23–013   **iv. Improper Sale of Authorised Investments.** When an authorised investment is improperly sold, the beneficiaries may require the trustees either to account for the proceeds of sale or to replace the investment, valued as at the date of judgment.[47] Thus where trustees sold Consols and invested in an unauthorised investment, the whole matter was treated as a single transaction and the trustees were held liable to replace the Consols at the higher price then prevailing.[48] This is so even though the improper investment was realised without loss.[49]

23–014   **v. Failure to Invest.** Trustees should invest within a reasonable time. Failure to do so will constitute a breach of the statutory duty of care.[50]

---

[42] *Fry v Fry* (1859) 27 Beav. 144.
[43] Above, para.18–016.
[44] Trustee Act 2000 s.1; Sch.1, para.1.
[45] [2011] W.T.L.R. 809.
[46] [2011] W.T.L.R. 809 at 838.
[47] *Re Bell's Indenture* [1980] 1 W.L.R. 1217 (overruled on another point in *Dubai Aluminium Co Ltd v Salaam* [2003] 2 A.C. 366). But where the asset sold in breach of trust would have been properly sold at a later date, the trustee is liable to replace it at its value on that date, and not as at the date of judgment.
[48] *Phillipson v Gatty* (1848) 7 Hare 516.
[49] *Re Massingberd's Settlement* (1890) 63 L.T. 296.
[50] Trustee Act 2000 s.1; Sch.1, para.1.

If a trustee is required to make a specific investment and fails to make any investment, and the price of the specific investment has risen, he will be liable to purchase as much of that investment as would have been purchased at the proper time.[51] Similarly if he chooses an investment other than that specified,[52] profit in the unauthorised investment being surrendered, of course, to the trust.[53] Where, as is nearly always the case in practice, the trustees may select investments at their discretion, it is not practicable to base recovery upon the price of a particular investment. The beneficiary will be entitled to any difference between the actual value of the trust fund and the value which a prudent trustee is likely to have achieved (by considering the average performance of ordinary shares during the period in question).[54]

vi. Employment of Trust Fund in Trade. A trustee who employs trust funds in his trade or business is liable to account for the profits he makes,[55] or for the sums involved with interest, whichever is the greater. Difficult questions arise when he employs a mixed fund, being partly his own and partly trust money. Here the rule is that the beneficiaries may claim a proportionate share of the profits[56] or demand the return of the trust money with interest.[57] **23–015**

vii. Interest. **23–016**

"It is well established in equity that a trustee who in breach of trust misapplies trust funds will be liable not only to replace the misapplied principal fund but to do so with interest from the date of the misapplication. This is on the notional ground that the money so applied was in fact the trustee's own money and that he has retained the misapplied trust money in his own hands and used it for his own purposes. Where a trustee has retained trust money in his own hands, he will be accountable for the profit which he has made or which he is assumed to have made with the use of the money. . . . The defaulting trustee is normally charged with simple interest only,[58] but if it is established that he has used the money in trade he may be charged compound interest. . . . Precisely similar equitable principles apply to an agent who has

[51] *Byrchall v Bradford* (1822) 6 Madd. 235.
[52] *Pride v Fooks* (1840) 2 Beav. 430.
[53] Below, para.23–017.
[54] *Nestlé v National Westminster Bank Plc* [1993] 1 W.L.R. 1260.
[55] *Re Davis* [1902] 2 Ch. 314; *Re Jarvis* [1958] 1 W.L.R. 815.
[56] Below, para.23–055.
[57] *Heathcote v Hulme* (1819) 1 Jac. & W. 122.
[58] *Belmont Finance Corp Ltd v Williams Furniture Ltd (No.2)* [1980] 1 All E.R. 393.

retained monies of his principal in his hands and used them for his own purposes.[59]" [60]

If the trustee or agent has received a sum in excess of what the court would impose, he is accountable for what he has actually received, or the beneficiaries may adopt the investment.[61]

The rate of interest, and the choice between simple and compound,[62] is in the discretion of the court. The 19th century cases laid down four per cent[63] as the general rule, with an increase to five per cent where the trustee or other fiduciary was guilty of fraud[64] or active misconduct,[65] at any rate where the fraud or misconduct involved a profit for the trustee,[66] or where he ought to have received more than four per cent.[67] These rates became out of line with commercial interest rates (although these are very low at the time of writing). More modern decisions have charged one per cent above the London clearing banks' base rate in force at the time[68]; or that allowed from time to time on the court's short-term investment account (now called the court special account).[69] Compound interest is charged where that fairly represents what the trustee may reasonably be treated as having received,[70] or where there is a duty to accumulate,[71] and sometimes in cases of fraud or misconduct.[72] The

[59] *Burdick v Garrick* (1870) 5 Ch.App. 233.

[60] *Wallersteiner v Moir (No.2)* [1975] Q.B. 373 at 397; *Guardian Ocean Cargoes Ltd v Banco do Brasil (No.3)* [1992] 2 Lloyd's Rep. 193 (presumed used in investment business); *Mathew v TM Sutton Ltd* [1994] 1 W.L.R. 1455; cf. *O'Sullivan v Management Agency and Music Ltd* [1985] Q.B. 428; W. Bishop and D. Prentice (1986) 49 M.L.R. 118, above, para.21–005 (simple interest where profits used in trade, but trade benefited claimant, being in the nature of a joint venture).

[61] *Re Jenkins' and Randalls' Contract* [1903] 2 Ch. 362; *Wright v Morgan* [1926] A.C. 788 at 799; above, para.23–010.

[62] With yearly rests (*Jones v Foxall* (1852) 15 Beav. 388 at 393; *Guardian Ocean Cargoes Ltd v Banco do Brasil (No.3)*, above, fn.60; *El Ajou v Dollar Land Holdings Plc (No.2)* [1995] 2 All E.R. 213); and sometimes half-yearly rests (*Re Emmet's Estate* (1881) 17 Ch.D. 142).

[63] *Att Gen v Alford* (1855) 4 De G.M. & G. 843; *El Ajou v Dollar Land Holdings Plc (No.2)* above, fn.62; *Fletcher v Green* (864) 33 Beav. 426 at 430.

[64] *Att Gen v Alford*, above, fn.63, at 852.

[65] *Jones v Foxall* (1852) 15 Beav. 388 at 393; *Gordon v Gonda* [1955] 1 W.L.R. 885.

[66] S. Elliott [2001] Conv. 313.

[67] *Jones v Foxall*, above, fn.65, at 388 (calling in a mortgage which was returning 5%); see *Re Waterman's WT* [1952] 2 All E.R. 1054.

[68] *Wallersteiner v Moir (No.2)* [1975] Q.B. 373; JTF [1982] Conv. 93; *Belmont Finance Corp v Williams Furniture Ltd (No.2)* [1980] 1 All E.R. 393; *O'Sullivan v Management Agency and Music Ltd* [1985] Q.B. 428; *Guardian Ocean Cargoes Ltd v Banco do Brasil (No.3)* [1992] 2 Lloyd's Rep. 193 (1% above New York prime rate); *Rama v Millar* [1996] 1 N.Z.L.R. 257; *Re Duckwari Plc (No.2)* [1999] Ch. 268.

[69] *Bartlett v Barclays Bank Trust Co Ltd (No.2)* [1980] Ch. 515; cf. *Re Evans* [1999] 2 All E.R. 777 (lower rate of 8% against non-professional administrator in times of "more gentle" inflation). For a full discussion, see S. Elliott [2001] Conv. 313. (The rate on the court special account is currently only 0.5%.)

[70] *Wallersteiner v Moir (No.2)*, above, fn.68.

[71] *Re Emmet's Estate* (1881) 17 Ch.D. 142.

[72] *Jones v Foxall*, above, fn.65; *Gordon v Gonda*, above, fn.65; cf. *O'Sullivan v Management Agency and Music Ltd*, above, fn.68. As to costs, see Snell, para.30–021.

traditional view, as mentioned above, has been that compound interest is awarded where the action is for disgorgement of profits but not in cases of compensation for loss, but the distinction is difficult to justify.[73]

The question which arose in *Westdeutsche Landesbank Girozentrale v Islington London Borough Council*[74] was whether the equitable jurisdiction to award compound interest could be invoked in a common law personal action. The House of Lords, by a majority, held that it could not. Their Lordships revisited the matter in *Sempra Metals Ltd (formerly Metallgesellschaft Ltd) v IRC*,[75] where the question was whether the court had jurisdiction to award compound interest in a common law claim for restitution. It had been conceded before the House of Lords in *Westdeutsche Landesbank* that no interest, compound or simple, was recoverable at common law in such a case, although either type could sometimes be recovered in equity. As the point had not been argued in the earlier case, their Lordships were free to re-examine the matter and held (by a majority) that compound interest could be awarded in the exercise of the common law restitutionary jurisdiction in appropriate circumstances. It is thus no longer necessary to consider whether equity should supplement the common law remedies to achieve full restitution.

viii. Profit in One Transaction: Loss in Another. Any gains made out of the trust property belong to the beneficiaries while a loss incurred by reason of a breach of trust must be made good by the trustee. A trustee cannot set off a gain in one transaction against a loss made in another unauthorised transaction. **23–017**

In *Dimes v Scott*[76] trustees retained an unauthorised mortgage returning 10 per cent all of which was paid to the tenant for life. When the mortgage was paid off, trustees were able to purchase more Consols than they would have done if the reinvestment had taken place at the end of a year from the testator's death. Lord Lyndhurst held the trustees liable for the excess interest paid to the tenant for life[77] over that which would have been payable if the capital of the unauthorised investment had been invested in Consols at the end of a year from the testator's death, and the trustees were unable to set off against this the gain arising from the fall in the price of Consols.

---

[73] S Elliott [2001] Conv. 313 at 332.
[74] [1996] A.C. 669.
[75] [2008] 1 A.C. 561; G. Virgo (2007) 66 C.L.J. 510; C. Nicholl (2008) 124 L.Q.R. 199; C. Mitchell (2008) 71 M.L.R. 290.
[76] (1828) 4 Russ. 195.
[77] The tenant for life was entitled only to 4% under the rule in *Howe v Earl of Dartmouth* (1802) 7 Ves.Jr. 137; above, para.19–002.

The rule is harsh though logical. It has not been applied where the court finds that the gain and loss were part of the same transaction. There is often difficulty in determining whether the matter should or should not be regarded as a single transaction.

In *Fletcher v Green*[78] trust money was lent on mortgage to a firm of which one trustee was a partner. The trustees reclaimed the money; the security was sold at a loss and the proceeds paid into court and invested in Consols. The question was whether the trustees' accounts should credit them with the amount of the proceeds of sale or with the value of the Consols, which had risen in price. They were held entitled to take advantage of the rise. No reasons were given. The case is usually explained on the ground that the whole matter was treated as one transaction. If that is so, they should logically have been at risk in relation to a possible fall in the price of Consols; the trustees can hardly be allowed to take advantage of a rise but not the burden of a fall; but it would be hard on the trustees if they have to run the risk of loss on an investment made by the court.

The difficulty of laying down a clear rule was recognised in *Bartlett v Barclays Bank Trust Co Ltd (No.1)*[79] where the defendant bank was held liable as trustee for failing to exercise proper supervision of the board of directors of a private company whose shares were almost wholly owned by the trust. The board embarked on speculative ventures in property development: the Old Bailey project was a disaster; the Guildford project was a success. In finding the bank liable, Brightman J. allowed the gain on the Guildford project to be set off against the Old Bailey. Without considering the cases in detail, he said,[80] after recognising the general rule:

"The relevant cases are, however, not altogether easy to reconcile. All are centenarians and none is quite like the present. . . . I think it would be unjust to deprive the bank of the element of salvage in the course of assessing the cost of the shipwreck."

Thus a gain can be set off against a loss if, even though not arising from the same transaction, they resulted from the same wrongful course of conduct; in the present case a policy of speculative investment.

---

[78] (1864) 33 Beav. 426. See also *Hulbert v Avens*, *The Times*, February 7, 2003 (trustees entitled to offset interest on trust money which would not have been earned but for the breach).
[79] [1980] Ch. 515; G. Shindler [1980] Conv. 155; above, para.18–021.
[80] [1980] Ch. 515, at 538.

2. LIABILITY INTER SE: CONTRIBUTION AND INDEMNITY

A. Joint and Several Liability

Where two or more trustees are liable for a breach of trust, their **23–018** liability is joint and several. Thus a beneficiary may claim the whole loss by suing all or some or any one of those who are liable; and may levy execution for the whole sum against any one.[81]

B. Contribution

The rule used to be that the joint liability of trustees required an **23–019** equal sharing of the liability, regardless of fault, and therefore that one trustee who had paid more than his share of the liability for a breach of trust was entitled to equal contribution from the other trustees who were also liable[82]; or from their estates after death.[83] The effect of this rule was shown dramatically in *Bahin v Hughes*,[84] where the Court of Appeal held that a passive trustee was liable with the active trustee. Cotton L.J. said[85]:

"Miss Hughes was the active trustee and Mr Edwards did nothing, and in my opinion it would be laying down a wrong rule to hold that where one trustee acts honestly, though erroneously, the other trustee is to be held entitled to indemnity who by doing nothing neglects his duty more than the acting trustee."

The Civil Liability (Contribution) Act 1978 gives the court a discretion in relation to the amount to be recovered against two or more defendants who are liable in respect of the damage. The amount recoverable against any defendant shall be "such as may be found by the court to be just and equitable having regard to the extent of that person's responsibility for the damage in question"[86]; and includes breach of trust as one of the forms of liability to which the Act applies.[87] It will be interesting to see how the passive trustee fares under this provision. The Act appears not to apply to situations in which one trustee is entitled to an indemnity.[88]

---

[81] *Fletcher v Green* (1864) 33 Beav. 426 at 430.

[82] *Fletcher v Green*, above, fn.81; *Ramskill v Edwards* (1885) 31 Ch.D. 100; *Robinson v Harkin* [1896] 2 Ch. 415.

[83] *Jackson v Dickinson* [1903] 1 Ch. 947.

[84] (1886) 31 Ch.D. 390; *Bishopsgate Investment Management Ltd v Maxwell (No.2)* [1994] 1 All E.R. 261 (no defence that blindly followed co-director's lead). See Goff and Jones, *The Law of Restitution*, 7th edn, p.417.

[85] (1886) 31 Ch.D. 390, at 396.

[86] s.2(1). This may extend to a complete indemnity; s.2(2). See generally C. Mitchell [1997] 5 R.L.R. 27.

[87] s.6(1). See *Dubai Aluminium Co Ltd v Salaam* [2003] 2 A.C. 366; C. Mitchell (2003) 119 L.Q.R. 364; *Charter Plc v City Index Ltd* [2008] Ch. 313; G. Virgo (2008) 67 C.L.J. 254.

[88] s.7(3); Law Commission Report on Contribution, No.79 (1977), para.26.

C. Indemnity

23–020 There are a few cases where one trustee is not liable to contribute; where, that is, he is entitled to an indemnity from his co-trustee against his own liability. Such cases are rare, for such relief:

> "[W]ould act as an opiate upon the consciences of the trustees; so that instead of the *cestui que trust* having the benefit of several acting trustees, each trustee would be looking to the other or others for a right of indemnity, and so neglect the performance of his duties."[89]

The situations are as set out below.

23–021 **i. Fraud.** In some cases where one trustee alone is fraudulent, the other will not be liable at all, and so no question of contribution or indemnity will arise.[90] If both are in breach but one alone has made personal use of trust money, the latter must indemnify his co-trustee.[91] If all are fraudulent the rule used to be that the one who has paid the damages could not claim contribution from the others,[92] because a claimant should not base his claim upon his wrong. No specific exception, however, is made under the modern legislation authorising the court to determine how liability will be shared, and the Civil Liability (Contribution) Act 1978 is applicable.[93]

23–022 **ii. Solicitor and Trustee.** Many of the cases of indemnity are cases where one trustee is a solicitor and has exercised such a controlling influence that the other trustee has been unable to exercise an independent judgment.[94] There is no rule, however, that:

> "[A] man is bound to indemnify his co-trustee against loss merely because he was a solicitor, when that co-trustee was an active participator in the breach of trust complained of, and is not proved to have participated merely in consequence of the advice and control of the solicitor."[95]

23–023 **iii. Beneficiary-Trustee.** When a person who is a trustee and beneficiary participates in a breach of trust, he may not claim any

---

[89] per Fry L.J. in *Bahin v Hughes*, above, fn.84, at 398.
[90] *Re Smith* [1896] 1 Ch. 71 was an exceptional case of two trustees who acted together, but only one of whom was liable to the beneficiaries for the consequences. One trustee had chosen an investment honestly but the other had received a bribe in order to induce him to make it.
[91] *Bahin v Hughes* (1886) 31 Ch.D. 390 at 395; *Thompson v Finch* (1856) 25 L.J.Ch. 681 (where trustee also a solicitor).
[92] *Att Gen v Wilson* (1840) Cr. & Ph. 1 at 28.
[93] See *K v P* [1993] Ch. 140 (not a case on trustees).
[94] *Re Partington* (1887) 57 L.T. 654.
[95] *Head v Gould* [1898] 2 Ch. 250 at 265, per Kekewich J.; above, para.17–007; *Lockhart v Reilly* (1856) 25 L.J. Ch. 697; *Re Turner* [1897] 1 Ch. 536.

share of the trust estate until he has made good his liability as trustee.[96] He will be required to indemnify his co-trustee to the extent of his beneficial interest; but this does not take away his right to contribution from his co-trustee. The rule in *Chillingworth v Chambers*[97] effects a compromise between these rules. A beneficiary-trustee must indemnify his co-trustee to the extent of his beneficial interest. That property is taken first to meet the claims; after that, their liability is shared equally. The non-beneficiary trustee is thus given a partial indemnity; partial in that it extends only to the value of the beneficiary-trustee's interest.

3. CRIMINAL LIABILITY[98]

Breach of trust was not, at common law, a crime at all. The trustee **23–024** was regarded as the owner of the trust property by the common law, which disregarded the rights of the beneficiary. But in 1857 breach of trust was made a statutory crime, and the law on the subject was incorporated in the Larceny Acts 1861 and 1916.

These Acts were repealed and replaced by the Theft Act 1968, which defines "theft" as the dishonest appropriation of property "belonging to another" with the intention of depriving the other of it permanently. By s.5(2) of the Act, "any person having a right to enforce the trust" is regarded as a person to whom the subject-matter of the trust "belongs" so that the criminal liability of trustees is in this way brought within the general law.[99] The objects of a discretionary trust can presumably be regarded as having a sufficient right of enforcement to bring s.5(2) into operation for such trusts. Section 4(2)(a) also brings within the definition of "theft" an appropriation by a trustee of "land or anything forming part of it," and s.2(1)(c) makes a trustee guilty of theft if he appropriates property though he believes that the equitable owners cannot be discovered.

The Fraud Act 2006 introduced a new criminal offence of fraud by abuse of position, which will be committed by a trustee who acts dishonestly for his own gain.[100]

---

[96] *Re Rhodesia Goldfields Ltd* [1910] 1 Ch. 239; *Selangor United Rubber Estates Ltd v Cradock (No.4)* [1969] 3 All E.R. 965.

[97] [1896] 1 Ch. 685; similarly if he becomes a beneficiary after the date of the breach, (1887) 37 Ch.D. 329, at 344.

[98] R. Brazier (1975) 39 Conv.(N.S.) 29.

[99] See *Re Att Gen's Reference (No.1 of 1985)* [1986] Q.B. 491; *R. v Clowes (No.2)* [1994] 2 All E.R. 316 (misappropriation of money held on trust for investors was theft).

[100] s.4.

4. PROTECTION OF TRUSTEES

23–025   A trustee who has committed a breach of trust may be able to escape personal liability by bringing the case within one of the categories discussed below. Many of the relevant points arose in *Re Pauling's Settlement Trusts*.[101]

> The children of the Younghusband family sued to recover from the trustees of their mother's marriage settlement various payments which were alleged to have been made in breach of trust. The Younghusbands were often in financial difficulties. Their main source of money was Mrs Younghusband's marriage settlement under which she was tenant for life. The trustees had power, with her consent, to advance up to one-half of the presumptive share of each child in the trust fund. Several advances were made under this power to the children when they had attained ages varying from 27 (Francis) to 21 (Ann and Anthony). In most cases the advances were, to the knowledge of everyone concerned, applied for family purposes and usually towards the reduction of Mrs Younghusband's overdraft. On several occasions, but not on all, independent legal advice was obtained. The trustees relied on the consent and acquiescence of the advanced beneficiaries, and claimed an indemnity under the Trustee Act 1925 s.62, and asked for relief under s.61. Several of the payments were held to be in breach of trust and the defences set up by the trustees are considered in the following sections.

A. Participation in, or Consent to, a Breach of Trust[102]

23–026   A beneficiary who has participated in, or consented to, a breach of trust may not sue. "It is clear to us," said Willmer L.J. in *Re Pauling's Settlement Trusts*,[103]

> "[T]hat if the [trustee] can establish a valid request or consent by the advanced beneficiary to the advance in question, that is a good defence on the part of the [trustee] to the beneficiary's claim, even though it be plain that the advance was made in breach of trust."

A reversioner is not "less capable of giving . . . assent when his interest is in reversion than when it is in possession,"[104] but he will

---

[101] [1964] Ch. 303.

[102] See generally J. Payne in Birks and Pretto (eds), *Breach of Trust*, 2002, Ch.10.

[103] [1964] Ch. 303, at 335; *Re Bucks Constabulary Widow's and Orphans' Fund Friendly Society (No.2)* [1979] 1 W.L.R. 936 at 955; *Allen v Rea Brothers Trustees Ltd* [2002] W.T.L.R. 625.

[104] *Life Association of Scotland v Siddal* (1861) 3 De G.F. & J. 58 at 73.

not be treated as having given consent wherever he fails to take steps to remedy a breach of trust of which he has knowledge.[105]

i. Knowledge. Consent is not a mere formality. It is a judgment **23–027** upon the propriety of the proposed transaction.[106] For, if mere knowledge and a passive assent constituted consent, then a trustee could always escape liability by informing a beneficiary of what he proposed to do. The consent must be given by an adult of full capacity in circumstances in which he had a free choice. However, a child beneficiary may exceptionally be taken to have assented to a breach, for instance where he fraudulently misstated his age[107]:

"The court has to consider all the circumstances in which the concurrence of the *cestui que trust* was given with a view to seeing whether it is fair and equitable that, having given his concurrence, he should afterwards turn around and sue the trustees: that, subject to this, it is not necessary that he should know what he is concurring in is a breach of trust, provided that he fully understands what he is concurring in, and that it is not necessary that he should himself have directly benefited by the breach of trust."[108]

Thus a beneficiary, who otherwise had a right to set aside a sale, was unable to do so when he had affirmed the sale, accepted part of the purchase money, and caused the purchaser to embark upon further liabilities which he could not repay.[109]

ii. Benefit. It is not necessary that the beneficiary should have **23–028** been motivated to derive a personal benefit from the breach, nor that he actually received one.[110] Where a beneficiary may recover even though he has received a benefit he must give credit for any benefit which he has received from the breach.[111]

iii. Freedom of Decision. The decision must be freely taken by **23–029** a person not under disability. Even where the beneficiary is an adult

---

[105] (1861) 3 De G.F. & J. 58.
[106] *Re Massingberd's Settlement* (1890) 63 L.T. 296 at 299.
[107] See *Overton v Bannister* (1884) 3 Hare 503.
[108] per Wilberforce J. in *Re Pauling's ST* [1962] 1 W.L.R. 86 at 108, accepted by counsel in the Court of Appeal but not commented on by the Court [1964] Ch. 303, at 339; approved in *Holder v Holder* [1968] Ch. 353 at 394, 399, 406. See also *Jeffery v Gretton* [2011] W.T.L.R. 809.
[109] *Holder v Holder*, above, fn.108.
[110] *Fletcher v Collis* [1905] 2 Ch. 24; *Allen v Rea Brothers Trustees Ltd* [2002] W.T.L.R. 625.
[111] *Re Pauling's ST* [1964] Ch. 303. (The £300 received by Ann; and the policies received by Francis and George). See 354 for the reasons why Anthony was not required to account for benefits received indirectly through his mother.

of full capacity, it may be possible to show that the consent was due
to undue influence. Thus, in *Re Pauling*,[112] the advancements were
in each case delayed until the child had become 21; but several of
the payments which had been made to, or indirectly for, the benefit
of the parents were presumed to have been the result of undue
influence exercised by them over the children. Indeed it was clear
that the advances were all made to meet the financial needs of the
father. The Court of Appeal refused to accept the trustees' argument
that undue influence was only relevant as between the children and
their parents where the parents had acquired the benefit; they suggested that:

> "[A] trustee carrying out a transaction in breach of trust may be
> liable if he knew, or ought to have known, that the beneficiary was
> acting under the undue influence of another, or may be presumed
> to have done so, but will not be liable if it cannot be established
> that he so knew, or ought to have known."[113]

It is impossible to say how long after the attainment of majority the
presumption continues; this depends upon the circumstances of each
case.[114]

B. Release and Acquiescence[115]

23–030   These defences relate to the conduct of the beneficiary after the
breach has taken place; where they apply, they become equivalent to
retrospective consent. A release may be, but need not be, formal; it
may be inferred from conduct, as where a beneficiary accepted
benefits under his mother's will which prohibited him from setting
up any claim in respect of the administration of his father's estate.[116]
Length of time in making a claim will not of itself be fatal, but will
assist the trustee by requiring less evidence to establish a release.[117]
Many of the points raised in connection with consent apply also
here:

> "I . . . agree that either concurrence in the act, or acquiescence
> without original concurrence, will release the trustees; but that is

---

[112] [1964] Ch. 303.

[113] [1964] Ch. 303, at 338.

[114] *Huguenin v Baseley* (1807) 14 Ves.Jr. 273; *Allcard v Skinner* (1887) 36 Ch.D. 145
at 171.

[115] See generally J. Payne in Birks and Pretto (eds), *Breach of Trust*, 2002, Ch.10.

[116] *Egg v Devey* (1847) 10 Beav. 444.

[117] *Stackhouse v Barnston* (1805) 10 Ves.Jr. 453; *Life Association of Scotland v Siddall*
(1861) 3 De G.F. & J. 58 at 77.

only a general rule, and the Court must inquire into the circumstances which induced concurrence or acquiescence."[118]

There will be no release for the trustees where the beneficiary acquiesced without knowledge of the facts; but, as with consent, it is not necessary that the beneficiary should have been aware of his legal rights.[119]

C. Impounding the Beneficiary's Interest: Trustee Act 1925 Section 62

i. Inherent Power. Independently of the Trustee Act 1925 s.62, the court has power to impound the interest of a beneficiary who has instigated or requested a breach of trust. The impounding of the beneficiary's interest means that it will be applied so far as it will go towards providing an indemnity to the trustee. The trustee must show that the beneficiary acted with knowledge of the facts, although he may not have known that these amounted to a breach of trust.[120] If the beneficiary instigated or requested the breach, it is not necessary to show that the beneficiary received a benefit[121]; but where a beneficiary merely concurred in or consented to a breach of trust, it seems necessary that a benefit be shown.[122] The trustee, as has been seen, is protected against an action from the consenting beneficiary in respect of the breach.   **23–031**

ii. Trustee Act 1925 Section 62. Section 62 extends this jurisdiction,[123] permitting the court to make an impounding order regardless of any question of benefit. As will be seen, consent, if it is to be effective, must be in writing.[124] Section 62(1) reads as follows: **23–032**

> "Where a trustee commits a breach of trust at the instigation or request or with the consent in writing of a beneficiary, the court may, if it thinks fit, . . . make such order as to the court seems just, for impounding all or any part of the interest of the beneficiary in

---

[118] *Walker v Symonds* (1818) 3 Swans. 1 at 64, per Lord Eldon; *Stackhouse v Barnston,* above, fn.117.

[119] *Holder v Holder* [1968] Ch. 353.

[120] See *Hillsdown Holdins Plc v Pensions Ombudsman* [1997] 1 All E.R. 862.

[121] *Fuller v Knight* (1843) 6 Beav. 205; *Chillingworth v Chambers* [1896] 1 Ch. 685 (a trustee beneficiary).

[122] *Chillingworth v Chambers,* above, fn.121. It has, however, been said that, even in the case of a beneficiary who requests a breach, the indemnity is limited to the benefit received by the beneficiary: *Raby v Ridehalgh* (1855) 7 De G.M. & G. 104.

[123] See Romer J. in *Bolton v Curre* [1895] 1 Ch. 544 at 549.

[124] The requirement of writing applies only to consent; per Lindley M.R. in *Re Somerset* [1894] 1 Ch. 231 at 265–266.

the trust estate by way of indemnity to the trustee or persons
claiming through him."

The effect of an impounding order is not only that the beneficiary
is unable to sue the trustee, but also that the liability to make up
losses suffered by other beneficiaries will fall on him, rather than on
the trustee. The liability cannot, however, be for a greater sum than
the subsisting value of his own interest in the trust, and it is subject
to the discretion of the court. The discretion is exercised in the light
of the earlier cases on which s.62 is founded,[125] and generally speaking an indemnity will be given to a trustee against a beneficiary who
has been at all active in inducing a breach. Again, however, the
knowledge of the beneficiary must amount to a definite appreciation
of what is being done. In *Re Somerset*,[126] an impounding order was
refused to trustees who had invested trust funds on a mortgage of a
particular property at the instigation of a beneficiary, since the beneficiary had no intention of being a party to a breach, which occurred
only because the loan exceeded the authorised limit. He had left it
entirely to the trustees to determine how much money to lend on the
security.

The principle applies to a beneficiary who, only subsequently to
the breach, became entitled to a beneficial interest.[127] The right to
indemnity by impounding is available to former trustees after their
resignation or replacement. The trustees in *Re Pauling's Settlement
Trusts (No.2)*[128] claimed an indemnity out of the life interest of the
parents of the claimants, and Wilberforce J. held that they were
entitled to it, and would remain so entitled, although, as was intended, they would at a future time be replaced by new trustees.

D. Statutory Relief: Trustee Act 1925 Section 61[129]

23–033   Under this section the court may excuse trustees from the consequences of a breach of trust. It reads:

"If it appears to the court that a trustee, . . . is or may be personally liable for any breach of trust . . . but has acted honestly and
reasonably, and ought fairly to be excused for the breach of trust

---

[125] See Romer J. in *Bolton v Curre* [1895] 1 Ch. 544 at 549.
[126] [1894] 1 Ch. 231; *Mara v Browne* [1895] 2 Ch. 69; cf. *Raby v Ridehalgh*, above,
fn.122.
[127] *Evans v Benyon* (1888) 37 Ch.D. 329.
[128] [1963] Ch. 576; *Re Bucks Constabulary Widow's and Orphans' Fund Friendly Society
(No.2)* [1979] 1 W.L.R. 936 at 955.
[129] L. Sheridan (1955) 19 Conv.(N.S.) 420n; D. Waters [1977] *Estates and Trusts Quarterly*
12; J. Lowry and R. Edmunds in Birks and Pretto (eds), *Breach of Trust*, Ch.9. The section
also applies to executors; TA 1925 s.68(17). The Charity Commission may relieve charity
trustees from liability; above, para.15–097.

and for omitting to obtain the directions of the court in the matter in which he committed such breach, then the court may relieve him either wholly or partly[130] from personal liability for the same."

The courts have preferred not to lay down formal rules for the application of the section. "It would be impossible," said Byrne J.:

"[T]o lay down any general rules or principles to be acted on in carrying out the provisions of the section, and I think that each case must depend upon its own circumstances."[131]

The only way to show how the discretion has been exercised is to catalogue the cases; but there is inadequate space here. A few general rules, however, can be extracted.

The jurisdiction is available where a trustee "is or may be personally liable" for a breach of trust. There is thus no need to establish the liability; indeed it would put a trustee in a strange position if he had to prove his own liability in order to obtain relief. Several cases allowing relief have done so without reaching a conclusion on the question of liability.[132] However, "'may be' has ... been interpreted as indicating doubt, not futurity"[133]; the court will not commit itself in advance to giving relief in the case of a future breach of trust.[134]

In exercising the discretion three factors must be considered[135]: the trustee's honesty, reasonableness, and the question whether he ought "fairly" to be excused. There is little authority on honesty; dishonest trustees do not apply. But Kekewich J. once characterised as dishonest "a trustee who does nothing, swallows wholesale what is said by his co-trustee, never asks for explanation, and accepts flimsy explanations."[136]

There is some uncertainty as to the standard to be applied in determining reasonableness, but the usual standard is that of a prudent man of business managing his own affairs.[137] (Compliance

---

[130] See *Re Evans* [1999] 2 All E.R. 777; below, para.23–034.

[131] *Re Turner* [1897] 1 Ch. 536 at 542; *Re Kay* [1897] 2 Ch. 518 at 524 (referring to the predecessor section).

[132] e.g. *Re Grindey* [1898] 2 Ch. 593.

[133] (1955) 19 Conv. (N.S.) 425.

[134] *Re Tollemache* [1903] 1 Ch. 457 at 465–466; affirmed at 953; *Re Rosenthal* [1972] 1 W.L.R. 1273. The court may, however, authorise an act so as to prevent it being a breach.

[135] *Marsden v Regan* [1954] 1 W.L.R. 423 at 434.

[136] *Re Second East Dulwich, etc., Building Society* (1899) 79 L.T. 726 at 727.

[137] See Chitty L.J. in *Re Grindey*, above, fn.132, at 601; *Re Turner* [1897] 1 Ch. 536 at 542; *Re Lord de Clifford's Estate* [1900] 2 Ch. 707 at 716; *Re Stuart* [1897] 2 Ch. 583 at 590; *Re Rosenthal*, above, fn.134; *Jeffery v Gretton* [2011] W.T.L.R. 809. The trustees in *Bartlett v Barclays Bank Trust Co Ltd (No.1)* [1980] Ch. 515, above, para.23–017, were unable to rely on the section because they had not acted reasonably.

with this standard may mean that there is no breach, but it is otherwise where, for example, payment has been made to the wrong person.)[138] The amount of money involved will be a relevant factor.[139] In *Re Stuart*[140] it was said that, in connection with lending trust money on mortgage, the statutory procedure for valuations and reports[141] "constitute a standard by which reasonable conduct will be judged"; but failure to follow this is "not necessarily a fatal objection to the application of the section."

23–034   The distinction between conduct that is reasonable and that for which a trustee ought fairly to be excused is a fine one. In *Davis v Hutchings*[142] trustees, on the distribution of the trust fund, paid the share of one beneficiary to the solicitor to the trust (employed by them) in reliance upon the solicitor's statement that he was the assignee of the share. The share had in fact been mortgaged and assigned to him subject to the mortgage. Kekewich J. held that the trustees were liable to the mortgagee. They had acted honestly and reasonably in relying on the solicitor, but they should not be excused.[143] Fairness should be considered in relation to all the parties, the trustees, the beneficiaries and the creditors, and is "essentially a matter within the discretion of the judge."[144] In *Re Evans*[145] the administratrix took out insurance to cover the share of a missing beneficiary and then distributed the estate. The beneficiary appeared and claimed his share, but the insurance covered only the capital sum to which he was entitled. The administratrix relied on s.61 as a defence to his claim for interest. It was held that she had acted reasonably, but ought fairly to be excused only to the extent that the claim could not be satisfied by assets retained by her which derived from the estate.

Little seems to be added to this section by the reference to omission to obtain the directions of the court:

> "I do not see how the trustee can be excused for the breach of trust without being also excused for the omission referred to, or how he can be excused for the omission without also being excused for the breach of trust."[146]

[138] See *Eaves v Hickson* (1861) Beav. 136.

[139] *Re Grindey* [1898] 2 Ch. 593; *Marsden v Regan*, above, fn.135.

[140] [1897] 2 Ch. 583.

[141] *Re Stuart*, above, fn.137, at 591–592; *Shaw v Cates* [1909] 1 Ch. 389; *Palmer v Emerson* [1911] 1 Ch. 758.

[142] [1907] 1 Ch. 356.

[143] Some of the dicta of Kekewich J. were disapproved in *Re Allsop* [1914] 1 Ch. 1 at 11, 12; see also *Marsden v Regan* [1954] 1 W.L.R. 423, at 434–435.

[144] *Marsden v Regan*, above, fn.143, at 435.

[145] [1999] 2 All E.R. 777.

[146] *Perrins v Bellamy* [1898] 2 Ch. 521 at 528.

The onus of showing that he acted honestly and reasonably is on the trustee.[147] Applications for relief have most commonly arisen in connection with unauthorised investments.[148] Another and common situation is that of payment of the funds to the wrong beneficiary,[149] or the payment of void claims by creditors.[150] The taking of legal advice is a relevant factor, but does not automatically entitle a trustee to relief.[151]

The section extends to professional trustees who are being paid for their services, but the court is less ready to grant relief in such cases.[152]

E. Limitation and Laches[153]

i. Six-Year Period under Limitation Act 1980, Section 21(3).[154] Subject to exceptions discussed below, the Limitation Act 1980 s.21(3), provides a six-year limitation for the protection of trustees. The subsection reads: 23–035

"Subject to the preceding provisions of this section, an action by a beneficiary[155] to recover trust property or in respect of any breach of trust, not being an action for which a period of limitation is prescribed by any other provision of this Act, shall not be brought after the expiration of six years from the date on which the right of action accrued.

---

[147] *Re Stuart* [1897] 2 Ch. 583.

[148] *Re Turner*, above, fn.137; *Re Stuart*, above, fn.147; *Re Dive* [1909] 1 Ch. 328; *Bartlett v Barclays Bank Trust Co Ltd (No.1)* [1980] Ch. 515.

[149] *Re Allsop* [1914] 1 Ch. 1; *National Trustees Co of Australasia v General Finance Co of Australasia* [1905] A.C. 373; *Re Wightwick's WT* [1950] Ch. 260; *Re Clapham* [2006] W.T.L.R. 203 (the section would not apply if the mistake was grossly negligent).

[150] *Re Lord de Clifford's Estate* [1900] 2 Ch. 707; *Re Mackay* [1911] 1 Ch. 300; cf. *Re Windsor Steam Coal Co Ltd* [1929] 1 Ch. 151.

[151] *National Trustees Co of Australasia v General Finance Co of Australasia* [1905] A.C. 373; *Marsden v Regan* [1954] 1 W.L.R. 423 at 434–435; *Re Evans* [1999] 2 All E.R. 777.

[152] *National Trustees Co of Australasia v General Finance Co of Australasia* [1905] A.C. 373; *Re Windsor Steam Coal Co* [1929] 1 Ch. 151; *Re Waterman's WT* [1952] 2 All E.R. 1054; *Re Pauling's ST* [1964] Ch. 303 at 356–359; *Martin v Triggs Turner Bartons* [2009] W.T.L.R. 1339.

[153] See Preston and Newsom's *Limitation of Actions*, 4th edn, Ch.7; Franks, *Limitation of Actions*, 1959, pp.62–80; H. McLean (1989) 48 C.L.J. 472; Prime and Scanlan, *The Modern Law of Limitations*, 1993; W. Swadling and G. Watt in Birks and Pretto (eds), *Breach of Trust*, 2002, Ch.11 and Ch.12 respectively.

[154] See Law Com. No.270 (2001), *Limitation of Actions*, proposing a three-year period from the date the breach was discoverable, applicable to all breaches of trust (and most other civil claims), with a long-stop of 10 years from the breach. The Government rejected the recommendations; Law Com. No.323, *Annual Report 2009/10*, para.3.14.

[155] The section does not apply to a claim by the Attorney General against the trustee of a charitable trust, which has no 'beneficiary"; *Att Gen v Cocke* [1988] Ch. 414; J. Warburton [1988] Conv. 292. For the position of beneficiaries of a discretionary trust, see D. Hayton (2010) *Trusts and Estates Law & Tax Journal* 18.

For the purposes of this subsection, the right of action shall not be treated as having accrued to any beneficiary entitled to a future interest in the trust property, until the interest fell into possession."

In this subsection, "trustee" includes personal representatives[156] and also certain fiduciary agents,[157] company directors[158] and a mortgagee in respect of the proceeds of sale,[159] but not a trustee in bankruptcy,[160] nor the liquidator of a company in voluntary liquidation.[161] It will also be noted that there is no distinction between the protection given to an express trustee and that given to an implied or constructive trustee; until the Trustee Act 1888 s.8, no protection based upon passage of time had been available to an express trustee.[162] It will be seen that the subsection only applies to cases where an action is brought by a beneficiary in respect of the trust property.[163] Under the proviso, time only begins to run against remaindermen or reversioners when their interest falls into possession; and it has been held that this does not occur when improper advancements are made in favour of remaindermen.[164] If a beneficiary is entitled to two interests in the property, one in possession and one in remainder, he does not lose a claim in respect of the latter where time has run against him in respect of the former.[165]

23–036   **ii. Exceptions to the Six-Year Rule.** There are some exceptions to the six-year rule.

(a) *Limitation Act 1980 Section 21(1).*[166]

"(1) No period of limitation prescribed by this Act shall apply to an action by a beneficiary under a trust, being an action—

    (a) in respect of any fraud or fraudulent breach of trust to which the trustee was a party or privy; or

---

[156] Limitation Act 1980 s.38(1); TA 1925 s.68(17).
[157] *Burdick v Garrick* (1870) L.R. 5 Ch.App. 233.
[158] *Belmont Finance Corp v Williams Furniture Ltd (No.2)* [1980] 1 All E.R. 393; *Gwembe Valley Development Company Ltd v Koshy* [2004] W.T.L.R. 97.
[159] *Thorne v Heard* [1895] A.C. 495.
[160] *Re Cornish* [1896] 1 Q.B. 99.
[161] *Re Windsor Steam Coal Co* [1928] Ch. 609; affirmed on other grounds [1929] 1 Ch. 151.
[162] Franks, *Limitation of Actions*, 1959, p.64.
[163] *Re Bowden* (1890) 45 Ch.D 444 at 451.
[164] *Re Pauling's ST* [1964] Ch. 303.
[165] *Mara v Browne* [1895] 2 Ch. 69, reversed on another point [1896] 1 Ch. 199.
[166] See H. McLean (1989) 48 C.L.J. 472 at 495.

(b) to recover from the trustee trust property or the proceeds of trust property in the possession of the trustee, or previously received by the trustee and converted to his use."[167]

This subsection reproduces in the situations to which it applies the rule of permanent liability which was applicable in equity to the case of express trustees.

In *North American Land Co v Watkins*,[168] an agent had been sent to America to buy land for his company. He bought it, and it was duly conveyed to the company, but the agent made and retained a profit for himself. After the expiration of the period applicable for the recovery of money had and received, the company successfully recovered the money on two grounds, first that the agent was in the position of a trustee and had retained trust money, and secondly that this conduct had been fraudulent.

It seems that the fraud must be that of the trustee himself.

In *Thorne v Heard*[169] a trustee was protected where he had negligently left funds in the hands of a solicitor who had embezzled them; for the trustee to come within s.21(1) he must be "party or privy" to the fraud.

Dishonesty is not relevant where a trustee is in possession of the trust property. **23–037**

In *James v Williams*[170] X, who was entitled to a one-third share of a house on the intestacy of Y, treated the house as his own and purported to leave it by will to Z. It was held that X had been in the position of a constructive trustee, so that an action brought against Z by one of the other intestacy beneficiaries more than 12 years after the death of Y was not barred.

In *Re Howlett*[171] a trustee, who was income beneficiary until remarriage, continued in possession of a wharf until he died, and the remainderman was held able to sue the life tenant's representatives after his death for an occupation rent for the premises.

Conversion to the trustee's own use requires some wrongful application in his own favour. A trustee was held to escape from the subsection where he applied the trust funds for the maintenance of a

---

[167] But where a trustee is also a beneficiary and has received his share on a distribution of the trust property, para.(b) shall only apply in respect of the excess over his share, so long as the trustee acted honestly and reasonably in making the distribution; s.21(2).

[168] [1904] 1 Ch. 242; [1904] 2 Ch. 233. See also *Statek Corp v Alford* [2008] W.T.L.R. 1089 (s.21(1) applied to de facto director).

[169] [1894] 1 Ch. 599; [1895] A.C. 495; *Re Fountaine* [1909] 2 Ch. 382.

[170] [2000] Ch. 1; cf. *Nolan v Nolan* [2004] W.T.L.R. 1261.

[171] [1949] Ch. 767. See also *Re Sharp* [1906] 1 Ch. 793.

child beneficiary,[172] or where the funds were dissipated by a co-trustee.[173]

It must be emphasised that s.21(1) cannot be relied upon where there is no trustee/beneficiary relationship beween the parties. Thus a personal action against a third party who has dishonestly assisted in a breach of trust does not fall within s.21(1)(a). Although such a third party is often (misleadingly) called a constructive trustee,[174] he is not a true trustee and has no trust property. Thus the action must be brought within the six-year period applicable to an action for damages for fraud.[175]

23–038   (b) *Claim to the Personal Estate of a Deceased Person.* Under s.22, which is subject to s.21(1), an action in respect of any claim to the personal estate of a deceased person must be brought within the period of 12 years from the date the right to receive the interest accrued. The better view is that this is the date on which the personal representatives are first in a position to distribute the residuary estate.[176] For historical reasons s.22 does not apply to land, as it re-enacts provisions dating from a time when realty did not vest in the personal representatives. Difficult questions on the inter-relation of this section and s.21(3) can arise where the personal representatives administering an estate would normally be treated as having become trustees. In that case the question is whether the 12-year or six-year rule is applicable.[177] It has recently been confirmed that s.22 does not apply to will trusts once the administration has been completed. The section deals with failures by personal representatives to administer the estate properly, but not with breaches of trust committed by trustees of the will trust (although they may be the same persons).[178]

23–039   (c) *Sections 28 and 32.* Section 28 allows an extension of the period of limitation in cases in which the claimant has been under disability. Section 32 provides that where any action is based upon fraud or where the right of action is concealed by fraud or where the action is for relief from the consequences of a mistake, "the period

---

[172] *Re Page* [1893] 1 Ch. 304; *Re Timmis* [1902] 1 Ch. 176.
[173] *Re Fountaine* [1909] 2 Ch. 382.
[174] Above, para.12–010.
[175] *Paragon Finance Plc v DB Thakerar & Co (A Firm)* [1999] 1 All E.R. 401; *Halton International Inc v Guernroy Ltd* [2006] W.T.L.R. 1241; *Cattley v Pollard* [2007] Ch. 353; *Peconic Industrial Development Ltd v Lau* [2009] W.T.L.R. 999; cf. *Statek Corp v Alford* [2008] W.T.L.R. 1089; C. Mitchell [2008] Conv. 226; D. Hayton (2008) 22 T.L.I. 81.
[176] *Re Loftus* [2007] 1 W.L.R. 591.
[177] *Re Timmis* [1902] 2 Ch. 176; *Re Richardson* [1920] 1 Ch. 423; *Re Oliver* [1927] 2 Ch. 323; *Re Diplock* [1948] Ch. 465; [1951] A.C. 251.
[178] *Davies v Sharples* [2006] W.T.L.R. 839.

of limitation shall not begin to run until the [claimant] has discovered the fraud, concealment or mistake . . . or could with reasonable diligence have discovered it."[179] This section applies to actions against trustees.[180]

iii. Assignees. A transferee from the trustee is in the same posi-   **23–040**
tion as the trustee was[181] unless he is bona fide purchaser for value
without notice in which case he will presumably be treated as if he
had purchased from someone who was not a trustee.

iv. Where No Period is Applicable. It has been seen that the   **23–041**
Limitation Act 1980 deals comprehensively with the running of
time in actions against trustees. In situations not covered, it is necessary to return to the law as it existed before the statutory protection
was given. No provision is made, for example, either for claims for
equitable relief by way of specific performance,[182] rescission or
rectification, or injunction,[183] or in cases of redemption of a mortgage of pure personalty,[184] or the setting aside of a purchase of trust
property by a trustee.[185] The rule of equity is that either no period is
applicable, or that the relevant common law period is applied by
analogy.[186] In any situation for which no period of limitation is
expressly applicable to an equitable claim, the defendant may rely
on the doctrine of laches.[187] Delay by a claimant in pursuing his
rights "may furnish a defence in equity to an equitable claim."[188]
Whether such a defence is available in a particular case is a matter
for the discretion of the court, and will depend to a large extent upon
the hardship caused to the defendant by the delay, and the effect
upon third parties; and generally upon the balance of justice in
granting or refusing relief.[189] Relief will only be refused in plain

---

[179] For limitation problems where the mistake was of law, see *Kleinwort Benson Ltd v
Lincoln CC* [1999] 2 A.C. 349.
[180] See *Kitchen v RAF Association* [1958] 1 W.L.R. 563; *Bartlett v Barclays Bank Trust Co
Ltd* [1980] Ch. 515 at 537.
[181] See *Baker v Medway Building and Supplies Ltd* [1958] 1 W.L.R. 1216; *Eddis v Chichester Constable* [1969] 2 Ch. 345.
[182] See *P & O Nedlloyd BV v Arab Metals Co (No.2)* [2007] 1 W.L.R. 2288; below,
para.24–036.
[183] See Limitation Act 1980 s.36(1); Law Com. C.P. 151 (1998), *Limitation of Actions*,
para.13.103. For criticisms of the present law, see *Cia de Seguros Imperio v Heath (REBX) Ltd*
[2001] 1 W.L.R. 112 at 124.
[184] *Weld v Petre* [1929] 1 Ch. 33.
[185] *Baker v Read* (1854) 18 Beav. 398; *Morse v Royal* (1806) 12 Ves.Jr. 355; Snell,
para.5–019.
[186] Limitation Act 1980 s.36(1). See *Knox v Gye* (1872) 5 App. Cas. 656 at 674.
[187] *Re Pauling's ST* [1964] Ch. 303. See also *Alec Lobb (Garages) Ltd v Total Oil GB Ltd*
[1985] 1 W.L.R. 173.
[188] *Re Sharpe* [1892] 1 Ch. 154 at 168; Franks, *Limitations of Actions*, 1959, p.233.
[189] *Lindsay Petroleum Co v Hurd* (1874) L.R. 5 P.C. 221 at pp.239–241; *Weld v Petre*
[1929] 1 Ch. 33 at 51, 52.

cases.[190] There is no maximum period beyond which the equitable relief cannot be sought but a period of 20 years may be taken as a convenient guide.[191] The defendant will be more likely to succeed if he can show not merely delay, but acquiescence. Both defences appear to have been retained by the Limitation Act 1980 which provides in s.36(2): "Nothing in this Act shall affect any equitable jurisdiction to refuse relief on the ground of acquiescence or otherwise."

These defences are therefore relevant to cases to which no period is applicable. There have been different views as to whether they apply to the cases within s.21(1). The Court of Appeal in *Gwembe Valley Development Co Ltd v Koshy*[192] considered that the defence of acquiescence could apply but laches could not. However, this distinction was doubted by the Court of Appeal in *Re Loftus*.[193] Although the defence of laches failed on the facts, the court considered that the effect of s.36(2) was that both laches and acquiescence could apply to cases within s.21(1). This appears to be the better view.

A question which has recently arisen is whether any limitation period applies to an action for an account. Section 23 of the 1980 Act provides that:

"[A]n action for an account shall not be brought after the expiration of any time limit under this Act which is applicable to the claim which is the basis of the duty to account."

This confirms that the period applicable to a particular cause of action (e.g. copyright infringement) applies equally to the relief by way of account which flows from it. In *Coulthard v Disco Mix Club Ltd*[194] an action for an account arising out of a contractual fiduciary relationship was brought more than six years after the alleged breaches. The claimant sought to overcome this by arguing that no period of limitation applied to a dishonest breach by a fiduciary of his duty to account. It was held that there was no distinction in the limitation period applicable to a common law fraud action for damages and an action in equity for dishonest breach of fiduciary duty, unless the defendant had misappropriated trust property, in which

---

[190] Franks, *Limitation of Actions*, p.261.

[191] *Weld v Petre*, above, fn.184, at 54, 55; *Kershaw v Whelan (No.2)*, *The Times*, February 10, 1997. See also *Humphreys v Humphreys* [2004] W.T.L.R. 1425 (in claims to set aside for undue influence, time does not run while the influence remains).

[192] [2004] W.T.L.R. 97.

[193] [2007] 1 W.L.R. 591.

[194] [2000] 1 W.L.R. 707. See also *Paragon Finance Plc v DB Thakerar & Co (A Firm)* [1999] 1 All E.R. 400; above, para.23–037; *Raja v Lloyds TSB Bank Plc*, *The Times*, May 16, 2000; *Cia de Seguros Imperio v Heath (REBX) Ltd* [2001] 1 W.L.R. 112.

case no period applied.[195] The present case involved no trust property, as the defendant was not obliged to keep the money in question separate from his own. The duty to account was contractual, even if owed by a fiduciary. It would have been "a blot on our jurisprudence" if the same facts gave rise to a time bar at common law but not in equity. The alleged dishonest breaches of fiduciary duty were simply the equitable counterparts of the common law claims, and so the common law period applied by analogy.

5. PROPRIETARY REMEDIES

A. Personal and Proprietary Actions

Most actions at law and in equity are personal. We now have to **23–042** consider the occasions on which a claimant has the right to proceed against a particular asset in the defendant's hands. Such proprietary claims exist to a very limited extent at law; and these, for convenience and for the sake of comparison, will be described here.[196] In equity the right to follow or trace property is more extensive. We will see that proprietary rights may be asserted where the claimant is making a claim at law or in equity to a specific piece of property, and also where he is making a claim in equity against a mixed fund to which property of his (in equity) has contributed. The tracing rules are also involved in personal actions based on receipt of property.[197] On a point of terminology, "tracing" is an identification process involved where one asset has been substituted for another; "following" is the process of establishing that a particular asset has passed from one person to another; while "claiming" is the next step once either process has been completed.[198]

There are two main advantages of a proprietary over a personal claim. First and foremost, satisfaction of the claimant's demand does not depend on the solvency of the defendant. If the property traced is the claimant's in equity, it escapes the defendant's bankruptcy.[199] Secondly, in some cases, the claimant will be able to take advantage of increases in the value of the property. This is obvious where specific property is treated as being the claimant's in equity, and is also established where a mixed fund is in question.[200]

---

[195] Limitation Act 1980 s.21(1); above, para.23–036.

[196] Below, 23–044.

[197] Above, Ch.12.

[198] Smith, *The Law of Tracing*, p.4; *Foskett v McKeown* [2001] 1 A.C. 102 at 127. As to whether confidential information is an asset for these purposes, see D. Sheehan [2005] 13 R.L.R. 82.

[199] Insolvency Act 1986 s.283.

[200] *Re Tilley's WT* [1967] Ch. 1179; *Foskett v McKeown*, above, fn.198; below, para.23–055.

B. Unjust Enrichment; Restitution[201]

23–043   Proprietary remedies cannot be fully understood without some appreciation of the doctrine of unjust enrichment. This is a doctrine which appears in nearly every system of law. It lays down as a general principle that where the defendant is unjustly enriched at the claimant's expense, the defendant must make restitution.[202] Such a principle has its greatest scope in common law actions, but it overlaps into many areas of equity. Even though there is no right to restitution in every case of unjust enrichment, all restitutionary claims are unified by the principle.[203]

Assume that A has a right to sue B on the ground that A has paid money to B by mistake, or under compulsion, or under a contract that was void, or in any other situation in which B is enriched at the expense of A. If B is solvent, a personal action will satisfy A's claim. What should be the effect on this situation if, (a) B is bankrupt, or (b) B invests the money and it doubles in value? In case (a) it is arguable that since B should never have had the money, nor should his creditors. In case (b) it can be argued that neither B nor his creditors should reap the full measure of the profit which B has made out of money which he should never have had. Should A have it? Would it make any difference if the invested funds were part A's and part B's? We might here pose a further case (c). If B uses the money to pay off a mortgage on his property and is insolvent, should A be placed in the position, by subrogation, of the mortgagee? These are all interesting and difficult questions, to most of which the English cases provide answers. But the principles which govern the availability of a proprietary remedy have not been fully worked out. Indeed, it has been said with some justification that the law in this area lacks all coherence.[204] What is clear is that the defendant's unjust enrichment is not of itself sufficient to give the claimant a proprietary remedy. Equally clearly, a claimant who can establish his proprietary rights by the tracing process may vindicate them without any need to rely on unjust enrichment.[205] Lord Neuberger

---

[201] Goff and Jones, *The Law of Restitution*, 7th edn; Birks, *An Introduction to the Law of Restitution*, revised edn, 1989.

[202] American Law Institute, *Third Restatement of the Law of Restitution and Unjust Enrichment* (2011), para.1. See M. Gergen (2003) 56 C.L.P. 289 and [2005] 13 R.L.R. 225, discussing the draft *Third Restatement of Restitution and Unjust Enrichment*.

[203] Goff and Jones, 7th edn, p.15; *Woolwich Equitable Building Society v IRC* [1993] A.C. 70 at 196.

[204] A. Burrows (1997) 50 C.L.P. 95 at 114. See also S. Evans (1999) 115 L.Q.R. 469; R. Goode in B. Rider (ed.), *Law at the Centre*, 1999, p.185; P. Jaffey (2002) 55 C.L.P. 263; G. Virgo in Getzler (ed.), *Rationalizing Property, Equity and Trusts*, 2003, Ch.5; R. Calnan [2004] 12 R.L.R. 1; R. Chambers in Burrows and Rodger (eds), *Mapping the Law*, 2006, Ch.13, examining the role of resulting trusts in restitution.

[205] *Foskett v McKeown* [2001] 1 A.C. 102.

has warned against extending the circumstances in which proprietary claims may be made in insolvency situations, bearing in mind the consequences to unsecured creditors.[206]

The account which follows shows that different rules currently operate at law and in equity, although Lord Millett took the opportunity in *Foskett v McKeown*[207] to say that there is no sense in this, although it was not the occasion to explore the matter further. A single set of rules should suffice to identify the claimant's property, although the distinction between law and equity may be relevant to his claim. It seems likely, therefore, that a unified tracing process may eventually evolve.

C. Tracing at Common Law[208]

A proprietary remedy is one which entitles a claimant to treat **23–044** specific property, or a portion thereof, as his own. If the common law had developed a real action for chattels which entitled a claimant to specific recovery, he would be able to demand the return of the chattel. But although the court recognised the claimant as being the owner, there was no such action at common law. The defendant had the choice of paying damages or returning the chattel. A discretion to award specific recovery in an action in detinue was given to the court in 1854.[209]

The claimant's ownership was relevant however in that his entitlement was to the chattel or to its value—its full value that is, even if the defendant was insolvent, and not merely to a dividend in the insolvency. In the case of a loan, the claim for the money lent to an insolvent defendant would abate; it was something owed. The position is different with the chattel; that was something owned.

The question then arises whether this right is limited to the case of a specific chattel. Should this right not continue if the defendant had exchanged one chattel for another; or the chattel for a sum of money; or had spent that money on another chattel? The answer was given by Lord Ellenborough in *Taylor v Plumer*[210]:

---

[206] *Re B A Peters Plc (in administration)* [2010] 1 B.C.L.C. 142 at 148.

[207] Above, fn.205, at 128. See his Lordship's extra-judicial views in (1998) 114 L.Q.R. 399 at 409 and [1999] 14 *Amicus Curiae* 4. See also Smith, *The Law of Tracing*, pp.278–279.

[208] M. Scott (1966) 7 W.A.L.R. 463; R. Pearce (1976) 40 Conv.(N.S.) 277; S. Khurshid and P. Matthews (1979) 95 L.Q.R. 78; R. Goode (1976) 92 L.Q.R. 360 at 364; P. Matthews in Birks (ed.), *Laundering and Tracing*, 1995, p.23; D. Fox, *Property Rights in Money* (2008). See Birks, *An Introduction to the Law of Restitution* (revised edn, 1989), p.358; Goff and Jones, 7th edn, pp.100–109.

[209] Common Law Procedure Act 1854 s.78. Detinue has been abolished: Torts (Interference with Goods) Act 1977 s.2; but the discretionary power of the court to order specific recovery is retained by s.3.

[210] (1815) 3 M. & S. 562 at 575.

"It makes no difference in reason or law into what other form, different from the original, the change may have been made, whether it be into that of promissory notes for the security of the money which was produced by the sale of the goods of the principal, as in *Scott v Surman*,[211] or into other merchandise, as in *Whitecomb v Jacob*,[212] for the product of or substitute for the original thing still follows the nature of the thing itself, as long as it can be ascertained to be such, and the right only ceases when the means of ascertainment fail, which is the case when the subject is turned into money, and mixed and confounded in a general mass of the same description. The difficulty which arises in such a case is a difficulty of fact and not of law, and the dictum that money has no ear-mark must be understood in the same way; *i.e.* as predicated only of an undivided and undistinguishable mass of current money. But money in a bag or otherwise kept apart from other money, guineas, or other coin marked (if the fact were so) for the purpose of being distinguished, are so far ear-marked as to fall within the rule on this subject, which applies to every other description of personal property whilst it remains (as the property in question did) in the hands of the factor [the bankrupt] or his general legal representatives."

23–045   In *Taylor v Plumer*,[213] the defendant handed money to a stockbroker, Walsh, to purchase bonds. Walsh instead purchased American investments and bullion and hurried off to Falmouth to sail to America. He was caught, and the investments and bullion were seized by the defendant. On Walsh's bankruptcy, his assignees in bankruptcy sought to recover them from the defendant. They failed. The investments were the ascertainable product of the defendant's money and owned by him. If the parties had been reversed, and the defendant had been suing for the recovery of the securities and bullion, his action would have succeeded, but the assignees would have had the choice of returning them or of paying their full value in damages; just as if Walsh had taken the defendant's coach and horses and had them in his possession on his bankruptcy.

It is important to appreciate that the common law action of conversion and the action for money had and received are personal actions as was detinue, though, as has been seen,[214] the court may exercise a discretionary power to order the specific recovery of a chattel. Personal actions as a general rule abate in a bankruptcy, which is the normal situation in which tracing is attempted. In the conversion cases, however, full damages without abatement may be

---

[211] (1742) Willes 400.
[212] (1710) Salk. 160.
[213] (1815) 3 M. & S. 562; *Re J Leslie Engineers Co Ltd* [1976] 1 W.L.R. 292 at 297.
[214] Above, para.23–044.

obtained against the trustee in bankruptcy if the chattel is not returned.[215] The claimant's proprietary rights are thus preserved to this extent.[216] A claimant who can establish by tracing that the defendant has received his money will be able to bring a personal action for money had and received, but, if he cannot identify his money or its product in the defendant's hands after receipt, he will not recover in full if the defendant is bankrupt. If he can still identify his money or its product, then he may assert a proprietary claim at common law against the defendant's trustee in bankruptcy on the basis of legal ownership.[217]

The crucial question at common law was whether there was identifiable property, the title to which did not pass to the defendant.[218] In *Banque Belge pour L'Etranger v Hambrouck*[219] money passing through substantially unmixed bank accounts was treated by the majority of the Court of Appeal as still identifiable. In *Lipkin Gorman v Karpnale Ltd*[220] the House of Lords considered that the claimant firm could have traced at common law where money was drawn out of its client account by a partner, Cass, and paid to the Playboy Club. Although the claimant had no proprietary interest in the money in the account, the bank's debt was a chose in action which was the legal property of the claimant. This could be traced into its product, the money withdrawn (apparently even though Cass had legal title to that), and followed into the hands of the volunteer recipient. In *Jones (FC) & Sons (Trustee) v Jones*[221] a partner withdrew £11,700 from a partnership account by cheques in favour of his wife after an act of bankruptcy on the part of the firm and the wife opened an account with a broker, into which the money was paid. The money was profitably invested and the wife received cheques from the broker for £50,760 which she paid into another account she had opened with R Bank. The wife conceded that the trustee in bankruptcy was entitled to £11,700 but claimed to keep

---

[215] S. Khurshid and P. Matthews (1979) 95 L.Q.R. 78; M. Scott (1966) 7 W.A.L.R. 463. See *Giles v Perkins* (1807) 9 East. 12; *Scott v Surman* (1742) Willes 400.

[216] R. Pearce (1976) 40 Conv.(N.S) 277; Goff and Jones, 7th edn, p.103, fn.39.

[217] *Jones (FC) & Sons (Trustee) v Jones* [1997] Ch. 159; below.

[218] See (1966) 7 W.A.L.R. 463 at 481.

[219] [1921] 1 K.B. 321.

[220] [1991] 2 A.C. 548 (a personal action); P. Watts (1991) 107 L.Q.R. 521; M. Halliwell [1992] Conv. 124; E. McKendrick (1992) 5 M.L.R. 377; W. Swadling All E.R.Rev 1992, p.262; L. Smith (2009) 125 L.Q.R. 338. It was conceded (p.572) that the claimant's legal title to the money was not defeated by any mixing by Cass with his own money before payment to the club (cf. *Bank of America v Arnell* [1999] Lloyd's Rep. Bank. 399). Presumably mixing by the club would defeat a common law tracing claim. The claimant could have traced in equity, as Cass held the withdrawn money on trust for the firm.

[221] [1997] Ch. 159; P. Birks and W. Swadling All E.R. Rev. 1996, p.366; N. Andrews and J. Beatson (1997) 113 L.Q.R. 21; P. Birks (1997) 11 T.L.I. 2; D. Fox (1997) 56 C.L.J. 30; R. Davern [1997] 5 R.L.R. 92; C. Mitchell (1997–98) 8 K.C.L.J. 123; D. Fox [1999] 7 R.L.R. 55; Smith, *The Law of Tracing*, pp.320–340; P. Millett in Burrows and Rodger (eds), *Mapping the Law*, Ch.14.

the profit. Her claim was rejected by the Court of Appeal. She had taken possession of money (£11,700) the legal title to which was vested in the trustee in bankruptcy under the insolvency legislation. He was entitled at common law not only to trace his property into its exchange product but also to trace any profit made from it.

23-046 It had been persuasively argued that *Taylor v Plumer*[222] was in fact a decision on tracing in equity and thus not authority for the proposition that tracing into an "exchange product" is possible at common law.[223] It is clear, however, that *Taylor v Plumer* has been accepted in the subsequent case law as authority for that proposition.[224] In the *Jones* case Millett L.J. acknowledged that *Taylor v Plumer* was concerned with the rules of equity but held that this did not mean that the common law did not recognise claims to substitute assets or their products. Thus the trustee in bankruptcy could follow the chose in action constituted by the partnership account into the cheques drawn on it, and could follow those cheques into the account with the broker, the cheques from the broker, and ultimately the chose in action constituted by the account with R Bank. He was entitled at law to the balance in that account, whether greater or less than the original amount withdrawn from the partnership account.[225]

What the common law could not do was to provide full protection to the claimant in the most important type of case in which these questions arise: where the defendant has received the claimant's money, mixed it with other money in a bank account, and has gone bankrupt.[226] In *Agip (Africa) Ltd v Jackson* the claimant sought to trace money transferred to the defendants as a result of the fraud of the claimant's accountant, who had changed the names on payment orders. The money had been paid out (to B Co and thence to the defendants) by a London bank on the telexed instructions of a Tunis bank (where the claimant maintained an account), which then instructed a New York bank to reimburse the London bank. The defendants had paid most of the money away, but part of it remained and was paid into court. Millett J.[227] rejected the common law tracing

---

[222] (1815) 3 M. & S. 562; above.

[223] S. Kurshid and P. Matthews (1979) 95 L.Q.R. 78; L. Smith [1995] L.M.C.L.Q. 240; P. Matthews and P. Birks in Birks (ed.), *Laundering and Tracing*, 1995, pp.49–51 and 297–298 respectively.

[224] *Banque Belge pour L'Etranger v Hambrouck*, above, fn.219; *Lipkin Gorman v Karpnale Ltd*, above, fn.220; *Agip (Africa) Ltd v Jackson* [1991] Ch. 547, below.

[225] cf. *SmithKline Beecham v Apotex Europe Ltd* [2007] Ch. 71 at 88, where Jacob L.J. said that he could not see why equity had no role to play in the *Jones* case: "it looks like a plain case of constructive trusteeship."

[226] P. Birks (1992) 45 C.L.P. 69. For the view that mixing does not prevent common law tracing, see Smith, *The Law of Tracing*, pp.162–174. For the position at common law in respect of mixed or improved goods, see P. Matthews (1981) 34 C.L.P. 159.

[227] [1990] Ch. 265 at 286; P. Birks (1989) 105 L.Q.R. 528; Sir Peter Millett (1991) 107 L.Q.R. 71. See also *Bank of America v Arnell* [1999] Lloyd's Rep. Bank. 399; D. Fox (2000) 59 C.L.J. 28.

claim on the ground that no physical asset of the claimant (such as a cheque or its proceeds) could be identified in the defendant's hands. Nothing but a stream of electrons passed between the banks as a result of the telegraphic transfers. The London bank paid with its own money, subject to reimbursement, and not with anything identifiable as the product of the claimant's property. It was not possible to show the source from which the London bank was reimbursed without tracing the money through the New York clearing system. There it was mixed, which defeated the common law claim. The decision was upheld on appeal on the basis that mixing defeated the claim, although Fox L.J. (giving the only reasoned judgment) thought it did not matter that no cheque was involved.[228] Lord Millett has restated the view that the common law cannot trace money transferred electronically both judicially and extra-judicially,[229] and it has found support elsewhere.[230] It may be, however, that such money remains traceable at common law if it has not been mixed by passing through an inter-bank clearing system.[231]

As we will see, mixing does not prevent tracing in equity, although other limitations upon the availability of the equitable remedy leave scope for tracing at common law. In practical terms, however, most of the situations in which a claim to trace arises are cases of money in mixed bank accounts, in which the common law remedy is not available. It has therefore limited practical importance at the present day.

D. Tracing in Equity

Equity has developed more sophisticated methods of tracing. The rules have developed, and are usually applied, in the context of property in the hands of trustees or other fiduciaries, and often on   **23–047**

---

[228] [1991] Ch. 547 at 565; C. Harpum (1991) 50 C.L.J. 409; S. Goulding [1992] Conv. 367; W. Swadling All E.R. Rev. 1992, 259. Tracing in equity was allowed; below, para.23–049. In *Jones (FC) & Sons (Trustee) v Jones*, above, fn.217, it was not necessary to trace the passage of the money through a clearing system.

[229] *El Ajou v Dollar Land Holdings Plc* [1993] 3 All E.R. 717 at 733 (not discussed on appeal at [1994] 2 All E.R. 685); (1991) 107 L.Q.R. 71 at 74; (1995) 9 T.L.I. 35 at 39; [1999] 14 *Amicus Curiae* 4.

[230] *Nimmo v Westpac Banking Corp* [1993] 3 N.Z.L.R. 218; *Bank Tejarat v Hong Kong and Shanghai Banking Corp (CI) Ltd* [1995] 1 Lloyd's Rep. 239; criticised P. Birks (1995) 9 T.L.I. 91. The position is otherwise in Canada; D. Fox (2010) 69 C.L.J. 28. Where a payment is made between two bank accounts telegraphically, electronically or by cheque, one chose in action is reduced or extinguished and another created, thus no property of the payer is obtained by the payee within the Theft Act 1968; *R. v Preddy* [1996] A.C. 815 (see now Theft (Amendment) Act 1996).

[231] A. Oakley (1995) 54 C.L.J. 377. See also Smith, *The Law of Tracing*, pp.253–258; L. Smith in F. Rose (ed.), *Restitution and Banking Law*, 1998, Ch.8; C. Mitchell (1997–98) 8 K.C.L.J. 123; J. Ulph [2007] 15 R.L.R. 76.

the bankruptcy of the fiduciary. But the rules apply also in a commercial context; as where a vendor, in order to protect himself in a customer's bankruptcy, provides expressly that property shall not pass in goods supplied until payment. Equity will assist in the location and preservation of traceable property by disclosure and injunctions.[232]

23–048   **i. Who is Entitled to Trace.** The remedy in equity is not confined to claims between trustee and beneficiary. *Re Hallett*[233] decided that the remedy was not restricted to such a case but was available against other fiduciaries.[234]

23–049   (a) *Requirement of Fiduciary Relationship.* The courts have insisted that the existence of a fiduciary relationship is a prerequisite to tracing in equity, although this relationship need not exist between the parties to the action. In *Re Diplock*[235] the action was not against the executors, but against the innocent volunteers (the charities) to whom they handed the money.

> By his will Diplock gave the residue of his property on trust for such "charitable or benevolent . . . objects in England as my . . . executors . . . may in their . . . absolute discretion select." He and the executors thought that this was a valid charitable gift, but it was not.[236] The executors distributed £203,000 among a considerable number of charitable institutions; and when the invalidity of the charitable gift was discovered, the next-of-kin claimed to recover the money from the charities. They succeeded in a personal claim[237] and were also entitled to trace, the Court of Appeal laying down as the test that[238]:
>
> > "[E]quity may operate on the conscience not merely of those who acquire a legal title in breach of some trust, express or constructive, or of some other fiduciary obligation, but of volunteers provided that as a result of what has gone before some

---

[232] *Bankers Trust Co v Shapira* [1980] 1 W.L.R. 1274; *A v C* [1981] Q.B. 956; *In re DPR Futures Ltd* [1989] 1 W.L.R. 778. For cross-border tracing, see G. Panagopoulos [1998] 6 R.L.R. 73.

[233] (1880) 13 Ch.D. 696 at 709.

[234] See Goff and Jones, 7th edn, p.112, fn.93, where they point out how difficult it is to define precisely who is a fiduciary. They refer to the analogy of decisions on the Statutes of Limitation, which suggest that "much depends on whether the agent is under a duty to keep separate his own money from his principal's money."

[235] [1948] Ch. 465.

[236] Above, para.15–058, *Chichester Diocesan Fund v Simpson* [1944] A.C. 341.

[237] [1951] A.C. 251. The appeal to the House of Lords concerned only the personal action; below, para.23–007.

[238] [1948] Ch. 465 at 530.

equitable proprietary interest has been created and attaches to the property in the hands of the volunteer."

Although a beneficiary is not normally regarded as the equitable owner of assets in an unadministered estate,[239] the "equitable proprietary interest" was established for present purposes by the equitable claim by the claimants as next-of-kin against the executors; and this gave the claimants the right to trace against the charities.

The requirement of a fiduciary relationship has been much criticised,[240] but has been accepted in modern decisions of the Court of Appeal[241] and (although somewhat ambiguously) by the House of Lords in *Westdeutsche Landesbank Girozentrale v Islington London Borough Council*,[242] where the principles established in *Re Diplock* were approved.[243] In *Foskett v McKeown*,[244] on the other hand, Lord Millett said that there was no logical justification for insisting on a fiduciary relationship as a precondition in equity, although such a relationship could be relevant to the claim. The issue, however, did not arise in that case. So long as the traditional approach prevails, the position may be relieved by the apparent ease with which a fiduciary relationship may be recognised, as in most cases of commercial fraud.[245]

(b) *Requirement of an Equitable Proprietary Interest.* In the **23–050** days before the fusion of the jurisdiction of law and equity, it was only possible to obtain equitable remedies if the litigation were "in equity". It is not therefore surprising that the test which has been laid down historically for the availability of equitable tracing is that the claimant should be entitled to an *equitable* proprietary interest; and this requirement of an equitable proprietary interest is distinct from absolute ownership at law.

There seems to be no reason at all on the merits why the equitable tracing process should not be available also to the beneficial legal owner. All that should be required is a proprietary base. Indeed, it was arguable, before *Re Diplock*[246] was decided, that this situation

---

[239] *Commissioner of Stamp Duties v Livingston* [1965] A.C. 694; above, para.2–020.

[240] P. Birks (1995) 9 T.L.I. 124 at 126; Goff and Jones, pp.110–112; *Bristol and West Building Society v Mothew* [1998] Ch.1 at 23; Smith, *The Law of Tracing*, pp.123–130, 340–347; cf. P. Kohler (2000) 53 C.L.P. 236 at 266–273.

[241] *Aluminium Industrie Vaassen BV v Romalpa Aluminium Ltd* [1976] 1 W.L.R. 676; *Agip (Africa) Ltd v Jackson* [1991] Ch. 547; *Boscawen v Bajwa* [1996] 1 W.L.R. 328 at 335; *Jones (FC) & Sons (Trustee) v Jones* [1997] Ch. 159.

[242] [1996] A.C. 669. See G. Jones (1996) 55 C.L.J. 432, pointing out inconsistencies.

[243] [1996] A.C. 669 at 714. But see P. Birks and W. Swadling All E.R. Rev. 1996, p.373; A. Oakley [1997] Conv. 1 at 4.

[244] [2001] 1 A.C. 102 at 128. See also Lord Millett [1999] 14 *Amicus Curiae* 4 and (2007) 123 L.Q.R. 159 at 164; *Smalley v Bracken Partners Ltd* [2004] W.T.L.R. 599.

[245] *Agip (Africa) Ltd v Jackson*, above, fn.241 (senior accountant and employer).

[246] [1948] Ch. 465; F. Babafemi (1971) 34 M.L.R. 12.

had been recognised by *Banque Belge v Hambrouck*.[247] Atkin L.J. treated equitable tracing as a means of overcoming the common law's difficulty in identifying the claimant's money in a mixed fund[248]:

> "The question always was, Had the means of ascertainment failed? But if in 1815 the common law halted outside the bankers' door, by 1879 equity had had the courage to lift the latch, walk in and examine the books: *Re Hallett's Estate*.[249] I see no reason why the means of ascertainment so provided should not now be available both for common law and equity proceedings."

It has been doubtful, since *Re Diplock*, whether equitable tracing will be available in the absence of some situation creating equitable as opposed to legal ownership.[250] In *Aluminium Industrie Vaassen BV v Romalpa Aluminium Ltd*[251] however, the Court of Appeal permitted tracing by a legal owner to whom a fiduciary duty was owed, although this point was not discussed.

Consider this case; B owes £1,000 to his creditors and has only £100. He steals £1,000 from A and mixes that money in his account which now has £1,100. He now "owes" £2,000. Should the available money be shared rateably between A and the creditors, or should A get back first his £1,000, which B should never have had? Common law tracing is not available because the funds are mixed; nor equitable tracing if there is no fiduciary relation between a thief and his victim. Fortunately Lord Templeman in *Lipkin Gorman v Karpnale Ltd*[252] has approved Australian authority[253] to the effect that a thief holds stolen money on trust for his victim, who can accordingly trace it. Similarly, Lord Browne-Wilkinson has confirmed that

---

[247] [1921] 1 K.B. 321.

[248] [1921] 1 K.B. 321 at 335; criticised in *Agip (Africa) Ltd v Jackson*, above, fn.238, for treating common law and equitable remedies as the same. See also *Chief Constable of Kent v V* [1983] Q.B. 34 at 41, per Lord Denning M.R.: "It may be that 150 year ago the common law halted outside the banker's door, but for the last 100 years, since the fusion of law and equity, it has had the courage to lift the latch, walk in and examine the books: see *Banque Belge pour l'Etranger v Hambrouck* [1912] 1 K.B. 321 at p.335, per Atkin L.J. and *Re Diplock's Estate, Diplock v Wintle* [1948] Ch. 465, per Lord Greene M.R."

[249] (1880) 13 Ch.D. 696.

[250] For arguments to the effect that legal, as opposed to equitable, ownership is a sufficient basis for a right to trace, see A. Oakley (1975) 28 C.L.P. 64; R. Pearce (1976) 40 Conv.(N.S.) 227; Goff and Jones, 7th edn, p.112.

[251] [1976] 1 W.L.R. 676, below, para.23–073; cf. *Re Andrabell Ltd* [1984] 3 All E.R. 407. See Heydon, Gummow and Austin, *Cases and Materials on Equity and Trusts*, 4th edn, pp.898, 906.

[252] [1991] 2 A.C. 548.

[253] *Black v S Freedman & Co* (1910) 12 C.L.R. 105. See also *Lennox Industries (Canada) Ltd v The Queen* (1987) 34 D.L.R. 297; *Bishopsgate Investment Management Ltd v Maxwell* [1993] Ch. 1 at 70; *Ghana Commercial Bank v C, The Times*, March 3, 1997.

the money is traceable on the ground that equity imposes a constructive trust on a fraudulent recipient.[254]

One question which came before the House of Lords in *West-* **23–051**
*deutsche Landesbank Girozentrale v Islington London Borough
Council*[255] was whether the claimant bank retained an equitable
proprietary interest in money paid to the defendant under a transaction (an "interest rate swap") which was ultra vires (so far as the
defendant was concerned) and void. Tracing would in any event
have been impossible because the money had been mixed with other
money in an account and used for general expenditure, the account
having been subsequently overdrawn several times.[256] The defendant now conceded personal liability to repay, the issue being
whether compound interest could be awarded to the bank. Their
Lordships unanimously agreed that the bank retained no equitable
proprietary interest in the money, which, according to the majority,
meant that there was no jurisdiction to award compound interest.[257]
Sinclair v Brougham,[258] where the House of Lords had permitted
tracing by creditors (depositors) of a bank whose business was ultra
vires, was overruled. Although in the present case the bank's belief
in the validity of the transaction was mistaken, it intended the
money to become the absolute property of the defendant and had
been prepared to take the risk of insolvency. As a general rule,
property in money passes even though a contract is void, although
there may be limited exceptions in the case of "fundamental mistake" in the orthodox sense.[259] Thus there was considered to be no
moral or legal reason why, had there been an insolvency, the claimant should have had priority over general creditors. The defendant
received the money neither as resulting trustee (because the property
had passed, as intended) nor as constructive trustee (because it was
unaware of the invalidity until after the money had been spent and
its conscience was thus unaffected) but was merely subject to personal liability at common law to repay.

[254] *Westdeutsche Landesbank Girozentrale v Islington LBC* [1996] A.C. 669 at pp.715–716
(but see doubts expressed in *Shalson v Russo* [2005] Ch. 281 at 317); cf. *Jones (FC) & Sons
(Trustee) v Jones* [1997] Ch. 159 (No constructive trust nor fiduciary relationship where wife
obtained possession of, but not title to, funds of bankrupt partnership. Thus only the common
law tracing rules applied). See also Chambers, *Resulting Trusts*, p.117, preferring a resulting
trust analysis; Smith, *The Law of Tracing*, pp.343–347.

[255] [1996] A.C. 669; M. Cope (1996) 112 L.Q.R. 521; P. Birks [1996] R.L.R. 3; G. Jones
(1996) 55 C.L.J. 432; C. Mitchell (1996) 10 T.L.I. 84; S. Gardner [2008] 16 R.L.R. 107.

[256] See below, paras 25–056, 25–057.

[257] This aspect has now been overtaken by the decision in *Sempra Metals Ltd (formerly
Metallgesellschaft Ltd) v IRC* [2008] 1 A.C. 561; above, para.23–016.

[258] [1914] A.C. 398. Lord Goff would have allowed it to stand in the confined area of ultra
vires loans. The present case did not involve loans. See A Burrows (1997) 50 C.L.P. 95. Lord
Millett has expressed the hope that *Sinclair* "can finally be relegated to the dustbin"; (2007)
123 L.Q.R. 159 at 164.

[259] [1996] A.C. 669 at 690 (Lord Goff); D. Fox [1996] 55 C.L.J. 547 and [1996]
R.L.R. 60.

Grave doubt was cast on the correctness of *Chase Manhattan Bank NA v Israel-British Bank (London) Ltd*,[260] where the claim to trace money paid by mistake of fact[261] to the defendant (now insolvent) was upheld on the basis that the claimant retained an equitable proprietary interest in the money. Lord Goff found it unnecessary to review that decision. Lord Browne-Wilkinson disagreed with the reasoning but considered that the result could be justified on the basis that the defendant bank became aware of the mistake within two days and retained the money in traceable form. Thus its conscience was sufficiently affected to found a constructive trust.[262] His Lordship could not have meant, however, that notice was sufficient to trigger a proprietary interest which the claimant could not otherwise have asserted.[263]

23–052   Essential to the reasoning in *Westdeutsche* was the fact that the bank intended the defendant to have the money. The position will be different in the absence of such an intention. In *Clark v Cutland*[264] a company director transferred company assets to trustees of a pension fund in breach of his fiduciary duty. As he acted without the company's authority, the transaction was void. It could not be said that the company intended the property to pass to the trustees. As the trustees were not purchasers, the company was entitled to trace into the pension fund assets.

In the case of a voidable transaction (such as a contract induced by misrepresentation or undue influence), it is established that a claimant who elects to rescind can trace on the basis that the property, having initially passed to the defendant, revests in equity in the claimant on rescission.[265] The consequence of the property having initially passed to the defendant is that no constructive trust or other

---

[260] [1981] Ch. 105; W. Swadling (1996) 16 L.S. 110; G. McCormack [1996] Conv. 86; A. Burrows (2001) 117 L.Q.R. 412 at 426. See further Lord Millett in Degeling and Edelman (eds), *Equity in Commercial Law*, 2005, Ch.12, for the view that there is no proprietary remedy in normal cases of mistaken transfers. On the possible role of resulting trusts see C. Webb in Mitchell (ed.), *Constructive and Resulting Trusts* (2009), Ch.11; R. Chambers (2010) 63 C.L.P. 631.

[261] The personal action (subject to solvency) would now lie in cases of payment by mistake of law; *Kleinwort Benson Ltd v Lincoln CC* [1999] 2 A.C. 349.

[262] [1996] A.C. 669 at 715. The correctness of *Chase Manhattan* had been left open by the Privy Council in *Re Goldcorp Exchange Ltd* [1995] 1 A.C. 74.

[263] See P. Birks [1996] R.L.R. 3 at 21; G. Jones (1996) 55 C.L.J. 432; P. Birks and W. Swadling All E.R. Rev. 1996 at 373; W. Swadling (1998) 12 T.L.I. 288; Sir Peter Millett (1998) 114 L.Q.R. 399; D. Hayton in P. Birks (ed.), *Privacy and Loyalty*, 1997, pp.301–304. cf. R Calnan [2004] 12 R.L.R. 1; *Papamichael v National Westminster Bank Plc* [2003] 1 Lloyd's Rep. 341 at 372; *Commerzbank Aktiengesellschaft v IMB Morgan Plc* [2005] W.T.L.R. 1485 at 1495.

[264] [2004] 1 W.L.R. 783. See also *Criterion Properties Plc v Stratford UK Properties LLC* [2004] 1 W.L.R. 1846 (Lord Nicholls).

[265] *Daly v Sydney Stock Exchange* (1986) 160 C.L.R. 371; *Lonrho Plc v Fayed (No.2)* [1992] 1 W.L.R. 1; *Halifax Building Society v Thomas* [1996] Ch. 217; *Shalson v Russo* [2005] Ch. 281; *Independent Trustee Services Ltd v G P Noble Trustees* [2011] 2 F.L.R. 174 at 182–189. D. Hayton in P. Birks (ed.), *Privacy and Loyalty*, p.304; Goff and Jones, 7th edn, pp.96–98.

proprietary claim may normally be asserted in respect of the period prior to rescission, nor would any third party rights arising prior to rescission be affected.[266] However, there appears to be some inconsistency in the principle that a party to a voidable transaction may trace on rescinding the contract, while a party to a void transaction is denied the right to trace, according to *Westdeutsche Landesbank Girozentrale v Islington LBC*,[267] on the basis that he intended the property to pass. As has been said, the concept of the property passing under a voidable transaction is inimical (in the absence of special circumstances) to the existence of either a constructive trust or a tracing claim.[268]

There are some situations in which an equitable proprietary interest has been held to remain in the transferor. Thus a payment induced by forgery may be traced on the basis that equity imposes a constructive trust on a fraudulent recipient.[269] An unusual situation arose in *Collings v Lee*,[270] where X agreed to find a buyer on behalf of the owners of land. He fraudulently procured registration in his own name, for no consideration and in breach of his fiduciary duty as agent, and mortgaged the land to Y. It was held that the equitable interest remained in the former owners, who never intended to transfer the property to X. As the owners remained in occupation, they had an overriding interest enforceable against Y under the principles of land registration. The case was distinguishable from those involving a voidable contract procured by fraudulent misrepresentation, where the transferor intended the property to pass pursuant to the contract notwithstanding the vitiating factor.

Many different views have been expressed by the judiciary and by academic commentators on the proprietary consequences of void and voidable transactions, and the principles have not yet been fully worked out. All that can be said with reasonable confidence is that rescission of a voidable contract revests the equitable interest in the claimant for tracing purposes.[271]

---

[266] See *Shalson v Russo*, above, fn.265.

[267] [1996] A.C. 669. The "revesting" theory was doubted by the Privy Council in *Re Goldcorp Exchange Ltd* [1995] 1 A.C. 74. See also P. Oliver (1997–98) 8 K.C.L.J. 147 at 152; M. Bridge (2004) 57 C.L.P. 277 at 294.

[268] *Re Ciro Citterio Menswear Plc* [2002] 1 W.L.R. 2217 (no tracing where money loaned by company to director under voidable transaction was used to purchase house).

[269] *Bankers Trust Co v Shapira* [1980] 1 W.L.R. 1274, as explained by Lord Brown-Wilkinson in the *Westdeutsche* case, at 716; cf. doubts expressed in *Shalson v Russo* [2005] Ch. 281.

[270] [2001] 2 All E.R. 332; D. O'Sullivan (2001) 117 L.Q.R. 381; R. Nolan (2001) 60 C.L.J. 477. See also *Halley v The Law Society* [2003] W.T.L.R. 845; T. Wu (2004) 63 C.L.J. 30.

[271] See S. Worthington [2002] R.L.R. 28. See also Lord Millett [1999] 14 *Amicus Curiae* 4, suggesting that a proprietary remedy in cases of voidable transactions should be available only where a money judgment would be inadequate; W. Swadling (2005) 121 L.Q.R. 123, suggesting title does not revest at common law on rescission; cf. B. Häcker [2006] 14 R.L.R. 106 and (2009) 68 C.L.J. 324.

As we have seen, the requirement of an equitable proprietary interest for tracing in equity is not satisfied in the case of bribes, because the defendant does not hold the bribe on constructive trust for his principal.[272] An equitable proprietary interest normally goes hand in hand with a fiduciary relationship, assuming the latter is still required. A fiduciary relationship alone, however, is not a sufficient basis for tracing. Thus, a person who dishonestly assists in a breach of trust is commonly called a constructive trustee, but no proprietary rights may be asserted against him if he has received no trust property.[273]

23–053   **ii. Unmixed Funds.** The easy case is that in which there has been no mixing of the trust funds with the trustee's own money. If the trustee has sold the trust property, the beneficiary may take the proceeds if he can identify them. (If the purchaser had notice, the beneficiary may elect to take either the property or the proceeds.[274]) If the proceeds of sale have been used to purchase other property the beneficiary may "follow" them and may:

> "[E]lect either to take the property purchased, or to hold it as a security for the amount of trust money laid out in the purchase; or, as we generally express it, he is entitled at his election either to take the property, or to have a charge on the property for the amount of the trust money."[275]

The beneficiary is entitled to any profit even though the trustee could have made the purchase with his own money.[276] Claims in equity will never, of course, be valid against a bona fide purchaser for value.[277] If, however, the property has come into the hands of an innocent volunteer, the tracing remedy lies against him while he retains it.[278]

23–054   **iii. Mixed Funds.** The position is more complicated where the trustee has mixed the trust funds with other money, and possibly converted the mixed funds into other property. The position differs

---

[272] *Sinclair Investments (UK) Ltd v Versailles Trade Finance Ltd (in administrative receivership)* [2011] 3 W.L.R. 1153, doubting *Att Gen for Hong Kong v Reid* [1994] 1 A.C. 324; above, para.21–026; D. Hayton (2011) 127 L.Q.R. 487; cf. R. Goode (2011) 127 L.Q.R. 493; G. Virgo (2011) 70 C.L.J. 502.

[273] Above, para.12–011; A. Oakley (1995) 54 C.L.J. 377 at 383.

[274] See P. Birks (1992) 45 C.L.P. 69 at 95; Smith, *The Law of Tracing*, pp.377–383; L. Smith in Burrows and Rodger (eds), *Mapping the Law*, 2006, Ch.7; *Jones (FC) & Sons (Trustee) v Jones* [1997] Ch. 159 (common law); C. Davis (2002) 61 C.L.J. 423 at 447.

[275] per Jessel M.R. in *Re Hallett's Estate* (1880) 13 Ch.D. 696 at 709.

[276] See the example of the winning lottery ticket in *Foskett v McKeown* [2001] 1 A.C. 102 at 134.

[277] Below, para.23–069.

[278] Below, para.23–066. As to whether he has any personal liability, see above, para.12–021.

according to whether the claim is against the trustee (or his successors), or whether the ownership of the mixed fund must be apportioned between two trusts or a trust and an innocent volunteer. Also, there are special rules applicable to cases of mixed funds in bank accounts.

(a) *Position as Against the Trustee.* The rule here is that the **23–055** beneficiaries have a first claim over the mixed fund or any property purchased with it. The onus is on the trustee to prove that part of the mixed fund is his own.

" . . . [I]f a trustee amalgamated [trust property] with his own, his beneficiary will be entitled to every portion of the blended property which the trustee cannot prove to be his own."[279]

Assuming the trustee can prove his contribution, the beneficiaries share any property purchased from the mixed fund with the trustee (or his successors), the shares being proportionate to the contributions. In *Foskett v McKeown*[280] the trustee used his own money to pay the first three premiums on a life assurance policy and trust money to pay the fourth and fifth, after which he died. It was held by a majority of the House of Lords that the beneficiaries were entitled to a 40 per cent share in the policy proceeds. The trustee had settled the policy on his children but they, being volunteer successors, could be in no better position than the trustee. Lord Millett expressed the rule as follows:

"Where a trustee wrongfully uses trust money to provide part of the cost of acquiring an asset, the beneficiary is entitled *at his option* either to claim a proportionate share of the asset or to enforce a lien upon it to secure his personal claim against the trustee for the amount of the misapplied money. It does not matter whether the trustee mixed the trust money with his own in a single fund before using it to acquire the asset, or made separate payments (whether simultaneously or sequentially) out of the

---

[279] *Lewin on Trusts*, 16th edn, 1964, p.223, quoted in *Re Tilley's WT* [1967] Ch. 1179 at 1182; *Lupton v White* (1808) 15 Ves.Jr. 432; *Indian Oil Corp Ltd v Greenstone Shipping SA* [1987] 2 Lloyd's Rep. 286; P. Stein (1987) 46 C.L.J. 369; *Coleman v Harvey* [1989] 1 N.Z.L.R. 723; *Glencore International AG v Metro Trading International Inc* [2001] 1 Lloyd's Rep. 284; *Sinclair Investments (UK) Ltd v Versailles Trade Finance Ltd (in administrative receivership)* [2011] 3 W.L.R. 1153 ("maelstrom account").

[280] [2001] 1 A.C. 102; P. Birks and W. Swadling All E.R. Rev. 2000 at 320; R. Grantham and C. Rickett (2000) 63 M.L.R. 905; C. Rotherham (2000) 59 C.L.J. 440; P. Jaffey (2000) 14 T.L.I. 194; Sir Robert Walker [2000] R.L.R. 573; J. Stevens [2001] Conv. 94; A. Burrows (2001) 117 L.Q.R. 412; D. Fox [2001] L.M.C.L.Q. 1; C. Rotherham [2003] 11 R.L.R. 57; Goff and Jones, 7th edn, p.88. The dissenting judgments proceeded on the basis that, on the particular facts, the premiums paid with trust money did not add to the value of the policy, so that the beneficiaries were entitled only to the return of the sums paid with their money.

differently owned funds to acquire a single asset . . . As against the wrongdoer and his successors, the beneficiary is entitled to locate his contribution in any part of the mixture and to subordinate their claims to share in the mixture until his own contribution has been satisfied. This has the effect of giving the beneficiary a lien for his contribution if the mixture is deficient."[281]

It has been held that the trustee is not to be treated as having made any contribution where he uses trust money in part payment for a property and provides the balance by borrowing on mortgage on the security of the property. Thus the beneficiaries take the whole of any profit.[282] Even where the trustee has contributed his own money, the trust should take all the profit if the asset (such as a house) could not have been bought without the trust contribution, in contrast with the case where a trustee buys shares and could have bought fewer with his funds alone.[283]

23–056   An extremely wide view of tracing into mixed funds emerged from dicta of the Privy Council in *Space Investments Ltd v Canadian Imperial Bank of Commerce Trust Co (Bahamas) Ltd*.[284] A bank trustee deposited trust money with itself under an express power to do so, and was then wound up. It was held that if a bank trustee misappropriated trust money for its own benefit, tracing would be possible. But where the mixing was done lawfully, as here, the trust money became the bank's, subject only to a personal obligation to pay. Hence the beneficiaries had no interest in the bank's assets and were unsecured creditors. The settlor had accepted the risk of insolvency by allowing the deposit. Lord Templeman went on to discuss the position if tracing had been available, saying that if the beneficiaries could not trace their money into any particular asset belonging to the trustee bank, equity would allow them:

> "[T]o trace the trust money to all the assets of the bank and to recover the trust money by the exercise of an equitable charge over all the assets of the bank."[285]

The difficulty with this is that it suggests that if a commingled fund has been lost, the beneficiaries still have a proprietary claim to the trustee's remaining assets, which are impressed with a charge. Such a view would be unfair to the general creditors, and is supported neither by principle nor by policy.[286]

---

[281] [2001] 1 A.C. 102 at 131.
[282] *Davies (Paul A) (Australia) Pty Ltd v Davies* [1983] 1 N.S.W.L.R. 440.
[283] See *Australian Postal Corp v Lutak* (1991) 21 N.S.W.L.R. 584; L. Aitken (1993) 13 L.S. 371. This distinction seems to have been overlooked in A. Berg (2001) 117 L.Q.R. 366.
[284] [1986] 1 W.L.R. 1072. See also *Ross v Lord Advocate* [1986] 1 W.L.R. 1077.
[285] [1986] 1 W.L.R. 1072 at 1074.
[286] See the cogent criticisms in R. Goode (1987) 103 L.Q.R. 433.

The point was discussed again by the Privy Council in *Re Gold-corp Exchange Ltd*,[287] where customers who had paid for bullion but had not taken delivery sought to trace into the assets of the now insolvent company. Save for one class of customers whose bullion had been segregated, the claim failed because the customers never had any proprietary rights in any bullion,[288] nor in the money paid over, which had never been impressed with any trust.[289] Thus they were simply unsecured creditors. As the customers had no proprietary rights in the purchase money, it was unnecessary to consider whether they could have traced into the company's assets. It was doubted, however, whether Lord Templeman's dicta in *Space Investments*[290] could overcome the difficulty that the money had been paid into an overdrawn account. The dicta, it was said, were concerned with tracing into a mixed fund, not a non-existent fund.

In the case of the customers whose bullion had been segregated, only a small amount could be traced because it had been mixed with other bullion, depleted by withdrawals, and not replaced by the addition of other bullion.[291] They could not improve their position by asserting an equitable lien over all the assets of the company in reliance on the dicta in *Space Investments*. It was accepted, however, that where a bank uses all borrowed money as a mixed fund for lending or investing, any trust money unlawfully borrowed by a bank trustee could be said to be latent in property subsequently acquired by the bank so that an equitable lien could be imposed on that property.[292] In the present case there was no evidence that the bullion of these customers continued to exist as a fund latent in property vested in the company's receivers and no reason to favour them above other customers by the grant of a lien. Thus it was not appropriate to consider the scope of *Space Investments* nor its application to trustees other than bank trustees.

Although the Privy Council did not expressly reject Lord Temple-man's observations (and it should be noted that his Lordship sat also in *Re Goldcorp Exchange Ltd*),[293] it has been said that after *Re* **23–057**

---

[287] [1995] 1 A.C. 74 (on appeal from New Zealand); E. McKendrick (1994) 110 L.Q.R. 509; N. Richardson (1994) 8 T.L.I. 91; L. Sealy (1994) 53 C.L.J. 443; N. Palmer All E.R. Rev. 1994 at 40; above, para.3–021.

[288] See now Sale of Goods (Amendment) Act 1995; T. Burns (1996) 59 M.L.R. 260; above, para.3–022 (co-ownership solution).

[289] In contrast with *Re Kayford Ltd* [1975] 1 W.L.R. 279; above, para.2–010. It is otherwise if a trust has been declared of money awaiting transfer to a segregated account (*Re Kaupthing Singer & Friedlander Ltd (in administration)* [2010] W.T.L.R. 79); or if a trust arises on receipt of client funds by an investment firm under a statutory regulatory regime (*Lehman Brothers International (Europe) (in administration) v CRC Credit Fund Ltd* [2011] Bus. L.R. 277).

[290] Above, fn.284.

[291] Applying *Roscoe v Winder* [1915] 1 Ch. 62; below, para.23–060.

[292] Criticised D. Hayton (1994–95) 5 K.C.L.J. 143.

[293] Above, fn.287.

Goldcorp the dicta are "now as good as dead".[294] This is reinforced
by *Bishopsgate Investment Management Ltd v Homan*,[295] where
Maxwell pension funds were wrongly paid into the overdrawn account of a company now found to be insolvent. The Court of Appeal
confirmed that there could be no tracing into an overdrawn bank
account (whether overdrawn at the payment or later) and that no
equitable charge could be imposed on the company's assets in reliance on the dicta in *Space Investments*. The Privy Council in *Re
Goldcorp Exchange Ltd*[296] had rejected a wide interpretation of
those dicta, which related specifically to tracing into a bank's credit
balances where a bank trustee had wrongfully deposited trust money
with itself.[297] More recently the Court of Appeal again rejected the
argument that a charge could be imposed on all of the defendant's
assets (including his share of the matrimonial home bought some
years earlier) where the trust funds could no longer be identified:

> "This cannot be right, in our view. For the equitable charge to
> attach it must attach to assets in existence which derive from the
> misappropriated trust funds. There must be a nexus. Were it other-
> wise the principles of following and tracing could become
> otiose."[298]

23–058   (b) *Position as Between Two Trusts, or Trust and Third Party.* It
may be, however, that the trustee has mixed the funds of two trusts,
whether or not with his own,[299] or has transferred the funds to an
innocent volunteer, who has mixed them with his own. The rule here
is that the two trusts, or the trust and the volunteer, share *pari passu*
(i.e. rateably) in the mixed funds or any property purchased out of
them.[300] The position of the innocent volunteer is further dealt with
below.

Where there have been several victims but there is no realistic
possibility that other claimants will seek to assert a charge ranking
rateably with the claimant's, the claimant may be permitted to trace
an amount in excess of that which he would obtain on a rateable
division. Whether the rights of third parties may be raised as a

---

[294] P. Birks (1995) 9 T.L.I. 43 at 45. See also P. Oliver (1995) 9 T.L.I. 43, p.78; S. Moriarty
and P. Birks in P. Birks (ed.), *Laundering and Tracing*, pp.82–88 and 294.
[295] [1995] Ch. 211; A. Jones [1996] Conv. 129; below, para.23–061. See also *Fortex Group
Ltd v MacIntosh* [1998] 3 N.Z.L.R. 171; *Box v Barclays Bank Plc* [1998] Lloyd's Rep. Bank.
185; *Shalson v Russo* [2005] Ch. 281; *Re B A Peters Plc (in administration)* [2010] 1
B.C.L.C. 142.
[296] Above, fn.287.
[297] [1995] Ch. 211 at 221–222.
[298] *Director of the Serious Fraud Office v Lexi Holdings Plc* [2009] Q.B. 376 at 393.
[299] Any claim to ownership by the trustee will be governed by the principle discussed in
para.(a) above.
[300] *Re Diplock* [1948] Ch. 465. The principle was affirmed in *Foskett v McKeown* [2001] 1
A.C. 102.

partial defence to a tracing claim depends on the circumstances of each case.[301]

(c) *Bank Accounts.* The mixing is likely, however, to occur in the **23–059** context of a banking account, to which special rules apply. Again, it is necessary to distinguish the position as between trustee and beneficiary and as between two trusts or trust and innocent volunteer. These rules govern the allocation of payments out of the mixed fund.[302] The principle as between trustee and beneficiary is that the trustee is presumed to spend his own money first.

In *Re Hallett's Estate*,[303] Hallett, a solicitor, mixed with his own money certain funds from two trusts, one his own marriage settlement of which he was trustee, and the other a trust of which a client, Mrs Cotterill, was beneficiary. At his death there were insufficient funds to pay his personal debts and to meet these claims.

Three questions arose; (i) whether Mrs Cotterill, not being a beneficiary of a trust of which Hallett was a trustee, was entitled to trace on the ground of the fiduciary relationship; (ii) (assuming that she was) how to allocate the payments from the fund as between Hallett and the claimants; and (iii) as between the claimants themselves.

The Court of Appeal held that Mrs Cotterill was entitled to trace, and that the payments out must be treated as payments of Hallett's own money. This left sufficient to satisfy the claims of Mrs Cotterill and of the beneficiaries under the marriage settlement, so the third question did not arise.[304]

We are at present concerned with (ii). The other matters are discussed elsewhere.[305] The reason given by Jessel M.R. for allocating payments to Hallett's money and not to the trust is that wherever an act, "can be done rightfully, [a man] is not allowed to say, against

---

[301] *El Ajou v Dollar Land Holdings Plc (No.2)* [1995] 2 All E.R. 213.

[302] In the case of insuperable accounting difficulties, these rules will not be applied. See *Cunningham v Brown*, 265 U.S. 1, 44 Sup Ct 424; 68 L.Ed. 873 (1923), where a tracing remedy was refused in respect of a mass of claims arising out of a fraud. Taft C.J. said "It would be running the fiction of *Knatchbull v Hallett* into the ground to apply it here." The claimants shared equally.

[303] (1880) 13 Ch.D. 696; see A. Oakley (1975) 28 C.L.P. 64. The principle has been applied to a common law claim to wrongly mixed oil; *Glencore International AG v Metro Trading International Inc* [2001] 1 Lloyd's Rep. 284; J. Ulph [2001] L.M.C.L.Q. 449.

[304] In the court below, where, on the view taken by Fry J., the third question did arise, it was solved by applying the rule in *Clayton's Case* (1817) 1 Mer. 572.

[305] Above, para.23–049; below, para.23–062.

the person entitled to the property or the right, that he has done it wrongfully."[306]

23–060   It should be appreciated, however, that this principle operates in the context of a claim against a balance in the account, and does not derogate from the general principle, described above, that the beneficiaries have a first claim on any property bought out of a mixed fund.[307]

In *Re Oatway*,[308] the trustee withdrew money from the mixed fund and invested it. Later he withdrew the balance of the fund and dissipated it. Joyce J. rejected the argument that the money drawn out first must be treated as his own, holding that the beneficiaries' claim must be satisfied from any identifiable part of the mixed fund before the trustee could set up his own claim. Thus the beneficiaries were entitled to the investments in priority to the creditors of the trustee.

It is arguable that *Re Oatway* merely gives the beneficiaries a charge over the property rather than a right to assert that it has been purchased with their money. On this approach, any increase in the value of the property will remain available for the claims of any other beneficiaries whose money may have been subsequently mixed in the account.[309] If the trustee is insolvent, this approach may also allow any increase in value to be available to the creditors, as there is little merit in permitting the beneficiaries to retrieve more than they have lost where the real contest is with the creditors.[310] This factor must always be borne in mind when considering whether, theoretically, the tracing remedy ought to be available. The question is essentially one of competition between the beneficiary and the creditors. The House of Lords in *Foskett v McKeown*[311] did not deal with the special rules relating to funds mixed in a current account, nor was the contest with creditors. The tenor of the majority judgments, however, lends support to the view that the beneficiaries may assert their property rights without regard to policy factors of this kind.

So far as claims against a bank balance are concerned, the rule is that tracing can succeed against a mixed fund in the bank account to the extent that the trust funds can still be shown to be there. If the account falls below that sum, that part of the trust money must have

---

[306] (1880) 13 Ch.D. 696 at 727.

[307] Thus it cannot be relied on in a criminal case to show that the accused was withdrawing his own money; *R. v Clowes (No.2)* [1994] 2 All E.R. 316.

[308] [1903] 2 Ch. 356; *Re Tilley's WT* [1967] Ch. 1179 at 1185.

[309] Such beneficiaries could not assert that the property was bought with their money if *Clayton's Case* applies, below, para.23–062.

[310] G. Jones (1988) 37 King's Counsel 15 at 16. The beneficiaries will be entitled to any profits if they can establish that the property was bought with their money; below para.23–065. On policy issues of this kind see *Re B A Peters Plc (in administration)* [2010] 1 B.C.L.C. 142 at 148.

[311] [2001] 1 A.C. 102.

been spent.[312] Later payments in are not treated as repayments of the trust fund unless the trustee shows an intention to do so.[313] It is essential therefore to ascertain from the accounts the lowest balance in the fund; to that extent the tracing remedy is available against that balance. Of course the personal claim remains as to any shortfall, in cases where the trust money withdrawn cannot be followed into other property. Where the money has been withdrawn from the account and paid into various different accounts, the beneficiaries can claim a charge over all such accounts and, as against the wrong-doer, are not bound to identify one.[314] This is because the payments derive from a fund which was subject to a charge in their favour.

We saw that the Privy Council in *Re Goldcorp Exchange Ltd*[315] **23–061** held that there could be no tracing of money paid into an overdrawn account, confirming the principle that later payments in are not normally treated as repayments to the trust.[316] A related question is whether "backwards tracing" is possible, as where a trustee borrows money to buy a car and then repays the loan with trust money.[317] May the trust trace the car? In *Bishopsgate Investment Management Ltd v Homan*[318] Leggatt L.J. firmly rejected the concept of tracing into an asset acquired by the trustee before the trust money was misappropriated and thus without its aid.[319] Dillon L.J., however, regarded it as arguable that the beneficiary could assert a charge over an asset if there was a connection between the misappropriated money and the acquisition of the particular asset, as where the asset was bought with borrowed money and at the time of the borrowing it could be inferred that the trustee intended to repay with trust money.[320] In this limited situation "backwards tracing" may be supportable, but to permit it on a wider basis would be contrary to the principles of tracing.[321]

---

[312] In *Roscoe v Winder* [1915] 1 Ch. 62, 69 Sargant J. said that the tracing remedy applied to "such an amount of the balance ultimately standing to the credit of the trustee as did not exceed the lowest balance of the account during the intervening period." It may be otherwise if "backwards tracing", below, becomes accepted; Smith, *The Law of Tracing*, p.354; S. Evans (1999) 115 L.Q.R. 469.

[313] *Roscoe v Winder*, above, fn.312. See also *Glencore International AG v Metro Trading International Inc* [2001] 1 Lloyd's Rep. 284, in the context of wrongly mixed oil.

[314] *El Ajou v Dollar Land Holdings Plc* [1993] 3 All E.R. 717 at 735 (not discussed on appeal at [1994] 2 All E.R. 685); P. Oliver (1995) 9 T.L.I. 78.

[315] [1995] 1 A.C. 74; above, para.23–056.

[316] *Roscoe v Winder*, above, fn.312 (applied also in *Bishopsgate Investment Management Ltd v Homan*, fn.318).

[317] If the loan was secured, subrogation to the security may assist; below, para.23–063.

[318] [1995] Ch. 211; above, para.23–057. Henry J., agreed with both judgments.

[319] [1995] Ch. 211 at 221–222.

[320] This view was favoured by Scott V.C. in *Foskett v McKeown* [1998] Ch. 265 at 283–284 (CA), but was not discussed on appeal. See also Sir Peter Millett (1995) 111 L.Q.R. 517; D. Hayton in Birks (ed.), *Laundering and Tracing* (1995), p.18; Smith, *The Law of Tracing*, pp.146–152, 354–356; *Shalson v Russo* [2005] Ch. 281.

[321] A. Oakley (1995) 54 C.L.J. 377 at 414; A. Tettenborn (1998) 57 C.L.J. 218 at 219; S. Evans (1999) 115 L.Q.R. 469 at 488; M. Conaglen (2011) 127 L.Q.R. 432; cf. Goff and Jones, 7th edn, p.123, giving some support to the theory.

There is little English authority on the question whether the beneficiaries may claim property purchased out of a mixed account when a sufficient balance remains to satisfy their claim. The point will be significant where the property purchased has increased in value, or it may be that the balance has been spent on a property which has made a smaller profit. Under *Re Hallett*[322] the first expenditure is presumed to have been the trustee's money. *Re Oatway*[323] is distinguishable because the balance has not been dissipated. *Re Tilley's Will Trusts*[324] suggests that the beneficiaries must be content with a claim to the balance (or the second property, as the case may be).[325] If the trustee is insolvent, the claims of the creditors must also be considered, as discussed above. In *Foskett v McKeown*,[326] where the point did not arise, Lord Millett said:

> "It is not necessary to consider whether there are any circumstances in which the beneficiary is confined to a lien in cases where the fund is more than sufficient to repay the contributions of all parties."

It could be argued that the beneficiary should be allowed to "cherry pick" if the only contest is between the beneficiary and the wrongdoer, to avoid the wrongdoer being "left with all the cherries".[327] However, it was recently held in the High Court that, where a trustee had mixed trust funds with her own in a deposit account and a sum equal to the trust fund remained in the account, the beneficiary had no beneficial interest in property purchased with funds from the account but could claim only against the account.[328]

23–062 It remains to consider the position where the mixed funds in the bank account represent the funds of two trusts,[329] or of a trust and an innocent volunteer. Here the rule in *Clayton's* case[330] lays down that in the case of a current bank account, the first payment in is appropriated to the earliest debt which is not statute-barred; in other words, first in, first out. This is a rule which has some relevance and convenience in commercial matters. We have seen that it does not

[322] (1880) 13 Ch.D. 696.
[323] [1903] 2 Ch. 356.
[324] [1967] Ch. 1179, below, para.23–065.
[325] See Birks, *An Introduction to the Law of Restitution*, 1995, p.370; A. Oakley (1995) 54 C.L.J. 377 at 416; cf. D. Hayton in P. Birks (ed.), *Laundering and Tracing* (1995), p.6.
[326] [2001] 1 A.C. 102 at 132.
[327] *Shalson v Russo* [2005] Ch. 281 at 329; D. Hayton in Birks and Pretto (eds), *Breach of Trust*, 2002, pp.386–387.
[328] *Turner v Jacob* [2008] W.T.L.R. 307.
[329] If the trustee's own money is also mixed, the principle of *Re Hallett's Estate*, above, fn.322, will apply to determine withdrawals to be allocated to the trustee; i.e. he is presumed to spend his own money before that of either trust.
[330] (1817) 1 Mer. 572; D. McConville (1963) 79 L.Q.R. 388; P. Higgins (1965) 6 W.A.L.R. 428, at 437. cf. *Re British Red Cross Balkan Fund* [1914] 2 Ch. 419 (where later subscribers to a fund could not claim surplus to the exclusion of earlier subscribers).

apply to accounts between trustee and beneficiary. Nor, it is submitted, should it appear in any aspect of the present subject,[331] but it has been applied as a means of determining entitlement in a mixed banking account between rival persons with a right to trace,[332] and also between a person with a right to trace and an innocent volunteer.[333] It never appears in any context other than that of a current bank account.[334] Although the rule has been much criticised, the Court of Appeal has confirmed it as settled law, although subject to a contrary intention, express or presumed, and subject to exceptions as established in the case law.[335] The modern approach is to distinguish *Clayton's* case rather than to apply it, so that in effect it has become the exception rather than the rule. Little is required to displace it in favour of the *pari passu* (rateable) approach, which is the "least unfair" method of apportioning loss.[336]

As has been said, the presumptions discussed above only work if the withdrawals and deposits are modest in number and amount.[337] If millions of pounds flow daily into and out of a bank, equity's rules and presumptions cannot identify the claimant's money.

iv. Subrogation. This is a doctrine with common law and equitable origins whereby one person is entitled to stand in the shoes of another and assert that other's rights.[338] The most common examples are insurance and suretyship. An insurer who pays the loss is entitled to stand in the shoes of the insured and assert his rights against the wrongdoer. The House of Lords in *Napier and Ettrick*

23–063

---

[331] D. McConville (1963) 79 L.Q.R. 401–402; D. Hayton in Birks (ed.), *Laundering and Tracing* (1995), p.14; Smith, *The Law of Tracing*, p.189. See the Report of the Review Committee on Insolvency Law and Practice (1982, Cmnd. 8558) paras 1076–1080, preferring a rateable distribution.

[332] *Re Hallett's Estate* (1879) 13 Ch.D. 696 (Fry J.); *Re Stenning* [1895] 2 Ch. 433; *Re Diplock* [1948] Ch. 465 (the National Institute for the Deaf). It was not applied in *Re Ontario Securities Commission* (1986) 30 D.L.R. (4th) 1; *Re Registered Securities* [1991] 1 N.Z.L.R. 545 or *Keefe v Law Society NSW* (1998) 44 N.S.W.L.R. 45.

[333] *Re Stenning* [1895] 2 Ch. 433; *Mutton v Peat* [1899] 2 Ch. 556 at 560, per Bryne J.; *Re Diplock*, above, fn.332.

[334] *Re Diplock* [1948] Ch. 465 at 554 (The Royal Sailors Orphan Girls' School and Home (Action 111C)).

[335] *Barlow Clowes International Ltd v Vaughan* [1992] 4 All E.R. 22 (rule displaced by contrary intention where investors knew their money would be pooled); P. Clarke All E.R. Rev. 1992, at 207; J. Martin [1993] Conv. 372; A. Jones (1993–94) 4 K.C.L.J. 86.

[336] *Russell-Cooke Trust Co v Prentis* [2003] 2 All E.R. 478; M. Pawlowski [2003] Conv. 339; P. Clarke All E.R. Rev. 2003, p.269; M. Conaglen (2005) 64 C.L.J. 45; *Re International Investment Unit Trust* [2005] 1 N.Z.L.R. 270; *Commerzbank Aktiengesellschaft v IMB Morgan Plc* [2005] W.T.L.R. 1485.

[337] See Goff and Jones, 7th edn, p.122. The rule was not applied in *Re Eastern Capital Futures Ltd* [1989] B.C.L.C. 371, where it was impossible to attribute particular sums to particular claimants.

[338] See Mitchell and Walterson, *Subrogation: Law and Practice*, 2007; Goff and Jones, 7th edn, Ch.3; L. Smith (1995) 54 C.L.J. 290; C. Mitchell in Burrows and Rodger (eds), *Mapping the Law*, 2006, Ch.6.

(Lord) v Hunter[339] held that an insurer's subrogation rights should have proprietary protection in the form of a lien (rather than a more onerous constructive trust) over damages paid to the insured by the wrongdoer. Thus unsecured creditors would not benefit from the double payment at the expense of the insurer on the bankruptcy of the insured.

In the insurance cases the payer is subrogated to the rights of the payee against third parties. In other cases the payer is subrogated to the rights of third parties against the payee, as where the payee has used the money to pay off creditors. Subrogation may assist where, because of the ultra vires doctrine, no direct action lies against the payee.[340] In such a case the payer cannot be subrogated to any securities of the repaid creditors, otherwise he would be in a better position than an intra vires creditor.[341]

In the context of tracing, the question is whether the claimant may be subrogated to the position of a secured creditor paid off by the defendant with the claimant's money. (If the creditor was unsecured, subrogation will not improve the claimant's position). In *Re Diplock*[342] the next-of-kin's money had been wrongly paid to hospital charities, two of which used it (innocently) to pay off secured and unsecured debts. It was held that there was no right of subrogation, because that would require reviving debts and securities which had been extinguished. This has long been criticised as allowing the unjust enrichment of the charities at the expense of the next-of-kin. The position was reviewed by the Court of Appeal in *Boscawen v Bajwa*.[343] A building society advanced money for the purchase of property and the discharge of a legal charge on that property. The society intended to have a first legal charge on completion. It sent the money to the solicitor[344] acting for itself and the purchaser, intending to retain the beneficial interest in the money until the security was in place, but its instructions were not carried out. The purchase was not completed, but the society's money was used to redeem the existing charge. It was held that the society was entitled to be subrogated to the position of the legal chargee. It would be

---

[339] [1993] A.C. 713; A. Jones [1993] Conv. 391; J. Martin (1993) 143 N.L.J. 1061; W. Gummow (1993) 109 L.Q.R. 159; Sir Peter Millett (1998) 114 L.Q.R. 399 at 406; R. Calnan [2004] 12 R.L.R. 1 at 19. See also *Lonrho Exports Ltd v Export Credits Guarantee Department* [1999] Ch. 158 (if insurer recovers from the third party a sum greater than its entitlement by subrogation, it holds the surplus on trust for the insured).

[340] See *Wenlock (Baroness) v River Dee Company* (1887) 19 Q.B.D. 155.

[341] See Goff and Jones, 7th edn, p.170; Birks, *Introduction to the Law of Restitution* (revised edn, 1989), pp.390–393. A surety, on the other hand, is entitled to be subrogated to any securities on paying the creditor.

[342] [1948] Ch. 465.

[343] [1996] 1 W.L.R. 328; P. Birks (1995) 9 T.L.I. 124; N. Andrews (1996) 55 C.L.J. 199; A. Oakley [1997] Conv. 1; P. Matthews (1997) 3 *Trusts & Trustees* 18. See also *Castle Phillips Finance v Piddington* [1995] 1 F.L.R. 783; *Anfield (UK) Ltd v Bank of Scotland Plc* [2011] 1 W.L.R. 2414.

[344] The sole partner was subsequently bankrupt.

unconscionable to assert that the charge had been redeemed for the landowner's benefit.

The application of the doctrine to a loan which is valid, intended **23–064** to be secured, and which is used to pay off a secured loan, is not surprising.[345] However, the Court of Appeal took the opportunity to state that the doctrine applied in circumstances such as those of *Re Diplock*.[346] The passage in that case which denied the remedy was considered difficult and in need of review in the light of later developments in the law of restitution. It could not be objected that the creditor's security had been extinguished: that was not a bar to subrogation but a precondition. What had motivated the Court of Appeal to deny the remedy in *Re Diplock* was a desire to avoid injustice to a charity which had redeemed a mortgage which the bank was content to leave outstanding indefinitely.

"It may be doubted whether in its anxiety to avoid injustice to the hospital the court may not have done an even greater injustice to the next of kin, who were denied even the interest on their money."[347]

Instead of denying a remedy, the solution should have been to delay enforcement of the revived security until the charity had had a reasonable opportunity to obtain a fresh loan on suitable terms, which would now be possible as an application of the defence of change of position.[348]

The House of Lords quite recently examined the role of intention in subrogation.[349] It was considered that in cases where the doctrine rested upon a contractual basis, as in the insurance cases, it was based on the common intention of the parties. However, no such intention was required where the claim was founded on the law of restitution (as in *Boscawen v Bajwa*[350]), where the aim was to reverse or prevent unjust enrichment. Where the claimant's money had been used to pay off a first chargee, the availability of subrogation did not depend on any common intention between the claimant and the second chargee or between the claimant and the payee that

---

[345] See Goff and Jones, 7th edn, p.165.

[346] Above, fn.342.

[347] [1996] 1 W.L.R. 328 at 341 (Millett L.J.).

[348] Below, para.23–070.

[349] *Banque Financière de la Cité v Parc (Battersea) Ltd* [1999] 1 A.C. 221. Subrogation was held to apply only as between the claimant and the second chargee. See P. Watts (1998) 114 L.Q.R. 341; C. Mitchell [1998] 6 R.L.R. 144; M. Bridge [1998] J.B.L. 323; D. Friedmann (1999) 115 L.Q.R. 195; D. Wright [1999] Conv. 113; T. Villiers [1999] L.M.C.L.Q. 233. See also *Cheltenham and Gloucester Plc v Appleyard*, *The Times*, March 29, 2004; K. Bracegirdle [2005] L.M.C.L.Q. 140.

[350] Above, fn.343. See also *Halifax Plc v Omar* (2002) 2 P. & C.R. 26, analysing the decision in *Banque Financière*; S. Midwinter [2003] L.M.C.L.Q. 6; *Anfield (UK) Ltd v Bank of Scotland Plc* [2011] 1 W.L.R. 2414 at 2417.

the claimant should be subrogated to the security of the first chargee. This issue was whether the second chargee would be unjustly en-riched at the claimant's expense in the absence of such subrogation. Intention was, however, relevant to the question whether the enrich-ment would be unjust: it would not be if the transaction had been intended to create merely an unsecured loan.

23–065   **v. Increase in Value.** We saw that Jessel M.R. said in *Re Hallett's Estate*[351] that where trust funds, unmixed, could be traced, the claimant could choose to take the property purchased with them, or to have a charge upon it for the amount; but that if property had been mixed with the trustee's own, and property purchased with the mixed fund, the claimant's remedy was that of a charge. Such a rule would mean, however, that the beneficiary would be able only to claim the original money taken (with interest, and in priority to the creditors) and that the trustee would keep all the profits. This would be a startling result; all the more so in view of the extreme strictness with which the courts deal with cases of profits made by trustees.[352]

It is now confirmed that the appropriate remedy in such a situation is to allow the beneficiary to claim a share of the fund in the proportion which the original trust funds bore to the mixed fund at the time of the mixing. If the fund increased in value, it would be in his interest to do so. If the fund decreased in value, it would be in his interest to have a charge. The principle of proportionate entitlement was conceded in *Re Tilley's Will Trusts*.[353] In that case an executrix had paid small sums from an estate (in which she had a life interest) into her account, from which, with the aid of an overdraft facility, she purchased properties which increased in value. On her death the remaindermen claimed a share of the profits. Although the principle of proportionate entitlement was conceded, it was surprisingly held that the trust money had not been used in the purchase of the properties, but merely went in reduction of the overdraft. On that basis the beneficiaries were entitled only to the return of the money with interest. The matter has now been put beyond doubt by the House of Lords in *Foskett v McKeown*.[354]

A trustee used £20,440 of trust money to pay for two of the five premiums on a life assurance policy which were paid prior to his death. On his death the proceeds of the policy were just over £1 million. It was held that the beneficiaries were entitled to 40 per cent of this sum. The windfall was attributable to their property

---

[351] (1880) 13 Ch.D. 696; above, para.23–059.
[352] *Boardman v Phipps* [1967] 2 A.C. 46; above, paras 21–022–21–025.
[353] [1967] Ch. 1179 at 1189; G. Jones (1968) 26 C.L.J. 28.
[354] [2001] 1 A.C. 102.

rights. *Re Hallett's Estate*[355] was not authority for any proposition that the beneficiaries should be confined to a charge, as the fund in that case had diminished and only a charge was claimed.

vi. The Innocent Volunteer. The tracing remedy is never avail-　**23–066** able against a bona fide purchaser for value. A volunteer of course is in a different position. The usual rule is that they take the property subject to any equitable interest affecting it. In the tracing situation, however, it appears from *Re Diplock*[356] that a person who receives a mixed fund bona fide[357] but without payment (the innocent volunteer) is raised to a position equal to that of the equitable owner who is entitled to trace:

"But this burden on the conscience of the volunteer is not such as to compel him to treat the claim of the equitable owner as paramount. That would be to treat the volunteer as strictly as if he himself stood in a fiduciary relationship to the equitable owner which *ex hypothesi* he does not. The volunteer is under no greater duty of conscience to recognise the interest of the equitable owner than that which lies upon a person having an equitable interest in one of two trust funds of 'money' which have become mixed towards the equitable owner of the other. Such a person is not in conscience bound to give precedence to the equitable owner of the other of the two funds."[358]

Thus the charities in *Re Diplock* were allowed to take rateably with the claimants; in other words, they were treated in the same way as they would have been if they had themselves been entitled to trace. This principle of rateable sharing applies whether the mixed property has increased or decreased in value.[359]

We will see that, as far as the personal action in *Re Diplock* was concerned, the action against the volunteer could be brought only after the remedies against the personal representatives had been exhausted.[360] Any money recovered from them reduced the sum recoverable from the volunteer. It is not clear whether the proprietary action against a third party is similarly limited. Without suggesting that there was any obligation to sue the executors before proceeding to trace against the volunteer, the Court of Appeal in *Re*

---

[355] Above, fn.351.

[356] [1948] Ch. 465.

[357] A recipient who, although not dishonest, ought to have known that the money was not his is not an innocent volunteer; *Boscawen v Bajwa* [1996] 1 W.L.R. 328 at 337.

[358] [1996] 1 W.L.R. 328 at 524.

[359] *Foskett v McKeown* [2001] 1 A.C. 102 at 132. Their Lordships distinguished innocent volunteers who were contributors from those who were merely successors in title to the wrongdoer and in no better position.

[360] Below, para.23–078.

Diplock took the preliminary view that "prima facie and subject to discussion"[361] the next-of-kin's proprietary claim should be reduced by any amounts recovered from the executors. It is difficult to see why this should be so. Of course, the beneficiary should not recover twice over, but:

> "[I]t should be no defence to the volunteer that the next-of-kin have recovered *in personam* against the executors. The executors should then be allowed to claim, as is an insurer in comparable circumstances, that part of the next-of-kin's fund which represents the difference between the total value of the sums recovered from the executors and the volunteer and the loss suffered by the next-of-kin."[362]

Another solution is to require the claimant to sue the volunteer before suing the executors, who are liable only for that which cannot be recovered from the volunteer.[363]

23–067   **vii. Loss of Right to Trace.** There are some situations in which the right to trace will be lost. Some of these have already been mentioned, but they will be included here for the sake of completeness.[364]

23–068   (a) *The Property Ceases to be Identifiable.* It is clear from the preceding discussion that tracing is not available to a claimant who cannot identify his property, for example where the trust funds or the proceeds of sale of trust assets have been dissipated or where his property never became part of the trust fund.[365] Of course, the personal action remains.

23–069   (b) *Bona Fide Purchaser.*[366] Where trust property has been transferred to a bona fide purchaser for value without notice, the latter must take free of the claims of the beneficiaries, which must be

---

[361] [1948] Ch. 465 at 556. The dictum may be confined to claims arising out of the administration of estates.

[362] Goff and Jones, 7th edn, p.122.

[363] This is the rule adopted by the New Zealand Administration Act 1952 s.30B(5) and the Western Australia Trustee Act 1962 s.65(7); cf. Trusts Act (Queensland) s.109, whereby the trustee must be sued before the third party.

[364] See also Goff and Jones, 7th edn, p.121, on the question how far the right to trace against an innocent volunteer is reduced by the amount recoverable from the trustee; *Re Diplock* [1948] Ch. 465 at 556.

[365] *Re B A Peters Plc (in administration)* [2010] 1 B.C.L.C. 142; cf. *Space Investments Ltd v Canadian Imperial Bank of Commerce Trust Co (Bahamas) Ltd* [1986] 1 W.L.R. 1072, above, para.23–056.

[366] See Smith, *The Law of Tracing*, pp.386–396; Lord Millett [1999] 14 *Amicus Curiae* at 4. See also *Independent Trustee Services Ltd v G P Noble Trustees* [2011] 2 F.L.R. 174 (money paid under consent order in divorce proceedings).

pursued against the proceeds of sale or against the trustee person-ally.[367] A purchaser in an arm's length transaction not involving investigation of title to land will not normally have constructive notice.[368] This is not a species of the change of position defence because the consideration does not need to be adequate.[369]

(c) *Change of Position.*[370] The doctrine of change of position **23-070** lays down that the right of a person to restitution from another because of a benefit received is terminated or diminished if, after the receipt of the benefit, circumstances have so changed that it would be inequitable to require the other to make full restitution.[371] It is the mechanism by which the tension between the right to restitution and the general interest in the protection of security of receipts is recon-ciled.[372] This doctrine, essential to any satisfactory system of restitu-tionary remedies, was accepted by the House of Lords in *Lipkin Gorman v Karpnale Ltd.*[373] That case involved a personal action, but it is clear that the defence will be generally available. Indeed, their Lordships envisaged that it would encourage a more consistent ap-proach to tracing at law and in equity. An earlier version of this defence can be seen in *Re Diplock,*[374] where innocent volunteers (charities) had spent the claimant's money on improvements and alterations to their own land. It was held that no charge should be imposed, because a charge is enforceable by sale and it would be harsh to make the volunteers sell their land. This has now been subsumed into the wider defence of change of position. It must be emphasised that there is no defence of "honest receipt".[375]

The defence is available to an innocent defendant but not to a wrongdoer.[376] Differing views have been expressed as to whether a

---

[367] *Thorndike v Hunt* (1859) 3 De G. & J. 563; *Thomson v Clydesdale Bank* [1893] A.C. 282.

[368] *Sinclair Investments (UK) Ltd v Versailles Trade Finance Ltd (in administrative receivership)* [2011] 3 W.L.R. 1153.

[369] *Lipkin Gorman v Karpnale Ltd* [1991] 2 A.C. 548; K. Barker [1999] 7 R.L.R. 75.

[370] See Smith, *The Law of Tracing*, pp.34–38; G. Virgo and J. Palmer [2005] 13 R.L.R. 34 and 53 respectively; C. Mitchell [2005] L.M.C.L.Q. 168; T. Wee [2006] 14 R.L.R. 55; G. Jones in Burrows and Rodger (eds), *Mapping the Law*, Ch.4; Bant, *The Change of Position Defence* (2009). For comparative studies, see P. Hellwege [1999] 7 R.L.R. 92 and M. Jewell [2000] 8 R.L.R. 1.

[371] American Law Institute, *Third Restatement of the Law of Restitution and Unjust Enrichment* (2011), para.65. It is no defence to the personal restitutionary claim that, because of transactions with third parties, the claimant has suffered no overall loss; *Kleinwort Benson Ltd v Birmingham CC* [1997] Q.B. 380.

[372] *National Bank of New Zealand Ltd v Waitaki International Processing (NI) Ltd* [1999] 2 N.Z.L.R. 211.

[373] [1991] 2 A.C. 548; G. Jones (1993–94) 4 K.C.L.J. 93; above, para.12–020.

[374] [1948] Ch. 465 at 546–548.

[375] *Kleinwort Benson Ltd v Lincoln Council* [1999] 2 A.C. 349.

[376] *Lipkin Gorman v Karpnale Ltd*, above, fn.373; *Cressman v Coys of Kensington (Sales) Ltd* [2004] 1 W.L.R. 2775 (no defence where property given away after knowledge of mistake).

defendant who, although honest, ought to have known that the property was not his is "innocent" for this purpose.[377] Mere carelessness on the part of the defendant is not a bar to the defence. Often the claimant has been careless in making the payment, and the court will not balance the fault of each party.[378] However, conduct short of dishonesty may bar the defendant from relying on the defence, as where he suspected a mistake but made no enquiries.[379] General suspicions unrelated to the transaction in question may not bar the defence.[380] The question is not whether he was dishonest but whether, in the circumstances, it would be inequitable to allow the recipient to deny restitution.[381] The recipient cannot rely on an illegal act as a change of position, even if he was unaware of the illegality.[382]

The defence will operate to eliminate or reduce the claim where the defendant has disposed of money or other property in an exceptional and irretrievable manner in reliance upon the validity of his receipt of the claimant's property.[383] The defence is not available where a lender, at the direction of the defendant, pays money directly to a third party who then fails to repay the defendant, as in such a case the defendant has taken the risk of loss.[384]

23–071   Where it is the claimant's property that has been disposed of, tracing will fail if neither the property nor anything representing it can be identified. The defence may then operate in the context of a personal claim against the defendant.[385] Where the defendant still

---

[377] Law Com. No.227 (1994), para.2.23; *South Tyneside Metropolitan Council v Svenska International Plc* [1995] 1 All E.R. 545 at 569; R. Nolan and P. Birks in P. Birks (ed.), *Laundering and Tracing* (1995), p.158 and 325; M. Jewell [2000] R.L.R. 1 at 16; cf. R. Chambers [1996] R.L.R. 103; P. Birks (2000) 14 T.L.I. 217 at 223–227.

[378] *Dextra Bank & Trust Co Ltd v Bank of Jamaica* [2002] 1 All E.R. (Comm) 193.

[379] See *Fea v Roberts* [2006] W.T.L.R. 255 (legacy paid to wrong person).

[380] *Abou-Rahmah v Abacha* [2007] W.T.L.R. 1 (suspicions of money-laundering); G. Virgo (2007) 66 C.L.J. 22; J. Lee [2007] 15 R.L.R. 135.

[381] *Niru Battery Manufacturing Company v Milestone Trading Ltd* [2004] Q.B. 895; A. Tettenborn [2003] 11 R.L.R. 98. The approach of the Court of Appeal is criticised as muddying the waters in P. Birks (2004) 120 L.Q.R. 373 at 377, and also in A. Burrows (2004) 63 C.L.J. 276; A. Tettenborn [2004] 12 R.L.R. 155; E. Ellinger (2005) 121 L.Q.R. 51.

[382] *Barros Mattos Jnr v MacDaniels Ltd* [2005] 1 W.L.R. 247; criticised in C. Mitchell All E.R. Rev. 2004, p.329; A. Tettenborn [2005] L.M.C.L.Q. 6; M. Halliwell [2005] Conv. 357.

[383] See *Philip Collins Ltd v Davis* [2000] 3 All E.R. 808 (overpaid royalties: partial defence where defendants had geared their outgoings to income over an extended period); cf. *Hillsdown Holdings Plc v Pensions Ombudsman* [1997] 1 All E.R. 862 at 904 (no defence where money used to pay tax which was recoverable).

[384] *Goss v Chilcott* [1996] A.C. 788. The case involved a restitutionary claim for money advanced under a mortgage instrument which had become unenforceable. See also *Rose v AIB Group (UK) Plc* [2003] 1 W.L.R. 2791; *Haugesund Kommune v Depfa ACS Bank* [2011] 1 All E.R. 190 (money paid under void loan spent by borrower on disastrous investments).

[385] Above, para.12–020.

has the proceeds of the claimant's property[386] but has disposed of his own in reliance upon ownership of the claimant's property, the defence may operate in the context of tracing. The payment of debts cannot normally be relied on as a change of position, as the defendant was obliged to pay them in any event and there is no hardship sufficient to deny the claim.[387] Where the defendant has used the claimant's money to pay off a secured debt, we have seen that the claimant may recover by being subrogated to the position of the repaid creditor.[388] The defence of change of position is not available in the usual sense of eliminating or reducing the claim,[389] but any hardship may be avoided by delaying enforcement by the claimant until the defendant has had a reasonable opportunity to obtain a fresh loan on suitable terms.[390] The defence is not confined to cases of disposal of money or other property. It could apply in rare cases where the defendant has given up his job[391] or performed services in reliance on entitlement to payment, although solicitors paid for services under the terms of an invalid will were not entitled to the defence when sued for recovery of the payment: they took the risk of invalidity in view of their knowledge of the law.[392]

The question which arose in *South Tyneside Metropolitan Bor-*   **23–072**
ough Council v Svenska International Plc[393] was whether the defence was available where the defendant had relied on the validity of certain ultra vires transactions (interest-rate "swaps") when entering into other irrevocable transactions ("hedges") *prior* to receipt of the claimant's money. It was held that the defence was not available, as, save in exceptional circumstances,[394] it required reliance on *actual receipt* and not merely on events before the receipt. On that approach an employee who spent money on a holiday in reliance on the promise of a forthcoming bonus would have no defence if the

---

[386] The defence would not apply where the defendant retains the claimant's actual property, such as a chattel. See Smith, *The Law of Tracing*, pp.35, 383–385; S. Worthington [2002] R.L.R. 28 at 55–59; G. Virgo [2005] 13 R.L.R. 34; L. Smith in Burrows and Rodger (eds), *Mapping the Law*, p.127; cf. J. Palmer [2005] 13 R.L.R. 53 at 80.

[387] *Scottish Equitable Plc v Derby* [2001] 3 All E.R. 818.

[388] *Boscawen v Bajwa* [1996] 1 W.L.R. 328; above, para.23–063.

[389] See *Scottish Equitable Plc v Derby* [2001] 3 All E.R. 818 (no defence where money used to pay off two-thirds of mortgage).

[390] *Boscawen v Bajwa* [1996] 1 W.L.R. 328 at 341; P. Birks (1995) 9 T.L.I. 124.

[391] See the discussion in *Commerzbank AG v Price-Jones* [2003] All E.R. (D) 303; P. Birks (2004) 120 L.Q.R. 373.

[392] *Gray v Richards Butler (A Firm)*, *The Times*, July 23, 1996.

[393] Above, fn.377; criticised A. Jones [1995] Conv. 490; A. Burrows [1995] 3 R.L.R. 15 at 21; R. Nolan and P. Birks in Birks (ed.), *Laundering and Tracing* (1995), p.168 and p.329; W. Swadling All E.R. Rev. 1995, at 455; Goff and Jones, 7th edn, p.857; M. Jewell [2000] 8 R.L.R. 1 at 7–16.

[394] See *Lipkin Gorman v Karpnale Ltd* [1991] 2 A.C. 548 (total receipts reduced by winnings paid to Cass regardless of order).

bonus turned out to be ultra vires after payment, whereas an employee who spent an ultra vires bonus on a holiday would have.[395]
This inflexible approach is now discredited. Lord Bingham and Lord
Goff, in a joint judgment of the Privy Council, suggested that acts
done in anticipation of the payment may give rise to the change of
position defence.[396] A wide view of the defence was also supported
by the Court of Appeal in *Scottish Equitable Plc v Derby*.[397] It was
said that the defence requires a causal link between the mistaken
payment and the change of position. An act by the defendant in
reliance on the receipt is not essential, as shown by the example of
the claimant's property being lost or stolen after receipt by the
defendant.

Another question which has recently been debated is whether the
development of the defence of change of position leaves any scope
for the defence of estoppel. Change of position can operate as a total
or partial defence, whereas traditionally estoppel operates as a complete defence. If the claimant mistakenly pays £10,000 to the defendant, making no representation to support an estoppel, and the
defendant changes his position as to £1,000 before the mistake is
discovered, his change of position defence will extend only to
£1,000. If the claimant had expressly represented that the £10,000
was correctly due to the defendant, it would be inequitable of the
defendant to rely on estoppel as to the whole amount, even though it
is normally a complete defence.[398] Tentative observations by the
Court of Appeal in *Scottish Equitable Plc v Derby*[399] support the
view that estoppel is too flexible to be regarded as an "all or nothing" defence. On this approach, estoppel is unlikely to have a role in
this area, especially now that the change of position defence is no
longer restricted to acts of reliance after receipt.

23–073   **viii. Retention of Title Clauses.** In recent years the rules of
equity have been utilised in the context of the supply of goods to
manufacturers. By means of a retention of title clause, the supplier
stipulates that the property in the goods shall not pass until payment.[400] He may also seek to reserve ownership where his goods

[395] [1995] 1 All E.R. 545 at 564–565.
[396] *Dextra Bank & Trust Co Ltd v Bank of Jamaica* [2002] 1 All E.R. (Comm) 193 at 203;
M. McInnes (2002) 118 L.Q.R. 209; P. Watts (2002) 61 C.L.J. 301; P. Birks and W. Swadling
All E.R. Rev. 2002, p.316; T. Akkouh and C. Webb [2002] 10 R.L.R. 107.
[397] [2001] 3 All E.R. 818. See also *Commerzbank AG v Price-Jones* [2003] All E.R.
(D) 303.
[398] *National Westminster Bank Plc v Somer International (UK) Ltd* [2002] Q.B. 1286; G
Virgo [2005] 13 R.L.R. 34 at 52.
[399] Above, fn.397; E. Fung and L. Ho (2001) 117 L.Q.R. 14; P. Key (2001) 60 C.L.J. 465; P.
Birks and W. Swadling All E.R. Rev. 2001, p.330 and 2002, p.318; P. Jaffey [2002]
L.M.C.L.Q. 1; G. McMeel [2002] 10 R.L.R. 174, 180. See also *Fea v Roberts* [2006]
W.T.L.R. 255 at 266.
[400] See Sale of Goods Act 1979 s.19.

have been mixed with others in a manufacturing process, or of the proceeds of sale by the manufacturer on a sub-sale. He may further, by means of an "all-monies" clause, stipulate that the property shall not pass until all the buyer's obligations to him have been satisfied, not merely as to the particular consignment. Retention of title clauses are often called "*Romalpa* clauses", and take their name from the leading case, *Aluminium Industrie Vaassen BV v Romalpa Aluminium Ltd.*[401]

> The claimant vendor sold aluminium foil to the defendant, a manufacturing company. One clause in the contract provided that legal ownership in the foil was not to pass to the defendant until payment. Until that time, the defendant could be required to store the foil in such a way that it was clearly the property of the claimant. Other clauses dealt with the position where the foil was mixed with other materials. The defendant company got into financial difficulties and a receiver was appointed at a time when over £122,000 was owing to the claimant. The receiver certified that £35,152 in his hands represented the proceeds of sale of unmixed foil sold by the defendant to third parties. The claimant claimed priority in respect of that sum over the secured and unsecured creditors. The Court of Appeal, applying *Re Hallett's Estate*,[402] upheld the claim. Although the third parties acquired title to the foil sold to them,[403] the position as between the claimant and defendant was that the foil was the claimant's property, which the defendant was selling as agent. The defendant's position as agent and bailee gave rise to a fiduciary relationship,[404] which entitled the claimant to trace the proceeds of the unmixed foil and recover in priority to the secured and unsecured creditors.

It was conceded in *Romalpa* that the defendant held the goods as bailee.[405] Normally, however, the relationship of the parties under a title retention clause hardly fits the concept of bailment or agency. It

---

[401] [1976] 1 W.L.R. 676; R. Goode (1976) 92 L.Q.R. 360, 528; R. Prior (1976) 39 M.L.R. 585; D. Donaldson and R. Goode (1977) 93 L.Q.R. 324 and 487 respectively; J. Farrow and N. Furey (1977) 36 C.L.J. 27; O. Wylie [1978] Conv. 37; J. Thornley (1980) 39 C.L.J. 48; W. Goodhart and G. Jones (1980) 43 M.L.R. 489; G McCormack [1994] Conv. 129. See Smith, *Property Problems in Sale*, 1978; Goode, *Proprietary Rights and Insolvency in Sales Transactions*, 2nd edn, 2008; McCormack, *Reservation of Title*, 1990; Worthington, *Proprietary Interests in Commercial Transactions*, 1997.

[402] (1880) 13 Ch.D. 696.

[403] See also *Four Point Garage Ltd v Carter* [1985] 3 All E.R. 12 (purchaser in good faith from buyer where resale in the ordinary course of business gets legal title even though, as between buyer and supplier, buyer did not get title); Sale of Goods Act 1979 ss.24, 25.

[404] Such relationships are not always fiduciary; *Hendy Lennox (Industrial Engines) Ltd v Grahame Puttick Ltd* [1984] 1 W.L.R. 485; *Re Andrabell Ltd* [1984] 3 All E.R. 407; *Napier and Ettrick (Lord) v Hunter* [1993] A.C. 713 at 744.

[405] See *Re Bond Worth Ltd*, below, fn.411.

has been held that if sub-sales are permitted, the normal implication is that the buyer will sell on his own account and not as fiduciary agent for the seller.[406] But where the sub-purchaser's contract also contains a reservation of title clause, the unpaid vendor may assert title against the sub-purchaser until the latter has paid the purchaser.[407]

23–074   (a) *Unmixed Goods.* Retention of title clauses have proved effective where, as in *Romalpa*, the property has retained its identity. In *Clough Mill Ltd v Martin*[408] the Court of Appeal held that a clause reserving legal title to yarn until payment entitled the seller, on the buyer's insolvency, to recover unused yarn which had not been paid for. As no title passed to the buyer, the buyer could not be regarded as having created a (registrable) charge over the yarn in favour of the seller. Similarly in *Hendy Lennox (Industrial Engines) Ltd v Grahame Puttick Ltd*,[409] where the seller reserved title to a diesel engine which had been used by the buyer as a major component of a diesel generating set. The seller's claim to ownership of the engine succeeded as the engine remained readily identifiable and could be disconnected quite easily from the generator. In *Re Peachdart Ltd*[410] on the other hand, where leather was supplied for the manufacture of handbags, it was not regarded as retaining its identity even though it remained recognisable in the product. Thus the claim fell to be considered under the following heading.

23–075   (b) *Incorporation into Manufacturing Process.* Vendors have been unsuccessful, however, where the property has been incorporated into a manufacturing process. In *Re Bond Worth Ltd*[411] the vendor supplied fibre to the purchaser, which was spun into yarn with other fibre and used in the manufacture of carpets, becoming an inseparable component of the yarn and the carpets. The contract provided that "equitable and beneficial ownership" should remain

---

[406] *E Pfeiffer Weinkellerei-Weineinkauf GmbH & Co v Arbuthnot Factors Ltd* [1988] 1 W.L.R. 150; *Compaq Computer Ltd v Abercorn Group Ltd* [1991] B.C.C. 484. See also *Fairfax Gerrard Holdings Ltd v Capital Bank Plc* [2008] 1 Lloyd's Rep 297; K. Loi [2008] L.M.C.L.Q. 427.

[407] *Re Highway Foods International Ltd* [1995] 1 B.C.L.C. 209; A. Tettenborn (1996) 55 C.L.J. 26.

[408] [1985] 1 W.L.R. 111, distinguishing *Re Bond Worth Ltd*, below, fn.411, as to unused material. See N. Palmer All E.R. Rev. 1984 at 31; S. Jones (1985) 135 N.L.J. 224, 271; McKee (1985) 36 N.I.L.Q. 165; J. Thornely (1985) 44 C.L.J. 33; J. Bradgate [1987] Conv. 434.

[409] [1984] 1 W.L.R. 485. The seller's proprietary claim to the engine was transferred to the proceeds of sale as the property in the engine had not passed to the defendant's customers at the time of receivership. As to other engines where the property had passed, see below.

[410] [1984] Ch. 131; N. Palmer All E.R. Rev. 1983, p.48; S. Whittaker (1984) 100 L.Q.R. 35; J. Thornely (1984) 43 C.L.J. 35; D. Milman [1984] Conv. 139. The contract expressly provided for a fiduciary relationship.

[411] [1980] Ch. 228. See also *Tatung (UK) Ltd v Galex Telesure Ltd* [1989] BCC 325.

with the vendor until payment. If resold, the vendor's rights should attach to the proceeds. If converted to other products, the vendor's rights should extend to those products. Upon the purchaser's insolvency £587,397 was owing to the vendor. The receiver held little raw fibre but much yarn and carpets. Slade J. rejected the vendor's claim to priority. The contract was primarily a contract of sale, whereby the legal title and the risk passed to the purchaser, who was at liberty to resell or use the fibre in the manufacturing process. The purchaser was neither an agent nor a bailee. The retention of title clause, upon its true construction, did not reserve full equitable ownership to the vendor, but gave the vendor an equitable charge over the fibre or its products. This charge, which was created by the purchaser company,[412] was void for non-registration under the Companies Act.[413] *Romalpa*[414] was distinguishable, primarily because there the clause reserved *legal* ownership to the vendor.[415]

The result was similar in *Borden UK Ltd v Scottish Timber Products Ltd*,[416] where the vendor supplied resin to the purchaser, to be used in the manufacture of chipboard, of which it became an inseparable component. The contract reserved legal ownership in the resin to the vendor until payment, but did not purport to give the vendor rights over the chipboard. Upon the purchaser's insolvency, £318,321 was owing to the vendor. The Court of Appeal held that the clause merely reserved rights over the resin, which had disappeared, leaving nothing to trace. There was no fiduciary relationship, as the contract was a contract of sale, giving the purchaser liberty to use the resin in the manufacturing process, destroying its very existence. It was doubted whether the tracing remedy could ever apply when heterogeneous goods were mixed in a manufacturing process wherein the original goods lost their character.[417] If there was such a remedy, how could the value of the original goods be quantified? There had been no mixing in issue in *Romalpa*, where it was conceded that the defendant was a bailee of the foil. In the present case, even if the vendor had acquired rights over the chipboard, the claim would have failed for non-registration under the Companies Act. The vendor was similarly unsuccessful in *Re Peachdart Ltd*,[418] where leather was supplied for the manufacture of handbags. The retention of title clause was held to create a charge over the handbags or their proceeds, which was void for non-registration. In *Chaigley Farms Ltd v Crawford, Kaye & Grayshire*

---

[412] See *Stroud Architectural Systems Ltd v John Laing Construction Ltd* [1994] BCC 18.
[413] Now Companies Act 2006 s.860.
[414] Above, fn.401.
[415] Might the claimant in *Romalpa* have succeeded at common law?
[416] [1981] Ch. 25; doubted in P. Birks (1992) 45 C.L.P. 69 at 98.
[417] This view is not inconsistent with the retention of proprietary rights prior to such mixing; *Clough Mill Ltd v Martin*, above, fn.408.
[418] Above, fn.410.

Ltd (T/A Leylands)[419] the claimant supplied live animals for slaughter and processing. The retention of title clause was held to cover
live animals only, as the claimant's title was extinguished on slaughter. The question of mixing was not in issue in *Clough Mill Ltd v
Martin*,[420] but the Court of Appeal there expressed the view that if
the material is incorporated into other goods, it is assumed that they
are owned by the buyer subject to a charge in favour of the seller,
unless they are still in a separate and identifiable state.

23-076   (c) *Proceeds of Sale.* Even where the seller's goods have not
been amalgamated with others, claims to proprietary rights in the
proceeds of sale have been unsuccessful.

First, the claimant may fail because he cannot establish a fiduciary relationship, which is necessary for tracing into a mixed fund.[421]
Such was the case in *Re Andrabell Ltd*,[422] where a claim to the
proceeds of sale of travel bags supplied by the claimant failed. The
rights and duties of the parties were inconsistent with a fiduciary
relationship and were merely those of debtor and creditor. Similarly
in *Hendy Lennox (Industrial Engines) Ltd v Grahame Puttick Ltd*,[423]
where the claimant supplied engines for incorporation into genera-
tors. Where the property in the engines had passed to the defendant's customers, the supplier's claim to the proceeds failed,
because the terms of the contract (in particular the granting of credit)
were inconsistent with a fiduciary relationship.

Secondly, even if a fiduciary relationship can be established, the
true analysis of the position is that the claimant has a charge over the
proceeds,[424] which will fail unless registered under the Companies Act.

The reform of this area of the law, which has been called "a maze
if not a minefield",[425] was considered by the Review Committee on
Insolvency Law and Practice.[426] Some of the Committee's proposals
were enacted by the Insolvency Act 1986 in the case of corporate
insolvency. The Act provides that an administrator may be appointed to manage the affairs of a company which is in financial

---

[419] [1996] BCC 957; L. Sealy (1997) 56 C.L.J. 28; J. de Lacy [1998] Conv. 52.
[420] Above, fn.408. See also *Specialist Plant Services Ltd v Braithwaite Ltd* [1987] B.C.L.C.
1 (retention of title clause concerning parts incorporated into machines, and expressed to be as
surety for debt, created charge which was void for non-registration).
[421] Above, para.23-049. The terms used in the documents are not conclusive; *Compaq
Computer Ltd v Abercorn Group Ltd* [1991] BCC 484.
[422] [1984] 3 All E.R. 407.
[423] [1984] 1 W.L.R. 485; above, para.23-074.
[424] *Re Peachdart Ltd* [1984] Ch. 131; *Re Weldtech Equipment Ltd* [1991] BCC 16; J. de
Lacy (1991) 54 M.L.R. 736; *Compaq Computer Ltd v Abercorn Group Ltd*, above, fn.421; L.
Sealy (1992) 51 C.L.J. 19.
[425] *Hendy Lennox (Industrial Engines) Ltd v Grahame Puttick Ltd* [1984] 1 W.L.R. 485
at 493.
[426] (1982 Cmnd. 8558), paras 1587–1651.

difficulties.[427] After the presentation of a petition for an administration order, no steps may be taken to enforce any security or to repossess goods under a retention of title agreement[428] without leave of the court.[429] Nor may any such steps be taken while an administration order is in force without the consent of the administrator or the leave of the court.[430] Where any property of the company is subject to a security or goods are subject to a retention of title agreement, the administrator may dispose of the property or goods as if they were not subject to the security or the agreement, if the court is satisfied that the disposal would be likely to promote the purposes specified in the administration order.[431] The net proceeds of the disposal must be applied towards discharging the sums secured by the security or payable under the retention of title agreement.[432] The object of these provisions is to enable the business to be kept as a going concern, for the benefit of all creditors.

The real question, however, is whether retention of title clauses are desirable as a matter of policy. Save where construed as creating charges and hence registrable, they effectively create a hidden security, enabling the seller to "leapfrog" other creditors.[433] This objection could be overcome if *all* retention of title clauses were registrable, but a proposal to this effect by the Law Commission met a mixed response and a decision on implementation is awaited.[434]

6. The Personal Action in Diplock

It will be recalled that in *Re Diplock*[435] executors distributed large sums of money to numerous charities under the terms of a residuary bequest which was subsequently held to be invalid. The misapplied money belonged, therefore, to the testator's next-of-kin, whose proprietary claim to the money has already been considered.[436] The next-of-kin claimed alternatively that a direct personal action lay against the innocent recipients in equity. This claim succeeded in the Court of Appeal, whose judgment was unanimously affirmed by the **23-077**

---

[427] Insolvency Act 1986 s.8.

[428] Defined in s.251 as an agreement which does not constitute a charge but which gives the seller priority over other creditors.

[429] Insolvency Act 1986 s.10.

[430] Insolvency Act 1986 s.11.

[431] Insolvency Act 1986 s.15. See also s.43.

[432] s.15(5).

[433] See J. Bradgate [1987] Conv. 434. For a recent overview, see K. Loi [2008] 16 R.L.R. 76.

[434] Law Com. No.296 (2005), *Company Security Interests*, paras 1.60–1.66; Law Com. No.328; *Annual Report 2010/11*, para.3.28.

[435] [1948] Ch. 465, [1951] A.C. 251. (Where the earlier authorities are extensively reviewed). For a historical survey, see S Whittaker (1983) 4 *Journal of Legal History* 3.

[436] Above, para.23–049.

House of Lords.[437] Such an action may be brought by an unpaid or underpaid creditor, legatee or next-of-kin against the recipient, whether the latter is an overpaid creditor or beneficiary or a "stranger" having no claim to any part of the estate.[438] While the common law action for money had and received was then confined to mistakes of fact,[439] it was held that the action in equity lay whether the mistake was of fact or, as in the present case, of law. The mistake in such a case is not that of the claimant, but that of the personal representative, who is not a party to the action. The claimant has no way of finding out whether the mistake was of fact or law, nor whether it was a mistaken or deliberate misapplication,[440] hence:

> "[I]t would be a strange thing if the Court of Chancery, having taken upon itself to see that the assets of a deceased person were duly administered, was deterred from doing justice to a creditor, legatee or next-of-kin because the executor had done him wrong under a mistake of law."[441]

23–078   The action will not lie against a bona fide purchaser without notice, but, as far as a volunteer is concerned, it is no defence that he was unaware of the mistake[442]:

> "[I]t is prima facie at least a sufficient circumstance that the defendant, as events have proved, has received some share of the estate to which he was not entitled."[443]

But the claim will fail if the claimant has acquiesced in the wrongful payment,[444] or has failed to bring his action within the time permitted by the Limitation Act 1980.[445] It is not settled whether the action lies against the recipient's successor in title.[446]

---

[437] [1951] A.C. 251 (sub nom. *Ministry of Health v Simpson*).

[438] [1948] Ch. 465 at 502; [1951] A.C. 251 at 269.

[439] The action now lies for recovery of money paid by mistake of law; *Kleinwort Benson Ltd v Lincoln CC* [1999] 2 A.C. 349.

[440] It seems that the action will lie where the wrongful payment was deliberate: [1951] A.C. 251 at 270.

[441] [1951] A.C. 251 at 270, per Lord Simonds. The personal representative can now himself recover from the recipient whether the mistake was of fact or law; above, fn.439.

[442] This was, however, a defence to an alternative claim based on constructive trusteeship; [1948] 1 Ch. 465 at 478.

[443] [1948] Ch. 465 at 503, per Lord Greene M.R.

[444] [1951] A.C. 251 at 276.

[445] By s.22, the period is 12 years. (For creditors the period is six years). See [1948] Ch. 465 at 514.

[446] Goff and Jones, 7th edn, p.707. See also para.12–020, fn.132, discussing the point in the context of personal liability for receipt of trust property.

The personal action in equity lies for the principal sum only, without interest,[447] and is subject to two further important qualifications. First, the direct claim against the recipient is limited to the amount which cannot be recovered from the personal representative, who is primarily liable.[448] Thus the recipient will only be liable in respect of the whole sum if nothing can be recovered from the personal representative, for example because he is insolvent, or acted under a court order,[449] or is protected by s.27 of the Trustee Act 1925.[450] This limitation has been criticised.[451] Why should the recipient's liability depend on the personal representative's solvency? The solution adopted in *Re Diplock*[452] benefits the recipient at the expense of the personal representative, who, on paying the claimant, should be subrogated to the claimant's right to sue the recipient. Another solution might be to require the claimant to exhaust his remedies against the recipient before suing the personal representative.[453]

The second qualification is that the action appears to be limited to claims arising out of the administration of estates.[454] The action originated at a time when the Court of Chancery was attempting to acquire the jurisdiction then exercised by the ecclesiastical courts over the administration of assets,[455] and is not necessarily available to beneficiaries of lifetime trusts.[456] But subsequent cases indicate that the court is not unwilling to extend the action beyond the administration of estates. This approach is consistent with the doctrine of unjust enrichment.[457] In *Butler v Broadhead*[458] it was suggested that the liquidator of a company had a sufficiently analogous position to that of an executor to allow a creditor of the company to recover from overpaid contributories in a winding-up, at any rate

---

[447] *Re Diplock*, above, fn.435. This is described as an anomaly by Lord Walker in *Sempra Metals Ltd (formerly Metallgesellschaft Ltd) v IRC* [2008] 1 A.C. 561 at 626.

[448] [1948] Ch. 465 at p.503. Here the executors paid £15,000 under a compromise approved by the court. For the position concerning the proprietary action, see above, para.23–049.

[449] For example, a *Benjamin* order (*Re Benjamin* [1902] 1 Ch. 723), giving him liberty to distribute on the footing that a particular person is dead.

[450] Above, para.17–014.

[451] See A. Denning (1949) 65 L.Q.R. 37 at 44; Goff and Jones, p.706; S. Whittaker (1983) 4 *Journal of Legal History* 3.

[452] [1948] Ch. 465, [1951] A.C. 251.

[453] See New Zealand Administration Act 1952; Western Australia Trustee Act 1962.

[454] See [1951] A.C. 251 at 265–266, per Lord Simonds.

[455] See C. Harpum (1990) 49 C.L.J. 217 at 219.

[456] Although if a trustee pays trust money under a mistake of fact (or now, by mistake of law) he may recover it, and may be compelled by the beneficiaries to do so: *Re Robinson* [1911] 1 Ch. 502.

[457] The question whether strict liability, subject to change of position, should apply to innocent receipt of trust property is discussed above, para.12–021.

[458] [1975] Ch. 97. See also *GL Baker Ltd v Medway Building and Supplies Ltd* [1958] 1 W.L.R. 1216; *Nelson v Larholt* [1948] 1 K.B. 339; *Eddis v Chichester Constable* [1969] 1 All E.R. 566 (affirmed, without discussing this point, [1969] 2 Ch. 345); *Davies v Sharples* [2006] W.T.L.R. 839 (will trust).

where the liquidator had not advertised for claims. But the action was held to be barred by the companies legislation.[459] In *Re J Leslie Engineers Co Ltd*[460] Oliver J. was prepared to allow a personal action where a liquidator claimed recovery of money paid to X after the commencement of a winding-up (the transaction being void under the Companies Act). But the claim failed because the liquidator had not exhausted his remedies against the person primarily responsible, and, in any event, it appeared that X had given consideration for the payment.

23–079   Much criticism has centred around the apparent refusal of the House of Lords in *Re Diplock*[461] to recognise the defence of change of position. Where the volunteer has received the money in good faith, his liability to repay it could cause hardship if he has acted to his detriment by spending the money in an exceptional and irretrievable manner. It will be recalled that in *Re Diplock* money had been paid to a hospital charity, and used in the erection of new buildings. This, it was considered, made it inequitable to allow tracing,[462] but was no defence to the personal action.[463] Now that the House of Lords in *Lipkin Gorman v Karpnale Ltd*[464] has accepted the defence of change of position, the *Diplock* personal action can develop on a fairer and more rational basis.

Finally, it seems that the action does not lie if there was a sufficiency of assets at the date of the payment to the defendant. Where the deficiency has arisen subsequently, the personal representative alone is liable.[465]

---

[459] Now Companies Act 1985 s.557.

[460] [1976] 1 W.L.R. 292.

[461] [1951] A.C. 251.

[462] Above, para.23–070.

[463] The Court of Appeal rejected the claim that the volunteers were personally liable *as constructive trustees*, holding that they were not under any duty to investigate the validity of the gift and were entitled to assume that the executors were acting properly; *Re Diplock* [1948] Ch. 465 at 477–479. A finding of constructive trusteeship would have resulted in liability to pay interest. See *Westdeutsche Landesbank Girozentrale v Islington LBC* [1996] A.C. 669.

[464] [1991] 2 A.C. 548; W. Cornish (1991) 50 C.L.J. 407; above, para.23–070.

[465] See *Peterson v Peterson* (1866) L.R. 3 Eq. 111.

PART IV

**MISCELLANEOUS EQUITABLE REMEDIES
AND DOCTRINES**

CHAPTER 24

SPECIFIC PERFORMANCE

1. GENERAL PRINCIPLES[1]

AN outline of the nature of equitable remedies has already been given.[2] Their characteristics, in relation to specific performance in particular, must now be examined.   **24–001**

[1] See Fry, *Specific Performance*, 6th edn, 1921; Spry, *Equitable Remedies*; Jones and Goodhart, *Specific Performance*, 2nd edn, 1996; Sharpe, *Injunctions and Specific Performance*, 1983.

[2] Above, para.1–037.

A. Discretionary

24–002   Specific performance, like other equitable remedies, is only given as a matter of discretion, although the discretion is exercised in accordance with settled principles.[3] Thus there are some cases, notably contracts for the sale of land,[4] where the claimant may expect to obtain specific performance as a matter of course, and other cases, such as contracts for personal services,[5] where he may expect not to. The discretionary nature of the remedy is well illustrated by a consideration of the matters, such as the conduct of the claimant, which the court may regard as a bar to specific performance.[6]

B. Common Law Remedies Inadequate

24–003   Equitable remedies are only available where common law remedies are inadequate[7]; for example where the obligation is a continuing one, necessitating a series of actions at law for damages,[8] or where the loss would be difficult to quantify.[9] But specific performance will not be available if, on the true construction of the contract, the parties have agreed that a specific sum of money is to be paid as an alternative to performing the contract.[10]

C. Specific Performance is a Remedy in Personam[11]

24–004   An order of specific performance issues against the individual defendant. If the defendant is within the jurisdiction of the court and can be compelled personally to carry out his obligation, the court may order him to do so even though the subject-matter of the contract is outside the jurisdiction of the court.

In *Penn v Lord Baltimore*[12] the parties had entered into a written agreement fixing the boundaries of Pennsylvania and Maryland, the former of which belonged to the claimants and the latter to the defendant. The claimants sued the defendant in England to

---

[3] *Lamare v Dixon* (1873) L.R. 6 H.L. 414; *Haywood v Cope* (1858) 25 Beav. 140 at 151 (Romilly M.R.).

[4] Below, para.24–014.

[5] Below, para.24–024.

[6] Below, para.24–033.

[7] *Beswick v Beswick* [1968] A.C. 58, below, para.24–047; *Tito v Waddell (No.2)* [1977] Ch. 106 at 327.

[8] [1968] A.C. 58, but see below, para.24–049.

[9] See, however, *Co-operative Insurance Society Ltd v Argyll Stores (Holdings) Ltd* [1998] A.C. 1.

[10] *Legh v Lillie* (1860) 6 H. & N. 165.

[11] Above, paras 1–008, 1–018.

[12] (1750) 1 Ves.Sen. 444; *Richard West and Partners (Inverness) Ltd v Dick* [1969] Ch. 424.

have the agreement specifically performed, and one of the objections taken by the defendant was to the jurisdiction of the court. This objection was overruled by Lord Hardwicke on the ground that:

> "[T]he conscience of the party was bound by this agreement; and being within the jurisdiction of this court, which acts *in personam*, the court may properly order it as an agreement."[13]

Although the land was not within the jurisdiction, the defendant was, and the court would hold him in contempt unless he complied.

But this jurisdiction is not, perhaps so wide as might at first appear. The land in question was subject at that time to the Crown. The court was invited in *Re Hawthorne*[14] to apply it to land in Saxony (not subject to the Crown) but refused to do so. It appears that the tendency of modern decisions is to restrict the limits within which this jurisdiction will be exercised.[15]

D. Ensuring Observance

Equitable remedies will never issue unless the court can ensure that they will be observed. As equity does not act in vain, specific performance will be ordered only where the defendant is in a position to comply.   **24–005**

In *Jones v Lipman*[16] the defendant entered into a contract to sell some land to the claimant, then sought to avoid specific performance by selling the land to a company acquired by him solely for this purpose and controlled by him. While specific performance would not normally be ordered against a vendor who no longer owned the property, here the defendant was still in a position to complete the contract, because the company was:

> "[T]he creature of the vendor, a device and a sham, a mask which he holds before his face in an attempt to avoid recognition by the eye of Equity."[17]

---

[13] (1750) 1 Ves. Sen. 444 at 447.
[14] (1883) 23 Ch.D. 743.
[15] See per Parker J. in *Deschamps v Miller* [1908] 1 Ch. 856, at 863; Dicey, Morris and Collins, *The Conflict of Laws*, 14th edn, 2006, p.1150. See also Civil Jurisdiction and Judgments Act 1982 s.30.
[16] [1962] 1 W.L.R. 832. See also *Elliott v Pierson* [1948] Ch. 452.
[17] [1962] 1 W.L.R. 832 at 836, per Russell J.

Thus specific performance was ordered against the vendor and the company.

E. The Enforcement of Positive Contractual Obligations

24–006   Unlike injunctions, the remedy of specific performance is confined to the enforcement of positive contractual obligations. A prohibitory injunction is appropriate to restrain the breach of a negative contract, while a mandatory injunction is used to force the defendant to take positive steps to undo an act already done in breach of contract. But this classification is not inflexible. Even where the claimant wishes to enforce a positive contractual obligation, he may ask for an injunction instead of specific performance. The advantage of such a course is that an injunction can be obtained on an interlocutory basis, while specific performance cannot.[18] It should also be added that specific performance does not lie against the Crown.[19]

F. Time for Performance

24–007   While specific performance is a remedy for breach of contract, it may in some circumstances be obtained before the time for performance has arrived. In *Marks v Lilley*[20] the claimant commenced an action for specific performance of a contract for the sale of land after the contractual completion date but without first having served a notice making time of the essence of the contract. It was held that this action was not premature, as the equitable right to specific performance, based on the defendant's equitable duty to perform his contract, had already accrued. But the court would not normally interfere before the time for performance had arrived, and a premature claimant may be penalised in costs. In *Hasham v Zenab*[21] specific performance of a contract for the sale of land was granted even before the contractual completion date where the defendant had been guilty of anticipatory breach of contract.[22] The order would not, of course, take effect before the fixed date.

---

[18] See *Sky Petroleum Ltd v VIP Petroleum Ltd* [1974] 1 W.L.R. 576; *Astro Exito Navegacion SA v Southland Enterprise Co Ltd (No.2)* [1983] 2 A.C. 787; *Peninsular Maritime Ltd v Padseal Ltd* (1981) 259 E.G. 860; *Parker v Camden LBC* [1986] Ch. 162.

[19] Crown Proceedings Act 1947 s.21(1)(a). The proper remedy is a declaration.

[20] [1959] 1 W.L.R. 749. There is a breach of contract at law and in equity if completion does not occur on the contractual date, even though time has not become of the essence: *Raineri v Miles* [1981] A.C. 1050, below, para.24–036.

[21] [1960] A.C. 316; REM (1960) 76 L.Q.R. 200. This is similar to the position at law, where an immediate right to damages accrues upon an anticipatory breach of contract: *Hochster v De la Tour* (1853) 2 E. & B. 678.

[22] Anticipatory breach is not essential, but there must be a sufficient likelihood of breach; Spry, *Equitable Remedies*, p.77. See further *Oakacre Ltd v Claire Cleaners (Holdings) Ltd* [1982] Ch. 197.

G. Specific Performance and Damages or Compensation

Damages may be awarded either in addition to or in substitution **24–008**
for specific performance.[23] Similarly, there are some cases, involving misdescription in contracts for the sale of land, where the court
may grant specific performance with compensation in the form of an
abatement of the purchase price.[24]

2. The Effect of an Order of Specific Performance on Other Remedies

If specific performance is granted, but enforcement subsequently **24–009**
becomes impossible, what remedies are available to the claimant?

A. Common Law Remedy not Excluded

In *Johnson v Agnew*[25] the claimant, having contracted to sell **24–010**
mortgaged properties to the defendant, obtained an order of specific
performance. Subsequently, owing to the defendant's delay, the
properties were sold by the mortgagees so that it became impossible
to comply with the order. The price obtained by the mortgagees was
lower than the contract price, so the claimant sought damages from
the defendant at common law for breach of contract.[26] The defendant claimed that the claimant's election to seek specific performance was irrevocable, so that he could not claim damages at
common law. The House of Lords found in favour of the claimant.
Lord Wilberforce explained the vendor's position as follows:

If a purchaser fails to complete, the vendor can treat this as a
repudiation and claim damages for breach of contract, or he may
seek specific performance. If he proceeds for these remedies in the
alternative, he must elect at trial.[27] If an order for specific performance is made, the contract still exists and is not merged in the
judgment. If the defendant then fails to comply with the order, the
claimant may apply either to enforce or to dissolve the contract. It
follows from the fact that the contract still exists that the claimant
can recover damages at common law. The argument based on irrevocable election is unsound:

---

[23] Lord Cairns' Act 1858; Judicature Act 1873; below, para.24–044.

[24] Below, para.24–044 (damages), and para.24–039 (compensation). See also *Seven Seas Properties Ltd v Al-Essa* [1988] 1 W.L.R. 1272 (specific performance and damages combined with asset-freezing injunction).

[25] [1980] A.C. 367; P. Baker (1979) 95 L.Q.R. 321; F. Crane [1979] Conv. 293; G. Wood-man (1979) 42 M.L.R. 696; M. Hetherington (1980) 96 L.Q.R. 403; A. Oakley (1980) 39 C.L.J. 58; D. Jackson (1981) 97 L.Q.R. 26.

[26] Or, alternatively, damages under Lord Cairns' Act, above.

[27] See further *Meng Leong Development Pte Ltd v Jip Hong Trading Co Pte Ltd* [1985] A.C. 511 (PC); (1985) 101 L.Q.R. 309.

"A vendor who seeks (and gets) specific performance is merely electing for a course which may or may not lead to implementation of the contract; what he elects for is not eternal and unconditional affirmation, but a continuance of the contract under control of the court, which control involves the power, in certain events, to terminate it. If he makes an election at all, he does so when he decides not to proceed under the order for specific performance; but to ask the court to terminate the contract."[28]

If the claimant accepts a repudiation, he cannot afterwards seek specific performance, because the defendant has been discharged from further performance by the claimant's acceptance of the repudiation. But if the claimant obtains an order of specific performance, and enforcement becomes impossible, there is no reason why the claimant should be precluded from seeking a remedy at common law.[29]

B. The Court's Discretion

24–011   The control of the court is exercised according to equitable principles: the relief sought by the claimant will be refused if it would be unjust to the other party to grant it. In *Johnson v Agnew*[30] it was the purchaser's fault that it had become impossible to enforce the order, therefore the vendor was entitled not only to its discharge and the termination of the contract, but to damages at common law for breach of contract.

C. Subsequent Performance Regulated by Terms of Order

24–012   Although the contract still exists after specific performance is granted and does not merge into the order until the legal title has been conveyed, the rights under the contract may be affected by the order. By applying for specific performance, the claimant puts into the hands of the court how the contract is to be carried out: the performance of the contract is regulated by the provisions of the order and not those of the contract. In *Singh v Nazeer*[31] a purchaser was granted specific performance of a contract for the sale of land. The purchaser then delayed, so the vendor served a completion notice and claimed damages and forfeiture of the deposit. Megarry J.

---

[28] [1980] A.C. 367 at 398 (per Lord Wilberforce). See also *Hillel v Christoforides* (1992) 63 P. & C.R. 301; *Homsy v Murphy* (1997) 73 P. & C.R. 26.
[29] Damages are also available in lieu of specific performance under Lord Cairns' Act (below, para.24–044); *Biggin v Minton* [1977] 1 W.L.R. 701.
[30] Above, fn.25.
[31] [1979] Ch. 474; criticised in M. Hetherington (1980) 96 L.Q.R. 403. cf. D. Jackson (1981) 97 L.Q.R. 26.

held that the completion notice was invalid. The machinery provisions of the contract, for example as to mode and date of completion, were intended to apply to performance out of court. Once specific performance was granted, they must yield to any directions in the order. Unless the parties agree, the working out, variation or cancellation of an order for specific performance is a matter for the court. Applying these principles, a vendor who obtains specific performance is not free to sell to a third party if the purchaser fails to comply with the order. Unless the purchaser agrees to the resale, the vendor's remedy in such a case is to apply to court either for enforcement of the order or for an order terminating the contract.[32]

3. Specific Performance in Particular Situations

It is a fundamental rule that specific performance will not be granted **24-013** where the claimant would be adequately compensated by the common law remedy of damages.[33] There are some situations, few in number, in which it is settled that the claimant may expect to obtain specific performance.[34] There are also numerous situations in which it can firmly be said that the claimant will *not* be awarded specific performance. It may be that many of the arguments for restricting specific performance are no longer wholly convincing, and that the trend is towards expansion of the remedy.[35]

A. Contracts for the Sale of Land[36]

A claimant seeking specific performance of a contract for the sale **24-014** (or other disposition) of land must first satisfy the requirements of s.2 of the Law of Property (Miscellaneous Provisions) Act 1989. These requirements apply also to a claim for damages. Section 2 provides that a contract for the sale or other disposition of an interest in land can only be made in writing incorporating all the terms which the parties have agreed. The document must be signed by or on behalf of each party. Under the previous law the contract needed

---

[32] *GKN Distributors Ltd v Tyne Tees Fabrication Ltd* [1985] 2 E.G.L.R. 181. (Vendor's claim against purchaser for declaration, forfeiture of deposit and damages dismissed.)

[33] *Hutton v Watling* [1948] Ch. 26 at 36, affirmed [1948] Ch. 398. On the effect on the defendant's insolvency, see *Freevale Ltd v Metrostore (Holdings) Ltd* [1984] Ch. 199; D. Milman and S. Coneys [1984] Conv. 446; *Amec Properties Ltd v Planning Research & Systems Plc* [1992] 1 E.G.L.R. 70 (insolvency of defendant before completion is no bar to specific performance).

[34] See *Haywood v Cope* (1858) 25 Beav. 140, per Romilly M.R. at 151; *Lamare v Dixon* (1873) L.R. 6 HL 414.

[35] See generally A. Burrows (1984) 4 L. S. 102. See, however, *Co-operative Insurance Society Ltd v Argyll Stores (Holdings) Ltd* [1998] A.C. 1; below, para.24–021.

[36] See R. Chambers in Degeling and Edelman (eds), *Equity in Commercial Law* (2005), Ch.17.

only to be *evidenced in* writing, and an oral contract could be enforced under the doctrine of part performance. The present rule leaves no scope for part performance, which can only cure *evidential* defects.[37]

Assuming s.2 is satisfied, specific performance is readily granted to enforce a contract to create or convey a legal estate in land (for example, to sell land[38] or to grant a lease) unless some special consideration arises to prevent it. It cannot however be said that the claimant is *entitled* to specific performance, as the order is always subject to the discretion of the court.

Each piece of land is unique, and it is accepted as a general rule that an award of damages is not adequate compensation for the purchaser or lessee.[39] If the purchaser does not acquire the land he will not have to pay the price, thus:

"[T]he damages for loss of such a bargain would be negligible and, as in most cases of breach of contract for the sale of land at a market price by refusal to convey it, would constitute a wholly inadequate and unjust remedy for the breach. That is why the normal remedy is by a order for specific performance by the vendor of his primary obligation to convey, on the purchaser's performing or being willing to perform his own primary obligations under the contract."[40]

The court, treating each party equally, will also give specific performance to the vendor or lessor,[41] although a monetary payment might be adequate compensation.

If a vendor fails to comply with the order, the purchaser may apply to the court for an order nominating some person to execute the conveyance in the vendor's name.[42]

B. Contractual Licences

24–015   It was at one time thought that specific performance would not be granted of a contractual licence to occupy land, on the ground that

---

[37] cf. *Singh v Beggs* (1996) 71 P. & C.R. 120 at 122, where this point is not taken.

[38] On specific performance of options and rights of pre-emption, see *Pritchard v Briggs* [1980] Ch. 338; *Sudbrook Trading Estate Ltd v Eggleton* [1983] 1 A.C. 444. See also *Berkley v Poulett* (1976) 120 S.J. 836, above, para.12–035 (sub-purchaser).

[39] cf. Heydon, Gummow and Austin, *Cases and Materials on Equity and Trusts*, 4th edn, p.946, preferring the explanation that "the process of looking for, negotiating for and completing the purchase of land is a lengthy and irritating one; . . . so that it is better to get specific performance . . . rather than get damages and use them to buy something similar." See also Law Com. No.238 (1996), para.9.3, fn.5.

[40] *Sudbrook Trading Estate Ltd v Eggleton*, above, fn.38 at 478.

[41] *Cogent v Gibson* (1864) 33 Beav. 557.

[42] Senior Courts Act 1981 s.39; Trustee Act 1925 ss.44(vi), 50; AEA 1925 s.43(2). For other remedies, see above, para.24–010.

the licence created no estate in the land.[43] This view has now been seen to be inconsistent with the court's power to grant an injunction to restrain the wrongful revocation of a contractual licence.[44] Thus in *Verrall v Great Yarmouth Borough Council*[45] the Court of Appeal affirmed the grant of specific performance to enforce a contractual licence whereby the National Front was to occupy the defendant's premises for the purpose of its annual conference. The remedy of damages would be inadequate as the claimant could not find any other premises. Roskill L.J. held it to be the duty of the court:

"[T]o protect, where it is appropriate to do so, any interest, whether it be an estate in land or a licence, by injunction or specific performance as the case may be."[46]

C. Contracts for the Sale of Personal Property

Chattels and stocks and shares do not usually possess such indi- **24–016** vidual character as land. Most commercial contracts for the purchase of goods,[47] or for a loan of money,[48] or contracts for the purchase of government stock, will not be specifically performed.[49] But if stocks or shares cannot always be bought in the market, the court may order specific performance[50]; or where a chattel has especial value by reason of its individuality, beauty or rarity.[51] Indeed, in such situations, there is an ancient jurisdiction to order the specific recovery of such a chattel if wrongly detained.[52] Where specific performance of a contract to sell a house is granted, the remedy is also available in respect of a related contract to sell the chattels in it.[53]

---

[43] *Booker v Palmer* [1942] 2 All E.R. 674 at 677, per Lord Greene M.R.

[44] *Winter Garden Theatre (London) Ltd v Millennium Productions Ltd* [1948] A.C. 173.

[45] [1981] Q.B. 202; A. Briggs [1981] Conv. 212. See also *Tanner v Tanner* [1975] 1 W.L.R. 1346 at 1350.

[46] [1981] Q.B. 202 at 220.

[47] *Dominion Coal Co Ltd v Dominion Iron and Steel Co Ltd* [1909] A.C. 293; *Cohen v Roche* [1927] 1 K.B. 169; *Société Des Industries Metallurgiques SA v The Bronx Engineering Co Ltd* [1975] 1 Lloyd's Rep. 465. See the examples given by Goff L.J. in *Price v Strange* [1978] Ch. 337 at 359.

[48] *South African Territories Ltd v Wallington* [1898] A.C. 309.

[49] *Cud (or Cuddee) v Rutter* (1720) 1 P.Wms. 570 (South Sea Bubble Stock); *Mason v Armitage* (1806) 13 Ves.Jr. 25.

[50] *Duncuft v Albrecht* (1841) 12 Sim. 189; A. Neef (1953) 51 Mich.L.R. 408; *Mills v Sportsdirect.com Retail Ltd* [2010] 2 B.C.L.C. 143.

[51] *Falcke v Gray* (1859) 4 Dr. 651; *Philips v Lamdin* [1949] 2 K.B. 33.

[52] *Pusey v Pusey* (1684) 1 Vern. 273 (an antique horn, supposedly given by King Canute); *Duke of Somerset v Cookson* (1735) 3 P.Wms. 390 (an altar piece); *Fells v Reed* (1796) 3 Ves.Jr. 70; (the tobacco box of a club).

[53] *Record v Bell* [1991] 1 W.L.R. 853.

Further, the Sale of Goods Act 1979[54] s.52 (replacing earlier legislation) enables the court to order specific performance of a contract for the sale of specific or ascertained goods, either unconditionally, or upon such terms as to damages, payment of the price or otherwise as to the court may seem just. The power is discretionary, and it must still be shown that the remedy of damages is inadequate. It was intended to broaden the scope of the remedy of specific performance in connection with the purchase of chattels, but less use has been made of it than might have been expected.[55] In *Cohen v Roche*,[56] the claimant agreed to purchase from the defendants a set of eight Hepplewhite chairs. This was a contract for the sale of specific goods; but McCardie J., finding that the chairs were "ordinary articles of commerce and of no special value or interest," refused to order specific performance and awarded damages. In *Behnke v Bede Shipping Co*,[57] Wright J. made an order for specific performance of a contract for the sale of a ship, being satisfied that the ship was of peculiar and practically unique value to the claimant.

The boldest exercise of jurisdiction was in *Sky Petroleum Ltd v VIP Petroleum Ltd*.[58]

A contract had been entered into whereby the claimant company would buy all the petrol needed for its garages from the defendant company, which would supply the claimant with all its requirements. The defendant, alleging breach, purported to terminate the contract in November 1973, at a time when petrol supplies were limited, so that the claimant would have little prospect of finding an alternative source. An interlocutory injunction was granted to restrain the withholding of supplies.

24–017   Goulding J. acknowledged that it amounted to specific performance, the matter being one of substance, and not of form; but held that the court had jurisdiction to order specific performance of a contract to sell chattels, although they were not specific or ascertained, where the remedy of damages was inadequate. The usual rule that specific performance was not available to enforce contracts for the sale of chattels was well established and salutary; but it was based on the adequacy of damages, and was therefore not applicable

---

[54] The Act has been amended to allow specific performance of the seller's duty to repair or replace goods (Pt 5A); D. Harris (2003) 119 L.Q.R. 541.

[55] [1969] J.B.L. 211; *Société Des Industries Metallurgiques SA v The Bronx Engineering Co Ltd*, above, fn.47.

[56] [1927] 1 K.B. 169.

[57] [1927] 1 K.B. 649 at 661; cf. *Hart v Herwig* (1873) L.R. 8 Ch.App. 680.

[58] [1974] 1 W.L.R. 576. See also *Howard E. Perry & Co Ltd v British Railways Board* [1980] 1 W.L.R. 1375; J. Thornely (1980) 39 C.L.J. 269.

to the present case, where the company might be forced out of business if the remedy was not granted.

D. Contracts to Pay Money

Contracts to pay money are normally not specifically enforceable, **24–018** because damages will usually be an adequate remedy. So, for example, specific performance of a contract of loan will not be awarded against the borrower, because the remedy of damages is adequate.[59] Exceptionally, however, specific performance may be obtainable in the following situations:

    i. where the contract is to pay money to a third party, so that any damages awarded would probably be nominal[60];

    ii. where the contract is for the payment of an annuity[61] or other periodical sums. This exception is based on two grounds: first that specific performance avoids the inconvenience of a series of actions for damages every time payment is not made; and, secondly, even if substantial damages were available, it has been suggested that the common law remedy would still be inadequate as the amount in the case of an annuity would be conjectural[62];

    iii. a contract with a company to take up and pay for debentures[63];

    iv. a contract of indemnity, if, on its true construction, the obligation is to relieve a debtor by preventing him from having to pay his debt. Instead of compelling the debtor first to pay the debt and perhaps to ruin himself in doing so, equity will order the indemnifier to pay the debt. It will be otherwise if the obligation is merely to repay the debtor a sum of money after he has paid it. Damages will then be an adequate remedy[64];

    v. as has been seen, in the case of a contract for the sale of land, the vendor will be granted specific performance of the purchaser's obligation to make a money payment. Although the remedy of damages may be adequate, specific performance is allowed because of the mutuality principle;

    vi. a contract to pay a debt out of specific property segregated by the debtor for that purpose is specifically enforceable,

---

[59] See *Locabail International Finance Ltd v Agroexport* [1986] 1 W.L.R. 657 (no mandatory injunction).

[60] *Beswick v Beswick* [1968] A.C. 58; below, para.24–047. The third party may now be able to enforce the contract under the Contracts (Rights of Third Parties) Act 1999.

[61] *Beswick v Beswick*, above, fn.60.

[62] *Adderly v Dixon* (1824) 1 Sim. & St. 607 at 611. But see below, para.24–049.

[63] Companies Act 2006 s.740 (re-enacting previous legislation).

[64] *McIntosh v Dalwood (No.4)* (1930) 30 S.R.(NSW) 415 at 418.

and creates an equitable interest in the specific property, unless there is evidence of a contrary intention.[65]

E. Volunteers

24–019   Specific performance will not be awarded to a volunteer. Indeed, unless the contract is by deed, consideration is necessary for the validity of the contract itself. Parties to a deed of covenant may sue at law, even though there is no consideration, but they will not be able to obtain specific performance.[66] Problems commonly arose in this connection in relation to covenants to make family settlements.[67] Inadequacy of consideration is not a bar to specific performance, but may be relevant to the exercise of the court's discretion.[68]

The Contracts (Rights of Third Parties) Act 1999 now permits a third party in certain circumstances to enforce a term of a contract which is for his benefit. Section 1(5) provides that:

> "[T]here shall be available to the third party any remedy that would have been available to him in an action for breach of contract if he had been a party to the contract (and the rules relating to damages, injunctions, specific performance and other relief shall apply accordingly)".

This provision arguably enables the third party to obtain specific performance in a case where the remedy of damages would be inadequate. However, the volunteer principle, which is one of the "rules relating to ... specific performance", may mean that the third party should be confined to damages, as in the case of a volunteer who is a party to a covenant.[69]

It is no objection, provided that the party seeking specific performance is not a volunteer, that the order will have the direct consequence of benefiting a volunteer[70]; nor, in the case of the due exercise of an option to purchase land, that the option was granted for a token payment or for no payment at all.[71]

---

[65] *Swiss Bank Corp v Lloyds Bank Ltd* [1982] A.C. 584 at 613 (per Lord Wilberforce); *Napier and Ettrick (Lord) v Hunter* [1993] A.C. 713.

[66] See *Cannon v Hartley* [1949] Ch. 213; cf. N. Andrews (2001) 60 C.L.J. 250, suggesting that s.1(5) is an exception to the volunteer rule.

[67] Above, para.4–017.

[68] Spry, *Equitable Remedies*, p.59, See below, para.24–038.

[69] *Cannon v Hartley*, above, fn.66.

[70] See *Beswick v Beswick* [1968] A.C. 58, below, para.24–047.

[71] *Mountford v Scott* [1975] Ch. 258, affirming on different grounds the decision of Brightman J.; F. Crane (1975) 39 Conv.(N.S.) 270; *Midland Bank Trust Co Ltd v Green* [1980] Ch. 590 CA; F. Crane [1979] Conv. 441.

F. Contracts Requiring Supervision

i. The Principle. It is settled law that a court will not grant **24–020**
specific performance where the order would require constant supervision by the court.[72] The reason is that supervision would be impracticable. Equity does nothing in vain; and will not issue orders
which it cannot be certain to enforce. Of course, the threat of imprisonment would be effective in many cases; but imprisonment of the
defendant for contempt, if he proves recalcitrant, is a "heavy-
handed" mechanism which will not get the duty performed.[73]

Orders for the specific performance of contracts to create or convey a legal estate in land do not meet with this difficulty. All that the
defendant needs to do to perform such a contract is to execute the
document; and, as has been seen, if he refuses, he may be threatened
with imprisonment for contempt; and if he still refuses, the court
may nominate any person to effect the conveyance.[74]

One important question is whether there is a sufficient definition
of what has to be done in order to comply with the order of the
court.[75]

In *Posner v Scott-Lewis*[76] a lease contained a landlord's covenant to employ a resident porter, whose duties were to clean the
common parts, to look after the heating and to carry rubbish to the
dustbins. Specific performance of this covenant was granted, to
procure the appointment of a porter. The earlier decision to the
contrary in *Ryan v Mutual Tontine Westminster Chambers Association*,[77] was difficult to distinguish, but the authority of that case
had been weakened by later decisions.[78] The relevant questions
were: (a) was there a sufficient definition of what had to be done?
(b) would an unacceptable degree of superintendence be involved? (c) what would be the respective hardship to the parties if
the order was made or refused? The answer to these questions
supported a grant of specific performance; the remedy of damages
was clearly inadequate.

---

[72] *Ryan v Mutual Tontine Westminster Chambers Association* [1893] 1 Ch. 116; *Blackett v Bates* (1865) L.R. 1 Ch. App. 117 (maintenance of railway); *Joseph v National Magazine Co* [1959] Ch. 14; *Re C (A Minor)* [1991] 2 F.L.R. 168 (schooling).

[73] *Co-operative Insurance Society Ltd v Argyll Stores (Holdings) Ltd* [1998] A.C. 1.

[74] Above, para.24–014.

[75] *Tito v Waddell (No.2)* [1977] Ch. 106 at 322, per Megarry V.C.; F. Crane (1977) 41 Conv.(N.S.) 432 at 436.

[76] [1987] Ch. 25; G. Jones (1987) 46 C.L.J. 21.

[77] [1893] 1 Ch. 116.

[78] *Giles (CH) & Co Ltd v Morris* [1972] 1 W.L.R. 307 at 318; *Shiloh Spinners Ltd v Harding* [1973] A.C. 691 at 724; *Tito v Waddell (No.2)* [1977] Ch. 106 at 321. The House of Lords in *Co-operative Insurance Society Ltd v Argyll Stores (Holdings) Ltd* [1998] A.C. 1, however, considered that the dicta in *Shiloh Spinners* had been too widely interpreted.

24–021   Other illustrations include *Beswick v Beswick*[79] where specific
performance was ordered of a contract to make a regular payment to
the claimant for life. In *Sky Petroleum Ltd v VIP Petroleum Ltd*[80] an
interlocutory injunction, which was regarded as tantamount to specific performance, was granted to enforce the defendant's obligation
to supply petrol regularly to the claimant. In the related area of
mandatory injunctions the requirement of supervision has not been
regarded as an unsurmountable obstacle.[81] Specific performance is
more likely to be granted, in spite of supervision difficulties, against
a defendant who has had some or all of the benefit to which he was
entitled under the contract.[82]

The principle was reviewed by the House of Lords in *Co-operative Insurance Society Ltd v Argyll Stores (Holdings) Ltd.*[83] The
question was whether specific performance should be granted of a
covenant in a lease of a supermarket (which was the focal point of a
shopping centre) to keep open during the usual hours of business.
The supermarket had been trading at a loss and the lease had 19
years to run. The House of Lords, reversing the Court of Appeal,
rejected the landlord's claim for specific performance, even though
any damages would be difficult to quantify. Although the breach was
deliberate, specific performance would be oppressive to the tenant,
whose loss in complying might be far greater than the loss to the
landlord should the covenant be broken. As in the analogous sphere
of mandatory injunctions, it was not in the public interest to require
the carrying on of a business at a loss if there was some other
plausible means of compensation. In any event, the covenant was
not sufficiently certain for an order of specific performance. The
supervision principle remained important, although there were
fewer objections where an order simply required the defendant to
achieve a specified result[84] (as in the repairs cases, discussed below)
than where an order was sought to require the defendant to carry on
an activity. The decision has been broadly welcomed in view of the
undoubted difficulties of supervision,[85] but another view is that the
House of Lords failed to liberalise the principles of specific performance and to grant an effective remedy to a landlord who was likely
to be "shortchanged" by any award of damages.[86]

[79] [1968] A.C. 58; below.
[80] [1974] 1 W.L.R. 576.
[81] *Redland Bricks Ltd v Morris* [1970] A.C. 652; *Gravesham BC v British Railways Board*
[1978] Ch. 379, below, para.25–018.
[82] *Tito v Waddell (No.2)*, above, fn.78, at 322.
[83] [1998] A.C. 1.
[84] This was the context of Lord Wilberforce's rejection of supervision difficulties in *Shiloh
Spinners Ltd v Harding* [1973] A.C. 691 at 724, which had been too widely interpreted in
other cases.
[85] See G. Jones (1997) 56 C.L.J. 488; A. Phang (1998) 61 M.L.R. 421; P. Luxton [1998]
Conv. 396.
[86] A. Tettenborn [1998] Conv. 23.

ii. The Construction Cases. The court does not, as a rule, order **24–022** specific performance of a contract to build or repair[87]; but there are certain exceptional cases.

"The first [requirement] is that the building work, of which he seeks to enforce the performance, is defined by the contract; that is to say, that the particulars of the work are so far definitely ascertained that the court can sufficiently see what is the exact nature of the work of which it is asked to order the performance. The second is that the claimant has a substantial interest in having the contract performed, which is of such a nature that he cannot adequately be compensated for breach of the contract by damages. The third is that the defendant has by the contract obtained possession of land on which the work is contracted to be done."[88]

In *Wolverhampton Corp v Emmons*[89] a plot of land had been sold by an urban sanitary authority, in pursuance of a scheme of street improvement, to the defendant, who agreed to erect buildings on it, and went into possession. A later agreement provided for the erection of the buildings in accordance with detailed plans. The Court of Appeal ordered specific performance.

This exception is said to be based on a "balance of convenience". Historically it originates in a series of cases relating to the early days of railways.[90] Where a railway was built through a farmer's land and the railway company undertook to provide a bridge or tunnel to connect the separated parts of the farmer's land, it would have been most unjust to leave the farmer to a remedy in damages. These specialised cases have been given more general application, and the formulation in *Wolverhampton Corp v Emmons*[91] was further extended in *Carpenters Estates v Davies*,[92] where Farwell J. held that it was sufficient that the defendant was in possession of the land, whether he came in by the contract or not. After all, the defendant's possession is the material factor; for the claimant cannot then enter to perform the construction or repair work himself.

iii. Enforcement of Leasehold Covenants. The "construction **24–023** contracts" exception was extended to cover a landlord's repairing

[87] *Wheatley v Westminster Brymbo Coal Co* (1869) L.R. 9 Eq. 538; *Haywood v Brunswick Building Society* (1881) 8 Q.B.D. 403.
[88] *Wolverhampton Corp v Emmons* [1901] 1 K.B. 515 at 525, per Romer L.J.; *Hounslow LBC v Twickenham Developments Ltd* [1971] Ch. 233.
[89] [1901] 1 K.B. 515. See also *Price v Strange* [1978] Ch. 337 at 359.
[90] *Ryan v Mutual Tontine Westminster Chambers Association* [1893] 1 Ch. 116 at 128.
[91] [1901] 1 K.B. 515.
[92] [1940] Ch. 160.

covenant in *Jeune v Queens Cross Properties Ltd*,[93] where a balcony
which was not part of the demised premises fell into disrepair. The
three conditions laid down in *Wolverhampton Corp v Emmons*[94]
were satisfied, as the landlord was in possession of the balcony, and
the work involved was specific. There was a clear breach, and no
doubt as to what was required to be done to remedy it. A mandatory
order was much more convenient than an award of damages, leaving
it to the tenant to do the work. The decision was extended by statute,
now Landlord and Tenant Act 1985 s.17, which provides that the
court may order specific performance of a landlord's repairing covenant relating to any part of the premises in which the tenant's
dwelling is comprised, notwithstanding any equitable rule restricting this remedy.

It has since been established that, contrary to the previous understanding, specific performance of a tenant's repair covenant may be
granted in rare cases where there is no other adequate remedy.
Rainbow Estates Ltd v Tokenhold Ltd[95] was such a rare case, as the
property (a listed building) was in serious disrepair and deteriorating
but the lease contained no right of forfeiture nor any right for the
landlord to have access to do the repairs at the tenant's expense. The
schedule of works was sufficiently certain to be enforceable, and
objections based on mutuality[96] or difficulties of supervision were of
little force. The order simply required the tenant to achieve a result
rather than carry on an activity.[97]

G. Contracts for Personal Services

24–024   It is well established that contracts which are personal in nature or
which involve the performance of personal services will not be
specifically enforced.[98] In this respect, it is necessary to distinguish
contracts of employment from other contracts for personal services.
The former are governed by a firm prohibition against specific enforcement by Trade Union and Labour Relations (Consolidation)
Act 1992 s.236, which provides that:

---

[93] [1974] Ch. 97; *Francis v Cowcliff Ltd* (1977) 33 P. & C.R. 368; *Gordon v Selico Ltd*
[1985] 2 E.G.L.R. 79; *Hammond v Allen* [1994] 1 All E.R. 307. If the matter is urgent, a
mandatory interlocutory injunction may be granted; *Parker v Camden LBC* [1986] Ch. 162
(boiler strike threatened tenants' health).

[94] [1901] 1 K.B. 515.

[95] [1999] Ch. 64; M. Pawlowski and J. Brown [1998] Conv. 495; S. Bridge (1999) 58
C.L.J. 283.

[96] Below, para.24–030.

[97] See *Co-operative Insurance Society Ltd v Argyll Stores (Holdings) Ltd* [1998] A.C. 1;
above, para.24–021.

[98] Fry, *Specific Performance*, 6th edn, 1921, pp.50–51; *Lumley v Wagner* (1852) 1 De G.M.
& G. 604, below, para.25–062; *Thomas Marshall (Exports) Ltd v Guinle* [1979] Ch. 227;
Provident Financial Group plc v Haywood [1989] 3 All E.R. 298 at 302. See A. Burrows
(1984) 4 L. S. 102 at 112–114.

"[N]o court shall . . . by way of an order for specific performance . . . compel an employee to do any work or to attend at any
place for the doing of any work."

A contract of employment is defined in s.295(1).[99] Not every contract for personal services constitutes a contract of employment; for
it may be a contract between an employer and an independent
contractor.

In cases of contracts not covered by the Act, or where enforcement is sought against an employer,[100] the equitable principle applies. The reasons traditionally given for the rule are first, that such
contracts would require constant supervision, and would in practice
be impossible to enforce; and secondly, that it is contrary to public
policy to compel one person to submit to the orders of another. "The
courts," said Fry L.J., "are bound to be jealous, lest they should turn
contracts of service into contracts of slavery."[101] Megarry J. hoped
that the court might look again at this "so-called rule". It was not
based on these difficulties alone; but was rather a question of human
nature.

"If a singer contracts to sing, there could no doubt be proceedings
for committal if, ordered to sing, the singer remained obstinately
dumb. But if instead the singer sang flat, or sharp, or too fast, or
too slowly, or too loudly, to too quietly, or resorted to a dozen of
the manifestations of temperament traditionally associated with
some singers, the threat of committal would reveal itself as a most
unsatisfactory weapon, for who could say whether the imperfec-
tions of performance were natural or self induced? To make an
order with such possibilities of evasion would be vain, and so the
order will not be made . . . the matter is one of balance and
advantage and disadvantage in relation to the particular obligations in question, and the fact that the balance will usually lie on
one side does not turn this probability into a rule."[102]

Nor, as we will see, can the rule be avoided by seeking an injunction
instead of specific performance, where the injunction would in effect compel performance.[103] However, this principle is not inflexible. An injunction may be granted where its effect would be to

---

[99] "Contract of employment" means "a contract of service or of apprenticeship".

[100] If an employee is unfairly dismissed the Employment Rights Act 1996 ss.114, 115
empower an employment tribunal to order reinstatement or re-engagement. But if the order is
not complied with the sanction is an award of compensation; s.117.

[101] *De Francesco v Barnum* (1890) 45 Ch.D. 430; below, para.25–062.

[102] *Giles (CH) & Co Ltd v Morris* [1972] 1 W.L.R. 307 at 318. This passage was approved
by Goff L.J. in *Price v Strange* [1978] Ch. 337 at 359; cf. Buckley L.J. at 369. But the House
of Lords in *Scandinavian Trading Tanker Co A/B v Flota Petrolera Ecuatoriana* [1983] 2
A.C. 694, concerning a time charter, took the view that there was no jurisdiction to grant
specific performance of a service contract.

[103] Below, para.25–062.

make performance of the contract the only realistic course open to the defendant, although not actually compelled.[104]

In *Giles (CH) & Co Ltd v Morris*,[105] a distinction was drawn between the performance of a contract of service and the execution of such a contract which provided for the claimant to be appointed managing director of a company for a period of five years. As we have seen, this approach was also adopted in *Posner v Scott-Lewis*,[106] where specific performance was granted of a covenant in a lease to appoint a resident porter. Nor should it be assumed that as soon as any element of personal service or continuous services can be discerned in a contract, the court will always refuse an order. In *Beswick v Beswick*,[107] Lord Upjohn said that a small element of personal services in a contract did not warrant the refusal of specific performance on the ground of want of mutuality.

In *Hill v CA Parsons & Co Ltd*[108] the claimant was a senior engineer in the employment of the defendant. In May 1970 a trade union successfully introduced a closed shop, under which it became a term of employment that all the defendant's employees were to be members of the union. The claimant refused, and received a month's notice of dismissal. He obtained an interlocutory injunction restraining the termination. The circumstances were special, in that the notice was short; a reasonable notice would probably have given him protection under the Industrial Relations Act 1971; and the employee and employer retained their mutual confidence.

Lord Denning M.R. said[109]:

"It may be said that, by granting an injunction in such a case, the court is indirectly enforcing specifically a contract for personal services. So be it. Lord St. Leonards L.C. did something like it in *Lumley v Wagner*.[110] And I see no reason why we should not do it here."

But Stamp L.J., dissenting, felt that the rule against specific performance of service contracts, while not without exceptions, was

---

[104] *Lauritzencool AB v Lady Navigation Inc* [2005] 1 W.L.R. 3686 (time charter); R. Grime All E.R. Rev. 2005, p.385; P. Devonshire (2005) 121 L.Q.R. 560.

[105] [1972] 1 W.L.R. 307.

[106] [1987] Ch. 25; G. Jones (1987) 46 C.L.J. 21; above, para.24–020.

[107] [1968] A.C. 58 at 97.

[108] [1972] Ch. 305; cf. *Chappell v Times Newspaper Ltd* [1975] 1 W.L.R. 482, where the employer "had every reason to suspect the plaintiff's loyalty"; *Wishart v National Association of Citizens Advice Bureaux Ltd* [1990] I.C.R. 794. It seems that injunctions of the kind granted in *Hill v Parsons* are not rare; see *Powell v London Borough of Brent* [1987] I.R.L.R. 466, *Hughes v London Borough of Southwark* [1988] I.R.L.R. 55, below, para.25–063.

[109] [1972] Ch. 305 at 315.

[110] (1852) 1 De G.M. & G. 604; below, para.25–062.

deeply embedded in the law. The rule, he said, was a salutary one, which benefited the employer and employee equally.[111]

H. Contracts for the Creation of Transient or Terminable Interests

As equity does not act in vain, specific performance will not be granted of an agreement for a lease which has already expired by the date of the hearing,[112] nor of an agreement for a tenancy at will or a partnership at will.[113]

24–025

An agreement for a tenancy from year to year is specifically enforceable,[114] but in *Lavery v Pursell*[115] specific performance of an agreement for a lease for one year was refused, one ground being that, although rights should not be prejudiced by delays in litigation, it was normally impossible to get the action heard and the order made within the year.

But the 19th century authorities on transient interests must now be treated with caution.

In *Verrall v Great Yarmouth Borough Council*[116] the defendant council had granted a contractual licence to the National Front to occupy its premises for two days (on a date which had not yet occurred) for an annual conference. The defendant wrongfully repudiated the contract, but sought to avoid specific performance, partly on the ground that the licence was a transient interest. This argument was rejected by the Court of Appeal. It was held that there was no reason why the court could not order specific performance of a contractual licence of short duration. Authorities to the contrary were inconsistent with the decision of the House of Lords in *Winter Garden Theatre (London) Ltd v Millennium Productions Ltd*,[117] whereby an injunction could be granted to restrain the wrongful revocation of the licence.

---

[111] [1972] Ch. 305 at 324.

[112] *Turner v Clowes* (1869) 20 L.T. 214. But the doctrine of *Walsh v Lonsdale* (1882) 21 Ch.D. 9, above, para.1–016, will govern the rights and obligations of the parties if specific performance of a contract for a lease would have been available during its currency, even though it has terminated by the date of the hearing: *Industrial Properties (Barton Hill) Ltd v Associated Electrical Industries Ltd* [1977] Q.B. 580; cf. P. Jackson (1977) 40 M.L.R. 718 at 720. See also *Tottenham Hotspur Football and Athletic Co v Princegrove Publishers* [1974] 1 W.L.R. 113; M. Albery (1974) 90 L.Q.R. 149.

[113] *Hercy v Birch* (1804) 9 Ves. 357. Even if not merely at will, a partnership agreement involves the difficulty of supervision.

[114] *Manchester Brewery Co Ltd v Coombs* [1901] 2 Ch. 608.

[115] (1888) 39 Ch.D. 508 at 519.

[116] [1981] Q.B. 202, above, para.24–015.

[117] [1948] A.C. 173.

"In my judgment the old view, such as it was, that courts of equity would not protect a so-called transient interest can no longer be supported, at any rate to its full extent."[118]

Thus while specific performance remains inappropriate in respect of an interest which has already expired or which is revocable at the will of the defendant, the mere fact that the interest is of short duration is no longer a bar to specific performance, which may be granted at the discretion of the court in an appropriate case.

I. Contracts to Leave Property by Will[119]

24–026   The remedy for breach of such a contract is normally damages, for any other result would amount to interference with testamentary freedom.[120] But specific performance might be ordered, as was indicated obiter by the Court of Appeal in *Synge v Synge*,[121] where the contract is in consideration of marriage, and the marriage takes place on the faith of it. The court has power to order a conveyance of a defined piece of real property after the death of the contracting party, against those who have acquired it as volunteers. While the court could not order the defendant to make a will in any particular terms,[122] it could order the executor or devisee to convey to the claimant.

In *Schaefer v Schuhmann*[123] Lord Cross treated it as established that where there is a contract to leave specific property by will, the claimant:

"[C]an obtain a declaration of his right to have it left to him by will and an injunction to restrain the testator from disposing of it in breach of contract: *Synge v Synge*.[124] No doubt if the property is land he could also register the contract or a caution against the title."[125]

If the testator retains the property until his death, but dies insolvent, the promisee can only rank as a creditor for value in competition with other such creditors.[126]

---

[118] [1981] Q.B. 202 at 220, per Roskill L.J. See also the comments of Lord Denning M.R. at 215.

[119] See W. Lee (1971) 87 L.Q.R. 358; Mellows, *The Law of Succession*, 5th edn, 1993; Ch.3.

[120] Above, para.12–028.

[121] [1894] 1 Q.B. 466. See also *Wakeham v Mackenzie* [1968] 1 W.L.R. 1175.

[122] *Re Dale (Deceased)* [1994] Ch. 31 (mutual wills); above, para.12–028.

[123] [1972] A.C. 572 (PC): see also Inheritance (Provision for Family and Dependants) Act 1975 s.11; Law Com. No.61 (1974), paras 222–242.

[124] [1894] 1 Q.B. 466.

[125] [1972] A.C. 572 at 586. If the contract relates to land, it must be writing, in order to satisfy s.2 of the Law of Property (Miscellaneous Provisions) Act 1989; *Taylor v Dickens* [1998] 1 F.L.R. 806.

[126] [1972] A.C. 572. See also *Beyfus v Lawley* [1903] A.C. 411.

Finally, it seems that specific performance will not be granted of a contract by the donee of a testamentary power of appointment to exercise the power in favour of the claimant.[127]

J. Contracts to Transfer Goodwill

A contract to sell the goodwill of a business alone is not specifi-   **24–027**
cally enforceable, because the subject-matter of the contract is too uncertain.[128] But specific performance will be granted of a contract to transfer the goodwill together with the premises or other assets of a business.[129]

K. Contracts to Refer to Arbitration

Such a contract is not specifically enforceable.[130] But if the claim-   **24–028**
ant sues on a contract which includes an arbitration provision, the defendant may ask for a stay of proceedings under Arbitration Act 1996 s.9 so that the claimant must proceed with the arbitration or be left with no remedy.[131] The court will, however enforce the arbitrator's award.[132]

L. No Specific Performance of Part of a Contract[133]

A court will not usually order specific performance of any part of   **24–029**
a contract unless it can order performance of the whole. In *Ogden v Fossick*,[134] an agreement between the parties provided that the defendant would grant to the claimant a lease of a coal wharf, and that the defendant should be appointed manager of the wharf. In an action for specific performance of the agreement to grant the lease, specific performance was denied on the ground that the part of the agreement which the court could enforce was inseparably connected with the contract of employment which it would not.

---

[127] *Re Parkin* [1892] 3 Ch. 510. The proper remedy is damages. See also *Robinson v Ommanney* (1883) 23 Ch.D. 285.

[128] *Darbey v Whitaker* (1857) 4 Drew. 134.

[129] (1857) 4 Drew. 134 at 140. And see *Beswick v Beswick* [1968] A.C. 58; below, para.24–048.

[130] *Doleman & Sons v Ossett Corp* [1912] 3 K.B. 257 at 268.

[131] See also s.86. As to the court's jurisdiction to intervene by way of injunction, see below, para.25–075.

[132] *Wood v Griffith* (1818) 1 Swans. 43. See also *Sudbrook Trading Estate Ltd v Eggleton* [1983] 1 A.C. 444, as to the possibility of specific performance of a contract to appoint a valuer or arbitrator to fix the price in an option to renew a lease.

[133] Fry, *Specific Performance*, 6th edn, 1921, Ch.16. Compare the doctrine of partial performance; *Thames Guaranty Ltd v Campbell* [1985] Q.B. 210.

[134] (1862) 4 De G.F. & J. 426.

But the rule is not absolute.[135] It may be possible to construe a contract which contains several parts as being in effect several separate and distinct contracts, so that the enforcement of one part is independent of the others.[136] This question often arises where several lots of land are sold and the question is whether there is one sale of several lots,[137] or several sales of individual lots.[138]

4. MUTUALITY

A. Refusal of Specific Performance for Lack of Mutuality[139]

24–030   It has been seen that where specific performance may be ordered in favour of a purchaser or lessee, the remedy will be available also in favour of the vendor or lessor.[140] Such a person can compel the other party to take the property even though in many cases an award of damages would be adequate compensation for his loss. He can obtain specific performance under a principle of mutuality.

A similar principle applies to deny specific performance, on grounds of lack of mutuality, where the situation is one in which that remedy could not be available to the other party.[141] "It is not disputed," said Leach M.R., "that it is a general principle of courts of equity to interpose only where the remedy is mutual."[142] Thus one party is not compelled specifically to perform his obligation if he would himself be left with only a remedy in damages. In *Flight v Bolland*,[143] the claimant failed to obtain specific performance because, as he was below the age of majority, it could not be obtained against him.[144] Nor can a person whose own obligation is to perform personal services obtain specific performance, as it could not be obtained against him.[145]

There is, however, a statutory exception to the mutuality principle in the Landlord and Tenant Act 1985 s.17, which allows a court to order specific performance of a landlord's repairing covenant, notwithstanding any equitable rule restricting this remedy, "whether

---

[135] *Beswick v Beswick* [1968] A.C. 58; *CH Giles & Co Ltd v Morris* [1972] 1 W.L.R. 307 at 317–318; *Astro Exito Navegacion SA v Southland Enterprise Co Ltd (No.2)* [1983] 2 A.C. 787.

[136] *Wilkinson v Clements* (1872) L.R. 8 Ch. App. 96, below, para.24–031.

[137] *Roffey v Shallcross* (1819) 4 Madd. 227.

[138] *Lewin v Guest* (1826) 1 Russ. 325.

[139] See Spry, *Equitable Remedies*, pp.7–12, 91–103.

[140] Above, para.24–014.

[141] This defence based on lack of mutuality may be waived by the conduct of the defendant: *Price v Strange* [1978] Ch. 337.

[142] (1828) 4 Russ. 298 at 301.

[143] (1828) 4 Russ. 298.

[144] *Lumley v Ravenscroft* [1895] 1 Q.B. 683.

[145] *Pickering v Bishop of Ely* (1843) 2 Y. & C. Ch. 249; *Ogden v Fossick* (1862) 4 De G.F. & J. 426; above, para.24–029.

based on mutuality or otherwise."[146] Now that it has been held that specific performance may be ordered against a tenant (although in rare cases), mutuality has been restored.[147] It might be added that the claimant may be able to overcome the absence of mutuality by waiving the benefit of a term,[148] or submitting to perform an obligation, which could not be specifically enforced against him.[149]

Finally, the mutuality principle goes only to discretion, not to jurisdiction. Thus the absence of mutuality does not deprive the court of jurisdiction to award damages in lieu of specific performance under Lord Cairns' Act 1858.[150]

B. The Time at which the Remedy must be Mutual

Must the requirement of mutuality be satisfied at the date of the contract, or will it suffice that the remedy has become mutually available by some later date, such as the date of the hearing? This question has been the source of much academic disagreement. Fry's proposition was that, subject to certain exceptions, the contract must be mutual when entered into.[151] Ames, on the other hand, considered that:

24–031

"Equity will not compel specific performance by a defendant if, after performance, the common law remedy of damages would be his sole security for the performance of the [claimant's] side of the contract."[152]

The courts, it must be said, had never applied a principle as rigid as that propounded by Fry. It was laid down in *Hoggart v Scott*[153] that a vendor may obtain specific performance if he can show a good title at the time of the hearing, even though he had none when the contract was made. We saw that there could be no specific performance of a contract where the obligation of one party was the performance of services. It was held, however, in *Wilkinson v Clements*[154] that if the claimant has already performed the services, he may enforce the contract.

---

[146] Above, para.24–027.
[147] *Rainbow Estates Ltd v Tokenhold Ltd* [1999] Ch. 64.
[148] *Heron Garage Properties Ltd v Moss* [1974] 1 W.L.R. 148.
[149] *Scott v Bradley* [1971] Ch. 850; REM (1951) 67 L.Q.R. 300.
[150] *Price v Strange* [1978] Ch. 337. For Lord Cairns' Act, see below, para.24–044.
[151] Fry, *Specific Performance*, 6th edn, 1921, p.219.
[152] Ames, *Lectures in Legal History*, 1913, p.370.
[153] (1830) 1 Russ. & M. 293; *Joseph v National Magazine Co Ltd* [1959] Ch. 14 (a case of personal property); *Price v Strange* [1978] Ch. 337 at 355 and 364. See C. Emery (1977) 41 Conv.(N.S.) 18.
[154] (1872) L.R. 8 Ch.App. 96. If the claimant has not performed all the obligations, justice can be done by granting specific performance on terms of a monetary readjustment. See also *Wakeham v Mackenzie* [1968] 1 W.L.R. 1175.

The formulation of Ames was adopted by the Court of Appeal in preference to Fry's rule.

24–032   In *Price v Strange*[155] D contracted to grant an underlease of a flat to P, and the agreement contained an undertaking by P to execute internal and external repairs. P did the internal repairs, and was ready and willing to complete the external; but D repudiated the contract, and did the external repairs herself. P sued for specific performance of the contract to grant the underlease. D claimed that P was not entitled to specific performance because, relying on Fry's rule, there was no mutuality at the date of the contract: P's repair obligations were not specifically enforceable. It was held that Fry's rule was wrong; the time for considering mutuality was the date of the judgment. If by that time those obligations which were not specifically enforceable had been performed, P could obtain specific performance.

The principle is that the court will not compel a defendant to perform his obligations specifically if it cannot at the same time ensure that any unperformed obligations of the claimant will be specifically performed, unless, perhaps, damages would be an adequate remedy to the defendant for any default on the claimant's part.[156] Specific performance was, accordingly, granted on terms that P should pay compensation to D for the cost of the repairs done by D.

5. DEFENCES TO SPECIFIC PERFORMANCE[157]

24–033 The situations discussed below are those in which the discretion of the court is unlikely to be exercised in favour of specific performance, although the contract is of a type to which the remedy is appropriate. Most of the illustrations relate to land, for, as we have seen, few contracts outside this area are specifically enforceable. It will be noted that, in some of the circumstances discussed below, such as hardship or delay, the contract is unaffected, and the defendant remains liable in damages; the claimant is merely denied specific performance. In others, as in some cases of mistake and

---

[155] [1978] Ch. 337; F. Glover (1978) 128 N.L.J. 569; applied in *Sutton v Sutton* [1984] Ch. 184 (wife agreed to consent to divorce and not to seek maintenance in return for a transfer of the home. Husband could not have enforced her promises, but once she had performed an appreciable part by giving formal consent to the petition, he could not rely on absence of mutuality).

[156] [1978] Ch. 337 at 367–378.

[157] See also *BICC v Burndy Corp* [1985] Ch. 232; (1985) 101 L.Q.R. 145; C. Harpum (1985) 44 C.L.J. 204; N. Palmer All E.R.Rev. 1985, at 36; discussing set-off as a defence to specific performance.

misrepresentation, the contract may be rescinded in equity, which is of course a defence to specific performance, and which will preclude enforcement at law.[158] In cases of substantial misdescription or lack of good title, the vendor may be in breach; not only is the vendor unable in such circumstances to obtain specific performance; he may be liable in damages to the purchaser.

A. Mistake and Misrepresentation

There are situations in which equity, although refusing to rescind **24–034** a contract or cancel a deed for mistake or misrepresentation, will not give the other party positive equitable help in enforcing it. The claimant will be left to his remedy in damages.[159] The court is not bound to order specific performance in every case in which it will not set aside the contract, nor to set aside every contract that it will not specifically enforce.[160]

A defendant cannot usually resist specific performance by alleging merely his own fault and mistake,[161] nor on the ground that he was mistaken as to the legal effect of the agreement,[162] although "unilateral mistake may, in some circumstances, afford an answer to a claim for specific performance."[163] Generally, equity will hold the defendant to enforcement of his bargain unless it can be shown that this would involve real hardship amounting to injustice.[164]

In *Webster v Cecil*[165] A, by letter, offered to sell some property to B. He intended to offer it at £2,250 but by mistake wrote £1,250. B agreed to buy at £1,250. A immediately gave notice of the error and was not compelled to carry out the sale.

In *Tamplin v James*[166] an inn was offered for sale, and was correctly described with reference to plans. At the rear of the inn

---

[158] Above, para.1–035.

[159] See per Lord Eldon in *Mortlock v Buller* (1804) 10 Ves.Jr. 292.

[160] e.g. *Wood v Scarth* (1855) 2 K. & J. 33 (in equity); 1 F. & F. 293 (at law). A modern example is *Heath v Heath* [2010] 1 F.L.R. 610 (both parties to a contract to sell the wife's share to the husband mistakenly thought that their son would inherit the property).

[161] *Duke of Beaufort v Neeld* (1845) 12 Cl. & F. 248 at 286.

[162] *Powell v Smith* (1872) L.R. 14 Eq. 85; *Hart v Hart* (1881) 18 Ch.D. 670.

[163] per Brightman J. in *Mountford v Scott* [1975] Ch. 258 at 261; *Malins v Freeman* (1837) 2 Keen 25; *Riverlate Properties Ltd v Paul* [1975] Ch. 133, per Russell L.J. at 140; *Watkin v Watson-Smith, The Times*, July 3, 1986.

[164] *Van Praagh v Everidge* [1902] 2 Ch. 266; reversed on another ground [1903] 1 Ch. 434.

[165] (1861) 30 Beav. 62; *Day v Wells* (1861) 30 Beav. 220; cf. *Hartog v Colin and Shields* [1939] 3 All E.R. 566. See also *Watkin v Watson-Smith, The Times*, July 13, 1986, below, para.26–014 (no specific performance where elderly vendor offered bungalow for sale at £2,950 by mistake, intending £29,500. There was no contract).

[166] (1880) 15 Ch.D. 215; cf. *Denny v Hancock* (1870) L.R. 6 Ch.App. 1, where specific performance was refused because the mistake was induced unintentionally by the claimant. See also *Bashir v Ali* [2011] 2 P. & C.R. 12 (specific performance ordered where common mistake as to inclusion of studio flat).

was a piece of land, not belonging to the vendors, and so not included in the sale, which had commonly been occupied with the inn. The defendant knew the premises, but did not consult the plans, and he agreed to purchase in the belief that he was buying both the inn and the land at the rear. Specific performance was ordered against him.

A case that goes further, and perhaps too far, is *Malins v Freeman*,[167] where an estate was purchased at an auction and the defendant bid under a mistake as to the lot put up for sale. Specific performance was refused although the mistake was due entirely to the defendant's fault and not in any way caused by the vendor; and the defendant waited until the auction was over before declaring the mistake.

Where the mistake is in the written record of the contract, the claimant may obtain rectification and specific performance in the same action.[168]

B. Conduct of the Claimant

24-035   The claimant must come to equity with clean hands.[169] Before specific performance can be ordered in his favour, he must show that he has performed all his own obligations under the contract,[170] or has tendered performance, or is ready and willing to perform them.[171] Thus a person holding under an agreement for a lease is not entitled to specific performance of the lease if he is himself in breach of one of its covenants.[172] Nor could a purchaser obtain specific performance if he had taken advantage of the illiteracy of a defendant who was not separately advised.[173] The conduct in question must be connected to the contract of which specific performance is sought.[174]

If both parties have "unclean hands", there is no question of balancing the misconduct of the one against that of the other. The

---

[167] (1837) 2 Keen 25.

[168] *Craddock Bros v Hunt* [1923] 2 Ch. 136.

[169] This doctrine cannot be ousted by the terms of the contract; *Quadrant Visual Communications Ltd v Hutchison Telephone (UK) Ltd, The Times*, December 4, 1991.

[170] Except the most trivial ones; *Dyster v Randall* [1926] Ch. 932 at 942–943. See also *Sport International Bussum BV v Inter-Footwear Ltd* [1984] 1 W.L.R. 776.

[171] *Lamare v Dixon* (1873) L.R. 6 HL 414; *Australian Hardwoods Pty Ltd v Railways Commissioner* [1961] 1 W.L.R. 425; *Cornish v Brook Green Laundry* [1959] 1 Q.B. 391. See also *Ailion v Spiekermann* [1976] Ch. 158.

[172] *Walsh v Lonsdale* (1882) 21 Ch.D. 9; *Coatsworth v Johnson* (1886) 55 L.J.Q.B. 220.

[173] *Mountford v Scott* [1975] Ch. 258.

[174] *van Gestel v Cann, The Times*, August 7, 1987 (no defence where alleged fraudulent expenses claims not connected to contract).

"clean hands" defence is concerned with the conduct of the claimant alone, although all the circumstances, including the conduct of
the defendant, are relevant to the exercise of the discretion.[175]

Where the contract, although not void, is affected by some element of illegality, it was initially proposed by the Law Commission
that legislation should be enacted to give the courts a discretion as to
enforcement. So far as equitable remedies such as specific performance (and injunctions) were concerned, it was proposed that this
statutory discretion would replace the "clean hands" doctrine.[176]
These proposals have since been dropped, and the current proposals
deal only with illegality in trusts.[177]

C. Laches or Delay

Generally, in equity, time is not held to be of the essence of a   **24–036**
contract,[178] thus specific performance may be ordered although the
contractual date for performance has passed. Failure to complete on
the contractual date may, however, render the delaying party liable
to damages for breach of contract. The fact that time is not of the
essence in equity does not negative a breach of contract in such a
case. It means that the breach does not amount to a repudiation of
the contract. Thus the delaying party, although liable to damages,
does not lose the right to seek specific performance, nor will he
forfeit his deposit, provided he is ready to complete within a reasonable time.[179]

There is no statutory period of limitation barring claims to specific performance or to the refusal of relief on the ground of acquiescence.[180] The six-year rule which governs claims for damages for
breach of contract does not apply by analogy to claims for specific
performance.[181] This means that a claim for specific performance
could be successful even if brought more than six years after the
breach of contract, although such cases would be rare in the absence
of fraud.[182] The defendant may rely on the doctrine of laches, so that

---

[175] *Sang Lee Investment Co Ltd v Wing Kwai Investment Co Ltd, The Times*, April 14, 1983.
See also *Wilton Group plc v Abrams, The Times*, February 23, 1990 (no specific performance
of "commercially disreputable" agreement).
[176] Law Com. C.P. No.154 (1999), *Illegal Transactions: The Effect of Illegality on Contracts and Trusts*, p.96.
[177] Law Com. No.320 (2010), *The Illegality Defence*.
[178] This rule now applies also at law; LPA. 1925 s.41. (Time may be made of the essence in
a contract for the sale of land by the service of a notice to complete.)
[179] *Raineri v Miles* [1981] A.C. 1050; *Oakacre Ltd v Claire Cleaners (Holdings) Ltd* [1982]
Ch. 197; cf. *United Scientific Holdings Ltd v Burnley BC* [1978] A.C. 904 (as to rent review
clauses). See J. Thomson (1980) 96 L.Q.R. 481; A. Samuels (1981) 44 M.L.R. 100.
[180] Limitation Act 1980 s.36(1), (2). For criticisms of the present law, see *Cia de Seguros
Imperio v Heath (REBX) Ltd* [2001] 1 W.L.R. 112 at 124.
[181] *P&O Nedlloyd BV v Arab Metals Co (No.2)* [2007] 1 W.L.R. 2288.
[182] [2007] 1 W.L.R. 2288.

a claimant who delays unreasonably in bringing an action for specific performance may lose his claim.[183] There is no rule to lay down what is meant by unreasonable delay. One relevant factor is the subject-matter of the contract. If it has a speculative or fluctuating value, the principle of laches will be especially applicable.[184] Another factor is whether cross-examination is still possible.[185] It was once thought that the claimant must normally seek specific performance well within one year,[186] but it is now clear that this approach was too strict.

In *Lazard Bros & Co Ltd v Fairfield Property Co (Mayfair) Ltd*[187] a contract was entered into on March 12, 1975. The claimants commenced an action for specific performance on May 14, 1977. In ordering specific performance, Megarry V.C. said that if specific performance was to be regarded as a prize, to be awarded by equity to the zealous and denied to the indolent, then the claimants should fail. But whatever might have been the position over a century ago that was the wrong approach today. If between the parties it was just that the claimant should obtain the remedy, the court ought not to withhold it merely because he had been guilty of delay. There was no ground here on which delay could properly be said to be a bar to a order of specific performance.

Thus the modern approach is not to look at the principles of previous cases to see if the circumstances fitted into them, but to ask whether, broadly considered, the claimant's actions were such as to render it unconscionable for him to assert his rights.[188] An exceptional case where delay will not be a bar is where the claimant has taken possession under the contract,[189] so that the purpose of specific performance is merely to vest the legal estate in him. In *Williams v Greatrex*[190] a delay of 10 years in such circumstances did not bar specific performance. But a significant factor there was that the transaction creating the proprietary interest was not in issue. It is

---

[183] *Southcomb v Bishop of Exeter* (1847) 6 H. 213; *Eads v Williams* (1854) 4 De G.M. & G. 674; *MEPC Ltd v Christian-Edwards* [1981] A.C. 205. Even a delay for which neither party is to blame may be a reason for leaving the purchaser to damages; *Patel v Ali* [1984] Ch. 283, below, para.24–038.

[184] *Mills v Haywood* (1877) 6 Ch.D. 196.

[185] *Heath v Heath* [2010] 1 F.L.R. 610 (one party deceased).

[186] *Huxham v Llewellyn* (1873) 21 W.R. 570 (delay of five months in the case of commercial premises prevented specific performance); cf. *Wroth v Tyler* [1974] Ch. 30.

[187] (1977) 121 S.J. 793; [1978] Conv. 184.

[188] *Frawley v Neill, The Times*, April 5, 1999.

[189] It is otherwise if possession has been taken other than pursuant to the contract: *Mills v Haywood*, fn.184, above. The principle applies, however, where the claimant remains in possession after buying the co-owner's share, but the legal title has not been conveyed into his sole name; *Frawley v Neill*, above, fn.188 (rights under 1975 contract not barred by laches).

[190] [1957] 1 W.L.R. 31.

otherwise where the contract itself is disputed. In such a case the doctrine of laches does apply.[191]

Where the claimant has delayed, but specific performance is re-   **24–037** fused for another reason, the effect of his delay may be that the date for assessing damages in lieu of specific performance under Lord Cairns' Act is moved back from the date of judgment to the date upon which the matter might have been disposed of.[192]

The situation discussed above is where the delay has occurred before the claimant has sought specific performance. Where the claimant commences the action for specific performance promptly but then delays in bringing the matter to trial, he may, in a clear case, be disentitled to the remedy.[193] Where he obtains an order for specific performance but then delays in enforcing it for a long period, leave to enforce it will be refused only if there is an insufficient explanation and detriment to the defendant. Thus, in *Easton v Brown*,[194] a delay of eight years in seeking to enforce the order was no bar where the defendant's former wife and children had remained in occupation and the claimant had been legally advised that it would be difficult to remove them. The claimant had an explanation for the delay and had acted reasonably; detriment to the defendant was not on its own a ground for refusing leave to enforce the order.

Finally, in cases where time is of the essence, specific performance is not normally available after the stipulated date. It has been held in Australia, however, that the court may, in the exercise of its equitable jurisdiction to relieve against forfeiture, grant specific performance to prevent the "forfeiture" of the purchaser's equitable interest under the contract.[195] The Privy Council has rejected the Australian approach, although leaving open the possibility of relief based on restitution or estoppel if injustice would otherwise result.[196]

D. Hardship

In general, specific performance may be refused in the discretion   **24–038** of the court where it would cause unnecessary hardship to either of

---

[191] *Joyce v Joyce* [1979] 1 W.L.R. 1170.

[192] *Malhotra v Choudhury* [1980] Ch. 52.

[193] *Du Sautoy v Symes* [1967] Ch. 1146 at 1168. *Towli v Fourth River Property Co Ltd, The Times*, November 24, 1976 (delay of nine years between writ and hearing) was such a clear case.

[194] [1981] 3 All E.R. 278. The claimant also obtained an order for inquiry as to damages arising from the defendant's failure to complete.

[195] *Legione v Hateley* (1983) 57 A.L.J.R. 292; (1983) 99 L.Q.R. 490.

[196] *Union Eagle Ltd v Golden Achievements Ltd* [1997] A.C. 514; J. Heydon (1997) 113 L.Q.R. 385; M. Thompson [1997] Conv. 382; J. Stevens (1998) 61 M.L.R. 255.

the parties,[197] or to a third party.[198] Inadequacy of price is not, standing by itself, a ground for refusing specific performance; but it may be evidence of other factors, such as fraud[199] or undue influence,[200] which would render enforcement inequitable.

These matters arose in *Patel v Ali*,[201] where the vendor and her husband were co-owners of a house which they contracted to sell in 1979. The husband's bankruptcy caused a long delay in completion, for which neither the vendor nor the purchaser was to blame. After the contract the vendor had a leg amputated. She later gave birth to her second and third children. The purchaser obtained an order for specific performance, against which the vendor appealed on the ground of hardship. She spoke little English, and relied on help from nearby friends and relatives, hence it would be a hardship to leave the house and move away. Goulding J. held that the court in a proper case could refuse specific performance on the ground of hardship subsequent to the contract, even if not caused by the claimant and not related to the subject-matter. On the facts, there would be hardship amounting to injustice, therefore the appropriate remedy was damages.

E. Misdescription of Subject-matter

24–039   **i. Specific Performance Subject to Compensation.**[202] If the property agreed to be sold is incorrectly described in the contract, the vendor cannot fulfil his promise to transfer property which corresponds exactly with that which he contracted to convey. A frequent instance is an inaccurate measurement in the plan.[203] A misdescription is a term of the contract; the vendor is therefore in breach. To

---

[197] *Denne v Light* (1857) 8 De G.M. & G. 774; *Warmington v Miller* [1973] Q.B. 877 (no specific performance of contract to sublet if result would be to expose tenant to liability for breach of covenant against subletting); *Mountford v Scott* [1975] Ch. 258; *Francis v Cowcliff Ltd* (1977) 33 P. & C.R. 368; *Shell UK Ltd v Lostock Garage Ltd* [1976] 1 W.L.R. 1187 at 1202. See Fry, *Specific Performance*, Ch.16; Spry, *Equitable Remedies*, p.196. See also A. Dowling [2011] Conv. 209, as to the position where the buyer cannot raise the money.

[198] *Earl of Sefton v Tophams Ltd* [1966] Ch. 1140; *Sullivan v Henderson* [1973] 1 W.L.R. 333; *Watts v Spence* [1976] Ch. 165; *Cedar Holdings Ltd v Green* [1981] Ch. 129 at 147; F. Crane [1979] Conv. 372; M. Prichard (1979) 38 C.L.J. 215. This case was disapproved on another point in *Williams and Glyn's Bank Ltd v Boland* [1981] A.C. 487 at 507. See also *Thames Guaranty Ltd v Campbell* [1985] Q.B. 210; cf. *Patel v Ali* [1984] Ch. 283, below, (interests of vendor's children in their own right not material, but relevant to hardship of vendor).

[199] *Coles v Trecothick* (1804) 9 Ves.Jr. 234 at 246; *Callaghan v Callaghan* (1841) 8 Cl. & F. 374.

[200] *Fry v Lane* (1888) 40 Ch.D. 312 (sale set aside).

[201] [1984] Ch. 283; (1984) 100 L.Q.R. 337. There was evidence that the Muslim community would pay the damages.

[202] See C. Harpum (1981) 40 C.L.J. 47, taking the view that this should not be distinguished from specific performance with damages under Lord Cairns' Act, below, para.24–044.

[203] See, e.g. *Watson v Burton* [1957] 1 W.L.R. 19; *Topfell Ltd v Galley Properties Ltd* [1979] 1 W.L.R. 446 (inability to give vacant possession); F. Crane [1979] Conv. 375.

deny him specific performance on that account would introduce a rigid rule capable of producing injustice. Equity adopts a more flexible approach; the circumstances may be such that justice will be done by compelling completion, notwithstanding the error, compensating the purchaser by allowing him a reduction in the price he had agreed to pay ("abatement").[204] This course will not be followed if it would prejudice the rights of a third party interested in the estate.[205] On the other hand the misdescription may be so serious that to order specific performance would be in effect to force the purchaser to take something wholly different from what he intended.[206] If so, the only way of achieving justice may be to permit the purchaser to rescind; or to refuse to grant specific performance to the vendor.

ii. Refusal of Specific Performance. The rule is thus that a **24–040** purchaser will not be forced to take something which is *different in substance* from that which he agreed to buy.[207] Differences of quality or quantity will not *by themselves* suffice as a defence to an action for specific performance (although of course they will give rise to a claim for compensation) unless they can fairly be said to make the property, as it in fact is, different in substance from that contracted to be sold.[208] A misdescription is substantial for this purpose if it so far affects:

"[T]he subject-matter of the contract that it may be reasonably supposed, that, but for such misdescription, the purchaser might never have entered into the contract at all."[209]

This will always be a question of fact in each case: obviously A, who has contracted to sell Blackacre to B, cannot force him to take Whiteacre, even if Whiteacre is larger, more valuable, and better suited to B's purposes. It is often difficult to say whether a misdescription of the area of land involves a difference of substance or of quantity; the rule is "easy to be understood, though often difficult of

---

[204] If the misdescription goes against the vendor, he cannot increase the price: *Re Lindsay and Forder's Contract* (1895) 72 L.T. 832. (But specific performance might be refused on the ground of hardship). See also *Seven Seas Properties Ltd v Al-Essa* [1988] 1 W.L.R. 1272.

[205] *Cedar Holdings Ltd v Green* [1981] Ch. 129.

[206] See *Cedar Holdings Ltd v Green*, above. (Specific performance with abatement not appropriate where vendor's interest merely a co-ownership share.)

[207] *Flight v Booth* (1834) 1 Bing.N.C. 370; *Watson v Burton* [1957] 1 W.L.R. 19.

[208] If a vendor contracts to sell a lease of Blackacre, a purchaser cannot be compelled to take an underlease; *Madeley v Booth* (1845) 2 De G & Sm. 718; nor if he contracts to sell a "registered freehold property," can he compel the purchaser to take a possessory (as distinct from *absolute*) freehold title; *Re Brine and Davies' Contract* [1935] Ch. 388.

[209] per Tindal C.J. in *Flight v Booth* (1834) 1 Bing.N.C. 370 at 377.

application."[210] However, although the vendor cannot compel a purchaser to take something different from that contracted to be sold, it is only just to give the purchaser the option of insisting on completion, and being paid compensation[211] for what he has lost. If it were not so, a person in default could in effect take advantage of his own wrong. Thus the purchaser has a choice: he may elect to take the property,[212] notwithstanding that it may be substantially different from the contract description.

24–041   **iii. Conditions of Sale.** The above is true of "open" contracts, but the parties are free to make their own conditions to regulate what is to happen if there is a misdescription. In the case of contracts for the sale of land, most contracts prepared by a solicitor will now be made subject to the Standard Conditions of Sale or the Standard Commercial Property Conditions. In every case, therefore, the first question must be: what does the contract provide? But even then caution is necessary, since the courts have been reluctant to permit either party to contract out of the rights conferred on him by equity.[213]

24–042   **iv. Want of Good Title.** The court will not force a doubtful title on a purchaser. The phrase "defect in title" is loosely used in some of the cases to indicate that the vendor, through some material error in description, fails in effect to convey to the purchaser the property he intended to buy. In other cases the expression may be used in a more literal sense; where, for example, the vendor's land is burdened with restrictive covenants.[214] Yet there are other cases where there is not merely a defect in the vendor's title, but no title at all. Clearly the purchaser cannot be compelled to take a bad title, nor be allowed to refuse a good one. Between the good and the bad is an infinite variety of doubtful titles, and the question inevitably arises of drawing a line between those titles which a purchaser will, and those which he will not, be compelled to accept. The test is whether there is likely to be litigation. If the doubt is one of law, the court

---

[210] per Lord Esher M.R. in *Re Fawcett and Holmes' Contract* (1889) 42 Ch.D. 150 at 156; cf. *Watson v Burton* [1957] 1 W.L.R. 19.

[211] *Mortlock v Buller* (1804) 10 Ves.Jr. 292 at 316. The compensation must generally be claimed before completion; *Joliffe v Baker* (1883) 11 Q.B.D. 255.

[212] In the absence of special circumstances, e.g. if he was himself aware of the misdescription at the date of the contract; *Castle v Wilkinson* (1870) L.R. 5 Ch. 534. See C. Emery [1978] Conv. 338 at 340.

[213] See *Topfell Ltd v Galley Properties Ltd* [1979] 1 W.L.R. 446; F. Crane [1979] Conv. 375; *Rignall Developments Ltd v Halil* [1988] Ch. 190. Conditions of sale are subject to the Unfair Contract Terms Act 1977; *Walker v Boyle* [1982] 1 W.L.R. 495.

[214] *Re Nisbet and Potts' Contract* [1906] 1 Ch. 386; *Faruqui v English Real Estates Ltd* [1979] 1 W.L.R. 963; F. Crane [1979] Conv. 444. See generally C. Emery [1978] Conv. 338.

will normally resolve it.[215] If the doubt is one of fact, it is the court's duty, unless there are exceptional circumstances, to decide the question of title as between the vendor and purchaser. If the court concludes that the purchaser will not be at risk of a successful assertion against him of an incumbrance, then the court should declare in favour of a good title, and should not be deterred by the mere possibility of future litigation by a claimant to an incumbrance who is not bound by the declaration.[216] But if good title is not shown, the purchaser will be entitled to rescind, unless the vendor removes the doubt. The court will not compel a party to purchase a law suit.[217]

F. Public Policy

The court will not order specific performance of a contract where **24–043** the result would be contrary to public policy.

In *Wroth v Tyler*,[218] a husband, the owner of the matrimonial home, entered into a contract to sell with vacant possession. Before completion, his wife registered a charge under the Matrimonial Homes Act 1967.[219] The purchasers sued for specific performance, and failed on two grounds:

i. the husband could only carry out his obligation by obtaining a court order terminating the wife's right of occupation, and this would depend on the discretion of the court. To grant specific performance would compel the husband to embark on difficult and uncertain litigation. He had attempted to obtain the wife's consent by all reasonable means short of litigation, and it would be most undesirable to require a husband to take proceedings against his wife, especially where they were still living together;

ii. nor could the purchasers get specific performance subject to the wife's right of occupation. The husband and daughter would remain liable to eviction by the purchasers, and the

---

[215] *Wilson v Thomas* [1958] 1 W.L.R. 422.

[216] *MEPC Ltd v Christian-Edwards* [1981] A.C. 205 (doubt as to abandonment of 1912 contract: good title established). See also *Re Handman and Wilcox's Contract* [1902] 1 Ch. 599; *Selkirk v Romar Investments Ltd* [1963] 1 W.L.R. 1415.

[217] *Re Nichols and Von Joel's Contract* [1910] 1 Ch. 43 at 46. See also *Pips (Leisure Productions) Ltd v Walton* (1981) 260 E.G. 601 (purchaser entitled to rescind contract for sale of lease which was already forfeited).

[218] [1974] Ch. 30. See also *Malhotra v Choudhury* [1980] Ch. 52 at 71; *Verrall v Great Yarmouth Borough Council* [1981] Q.B. 202, above, para.24–015 (specific performance of contract to hire conference hall to National Front), where this defence failed: the risk of public disorder was outweighed by the freedom of speech and assembly and the sanctity of contract.

[219] Now Family Law Act 1996.

family would be split up. The court would be slow to order specific performance in such circumstances.

6. DAMAGES IN SUBSTITUTION FOR, OR IN ADDITION TO, SPECIFIC PERFORMANCE

A. Chancery Amendment Act 1858. Lord Cairns' Act[220]

24–044   Section 2 of Lord Cairns' Act gave to the Court of Chancery discretionary power to award damages either in addition to or in substitution for specific performance, the damages to be assessed in such manner as the court shall direct.

Before this Act, it was only in the common law courts that damages were awarded.[221] The Act gave power to award damages where none would be available at law.[222] But it did not give the Court of Chancery power to award common law damages.[223] It applied only to cases where the court had jurisdiction to award specific performance. Thus Lord Cairns' Act does not apply where the contract is of a type which is not specifically enforceable[224]; but it does apply where the contract is of a type which is, even though specific performance is refused on some discretionary ground, such as the absence of mutuality.[225] There is no jurisdiction under Lord Cairns' Act if specific performance is no longer possible, as where the land has been sold to a third party.[226] However, the jurisdiction exists if, when the proceedings were begun, the court could have granted

---

[220] See generally J. Jolowicz (1975) 34 C.L.J. 224; T. Ingman and J. Wakefield [1981] Conv. 286; T. Ingman [1994] Conv. 110; McDermott, *Equitable Damages* (1994).

[221] It appears that the Court of Chancery had inherent power to award damages in equity, but this was rarely exercised. See Spry, *Equitable Remedies*, p.623; P McDermott (1992) 108 L.Q.R. 652; cf. *Surrey v Bredero Homes Ltd* [1993] 1 W.L.R. 1361 at 1368, where Dillon L.J. said that the Court of Chancery had "no power to award damages" before the 1858 Act. For the Court of Chancery's ancient statutory jurisdiction to award damages, see McDermott, *Equitable Damages*, 1994, p.8.

[222] See *Johnson v Agnew* [1980] A.C. 367 (Lord Wilberforce); *Price v Strange* [1978] Ch. 337; *Oakacre Ltd v Claire Cleaners (Holdings) Ltd* [1982] Ch. 197 (cause of action for damages at law not accrued when action commenced).

[223] But see *Price v Strange* [1978] Ch. 337 at 358, where Goff L.J. said "One purpose and a very important purpose of that Act was, of course, to avoid circuity of action by enabling the old Court of Chancery to award damages at law. . . . "

[224] *Lavery v Pursell* (1888) 39 Ch.D. 508 (tenancy for one year; above para.24–025). As to whether contracts for personal services come into this category, see the different views expressed in *Price v Strange* [1978] Ch. 337 at 359 (Goff L.J.) and at 369 (Buckley L.J.). The House of Lords in *Scandinavian Trading Tanker Co AB v Flota Petrolera Ecuatoriana* [1983] 2 A.C. 694 took the view that there was no jurisdiction to grant specific performance of a contract for services.

[225] *Price v Strange* [1978] Ch. 337. Even where the contract concerns building or repair works, the court has jurisdiction under the 1858 Act: at 359. See also *Wroth v Tyler* [1974] Ch. 30; *Malhotra v Choudhury* [1980] Ch. 52; D. Hayton (1979) 38 C.L.J. 35; and the cases on injunctions, below, paras 25–048–25–050.

[226] *Surrey County Council v Bredero Homes Ltd* [1993] 1 W.L.R. 1361.

specific performance, notwithstanding that thereafter, but before judgment, specific performance has become impossible.[227]

It was not until the Judicature Act 1873 that common law damages were available in the Chancery Division. Today it is only necessary to rely on Lord Cairns' Act if no damages would be available at law.[228] It was at one time thought that it could be advantageous to the claimant to rely on Lord Cairns' Act even where common law damages were available, as the measure of damages might be different.[229] This is now discredited.[230]

Lord Cairns' Act was repealed in 1883 by the Statute Law Revision Act, but s.5 of that Act preserved its general effect,[231] although that section was unnecessary because s.16 of the Judicature Act 1873 had transferred all Chancery jurisdiction to the High Court.[232] Its provisions are now found in s.50 of the Senior Courts Act 1981.

B. Measure of Damages under Lord Cairns' Act

Where a purchaser claims damages for breach of a contract for the 24–045 purchase of land, he is normally entitled to damages for any loss of bargain. In *Wroth v Tyler*[233] the purchasers contracted to buy a bungalow for £6,000. Contracts were exchanged on May 27, 1971, but on May 28 the vendor's wife registered a charge under the Matrimonial Homes Act 1967,[234] and refused to remove it. The vendor was thus unable to pass a clear title. At the date at which completion was due, the property was worth £7,500, but at the date of the judgment in January 1973, its value had risen to £11,500.

Megarry J. refused specific performance for reasons mentioned above.[235] Therefore the main issue was the measure of damages. It was "common ground" that the normal rule is that damages for breach of a contract for the sale of land are measured by the difference (if any) between the contract price and the market price at the date of the breach, which is normally the completion date (with interest from that date until judgment). Applying that rule, damages would be £1,500. Although Fry had said that "the measure would be

---

[227] *Johnson v Agnew* [1978] Ch. 176, CA.
[228] See *Oakacre Ltd v Claire Cleaners (Holdings) Ltd* [1982] Ch. 197 (cause of action for damages not yet accrued).
[229] *Wroth v Tyler* [1974] Ch. 30, below.
[230] *Johnson v Agnew* [1978] Ch. 176, below, para.24–046.
[231] See *Leeds Industrial Co-operative Society Ltd v Slack* [1924] A.C. 851.
[232] McDermott, *Equitable Damages*, 1994, pp.41–44.
[233] [1974] Ch. 30; applied in *Grant v Dawkins* [1973] 1 W.L.R. 1406. See also *Oakacre Ltd v Claire Cleaners (Holdings) Ltd* [1982] Ch. 197 (damages awarded in addition to specific performance not limited to those accrued when action commenced).
[234] Now Family Law Act 1996.
[235] Above, para.24–043.

the same under Lord Cairns' Act",[236] Megarry J. held that damages under the Act may be assessed on a basis which is not identical with that of the common law[237]: they should be a true substitute for specific performance, and must put the claimants in as good a position as if the contract had been performed. Damages could be measured as at the date of judgment, and the purchasers were awarded £5,500.

It has since been doubted by the House of Lords[238] whether Lord Cairns' Act permits a departure from the common law rule on the quantum of damages, and, indeed, whether the damages awarded in *Wroth v Tyler*[239] could not have been equally available at common law. There is no inflexible rule at common law that damages must be assessed as at the date of the breach of contract.[240] The principle is that the claimant should be put in the same position as if the contract had been duly performed. The rule that damages are to be assessed as at the date of the breach evolved in times of financial stability when the subject-matter was unlikely to have increased in value between the breach and the judgment. The position at common law will be more readily appreciated by considering the doctrine of mitigation of damages. The principle that the claimant is to be put in the same position as if the contract had been performed is subject to the principle of mitigation.[241] Thus in the case of chattels, damages will usually be assessed at the breach, because at that date the claimant could have acquired an equivalent chattel elsewhere. But in the case of a specifically enforceable contract, such as a contract to buy land, the purchaser cannot reasonably be expected to mitigate the damages by seeking an equivalent property elsewhere as soon as the breach occurs, because he will normally wish to wait and see if specific performance is obtainable. In such a case, the common law principle of putting the claimant in the same position as if the contract had been performed is only adhered to in times of rising property prices by assessing the damages at a date subsequent to the breach.[242]

---

[236] Fry, *Specific Performance*, 6th edn, 1921, p.602.

[237] [1974] Ch. 30 at 58–60.

[238] In *Johnson v Agnew*, below, para.24–046. The reasoning in *Wroth v Tyler* is preferred in McDermott, *Equitable Damages*, 1994, p.108; cf. T Ingman [1994] Conv. 110.

[239] [1974] Ch. 30, above.

[240] *Wroth v Tyler* [1974] Ch. 30 at 57; *Radford v De Froberville* [1977] 1 W.L.R. 1262; A. Zuckerman (1978) 94 L.Q.R. 327; F. Crane [1978] Conv. 163; *Malhotra v Choudhury* [1980] Ch. 52; D. Hayton (1979) 38 C.L.J. 35; *Johnson v Agnew* [1980] A.C. 367; *Suleman v Shahsavari* [1988] 1 W.L.R. 1181.

[241] *Wroth v Tyler* [1974] Ch. 30 at 57; *Radford v De Froberville* [1977] 1 W.L.R. 1262; *Malhotra v Choudhury*, above, fn.240; cf. *Kaunas v Smyth* (1977) 75 D.L.R. 368.

[242] See generally D. Feldman and D. Libling (1979) 95 L.Q.R. 270; S. Waddams (1981) 97 L.Q.R. 445; I. Duncan Wallace (1982) 98 L.Q.R. 406; A. Burgess (1985) 34 I.C.L.Q. 317. If the market is falling, damages will be assessed at the date of breach; *Woodford Estates Ltd v Pollack* (1979) 93 D.L.R. (3d) 350.

In *Johnson v Agnew*[243] Lord Wilberforce rejected the view that **24–046** damages under Lord Cairns' Act could be assessed on a different basis from that of the common law. Subject to the point that in some cases damages would be available under the Act where none at all would be available at common law, the quantum is the same. The words in s.2 that damages "may be assessed in such manner as the court shall direct" relate only to procedure.[244] *Wroth v Tyler*[245] could not be supported in so far as it suggested that damages under the Act may be assessed on a different basis than at common law. Where, after the breach, the innocent party has reasonably continued to try for completion, the damages, however awarded should be assessed as at the date the contract was lost.[246] This will normally be the date of the hearing, provided the proceedings have been conducted with due expedition: an earlier date will be substituted if the claimant has delayed.[247]

The assessment of damages under Lord Cairns' Act has been more recently reviewed in the context of injunctions,[248] and is further considered in Ch.25.

7. SPECIFIC PERFORMANCE AND THIRD PARTIES

Claims for specific performance are usually made between the par- **24–047** ties to the contract.[249] In such a case, all the parties to the contract must be parties to the action.[250] Other difficulties arise where the issue is between assignees, or where the person to be benefited was not a party to the contract.

Difficulties have arisen as to whether the right to (or liability to) specific performance passes to an assignee of the agreement. These problems mainly arose in the context of agreements for leases, where the question was whether the assignee of either party could sue or be sued on the obligations of the agreed lease. These matters are now dealt with by the Landlord and Tenant (Covenants) Act

---

[243] [1980] A.C. 367. The facts have been given, above, para.24–010. See also *William Sindall Plc v Cambridgeshire County Council* [1994] 1 W.L.R. 1016 at 1037.

[244] This phrase does not appear in Senior Courts Act 1981 s.50.

[245] [1974] Ch. 30.

[246] This was the date on which the vendor's mortgagees contracted to sell the property; above, para.24–010. See also *Domb v Isoz* [1980] Ch. 548; *Suleman v Shahsavari* [1988] 1 W.L.R. 1181 (£29,500 awarded where property worth £76,000 at hearing but contract price £46,500); *Johnson & Co (Barbados) Ltd v NSR Ltd* [1997] A.C. 400.

[247] *Radford v De Froberville* [1977] 1 W.L.R. 1262 (assuming a rising market); *Malhotra v Choudhury* [1980] Ch. 52.

[248] Below, para.25–051.

[249] For the rights of a sub-purchaser to obtain specific performance of the head contract, see *Berkley v Poulett* (1976) 120 S.J. 836, above para.12–035.

[250] See *Tito v Waddell (No.2)* [1977] Ch. 106 at 324 (Megarry V.C.).

1995,[251] and will not be further discussed here. As far as contracts for the sale of land are concerned, such a contract confers an equitable interest on the purchaser. Whether specific performance is available against an assignee of the vendor will depend on the registration rules.[252]

A different question is whether specific performance may be obtained for the benefit of a third party, as where A has contracted with B to confer a benefit on C. As discussed below, C may now be able to enforce the contract in his own right under the Contracts (Rights of Third Parties) Act 1999. If, however, because the contract was entered into before the application of the 1999 Act, C cannot enforce the contract himself, the question is whether B may obtain specific performance, compelling A to confer the benefit on C.

In *Beswick v Beswick*,[253] one Peter Beswick, a coal merchant who wished to retire, made an arrangement with his nephew under which the business was transferred to the nephew, and the nephew promised to employ Peter as consultant for a weekly wage, and after his death to pay to Peter's widow £5 per week for her life. Payments were made to Peter during his lifetime, but soon after his death ceased to be paid to his widow. The widow took out letters of administration of Peter's estate and sued both as administratrix and in her own right under the contract.

The House of Lords held that she was entitled as administratrix to specific performance of the promise to make the weekly payments to her as Peter's widow. She was unable to sue in her own right because of the rule of privity.

24–048   The difficulties which faced the widow in her action as administratrix were essentially threefold: (a) Peter's estate, which she represented, had lost nothing by the breach; (b) the widow, in her own capacity, had suffered the loss but had no right of action; and (c) the agreement was for the payment of money and was not the type of agreement where breach is usually remedied by an order of specific performance.[254]

The widow, as administratrix, overcame them all. Lord Upjohn thought that (a) was an argument in favour of specific performance; " . . . the court ought to grant a specific performance order all the more because damages *are* nominal."[255] She had no other effective remedy; "justice demands that [the promisor] pay the price and this

---

[251] The Act extends to agreements for leases and equitable assignments of leases; s.28(1).
[252] Land Charges Act 1972 s.2(4); Land Registration Act 2002 s.32 (estate contracts).
[253] [1968] A.C. 58; N. Andrews (1988) 8 L.S. 14.
[254] Above, para.24–018.
[255] [1968] A.C. 58 at 102; cf. *Re Cook's ST* [1965] Ch. 902; above, para.4–021.

can only be done in the circumstances by equitable relief."[256] This disregards the principle that equitable remedies are available where the legal remedy is inadequate to compensate for the loss. It is not that equitable remedies are available where the claimant has suffered no loss,[257] nor where an independent person has suffered a loss for which there is no cause of action.

Their Lordships found no difficulty in treating the case as a suitable one for specific performance. "Had [the promisor] repudiated the contract in the lifetime of [the promisee] the latter would have had a cast-iron case for specific performance."[258] The orthodox view has been that specific performance will not be ordered in cases where the promise is to pay money unless the claimant is a vendor or lessor against whom the purchaser or lessee could have demanded specific performance. *Beswick v Beswick*[259] may have been regarded as such a case, for the nephew "could on his part clearly have obtained specific performance of it if Beswick senior or his administratrix had defaulted."[260] That, it is submitted, is questionable; for the contract was essentially for the sale of the goodwill of the business; such a contract is not normally specifically enforceable, in contrast to a contract to sell premises along with the goodwill.[261]

It was said also that a contract to pay an annuity is specifically enforceable. In *Adderly v Dixon*,[262] Leach M.R. gave the reason that the amount of damages would be conjectural. While such a proposition may have been sound in 1824, the development of life assurance and of actuarial valuation of life interests has made an annuity and a capital sum in effect interchangeable. Annuities are freely purchased from insurance companies in exchange for capital payments and can similarly be freely sold for a capital sum. Thus the conjectural element is less marked than it was in earlier times. If the claimant was awarded damages, and desired the annuity, all he has to do is to buy one.

24-049

The cases on which their Lordships relied to support the view that the contract to pay was specifically enforceable, at the instance of a personal representative, were all cases either of a contract to transfer land or contracts to pay an annuity. It is possible to treat *Beswick v Beswick*[263] as consistent with authority by saying that there was mutuality, that the contract (being to pay an annuity) was capable of

[256] [1968] A.C. 58.

[257] cf. *Marco Productions Ltd v Pagola* [1945] 1 K.B. 111; injunction available to restrain breach of negative covenant even though the breach causes no loss to claimant; or if only nominal damages would be available at law; *Rochdale Canal Co v King* (1851) 2 Sim.(N.S.) 78.

[258] [1968] A.C. 58 at 98.

[259] [1968] A.C. 58.

[260] [1968] A.C. 58 at 89, per Lord Pearce.

[261] *Darbey v Whitaker* (1857) 4 Drew. 134 at 139, 140; above, para.24-027.

[262] (1824) 1 Sim. & St. 607 at 611; G Treitel (1966) 29 M.L.R. 657 at 663.

[263] [1968] A.C. 58.

specific performance, and that the common law remedy of damages (assuming them to be nominal) was inadequate. The claimant barely succeeds on the first two; and only on the third by relying on cases which uphold it without explaining the logical dilemma of holding an award of nominal damages inadequate where no loss was suffered by the party able to sue.

In spite of these criticisms, the House of Lords should be applauded for taking a broad equitable view of the situation. There was "an unconscionable breach of faith [and] the equitable remedy sought is apt."[264] Lord Pearce and Lord Upjohn both approved the dictum of Windeyer J. in *Coulls v Bagot's Executor and Trustee Co Ltd* in which he said[265]:

> "It seems to me that contracts to pay money or transfer property to a third person are always, or at all events very often, contracts for breach of which damages would be an inadequate remedy—all the more so if it be right (I do not think it is) that damages recoverable by the promisee are only nominal . . . I see no reason why specific performance should not be had in such cases . . . There is no reason today for limiting by particular categories, rather than by general principle, the cases in which orders for specific performance will be made."

24–050   There were no technical or practical difficulties preventing an award of specific performance and "justice demands that [the promisor] pay the price and this can only be done in the circumstances by equitable relief."[266] Perhaps the correct explanation is that damages must be considered from the point of view of both claimant and defendant. Thus the remedy of damages is inadequate if it would lead to the unjust enrichment of the wrongdoer. Substantial damages have been awarded under Lord Cairns' Act for this reason.[267]

Now the widow Beswick would be able to enforce the contract in her own right if it were entered into after the Contracts (Rights of Third Parties) Act 1999. Whether she would be able to obtain specific performance by virtue of s.1(5) is less clear.[268] This depends on whether the subsection must be taken to override the principle that specific performance is not available to a volunteer. The Law Commission simply stated that the widow would have "the right of enforcement", without reference to specific performance.[269] Even if specific performance would not be available, at least the widow

[264] [1968] A.C. 58, per Lord Hodson at 83.
[265] (1967) 40 A.L.J.R. at 487. See also *Staden v Jones* [2008] 2 F.L.R. 1931.
[266] *Beswick v Beswick* [1968] A.C. 58 at 102, per Lord Upjohn.
[267] *Wrotham Park Estate Co v Parkside Homes Ltd* [1974] 1 W.L.R. 798. For further developments in the context of injunctions, see para.25–052, below.
[268] Discussed above, para.24–048.
[269] Law Com. No.242, para.7.46.

would be able to obtain substantial damages, being a person with a cause of action who has suffered a loss by the breach. To that extent, the remedy of damages is adequate.

This chapter began by indicating how narrow the scope of the remedy of specific performance was in practice. Other systems of law tend to be much more free in their use of this type of remedy. *Beswick v Beswick*[270] indicated a willingness in the House of Lords to make freer use of the remedy in the interests of justice. The case is however concerned with its own particular problem, now resolved by legislation, of the contract to pay to a third party. We have seen that their Lordships were subsequently more orthodox in the context of the supervision principle, refusing to extend the remedy of specific performance to a landlord seeking to enforce a "keep open" covenant in a lease.[271]

8. JURISDICTION

Both the High Court and the county court have jurisdiction to grant **24–051** specific performance, but the jurisdiction of the county court, in cases of specific performance of contracts to sell or to let land, is limited to cases where the purchase money, or the value of the property in the case of a lease, does not exceed the county court limit.[272]

The county court must give effect to every defence or counter-claim to which effect would be given in the High Court.[273] Thus, in *Kingswood Estate Co Ltd v Anderson*,[274] where the landlord brought an action for possession based on the termination of a common law periodic tenancy, the county court gave effect to the tenant's defence that she held the property under a specifically enforceable agreement for a lease for life, even though it had no jurisdiction to grant specific performance of that agreement. Similarly, in *Rushton v Smith*,[275] the county court had no jurisdiction to grant specific performance of an agreement for a business tenancy where the value of the property exceeded the county court limit, but it nevertheless had jurisdiction to decide whether or not the tenant would be entitled to such an order.

---

[270] [1968] A.C. 58.

[271] *Co-operative Insurance Society Ltd v Argyll Stores (Holdings) Ltd* [1998] A.C. 1; above, para.4–016.

[272] County Courts Act 1984 s.23. The current limit is £30,000, although the parties may agree to submit to the jurisdiction of the county court in cases above the limit. The High Court has power to transfer any proceedings to the county court under s.40(2) of the 1984 Act. See also *Joyce v Liverpool City Council* [1996] Q.B. 252 (small claims).

[273] County Courts Act 1984 s.38.

[274] [1963] 2 Q.B. 169. See also *Cornish v Brook Green Laundry Ltd* [1959] 1 Q.B. 394.

[275] [1976] Q.B. 480.

Chapter 25

INJUNCTIONS

1. JURISDICTION

25–001 AN injunction is an order by the court to a party to do or refrain from doing a particular act. Originally the Court of Chancery alone[1] had jurisdiction to grant an injunction. This inevitably led to much duplication of proceedings; as where a claimant required an injunction as a remedy for a legal right. The Common Law Procedure Act 1854 gave to common law courts a power to grant injunctions in certain cases. The present jurisdiction is governed by the Senior Courts Act 1981, replacing the Judicature Acts, which vested the jurisdiction of the Court of Chancery and of the common law courts in the High Court.

A. The High Court

25–002 Section 37(1) of the Senior Courts Act 1981 provides that:

> "The High Court may by order (whether interlocutory or final) grant an injunction . . . in all cases in which it appears to the court to be just and convenient to do so."[2]

The jurisdiction is however not so wide as would appear from a first reading of the section. It is exercised, not on the individual preference of the judge, but "according to sufficient legal reasons or on settled legal principles."[3] There have been differences of opinion as to whether s.25(8) of the Judicature Act 1873, which introduced the provision similar to that now contained in the Act of 1981, gave the court power to grant injunctions in cases where they had not previously been granted.[4] It has been said that the Act of 1873 "has not revolutionised" but "has to some extent enlarged" the jurisdiction.[5] The restrictive approach, namely that the court's jurisdiction has not

---

[1] Or the Court of Exchequer in its equity jurisdiction, above, para.1–002. See generally Sharpe, *Injunctions and Specific Performance*.

[2] This consolidates the previous legislation. (The 1981 Act was formerly the Supreme Court Act but was renamed by the Constitutional Reform Act 2005). Compare the wording of s.25(8) of the Supreme Court of Judicature Act 1873 and s.45 of the Act of 1925: "just *or* convenient"; *Day v Brownrigg* (1878) 10 Ch.D. 294; *L v L* [1969] P. 25.

[3] per Jessel M.R. in *Beddow v Beddow* (1878) 9 Ch.D. 89 at 93. Thus a claimant with no "rights" cannot obtain an injunction, however "just and convenient" it may be: *Gouriet v Union of Post Office Workers* [1978] A.C. 435; *Paton v Trustees of British Pregnancy Advisory Service* [1979] Q.B. 76, below, para.25–015.

[4] See the different views of Lord Esher M.R. and Cotton L.J. in *North London Ry v Great Northern Ry* (1883) 11 Q.B.D. 30. See also *The Siskina* [1979] A.C. 210; *Maclaine Watson & Co Ltd v International Tin Council (No.2)* [1989] Ch. 286; *Channel Tunnel Group Ltd v Balfour Beatty Construction Ltd* [1993] A.C. 334.

[5] *Cummins v Perkins* [1899] 1 Ch. 16 at 20.

been extended, was affirmed by the House of Lords in *Gouriet v Union of Post Office Workers*.[6] Lord Edmund-Davies said that s.25(8) of the Act of 1873 "dealt only with procedure and had nothing to do with jurisdiction."[7] But former rules of practice no longer hamper the exercise of discretion; thus enabling the merits of new situations to be dealt with as they arise.[8] A similar question is whether the Act of 1981 enlarged the previous jurisdiction, but the better view is that it did not.[9] A claimant with no cause of action cannot invoke s.37(1).[10]

B. The County Court

The jurisdiction of the county court, which is wholly statutory, was enlarged by the Courts and Legal Services Act 1990.[11] Under s.38 of the County Courts Act 1984 the court could only grant an injunction if it was ancillary to a claim for some other specific relief, such as damages, within its jurisdiction. The amended s.38 provides that (subject to exceptions) the court may make an order which could be made by the High Court. It appears, therefore, that no other relief need be claimed. The county court has no jurisdiction, however, to grant a search order[12] or a freezing injunction[13] (other than in family proceedings or in aid of execution of a county court judgment).[14]

25–003

2. Types of Injunctions

A. Prohibitory and Mandatory Injunctions

The most common form of an injunction, as the name implies, is one which is prohibitory or restrictive. However, if the unlawful act has been committed and an order restraining its commission is therefore meaningless, justice can sometimes be done by issuing a mandatory injunction ordering the act to be undone. At one time the

25–004

---

[6] [1978] A.C. 435. See also *Bremer Vulkan Schiffbau und Maschinenfabrik v South India Shipping Corp* [1981] A.C. 909.

[7] [1978] A.C. 435 at 516. cf. the wider views of Lord Denning M.R. in *Rasu Maritima SA v Perusahaan* [1978] Q.B. 644 at 659–660.

[8] *Argyll v Argyll* [1967] Ch. 302 at 345; *Rasu Maritima SA v Perusahaan*, above, fn.7. See generally search orders and freezing injunctions, below, paras 25–077, 25–080.

[9] Contrast the views of Lord Denning M.R. with those of Donaldson and Slade L.JJ. in *Chief Constable of Kent v V* [1983] Q.B. 34; (1983) 99 L.Q.R. 1; A. Tettenborn (1983) 42 C.L.J. 51; G. Zellick All E.R. Rev. 1982, at 205; *Richards v Richards* [1984] A.C. 174. The wording of the 1981 Act and its predecessors is not identical.

[10] *Ainsbury v Millington* [1986] 1 All E.R. 73.

[11] s.3. In the case of land, its value must be within the county court limits (currently £30,000). See also *Joyce v Liverpool City Council* [1996] Q.B. 252 (small claims).

[12] Below, para.25–077.

[13] Below, para.25–080.

[14] County Courts Remedies Regulations 1991 (SI 1991/1222). See *Schmidt v Wong (Practice Note)* [2006] 1 W.L.R. 561.

negative character of an injunction used to be insisted upon; if the court intended to order a party to pull down a building, the order would be that he should refrain from permitting the building to remain on his land. Such an injunction may have a positive effect, as in *Sky Petroleum Ltd v VIP Petroleum Ltd*,[15] where an injunction restraining the defendant from withholding supplies of petrol was equivalent to specific performance of the contract. But a mandatory injunction is now couched in positive form,[16] but just for this reason it may be harder to obtain. For example, it has been held that it ought not to issue to compel a ferry owner to run a ferry when it could only be run at a loss.[17] But the fact that a local authority may have to borrow money, or get a building licence to comply with a mandatory injunction may be a ground, not for refusing the remedy, but for granting it subject to a suspension.[18]

B. Perpetual and Interlocutory (or Interim) Injunctions

25–005   Prohibitory or mandatory injunctions may be perpetual or interlocutory. "Perpetual" does not mean necessarily that the effect of the order must endure forever; it means that the order will finally settle the present dispute between the parties, being made as the result of an ordinary action, the court having heard in the ordinary way the arguments on both sides. But a claimant may not always be able to wait for the action to come on in the normal course; it may be that irreparable damage will be done if the defendant is not immediately restrained. If such is the case, the claimant will serve on him a notice that an application is being made to the court for an interlocutory injunction. The service of this notice will enable the defendant also to be heard, if he wishes, but the hearing will not be a final decision on the merits of the case. If the claimant has made out a sufficient case, the judge will grant an interlocutory injunction, which is effective only until the trial of the action or some earlier specified date.

C. Injunctions Without Notice[19]

25–006   An application may be made without notice if notice would enable the defendant to take steps to defeat the purpose of the injunction, for example by taking assets out of the jurisdiction, or if the claimant had no time to give notice before the threatened wrongful

---

[15] [1974] 1 W.L.R. 576.
[16] *Jackson v Normanby Brick Co* [1899] 1 Ch. 438.
[17] *Att Gen v Colchester Corp* [1955] 2 Q.B. 207; *Gravesham Borough Council v British Railways Board* [1978] Ch. 379; *Morris v Redland Bricks Ltd* [1970] A.C. 652; *Co-operative Insurance Society Ltd v Argyll Stores (Holdings) Ltd* [1998] A.C. 1, above, para.24–021.
[18] *Pride of Derby Angling Association v British Celanese Co* [1953] Ch. 149.
[19] Called ex parte injunctions before the CPR 1998 came into operation.

act. But the latter would be rare, as he could normally at least give notice by telephone: "Any notice is better than none."[20] If an injunction is granted without notice, notice will then be served on the defendant, who will then have a chance of having the order set aside or varied.[21]

D. *Quia Timet* Injunctions

A *quia timet* injunction is one which issues to prevent an infringement of the claimant's rights where the infringement is threatened, but has not yet occurred. The jurisdiction is one of long standing, and exists in relation to both perpetual and interlocutory injunctions, and to both prohibitory and mandatory injunctions. The claimant must show a very strong probability of a future infringement, and that the ensuing damage will be of a most serious nature.[22]

25–007

3. PRINCIPLES APPLICABLE TO THE ISSUE OF INJUNCTIONS

A. General

i. Discretionary Remedy. While the injunction is a much wider remedy than specific performance, the characteristics of the two remedies are similar. Thus, the injunction is a discretionary remedy,[23] based on the inadequacy of common law remedies. As will be seen, similar principles apply to the exercise of the discretion of the court. As in the case of specific performance, the court may award damages under Lord Cairns' Act, either in lieu of, or in addition to, an injunction.[24] In a rare case the court will grant a declaration that a person who has yet to seek an injunction has no entitlement to it.[25]

25–008

ii. Remedy in Personam.[26] Like specific performance, the injunction is a remedy *in personam*. It is possible to enjoin a defendant

25–009

---

[20] *National Commercial Bank Jamaica Ltd v Olint Corporation Ltd (Practice Note)* [2009] 1 W.L.R. 1405 at 1408 (PC).

[21] CPR 23.9, 23.10.

[22] *Fletcher v Bealey* (1885) 28 Ch.D. 688; *Att Gen v Nottingham Corp* [1904] 1 Ch. 673; *Redland Bricks Ltd v Morris* [1970] A.C. 652; below, para.25–042.

[23] Unless it is a statutory remedy to enforce a right for which there is no common law remedy; *Bristol City Council v Lovell* [1998] 1 W.L.R. 446 at 453 (right to buy). Similarly, a claimant who has been totally dispossessed by trespass is entitled to an injunction as of right; *Harrow LBC v Donohue* [1995] 1 EGLR 257; below, para.25–067.

[24] Below, para.25–041, Spry, *Equitable Remedies*, p.625.

[25] *Greenwich Healthcare NHS Trust v London Quadrant Housing Trust* [1998] 1 W.L.R. 1749.

[26] Above, para.24–004.

who is not personally within the jurisdiction, provided service out of the jurisdiction can properly be done under the civil procedure rules.[27] But, as a general rule, no injunction will be granted in connection with the title to land outside the jurisdiction, even if the defendant is within the jurisdiction.[28] It is otherwise in the case of chattels, and, even in the case of land, the rule is subject to exceptions.[29] Finally, an injunction may be granted against an unnamed defendant,[30] or against all the members of a class or organisation to restrain the unlawful acts of unidentified members.[31]

25–010   **iii. The Public Interest.** Divergent views have been expressed in the Court of Appeal on the question whether the court, in considering an application for an injunction to protect a private right, has a duty to take into account the interests of the general public. In *Miller v Jackson*[32] a cricket club committed the torts of nuisance and negligence in allowing cricket balls to land on the claimants' property. An injunction was refused by the Court of Appeal. The public interest in enabling the inhabitants to enjoy the benefits of outdoor recreation prevailed over the claimants' private right to quiet enjoyment of their house and garden. But in *Kennaway v Thompson*,[33] where the claimant sought an injunction to restrain a motor boat racing club from committing nuisance by excessive noise, the Court of Appeal granted the injunction, holding that the rights of the claimant should not be overridden by the interests of the club or of the general public. In considering whether to grant an injunction or damages in lieu under Lord Cairns' Act,[34] the public interest does not prevail over private rights. The views expressed in *Miller v Jackson* ran counter to the well-established principles laid down in *Shelfer v City of London Electric Lighting Co.*[35] However, *Miller*

[27] CPR 1998, Pt 6.30–6.47. See *Re Liddell's ST* [1936] Ch. 365.

[28] *Deschamps v Miller* [1908] 1 Ch. 856; *Re Hawthorne* (1883) 23 Ch.D. 743. See Dicey, Morris and Collins, *The Conflict of Laws*, 14th edn, 2006, p.1150, discussing also the effect of Civil Jurisdiction and Judgments Act 1982 s.30. This principle applies also to foreign intellectual property; *Tyburn Productions Ltd v Conan Doyle* [1991] Ch. 75.

[29] See *Penn v Lord Baltimore* (1750) 1 Ves.Sen. 444, above, para.24–004; *Hamlin v Hamlin* [1986] Fam. 11.

[30] *Bloomsbury Publishing Group Plc v News Group Newspapers Ltd* [2003] 1 W.L.R. 1633.

[31] *M. Michaels (Furriers) Ltd v Askew, The Times*, June 25, 1983 (nuisance by members of "Animal Aid"); cf. *United Kingdom Nirex Ltd v Barton, The Times*, October 14, 1986. See further J. Seymour (2007) 66 C.L.P. 605.

[32] [1977] Q.B. 966. For interlocutory injunctions, see below, para.25–032. See also the cases on libel and breach of confidence, below, paras 25–068, 25–069.

[33] [1981] Q.B. 88; (1981) 97 L.Q.R. 3; R. Buckley (1981) 44 M.L.R. 212; *Sevenoaks District Council v Pattullo & Vinson Ltd* [1984] Ch. 211; *Elliott v Islington London LBC* [1991] 1 E.G.L.R. 167; *Watson v Croft Promosport Ltd* [2009] 3 All E.R. 249.

[34] Below, para.25–045.

[35] [1895] 1 Ch. 287, below, para.25–048. See S. Tromans (1982) 41 C.L.J. 87.

has recently been cited by the Court of Appeal as authority for taking the public interest into account in limited circumstances.[36]

iv. Contempt. Non-compliance with an injunction (or an under-   **25–011** taking given in lieu[37]) is a contempt of court,[38] punishable by imprisonment, sequestration of property (in the case of a corporation) or a fine.[39] Acts done in breach of an injunction may be void for illegality.[40] As disobedience may lead to imprisonment, the injunction must be expressed in exact terms, so that the defendant knows precisely what to do, or refrain from doing.[41] As committal proceedings are equivalent to a criminal charge, the breach of injunction must be established beyond reasonable doubt.[42]

In matrimonial cases, committal orders should be made very reluctantly. As Ormrod L.J. said in *Ansah v Ansah*,[43] "Committal orders are remedies of last resort; in family cases they should be the very last resort." It should be added that a power of arrest may be attached to occupation or non-molestation orders granted under the Family Law Act 1996.

A question which has become prominent is whether third parties commit contempt if they knowingly act contrary to an injunction. A third party who aids and abets a breach of injunction is guilty of contempt.[44] An agent of the party enjoined is also bound by the injunction.[45] The court has jurisdiction in wardship and other special cases to make an injunction against the world at large,[46] although a person who contravened the order in good faith and without notice

---

[36] *SmithKline Beecham Plc v Apotex Europe Ltd* [2007] Ch. 71. *Kennaway* was not cited.

[37] *Hussain v Hussain* [1986] Fam. 134; *Roberts v Roberts* [1990] 2 F.L.R. 111.

[38] Contempt of Court Act 1981. See also *Parker v Camden LBC* [1986] Ch. 162. As to children and persons who lack capacity, see *Wookey v Wookey* [1991] Fam. 121; *Re H (Respondent under 18: Power of Arrest)* [2001] 1 F.L.R. 641.

[39] As to a company's liability for employee's breach, see *Re Supply of Ready Mixed Concrete (No.2)* [1995] 1 A.C. 456. For liability of directors, see *Director General of Fair Trading v Buckland* [1990] 1 W.L.R. 920; *Att Gen for Tuvalu v Philatelic Distribution Corp Ltd* [1990] 1 W.L.R. 926. Non-compliance with an injunction may be an element in a subsequent award of exemplary damages: *Drane v Evangelou* [1978] 1 W.L.R. 455.

[40] *Clarke v Chadburn* [1985] 1 W.L.R. 78 (union rules); C Miller All E.R. Rev. 1985 at 76; cf. *Harrow LBC v Johnstone* [1997] 1 W.L.R. 459 (notice to quit). Compliance with a statute affords a defence; *A v B Bank (Governor and Company of the Bank of England intervening)* [1993] Q.B. 311.

[41] *Redland Bricks Ltd v Morris* [1970] A.C. 652; *Co-operative Insurance Society Ltd v Argyll Stores (Holdings) Ltd* [1998] A.C. 1.

[42] *Re Bramblevale Ltd* [1970] Ch. 128; *Kent County Council v Batchelor* (1977) 33 P. & C.R. 185.

[43] [1977] Fam. 138 at 144. See also P. Pettit (1977) 40 M.L.R. 220; *Hale v Tanner (Practice Note)* [2000] 1 W.L.R. 2377.

[44] *Acro (Automation) Ltd v Rex Chainbelt Inc* [1971] 1 W.L.R. 1676.

[45] *Cretanor Maritime Co Ltd v Irish Marine Management Ltd* [1978] 1 W.L.R. 966. See the asset-freezing cases, below, para.25–080, particularly the "world-wide assets" cases.

[46] Below, para.25–069.

of its terms would not commit contempt.[47] In *Att Gen v Times Newspapers Ltd*[48] newspapers which published confidential material which other newspapers had been enjoined from publishing were guilty of contempt. The House of Lords held that strangers who knowingly took action to damage or destroy confidentiality before the trial committed contempt by nullifying the purpose of the trial. The question was not whether third parties were bound by the injunction, but whether they could commit contempt even though they were not bound. As they were not parties to the order, the basis of the contempt would not be a breach of the order (unless they had aided and abetted a breach) but knowing interference with the administration of justice.[49]

25–012   **v. Crown Proceedings.** An injunction will not normally lie against the Crown.[50] The proper remedy in such a case is the declaration. A former disadvantage that an interim declaration could not be granted has now gone.[51] An interlocutory injunction may, exceptionally, be granted against the Crown to protect rights enforceable under European Community law.[52] Further, an injunction, final or interlocutory, may be granted against ministers and other officers of the Crown, and a minister can be liable for contempt.[53]

B. Protection of Rights

25–013   **i. Locus Standi.** "It is a fundamental rule that the court will only grant an injunction at the suit of a private individual to support a legal right."[54] The type of right which may be protected by injunction in the field of private law is dealt with below, but the question

---

[47] *Re X (A Minor)* [1984] 1 W.L.R. 1422; *Att Gen v Times Newspapers Ltd* [1992] 1 A.C. 191 at 224; *Kelly v BBC* [2001] Fam. 59; *Att Gen v Harris* [2001] 2 F.L.R. 895; *BBC v CAFCASS Legal* [2007] 2 F.L.R. 765.

[48] [1992] 1 A.C. 191 (the *Spycatcher* case). See also *Bank Mellat v Kazmi* [1989] Q.B. 541; *Derby & Co Ltd v Weldon (Nos 3 and 4)* [1990] Ch. 65; *Re C (Adult: Refusal of Treatment)* [1994] 1 W.L.R. 290; *Harrow LBC v Johnstone* [1997] 1 W.L.R. 459.

[49] *Att Gen v Punch* [2003] 1 A.C. 1046; P. Devonshire (2003) 119 L.Q.R. 384. For the position of third parties in relation to final injunctions, see *Jockey Club v Buffham* [2003] Q.B. 462; A. Smith (2003) 62 C.L.J. 241.

[50] Crown Proceedings Act 1947 s.21; *R. v Secretary of State for Transport, Ex p. Factortame Ltd* [1990] 2 A.C. 85.

[51] CPR 25.1. See *R. v R. (Interim Declaration: Adult's Residence)* [2000] 1 F.L.R. 451; *Bank of Scotland (Governor and Company) v A Ltd* [2001] 1 W.L.R. 751; *NHS Trust v T (Adult Patient: Refusal of Medical Treatment)* [2005] 1 All E.R. 387.

[52] *R. v Secretary of State for Transport, Ex p. Factortame Ltd (No.2)* [1991] 1 A.C. 603; H. Wade (1991) 107 L.Q.R. 4.

[53] *M v Home Office* [1994] 1 A.C. 377; C. Harlow (1994) 57 M.L.R. 620; T. Allen (1994) 53 C.L.J. 1.

[54] per Lord Denning M.R. in *Thorne v British Broadcasting Corporation* [1957] 1 W.L.R. 1104 at 1109. But compare the different views expressed in *Chief Constable of Kent v V* [1983] Q.B. 34.

also arises as to who may seek an injunction to protect a public right. This requires a consideration of the extent to which the civil courts may restrain a breach of the criminal law by injunction. The general rule is that public rights are protected by the Attorney General, acting either on his own initiative or on the relation of a member of the public. He may obtain an injunction to restrain breaches of the criminal law even if there is a statutory remedy, where that remedy is inadequate,[55] and the view of the court is that injunctions should be granted at his request to prevent clear breaches of the law irrespective of the weighing of benefits and detriments which characterises most other injunctions.[56]

By way of exception to this general rule, an individual may seek an injunction if interference with a public right, created by statute or existing at common law, would also infringe some private right of his or would inflict special damage on him,[57] save where statute has, for instance by providing an exclusive remedy, excluded it.[58] But an individual who does not come within the established exceptions has no remedy, for it is no part of English law that a person who suffers damage by reason of another person's breach of statute has a civil action against that person.[59] Thus a record company could not get an injunction against a defendant who traded in "bootleg" records in breach of statute, as there is no principle that a person can restrain a crime affecting his property rights by injunction where the statute was not designed for the protection of the class of which he is a member.[60]

Another important question is whether a private individual may obtain an injunction to restrain a threatened criminal offence which would interfere with a public right when the Attorney General has refused his consent to a relator action, the case not being one where private rights or special damage to the claimant are involved.[61]

---

[55] *Att Gen v Sharp* [1931] 1 Ch. 121; *Att Gen v Chaudry* [1971] 1 W.L.R. 1623.

[56] *Att Gen v Bastow* [1957] 1 Q.B. 514; *Att Gen v Harris* [1961] 1 Q.B. 74; below, para.25–071. The role of the Attorney General was reviewed in 2007 but the law was not changed.

[57] *Gouriet v Union of Post Office Workers* [1978] A.C. 435; *Lonrho Ltd v Shell Petroleum Co Ltd* [1982] A.C. 173; *RCA Corp v Pollard* [1983] Ch. 135. An action also lies if the claimant can show that he is a member of the class for whose benefit the statute was passed and upon whom Parliament intended to confer a cause of action; *R. v Deputy Governor of Parkhurst Prison, Ex p. Hague* [1992] 1 A.C. 58. See also *Francome v Mirror Group Newspapers* [1984] 1 W.L.R. 892; *Barrs v Bethell* [1982] Ch. 294.

[58] *Stevens v Chown* [1901] 1 Ch. 894; cf. *Meade v London Borough of Haringey* [1979] 1 W.L.R. 637; Spry, p.365.

[59] *Lonrho Ltd v Shell Petroleum Co Ltd*, above, fn.57; *CBS Songs Ltd v Amstrad Consumer Electronics Plc* [1988] A.C. 1013; *P v Liverpool Daily Post and Echo Newspapers Plc* [1991] 2 A.C. 370.

[60] *RCA Corp v Pollard* [1983] Ch. 135; *Rickless v United Artists Corp* [1988] Q.B. 40. See now Copyright, Designs and Patents Act 1988 s.194.

[61] The right to bring a private prosecution, once the offence is committed, is a different matter, but the Attorney General has power to veto such proceedings.

In *Gouriet v Union of Post Office Workers*[62] the claimant, a member of the public, sought an injunction to restrain a threatened boycott of postal communications between Britain and South Africa, in breach of statute. The Attorney General had refused consent to a relator action, without giving reasons. It was unanimously held in the House of Lords that the court had no jurisdiction to grant such an injunction, nor to control the exercise of the Attorney General's discretion in any way.

25–014 It was a fundamental principle that private rights could be asserted by the individual and public rights by the Attorney General, and that, "the criminal law is enforced in the criminal courts by the conviction and punishment of offenders, not in the civil courts."[63] Any interference by the civil courts exposes the defendant to "double jeopardy"; the penalty of imprisonment for contempt of court, if the offence is committed, is added to the criminal penalties fixed by Parliament.[64] Not only are the punishments different, but the contempt proceedings will be decided by a judge alone while the defendant may be entitled to a jury in the criminal proceedings.[65] These considerations are, of course, also present in cases where injunctions may be granted to enforce the criminal law. No doubt for this reason the House of Lords expressed the view that the cases where the Attorney General can seek an injunction to restrain the commission of an offence are narrow and not to be extended. The jurisdiction is "of great delicacy and is one to be used with caution." The Attorney General's power is "not without its difficulties and these may call for consideration in the future."[66]

But the effect of the decision may not be so great as first appears. The prerogative remedies, with their broader concept of standing,[67] may be available where the defendant is a public authority.[68] Here the court feels able to judge on matters of public interest, even

---

[62] [1978] A.C. 435; D. Williams (1977) 36 C.L.J. 201; HWRW (1978) 94 L.Q.R. 4; T. Hartley (1978) 41 M.L.R. 58; R. Simpson (1978) 41 M.L.R. 63; D. Feldman (1979) 42 M.L.R. 369. See also Lord Denning's observations in *The Discipline of Law*, 1979, pp.137–144.

[63] [1978] A.C. 435 at 490 (per Viscount Dilhorne). Although the case concerned criminal law enforcement, many statements in the House of Lords were wide enough to cover all public law actions. See also *Ashby v Ebdon* [1985] Ch. 394; J. Jolowicz (1985) 44 C.L.J. 6.

[64] [1978] A.C. 435 at 498, per Lord Diplock. See *Kent County Council v Batchelor* [1979] 1 W.L.R. 213. But in other areas the civil court adds to the criminal penalty; see para.12–038, above, (forfeiture of property acquired by killing).

[65] But the standard of proof will be the same; see D. Feldman (1979) 42 M.L.R. 369.

[66] See also *Stoke-on-Trent City Council v B&Q (Retail) Ltd* [1984] A.C. 754; *Waverley Borough Council v Hilden* [1988] 1 W.L.R. 246; *Kirklees Borough Council v Wickes Building Supplies Ltd* [1993] A.C. 227, para.25–071.

[67] Below, para.25–072.

[68] See *R. v Commissioner of Police of the Metropolis* [1968] 2 Q.B. 118; *R. v IRC, Ex p. National Federation of Self-Employed and Small Businesses Ltd* [1982] A.C. 617 at 640, below, para.25–072; *R. v Her Majesty's Treasury, Ex p. Smedley* [1985] Q.B. 657.

where there are political implications,[69] but the House of Lords has doubted the analogy.[70]

In the case of a crime which has already been committed, it has been held that the police have locus standi to seek an injunction to "freeze" money in a bank account which is reasonably believed to be the proceeds of a crime.[71] This principle is not without difficulty, and is confined to an asset which can be identified as the stolen item or as property representing it.[72] No such injunction is available in respect of moneys not themselves obtained by fraud but which were profits made by means of a loan obtained by fraud.[73] The House of Lords in *Att Gen v Blake*[74] considered that the Attorney General had no entitlement to an injunction which effectively froze the proceeds of crime (royalties from a book written by a former KGB spy), because this would amount to confiscation outside the statutory provisions permitting confiscation orders. Their Lordships decided that the private law remedy of an account of profits was available,[75] and thus the point did not arise. No view was expressed as to the correctness of the police cases, which were distinguishable.

Finally, the rule that only the Attorney General may enforce public rights is subject to certain limited statutory exceptions, enabling a local authority to seek an injunction in its own name to protect public rights in the locality or to enforce planning control.[76]

ii. Legal and Equitable Rights. A right that is to be protected by **25–015** an injunction must be one that is known to law or equity.[77] The point was firmly made in *Day v Brownrigg*.[78]

The claimant lived in a house that had been called "Ashford Lodge" for 60 years. The defendant lived in a smaller neighbouring house called "Ashford Villa". The defendant started to call

[69] See, for example, *Secretary of State for Education and Science v Tameside Metropolitan Borough Council* [1977] A.C. 1014.

[70] *Gouriet v Union of Post Office Workers* [1978] A.C. 435 at 483.

[71] *Chief Constable of Kent v V* [1983] Q.B. 34; *West Mercia Constabulary v Wagener* [1982] 1 W.L.R. 127; D. Feldman (1982) 98 L.Q.R. 190; G. Zellick All E.R. Rev. 1982 at 205; (1983) 99 L.Q.R. 1; A. Tettenborn (1983) 42 C.L.J. 51.

[72] *Chief Constable of Hampshire v A Ltd* [1985] Q.B. 132; G. Samuel (1984) 100 L.Q.R. 537. See also *Malone v Metropolitan Police Commissioner* [1980] Q.B. 49.

[73] *Chief Constable of Leicestershire v M* [1989] 1 W.L.R. 20; cf. *Securities and Investments Board v Pantell SA* [1990] Ch. 426.

[74] [2001] 1 A.C. 268.

[75] Above, para.1–022.

[76] Local Government Act 1972 s.222; Town and Country Planning Act 1990 s.187B; below, para.25–071.

[77] In *Chief Constable of Kent v V* [1983] Q.B. 34, Lord Denning M.R. considered that this was no longer the case after the Supreme Court Act 1981 (now the Senior Courts Act 1981), but this was firmly rejected by the House of Lords in *P v Liverpool Daily Post and Echo Newspapers Plc* [1991] 2 A.C. 370. A broad approach is favoured in *Broadmoor Hospital Authority v Robinson* [2000] 1 W.L.R. 1590.

[78] (1878) 10 Ch.D. 294; *Beddow v Beddow* (1878) 9 Ch.D. 89 at 93.

his house "Ashford Lodge" and the claimant sought an injunction to restrain him from doing so. The Court of Appeal took the view that there was no violation of a legal or equitable right of the claimant so that no injunction would be granted.[79]

Similarly, in *Paton v Trustees of British Pregnancy Advisory Service*[80] it was held that a husband could not obtain an injunction to prevent his wife from having, or a registered medical practitioner from performing, a legal abortion: the husband had "no legal right enforceable at law or in equity."

Injunctions have proved valuable in protecting confidential material.[81] Before 1875, it was accepted that equity would, in suitable cases, restrain a defendant from revealing or distributing information or other material obtained in confidence,[82] regarding the breach of confidence as an equitable wrong needing protection by injunction. It is now accepted[83] that the jurisdiction in this type of case does not depend on any notion of property or contract, but that an obligation of confidence can exist by virtue of the circumstances, and independently of any actual agreement to that effect. Confidential commercial information will be restrained from publication along similar lines.

Other rights which may be protected by injunction include the right (contractual or otherwise) not to be subjected to arbitration proceedings which could not lead to a fair trial[84]; the right (contractual or otherwise) not to be sued in a foreign court[85]; the right of the police to "freeze" money in a bank account which is reasonably believed to be the identifiable proceeds of crime[86]; the right to restrain a breach of European Community law[87]; the right to restrain the export of works of art by means of forged documents[88]; the right to refuse surgery[89]; the right not to be harassed[90]; the right of a

---

[79] See also *Montgomery v Montgomery* [1965] P. 46.

[80] [1979] Q.B. 276; J. Phillips (1979) 95 L.Q.R. 332; C. Lyon and G. Benett (1979) 30 C.L.P. 217. For a discussion of the position if the proposed abortion would be illegal, see I. Kennedy (1979) 42 M.L.R. 324; *C v S* [1988] Q.B. 135; A. Grubb and D. Pearl (1987) 103 L.Q.R. 340.

[81] Below, para.25–069.

[82] *Prince Albert v Strange* (1849) 1 H. & T. 1 (copies of etchings made by the Prince and Queen Victoria: distribution restrained).

[83] See particularly *Argyll v Argyll* [1967] Ch. 302 at 322; *Fraser v Evans* [1969] 1 Q.B. 349 at 361.

[84] *Bremer Vulkan Schiffbau und Maschinenfabrik v South India Shipping Corp* [1981] A.C. 909.

[85] *British Airways Board v Laker Airways Ltd* [1985] A.C. 58; *South Carolina Insurance Co v Assurantie Maatschappij "De Zeven Provincien" NV* [1987] A.C. 24.

[86] Above, para.25–014.

[87] *Cutsforth v Mansfield Inns Ltd* [1986] 1 W.L.R. 558; *Taittinger v Allbev Ltd* [1994] 4 All E.R. 75.

[88] *Kingdom of Spain v Christie, Manson & Woods Ltd* [1986] 1 W.L.R. 1120.

[89] *Re C (Adult: Refusal of Treatment)* [1994] 1 W.L.R. 290.

[90] Protection from Harassment Act 1997 s.3.

public body to prevent interference with the performance of its statutory responsibilities[91]; and the right to ensure the effectiveness of a court order.[92] The latter right is the basis of the novel use of the injunction to prevent the defendant from leaving the country,[93] although this has been described as draconian and requiring careful examination.[94] Such an injunction may be granted even though there is no pre-existing cause of action.[95] The jurisdiction, which arises under s.37(1) of the Senior Courts Act 1981, is in aid of the court's procedures leading to the disposal of proceedings, and is available after judgment to aid enforcement. The injunction is ancillary to other powers of the court and is not a free-standing enforcement procedure in its own right.[96]

C. Perpetual Injunctions

It is axiomatic that the jurisdiction to grant injunctions is purely discretionary. But, as with specific performance, the court, in exercising its discretion, pays attention to certain factors established by the precedents as being of particular relevance.   **25–016**

i. Prohibitory Injunctions. If a claimant has established the existence of a right, infringement of that right should be restrained, but injunctions will not be granted where an award of damages[97] would be sufficient. Damages will not be an adequate remedy if they are not quantifiable, or if money could not properly compensate the claimant, as in the case of nuisance and other continuous or repeated injuries requiring a series of actions for damages, or even where the remedy would be ineffective because the defendant is a pauper.[98]   **25–017**

The extent of the damage is not the crucial point. An injunction may be granted even if only nominal damages would be recoverable at law.[99] The smallness of the damage and the fact that a monetary sum could easily be assessed to compensate for it, is no reason for

[91] *Broadmoor Hospital Authority v Robinson* [2000] 1 W.L.R. 1590.

[92] *Maclaine Watson & Co Ltd v International Tin Council (No.2)* [1989] Ch. 286 (unpaid judgment debt).

[93] *Bayer AG v Winter* [1986] 1 W.L.R. 497 below, para.25–080; *Arab Monetary Fund v Hashim* [1989] 1 W.L.R. 565; *Ali v Naseem, The Times,* October 3, 2003; cf. *Al Nahkel for Contracting and Trading Ltd v Lowe* [1986] Q.B. 235 and *Allied Arab Bank Ltd v Hajjar* [1988] Q.B. 787; N. Andrews (1988) 47 C.L.J. 364 (ne exeat regno). See also *Re I (A Minor), The Times,* May 22, 1987.

[94] *Bayer AG v Winter (No.2)* [1986] 1 W.L.R. 540; J. Martin (1990) 20 U.W.A.L.R. 143.

[95] *Re Oriental Credit Ltd* [1988] Ch. 204 (to prevent director leaving the country prior to examination under insolvency legislation powers); criticised in C. Forsyth (1988) 47 C.L.J. 177; *Morris v Murjani* [1996] 1 W.L.R. 848 (to prevent bankrupt leaving the country without complying with Insolvency Act 1986 s.333).

[96] *B v B (Injunction: Jurisdiction)* [1998] 1 W.L.R. 329 (judgment debtor).

[97] The jurisdiction to award damages under Lord Cairns' Act is considered below, below, para.25–048.

[98] *Hodgson v Duce* (1856) 28 L.T.(O.S.) 155.

[99] *Rochdale Canal Co v King* (1851) 2 Sim.(N.S.) 78; *Woollerton and Wilson Ltd v Richard Costain Ltd* [1970] 1 W.L.R. 411.

withholding an injunction if the consequence is that the defendant is in effect compulsorily "buying" a right which is the claimant's to sell only if he wants to.[100] This principle was applied in *Express Newspapers Ltd v Keys*.[101]

Certain trade unions had issued instructions to their members to support a "Day of Action" in protest against Government policies. The claimants sought an injunction to restrain the unions from inducing a breach of contract between the members and their employers. Griffiths J., in granting the injunction, held that damages would be inadequate. The employers did not want money; they wanted their newspapers to be published. To refuse the injunction would be giving a licence to the unions to commit an unlawful act merely because they could afford to pay the damages.

Similarly in cases in which the defendant has trespassed on the claimant's property: actual loss does not need to be shown before an injunction is granted.[102] But there may be cases in which injunctions will be refused, for example if the infringement is occasional or temporary, or if it is a trivial matter. One such case was *Armstrong v Sheppard and Short*,[103] where the claimant had misled the court and had suffered no real damage. Lord Evershed M.R. said:

"A proprietor who establishes a proprietary right is ex debito justitiae entitled to an injunction unless it can be said against him that he has raised such an equity that it is no longer open to him to assert his legal or proprietary rights."[104]

Similarly, in *Behrens v Richards*[105] an injunction was not granted to restrain the public from using tracks on the claimant's land on an unfrequented part of the coast, causing no damage to him. Such cases are, however, to be regarded as exceptional.[106]

It is obvious that these various factors are not to be considered in isolation and no complete list can be given of instances where an

---

[100] *Wood v Sutcliffe* (1851) 2 Sim.(N.S.) 163. In *Express Newspapers Ltd v Keys* [1980] I.R.L.R. 247, and *Patel v WH Smith (Eziot) Ltd* [1987] 1 W.L.R. 853, it was held that this principle applied equally to interlocutory injunctions, and was not affected by *American Cyanamid Co v Ethicon Ltd* [1975] A.C. 396, below, para.25–029.

[101] [1980] I.R.L.R. 247. The injunction in this case was interlocutory but the judgment on this aspect is of general application.

[102] *Goodson v Richardson* (1874) L.R. 9 Ch.App. 221; *Trenberth (John) Ltd v National Westminster Bank Ltd* (1979) 39 P. & C.R. 104. See also *Marco Productions Ltd v Pagola* [1945] K.B. 111 on breach of contract.

[103] [1959] 2 Q.B. 384.

[104] [1959] 2 Q.B. 384 at 394. See *Harrow LBC v Donohue* [1995] 1 E.G.L.R. 257.

[105] [1905] 2 Ch. 614.

[106] *Patel v WH Smith (Eziot) Ltd* [1987] 1 W.L.R. 853; *Anchor Brewhouse Developments Ltd v Berkley House (Docklands Developments) Ltd* [1987] 2 E.G.L.R. 173; E. McKendrick and H. Wilkinson (1988) 138 N.L.J. 23 and 385.

injunction will be refused. The principle applied by the courts is the protection of existing rights which are recognised by the law. But an injunction will not issue in every such case; it may be refused where damages are an adequate remedy, or where the claimant has by his conduct disentitled himself from injunctive relief,[107] or where the defendant gives to the court an undertaking not to do the act complained of[108]; or where, even if there is no other suitable remedy, the court considers that the claimant has suffered no injustice.[109]

ii. Mandatory Injunctions. These are governed by the same **25–018** general principles as prohibitory injunctions, save that the problems of enforcement, supervision and hardship may be more acute. Mandatory injunctions are less frequently granted than prohibitory injunctions, and, as Lord Upjohn stated in *Redland Bricks Ltd v Morris*,[110] are entirely discretionary, although it has been held that the court has no real discretion in cases involving trespass by total dispossession.[111]

There are two broad categories of mandatory injunctions: the first is the "restorative" injunction, requiring the defendant to undo a wrongful act in situations where a prohibitory injunction might have been obtained to prevent the commission of the act.[112] In such a case failure to seek a prohibitory injunction does not preclude the subsequent grant of a mandatory injunction, but it is a factor to be taken into account: a final injunction is unlikely if the claimant "stood by" during building works in breach of covenant, but he may succeed if he made his objections clear.[113] The other category is the mandatory injunction to compel the defendant to carry out some positive obligation. If the matter is one of contract, specific performance is more usual in the latter situation, but an injunction may be granted.[114] We have already seen that the terms of an injunction must be certain. It follows from this that a duty which is itself uncertain cannot be enforced by injunction.[115]

---

[107] Discretionary bars are considered below, below, para.25–043.
[108] *Halsey v Esso Petroleum Co Ltd* [1961] 1 W.L.R. 683; *British Broadcasting Corp v Hearn* [1977] 1 W.L.R. 1004.
[109] See *Glynn v Keele University* [1971] 1 W.L.R. 487.
[110] [1970] A.C. 652 at 655. See also *Leakey v National Trust for Places of Historic Interest or Natural Beauty* [1980] Q.B. 485; *Re C (A Minor)* [1991] 2 F.L.R. 168.
[111] *Harrow LBC v Donohue* [1995] 1 E.G.L.R. 257.
[112] *Charrington v Simons & Co Ltd* [1971] 1 W.L.R. 598; *Pugh v Howells* (1984) 48 P. & C.R. 29; *Jones v Stones* [1999] 1 W.L.R. 1739.
[113] See *Wrotham Park Estate v Parkside Homes Ltd* [1974] 1 W.L.R. 798, below; *Gafford v Graham* (1999) 77 P. & C.R. 73; *Mortimer v Bailey* [2005] 1 E.G.L.R. 75; G. Watt [2005] Conv. 460.
[114] See *Evans v BBC and IBA*, *The Times*, February 26, 1974 (interlocutory).
[115] *Bower v Bantam Investments Ltd* [1972] 1 W.L.R. 1120 (interlocutory); cf. *Acrow (Automation) Ltd v Rex Chainbelt Inc* [1971] 1 W.L.R. 1676; *Peninsular Maritime Ltd v Padseal Ltd* (1981) 259 E.G. 860.

Problems of supervision may arise with mandatory injunctions as with specific performance.[116] This will not normally prevent the grant of a "restorative" mandatory injunction, which merely requires an act of restoration, but a mandatory injunction is unlikely to be granted in cases involving the continuous performance of a positive obligation.

In *Gravesham Borough Council v British Railways Board*,[117] the defendant planned to curtail the services of its ferry. As this would cause inconvenience to some local workers, a mandatory injunction was sought to compel the defendant to maintain existing timetables, even though this would cause the ferry to be run at a loss. It was held that in fact there was no breach of the defendant's common law duty to operate the ferry, but even if there had been, a mandatory injunction would not be appropriate, because of enforcement difficulties and financial hardship to the defendant. Slade J. said that there was no absolute and inflexible rule that the court will never grant an injunction requiring a series of acts involving the continuous employment of people over a number of years. But the jurisdiction to grant such an injunction would be exercised only in exceptional circumstances.

25–019   As in the case of prohibitory injunctions, it is not necessary for the claimant to show grave damage or inconvenience. In *Kelsen v Imperial Tobacco Co Ltd*[118] a mandatory injunction was granted to enforce the removal of a sign which trespassed in the airspace above the claimant's premises, causing no real damage to him, save in so far as he could have charged for the use of the space.

While the extent of the damage is not crucial, the question of hardship to the defendant is more significant.[119] In *Charrington v Simons & Co Ltd*,[120] Buckley J. thought that the criterion for the grant of a mandatory injunction was a fair result, taking into consideration the benefit which the order would confer on the claimant and the detriment which it would cause the defendant. But the Court of Appeal doubted the usefulness of the "fair result" test.[121]

---

[116] Above, para.24–020.

[117] [1978] Ch. 379. See also *Dowty Boulton Paul Ltd v Wolverhampton Corp* [1971] 1 W.L.R. 204 (no injunction to enforce a covenant to maintain land as an airfield); cf. *Co-operative Insurance Society Ltd v Argyll Stores (Holdings) Ltd* [1998] A.C. 1 (no specific performance of covenant in lease to keep open in trading hours as a retail shop); above, para.25–021.

[118] [1957] 2 Q.B. 334.

[119] *Gravesham BC v British Railways Board*, above, fn.117; *Jordan v Norfolk CC* [1994] 1 W.L.R. 1353 (disproportionate cost). See also *Colls v Home and Colonial Stores Ltd* [1904] A.C. 179, and other cases on Lord Cairns' Act, below, para.25–048.

[120] [1970] 1 W.L.R. 725 at 730. See also *Shepherd Homes Ltd v Sandham* [1971] Ch. 340.

[121] [1971] 1 W.L.R. 598, below, para.25–056.

In *Wrotham Park Estate v Parkside Homes Ltd*,[122] the defendant had erected houses in breach of a restrictive covenant which it had thought was unenforceable. Although purchasers were now in occupation, the claimants sought a mandatory injunction for the demolition of the houses. For various reasons, they had not sought interlocutory relief to prevent the erection of the houses, but this was not fatal to the grant of a mandatory injunction.[123] The fact that the action was commenced before much building had been done was a relevant but not a conclusive factor. The injunction was refused, as it would result in the unpardonable waste of needed houses. Instead, damages were awarded under Lord Cairns' Act.

Finally, it has been held that the court should be reluctant to intervene in industrial disputes by the grant of a mandatory injunction.　　**25–020**

In *Harold Stephen and Co Ltd v Post Office*,[124] an industrial dispute had arisen whereby postal workers were suspended. This resulted in the claimant company's mail being held up and its business seriously disrupted. The company sought a mandatory injunction against the Post Office to release its mail. The Court of Appeal refused the injunction, which would require the Post Office to take back the suspended workers, who would be likely to continue the unlawful action. The injunction would, therefore, have the effect of revoking the Post Office's disciplinary measures.

> "It can only be in very rare circumstances and in the most extreme circumstances that this court should interfere by way of mandatory injunction in the delicate mechanism of industrial disputes and industrial negotiations."[125]

Such an extreme case was *Parker v Camden LBC*,[126] where a strike of boilermen employed by the landlord council meant that the tenants, many of whom were elderly or had young children, had no heating or hot water. In these exceptional circumstances, involving risk to life and health, the court was prepared to grant a mandatory

---

[122] [1974] 1 W.L.R. 798; F. Crane (1974) 39 Conv.(N.S.) 289; J. Jolowicz (1975) 34 C.L.J. 224; distinguished in *Wakeham v Wood* (1982) 43 P. & C.R. 40, where the building was in flagrant disregard of the covenant.
[123] See also *Shaw v Applegate* [1977] 1 W.L.R. 970 at 978.
[124] [1977] 1 W.L.R. 1172.
[125] [1977] 1 W.L.R. 1172 at 1180. See also *Meade v London Borough of Haringey* [1979] 1 W.L.R. 637.
[126] [1986] Ch. 162 (interlocutory).

injunction to turn on the boiler even though industrial action was involved.

The principles applicable to the grant of mandatory interlocutory injunctions and mandatory *quia timet* injunctions are discussed below.[127]

25–021		**iii. Suspension of Injunctions.** If it would be very difficult for the defendant to comply immediately with the injunction, he will not be made to do the impossible. The injunction may be granted but suspended for a reasonable period, particularly if such a course will not result in financial damage to the claimant. The defendant may be required to undertake to pay damages to the claimant for any loss. Suspension is not unusual where the defendant is a local authority, which must make alternative arrangements for the performance of its duties. Thus, in *Pride of Derby Angling Association v British Celanese and Others*[128] an injunction was granted against a local authority to restrain the pollution of a river, but was suspended for a reasonable time, with the possibility of further suspension should the circumstances require it.

The courts have sometimes suspended injunctions not in order to give the defendant time to comply, but rather to enable him to continue his wrongful activity in cases involving no substantial injury to the claimant. Thus, in *Woollerton and Wilson Ltd v Richard Costain Ltd*[129] an injunction to restrain aerial trespass (causing no danger or damage) by a crane during building works was granted but suspended until a date when the crane would no longer be needed. This was doubted by the Court of Appeal in *Charrington v Simons & Co Ltd*,[130] where a three-year suspension of an injunction to reinstate a track (which had been resurfaced in breach of covenant) was held improper.

D. Interlocutory (or Interim) Injunctions

25–022		**i. General.** Interlocutory injunctions raise somewhat different considerations. The object of an interlocutory injunction is "to prevent a litigant, who must necessarily suffer the law's delay, from

---

[127] Below, paras 25–040, 25–042.
[128] [1953] Ch. 149. See also *Halsey v Esso Petroleum Co Ltd* [1961] 1 W.L.R. 683 (suspension for six weeks in nuisance case); *Miller v Jackson* [1977] Q.B. 966; *Waverley BC v Hilden* [1988] 1 W.L.R. 246.
[129] [1970] 1 W.L.R. 411; G. Dworkin (1970) 33 M.L.R. 552.
[130] [1971] 1 W.L.R. 598; J. Jolowicz (1975) 34 C.L.J. 224. See also *Trenberth (John) Ltd v National Westminster Bank Ltd* (1979) 39 P. & C.R. 104; H. Street [1980] Conv. 308; *Jaggard v Sawyer* [1995] 1 W.L.R. 269; *Mid Bedfordshire DC v Brown* [2005] 1 W.L.R. 1460.

losing by that delay the fruit of his litigation."[131] Or, as more recently expressed by the Privy Council, its purpose is "to improve the chances of the court being able to do justice after a determination of the merits at the trial."[132]

Interlocutory injunctions may be prohibitory, mandatory, or *quia timet*. Normally such an injunction remains in force until the trial of the action, but it may be granted for some shorter specified period. If the parties consent, the interlocutory hearing may be treated as a final trial if the dispute is of law. But this will not be possible if the dispute is of fact, as affidavit evidence is unsuitable for such issues.

As we have seen, failure to seek an interlocutory injunction to restrain the commission of a wrongful act will not necessarily preclude the claimant from later obtaining a final mandatory injunction to compel the defendant to undo the act.[133]

(a) *Without Notice Procedure.* The claimant should give at least three clear days' notice, so that, when the application is heard, the defendant can oppose it. But exceptionally an injunction may be granted without serving notice on the defendant, if the matter is one of such urgency that irreparable damage would be caused if the claimant had to go through the normal procedure.[134] The "without notice" injunction may be subsequently set aside or varied on the defendant's application.[135] Such an injunction may be granted even before the proceedings have started. In *Re N (No.2)*,[136] an injunction was granted without notice by a High Court judge at his residence on a Sunday, to prevent the applicant's husband from taking their children to Australia.

In family matters injunctions should not be granted without notice unless there is real immediate danger of serious injury or irreparable damage.[137] Only in the most exceptional circumstances will an injunction be granted without notice requiring a spouse to leave the matrimonial home.[138]

25–023

---

[131] *Hoffman-La Roche (F) & Co v Secretary of State for Trade and Industry* [1975] A.C. 295 at 355 (Lord Wilberforce).

[132] *National Commercial Bank Jamaica Ltd v Olint Corporation Ltd (Practice Note)* [2009] 1 W.L.R. 1405 at 1409.

[133] *Wrotham Park Estate v Parkside Homes Ltd* [1974] 1 W.L.R. 798. But such an omission may be relevant to the defence of acquiescence: *Shaw v Applegate* [1977] 1 W.L.R 970, below, para.25–045.

[134] CPR 25.3. See *National Commercial Bank Jamaica Ltd v Olint Corporation Ltd (Practice Note)* [2009] 1 W.L.R. 1405 at 1408. Where a trade dispute is involved, see the Trade Union and Labour Relations (Consolidation) Act 1992 s.221(2), below, para.25–034.

[135] CPR 23.9, 23.10.

[136] [1967] Ch. 512.

[137] *Ansah v Ansah* [1977] Fam. 138; *G v G* [1990] 1 F.L.R. 395; applied in *Moat Housing Group South Ltd v Harris* [2006] Q.B. 606 in the context of anti-social behaviour injunctions ousting tenants from property.

[138] *Masich v Masich* (1977) 121 S.J. 645; (1977) 7 Fam. Law 245.

In the commercial sphere, injunctions should not normally be granted without notice where they would prevent banks from honouring contractual obligations, such as payouts under letters of credit.[139]

The "without notice" procedure has been found most useful in the search order and asset-freezing cases, where there is a danger that the defendant, if aware of the application, would destroy or remove vital evidence, or move assets out of the jurisdiction. These developments are discussed below.[140]

25–024   (b) *Discharge of Interlocutory Injunctions.* The court has inherent jurisdiction to discharge an interlocutory injunction, even when the defendant has not applied for its discharge.[141] Furthermore, where an injunction has been granted which affects someone who was not a party to the action, he can apply to court for the variation or discharge of the injunction.[142]

25–025   (c) *Injunctions Pending Appeal.* Where a claim for an interlocutory injunction is dismissed, the judge has jurisdiction to grant a limited injunction pending an appeal, on the claimant's without notice application.[143] Such an injunction may be granted in order that the appeal, if successful, is not nugatory.

25–026   (d) *Complete Relief.* It is no objection that the grant of an interlocutory injunction gives complete relief to the claimant without requiring him to prove his case, so that he need bring no final action.[144] In *Woodford v Smith*,[145] Megarry J. granted an interlocutory injunction to restrain a residents' association from breaking its contract by holding a meeting without the claimant members. There was nothing to prevent the court in a proper case from granting on an interim application all the relief claimed in the action. It may be a more serious objection in the case of mandatory interlocutory injunctions,[146] where positive action is required, but in *Evans v BBC*

---

[139] *Bolivinter Oil SA v Chase Manhattan Bank* [1984] 1 W.L.R. 392n.

[140] Below, paras 25–077, 25–080.

[141] *RD Harbottle (Mercantile) Ltd v National Westminster Bank Ltd* [1978] Q.B. 146.

[142] *Cretanor Maritime Co Ltd v Irish Marine Management Ltd* [1978] 1 W.L.R. 966; *Iraqi Ministry of Defence v Arcepey Shipping Co SA* [1981] Q.B. 65, below, para.25–085 (asset-freezing injunctions).

[143] *Erinford Properties Ltd v Cheshire CC* [1974] Ch. 261; *Chartered Bank v Daklouche* [1976] 1 W.L.R. 107. See also *Ketchum International Plc v Group Public Relations Holdings Ltd* [1997] 1 W.L.R. 4 (jurisdiction to restrain disposal of assets pending appeal if good arguable appeal); *Belize Alliance of Conservation Non-Govermental Organisations v Department of the Environment of Belize* [2003] 1 W.L.R. 2839 (Privy Council has such jurisdiction).

[144] As to whether the principle of *American Cyanamid Co v Ethicon Ltd* [1975] A.C. 396, applies in such cases, see below, para.25–035.

[145] [1970] 1 W.L.R. 806; see also *Manchester Corp v Connolly* [1970] Ch. 420, where there was plainly no defence.

[146] *Locabail International Finance Ltd v Agroexport* [1986] 1 W.L.R. 657.

and IBA[147] a mandatory interlocutory injunction was granted to enforce the Welsh Nationalist Party's alleged contractual right to a Party Political Broadcast on television just before an election. The interlocutory injunction was thus a complete remedy, making it unnecessary to continue to trial and prove the case.

(e) *Injunction Ineffective.* As equity does not act in vain, an inter- **25–027** locutory injunction will not be granted where it would be of no effect.[148] In *Bentley-Stevens v Jones*[149] a director was removed by irregular proceedings. This was not a case for an interlocutory injunction, as the irregularities could be cured by going through the proper processes; the result therefore would be the same.

ii. Principles Applicable to the Issue of Interlocutory Injunc- **25–028** tions. As in the case of mandatory injunctions, the interlocutory injunction is discretionary and is never granted as of course. Prior to the decision of the House of Lords in *American Cyanamid Co v Ethicon Ltd*,[150] discussed below, it was well established that the claimant had to show a strong prima facie case that his rights had been infringed.[151] He was then required to show that damages would not be an adequate remedy if he succeeded at the trial, and that the balance of convenience favoured the grant. In other words, an interlocutory injunction would not be granted unless the claimant could show that it was more likely than not that he would succeed in obtaining a final injunction at the trial.

(a) *American Cyanamid Co v Ethicon Ltd.*[152] The principles **25–029** mentioned above were replaced by the rules laid down by Lord Diplock in *American Cyanamid*, which were designed to circumvent the necessity of deciding disputed facts or determining points of law without hearing sufficient argument.[153] The case concerned an application for a *quia timet* interlocutory injunction to restrain the infringement of a patent. It was unanimously held that there was no rule requiring the claimant to establish a prima facie case.[154] The

---

[147] *The Times*, February 26, 1974. See also *Shepherd Homes Ltd v Sandham* [1971] Ch. 340 at 347, and *Acrow (Automation) Ltd v Rex Chainbelt Inc* [1971] 1 W.L.R. 1676 at 1683.

[148] Similarly with final injunctions; *Att Gen v Guardian Newspapers Ltd (No.2)* [1990] 1 A.C. 109. A declaration may be appropriate; *Love v Herrity* (1991) 23 H.L.R. 217.

[149] [1974] 1 W.L.R. 638.

[150] [1975] A.C. 396; A. Gore (1975) 38 M.L.R. 672; P. Wallington (1976) 35 C.L.J. 82; P. Prescott (1975) 91 L.Q.R. 168; C. Gray (1981) 40 C.L.J. 307.

[151] See *J T Stratford & Son Ltd v Lindley* [1965] A.C. 269, especially at 338 (Lord Upjohn). The contrary was not there argued. The decision was not cited in *American Cyanamid*.

[152] [1975] A.C. 396.

[153] *Smith v Inner London Education Authority* [1978] 1 All E.R. 411, at 426.

[154] But Lord Diplock himself had said that an applicant for an interlocutory injunction had to show a "strong prima facie case" that he would succeed at trial: *Hoffman-LaRoche (F) & Co v Secretary of State for Trade and Industry* [1975] A.C. 295 at 360. For an explanation, see *Series 5 Software Ltd v Clarke* [1996] 1 All E.R. 853; A. Zuckerman All E.R. Rev. 1996, p.327.

rule is that the court must be satisfied that the claimant's case is not frivolous or vexatious and that there is a serious question to be tried. Once that is established, the governing consideration is the balance of convenience. The court should not embark on anything resembling a trial of the action. At the interlocutory stage it is no part of the court's function to resolve conflicts of evidence on affidavit nor to resolve difficult questions of law.[155] These are matters for the trial. At the interlocutory stage the facts may be disputed and the evidence incomplete and there is no cross-examination; the court's discretion would be stultified if, on untested and incomplete evidence, it could only grant the injunction if the claimant had shown that he was more than 50 per cent likely to succeed at trial.

While the balance of convenience is the governing consideration, a significant factor in assessing it is the inadequacy of damages to each party. If that does not provide an answer, then other aspects of the balance of convenience will arise. If the balance of convenience does not clearly favour either party, then the preservation of the status quo will be decisive. Only as a last resort is it proper to consider the relative strength of the cases of both parties, and only then if it appears from the facts set out in the affidavit evidence, as to which there is no credible dispute, that the strength of one party's case is disproportionate to that of the other.[156] Finally, other special factors may have to be considered in individual cases. More recently the Privy Council restated the position as follows: "The basic principle is that the court should take whichever course seems likely to cause the least irremediable prejudice to one party or the other."[157]

Thus it will be seen that there is a series of rules, most of which will apply only if the previous one has not afforded a solution. But, as Browne L.J. stated in *Fellowes & Son v Fisher*,[158] the remedy is discretionary and the principles enunciated by Lord Diplock contain some elements of flexibility. The House of Lords cannot have intended to lay down rigid rules.[159] They are best described as guidelines,[160] which "must never be used as a rule of thumb, let alone as a strait-jacket."[161]

---

[155] *Derby & Co Ltd v Weldon* [1990] Ch. 48.

[156] See *Cambridge Nutrition Ltd v British Broadcasting Corp* [1990] 3 All E.R. 523; cf. *Series 5 Software Ltd v Clarke*, above, fn.154.

[157] *National Commercial Bank Jamaica Ltd v Olint Corporation Ltd (Practice Note)* [2009] 1 W.L.R. 1405 at 1409.

[158] [1976] Q.B. 122 at 139.

[159] See *Hubbard v Vosper* [1972] 2 Q.B. 84, advocating the flexibility of the remedy, and referred to with apparent approval by Lord Diplock in *American Cyanamid* [1975] A.C. 396 at 407; *Kirklees BC v Wickes Building Supplies Ltd* [1993] A.C. 227.

[160] *Cayne v Global Natural Resources Plc* [1984] 1 All E.R. 225.

[161] *Cambridge Nutrition Ltd v British Broadcasting Corp*, above, fn.156, at 535.

But the *American Cyanamid* principles have not satisfied everybody. Lord Denning M.R. in *Fellowes & Son v Fisher*[162] expressed a preference for the "prima facie case" approach, which had been required for a century, because most cases never went to trial,[163] as the parties usually accepted the court's prima facie view, which was a sensible and convenient practice. The other members of the Court of Appeal expressed the need for further guidance, as the new rules were a complete departure from previous practice. But the majority of the Court of Appeal in *Hubbard v Pitt*[164] considered that the *American Cyanamid* principles were convenient and had often been adopted.

The principles laid down by Lord Diplock in *American Cyanamid* were these:

(i) CLAIMANT'S CASE NOT FRIVOLOUS OR VEXATIOUS. This requirement was designed to remove "any attempt by [claimants] to harass defendants, any case which was futile and any case which was misconceived or an abuse of the process of the court."[165] Such claims fail at the threshold. The claimant must also show that there is a serious question to be tried, which means that he must have a good arguable case,[166] or, in other words, a real prospect of success at the trial.[167] **25–030**

(ii) THE BALANCE OF CONVENIENCE. This concept was well known before the decision in *American Cyanamid*,[168] thus the earlier cases remain useful illustrations, but it must be borne in mind that this is now the governing consideration, assuming that the preliminary requirement outlined above is satisfied. **25–031**

We have seen that the inadequacy of damages is a significant factor in assessing the balance of convenience. The court must first of all consider the adequacy of damages to each party, namely whether damages would adequately compensate the claimant for any loss caused by the acts of the defendant prior to the trial[169] and whether, should the claimant fail at the trial, any loss caused to the

---

[162] [1976] Q.B. 122.
[163] See *British Broadcasting Corp v Hearn* [1977] 1 W.L.R. 1004; *Dunford & Elliott Ltd v Johnson & Firth Brown Ltd* [1977] 1 Lloyd's Rep. 505 at 513; *Cayne v Global Natural Resources Plc* [1984] 1 All E.R. 225.
[164] [1976] Q.B. 142. Lord Denning M.R. dissented.
[165] *Honeywell Information Systems Ltd v Anglian Water Authority, The Times,* June 29, 1976 (Geoffrey Lane L.J.).
[166] *Morning Star Cooperative Society Ltd v Express Newspapers Ltd, The Times,* October 18, 1978; cf. *Derby & Co Ltd v Weldon* [1990] Ch. 48; below, para.25–084.
[167] *Re Lord Cable* [1977] 1 W.L.R. 7 at 20; *Smith v Inner London Education Authority* [1978] 1 All E.R. 411; *Cayne v Global Natural Resources Plc,* above, fn.163.
[168] [1975] A.C. 396. The "balance of justice" was preferred in *Att Gen v Barker* [1990] 3 All E.R. 257 at 260.
[169] See *Lion Laboratories Ltd v Evans* [1985] Q.B. 526.

defendant by the grant of the injunction could be adequately compensated by the claimant's undertaking in damages.[170]

An example of irreparable loss is the distribution of a dividend to shareholders on the basis of supposedly erroneous calculations.[171] Another is the loss of trade when members of the public "picketed" the claimant's business premises,[172] or when a trade union proposed unlawfully to induce the claimant's employees to break their contracts by supporting a political strike[173]; the loss cannot be measured, but it may be great. Similarly, the publication of confidential material,[174] or the loss of a job with good prospects.[175] Damages will also be inadequate where, if a doctor did not obtain an injunction to restrain the termination of his contract, he would lose the chance to clear his name at disciplinary proceedings.[176] Likewise if the defendant does not have the means to pay any appreciable damages,[177] or if the damages would be unquantifiable,[178] as in the case of injury to goodwill[179] or reputation.[180]

While the adequacy of damages is a most significant factor, other considerations may be taken into account in assessing the balance of convenience. Where the dispute between the parties is a political one, the damage to both parties may not be calculable in monetary terms.[181] All the circumstances must be considered, including difficulties of compliance or enforcement, and the principle that the

---

[170] *Chancellor, Masters and Scholars of the University of Oxford v Pergamon Press Ltd* (1977) 121 S.J. 758. See also *Laws v Florinpace Ltd* [1981] 1 All E.R. 659 (injunction to restrain nuisance by running "sex shop" in residential area).

[171] *Bloxham v Metropolitan Ry* (1868) L.R. 3 Ch.App. 337.

[172] *Hubbard v Pitt* [1976] Q.B. 142, below, para.25–032. See also *Cutsforth v Mansfield Inns Ltd* [1986] 1 W.L.R. 558.

[173] *Express Newspapers Ltd v Keys* [1980] I.R.L.R. 247.

[174] *Att Gen v Guardian Newspapers Ltd* [1987] 1 W.L.R. 1248 (*Spycatcher*). But the perpetual injunction was refused: *Att Gen v Guardian Newspapers (No.2)* [1990] 1 A.C. 109.

[175] *Fellowes & Son v Fisher* [1976] Q.B. 122, below, para.25–032; *Powell v London Borough of Brent* [1987] I.R.L.R. 466.

[176] *Kircher v Hillingdon Primary Care Trust* [2006] Lloyd's Rep. Med. 215.

[177] *Morning Star Cooperative Society Ltd v Express Newspapers Ltd*, *The Times*, October 18, 1978; *De Falco v Crawley BC* [1980] Q.B. 460 (no injunction where claimant could not give worthwhile undertaking in damages); cf. *Bunn v British Broadcasting Corp* [1998] 3 All E.R. 552 at 558. See also *Thomas Marshall (Exports) Ltd v Guinle* [1979] Ch. 227; *Araci v Fallon* [2011] EWCA Civ 668, [2011] All E.R. (D) 37.

[178] *Morning Star Cooperative Society Ltd v Express Newspapers Ltd*, above, fn.177. See also *Express Newspapers Ltd v Keys*, above, fn.173; *Araci v Fallon*, above, fn.177 (breach of contract not to ride horse other than claimant's in the Derby).

[179] *Chancellor, Masters and Scholars of the University of Oxford v Pergamon Press Ltd* (1977) 121 S.J. 758.

[180] *British Broadcasting Corp v Hearn* [1977] 1 W.L.R. 1004. (Injunction to restrain interference with claimant's broadcast of the Cup Final to South Africa); *Schering Chemicals Ltd v Falkman Ltd* [1982] Q.B. 1.

[181] See *Lewis v Heffer* [1978] 1 W.L.R. 1061. Geoffrey Lane L.J., at 1078, found great difficulty in applying *American Cyanamid* in such a case.

court should be reluctant to interfere in industrial disputes or politi-cal decisions by injunction.[182] In *Smith v Inner London Education Authority*,[183] where an interlocutory injunction was sought to re-strain an alleged breach of statutory duty, it was said that where the defendant is a public body, the balance of convenience must be looked at more widely; the court must consider the interests of the general public to whom the duty is owed. The public interest was also a relevant consideration in *Express Newspapers Ltd v Keys*,[184] where an interlocutory injunction was granted to restrain a trade union from unlawfully inducing a breach of contract by the claim-ant's employees, by persuading them to support a political strike. If the injunction was refused, the employer would suffer unquantifi-able damage, whereas if it was granted, the union would suffer no harm save political embarrassment. It was in the interest of the members of the union and of the public that the injunction be granted.

If the balance of convenience does not clearly favour either party, then, as we have seen, the deciding factor will be the preservation of the status quo.[185] This means the circumstances prevailing when the defendant began the activity which the claimant seeks to restrain,[186] "but it is of course impossible to stop the world pending trial."[187]

We have also seen that the relative strength of each party's case is a factor to be considered as a last resort, and only then if the strength of one party's case is disproportionate to that of the other.[188] Prior to the decision in *American Cyanamid*,[189] however, this was a vital consideration: the claimant had to show a strong prima facie case. This departure from the previous practice was regarded as a source of difficulty by the Court of Appeal in *Fellowes & Son v Fisher*,[190] where it was felt that the relative strength of the parties must be a

---

[182] *Meade v London Borough of Haringey* [1979] 1 W.L.R. 637, above, para.25–020; *Jakeman v South West Thames Regional Health Authority and London Ambulance Service* [1990] I.R.L.R. 62.

[183] [1978] 1 All E.R. 411. (Injunction to restrain phasing out of grammar schools refused.) See also *R. v Ministry of Agriculture Fisheries and Food, Ex p. Monsanto Plc* [1999] Q.B. 116.

[184] [1980] I.R.L.R. 247, above, para.25–017.

[185] See *Lewis v Heffer* [1978] 1 W.L.R. 1061; *Chancellor, Masters and Scholars of the University of Oxford v Pergamon Press Ltd* (1977) 121 S.J. 758.

[186] *Fellowes & Son v Fisher* [1976] Q.B. 122 at 141; *Garden Cottage Foods Ltd v Milk Marketing Board* [1984] A.C. 130. But delay by the claimant will be taken into account in considering this principle: *Shepherd Homes Ltd v Sandham* [1971] Ch. 340, below, para.25–043.

[187] *National Commercial Bank Jamaica Ltd v Olint Corporation Ltd (Practice Note)* [2009] 1 W.L.R. 1405 at 1409.

[188] Relative strength was decisive in *Cambridge Nutrition Ltd v British Broadcasting Corp* [1990] 3 All E.R. 523, where the timing of a broadcast was vital and a contract to restrain it was doubtful.

[189] [1975] A.C. 396.

[190] [1976] Q.B. 122, below. See further *Series 5 Software Ltd v Clarke* [1996] 1 All E.R. 853; *Intelsec Systems Ltd v Grech-Cini* [2000] 1 W.L.R. 1190.

factor in assessing the balance of convenience, and that sometimes
the court could not do justice without considering the merits. The
view was expressed that perhaps the House of Lords had not had all
types of cases in mind.[191]

25–032   (iii) OTHER SPECIAL FACTORS. Lord Diplock in *American
Cyanamid* concluded his exposition of the guiding principles by
saying that "other special factors" may have to be considered in
individual cases. A question which arises is whether these special
factors are merely an aspect of the balance of convenience, or
whether they justify a departure from the principles laid down in
American Cyanamid and a return to the previous practice of requiring a prima facie case.

> In *Fellowes & Son v Fisher*,[192] the claimants, a firm of solici-
> tors, sought to restrain the breach of a restrictive covenant in the
> contract of a former employee. The covenant was of doubtful
> validity, but there was a serious question to be tried. As there was
> no evidence as to the adequacy of damages to either party, the
> decisive factor, according to the majority of the Court of Appeal,
> was the balance of convenience, which favoured refusal of the
> injunction.

Lord Denning M.R., refusing the injunction on different grounds,
did not feel bound by *American Cyanamid*.[193] There were two escape routes from it. First, Lord Diplock had indicated that other
special factors could be considered in individual cases. These "individual cases" were numerous and important, and included the present case. Secondly, the relative strength of the parties could be
looked at where the court found that there was little difference in the
uncompensatable disadvantages to both sides. Thus the injunction
should be refused because there was no prima facie case.

The question next arose in *Hubbard v Pitt*.[194]

> Certain members of the public disapproved of the extensive
> development which had taken place in Islington, and they pick-
> eted a leading firm of estate agents which had acted in connection
> with many developments in the area. The pickets held placards
> and distributed leaflets to passers-by, thus impeding access to the
> premises, and deterring potential clients. The estate agents ob-
> tained an injunction to restrain them and this was upheld by the
> majority of the Court of Appeal.

[191] Possible special cases are dealt with below.
[192] [1976] Q.B. 122.
[193] [1975] A.C. 396.
[194] [1976] Q.B. 142; P. Wallington (1976) 35 C.L.J. 82.

There was a serious question to be tried, and the balance of convenience favoured the grant. Damages could not compensate the claimants for loss of business, even if the defendants could pay, whereas the injunction would not prevent a legitimate campaign. The majority held that there were no circumstances in which "special factors" would take a case out of the general rule that no prima facie case was required.

> "It appears to me clear beyond peradventure that Lord Diplock was there referring to special factors affecting the balance of convenience and not to special factors enabling the court to ignore the general principles laid down or, more particularly, to ignore ... the admonition not to require of a party seeking an interlocutory injunction that he should have made out a prima facie case." [195]

But Lord Denning M.R. again held that "special factors" took the case out of the *American Cyanamid* rules. In his view a prima facie case was required. The appeal should be allowed because the injunction would interfere with free speech and the right to demonstrate and protest.

The better view, it is submitted, is that "special factors" are merely an aspect of the balance of convenience. In *Smith v Inner London Education Authority* [196] it was held, as we have seen, that where the defendant is a public body, the balance of convenience must be looked at more widely, and the interests of the general public, to whom the defendant's duties are owed, must be considered. This was treated as a "special factor". Similarly where an injunction is sought to prevent a public authority from enforcing a law which is claimed to be invalid (as being incompatible with European Community law). In such an exceptional case an injunction should not be granted unless there is firm ground for the challenge, and the public interest must be considered when assessing the balance of convenience. [197]

It has long been established that interlocutory injunctions will rarely be granted in libel cases where the defendant intends to justify. [198] It has been held that *American Cyanamid* has not affected

---

[195] [1976] Q.B. 142 at 185, per Stamp L.J.

[196] [1978] 1 All E.R. 411. See also *Lewis v Heffer* [1978] 1 W.L.R. 1061, above; *Bryanston Finance Ltd v de Vries (No.2)* [1976] Ch. 63, below; *Belize Alliance of Conservation Non-Governmental Organisations v Department of the Environment of Belize* [2003] 1 W.L.R. 2839.

[197] *R. v Secretary of State for Transport, Ex p. Factortame (No.2)* [1991] 1 A.C. 603; A. Zuckerman (1991) 107 L.Q.R. 196.

[198] *Bonnard v Perryman* [1891] 2 Ch. 269, below, para.25–068; *Greene v Associated Newspapers Ltd* [2005] Q.B. 972. See also *Hubbard v Vosper* [1972] 2 Q.B. 84 (similarly in copyright actions where reasonable defence of fair dealing). See further para.25–037, below, on human rights considerations.

this principle,[199] which might, therefore, be regarded as a "special factor". Similarly the rule that a bank will not be enjoined from paying under a letter of credit unless there is a clear prima facie case of fraud by the beneficiary.[200] Special considerations affecting the grant of search orders and asset-freezing interlocutory injunctions are discussed elsewhere.[201]

25–033   (b) *Exceptional cases*. The following are cases where the *American Cyanamid* principles do not apply, or apply in modified form. Other exceptional cases may arise outside these categories.[202] Thus it has been held that *American Cyanamid* is inapplicable to an order to give life-sustaining treatment to a child.[203] Nor does it apply where there is a clear statutory power to grant an injunction.[204] Indeed, the growing number of exceptions may indicate that the principles are flawed.[205]

25–034   (i) TRADE DISPUTES. After the decision in *American Cyanamid*, provisions now found in s.221(2) of the Trade Union and Labour Relations (Consolidation) Act 1992[206] were enacted, providing that where, in an application for an interlocutory injunction, the defendant claims that he acted in contemplation or furtherance of a trade dispute, the court in exercising its discretion is to have regard to the likelihood of the defendant's establishing at the trial any of the matters which, under the Act, confer immunity from tortious liability.[207] Thus *American Cyanamid* is modified in trade dispute cases by the opportunity for the defendant to prove a prima facie defence under the labour relations legislation.

The reason for this amendment was that applications for injunctions in industrial disputes rarely went beyond the interlocutory stage, and if *American Cyanamid* was applied without modification, the balance of convenience would invariably favour the claimant

---

[199] *J Trevor & Sons v P R Solomon* (1978) 248 E.G. 779 (per Lord Denning M.R.); *Bestobell Paints Ltd v Bigg* (1975) 119 S.J. 678; *Herbage v Pressdram Ltd* [1984] 1 W.L.R. 1160; *Att Gen v British Broadcasting Corp* [1981] A.C. 303 at 342 (expressing a similar principle as to contempt in civil actions); *Gulf Oil (Great Britain) Ltd v Page* [1987] Ch. 327; *Holley v Smyth* [1998] Q.B. 726.

[200] See *Group Josi Re v Walbrook Insurance Co Ltd* [1996] 1 W.L.R. 1152.

[201] Below, para.25–084.

[202] *R. v Secretary of State for Health, Ex p. Generics (UK) Ltd, The Times*, February 25, 1997. For community law considerations, see *R. v Secretary of State for Health, Ex p. Imperial Tobacco Ltd* [2001] 1 W.L.R. 127.

[203] *Re J (A Minor) (Medical Treatment)* [1993] Fam. 15.

[204] *Runnymede BC v Harwood* (1994) 68 P. & C.R. 300 (Town and Country Planning Act 1990 s.187B).

[205] See J. Martin (1993) 3 Carib. L.R. 76 and (1993–94) 4 K.C.L.J. 52; A. Zuckerman (1993) 56 M.L.R. 325 at 328.

[206] The amendments have been said to have made little impact; B. Simpson (1987) 50 M.L.R. 506. See also s.221(1) (orders without notice).

[207] See s.219 of the 1992 Act.

(i.e. the employer),[208] thus denying the trade unions their power to pressurise employers. Industrial action is unlikely to be effective if it has to be postponed, thus the unions' bargaining counter would disappear. In view of the immunity from liability in tort mentioned above, this might be thought to be unfair.[209] But trade dispute cases should not be approached on the basis that they will not go to trial.[210] Since the Employment Act 1982 the injunction may be sought against the union itself, as opposed to an office-holder personally, which increases the likelihood of a trial.[211]

A question which arises is whether the predecessor to s.221(2) restored the previous law, requiring a prima facie case, to interlocutory injunctions concerning trade disputes,[212] or whether it merely added an extra element to the *American Cyanamid*[213] principles. It is submitted that the latter is the correct approach.[214] Sometimes the likelihood of the defendant's establishing the defence of statutory immunity has been regarded simply as an aspect of the balance of convenience.[215] Perhaps the better view[216] is that it adds a third stage to the enquiry. Thus the court must consider first whether there is a serious question to be tried, secondly the balance of convenience, and thirdly the likelihood of the establishment of the defence of statutory immunity.[217]

Section 221(2) requires the court to "have regard" to the likelihood of the defence of statutory immunity succeeding at the trial. Thus the injunction will not normally be granted where the likelihood is that this defence would succeed.[218] But even in such a case the court retains a residual discretion which it may exercise in favour of granting the injunction, for example if the industrial action "endangers the nation or puts at risk such fundamental rights as the

---

[208] Especially in public service disputes, where public interest is relevant to the balance of convenience; see *Beaverbrook Newspapers Ltd v Keys* [1978] I.R.L.R. 34.

[209] See *NWL Ltd v Woods* [1979] 1 W.L.R. 1294; R. Simpson (1980) 43 M.L.R. 327; A. Clarke and J. Bowers (1980) 96 L.Q.R. 189. *Woods* was regarded as of general application and not confined to trade disputes in *Cayne v Global Natural Resources Plc* [1984] 1 All E.R. 225; below, para.25–035.

[210] *Hadmor Productions Ltd v Hamilton* [1983] 1 A.C. 191; *Dimbleby & Sons Ltd v National Union of Journalists* [1984] 1 W.L.R. 427; H. Carty (1984) 100 L.Q.R. 342.

[211] Below, para.25–035.

[212] See *The Camilla M* [1979] 1 Lloyd's Rep. 26; B. Doyle (1979) 42 M.L.R. 458.

[213] [1975] A.C. 396.

[214] See *NWL Ltd v Woods* [1979] 1 W.L.R. 1294; *British Broadcasting Corp v Hearn* [1977] 1 W.L.R. 1004; Lord Wedderburn (1978) 41 M.L.R. 80; R. Kidner (1977) 127 N.L.J. 654; *Hadmor Productions Ltd v Hamilton*, above, fn.210.

[215] *NWL Ltd v Woods*, above, fn.214 (Lords Diplock and Fraser).

[216] So considered by Lord Wedderburn in (1978) 41 M.L.R. 80 and (1980) 43 M.L.R. 319. See also R. Simpson (1980) 43 M.L.R. 372.

[217] *British Broadcasting Corp v Hearn* [1977] 1 W.L.R. 1004 at 1016 (Scarman L.J.); *NWL Ltd v Woods*, above, fn.214, at 1315 (Lord Scarman).

[218] As to the degree of likelihood necessary to produce this result, see *Duport Steels Ltd v Sirs* [1980] 1 W.L.R. 142; *Hadmor Productions Ltd v Hamilton* [1983] 1 A.C. 191.

right of the public to be informed and the freedom of the Press,"[219]
or "would probably have an immediate and devastating effect on the
applicant's person or property" or would "cause immediate serious
danger to public safety or health."[220] But such cases would be
"altogether exceptional", because, "When disaster threatens, it is
ordinarily for the government, not the courts, to act to avert it."[221]
Where it is unlikely that the defence of statutory immunity will be
established, it does not always follow that an injunction is appropriate, for example if it would be of no practical use.[222]

25–035   (ii) WHERE TRIAL OF THE ACTION UNLIKELY OR DELAYED. We
have seen that Lord Denning M.R. in *Fellowes & Son v Fisher*[223]
preferred the "prima facie case" approach to the principles laid
down in *American Cyanamid* because most cases never went to trial;
and also that amendment was required in the area of trade disputes
for the same reason.[224] It has since been held by the Court of Appeal
in *Cayne v Global Natural Resources Plc*[225] that the *American Cyanamid* principles do not apply to cases where no trial is likely to take
place. Likewise in a restraint of trade case if the trial is unlikely to
come on before the end of the period of the restraint.[226] Where the
question is whether information can be published in spite of its
confidentiality, delay in coming to trial could result in the stifling of
legitimate comment until it is no longer important if only an arguable case is required.[227] In these cases it is best to decide on the basis
of relative strength, otherwise the defendant might be effectively
precluded at the interlocutory stage from disputing the claim at
trial.

In the area of trade disputes, however, it is possible to obtain an
injunction and damages against the union itself as opposed to an
office-holder personally, and to obtain substantial damages.[228] This
means that there is no reason for a judge to exercise his discretion on

---

[219] *Express Newspapers Ltd v MacShane* [1980] A.C. 672 at 695 (Lord Scarman). See also
the views of Lords Diplock and Scarman in *NWL Ltd v Woods* [1979] 1 W.L.R. 1294.

[220] *Duport Steels Ltd v Sirs* [1980] 1 W.L.R. 142 at 166 (Lord Fraser).

[221] [1980] 1 W.L.R. 142 at 171. The existence of this residual discretion has been challenged; Lord Wedderburn and R. Simpson (1980) 43 M.L.R. 319 at 326, and at 327.

[222] *Hadmor Productions Ltd v Hamilton*, above, fn.210; R. Simpson (1982) 45
M.L.R. 447.

[223] [1976] Q.B. 122; above, para.25–032.

[224] Above, para.25–034.

[225] [1984] 1 All E.R. 225, applying *NWL Ltd v Woods* [1979] 1 W.L.R. 1294; *Thomas v
National Union of Mineworkers (South Wales Area)* [1986] Ch. 20; K. Ewing (1985) 44 C.L.J.
374; *Cambridge Nutrition Ltd v British Broadcasting Corp* [1990] 3 All E.R. 523. See also
Araci v Fallon [2011] EWCA Civ 668, [2011] All E.R. (D) 37 (to restrain breach of contract
not to ride horse other than claimant's in the Derby).

[226] *David (Lawrence) Ltd v Ashton* [1991] 1 All E.R. 385; *Lansing Linde Ltd v Kerr* [1991]
1 W.L.R. 251 (treated as a "wider view of the balance of convenience").

[227] *Att Gen v Times Newspapers Ltd* [1992] 1 A.C. 191 at 226.

[228] Trade Union and Labour Relations (Consolidation) Act 1992 ss.20–23.

the assumption that the case will not proceed to trial in cases where the union itself is the defendant.[229]

(iii) WHERE NO ARGUABLE DEFENCE. It has been held that the **25–036** *American Cyanamid*[230] rules do not apply where the defendant has no arguable defence.[231] In such a case it is not necessary to consider the balance of convenience. Thus the claimant may obtain an interlocutory injunction to restrain a clear trespass even where it causes no damage[232]; or to restrain a clear misapplication of union funds.[233] The principle that the claimant is entitled almost as of right to an injunction to restrain a plain breach of a negative contract provides another example.[234]

(iv) HUMAN RIGHTS ACT 1998: FREEDOM OF EXPRESSION. Article **25–037** 10 of the European Convention on Human Rights protects the right to freedom of expression, subject to certain qualifications. Section 12 of the Human Rights Act 1998 applies where a court is considering whether to grant any relief which, if granted, might affect the exercise of the Convention right to freedom of expression. Section 12(3) provides that no such relief is to be granted so as to restrain publication before trial unless the court is "satisfied that the applicant is likely to establish that publication should not be allowed". Under s.12(4) the court must have particular regard to the importance of the Convention right to freedom of expression and, where the proceedings relate to material which appears to be journalistic, literary or artistic, to the extent to which the material has or is about to become available to the public, or to which publication is or would be in the public interest, and to any relevant privacy code.

Thus where interlocutory injunctions are sought to restrain publication before trial in cases involving breach of confidence, privacy or libel,[235] the court must look at the strength of the case and not

---

[229] *Dimbleby & Sons Ltd v National Union of Journalists* [1984] 1 W.L.R. 427; H. Carty (1984) 100 L.Q.R. 342; B Simpson (1984) 47 M.L.R. 577; *Hadmor Productions Ltd v Hamilton* [1983] 1 A.C. 191.

[230] [1975] A.C. 396.

[231] *Official Custodian for Charities v Mackey* [1985] Ch. 168; *Love v Herrity* (1991) 23 H.L.R. 217.

[232] *Patel v WH Smith (Eziot) Ltd* [1987] 1 W.L.R. 853; *Anchor Brewhouse Developments Ltd v Berkley House (Docklands Developments) Ltd* [1987] 2 E.G.L.R. 173; *London & Manchester Assurance Co Ltd v O & H Construction Ltd* [1989] 2 E.G.L.R. 185.

[233] *Taylor v National Union of Mineworkers (Derbyshire Area), The Times*, December 29, 1984.

[234] *Doherty v Allman* (1878) 3 App.Cas. 709; below, para.25–054, applied to interlocutory injunctions in *Hampstead & Suburban Properties Ltd v Diomedous* [1969] 1 Ch. 248; *Att Gen v Barker* [1990] 3 All E.R. 257; *Araci v Fallon* [2011] EWCA Civ 668, [2011] All E.R. (D) 37.

[235] For special factors relating to interlocutory injunctions in libel cases, see para.25–032, above. The principles applicable in these cases are not affected by s.12(3); *Greene v Associated Newspapers Ltd* [2005] Q.B. 972.

apply *American Cyanamid*. The word "likely" in s.12(3) means that the claimant must normally show that he will probably succeed at the trial, although a lesser degree of likelihood will suffice in some cases, for example where the consequences of publication would be particularly grave.[236] In any event, even if the claimant does satisfy this test, it does not follow that the injunction must be granted, as factors such as the balance of convenience must still be considered. So in *Douglas v Hello! Ltd*,[237] where a celebrity couple sought to restrain publication of wedding photographs by the defendant magazine in breach of exclusive rights agreed with a rival magazine, they were left to their remedy in damages. Although the test in s.12(3) was satisfied, the balance of convenience favoured the defendant in view of the publicity organised by the claimants. However, this result has been criticised.[238]

25–038   (v) INJUNCTIONS TO RESTRAIN THE PRESENTATION OF A WINDING-UP PETITION. It has been held that a prima facie case (of abuse of process) is still required where a company seeks to restrain a creditor from presenting a winding-up petition.[239] If a prospective petitioner intends to petition on the basis of a debt alleged to be presently due, and there is a bona fide dispute as to whether it is presently due, it has been held by the Court of Appeal that the company is entitled as of right to an interlocutory injunction restraining the presentation of the petition, other than on the basis of a contingent or future debt.[240]

Difficulty was also experienced in applying the *American Cyanamid* rules where a company sought an interlocutory injunction to restrain a takeover bid.[241]

25–039   (vi) MANDATORY INTERLOCUTORY INJUNCTIONS. *American Cyanamid* itself involved a prohibitory injunction, but the principles there expressed were not intended to be confined to such applications, as has recently been confirmed by the Privy Council.[242] But it

---

[236] *Cream Holdings Ltd v Banerjee* [2005] 1 A.C. 253; A. Zuckerman All E.R. Rev. 2004 p.296; A. Smith (2005) 64 C.L.J. 4; *CC v AB* [2007] 2 F.L.R. 301; *Browne of Madingley (Lord) v Associated Newspapers Ltd* [2008] Q.B. 103.

[237] [2001] Q.B. 967; N. Moreham (2001) 64 M.L.R. 767.

[238] *Douglas v Hello! Ltd (No.3)* [2006] Q.B. 125.

[239] *Bryanston Finance Ltd v De Vries (No.2)* [1976] Ch. 63. But Buckley L.J., at 78, regarded this as a "special factor". The other members of the Court of Appeal said that *American Cyanamid* did not apply. See P. Wallington (1976) 35 C.L.J. 82 at 86. *American Cyanamid* was applied, albeit with difficulty, in *Re Euro Hotel (Belgravia) Ltd* [1975] 3 All E.R. 1075.

[240] *Stonegate Securities Ltd v Gregory* [1980] Ch. 576 (*American Cyanamid* was not cited).

[241] *Dunford & Elliott Ltd v Johnson & Firth Brown Ltd* [1977] 1 Lloyd's Rep. 505. Lord Denning M.R. held that the *American Cyanamid* principles did not apply, but Lawton and Roskill L.JJ. preferred to apply those principles, notwithstanding the difficulties.

[242] *National Commercial Bank Jamaica Ltd v Olint Corporation Ltd (Practice Note)* [2009] 1 W.L.R. 1405.

may still be said that mandatory interlocutory injunctions, which are discussed below,[243] will be granted less readily than the prohibitory, as was the case before *American Cyanamid*,[244] because the balance of convenience is likely to favour the refusal more often than the grant.[245]

The *American Cyanamid* principles have been applied to mandatory injunctions,[246] but a strong prima facie case was required in *De Falco v Crawley BC*,[247] where the claimant sought a mandatory interlocutory injunction to secure the provision of housing by the defendant. The Court of Appeal, refusing the injunction, held that the claimant had to show a strong prima facie case that the defendant's decision was invalid. Lord Denning M.R. held *American Cyanamid* to be inapplicable because the claimant could not give a worthwhile undertaking in damages.[248]

If the defendant was wrong, the claimant would suffer homelessness which was not compensatable in damages. But if the claimant was wrong, a heavy financial burden, with no prospect of recovery, would fall on the ratepayers, and there would also be a detriment to others on the housing list.[249] Therefore such an injunction should be granted only if the claimant had a strong prima facie case. *De Falco* could be regarded as a special case because of the public law element.

Finally, the search order, formerly known as an *Anton Piller* injunction,[250] which is partly mandatory, has been held to require an extremely strong prima facie case.[251] This, it is submitted, is an exceptional case because such applications are usually without notice, and because of the "draconian" nature of the injunction.[252]

iii. Mandatory Interlocutory Injunctions. These are less readily granted than prohibitory interlocutory injunctions,[253] especially

25–040

---

[243] Below, para.25–040.

[244] [1975] A.C. 396.

[245] See *Shotton v Hammond* (1976) 120 S.J. 780.

[246] *Meade v London Borough of Haringey* [1979] 1 W.L.R. 637.

[247] [1980] Q.B. 460; overruled in *Cocks v Thanet DC* [1983] 2 A.C. 286, on another point. The requirement of a strong prima facie case was upheld in *R. v Kensington and Chelsea RLBC, Ex p. Hammell* [1989] Q.B. 518 and *R. v Westminster City Council, Ex p. Augustin* [1993] 1 W.L.R. 730, regarding *De Falco* as still good law on the point.

[248] [1980] Q.B. 460 at 478. This, it is submitted, might more properly be regarded as a factor in assessing the balance of convenience.

[249] This, again, might be regarded simply as an aspect of the balance of convenience, without departing from *American Cyanamid*.

[250] *Anton Piller KG v Manufacturing Processes Ltd* [1976] Ch. 55.

[251] Below, para.25–077. See also L. Anderson (1987) 103 L.Q.R. 246, suggesting likewise in the case of an injunction against leaving the country.

[252] See *Yousif v Salama* [1980] 1 W.L.R. 1540 at 1544; below, para.25–077; *Derby & Co Ltd v Weldon (No.7)* [1990] 1 W.L.R. 1156 at 1173.

[253] *Daniel v Ferguson* [1891] 2 Ch. 27; *Shotton v Hammond* (1976) 120 S.J. 780.

on an application without notice, because the mandatory order may be more drastic in effect. If the defendant has been required to do some positive act, it may not be easy to restore the parties to their previous position if the claimant turns out to be wrong at the trial.[254]

Mandatory interlocutory injunctions will be granted in a suitable case, for example, to compel the demolition of a building where the defendant has deliberately hurried on with the building,[255] to re-instate a wrongfully evicted occupier to possession[256]; to enforce the return of passports wrongfully detained by the police[257]; to compel performance of a landlord's obligations[258]; to enforce the planning legislation[259]; to compel surrender of an unlawful sublease[260]; or in the search order cases,[261] to compel the defendant to submit articles for inspection.

The court will be reluctant to grant such an injunction where the case involves an industrial dispute,[262] but will do so in exceptional circumstances if the balance of convenience so requires. Such a case was *Parker v Camden LBC*,[263] where a strike of boilermen was endangering the life and health of council tenants. The court was prepared to grant a mandatory interlocutory injunction to resume the supply of heating and hot water.

It has been held, in a case concerning trespass by building opera-tions, that if the claimant could have got a prohibitory *quia timet* injunction to restrain the commission of the wrongful act, had he known about it in time, then the defendant should be in no better position if he in fact commits the act: a mandatory interlocutory injunction should be granted to enforce the removal of the building works.[264]

Modern decisions illustrate an increasing readiness to grant man-datory interlocutory injunctions. The principles were reviewed in

---

[254] See *Shepherd Homes Ltd v Sandham* [1971] Ch. 340 at 349.

[255] *Von Joel v Hornsey* [1895] 2 Ch. 774; *London & Manchester Assurance Co Ltd v O & H Construction Ltd* [1989] 2 E.G.L.R. 185.

[256] *Luganda v Service Hotels* [1969] 2 Ch. 209; *Parsons v Nasar* (1991) 23 H.L.R. 1.

[257] *Ghani v Jones* [1970] 1 Q.B. 693; cf. *Malone v Metropolitan Police Commissioner* [1980] Q.B. 49.

[258] *Hart v Emelkirk Ltd* [1983] 1 W.L.R. 1289; *Peninsular Maritime Ltd v Padseal Ltd* (1981) 259 E.G. 860. See also *Cork v Cork* [1997] 1 E.G.L.R. 5.

[259] *Croydon LBC v Gladden* (1994) 68 P. & C.R. 300 (removal of replica spitfire from roof).

[260] *Hemingway Securities Ltd v Dunraven Ltd* [1995] 1 E.G.L.R. 61.

[261] Below, para.25–077.

[262] *Meade v London Borough of Haringey* [1979] 1 W.L.R. 637; J. Griffiths (1979) 38 C.L.J. 228. (No injunction to reopen schools closed by a strike.) See also *Harold Stephen and Co Ltd v Post Office* [1977] 1 W.L.R. 1172, above, para.25–020. cf. *Express Newspapers Ltd v Keys* [1980] I.R.L.R. 247, where the dispute was political.

[263] [1986] Ch. 162; above, para.25–020.

[264] *Trenberth (John) Ltd v National Westminster Bank Ltd* (1979) 39 P. & C.R. 104.

Shepherd Homes Ltd v Sandham,²⁶⁵ where the defendant erected a fence in breach of covenant, which the claimant sought to have removed. Megarry J. said that the case has to be unusually strong and clear before a mandatory interlocutory injunction will be granted. The court must feel "a high degree of assurance" that at the trial it will appear that the injunction was rightly granted, and this is a higher standard than is required for a prohibitory injunction. In view of the claimant's delay, the injunction was refused.

The "high degree of assurance" test was approved by the Court of Appeal,²⁶⁶ holding that although the test was formulated before *American Cyanamid Co v Ethicon Ltd*,²⁶⁷ it was unaffected by that case. It was added that the application should be approached with caution where the relief sought on the interim application would amount to a major part of the relief claimed at the trial. The matter was recently reviewed by the Privy Council, where it was held that the underlying principles were the same whether the interlocutory injunction was mandatory or prohibitory, and indeed that arguments over the classification were "barren".²⁶⁸ The "least irremediable prejudice" principle applies to both.²⁶⁹ "What is true is that the features which ordinarily justify describing an injunction as mandatory are often more likely to cause irremediable prejudice than in cases in which a defendant is merely prevented from taking or continuing with some course of action."²⁷⁰ If it appeared likely that the injunction would cause irremediable prejudice to the defendant, the court would be reluctant to grant it unless satisfied that the chances that it would turn out at the trial to have been wrongly granted were low. In other words, the court would need to feel a "high degree of assurance" that it would appear at the trial that it had been rightly granted.

The following are cases where a mandatory interlocutory injunction was clearly required:

In *Esso Petroleum Co Ltd v Kingswood Motors*,²⁷¹ the defendant agreed with the claimant not to sell a garage without first procuring that the purchaser would enter a solus agreement with the claimant. The land was sold to a purchaser who conspired with the defendant to effect a breach. A mandatory interlocutory injunction was granted to compel a retransfer of the land to the

---

²⁶⁵ [1971] Ch. 340. See also *Astro Exito Navegacion SA v Southland Enterprise Co (No.2)* [1982] Q.B. 1248 CA; *Minja Properties Ltd v Cussins* [1998] 2 E.G.L.R. 52.
²⁶⁶ *Locabail International Finance Ltd v Agroexport* [1986] 1 W.L.R. 657.
²⁶⁷ [1975] A.C. 396; above, para.25–029.
²⁶⁸ *National Commercial Bank Jamaica Ltd v Olint Corporation Ltd (Practice Note)* [2009] 1 W.L.R. 1405.
²⁶⁹ Above, para.25–029.
²⁷⁰ [2009] 1 W.L.R. 1405 at 1409.
²⁷¹ [1974] Q.B. 142; *Hemingway Securities Ltd v Dunraven Ltd* [1995] 1 E.G.L.R. 61.

defendant. There could be no clearer case of inducing breach of contract, and damages would be wholly inadequate.

In *Sky Petroleum v VIP Petroleum Ltd*,[272] such an injunction was granted to enforce a contract to supply petrol to the claimant. As there was no alternative supply, damages would be inadequate, and the claimant might be forced out of business unless the court intervened.

In *Evans v BBC and IBA*,[273] an order was made to compel the television authorities to show a party political broadcast. On the balance of probabilities[274] there was a contract with the Welsh Nationalist Party to broadcast it. Damages would be manifestly useless, as the election was about to take place. In such a case the court should take the risk of it turning out that there was no contract.

25–041   **iv. Conditions and Undertakings.** On the grant of an interlocutory injunction, the claimant is normally required to give an undertaking in damages[275] in the event that the injunction is discharged at the trial as having been granted without good cause[276]; but a defendant may also be put on similar terms as a condition of an injunction not being granted.[277] One reason for the practice of undertakings is that it aids the court in achieving its object of abstaining from expressing any opinion on the merits until the hearing.[278] While an undertaking by the claimant is exacted for the benefit of the defendant, it is not a contract with the defendant. The undertaking is given to the court, so that non-performance is a contempt of court and not a breach of contract.[279] Enforcement is at the court's discretion.[280] Damages will normally become payable if the claimant is unsuccessful at the trial, either because he cannot establish his case or because the judge who granted the interlocutory injunction took a wrong view of the law. The claimant may be required to give security or to pay the money into court. Any damages will be assessed on the same basis as damages for breach of contract.[281] Aggravated and

---

[272] [1974] 1 W.L.R. 576. (The injunction was negative in form, but mandatory in substance.)

[273] *The Times*, February 26, 1974.

[274] cf. Megarry J.'s requirement of a "high degree of assurance", above.

[275] Or to do some other act; *PS Refson & Co Ltd v Saggers* [1984] 1 W.L.R. 1025. See generally A. Zuckerman (1994) 53 C.L.J. 546; S. Gee [2006] L.M.C.L.Q. 181.

[276] Search orders and asset-freezing injunctions, below, paras 25–077, 25–080, provide good examples of the need for undertakings. See *Digital Equipment Corp v Darkcrest Ltd* [1984] Ch. 512.

[277] *Elwes v Payne* (1879) 12 Ch.D. 468.

[278] *American Cyanamid Co v Ethicon Ltd* [1975] A.C. 396 at 407.

[279] See *Hussain v Hussain* [1986] Fam. 134; *Mid Suffolk DC v Clarke* [2007] 1 W.L.R. 980. But the undertaking may include a contractual obligation to the other party; *Midland Marts Ltd v Hobday* [1989] 1 W.L.R. 1143.

[280] *Cheltenham and Gloucester Building Society v Ricketts* [1993] 1 W.L.R. 1545.

[281] *Hoffman-La Roche (F) & Co v Secretary of State for Trade and Industry* [1975] A.C. 295 at 361, per Lord Diplock. See generally S. Ralston (2011) 127 L.Q.R. 180.

exemplary damages may be awarded if appropriate.[282] Undertakings may also extend to paying damages to third parties.[283] A claimant's refusal to seek an interlocutory injunction, in order to avoid the need to give an undertaking, is not a ground for striking out his application for a final injunction,[284] but is a factor to be taken into account.[285]

Where interlocutory injunctions are sought in matrimonial and children's matters, undertakings may be required if the claim concerns the protection of property rights, but will not be required in respect of matters concerning personal conduct.[286]

In *Hoffman-La Roche (F) & Co v Secretary of State for Trade and Industry*[287] the question arose whether the Crown should be required to give an undertaking as a condition of the grant of an interlocutory injunction to restrain the company from charging prices for drugs in excess of those specified in an order (which the company claimed was ultra vires). The House of Lords held that the undertaking should not be required.

A distinction had to be drawn between two cases: first, where the Crown was asserting a proprietary or contractual right, the ordinary rule applied and the Crown should give an undertaking; but, secondly, where an injunction was sought to enforce the law, the defendant must show special reason why justice required that it should not be granted, or should only be granted on terms. The present case was within the second category. The reason for this distinction is that where a person is prosecuted and acquitted, he may suffer loss but cannot normally recover from the prosecutor. There is therefore no reason why the Crown should incur liability when an injunction is sought to enforce the law.

This principle applies also to a local authority seeking a law-enforcement injunction[288] and to a foreign regulatory body[289]; likewise where the Attorney General acts ex officio to enforce the law by injunction. But where the Attorney General brings the action

---

[282] *Al-Rawas v Pegasus Energy Ltd* [2009] 1 All E.R. 346; A. Zuckerman All E.R. Rev. 2009, p.370.

[283] CPR 25 *Practice Direction* 5.1A. See generally *SmithKline Beecham Plc v Apotex Europe Ltd* [2007] Ch. 71; A. Zuckerman All E.R. Rev. 2006, p.312.

[284] *Oxy Electric Ltd v Zainuddin* [1991] 1 W.L.R. 115, doubting *Blue Town Investments Ltd v Higgs & Hill Plc* [1990] 1 W.L.R. 696; A. Zuckerman All E.R. Rev. 1990, p.201; R. Chaplin (1991) 141 N.L.J. 243. The final injunction in *Oxy Electric* was later refused; [1990] E.G.C.S. 128.

[285] *Snell & Prideaux Ltd v Dutton Mirrors Ltd* [1995] 1 E.G.L.R. 259.

[286] *Practice Direction* [1974] 1 W.L.R. 576.

[287] [1975] A.C. 295. The statute in question expressly provided for the grant to the Crown of an injunction as the only means of enforcing the statute.

[288] *Kirklees BC v Wickes Building Supplies Ltd* [1993] A.C. 227 (Sunday trading); criticised A. Zuckerman All E.R. Rev. 1992 at 319; *Director General of Fair Trading v Tobyward Ltd* [1989] 1 W.L.R. 517. See also *Securities and Investments Board v Lloyd-Wright* [1993] 4 All E.R. 210; *Customs and Excise Commissioners v Anchor Foods Ltd* [1999] 1 W.L.R. 1139.

[289] *United States Securities & Exchange Commission v Manterfield* [2010] 1 W.L.R. 172; P. Rogerson All E.R. Rev. 2009, p.98.

under the relator procedure, the relator must give the usual undertaking,[290] as must a local authority acting as a relator.[291]

E. *Quia Timet* Injunctions

25–042   A *quia timet* injunction may be available where the injury to the claimant's rights has not yet occurred, but is feared or threatened.[292] The injunction may be perpetual or interlocutory, prohibitory or mandatory. It may further be subdivided into two broad categories:

"[F]irst, where the defendant[293] has as yet done no hurt to the [claimant] but is threatening and intending (so the [claimant] alleges) to do works which will render irreparable harm to him or his property if carried to completion . . . those cases are normally, though not exclusively, concerned with negative injunctions. Secondly, the type of case where the [claimant] has been fully recompensed both at law and in equity for the damage he has suffered but where he alleges that the earlier actions of the defendant may lead to future causes of action . . . It is in this field that the undoubted jurisdiction of equity to grant a mandatory injunction . . . finds its main expression."[294]

How serious must the fears of the claimant be, and how grave the suspected damage? As Lord Dunedin has said, it is not sufficient to say "timeo".[295] The requirements have been described in the following terms: a strong case of probability[296]; proof of imminent danger, and there must also be proof that the apprehended damage will, if it comes, be very substantial.[297] Thus in *Att Gen v Nottingham Corp*[298] a *quia timet* injunction was not granted to restrain the

---

[290] *Hoffman-La Roche (F) & Co v Secretary of State for Trade and Industry*, above, fn.281, at 363.

[291] *Kirklees BC v Wickes Building Supplies Ltd*, above, fn.288.

[292] For different views on the meaning of *quia timet*, see J. Jolowicz (1975) 34 C.L.J. 224; cf. P. Pettit (1977) 36 C.L.J. 369, (1978) 37 C.L.J. 51; Spry, p.377.

[293] The defendant must himself have threatened the act in question. See *Celsteel Ltd v Alton House Holdings Ltd* [1986] 1 W.L.R. 512 (no injunction against freeholder where act threatened by tenant).

[294] *Redland Bricks Ltd v Morris* [1970] A.C. 652 at 665, per Lord Upjohn. See also *Hooper v Rogers* [1975] Ch. 43; *Allen v Greenhi Builders Ltd* [1979] 1 W.L.R. 136 (registration as "pending land action").

[295] *Att Gen for the Dominion of Canada v Ritchie Contracting and Supply Co Ltd* [1919] A.C. 999 at 1005.

[296] *Att Gen v Manchester Corp* [1893] 2 Ch. 87 at 92.

[297] *Fletcher v Bealey* (1885) 27 Ch.D. 688 at 698. cf. *Trenberth (John) Ltd v National Westminster Bank Ltd* (1979) 39 P. & C.R. 104.

[298] [1904] 1 Ch. 673; *Att Gen v Guardian Newspapers (No.2)* [1990] 1 A.C. 109 (no general injunction against publication of any material the media might obtain from Crown servants in breach of confidence). See also *British Data Management Plc v Boxer Commercial Removals Plc* [1996] 3 All E.R. 707 (libel); *Re Q's Estate* [1997] 1 Lloyd's Rep. 931 (asset freezing).

corporation from building a smallpox hospital, as there was no proof of genuine danger to nearby residents.

The principles applicable to the grant of a mandatory *quia timet* injunction were laid down by the House of Lords in *Redland Bricks Ltd v Morris*.[299]

> The defendant company's digging activities caused landslips on the claimants' adjoining property, which they used as a market garden. The claimants' land, of which about one-tenth of an acre was affected, was worth about £12,000, but the cost of remedying the landslips would be about £30,000. The claimants were awarded damages, a prohibitory injunction to restrain further withdrawal of support, and a mandatory injunction that the defendants "take all necessary steps to restore support within six months." But the House of Lords allowed the defendant's appeal against the grant of the mandatory injunction on the ground that it did not specify exactly what it had to do. Lord Upjohn set out the following four principles applicable to the grant of a mandatory *quia timet* injunction.
>
> i.   The claimant must show a very strong probability that grave damage will accrue to him in the future. It is a jurisdiction to be exercised sparingly and with caution, but, in the proper case, unhesitatingly.
> ii. Damages will not be an adequate remedy if such damage does happen, applying the general principle of equity.
> iii. Unlike the case where a negative injunction is granted to prevent the continuance or recurrence of a wrongful act, the cost to the defendant to do works to prevent or lessen the likelihood of a future apprehended wrong must be taken into account:
>
>   (a) where the defendant has acted wantonly and quite unreasonably, he may be ordered to do positive work even if the expense to him is out of all proportion to the advantage thereby accruing to the claimant;
>   (b) but where the defendant has acted reasonably, although wrongly, the cost of remedying his earlier activities is most important. If it seems unreasonable to inflict such expenditure on one who is no more than a potential wrongdoer the court must exercise its jurisdiction accordingly. The court may order works which may not remedy the wrong but may lessen the likelihood of further injury. It must be borne in mind that the injury may

---

[299] [1970] A.C. 652. See critical commentary in Heydon, Gummow and Austin, *Cases and Materials on Equity and Trusts*, 4th edn, p.1050.

never in fact occur, and that, if it does, the claimant may then seek the appropriate legal or equitable remedy.

iv. If a mandatory injunction is granted, the court must see that the defendant knows exactly in fact what he has to do.[300] It was later added that, in the issue of mandatory *quia timet* injunctions, "what is aimed at is justice between the parties, having regard to all the relevant circumstances."[301]

4. Defences to Perpetual and Interlocutory Injunctions

A. Delay

25–043   As in the case of specific performance, laches may be a defence even though the claimant's rights have not become statute-barred.[302] But a smaller degree of delay will defeat a claim for an interlocutory injunction than is necessary in the case of a perpetual injunction.[303] This is because, if an interlocutory claim is dismissed, the claimant is not unduly prejudiced, as he can still seek a perpetual injunction. But the refusal of a perpetual injunction amounts to a final dismissal.

As we have seen, the claimant must act promptly in the case of an injunction without notice, as any delay illustrates that his case is not urgent.[304] Where the claimant has delayed his application for an interlocutory injunction, he is unlikely to establish that it would be unreasonable to make him wait until trial. An unexplained delay of five months prevented the grant of an interlocutory injunction in *Shepherd Homes Ltd v Sandham*,[305] where Megarry J. explained that if the injunction is also mandatory, any delay by the claimant will mean that the injunction, if granted, would disturb rather than preserve the status quo.[306] It may be otherwise, however, if there is no arguable defence.[307]

The authorities are not reconcilable on the question of delay in perpetual injunctions. It is sometimes said that laches is no defence,[308] or, to go to the other extreme, that mere lapse of time is a

---

[300] See also *Harold Stephen & Co Ltd v Post Office* [1977] 1 W.L.R. 1172; *Parsons v Nasar* (1991) 23 H.L.R. 1; *Co-operative Insurance Society Ltd v Argyll Stores (Holdings) Ltd* [1998] A.C. 1.

[301] *Hooper v Rogers* [1975] Ch. 43 at 50, per Russell L.J.

[302] See Limitation Act 1980 s.36.

[303] *Johnson v Wyatt* (1863) 2 De G.J. & S. 18.

[304] *Bates v Lord Hailsham of St Marylebone* [1972] 1 W.L.R. 1373.

[305] [1971] Ch. 340; above, para.25–040; cf. *Texaco Ltd v Mulberry Filling Station Ltd* [1972] 1 W.L.R. 814; *Express Newspapers Plc v Liverpool Daily Post and Echo Plc* [1985] 1 W.L.R. 1089; *Newport Association Football Club Ltd v Football Association of Wales Ltd* [1995] 2 All E.R. 87 (explanation for delay).

[306] See *Shotton v Hammond* (1976) 120 S.J. 780: mandatory interlocutory injunction granted in spite of delay of six weeks by the claimant, who was not legally aided.

[307] See *Patel v WH Smith (Eziot) Ltd* [1987] 1 W.L.R. 853.

[308] *Archbold v Scully* (1861) 9 H.L.C. 360 at 383.

bar.[309] In *Kelsen v Imperial Tobacco Co Ltd*[310] a mandatory injunction was granted to restrain a trespass even though it appeared that the state of affairs had existed for seven years. In *Fullwood v Fullwood*,[311] Fry J. held that a delay of two to three years was no defence, on the ground that mere lapse of time unaccompanied by acquiescence was no bar unless the legal right itself was barred.

In *HP Bulmer Ltd & Showerings Ltd v Bollinger SA*[312] the appel-   **25–044** lants had described their products as "champagne perry" and "champagne cider" since 1950 and 1906 respectively. The latter usage had been known to the respondents since about 1930. Injunctions were granted in the High Court to restrain both descriptions. The defence of delay failed. This was a continuing wrong, and the right in question was legal. Whitford J. held that in such a case the delay must be "inordinate" if it is to prevent the grant of an injunction. Here it was not, because advice had to be sought, and interests consulted. One injunction was discharged by the Court of Appeal because passing-off was not established, but their Lordships considered that the injunction would not have been refused on account of delay. Goff L.J. thought that "inordinate" delay would be a ground for refusing an injunction, even in the case of a legal right, but that delay in the present case was not of that order. The issue was more recently aired in the House of Lords in a case where the claimant sought a declaration to recognise his entitlement to royalties in connection with his organ solo in 1967 in the highly successful recording of the song "A Whiter Shade of Pale".[313] There was no statutory limitation period, but he had delayed 38 years in making the claim. As a declaration as to the existence of a long term property right was not equitable relief, it could not be barred by laches or acquiescence. In any event, no prejudice to the defendants resulting from the delay, which would be necessary if the defence had been available, had been shown.

Laches may be regarded more strictly if third parties would be affected. It is possible that a claimant who has delayed will be awarded damages in lieu of an injunction under Lord Cairns' Act.[314]

It has been suggested that a longer delay is required before a claimant will be refused an injunction where the right is legal than

---

[309] *Brooks v Muckleston* [1909] 2 Ch. 519.

[310] [1957] 2 Q.B. 334; cf. *Lester v Woodgate* [2010] 2 P. & C.R. 21.

[311] (1878) 9 Ch.D. 176.

[312] [1977] 2 C.M.L.R. 625, CA. cf. *Vine Products Ltd v McKenzie & Co Ltd* (1969) R.P.C. 1 (no injunction to restrain description as "sherry", the usage having been common knowledge for 100 years). See also *Erlanger v New Sombrero Phosphate Co* (1873) 3 App.Cas. 1218 at 1279–1280.

[313] *Fisher v Brooker* [2009] 1 W.L.R. 1764.

[314] *Shelfer v City of London Electric Lighting Co* [1895] 1 Ch. 287 at 322; see also *Bracewell v Appleby* [1975] Ch. 408; *Ketley v Gooden* (1997) 73 P. & C.R. 305.

where it is equitable[315]; or alternatively that a less strict view of laches might be taken as to matters within equity's exclusive jurisdiction, such as a breach of trust, where there is no alternative remedy at law.[316] But the Court of Appeal has described the distinction between legal and equitable rights in this context as archaic and arcane.[317]

Finally, where an injunction is sought in a claim for judicial review,[318] it is provided that, in the case of "undue delay", the injunction may be refused if the granting of relief "would be likely to cause substantial hardship to, or substantially prejudice the rights of, any person or would be detrimental to good administration."[319]

B. Acquiescence[320]

25–045   Lapse of time will be taken into account in that it may indicate acquiescence. It is, of course, possible to find acquiescence without delay and delay without acquiescence but there is normally some overlap.[321] As in the case of laches, a greater degree of acquiescence is needed to defeat a claim for a final injunction than an interlocutory injunction. It has also been suggested that acquiescence is easier to establish where the right in question is equitable only,[322] but this is now discredited.[323] In *Richards v Revitt*[324] it was said that the fact that the claimant has previously overlooked trivial breaches of covenant does not debar him, on the ground of acquiescence, from acting on a serious breach. A leading authority is *Sayers v Collyer*,[325] where a house was being used as a beershop in breach of covenant. The claimant could not get an injunction, as he had known of the breach for three years, and, furthermore, had bought beer there. This was sufficient to bar any remedy. But a lesser degree of acquiescence, while not sufficient to bar the action completely,

---

[315] *Cluett Peabody & Co Inc v McIntyre Hogg Marsh and Co Ltd* [1958] R.P.C. 335 at 354, per Upjohn J.; *HP Bulmer and Showerings Ltd v J Bollinger SA*, above, fn.312.

[316] See Spry, *Equitable Remedies*, p.437; *Knight v Bowyer* (1858) 2 De G. & J. 421; cf. *Oxy Electric Ltd v Zainuddin* [1990] E.G.C.S. 128 (final injunction to enforce restrictive covenant refused because of seven month delay).

[317] *Habib Bank Ltd v Habib Bank AG Zurich* [1981] 1 W.L.R. 1265 at 1285 and 1287; cf. Spry, p.437.

[318] Below, para.25–072.

[319] Senior Courts Act 1981 s.31(6); CPR 1998, Pt 54.5.

[320] See Limitation Act 1980 s.36(2). The Act does not affect this defence.

[321] See the discussion in *Fisher v Brooker* [2009] 1 W.L.R. 1764; above, para.25–045.

[322] *Shaw v Applegate* [1977] 1 W.L.R. 970 at 979 (the right in this case was legal).

[323] *Habib Bank Ltd v Habib Bank AG Zurich*, above, fn.317; *Gafford v Graham* (1999) 77 P. & C.R. 73 at 80–81.

[324] (1877) 7 Ch.D. 224 at 226.

[325] (1885) 28 Ch.D. 103.

might be a reason for giving damages in lieu of an injunction under Lord Cairns' Act.

In *Shaw v Applegate*[326] the claimant sought to enforce a covenant entered into by the defendant in 1967 not to use his land as an "amusement arcade". Breaches of covenant occurred from about 1971. The claimant was aware of the facts but was unsure whether they constituted a breach of covenant. He began proceedings for an injunction in 1973, but did not seek interlocutory relief, so that the defendant continued to carry on his business, investing money and building up goodwill, until the trial in 1976. It was held that the claimant was not guilty of such a degree of acquiescence as to bar all remedies, the real test being whether, on the facts of the particular case, it would be dishonest or unconscionable for him to seek to enforce his rights.[327] This was not the case, because of the claimant's doubts as to his legal rights. But there was sufficient acquiescence to bar the remedy of an injunction because the defendant had been lulled into a false sense of security by the claimant's inactivity and failure to seek interlocutory relief. Thus the appropriate remedy was damages in lieu of an injunction under Lord Cairns' Act.

Similarly in *Gafford v Graham*,[328] where the claimant sought mandatory and prohibitory injunctions to demolish a building erected in breach of covenant and to restrain an unlawful use of the land. In the case of one breach where, knowing of his rights, he had failed to complain for three years, all relief was barred by acquiescence. In the case of another breach, the claimant had acted promptly but had not sought interlocutory relief. This was an important factor which made a final injunction inappropriate, thus damages were awarded. The modern approach to acquiescence is to enquire:

(a) whether the defendant was encouraged to believe he was entitled to act as he did; and
(b) if so, whether the encouragement caused detriment; and
(c) if so, whether it was unconscionable in all the circumstances for the claimant to assert his legal rights.[329]

---

[326] [1977] 1 W.L.R. 970; F. Crane (1977) 41 Conv.(N.S.) 355. See also on this point *Sayers v Collyer* (1885) 28 Ch.D. 103 at 110.

[327] [1977] 1 W.L.R. 970 at 978. See also *HP Bulmer & Showerings Ltd v J Bollinger SA* [1977] 2 C.M.L.R. 625 at 682; *Blue Town Investments Ltd v Higgs and Hill Plc* [1990] 1 W.L.R. 696.

[328] (1999) 77 P.& C.R. 73; P. Milne (1998) 114 L.Q.R. 555, below, para.25–049.

[329] *Jones v Stones* [1999] 1 W.L.R. 1739; *Harris v Williams-Wynne* [2006] 2 P. & C.R. 27.

C. Hardship

25–046 Hardship to the defendant is a relevant consideration in injunctions as in specific performance.[330] It is perhaps of more weight in the case of an interlocutory injunction[331] than in the case of a final injunction, where the infringement of the claimant's rights has been established. Hardship may also carry more weight in the case of mandatory injunctions,[332] where it has been said that the benefit to the claimant in granting the injunction must be balanced against the detriment to the defendant.[333] As we shall see, damages may be awarded in lieu of an injunction under Lord Cairns' Act if the injunction would be oppressive to the defendant.[334]

The element of hardship to the defendant might be overcome in appropriate cases by granting an injunction but suspending its operation.[335] Even if there is no hardship to the defendant, an injunction may be refused if it would prejudice an innocent third party.[336]

It has previously been noted that the disproportionate cost of complying with a mandatory *quia timet* injunction may be a ground for refusing the grant if the defendant has acted reasonably.[337] Lord Upjohn, however, thought that such considerations would not be taken into account in the case of a negative injunction to prevent the continuance or recurrence of a wrongful act; any argument by the wrongdoer that the injunction would be very costly to him, perhaps by preventing him from carrying out a contract with a third party, would carry little weight.

D. Conduct of the Claimant

25–047 The claimant must come to equity with clean hands.[338] If, therefore, he is in breach of his own obligations, or otherwise guilty of

---

[330] See *Shell UK Ltd v Lostock Garages Ltd* [1976] 1 W.L.R. 1187. As to difficulty in compliance, see generally *Att Gen v Colney Hatch Lunatic Asylum* (1868) L.R. 4 Ch.App. 146.

[331] See the "balance of convenience" requirement, above.

[332] *Att Gen v Colchester Corp* [1955] 2 Q.B. 207; *Gravesham BC v British Railways Board* [1978] Ch. 379 (A mandatory injunction would not be granted to compel the running of a ferry at a heavy loss, which would benefit few passengers).

[333] *Shepherd Homes Ltd v Sandham* [1971] Ch. 340; *Charrington v Simons & Co Ltd* [1970] 1 W.L.R. 725.

[334] There are other conditions: see *Shelfer v City of London Electric Lighting Co* [1895] 1 Ch. 287. See also *Shaw v Applegate*, above, fn.326, at 978–979.

[335] Above, para.25–021.

[336] *Maythorn v Palmer* (1864) 11 L.T. 261; cf. *PSM International Plc v Whitehouse and Willenhall Automation Ltd* [1992] I.R.L.R. 279.

[337] *Redland Bricks Ltd v Morris* [1970] A.C. 652 at 666.

[338] See *Malone v Metropolitan Police Commissioner* [1980] Q.B. 49 at p.71. In cases of illegality it was proposed that the principle be replaced by a statutory discretion; Law Com. C.P. No.154 (1999), *Illegal Transactions: The Effect of Illegality on Contracts and Trusts*. However, current proposals focus solely on trusts; Law Com. No.320, (2010), *The Illegality Defence*.

unfair conduct,[339] he will not be granted an injunction, although trifling breaches may not disentitle him.[340] Similarly, he who comes to equity must do equity, therefore the claimant will not succeed if he is unable or unwilling to carry out his own future obligations.[341]

But the defence of "clean hands" must be related to the subject-matter of the dispute, and does not embrace the claimant's general conduct. Thus in *Argyll v Argyll*,[342] the fact that the wife's conduct had caused the divorce was no answer to her claim to an injunction to restrain a breach of confidence by her husband. In *Hubbard v Vosper*,[343] one reason for refusing the interlocutory injunction was that the claimant had not come with clean hands, in that he had protected his secrets by deplorable means, namely by a private criminal code for dealing with the "enemies" of scientology.

Similarly, the injunction may be refused if the court is not impressed with the claimant on the merits.[344]

5. THE JURISDICTION UNDER LORD CAIRNS' ACT

The Chancery Amendment Act 1858[345] allowed damages to be awarded in lieu of, or in addition to, an injunction or specific performance. The Chancery Division has, of course, been able, since the Judicature Act 1873, to award damages in any case where the common law courts could have done so, but these are common law damages. It will still be necessary to rely on Lord Cairns' Act where no damages would be available at law, for example in lieu of a *quia timet* injunction where no legal injury has yet occurred[346]; or if some damage has occurred but may continue in the future, and damages

25–048

---

[339] *Shell UK Ltd v Lostock Garages Ltd* [1976] 1 W.L.R. 1187.

[340] *Besant v Wood* (1879) 12 Ch.D. 605.

[341] *Measures v Measures* [1910] 2 Ch. 248; *Chappell v Times Newspapers Ltd* [1975] 1 W.L.R. 482 (employees failed to obtain injunction to restrain their dismissal where they refused to give an undertaking not to strike).

[342] [1967] Ch. 302.

[343] [1972] 2 Q.B. 84.

[344] See *Glynn v Keele University* [1971] 1 W.L.R. 487; *Shelfer v City of London Electric Lighting Co* [1895] 1 Ch. 287 at 317.

[345] Above, para.24–044; repealed and replaced by Statute Law Revision Act 1883 and Judicature Act 1873. The jurisdiction now derives from Senior Courts Act 1981 s.50. In *Leeds Industrial Co-operative Society v Slack* [1924] A.C. 851 Viscount Finlay suggested that the repeal may have been a mistake, made under the false impression that it dealt only with common law damages, and was therefore redundant after the Judicature Act 1873. The better view is that s.16 of the 1873 Act, which transferred all Chancery jurisdiction to the High Court, made the 1858 Act redundant. See McDermott, *Equitable Damages* (1994), pp.44–45.

[346] *Leeds Industrial Co-operative Society v Slack*, above, fn.345; establishing the point after some doubt; *Hooper v Rogers* [1975] Ch. 43; *Johnson v Agnew* [1980] A.C. 367 at 400.

are awarded to cover future loss[347]; or where the claimant's right is exclusively equitable, as in the case of a restrictive covenant.[348] In other cases, it will not be necessary to invoke Lord Cairns' Act, and damages may be awarded at common law; but there is no need to distinguish the ground of jurisdiction. The discretion exercisable under Lord Cairns' Act is similar to the discretion which the court has had since the Judicature Act to grant injunctions or damages at common law, in cases where they are available. The principle is the same; the court will not give damages instead of an injunction if damages will not be adequate to protect the claimant's rights. It seems that the court will consider the principles set out in *Shelfer v City of London Electric Lighting Co*[349] governing the award of damages under Lord Cairns' Act even where the claimant has a cause of action at law, and there is jurisdiction to award damages at law.[350]

Lord Cairns' Act enables the award of damages in lieu of a final (not interlocutory) injunction only if there is *jurisdiction* to grant one,[351] in the sense that the claimant has established a prima facie case for equitable relief. It does not matter that the injunction is refused on some discretionary ground, such as, for example, delay or acquiescence,[352] although delay may be a reason for moderation when assessing the damages.[353] Nor is it necessary for an injunction to have been claimed.[354] If, on the other hand, the claimant has no case at all for an injunction, then damages cannot be awarded under Lord Cairns' Act, but, as we have seen, such a claimant can be awarded common law damages, provided he has a cause of action at law.

A. Award of Damages under Lord Cairns' Act

25–049   If the claimant can establish that his rights have been infringed, he is prima facie entitled to an injunction. Damages will only be

---

[347] See *Kennaway v Thompson* [1981] Q.B. 88. For the position under the Human Rights Act 1998 where the defendant is a public authority, see *Marcic v Thames Water Utilities Ltd (No.2)* [2002] Q.B. 1003.

[348] *Baxter v Four Oaks Properties Ltd* [1965] Ch. 816; *Wrotham Park Estate Ltd v Parkside Homes Ltd* [1974] 1 W.L.R. 798.

[349] [1895] 1 Ch. 287; below.

[350] See *Kelsen v Imperial Tobacco Co Ltd* [1957] 2 Q.B. 334; *Woollerton and Wilson Ltd v Richard Costain Ltd* [1970] 1 W.L.R. 411.

[351] *Hooper v Rogers* [1975] Ch. 43; *Wrotham Park Estate Ltd v Parkside Homes Ltd*, above, fn.348.

[352] *Shaw v Applegate* [1977] 1 W.L.R. 970; *Gafford v Graham* (1999) 77 P. & C.R. 73. Distinguish a case of *jurisdiction* being lost through the passage of time. See generally *Lavery v Pursell* (1883) 39 Ch.D. 508 at 519. The position is the same for specific performance, above, para.24–044.

[353] *Pell Frischmann Engineering Ltd v Bow Valley Iran Ltd* [2011] 1 W.L.R. 2370.

[354] *Pell Frischmann*, above, fn.353.

awarded in lieu in special circumstances; otherwise the defendant would be allowed to "buy" the right to continue the wrongful act.[355]

The leading case is *Shelfer v City of London Lighting Co*,[356] a case of nuisance. AL Smith L.J. laid down a "good working rule", that damages should only be awarded in lieu if all the following requirements were satisfied:

(i) the injury to the claimant is small; and

(ii) the injury is capable of being estimated in monetary terms; and

(iii) the injury would be adequately compensated by a small payment[357]; and

(iv) it would be oppressive to grant an injunction.[358]

Lindley L.J. said[359] that the injunction should not be refused merely because it would not greatly benefit the claimant, as the court is not a tribunal for legalising wrongful acts where the wrongdoer is able and willing to pay. Damages will not normally be substituted in a case of nuisance, as they cannot be easily estimated, but it was suggested that damages would be appropriate if it was a trivial or occasional nuisance, or if it is a vexatious case, or if the claimant has shown that he only wants money.[360] If damages are awarded in a case where the wrong is continuing, they must include a sum for the future as well as the past.

Even if the above four principles are satisfied, an injunction may still be awarded if the defendant has acted in reckless disregard of the claimant's rights,[361] or has acted in a high-handed manner, or

---

[355] See *Wakeham v Wood* (1982) 43 P. & C.R. 40; *Sampson v Hodson-Pressinger* [1981] 3 All E.R. 710; *Oxy Electric Ltd v Zainuddin* [1991] 1 W.L.R. 115; *Elliott v Islington LBC* [1991] 1 E.G.L.R. 167; *Harrow LBC v Donohue* [1995] 1 E.G.L.R. 257.

[356] [1895] 1 Ch. 287. See Viscount Finlay's valuable account of the Act in *Leeds Industrial Co-operative Society v Slack* [1924] A.C. 851 at 856–863. Damages are not appropriate where the nuisance is actionable without proof of damage; *Sevenoaks DC v Pattullo & Vinson Ltd* [1984] Ch. 211 (right to hold market).

[357] The jurisdiction to grant injunctions is based on the inadequacy of common law damages. It might be argued that compliance with the third requirement should alone be sufficient to prevent the grant of an injunction. But common law damages may not be available, and cannot be awarded for the future; *Jaggard v Sawyer* [1995] 1 W.L.R. 269. See J. Jolowicz (1975) 34 C.L.J. 224.

[358] See *Jaggard v Sawyer*, above, fn.357 (injunction would prevent access to defendants' house); *Watson v Croft Promosport Ltd* [2009] 3 All E.R. 249 (court must not slide into applying a balance of convenience test).

[359] [1895] 1 Ch. 287 at 315–316.

[360] See *Gafford v Graham* (1999) 77 P. & C.R. 73; *Marcic v Thames Water Utilities Ltd (No.2)* [2002] Q.B. 1003.

[361] *Shelfer v City of London Electric Lighting Co* [1895] 1 Ch. 287; *Pugh v Howells* (1984) 48 P. & C.R. 298; cf. *Ketley v Gooden* (1997) 73 P. & C.R. 305; *Gafford v Graham* (1999) 77 P. & C.R. 73.

tried to steal a march on the claimant, or to evade the jurisdiction of the court.[362]

The Court of Appeal in *Redland Bricks Ltd v Morris*,[363] while accepting the principles of *Shelfer's* case, disagreed on the question whether the injury could be regarded as small, or could be adequately compensated in money. The defendant's excavations caused damage by subsidence to the value of £1,500, but the correction of the situation, if an injunction was issued, would require expenditure of some £30,000. An injunction was granted, but the House of Lords reversed on a different ground, and Lord Upjohn rejected the applicability of Lord Cairns' Act to the case. But the reasons for his Lordship's rejection of the Act are unclear and, it is submitted, unconvincing.[364]

It has more recently been emphasised that *Shelfer's* case provides only a "working rule", and that the principles must be adaptable to the facts of individual cases. Thus damages could be awarded in lieu of an injunction to demolish a building put up in breach of covenant and to restrain a prohibited use of the land, even though the injury was not "small", nor could it be remedied by a "small payment".[365] Thus damages of £25,000 were awarded, as the essential prerequisite that it would be oppressive to grant an injunction was satisfied. The claimant had previously shown that he was willing to settle for money, and this tipped the balance in favour of damages.

25–050   The four principles of *Shelfer's* case have not always met with approval, notably in cases concerning rights to light and trespass, where the burden of remedying the situation will often be out of all proportion to the injury to the claimant. In *Fishenden v Higgs and Hill Ltd*[366] the defendant erected a building which obstructed the claimant's light in a manner that justified substantial damages, but not, by reason of the very high property values involved and the conduct of the defendant, an injunction. The Court of Appeal said that the principles of *Shelfer's* case were a useful guide, but not intended to be exhaustive or rigidly applied, and not a universal or even a sound rule in the case of rights to light. The Court of Appeal recently reviewed the authorities on *Shelfer's* case, in circumstances where the defendant's building significantly reduced the light to the

---

[362] *Colls v Home and Colonial Stores Ltd* [1904] A.C. 179 at 193, a case on an easement of light, where it was suggested that the court should incline to damages if there is any doubt, and the defendant has not acted in an unneighbourly spirit. See also *Pugh v Howells*, above, fn.361 (injunction to remove extension interfering with easement of light, where built quickly over a bank holiday, although warning given); *Daniells v Mendonca* (1999) 78 P. & C.R. 401.

[363] [1967] 1 W.L.R. 967; above, para.25–042.

[364] See J. Jolowicz (1975) 34 C.L.J. 224; (1977) 36 C.L.J. 369; P. Pettit (1978) 37 C.L.J. 51. See also *Hooper v Rogers* [1975] Ch. 43.

[365] *Gafford v Graham*, above, fn.361; P. Milne (1998) 114 L.Q.R. 555.

[366] (1935) 153 L.T. 128; *Colls v Home and Colonial Stores Ltd*, above, fn.362; *Lyme Valley Squash Club Ltd v Newcastle under Lyme BC* [1985] 2 All E.R. 405.

claimant's living room.[367] This interference reduced the value of the property by only £5,000, but it would cost the defendant £175,000 to comply with an injunction to remove the upper level of the building, which had been constructed after the claimant had protested. The injunction was granted, because the injury was not "small", nor would the loss to the defendant make it oppressive to grant the injunction. It was still the law that damages in lieu of an injunction to restrain a continuing wrong should be granted only in very exceptional cases, and there was no onus on the claimant to persuade the court that damages would be inadequate. This serves as a warning to developers who have taken a calculated risk: there is no principle that injunctions are less readily granted in rights of light cases.

Similar issues arise in the case of trespass, where the injury to the claimant may bear no relationship to that imposed on the defendant by the grant of an injunction. It was assumed in *Kelsen v Imperial Tobacco Co Ltd*[368] that *Shelfer's* case applied to trespass. The question was whether the defendant should be required to remove an advertisement which trespassed upon the claimant's airspace. The injury was minimal, but an injunction was granted. In *Woollerton and Wilson Ltd v Richard Costain Ltd*[369] Stamp L.J. doubted whether *Shelfer's* case could apply to trespass involving nominal damage, as the award of damages would amount to a licence to continue the trespass. An injunction was granted although the four principles were satisfied, but the injunction was suspended.[370] That decision was considered wrong in *Jaggard v Sawyer*,[371] where *Shelfer's* case was applied to a trespass which caused little injury and the other conditions were satisfied. The damages could reflect the amount the defendants should have been prepared to pay for a right of way. Thus *Shelfer's* case remains good law in relation to trespass, rights to light and nuisance.

In *Kennaway v Thompson*[372] the claimant sought an injunction to restrain a nuisance by excessive noise against a motor boat racing club. The Court of Appeal granted the injunction, holding that the jurisdiction to award damages in lieu of an injunction should be exercised only in very exceptional circumstances in

[367] *Regan Paul Properties DPF No.1 Ltd* [2007] Ch. 135; P. Chynoweth [2007] Conv. 175; cf. *Tamares (Vincent Square) Ltd v Fairpoint Properties (Vincent Square) Ltd* [2007] 1 W.L.R. 2148 (no injunction for loss of light to office building).

[368] [1957] 2 Q.B. 334.

[369] [1970] 1 W.L.R. 411.

[370] Above, para.25–021; criticised in J. Jolowicz (1975) 34 C.L.J. 224. Trespass is an exception to the rule that damages require proof of loss; *Stoke-on-Trent City Council v W & J Wass Ltd* [1988] 1 W.L.R. 1406.

[371] [1995] 1 W.L.R. 269; below, para.25–052; *Ketley v Gooden* (1997) 73 P. & C.R. 305 (no injunction if injury small, even if reckless disregard by defendant).

[372] [1981] Q.B. 88; (1981) 97 L.Q.R. 3; R. Buckley (1981) 44 M.L.R. 212; *Elliott v Islington LBC* [1991] 1 E.G.L.R. 167; *Watson v Croft Promosport Ltd* [2009] 3 All E.R. 249.

cases of continuing nuisance. In the present case the injury to the claimant was not small, nor was it capable of estimation in monetary terms, nor could the sum awarded in the High Court (£16,000) be called a "small payment". In considering whether to award damages in lieu of an injunction, the public interest does not prevail over the private rights of the claimant. Any statements to the contrary in *Miller v Jackson*[373] ran counter to the principles of *Shelfer's* case and were based on old authorities decided before *Shelfer's* case and now subject to it.

B. The Measure of Damages under Lord Cairns' Act

25–051   In *Leeds Industrial Co-operative Society v Slack*,[374] Lord Sumner said[375]:

"No money awarded in substitution can be justly awarded, unless it is at any rate designed to be a preferable equivalent to an injunction and therefore an adequate substitution for it."

This principle was re-echoed in *Wroth v Tyler*[376] in respect of specific performance. This decision was once regarded as authority for the proposition that greater damages may be awarded under Lord Cairns' Act than would be available at law. But in *Johnson v Agnew*[377] the House of Lords held, in a case concerning specific performance, that there is no difference in the measure of damages obtainable under Lord Cairns' Act and at common law. Of course, damages may be recoverable under Lord Cairns' Act where none at all would be obtainable at law,[378] but in general equity follows the law, and it may generally be expected that if only nominal damages would be available at law, then no more will be awarded in equity.[379] A different view had been taken in *Wrotham Park Estate Ltd v Parkside Homes Ltd*,[380] a case where no damages were available at law.

The defendant had erected houses in breach of covenant. There was jurisdiction to grant a mandatory injunction against the defendant and the purchasers, who had aided and abetted the breach;

[373] [1977] Q.B. 966; above, para.25–010. The principle of *Miller v Jackson* was also rejected in *Webster v Lord Advocate* (1984) S.L.T. 13. See also *Sevenoaks DC v Pattullo & Vinson Ltd* [1984] Ch. 211.
[374] [1924] A.C. 851.
[375] [1924] A.C. 851, at 870.
[376] [1974] Ch. 30.
[377] [1980] A.C. 367, above, para.24–010.
[378] As in *Hooper v Rogers* [1975] Ch. 43 (*quia timet*).
[379] *Johnson v Agnew* [1980] A.C. 367.
[380] [1974] 1 W.L.R. 798; not cited in *Johnson v Agnew*, above, fn.379. See also *Amec Developments Ltd v Jury's Hotel Management (UK) Ltd* (2001) 82 P. & C.R. 286; D. Halpern [2001] Conv. 453.

but the injunction was refused, in order to avoid the demolition of valuable houses. As a restrictive covenant was involved, damages were available only under Lord Cairns' Act. The value of the claimant's estate was not diminished by the breach, but it did not follow that only nominal damages were available. It would not be right to leave the defendants in possession of the fruits of their wrongdoing. Brightman J. held that a just substitute would be such sum as the claimant could reasonably have demanded to relax the covenant, assessed at £2,500.

The question whether substantial damages may be awarded under Lord Cairns' Act (or at common law) in the absence of loss cannot be answered without distinguishing various causes of action. Clearly damages cannot be awarded on the *Wrotham Park* basis in all cases, because to do so would be inconsistent with the principle expressed in *Johnson v Agnew*[381] that the measure of damages under Lord Cairns' Act is the same as at common law. The basic principle at common law is that damages are to compensate for loss suffered. One exception is trespass, where substantial damages may be awarded without proof of loss.[382] Thus an award of substantial damages (including such sum as the claimant might reasonably have charged to permit the otherwise tortious act) may be awarded in lieu of an injunction under Lord Cairns' Act.[383]

25–052

In cases of nuisance it is essential to prove damage, but once that is established, any damages awarded in lieu of an injunction may properly include such sum as the claimant could reasonably have charged to permit the nuisance.[384] Indeed, tort damages at common law may include this element.[385] When assessing the damages, the court will take into account the fact that the claimant would have bargained for a fair share of any profit made by the defendant in the hypothetical negotiation. The guiding principle when fixing the amount is "whether the deal feels right".[386]

So far as contract actions are concerned, a claimant who cannot establish loss is not traditionally entitled to damages at common law

---

[381] [1980] A.C. 367.

[382] See *Inverugie Investments Ltd v Hackett* [1995] 1 W.L.R. 713 (claimant entitled to reasonable rent for wrongful use whether or not he would have let the property to a third party or used it himself).

[383] *Bracewell v Appleby* [1975] Ch. 408; *Jaggard v Sawyer* [1995] 1 W.L.R. 269; below. Doubts expressed in *Anchor Brewhouse Developments Ltd v Berkley House (Docklands Developments) Ltd* [1987] 2 E.G.L.R. 173 were considered misplaced in *Jaggard v Sawyer*. See also *Bosomworth v Faber* (1995) 69 P. & C.R. 288.

[384] *Carr-Saunders v Dick McNeill Associates Ltd* [1986] 1 W.L.R. 922; *Stoke-on-Trent City Council v W & J Wass Ltd* [1988] 1 W.L.R. 1406.

[385] So considered in *Surrey CC v Bredero Homes Ltd* [1993] 1 W.L.R. 1361 and *Jaggard v Sawyer* [1995] 1 W.L.R. 269, below.

[386] *Tamares (Vincent Square) Ltd v Fairpoint Properties (Vincent Square) Ltd (No.2)* [2007] 1 W.L.R. 2167 at 2172 (damages of £50,000 "felt right" where developer's profit was £174,500 in right to light case).

to reflect the sum he might have charged to release the defendant from the contract. However, the House of Lords has now held that, in exceptional cases, the remedy of an account of profits is available for breach of contract.[387]

The *Wrotham Park* principle was reviewed by the Court of Appeal in *Surrey CC v Bredero Homes Ltd*,[388] where the defendant, a property developer, increased its profits by building five extra houses in breach of covenant. The claimant sued for damages, and did not seek an injunction because the defendant had sold all the houses. For that reason it was considered that Lord Cairns' Act did not apply.[389] The claimant could not establish that the breach of covenant caused it any loss, but sought such part of the profits made from the breach as would reflect a reasonable payment for release of the covenant, relying on *Wrotham Park*. It was held that only nominal damages could be awarded, under the ordinary contract principle. *Wrotham Park* was distinguished as a decision on Lord Cairns' Act.

The matter arose again in *Jaggard v Sawyer*,[390] where the defendant built a house in breach of covenant and trespassed upon a private road to gain access to it. The claimant sought an injunction to restrain the trespass (which caused little injury) or damages in lieu. The judge below refused the injunction, which would have rendered the property landlocked, and awarded a sum reflecting what the defendant should have paid for a right of way and a release of the covenant. This was upheld by the Court of Appeal, applying *Wrotham Park*.

The matter has since been resolved by the House of Lords in favour of the *Wrotham Park* principle. In *Att Gen v Blake*[391] the issue was whether the remedy of an account of profits was available for breach of contract.[392] In that case the Attorney General sought to recover the royalties from the publication of a book in breach of contract by the defendant, a former KGB spy. The House of Lords held that this remedy was available in exceptional circumstances, where the remedy of damages was inadequate. Although the case

---

[387] *Att Gen v Blake* [2001] 1 A.C. 268. See also Law Com. No.247 (1997), *Aggravated Exemplary and Restitutionary Damages*.

[388] [1993] 1 W.L.R. 1361.

[389] See the discussion of this aspect in *Jaggard v Sawyer* [1995] 1 W.L.R. 269.

[390] [1995] 1 W.L.R. 269; W. Goodhart [1995] 3 R.L.R. 3; W. Swadling All E.R. Rev. 1995, p.453. The decision was applied in *Gafford v Graham* (1999) 77 P. & C.R. 73; above, para.25–049.

[391] [2001] 1 A.C. 268; P. Jaffey [2000] R.L.R. 578; D. Fox (2001) 60 C.L.J. 33; D. Campbell and D. Harris (2002) 22 L.S. 208; D. Campbell (2002) 65 M.L.R. 256; M. McInnes [2006] 14 R.L.R. 76; K. Barnett [2009] 17 R.L.R. 79; O. Odudu and G. Virgo [2009] 17 R.L.R. 112.

[392] The remedy may also be available in some tort cases; *Devenish Nutrition Ltd v Sanofi-Aventis SA* [2009] Ch. 390.

did not concern Lord Cairns' Act, their Lordships reviewed the modern decisions on the Act and confirmed that in cases such as *Wrotham Park* and *Jaggard v Sawyer*[393] the correct analysis was that the claimant was compensated for the loss of a bargaining opportunity, or, to put it another way, for the compulsory acquisition of his rights. *Surrey County Council v Bredero Homes Ltd*[394] was a "difficult decision". If the defendant could escape with impunity, that would be a sorry reflection on the law. To the extent that it conflicted with *Wrotham Park*, the latter was to be preferred. In the words of Lord Nicholls:

> "The *Wrotham Park* case, therefore, still shines, rather as a solitary beacon, showing that in contract as well as tort damages are not always narrowly confined to recoupment of financial loss. In a suitable case damages for breach of contract may be measured by the benefit gained by the wrongdoer from the breach."[395]

Thus a claimant may, in an appropriate case, obtain a remedy for breach of contract or covenant without establishing loss, whether the case is decided under the Lord Cairns' Act jurisdiction or the general law. Even if the circumstances do not warrant the remedy of an account of profits, the law on damages for breach of contract is now sufficiently flexible to allow assessment on the *Wrotham Park* principle, whether in relation to past or future breaches.[396]

A question which has proved controversial is whether damages assessed under this principle are compensatory (loss-based) or restitutionary (gains-based). Bearing in mind that the claimant does not need to establish loss, the award appears restitutionary. However, the Court of Appeal has expressed the view that such damages are not gains-based, but are a flexible response to the need to compensate for a wrong where identifiable loss has not been shown.[397] This analysis has been convincingly criticised.[398] Arden L.J. subsequently adopted a middle way, considering that damages assessed on the *Wrotham Park* principle had an element of compensation (for

---

[393] Above, fn.390.

[394] [1993] 1 W.L.R. 1361.

[395] [2001] 1 A.C. 268 at 283.

[396] *Experience Hendrix LLC v PPX Enterprises Inc* [2003] 1 All E.R. (Comm) 830; J. Edelman [2003] 11 R.L.R. 101; M. Graham (2003) 119 L.Q.R. 26; P.-W. Lee [2003] L.M.C.L.Q. 301; D. Campbell and P. Wylie (2003) 62 C.L.J. 605; M. Graham (2004) 120 L.Q.R. 26; *Field Common Ltd v Elmbridge BC* [2009] 1 P. & C.R. 1.

[397] *WWF World Wide Fund for Nature v World Wrestling Federation Entertainment Inc* [2008] 1 W.L.R. 445.

[398] R. Cunnington (2007) 66 C.L.J. 507 and (2008) 71 M.L.R. 559; J. Edelman and C. Mitchell All E.R. Rev. 2007, p.350 and C. Rotherham [2008] L.M.C.L.Q. 25. See also Lord Scott [2007] L.M.C.L.Q. 465.

invasion of rights), but were not purely compensatory.[399] The principles were reviewed by the Privy Council in *Pell Frischmann Engineering Ltd v Bow Valley Iran Ltd*,[400] where it was said that the recent cases were not completely consistent. The Privy Council did not expressly resolve the question whether damages of this nature are loss-based or gains-based. The claimant was held entitled on the facts to a sum greater than the defendant's actual profit, which would be inconsistent with a purely restitutionary analysis.

6. INJUNCTIONS IN PARTICULAR SITUATIONS

A. To Restrain a Breach of Contract

25–053   An injunction is the appropriate remedy to restrain the breach of a negative undertaking in a contract. In some measure it corresponds to specific performance in the area of positive undertakings.[401] But, as will be seen,[402] the jurisdiction to grant an injunction is wider.

i. Contract Wholly Negative

25–054   (a) *Perpetual Injunctions.* Where the essence of the contractual undertaking is negative, the court will grant an injunction to restrain a breach almost as a matter of course. As Lord Cairns L.C. explained in *Doherty v Allman and Dowden*,[403] if the parties:

> "[C]ontract that a particular thing shall not be done, all that a Court of Equity has to do is to say, by way of injunction, that which the parties have already said by way of covenant, that the thing shall not be done ... ".

It is not necessary even to prove damage,[404] except where the action is by a reversioner.[405]

---

[399] *Devenish Nutrition Ltd v Sanofi-Aventis SA* [2009] Ch. 390, where the *WWF* case (above, fn.397) was said to be "difficult". See C. Rotherham (2010) 126 L.Q.R. 102; J. Edelman [2010] 18 R.L.R. 1.

[400] [2011] 1 W.L.R. 2370; J. Edelman All E.R. Rev. 2009, p.403; T. Cutts [2010] L.M.C.L.Q. 215. See also *Vercoe v Rutland Fund Management Ltd* [2010] EWHC 424 (Ch); [2011] Bus. L.R. D141; P. Devonshire (2010) 126 L.Q.R. 526.

[401] Above, para.24–006. Mandatory injunctions may also be available.

[402] Below, para.25–057.

[403] (1878) 3 App.Cas. 709 at 720; *Sefton v Tophams Ltd* [1967] A.C. 50; *Sutton Housing Trust v Lawrence* (1988) 55 P. & C.R. 320 (granted to prevent tenant keeping dog in breach of covenant).

[404] *Grimston v Cuningham* [1894] 1 Q.B. 125; *Marco Productions Ltd v Pagola* [1945] K.B. 111, where dancers agreed not to perform for another producer; injunction granted although the claimants could not show that they would suffer greater damage if the dancers performed elsewhere than if they remained idle; cf. *Provident Financial Group Plc v Hayward* [1989] I.C.R. 160.

[405] *Johnstone v Hall* (1856) 2 K. & J. 414; *Martin v Nutkin* (1724) 2 P.Wms. 266 (injunction to restrain ringing of church bells at 5 am).

But the *Doherty v Allman* principle must be applied "in the light of the surrounding circumstances in each case,"[406] and it does not prevent the court from considering the effect of delay or other supervening circumstances.[407]

Thus an injunction was refused in *Baxter v Four Oaks Properties Ltd*,[408] where the defendants, innocently, but in breach of the covenant, intended to use a new building as flats.

"The effect of granting such an order would ... be to put the [claimants] in a very strong bargaining position, for unless the defendants were prepared to leave the building unused, they would be forced to buy a release of the injunction ... what the [claimants] would get in the end would be damages—though, no doubt, more damages than they would get if no injunction were granted."[409]

(b) *Interlocutory Injunctions*. Interlocutory injunctions are not **25–055** granted as a matter of course, but it was said in *Hampstead and Suburban Properties Ltd v Diomedous*[410] that the *Doherty v Allman*[411] principle applied where there was a plain breach of a clear negative covenant. In such a case, there was no reason why the defendant "should have a holiday from the enforcement of his obligation until the trial."[412] This principle was recently applied by the Court of Appeal in *Araci v Fallon*.[413] The defendant, a famous jockey, had contracted to ride the claimant's horse when asked, and not to ride a rival owner's horse. An interlocutory injunction was granted to prevent him from riding a rival owner's horse in the Derby. But where the validity of the covenant is in dispute, *Doherty v Allman* cannot apply to interlocutory injunctions.[414]

(c) *Mandatory Injunctions*. Mandatory injunctions are entirely **25–056** discretionary, and can never be granted automatically, even if a negative covenant is involved.[415] It is not possible to give precise

---

[406] *Shaw v Applegate* [1977] 1 W.L.R. 970 at 975, per Buckley L.J.
[407] [1977] 1 W.L.R. 970 at 980, per Goff L.J.
[408] [1965] Ch. 816.
[409] [1965] Ch. 816 at 829, per Cross J.
[410] [1969] 1 Ch. 248 (excessive noise made in breach of covenant by restaurant).
[411] (1878) 3 App.Cas. 709.
[412] [1969] 1 Ch. 248 at 259; *Att Gen v Barker* [1990] 3 All E.R. 257 (proposed publication, in breach of contract, of book about royal family).
[413] [2011] EWCA Civ 668, [2011] All E.R. (D) 37.
[414] *Texaco Ltd v Mulberry Filling Station Ltd* [1972] 1 W.L.R. 814 at 831.
[415] See *Wrotham Park Estate Ltd v Parkside Homes Ltd* [1974] 1 W.L.R. 798. But the claimant may obtain summary judgment in a flagrant case; *Chelsea (Viscount) v Muscatt* [1990] 2 E.G.L.R. 48.

guidance as to the way in which the discretion will be exercised. In *Shepherd Homes Ltd v Sandham*,[416] Megarry J. said of *Doherty v Allman*[417] that:

"[A] court of equity which says by way of injunction 'that which the parties have already said by way of covenant that the thing shall not be done,' is not thereby in the same breath adding 'and what is more, if it has been done, it shall be undone.' "[418]

The application of the principle of *Doherty v Allman* is tempered by a judicial discretion which withholds a mandatory injunction more readily than a prohibitory injunction, even where the claimant is blameless. Benefit to the claimant must be balanced against detriment to the defendant. But the search is not merely for "a fair result".[419]

25–057 **ii. Positive and Negative Terms.** Where a contract contains both positive and negative stipulations, and the positive ones are not susceptible to specific performance, the question arises whether the claimant can restrain the breach of the negative stipulation by injunction. In suitable cases, this can be done. The jurisdiction to grant an injunction is wider than that to order specific performance.[420]

The principle is that an injunction will not be granted if that would amount to indirect specific performance of the positive terms. Thus, it used to be said with confidence that no injunction would lie to restrain the termination of employment in breach of contract, for this would indirectly enforce the contract.[421] It has been seen, however, that in the special circumstances of *Hill v CA Parsons & Co Ltd*,[422] where an employer was reluctantly obliged to terminate the employment of a senior engineer who refused to join a trade union operating a closed shop principle, an interim injunction was issued to restrain the termination.

25–058 **iii. No Express Negative Stipulation.** Where a contract, drafted in positive form, contains no express negative stipulation, it may be possible to discover in the contract, on its proper construction, an

---

[416] [1971] Ch. 340; *Sharp v Harrison* [1922] 1 Ch. 502 at 512.
[417] (1878) 3 App.Cas. 709.
[418] [1971] Ch. 340 at 346.
[419] *Charrington v Simons & Co Ltd* [1971] 1 W.L.R. 598 at 603, per Russell L.J.
[420] See *Thomas Marshall (Exports) Ltd v Guinle* [1979] Ch. 227 at 243.
[421] *Davis v Foreman* [1894] 3 Ch. 654.
[422] [1972] 1 Ch. 305; *CH Giles & Co Ltd v Morris* [1972] 1 W.L.R. 307; B. Napier (1975) 34 C.L.J. 36.

implied negative undertaking which can be remedied by injunc-tion.[423] This is especially important where the positive obligation is not specifically enforceable. It is not possible to lay down a rule to determine the circumstances in which an injunction may be ob-tained. The question in each case depends upon the construction which the court places upon the particular contract.

The principle was laid down by Lord Selborne in *Wolverhampton and Walsall Railway Co Ltd v LNW Ry Ltd*[424] as being that the court should:

> "[L]ook in all such cases to the substance and not to the form. If the substance of the agreement is such that it would be violated by doing the thing sought to be prevented, then the question will arise, whether this is the court to come to for a remedy. If it is, I cannot think that ought to depend on the use of a negative rather than an affirmative form of expression."

A negative stipulation is rarely implied in contracts of personal service, for to do so might allow the indirect enforcement of a contract which is not specifically enforceable.[425] Thus, it will not be implied although the servant has contracted to devote the whole of his time to his employer,[426] nor where there was a contract to sell to a purchaser all the "get" of a colliery for five years[427]; nor where a boxer agreed that his manager should have the "sole arrangements" for his boxing and other engagements.[428] However, in *Metropolitan Electric Supply Co v Ginder*,[429] the defendant applied for a supply of electricity on terms which provided that the defendant agreed to take all the electricity required by his premises from the claimant for a stated period. The claimant was not bound to supply, nor the defen-dant to take, any electricity. The contract was construed as an under-taking not to take electricity from any other persons, and the defendant was restrained by injunction from doing so. In

---

[423] *Tulk v Moxhay* (1848) 2 Ph. 774; *Jones & Sons Ltd v Tankerville* [1909] 2 Ch. 440. Breach of an obligation imposed by law can be restrained by injunction even though the contract contains no express negative term: *Hivac v Park Royal Scientific Instruments* [1946] Ch. 169; *Provident Financial Group Plc v Hayward* [1989] I.C.R. 160 (confidential in-formation).

[424] (1873) L.R. 16 Eq. 433 at 440; *Whitwood Chemical Co Ltd v Hardman* [1891] 2 Ch. 416 at 441, per Lindley L.J.; *Bower v Bantam Investments Ltd* [1972] 1 W.L.R. 1120.

[425] Above, para.24–024.

[426] *Whitwood Chemical Co Ltd v Hardman* [1891] 2 Ch. 416; *Bower v Bantam Investments Ltd* [1972] 1 W.L.R. 1120.

[427] *Fothergill v Rowland* (1873) L.R. 17 Eq. 132.

[428] *Mortimer v Beckett* [1920] 1 Ch. 571. See also *Fraser v Thames Television Ltd* [1984] Q.B. 44.

[429] [1901] 2 Ch. 799. See also *Sky Petroleum Ltd v VIP Petroleum Ltd* [1974] 1 W.L.R. 576.

Manchester Ship Canal v Manchester Racecourse Co[430] the grant of a "first refusal" was construed as an undertaking enforceable by injunction, not to sell to anyone else in contravention of the undertaking.

It is established that a negative term may be implied in the following types of case.

25–059   (a) *Contracts Affecting the Use of Land.* A covenant which touches and concerns the land so as to be binding in equity upon successors in title under the doctrine of *Tulk v Moxhay*[431] will be construed as negative and subjected to an injunction if it is negative in substance although positive in form. Indeed, in *Tulk v Moxhay* itself, the covenant was to:

> "[K]eep and maintain the said piece of ground in its then form, and in sufficient and proper repair . . . in an open state, uncovered with any buildings in neat and ornamental order."[432]

The fact that a court was powerless to interfere against third parties except by the use of an injunction no doubt encouraged the courts to extend its use of the concept.

25–060   (b) *Contractual Licences.* After a long search for the proper solution to the problem of the revocation by a licensor of a contractual licence in breach of contract, the courts found it in the issue of an injunction to restrain the breach of contract.[433] Where the wrongful revocation occurs before the licensee has entered, the court may, in an appropriate case, grant specific performance or a mandatory injunction to compel performance of the licensor's obligations.[434] A contractual licence is commonly in positive form—permitting the licensee to occupy premises. But where the licence on its proper construction gives no right to the licensor to revoke in the way in which he has purported to do, the court will treat the matter as one in which the licensor has contracted not to revoke inconsistently with the terms of the licence, and will restrain him from doing so.[435]

25–061   iv. Contracts for Personal Services. It has been seen that contracts for personal services would not be specifically enforced either

---

[430] [1901] 2 Ch. 37. See also *Gardner v Coutts & Co* [1968] 1 W.L.R. 173 (implied term in right of pre-emption that property will not be given to another); cf. *Pritchard v Briggs* [1980] Ch. 338.

[431] (1848) 2 Ph. 774.

[432] (1848) 2 Ph. 774 at 775.

[433] Below, para.27–009.

[434] *Verrall v Great Yarmouth BC* [1981] Q.B. 202, above, para.24–015.

[435] See *Jones (James) and Sons Ltd v Earl of Tankerville* [1909] 2 Ch. 440.

by specific performance or by an injunction.[436] In the case of contracts of employment, the Trade Union and Labour Relations (Consolidation) Act 1992 s.236 provides that:

"[N]o court shall . . . by way of . . . injunction . . . restraining a breach or threatened breach of [a contract of employment] compel an employee to do any work or to attend at any place for the doing of any work."

This provision, as with the corresponding provision relating to specific performance, applies only to contracts of employment[437] and only to enforcement against an employee. The equitable principle which denies specific enforcement of contracts of service has in appropriate circumstances permitted the issue of an injunction to restrain a negative undertaking in a contract for personal services, and this may have the effect indirectly of causing a contract to be performed. It remains to be determined whether and how far the provision now found in s.236 affects the operation of this principle. Two aspects of the question of the issue of an injunction in this circumstance need to be examined.

(a) *Restraining Breach by Employee or Independent Contractor.* **25–062**

In *Lumley v Wagner*,[438] Miss Wagner, an opera star, had agreed with Lumley that she would sing at Her Majesty's Theatre during a certain period, and would not sing anywhere else without his written permission. She made another engagement with Gye to sing at Covent Garden and abandoned her previous commitment to Lumley, who sought an injunction to restrain her from singing for Gye. Lord St Leonards held that an injunction should be granted to restrain the breach of the negative stipulation; it would not of course have been possible to obtain specific performance of the promise to sing.

The principle of *Lumley v Wagner* has been much criticised.[439] It is said that the issue of an injunction in this situation is the equivalent of specific performance; and that a number of principles are

[436] Above, para.24–024.
[437] cf. independent contractors.
[438] (1852) 1 De G.M. & G. 604; S. Waddams (2001) 117 L.Q.R. 431. The injunction may be granted even though it interferes with the contractual rights of innocent third parties; *PSM International Plc v Whitehouse and Willenhall Automation Ltd* [1992] I.R.L.R. 279; cf. *Maythorn v Palmer* (1864) 11 L.T. 261. See also *Thomas Marshall (Exports) Ltd v Guinle* [1979] Ch. 227 at 240–242.
[439] Ames, *Lectures on Legal History*, 1913, p.370; per Lindley L.J. in *Whitwood Chemical Co v Hardman* [1891] 2 Ch. 416 at 428; "I think that the court . . . will generally do much more harm by attempting to decree specific performance in cases of personal service than by leaving them alone; and whether it is attempted to enforce these contracts directly by a decree of specific performance, or indirectly by an injunction, appears to me to be immaterial."

thereby disregarded, especially the rule that the court will not supervise the performance of contracts; and the principle that the contracting parties must not become tied together in a relationship involving a status of servitude. However, where the contract does not involve very personal skills or talents, there is no objection to an injunction which might indirectly compel performance.[440]

It is submitted that the correct approach in these situations, as in other cases of injunctions, is that the injunction should issue to restrain the breach of a negative undertaking, unless the defendant can show that the court should in its discretion refuse on the ground that undesirable consequences may follow. Each case, in other words, should be treated on its merits.

Thus an employee should not be put into a position in which he must either perform the contract or do nothing.

> In *Rely-a-Bell Burglar and Fire Alarm Co v Eisler*[441] the employee had contracted to serve the employer and to take no other employment for the period of the contract of service. An injunction was refused, and damages awarded.
>
> In *Warner Bros v Nelson*,[442] a well-known actress, Bette Davis, contracted to work for the claimants and not to work as a film actress for any other film company for the period of her contract, "or to be engaged in any other occupation." The term was not void under the restraint of trade doctrine,[443] and the question was whether an injunction was an appropriate remedy.

> "[I]t would, of course, be impossible to grant an injunction covering all the negative covenants in the contract. That would, indeed, force the defendant to perform her contract or remain idle; but this objection is removed by the restricted form in which the injunction is sought. It is confined to forbidding the defendant, without the consent of the [claimants], to render any services for or in any motion picture or stage production for any one other than the [claimants]."[444]

> An injunction was given on these terms.[445] Miss Davis was still free to earn a living in other ways, even if they were less lucrative.

---

[440] *Lauritzencool AB v Lady Navigation Inc* [2005] 1 W.L.R. 3686 (time charter); P. Devonshire (2005) 121 L.Q.R. 560; R. Grime All E.R. Rev. 2005 p.385.

[441] [1926] Ch. 609.

[442] [1937] 1 K.B. 209.

[443] per Russell L.J. in *Instone v A Schroeder Music Publishing Co Ltd* [1974] 1 All E.R. 171 at 178, CA. He also criticised Branson J. who suggested in *Warner Bros v Nelson* [1937] 1 K.B. 209 at 214 that the doctrine of restraint of trade could not apply during the continuance of the contract; see also *Clifford Davis Management Ltd v WEA Records Ltd* [1975] 1 W.L.R. 61.

[444] [1937] 1 K.B. 209 at 219, per Branson J.

[445] *Robinson & Co Ltd v Heuer* [1898] 2 Ch. 451.

In *Evening Standard Co Ltd v Henderson*[446] an employee had failed to give the required notice. The Court of Appeal was prepared to grant an interlocutory injunction to prevent him from working for a rival paper during the notice period. As the employer had undertaken to pay his salary for that period even if he did not work ("garden leave"), the injunction did not compel him to perform the contract or starve, but was rather a means of enforcing the notice requirement. It may be otherwise if the "garden leave" is so long that the employee may lose his skills.[447]

(b) *Compelling Employer to Employ.*   **25–063**

In *Page One Records v Britton*,[448] a group of musicians appointed the claimant as their manager for five years, contracting not to engage anyone else as manager. They wished to change, and the claimant sought an injunction to prevent the employment of another manager, arguing, on the lines of *Warner Bros v Nelson*[449] that the defendants could retain him or continue without a manager. The injunction was refused, as it would *persuade* them to retain the claimant, which would be undesirable in a personal and fiduciary relationship in which the defendants had lost confidence in him.

Although the group could have earned their living in another way, just as Bette Davis could have done, it would be unrealistic to expect any of them to do so. Unless the period of the injunction is short, it puts economic pressure on the defendant to perform an obligation which is not specifically enforceable. The Court of Appeal has since held in *Warren v Mendy*[450] that *Page One Records* is preferable to *Warner*. The claimant was refused an injunction which in effect would have compelled a boxer to retain him as manager for at least two years. In relationships involving skill or talent and a high degree of mutual confidence,[451] the court should not enforce negative terms of a contract if this would in effect compel performance of the positive terms.

In *Hill v CA Parsons & Co Ltd*,[452] we saw that the Court of Appeal granted an injunction restraining an employer from acting on

---

[446] [1987] I.R.L.R. 64; J. Hand and P. Smith (1989) 139 N.L.J. 1716.

[447] *Provident Financial Group Plc v Hayward* [1989] I.C.R. 160; *William Hill Organisation Ltd v Tucker* [1999] I.C.R. 291.

[448] [1968] 1 W.L.R. 157.

[449] [1937] 1 K.B. 209.

[450] [1989] 1 W.L.R. 853; H. McLean (1990) 49 C.L.J. 28; A. Burrows (1990) 140 N.L.J. 1007; J. McCutcheon (1997) 17 L.S. 65.

[451] The obligation of the claimants in *Warner Bros v Nelson*, above, fn.449, and *Lumley v Wagner*, fn.439, above, para.25–062, was merely to pay money.

[452] [1972] Ch. 305; above, para.24–024. See also *Jones v Lee* [1980] I.R.L.R. 67.

a wrongful dismissal. This amounted to indirect specific performance of a service contract; but the circumstances were special. Personal confidence still existed between the parties; a proper length of
notice would have safeguarded the claimant's right under the Industrial Relations Act 1971; also the claimant was due to retire in two
years, and his pension depended on his average salary during the last
three years of employment. Stamp L.J. dissented, and would have
allowed the pension claim to be included in an award of damages.
The question arose again in *Chappell v Times Newspapers Ltd*,[453]
where employees sought an injunction to restrain their dismissal
during an industrial dispute. As mutual confidence no longer existed
between the parties, the case was not within the *Hill v Parsons*
exception. The fact that unfair dismissal was unlawful did not mean
that a service contract was enforceable by injunction. That would be
a "plain recipe for disaster".[454]

It appears that the grant of an injunction within the *Hill v Parsons*
exception is not a rarity. Although the claimant must normally show
that mutual confidence still exists,[455] this is not inevitably precluded
by the fact that the employer opposes the claim. It suffices to establish that the employer has no rational ground to lack confidence, as
where there has been no friction at the workplace.[456]

B. To Restrain a Breach of Trust

25–064   There are many examples of the issue of an injunction to restrain
a breach of an equitable obligation, and a few must suffice here.
Trustees have been restrained from distributing an estate inconsistently with the terms of the instrument,[457] or from selling under
depreciatory conditions of sale[458]; or for a price below that offered
firmly by a prospective purchaser[459]; or selling land without appointing a second trustee and without consulting the beneficiary.[460]

---

[453] [1975] 1 W.L.R. 482; see also *GKN (Cwmbran) Ltd v Lloyd* [1972] I.C.R. 214; *Ali v London Borough of Southwark* [1988] I.R.L.R. 100; *Wishart v National Association of Citizens Advice Bureau Ltd* [1990] I.C.R. 794.

[454] [1975] 1 W.L.R. 482 at 506. See also the Employment Rights Act 1996 s.117: an employment tribunal may order reinstatement, but the sanction in the event of non-compliance is an award of compensation.

[455] cf. *Robb v London Borough of Hammersmith and Fulham* [1991] I.R.L.R. 72 (no dismissal prior to disciplinary procedure even though loss of confidence); *Jones v Gwent CC* [1992] I.R.L.R. 521; *Gryf-Lowczowski v Hinchingbrooke Healthcare NHS Trust* [2006] Lloyd's Rep. Med. 199.

[456] *Powell v London Borough of Brent* [1987] I.R.L.R. 466; *Hughes v London Borough of Southwark* [1988] I.R.L.R. 55; J. Hendy and J. McMullen (1988) 85/5 L.S.Gaz. 28; K. Ewing (1989) 48 C.L.J. 28 and (1993) 52 C.L.J. 405; H. Carty (1989) 52 M.L.R. 449.

[457] *Fox v Fox* (1870) L.R. 11 Eq. 142.

[458] *Dance v Goldingham* (1873) L.R. 8 Ch.App. 902.

[459] *Buttle v Saunders* [1950] 2 All E.R. 193 (above, para.18–002) where the trustee had promised (but not in binding form) to sell land to another purchaser.

[460] *Waller v Waller* [1967] 1 W.L.R. 451.

Where the claimant has a claim to trace property in equity,[461] an injunction may be granted to restrain the defendant from disposing of the property.[462]

C. To Restrain the Commission or Continuance of a Tort

In each of the many cases in which an injunction issues to restrain **25–065** the commission of a tort, equity is exercising its "concurrent" jurisdiction. Equity plays no part in determining whether a wrong has been committed; that is a matter solely of law. It is the remedy alone that is equitable. Thus the claimant must first establish the commission or threat of something which constitutes a tort at law. If it is, the court may, in its discretion, grant an injunction. The rules and practice vary with the tort in question.

i. Nuisance.[463] The act complained of must constitute a nuisance **25–066** at law. "There is no such thing as an equitable nuisance."[464] The interference must cause or threaten damage.[465] No injunction will issue to deal with a trifling interference[466]; and even if damage is proved, equity will not grant an injunction in every case in which the common law would award damages. The remedy is discretionary, and is particularly appropriate in cases of nuisance.[467] Damages may be awarded in lieu under Lord Cairns' Act.[468]

It was held in *Miller v Jackson*,[469] by a majority of the Court of Appeal, that the court should weigh the interests of the public against those of the individual, and should refuse the injunction if, on balance, it was felt that the interest of the public should prevail. This proposition was doubted in *Kennaway v Thompson*[470] by the Court of Appeal. It was there held that, when considering whether to award damages in lieu of an injunction under Lord Cairns' Act in a

---

[461] Above, para.23–047.

[462] *A v C* [1981] Q.B. 956n.; *Polly Peck International Plc v Nadir (No.2)* [1992] 4 All E.R 769.

[463] See generally S. Tromans (1982) 41 C.L.J. 87.

[464] per Kindersley V.C. in *Soltau v de Held* (1851) 2 Sim.(N.S.) 133 at 151.

[465] It is otherwise where the nuisance is actionable without proof of damage; *Sevenoaks DC v Pattullo & Vinson Ltd* [1984] Ch. 211; *Halton BC v Cawley* [1985] 1 W.L.R. 15 (right to hold market).

[466] *Ankerson v Connelly* [1907] 1 Ch. 678.

[467] *Halsey v Esso Petroleum Co Ltd* [1961] 1 W.L.R. 683; *Leakey v National Trust for Places of Historic Interest or Natural Beauty* [1980] Q.B. 485; *Laws v Florinpace* [1981] 1 All E.R. 659; *Pugh v Howells* (1984) 48 P. & C.R. 298.

[468] Above, para.25–048.

[469] [1977] Q.B. 966, above, para.25–010; *Tetley v Chitty* [1986] 1 All E.R. 663.

[470] [1981] Q.B. 88. It was also rejected in *Webster v Lord Advocate* (1984) S.L.T. 13. See also *Sevenoaks DC v Pattullo & Vinson Ltd*, above, fn.465; *Rosling v Pinnegar* (1987) 54 P. & C.R. 124.

nuisance case, the public interest does not prevail over the private interest of the claimant.[471]

25–067   **ii. Trespass.** An injunction will issue to restrain a threatened or existing trespass. In minor cases, the court will leave the claimant to such remedy as he has at law; as where a clergyman of the Church of England held services on the seashore between high and low water mark which was leased by the Crown to the Corporation[472]; or where collectors chased a butterfly on to the claimant's land.[473] Where, however, the defendant entered the claimant's wood, cut down trees and clearly intended to cut more, he was restrained.[474] Indeed, there is no real discretion to refuse in cases of total dispossession.[475] Even if the injunction would be difficult to enforce, as where the defendants had no assets and imprisonment would be disproportionate, it may still be granted if it could have a real deterrent effect.[476]

Where the defendant has no arguable defence, the claimant may be granted an interlocutory injunction even where the trespass has caused no damage.[477]

A mandatory injunction will be granted where necessary, for example requiring the removal of an advertising sign which projected into the airspace above the claimant's single-storey shop.[478]

25–068   **iii. Libel.** The granting of injunctions to restrain the publication of a libel has caused particular difficulty, partly because of the complexity of proof of the tort, but largely because of the importance of allowing to be said things that ought to be said. It was not until *Quartz Hill Consolidated Gold Mining Co v Beall* in 1882[479] that the courts positively asserted a jurisdiction to restrain publication. The matter is usually one of urgency, requiring an interlocutory injunction, and Jessel M.R. was careful to point out the need for great caution in its exercise.

---

[471] Authorities supporting the contrary proposition were decided before *Shelfer v City of London Electric Lighting Co* [1895] 1 Ch. 287, above, para.25–049.

[472] *Llandudno Urban District Council v Woods* [1899] 2 Ch. 705. Refusal terminates self-help remedies; *Burton v Winters* [1993] 1 W.L.R. 1077.

[473] *Fielden v Cox* (1906) 22 T.L.R. 411; *Behrens v Richards* [1905] 2 Ch. 614.

[474] *Stanford v Hurlstone* (1873) L.R. 9 Ch.App. 116. See also *League Against Cruel Sports Ltd v Scott* [1986] Q.B. 240 (persistent trespass by hunt).

[475] *Harrow LBC v Donohue* [1995] 1 E.G.L.R. 257.

[476] *Secretary of State for the Environment, Food and Rural Affairs v Meier* [2009] 1 W.L.R. 2780 (gypsies).

[477] *Patel v WH Smith (Eziot) Ltd* [1987] 1 W.L.R. 853; *Anchor Brewhouse Developments Ltd v Berkley House (Docklands Developments) Ltd* [1987] 2 E.G.L.R. 173.

[478] *Kelsen v Imperial Tobacco Co Ltd* [1957] 2 Q.B. 334. See also *Trenberth (John) Ltd v National Westminster Bank Ltd* (1979) 39 P. & C.R. 104; *London & Manchester Assurance Company Ltd v O & H Construction Ltd* [1989] 2 E.G.L.R. 185 (interlocutory).

[479] (1882) 20 Ch.D. 501.

The claimant must satisfy the court of the falsity of the statements and, where they are privileged, the presence of malice.

"The court will not restrain the publication of an article, even though it is defamatory, when the defendant says that he intends to justify it or to make fair comment on a matter of public interest. . . . The reason sometimes given is that the defences of justification and fair comment are for the jury, which is the constitutional tribunal, and not for a judge; but a better reason is the importance in the public interest that the truth should out."[480]

The interest of the public in knowing the truth outweighs the interest of a claimant in maintaining his reputation.[481] Thus, it was laid down in *Bonnard v Perryman*[482] as a working rule that an interlocutory injunction ought never to be granted except in the clearest cases, in which, if a jury did not find the matter complained of to be libellous, the court would set aside the verdict as unreasonable. Lord Denning M.R. stated that all requests for "gagging injunctions" which seek to prevent true and fair comment on matters of public interest should fail.[483] But in *Hubbard v Pitt*[484] the Court of Appeal upheld the grant of an interlocutory injunction to restrain, amongst other things, the display of allegedly libellous placards and leaflets outside the claimants' business premises. The necessity of preserving the freedoms of speech, assembly and demonstration should "not constrain the court to refuse a [claimant] an injunction to prevent defendants exercising these liberties in his front garden."[485] The injunction may also be granted if there is a clear case that publication is part of a concerted plan to inflict deliberate damage without just cause.[486] In *Monson v Tussaud's*,[487] an injunction was refused because it appeared that there might be a question at the trial whether the claimant had agreed to the publication. The court will only intervene where the issue is clear and certain. It "will not

[480] *Fraser v Evans* [1969] 1 Q.B. 349 at 360, per Lord Denning M.R.; *Bryanston Finance Ltd v de Vries* [1975] Q.B. 703 (privileged occasions); *Crest Homes Ltd v Ascott, The Times,* February 4, 1975 (no injunction when defendant chose "flamboyant and vulgar method of airing his complaints"); *Khashoggi v IPC Magazines Ltd* [1986] 1 W.L.R. 1412; *Att Gen v News Group Newspapers Ltd* [1987] Q.B. 1; *Holley v Smyth* [1998] Q.B. 726.

[481] *Woodward v Hutchins* [1977] 1 W.L.R. 760, at 764 (per Lord Denning M.R.).

[482] [1891] 2 Ch. 269.

[483] *Att Gen v British Broadcasting Corp* [1981] A.C. 303 at 311 CA.

[484] [1976] Q.B. 142; (Lord Denning M.R. dissenting). See P. Wallington (1976) 35 C.L.J. 82.

[485] [1976] Q.B. 142 at 187, per Stamp L.J.

[486] *Gulf Oil (Great Britain) Ltd v Page* [1987] Ch. 327 (airborne sign over Cheltenham racecourse); *Femis-Bank (Anguilla) Ltd v Lazar* [1991] Ch. 391.

[487] [1894] 1 Q.B. 671. The claimant, who had been tried in Scotland for murder, where the jury had returned a verdict of "not proven", complained of the exhibition of a figure of himself in a room next to the "Chamber of Horrors".

prejudice the issue by granting an injunction in advance of publication."[488] It has been held that the principles laid down in *American Cyanamid Co v Ethicon Ltd*[489] governing the grant of an interlocutory injunction have no application to libel injunctions, thus preserving the rule in *Bonnard v Perryman*.[490] This rule is unaffected by s.12(3) of the Human Rights Act 1998, which has already been considered.[491]

Once libel has been proved at the trial, the claimant may obtain an injunction to restrain its repetition.

D. Breach of Confidence

25–069   An injunction will be available to restrain a breach of confidence, whether arising out of a personal, commercial or other relationship.[492] An initial confidential relationship is not required: a duty of confidence arises where a person receives information he knows or should know is confidential. The essence of the action is misuse of private information.[493] Many of the questions which arise are similar to those discussed in connection with the cases on libel, but the principle of freedom of speech plays a less dominant part here. Unlike libel, the truth of the statement is no defence to a breach of confidence. As will be seen, the search order[494] has evolved to protect the victims of commercial malpractice and espionage. Also in the commercial context, an injunction may be granted to restrain a firm of solicitors or accountants from acting for one client against another client in respect of whom confidential information is retained, unless a clearly effective "Chinese wall" is in place.[495]

An obligation of confidence exists in respect of communications between husband and wife.

> "It is the policy of the law (which is the basis of the court's jurisdiction) to preserve the close confidence and mutual trust between husband and wife."[496]

[488] *Fraser v Evans*, above, fn.480, at 361, per Lord Denning M.R.

[489] [1975] A.C. 396, above, para.25–029.

[490] *Bestobell Paints Ltd v Bigg* (1975) 119 S.J. 678; *J Trevor & Sons v PR Solomon* (1978) 248 E.G. 779 (per Lord Denning M.R.); *Herbage v Pressdram Ltd* [1984] 1 W.L.R. 1160; *Gulf Oil (Great Britain) Ltd v Page* [1987] Ch. 327.

[491] Above, para.25–037; *Greene v Associated Newspapers Ltd* [2005] Q.B. 972. See also I. Leigh and L. Lustgarten (1999) 58 C.L.J. 509 at 531–536.

[492] See generally M. Bryan (1977) 30 C.L.P. 191 and (1976) 92 L.Q.R. 180; Goff and Jones, *The Law of Restitution*, 7th edn, Ch.34.

[493] *Campbell v MGN Ltd* [2004] A.C 457.

[494] Below, para.25–077. See *Lock International Plc v Beswick* [1989] 1 W.L.R. 1268.

[495] *Bolkiah (Prince Jefri) v KPMG* [1999] 2 A.C. 222; *Young v Robson Rhodes (A Firm)* [1999] 3 All E.R. 524; H. McVea (2000) 59 C.L.J. 370; *Marks & Spencer Plc v Freshfields Bruckhaus Deringer* [2004] 1 W.L.R. 233; *Re Z (Restraining solicitors from acting)* [2010] 2 F.L.R. 132.

[496] *Argyll v Argyll* [1967] Ch. 302 at 332.

The same applies to stable relationships but not to transient sexual relationships.[497] Other kinds of confidential information will be restrained from publication along similar lines,[498] and even, in some cases, where the information is available from other public sources,[499] but not if it has already been disseminated worldwide, for in such a case the injunction would be futile.[500] It is necessary that the claimant should himself have an interest in preventing the disclosure,[501] although he need not show that the use of the information would cause him detriment.[502] Even where the injunction is granted, it may be that the defendant is enjoined from making use of the confidential information only for a limited period rather than for all time.[503] However, in exceptional cases an injunction may be granted against the whole world restraining publication of confidential information indefinitely, to protect those who would be seriously at risk of injury or death if their identity or whereabouts were to become public knowledge, if there is no other way to ensure protection of their right to life under the European Convention on Human Rights as given effect by the Human Rights Act 1998.[504]

It has been confirmed by the House of Lords that infringement of privacy is not a cause of action in English law.[505] However, the right to privacy underlies the action for breach of confidence. This fast developing area has been influenced and reinforced by the European Convention on Human Rights and the Human Rights Act 1998. Article 8 of the Convention protects the right to respect for private and family life, while art.10 protects the right to freedom of expression, in both cases subject to qualifications.[506] The values enshrined in arts 8 and 10 are now embedded in the action for breach of confidence. The right to privacy has to be balanced against the media's right to give information to the public, but neither article

---

[497] *A v B Plc* [2003] Q.B. 195; D. Howarth (2002) 61 C.L.J. 264.

[498] *Saltman Engineering Co Ltd v Campbell Engineering Co Ltd* [1963] 3 All E.R. 413; *Peter Pan Manufacturing Corp v Corsets Silhouette Ltd* [1964] 1 W.L.R. 96; *Seager v Copydex* [1967] 1 W.L.R. 923; *Thomas Marshall (Exports) Ltd v Guinle* [1979] Ch. 227; *Fraser v Thames Television Ltd* [1984] Q.B. 44; A. Tettenborn (1983) 42 C.L.J. 209.

[499] *Schering Chemicals Ltd v Falkman Ltd* [1982] Q.B. 1; *Att Gen v Guardian Newspapers Ltd* [1987] 1 W.L.R. 1248 (*Spycatcher* at the interlocutory stage).

[500] *Att Gen v Guardian Newspapers Ltd (No.2)* [1990] 1 A.C. 109 (*Spycatcher* final injunction refused). The European Court of Human Rights held that the Government had violated art.10 of the Convention in maintaining the injunctions after publication abroad.

[501] *Fraser v Evans* [1969] 1 Q.B. 349; *Hubbard v Vosper* [1972] 2 Q.B. 84.

[502] *X v Y* [1988] 2 All E.R. 648. See the varying views in *Att Gen v Guardian Newspapers Ltd (No.2)*, above, fn.500.

[503] This is the "springboard" doctrine. See W. Braithwaite (1979) 42 M.L.R. 94; M. Bryan (1976) 92 L.Q.R. 180.

[504] *Venables v News Group Newspapers* [2001] Fam. 430.

[505] *Wainwright v Home Office* [2004] 2 A.C. 430; *Campbell v MGN Ltd* [2004] 2 A.C. 457; J. Morgan (2004) 120 L.Q.R. 563; N. Moreham (2004) 63 C.L.J. 555.

[506] See *H v N (A Health Authority)*, *The Times*, March 19, 2002.

prevails over the other.[507] The provisions of the Human Rights Act 1998 affecting the grant of interlocutory injunctions in the area of breach of confidence and privacy have already been noted.[508]

It has been said that the right to privacy has been "shoehorned" into the action for breach of confidence,[509] thus becoming "the tort that dares not speak its name".[510] The discomfort in using breach of confidence in cases where there was no pre-existing relationship of confidence between the parties has been avoided by re-christening it "misuse of private information".[511] The test is whether the claimant had a reasonable expectation of privacy.[512] In this way the law of confidence has developed so as to prevent the publication of unauthorised photographs of celebrities or their children,[513] even in public places.[514] It has further developed so that a publisher who has paid the celebrity for exclusive rights to publish the photographs may obtain a remedy against third parties who publish them. So the House of Lords held in a dispute between rival publishers of photographs of a celebrity wedding, where it was considered that there was no public policy reason why the law of confidence should not protect information of this kind.[515] It has been said, however, that "The Law Lords have succeeded in bringing absolutely no clarity whatsoever into the muddy waters of the law of confidence".[516] In spite of this "shoehorning", differences remain between breach of privacy and breach of confidence when weighing the balance between art.8 and art.10 rights, as art.10(2) expressly recognises confidence as qualifying the right to freedom of expression.[517]

There has been much recent litigation in which celebrities have sought to restrain publication of information concerning their private lives. Some have sought anonymity, while others have gone further and asked the court to prohibit disclosure of the very existence of the proceedings (a "super-injunction"). There is no room to deal with the cases here, but the general principle is that, if the

---

[507] *Campbell v MGN Ltd*, above, fn.505. See also *Re S (A Child) (Identification: Restrictions on Publication)* [2005] 1 A.C. 593; *K v News Group Newspapers Ltd* [2011] 1 W.L.R. 1827 (Article 8 rights of children carry particular weight); T. Bennett (2011) 127 L.Q.R. 531.

[508] Above, para.25–037.

[509] *Douglas v Hello! Ltd (No.3)* [2006] Q.B. 125; D. Friedman, R. Bagshaw and N. Moreham (2005) 121 L.Q.R. 400, 550 and 628 respectively; R. Mulheron (2006) 69 M.L.R. 679; *McKennitt v Ash* [2008] Q.B. 73.

[510] J. Morgan (2005) 64 C.L.J. 549.

[511] *McKennit v Ash*, above, fn.509, referring to *Campbell v MGN Ltd* [2004] 2 A.C. 457; N. Moreham (2007) 123 L.Q.R. 373; *Mosley v News Group Newspapers Ltd, The Times*, July 30, 2008.

[512] *Imerman v Tchenguiz* [2011] Fam. 116; R. Probert (2011) 127 L.Q.R. 28.

[513] *Murray v Express Newspapers Plc* [2009] Ch. 481 (child of "Harry Potter" author).

[514] *Campbell v MGN Ltd*, above, fn.511.

[515] *Douglas v Hello! Ltd (No.3)* [2008] A.C. 1 (heard with *OBG Ltd v Allan*).

[516] A. Caddick (2007) 157 N.L.J. 805.

[517] *Prince of Wales v Associated Newspapers Ltd* [2008] Ch. 57 (injunction granted to restrain publication of Prince's journals recording his views on foreign visits).

court considers that an injunction should be granted, it may (if there is no acceptable alternative) either anonymise the claimant's name and allow the nature of the information to be disclosed, or may direct that the claimant's name may be disclosed but not the nature of the information.[518] This whole area has recently been examined by the Committee on Super-Injunctions, chaired by Lord Neuberger M.R.[519] The Committee's recommendations are intended to ensure that the exceptions to the principle of open justice will only be allowed when they are strictly necessary in the interests of justice, so that super-injunctions will only be granted in very limited circumstances and normally for a very short period.

Injunctions may be granted against a party to a confidential rela- **25–070** tionship or against third parties, such as the press, who seek to publish confidential information knowing it to be such.[520] The third party, however, is not necessarily in the same position as the original confidant, as their respective duties may be different.[521] Worldwide publication releases third parties[522] (but probably not the original confidant[523]) from any duty of confidence, although in exceptional cases publication on the internet after the injunction has been issued may not bring this principle into play, as the injunction could prevent wider circulation of the information.[524]

The injunction will be refused if the public interest in the preservation of confidence is overridden by some other public interest. It is not enough that the information is a matter of public interest. The test is whether it is in the public interest that the duty of confidence should be breached.[525] While the precise scope of the "public interest" defence remains uncertain,[526] it is clear that matters such as confidentiality or national security[527] must be balanced against the public interest in freedom of speech and the press and the right to

---

[518] *H v News Group Newspapers Ltd (Practice Note)* [2011] 1 W.L.R. 1645.

[519] *Super-Injunctions, Anonymised Injunctions and Open Justice* (May 21, 2011).

[520] *Att Gen v Guardian Newspapers Ltd* [1987] 1 W.L.R. 1248, and *(No.2)* [1990] 1 A.C. 109 (*Spycatcher*); J. Michael (1989) 52 M.L.R. 389; G. Jones (1989) C.L.P. 49; *Douglas v Hello! Ltd (No.3)*, above, fn.515.

[521] *Att Gen v Guardian Newspapers Ltd (No.2)*, above, fn.500.

[522] *Att Gen v Guardian Newspapers Ltd (No.2)*, above, fn.500. (*Spycatcher* final injunction refused). See also *Lord Advocate v The Scotsman Publications Ltd* [1990] 1 A.C. 812.

[523] *Att Gen v Guardian Newspapers Ltd (No.2)*, above, fn.500 (because he must not profit from his own wrong).

[524] *Venables v News Group Newspapers* [2001] Fam. 430, above.

[525] *Prince of Wales v Associated Newspapers Ltd*, above, fn.517; *Mosley v News Group Newspapers Ltd, The Times*, July 30, 2008 (no public interest in disclosure of sado-masochistic activities); K. Hughes (2009) 125 L.Q.R. 244.

[526] Goff and Jones, pp.791–797. See also *Att Gen v Jonathan Cape Ltd* [1976] Q.B. 752; *Schering Chemicals Ltd v Falkman Ltd* [1982] Q.B. 1; G. Jones (1982) 41 C.L.J. 40; A. Tettenborn (1982) 98 L.Q.R. 5.

[527] *Att Gen v Guardian Newspapers Ltd* [1987] 1 W.L.R. 1248, and *(No.2)* [1990] 1 A.C. 109 (*Spycatcher*). The latter decision, however, is not based on the balancing of public interests but on the fact that no further damage could be caused by publication. See generally *X Ltd v Morgan Grampian (Publishers) Ltd* [1991] 1 A.C. 1.

receive information. More particularly, there is no confidence as to the disclosure of "iniquity". This principle was discussed by the House of Lords in *Att Gen v Guardian Newspapers Ltd (No.2)*,[528] where the question was whether newspapers should be enjoined from publishing *Spycatcher* (the Peter Wright memoirs). It was said that the "iniquity" defence was subject to two limitations. First, the disclosure of confidential information revealing wrong-doing should in some cases be to interested parties such as the police rather than to the public at large.[529] Secondly, the duty of confidence was not overridden by mere allegations of wrong-doing. While the wrong-doing need not be proved, there must be at least a prima facie case. Further, it was not the case that *any* breach of the law was within the "iniquity" defence. In the present case, the publication of the entire book or substantial extracts could not be within this defence when the allegations of "iniquity" covered only a few pages. The final injunction was, however, refused because the information was by this time within the public domain.

Where there is no wrong-doing by the claimant the public interest defence will succeed only in exceptional cases. Such a case was *Lion Laboratories Ltd v Evans*,[530] where the claimant failed to restrain the publication of confidential documents concerning the accuracy of a "breathalyser" device manufactured by the claimant. The public interest in confidentiality had to be weighed against its interest in the accuracy of a device upon which depended liability to criminal penalties.

We saw above that celebrities and other public figures are entitled to have their privacy respected in appropriate circumstances. However, where a public figure deceives the public about his or her private life, publication of the truth is justified in the public interest.[531] The defence succeeded in *W v Egdell*,[532] where a prisoner in a

---

[528] Above. The "iniquity" involved alleged plots to overthrow the Wilson government and to kill President Nasser. See also *Finers v Miro* [1991] 1 W.L.R. 35 (fraud); *Commissioner of Police of Bermuda v Bermuda Broadcasting Co Ltd*, *The Times*, January 24, 2008 (corruption allegations about public figures).

[529] See *Francome v Mirror Group Newspapers* [1984] 1 W.L.R. 892 (injunction to restrain publication of illegally taped telephone conversations revealing possible criminal offences and breaches of Jockey Club regulations. Public interest could be served by making tapes available to police or Jockey Club); cf. *Cork v McVicar*, *The Times*, October 31, 1984 (Exposure of corrupt practices in the administration of justice not to be restrained by injunction. Argument that disclosure should only be to the appropriate authorities rejected). See also *Re a Company's Application* [1989] Ch. 477; E. Lomnicka (1990) 106 L.Q.R. 42; (no injunction to restrain disclosure to tax and regulatory authorities); *Woolgar v Chief Constable of Sussex Police* [2000] 1 W.L.R. 25 (no injunction to restrain disclosure to nursing regulatory body).

[530] [1985] Q.B. 526 (interlocutory); (1984) 100 L.Q.R. 517; Y. Cripps (1985) 44 C.L.J. 35; N. Lowe and C. Willmore (1985) 48 M.L.R. 592.

[531] *Campbell v MGN Ltd* [2004] 2 A.C. 457 (but the majority of the House of Lords upheld a damages award because the publication of a photograph of a "supermodel" leaving a Narcotics Anonymous meeting was unjustified).

[532] [1990] Ch. 395.

secure hospital failed to enjoin the disclosure by a doctor to the authorities having power to discharge him of a confidential report on his mental state. In *X v Y*,[533] on the other hand, the defence failed when a health authority sought to prevent publication of the identity of two doctors suffering from AIDS, disclosed by its employee in breach of contract and confidence.

In the sphere of judicial proceedings, the public interest requiring the truth to be disclosed in the administration of justice does not override the confidentiality of matters disclosed in other proceedings, which may be protected by injunction.[534]

E. Public Wrongs

Although an injunction normally issues to prevent a breach of the claimant's own rights, it is available, at the suit of the Attorney General, to restrain an act which is illegal or detrimental to the public. Thus the Attorney General may obtain an injunction to restrain a public nuisance, either on his own initiative, or on the relation of some other person.[535] A private individual may only sue in respect of public wrongs where a private right of his own is interfered with,[536] or where he suffers special damage from the interference with the public right.[537] We have seen that, subject to this exception, the individual cannot sue in his own name to enforce a public right. He must bring a relator action, with the consent of the Attorney General.[538]

25–071

An injunction may issue in circumstances where it is the only effective way of protecting the interests of the public, or where the criminal penalty has proved inadequate to prevent continuous breaches of the law. It should be added that where the Attorney General brings such an action, the injunction is almost always granted. Thus injunctions were issued where the defendant ran buses in Manchester without licence and in defiance of the corporation's

---

[533] [1988] 2 All E.R. 648; A. Grubb All E.R. Rev. 1988 at 214.

[534] *Medway v Doublelock Ltd* [1978] 1 W.L.R. 710. See also *Distillers Co (Biochemicals) Ltd v Times Newspapers Ltd* [1975] Q.B. 613. But the Banking Act 1987 overrides the duty of confidence; *A v B Bank (Governor and Company of the Bank of England intervening)* [1993] Q.B. 311.

[535] *Att Gen v PYA Quarries* [1975] 2 Q.B. 169.

[536] *Lyon v Fishmongers Co* (1876) 1 App.Cas. 662.

[537] *Meade v London Borough of Haringey* [1979] 1 W.L.R. 637; *Gravesham BC v British Railways Board* [1978] Ch. 379; *Barrs v Bethell* [1982] Ch. 294; *Lonrho Ltd v Shell Petroleum Co Ltd* [1982] A.C. 173; *Ashby v Ebdon* [1985] Ch. 394; *Rickless v United Artists Corp* [1988] Q.B. 40; *CBS Songs Ltd v Amstrad Consumer Electronics Plc* [1988] A.C. 1013; *P v Liverpool Daily Post and Echo Newspapers Plc* [1991] 2 A.C. 370; *R. v Deputy Governor of Parkhurst Prison, Ex p. Hague* [1992] 1 A.C. 58.

[538] *Gouriet v Union of Post Office Workers* [1978] A.C. 435, above, para.25–013.

objections, the profits being greater than the fines,[539] and where the defendant operated a hotel without a fire certificate, causing danger to the public.[540] The Attorney General may not, however, obtain an injunction to "freeze" the proceeds of crime, as that would amount to confiscation outside the statutory provisions permitting confiscation orders.[541]

We have already seen that the view of the House of Lords was that the cases where the Attorney General can invoke the aid of the civil courts to restrain the commission of a criminal offence are narrow and not to be extended, and may require reconsideration.[542]

Some statutory provisions enable local authorities to seek injunctions in their own name to enforce public rights, without the concurrence of the Attorney General. For example, the Local Government Act 1972 s.222[543] enables the local authority to act where it is "expedient for the promotion or protection of the interests of the inhabitants of their area." Applications under s.222 are usually successful. Although the Attorney General's power to seek injunctions to restrain criminal offences is limited to cases of emergency or inadequate criminal penalty, it has been held that the local authority's power under s.222 is not limited in this way: the only limitation is that the action must promote or protect the interests of the inhabitants.[544] But the court will be reluctant to grant an injunction if the sanctions for disobeying it would be more onerous than the criminal penalty.[545] Nor should the court "indulge in parallel creativity" by granting injunctions in areas such as restraining anti-social behaviour, where Parliament had recently made a detailed statutory scheme designed to deal with the situation.[546]

---

[539] *Att Gen v Sharp* [1931] 1 Ch. 121; *Att Gen v Harris* [1961] 1 Q.B. 74 (selling flowers illegally from stalls); *Att Gen v Bastow* [1957] 1 Q.B. 514; *Att Gen v Smith* [1958] 2 Q.B. 173. Such cases could now be dealt with by an action by the local authority under the Local Government Act 1972 s.222, below.

[540] *Att Gen v Chaudry* [1971] 1 W.L.R. 1623.

[541] *Att Gen v Blake* [2001] 1 A.C. 268 (no injunction to prevent receipt of royalties by KGB spy for his autobiography, but private law action for account of profits available).

[542] *Gouriet v Union of Post Office Workers* [1978] A.C. 435.

[543] This exception was described as "limited" in *Gouriet v Union of Post Office Workers*, above, fn.542. For limitations, see *Worcestershire CC v Tongue* [2004] Ch. 236. See also the wider provisions of Town and Country Planning Act 1990 s.187B; *South Bucks DC v Porter* [2003] 2 A.C. 558.

[544] *Kent County Council v Batchelor* [1979] 1 W.L.R. 213 (breach of tree preservation order); D. Feldman (1979) 95 L.Q.R. 174. See also *Thanet DC v Ninedrive Ltd* [1978] 1 All E.R. 703 (Sunday trading); *Hammersmith BC v Magnum Automated Forecourts Ltd* [1978] 1 W.L.R. 50 (nuisance). See also *Re L (Vulnerable Adults with Capacity: Court's Jurisdiction)* [2011] Fam. 189.

[545] *Stoke-on-Trent City Council v B&Q (Retail) Ltd* [1984] A.C. 754. See also *Nottingham City Council v Zain (A Minor)* [2002] 1 W.L.R. 607 (injunction against alleged drug-dealer).

[546] *Birmingham City Council v Shafi* [2009] 1 W.L.R. 1961 at 1982.

Where the defendant is flouting a statute, an injunction may be sought before the statutory remedies have been exhausted.[547] In exceptional cases, involving a plain breach and a clear intention to continue with it, the injunction may be granted before proceedings for the statutory remedy have even been commenced.[548]

Although injunctions under s.222 are typically granted in cases of deliberate flouting or where the criminal penalty is inadequate, the jurisdiction is not confined to these circumstances.[549] Flagrant breaches of the criminal law need not be shown where there is clear evidence of persistent and serious conduct.[550] However, an injunction in aid of the criminal law is a remedy of last resort and should not be granted if a less draconian means of securing obedience is available.[551] Nor should it be granted where adequate powers are vested in the criminal justice agencies.[552]

In the sphere of public law an injunction, declaration or preroga-   **25–072**
tive order may be sought, with the permission of the court, in a claim for judicial review. This is now governed by Pt 54 of the Civil Procedure Rules 1998. The court may grant the injunction or declaration if, in all the circumstances, it is "just and convenient" to do so.[553] On the question of locus standi, the claimant must have a sufficient interest in the matter.[554] In a case concerning a declaration and a mandatory order, then called mandamus, it was held that one taxpayer had no sufficient interest to ask the court to investigate the tax affairs of another taxpayer or to complain that the latter had been under or over-assessed.[555]

The question arose whether, in the field of administrative law, the claim for judicial review was an exclusive remedy, so that the claimant could not seek an injunction in the ordinary way. In *O'Reilly v Mackman*[556] the House of Lords held that, as a general rule, it would be contrary to public policy and an abuse of process for a claimant complaining of a public authority's infringement of his public law

[547] *Runnymede BC v Ball* [1986] 1 W.L.R. 353.
[548] *Stafford BC v Elkenford Ltd* [1977] 1 W.L.R. 324; *Stoke-on-Trent City Council v B&Q (Retail) Ltd*, above, fn.545 (Sunday trading).
[549] *Runnymede BC v Ball* [1986] 1 W.L.R. 353; *Kirklees BC v Wickes Building Supplies Ltd* [1993] A.C. 227; *Guildford BC v Hein* [2005] L.G.R. 797.
[550] *City of London Corp v Bovis Construction Ltd* [1992] 3 All E.R. 697.
[551] *Waverley BC v Hilden* [1988] 1 W.L.R. 246; *Newport Borough Council v Khan* [1990] 1 W.L.R. 1185. See also *Mayor of London (on behalf of the Greater London Authority) v Hall* [2011] 1 W.L.R. 504 (injunction against demonstrators camped opposite Parliament).
[552] *Re Z (Local Authority: Duty)* [2005] 1 W.L.R. 959 (no injunction to restrain travel to Switzerland for purpose of euthanasia although offence of aiding and abetting suicide could be committed).
[553] Senior Courts Act 1981 s.31(2).
[554] See the comments of Lord Denning in *The Discipline of Law*, 1979, p.133.
[555] *R. v IRC, Ex p. National Federation of Self-Employed and Small Businesses Ltd* [1982] A.C. 617; D. Feldman (1982) 45 M.L.R. 92; J. Griffiths (1982) 41 C.L.J. 6. cf. *R. v Her Majesty's Treasury, Ex p. Smedley* [1985] Q.B. 657.
[556] [1983] 2 A.C. 237; HWRW (1983) 99 L.Q.R. 166; J. Jolowicz (1983) 42 C.L.J. 15; M. Sunkin (1983) 46 M.L.R. 645; J. Beatson (1987) 103 L.Q.R. 34.

rights to seek redress by an ordinary action and thus avoid the protection afforded to statutory tribunals.[557] It is otherwise where the claimant's private law rights have been infringed.[558] The Civil Procedure Rules 1998 now provide more flexibility where the claimant has used the wrong procedure.[559]

An ordinary injunction is appropriate where the defendant is a domestic body with no public role. Where the defendant is a public body, a distinction is drawn between its public and private law functions. Thus a local authority's decision as to whether it has a duty to house a homeless person is a public law function, while its functions as landlord or licensor once it has implemented its duty are matters of private law.[560]

Even before the Civil Procedure Rules 1998, the House of Lords favoured a broader approach, namely that a litigant could seek to enforce a private law right by ordinary action, notwithstanding that the proceedings involved a challenge to a public law act or decision, judicial review being necessary only when private law rights were not at stake.[561] It was concluded that, unless the procedure was ill suited to dispose of the question at issue:

> "[T]here is much to be said in favour of the proposition that a court having jurisdiction ought to let a case be heard rather than entertain a debate concerning the form of the proceedings."[562]

This flexible approach was developed by the Court of Appeal in *Clark v University of Lincolnshire and Humberside*,[563] which involved a dispute as to whether an action for breach of contract brought by a student against the university should properly have been commenced as judicial review. It was held that, in cases where judicial review would have been more appropriate, the court would not strike out the action merely because of the procedure adopted. Under the Civil Procedure Rules 1998 the court could prevent unfair exploitation of the longer limitation period applicable to private law actions without resorting to a rigid exclusionary rule capable of doing equal injustice:

---

[557] Which includes the requirement of the permission of the court, and a three-month time limit.

[558] No private right was involved in a decision as to remission of a prison sentence. There may be other exceptions, such as where none of the parties objects.

[559] CPR Pt 54.20. See also Pt 30, as to transfers to and from the Administrative Court.

[560] *O'Rourke v Camden LBC* [1998] A.C. 188. See the review by the House of Lords in *X (Minors) v Bedfordshire CC* [1995] 2 A.C. 633.

[561] *Roy v Kensington and Chelsea and Westminster Family Practitioner Committee* [1992] 1 A.C. 624; S. Fredman and G. Morris (1992) 108 L.Q.R. 353; I. Hare (1992) 51 C.L.J. 201; *Mohram Ali v Tower Hamlets LBC* [1993] Q.B. 407.

[562] [1992] 1 A.C. 624 at 655.

[563] [2000] 1 W.L.R. 1988 (decided before the introduction of CPR Pt 54).

"The intention of the Civil Procedure Rules is to harmonise procedures as far as possible and to avoid barren procedural disputes which generate satellite litigation."[564]

Thus the emphasis has changed since *O'Reilly v Mackman*.[565]

F. Family Matters

The court has a statutory jurisdiction to grant injunctions to restrain a husband from dealing with property so as to defeat his wife's claim to maintenance.[566] Injunctions are commonly granted in relation to occupation of the home under the provisions of the matrimonial homes legislation.[567] Thus injunctions have been granted to restrain a husband from installing his lover in the matrimonial home,[568] or to exclude the husband from the home,[569] or to restrain a man from living near his former wife,[570] or, in a grave case, to exclude an adult child from his parents' home.[571] But the jurisdiction is sparingly exercised; it must be necessary to protect the applicant or a relevant child and should never be regarded as routine.[572]

25–073

Orders may be made under the Family Law Act 1996 (replacing and extending earlier legislation) to regulate the occupation of the family home.[573] The jurisdiction extends to spouses, former spouses, cohabitants and former cohabitants, but the details are outside the scope of this book. Non-molestation orders may be granted under the 1996 Act,[574] and under the court's general jurisdiction. They should not normally be granted against persons who lack mental capacity, nor against children where there is not usually any effective means of enforcement.[575] It should be added that injunctions of this kind should not be granted without notice unless there is real danger of serious injury or damage.[576]

---

[564] [2000] 1 W.L.R. 1988 at 1998, per Lord Woolf M.R.

[565] [1983] 2 A.C. 237, above.

[566] Matrimonial Causes Act 1973 s.37; Matrimonial and Family Proceedings Act 1984 s.24.

[567] Now the Family Law Act 1996.

[568] *Pinckney v Pinckney* [1966] 1 All E.R. 121.

[569] *Hall v Hall* [1971] 1 W.L.R. 404; *Phillips v Phillips* [1973] 1 W.L.R. 615.

[570] *M v M* (1983) 13 Fam.Law 110; *Burris v Azadani* [1995] 1 W.L.R. 1372.

[571] *Egan v Egan* [1975] Ch. 218 (a clear history of assaults, and threats of more). See also *Re L (Vulnerable Adults with Capacity: Court's Jurisdiction)* [2011] Fam. 189.

[572] *Des Salles d'Epinoix v Des Salles d'Epinoix* [1967] 1 W.L.R. 553; *Wiseman v Simpson* [1988] 1 W.L.R. 35; Family Law Act 1996, ss.33, 35, 36.

[573] See ss.33, 35, 36.

[574] See ss.42, 45 (orders without notice), 47 (power of arrest).

[575] *Wookey v Wookey* [1991] Fam. 121. See also *G v Harrow LBC* (2004) 1 P. & C.R. DG 17 (minors).

[576] *Ansah v Ansah* [1977] Fam. 138.

The remedy of injunction is also employed in the protection of children[577]; for example, to restrain persons who had enticed a girl of 16 away from her father, from continuing to harbour her[578]; in support of a custody order[579]; to protect a child from publicity[580] (although press freedom should not be restricted any more than is essential); or to restrain the mother of a ward from leaving the jurisdiction before submitting to a test to establish its paternity.[581] It is in connection with equity's special care concerning children that most risks are taken with regard to the issue of injunctions against persons outside the jurisdiction.[582]

As we have seen, a husband cannot obtain an injunction to prevent his wife from having an abortion.[583]

Finally, the use of search orders and asset-freezing injunctions in family matters is dealt with below.[584]

G. Trade Unions, Clubs and Colleges

25–074   Some use of the injunction has been made as a remedy against trade unions.[585] Perhaps the most important use of the injunction in this field has been to restrain the expulsion of a member by his union where such expulsion is contrary to the rules of the union,[586] or the rules of natural justice.[587]

The right of a member of an association to invoke the assistance of the courts in resisting expulsion is essentially a contractual right.[588] Modern decisions have established that the right to an injunction is not confined to cases where the claimant has some proprietary right. A member may seek an injunction, for example, to

---

[577] For the practical limitations on the exercise of the jurisdiction, see *Re C (A Minor)* [1991] 2 F.L.R. 168. For the protection of vulnerable adults, see *Re HM (Vulnerable Adult: Abduction) (No.2)* [2011] 1 F.L.R. 97.

[578] *Lough v Ward* [1945] 2 All E.R. 338.

[579] *Re W (A Minor)* [1981] 3 All E.R. 401; doubted G. Douglas (1982) 45 M.L.R. 468. As to adoption orders, see *Re D (A Minor)* [1991] Fam. 137.

[580] The extensive case law cannot be cited here, but the leading case is *Re S (A Child) (Identification: Restrictions on Publication)* [2005] 1 A.C. 593.

[581] *Re I (A Minor)*, *The Times*, May 22, 1987.

[582] *Re Liddell's ST* [1936] Ch. 365; *Harben v Harben* [1957] 1 W.L.R. 261; *Re O* [1962] 1 W.L.R. 724. See also *Practice Direction* [1983] 1 W.L.R. 558 (injunctions to restrain removal of child from jurisdiction).

[583] *Paton v Trustees of British Pregnancy Advisory Service* [1979] Q.B. 276; above, para.25–015; *C v S* [1988] Q.B. 135.

[584] Below, para.25–077.

[585] See also Trade Union and Labour Relations (Consolidation) Act 1992 s.176, providing additional remedies against unreasonable exclusion or expulsion.

[586] See *Osborne v Amalgamated Society of Railway Servants* [1911] 1 Ch. 540; *Lee v Showmen's Guild* [1952] 2 Q.B. 329. The claimant should normally, however, first exhaust other remedies available under the rules: *White v Kuzych* [1951] A.C. 585; but cf. *Lawlor v Union of Post Office Workers* [1965] Ch. 712.

[587] *Edwards v SOGAT* [1971] Ch. 354; *Breen v AEU* [1971] 2 Q.B. 175; *Shotton v Hammond* (1976) 120 S.J. 780.

[588] *White v Kuzych*, above, fn.586; *Bonsor v Musicians' Union* [1956] A.C. 104.

protect his "right to work",[589] or where matters of public importance are concerned.[590] But the mere fact of membership is not, in
the absence of these special considerations, sufficient to found a
claim to an injunction.[591] Equity will not compel persons to remain
in continual and personal relations with one another.[592]

Injunctions have also been granted to professional people who
have been dismissed contrary to the rules of their profession, though
usually only where improper motive or bad faith can be shown,[593]
and to members expelled by social clubs, either in breach of the
rules of the club, or where the club has acted in breach of natural
justice. Thus, in *Labouchere v Earl of Wharncliffe*,[594] the general
meeting of a club, summoned without proper notice, expelled the
claimant without full inquiry, without giving him notice of any
definite charge, and by a resolution carried by an insufficient majority. The court granted an injunction against such purported expulsion.

Injunctions have sometimes been sought by students or teachers
dismissed from a university without a fair hearing, in breach of the
rules of natural justice, to restrain the university authorities from
acting on the dismissal, but most complaints of this kind are now
dealt with by the Office of the Independent Adjudicator for Higher
Education.[595]

H. Judicial Proceedings

In proper cases, judicial proceedings in inferior courts[596] and
private prosecutions[597] may be restrained. So also the initiation of
proceedings in the High Court,[598] but once commenced, proceedings
in the High Court are not subject to injunction; indeed interference
with such proceedings may itself be restrained by injunction as a

25–075

---

[589] *Edwards v SOGAT*, above, fn.587; cf. *Gaiman v National Association for Mental Health*
[1971] Ch. 317 (no injunction as membership involved no question of property, livelihood or
reputation).

[590] *Woodford v Smith* [1970] 1 W.L.R. 806, concerning membership of a ratepayers' association, where an injunction was granted to restrain the holding of a meeting without permitting the claimant members to attend and vote.

[591] *Baird v Wells* (1890) 44 Ch.D. 661.

[592] *Lumley v Wagner* (1852) 1 De G.M. & G. 604.

[593] *Hayman v Governors of Rugby School* (1874) L.R. 18 Eq. 28; *Cassel v Inglis* [1916] 2
Ch. 211; *Weinberger v Inglis* [1919] A.C. 606.

[594] (1879) 13 Ch.D. 346; and see *Harington v Sendall* [1903] 1 Ch. 921; cf. *Dawkins v
Antrobus* (1881) 17 Ch.D. 615.

[595] This is governed by the Higher Education Act 2004.

[596] *Re Connolly Bros Ltd* [1911] 1 Ch. 731 (Lancaster Palatine Court); *Thames Launches v
Trinity House Corp (Deptford Strond)* [1966] Ch. 197 (magistrates' court); *Murcutt v Murcutt*
[1952] P. 266 (county court).

[597] *Thames Launches v Trinity House Corp (Deptford Strond)* [1966] Ch. 197.

[598] *McHenry v Lewis* (1882) 22 Ch.D. 397; *Ellerman Lines v Read* [1928] 2 K.B. 144;
Settlement Corp v Hochschild [1966] Ch. 10. See also *Bryanston Finance Ltd v de Vries
(No.2)* [1976] Ch. 63 (winding-up petition).

contempt of court.[599] Where a dispute is subject to an arbitration agreement, the court may not grant an injunction to restrain judicial proceedings in another Member State.[600] The court has limited jurisdiction to grant injunctions before the commencement of the arbitration proceedings.[601]

Judicial proceedings in foreign courts may be restrained by injunction, where this is appropriate to avoid an injustice, but this is a jurisdiction to be exercised with great caution. Such an injunction will only be issued against a party who is amenable to the jurisdiction of the English court. It is directed not to the foreign court, but to the parties.[602] Generally comity requires that the English court should have a sufficient interest in, or connection with, the matter to justify indirect interference.[603] An anti-suit injunction may not be granted to restrain proceedings in another Member State.[604]

I. Legislative Proceedings

25–076   It is very doubtful whether an injunction will lie to restrain the introduction or enactment of a Bill,[605] or to restrain the making of a subordinate legislative instrument.[606] It is, however, possible that an injunction may be granted to restrain the breach of contractual obligations not to promote or to petition against a private Bill,[607] or to restrain unauthorised expenditure of public funds in promoting or opposing a private Bill.[608] But no injunction will lie to restrain any procedure concerning a public Bill.[609]

---

[599] *Att Gen v Times Newspapers Ltd* [1974] A.C. 273. But this decision was held by the European Court (April 26, 1979) to infringe art.10 of the European Convention on Human Rights, which guarantees freedom of expression. See F. Mann (1979) 95 L.Q.R. 348; C. Gray (1979) 38 C.L.J. 242; Lord Denning, *The Due Process of Law*, 1980, pp.45–49. See also *Att Gen v London Weekend Television Ltd* [1973] 1 W.L.R. 202; *Att Gen v Ebert* [2002] 2 All E.R. 789 (injunction to prevent vexatious litigant from interfering with the proper administration of justice).

[600] *West Tankers Inc v Ras Riunione Adriatica Di Sicurta SpA* [2009] 1 A.C. 1138 (European Court of Justice); E. Peel (2009) 125 L.Q.R. 365; R. Fentiman (2009) 68 C.L.J. 278.

[601] *Cetelem SA v Roust Holdings Ltd* [2005] 1 W.L.R. 3555; *Econet Wireless Ltd v Vee Networks Ltd* [2006] 2 Lloyd's Rep. 428.

[602] *Société Nationale Industrielle Aerospatiale v Lee Kui Jak* [1987] A.C. 871; *Donohue v Armco Inc* [2002] 1 All E.R. 749. See Civil Jurisdiction and Judgments Act 1982, s.49.

[603] *Airbus Industrie GIE v Patel* [1999] 1 A.C. 119.

[604] The European Court of Justice so held on a reference by the House of Lords in *Turner v Grovit* [2005] 1 A.C. 101; A. Briggs (2004) 120 L.Q.R. 529; A. Dickinson [2004] L.M.C.L.Q. 273; C. Hare (2004) 63 C.L.J. 570.

[605] Bill of Rights 1688 s.1, art.9; see de Smith, *Judicial Review*, 6th edn, 2007, pp.118–119.

[606] *Harper v Secretary of State for Home Affairs* [1955] Ch. 238; see also *Bates v Lord Hailsham of St Marylebone* [1972] 1 W.L.R. 1373.

[607] *Bilston Corp v Wolverhampton Corp* [1942] Ch. 391.

[608] *Att Gen v London and Home Counties Joint Electricity Authority* [1929] 1 Ch. 513.

[609] *Att Gen for New South Wales v Trethowan* [1932] A.C. 526.

J. To Prevent Removal or Destruction of Evidence: Search Orders

This type of injunction is designed to secure that pending trial[610] **25–077**
the defendant does not dispose of any articles in his possession
which could be prejudicial at the trial. It is "an illustration of the
adaptability of equitable remedies to new situations."[611] It is particularly useful to the victims of commercial malpractice, such as
breach of confidence, breach of copyright and passing off. It has also
been used in the family context, as in *Emanuel v Emanuel*,[612] where
a husband had been ordered in matrimonial proceedings to transfer
properties to his wife. He failed to comply, and had sold a property
and spent the proceeds. An order was granted to allow the wife's
solicitors to enter his home to inspect documents relating to his
finances. It is essential that such an order be available without
notice, so that the defendant is not forewarned:

"If the stable door cannot be bolted, the horse must be secured.
. . . If the horse is liable to be spirited away, notice of an intention
to secure the horse will defeat the intention."[613]

Search orders were formerly known as *Anton Piller* orders, taking
their name from the case (discussed below) in which the Court of
Appeal confirmed the practice over 30 years ago. They were put on
a statutory footing by s.7 of the Civil Procedure Act 1997, and are
governed also by the Civil Procedure Rules 1998.[614] They are now
called "search orders", although of course they are referred to as
Anton Piller orders or injunctions in the case law preceding these
developments.

The search order has been variously described as "a draconian
power which should be used only in very exceptional cases",[615] and
as "an innovation which has proved its worth time and time
again".[616] The first reported decision was *EMI Ltd v Pandit*,[617]
where an order was made without notice in a breach of copyright
action to enable the claimant to enter the defendant's premises to
inspect, photograph and remove infringing articles. The jurisdiction

---

[610] Or after judgment, in aid of execution; CPR 25.2.

[611] *Rank Film Distributors Ltd v Video Information Centre* [1982] A.C. 380 at 439 (per
Lord Wilberforce).

[612] [1982] 1 W.L.R. 669. It remains a rare weapon in family cases; *Burgess v Burgess*
[1996] 2 F.L.R. 34.

[613] *Rank Film Distributors Ltd v Video Information Centre* [1982] A.C. 380 at 418.

[614] Part 25 (Interim Remedies). See also Senior Courts Act 1981 s.33(1).

[615] *Yousif v Salama* [1980] 1 W.L.R. 1540 at 1544, per Donaldson L.J. His Lordship,
dissenting, regarded the order granted by the majority as a power to "take" disclosure.

[616] *Rank Film Distributors Ltd v Video Information Centre* [1982] A.C. 380 at 406 (Lord
Denning M.R.).

[617] [1975] 1 W.L.R. 302.

to make such an order was confirmed by the Court of Appeal in *Anton Piller KG v Manufacturing Processes Ltd.*[618]

The defendants had received confidential information and plans concerning the claimant's electrical equipment in their capacity as the claimant's selling agents in England. The claimant had reason to believe that the defendants were selling the information to competitors, but were unable to prove this without access to documents situated on the defendants' premises.

The Court of Appeal made an order without prior notice to the defendants, requiring them to permit the claimant to enter their premises and inspect documents relating to the equipment. Such an order would only be made in exceptional circumstances, where it was essential that the claimant should inspect the documents to enable justice to be done between the parties, and there was a danger that vital evidence would otherwise be destroyed.

25–078 Unlike a search warrant, the order does not authorise the claimant to enter against the defendant's will. But it does order him to permit the claimant to enter, so that, if the defendant does not comply, not only does he commit a contempt of court, but adverse inferences will be drawn against him at the trial. Ormrod L.J. laid down three conditions for the grant of the order.[619] The claimant must:

(i) have an extremely strong prima facie case;
(ii) show actual or potential damage of a very serious nature;
(iii) have clear evidence that the defendant has incriminating documents or things and a real possibility of their destruction before an application with notice can be made.[620]

It might be added that the order should not be sought as a "fishing expedition".[621]

In the enforcement of the order, the claimant must act with circumspection. He should be attended by his solicitor, and must undertake in damages (giving security in appropriate cases), so as to safeguard the defendant's rights. Because of the draconian nature of the order, the applicant is under a strict duty to make full and frank disclosure of all relevant matters to the court.[622] Strict requirements

---

[618] [1976] Ch. 55; Lord Denning, *The Due Process of Law*, 1980, pp.123–130.

[619] In *Anton Piller KG v Manufacturing Processes Ltd*, above, fn.618. For further guidelines, see *CBS United Kingdom Ltd v Lambert* [1983] Ch. 37; *Digital Equipment Corp v Darkcrest Ltd* [1984] Ch. 512.

[620] See *Yousif v Salama*, above, fn.615.

[621] i.e. as a means of finding out what charges can be made.

[622] *Behbehani v Salem* [1989] 1 W.L.R. 723; *Lock International Plc v Beswick* [1989] 1 W.L.R. 1268; *Tate Access Floors Inc v Boswell* [1991] Ch. 512.

have been developed to avoid oppression.[623] For example, the order must be executed in office hours so that legal advice is available; a woman must be present at a search of a private house where a woman may be alone; and a list of items must be prepared before they are removed, which the defendant may check. Where the claimant or his solicitor has acted improperly the court may set aside the order. Even if it is not set aside, the defendant may be entitled to exemplary damages.[624]

As the practice became established, grave disquiet was expressed **25-079** that it had gone too far in favour of claimants,[625] and was "inherently oppressive".[626] An example of its abuse is *Lock International Plc v Beswick*,[627] where the claimant's solicitors searched the business premises and homes of the defendants and removed not only documents containing confidential information but nearly all their commercial papers, computer records and prototypes. The search order, which should never have been granted, was discharged. Commentators said that "an exceptional device intended to avoid injustice has become almost a routine method of creating it."[628] It seems that these warnings have been heeded.[629]

The utility of the search order suffered a set-back when the House of Lords held in *Rank Film Distributors Ltd v Video Information Centre*,[630] a copyright case, that the defendant could invoke the privilege against self-incrimination. But the privilege was subsequently withdrawn by s.72 of the Senior Courts Act 1981, in the case of proceedings to obtain disclosure of information relating to the infringement of rights pertaining to any intellectual property[631] or passing-off. Matters disclosed as a result of such proceedings are not admissible in evidence against the defendant in proceedings against him for a related offence.[632] Other exceptions have been added.[633] The defendant may still invoke the privilege against self-

---

[623] *Universal Thermosensors Ltd v Hibben* [1992] 1 W.L.R. 840; CPR 25A *Practice Direction*, para.7.

[624] *Columbia Picture Industries Inc v Robinson* [1987] Ch. 38.

[625] *Columbia Picture Industries Inc v Robinson* [1987] Ch. 38; A. Zuckerman All E.R. Rev. 1986, p.225; N. Andrews (1987) 46 C.L.J. 50; C. Bell (1987) 1 *Trust Law & Practice* 146.

[626] *Bhimji v Chatwani* [1991] 1 W.L.R. 989 at 1002; A. Zuckerman All E.R. Rev. 1991, p.263.

[627] [1989] 1 W.L.R. 1268; A. Zuckerman All E.R. Rev. 1989, p.221.

[628] M. Dockray and H. Laddie (1990) 106 L.Q.R. 601 at 620; J. Martin (1990) 20 U.W.A.L.R. 143.

[629] See CPR 25A *Practice Direction*, para.7.

[630] [1982] A.C. 380. Templeman L.J. in the Court of Appeal, at 423, thought the court would award high damages where the defendant sought to rely on the privilege.

[631] Defined by s.72(5). See *Cobra Golf Inc v Rata* [1998] Ch. 109; *Gray v News Group Newspapers Ltd* [2011] 2 W.L.R. 1401.

[632] s.72(3). It is otherwise in the case of proceedings for contempt or perjury, s.72(4).

[633] See CPR 25A *Practice Direction* 7.9; *Kensington International Ltd v Republic of Congo* [2008] 1 W.L.R. 1144 (Fraud Act 2006, s.13).

incrimination in a case outside the statutory exceptions.[634] The House of Lords has suggested further reforms.[635] Although the privilege may still be invoked in many areas, it does not extend to "independent matters" coming to light in the course of executing a search order, as where pornographic material was found during a search for other items.[636]

K. To Prevent Removal of Assets: Freezing Injunctions

25–080   **i. General Principles.** This injunction was for many years known as a *Mareva* injunction, taking its name from *Mareva Compania Naviera SA v International Bulkcarriers SA*,[637] although the first reported exercise of this novel jurisdiction occurred in *Nippon Yusen Kaisha v Karageorgis*.[638] It is now called a freezing injunction.[639] It was described by Lord Denning M.R. as "the greatest piece of judicial law reform in my time."[640]

> "A *Mareva* injunction is interlocutory, not final; it is ancillary to a substantive pecuniary claim for debt or damages; it is designed to prevent the judgment . . . for a sum of money being a mere 'brutum fulmen.' "[641]

The usual purpose of a freezing injunction is to prevent the dissipation or removal of assets before trial, so that if the claimant succeeds in the action, there will be property of the defendant available to satisfy the judgment. It may also be granted after final judgment if the claimant can show grounds for believing that the defendant will dispose of his assets to avoid execution.[642] In such a case the injunction may even be granted against the defendant's wife.[643] In view of

---

[634] *Emanuel v Emanuel* [1982] 1 W.L.R. 669 (Revenue offences); *Tate Access Floors Inc v Boswell* [1991] Ch. 512; *IBM United Kingdom Ltd v Prima Data International Ltd* [1994] 1 W.L.R. 719 (conspiracy).

[635] *Istel (AT & T) Ltd v Tully* [1993] A.C. 45. The position is not changed by the Civil Procedure Act 1997; s.7(7).

[636] *C Plc v P (Att Gen intervening)* [2008] Ch. 1; R. Moules (2007) 66 C.L.P. 528.

[637] [1975] 2 Lloyd's Rep. 509; D. Powles (1978) J.B.L. 11; A. Bland (1980) 2 W.I.L.J. 60; R. Horsfall [1982] Conv. 265; C. Hodgekiss (1982) 99 L.Q.R. 7; A. Zuckerman (1993) 56 M.L.R. 325 and (1993) 109 L.Q.R. 432.

[638] [1975] 1 W.L.R. 1093. See *The Siskina* [1979] A.C. 210 at 229, where Lord Denning M.R. described this injunction as a "rediscovery" of the procedure known as foreign attachment; *Z Ltd v A-Z and AA-LL* [1982] Q.B. 558.

[639] CPR 25.1(1)(f).

[640] *The Due Process of Law*, 1980, p.134; Lord Denning, *The Closing Chapter*, 1983, p.225. See also Donaldson L.J. in *Bank Mellat v Nikpour* [1985] F.S.R. 87 at 91–92, describing the freezing injunction, along with the search order, as "one of the law's two 'nuclear' weapons."

[641] *The Siskina* [1979] A.C. 210 at 253 (Lord Diplock).

[642] *Babanaft International Co SA v Bassatne* [1990] Ch. 13; CPR 25.2.

[643] *Mercantile Group (Europe) AG v Aiyela* [1994] Q.B. 366.

the advent of electronic banking, the significance of the injunction will be readily appreciated. Its effectiveness is assisted by ancillary orders to enable the claimant to obtain disclosure of documents and information as to assets,[644] and by the availability of contempt proceedings against third parties.

The freezing injunction is always interlocutory, and usually without notice: speed is of the essence.[645] It is frequently sought in conjunction with a search order. The basis of the jurisdiction is now the Senior Courts Act 1981 s.37: the injunction may be granted whenever it is "just and convenient" to do so,[646] but with "great circumspection".[647] It is unlimited as to its subject-matter and the nature of the proceedings.[648] It may be granted, although rarely, in matrimonial cases.[649] As in the case of interlocutory injunctions generally, the claimant must satisfy the conditions laid down by the House of Lords in *American Cyanamid Co v Ethicon Ltd*[650]: he must have a good arguable case and the balance of convenience must favour the grant.[651] The claimant must give an undertaking in damages in case he should be unsuccessful at the trial, and the defendant may apply within seven days of service of the order on him for it to be discharged.[652] The defendant may be able to rely on the privilege against self-incrimination to avoid compliance with the injunction or a disclosure order, unless he is adequately protected by a term of the order preventing the use of the disclosures in a prosecution. The application of the privilege has already been discussed.[653]

It has been held that the old writ ne exeat regno[654] may be granted in support of a freezing injunction,[655] or, if its requirements are not satisfied, an interlocutory injunction under s.37(1) of the Senior

---

[644] *Bekhor (AJ) & Co Ltd v Bilton* [1981] Q.B. 923; *Bankers Trust Co v Shapira* [1980] 1 W.L.R. 1274; CPR 25.1(1)(g).

[645] *Third Chandris Shipping Corp v Unimarine SA* [1979] Q.B. 645.

[646] *Mareva Compania Naviera SA v International Bulkcarriers SA*, above, fn.637; *Nippon Yusen Kaisha v Karageorgis* [1975] 1 W.L.R. 1093; *Third Chandris Shipping Corp v Unimarine SA*, above, fn.645; *Rasu Maritima SA v Perusahaan Pertambangan Minyak Dan Gas Bumi Negara (Pertamina)* [1978] Q.B. 644.

[647] *Mercedes-Benz AG v Leiduck* [1996] 1 A.C. 284 at 297 (Lord Mustill).

[648] *Z Ltd v A-Z and AA-LL* [1982] Q.B. 558. It may be combined with specific performance; *Seven Seas Properties Ltd v Al-Essa* [1988] 1 W.L.R. 1272.

[649] *C v C (Without Notice Orders)* [2006] 1 F.L.R. 936; *Re M (Freezing Injunction)* [2006] 1 F.L.R. 1031.

[650] [1975] A.C. 396; cf. *Polly Peck International Plc v Nadir (No.2)* [1992] 4 All E.R. 769 at 786.

[651] *Rasu Maritima SA v Perusahaan, etc.* above, fn.646; *Third Chandris Shipping Corp v Unimarine SA*, above, fn.645; *Allen v Jambo Holdings Ltd* [1980] 1 W.L.R. 1252; *Derby & Co Ltd v Weldon* [1990] Ch. 48. See M. Kerr (1978) 41 M.L.R. 1 and fn.659, below.

[652] *Mareva Compania Naviera SA v International Bulkcarriers SA*, above, fn.637; CPR 23.10.

[653] Above, para.25–079.

[654] Above, para.1–037. "Writ" has now been replaced by "claim form"; CPR 7.

[655] *Al Nahkel for Contracting and Trading Ltd v Lowe* [1986] Q.B. 235; cf. *Allied Arab Bank Ltd v Hajjar* [1988] Q.B. 787. This is doubtful, as ne exeat regno is to assist prosecution of an action, not execution of a judgment.

Courts Act 1981 to restrain the defendant from leaving the country.[656] While this development increases the efficacy of the freezing injunction, it has been criticised as an unjustified restriction on individual liberty.[657]

25–081   **ii. Guidelines for the Grant of the Injunction.** While the discretion of the court is not fettered by rigid rules, Lord Denning M.R. suggested the following guidelines[658]:

(a) the claimant must have a good arguable case[659];

(b) where the injunction applies to goods, caution is required to avoid bringing the defendant's business to a standstill[660];

(c) the court should favour the grant if it would be likely to compel the defendant to provide security;

(d) the claimant must make full and frank disclosure of all material matters[661];

(e) he should give particulars of his claim and its amount, and (in an application without notice) he should fairly state the points made against it by the defendant;

(f) he must undertake in damages, giving security in suitable cases, in case he is unsuccessful in the action.[662]

Lord Denning added that the claimant had to establish that there was a risk of the removal of assets from the jurisdiction. It is no longer necessary for the claimant to establish in all cases that there is such a risk, as s.37(3) of the Senior Courts Act 1981 provides that the injunction may be granted to prevent the defendant from removing from the jurisdiction "or otherwise dealing with" the assets. Thus a risk of dissipation within the jurisdiction[663] (or, in an extreme

---

[656] Above, para.25–015.

[657] C. Harpum (1986) 45 C.L.J. 189; A. Zuckerman All E.R. Rev. 1986 at 225; L. Anderson (1987) 104 L.Q.R. 246; J. Martin (1990) 20 U.W.A.L.R. 143.

[658] *Rasu Maritima SA v Perusahaan, etc.* [1978] Q.B. 644; *Third Chandris Shipping Corp v Unimarine SA* [1979] Q.B. 645. See also *Barclay-Johnson v Yuill* [1980] 1 W.L.R. 1259; (1981) 97 L.Q.R. 4; *Z Ltd v A-Z and AA-LL* [1982] Q.B. 558; *Derby & Co Ltd v Weldon*, above, fn.651; *Flightwise Travel Services Ltd v Gill*, *The Times*, December 12, 2003. See *Practice Direction* [1996] 1 W.L.R. 1552.

[659] See *Etablissement Esefka International Anstalt v Central Bank of Nigeria* [1979] 1 Lloyd's Rep. 445; *Barclay-Johnson v Yuill*, above, fn.658.

[660] As to chattels, see *CBS United Kingdom Ltd v Lambert* [1983] Ch. 37.

[661] Failure to make full disclosure may result in discharge. See *Columbia Picture Industries Inc v Robinson* [1987] Ch. 38; *Lloyds Bowmaker Ltd v Britannia Arrow Holdings Plc* [1988] 1 W.L.R. 1337; *Brink's-MAT Ltd v Elcombe* [1988] 1 W.L.R. 1350; *Behbehani v Salem* [1989] 1 W.L.R. 723; *Memory Corp Plc v Sidhu (No.2)* [2000] 1 W.L.R. 1443.

[662] This will not normally be required in a post-judgment case unless leave to appeal has been granted; *Gwembe Valley Development Co Ltd v Koshy (No.4)*, *The Times*, February 28, 2002.

[663] See *Z Ltd v A-Z and AA-LL* [1982] Q.B. 558.

case, damage or destruction[664]) is sufficient. The developments as to foreign assets are discussed below.

Exceptionally, the injunction may be made against all the defendant's assets; but usually a limit will be specified.[665] In rare cases it may be made in respect of a joint account,[666] but not assets of the defendant's wife or another third party,[667] save in aid of enforcement of a judgment.[668] An order made in relation to "his assets" does not include those of which the defendant is legal owner, but which he holds on trust for a third party.[669] The injunction may be granted to restrain a sale of assets at an independently assessed price, although this will rarely be done in the case of a transaction in good faith in the ordinary course of business.[670] The injunction should rarely be granted where the defendant is a bank, otherwise its business could be irreparably harmed.[671]

iii. The Jurisdiction of the Court. The House of Lords in *The Siskina*[672] emphasised that the injunction had to be ancillary to substantive relief which the High Court had jurisdiction to grant; and that there was no power to grant the injunction save in protection or assertion of some legal or equitable right which the High Court had jurisdiction to enforce by final judgment. *The Siskina* was reversed on this point for cases within s.25 of the Civil Jurisdiction and Judgments Act 1982,[673] "but it remains an influential and controversial decision, and has had considerable effect on the development of the law of anti-suit injunctions."[674] Section 25 was originally confined to proceedings in countries which were parties to the Brussels and Lugano Conventions,[675] but was extended in   **25–082**

---

[664] *Standard Chartered Bank v Walker* [1992] 1 W.L.R. 561.

[665] *Z Ltd v A-Z and AA-LL*, above, fn.663; See also *Oceanica Castelana Armadora SA of Panama v Mineralimportexport* [1983] 1 W.L.R. 1294. After-acquired assets may be included; *TDK Tape Distributors (UK) Ltd v Videochoice Ltd* [1986] 1 W.L.R. 141.

[666] *Z Ltd v A-Z and AA-LL* [1982] Q.B. 558.

[667] *SCF Finance Co Ltd v Masri* [1985] 1 W.L.R. 876; *Allied Arab Bank Ltd v Hajjar* (1989) 19 Fam.Law 68; cf. *TSB Private Bank International SA v Chabra* [1992] 1 W.L.R. 231.

[668] *Mercantile Group (Europe) AG v Aiyela* [1994] Q.B. 66. See also *C Inc Plc v L* [2001] 2 Lloyd's Rep. 459.

[669] *Federal Bank of the Middle East v Hadkinson* [2000] 1 W.L.R. 1695. The order could be worded differently, so as to cover all assets in his name, although it would be varied if it later became clear that certain assets were held on trust. See *JSC BTA Bank v Solodchenko* [2011] 1 W.L.R. 888.

[670] *Customs and Excise Commissioners v Anchor Foods Ltd* [1999] 1 W.L.R. 1139; A. Zuckerman All E.R. Rev. 1999 at 283.

[671] *Polly Peck International Plc v Nadir (No.2)* [1992] 4 All E.R. 769; A. Zuckerman (1992) 108 L.Q.R. 559. See also *Themehelp Ltd v West* [1996] Q.B. 84 (guarantee).

[672] [1979] A.C. 210.

[673] See *Haiti (Republic of) v Duvalier* [1990] 1 Q.B. 202.

[674] *Masri v Consolidated Contractors International (UK) Ltd (No.3)* [2009] Q.B. 503 at 518.

[675] These Conventions were superseded (subject to certain exceptions) by the Judgments Regulation, with effect from March 1, 2002.

1997[676] to proceedings in countries which are party to neither Convention. In cases where the court has no independent jurisdiction as to the subject-matter of the proceedings, it may refuse to grant the injunction on the basis of inexpedience.[677]

It has been held that a freezing injunction may not be granted unless the cause of action has accrued,[678] but the current view is that equity will "lend a hand" in advance of the appropriate time at law, to prevent injustice.[679] However, the claimant must at least have formulated a case for substantive relief which he intends to seek.[680]

25–083   **iv. The English-based Defendant.** The freezing injunction evolved as a remedy against a foreign-based defendant having assets within the jurisdiction. It was assumed in the earlier decisions that there was no power to grant such an injunction against an English-based defendant, although the merit of such a distinction was questioned.[681]

The difficulty in the way of extending the freezing injunction to English-based defendants was the clear line of authority to the effect that there is:

> "[N]o statutory or other power in the Court to restrain a person from dealing with his property at a time when no order against him has been made."[682]

It must be said, however, that this principle had already been eroded by the development of the injunction against foreign-based defendants.

Eventually the jurisdiction to enjoin an English-based defendant became established.[683] It was confirmed by s.37(3) of the Senior Courts Act 1981, providing that the court's power to grant an interlocutory injunction restraining a party to any proceedings from removing from the jurisdiction, or otherwise dealing with, assets

---

[676] Civil Jurisdiction and Judgments Act 1982 (Interim Relief) Order 1997 (SI 1997/302). See also Civil Jurisdiction and Judgments Regulation 2009 (SI 2009/3131).

[677] Civil Jurisdiction and Judgments Act 1982 s.25(2); *Crédit Suisse Fides Trust SA v Cuoghi* [1998] Q.B. 818 at 829, 831; A. Lenon (1997) 147 N.L.J. 1234. See also *Refco Inc v Eastern Trading Co* [1999] 1 Lloyd's Rep. 159; *Motorola Credit Corp v Uzan (No.2)* [2004] 1 W.L.R. 113; *Rhode v Rhode and Pembroke Square Ltd* [2007] 2 F.L.R. 971.

[678] *Veracruz Transportation Inc v VC Shipping Co Inc* [1992] 1 Lloyd's Rep. 353, criticised L. Collins (1992) 108 L.Q.R. 175.

[679] *Re Q's Estate* [1999] 1 Lloyd's Rep. 931.

[680] *Fourie v Le Roux* [2007] 1 W.L.R. 320; P. Devonshire (2007) 123 L.Q.R. 361.

[681] See *The Siskina* [1979] A.C. 210.

[682] *Jagger v Jagger* [1926] P. 93 at 102, per Scrutton L.J. See also *Lister & Co v Stubbs* (1890) 45 Ch.D. 1.

[683] See *AJ Bekhor & Co Ltd v Bilton* [1981] Q.B. 923; Lord Denning, *The Due Process of Law*, pp.147–149.

located within the jurisdiction shall be exercisable whether or not that party is domiciled, resident or present within the jurisdiction.

v. Assets outside the Jurisdiction. The freezing injunction was **25–084** originally confined to assets within the jurisdiction. It is now established that the injunction (and ancillary disclosure order) may be granted against a defendant who is amenable to the jurisdiction[684] of the court in respect of assets outside the jurisdiction, even on a worldwide basis. The objections to extending the injunction to foreign assets were that the order would be oppressive and unenforceable, and that the territorial limitations were confirmed by s.37(3) of the Senior Courts Act 1981.[685] But the Court of Appeal held in *Babanaft International Co SA v Bassatne*[686] that s.37(3) did not restrict the scope, geographical or otherwise, of s.37(1). This case involved a post-judgment freezing injunction. Such an order would more readily be made against assets abroad than in a pre-judgment case, but would nevertheless be rare. A personal order binding the defendant alone was made. It is now provided in the Civil Procedure Rules that the injunction may be granted in relation to assets "whether located within the jurisdiction or not",[687] but the decisions on "world-wide assets" remain important.

The issue next arose in the Court of Appeal in *Haiti (Republic of) v Duvalier*,[688] which concerned the alleged embezzlement of $120m from the Republic during the presidency of Jean-Claude Duvalier. No substantive relief in England was sought. The court granted a pre-judgment freezing injunction in respect of worldwide assets, although recognising that this was a most unusual measure which should very rarely be granted. While the court would be more willing in a post-judgment case, or where the claimant had a tracing or other proprietary claim, the injunction could be granted in respect of a pre-judgment money claim such as the present case, where international co-operation was demanded. Previous limitations arose from practice rather than from any restriction on the court's power. The injunction was granted subject to a *"Babanaft* proviso"[689] in respect of the foreign assets, to protect third parties outside the

---

[684] See L. Collins (1989) 105 L.Q.R. 262; P. Friedman (1994) 144 N.L.J. 932.
[685] Above.
[686] [1990] Ch. 13.
[687] CPR 25.1(1)(f).
[688] [1990] 1 Q.B. 202. It has been said that *Duvalier* "goes to the very edge of what is permissible"; L. Collins (1989) 105 L.Q.R. 262 at 281. This comment was noted by Millett L.J. in *Crédit Suisse Fides Trust SA v Cuoghi* [1998] Q.B. 818. For other criticisms of worldwide orders, see T. Hartley (2010) 126 L.Q.R. 194 at 210–221.
[689] For the current form of the proviso, see CPR 25A *Practice Direction (Annex)*. The applicant must undertake not to enforce outside the jurisdiction without permission of the court. Guidelines for the grant of permission were given in *Dadourian Group International Inc v Simms (Practice Note)* [2006] 1 W.L.R. 2499.

jurisdiction save to the extent that the order might be enforced by the local court. Even stricter safeguards were required by the Court of Appeal in *Derby & Co Ltd v Weldon*,[690] where a pre-judgment worldwide freezing injunction was granted. It was emphasised that, in addition to a good arguable case, the claimant must show that any English assets are insufficient, that there are foreign assets, and that there is a real risk of disposal of the latter. The injunction will not be granted if it would be oppressive. The court must be satisfied, by means of undertaking or proviso, that (a) the defendant will not be oppressed by exposure to a multiplicity of proceedings[691]; (b) the defendant will be protected against misuse of information gained from the order for disclosure of assets; and (c) third parties are protected. The present case was sufficiently exceptional because a very large sum was involved (£15m), the English assets were totally inadequate, and there was a high risk of dissipation of the foreign assets through inaccessible overseas companies. In *Derby & Co Ltd v Weldon (No.3 and No.4)*[692] a similar injunction was granted against companies in Luxembourg and Panama which had no assets within the jurisdiction. The Luxembourg company was subject to the jurisdiction of a court which would enforce the orders of the English court under the Civil Jurisdiction and Judgments Act 1982. Concerning the Panama company, the fact that the order could not be specifically enforced was no bar. The order would not be made if there was no effective sanction, but the sanction of being debarred from defending in the event of disobedience normally sufficed.[693] It has since been explained that, where an injunction is sought in aid of foreign proceedings, the focus is on whether it is expedient to grant it, in view of the court's lack of jurisdiction over the subject-matter of the proceedings, and not whether the circumstances are exceptional.[694] However, a worldwide order should not be granted routinely or without very careful consideration. Indeed, the Court of Appeal has recently emphasised that a worldwide order should not be made in the absence of a "real connecting link" between the defendant and the territorial jurisdiction of the court, such as the defendant being a British national or based in the jurisdiction or where the main proceedings will be in this jurisdiction.[695] Finally,

---

[690] [1990] Ch. 48.

[691] See *Re Bank of Credit and Commerce International SA* [1994] 1 W.L.R. 708; A. Zuckerman All E.R. Rev. 1994 at 305.

[692] [1990] Ch. 65.

[693] See L. Collins (1989) 105 L.Q.R. 262 at 296.

[694] *Crédit Suisse Fides Trust SA v Cuoghi* [1998] Q.B. 818; Civil Jurisdiction and Judgments Act 1982, s.25(2); *Motorola Credit Corp v Uzan (No.2)* [2004] 1 W.L.R. 113.

[695] *Banco Nacional De Comercio Exterior SNC v Empresa De Telecommunicaciones De Cuba SA* [2008] 1 W.L.R. 1936; L Merrett (2007) 66 C.L.J. 495 and (2008) L.M.C.L.Q. 71.

the court may, in exceptional cases, order the transfer of assets from one foreign jurisdiction to another to prevent their dissipation.[696]

vi. Operation *in Personam*. The usual subject-matter of a freezing injunction is a sum of money, often in a bank account. But there is no reason why other assets, such as a ship,[697] or an aeroplane,[698] should not be "frozen" by this method. It is important to note, however, that such an injunction, even if related to a specified asset, operates only *in personam*.[699] It is not a form of pre-trial attachment. It does not effect seizure of the asset, nor is it analogous to a lien. It merely prohibits the defendant personally from removing or transferring the asset. It gives no proprietary right in the asset, nor priority over other creditors.[700] The claimant's right is merely to have the asset preserved so that, if he succeeds in his action, judgment may be executed against it, but the rights of a third party with an interest in the asset will not be prejudiced.[701] The injunction may (initially or by variation) permit the assets to be used for living expenses or to make payments in good faith in the ordinary course of business.[702] Such a term does not protect the recipient of the payments in a case where the claimant establishes proprietary rights over the assets.[703]

25–085

vii. Position of Third Parties.[704] As far as the liabilities of a third party are concerned, we have seen that a third party who aids and abets the breach of an injunction by the defendant is guilty of contempt.[705] So in the case of a freezing injunction against a sum of money in a bank account, the bank, once it has notice, must not

25–086

---

[696] *Derby & Co Ltd v Weldon (No.6)* [1990] 1 W.L.R. 1139.

[697] *The Rena K* [1979] Q.B. 377. There is no conflict here with the jurisdiction to arrest ships. See R. Horsfall [1982] Conv. 265 at 270.

[698] *Allen v Jambo (Holdings) Ltd* [1980] 1 W.L.R. 1252 (A fatal accident case).

[699] cf. *Z Ltd v A-Z and AA-LL* [1982] Q.B. 558 at 573 "it operates *in rem* just as the arrest of a ship does.", per Lord Denning M.R. This was per incuriam; *Att Gen v Times Newspapers Ltd* [1992] 1 A.C. 191 at 215.

[700] See *Sanders Lead Co Inc v Entores Metal Brokers Ltd* [1984] 1 W.L.R. 452; *Bank Mellat v Kazmi* [1989] Q.B. 541. Assets subject to a tracing claim may be protected by an ordinary interlocutory injunction; *Polly Peck International Plc v Nadir (No.2)* [1992] 4 All E.R. 769; P. Devonshire (1999) 62 M.L.R. 539.

[701] *Cretanor Maritime Co Ltd v Irish Marine Management Ltd* [1978] 1 W.L.R. 966.

[702] *Iraqi Ministry of Defence v Arcepey Shipping Co SA* [1981] Q.B. 65; *Z Ltd v A-Z and AA-LL* [1982] Q.B. 558; *TDK Tape Distributors (UK) Ltd v Videochoice Ltd* [1986] 1 W.L.R. 141; *Law Society v Shanks* [1988] 1 F.L.R. 504; *Atlas Maritime Co SA v Avalon Maritime Ltd* [1991] 4 All E.R. 769 and *(No.3)* [1991] 1 W.L.R. 917.

[703] *United Mizrahi Bank Ltd v Doherty* [1998] 1 W.L.R. 435; A. Zuckerman All E.R. Rev. 1998 at 341.

[704] See P. Devonshire (1999) 62 M.L.R. 539 and (2002) 118 L.Q.R. 124.

[705] Above, para.25–011. See *Bank Mellat v Kazmi* [1989] Q.B. 541. A post-judgment freezing injunction may be granted against the defendant's wife; *Mercantile Group (Europe) AG v Aiyela* [1994] Q.B. 366; above, para.25–081.

facilitate the disposal of the money without a court order.[706] If it does so, it may commit contempt but the claimant has no action against the bank in negligence.[707] It is clear that any expenses incurred by a bank or other third party in complying with the injunction must be met by the claimant.[708] Furthermore, a bank can exercise any right of set-off it had before notification of the injunction.[709]

Similarly, the injunction must not interfere with the convenience or freedom of action of a third party. So in *Galaxia Maritime SA v Mineralimportexport*,[710] where a freezing injunction had been obtained as to a ship's cargo, the shipowner obtained its discharge, as it would interfere with the crew's arrangements for Christmas.

The protection of third parties where a worldwide freezing injunction is granted has already been considered.[711]

---

[706] *Z Ltd v A-Z and AA-LL* [1982] Q.B. 558; cf. *Law Society v Shanks*, above, fn.702. The injunction should not be granted against a bank as defendant; above, para.25–081.

[707] *Commissioners of Customs and Excise v Barclays Bank Plc* [2007] 1 A.C. 181; S. Gee (2006) 122 L.Q.R. 535.

[708] *Rahman (Prince Abdul) Bin Turki Al Sudairy v Abu-Taha* [1980] 1 W.L.R. 1268; *Searose Ltd v Seatrain (UK) Ltd* [1981] 1 W.L.R. 894. Undertakings will normally be given in this respect; *Z Ltd v A–Z and AA–LL*, above, fn.706. The undertaking may provide for damages to be paid to third parties; CPR 25A *Practice Direction* 5.1A.

[709] *Oceanica Castelana Armadora SA of Panama v Mineralimportexport* [1983] 1 W.L.R. 1294; A. Zuckerman All E.R. Rev. 1983 at 262.

[710] [1982] 1 W.L.R. 539. See also *Clipper Maritime Co Ltd of Monrovia v Mineralimportexport* [1981] 1 W.L.R. 262; *Arab Monetary Fund v Hashim (No.2)* [1990] 1 All E.R. 673 (where compliance with disclosure order might incriminate third parties abroad).

[711] Above, para.25–084.

CHAPTER 26

RESCISSION AND RECTIFICATION

1. RESCISSION

A. General

The right to rescind is the right of a party to a contract to have it **26–001** set aside and to be restored to his former position. The contract remains valid unless and until rescinded, so that, as we shall see, third parties may acquire interests under it in the meantime. This is rescission in the strict sense, and must be distinguished on the one hand from contracts void ab initio, for example on the ground of illegality, and on the other hand from contracts with no inherent invalidity which are subsequently discharged by breach.[1] Rescission is not a judicial remedy as such, for it may be achieved by act of the parties, nevertheless the assistance of the court is often invoked, for example to secure restitution of any property. Equity has traditionally been more flexible than the common law in its view of restitutio in integrum, although the distinction is becoming harder to main-

---

[1] See *Johnson v Agnew* [1980] A.C. 367. On the right to rescind for fraud, see *Logicrose Ltd v Southend United Football Club Ltd* [1988] 1 W.L.R. 1256.

tain.[2] Equity can effect what is necessary, for example by ordering accounts and inquiries[3] or an allowance for services rendered.[4]

The party rescinding is entitled to be restored to the position he would have been in had the contract not been entered into. He cannot recover damages, as that would put him in the position he would have been in had the contract been performed.[5]

B. Grounds for Rescission

i. Mistake.

26–002   (a) *Voluntary Dispositions.* A voluntary disposition, such as a gift or settlement, may be set aside in equity on the ground of mistake. The principles were recently reviewed by the Court of Appeal in *Pitt v Holt*.[6]

> The settlor, who had a personal injury award, created a "special needs" discretionary trust, of which he was the primary beneficiary, but professional advisers did not appreciate that inheritance tax would be payable. This could have been avoided if a different form of trust had been used. An application was made to set aside the settlement on the ground of mistake, and HMRC joined the proceedings. It was held that the settlement could not be set aside, as the mistake was not as to its effect, but only as to its consequences.

> Lloyd L.J. emphasised the need to protect a recipient of property in his possession and enjoyment, resulting in a very high test as to the gravity of a mistake justifying the setting aside of a voluntary disposition. Clearly a gift or settlement could not be set aside simply because donors wished that they had not made them, in the absence of special factors.[7] Modern cases drew a distinction between mistakes as to the legal effect of the disposition,[8] which may be sufficient, and as to its consequences, which is not. The impact of

---

[2] *Halpern v Halpern (Nos 1 and 2)* [2008] Q.B. 195; L. Pearce [2008] 16 R.L.R. 124. See generally O'Sullivan, Elliott and Zakrzwski, *The Law of Rescission*, 2007.

[3] *Erlanger v New Sombrero Phosphate Co* (1878) 3 App.Cas. 1218. If all that was required was a return of money or other property without any adjustments, this could be achieved by the common law action for money had and received.

[4] *Guinness Plc v Saunders* [1990] 2 A.C. 663 at 698.

[5] *Redgrave v Hurd* (1881) 20 Ch.D. 1.

[6] [2011] 3 W.L.R. 19; R. Chambers [2011] 25 T.L.I. 17; M. Conaglen (2011) 70 C.L.J. 301; R. Nolan and A. Cloherty (2011) 127 L.Q.R. 499; P. Davies [2011] Conv. 406. Leave to appeal to the Supreme Court was granted on August 1, 2011.

[7] *Ogilvie v Littleboy* (1897) 13 T.L.R. 399 at 400.

[8] *Gibbon v Mitchell* [1990] 1 W.L.R. 1304; *Anker-Petersen v Christensen* [2002] W.T.L.R. 313; *Wolff v Wolff* [2004] W.T.L.R. 1349.

taxation on a transaction is a consequence rather than a legal effect, and so is outside the scope of factors enabling a disposition to be set aside. In the present case there was a mistaken belief that the settlement would have no adverse tax consequences. This was a mistake as to consequence, and there was no mistake as to the legal effect of the disposition, which was to create a "special needs" discretionary trust. Thus the settlement could not be set aside, and the remedy (if any) would be against professional advisers.

A voluntary disposition may also be set aside if there was a fundamental mistake as to an existing fact which was basic to the transaction. An example is *Re Griffiths*,[9] where a gift was set aside where the donor would not have made it had he been aware of his terminal illness, which made the intended tax saving impossible to achieve.

(b) *Contracts.* While mistake alone may justify refusal of an **26–003** order for specific performance,[10] mistake alone is not an automatic ground for rescission, although a mistake induced by fraud, or by misrepresentation, or deliberately not corrected in a situation that called for full disclosure[11] is a more compelling case than a mistake arising without the responsibility of the other party. If two parties enter into a contract and one makes a mistake concerning it, the general principle is that behind the maxim caveat emptor; a party who knows he is making a better bargain than the other is under no duty to divulge the fact. A party who wishes to secure a form of guarantee as to any aspect of the transaction must raise the matter at the time and have it dealt with on the basis of representation or a term of the contract. All this is inherent in freedom of contract; but it is subject to some limits even at common law. For instance, a party cannot remain silent when he knows the other party is mistaken as to what the actual terms of the contract are[12]; or in certain cases of mistake as to the identity of the person contracted with.[13]

It was until quite recently established that there was a jurisdiction in equity to rescind a contract on the ground of mistake common to both parties in circumstances where the contract was valid at common law. This has now been discredited as inconsistent with the decision of the House of Lords in *Bell v Lever Bros Ltd*.[14] In that

[9] [2009] Ch. 162. The Court of Appeal in *Pitt v Holt* [2011] 3 W.L.R. 19 had reservations about the result (although not the principle) because the donor had not followed advice to take out insurance. As he had taken the risk, it would not be against conscience for the recipient to retain the gift.

[10] e.g. *Wood v Scarth* (1855) 2 K. & J. 33, above, para.24–034.

[11] e.g. *Gordon v Gordon* (1816) 3 Swan. 400, below, para.26–005.

[12] *Smith v Hughes* (1871) L.R. 6 Q.B. 597; *Hartog v Colin & Shields* [1939] 3 All E.R. 566.

[13] *Cundy v Lindsay* (1878) 3 App.Cas. 459; *Ingram v Little* [1961] 1 Q.B. 31; *Lewis v Averay* [1972] 1 Q.B. 198.

[14] [1932] A.C. 161; C. MacMillan (2003) 119 L.Q.R. 625.

case a company gave Bell a "golden handshake" to compensate him for the early termination of his contract of service. The company then discovered that the contract of service was voidable by reason of Bell's breach of fiduciary duty, so that he could have been dismissed without compensation. There was no fraudulent concealment, as Bell's mind was not directed to his breach of duty at the time of the compensation agreement. The House of Lords declined to rescind the latter agreement.

After *Bell* the Court of Appeal, in particular Lord Denning, asserted a wide equitable jurisdiction to rescind a contract where the mistake was not of a character to make the contract void at law. The leading case was *Solle v Butcher.*[15]

> A flat was leased for seven years on an erroneous assumption (made by both parties) that structural alterations had taken the premises out of the provisions of the Rent Restriction Acts imposing rent control. The lessee sued to recover rent paid in excess of the amount permitted by the Act. He failed. The landlord obtained rescission of the lease on "just and equitable" terms on the ground of mistake.

For the next half century the courts struggled to define equity's supposed jurisdiction, which required the mistake to be common and sufficiently fundamental, and the claimant not to have been "at fault". The decision in *Bell v Lever Bros Ltd*[16] was treated as dealing only with the position at common law. However, it did not prove possible to define the two different kinds of mistake, one operating at law and one in equity, and the attempts to do so merely emphasised the confusion. The Court of Appeal rejected equity's supposed jurisdiction in *Great Peace Shipping Ltd v Tsavliris Salvage (International) Ltd.*[17]

> The parties entered into a contract to hire a ship to escort a damaged ship to port. Both parties wrongly thought that the two ships were in close proximity. On discovering that this was not so, the defendant repudiated the contract and hired a closer ship, refusing to pay the claimant the contractual cancellation fee on the ground that the contract could be set aside in equity. The Court of Appeal held that equity had no jurisdiction to rescind a

---

[15] [1950] 1 K.B. 671.
[16] [1932] A.C. 161.
[17] [2003] Q.B. 679. See also *Statoil ASA v Louis Dreyfus Energy Services LP* [2008] 2 Lloyd's Rep. 685 (unilateral mistake).

contract for common mistake. The cancellation fee was, there-fore, payable.

A review of the authorities showed that the courts had wrestled to reconcile *Solle v Butcher*[18] with *Bell v Lever Bros Ltd*.[19] The mis-take in the present case was of the same type as in *Bell*: the parties had agreed on the terms of the contract but had a mistaken assump-tion. Such a mistake was not enough to make the contract void at law. Lord Denning in *Solle v Butcher*,[20] where the contract was likewise not void at law, had sought to "outflank" *Bell*. It was, however, inconceivable that the House of Lords in that case would have overlooked a right to rescind in equity. The reality was that equity had no such jurisdiction.[21] It was not possible to distinguish Lord Denning's "fundamental mistake" from Lord Atkin's test in *Bell* for the type of common mistake sufficient to render a contract void at law. The effect of *Solle v Butcher* was not to supplement or mitigate *Bell*, but to say that it was wrongly decided. Thus *Solle v Butcher* could not stand with *Bell*. While Lord Denning's doctrine that equity could rescind on terms was more flexible than the com-mon law doctrine, legislation would be necessary to achieve this.

This rejection of equity's "intrusion" into the law on rescission of a contract for mistake has been welcomed, although the decision in *Great Peace Shipping*[22] has been considered doubtful in terms of the doctrine of precedent.[23]

ii. Other Grounds. Mistake in a wider sense may give rise to the right to rescind, as where the mistake results from a misrepresenta-tion; similarly in a case of constructive fraud, which embraces the doctrines of undue influence and unconscionable bargains. These will be discussed below. The right to rescind may also be granted expressly by the terms of the contract, which will then govern its exercise.[24] The right to rescind where there has been a substantial misdescription in a contract for the sale of land has already been discussed.[25]

26–004

---

[18] [1950] 1 K.B. 671.
[19] Above, fn.16.
[20] Above, fn.18.
[21] Lord Millett recently described Lord Denning's principle as "heresy", saying "The less said about it the better." See (2007) 123 L.Q.R. 159 at 163.
[22] Above, fn.17.
[23] G. McMeel [2002] L.M.C.L.Q. 449; F. Reynolds and S. Midwinter (2003) 119 L.Q.R. 177 and 180 respectively; C. Hare (2003) 62 C.L.J. 29; A. Phang [2003] Conv. 247; J. Cartwright [2003] 11 R.L.R. 93; T. Yeo (2005) 121 L.Q.R. 393; G. McMeel [2006] L.M.C.L.Q. 49 at 62.
[24] See Pettit, p.690.
[25] Above, para.24–039.

26–005 (a) *Misrepresentation.*[26] Where the misrepresentation was fraudulent, the contract could be set aside both at common law and in equity. "Fraudulent" here means that the misrepresentation was made knowingly or recklessly.[27] It must have been intended to be acted upon, and actually have had this result. Equity alone, however, gave relief where the misrepresentation was not fraudulent. Such an "innocent misrepresentation" was not recognised at common law unless it had become a term of the contract.[28]

It should be noted that mere silence does not constitute a misrepresentation unless it creates a false impression by distorting the meaning of any positive statement.[29] Further, there is a duty of disclosure in the case of a contract uberrimae fidei (of the utmost good faith),[30] such as contracts of insurance of all kinds,[31] and contracts for family settlements. Breach of such a duty of disclosure is not a misrepresentation within the Misrepresentation Act 1967,[32] nor does it sound in damages,[33] the proper remedy being rescission. Thus in *Gordon v Gordon*[34] a deed of settlement of property within a family was entered into by an eldest son in the belief that he was illegitimate, though a younger son knew of a secret marriage of his parents by virtue of which the eldest son was legitimate. Lord Eldon held that a duty of candour recognised in equity had been breached so that the settlement should be set aside.

Similar duties may be owed to the court. In *Jenkins v Livesey (formerly Jenkins),*[35] a divorcing couple agreed that the husband would transfer his half-share of the home to the wife, who would give up all claims to financial provision. Shortly after this agreement, the wife became engaged to marry a man she had met before

[26] Only an outline can be given here, and reference should be made to the standard works on contract.

[27] *Derry v Peek* (1889) 14 App.Cas. 337. Damages for deceit are also available: *Archer v Brown* [1985] Q.B. 401; *Saunders v Edwards* [1987] 1 W.L.R. 1116.

[28] See *Heilbut Symons & Co v Buckleton* [1913] A.C. 30.

[29] *Oakes v Turquand* (1867) L.R. 2 H.L. 325.

[30] Or where a fiduciary or other similar special relationship exists between the contracting parties; *van Gestel v Cann, The Times*, August 7, 1987; *Guinness Plc v Saunders* [1990] 2 A.C. 663; *Conlon v Simms* [2008] 1 W.L.R. 848 (partnership agreement).

[31] Also company prospectuses. See *London Assurance Co v Mansel* (1879) 11 Ch.D. 363, and Kindersley V.C.'s well-known judgment in *The New Brunswick and Canada Railway and Land Company v Muggeridge* (1860) 1 Dr. & Sm. 363 at 381. Insurance contracts have been reviewed by the Law Commission; Law Com. No.319 (2009); *Consumer Insurance Law: Pre-Contract Disclosure and Misrepresentation*. The Consumer Insurance (Disclosure and Representations) Bill was introduced in May 2011.

[32] *Banque Keyser Ullman SA v Skandia (UK) Insurance Co Ltd* [1990] 1 Q.B. 665 at 789–790; affirmed [1991] 2 A.C. 249.

[33] [1990] 1 Q.B. 665; *Bank of Nova Scotia v Hellenic Mutual War Risks Association (Bermuda) Ltd* [1990] 1 Q.B. 818. Damages are recoverable in cases of fraud; *Conlon v Simms*, above, fn.30.

[34] (1816) 3 Swan 400.

[35] [1985] A.C. 424. See R. Ingleby (1985) 44 C.L.J. 202; S. Cretney All E.R.Rev. 1985 at 175. The decision is based on the requirements of s.25, rather than the concept of uberrima fides in the agreement for a consent order.

the agreement. This was not disclosed to the husband nor to her own solicitor. The agreement was then embodied in a consent order under s.25(1) of the Matrimonial Causes Act 1973. Two days after the husband conveyed his share of the home, the wife remarried. The House of Lords set aside the consent order. The remarriage ended the wife's right to financial provision, thus the husband would not have entered into the agreement had it been disclosed. Under s.25(1) the court must have regard to all the circumstances, and therefore a duty is owed to the court to make full and frank disclosure of material facts to the other party and to the court. But not every failure to disclose would result in the setting aside of the order. The test was whether the order was substantially different from that which would have been made upon full disclosure.

As far as innocent misrepresentation was concerned, equity's jurisdiction depended on the force of the misrepresentation on the claimant's mind rather than the mental state of the defendant when he made it, or on the relative importance of the fact misrepresented to the contract as a whole. Thus a claimant seeking rescission on this ground did not have to prove negligence or any other degree of fault in the defendant but only the fact of his own reliance on the statement, and its untruth.

Until the Misrepresentation Act 1967 the claimant could re- **26–006** scind,[36] or possibly resist specific performance, but he could not recover damages on the basis of an innocent misrepresentation. Since that Act, however, the claimant may recover damages under s.2(1) for an innocent misrepresentation unless the defendant had reasonable grounds to believe and did believe that the statement was true.[37] The measure of damages is the same as that which applies to a fraudulent misrepresentation.[38] By s.2(2), damages may be awarded in lieu of rescission wherever the court thinks it would be equitable to do so, having regard to the nature of the misrepresentation and the loss that would be caused by it if the contract were upheld, as well as the loss that rescission would cause to the defendant. Damages may be awarded under s.2(2) although the misrepresentation was wholly innocent, (i.e. non-negligent). The measure is as in contract, and is thus different from the measure of damages

---

[36] See generally *Redgrave v Hurd* (1881) 20 Ch.D. 1.

[37] See *Laurence v Lexcourt Holdings Ltd* [1978] 1 W.L.R. 1128; *Walker v Boyle* [1982] 1 W.L.R. 495; *Government of Zanzibar v British Aerospace (Lancaster House) Ltd* [2000] 1 W.L.R. 2333.

[38] *Royscot Trust Ltd v Rogerson* [1991] 2 Q.B. 297; R Hooley (1991) 107 L.Q.R. 547. But the correctness of *Royscot* was left open in *Smith New Court Securities Ltd v Scrimgeour Vickers (Asset Management) Ltd* [1997] A.C. 254; J. Payne (1997) 56 C.L.J. 17. See also *East v Maurer* [1991] 1 W.L.R. 461 (loss of profits); J. Marks (1992) 108 L.Q.R. 386; P. Chandler (1994) 110 L.Q.R. 35; *Clef Aquitaine SARL v Laporte Materials (Barrow) Ltd* [2001] Q.B. 488 (reduced profits).

under subs.(1).[39] The result intended would seem to be that damages
are the most suitable remedy in cases of misrepresentations inducing
a contract, save where the facts reveal a real justification for there
being rescission of the contract as well. A term in the contract
purporting to restrict or exclude liability for misrepresentation is of
no effect except insofar as it satisfies the requirement of reasonableness as stated in s.11(1) of the Unfair Contract Terms Act 1977.[40]

Equity's remedy of rescission now forms part of a hierarchy of
remedies for misrepresentation that are available generally to a
claimant, instead of being the only and not always very apposite
remedy available in the absence of fraud. It is thus now more important as a supplementary than as a basic remedy. The history and
rationale of the remedy are, however, of interest in considering
rescission for mistakes not induced by misrepresentation, discussed
in the earlier part of this section.

26–007   (b) *Undue Influence.*[41] Under the head of constructive fraud,[42]
equity recognises a wide variety of situations in which intervention
is justified by reason of a defendant's influence or dominance over
the claimant in procuring his execution of a document (such as a
settlement) or his entering into an obligation; equity's intervention
here is independent of any question of the accuracy of information
supplied to the claimant. Equity intervenes in such cases, not because, as is the case with misrepresentations, the defendant has
positively (albeit innocently) misled the claimant on a particular and
relevant point of fact, but because the defendant had caused the
claimant's judgment to be clouded, with the result that he has failed
to consider the matter as he ought. The right to set aside the transaction arises without the claimant having to show that he or she would
have acted differently in the absence of undue influence.[43]

Actual threats, or physical duress, are remedied both at law and in
equity, but equity's view is the wider. Where threats have made it
impossible for the claimant either to consider the relevant matter
normally or to feel a free agent, as when a son was threatened with
disclosure to his sick father of the forging of the father's signature

---

[39] *William Sindall Plc v Cambridgeshire CC* [1994] 1 W.L.R. 1016; H. Beale (1995) 111
L.Q.R. 60; A. Oakley (1995) 54 C.L.J. 17.

[40] s.3, as amended by the 1977 Act. See *Walker v Boyle* [1982] 1 W.L.R. 495.

[41] See generally Halliwell, *Equity and Good Conscience in a Contemporary Context*, 1997,
Ch.3; Enonchong, *Duress, Undue Influence and Unconscionable Dealing*, 1998; K. Lewison
[2011] 19 R.L.R. 1.

[42] See *O'Sullivan v Management Agency and Music Ltd* [1985] Q.B. 428, at 455; *Mander v
Evans* [2001] 1 W.L.R. 2378. See also *Re Edwards* [2007] W.T.L.R. 1387 (will may be set
aside in equity on the ground of "fraudulent calumny").

[43] *UCB Corporate Services Ltd v Williams* (2003) 1 P. & C.R. 12. However, this question is
relevant to the quantification of any loss.

by his brother, equity will intervene.[44] But influence by means other than threats is the more usual type of case. It is possible for a defendant to have obtained almost complete domination over the mind of another,[45] but in most cases the undue influence is exerted only to secure a specific objective.[46] The varieties of methods are infinite also; they may range from developing a sense of complete confidence[47] over many years to quick seizure of an opportunity presented by a defendant's weakness. In *Tufton v Sperni*,[48] the claimant was prevailed upon to buy a house from the defendant at an over-value and at the same time to make it available to the defendant on a lease on absurdly favourable terms. The Court of Appeal, in rescinding the transaction, emphasised that these cases cannot be categorised, but are all variations on the one theme of undue[49] use of a mental domination possessed or gained over another. Undue influence may be exercised by a corporation, although there may be no special personal relationship with any individual representative.[50] The novel point as to whether undue influence could be exercised by an unincorporated association arose in *Roche v Sherrington*,[51] where the claimant had been a member of Opus Dei (an international Roman Catholic association) for some years. After leaving, he sought repayment of gifts to the association on the basis of undue influence. Slade J. held it to be arguable that a transaction between an individual and an unincorporated association might give rise to a presumption of undue influence on the part of the members. But the action was dismissed as it had been brought against the defendant as representative of all present members, including many persons who were not members at the time of the gifts.

There are two categories of cases; first, those in which equity **26–008** presumes undue influence. While the presumption does not apply to every relationship of trust and confidence,[52] it does arise in certain well defined cases such as parent and child, guardian and ward, doctor and patient, solicitor and client, religious adviser and pupil,[53]

---

[44] *Mutual Finance Co v Wetton* [1937] 2 K.B. 389; *Barton v Armstrong* [1976] A.C. 104. See W Winder (1939) 3 M.L.R. 97.

[45] *Smith v Kay* (1875) 7 H.L.Cas. 750; *Morley v Loughnan* [1893] 1 Ch. 736.

[46] *Lyon v Home* (1868) L.R. 6 Eq. 655.

[47] *Tate v Williamson* (1866) L.R. 2 Ch.App. 55.

[48] [1952] 2 T.L.R. 516. See also *Langton v Langton* [1995] 2 F.L.R. 890 (father pressured to make gift of house).

[49] It may be undue without being for personal gain, as where a parent's influence leads to an improvident settlement by a child that is only of marginal benefit to the parent: *Bullock v Lloyds Bank* [1955] Ch. 317.

[50] See *Lloyds Bank Ltd v Bundy* [1975] Q.B. 326.

[51] [1982] 1 W.L.R. 599.

[52] *National Westminster Bank Plc v Morgan* [1985] A.C. 686; *Goldsworthy v Brickell* [1987] Ch. 378.

[53] *Allcard v Skinner* (1887) 36 Ch.D. 145 (nun and mother superior); *Huguenin v Baseley* (1807) 14 Ves. 273. For the view that there are not two categories, see K. Lewison [2011] 19 R.L.R. 1.

and other situations where it is shown that a similar relationship of confidence existed.[54] Here equity requires positive evidence that no undue influence was in fact exerted, and it is not enough to show that there was no "sinister" conduct on the part of the defendant.[55] Secondly, in cases outside this category equity requires positive proof of influence having actually been exerted.[56] But in all cases the question is whether a defendant has taken advantage of his position, which includes breaching a duty of candour and fairness arising from the relationship,[57] or has been assiduous not to do so. Many cases turn on whether a defendant discouraged independent legal advice or proceeded in such a way as to make it unlikely that the claimant would think of taking it.[58] For, as with many of the flexible remedies of equity, a defendant is not placed under an absolute bar by virtue of this equitable obligation, but has to adopt proper steps, in view of the obligation, if he wishes to proceed in certain ways. So a genuine insistence on independent legal advice from a fully informed adviser is a natural means of repudiating a charge of having exerted undue influence, even in a case where the possibility of influence was strong[59] and especially where there is a

[54] *Re Craig* [1971] Ch. 95 (aged widower and secretary); *Lloyd's Bank Ltd v Bundy* (above, fn.50), (banker and aged customer); *O'Sullivan v Management Agency and Music Ltd* [1985] Q.B. 428 (manager and entertainer); *Re Brocklehurst* [1978] Ch. 14 at 42; *Simpson v Simpson* [1992] 1 F.L.R. 601 (incapacitated elderly husband and younger wife); *Goldsworthy v Brickell* [1987] Ch. 378 (elderly farmer and manager); *Cheese v Thomas* [1994] 1 W.L.R. 129 (elderly uncle and great nephew); *Langton v Langton* [1995] 2 F.L.R. 890 (vulnerable ex-convict and son); *Mahoney v Purnell* [1996] 3 All E.R. 61 (elderly father-in-law and son-in-law); *Hammond v Osborn* [2002] W.T.L.R. 1125 (elderly man and carer); *Walker v Walker* [2010] W.T.L.R. 1617 (father and daughter). See also *Mathew v Bobbins* (1980) 41 P. & C.R. 1 (there is no presumption of undue influence arising from the relationship of master and servant or landlord and tenant).

[55] *Hammond v Osborn* [2002] W.T.L.R. 1125; K. Scott [2003] L.M.C.L.Q. 145; P. Birks (2003) 119 L.Q.R. 34 at 36 and (2004) 120 L.Q.R. 34; *Niersmans v Pesticcio* [2004] W.T.L.R. 699; N. Enonchong (2005) 121 L.Q.R. 29. See generally M. Chen-Wishart (2006) 59 C.L.P. 231.

[56] As in the case of gifts by will, where no presumption of undue influence arises by reason of the relationship of the parties. See Mellows, *The Law of Succession*, 5th edn, 1993, pp.53–55; P. Ridge (2004) 120 L.Q.R. 617; L. Mason [2011] Conv. 115; *Cattermole v Prisk* [2006] 1 F.L.R. 693. There is no presumption of undue influence between husband and wife, although a transaction may be set aside if a relationship of confidence is shown to have existed, or failing that, on proof of undue influence; *Bank of Montreal v Stuart* [1911] A.C. 120; *Kingsnorth Trust Ltd v Bell* [1986] 1 W.L.R. 119; *Simpson v Simpson*, above, fn.54; *Midland Bank Plc v Shephard* [1988] 3 All E.R. 17; B. Dale [1989] Conv. 63. On engaged couples, see N. Enonchong (2005) 121 L.Q.R. 567.

[57] *Hewett v First Plus Financial Group Plc* [2010] 2 F.L.R. 177 (husband concealed affair when persuading wife to charge family home). Non-disclosure of material facts, as opposed to deliberate concealment, does not amount to undue influence; *Royal Bank of Scotland Plc v Chandra* [2011] EWCA Civ 192; [2011] 2 P. & C.R. DG 1.

[58] *Baker v Monk* (1864) 4 De G.J. & S. 388; *Backhouse v Backhouse* [1978] 1 W.L.R. 243; *Cresswell v Potter* (1968); [1978] 1 W.L.R. 255n.

[59] See *Zamet v Hyman* [1961] 1 W.L.R. 1442 at 1445–1446; *Banco Exterior Internacional SA v Thomas* [1997] 1 W.L.R. 221.

conflict of interest and duty.[60] But the presumption of undue influence is not rebuttable only by establishing insistence on independent legal advice (which, however, does not always suffice to rebut the presumption[61]); it may also be rebutted by showing that a gift was a "spontaneous and independent act".[62] In any event, the presumption will not operate unless the gift is so large or the transaction so improvident that it cannot reasonably be accounted for on grounds of friendship, relationship, charity or other motives.[63]

Most of the illustrations relate to situations of special relationship existing between particular people, and often involve settlements of property. The principle is less often seen in operation in commercial matters, where it has had little impact in derogating from the more widely applicable principle that lies behind the maxim caveat emptor.[64] Mere inequality of bargaining power, which is a relative concept, does not justify interference with a commercial transaction. There is rarely absolute equality, and the court only interferes in exceptional cases as a matter of common fairness.[65] The principles of undue influence have generally been discussed in the types of transaction which attracted equity's particular attention in the 19th century, such as the cases on bargains with expectant heirs, and the modern form of such cases. These include cases where a beneficiary under a trust, who, although past the age of majority, is still subject to parental influence, and is persuaded to use his fortune to support the family finances[66]; or where a secretary companion takes advantage of her dominance of a vulnerable old man[67]; or where an elderly farmer grants a tenancy on terms disadvantageous to himself to the manager upon whom he relies.[68] Bridge L.J. summarised these cases as those in which there is a "duty on the donee to advise the donor, or a position of actual or potential dominance of the

---

[60] *Lloyds Bank Ltd v Bundy* [1975] Q.B. 326.

[61] *Credit Lyonnais Bank Nederland NV v Burch* [1997] 1 All E.R. 144 (because the influence may cause the advice to be disregarded); *Claughton v Price* (1998) 30 H.L.R. 396; *Niersmans v Pesticcio*, above, fn.55; cf. *Banco Exterior Internacional SA v Thomas*, above, fn.59 at 230; *Smith v Cooper* [2010] 2 F.L.R. 1521.

[62] *Re Brocklehurst* [1978] Ch. 14. See also *Simpson v Simpson* [1992] 1 F.L.R. 601; *Goldsworthy v Brickell* [1987] Ch. 378.

[63] *Goldsworthy v Brickell* [1987] Ch. 378; (1987) 104 L.Q.R. 160; M. Furmston All E.R. Rev. 1987, p.311; *Turkey v Awadh* [2006] W.T.L.R. 553.

[64] "Extravagant liberality and immoderate folly do not provide a passport to equitable relief," per Evershed M.R. in *Tufton v Sperni* [1952] 2 T.L.R. 516 at 519.

[65] *Alec Lobb (Garages) Ltd v Total Oil GB Ltd* [1985] 1 W.L.R. 173; (1985) 101 L.Q.R. 306. The cases where a commercial transaction such as a mortgage may be set aside because the mortgagee has constructive notice of undue influence exerted by a third party are discussed below; paras 26–010–26–013.

[66] *Re Coomber* [1911] 1 Ch. 732 at 726, 727; *Bullock v Lloyds Bank Ltd* [1955] Ch. 317; *Re Pauling's ST* [1964] Ch. 303.

[67] *Re Craig* [1971] Ch. 95; *Hammond v Osborn* [2002] W.T.L.R. 1125 (large gifts by elderly man to his carer).

[68] *Goldsworthy v Brickell* [1987] Ch. 378. See also *Dalgleish Wright v Hodgkinson* [2005] W.T.L.R. 435.

donee over the donor."[69] But there was no such position of dominance in *Re Brocklehurst*,[70] where an "autocratic and eccentric old
gentleman" made a valuable gift of shooting rights to the defendant,
a "subservient garage proprietor". The relationship was not one of
confidence and trust such as to give rise to a presumption of undue
influence.

26–009   The House of Lords reviewed the doctrine in *National Westminster Bank v Morgan*,[71] where a husband and wife mortgaged their
home to the bank to secure a loan to the husband, who was in
difficulties with his business. The wife claimed that the bank manager had exercised undue influence in obtaining her signature during
a visit to the home. Although the wife had not received independent
legal advice before signing, her claim failed because the relationship
never went beyond the normal business relationship of banker and
customer, nor was the transaction disadvantageous to the wife. The
principle which justifies setting a transaction aside for undue influence is the victimisation of one party by the other. The party alleging
undue influence must show, it was said, that the transaction was
manifestly disadvantageous to him (which will, of course, be easier
to establish in cases of gifts). While there are no precisely defined
limits to the equitable jurisdiction to relieve against undue influence,
the doctrine is sufficiently developed not to need the support of a
principle of inequality of bargaining power. This decision, in rejecting the broad approach of inequality of bargaining power, restricted
the scope of the doctrine of undue influence.

The requirement of manifest disadvantage proved troublesome,
especially where a wife was seeking to set aside (on the basis of
undue influence) a charge over the matrimonial home to secure a
loan made to assist the husband's business. If the loan was the only
way to keep the business afloat, the wife had difficulty in showing
that it was to her manifest disadvantage even though the business
ultimately failed.[72] "Manifest" means "clear and obvious", on an
objective view as at the date of the transaction. It may be small, so
long as it is more than de minimis. The House of Lords has held that
manifest disadvantage need not be shown in cases of actual, as
opposed to presumed, undue influence.[73] It was considered that
National Westminster Bank v Morgan[74] did not intend to lay it down
as a universal requirement, and that there was no logic in requiring it
in a case of actual undue influence, which is a species of fraud. The

---

[69] *Re Brocklehurst* [1978] Ch. 14 at 41.
[70] [1978] Ch. 14 (Lord Denning M.R. dissented).
[71] [1985] A.C. 686; N. Andrews (1985) 101 L.Q.R. 305 and (1985) 44 C.L.J. 192; D.
Tiplady (1985) 48 M.L.R. 579; N. Palmer and M. Furmston All E.R. Rev. 1985 at 20 and
at 89.
[72] See *National Westminster Bank Plc v Leggatt* [2001] 1 F.L.R. 563.
[73] *CIBC Mortgages Plc v Pitt* [1994] 1 A.C. 200.
[74] [1985] A.C. 686.

requirement of manifest disadvantage remains in cases of presumed undue influence.[75] Lord Nicholls, however, has said that the "manifest disadvantage" terminology should be discarded. The necessary element is that the transaction is not readily explicable by the relationship of the parties.[76] The Court of Appeal has more recently confirmed that manifest disadvantage is relevant at the stage of considering whether the presumption of undue influence has arisen. It is not relevant at the second stage of considering whether the presumption has been rebutted: it is not sufficient at that stage to show that there was no manifest disadvantage.[77]

An important question which has arisen in the context of mort- **26–010**
gages and guarantees is whether the creditor should be prejudiced by any misrepresentation or undue influence exercised by the debtor over a third party who executes the mortgage or guarantee in favour of the creditor, or agrees to give priority to the mortgagee. As a general rule, a creditor owes no duty to the debtor's surety or guarantor to ensure that the third party understands the transaction and has given a free and informed consent. The transaction will, however, be set aside if the creditor had actual or constructive notice at the time of the execution of the security that the third party's consent was procured by the undue influence or misrepresentation of the debtor. Likewise in the very rare case where the creditor has made the debtor its agent in procuring the execution of the security by the third party (agency not being established merely by reason that the creditor has left it to the debtor to procure the execution), and the debtor has been guilty of undue influence or misrepresentation.

These propositions were confirmed by the House of Lords in *Barclays Bank Plc v O'Brien*,[78] where the principles were fully reviewed. In that case a wife (who was neither uneducated nor vulnerable) executed a charge securing her husband's unlimited guarantee of a company's liability to the bank. Owing to her husband's misrepresentation, she thought it was a temporary security for the sum of £60,000. The wife did not read the documents before signing. It was held that the bank could not enforce the charge because it had constructive notice of the wife's right to set aside the

---

[75] See *Cheese v Thomas* [1994] 1 W.L.R. 129, below, para.26–017 (transaction set aside where elderly man aged 86 spent £43,000 to buy an insecure right to reside in a particular house for life); *Mahoney v Purnell* [1996] 3 All E.R. 61; *Dunbar Bank Plc v Nadeem* [1998] 3 All E.R. 876; A. Chandler (1999) 115 L.Q.R. 213; *Vale v Armstrong* [2004] W.T.L.R. 1471; *Curtis v Pulbrook* [2011] W.T.L.R. 1503.

[76] *Royal Bank of Scotland Plc v Etridge (No.2)* [2002] 2 A.C. 773.

[77] *Smith v Cooper* [2010] 2 F.L.R. 1521.

[78] [1994] 1 A.C. 180. The bank had recovered £60,000, and the appeal did not deal with that. See generally F. Rose (ed.), *Restitution and Banking Law*, 1998, Chs 3, 4; J. Cartwright [1999] R.L.R. 1; M. Draper [1999] Conv. 176; Fehlberg, *Sexually Transmitted Debt*, 1997.

transaction. Such cases involved a consideration of two questions: was the creditor put on inquiry as to the existence of undue influence, misrepresentation or other legal wrong and, if so, had the creditor taken reasonable steps to ensure that the third party understood the transaction? If reasonable steps had not been taken, the creditor would have constructive notice of the third party's right to set aside the transaction, which would be accordingly unenforceable by the creditor. Where a wife charged her property or stood surety for her husband's debt, the creditor would be put on inquiry by a combination of two factors: first, the transaction on its face was not to the wife's financial advantage; secondly, although there was no presumption of undue influence between husband and wife, there was a substantial risk that the husband had committed a legal or equitable wrong entitling the wife to set aside the transaction.[79] The principle was not confined to wives, but extended to cohabitants[80] (including homosexual couples), provided the creditor was aware of the cohabitation, and other relationships may be included.[81] It was emphasised, however, that the principle did not apply to a third party who merely misunderstood the transaction, without wrongdoing by the debtor. It has since been confirmed that the doctrine may be invoked by husbands also, although as a matter of evidence a husband may find it harder to persuade the court that he left his affairs to his wife.[82]

Where the creditor is put on inquiry,[83] the next question, as mentioned above, is whether it can prove that it has taken reasonable steps to ensure that the third party understood the transaction. The guidelines given in *O'Brien* were that, unless the circumstances were exceptional, the creditor must warn the third party, at a meeting not attended by the debtor, of the potential liability and risks, and must advise the third party to take independent legal advice. Cases involving transactions entered into before the formulation of these guidelines are dealt with on their merits. As we will see, the House of Lords subsequently revised the guidelines.[84]

---

[79] A recent example is *Hewett v First Plus Financial Group Plc* [2010] 2 F.L.R. 177.

[80] See also *Massey v Midland Bank Plc* [1995] 1 All E.R. 929 (couple not cohabiting but longstanding relationship); *Allied Irish Bank Plc v Byrne* [1995] 2 F.L.R. 325 (divorced but partly reconciled). This reflects the Code of Banking Practice.

[81] The House of Lords approved *Avon Finance Ltd v Bridger* [1985] 2 All E.R. 281 (vulnerable elderly parents and adult son). See also *Credit Lyonnais Bank Nederland NV v Burch* [1997] 1 All E.R. 144 and *Steeples v Lea* (1998) 76 P. & C.R. 157 (employer and employee whose relationship gave rise to a presumption of undue influence); *National Westminster Bank Plc v Amin* [2002] 1 F.L.R. 735; M. Haley [2002] Conv. 499; J. Holland All E.R. Rev. 2002, p.342 (parents who secured son's debt spoke only Urdu).

[82] *Barclays Bank Plc v Rivett* [1999] 1 F.L.R. 730.

[83] The burden of proving constructive notice is on the wife; *Barclays Bank v Boulter* [1999] 1 W.L.R. 1919; M. Thompson [2000] Conv. 43; K. Barker [2000] R.L.R. 114.

[84] Below, para.26–012.

Some older authorities had treated the wife as having a "special equity" deserving of extra protection. Lord Browne-Wilkinson in *Barclays Bank Plc v O'Brien*,[85] rejecting this theory, considered the true basis to be the doctrine of notice, which "lies at the heart of equity".[86] Although his Lordship spoke in terms of earlier rights prevailing against later rights, it must be emphasised that it is not the traditional doctrine of notice which is at work here, because there is only one transaction, and not a contest between a prior interest and a later one. The concept is that a party to a contract may lose the benefit of his contract, entered into in good faith, if he ought to have known that the other's concurrence had been procured by the misconduct of a third party.[87] The doctrine of notice is applied in this extended sense, and for that reason is equally applicable to cases of registered title.[88]

Lord Browne-Wilkinson was concerned to hold a fair balance **26–011** between the vulnerability of wives (and others) and the practical problems of lenders. This factor was particularly significant in the contemporaneous decision of the House of Lords in *CIBC Mortgages Plc v Pitt*,[89] where a husband exercised undue influence in relation to a mortgage to secure a joint loan of £150,000 to himself and his wife. The loan application stated that the money was required to pay off an existing mortgage and to buy a holiday home. After paying off the prior mortgage the husband used the surplus in unsuccessful speculation on the stock market. The wife, who had not read the documents nor received separate advice, failed to set aside the mortgage. The bank was not put on inquiry because it was a joint loan and, in contrast with the surety cases, there was nothing to indicate that it was not for their joint benefit. To have decided otherwise would have had the detrimental result in practice of restricting the availability of joint mortgage loans for the purchase of homes. The mere fact that the loan is joint will not, however, automatically disapply the principle of *Barclays Bank Plc v O'Brien*,[90] if

---

[85] Above. The "special equity" approach has been preferred in Australia; *Garcia v National Australia Bank Ltd* (1998) 72 A.L.J.R. 1243; S. Gardner (1999) 115 L.Q.R. 1; E. Stone (1999) 62 M.L.R. 604; M. Bryan [1999] L.M.C.L.Q. 327; M. Brown [2000] R.L.R. 152.

[86] [1994] 1 A.C. 180 at 195.

[87] *Royal Bank of Scotland Plc v Etridge (No.2)* [2002] 2 A.C. 773.

[88] Above, para.1–048. See W. Swadling All E.R. Rev. 1993, 367; P. O'Hagan (1994) 144 N.L.J. 765; M. Dixon and C. Harpum [1994] Conv. 421; P. Sparkes [1995] Conv. 250; A. Lawson and J. Mee (1995) 54 C.L.J. 280 and 536 respectively; G. Battersby (1995) 15 L.S. 35; J. Howell [1996] Conv. 34. For the position where the debtor was not a party to the transaction in question, see *Banco Exterior Internacional SA v Thomas* [1997] 1 W.L.R. 221.

[89] [1994] 1 A.C. 200; B. Fehlberg (1994) 57 M.L.R. 467; S. Cretney [1994] 2 R.L.R. 3. See also *Britannia Building Society v Pugh* [1997] 2 F.L.R. 7; *Scotlife Home Loans (No.2) Ltd v Hedworth* (1996) 28 H.L.R. 771 (not set aside where in fact used for joint benefit, contrary to stated purpose); *Chater v Mortgage Agency Services Number Two Ltd* (2004) 1 P. & C.R. 4.

[90] [1994] 1 A.C. 180.

in substance the situation is one of suretyship,[91] or if the stated purpose is for the couple's joint benefit but the creditor knows that the money will be used for the husband's sole benefit,[92] or knows that the benefit to the wife is disproportionately small in comparison with her potential liability.[93] A loan to a company whose shares are held by the husband and wife is not to be treated as a joint loan.[94]

It was held by the Court of Appeal in *TSB Bank Plc v Camfield*[95] that where a third party has established the right to set aside a transaction against the creditor, the right is absolute. The court will not impose terms which make the security or guarantee partially enforceable. Thus where the husband misrepresented that the security was limited to £15,000, but in fact it was unlimited, the wife had no liability even as to the £15,000. Although the court recognised the "abstract justice" of partial enforcement, the position was the same as any other case where a person was affected by notice of another's rights. The right to rescind is that of the third party, who does not need to ask the court for equitable relief, to which terms may be attached. In *Camfield*, however, the wife received no benefit from the transaction and thus had nothing to restore under the restitutio in integrum principle.[96] The Court of Appeal subsequently confirmed in *Dunbar Bank Plc v Nadeem*[97] that the restitutio principle applies in these cases where the wife has received a benefit, although on the facts it did not arise because the wife failed to set aside the mortgage. Where, however, a joint mortgage on the home

---

[91] *Allied Irish Bank Plc v Byrne* [1995] 2 F.L.R. 325 (joint loan but bank aware that for benefit of husband). See also M. Thompson [1994] Conv. 140; M. Dixon (1994) 53 C.L.J. 21.

[92] *Halifax Mortgage Services Ltd v Stepsky* [1996] Ch. 207 (not set aside because knowledge of borrowers' solicitor acquired before instructed by lender not imputed to lender).

[93] *Goode Durrant Administration v Biddulph* (1994) 26 H.L.R. 625 (joint loan to spouses and company but wife entitled only to 2.5% shareholding); S. Cretney (1994) 24 Fam. Law 675.

[94] *Royal Bank of Scotland Plc v Etridge (No.2)* [2002] 2 A.C. 773. See also *Bank of Cyprus (London) Ltd v Markou* [1999] 2 All E.R. 707.

[95] [1995] 1 W.L.R. 430; A. Dunn [1995] Conv. 325; P. Ferguson (1995) 111 L.Q.R. 555; W. Swadling All E.R. Rev. 1995, 450; L. Proksch [1996] R.L.R. 71; P. Watts (2002) 61 C.L.J. 301 at 309; *Castle Phillips Finance v Piddington* (1995) 70 P. & C.R. 592; *De Molestina v Ponton* [2002] 1 Lloyd's Rep. 271. The point did not arise in *Barclays Bank Plc v O'Brien* [1994] 1 A.C. 180; above, para.26–010, fn.78. *Camfield* has been rejected in Australia; *Vadasz v Pioneer Concrete (SA) Pty Ltd* (1995) 184 C.L.R. 102; D. O'Sullivan (1997) 113 L.Q.R. 16; J. O'Sullivan (2000) 59 C.L.J. 509. See generally J. Poole and A. Keyser (2005) 121 L.Q.R. 273 supporting partial rescission.

[96] Below, para.26–017.

[97] [1998] 3 All E.R. 876 (loan for purpose of acquiring lease in joint names); criticised in P. Birks and W. Swadling All E.R. Rev. 1998, pp.407–8, where the result is said to be "barely intelligible". See also *Barclays Bank Plc v Caplan* (1999) 78 P. & C.R. 153 (a mortgage not vitiated by undue influence could be severed from later extensions of the liability which were so vitiated); *Yorkshire Bank Plc v Tinsley* [2004] 1 W.L.R. 2380 (remortgage with same lender after undue influence ended); M. Thompson [2004] Conv. 399; N Gravells (2005) 64 C.L.J. 42.

is set aside by the wife, it may take effect as a charge on the husband's equitable interest, and in any event the creditor may bring about a sale of the home by making the husband bankrupt.[98] A wife who has recognised the validity of the charge in matrimonial proceedings is precluded from asserting its invalidity in possession proceedings.[99]

As stated above, the requirements laid down in *Barclays Bank Plc v O'Brien*, which a creditor with constructive notice must satisfy in order to establish that reasonable steps have been taken to ensure that the third party understood the transaction, apply in their full rigour only to post-*O'Brien* transactions. Subsequent decisions treated creditors somewhat leniently in this regard.[100] **26–012**

The House of Lords reviewed the principles again in *Royal Bank of Scotland Plc v Etridge (No.2)*,[101] setting out clear and simple procedures to be operated by banks (and other lenders) in these cases. Where the circumstances are such that the bank has been put on enquiry, it must take reasonable steps to satisfy itself that the implications of the proposed transaction have been meaningfully explained to the wife. The bank should ask the wife who she wants to act for her, and should explain that it will require confirmation from the solicitor that he has advised her. It must always obtain such confirmation in writing. What must be confirmed is that the solicitor has explained the nature, effect and risks of the transaction, not that he has satisfied himself that there has been no undue influence or misrepresentation. If the bank does not itself wish to have a meeting with the wife, it must provide the relevant financial information to the solicitor. If the bank suspects wrongdoing, it must tell the solicitor. The solicitor who advises the wife may also be acting for the husband or the bank, but when advising the wife (at a meeting not attended by the husband), he will be concerned only with her interests. The bank is entitled to assume that the solicitor has done his job properly. If he has not, the wife's remedy is against him.

Thus the emerging principle is that a wife who has received independent legal advice will rarely succeed in setting aside the

---

[98] *Zandfarid v Bank of Credit and Commerce International SA (In Liquidation)* [1996] 1 W.L.R. 1420; *Alliance & Leceister Plc v Slayford* [2001] 1 All E.R. (Comm) 1; *Hewett v First Plus Financial Group Plc* [2010] 2 F.L.R. 177. See also *Albany Home Loans Ltd v Massey, The Times*, February 14, 1997 (possession proceedings against H to be adjourned where W has arguable *O'Brien* defence).

[99] *First National Bank Plc v Walker* [2001] 1 F.L.R. 505; M. Oldham (2001) 60 C.L.J. 250.

[100] S. Cretney (1994) 24 Fam. Law 563; A. Chandler (1995) 111 L.Q.R. 51; J. Mee [1995] Conv. 148; M. Oldham [1995] 7 C.F.L.Q. 104; P. Giliker (1995–96) 6 K.C.L.J. 108; B. Fehlberg (1996) 59 M.L.R. 675.

[101] [2002] 2 A.C. 773; M. Oldham (2002) 61 C.L.J. 29; R. Bigwood (2002) 65 M.L.R. 435; M. Thompson and G. Andrews [2002] Conv. 174 and 456 respectively; D. O'Sullivan (2002) 118 L.Q.R. 337; A. Phang and H. Tjio [2002] L.M.C.L.Q. 231; D. Capper [2002] 10 R.L.R. 100; K. Lewison [2011] 19 R.L.R. 1.

security. On the other hand, the terms of the transaction may be so manifestly disadvantageous (as where a junior employee mortgaged her home to the bank to secure an unlimited guarantee of her employer's overdraft) that the creditor cannot be said to have taken reasonable steps even if it ensured that the third party took independent legal advice, if it must have known that no competent solicitor could have advised the third party to enter into the transaction.[102]

One significant feature of *Royal Bank of Scotland Plc v Etridge (No.2)*[103] was the extension by Lord Nicholls of the principles discussed above to all "non-commercial" relationships. His Lordship considered that in future banks should regulate their affairs on the basis that they would be put on enquiry where the relationship between the surety and the debtor was non-commercial, and that this would impose only a modest burden on them.

26–013   After previous doubts it has been held by the House of Lords in *Smith v Governor and Company of Bank of Scotland*[104] that these principles apply also in Scotland, although Lord Jauncey distinguished undue influence and misrepresentation, doubting whether it can be said in Scots law that one class of persons is more likely than any other to make a misrepresentation.[105] It was suggested that the doctrine rests on the principle of good faith rather than notice: good faith requires a creditor to give advice where it should reasonably suspect that the intimate relationship might undermine the validity of the transaction. Another view is that the courts are simply laying down a code of practice for a species of transaction which is regarded as unsafe to leave to the normal bargaining process.[106]

The review of this area by the House of Lords in *Barclays Bank Plc v O'Brien*[107] and *Royal Bank of Scotland Plc v Etridge (No.2)*[108] leaves some matters still uncertain, in particular the relationship between cases of presumed undue influence, where "manifest disadvantage" is still required, and cases of breach of fiduciary duty, where transactions can be set aside without proof of disadvantage. Likewise the distinction between cases of actual undue influence

---

[102] *Credit Lyonnais Bank Nederland NV v Burch* [1997] 1 All E.R. 144; H. Tjio (1997) 113 L.Q.R. 10; A. Pugh-Thomas (1997) 147 N.L.J. 726, 767; J. Phillips (1997–98) 8 K.C.L.J. 139; M. Chen-Wishart (1997) 56 C.L.J. 60; M. Haley (1997) 9 C.F.L.Q. 173; *National Westminster Bank Plc v Breeds* [2001] Lloyd's Rep. Bank 98.

[103] Above, fn.101.

[104] [1997] 2 F.L.R. 862.

[105] [1997] 2 F.L.R. 862 at 866. See also C. Rickett (1998) 114 L.Q.R. 17, suggesting that the doctrine could be based on the creditor's equitable duty of care to safeguard the interests of persons with whom it deals who come from a particular class at risk.

[106] P. Birks and W. Swadling All E.R. Rev. 1997, pp.390–397. See also J. Wadsley [2003] L.M.C.L.Q. 341.

[107] [1994] 1 A.C. 180.

[108] [2002] 2 A.C. 773; K. Lewison [2011] 19 R.L.R. 1.

and "unconscionable bargains", discussed below, needs to be clarified.[109]

(c) *Unconscionable Bargains.* Equity intervenes to set aside un- **26–014** fair transactions made with "poor and ignorant" persons. The doctrine does not apply to gifts.[110] It is not enough to show that the transaction was hard and unreasonable.[111] Three elements must be established.[112] First, that one party was at a serious disadvantage to the other by reason of poverty, ignorance or otherwise,[113] so that circumstances existed of which unfair advantage could be taken[114]; secondly, that the transaction was at an undervalue; and thirdly, that there was a lack of independent legal advice.[115] A similar principle applies in the case of unconscionable bargains with reversioners or "expectant heirs".[116] The Court of Appeal has stated that the doctrine needs careful confinement if it is not itself to become an instrument of oppression.[117] It was held that a bank guarantee could not be set aside on the basis of illiteracy or unfamiliarity with English in the absence of substantial unfairness in the transaction itself, otherwise banks would not lend to those in a weak bargaining position. An example of substantial unfairness readily justifying the setting aside of a transaction was where a junior employee mortgaged her home to secure an unlimited guarantee of her employer's

---

[109] J. Lehane (1994) 110 L.Q.R. 167, considering Lord Browne-Wilkinson's comments in *CIBC Mortgages Plc v Pitt* [1994] 1 A.C. 200; Sir Anthony Mason (1994) 110 L.Q.R. 238 at 249; cf. Sir Peter Millett (1995) 9 T.L.I. 35 at 37. See also D. Capper (1998) 114 L.Q.R. 479 and (2010) 126 L.Q.R. 403 and A. Phang and H. Tjio [2003] 11 R.L.R. 110, advocating merger of the two doctrines.

[110] *Langton v Langton* [1995] 2 F.L.R. 890 (set aside only if undue influence or equitable fraud); S. Cretney (1996) 26 Fam. Law 87; D. Capper [1996] Conv. 308 and (1998) 114 L.Q.R. 479.

[111] *Alec Lobb (Garages) Ltd v Total Oil GB Ltd* [1985] 1 W.L.R. 173; *Boustany v Piggott* (1995) 69 P. & C.R. 298; J. Cartwright (1993) 109 L.Q.R. 530; M. Pawlowski [1996] Conv. 454; *Jones v Morgan* [2001] Lloyd's Rep. Bank 323; *Kalsep Ltd v X-Flow BV, The Times*, May 3, 2001; *Fineland Investments Ltd v Pritchard* [2011] 6 E.G. 102 ("undertones of constructive fraud" required).

[112] *Fry v Lane* (1888) 40 Ch.D. 312. The list is not exhaustive; *Cresswell v Potter* [1978] 1 W.L.R. 255.

[113] See *Watkin v Watson-Smith, The Times*, July 3, 1986 (old age with diminution of capacity and judgment, together with a desire for a quick sale, satisfied the requirement). See also *Mountford v Scott* [1975] Ch. 259. The modern equivalent of "poor and ignorant" is a member of the lower income group or a "less highly educated" person; *Cresswell v Potter*, above, fn.112, at 257; *Credit Lyonnais Bank Nederland NV v Burch* [1997] 1 All E.R. 144.

[114] This requirement is not satisfied where, unknown to the purchaser, the vendor is of unsound mind; *Hart v O'Connor* [1985] A.C. 1000; A. Hudson [1986] Conv. 178.

[115] See *Butlin-Sanders v Butlin* (1985) 15 Fam. Law 126, where the claim was in any event barred by laches and acquiescence.

[116] Mere undervalue is not sufficient. See LPA 1925 s.174(1).

[117] *Barclays Bank Plc v Schwartz, The Times*, August 2, 1995. See also *Portman Building Society v Dusangh* [2001] W.T.L.R. 117; L McMurtry [2000] Conv. 573; where a mortgage by an elderly, illiterate man for the benefit of his son was not set aside, as there was no unconscionable conduct by the son or the lender.

debts to a bank without receiving independent legal advice.[118] It seems that the unconscionable bargain cases should now be treated as cases where a presumption of undue influence arises from the facts.[119]

There are also at the present time other types of situation which call for relief. Oppressive hire purchase contracts and other credit arrangements are controlled by legislation,[120] and statutory protection is given to unfair contractual terms, especially in the field of exemption clauses, by the Unfair Contract Terms Act 1977. Relief has long been given against oppressive provisions in mortgages,[121] and a similar general principle is evident in the protection of the weak against the strong in the context of relief against forfeiture, in the development of the principles of restraint of trade, and in certain other contexts.[122] The view of the House of Lords was that there is no need to erect a general principle of relief against inequality of bargaining power. Parliament has undertaken this essentially legislative task, and the courts should not formulate further restrictions.[123]

C. Loss of the Right to Rescind

26–015   Formerly a contract entered into in reliance upon an innocent misrepresentation could not be rescinded after execution of the contract by the transfer of property under it. This rule was abrogated by the Misrepresentation Act 1967 s.1. However, the court has a discretion under s.2(2) to award damages in lieu of rescission in any case of innocent misrepresentation if it would be equitable to do so.[124] This discretion is more likely to be exercised where the contract has been executed than where it remains executory.

More generally, the right to rescind may be lost in any of three ways.

26–016   **i. Affirmation.** Where the party entitled to rescind affirms the contract, for example by taking a benefit under it, with knowledge of the facts giving rise to the right to rescind and of his legal rights,[125] he will be taken to have waived that right.[126] Affirmation may be

---

[118] *Credit Lyonnais Bank Nederland NV v Burch* [1997] 1 All E.R. 144 (decided on the basis of undue influence, however).

[119] *Langton v Langton*, above, fn.110.

[120] Consumer Credit Act 1974 (as amended by Consumer Credit Act 2006); S. Brown [2007] Conv. 316.

[121] See *Cityland and Property (Holdings) Ltd v Dabrah* [1968] Ch. 166; cf. *Multiservice Bookbinding Ltd v Marden* [1979] Ch. 84.

[122] e.g. salvage agreements; *The Port Caledonia and The Anna* [1903] P. 184.

[123] *National Westminster Bank Plc v Morgan* [1985] A.C. 686, disapproving wider statements in *Lloyds Bank Ltd v Bundy* [1975] Q.B. 326.

[124] G. Treitel and P. Atiyah (1967) 30 M.L.R. 369.

[125] *Peyman v Lanjani* [1985] Ch. 457; L Anderson [1985] Conv. 408; K Handley (2006) 122 L.Q.R. 82; *Stevens & Cutting Ltd v Anderson* [1990] 1 E.G.L.R. 95; cf. *Goldsworthy v Brickell* [1987] Ch. 378.

[126] *Clough v London and North Western Rail Co* (1871) L.R. 7 Ex.Ch. 26.

shown by words or acts, or may be indicated by lapse of time, the remedy being subject to the doctrine of laches.[127]

ii. Restitutio in Integrum not Possible. A contract will cease to **26–017** be capable of rescission if the parties can no longer be restored to their original position.[128] Any money paid or other property transferred under the contract must be restored. But a precise restoration is not required, particularly in cases involving fraud or duress.[129] Equity is concerned to restore the parties, and especially the defendant, to their former positions so far as practically possible.[130] This might be achieved by, for example, ordering an account of profits and making allowances for deterioration of the property,[131] or by ordering fair compensation in equity where it is not possible to restore the property nor (because its value has since been lost) to account for profits.[132]

In *Cheese v Thomas*[133] the claimant, aged 86, and the defendant, his great nephew, agreed to buy a house for £83,000 in the defendant's name, where the claimant would reside for life, after which it would belong to the defendant. The claimant contributed £43,000 and the defendant raised the balance on mortgage. When the mortgage payments fell into arrears, the claimant sought to set aside the transaction and to recover £43,000. The relationship of the parties was one of confidence, giving rise to a presumption of undue influence, but there was no evidence of impropriety. The lower court ordered a sale and division of the proceeds in the proportions of 43:40. Owing to the property slump, the sale realised only £55,000. The Court of Appeal held that the claimant

---

[127] *Life Association of Scotland v Siddal* (1861) 3 De G.F. & J. 58; *Alec Lobb (Garages) Ltd v Total Oil GB Ltd*, above, fn.111. In the case of company shares it seems that delay is viewed more strictly; *Re Scottish Petroleum Co* (1883) 23 Ch.D. 434. See also *Leaf v International Galleries* [1950] 2 K.B. 86. For the application of the Limitation Act 1980 s.32(1)(c), see *Peco Arts Inc v Hazlitt Gallery Ltd* [1983] 1 W.L.R. 1315.

[128] *Thorpe v Fasey* [1949] Ch. 649; *Erlanger v New Sombrero Phosphate Co* (1873) 3 App.Cas. 1218.

[129] See *Halpern v Halpern (Nos 1 and 2)* [2008] Q.B. 195, discussing rescission for common law duress; L. Pearce [2008] 16 R.L.R. 124.

[130] *Spence v Crawford* [1939] 3 All E.R. 271; *Newbigging v Adam* (1886) 34 Ch.D. 582. See also *Logicrose Ltd v Southend United Football Club Ltd* [1988] 1 W.L.R. 1256.

[131] *Erlanger v New Sombrero Phosphate Co*, above, fn.128. See also *O'Sullivan v Management Agency and Music Ltd* [1985] Q.B. 428 (contracts between manager and entertainer rescinded for undue influence; restitutio principle not applied with full rigour in cases of breach of fiduciary relationship; practical justice achieved by ordering account of profits, giving credit for defendant's labour and skill).

[132] *Mahoney v Purnell* [1996] 3 All E.R. 61 (sale of shares in company now in liquidation); J. Heydon (1997) 113 L.Q.R. 8; P. Birks [1997] 5 R.L.R. 72; T. Akkouh (2002) 16 T.L.I. 151.

[133] [1994] 1 W.L.R. 129; J. Martin (1994) 144 N.L.J. 264; M. Dixon (1994) 53 C.L.J. 232; M. Chen-Wishart (1994) 110 L.Q.R. 173, considering change of position a preferable basis. See also *Niersmans v Pesticcio* [2004] W.T.L.R. 699.

was entitled only to a proportionate share, and not £43,000. Justice required each party to be restored to his original position so far as possible; it would be harsh to make the defendant stand all the loss.

If the parties were cohabitants, unraveling the transactions is more difficult. The court should take a broad approach aimed at reversing the property transactions in substance, not rewriting the history of the relationship.[134]

26–018 **iii. Third Party Acquiring Rights.** The right to rescind is lost if an innocent third party acquires an interest under the contract for value before the claimant seeks to set it aside,[135] although a remedy may be available against the other party to the original transaction.[136] There is no bar to rescission if the third party is a volunteer, such as the defendant's trustee in bankruptcy.[137]

2. RECTIFICATION

A. Nature of the Remedy[138]

26–019 Rectification is a discretionary equitable remedy whereby an instrument[139] which does not accord with the intentions of the parties to it may be corrected. It operates as an exception to the "parol evidence rule", whereby oral evidence is not admissible to alter a written instrument. It must be emphasised that the court does not rectify a mistake in the contract itself, but only a mistake in the instrument recording the contract (or other transaction). It must be very clearly shown that the parties had come to a genuine agreement and that the instrument had failed to record it. Thus where both a written agreement to sell land and the ensuing conveyance incorrectly described the land which it had been agreed to sell, it was possible to obtain rectification on proof of the real oral agreement.[140]

It is no objection that the rectification may have the effect of saving tax[141]; nor that the mistake arose through the negligence of

---

[134] *Smith v Cooper* [2010] 2 F.L.R. 1521.
[135] *Oakes v Turquand* (1867) L.R. 2 H.L. 325.
[136] See *Niersmans v Pesticcio*, above, fn.133 (remedy against proceeds of sale of gifted house). See also B. Häcker [2006] 14 R.L.R. 21.
[137] *Re Eastgate* [1905] 1 K.B. 465.
[138] See Goff and Jones, pp.295–302.
[139] Distinguish cancellation of an instrument that is void or voidable on some ground, e.g. forgery: *Peake v Highfield* (1826) 1 Russ. 559. For the effect of an unexecuted alteration to a deed, see *Co-operative Bank Plc v Tipper* [1996] 4 All E.R. 366.
[140] *Craddock Bros v Hunt* [1923] 2 Ch. 136.
[141] *Re Colebrook's Conveyance* [1972] 1 W.L.R. 1397; *Re Slocock's WT* [1979] 1 All E.R. 358; *Lake v Lake* [1989] S.T.C. 865; *Seymour v Seymour, The Times*, February 16, 1989; *Ashcroft v Barnsdale* [2010] W.T.L.R. 1675.

the claimant or his legal advisers[142]; nor that one of the parties has since died.[143]

When rectification is ordered, a copy of the order may be indorsed on the instrument. There is no need to execute a new document.[144] Rectification is retrospective, and affects steps taken by the parties in the meantime.[145] But the instrument remains binding in its uncorrected form until rectification is actually ordered. The claimant may obtain rectification and specific performance in the same action.[146]

Rectification must be distinguished from the court's power to correct an obvious error as a matter of construction. If an instrument contains a manifest mistake in its drafting, neither common law nor equity is prevented from discerning the fact and substituting the words that were intended to be there. But this is a limited jurisdiction for it applies only when the mistake is obvious from the instrument itself and what should have been written is obvious too.[147] Extrinsic evidence is not admissible. This jurisdiction is one based on the duty of the court to construe documents correctly and is not a jurisdiction to rectify as such.

B. The Nature of the Mistake

i. Common Mistake. The general rule is that rectification re-   **26–020**
quires a mistake common to both parties, whereby the instrument records the agreement in a manner contrary to the intention of both.[148] It must be shown that there was some prior agreement, although not necessarily an enforceable contract, whereby the parties expressed a common intention regarding the provisions in question.[149] The question is what an objective observer would have

---

[142] *Weeds v Blaney* (1977) 247 E.G. 211 (discussing also the position as to costs); *Central & Metropolitan Estates Ltd v Compusave* (1983) 266 E.G. 900 (rectification ordered on terms in such a case); *Boots The Chemist Ltd v Street* (1983) 268 E.G. 817.

[143] *Johnson v Bragge* [1901] 1 Ch. 28; *Allnutt v Wilding* [2007] W.T.L.R. 941 (action by settlor's executors failed on the facts).

[144] *White v White* (1872) L.R. 15 Eq. 247.

[145] *Malmesbury v Malmesbury* (1862) 31 Beav. 407. See also *Freer v Unwins Ltd* [1976] Ch. 288, contrasting rectification under the Land Registration Act 1925 (now the Act of 2002).

[146] *Craddock Bros v Hunt* [1923] 2 Ch. 136.

[147] *Re Bacharach's WT* [1959] Ch. 245; *Re Doland* [1970] Ch. 267; *Schnieder v Mills* [1993] 3 All E.R. 377.

[148] *Murray v Parker* (1854) 19 Beav. 305. See also *Fowler v Fowler* (1859) 4 De G. & J. 250.

[149] *Joscelyne v Nissen* [1970] 2 Q.B. 86. See also *Shipley UDC v Bradford Corp* [1936] Ch. 375; *Crane v Hegeman-Harris Co Inc* [1939] 1 All E.R. 662, [1939] 3 All E.R. 68, [1971] 1 W.L.R. 1390; *CH Pearce & Sons Ltd v Stonechester Ltd, The Times,* November 17, 1983 (a claimant who pleads two claims for rectification in the alternative based on inconsistent assertions of the parties' common intentions demonstrates at the outset that there was no certain intention which would found such a claim).

thought their intentions to be.[150] It must also be shown that the common intention continued until the execution of the instrument. Rectification is not possible where the instrument departs from the prior agreement because the parties had agreed to vary the terms.[151] Next, it must be established that the instrument is not in accordance with the true agreement of the parties, and that, if rectified in the manner claimed, it will represent the agreement. But only the actual agreement of the parties is relevant, not what they would have agreed if they had not been under a misapprehension. Thus in *Frederick E Rose (London) Ltd v William H Pim Jnr & Co Ltd*,[152] rectification was not possible where the parties agreed to buy and sell horsebeans, and the written contract referred to horsebeans, but the parties mistakenly believed that horsebeans were the same as feveroles. The mistake was made when entering into the contract in the first place. The crux of the remedy is proof of what the parties actually had decided at the time of reaching their agreement and not what they, or one of them, had thought at a later date, or what they might have thought if they had considered the matter in greater detail or in the light of more information than that available to them. In other words, the remedy exists to correct, but not to improve, an instrument. It is about "putting the record straight".[153]

The mistake is usually one of fact, but relief may be possible where the mistake is of law. In *Re Butlin's Settlement Trust*,[154] rectification was ordered where the settlor and his solicitor were mistaken as to the effect of a clause giving power to the trustees to decide by a majority. Rectification has been granted where the parties used the then ineffective phrase "free of tax" to carry out their agreement to pay such sum as after deduction of tax would leave the sum in question.[155] It is no bar to rectification that the parties are in agreement and there is thus no dispute, but there must be an issue capable of being contested between the parties.[156] The remedy was accordingly refused in *Whiteside v Whiteside*[157] as the parties had already corrected the error by executing a supplemental deed.

---

[150] *Chartbrook Ltd v Persimmon Homes Ltd* [2009] 1 A.C. 1101; J. O'Sullivan (2009) 68 C.L.J. 510; R. Buxton (2010) 69 C.L.J. 253; D. McLauchlan (2010) 126 L.Q.R. 8.

[151] *Breadalbane v Chandos* (1837) 2 My. & Cr. 711.

[152] [1953] 2 Q.B. 450. (Lord Denning's dicta on rescission were disapproved in *Great Peace Shipping Ltd v Tsavliris Salvage (International) Ltd* [2003] Q.B. 679). See also *London Regional Transport v Wimpey Group Services Ltd* (1987) 53 P. & C.R. 356.

[153] *Allnutt v Wilding* [2007] W.T.L.R. 941 at 944.

[154] [1976] Ch. 251.

[155] *Burroughes v Abbott* [1922] 1 Ch. 86; *Seymour v Seymour, The Times,* February 16, 1989; *Lake v Lake* [1989] S.T.C. 865.

[156] *Seymour v Seymour*, above, fn.155; *Lake v Lake*, above, fn.155; J. Tiley All E.R.Rev. 1989, p.320; *Racal Group Services Ltd v Ashmore* [1995] S.T.C. 1151; *Ashcroft v Barnsdale* [2010] W.T.L.R. 1675.

[157] [1950] Ch. 65. The claimant's purpose in seeking the order was to improve his tax position. Such a motive is immaterial if the requirements of rectification are satisfied.

ii. Unilateral Mistake. Where one party incorrectly records a **26–021** term of the agreement, but it is bona fide accepted as it is written by the other party, the mistake is unilateral and there is no ground for rectification. Thus, the rent may be incorrectly stated, or the lessor's obligations, or the land or buildings incorrectly described. The party making the mistake can only obtain rectification if he can show that the mistake is due to the fraud[158] of the other party, or that the other party was aware of the mistake.

In *Riverlate Properties Ltd v Paul*,[159] the claimant, who was the landlord of property in London, intended to provide in the lease that the defendant should be liable to contribute one half of the landlord's expenditure on matters contained in cll.6(a), (b), (c). By mistake, the lease referred to 6(b), (c), (d). The defendant and her solicitors were unaware of the mistake. The lease stood, as signed.

On the other hand, in *A Roberts and Co Ltd v Leicestershire CC*,[160] the claimant had undertaken to build a school for the defendants. The agreement provided that the school should be completed within 18 months, but the officers of the Council altered the period to 30 months in the draft contract, not drawing the company's attention to the alteration. The company signed the contract without noticing the change, and one of the defendant's officials was aware of the mistake. Rectification was ordered.

The Court of Appeal has held[161] that, in order for the *Roberts* doctrine to apply, it must be shown first that one party, A, erroneously believed[162] that the document sought to be rectified contained a particular provision; secondly, that the other party, B, was aware of the mistake and that it was due to an error on the part of A; thirdly, that B had omitted to draw the mistake to the notice of A; fourthly, that the mistake must be one calculated to benefit B.[163] Although it need not amount to sharp practice, the conduct of B must be such as to make it inequitable that he should be allowed to

---

[158] Constructive fraud suffices. See *Lovesy v Smith* (1880) 15 Ch.D. 655.

[159] [1975] Ch. 133; (1974) 90 L.Q.R. 439; S. Waddams (1975) 53 Can.Bar.Rev. 339; *Agip SpA v Navigazione Alta Italia SpA* [1984] 1 Lloyd's Rep. 353.

[160] [1961] Ch. 555. See Goff and Jones, p.298, expressing the view that the principle is akin to estoppel. See also D. McLauchlan (2008) 124 L.Q.R. 608, suggesting that the courts have been too restrictive in their requirements.

[161] *Bates (Thomas) & Son Ltd v Wyndham's (Lingerie) Ltd* [1981] 1 W.L.R. 505; *Kemp v Neptune Concrete Ltd* (1989) 57 P. & C.R. 369. See also *Central & Metropolitan Estates Ltd v Compusave* (1983) 266 E.G. 900 (20 year lease rectified to include rent review clause. Negotiations contemplated such a provision, but mistakenly omitted from lease. Tenant aware of landlord's mistake. Rectification on terms that tenant should have opportunity to surrender lease after first review).

[162] The belief need not have been induced by any misrepresentation by the other party; *Commission for the New Towns v Cooper (Great Britain) Ltd* [1995] Ch. 259.

[163] Or, per Eveleigh L.J., be detrimental to A.

object to rectification. The graver the character of the conduct involved, the heavier the burden of proof, but the conduct must be such as to affect the conscience of the party who had suppressed the fact that he had recognised the presence of a mistake. Thus, rectification was ordered where a rent review clause in a lease failed to provide machinery for determining the rent in default of agreement. The landlord realised the omission only when the time for review arrived, whereas the tenant had been aware of the mistake at all times. An arbitration clause was ordered to be inserted into the lease, according to the original mutual intention of the parties. Similarly where the defendant "put up a smokescreen" during negotiations to divert the claimant from discovering its mistake.[164] In such a case it suffices that the defendant merely suspected the claimant's mistake, without proof of actual knowledge of it.

It was at one time thought that the court could give the defendant a choice of submitting to rescission or rectification, even though the mistake was unilateral and the court was unable to satisfy itself that the defendant was aware of the mistake. A practice developed of imposing such an option,[165] but this was firmly disapproved by the Court of Appeal in *Riverlate Properties Ltd v Paul*.[166] Unilateral mistake can only give rise to rectification in cases of fraud or upon the principle of *A Roberts and Co Ltd v Leicestershire CC*,[167] where rectification was particularly appropriate, for the school had been built at the time of the action; and if the contract had been rescinded or held void at law, the claimant would have been forced to bring a restitutionary claim.

Where the transaction is unilateral, a unilateral mistake is sufficient. This is discussed below.

C. Proof of the Mistake

26–022   The burden of proof on the party seeking rectification is a heavy one. According to older authority, the claimant must establish the mistake with a "high degree of conviction".[168] A more modern description is "convincing proof".[169] Oral evidence is admissible to

---

[164] *Commission for the New Towns v Cooper (Great Britain) Ltd*, above, fn.162. See also *George Wimpey UK Ltd v V I Construction Ltd*, The Times, February 16, 2005; E. Palser [2006] L.M.C.L.Q. 139.

[165] See *Paget v Marshall* (1882) 28 Ch.D. 255.

[166] [1975] Ch. 133 at 145; in the absence of fraud or sharp practice, mere unilateral mistake was not a ground for rescission "either with or without the option to the [defendant] to accept rectification to cure the [claimant's] mistake." Rectification may, however, be ordered on terms. See *Central & Metropolitan Estates Ltd v Compusave*, above, fn.161.

[167] [1961] Ch. 555.

[168] *Crane v Hegeman-Harris Co Inc* [1939] 4 All E.R. 68 at 71.

[169] *Joscelyne v Nissen* [1970] 2 Q.B. 86 at 98. See also *Bates (Thomas) and Son Ltd v Wyndham's (Lingerie) Ltd* [1981] 1 W.L.R. 505 at 514; *Racal Group Services Ltd v Ashmore* [1995] S.T.C. 1151.

prove the agreement, and there is no need to show anything in the nature of error on the face of the instrument. It is no objection that the transaction is one required by statute to be evidenced in writing; it suffices that the rectified instrument will comply with the statute.[170]

In the case of a settlement, the settlor's evidence alone,[171] or even a mere perusal of the document[172] may suffice to establish the mistake, but the court is slow to act without the support of other evidence such as any written instructions given by the settlor prior to the execution of the settlement. In the case of a will (discussed below) extrinsic evidence of the testator's intentions is admissible but, although the standard of proof is the balance of probabilities, convincing proof is needed to rectify a formally executed will.[173]

D. Instruments which may be Rectified

The remedy is widely available, being applicable to leases and **26–023** other conveyances of land,[174] insurance policies,[175] bills of exchange[176] and many other instruments; but not the articles of a company.[177]

Rectification can also be obtained of a voluntary deed, such as a deed of gift[178] or a settlement,[179] if the court is satisfied on the evidence that the donor's real intent at the time of entering into it was not accurately reflected in the instrument.[180] It is not necessary to show that the intent of the trustees was inaccurately reflected.[181] Clearly the requirement of a common mistake has no application to unilateral transactions.[182] Rectification of a settlement may be ordered not only at the instance of the settlor but also at the instance of

---

[170] *Craddock Bros v Hunt* [1923] 2 Ch. 136.

[171] *Hanley v Pearson* (1870) 13 Ch.D. 545.

[172] *Banks v Ripley* [1940] Ch. 719.

[173] *Re Segelman* [1996] Ch. 171; E. Histed [1996] Conv. 379.

[174] *Bates (Thomas) and Son Ltd v Wyndhams (Lingerie) Ltd* [1981] 1 W.L.R. 505.

[175] *Collett v Morrison* (1851) 9 Hare 162.

[176] *Druiff v Lord Parker* (1868) L.R. 5 Eq. 131.

[177] *Scott v Frank F Scott (London) Ltd* [1940] Ch. 794.

[178] *Glass v Segerman* [2008] W.T.L.R. 1615.

[179] Similarly a unilateral deed of variation; *Martin v Nicholson* [2005] W.T.L.R. 175; or a deed of appointment executed by trustees; *Price v Williams-Wynn* [2006] W.T.L.R. 1633.

[180] *Lackersteen v Lackersteen* (1864) 30 L.J. Ch. 5; *Bonhote v Henderson* [1895] 1 Ch. 742; [1895] 2 Ch. 202 (where rectification was refused); *Tankel v Tankel* [1999] 1 F.L.R. 676; *Bartlam v Coutts & Co* [2006] W.T.L.R. 1165; *Stephenson v Stephenson* [2009] W.T.L.R. 1467 (settlor's right to capital); *Whalen v Kelsey* [2009] W.T.L.R. 1297. Such a deed may be set aside for mistake if rectification would not be appropriate; *Gibbon v Mitchell* [1990] 1 W.L.R. 1304; *Anker-Petersen v Christensen* [2002] W.T.L.R. 313; *Wolff v Wolff* [2004] W.T.L.R. 1349. This principle does not apply to pension trusts, which are not voluntary deeds; *Smithson v Hamilton* [2008] 1 W.L.R. 1453.

[181] *Re Butlin's Settlement* [1976] Ch. 251 at 262.

[182] *Wright v Goff* (1856) 22 Beav. 207.

a volunteer beneficiary, although this will not be done during the settlor's lifetime without his agreement.[183] A unilateral document may not be rectified so as to make it into a document effecting something other than was intended at the time.[184] For example, a settlement creating a discretionary trust cannot be rectified so as to create a wholly different settlement with an interest in possession.[185] If an omitted term invalidates the document, rectification requires clear and convincing evidence of the missing term.[186]

Formerly it was not possible to rectify a will except in the case of fraud,[187] although the court could, as a matter of construction, correct a manifest error in drafting.[188] It is now provided by s.20 of the Administration of Justice Act 1982[189] that a will may be rectified if the court is satisfied that it fails to carry out the testator's intentions in consequence of a clerical error or a failure to understand his instructions,[190] as where a solicitor failed to delete a clause for which the testator had not given instructions and which restricted the class of beneficiaries intended by the testator.[191] There is no rule that rectification must be sought before suing the solicitor for negligence.[192] The statutory power does not permit rectification where the testator himself has misunderstood the legal effect of the wording used,[193] nor where the wrong will has been signed.[194]

E. Defences

26–024   The remedy of rectification, which, like other equitable remedies, is discretionary, will not be granted where a bona fide purchaser for

---

[183] *Thompson v Whitmore* (1860) 1 J. & H. 268; *Lister v Hodgson* (1867) L.R. 4 Eq. 30.
[184] *Collins v Jones, The Times*, February 3, 2000 (ineffective nomination under pension scheme).
[185] *Allnutt v Wilding* [2007] W.T.L.R. 941 (settlor mistaken as to inheritance tax implications); distinguished in *Chisholm v Chisholm* [2011] W.T.L.R. 187.
[186] *Pappadakis v Pappadakis, The Times*, January 19, 2000 (no rectification of purported assignment of policy to unidentified trustees).
[187] *Collins v Elstone* [1893] P. 1.
[188] *Re Bacharach's WT* [1959] Ch. 245; *Re Doland* [1970] Ch. 267; above, para.26–019.
[189] For time limits and the position of the personal representatives, see s.20(2), (3). See generally A. Borkowski and K. Stanton (1983) 46 M.L.R. 191 at 201; R. Kerridge and A. Brierley (2003) 62 C.L.J. 750.
[190] See *Wordingham v Royal Exchange Trust Co Ltd* [1992] Ch. 412; *Goodman v Goodman* [2006] W.T.L.R. 1807; *Price v Craig* [2006] W.T.L.R. 1873; *Re Martin* [2007] W.T.L.R. 329; R. Kerridge and A. Brierley [2007] Conv. 558; *Pengelly v Pengelly* [2008] Ch. 375; *Sprackling v Sprackling* [2009] W.T.L.R. 897; *Re Ryan* [2011] W.T.L.R. 1029.
[191] *Re Segelman* [1996] Ch. 171.
[192] *Horsfall v Haywards (A Firm)* [1999] 1 F.L.R. 1182, distinguishing *Walker v GH Medlicott & Son (A Firm)* [1999] 1 W.L.R. 727; E O'Dell (2002) 65 M.L.R. 360.
[193] See *Collins v Elstone* [1893] P. 1.
[194] *Marley v Rawlings* [2011] 1 W.L.R. 2146 (spouses signed each other's "mirror" will by mistake).

value without notice has acquired an interest under the instrument.[195] Laches or acquiescence will bar the claim[196]; similarly if the contract is no longer capable of performance,[197] or has been fully performed under a judgment of the court.[198] In the case of a voluntary settlement, it has been held that the court may decline to rectify if a trustee, having taken office in ignorance of the mistake, has a reasonable objection to the rectification.[199]

---

[195] *Smith v Jones* [1954] 1 W.L.R. 1089; *Lyme Valley Squash Club Ltd v Newcastle under Lyme BC* [1985] 2 All E.R. 405. In the case of registered land, the right to rectify may be asserted against the purchaser as an overriding interest under the provisions now found in s.11 and Sch.1, para.2, of the Land Registration Act 2002: *Blacklocks v JB Developments (Godalming) Ltd* [1982] Ch. 183; *Ramsden (DB) & Co Ltd v Nurdin & Peacock Plc, The Times,* September 14, 1998. The benefit of the right to rectify in cases concerning land will pass with the land; *Boots The Chemist Ltd v Street* (1983) 268 E.G. 817; LPA 1925, s.63.

[196] *Beale v Kyte* [1907] 1 Ch. 564; cf. *KPMG LLP v Network Rail Infrastructure Ltd* [2006] 2 P. & C.R. 7 (six-year delay no bar).

[197] *Borrowman v Rossell* (1864) 16 C.B.(N.S.) 58.

[198] *Caird v Moss* (1886) 33 Ch.D. 22.

[199] *Re Butlin's ST* [1976] Ch. 251 (where rectification was granted).

CHAPTER 27

LICENCES AND ESTOPPEL

1. GENERAL

A LICENCE is a permission. We are here concerned with licences to **27–001**
enter land.[1] The licence makes lawful what would otherwise be a
trespass.[2] The licence may be express; or it may be implied; as in the
case of a shopkeeper's invitation to enter the premises to do
business.

Express licences arise in a myriad of factual situations, as where
the owner invites guests to dinner; or to stay in a room in his hotel.
Some of these situations will be expected to give minimal rights to a
licensee. He has no interest in the land. The licence prevents him

---

[1] A licence, however, may be a permission to a neighbour to do on his own land something
which would otherwise be a wrong to the licensor; *Hopgood v Brown* [1955] 1
W.L.R. 213.

[2] *Winter Garden Theatre (London) Ltd v Millennium Productions Ltd* [1946] 1 All E.R. 678
at 680.

from being a trespasser, and no more. In other situations there will be a contract which gives certain rights to the licensee; and some situations create difficulties in determining whether a person is a contractual licensee or a lessee.[3] Different situations create different types of licences; and different levels of protection to the licensee.

The main question for discussion in this chapter is the protection of the licensee; as where the licensor purports to revoke the licence. The common law cases prior to the Judicature Acts will demonstrate what difficulties the common law met in dealing with this question; largely through the inadequacy of the remedies available at common law. If the licence was coupled with a proprietary interest, the licensor clearly could not revoke; but, as a licence was not a proprietary interest, it was difficult to see how the licensee could be protected. The common law judges found themselves saying that if a licence were granted by deed, it would not be revocable; which still leaves open the question of finding a proper remedy available to the licensee.

Equity provided the remedies. If the licensor could not lawfully revoke the licence, equity could grant an injunction to restrain him. The licence may be irrevocable for various reasons; most commonly because the terms of the contractual licence make it irrevocable; or because an estoppel has worked in favour of the licensee. Thus, the licensee would enjoy the licence for the period covered by the injunction.

The protection of the licensee against the licensor soon raised the question of whether the licensee should be protected against a third party; not being a bona fide purchaser of the legal estate for value without notice. Where the licensee is protected against third parties, the question arises whether the licence has, by this roundabout route, become an interest in land.

Another question is whether the licensee can only properly be satisfied by a permanent right, and not merely by an injunction. The doctrine known as "proprietary estoppel" has developed, allowing the courts to exercise a wide range of remedies in favour of the licensee, including the award of a proprietary interest in the land, with or without monetary compensation; and intended to provide the solution which is the most just and proper in all the circumstances.

2. The Situation at Common Law

27–002 The common law never reached a satisfactory solution to the problem of the protection of the licensee. Essentially, this was because

---

[3] *Street v Mountford* [1985] A.C. 809.

the inquiry was to see what it was that the licensor had *granted* to the licensee; and a licence *grants* nothing. The true issue is the extent of the protection which should be given against the licensor or against a third party; and, without the remedy of an injunction to restrain interference, the common law had no adequate means of protection. A number of propositions were, however, established prior to 1875.

A. Bare or Gratuitous Licence

A simple permission to enter the licensor's land gives no contrac- **27–003** tual or proprietary right to the licensee. The permission may be withdrawn at any time by the licensor. On revocation, the licensee becomes a trespasser, but is allowed a reasonable time to leave the land.[4]

B. Licence Coupled with a Grant (or an Interest)

It has long been established that a licence coupled with a grant of **27–004** a proprietary interest is irrevocable[5]; where for example an occupier sells some cut timber,[6] and expressly or by implication gives the purchaser permission to enter the land to collect it. Such a licence is irrevocable. Similarly where there is a grant of a right to take away part of the realty, as with a *profit à prendre*. The grant carries with it an irrevocable licence to enter. We do not speak of a licence coupled with a grant where the proprietary interest is one which itself includes a presence on the land; with a lease or an easement, the grantee enters by force of the grant and not under any licence.

C. Contractual Licences

Most of the difficulties which arose at common law were con- **27–005** cerned with contractual licences. If the licensor (A) contracted to allow the licensee (B) to enter his land for a particular purpose or for a particular period of time, and A, in breach of contract, ordered B to leave, and perhaps forcibly ejected him, the common law held that B had become a trespasser and could be ejected.

In *Wood v Leadbitter*,[7] the claimant purchased a ticket for the grandstand at Doncaster Racecourse. The defendant, on the orders

---

[4] *Winter Garden Theatre (London) Ltd v Millennium Productions Ltd* [1948] A.C. 173 at p.199. See J. Hill (2001) 60 C.L.J. 89.

[5] *Webb v Paternoster* (1619) Palm 71; *James Jones & Son Ltd v Tankerville* [1909] 2 Ch. 440.

[6] *James Jones & Son Ltd v Tankerville*, above, fn.5.

[7] (1845) 13 M. & W. 838.

of the steward, required him to leave. He refused to go, and was physically removed, no more force being used than was reasonably necessary. He sued for assault and false imprisonment, and failed. The Court of Exchequer distinguished between a mere licence, such as this, which was revocable; and a licence coupled with an interest, which was not.

In the circumstances, nothing had been *granted*. As Latham C.J. said in *Cowell v Rosehill Racecourse Co*[8]: "50,000 people who pay to see a football match do not obtain 50,000 interests in the football ground." An action for breach of contract no doubt lay,[9] but that was not the issue. Whether or not the defendant had the *right*, under the terms of the contract, to eject the claimant, he had a *power* to do so.[10]

The conclusion must be that the common law provided no adequate doctrine nor any adequate remedies to deal with the problem of protection of licensees.

3. CONTRACTUAL LICENCES AFTER THE JUDICATURE ACTS

27–006　　The treatment of contractual licences at common law was clearly unsatisfactory. This situation, and that of licences generally, has been transformed by the application of equitable remedies, not available to common law courts; by the recognition of the part that estoppel has to play; and finally by the willingness of modern courts to seek the most appropriate remedy for the particular situation. "It is for the court in each case to decide in what way the equity can be satisfied."[11]

A. Injunction to Restrain a Licensor from Breaking a Contractual Licence

27–007　　The reasoning of the common law, established in *Wood v Leadbitter*,[12] was that a licence was revocable unless it validly granted a proprietary interest. In the absence of such a grant, it was said, even as late as 1944,[13] that, though the licensor had no *right* to revoke, he had a *power* to revoke, and could then turn the licensee into a trespasser. The opposite conclusion had been reached in 1915 in

---

[8] (1937) 56 C.L.R. 605 at 616.
[9] per Viscount Simon L.C. in *Winter Garden Theatre (London) Ltd v Millennium Productions Ltd* [1948] A.C. 173 at 190.
[10] per Goddard L.J. in *Thompson v Park* [1944] K.B. 408 at 410; later disapproved in *Verrall v Great Yarmouth BC* [1981] Q.B. 202.
[11] Lord Denning M.R. in *Ives (ER) Investments Ltd v High* [1967] 2 Q.B. 379 at 395.
[12] (1845) 13 M. & W. 838.
[13] *Thompson v Park* [1944] K.B. 408 at 412.

Hurst v Picture Theatres Ltd,[14] but on grounds that show that the courts still thought that it was the grant of a proprietary interest which made the licence irrevocable. In that case the claimant paid to watch a cinema show in the defendants' theatre. The defendants mistakenly thought that he had entered without paying. On being requested to leave, he refused and was ejected. He sued for assault and false imprisonment and succeeded.

Buckley L.J. gave two grounds for distinguishing the case from *Wood v Leadbitter,*[15] both based upon the availability of equitable doctrine, the first reason being, it is submitted, clearly wrong, and the second being the basis of the modern doctrine protecting contractual licensees. The first ground was that the claimant had a licence coupled with an interest—"the right to see"—and that the interest could now be granted in equity by a contract, whereas before 1875 a deed was required. The fallacy in this reasoning is that there was no identifiable proprietary interest to be granted.[16]

As a second ground for the decision, Buckley L.J. treated the matter as one of construing the parties' rights under the contract. Here, "there was included in that contract a contract not to revoke the licence until the play had run to its termination".[17] This is the germ of the later development; and the significance of the Judicature Act in this context is that it makes available the equitable remedy of an injunction to restrain the breach of contract by the licensor. This precludes the argument that he has no right to revoke, but has a power to do so; he has no power if an injunction is available to restrain him.

Winter Garden Theatre (London) Ltd v Millennium Productions Ltd[18] finally established that the rights of the parties must be determined upon the proper construction of the contract. In that case, as the licence was held to have been revoked in accordance with its terms, the problem in *Hurst's* case[19] did not arise. In the Court of Appeal, however, the contract had been construed as irrevocable by the licensor. In that situation, they held, the licensee would be protected by the issue of an injunction to restrain a breach of contract by the licensor. Lord Greene M.R., in words referred to with approval in the House of Lords, explained that the revocation of the licence was a breach[20]:

---

[14] [1915] 1 K.B. 1.

[15] (1845) 13 M. & W. 838.

[16] These matters are demonstrated by Phillimore L.J. in his dissenting judgment; see *Hounslow LBC v Twickenham Garden Developments Ltd* [1971] Ch. 233 at 244; cf. *Cowell v Rosehill Racecourse* (1937) 56 C.L.R. 605.

[17] *Hurst v Picture Theatres Ltd* [1915] 1 K.B. 1 at 10; see also Kennedy L.J. at 14.

[18] [1948] A.C. 173.

[19] [1915] 1 K.B. 1.

[20] [1946] 1 All E.R. 678 at 648.

"It may well be that, in the old days, that would only have given rise to a right to sue for damages. The licence would have stood revoked, but after the expiration of what was the appropriate period of grace the licensees would have been trespassers and could have been expelled, and their right would have been to sue for damages for breach of contract . . . But the matter requires to be considered further, because the power of equity to grant an injunction to restrain a breach of contract is, of course, a power exercisable in any court. The general rule is that, before equity will grant such an injunction, there must be, on the construction of the contract, a negative clause express or implied. In the present case it seems to me that the grant of an option which, if I am right, is an irrevocable option, must imply a negative undertaking by the licensor not to revoke it. That being so, in my opinion, such a contract could be enforced in equity by an injunction."

B. The Licensee's Remedy for the Breach

27–008   **i. Damages.** The normal remedy for breach of contract is, of course, damages; and there is little doubt that this was recognised even in the old common law cases which held that the licensee could be evicted. The question did not arise in *Wood v Leadbitter*,[21] because the form of action was for assault and not for breach of contract.

In *Tanner v Tanner*,[22] the defendant had a relationship with the claimant. She lived in a rent-controlled flat, which she left in 1970, when the claimant purchased a house for her and for their children. The relationship ended, and in 1973 the claimant offered her £4,000 to vacate. She refused, claiming that she could stay in the house until the children left school. The Court of Appeal would have permitted her to stay, but she had been rehoused by the local authority before the appeal. The defendant's remedy was compensation for the loss of the licence, which was quantified at £2,000.

27–009   **ii. Injunction.** The normal way of protecting a contractual licensee against improper revocation is by issuing an injunction to restrain the breach by the licensor. A number of questions arise.

27–010   (a) *The Judge at your Elbow.* It was said in 1915[23] in connection with *Hurst's* case, that an injunction would be a useless remedy unless a Chancery judge was sitting at your elbow, because the

---

[21] (1845) 13 M. & W. 838.
[22] [1975] 1 W.L.R. 1346.
[23] See Sir John Miles (1915) 31 L.Q.R. 217 at 221; and Lord Greene M.R. in *Millennium Productions Ltd v Winter Garden Theatre (London) Ltd* [1946] 1 All E.R. 678 at 685.

breach and ejection would take place before the injunction could issue. But the court will treat the licence as not revoked in circumstances in which an injunction would issue, and this will prevent the licensee from being a trespasser. As has been seen, monetary compensation was awarded in *Tanner v Tanner*[24] where it was no longer practicable to issue an injunction. Moreover, a mandatory injunction may be obtained, in a suitable case, to enable the licensee to re-enter.[25]

(b) *Discretionary Nature of the Remedy.* An injunction, like all **27–011** equitable remedies, is discretionary. An injunction will not therefore be available to a licensee who is himself in breach of the terms of the licence. A licensee who himself misbehaves will not be protected.[26] Further, an injunction will not be granted where it will have the effect of compelling persons to live together in circumstances which are intolerable. If this situation arises in the case of a licence, an injunction may be refused, and the parties may be left to their rights at common law to sue for breach of contract.[27]

iii. Specific Performance. The Court of Appeal had no hesita- **27–012** tion in holding in *Verrall v Great Yarmouth BC*[28] that a contractual licence was enforceable by specific performance.

The National Front entered into a contract in April 1979 with the Council to hire a hall for a conference. In May 1979, after local authority elections, the new Labour controlled Council purported to revoke the licence; on the ground that the Front's extremist political stance would create unrest in the borough. Specific performance of the contract was granted.

The old argument that a licence can be revoked by the licensor on payment of damages was firmly and finally disposed of. The Front was entitled to the benefits of the contractual licence.

The issue of an order for specific performance raised a number of questions of principle. It used to be said that specific performance would not issue in relation to a transient matter; because the issue

---

[24] [1975] 1 W.L.R. 1346.

[25] As in *Luganda v Services Hotels Ltd* [1969] 2 Ch. 209.

[26] *Thompson v Park* [1944] K.B. 408. For a consideration of the question of the circumstances in which misbehaviour by a licensee by estoppel will allow his licence to be terminated, see *Williams v Staite* [1979] Ch. 291; M Thompson [1986] Conv. 406, suggesting that termination is only possible where the previous court order was not the grant of an estate in the land. A smaller degree of misconduct will prevent an estoppel licence arising, under the "clean hands" principle, than will cause it to terminate; *J Willis & Son v Willis* [1986] 1 E.G.L.R. 62.

[27] *Thompson v Park* [1944] K.B. 408 at 409.

[28] [1981] Q.B. 202; A. Briggs [1981] Conv. 212.

may not come to the court in time.[29] That view was held to be out of date. Presumably, however, it would have been a defence if the date of the conference had passed before the issue was tried. Another possible difficulty might be the question of the continued supervision by the court, although, as we have seen,[30] inroads have already been made into the supervision principle. A further question is whether specific performance is available to enforce a contract which does not create a proprietary interest. The older view was that the order would not be made in such a case.[31] But more recent authorities indicate that specific performance is a remedy based on the inadequacy of damages rather than on the vindication of some proprietary interest.[32] This, it is submitted, is the correct approach today:

> "[I]t is the duty of the court to protect, where it is appropriate to do so, any interest, whether it be an estate in land or a licence, by injunction or specific performance as the case may be."[33]

Such an approach is consistent with the court's power to grant a prohibitory injunction to restrain the wrongful revocation of a contractual licence, or to grant a mandatory injunction to reinstate a licensee whose licence has been revoked in breach of contract.[34]

C. Express or Implied Contracts

27–013   The contract may be express or implied. In the older cases, which dealt mainly with commercial transactions, it was not difficult to recognise the existence of a contract, though its terms may have been difficult to construe. Many of the recent cases concern arrangements within the family. These are situations in which the terms of an agreement are usually not spelled out; and a contract may in any case fail because of a lack of intention to create legal relations.

In these circumstances, it is not surprising that it is difficult to distinguish clearly between cases in which a contract has been found and those where it has not. As has been seen, a contractual licence was implied in *Tanner v Tanner*.[35] That indeed was the only way to find an adequate remedy; and Lord Denning M.R., conscious of the

---

[29] Above, para.24–025.
[30] Above, para.24–020.
[31] *Booker v Palmer* [1942] 2 All E.R. 674 at 677, per Lord Greene M.R. This was the view that prevailed at the time of *Hurst's* case.
[32] *Beswick v Beswick* [1968] A.C. 58; *Tanner v Tanner* [1975] 1 W.L.R. 1346 at 1350; *Hutton v Watling* [1948] Ch. 26 at 36 (affirmed at 398); (1980) 96 L.Q.R. 483.
[33] [1981] Q.B. 202 at 220, per Roskill L.J.
[34] *Winter Garden Theatre (London) Ltd v Millennium Productions Ltd* [1948] A.C. 173 (prohibitory); *Luganda v Service Hotels Ltd* [1969] 2 Ch. 209 (mandatory).
[35] [1975] 1 W.L.R. 1346; J. Barton (1976) 92 L.Q.R. 168.

difficulty of finding a contract in the circumstances, went so far as to say that the court should "imply a contract by him—or if need be impose the equivalent of a contract by him."[36] In *Coombes v Smith*,[37] the court failed to find a contract in circumstances which were basically similar. There the defendant bought a house into which the claimant, his lover, moved. As she was pregnant, she gave up her job, the defendant assuring her that he would always provide for her. The defendant paid the outgoings, but the claimant did some decorating and gardening. When the couple separated 10 years later, the defendant offered her £10,000 to move out, but she claimed a contractual licence for life. Her claim failed, as she had provided no consideration, and it was impossible to infer a contract. *Tanner v Tanner*[38] was distinguished as the claimant there had provided consideration in giving up her rent-controlled flat and was not claiming a licence for life. The defendant, however, conceded that the claimant could remain until the child was 17. It is indeed easier to see why there was not a contract in *Coombes v Smith*,[39] than it is to see how one could be implied in *Tanner v Tanner*.[40]

In other cases the occupier has received protection by the court's finding that there was a contractual licence which was irrevocable for a period of time.

In *Hardwick v Johnson*,[41] a mother purchased a house, on her son's marriage, for occupation by him and his bride. The young couple were to pay £7 a week as rent to the mother. But this soon ceased to be paid, and the mother did not demand it because the couple had little money.

The son left his bride, now pregnant, for another woman. The mother sued for possession. The wife claimed to be entitled to remain in possession on payment of £7 per week.

The Court of Appeal found a contractual licence. The daughter-in-law was held entitled, subject to resuming the weekly payments, to protection by injunction for an indefinite period of time. Lord Denning M.R. thought, however, that no enforceable contract could arise in a family situation of this kind,[42] preferring to find a licence by estoppel. On the face of it, it would seem to be unlikely that the

---

[36] [1975] 1 W.L.R. 1346 at 1350.
[37] [1986] 1 W.L.R. 808; D. Hayton (1986) 45 C.L.J. 394; below, para.27–023. See also *Horrocks v Forray* [1976] 1 W.L.R. 230; M. Richards (1976) 40 Conv.(N.S.) 362.
[38] See fn.40.
[39] Above, fn.37.
[40] [1975] 1 W.L.R. 1340.
[41] [1978] 1 W.L.R. 683. See also *Chandler v Kerley* [1978] 1 W.L.R. 693 ("mistress" entitled to remain for a period determinable upon 12 months' notice).
[42] [1978] 1 W.L.R. 683 at 688.

parties would intend to bind themselves contractually in a situation of this type.

D. Contractual Licences and Third Parties

27–014   Protection of the licensee against the licensor inevitably gives rise to the question whether a licensee will be protected also against an assignee of the licensor. On the one hand, protection given to a licensee is in many cases of little use if the licensor can transfer the land and leave the licensee helpless. On the other hand, if a licensee is protected against third parties, the licence begins to look like some sort of proprietary interest.[43]

The extent to which a licence is binding on a third party will vary with the type of licence. Bare licences are obviously not binding. The question whether a contractual licence can bind a purchaser under a constructive trust is considered later[44]; likewise whether an estoppel licence can bind third parties.[45] First the position as to contractual licences outside these situations will be examined.

It is important to appreciate that there is no principle which requires that the availability of an injunction against one contracting party will make it available against third parties coming to the land. The jurisdiction to apply an injunction against a third party was demonstrated by the development of the law of restrictive covenants from *Tulk v Moxhay*.[46] The policy decision to refuse an injunction against third parties was shown by the unsuccessful attempts to make covenants run with chattels.[47]

As far as contractual obligations are concerned, the estate of a deceased party to the contract is not properly a third party. The devisee of the licensor is a third party, but takes as a volunteer. One of the landmark cases on the enforcement of licences against third parties, *Errington v Errington and Woods*,[48] is such a case; the report fails to say whether the licensor's widow, who was the devisee, was also his executrix; but both Lord Denning M.R. and Hodson L.J. refer to her as successor in title. Such a person is in a different position from a purchaser.

Authority leads to the conclusion that contractual licences are not ordinarily binding on third parties.

---

[43] See, however, J. Dewar (1986) 49 M.L.R. 741, suggesting that it is wrong to attempt to fit licences into traditional academic land law.

[44] Below, para.27–016.

[45] Below, para.27–030.

[46] (1848) 2 Ph. 774.

[47] *Port Line v Ben Line Steamers* [1958] 2 Q.B. 146; *Lord Strathcona SS Co v Dominion Coal Co* [1926] A.C. 108; B. McFarlane (2004) 120 L.Q.R. 667.

[48] [1952] 1 K.B. 290.

In *King v David Allen & Sons, Billposting Ltd*,[49] the licensor agreed that the licensees should have the exclusive right of affixing advertisements upon a building. Later the licensor leased the building to a cinema company, no provision being made to protect the rights of the licensees. The licensees sued the licensor for breach of contract. The licensor was liable if the lease to the company deprived the licensees of their contractual right. The House of Lords held that it did.

In *Clore v Theatrical Properties Ltd*,[50] a deed which was drafted in the form of a lease purported to grant the lessee the "front of the house" rights in a theatre; that is, the right to use refreshment rooms, etc. to provide for the needs of patrons. The instrument provided that the terms "lessor" and "lessee" should include their executors, administrators and assigns.

It was held to be a licence and not a lease. The "lessor" and "lessee" both assigned; and the question was whether the "lessee's" assignee could enforce the right under the agreement. He failed; because the licence was a personal contract and enforceable only between the parties to it.

As has since been reaffirmed,[51] these cases lay down a correct **27–015** doctrine relating to contractual licences. Licences were indeed treated as binding on third parties in a number of cases decided in the days when a deserted wife was treated as a licensee protected by injunction[52]; and these provided a very compelling case for applying the injunction also against the party to whom the deserting husband sold the house. But these cases were incorrect; because the House of Lords decided that a deserted wife was not a licensee of her husband, and had no interest capable of binding the land.[53] Legislation followed.[54] There are some cases in which a contractual arrangement, outside the context of a deserted wife, was held to bind a third party, but they are best explained as being decided on other grounds.

In *Errington v Errington and Woods*[55] the father, A, of a young man who was about to be married purchased a house through a building society, made a down-payment and told the young couple that the house would be theirs when they paid all the instalments due under the mortgage. They went into possession and

[49] [1916] 2 A.C. 54.
[50] [1936] 3 All E.R. 483.
[51] *Ashburn Anstalt v Arnold* [1989] Ch. 1; below, para.27–017.
[52] *Bendall v McWhirter* [1952] 2 Q.B. 466; *Lee v Lee* [1952] 2 Q.B. 489n; *Ferris v Weaven* [1952] 2 All E.R. 233.
[53] *National Provincial Bank Ltd v Ainsworth* [1965] A.C. 1175.
[54] Matrimonial Homes Act 1967 (now Family Law Act 1996).
[55] [1952] 1 K.B. 290; *Duke of Beaufort v Patrick* (1853) 17 Beav. 60.

paid all the instalments which fell due. Nothing was stated concerning the rights of the young couple during the currency of the mortgage payments. A died, leaving all his property to Mrs A. The son returned to his mother, who took steps to evict the daughter-in-law. She failed. The daughter-in-law was held to be a licensee who was entitled to protection not only against A in his lifetime, but also against Mrs A, taking as a volunteer.

There was clearly a flavour of contract in the licence, and the case is usually treated as one of contractual licence. But the wide views expressed in the case as to the enforceability of such licences were disapproved, obiter, by the House of Lords in *National Provincial Bank Ltd v Ainsworth*,[56] and have since been said by the Court of Appeal in *Ashburn Anstalt v Arnold*[57] to be neither practically necessary nor theoretically convincing. They could not be reconciled with *King*[58] and *Clore*,[59] but the decision was, however, correct on the facts. It could be justified on any of three grounds:

   (i) there was a contract to convey on completion of the payments, giving rise to an equitable interest in the form of an estate contract which would bind the widow as a volunteer;

  (ii) the daughter-in-law had changed her position in reliance upon a representation by the deceased, the estoppel binding the widow;

 (iii) the payment of instalments gave rise to a direct proprietary interest by way of a constructive trust under the principle later formulated in *Gissing v Gissing*.[60]

Thus the result could have been achieved without accepting Lord Denning's broad principles, which were unnecessary and per incuriam. The correct principle is that a contractual licence cannot bind a third party unless the circumstances are such that a constructive trust has arisen. Further examination of this principle will be deferred until the development of the constructive trust solution has been outlined.

4. Constructive Trusts

27–016 A few cases in this field have been decided on the basis of a constructive trust. Lord Denning has described a constructive trust as one:

---

[56] [1965] A.C. 1175.
[57] [1989] Ch. 1, below.
[58] Above, see fn.49.
[59] Above, see fn.50.
[60] [1971] A.C. 886, above, para.11–011.

"[I]mposed by law whenever justice and good conscience require it. It is a liberal process, founded upon large principles of equity, to be applied in cases where the legal owner cannot conscientiously keep the property for himself alone, but ought to allow another to have the property or the benefit of it or a share of it."[61]

In those terms, the constructive trust solution is at once too vague and too far-reaching. Too vague in that such broad statements provide no way of determining when such a trust will be held to exist.[62] It may be unobjectionable in cases such as *DHN Food Distributors Ltd v Tower Hamlets LBC*,[63] where the issue was whether a contractual licensee could claim compensation for disturbance upon compulsory purchase. But it is not appropriate where title to land is at stake.

Lord Denning M.R. pioneered this solution in *Binions v Evans*.[64]

Mrs Evans was the widow of an employee of the Tredegar Estate. The trustees made an agreement with her, under which she would be allowed to reside in a cottage, free of rent and rates, for life. She undertook to keep the cottage in repair.

Two years later, the trustees sold the cottage to Mr and Mrs Binions, expressly subject to the agreement, the purchase price being reduced accordingly. The purchasers claimed possession of the cottage. Lord Denning M.R. held that the purchasers were bound by Mrs Evans' contractual licence and also by a constructive trust in her favour, whereas Megaw and Stephenson L.JJ. relied upon the agreement as creating a life interest.[65]

Clearly, the case provides no support for the view that contractual licences generally are binding on third parties. Nevertheless, it was cited subsequently as authority for the proposition that a contractual licence is capable of binding a third party.

In *Re Sharpe*[66] an elderly aunt lent money to her nephew towards the purchase of a house on the understanding that she

---

[61] *Hussey v Palmer* [1972] 1 W.L.R. 1286, at 1290.

[62] R. Smith (1973) 32 C.L.J. 123 at 142.

[63] [1976] 1 W.L.R. 852; D. Hayton (1977) 36 C.L.J. 12. See also *Pennine Raceway Ltd v Kirklees Metropolitan Council* [1983] Q.B. 382 (Licensee a "person interested in the land" within Town and Country Planning Act 1971, s.164).

[64] [1972] Ch. 359; PVB (1972) 88 L.Q.R. 336; J. Martin (1972) 36 Conv.(N.S.) 266; R. Smith (1973) 32 C.L.J. 123; S. Bright [2000] Conv. 398.

[65] Applying *Bannister v Bannister* [1948] 2 All E.R. 133. See also *Costello v Costello* (1995) 70 P. & C.R. 297.

[66] [1980] 1 W.L.R. 219; J. Martin [1980] Conv. 207.

would live there with the nephew and his wife for the rest of her life. The nephew subsequently went bankrupt, and his trustee in bankruptcy contracted to sell the house to a purchaser. The trustee failed in his claim to recover possession of the house from the aunt. Her rights were held to be more than merely contractual, and gave rise to a constructive trust binding upon the trustee in bankruptcy. The purchaser was not a party to the action, and it was left open whether he would also be bound. However, as the aunt had sold her home and paid for improvements to the nephew's house, a preferable basis for the decision might have been proprietary estoppel.

27–017 The position has since been clarified by the Court of Appeal in *Ashburn Anstalt v Arnold*,[67] which has "put the *quietus* to the heresy that a mere licence creates an interest in land."[68] The claimant purchaser sought possession against the defendant, who was in occupation under an agreement with the purchaser's predecessor in title. The claimant had been aware of the agreement and had purchased expressly subject to its provisions "so far as the same are enforceable against the Vendor." In fact it was held that the defendant had a tenancy which was binding on the purchaser under the Land Registration Act 1925. However, the Court of Appeal proceeded to consider the position if the defendant had been a contractual licensee. On the clear authority of *King v David Allen & Sons, Billposting Ltd*,[69] the correct principle was that a contractual licence could not normally bind a third party. However, the law must be free to develop, and the finding of a constructive trust was considered a beneficial adaptation of old rules to new situations in appropriate circumstances. But there could be no bare assertion that a licence gives rise to a constructive trust. It would arise only if the conscience of the third party was affected. Mere notice would not be sufficient,[70] nor the fact that the property was conveyed "subject to" the interest. Such a term does not mean that the grantee is necessarily intended to be under an obligation to give effect to the interest, but may be merely to protect the grantor against claims by the grantee (for example as in the case of an old restrictive covenant which may or may not be enforceable). The question is whether the grantee has acted in such a way that, as a matter of justice, a trust

---

[67] [1989] Ch. 1; J. Hill (1988) 51 M.L.R. 226; P. Sparkes (1988) 104 L.Q.R. 175; M. Thompson [1988] Conv. 201; A. Oakley (1988) 47 C.L.J. 353; P. Clarke All E.R. Rev. 1988 at 177; B. McFarlane (2004) 120 L.Q.R. 667.
[68] *IDC Group Ltd v Clarke* [1992] 1 E.G.L.R. 187 at 189, upheld (1993) 65 P. & C.R. 172 (where the issue was not discussed).
[69] [1916] 2 A.C. 54, above, para.27–014.
[70] See *IDC Group Ltd v Clark* [1992] 1 E.G.L.R. 187 at 190 (in the High Court); *Chattey v Farndale Holdings Inc* (1998) 75 P. & C.R. 298; *Lloyd v Dugdale* (2002) 2 P. & C.R. 13; M Dixon [2002] Conv. 584.

must be imposed on him. In the present case there would be no constructive trust because the transfer "subject to" the defendant's rights was done to protect the vendor, and the purchaser had not paid a reduced price. As far as the previous cases were concerned, *Binions v Evans*[71] was a legitimate application of the constructive trust doctrine because the parties intended the purchaser to give effect to the interest and the price was reduced accordingly. Also approved was *Lyus v Prowsa Ltd*,[72] where the intention had been similar and the purchaser had given assurances. The doctrine was not, however, appropriate in *Re Sharpe*,[73] where the aunt had not replied to the trustee in bankruptcy's enquiries as to her interest.

The Court of Appeal added that certainty was of prime importance as far as title to land was concerned, and it was not desirable to impose a constructive trust on slender materials.[74] One difficulty is that the imposition of a constructive trust, in the case of a fee simple, creates an equitable interest which is not registrable (in unregistered land).[75] If the interest protected by a constructive trust is for life only, problems once arose with the Settled Land Act, but settlements cannot now be created.[76] Similar points arise with the doctrine of proprietary estoppel, as discussed below.[77] In that context also the constructive trust has been invoked in order to achieve a just result.[78]

The latest formulation, it is submitted, provides welcome guidelines as to the circumstances in which a constructive trust will be imposed, and thereby achieves a compromise between the sometimes divergent goals of certainty and justice.

5. Licences by Estoppel

The doctrine of estoppel has played a significant part in the modern development of the law of licences.[79] A situation in which a licensee has acted to his detriment in reliance upon a representation or promise by the licensor presents a compelling case for the intervention of **27–018**

---

[71] [1972] Ch. 359, above.

[72] [1982] 1 W.L.R. 1044; distinguished in *Chaudhary v Yavuz* [2011] EWCA Civ 1314; *The Times*, December 29, 2011.

[73] [1980] 1 W.L.R. 219, above.

[74] Reiterated in *IDC Group Ltd v Clark*, above, fn.70 (in the High Court).

[75] Formerly the interest of a beneficiary absolutely entitled under a constructive trust was not overreachable, but this has been changed by the Trusts of Land and Appointment of Trustees Act 1996; above, para.11–017. Overreaching, however, requires two trustees.

[76] Life interests now give rise to the less complex trust of land under the 1996 Act, above.

[77] Below, para.27–034.

[78] *Re Basham* [1986] 1 W.L.R. 1498, below, para.27–028.

[79] It seems that a licence by estoppel was first so referred to judicially in *Inwards v Baker* [1965] 2 Q.B. 29, per Danckwerts L.J. at 38, below, para.27–025.

equity in order to protect the licensee; more compelling, in a sense, than the case of a contractual licence, because the licensee by estoppel has no alternative remedy in damages.[80] The doctrine of estoppel by encouragement or acquiescence has found a fruitful area of operation in the field of licences, under the name of proprietary estoppel; its success in this area has been largely due to the fact that, unlike estoppel by representation or promissory estoppel, it can found a cause of action and, in the licence context, enables the court to award a proprietary interest to the licensee. In the enthusiasm for the application of this doctrine, it has become confused with other estoppels, and has been credited with the solution to many cases in which it is quite clear that the judges reached their decision on other grounds. The utility of the doctrine stems from the fact that the court will "look at all the circumstances in each case to decide in what way the equity can be satisfied"[81]; and the most suitable solution is often an award to the licensee of a proprietary interest, rather than merely an injunction. A sword and not a shield is sometimes required.

A. Types of Estoppel

27–019   There are many different types of estoppel at law and in equity. We are concerned with three of these, each having a separate origin and history.[82] The Australian courts have asserted that distinctions should not be drawn between the various categories of estoppel, nor between their common law or equitable origin.[83] The courts in this country have not yet reached this conclusion, although there have been dicta to the effect that it is undesirable to distinguish between types of estoppel.[84] If this view prevails, the existing differences (such as whether the type of estoppel operates as a sword or a shield) will have to be modified in order to achieve a coherent unified

---

[80] As to how far a contractual licence may also be a licence by estoppel, see M. Thompson and A. Briggs [1983] Conv. 50 and 285 respectively.

[81] *Plimmer v Wellington Corp* (1884) 9 App.Cas. 699 at 714; *Greasley v Cooke* [1980] 1 W.L.R. 1306 at 1312. It may be held that the claimant has already had sufficient satisfaction for his expenditure; *Sledmore v Dalby* (1996) 72 P. & C.R. 196.

[82] For estoppel by convention, i.e. by a course of dealing, see *Amalgamated Investment and Property Co (In Liquidation) v Texas Commerce International Bank Ltd* [1982] Q.B. 84; *Pacol Ltd v Trade Lines Ltd* [1982] 1 Lloyd's Rep. 456; P. Matthews (1982) 79 L.S.Gaz. 662. See generally Wilken and Villiers, *Waiver, Variation and Estoppel*, 2nd edn, 2002; Cooke, *The Modern Law of Estoppel*, 2000.

[83] *Waltons Stores (Interstate) Ltd v Maher* (1988) 62 A.L.J.R. 110 at 123; A. Duthie (1988) 104 L.Q.R. 362; *Commonwealth of Australia v Verwayen* (1990) 65 A.L.J.R. 540 at 546; M. Spence (1991) 107 L.Q.R. 221; M. Lunney [1992] Conv. 239. Likewise in New Zealand: *Gillies v Keogh* [1989] 2 N.Z.L.R. 327 at 331. See Halliwell, *Equity and Good Conscience in a Contemporary Context*, 1997, Ch.2.

[84] *Crabb v Arun DC* [1976] Ch. 179 at 193; *Amalgamated Investment and Property Co Ltd (In Liquidation) v Texas Commerce International Bank Ltd* [1982] Q.B. 84 at 103; cf. JMT (1981) 97 L.Q.R. 513; P. Evans [1988] Conv. 46; *JT Developments Ltd v Quinn* (1991) 62 P. & C.R. 33 at 45; *First National Bank Plc v Thompson* [1996] Ch. 231.

doctrine.[85] More recent pronouncements, however, are against the idea of "an overarching principle" which would blur the distinctions.[86] Lord Scott in *Yeoman's Rowe Management Ltd v Cobbe*[87] expressed the view that proprietary estoppel was a sub-species of promissory estoppel, but this is at variance with the origin and development of the doctrines and was doubted by Lord Walker in *Thorner v Major.*[88]

i. Estoppel by Representation. Estoppel by representation op-   **27–020**
erates over a wide field of common law and equity. The basic principle is that a person who makes an unambiguous[89] representation, by words,[90] or conduct,[91] or by silence,[92] of an existing fact, and causes another party to act to his detriment in reliance on the representation will not be permitted subsequently to act inconsistently with that representation. The doctrine was originally applied only where there was a representation of existing fact,[93] and not where the representation was one of law or of intention. The representor could not subsequently allege, in dealing with the representee, that the facts were different from those represented. Apart from a few long-established exceptions,[94] such an estoppel works negatively. It is not capable of creating a cause of action. It works like a rule of evidence, a rule which excludes a particular defence or line of argument.

This is not to say that estoppel is available only to a defendant. A claimant may take advantage of the doctrine if he has an independent cause of action, and can show that the defence is inconsistent with a representation of the defendant on which he relies.[95]

---

[85] See M. Halliwell (1994) 14 L.S. 15, suggesting the remedying of unconscionable conduct as the unifying factor. See generally Pawlowski, *The Doctrine of Proprietary Estoppel* (1996).

[86] *Republic of India v India Steamship Co Ltd (No.2)* [1998] A.C. 878 at 914; R. Halson [1999] L.M.C.L.Q. 256; *National Westminster Bank Plc v Somer International (UK) Ltd* [2002] Q.B. 1286 at 1303.

[87] [2008] 1 W.L.R. 1752; below, para.27–022.

[88] [2009] 1 W.L.R. 776; below, para.27–022.

[89] *Low v Bouverie* [1891] 3 Ch. 82.

[90] *Hunt v Carew* (1649) Nels. 46; or through an agent; *Moorgate Mercantile Ltd v Twitchings* [1977] A.C. 890.

[91] *Waldron v Sloper* (1852) 1 Drew. 193.

[92] *Fung Kai Sun v Chan Fui Hing* [1951] A.C. 489; *Pacol Ltd v Trade Lines Ltd* [1982] 1 Lloyd's Rep. 456.

[93] *Jorden v Money* (1845) 5 H.L.C. 185; not followed in Australia; *Legione v Hateley* (1983) 57 A.L.J.R. 292; *Foran v Wight* (1989) 168 C.L.R. 385.

[94] e.g. a tenancy by estoppel, M. & W., p.778; see also *Ramsden v Dyson* (1866) L.R. 1 H.L. 129; below, para.27–026.

[95] Similarly with promissory estoppel; *Amalgamated Investment and Property Co (In Liquidation) v Texas Commerce International Bank Ltd* [1982] Q.B. 84; *Pacol Ltd v Trade Lines Ltd* [1982] 1 Lloyd's Rep. 456. See M. Barnes [2011] L.M.C.L.Q. 372.

A well-known example is *Roberston v Minister of Pensions*,[96] where an officer claimed a pension, relying upon a statement by the War Office that his disability had been accepted as due to military service, and forbore to obtain an independent medical opinion. It was held that the Crown, through the Minister of Pensions, could not go back on the statement previously made. The officer was no longer in a position to supply the necessary evidence; but the Minister was estopped from denying that he qualified.

27–021   **ii. Promissory Estoppel.** The doctrine is expanded in equity, so as to include not only representations of fact, but also representations of intention; or promises. The doctrine came into prominence with the decision of Denning J. in *Central London Property Trust Ltd v High Trees House Ltd* in 1947,[97] and became firmly established in later cases.[98]

Where, by words or conduct, a person makes an unambiguous representation as to his future conduct, intending the representation to be relied on, and to affect the legal relations between the parties, and the representee alters his position in reliance on it, the representor will be unable to act inconsistently with the representation if by so doing the representee would be prejudiced.[99]

The doctrine emerged in *Loffus v Maw*[100] and *Hughes v Metropolitan Railway Co*,[101] and developed through a line of cases which was little known until 1947. Denning J. then applied it in *Central London Property Trust Ltd v High Trees House Ltd*.[102]

> The landlord company in 1937 leased to the defendant a block of flats for 99 years at a rent of £2,500 a year. Early in 1940, because of the war, the defendants were unable to find sub-tenants for the flats, and unable in consequence to pay the rent. The landlord agreed to reduce the rent to £1,250 from the beginning of the term. By the beginning of 1945 all the flats were let, and the landlord was held entitled to the full rent as from the middle of that year. Denning J., however, stated that the landlord would have been estopped from claiming the full rent for the period from 1940 to 1945, on the ground that though not technically bound because of the lack of consideration, the landlord had intended the

---

[96] [1949] 1 K.B. 227; *Combe v Combe* [1951] 2 K.B. 215 at 219, per Denning L.J. See also *Western Fish Products Ltd v Penwith DC* [1981] 2 All E.R. 204.

[97] [1947] K.B. 130. For a recent discussion of the principle, see *Collier v P & MJ Wright (Holdings) Ltd* [2008] 1 W.L.R. 643

[98] *Combe v Combe* [1951] 2 K.B. 215; *Ajayi v RT Briscoe (Nigeria) Ltd* [1964] 1 W.L.R. 1326; *WJ Alan & Co Ltd v El Nasr Export and Import Co* [1972] 2 Q.B. 189.

[99] See *Combe v Combe* [1951] 2 K.B. 215 at 220.

[100] (1862) 3 Giff. 592.

[101] (1877) 2 App.Cas. 439.

[102] [1947] K.B. 130.

defendants to rely on the promise and the defendants had acted on the faith of it.

Promissory estoppel contains a number of features which distinguish it from estoppel by representation of fact.[103] First, in that the representation may be one of intention and not one of fact; which raises the question whether it is inconsistent with the House of Lords decision in *Jorden v Money*.[104] But the doctrine is now well established.[105] Secondly, the requirement of detriment to the representee is less stringent in the case of promissory estoppel. Financial loss or other detriment is of course sufficient; but it seems that it is not necessary to show more than that the representee committed himself to a particular course of action as a result of the representation.[106] Thirdly, the effect of the estoppel may not be permanent. The representor may escape from the burden of the equity if he can ensure that the representee will not be prejudiced.[107] But, consistently with estoppel by representation, promissory estoppel does not create a cause of action. It is a shield and not a sword.[108]

iii. Proprietary Estoppel.

(a) *General Principles.* This doctrine is applicable where one 27–022 party knowingly encourages another to act, or acquiesces in the other's actions, to his detriment in the belief that he has or will have some property right against the first party. The latter may be required to make good the expectation which he encouraged in the other party. Unlike other estoppels, therefore, this doctrine may, in some circumstances, create a claim, and an entitlement to positive proprietary rights; in others, it can operate negatively, or can produce a compromise situation appropriate to the particular circumstances.

The doctrine was restrictively interpreted by the House of Lords in *Yeoman's Row Management Ltd v Cobbe*,[109] where the claimant, a property developer, made an oral "in principle" agreement to buy

---

[103] See generally G. Cheshire and C. Fifoot (1947) 63 L.Q.R. 283; J. Wilson (1951) 67 L.Q.R. 330; Denning L.J. (1952) 15 M.L.R. 1; L. Sheridan (1952) 15 M.L.R. 325.

[104] (1854) 5 H.L.Cas. 185. See *Foran v Wight* (1989) 168 C.L.R. 385 at 411.

[105] But it "may need to be reviewed and reduced to a coherent body of doctrine by the Courts": *Woodhouse AC Israel Cocoa Ltd v Nigerian Produce Marketing Co Ltd* [1972] A.C. 741 at p.758 (per Lord Hailsham).

[106] *Central London Property Ltd v High Trees House Ltd* [1947] K.B. 130; *WJ Alan & Co Ltd v El Nasr Export and Import Co* [1972] 2 Q.B. 189; *Ajayi v RT Briscoe (Nigeria) Ltd* [1964] 1 W.L.R. 1326.

[107] *Tool Metal Manufacturing Co Ltd v Tungsten Electric Co Ltd* [1955] 1 W.L.R. 766.

[108] *Combe v Combe* [1951] 2 K.B. 215 at 224. See generally M. Thompson (1983) 42 C.L.J. 257; cf. *Waltons Stores (Interstate) v Maher* (1988) 62 A.L.J.R. 110.

[109] [2008] 1 W.L.R. 1752.

the defendant's land. Section 2 of the Law of Property (Miscellaneous Provisions) Act 1989 requires contracts relating to land to be
made in writing. Although the claimant was aware that there was no
binding contract, he spent time and money on obtaining planning
permission in the expectation that the contract would be finalised,
but it was not. His claim to an interest in the property under the
doctrines of proprietary estoppel or constructive trust failed. (He
was entitled to compensation under the quantum meruit principle for
the value of his services.) Lord Scott explained that the doctrine
could not normally arise in the "subject to contract" cases, as the
claimant's expectation was always subject to a contingency controlled by the other party. The vendor had taken advantage of him,
but he knew all along that there was no contract and took a commercial risk.[110]

> "Proprietary estoppel requires, in my opinion, clarity as to what it
> is that the object of the estoppel is to be estopped from denying,
> or asserting, and clarity as to the interest in the property in ques-
> tion that that denial, or assertion, would otherwise defeat. If these
> requirements are not recognised, proprietary estoppel will lose
> contact with its roots and risk becoming unprincipled and there-
> fore unpredictable, if it has not already become so."[111]

Section 2(5) of the 1989 Act provided an exception for constructive
trusts,[112] but not for estoppel, and it was considered that proprietary
estoppel could not be prayed in aid to render enforceable an agreement that the statute has declared to be void. This view is open to
question, and it has since been doubted in the High Court.[113] Lord
Neuberger, writing extra-judicially, described s.2 of the 1989 Act as
"that misconceived piece of legislation", and suggested that "section 2 offers no bar to a claim based in equity".[114]

The approach of the House of Lords, although not the result,
attracted considerable academic criticism, and was viewed as a set-
back which had curtailed or even extinguished the doctrine.[115] However, these fears have been allayed by the decision of the House of

---

[110] See also *Att Gen of Hong Kong v Humphreys Estate (Queen's Gardens) Ltd* [1987] A.C.
114, where the claim failed on similar grounds; *Haq v Island Homes Housing Association*
[2011] 2 P. & C.R. 17.
[111] [2008] 1 W.L.R. 1752 at 1768.
[112] The exception may be relied on where estoppel gives rise to a constructive trust. See
Yaxley v Gotts [2000] Ch. 162; *Kinane v Mackie-Conteh* [2005] W.T.L.R. 345; *S v S and M*
[2007] 1 F.L.R. 1123.
[113] *Herbert v Doyle* [2009] W.T.L.R. 589.
[114] (2009) 68 C.L.J. 536 at 546. See also G. Owen and O. Rees [2011] Conv. 495.
[115] B. McFarlane and A. Robertson [2008] L.M.C.L.Q. 449. In similar vein, see also P.
Clarke All E.R. Rev. 2008, 286; A. Goymour (2009) 68 C.L.J. 37; J. Getzler (2009) 125
L.Q.R. 196; G. Griffiths [2009] Conv. 141.

Lords in *Thorner v Major*,[116] where the doctrine was again reviewed in the context of an expectation of inheritance.

> Peter, a man of few words, owned a farm. His cousin's son, David, worked on the farm without pay for 29 years until Peter died. Peter never expressly promised to leave the farm to David, but that was the understanding between them. In 1990 Peter gave David some papers on his life policies worth £20,000, saying that David should use them to pay death duties. This was part of a pattern of conduct over many years indicating his intention to leave David the farm. In 1997 Peter made a will leaving David his estate apart from some pecuniary legacies. He later fell out with a pecuniary legatee and revoked the will, but he never made another and died intestate. The House of Lords, reversing the Court of Appeal, held that David was entitled to the farm.

> It was held that, in the appropriate context, "oblique assurances" could constitute a sufficiently clear and unequivocal representation. The representation had to be "clear enough", and that was hugely dependent on context. While the representations had to relate to identified property owned, or perhaps about to be owned, by the defendant, changes in its character or extent over time did not exclude a remedy if it was still identifiable. Lord Scott considered that proprietary estoppel provided a remedy if assurances related to the acquisition of an immediate interest, but preferred to regard representations as to inheritance prospects as giving rise to a "remedial constructive trust".[117] As the remedial constructive trust is not yet established in this jurisdiction, his Lordship's analysis was surprising.

> The approach of the House of Lords in *Yeoman's Rowe Management Ltd v Cobbe*[118] was regarded as confined to the commercial context of a situation in which the parties were at arm's length and knew that neither was yet bound by any contract. It was very different from a case concerning assurances of inheritance by one family member to another.

> *Thorner v Major*[119] has generally been welcomed as having restored the flexibility of the doctrine, but it has not resolved every issue, and the volume of litigation in this area is unlikely to diminish.[120]

---

[116] [2009] 1 W.L.R. 776. See also *Suggitt v Suggitt* [2011] W.T.L.R. 1841.

[117] Above, paras 12–006–12–007.

[118] [2008] 1 W.L.R. 1752.

[119] [2009] 1 W.L.R. 776.

[120] B. McFarlane and A. Robertson (2009) 125 L.Q.R. 535; N. Piska (2009) 72 M.L.R. 998; M. Dixon [2009] Conv. 260; J. Uguccioni [2009] L.M.C.L.Q. 463; B. McFarlane All E.R. Rev. 2009, 301; B. Sloan (2009) 68 C.L.J. 518; Lord Neuberger (2009) 68 C.L.J. 536.

27–023   As far as interests in the home are concerned, the modern tendency has been to assimilate proprietary estoppel and common intention constructive trusts, but there has recently been a retreat from
this.[121]

One question which arises is whether the courts should award a
remedy which fufils the expectations of the claimant[122] or one which
merely reverses the detriment or, to put it another way, is the minimum award to do justice. The latter is all that is required to avoid
unjust enrichment, whereas the former might be said to give a promise unsupported by consideration the effect of a contract. The better
view, which was favoured by the House of Lords,[123] is that the aim
should be the reversal of detriment, as it would normally be inequitable to insist on a remedy which is disproportionate to the detriment.[124] There may, however, be special reasons for going further in
some cases.[125] The Court of Appeal in *Jennings v Rice*[126] reviewed
the authorities and concluded that the claimant's expectation was no
more than a starting point: the most essential requirement was proportionality between the expectation and the detriment. Other factors included any misconduct of either party, changes in the
benefactor's circumstances, and the existence of other legal or moral
claims against the benefactor. On this approach £200,000 was
awarded to the claimant who had acted as a carer in the expectation
of inheriting a house worth £435,000. "Proportionality lies at the
heart of the doctrine of proprietary estoppel and permeates its every
application."[127] The range of remedies is further discussed
below.[128]

---

[121] *Stack v Dowden* [2007] 2 A.C. 432 at 448; above, para.11–013; *Thorner v Major* [2009]
1 W.L.R. 776 (Lord Scott).

[122] *Pascoe v Turner* [1979] 1 W.L.R. 431, below, para.27–025; S. Moriarty (1984) 100
L.Q.R. 376; M. Thompson [1986] Conv. 406; *Re Basham* [1986] 1 W.L.R. 1498, below,
para.27–028; *Wayling v Jones* (1995) 69 P. & C.R. 170; *Yaxley v Gotts*, above, fn.112; *Kinane
v Mackie-Conteh* [2005] W.T.L.R. 345 at 354. For the view that this approach is correct, see E.
Cooke (1997) 17 L.S. 258; cf. A. Robertson (1998) 18 L.S. 360.

[123] *Stack v Dowden* [2007] 2 A.C. 432 at 448.

[124] *Waltons Stores (Interstate) Ltd v Maher* (1988) 62 A.L.J.R. 110 at 126; *Commonwealth
of Australia v Verwayen* (1990) 64 A.L.J.R. 540 at 546; cf. *Giumelli v Giumelli* (1999) 161
A.L.R. 473; D. Wright (1999) 58 C.L.J. See also *Crabb v Arun DC* [1976] Ch. 179 at 198;
Baker v Baker [1993] 2 F.L.R. 247 (an unusual case where the detriment exceeded the value of
the expected interest); *Sledmore v Dalby* (1996) 72 P. & C.R. 196; *Gillett v Holt* [2001] Ch.
210; *Evans v HSBC Trust Company (UK) Ltd* [2005] W.T.L.R. 1289. See generally A.
Robertson [2008] Conv. 295.

[125] *Pascoe v Turner*, above (interest less than fee simple considered insecure against future
purchasers); *Holman v Howes* [2007] W.T.L.R 1539. See generally S. Gardner (1999) 115
L.Q.R. 438 and (2006) 122 L.Q.R. 492.

[126] (2003) 1 P. & C.R. 8; M. Pawlowski (2002) 118 L.Q.R. 519; M. Thompson [2003]
Conv. 225. See also *Campbell v Griffin* [2001] W.T.L.R. 981; M. Thompson [2003] Conv.
157; *Grundy v Ottey* [2003] W.T.L.R. 1253; M. Thompson [2004] Conv. 137.

[127] *Henry v Henry* [2010] 1 All E.R. 988 at 1002 (P.C.).

[128] Para.27–025.

Detrimental reliance need not involve the expenditure of money **27–024**
on the land.[129] In *Greasley v Cooke*,[130] the claimant served notice to
quit on the defendant, who had moved into the property as a servant,
but had cohabited with the owner's son, K, and had stayed on after
the owner's death, continuing to care for the family, which included
a mentally-ill daughter. She had remained without payment since
1948, encouraged by K, now deceased, and his brother (the claimant) to believe that it was her home for life. The Court of Appeal
held that she was entitled to remain as long as she wished. Lord
Denning M.R. appeared to suggest that it was not necessary that the
claimant should have acted to her detriment[131]:

> "[I]t is sufficient if the party, to whom the assurance is given, acts
> on the faith of it—in such circumstances that it would be unjust
> and inequitable for the party making the assurance to go back on
> it. . . . There is no need for her to prove that she acted to her
> detriment or to her prejudice."[132]

Subsequent cases, however, have made it clear that these comments related only to the burden of proving reliance. In *Coombes v
Smith*[133] (the facts of which have already been given[134]) Lord Denning's statement was interpreted as meaning merely that where the
claimant has adopted a detrimental course of conduct after the defendant's assurances, there is a rebuttable presumption that this was
done in reliance upon the assurances. Here the claim based on
proprietary estoppel failed. The claimant had no mistaken belief that
she had a right to remain indefinitely, and in any event there was no
detrimental act. Her acts in leaving her husband, becoming pregnant
and looking after the house were not done in reliance on any expectation of an interest and were not detrimental.[135] Other decisions

---

[129] For the application of the doctrine to property other than land, see *Western Fish Products Ltd v Penwith DC* [1981] 2 All E.R. 204 at 218; *Moorgate Mercantile Co Ltd v Twitchings* [1976] Q.B. 225 at 242; P. Matthews (1981) 40 C.L.J. 340.

[130] [1980] 1 W.L.R. 1306; G. Woodman (1981) 44 M.L.R. 461. See also *Stallion v Albert
Stallion Holdings (Great Britain) Ltd* [2010] 2 F.L.R. 78 (foregoing ancillary relief on divorce).

[131] Here in any event the claimant had foregone wages and perhaps lost job opportunities.

[132] [1980] 1 W.L.R. 1306 at 1311–1312. This resembles the requirements of promissory
estoppel (above, para.27–021).

[133] [1986] 1 W.L.R. 808; D. Hayton (1986) 45 C.L.J. 394; *Wayling v Jones* (1995) 69 P. &
C.R. 170. See also *Stevens & Cutting Ltd v Anderson* [1990] 1 E.G.L.R. 95, suggesting that
the headnote in *Greasley* is wrong: the decision was on the burden of proof of reliance, not of
detriment.

[134] Above, para.27–015 (the contract claim).

[135] cf. *Grant v Edwards* [1986] Ch. 638, above, para.11–008. See also *Walsh v Singh* [2010]
1 F.L.R. 1658 (no estoppel where woman's contributions were in expectation of a long term
relationship, not a property interest).

have shown more lenience on "reliance". In *Matharu v Matharu*[136] a married couple had improved property owned by the husband's father, who had encouraged the wife to believe that it belonged to her husband. She was granted a licence to occupy for life even though some of the improvements were done after she discovered the truth. In *Wayling v Jones*[137] the claimant helped the deceased, with whom he cohabited, to run a café merely for pocket money, and acted as his chauffeur and companion. The deceased promised to leave him a house and business, but all he received by will was a car and furniture. The café had been sold and at his death the deceased owned a hotel. The claimant was awarded the proceeds of sale of the hotel (over £72,000), even though his evidence was that he would have stayed with the deceased if no promise had been made. It was held that the promise did not need to be the sole inducement for the claimant's conduct.

27–025   (b) *Remedies.*[138] Early illustrations of the doctrine dealt with the protection of a lessee; as where a life tenant granted a 30-year lease, to the knowledge of remainderman who "stood by and encouraged" the tenant to take the lease and incur expenditure. Lord Hardwick confirmed the tenant in the balance of his lease after the life tenant's death.[139]

Other cases deal with activities on a party's own land which require facilities from a neighbour; allowing that party to acquire a right in the nature of an easement; as where a millowner erects a mill on the understanding, to the knowledge of a canal owner, that he could use canal water to generate steam[140]; or where the defendants constructed a sewer over a strip of the claimant's land, and the claimant failed to complain until the construction of the sewer was complete,[141] or where a landowner subdivides his land in reliance on a right of way being granted by a neighbour (the local authority) through a specified outlet[142]; or where one party with the knowledge and consent of his neighbour, builds so as to encroach on the neighbour's land.[143] The doctrine does not, however, apply where the

---

[136] (1994) 68 P. & C.R. 93; J. Dewar (1994) 24 Fam. Law. 625; M. Welstead [1995] Conv. 61; P. Milne (1995) 58 M.L.R. 411; G. Battersby [1995] 7 C.F.L.Q. 59.

[137] Above; E. Cooke (1995) 111 L.Q.R. 389; C. Davis [1995] Conv. 409; A. Lawson (1996) 16 L.S. 218.

[138] See generally S. Bright and B. McFarlane (2005) 64 C.L.J. 449; S. Gardner (2006) 122 L.Q.R. 492.

[139] *Huning v Ferrers* (1711) Gilb.Eq. 85; *Jackson v Cator* (1800) 5 Ves. 688 (tenant making alterations to landlord's knowledge).

[140] *Rochdale Canal Co v King* (1853) 16 Beav. 630.

[141] *Armstrong v Sheppard & Short Ltd* [1959] 2 Q.B. 384.

[142] *Crabb v Arun DC* [1976] Ch. 179.

[143] *Hopgood v Brown* [1955] 1 W.L.R. 213; *Ives (ER) Investments Co v High* [1967] 2 Q.B. 379.

claimant does acts on his own land which are not done in the expectation of acquiring rights over the land of another.[144]

The most extreme cases are those where a non-owner, in reliance upon a gratuitous promise of a gift of the land, has built on or improved the land. Clearly some remedy is required. In some cases the licensee has been protected from eviction without obtaining a proprietary interest in the land.

In *Inwards v Baker*,[145] Mr Baker's son, Jack, decided to build a bungalow upon land which he hoped to purchase, but the project proved to be too expensive. Mr Baker suggested that Jack should put the bungalow on land already owned by him; that would save some expense, and Jack could build a bigger bungalow. This was done. Jack lived there some 40 years before the proceedings began in 1963. The father died in 1951, leaving a will dated 1922, under which the land was left to others.

The Court of Appeal held that the son should not be disturbed as long as he wished to stay. This is the first case, as far as is known, in which a licence is expressly referred to as one "created by estoppel".[146] Negative protection only was considered, because "proprietary estoppel" had not yet been introduced into the licence cases.

On other occasions, the non-owner has been given a lien on the land for his expenditure[147]; or compensation for the value of the improvements[148]; or awarded the improved land on payment of a reasonable price for the site[149]; or a right to occupy until expenditure on improvements has been reimbursed[150]; or a non-assignable lease at a nominal rent, determinable on death.[151] A monetary award may

---

[144] *Western Fish Products Ltd v Penwith DC* [1981] 2 All E.R. 204 (no estoppel where claimant spent money on own land relying on planning officer's assurance that planning permission would be granted; doctrine in any event not available against planning authority); *R. v East Sussex CC Ex p. Reprotech (Pebsham) Ltd* [2002] 4 All E.R. 58; *Lloyds Bank Plc v Carrick* [1996] 4 All E.R. 630; M. Thompson [1996] Conv. 295; P. Clarke All E.R. Rev. 1996 at 257; M. Oldham (1997) 56 M.L.R. 32; N. Hopkins (1998) 61 M.L.R. 486. cf. *Lim Teng Huan v Ang Swee Chuan* [1992] 1 W.L.R. 113 (co-owned land).

[145] [1965] 2 Q.B. 29; *Jones v Jones* [1977] 1 W.L.R. 438; *Matharu v Matharu* (1994) 68 P. & C.R. 93; *Thompson v Foy* [2010] 1 P.& C.R. 16.

[146] By Danckwerts L.J. at 38.

[147] *Unity Joint Stock Mutual Banking Association v King* (1858) 25 Beav. 72; *McGuane v Welch* [2009] W.T.L.R. 1201.

[148] *Raffaele v Raffaele* [1962] W.A.R. 29. See also *Plimmer v Wellington Corp* (1884) 9 App.Cas. 699.

[149] *Duke of Beaufort v Patrick* (1853) 17 Beav. 60; *Lim Teng Huan v Ang Swee Chuan* [1992] 1 W.L.R. 113 (house built on land co-owned by parties, but contract to build house void for uncertainty).

[150] *Dodsworth v Dodsworth* (1973) 228 E.G. 1115.

[151] *Griffiths v Williams* (1977) 288 E.G. 947.

be given where a right to occupy would be oppressive or unwork-able,[152] or where the land in question has been sold.[153] In some cases, however, the minimum equity to do justice may have expired, so that it is no longer inequitable to enforce legal rights.[154] In other cases a conveyance of the freehold has been ordered.

In *Dillwyn v Llewelyn*[155] a father encouraged his son to build a house on the father's land, and signed a memorandum purporting to convey the land to the son; but it was not by deed. The father's will left all his land upon certain trusts in favour of others. The son spent some £14,000 in building a house on the land, with his father's knowledge and approval. On the father's death, it was held that the son was entitled to a conveyance of the land.

On its face, the decision is inconsistent with two basic rules, namely that a gratuitous promise is not enforceable, and that an incomplete gift will not be completed in favour of a volunteer.[156] Detrimental reliance is not consideration under English law. There was no compelling reason why the son should have a transfer of the land at the expense of the father's estate. However, the decision was recently referred to with apparent approval by the House of Lords.[157]

Perhaps the most extreme of the cases on proprietary estoppel, resulting in an extraordinary windfall for the licensee, is *Pascoe v Turner*.[158]

The claimant and defendant lived together in the claimant's home. Later the claimant purchased another house and the couple moved in. When the relationship ended he told the defendant that the house was hers and everything in it. In reliance on this gratui-tous promise, she expended, to the claimant's knowledge, her own money on repairs, improvements and redecoration, and also on furniture. Later the claimant gave the defendant two months' notice to determine the licence. Even though the defendant never sought to establish that she had spent more money on the house than she would have done had she believed that she only had a licence to live there for her lifetime, the Court of Appeal felt that

---

[152] *Baker v Baker* [1993] 2 F.L.R. 247; *Campbell v Griffin* [2001] W.T.L.R. 981.

[153] *Wayling v Jones* (1995) 69 P. & C.R. 170. See further S. Bright and B. McFarlane [2005] Conv. 14.

[154] *Sledmore v Dalby* (1996) 72 P. & C.R. 196 (rent-free occupation for past 18 years sufficient recompense for improvements); J. Adams [1997] Conv. 458; M. Pawlowski (1997) 113 L.Q.R. 232. See also *Clark v Clark* [2006] W.T.L.R. 823.

[155] (1862) 4 De G.F. & J. 517; *Chalmers v Pardoe* [1963] 1 W.L.R. 677; *Raffaele v Raffaele*, above, fn.148; D. Allen (1963) 79 L.Q.R. 238.

[156] See S. Naresh (1980) 96 L.Q.R. 534 at 539–542.

[157] *Yeoman's Rowe Management Ltd v Cobbe* [2008] 1 W.L.R. 1752 at 1776.

[158] [1979] 1 W.L.R. 431; *Voyce v Voyce* (1991) 62 P. & C.R. 290.

protection for her lifetime was insecure, and awarded a conveyance of the house.

Finally, the court will not make an order which would be unworkable in view of family discord. In such a case a clean break may be
the best solution, involving an award of compensation rather than a
proprietary interest.[159] Thus the equity may be satisfied in a different
way from that which the parties intended when on good terms. The
requirement of proportionality has already been discussed.[160]

(c) *Judicial Formulations.* Two early judicial formulations of **27–026**
the doctrine come from statements of Lord Kingsdown and Fry J.
Lord Kingsdown, with the old cases of disappointed lessees in mind,
explained the doctrine as follows[161]:

"If a man, under a verbal agreement with a landlord for a certain
interest in land, or, what amounts to the same thing, under an
expectation, created or encouraged by the landlord, that he shall
have a certain interest, takes possession of such land, with the
consent of the landlord, and upon the face of such promise or
expectation, with the knowledge of the landlord, and without
objection by him, laid out money on the land, a Court of Equity
will compel the landlord to give effect to such promise or expectation."

Fry J. in *Willmott v Barber*[162] laid down the principle in more
specific detail, in what have been called the "five probanda":

"In the first place the [claimant] must have made a mistake as to
his legal rights. Secondly, the [claimant] must have expended
some money or must have done some act (not necessarily upon
the defendant's land) on the faith of his mistaken belief. Thirdly,
the defendant, the possessor of the legal right, must know of the
existence of his own right which is inconsistent with the right
claimed by the [claimant]. If he does not know of it he is in the
same position as the [claimant], and the doctrine of acquiescence
is founded upon conduct with a knowledge of your legal rights.
Fourthly, the defendant, the possessor of the legal right, must
know of the [claimant's] mistaken belief to his rights. If he does

---

[159] *Burrows v Sharp* (1991) 23 H.L.R. 82; J. Martin [1992] Conv. 54; *Baker v Baker* [1993]
2 F.L.R. 247; J. Martin (1994) 144 N.L.J. 264.
[160] Above, para.27–023.
[161] *Ramsden v Dyson* (1866) L.R. 1 H.L. 129 at 170. It would be otherwise if the expectation was not created nor encouraged by the landlord; at 171. The House of Lords in *Yeoman's
Row Management Ltd v Cobbe* [2008] 1 W.L.R. 1752 made it clear that the "verbal agreement" did not include an oral contract made void by statute.
[162] (1880) 15 Ch.D. 96 at 105–106.

not, there is nothing which calls upon him to assert his own rights. Lastly, the defendant, the possessor of the legal right, must have encouraged the [claimant] in his expenditure of money or in the other acts which he has done, either directly or by abstaining from asserting his legal right."[163]

27–027   Modern judicial formulations of the doctrine have moved away from the inflexibility of the "five probanda". In *Taylors Fashions Ltd v Liverpool Victoria Trustees Co Ltd*,[164] Oliver J. held that estoppel by acquiescence was not restricted to cases where the defendant knew his rights. There were many circumstances of estoppel, and it was not possible to lay down strict and inflexible rules. The application of the *Ramsden v Dyson*[165] principle:

"[R]equires a very much broader approach which is directed to ascertaining whether, in particular individual circumstances, it would be unconscionable for a party to be permitted to deny that which, knowingly or unknowingly, he has allowed or encouraged another to assume to his detriment rather than to inquiring whether the circumstances can be fitted within the confines of some preconceived formula serving as a universal yardstick for every form of unconscionable behaviour[166] . . . The inquiry which I have to make therefore . . . is simply whether, in all the circumstances of the case, it was unconscionable for the defendants to seek to take advantage of the mistake, which, at the material time, everybody shared. . . . "[167]

This broad approach was adopted in *Amalgamated Investment and Property Co Ltd (In Liquidation) v Texas Commerce International Bank Ltd*,[168] where Robert Goff J. said that, "Of all doctrines, equitable estoppel is surely one of the most flexible . . . it

---

[163] See *Brinnand v Ewens* (1987) 19 H.L.R. 415 (tenant had no claim for voluntary improvements where no reliance on any interest and no encouragement or acquiescence by landlord).

[164] [1981] 2 W.L.R. 576; [1982] Q.B. 133n.; P. Jackson [1982] Conv. 450. See also *Lester v Woodgate* [2010] 2 P. & C.R. 21.

[165] Above, fn.161. See generally K. Handley [2008] Conv. 382; H. Delaney and D. Ryan [2008] Conv. 401.

[166] [1981] 2 W.L.R. 576 at 593. See also *Ives (ER) Investments Co v High* [1967] 2 Q.B. 379; *Shaw v Applegate* [1977] 1 W.L.R. 970 at 977–978, 980; *Jones v Stones* [1999] 1 W.L.R. 1739 at 1743. See also M. Balen and C. Knowles [2011] Conv. 176, preferring "failure of basis" to unconscionability.

[167] [1981] 2 W.L.R. 576 at 596. It was suggested that the "five probanda" might be necessary in a case of "standing by", where the defendant has done no positive act. This was accepted by the House of Lords in *Yeoman's Row Management Ltd v Cobbe* [2008] 1 W.L.R. 1752. See generally K. Low (2012) 128 L.Q.R. 63.

[168] [1982] Q.B. 84; *Pacol Ltd v Trade Lines Ltd* [1982] 1 Lloyd's Rep. 456; *Lloyds Bank Plc v Carrick* [1996] 4 All E.R. 630.

cannot be right to restrict [it] to certain defined categories."[169] How-ever, we saw that the House of Lords recently emphasised that the doctrine required more than unconscionable behaviour.[170] Proprietary estoppel:

"[I]s not a sort of joker or wild card to be used whenever the Court disapproves of the conduct of a litigant who seems to have the law on his side. Flexible though it is, the doctrine must be formulated and applied in a disciplined and principled way. Certainty is important in property transactions."[171]

This case arose in a commercial context. Although the actual decision has not been questioned, we saw that, when the doctrine was again before the House of Lords a short time later, a more flexible approach was taken in the family context.[172]

It is clear that we have moved away from the basic rule that an estoppel is a shield and not a sword. If an injunction suffices as the remedy, the estoppel operates in the traditional way as a shield and not a sword. But if something more is justified, like the grant of a proprietary interest, then proprietary estoppel provides additional remedies. The constructive trust has also been called upon to fill in possible gaps in the estoppel doctrine. **27–028**

In *Re Basham*[173] the claimant's mother married her stepfather in 1936 when the claimant was aged 15. The claimant lived with them until her marriage in 1941, helping to run the business without pay on the understanding that she would inherit from her stepfather. He dissuaded her husband from taking a job with a tied cottage, saying he would help them to get a house. After the mother's death in 1976, the claimant and her husband helped her stepfather in his house and garden, prepared his meals, bought carpets for the house, and paid solicitors for advice over a boundary dispute. The stepfather constantly assured her that the house would be hers, but he died intestate. The claimant, who did not benefit under the intestacy, succeeded in her claim to the whole estate under the doctrine of proprietary estoppel. It was held that the doctrine was not confined to a case where the claimant's belief

---

[169] [1982] Q.B. 84 at 103. See also *Lim Teng Huan v Ang Swee Chuan* [1992] 1 W.L.R. 113 (where both parties wrongly assumed they had a contract); S. Goo [1993] Conv. 173; *John v George* (1996) 71 P. & C.R. 375.
[170] *Yeoman's Row Management Ltd v Cobbe* [2008] 1 W.L.R. 1752; above, para.27–022.
[171] [2008] 1 W.L.R. 1752 at 1775 (Lord Walker).
[172] *Thorner v Major* [2009] 1 W.L.R. 776; above, para.27–022.
[173] [1986] 1 W.L.R. 1498; *Wayling v Jones* (1995) 69 P. & C.R. 170. The decision was discussed by the House of Lords in *Thorner v Major* [2009] 1 W.L.R. 776; below, para.27–029.

related to an existing right and to specific assets.[174] Where the belief related to a future right, a species of constructive trust arose. The doctrines of estoppel, mutual wills[175] and secret trusts[176] had a common theme, and thus reliance could be placed on cases such as *Re Cleaver*,[177] where an expectation of inheritance of non-specific assets gave rise to a constructive trust under the mutual wills doctrine. The proper remedy was an award of the entire estate, to satisfy the expectations encouraged by the deceased.

Clearly the claimant should have some remedy, however it is doubtful whether the introduction of the constructive trust is either necessary or desirable.[178] Under modern formulations of the doctrine of proprietary estoppel,[179] the claimant may succeed without a constructive trust. If that is not so, the claimant should not succeed under estoppel but should look to other remedies.[180]

27–029   Subsequently a restrictive approach was taken in relation to promises to leave property by will, on the basis that it is well known that a testator is free to change his testamentary intentions. In *Taylor v Dickens*[181] the testatrix told her gardener that she planned to leave him her house by will, whereupon he said that he would no longer accept wages for his work. In her last will the testatrix left the property elsewhere but did not tell the gardener of her change of mind. His claim under the proprietary estoppel doctrine (and also in contract) failed on the ground that an unconscionable broken promise was insufficient. It was held that in the case of a promised legacy, it must be shown that the promisor created or encouraged a belief that he would not exercise his right to change his mind and that the promisee relied on that belief. This was criticised as too rigid a view of proprietary estoppel.[182] The criticisms were held to be well

---

[174] cf. *Layton v Martin* (1986) 16 Fam. Law. 212, where the deceased's assurances that he would provide for the claimant by will could not found a claim to proprietary estoppel, which arose only in connection with specific assets; C. Davis [1996] Conv. 193; *Lissimore v Downing* [2003] 2 F.L.R. 38 (estoppel may relate to whole estate but not to unascertainable property).

[175] Above, para.12–026.

[176] Above, Ch.5.

[177] [1981] 1 W.L.R. 939, above, para.12–032. If the analogy with the surviving testator in *Re Cleaver* is taken too far, a finding that the estopped party holds his estate on constructive trust seems to restrict the choice of discretionary remedies open to the court.

[178] See J. Martin [1987] Conv. 211; D. Hayton (1987) 46 C.L.J. 215; P. Clarke and C. Sherrin All E.R. Rev. 1987 at 156 and 263; M. Davey (1988) 8 L.S. 92 at 101 et seq. See, however, *Sen v Headley* [1991] Ch. 425 at 440.

[179] Above, para.27–027.

[180] For example, under the Inheritance (Provision for Family and Dependants) Act 1975.

[181] [1998] 1 F.L.R. 806, distinguishing *Re Basham*, above, fn.173, and *Wayling v Jones* (1995) 69 P. & C.R. 170, above, para.27–024. An appeal in *Taylor* was settled.

[182] G. Douglas (1998) 28 Fam.Law 192; M. Thompson [1998] Conv. 210; M. Pawlowski (1998) 114 L.Q.R. 351.

founded by the Court of Appeal in *Gillett v Holt*,[183] where the defendant over many years had indicated that he would leave his farm to the claimant, who had worked there since the age of 16 in 1956, depriving himself of the opportunity of trying to better himself in other ways. In 1995 the friendship broke down and the defendant made a new will in favour of another. The proprietary estoppel claim against the defendant (who was still living) was upheld. In a case where assurances had been given over many years, the court should look at the matter in the round. If the assurances were intended to be relied on and had been relied on, it was not necessary to look for an *irrevocable* promise, as it was the other party's detrimental reliance which made it irrevocable. The inherent revocability of testamentary dispositions was irrelevant to an assurance that "all this will be yours". The question of detriment should be approached as part of a broad inquiry as to whether repudiation of an assurance was unconscionable. A quantifiable financial detriment was not required, so long as the detriment was substantial. In this case the equity was satisfied by a transfer to the claimant of one of the three farms and £100,000 to compensate him for exclusion from the rest of the farming business.

We saw that the House of Lords in *Thorner v Major*[184] preferred a flexible approach in the context of assurances to leave property by will. An oblique assurance could be sufficiently unequivocal so long as it was "clear enough". Lord Scott considered *Gillett v Holt*[185] and *Re Basham*[186] to be constructive trust cases, but that was in the context of his view, not shared by the other members of the House of Lords, that representations relating to inheritance prospects gave rise to a remedial constructive trust. However, it was left open whether *Re Basham*[187] was correctly decided in so far as the claimant was awarded the whole estate.

B. Conveyancing Problems Caused by Licences by Estoppel[188]

The question to be considered in this section is whether a licence by estoppel has the status of a proprietary interest prior to the   **27–030**

---

[183] [2001] Ch. 210; M. Dixon (2000) 59 C.L.J. 453; R. Wells and M. Thompson [2001] Conv. 13 and 78. See also *Campbell v Griffin* [2001] W.T.L.R. 981; *Jennings v Rice* (2003) 1 P. & C.R. 8; *Jiggins v Brisley* [2003] W.T.L.R. 1141; *Uglow v Uglow* [2004] W.T.L.R. 1153; *Evans v HSBC Trust Company (UK) Ltd* [2005] W.T.L.R. 1289.

[184] [2009] 1 W.L.R. 776. The facts were given above, para.27–022.

[185] [2001] Ch. 210.

[186] [1986] 1 W.L.R. 1498; above, para.27–028.

[187] [1986] 1 W.L.R. 1498. See further criticisms of *Re Basham* in *Macdonald v Frost* [2009] W.T.L.R. 1815.

[188] See generally S. Moriarty (1984) 100 L.Q.R. 376; A. Briggs and P. Todd [1981] Conv. 212 and 347; M. Thompson and A. Briggs [1983] Conv. 50 and 285 respectively; J. Hill (1988) 51 M.L.R. 226; M. Pawlowski (2011) 41 Fam. Law 1251.

litigation, and, if so, how it may be protected against successors in title of the estopped party.

27–031   **i. Status Prior to Court Order.** Clearly a recognised proprietary interest may be conferred by the court, such as the conveyance of the fee simple or the grant of a life interest. More difficult is the question whether the estoppel licensee has an interest capable of binding a third party prior to the order of the court. What would have happened, for example, if the legal owner in *Pascoe v Turner*[189] had conveyed the house to a purchaser before the matter came to court? Before the matter was clarified by legislation, one view was that the estoppel interest was too uncertain and unstable to qualify as a proprietary interest, even a "mere equity", before the court's decision. Another view was that the interest was a "mere equity" capable of binding third parties, at any rate volunteers and purchasers with actual notice. Another was that it could bind third parties under the ordinary rules of priorities, even though the interest was inchoate and did not "crystallise" until the court order.

The weight of authority supported the view that an estoppel interest had proprietary status before the court order, and this was confirmed by the Land Registration Act 2002. Section 116 provides as follows:

> "It is hereby declared for the avoidance of doubt that, in relation to registered land . . . an equity by estoppel . . . has effect from the time the equity arises as an interest capable of binding successors in title (subject to the rules about the effect of dispositions on priority)."

Although this provision applies only to registered land, it would now be difficult to argue for a different position in unregistered land. In most cases the equity will be treated as having arisen when the other party acts to his detriment. At the latest, it will be when the circumstances make it unconscionable for the owner to go back on the expectation.

How the interest may be protected against a third party is discussed in the next section. Section 116 does not operate to pre-empt the court's decision as to the appropriate remedy, which could still be a money payment rather than some right over the land.[190] There is nothing in s.116 to compel the conclusion that the estoppel right must give rise in all cases to a proprietary interest.

---

[189] [1979] 1 W.L.R. 431; above, para.27–025.
[190] See B. McFarlane (2003) 62 C.L.J. 661, doubting whether, in such a case, the obligation to pay would be imposed on the purchaser. See also M. Dixon (2009) 125 L.Q.R. 401.

ii. Registered and Unregistered Land. As it is now clear that **27–032** estoppel interests are capable of binding successors in title, the next point to consider is how they may be protected. In unregistered land such interests are not registrable under the Land Charges Act 1972[191] and, therefore, depend on the doctrine of notice. Occupation will normally give constructive notice. In registered land, estoppel interests would be overriding if coupled with occupation,[192] or could be protected by a notice.[193]

The Court of Appeal has stated that estoppel interests of a "family" nature are overreachable by a disposition by two trustees.[194] In cases where capital money is paid to a sole trustee, so that overreaching cannot occur, the interest will depend on the doctrine of notice in unregistered land or may be an overriding interest in registered land if coupled with occupation, as mentioned above. Estoppel interests of a commercial nature are not overreachable.[195]

iii. Other Problems Arising Under the Doctrine of Proprietary Estoppel.

(a) *Necessity for Litigation.* The problems here are the same as **27–033** those met in the context of licences giving rise to a constructive trust. No one knows, without the court's decision, whether or not the licensee is entitled to have an interest in the land transferred to him, nor what the interest will be. If the court orders the transfer of any interest, the documentation will be completed.

(b) *Effect of Life Interest.* Where the expectation of the licensee **27–034** was to occupy the licensor's property for life, as is not uncommon in the family context, the award of a life interest to the licensee used to cause problems. The difficulty was that such a life interest brought the complex provisions of the Settled Land Act 1925 into play, under which the life tenant acquired the legal estate and extensive powers of sale and leasing. Thus in *Ungurian v Lesnoff*[196] a life interest under the Settled Land Act arose (either on the basis of estoppel or a common intention constructive trust[197]) in favour of the defendant, who had given up her flat, nationality and career to

---

[191] s.2 (easement, right or privilege, being merely equitable) has been narrowly construed; *Shiloh Spinners Ltd v Harding* [1973] A.C. 691.

[192] LRA 2002 s.29 and Sch.3, para.2. In the case of first registration of title, the overriding interests are set out in Sch.1, which includes the interest of an occupier (para.2).

[193] If the registered proprietor does not consent, a unilateral notice may be entered; LRA 2002 ss.34, 35.

[194] *Birmingham Midshires Mortgage Services Ltd v Sabherwal* (2000) 80 P. & C.R. 256; C Harpum (2000) 116 L.Q.R. 341.

[195] (2000) 80 P. & C.R. 256.

[196] [1990] Ch. 206. The 1925 Act was also applied in *Costello v Costello* (1995) 70 P. & C.R. 297, where a deed provided that parents could occupy rent free for life.

[197] Above, para.11–008.

live with the claimant. He bought a house for them to live in, which the defendant improved, but they separated after four years. An irrevocable licence was considered inadequate, but an outright conveyance would have gone beyond what the parties intended.

Most modern cases, however, have avoided a solution involving the Settled Land Act. In *Dodsworth v Dodsworth*[198] the defendants had spent over £700 on improvements in the belief that they would have a right to occupy for life. They were held entitled to occupy until the expenditure had been reimbursed. Similarly in *Griffiths v Williams*,[199] where a daughter looked after her mother and spent money on repairs and improvements to the house in the belief that she had a home there for life, but the house was left to another relative. In order to avoid the complications of the Settled Land Act, she was awarded a non-assignable lease at a nominal rent, determinable on death.

Since the Trusts of Land and Appointment of Trustees Act 1996 came into operation it is no longer possible to create a settlement under the 1925 Act. The problem discussed above has diminished because the award of a life interest will now bring into play the less complex "trust of land", which was explained in Ch.11. A different remedy may, however, be preferred.[200]

---

[198] (1973) 228 E.G. 1115.

[199] (1977) 248 E.G. 947.

[200] *Campbell v Griffin* [2001] W.T.L.R. 981 (money award preferred to life interest under trust of land).

INDEX

FROM SWEET & MAXWELL

This index has been prepared using Sweet & Maxwell's Legal Taxonomy. Main index entries conform to keywords provided by the Legal Taxonomy except where references to specific documents or non-standard terms (denoted by quotation marks) have been included. These keywords provide a means of identifying similar concepts in other Sweet & Maxwell publications and online services to which keywords from the Legal Taxonomy have been applied. Readers may find some minor differences between terms used in the text and those which appear in the index. Suggestions to *sweet&maxwell.taxonomy@thomson.com.*

[all references are to paragraph number]